Paris Metro

*The stations Liège and Rennes are closed after 8pm and on Sundays and holidays.

Beyond the city limits, *Métro Urbain* tickets are not valid on the RER

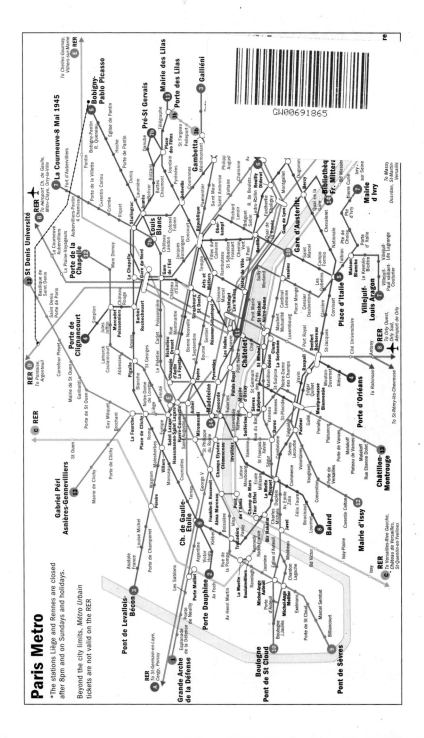

GW00691865

Paris: Overview and Arrondissements

1 Cimetière de Montmartre
2 Sacré Coeur Basilica
3 Parc La Villette
4 Parc des Buttes Chaumont
5 Jardins du Trocadero
6 Palais Chaillot
7 Cimetière de Passy
8 American Embassy
9 British Embassy
10 Petit Palais
11 Grand Palais
12 Arc de Triomphe
13 Madeleine
14 Gare St-Lazare
15 Parc Monceau
16 Palais de la Découverte
17 Opéra Garnier
18 Galeries Lafayette
19 Printemps
20 Gare du Nord
21 Gare de l'Est
22 Opéra Bastille
23 Palais Omnisports de Bercy
24 Ministère des Finances
25 Gare de Lyon
26 Parc de Montsouris
27 Cité Universitaire
28 Cimetière Montparnasse
29 Gare Montparnasse

30 Bureau des Objets Trouvés (Lost and Found)
31 Louvre
32 Palais Royale
33 Forum des Halles
34 Musée de l'Orangerie
35 Central Post Office
36 Bourse
37 Bibliothèque Nationale
38 Ecole des Arts et Métiers
39 Archives Nationales
40 Musée Carnavalet
41 Musée Picasso
42 Centre George Pompidou
43 place des Vosges
44 Musée Victor Hugo
45 Notre Dame
46 Mémorial de la Déportation
47 Université de Paris (Sorbonne)

48 Ecole Normal Supérieure
49 Musée de Cluny
50 Museum Nationale d'Histoire Naturelle
51 Panthéon
52 Eglise St-Etienne du Mont
53 La Mosquée
54 Jardin des Plantes
55 Jardins du Luxembourg
56 Eglise St-Sulpice
57 Théâtre Nationale de l'Odéon
58 Eiffel Tower
59 Champs de Mars

60 Ecole Militaire
61 UNESCO
62 Hôtel des Invalides
63 Assemblée Nationale
64 Musée d'Orsay
65 Cimetière de l'Est du Pere Lachaise

Bois de Boulogne

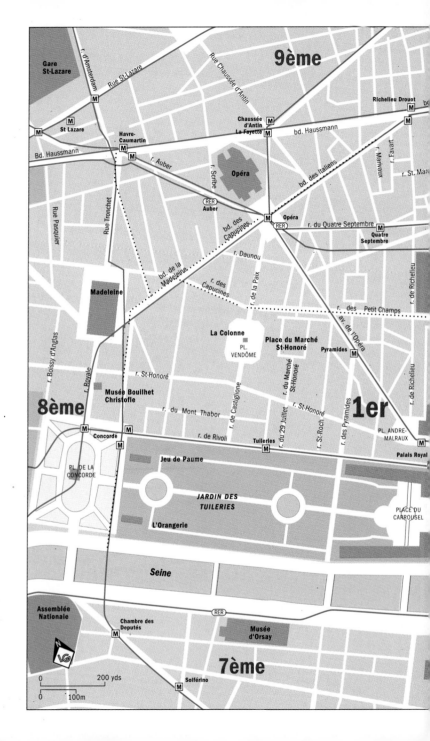

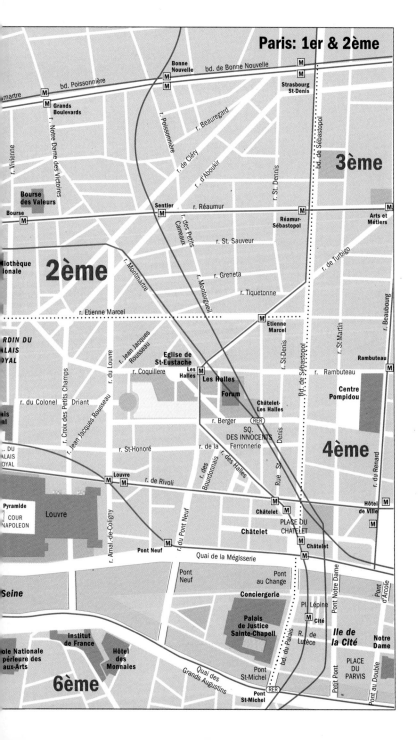

Paris: 1er & 2ème

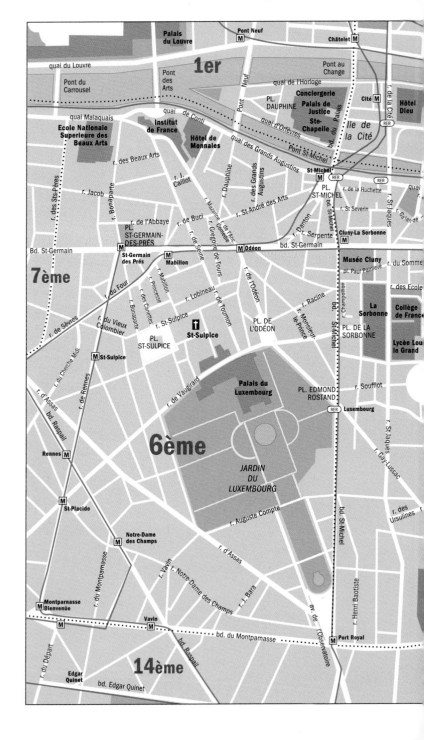

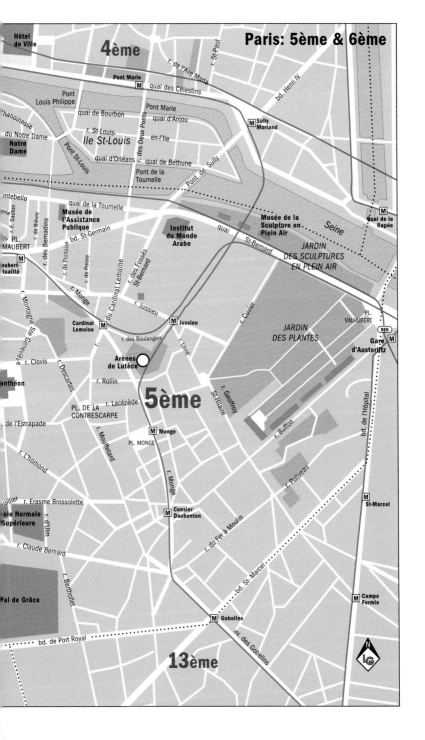

Paris: 5ème & 6ème

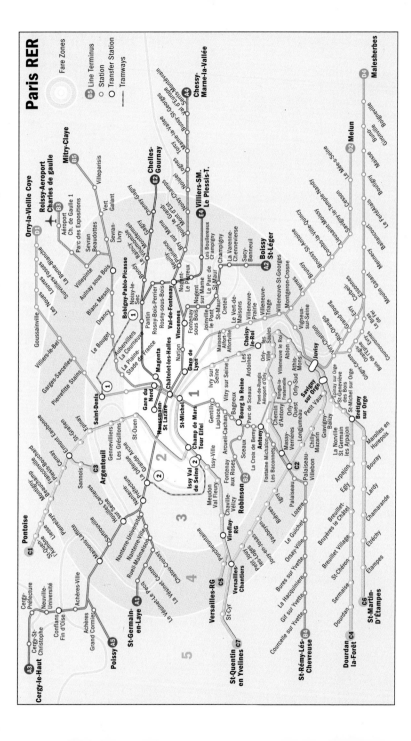

Paris RER

LET'S GO

■ THE RESOURCE FOR THE INDEPENDENT TRAVELER

"The guides are aimed not only at young budget travelers but at the indepedent traveler; a sort of streetwise cookbook for traveling alone."

—*The New York Times*

"Unbeatable; good sight-seeing advice; up-to-date info on restaurants, hotels, and inns; a commitment to money-saving travel; and a wry style that brightens nearly every page."

—*The Washington Post*

"Lighthearted and sophisticated, informative and fun to read. [Let's Go] helps the novice traveler navigate like a knowledgeable old hand."

—*Atlanta Journal-Constitution*

"A world-wise traveling companion—always ready with friendly advice and helpful hints, all sprinkled with a bit of wit."

—*The Philadelphia Inquirer*

■ THE BEST TRAVEL BARGAINS IN YOUR PRICE RANGE

"All the dirt, dirt cheap."

—*People*

"Anything you need to know about budget traveling is detailed in this book."

—*The Chicago Sun-Times*

"Let's Go follows the creed that you don't have to toss your life's savings to the wind to travel—unless you want to."

—*The Salt Lake Tribune*

■ REAL ADVICE FOR REAL EXPERIENCES

"The writers seem to have experienced every rooster-packed bus and lunar-surfaced mattress about which they write."

—*The New York Times*

"A guide should tell you what to expect from a destination. Here Let's Go shines."

—*The Chicago Tribune*

"[Let's Go's] devoted updaters really walk the walk (and thumb the ride, and trek the trail). Learn how to fish, haggle, find work—anywhere."

—*Food & Wine*

LET'S GO PUBLICATIONS

TRAVEL GUIDES
Alaska 1st edition **NEW TITLE**
Australia 2004
Austria & Switzerland 2004
Brazil 1st edition **NEW TITLE**
Britain & Ireland 2004
California 2004
Central America 8th edition
Chile 1st edition
China 4th edition
Costa Rica 1st edition
Eastern Europe 2004
Egypt 2nd edition
Europe 2004
France 2004
Germany 2004
Greece 2004
Hawaii 2004
India & Nepal 8th edition
Ireland 2004
Israel 4th edition
Italy 2004
Japan 1st edition **NEW TITLE**
Mexico 20th edition
Middle East 4th edition
New Zealand 6th edition
Pacific Northwest 1st edition **NEW TITLE**
Peru, Ecuador & Bolivia 3rd edition
Puerto Rico 1st edition **NEW TITLE**
South Africa 5th edition
Southeast Asia 8th edition
Southwest USA 3rd edition
Spain & Portugal 2004
Thailand 1st edition
Turkey 5th edition
USA 2004
Western Europe 2004

CITY GUIDES
Amsterdam 3rd edition
Barcelona 3rd edition
Boston 4th edition
London 2004
New York City 2004
Paris 2004
Rome 12th edition
San Francisco 4th edition
Washington, D.C. 13th edition

MAP GUIDES
Amsterdam
Berlin
Boston
Chicago
Dublin
Florence
Hong Kong
London
Los Angeles
Madrid
New Orleans
New York City
Paris
Prague
Rome
San Francisco
Seattle
Sydney
Venice
Washington, D.C.

COMING SOON:
Road Trip USA

LET'S GO

FRANCE

2004

BRIANA CUMMINGS EDITOR
TIM CAITO ASSOCIATE EDITOR
EMILY PORTER ASSOCIATE EDITOR

RESEARCHER-WRITERS
GILMARA AYALA
MARIT DEWHURST
ROBERT HODGSON
IAN MACKENZIE
ROBIN MCNAMARA
PRIYA MEHTA
SARAH SELTZER

TZU-HUAN LO MAP EDITOR
SARAH ROBINSON MANAGING EDITOR

MACMILLAN

HELPING LET'S GO If you want to share your discoveries, suggestions, or corrections, please drop us a line. We read every piece of correspondence, whether a postcard, a 10-page email, or a coconut. **Address mail to:**

Let's Go: France
67 Mount Auburn Street
Cambridge, MA 02138
USA

Visit Let's Go at **http://www.letsgo.com,** or send email to:

feedback@letsgo.com
Subject: "Let's Go: France"

In addition to the invaluable travel advice our readers share with us, many are kind enough to offer their services as researchers or editors. Unfortunately, our charter enables us to employ only currently enrolled Harvard students.

Published in Great Britain 2004 by Macmillan, an imprint of Pan Macmillan Ltd.
20 New Wharf Road, London N1 9RR
Basingstoke and Oxford
Associated companies throughout the world
www.panmacmillan.com

Maps by David Lindroth copyright © 2004 by St. Martin's Press.

Published in the United States of America by St. Martin's Press.

ISBN:1 4050 3304 5
First edition
10 9 8 7 6 5 4 3 2 1

Let's Go: France is written by Let's Go Publications, 67 Mount Auburn Street, Cambridge, MA 02138, USA.

Let's Go® and the LG logo are trademarks of Let's Go, Inc.
Printed in the USA.

HOW TO USE THIS BOOK

ORGANIZATION. This book is divided into 17 regions, which generally correspond to French governmental divisions and local identities. Our coverage begins in Paris and the Ile-de-France, moving up to the northeast coast and sweeping south through the country. The introduction to each region outlines its major areas of interest and gives a brief summary of the region's history and cuisine.

PRICE RANGES & RANKINGS. Our researchers list establishments in order of value, starting with the best. Our absolute favorites are denoted by the *Let's Go* thumbs-up (🖐). Since the best value does not always mean the cheapest price, we have incorporated a system of price ranges in the guide. The table below lists how prices fall within each bracket.

FRANCE	❶	❷	❸	❹	❺
ACCOMM.	€1-15	€16-25	€26-35	€36-55	€56-100
FOOD	€1-6	€7-10	€11-15	€16-25	€26-50

WHEN TO USE IT

TWO MONTHS BEFORE. The first chapter, **Discover France,** contains highlights of the region, including **Suggested Itineraries** (p. 5) that can help you plan your trip. For itineraries farther off the beaten path, check out the **Alternatives to Tourism** chapter, with listings for schools, volunteer activities, and teaching opportunities in France. The **Essentials** (p. 8) chapter has practical information on arranging transportation, planning a budget, making reservations, and renewing a passport.

ONE MONTH BEFORE. Take care of insurance. Make a list of packing essentials (see **Packing,** p. 22) and shop for anything you are missing. Read through the coverage and make sure you understand the logistics of your itinerary (catching trains, ferries, and buses). Make reservations if necessary.

TWO WEEKS BEFORE. Leave an itinerary and a photocopy of important documents with someone at home. Take some time to peruse the **Life and Times** section (p. 69), which has info on history, the arts, recent political events, and cuisine.

ON THE ROAD. The **Appendix** contains a French glossary, a temperature chart, and a measurement converter. As you wait to catch your train, take a cultural crash course with one of our in-depth articles on French regionalism (p. 77) and urban development in Paris (p. 133), and check out our exclusive interviews with locals—from a monk in Mont-St-Michel (p. 228) to France's premier chef (p. 442). Now, grab your travel journal and hit the road!

A NOTE TO OUR READERS The information for this book was gathered by *Let's Go* researchers from May through August of 2003. Each listing is based on one researcher's opinion, formed during his or her visit at a particular time. Those traveling at other times may have different experiences since prices, dates, hours, and conditions are always subject to change. You are urged to check the facts presented in this book beforehand to avoid inconvenience and surprises.

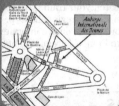

CONTENTS

PRICE RANGES >> FRANCE

Our researchers list establishments in order of value, starting with the best; our favorites get the *Let's Go* 🖒thumbs-up. Since the best value is not always the cheapest price, we have a system of price ranges for quick reference, based on a rough expectation of what you will spend. For **accommodations**, it's based on the cheapest price a solo can pay for one night. For **restaurants** and other dining establishments, we estimate the cost of a meal. The table below gives an idea of what one will typically find in France in the corresponding price range. Numbers are assigned based on actual cost, not value or prices relative to those of similar establishments. Thus, a very expensive *crêperie* may still only be a ❶.

ACCOMMODATIONS	RANGE	WHAT YOU'RE *LIKELY* TO FIND
❶	under €15	Camping; most dorm rooms, such as HI or other hostels or university dorm rooms. Expect bunk beds and a communal bath; you may have to provide or rent towels and sheets.
❷	€16-25	Upper-end hostels or small hotels. You may have a private bathroom, but most likely there will be a sink in your room and communal shower in the hall.
❸	€26-35	A small room with a private bath and some amenities, such as phone and TV. Breakfast may be included in the price of the room. Prices uniformly higher on the Côte d'Azur and in Corsica.
❹	€36-55	You'll have more amenities or be in a more touristed area. You'll usually have TV, A/C, phone, shower, and toilet.
❺	above €55	Large hotels or upscale chains. If it's a ❺ and it doesn't have the perks you want, you've paid too much.

FOOD	RANGE	WHAT YOU'RE *LIKELY* TO FIND
❶	under €7	Street-corner stands, *sandwicheries*, *crêperies*, bakery *quiches* or fast-food joints. Rarely ever a sit-down meal.
❷	€7-10	Sandwiches, appetizers at a bar, or low-priced entrees. You may have the option to sit down or take out.
❸	€11-15	Mid-priced entrees, possibly coming with a soup or salad, and some *prix-fixe menus*. Tip'll bump you up a couple dollars, since you'll probably have a waiter or waitress.
❹	€16-25	Somewhat fancier, usually because of amazing French sauces. Expect large portions or multiple courses for this price range, or you've paid too much. Tip is usually *compris*.
❺	above €25	High cuisine and a decent wine list. Slacks and dress shirts may be expected. Don't order PB&J.

RESEARCHER-WRITERS

Gilmara Ayala   *Loire Valley, Dordogne, Périgord, Poitou-Charentes*

Exhibiting Texan style and stoicism, this former ROTC cadet deftly handled sweltering bike rides between the châteaux of the Loire and treks through the prehistoric caves of Périgord without ever breaking a nail. A one-time designer of wedding cakes, Gilmara had dreams of becoming a French pastry chef—until her taste of France's other major culinary contribution changed her mind. She now wants to work for a vineyard.

Marit Dewhurst   *Provence, Massif Central, Berry-Limousin*

With a jar of Nutella by her side and chèvre on the dinner horizon, Marit couldn't have been happier driving through the small towns of Provence. She always pushed herself to find the perfect restaurant or hotel, adding several North African and Middle Eastern treasures. Ebullient and persistent, she managed to nab an interview with the Queen of Arles and treat herself to a spa in the Auvergne, reporting everything in funny—and extremely thorough— accounts.

Robert Hodgson   *Alsace-Lorraine, Champagne, Flanders, Burgundy*

From the northern reaches of France to the land of bubbly itself, this indomitable young researcher rarely found a place he didn't like, and endured raucous German school groups in Alsace and hordes of British tourists on the coast of Flanders with unshakable calm. Used to entertaining people from the stage, Bobby proved his skill to amuse through a different medium, sending back an endless supply of humorous observations from his travels.

Ian MacKenzie   *Brittany, Normandy*

A veteran of *Let's Go: Amsterdam*, this brooding writer was in his element among the misty isles and forests of fiercely Celtic Brittany. After touring the D-Day landing beaches and Holocaust memorials in Normandy for *Let's Go*, he went on to Poland to do research for his first novel, which is set during World War II. When not tearing through northwest France with his trenchant wit, he managed to charm a few cute French girls.

Robin McNamara   *Languedoc, Aquitaine, Pays Basque, Côte d'Azur*

The Côte d'Azur is like a second home to Robin, but this freshman lacrosse player took on the challenge of covering France's other major coast for *Let's Go*. From La Rochelle to Biarritz, she braved hostel room break-ins, midnight hitched rides amid transportation strikes, and near-constant harassment from the overly amorous men of southwestern France, handling it all with grace and finesse. No distance was too great to walk, no hotel owner too rude to question.

Priya Mehta *Côte d'Azur*

Despite many a late night, Priya beat off drunken men to send back beautiful coverage of the Côte d'Azur and the rugged island of Corsica. In the spirit of adventure and in the name of thorough research, she hopped motorcycle rides along clifftops overlooking the sparkling Mediterranean, attended a party with a pair of French celebrities, and found herself applauded by twenty-five celebrating young men in Nice.

Sarah Seltzer *Burgundy, Alps, Languedoc-Roussillon*

A New Yorker through and through, Sarah beefed up our coverage of trendy wine bars and bohemian hangouts and lived it up biking through the vineyards of Burgundy, hiking through the French Alps, and rambling through the streets of Toulouse. She eagerly quizzed locals on current hotspots, snapped photos of everything along the way, and succeeded in nabbing more than a few free glasses of wine from some of her many new-found friends.

William Lee Adams *Paris*

Neasa Coll *Paris*

Brendan McGeever *Paris*

Abigail K. Joseph *Editor, Let's Go: Paris*

Megan Moran-Gates *Associate Editor, Let's Go: Paris*

CONTRIBUTING WRITERS

Matthew Lazen spent two years in Brittany and Alsace on a Chateaubriand Fellowship for dissertation research on regional cultures in modern France. He is currently revising his dissertation for publication and organizing a conference on post-WWII French regionalism at Harvard University.

Charlotte Houghteling has worked on Let's Go's *Middle East*, *Egypt*, and *Israel* titles. She wrote her senior thesis on the development of department stores during the Second Empire and will complete her M.Phil at Cambridge on the consumer society of Revolutionary Paris.

Sarah Houghteling was a researcher-writer for *Let's Go: France 1999*. She taught at the American School in Paris for a year. Now a graduate student in creative writing at the University of Michigan, she is currently in Paris researching Nazi art theft during World War II.

ABOUT LET'S GO

GUIDES FOR THE INDEPENDENT TRAVELER

Budget travel is more than a vacation. At *Let's Go*, we see every trip as the chance of a lifetime. If your dream is to grab a knapsack and a machete and forge through the jungles of Brazil, we can take you there. Or, if you'd rather enjoy the Riviera sun at a beachside cafe, we'll set you a table. If you know what you're doing, you can have any experience you want—whether it's camping among lions or sampling Tuscan desserts—without maxing out your credit card. We'll show you just how far your coins can go, and prove that the greatest limitation on your adventure is not your wallet, but your imagination. That said, we understand that you may want the occasional indulgence after a week of hostels and kebab stands, so we've added "Big Splurges" to let you know which establishments are worth those extra euros, as well as price ranges to help you quickly determine whether an accommodation or restaurant will break the bank. While we may have diversified, our emphasis will always be on finding the best values for your budget, giving you all the info you need to spend six days in London or six months in Tasmania.

BEYOND THE TOURIST EXPERIENCE

We write for travelers who know there's more to a vacation than riding double-deckers with tourists. Our researchers give you the heads-up on both world-renowned and lesser-known attractions, on the best local eats and the hottest nightclub beats. In our travels, we talk to everybody; we provide a snapshot of real life in the places you visit with our sidebars on topics like regional cuisine, local festivals, and hot political issues. We've opened our pages to respected writers and scholars to show you their take on a given destination, and turned to lifelong residents to learn the little things that make their city worth calling home. And we've even given you Alternatives to Tourism—ideas for how to give back to local communities through responsible travel and volunteering.

OVER FORTY YEARS OF WISDOM

When we started, way back in 1960, Let's Go consisted of a small group of well-traveled friends who compiled their budget travel tips into a 20-page packet for students on charter flights to Europe. Since then, we've expanded to suit all kinds of travelers, now publishing guides to six continents, including our newest guides: *Let's Go: Japan* and *Let's Go: Brazil*. Our guides are still annually researched and written entirely by students on shoe-string budgets, adventurous travelers who know that train strikes, stolen luggage, food poisoning, and marriage proposals are all part of a day's work. Even as you read this, work on next year's editions is well underway. Whether you're reading one of our new titles, like *Let's Go: Puerto Rico* or *Let's Go Adventure Guide: Alaska*, or our original best-seller, *Let's Go: Europe*, you'll find the same spirit of adventure that has made *Let's Go* the guide of choice for travelers the world over since 1960.

GETTING IN TOUCH

The best discoveries are often those you make yourself; on the road, when you find something worth sharing, please drop us a line. We're Let's Go Publications, 67 Mt. Auburn St., Cambridge, MA 02138, USA (feedback@letsgo.com).

For more info, visit our website: www.letsgo.com.

ACKNOWLEDGMENTS

Team France thanks: Our truly amazing researchers, Scrobins for stellar managing, Abigail for super crunching, Dusty, Jeff, Tom, and Peyton, the Axis pod for entertaining poetry readings, SPAM for pizza, the Europe peeps for keeping us company at night, Tzu-Huan and the rest of the mapping team, and Jan Ziolkowski.

Briana thanks: Tim and Emily for constantly blowing me away with their work, Scrobs for sarcasm and unexpected photos and cookies, Matty for his smiles and the "mime features" that kept me sane, Christine for bagels, Dunia for the kittens and Sex in the City, Teri, Leslie and Josh for feeding me, the whole C-entry crew for giving me something to look forward to every day, and my wonderful family.

Tim thanks: Brie, Emily, and Scrobins for making it through the summer and for always keeping me laughing despite the pressure. Abigail, Dan, Mike, and Oussama for not getting evicted, and Dane Street in general for existing after late nights at the office. Blake, Jason, and Will, without whom I can't imagine the last four years. Emily and Jess for the (final) night trip to Walden. Sarah for her expert fajita advice, and Catherine for many late-night calls. My family, for supporting me and for being first in line at the bookstore the day that this baby is published.

Emily thanks: Brie for your sweetness and for being the most amazing editor; Tim for your enduring cheer; Sarah for always brightening my day; Mom, Daddy, and Adam for their love and everything else important; Teri for our breakfast at Johnny's; Dunia, Matty, Maya, and Molly for being breaths of fresh air; Joy for our Southern belle-ness and raining on our own parade; Team Italy for spicing up the workdays; my girls, the DGs, and all my friends for all the pictures so far and all the ones to come.

Tzu-Huan thanks: Special thanks to Brie and Tim for invaluable assistance in this massive undertaking, the accented French language for increasing my risk of RSI, and Brian and Christine of mapland for proofing at the last minute. A.M.D.G.

LET'S GO

Publishing Director
Julie A. Stephens
Editor-in-Chief
Jeffrey Dubner
Production Manager
Dusty Lewis
Cartography Manager
Nathaniel Brooks
Design Manager
Caleb Beyers
Editorial Managers
Lauren Bonner, Ariel Fox,
Matthew K. Hudson, Emma Nothmann,
Joanna Shawn Brigid O'Leary,
Sarah Robinson
Financial Manager
Suzanne Siu
Marketing & Publicity Managers
Megan Brumagim, Nitin Shah
Personnel Manager
Jesse Reid Andrews
Researcher Manager
Jennifer O'Brien
Web Manager
Jesse Tov
Web Content Director
Abigail Burger
Production Associates
Thomas Bechtold, Jeffrey Hoffman Yip
IT Directors
Travis Good, E. Peyton Sherwood
Financial Assistant
R. Kirkie Maswoswe
Associate Web Manager
Robert Dubbin
Office Coordinators
Abigail Burger, Angelina L. Fryer,
Liz Glynn

Director of Advertising Sales
Daniel Ramsey
Senior Advertising Associates
Sara Barnett, Daniella Boston
Advertising Artwork Editors
Julia Davidson, Sandy Liu

President
Abhishek Gupta
General Manager
Robert B. Rombauer
Assistant General Manager
Anne E. Chisholm

Editor Briana Cummings
Associate Editors Timothy Caito, Emily Porter
Map Editor Tzu-Huan Lo
Managing Editor Sarah Robinson
Typesetter Ankur Ghosh

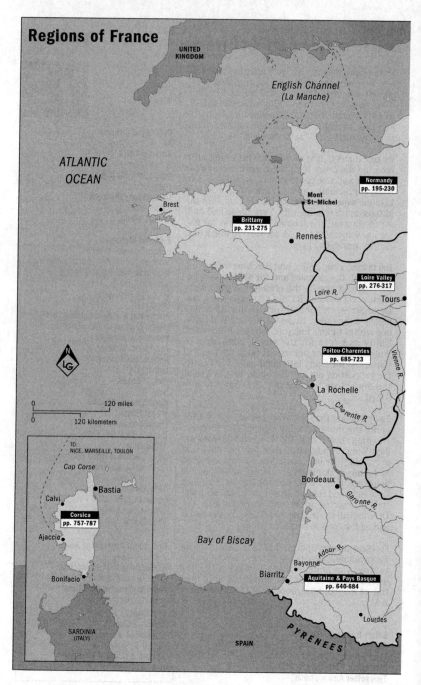

Regions of France

UNITED KINGDOM

English Channel (La Manche)

ATLANTIC OCEAN

Normandy
pp. 195-230

Mont St-Michel

Brest

Brittany
pp. 231-275

Rennes

Loire Valley
pp. 276-317

Loire R.

Tours

Poitou-Charentes
pp. 685-723

Vienne R.

La Rochelle

Charente R

Bordeaux

Garonne R.

Bay of Biscay

Adour R.

Bayonne

Biarritz

Aquitaine & Pays Basque
pp. 640-684

Lourdes

PYRENEES

SPAIN

120 miles

120 kilometers

TO: NICE, MARSEILLE, TOULON

Cap Corse

Bastia

Calvi

Corsica
pp. 757-787

Ajaccio

Bonifacio

SARDINIA (ITALY)

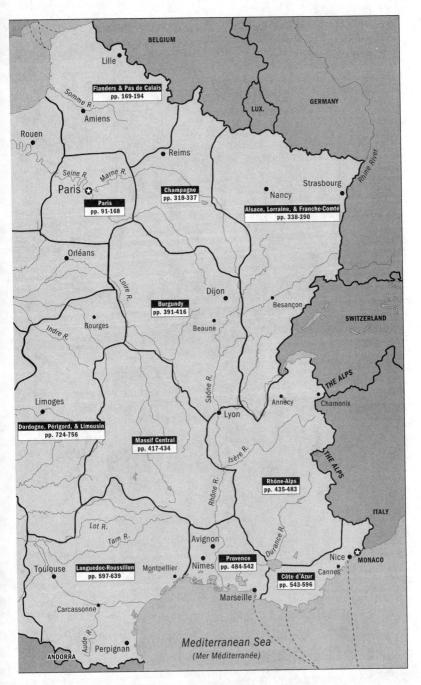

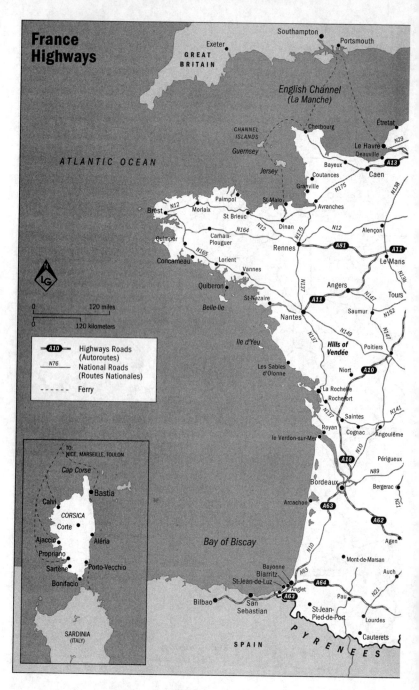

France Highways

GREAT BRITAIN

Exeter

Southampton   Portsmouth

English Channel
(La Manche)

CHANNEL ISLANDS

Cherbourg   Étretat

Guernsey   Le Havre   N29
Deauville   A13

ATLANTIC OCEAN

Jersey   Bayeux   Caen

Coutances   N175   N138

Granville   Alençon

Paimpol   St-Malo   Avranches   A11

Brest   N12   Morlaix   St Brieuc   Dinan   N175   N12   Le Mans

Quimper   Carhaix-Plouguer   N164   Rennes   A81   Angers   N147   Tours   N38

Concameau   N165   Lorient   Vannes   N137   A11   Saumur   N152

Quiberon   St-Nazaire   Angers   N149   Poitiers   N147

Belle-Ile   Nantes   Hills of Vendée

Ile d'Yeu   N137

N
LG

0 ———— 120 miles
0 ———— 120 kilometers

A10 —— Highways Roads
(Autoroutes)

N76 —— National Roads
(Routes Nationales)

------ Ferry

Les Sables d'Olonne   Niort   A10

La Rochelle
Rochefort   N141

Saintes

Royan   Cognac   Angoulême

le Verdon-sur-Mer   N137

A10   Périgueux

N89   Bergerac   N21

TO:
NICE, MARSEILLE, TOULON

Cap Corse   Bordeaux

Bastia   A63

Calvi   Arcachon   A62

CORSICA   Corte   N10   Agen

Ajaccio   Aléria   Bay of Biscay   Mont-de-Marsan   Auch

Propriano   Sartène   Porto-Vecchio   Bayonne   A63   N21

Bonifacio   Biarritz   Anglet   A64   Pau
St-Jean-de-Luz   A63   Lourdes

SARDINIA
(ITALY)   Bilbao   San
Sebastian   St-Jean-Pied-de-Port   Cauterets

SPAIN   P Y R E N E E S

XVI

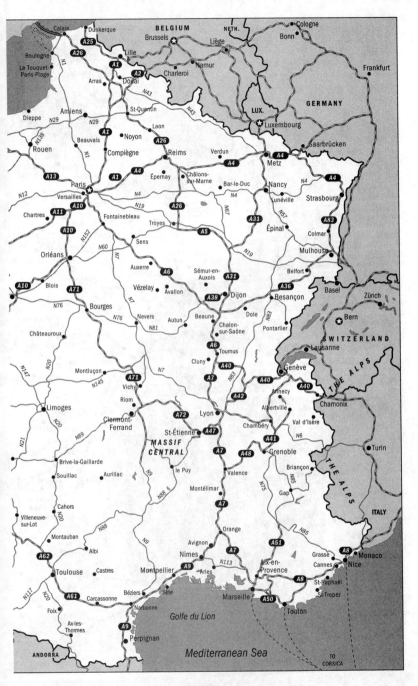

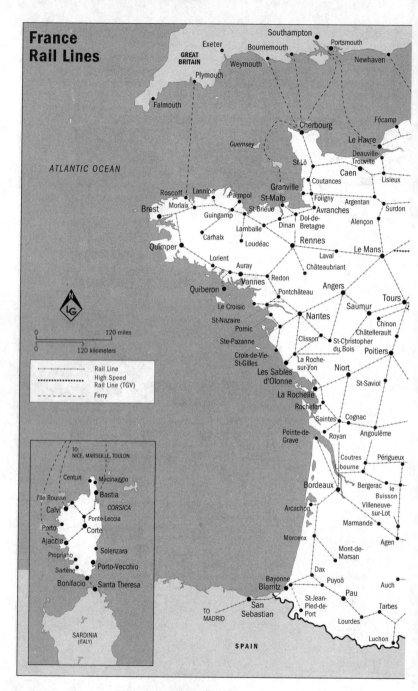

France Rail Lines

GREAT BRITAIN

Exeter
Southampton
Bournemouth
Portsmouth
Weymouth
Newhaven
Plymouth

Falmouth

Fécamp

Cherbourg
Le Havre

ATLANTIC OCEAN

Guernsey
St-Lô
Deauville-Trouville
Caen
Lisieux

Roscoff
Lannion
Paimpol
Granville
St-Malo
Coutances
Foligny
Argentan
Surdon

Brest
Morlaix
St-Brieuc
Avranches
Alençon

Guingamp
Dol-de-Bretagne
Dinan

Quimper
Carhaix
Lamballe
Loudéac
Rennes
Laval
Le Mans

Lorient
Auray
Châteaubriant

Quiberon
Vannes
Redon
Angers
Tours

Le Croisic
Pontchâteau
Saumur

St-Nazaire
Nantes
Chinon

Pornic
Clisson
Châtellerault

Ste-Pazanne
St-Christopher du Bois
Poitiers

Croix-de-Vie-St-Gilles
La Roche-sur-Yon
Niort

Les Sables d'Olonne
St-Saviol

La Rochelle
Rochefort
Cognac

Saintes
Angoulême

Pointe-de-Grave
Royan

Coutras
Périgueux

Libourne

Bordeaux
Bergerac
le Buisson

Arcachon
Villeneuve-sur-Lot

Morcenx
Marmande
Agen

Mont-de-Marsan

Dax
Puyoô
Auch

Bayonne
Pau
Tarbes

Biarritz

St-Jean-Pied-de-Port
Lourdes
Luchon

San Sebastian

SPAIN

TO MADRID

Legend

	Rail Line
	High Speed Rail Line (TGV)
	Ferry

120 miles
120 kilometers

Corsica inset

TO: NICE, MARSEILLE, TOULON

Centuri
Macinaggio
l'Ile Rousse
Bastia
Calvi
CORSICA
Porto
Ponte-Leccia
Corte
Ajaccio
Solenzara
Propriano
Porto-Vecchio
Sartène
Bonifacio
Santa Theresa

SARDINIA (ITALY)

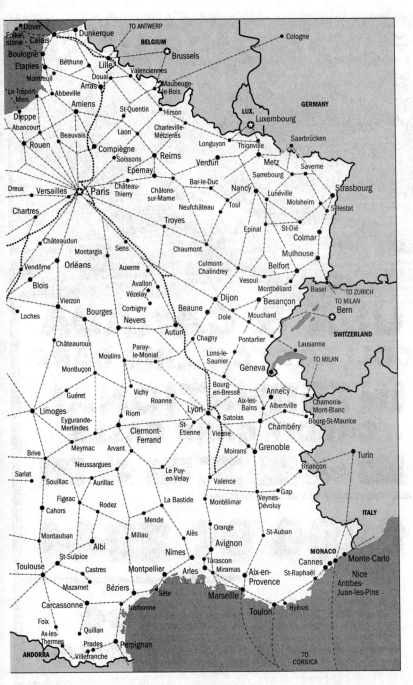

XIX

DISCOVER
FRANCE

With the grandest art museums, exorbitant châteaux, and many other vestiges of aristocracy, France arguably remains the cultural capital of the world. It is especially in the smaller details of life, however, that the French reign supreme. France has always been a magnet for artists, but visitors of all kinds find the slow and sensuous French lifestyle irresistible. From their pungent cheeses to their elaborate fashions, the French have that certain *je ne sais quoi*. It makes their pastries impossibly intricate, their cuisine exquisite, their craftsmanship impeccable, and their wines divine. You might experience it as you watch a fierce, high-stakes game of *pétanque* in a Provençal village or eavesdrop on the low conversation of the elegant Parisian couple beside you at a bistro; or it might come to you in a single impression as you bite into a warm chocolate croissant at dawn after a night of clubbing in Lille or as you haggle for the perfect piece of *batik* in a North African market in Marseille.

Part of the secret of France's success in living *la vie douce* is its strong adherence to tradition—a way of life that is nicely complemented by the centuries-old farms and churches and labyrinthine medieval streets that characterize much of its landscape. Equally well preserved is the incomparable beauty of the French countryside, from the misty islands off the coast of Brittany and lush vines amidst the sleepy towns of Alsace to the dazzling turquoise beaches of the Riviera and the fields of lavender and poppies in Provence. From countless sandy shores and craggy Alpine cliffs that cater to everyone from beachbums to thrill-seeking adventurers, France has something for everyone.

FACTS & FIGURES

OFFICIAL NAME: République Française

POPULATION: 60,100,000

CAPITAL: Paris

GDP PER CAPITA: US$24,400

PRESIDENT: Jacques Chirac

MAJOR RELIGIONS: 90% Catholic, 3% Muslim, 2% Protestant, 1% Jewish

AVERAGE LIFE EXPECTANCY: 78.9 years

LITERACY RATE: 99% of those over 15

WINE PRODUCED PER YEAR: Equivalent to 1927 Olympic-size pools.

BAGUETTES CONSUMED PER YEAR: Laid end-to-end, they would span the Earth's circumference 1.14 times.

ESTIMATED NUMBER OF ROMANTIC ENCOUNTERS PER DAY: 4,959,476 in Paris alone. *Ah, l'amour!*

WHEN TO GO

In July, Paris starts to shrink; in August, it positively shrivels. The city in August is devoid of Parisians, animated only by tourists and the pickpockets who love them. At the same time, the French themselves hop over to the Norman coast, swell the beaches of the western Atlantic coast from La Rochelle down to Biarritz, and move along the shores of rocky Corsica. From June to September, the Côte d'Azur becomes one long tangle of halter-topped, khaki-shorted anglophones; a constant, exhausting party. Early summer and autumn are the best times to visit Paris, while winter there can be abominable, presided over by a terrible *grisaille*—chill "grayness." The north and west of France are prone to wet but mild winters and springs, while summers are warm but undependable. The center and east of the country have a more continental climate, with harsh winters and long, dry summers; these are also generally the least crowded and most unspoiled regions. During the winter, the Alps provide some of the best skiing in the world, while the Pyrénées offer a calmer, if less climatically dependable, alternative.

As a general rule, the farther south you travel in the summer, the more crucial hotel reservations become. Reserve a month in advance for the Côte d'Azur, Corsica, Provence, Languedoc, and the Pays Basque.

THINGS TO DO

WHERE ALL THE LIGHTS ARE BRIGHT

While **Paris** (p. 91) is one of the world's great cities, you'll find plenty to do in France's major regional centers. **Lyon** (p. 417), France's second city, has had a reputation for staid *bourgeoisie*, but today it provides non-stop action and France's best cuisine. In **Marseille's** (p. 484) 2600-year history, this multicultural working city has never failed to make itself heard. **Nice** (p. 545) is a party town packed with museums, and only a pebble's throw from the rest of the sandy Côte d'Azur. With a hybrid Franco-German culture, **Strasbourg** (p. 354) is the obvious home for the European Parliament. In Brittany, **Rennes** (p. 231) mixes a medieval *vieille ville* and major museums with frenzied party kids. In the southwest, sophisticated **Montpellier** (p. 630) is the gay capital of France, while rosy **Toulouse** (p. 597) holds Languedoc together with student-filled nightlife and modern art.

ONCE UPON A TIME...

French châteaux range from imposing feudal ruins to the well-preserved country homes of 19th-century industrialists. The greatest variety and concentration is found in the **Loire Valley** (p. 276), where the defensive hilltop fortresses of **Chinon** (p. 297) and **Saumur** (p. 302) contrast with the Renaissance grace of **Chenonceau** (p. 299) and **Chambord** (p. 288). **Ussé** (p. 301) inspired Charles Perrault to pen "Sleeping Beauty," and **Villandry** (p. 300) has been called "the most beautiful garden of the garden that is France."

The Loire has no monopoly on châteaux, however. Right near Paris you can find a tribute to the great "Sun King" Louis XIV's even greater ego at **Versailles** (p. 157), and the masterpiece that inspired it at **Vaux-le-Vicomte** (p. 164). In Provence, you'll be hard-pressed to decide whether the Palais des Papes in **Avignon** (p. 504) is a castle or a palace, while nearby the craggy ruins of **Les Baux** (p. 526) will take you back to the age of chivalry. Perhaps the most impressive château is the fortress of **Carcassonne** (p. 609), a medieval citadel which still stands guard over the Languedoc. If you prefer smaller, less-touristed castles, head to the **Route Jacques Cœur** near **Bourges** (p. 730).

Paris's **Notre Dame** (p. 123) is the most famous Church building in France, but a more exquisite Gothic jewel is the nearby **Sainte-Chapelle** (p. 124). The Gothic style of architecture first reached maturity in the majestic cathedral at **Chartres** (p. 161), while several other medieval masterpieces await at **Strasbourg** (p. 354) and **Reims** (p. 318). A more modern sensibility animates Le Corbusier's post-war masterpiece at **Ronchamp** (p. 376).

AU NATUREL

Everyone's heard about the **Alps,** where some of the best hiking and skiing in the world can be found around **Val d'Isère** (p. 477) and **Chamonix** (p. 468). But the Alps are just one of France's four major mountain ranges. To the north, you'll find the rolling **Jura** mountains (p. 384) in Franche-Comté, while **Le Mont-Dore** (p. 423), in the **Massif Central,** provides spectacular hiking near extinct volcanoes. To the southwest, you can climb into Spain from the western **Pyrénées** (p. 667). If snow-capped peaks aren't your thing, lowland pleasures can be found exploring the flamingo-filled plains of the **Camargue** (p. 530). For advanced hikers, it's possible to trek the length of rugged **Corsica's** interior (p. 757), but those less advanced can find great day and overnight hikes everywhere on the island, especially on the **Cap Corse** (p. 782).

LA VIE EN *ROSÉ*

France produces some of the finest wines and inebriants in the world. Start with an apéritif of a champagne cocktail from one of **Reims's** spectacular *caves* (p. 318). To try a little bit of everything, check out the red wines in **Bordeaux** (p. 640) and **Burgundy** (p. 391), or the whites of Alsace's **Route du Vin** (p. 363) and the **Loire Valley** (p. 276). Top it all off with an after-dinner drink—either **Cognac** in the eponymous town (p. 698) or Calvados, made throughout **Normandy** (p. 195).

HERE COMES THE SUN

The Côte d'Azur attracts two types of people—the stars who create its glamor, and the masses who come looking for it. You'll party among the tanned youth of Europe in **Nice** (p. 545) and **Juan-les-Pins** (p. 575). Surfers should head straight for the big rollers of the Atlantic coast in **Anglet** (p. 662). If sun and sand are your only desires, try **Ile Rousse** (p. 772) in Corsica or the dune beaches near **Arcachon** (p. 650). Some of France's most beautiful beaches await in foggy Brittany, at **Belle-Ile** (p. 267) and **St-Malo** (p. 239). Find solitude on the pristine untouched *plages* of **Ile de Ré** and **Ile d'Aix** (p. 711).

FINE FRENCH WARES

Those with the most refined taste decorate their homes with Brittany's *faïence,* brightly painted French porcelain, the bubble glass unique to **Biot** (p. 574), and linen from **Alençon** (p. 316), the lace capital of France. **Strasbourg** (p. 354), the birthplace of the Christmas tree, is a one-stop shopping center for the

TOP TEN LIST

FRANCE'S BEST HIKING

1. Mt. Blanc (p. 476). Only for experienced climbers, the two- or three-day excursion will leave you chilled and speechless.

2. Porto (p. 765). Corsica's rugged hiking paradise is spotted with coastal gorges and grottos for impromptu swimming, as well as wandering pigs.

3. Massif Central (p. 426). Volcanos and several breathtaking waterfalls make the Massif Central a surreal hiking hotspot.

4. Parc National des Pyrénées (p. 680). Mountain trails pass from misty French forests to dessicated Spanish red rock, with opportunities to camp in the clouds.

5. Parc Naturel Régional des Grands Causses (p. 629). Outside Millau, this expansive park, filled with prehistoric art, is a center for hiking, biking, gliding, and rafting.

6. St-Malo (p. 242). Low tides allow strolls or swims to island forts and tombs around this Breton town.

7. The Camargue (p. 530). By safari, horseback, or bike, travelers flock to this marshland and wildlife preserve.

8. Val d'Isère (p. 480). Alpine hikes for all abilities lead past ibexes, *chamois,* and marmots.

9. Cap Corse (p. 782). Secluded beach hikes pass Corsican ruins and precarious mountain chapels.

10. Jura Mountains (p. 384). Older than the Alps, the mild Jura range is perfect for hiking, biking, or skiing.

most charming Christmas decorations of all kinds. For a sample of the highest names in France's haute couture, visit the high-end boutiques in **Nice** (p. 545). Stop by nearby Grasse (p. 583), the capital of the world's perfume industry, where even the notoriously bath-phobic French smell sweet.

LET'S GO PICKS

BEST PLACE TO KISS: Dusk on **Pont Neuf** (p. 125), on Paris's Ile de la Cité.

BEST MUSES: The gorgeous orchards and harbor of **Collioure** (p. 618) inspired Matisse, Dalí, and Picasso. Van Gogh left his heart and his ear in **Arles** (p. 519), where he painted cafés and starry nights. Follow in the footsteps of Cézanne in **Aix-en-Provence** (p. 498).

LONGEST SHOTS: The **bar-o-mètre** in Nice's Tapas la Movida (p. 554); the still-loaded **German artillery** in Longues-sur-Mer (p. 220); your chances at the famous **Monte-Carlo Casino** (p. 563).

BEST INDOOR RAINSHOWERS: Inside the funky **Maison Satie** in Honfleur (p. 207). Each room is a surprise!

BEST EXCUSE FOR DRINKING WINE: The therapeutic waters from Vichy's sulfuric *sources* (p. 434). Don't say we didn't warn you!

BEST ISLANDS: White homes with blue shutters cover idyllic **Ile d'Yeu** (p. 721). Sheep and stone crosses are the main inhabitants of **Ile d'Ouessant** (p. 259). Neither island is larger than a Peugeot.

BEST REASONS FOR WORLD PEACE: Normandy's World War II **D-Day beaches** (p. 217); tiny **Oradour-sur-Glane** (p. 737), untouched since Nazis massacred its entire population; the bones of 130,000 unknown soldiers at the **Ossuaire** outside Verdun (p. 353).

MOST INTRIGUING PALACE: Le **Palais Idéal** in Hauterives (p. 459), assembled stone by stone over 33 years by the local postman, Ferdinand Cheval.

SCARIEST GARGOYLES: Viollet-le-Duc's *chimera* on the **Cathédrale de Notre-Dame** in Paris (p. 123); Front Nationale leader and defeated presidential candidate **Jean-Marie Le Pen** (p. 74).

SUGGESTED ITINERARIES

The following itineraries are designed to give you the highlights of France's distinct regions, from its cosmopolitan hubs to its sleepy villages. While these itineraries are intended for those who haven't traveled around France very much, even initiated Francophiles can use them as a template for additional daytrips and excursions. There are many Frances, however, and these are not the only ones; in fact, we've left out more than half the country. For more ideas, see "Other Trips," below, or the regional chapter introductions.

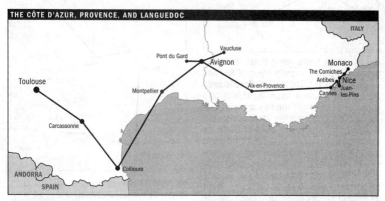

THE CÔTE D'AZUR, PROVENCE, AND LANGUEDOC

COTE D'AZUR, PROVENCE, & LANGUEDOC (3 WEEKS)

Visit the Côte d'Azur for beaches and glamor, inland Provence for scented fields and sun-drenched villages, and Languedoc for orchards and crumbling monuments. **Nice** is the unofficial capital of the Côte d'Azur, a nonstop anglophone beach party with more beaches, nightlife, and budget housing than you can shake a glowstick at (2 days; p. 545). Don't neglect the nearby clifftop villages of the **Corniches** (2 days; p. 556). If you have any money left, you'll want to daytrip east to the micro-state of **Monaco,** which is absolutely the richest place on the Riviera (1 day; p. 559). Twin towns **Antibes** and **Juan-les-Pins** have enough beauty and nightlife for ten towns; don't miss them (1 day; p. 569). **Cannes,** home to the famous and exclusive film festival, is star-packed all year round, and has some of the cheapest housing on the coast (1 day; p. 577). **Aix-en-Provence** is a slow Provençal city full of fountains, twisty streets, and Cézanne paintings (2 days; p. 498). **Avignon,** city of Popes, hosts a yearly drama festival (2 days; p. 504). It's also the closest city to the lovely **Vaucluse,** a group of sleepy, ruin-dotted, quintessen-

tially Provençal little towns, and the Roman aqueduct, **Pont du Gard** (2 days; p. 513 and p. 504). **Montpellier** is a city with intellectual and cultural sophistication and unbeatable gay nightlife (3 days; p. 630). Tiny **Collioure,** sandwiched between the Pyrénées and the Mediterranean, is a paradise of vineyards and orchards (1 day; p. 618). Brave the hordes of tourists to climb the ancient ramparts of **Carcassonne** (1 day; p. 609), and top it all off in **Toulouse,** the pink-bricked capital of the southwest (3 days; p. 597).

LOIRE VALLEY, BRITTANY, & NORMANDY (2 WEEKS)

The northeast has it all: from vibrant student cities to isolated rugged coasts, from the monastic austerity of Mont St-Michel to the monarchial decadence of the Loire châteaux. **Blois** houses one of France's most famous châteaux and serves as a base for the magnificent many-chimneyed **Chambord** (2 days; p. 284). The bustling, student-filled **Tours** serves as a daytrip hub for the medieval town of **Chinon** and the graceful lines of the river-spanning Renaissance chateau of **Chenonceau** (2 days; p. 292).

DISCOVER

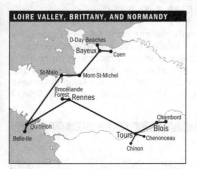

LOIRE VALLEY, BRITTANY, AND NORMANDY

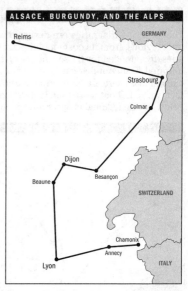

ALSACE, BURGUNDY, AND THE ALPS

Check out all the student hotspots in the bustling Breton university town of **Rennes** (3 days; p. 231). The nearby **Brocéliande forest,** the ancient haunt of Merlin and Guinevere, is one of Brittany's most legend-steeped sites. Just off the Western coast of Brittany, the windswept cliffs of **Belle Ile** (reached by ferry from mainland **Quiberon**) set the scene for a perfect day-long bike ride (2 days; p. 267). Soak your tired muscles at the sandy beaches of the seaside resort town **St-Malo** (1 day; p. 239). **Mont St-Michel** simply can't be missed for the breathtaking view of sunlight on the monastery's stark walls (1 day; p. 226). Visit **Bayeux,** home of the 1000-year-old tapestry that recounts William the Conqueror's invasion of England, then head to the **D-Day beaches,** which memorialize the events of 1944 with striking honesty (2 days; p. 214). Another springboard for many of the D-Day beaches, **Caen** holds a wealth of fascinating museums (1 day; p. 208).

ALSACE, BURGUNDY, & THE ALPS (2 WEEKS)

Spanning from the gentle Vosges mountains to the peak of Mont Blanc, France's eastern border is the perfect destination for history buffs, nature enthusiasts, and wine connoisseurs alike. While **Reims's** architectural claim to fame is its immense medieval cathedral, no traveller will want to miss a light-headed tour of the city's palatial *maisons de champagne* (2 days; p. 318). **Strasbourg** is a cosmopolitan center of Alsatian culture, and serves as the hub for the tiny villages amidst the vineyards of the *Route du Vin* (3 days; p. 354). **Colmar** stands at the heart of the Route with pastel half-timbered houses and an exquisite

museum (1 day; p. 368). Bustling student center **Besançon** entertains a diverse international crowd with several interesting museums and a hopping nightlife (2 days; p. 378). Fill up on *boeuf bourgignon* and scrutinize the winning wines of the Cote d'Or in the city of **Dijon,** and glimpse glazed-tile roofs in nearby **Beaune** (3 days; p. 398). **Lyon** serves up world-class cuisine in a capital city second only to Paris (2 days; p. 435). Nestled in the Alps and perched on a pristine lake, **Annecy** belongs in a fairy tale (1 day; p. 498), while **Chamonix** is the gateway to the majestic Mont Blanc (2 days; p. 504).

LA CRÈME DE LA CRÈME (1 MONTH)

To see everything worth seeing in France in only a few weeks is impossible, but you can still try. You'll need at least 4-5 days to see the sights and shops of **Paris** (p. 91)—be sure to make time for a daytrip to **Versailles** (p. 157). **Caen** is the quintessential stop for World War II history buffs, which makes it a worthwhile stop on France's lovely northwest coast (1 day; p. 210). While in the area, travel to the island abbey of **Mont-St-Michel** (1 day; p. 226) and **St-Malo** (1 day; p. 239), popular for its ram-

LA CRÈME DE LA CRÈME

parts, beaches, and fantastic seafood. Head down to **Rennes** (2 days; p. 231) for medieval sights and modern nightlife. Next, slip down to the Loire Valley. **Chambord** (1 day; p. 288), which is perhaps as grand as Versailles, has as many chimneys as there are days in a year. The château of **Amboise** (1 day; p. 290) was home to four French kings, while **Saumur** (1 day; p. 297) is famous for its castle, riding school, and sparkling wines. For a change of pace, soak up the sun in beach-blessed, historical **La Rochelle** (1 day; p. 705) or contemplate times past in the 17,000-year-old cave paintings of **Les-Eyzies-de-Tayac** (1 day; p. 742). Test your taste buds in the vineyards of **Bordeaux** (2 days; p. 640) before zipping southward to *basque* on the beach in **Biarritz** (1 day; p. 652). Keep heading east to reach the stunning walls of **Carcassonne**

(1 day; p. 609), guarding the town as they have done for centuries. No less formidable are the fortifications of the Palais-des-Papes in festive **Avignon** (1 day; p. 504). Students have been partying in elegant **Aix-en-Provence** (1 day; p. 498) for 600 years, but for non-stop action go to **Cannes**, one of the more fun, laid-back stops on the Côte d'Azur. Complete your tour of the Riviera in **Nice** (2 days; p. 545), its undisputed capital. From there, climb into the Alps to reach dynamic **Grenoble** (2 days; p. 452) and breathtaking **Chamonix** (1 day; p. 468), home to Europe's tallest peak, Mt. Blanc. You'll find highs of a very different sort in the town of **Beaune** (1 day; p. 398), home of Burgundy's most precious wines, while to the northeast, international **Strasbourg** (2 days; p. 354) offers a variety of Alsatian wines and an interesting hybrid Franco-German culture. Finally, finish off in style with a tasting at one of the champagne *caves* in **Reims** (1 day; p. 318).

OTHER TRIPS

France's best hiking and windsurfing are in the rugged, rocky, sun-blasted island of **Corsica** (p. 757), ringed with beautiful beaches and crumbling Genoese watchtowers. **Burgundy** (p. 391) is known for great wines and sleepy villages, as are the towns around **Bordeaux** (p. 640), in the southwest. Don't forget the exquisite **Dordogne,** a river-cut valley of walnut trees, lazy flowing water, and enough pâté for several coronaries (p. 748).

DISCOVER

ESSENTIALS

FACTS FOR THE TRAVELER

ENTRANCE REQUIREMENTS
Passport (p. 10). Required of all non-EU citizens, plus UK and Irish citizens.
Visa (p. 11). Required of citizens of South Africa for all stays. Required of Australian, Canadian, New Zealand, and US citizens for stays of over 90 days.
Work Permit (p. 11). Required of Australian, Canadian, New Zealand, South African, and US citizens.

EMBASSIES & CONSULATES

FRENCH CONSULAR SERVICES ABROAD

All consulates will provide information on obtaining visas or travel to France in general. Different services have different opening hours; the hours listed below are for visa concerns, unless otherwise stated. Most consulates will receive inquiries by appointment.

Australia: Consulate General, Level 26, St. Martins Tower, 31 Market St., Sydney NSW 2000 (☎02 92 61 57 79; www.consulfrance-sydney.org). Open M-F 9am-1pm.

Canada: Consulat général de France à Montréal, 1 pl. Ville-Marie, ste. 2601, 26th floor, **Montréal**, QC H3B 4S3 (☎514-878-4385; www.consulfrance-montreal.org). Open M-F 8:30am-noon. Consulat général de France à Québec, Maison Kent, 25 rue Saint-Louis, **Québec,** QC G1R 3Y8 (☎418-694-2294; www.consulfrance-quebec.org). Open M-F 9am-noon. Consulat Général de France à Toronto, 130 Bloor St. West, ste. 400, **Toronto,** ON M5S 1N5 (☎416-925-8041; www.consulfrance-toronto.org). Open M-F 9am-1pm.

Ireland: French Embassy, Consulate Section, 36 Ailesbury Rd., Ballsbridge, Dublin 4 (☎01 260 16 66; www.ambafrance.ie). Open M-F 9:30am-11:30pm.

New Zealand: New Zealand Embassy and Consulate, 34-42 Manners St., P.O. Box 11-343, **Wellington** (☎04 384 25 55; fax 04 384 25 77). Open M-F 9am-1pm. French Honorary Consulate in Auckland, P.O. Box 1433, **Auckland** (☎09 379 58 50; www.ambafrance-nz.org).

South Africa: Consulate General at **Johannesburg,** 191 Jan Smuts Ave., Rosebank. If you live in Gauteng, KwaZuluNatal, Free State, Mpumalanga, Northern Province, North West Province or Lesotho, mail inquiries to P.O. Box 1027, Parklands 2121 (☎011 778 56 00, visas 011 778 56 05; www.consulfrance-jhb.org). Open M-F 8:30am-1pm. If you live in the Northern Cape, Eastern Cape, or Western Cape, inquire at the Consulate General, 2 Dean St., Gardens, 8001 **Cape Town** (☎021 423 15 75; www.consulfrance-lecap.org). Open M-F 9am-1pm. Send mail to P.O. Box 1702 Cape Town 8000.

United Kingdom: Consulate General, P.O. Box 520, 21 Cromwell Rd., London SW7 2EN (☎020 7073 1200; www.ambafrance-uk.org). Open M-W 8:45am-3pm, Th-F 8:45am-noon. Visa service: P.O. Box 57, 6a Cromwell Pl., London SW7 2EW (☎020 7073 1250). Open M-F 8:45-11:30am.

United States: Consulate General, 4101 Reservoir Rd. NW, Washington, D.C. 20007-2185 (☎202-944-6195; www.consulfrance-washington.org). Open M-F 8:45am-12:45pm. Visa service ☎202-944-6200 M-F 2-5pm, answering machine 8:45am-12:45pm; fax 944-6212. Consulates also in Atlanta, Boston, Chicago, Houston, Los Angeles, Miami, New Orleans, New York, and San Francisco. See www.info-france-usa.org/intheus/consulates.asp for more info.

CONSULAR SERVICES IN FRANCE

Travelers visit these embassies only when they encounter trouble and need assistance. The most common concern is a loss of passport or worry about potentially dangerous local conditions. In serious trouble, your home country's embassy or consulate usually can provide legal advice, and may even be able to advance you money in emergency situations. But don't expect them to get you out of every scrape: you must always follow French law in France. In the case of arrest, your consulate can do little more than suggest a lawyer. Dual citizens of France cannot call on the consular services of their second nationality for assistance. Call before visiting any of these embassies, as hours vary. Visa services tend to be available only in the morning.

Australia: Australian Embassy and Consulate, 4 rue Jean Rey, 75724 Paris Cédex 15 (☎01 40 59 33 00, after-hours emergency 01 40 59 33 01; www.austgov.fr). Open daily 9:15am-noon and 2-4:30pm.

Canada: Canadian Embassy and Consulate, 35 av. Montaigne, 75008 Paris (☎01 44 43 29 00; www.amb-canada.fr). Open daily 9am-noon and 2-5pm. General Delegation of **Quebec,** 66 rue Pergolèse, 75116 Paris (☎01 40 67 85 00; www.mri.gouv.qc.ca/paris).

Ireland: Embassy of Ireland, 4 rue Rude, 75016 Paris (☎01 44 17 67 00, emergencies 01 44 17 67 67; fax 01 44 17 67 60; www.irlande.tourisme.fr). Open M-F 9:30am-noon. Also in Antibes, Cherbourg, Lyon, and Monaco.

New Zealand: New Zealand Embassy and Consulate, 7ter rue Leonardo de Vinci, 75116 Paris (☎01 45 00 24 11; fax 01 45 01 26 37; nzembassy.paris@wanadoo.fr). Open July-Aug. M-Th 8:30am-1pm and 2-5:30pm, F 8:30am-2pm; Sept.-June M-F 9am-1pm and 2-5:30pm.

South Africa: South African Embassy, 59 quai d'Orsay, 75343 Paris Cédex 07 (☎01 53 59 23 23, emergencies 86 09 67 06 93; www.afriquesud.net). Open M-F 8:30am-5:15pm; consular services M-F 9am-noon.

United Kingdom: British Embassy, Consulate Section, 18bis rue d'Anjou, 75008 Paris (☎01 44 51 31 00; www.amb-grandebretagne.fr). Open M and W-F 9:30am-12:30pm and 2:30-5pm, Tu 9:30am-4:30pm. Also in **Bordeaux, Lille, Lyon,** and **Marseille.**

United States: Consulate General, 2 rue St-Florentin, 75001 Paris (☎01 43 12 22 22; www.amb-usa.fr). Send mail to 2 rue St-Florentin, 75382 Paris Cédex 08. Open M-F 9am-12:30pm and 1-3pm, notarial services Tu-F only. Don't wait in line; tell the guard that you desire American services. Also in **Bordeaux, Lille, Lyon, Marseille, Nice, Rennes, Strasbourg,** and **Toulouse;** visa services only in Paris.

TOURIST OFFICES

The **French Government Tourist Office (FGTO),** also known as Maison de la France, runs tourist offices in French cities and offers tourist services to travelers abroad. The FGTO runs the website **www.franceguide.com,** which offers very useful info for travelers from many countries. *Let's Go* lists the tourist office in every town where one exists.

DOCUMENTS & FORMALITIES

ESSENTIALS

 ONE EUROPE. The idea of European unity has come a long way since 1958, when the European Economic Community (EEC) was created in order to promote solidarity and cooperation. Since then, the EEC has become the European Union (EU), with political, legal, and economic institutions spanning 15 members: Austria, Belgium, Denmark, Finland, France, Germany, Greece, Ireland, Italy, Luxembourg, the Netherlands, Portugal, Spain, Sweden, and the UK. What does this have to do with the average non-EU tourist? In 1999, the EU established **freedom of movement** across 14 European countries–the entire EU minus Ireland and the UK, plus Iceland and Norway. This means that border controls between participating countries have been abolished, and visa policies harmonized. While you're still required to carry a passport (or government-issued ID card if you're an EU citizen) when crossing an internal border, once you've been admitted into one country, you're free to travel to all participating states. Britain and Ireland have also formed a **common travel area,** abolishing passport controls between the UK and the Republic of Ireland. The only times you'll see a border guard within the EU are while traveling between the British Isles and the Continent. For more important consequences of the EU for travelers, see **The Euro** (p. 13) and **European Customs** and **EU Customs Regulations** (p. 12).

PASSPORTS

REQUIREMENTS. Citizens of Australia, Canada, Ireland, New Zealand, South Africa, the UK, and the US need valid passports to enter France and to re-enter their own country. France does not allow entrance if the holder's passport expires in under three months after the expected date of departure from France; returning home with an expired passport is illegal and may result in a fine.

NEW PASSPORTS. Citizens of Australia, Canada, Ireland, New Zealand, the United Kingdom, and the United States can apply for a passport at any post office, passport office, or court of law. Citizens of South Africa can apply for a passport at any Home Affairs office. Any new passport or renewal applications must be filed well in advance of the departure date, although most passport offices offer rush services for a very steep fee. Citizens living abroad who need a passport or renewal services should contact the nearest consular service of their home country. Passport office hours vary greatly, so call ahead.

PASSPORT MAINTENANCE. Be sure to photocopy the page of your passport with your photo, as well as your visas, traveler's check serial numbers and any other important documents. Carry one set of copies in a safe place, apart from the originals, and leave another set at home. Consulates also recommend that you carry an expired passport or an official copy of your birth certificate in a part of your baggage separate from other documents.

If you lose your passport, immediately notify the local police and the nearest embassy or consulate of your home government. To expedite its replacement, you will need to know all information previously recorded and show ID and proof of citizenship. In some cases, a replacement may take weeks to process, and it may be valid only for a limited time. Any visas stamped in your old passport will be irretrievably lost. In an emergency, ask for immediate temporary traveling papers that will permit you to re-enter your home country.

VISAS, INVITATIONS, & WORK PERMITS

In certain cases of travel or short residence, the government of France requires the traveler to obtain a visa. French visas are valid for travel in any of the states of the EU common travel area (see **One Europe,** above), but if your primary destination is a country other than France, you should apply to that country's consulate for a visa. All visitors to France are required to register with the police in the town in which they plan to reside; you are automatically registered when you rent a hotel or hostel room or sign a lease. Before departure, check at the nearest French embassy or consulate (listed under **Embassies & Consulates,** on p. 8) for up-to-date info on entrance requirements. US citizens can also consult the website at www.pueblo.gsa.gov/cic_text/travel/foreign/foreignentryreqs.html.

VISITS OF UNDER 90 DAYS. Citizens of South Africa need a **short-stay visa** *(visa de court séjour)*. In order for you to obtain this visa, your passport must be valid for three months past the date you intend to leave France. You must submit two passport-sized photos, a return ticket, proof of medical insurance, and documentary evidence of your professional situation and means of support in France. You will also need to provide either a certificate of accommodation stamped by a police station or town hall (2 copies) if you plan to stay with friends, a letter from your employer if you plan to work, or evidence of a hotel reservation or organized tour. Apply at your nearest French consulate; short-stay visas for South African nationals take up to 2 weeks to process. (Transit visa—1 or 2 entries of 1 or 2 days each—ZAR95; single/multiple entry visa up to 30 days ZAR239; single entry visa for 31-90 days ZAR286.)

VISITS OF OVER 90 DAYS. All non-EU citizens need a long-stay visa *(long séjour)* for stays of over 90 days. You must present the same info as for the *court séjour* (see above). The visa can take two months to process and costs €100.90. US citizens can take advantage of the Center for International Business and Travel (**CIBT;** ☎800-925-2428), which secures visas for travel to almost all countries for a variable service charge. All foreigners (including EU citizens) who plan to stay over 90 days must apply for a temporary residence permit *(carte de séjour temporaire)* at the prefecture in their town of residence within eight days of their arrival in France.

STUDY & WORK PERMITS. Admission as a visitor does not include the right to work, which is authorized only by a work permit. Entering France to study requires a special student visa. For more information, see the **Alternatives to Tourism** chapter (p. 56).

IDENTIFICATION

French law requires that all people carry an official form of identification, either a passport or an EU government-issued identity card. The police have the right to demand identification at any time; refusal or lack of identification can result in a large fine. Minority travelers, particularly black and Arab travelers, should be especially mindful of this. It is advisable to carry two or more forms of photo identification. Many establishments, like banks, demand several forms of ID to cash traveler's checks. A passport combined with a driver's license or birth certificate is almost always adequate. Never carry all your IDs together, in case of theft, and keep photocopies of them in your luggage and at home. You may want to bring a supply of passport-size photos to affix to the railpasses or other IDs you acquire in France; you can also find photo booths at almost every metro station.

ESSENTIALS

TEACHER, STUDENT, & YOUTH IDENTIFICATION. The **International Student Identity Card (ISIC)**, the most widely accepted form of student ID, provides discounts on some sights, accommodations, food, and transport; access to 24hr. emergency helpline (in North America call ☎877-370-ISIC or 877-370-4742; elsewhere call US collect ☎+1 715-345-0505); and insurance benefits for US cardholders (see **Insurance,** p. 22). Many museums in France offer admission discounts of 20-50% to cardholders. Applicants must be degree-seeking students of a secondary or post-secondary school and must be of at least 12 years of age. Because of the proliferation of fake ISICs, some services (particularly airlines) require additional proof of student identity.

The **International Teacher Identity Card (ITIC)** offers teachers the same insurance coverage as well as similar but limited discounts. For travelers who are 25 years old or under but are not students, the **International Youth Travel Card (IYTC)** also offers many of the same benefits as the ISIC. Similarly, the **International Student Exchange ID Card (ISE)** provides discounts, medical benefits, and the ability to purchase student airfares.

Each of these identity cards costs US$22 or equivalent. ISICs and ITICs are valid for roughly one-and-a-half academic years; IYTCs are valid for one year from the date of issue. Many student travel agencies (see p. 35) issue the cards; for more information, contact the **International Student Travel Confederation (ISTC),** Herengracht 479, 1017 BS Amsterdam, The Netherlands (☎+31 20 421 28 00; www.istc.org).

CUSTOMS

CUSTOMS IN THE EU. As well as freedom of movement of people within the EU (see p. 127), travelers in the member countries (Austria, Belgium, Denmark, Finland, France, Germany, Greece, Ireland, Italy, Luxembourg, the Netherlands, Portugal, Spain, Sweden, and the UK) can also take advantage of the freedom of movement of goods. This means that there are no customs controls at internal EU borders, and travelers are free to transport whatever legal substances they like as long as it is for their own personal (non-commercial) use—up to 800 cigarettes, 10L of spirits, 90L of wine (60L of sparkling wine), and 110L of beer.

Upon entering France, you must declare certain items from abroad and pay a duty on the value of those articles if that value exceeds the allowance established by France's customs service. Note that goods purchased at **duty-free** shops abroad are not exempt from duty or sales tax; "duty-free" merely means that you need not pay a tax in the country of purchase. Duty-free allowances were abolished for travel between EU member states in July 1999 but still exist for those arriving from outside the EU. Upon returning home, you must likewise declare all articles acquired abroad and pay a duty on the value of articles in excess of your home country's allowance. In order to expedite your return, make a list of any valuables brought from home and register them with customs before traveling abroad, and be sure to keep receipts for all goods acquired abroad.

RECLAIMING THE VALUE-ADDED TAX. Most purchases in France include a 19.6% value-added tax (**TVA** is the French acronym, VAT the English). Non-EU citizens residing in France for less than six months can reclaim the tax for purchases made over €175 in one store. Only certain stores participate in this **vente en détaxe** refund program. You must show a non-EU passport or proof of non-EU residence at the time of purchase, and ask the vendor for a *bordereau de détaxe* form in triplicate; make sure that the vendor fills out his part. Present the purchase receipt and the completed form to a French customs official within three months of the purchase. Have the purchased goods at hand. At an airport, look for the window labeled *douane de détaxe*. On a train, find an official or get off at a station close to the border. Budget at least two hours for this exquisitely painful encounter with French bureaucracy. Some shops will exempt you from paying the tax at the time of purchase, but you must still complete the above process. Food products, tobacco, medicine, firearms, unmounted precious stones, cars (sorry!), and "cultural goods" do not qualify for a refund. For more information, contact the Europe Tax-Free Shopping office in France, 4 pl. de l'Opéra, Paris 75002 (☎ 01 42 66 24 14).

MONEY

 THE EURO. The official currency of 12 members of the European Union—Austria, Belgium, Finland, France, Germany, Greece, Ireland, Italy, Luxembourg, the Netherlands, Portugal, and Spain—is now the euro.

The currency has some important—and positive—consequences for travelers hitting more than one euro-zone country. For one thing, money-changers across the euro-zone are obliged to exchange money at the official, fixed rate (see below), and at no commission (though they may still charge a small service fee). Second, euro-denominated traveler's checks allow you to pay for goods and services across the euro-zone, again at the official rate and commission-free.

CURRENCY & EXCHANGE

EUROS (€)		
AUS$1 = €0.59	€1 = AUS$1.70	
CDN$1 = €0.66	€1 = CDN$1.52	
NZ$1 = €0.53	€1 = NZ$1.90	
ZAR1 = €0.12	€1 = ZAR8.04	
UK£1 = €1.43	€1 = UK£0.68	
US$1 = €0.91	€1 = US$1.10	

The chart above is based on August 2003 exchange rates between European Union euros (EUR€) and Australian dollars (AUS$), Canadian dollars (CDN$), Irish pounds (IR£), New Zealand dollars (NZ$), South African Rand (ZAR), British pounds (UK£), and US dollars (US$). Check the currency converter on financial websites such as www.xe.com, or a large newspaper, for the latest exchange rate.

As a general rule, it's cheaper to convert money in France than at home. While currency exchange will probably be available in your arrival airport, it's wise to bring enough foreign currency to last for the first 24 to 72 hours of a trip.

When changing money abroad, try to go only to banks or *bureaux de change* that have at most a 5% margin between their buy and sell prices. Since you lose money with every transaction, **convert large sums** (unless the currency is depreciating rapidly), **but no more than you'll need.** Exchange money early in the day, as some banks only have window hours Tu-Sa 9am-noon.

If you use traveler's checks or bills, carry some in small denominations (the equivalent of US$50 or less) for times when you are forced to exchange money at disadvantageous rates, but bring a range of denominations since charges may be levied per check cashed. Store your money in a variety of forms; ideally, at any given time you will be carrying some cash, some traveler's checks, and an ATM and/or credit card. All travelers should also consider carrying some US dollars (about US$50 worth), which are often preferred by local tellers.

TRAVELER'S CHECKS

Traveler's checks are one of the safest and least troublesome means of carrying funds. American Express and Visa are the most widely recognized brands. Many banks and agencies sell them for a small commission. Check issuers provide refunds if the checks are lost or stolen, and many provide additional services like toll-free refund hotlines, emergency message services, and stolen credit card assistance. They are readily accepted in France, though some establishments only take checks in euros; a passport is often required to cash them. Always carry emergency cash.

American Express: Checks available with commission at select banks, at all AmEx offices, and online (www.americanexpress.com; US residents only). American Express cardholders can also purchase checks by phone (☎888-269-6669). AAA (see p. 49) offers commission-free checks to its members. Available in US, Australian, British, Canadian, Japanese, and EU currencies. *Cheques for Two* can be signed by either of two people traveling together. For more information contact AmEx's service centers: in the US and Canada ☎800-221-7282; in the UK 0800 587 6023; in Australia 800 68 80 22; in New Zealand 0508 555 358; elsewhere US collect +1 801-964-6665.

Visa: Checks available (generally with commission) at banks worldwide. For the location of the nearest office, call Visa's service centers: In the US ☎800-227-6811; in the UK 0800 51 58 84; elsewhere UK collect +020 7937 8091. Checks available in US, British, Canadian, Japanese, and EU currencies.

Travelex/Thomas Cook: In the US and Canada call ☎800-287-7362; in the UK call 0800 62 21 01; elsewhere call UK collect +1733 31 89 50.

CREDIT, ATM, & DEBIT CARDS

Credit cards are generally accepted in France for purchases over €15. Where they are accepted, credit cards often offer superior exchange rates—up to 5% better than the retail rate used by banks and other establishments. Credit cards may also offer services such as insurance or emergency help, and are sometimes required to reserve hotel rooms or rental cars. **MasterCard (EuroCard)** and **Visa (Carte Bleue)** are the most welcomed; American Express cards work at some ATMs and at AmEx offices and major airports. French-issued credit cards are fitted with a microchip (and are known as *cartes à puce*) rather than a magnetic strip *(cartes à piste*

PINS & ATMS. To use a cash or credit card to withdraw money from a cash machine (ATM) in Europe, you must have a four-digit **Personal Identification Number (PIN).** If your PIN is longer than four digits, ask your bank whether you can just use the first four, or you need a new one PIN. **Credit cards** don't usually come with PINs, so if you intend to hit up ATMs in Europe with a credit card to get cash advances, call your credit card company before leaving.

People with alphabetic rather than numerical PINs may also be thrown off by the lack of letters on European cash machines. The following chart gives the corresponding numbers to use: 1=QZ; 2=ABC; 3=DEF; 4=GHI; 5=JKL; 6=MNO; 7=PRS; 8=TUV; and 9=WXY. Note that if you mistakenly punch the wrong code into the machine three times, it will swallow your card for good.

magnétique); in untouristed areas, cashiers may attempt to scan the card with a microchip reader. In such circumstances you should explain: *"Ceci n'est pas une carte à puce, mais une carte à piste magnétique."* Self-service and cash machines should have no problem scanning magnetic cards.

24hr. **ATMs** (cash machines) are widespread in France. Depending on the system that your home bank uses, you can most likely access your personal bank account from abroad. ATMs get the same wholesale exchange rate as credit cards, but there is often a limit on the amount of money you can withdraw per day (around US$500), and unfortunately computer networks sometimes fail. There is typically also a surcharge of US$1-5 per withdrawal.

The two major international money networks are **Cirrus** (to locate ATMs call US ☎800-424-7787 or visit www.mastercard.com) and **Visa/PLUS** (to locate ATMs call US ☎800-843-7587 or visit www.visa.com). Most ATMs charge a transaction fee that is paid to the bank that owns the ATM.

GETTING MONEY FROM HOME

If you run out of money while traveling, the easiest and cheapest solution is to have someone back home make a deposit to your credit card or cash (ATM) card. Failing that, consider one of the following options.

WIRING MONEY. It is possible to arrange a **bank money transfer,** which means asking a bank back home to wire money to a bank in France. This is the cheapest way to transfer cash, but it's also the slowest, usually taking several days or more. Note that some banks may only release your funds in local currency, potentially sticking you with a poor exchange rate; inquire about this in advance. Money transfer services like **Western Union** are faster and more convenient than bank transfers— but also much pricier. Western Union offers services in many French post offices. To locate a service station, visit www.westernunion.com, or call: in the US ☎800-325-6000, in Canada 800-235-0000, in the UK 0800 83 38 33, in Australia 800 501 500, in New Zealand 800 27 0000, in South Africa 0860 100031. Money transfer services are also available at **American Express** and **Thomas Cook** offices.

US STATE DEPARTMENT (US CITIZENS ONLY). In dire emergencies only, the US State Department will forward money within hours to the nearest consular office, which will then disburse it for a US$15 fee. If you wish to use this service, you must contact the Overseas Citizens Service division of the US State Department (☎202-647-5225; nights, Sundays, and holidays 202-647-4000).

COSTS

The cost of your trip will vary considerably, depending on the region of France you visit, your method of travel, and the types of accommodations you choose. The most significant expenses will be your round-trip **airfare** to France (see **Getting to France: By Plane,** p. 33) and a **railpass** (p. 41) or **bus pass** (p. 46). Before you go, calculate a reasonable per-day **budget** that will meet your needs.

STAYING ON A BUDGET. A bare-bones day traveling in France (camping or sleeping in hostels or guesthouses, buying all your food at supermarkets) costs about €20 (US$20); a slightly more comfortable day (sleeping at budget hotels, eating one meal a day at a restaurant, going out at night) runs about €45 (US$45); and for a day of luxury, the sky's the limit. Visits to Paris are typically more expensive. Also, don't forget to factor reserve funds for emergencies (bring at least US$200) when deciding how much money to bring.

TIPPING & BARGAINING

By law, service must be included at all **restaurants, bars,** and **cafés** in France. Look for the phrase *service compris* on the menu. If service is not included, tip 15-20%. Even when service is included, it is polite to leave a *pourboire* at a café, bistro, restaurant, or bar—from half a euro to 5% of the bill. Do tip your hairdresser well; do not tip taxis more than a euro. People such as concierges may also expect to be tipped for services beyond the call of duty, never less than €1.50.

Though you should inquire about discounts and less pricey options, do not try to bargain at established places—i.e., hotels, hostels, restaurants, cafés, museums, nightclubs. Although not encouraged, bargaining is acceptable at outdoor markets, but you shouldn't expect to get any deals.

TAXES

The **value-added tax (VAT)** is a general tax on doing business in France; it applies to a wide range of goods (entertainment, food, accommodations) and services. The tax can be up to 19.6% of the price of the good. Some of the VAT can be recovered (see **Reclaiming Value-Added Tax,** p. 12). There is a also tax on staying at a hotel, hostel, or other accommodation *(taxe de séjour)*, which is typically included in the price of a stay and the price quoted in *Let's Go: France.*

SAFETY & SECURITY

EMERGENCY & CRISIS NUMBERS

MEDICAL EMERGENCY: Dial ☎ **15.**

POLICE EMERGENCY: Dial ☎ **17.**

FIRE EMERGENCY: Dial ☎ **18.**

NATIONAL ENGLISH-LANGUAGE CRISIS LINE: In Paris dial ☎ **01 47 23 80 80** (3-11pm).

DIRECTORY ASSISTANCE: Dial ☎ **12.**

SNCF RESERVATIONS AND INFORMATION: Dial ☎ **08 91 67 68 69.**

Tourists are the biggest targets for crime in France. When confronted by a suspicious individual, do not respond or make eye contact. Walk quickly away, and keep a solid grip on your belongings. Contact the police if a hustler is insistent or aggressive. When driving, lock your doors and keep bags away from windows; scooter-borne thieves often snatch purses and bags from cars stopped at lights. In **Paris,** be especially careful on public transportation at rush hour and traveling to and from the airport. Pick-pocketing is common on the Paris metro, especially on line #1 and the RER B line to De Gaulle Airport, and at department stores, particularly on the escalators. Be vigilant with your baggage at **airports** and **train stations.** Take a **licensed taxi.** Outside Paris, tourist-related crime is most prevalent on the **Côte d'Azur,** in **Marseille,** and in **Montpellier.**

PERSONAL SAFETY

EXPLORING. To avoid unwanted attention, blend in. What may look perfectly innocuous in Miami will stick out instantly in Menton. The French are known for their conservative stylishness. Go for restrained sneakers or closed shoes, solid-color pants or jeans, and plain T-shirts or button-down shirts. Avoid sport sandals, baggy pants, or torn jeans. French people rarely wear shorts, and only long ones. For women, skirts or dresses are more appropriate. Carrying a large bag with you everywhere will reveal your true identity as a tourist. Dress especially conservatively when visiting churches. Women should wear long pants or a long skirt and cover their shoulders; men should remove their hats.

DRIVING. Despite being blessed with excellent roads, the French have deservedly earned a reputation for aggressive and dangerous driving. They regularly flout the speed limit, often while drunk. Corsica's narrow and twisting roads are among the most lethal in Europe, often because cars try to pass in dangerous situations. Watch out for mopeds, especially in the south; they sometimes speed out from alleys or sidewalks. By law, all passengers must wear a seatbelt. Children under 40 lbs. must ride in a specially designed carseat, available at a small fee from most car rental agencies. In cities, and especially on the Côte d'Azur, park your car in a well-lit area and secure it with a steering wheel locking device. **Sleeping in your car** is one of the most dangerous (and often illegal) ways to get your rest.

For info on the perils of **hitchhiking**, see p. 41.

TERRORISM. Terrorism has not been as serious a problem in France as in other European countries, but after September 11, 2001, the French government heightened security at public places. Many train stations no longer permit luggage storage, for example. France contains cells of al Qaeda and other terrorist groups. Many cities have recently experienced unrest, but because of immigrant conditions rather than terrorism. Since its colonial period, France has always been an enemy of unstable Algeria. Domestic anti-Semites firebombed several Jewish synagogues in the last couple of years.

TRAVEL ADVISORIES. The following government offices provide travel information and advisories by telephone, by fax, or via the Web:

Australian Department of Foreign Affairs and Trade: ☎13 00 555135; faxback service 02 6261 1299; www.dfat.gov.au.

Canadian Department of Foreign Affairs and International Trade (DFAIT): In Canada and the US call ☎800-267-8376, elsewhere call +1 613-944-4000; www.dfait-maeci.gc.ca. Call for their free booklet, *Bon Voyage...But.*

New Zealand Ministry of Foreign Affairs: ☎04 439 8000; fax 04 494 8506; www.mft.govt.nz/travel/index.html.

United Kingdom Foreign and Commonwealth Office: ☎020 7008 0232; fax 020 7008 0155; www.fco.gov.uk.

US Department of State: ☎202-647-5225, faxback service 647-3000; http://travel.state.gov. For *A Safe Trip Abroad*, call ☎202-512-1800.

FINANCIAL SECURITY

PROTECTING YOUR VALUABLES. To minimize the financial risk associated with traveling, **bring as little with you as possible.** Second, buy a few combination **padlocks** to secure your belongings either in your pack or in a hostel locker. Don't expect train stations in France to have locker storage facilities, as most have closed them due to new security laws. Third, **carry as little cash as possible.** Keep your traveler's checks and ATM/credit cards in a **money belt**—not a "fanny pack"—along with your passport and ID cards. Fourth, **keep a small cash reserve separate from your primary stash.** This should be about US$50 (US$ or Euros are best) sewn into or stored in the depths of your pack along with your traveler's check numbers and important photocopies.

ESSENTIALS

CON ARTISTS & PICKPOCKETS. In large cities **con artists** often work in groups, and children are among the most effective. Beware certain classics: sob stories that require money, rolls of bills "found" on the street, mustard spilled (or saliva spit) onto your shoulder to distract you while they snatch your bag. **Never let your passport and your bags out of your sight.** Beware **pickpockets** in city crowds, especially on public transportation. Also, be alert in public telephone booths. If you must say your calling card number, do so very quietly; if you punch it in, make sure no one can look over your shoulder.

DRUGS, DRINKS, & SMOKES

Possession of **illegal drugs** (including marijuana) in France can result in a substantial jail sentence or fine. Drug dealers often sell drugs to tourists and then turn them in to authorities for a reward. In France, police may arbitrarily stop and search anyone on the street. **Prescription drugs,** particularly insulin, syringes, or narcotics, should be left in their original, labeled containers and accompanied by their prescriptions and a doctor's statement. In case of arrest, your home country's consulate can suggest attorneys and inform your family and friends but can't get you out of jail. For more info, contact the Office of Overseas Citizens Services (US ☎ 202-647-5225; after-hours 647-4000; http://travel.state.gov).

The French love alcohol, but they drink carefully. Virtually no one drinks "to get drunk." Drinking on the street is uncouth. Restaurants may serve alcohol to anyone 14 or over. Smoking is banned in public places, but people light up almost anywhere. Some eateries have non-smoking sections, but they're often not respected.

HEALTH

Use common sense: drink lots of fluids to prevent dehydration and constipation, and wear sturdy, broken-in shoes and clean socks.

BEFORE YOU GO

In your **passport,** write the names of any people you wish to be contacted in case of a medical emergency, and list any allergies or medical conditions. Matching a prescription to a foreign equivalent is not always easy, safe, or possible, so carry up-to-date, legible prescriptions or a statement from your doctor stating the medication's trade name, manufacturer, chemical name, and dosage. Keep all medication with you in carry-on luggage. For tips on packing a basic **first-aid kit** and other health essentials, see p. 18. Women report having difficulty finding applicator **tampons** in France, though other kinds are available at pharmacies and supermarkets.

IMMUNIZATIONS & PRECAUTIONS

Travelers over two years old should make sure the following vaccines are up to date: MMR (for measles, mumps, and rubella); DTaP or Td (for diptheria, tetanus, and pertussis); OPV (for polio); HbCV (for haemophilus influenza B); and HBV (for hepatitis B). For immunization and prophylaxis recommendations, consult the CDC (see below) in the US or the equivalent in your home country, and check with a doctor.

USEFUL ORGANIZATIONS & PUBLICATIONS

The US **Centers for Disease Control and Prevention** (CDC; ☎ 877-FYI-TRIP; toll free fax 888-232-3299; www.cdc.gov/travel) maintains an international travelers' hotline and an informative website. The CDC's comprehensive booklet *Health Information for International Travel*, an annual rundown of disease, immunization, and general health advice, is free online or US$30 via the Public Health Foundation (☎877-252-1200). Consult the appropriate government agency of your home country for consular information sheets on health and entry requirements, and other issues for various countries (see the listings in the box on **Travel Advisories,** p. 17). For quick information on health and other travel warnings, call the **Overseas Citizens Services** (☎202-647-5225, after-hours 647-4000), or contact a passport agency, embassy, or consulate abroad. US citizens can send a self-addressed, stamped envelope to the Overseas Citizens Services, Bureau of Consular Affairs, #4811, US Department of State, Washington, D.C. 20520. For info on medical evacuation services and travel insurance, see the US government's site at http://travel.state.gov/medical.html or the **British Foreign and Commonwealth Office** (www.fco.gov.uk).

For detailed information on travel health, including a country-by-country overview of diseases, try the **International Travel Health Guide,** by Stuart Rose, MD (US$25; www.travmed.com). For general health info, contact the **American Red Cross** (☎800-564-1234; www.redcross.org).

MEDICAL ASSISTANCE ON THE ROAD

Medical care in France is as good (and as expensive) as anywhere in the world. All but the smallest towns have a hospital, generally with English-speaking staff, which is listed under the Practical Information in each city listing. Every town has a **24hr. pharmacy** *(pharmacie de garde)*. Different pharmacies assume this duty at different times. The police can direct you to the right one. Pharmacies also post this info on their doors each Sunday.

EU citizens get "reciprocal health benefits" (including immediate urgent care) if they fill out an **E-111** form, available at most post offices, before departure. EU citizens studying in France qualify for long-term care. Other travelers should get adequate medical insurance before leaving; regular **insurance** policies may require you to purchase additional coverage for travel abroad. Medicare does not cover travel abroad. For more info, see **Insurance,** p. 22.

If you need a **doctor** *(un médecin),* call the local hospital for a list of nearby practitioners or inquire at a pharmacy. If you are receiving reciprocal health care, make sure you call an **honoraires opposables** doctor (linked to the state health care system). Legally, they may not charge more than €17 for a consultation. Doctors registered as **honoraires libres** can charge whatever they like, and their fees will not be reimbursed under reciprocal health care agreements.

If you are concerned about obtaining medical assistance while traveling, you may wish to employ special support services. The *MedPass* from **GlobalCare, Inc.,** 6875 Shiloh Rd. East, Alpharetta, GA 30005, USA (☎800-860-1111; fax 678-341-1800; www.globalems.com), provides 24hr. international medical assistance, support, and medical evacuation resources. The **International Association for Medical Assistance to Travelers (IAMAT;** US ☎716-754-4883, Canada ☎519-836-0102; www.cybermall.co.nz/nz/iamat) has free membership, lists English-speaking doctors worldwide, and offers detailed info on immunization requirements and sanitation. If your regular **insurance** policy does not cover travel abroad, you may wish to purchase additional coverage (see p. 22).

ONCE IN FRANCE

ENVIRONMENTAL HAZARDS

Hikers should be especially attentive to their health. The summer heat can cause rapid dehydration and sunburn, especially in the south. In the Alps, the Pyrénées, and Corsica, storms strike unpredictably, killing several hikers each year.

Heat exhaustion and dehydration: Heat exhaustion leads to nausea, excessive thirst, headaches, and dizziness. Avoid it by drinking plenty of fluids, not eating salty foods (e.g. crackers), and abstaining from dehydrating beverages (e.g. alcohol and caffein- ated beverages). Continuous heat stress can eventually lead to heatstroke, character- ized by a rising temperature, severe headache, delirium, and cessation of sweating. Victims should be cooled off with wet towels and taken to a doctor.

Hypothermia and frostbite: A rapid drop in body temperature is the clearest sign of overexposure to cold. Victims may also shiver, feel exhausted, have poor coordination or slurred speech, hallucinate, or suffer from amnesia. *Do not let hypothermia victims fall asleep.* To avoid hypothermia, keep dry, wear layers, and stay out of the wind. When the temperature is below freezing, watch out for frostbite. If skin turns white or blue, waxy, and cold, do not rub the area. Drink warm beverages, stay dry, and slowly warm the area with dry fabric or steady body contact until a doctor can be found.

High altitude: Allow your body a couple of days to adjust to less oxygen before exerting yourself. Note that alcohol is more potent and UV rays are stronger at high elevations.

INSECT-BORNE DISEASES

Many diseases are transmitted by insects, especially mosquitoes, fleas, ticks, and lice. Protect against them in wet or forested areas, especially while hiking and camping: wear long pants and long sleeves, tuck your pants into your socks, and always use a mosquito net. Use insect repellents such as DEET, and soak or spray your gear with permethrin (licensed in the US for use on clothing). **Ticks**—respon- sible for Lyme disease and other diseases—can be particularly dangerous in rural and forested regions.

Tick-borne encephalitis: This viral infection of the central nervous system is transmitted during the summer by tick bites (primarily in wooded areas) or by consumption of unpasteurized dairy products. The risk of contracting the disease is relatively low, espe- cially if precautions are taken against tick bites.

Lyme disease: This bacterial infection is carried by ticks and marked by a circular bull's- eye rash of 2 in. or more. Later symptoms include fever, headache, fatigue, and aches and pains. Antibiotics are effective if administered early. Left untreated, Lyme can cause problems in joints, the heart, and the nervous system. If you find a tick attached to your skin, grasp the head with tweezers as close to your skin as possible and apply slow, steady traction. Removing a tick within 24hr. greatly reduces the risk of infection. Do not try to remove ticks by burning them or coating them with nail polish remover or petroleum jelly.

Other insect-borne diseases: Filariasis is a roundworm infestation transmitted by mos- quitoes. Infection causes enlargement of extremities and has no vaccine. **Leishmania- sis,** a parasite transmitted by sand flies, can occur in Central and South America, Europe, Africa and the Middle East, and the Indian subcontinent. Common symptoms of this disease are fever, weakness, and excessive swelling of the spleen. There is a treat- ment, but no vaccine.

FOOD- & WATER-BORNE DISEASES

Cook everything properly and thoroughly and drink clean water. Clean water is not usually a problem in France, though most French people drink mineral water as a matter of taste and style.

Traveler's diarrhea in France is usually only the body's temporary reaction to bacteria in unfamiliar food ingredients; it tends to last 3-7 days and causes nausea, bloating, and urgency. Try quick-energy, non-sugary foods with protein and carbohydrates to keep your strength up. Over-the-counter anti-diarrheals (e.g. Immodium) may counteract the problems. The most dangerous side effect is dehydration; drink 8 oz. of water with ½ tsp. of sugar or honey and a pinch of salt, and try uncaffeinated soft drinks. If you develop a fever or your symptoms don't go away after 4-5 days, consult a doctor. Consult a doctor immediately for treatment of diarrhea in children.

INFECTIOUS DISEASES

Rabies: This disease is transmitted through the saliva of infected animals and fatal if untreated. By the time symptoms (thirst and muscle spasms) appear, the disease is in its terminal stage. If you are bitten, wash the wound thoroughly, seek immediate medical care, and try to have the animal located. A rabies vaccine, which consists of three shots given over a 21-day period, is available but only semi-effective.

Hepatitis B: A viral infection of the liver transmitted via bodily fluids or needle-sharing. Symptoms, which may not surface until years after infection, include jaundice, loss of appetite, fever, and joint pain. A three-shot vaccination sequence is recommended for health-care workers, sexually active travelers, and anyone planning to seek medical treatment abroad; it must begin six months before traveling.

Hepatitis C: This infection is like Hepatitis B, but the mode of transmission differs. IV drug users, those with occupational exposure to blood, hemodialysis patients, and recipients of blood transfusions are at the highest risk, but the disease can also be spread through sexual contact or sharing items like razors and toothbrushes that may have traces of blood on them.

AIDS, HIV, & STDS

Acquired Immune Deficiency Syndrome (**AIDS; SIDA** in French) is a major problem in France; Paris has the largest HIV-positive community in Europe. France has only recently lifted immigration bans on HIV-positive individuals. In France, there are as many heterosexuals infected as homosexuals.

For detailed information on **Acquired Immune Deficiency Syndrome (AIDS)** in France, call the **US Centers for Disease Control's** 24hr. hotline at ☎800-342-2437, or contact the **Joint United Nations Programme on HIV/AIDS (UNAIDS),** 20 av. Appia, CH-1211 Geneva 27, Switzerland (☎22 791 3666; fax 22 791 4187). France's AIDS hotline is ☎01 44 93 16 16. Contact the consulate of France for more information.

Sexually transmitted diseases (STDs) such as gonorrhea, chlamydia, genital warts, syphilis, and herpes are easier to catch than HIV but can be just as deadly. **Hepatitis** B and C can also be transmitted sexually (see p. 21). Though condoms may protect you from some STDs, oral or even tactile contact can lead to transmission. If you think you may have contracted an STD, see a doctor immediately.

Contraception is readily available in most pharmacies and supermarkets. To obtain **condoms** in France, visit a pharmacy and tell the clerk, "*Je voudrais une boîte de préservatifs*" (zhuh-voo-DRAY oon BWAHT duh PREY-zehr-va-TEEF).

WOMEN'S HEALTH

Recent changes have relaxed restrictions on surgical and pharmaceutical **abortions,** permitting them up to 12 weeks into pregnancy. Minors now need the permission of a legal adult rather than their parent or guardian. EU citizens have a reciprocal health care agreement whereby abortions are covered if deemed medically necessary. Non-EU citizens should check with their home insurance provider to ascertain whether abortions are covered. Contact the French branch of the International Planned Parenthood Federation, the **Mouvement Français pour le Planning Familial (MFPF),** which can supply the names of French hospitals and OB/GYN clinics performing abortions. (☎01 48 07 29 10. €550 if not covered by insurance.) More info about family planning centers can also be obtained through the **International Planned Parenthood Federation,** European Regional Office, Regent's College Inner Circle, Regent's Park, London NW1 4NS, England (☎020 7487 7900).

INSURANCE

Travel insurance generally covers four basic areas: medical/health problems, property loss, trip cancellation/interruption, and emergency evacuation. Although your regular insurance policies may well extend to travel-related accidents, you may consider purchasing travel insurance if the cost of potential trip cancellation/interruption or emergency medical evacuation is greater than you can absorb. Prices for travel insurance purchased separately generally run about US$50 per week for full coverage, while trip cancellation/interruption may be purchased separately at a rate of about US$5.50 per US$100 of coverage.

Medical insurance (especially university policies) often covers costs incurred abroad; check with your provider. **US Medicare** does not cover foreign travel. **Canadians** are protected by their home province's health insurance plan for up to 90 days after leaving the country; check with the provincial Ministry of Health or Health Plan Headquarters for details. **Homeowners' insurance** (or your family's coverage) often covers theft during travel and loss of travel documents (passport, plane ticket, railpass, etc.) up to US$500.

ISIC and **ITIC** (see p. 11) provide basic insurance benefits, including US$100 per day of in-hospital sickness for up to 60 days, US$3000 of accident-related medical reimbursement, and US$25,000 for emergency medical transport. Cardholders have access to a toll-free 24hr. helpline (run by the insurance provider **TravelGuard**) for medical, legal, and financial emergencies overseas (US and Canada ☎ 877-370-4742, elsewhere call US collect +1 715-345-0505). **American Express** (US ☎ 800-528-4800) grants most cardholders automatic car rental insurance (collision and theft, but not liability) and ground travel accident coverage of US$100,000 on flight purchases made with the card.

INSURANCE PROVIDERS. STA (see p. 35) offers a range of plans that can supplement your basic coverage. Other private insurance providers in the US and Canada include: **Access America** (☎ 800-284-8300); **Berkely Group/Carefree Travel Insurance** (☎ 800-323-3149; www.berkely.com); **Globalcare Travel Insurance** (☎ 800-821-2488; www.globalcare-cocco.com); and **Travel Assistance International** (☎ 800-821-2828; www.europ-assistance.com). Providers in the **UK** include **Columbus Direct** (☎ 020 7375 0011). In **Australia,** try **AFTA** (☎ 02 9264 3299).

PACKING

LUGGAGE. If you plan to cover most of your itinerary by foot, a sturdy **frame backpack** is unbeatable. (For the basics on buying a pack, see p. 22.) Toting a **suitcase** or **trunk** is fine if you plan to live in one or two cities and explore from there, but not a great idea if you plan to move around frequently. In addition to your main piece of luggage, a **daypack** (a small backpack or courier bag) is useful.

CLOTHING. France's weather is highly variable. Take a **warm jacket** or wool sweater, a **rain jacket** (Gore-Tex™ is waterproof and breathable), sturdy shoes or **hiking boots,** and **thick socks. Flip-flops** or waterproof sandals make grubby hostel showers more bearable. You may want to add one outfit beyond the jeans and T-shirt uniform, and maybe a nicer pair of shoes. If you plan to visit any religious or cultural sites, you'll need something besides tank tops and shorts, to be respectful.

SLEEPSACK. Some hostels require that you either provide your own linen or rent sheets from them. Save cash by making your own sleepsack: fold a full-size sheet in half the long way, then sew it closed along the long side.

CONVERTERS & ADAPTERS. In France, electricity is 220 volts AC, enough to fry any 110V North American appliance. **Americans** and **Canadians** should buy an **adapter** (which changes the shape of the plug) and a **converter** (which changes the voltage; US$20). Don't make the mistake of using only an adapter (unless appliance instructions explicitly state otherwise). **New Zealanders** and **South Africans** (who both use 220V at home) as well as **Australians** (who use 240/250V) won't need a converter, but will need a set of adapters to use anything electrical. For more on all things adaptable, check out http://kropla.com/electric.htm.

FIRST-AID KIT. For a basic first-aid kit, pack: bandages, pain reliever, antibiotic cream, a thermometer, a Swiss Army knife, tweezers, moleskin, decongestant, motion sickness remedy, diarrhea or upset-stomach medication (Pepto Bismol or Immodium), an antihistamine, sunscreen, insect repellent, burn ointment, and a syringe for emergencies (get an explanatory letter from your doctor).

OTHER USEFUL ITEMS. For safety purposes, you should bring a **money belt** and small **padlock**. Basic **outdoors equipment** (plastic water bottle, compass, waterproof matches, pocketknife, sunglasses, sunscreen, hat) may also prove useful. **Other things** you're liable to forget are an umbrella, sealable **plastic bags** (for damp clothes, soap, food, shampoo, and other spillables), an **alarm clock,** safety pins, rubber bands, a flashlight, earplugs, garbage bags, and a small **calculator.**

IMPORTANT DOCUMENTS. Don't forget your passport, traveler's checks, ATM and/or credit cards, adequate ID, and photocopies of all of the aforementioned in case these documents are lost or stolen (see p. 11). Also check that you have any of the following that might apply to you: a hosteling membership card (see p. 23); driver's license (see p. 11); travel insurance forms; and rail or bus pass (see p. 41).

ACCOMMODATIONS

HOSTELS

Hostels are generally laid out dorm-style, often with large single-sex rooms and bunk beds, although some offer private rooms for families and couples. They sometimes have kitchens and utensils for your use, bike or moped rentals, storage areas, transportation to airports, breakfast, and laundry facilities. There can be drawbacks: some hostels close during certain daytime "lockout" hours, have a curfew, don't accept reservations, impose a maximum stay, or, less frequently, require that you do chores. In France, a dorm bed in a hostel will average around €8-15 and a private room around €12-22.

HOSTELLING INTERNATIONAL

Joining the youth hostel association in your own country (listed below) automatically grants you membership privileges in **Hostelling International (HI),** a federation of national hosteling associations. In France, Hostelling International's affiliate, the **Fédération Unie des Auberges de Jeunesse (FUAJ),** operates 178 hostels. Many accept reservations via the **International Booking Network,** which takes worldwide reservations online and over the phone (US☎202-783-6161; www.hostelbooking.com). HI's umbrella organization's web page (www.iyhf.org), which lists the web addresses and phone numbers of all national associations, can be a great place to begin researching hostelling in a specific region. Other comprehensive hostelling websites include www.hostels.com and www.hostelplanet.com.

Most HI hostels also honor **guest memberships**—you'll get a blank card with space for six validation stamps. Each night you'll pay a nonmember supplement (one-sixth the membership fee) and earn one guest stamp; get six stamps, and you're a member. This system works well in most of Western Europe, but in some countries you may need to remind the hostel reception. A new membership bene-

fit is the Free Nites program, which allows hostelers to gain points toward free rooms. Most student travel agencies (see p. 35) sell HI cards, as do all of the national hosteling organizations listed below. All prices listed below are valid for **one-year memberships** unless otherwise noted.

Australian Youth Hostels Association (AYHA), Level 3, 10 Mallett St., Camperdown NSW 2050 (☎02 9565 1699; www.yha.org.au). AUS$52, under 18 AUS$16.

Hostelling International-Canada (HI-C), 205 Catherine St. #400, Ottawa, ON K2P 1C3 (☎613-237-7884; www.hihostels.ca). CDN$35, under 18 free.

An Óige (Irish Youth Hostel Association), 61 Mountjoy St., Dublin 7 (☎830 4555; www.irelandyha.org). IR£15, under 18 IR£7.5.

Youth Hostels Association of New Zealand (YHANZ), P.O. Box 436, 193 Cashel St., 3rd floor Union House, Christchurch (☎03 379 9970; www.stayyha.org). NZ$40, under 18 free.

Hostels Association of South Africa, 3rd fl., 73 St. George's House, Cape Town 8001 (☎021 424 2511; www.hisa.org.za). R70, under 18 R40.

Scottish Youth Hostels Association (SYHA), 7 Glebe Crescent, Stirling FK8 2JA (☎+44 08701 55 32 55; fax 08713 30 85 62; www.syha.org.uk). UK£6.

Youth Hostels Association (England and Wales), Trevelyon House, Dimple Rd., Matlock, Derbyshire DE4 3YH, UK (☎+44 1629 592 708; www.yha.org.uk). UK£13, under 18 UK£6.50.

Hostelling International Northern Ireland (HINI), 22 Donegall Rd., Belfast BT12 5JN (☎02890 31 54 35; www.hini.org.uk). UK£10, under 18 UK£6.

Hostelling International-American Youth Hostels (HI-AYH), 733 15th St. NW, #840, Washington, D.C. 20005 (☎202-783-6161; www.hiayh.org). US$25, under 18 free.

ESSENTIALS

HOTELS

Two or more people traveling together can save money by staying in cheap hotels rather than hostels. All accredited hotels are ranked with between zero and four stars by the French government, according to various factors such as room size, facilities, and plumbing. Prices are generally per room, although *demi-pension* (half-board; includes room and breakfast) and *pension* (room and all meals) are quoted per person.

Expect to pay at least €18 for a single room and €25 for a double. If you want a room with twin beds, ask for *une chambre avec deux lits* (oon chAMBR-avEK DUH LEE); otherwise you may find yourself in *une chambre avec un grand lit* (oon chAMBR avEK anh grANH LEE; a room with a double bed). A **taxe de séjour** (residency tax) of €0.25-1.50 per person per night is generally included in the quoted price. French hotels must display a list of the prices of rooms, breakfast, and any residency tax on the back of each room's door. It is illegal to charge more than shown. Rooms in cheap hotels normally have no *en suite* facilities—even the sink is in the hall. Occasionally you must pay extra for a hot shower (€2.30-3.80). Some very cheap hotels have no washing facilities at all. Otherwise, rooms can come *avec WC* or *avec cabinet* (with sink and toilet), *avec douche* (with shower), and *avec salle de bain* (with full bathroom). Many bathrooms also have a *bidet*, a low toilet-like apparatus used to clean your unmentionables. "Turkish toilets"— porcelain-rimmed holes in the floor—still exist in parts of France; put your feet where indicated, don't fall over, and make sure the light timer doesn't run out.

Hotels listed in *Let's Go* are generally small, family-run establishments close to sights of interest. *Let's Go* doesn't list the budget chains like *Hôtels Formule 1*, *Etap Hôtel*, and *Hôtels Première Classe*, which can usually be found on the out-

skirts of town. These typically charge €27-31 for one- to three-person rooms, have rooms with sink, TV, hall showers, toilets, and telephones, and allow you to rent with a credit card when the reception is closed.

OTHER OPTIONS

GÎTES D'ETAPE & MOUNTAIN REFUGES

Gîtes d'étape are rural accommodations for cyclists, hikers, and other outdoors people. These farmhouses, cottages, and campgrounds are located in less populated areas, normally beside major biking and hiking trails. Though they vary widely in price (averaging €10) and quality, *gîtes* generally have beds, kitchen facilities, and a resident caretaker. During the high season, *gîtes* in resort towns fill up quickly; reserve in advance. Don't confuse *gîtes d'étapes* with *gîtes ruraux*, country houses rented by the week.

Hikers and skiers on extended treks frequently make use of the *refuge*, a rustic shelter overseen by a do-it-all caretaker. *Refuge* accommodations range in price from €6.50-12.50. Hot, home-cooked meals typically cost up to €12. *Refuges* are not always guarded year-round, but their doors generally remain open all year for hikers and skiers on the road.

CHAMBRES D'HÔTE (BED & BREAKFASTS)

Some French house-owners supplement their income by letting rooms to travelers. These **chambres d'hôte**, or bed-and-breakfasts, range from acceptable rooms in modern townhouses to palatial chambers in Baroque châteaux. Most cost €30-45 per night. For a comprehensive listing of *chambres d'hôte* in France, buy **Selected Bed & Breakfasts in France 2003** in a bookstore or from Thomas Cook Publishing, P.O. Box 227, Units 19-21, Thomas Cook Business Park, Peterborough PE3 8XX, UK (☎1733 416477; www.thomascookpublishing.com/books). **Fleurs de Soleil** (www.fleurs-soleil.tm.fr) and **B&B** (www.bedbreak.com) list *chambres d'hôte* throughout France. For more info on B&Bs around the world and in France, contact **InnFinder**, 6200 Gisholt Dr., #105 Madison, WI 53713 (www.inncrawler.com), or **InnSite** (www.innsite.com).

UNIVERSITY HOUSING

Many universities open their residence halls to travelers when classes are out, and occasionally during term-time. Getting a room may take a couple of phone calls and require advanced planning, but rates tend to be low, and many offer free local calls and Internet access.

HOME EXCHANGE & RENTALS

In a **home exchange** program, you get to live for free in a French residence (a house, apartment, villa, even a castle) while a French family lives in yours. Some exchange services are listed below. It is also possible to **rent homes**, which can be a cheap bet for large groups.

HomeExchange, P.O. Box 30085, Santa Barbara, CA 93130, USA (☎310-798-3864; www.homeexchange.com). US$50 for a 1yr. listing.

Intervac International Home Exchange, 230 bd. Voltaire, 75011 Paris (☎01 43 70 21 22; www.intervac.org/france). 4-day listings are free and renewable.

The Invented City: International Home Exchange, 41 Sutter St., San Francisco, CA 94404, USA (☎415-252-1141; www.invented-city.com). US$50 for the first year to list your home and gain unlimited access to a database of thousands of homes.

FURTHER READING

The Complete Guide to Bed and Breakfasts, Inns and Guesthouses in the US, Canada, and Worldwide, by Pamela Lanier (Lanier Publishing Intl., Ltd.; US$15).

CAMPING & THE OUTDOORS

The French are avid campers, but not in the sense you might be used to. After 3000 years of settled history, there is little wilderness in France. It is illegal to camp in public spaces or light your own fires. Forget those romantic dreams of roughing it and prepare to share organized *campings* (campsites) with hundreds of fellow campers. Sites generally cost around €3. Most campsites have toilets, showers, and electrical outlets, though often at extra expense (€1.50-6). Cars may incur an additional €3-7.50 charge.

PUBLICATIONS & WEB RESOURCES

For info about camping, hiking, and biking, write or call the publishers listed below. The **Great Outdoor Recreation Pages** (www.gorp.com) is also an excellent resource for travelers in the outdoors. Campers heading to Europe should consider buying an **International Camping Carnet.** Like the hostel membership card, it's required at a few campgrounds and provides discounts or preferred camping at others. It also provides third-party insurance. It is available to AAA members in North America from the **Canadian Automobile Association** (www.caa.ca) and in the UK from **The Caravan Club** (see below).

AUTOMOBILE ASSOCIATIONS

Automobile Association, Contact Centre, Car Ellison House, William Armstrong Drive, Newcastle-upon-Tyne NE4 7YA, UK. (General info ☎0870 600 0371; www.theaa.com). Publishes Big Road Atlases for France and its regions, as well as the rest of Europe.

The Caravan Club, East Grinstead House, East Grinstead, West Sussex, RH19 1UA, UK (☎01342 326 944; www.caravanclub.co.uk). For UK£30, members get special deals on ferries, insurance services, and monthly magazine.

The Mountaineers Books, 1001 SW Klickitat Way, #201, Seattle, WA 98134, USA (☎800-553-4453 or 206-223-6303; www.mountaineersbooks.org). Over 400 titles on hiking, biking, mountaineering, natural history, and conservation.

GUIDEBOOKS

Hikers will want to bring or acquire guidebooks for their travels. The **Institut Géographique National (IGN)** publishes the acclaimed **Blue Series** of maps for hikers, as well as many road maps. The Blue Series is sold throughout France; for more info contact their map superstore in Paris: **Espace IGN,** 107 rue La Boétie, 75008 Paris (☎01 43 98 84 10; www.ign.fr). You can buy IGN maps in **Australia** from **Hema maps,** P.O. Box 4365, Eight Mile Plains QLD 4113 Australia (☎07 33 40 00 00; www.hemamaps.com.au); in **Canada** from **Ulysse,** 4176 rue St-Denis, Montreal, Québec H2W 2M5 (☎514-843-9447; www.ulysse.ca); in the **UK** from **Footprint Maps,** 25 Saltesford Lane, Alton, Staffordshire, ST10 4AY (☎0153 870 3642; fax 870 2019; www.lynx.net.uk/aspidistra); and in the **US** from Map Link Inc., 30 S. La Patera Lane, Unit #5, Santa Barbara, CA 93117 (☎800-962-1394 or 805-692-6777; www.maplink.com). Maps can be ordered by mail from IGN Sologne, Administration des ventes, 41200 Romorantin-Lanthenay, France.

CAMPING & HIKING EQUIPMENT

Stores with camping and outdoor equipment abound in hiker-friendly towns in the Alps and Pyrénées but may be difficult to find elsewhere, so plan ahead if purchasing equipment in France.

Sleeping Bag: Sleeping bags are identified by the season they are designed for ("summer" means 30-40°F at night; "four-season" or "winter" means below 0°F). They are made either of **down** (warm and light, but disgusting when wet) or **synthetic** material (durable and less soggy when wet). Prices range US$80-210 for a summer synthetic, US$250-300 for a quality down winter bag. Sleeping bags can be accompanied by foam pads (US$10-20), air mattresses (US$15-50), and Therm-A-Rest self-inflating pads (US$45-80). A **stuff sack** stores your sleeping bag and keeps it dry.

Tent: The best tents, especially low-profile dome tents, are free-standing, set up quickly, and only require staking in high winds. Good 2-person tents start at US$90, 4-person US$300. Seal the seams of your tent with **waterproofer**, and bring a **battery-operated lantern**, a plastic **groundcloth**, and a **nylon tarp**.

Backpack: Flexible **internal-frame packs**, better for difficult hikes, mold to your back and maintain a low center of gravity. Less flexible **external-frame packs** are more comfortable for long hikes over even terrain; they keep weight higher and distribute it more evenly. Your pack should have a strong, padded hip-belt to transfer weight to your legs. Serious backpackers need at least 4000 inches cubed (16,000cc) of pack space. Sturdy backpacks cost US$125-420.

Boots: Bring hiking boots with good **ankle support** that fit snugly and comfortably over two pairs of socks (wool and thin liner). Break in your boots before hiking.

Other Necessities: Synthetic layers (like polypropylene) and a **pile jacket** maintain warmth close to the body, even when wet. A **space blanket** (US$5-15) retains your body heat and doubles as a groundcloth when camping. Be sure to bring shatter- and leak-proof plastic **water bottles** and **water-purification tablets** in case you cannot boil water in the outdoors. Since most French campgrounds forbid making fires, you'll also definitely need a **camp stove** for cooking food (the classic Coleman starts at US$45) and a propane **fuel bottle** to get the stove going. When going camping and hiking, also don't forget a **first-aid kit, pocketknife, insect repellent, calamine lotion,** and **waterproof matches** or a **lighter**.

CAMPERS & RVS

Renting an RV or campervan is more expensive than tenting or hosteling in France, but it is cheaper than staying in hotels and renting a car to get around. With RVs, you also get to have your own bedroom, bathroom, and kitchen. Rates vary widely by region, season (July and August are most expensive, as that is when many French people go on vacation), and type of RV. Rental prices for a standard RV are around US$1200. **Auto Europe** rents RVs out of Paris, Lyon, and Marseilles. (US ☎ 888-223-5555, UK toll-free 0191 247 8501; www.autoeurope.com.)

ORGANIZED ADVENTURE TRIPS

Organized adventure tours are structured ways of exploring the wild through organized activities like hiking, biking, skiing, canoeing, kayaking, rafting, and climbing. Tourism bureaus and outdoor stores will have info about these tours (see p. 28). **Specialty Travel Index** offers tours worldwide. (☎ 888-624-4030 or 415-455-1643; www.specialtytravel.com.)

ESSENTIALS

ESSENTIALS

WILDERNESS SAFETY

Stay warm, stay dry, and stay hydrated. The weather can change suddenly, so pay attention to the sky and check **weather forecasts:** www.intellicast.com/Local-Weather/World/Europe and www.meteo.fr provide up-to-date meteorological info. Dress in wool or warm synthetic layers and pack raingear, a hat, and mittens. Also pack a first-aid kit, a reflector, a whistle, high-energy food, and extra water. Let a friend, hostel owner, park ranger, or local hiking organization know when and where you are hiking. Do not attempt a hike that is beyond your ability. See **Health,** p. 18, for info about outdoor ailments and medical concerns.

KEEPING IN TOUCH

MAIL

SENDING MAIL FROM FRANCE

Surface mail saves a lot of money, but it takes one to three months to cross the Atlantic and two to four to cross the Pacific. **Airmail** is the fastest way to send mail home. **Aerogrammes,** printed sheets that fold into envelopes, more private versions of post cards, travel by air and are faster than regular airmail. Purchase an aerogramme at a post office and write *par avion* on the front. It is usually impossible or expensive to send enclosures with aerogrammes.

SENDING MAIL TO FRANCE

Mark envelopes *air mail* or *par avion*. In addition to the standard postage system, **Federal Express** (US and Canada ☎ 800-247-4747, Australia 13 26 10, New Zealand 0800 73 33 39, UK 0800 12 38 00; www.fedex.com) handles express mail services from many countries to France; they can get a letter from New York to France in two days for US$50 and from London to Paris in two days for US$30.

RECEIVING MAIL IN FRANCE

Mail can be sent Poste Restante (General Delivery) to be picked up by the addressee. We list post offices and postal codes and note when a town's Poste Restante code differs from its postal code. To pick up Poste Restante mail, bring a passport, €0.25 for periodicals, and €0.50 for packages. Mail is held for up to 15 days. Offices will not accept courier service deliveries (e.g. Federal Express) or anything requiring a signature for *Poste Restante*. Address letters in this format:

> PICARD, Jean-Luc
> Poste Restante: [post office address]
> [5-digit postal code] [TOWN]
> FRANCE.
> HOLD.

BY TELEPHONE

CALLING HOME FROM FRANCE

A calling card is the cheapest way to make international calls. Cards are either billed or prepaid. **Billed** cards cost a small fee and charge the recipient of your call or bill you upon your return home. A cheaper but less convenient option is a prepaid calling card. You can frequently call collect without buying a company's calling card by dialing their access number and following the instructions (see **International Direct Dial,** below). To obtain a calling card or the access number, contact your national telecommunications service.

COMPANY	TO OBTAIN A CARD, DIAL:	TO CALL ABROAD, DIAL:
AT&T (US)	800-361-4670	0 800 99 00 11
British Telecom Direct	800 34 51 44	0 800 99 02 44
Canada Direct	800-668-6878	0 800 99 00 16 or 0 800 99 02 16
Ireland Direct	800 40 00 00	0 800 58 05 00
MCI (US)	800-444-3333	0 800 99 00 19
New Zealand Direct	0800 00 00 00	0 800 99 00 64
Sprint (US)	800-877-4646	0 800 99 00 97
Telkom South Africa	10 219	0 800 99 00 27
Telstra Australia	13 22 00	0 800 99 00 61

Let's Go has recently partnered with **ekit.com** (www.letsgo.ekit.com) to provide a calling card that offers a number of services, including email and voice messaging. Always compare rates before buying a calling card.

PLACING INTERNATIONAL CALLS. To call France from home or to call home from France, dial:

1. The **international direct dialing prefix.** To call out of **France,** dial ☎ 00; **Australia,** 0011; **Canada** or the **US,** 011; the **Republic of Ireland, New Zealand,** or the **UK,** 00; **South Africa,** 09.
2. The **country code** of the country you want to call. For **Australia,** dial ☎ 61; **Canada** or the **US,** 1; the **Republic of Ireland,** 353; **New Zealand,** 64; **South Africa,** 27; the **UK,** 44; **France,** 33.
3. The **city/area code.** *Let's Go* lists the city/area codes for each French city and town; find it directly after the ☎ symbol in each phone number. Omit the first zero of this number when calling from abroad (e.g. dial 20, not 020, to reach London from Canada).
4. The 8-digit **local number.**

CALLING WITHIN FRANCE

Coin-operated phones are nearly impossible to find in France. Most public phones require a **prepaid phone card,** or *Télécarte* (available at post offices and *tabacs*). One kind of card is inserted into the phone to place calls. Another kind of card comes with a Personal Identification Number (PIN) and a toll-free access number: with these cards, you call the access number and follow the directions on the card. These cards can be used to make international as well as domestic calls. *Télécartes* are available in 50-unit (€7.50) and 120-unit (€15) denominations; one minute of a local call uses about one unit. Sometimes certain credit cards (Visa, Mastercard/Eurocard) can be used in place of a *Télécarte*. Do not use long-distance calling cards to call within France—the company will bill you for the call to the overseas access number and then for the call from the access number to France. Emergency numbers, directory information (☎ 12), and toll-free numbers *(numéros verts)* beginning with 0800 can be dialed without a card or coins.

If the phone you use does not provide English commands, proceed with caution, since French payphones are notoriously unforgiving. *Décrochez* means pick up; *patientez* means wait. Do not dial until you see *numérotez* or *composez. Raccro-*

chez means "hang up." To make another call, press the green button instead of hanging up. Rates tend to be high in the morning, intermediate in the evening, and low on Sundays and late at night. Calls with a 120-unit card are 50% cheaper after 7pm Monday-Friday, from noon to midnight Saturday, and all day Sunday. Expect to pay about €0.45 per minute to the UK, Ireland, and North America and about €1.50 per minute to Australia, New Zealand, and South Africa.

Calling collect *(faire un appel en PCV)* is an expensive alternative to the calling card. Though convenient, in-room hotel calls often incur arbitrary and pricey surcharges (as much as US$10).

CELL PHONES

Most American cell phones do not work in France. Check with your service provider to see if your phone's band can be switched to 900/1800, which will register your phone with one of the three French servers: **Bouygue** (www.bouygtel.com), **Itineris** (www.ifrance.com/binto/itineris.htm), or **France Télécom** (www.francetele-com.com/fr/). Phones can also be rented for delivery or airport pickup: try **Ellinas Phone Rental** (☎01 48 16 10 99), **Rent a Cell** (☎01 53 93 78 09; www.rentacell.com), or **Cellular Abroad** (http://cellularabroad.com/franceRcell.html). If you plan to stay in France for several months, buy a French cell phone. In France, incoming calls to cell phones are free (even from abroad), local calls are charged the local rate, and cell phone service is free. Cell phone calls are paid for with a **Mobicarte**, a prepaid card. Mobicartes are available in denominations of €15, €25, or €35.

EMAIL

Most major **post offices** and some branches now offer Internet access at special "cyberposte" terminals. Rechargeable cards provide 1hr. of access at the post office for €7. Every hour after that is €4. Most large towns in France have at least

one cybercafé, the listing for which can be found in the Practical Information section of the town chapter. **Cybercafes.com** can find a cybercafé near you.

Though in some places it's possible to forge a remote link with your home server, in most cases this is a much slower (and thus more expensive) option than taking advantage of free **web-based email accounts** (e.g., www.hotmail.com and www.yahoo.com). Travelers with laptops can call an Internet service provider via a modem. The cost of a modem call is steep, but some long-distance cards can defray the cost. Also be aware that many hotel switchboards use the **PBX** system, which fries modems without a **converter** (US$50).

MEDIA IN FRANCE

LES JOURNAUX. Most French papers are politically oriented. *Le Monde* is France's most well known newspaper and leans slightly to the left. Popular *Le Figaro* is slightly right-of-center. *Le Parisien* targets readers in the capital. *Le Libération* ("Libé") is big among left-wingers, *L'Humanité* among the Communist fringe. Many French read news magazines, including the liberal *Nouvel Observateur;* conservative *L'Express;* the vacuous *Paris-Match;* and the witty, complex *le Canard Enchainé*. The *New York Times*, the *Times of London*, and the *International Herald Tribune* can be purchased in major cities.

LA RADIO. Most corporate and public radio stations are national. Popular national stations are *Fun Radio, NRJ, RTL*, and *Skyrock* for teens; *Nostalgie* for older listeners; and *Europe 1* for news. Public stations include *France Inter*, a general-interest station, and *France Info*, a news channel. Most music played is anglophone; a French law requires that radios play 40% francophone music, but stations typically fill the quota between 1 and 6am. Check local radio frequencies at http://schoop.free.fr/nvfreqs.shtml.

TELEVISION. France has six major national TV channels. Three are public: **France 2** with news, educational, and entertainment shows; **France 3** with regional programs and occasional news; **La Cinquième** with cartoons, game shows, and documentaries until 7pm, when it becomes **Arte,** a cultural channel. Three channels are private. **Canal+** exhibits foreign and French films; **TF1,** the most popular station in France, produces news, sports, and general-interest programs; **M6,** a more vacuous version of the American MTV, is geared towards teenagers and young adults. France has 25 cable channels, as well as numerous local stations. Two popular cable news stations are **Canal France International** and **La Chaine Info.**

GETTING TO FRANCE

BY PLANE

A little effort searching for flights can save you a bundle. If you are able to tolerate certain restrictions, courier fares are the cheapest. Good deals can be found from consolidators, by flying standby, from last-minute specials, or charter flights. Students, seniors, and those under 26 should never pay full price for a ticket.

AIRFARES

Airfares to France peak between June and September and at Easter and Christmas. The cheapest fares involve a Saturday night stay. Traveling with an "open return" ticket is pricier than fixing a return date. Most fixed budget tickets don't

allow date or route changes. Round-trip flights are much cheaper than "open-jaw" trips (arriving and departing from different cities). Flights between capitals or regional hubs have the cheapest fares. Paris is the most affordable point of entry from outside Europe, though other cities offer good fares to travelers from Ireland and the UK. Globe-hoppers should consider a **Round-the-World (RTW)** ticket, which includes at least 3 stops, is priced by total mileage, and remains valid for a year after purchase. Prices range US$3500-5000. Try **Northwest Airlines/KLM** (US ☎800-447-4747; www.nwa.com) or **Star Alliance,** a consortium of 22 airlines including United Airlines (US ☎800-241-6522; www.star-alliance.com). Round-trip fares to Paris from the US range from US$250-500 (low season) to US$300-800 (high season); from Australia, between AUS$1600 and AUS$2500; from New Zealand, NZ$5000-9000; from Britain, UK£60-80; from Dublin to Paris, as little as IR£120.

BUDGET & STUDENT TRAVEL AGENCIES

Though travel agencies can make your life easier, they may not always find the lowest possible fare since they get paid on commission. Travelers holding **ISICs** and **IYTCs** (see p. 11) can get discounts on student travel agency services.

USIT, 19-21 Aston Quay, Dublin 2 (☎01 602 1600; www.usitworld.com). Ireland's leading student/budget travel agency has 22 offices throughout Northern Ireland and the Republic of Ireland.

CTS Travel, 30 Rathbone St., **London** W1T IGO, UK (☎0207 290 0630; www.ctstravel.co.uk). A British student travel agent with offices in 39 countries including at the Empire State Building, 350 Fifth Ave., ste. 7813, New York, NY 10118 (☎877-287-6665; www.ctstravelusa.com).

STA Travel, 7890 S. Hardy Dr., ste. 110, Tempe, AZ 85284, USA (24hr. reservations and info ☎800-781-4040; www.sta-travel.com). A student and youth travel organization with over 150 offices worldwide, including US offices in Boston, Chicago, L.A., New York, San Francisco, Seattle, and Washington, D.C. Ticket booking, travel insurance, railpasses, and more. In the UK, walk-in office 11 Goodge St., **London** W1T 2PF (☎0207 436 7779). In New Zealand, Shop 2B, 182 Queen St., **Auckland** (☎09 309 0458). In Australia, 366 Lygon St., **Carlton** Vic 3053 (☎03 9349 4344).

Travel CUTS (Canadian Universities Travel Services Limited), 187 College St., **Toronto,** ON M5T 1P7 (☎416-979-2406; www.travelcuts.com). 60 offices across Canada and the US. Also in the UK, 295-A Regent St., **London** W1B 2H9 (☎02072 255 2191).

Wasteels, Skoubogade 6, 1158 Copenhagen K. (☎3314 4633; www.wasteels.com). A chain with 180 locations across Europe. Sells BIJ tickets discounted 30-45% off regular fare, 2nd-class international train tickets with unlimited stopovers for those under 25.

Contiki Travel (☎1-888-CONTIKI/1-888-266-8454; www.contiki.com) offers comprehensive bus tour packages. They run 13-day tours starting at $959.

COMMERCIAL AIRLINES

The commercial airlines' lowest regular offer is the **APEX** (Advance Purchase Excursion) fare, which provides confirmed reservations and allows "open-jaw" tickets. Generally, reservations must be made seven to 21 days ahead of departure, with seven- to 14-day minimum-stay and up to 90-day maximum-stay restrictions. These fares carry hefty cancellation and change penalties (fees rise in summer). Book peak-season APEX fares early; by May you will have a hard time getting your desired departure date.

TRAVELING FROM NORTH AMERICA

Basic round-trip fares to Western Europe range roughly US$200-750; to Frankfurt, US$300-750; London, US$200-600; Paris, US$250-700. Standard commercial carri-

FLIGHT PLANNING ON THE INTERNET. Many airline sites offer special last-minute deals on the Web. Other sites compile the deals for you—try www.bestfares.com, www.flights.com, www.hotdeals.com, www.lowestfare.com, www.onetravel.com, and www.travelzoo.com.

StudentUniverse (www.studentuniverse.com), **STA** (www.sta-travel.com), Council (www.counciltravel.com) and **Orbitz.com** provide quotes on student tickets. **Expedia** (www.expedia.com) and **Travelocity** (www.travelocity.com) offer full travel services. **Priceline** (www.priceline.com) has you specify your desired price and obligates you to buy any ticket that meets or beats it, including ones with late hours and odd routes. **Skyauction** (www.skyauction.com) allows you to bid on both last-minute and advance-purchase tickets.

An indispensable Internet resource is the *Air Traveler's Handbook* (www.cs.cmu.edu/afs/cs/user/mkant/Public/Travel/airfare.html), a comprehensive listing of links to everything you need to know before you board a plane.

ers like **American** (☎800-433-7300; www.aa.com) and **United** (☎800-241-6522; www.ual.com) offer the most convenient flights, but rarely the cheapest. If any of their limited departure points is convenient for you, you might find a better deal on **Icelandair** (☎800-223-5500; www.icelandair.com), **Finnair** (☎800-950-5000; www.us.finnair.com), or **Martinair** (☎800-627-8462; www.martinair.com). Icelandair offers stopovers in Iceland for no extra cost on most transatlantic flights. Other places to look for cheap fares are **Air France** (☎802-802-802; www.airfrance.com), **British Airways** (☎800-403-0882; www.britishairways.com), **Scandinavian Airways** (☎800-221-2350; www.scandinavian.net), **Air Canada** (☎888-422-7533; www.aircanada.ca/e-home.html), and **US Airways** (☎800-428-4322; www.usairways.com). It may also be worthwhile to check United's last-minute special e-fares deals, available online.

TRAVELING FROM THE UK & IRELAND

The **Air Travel Advisory Bureau** in London (☎020 7636 5000; www.atab.co.uk) refers you to travel agencies and consolidators with discounted airfares from the UK. Although there is never a shortage of flights from the British Isles to the continent, you might find especially sweet deals from some of the following.

Aer Lingus: Ireland ☎0818 365 000; www.aerlingus.ie. Ireland to Paris (€49).

British Midland Airways: UK ☎0870 607 05 55; www.flybmi.com. Departures from throughout the UK. London to Paris (UK£71).

easyJet: UK ☎0870 600 00 00; www.easyjet.com. London to Nice (UK£50-90). Online tickets.

KLM: UK ☎0870 507 40 74; www.klmuk.com. Roundtrip London to Paris (UK£135).

Ryanair: Ireland ☎0818 303 030, UK 0870 156 95 69; www.ryanair.ie. From Dublin, London, and Glasgow to destinations throughout France for €20-30. They offer deals from as low as €3 on limited weekend specials.

TRAVELING FROM AUSTRALIA & NEW ZEALAND

In addition to the airlines listed below, good deals may be found from **Austrian Airlines** (www.aua.com).

Air New Zealand, New Zealand ☎0800 73 70 00; www.airnz.co.nz. Auckland to London and Frankfurt.

Qantas Air, Australia ☎13 13 13, New Zealand ☎0800 808 767; www.qantas.com.au. Flights from Australia and New Zealand to London around AUS$2400.

Singapore Air, Australia ☎13 10 11, New Zealand ☎0800 808 909; www.sin-gaporeair.com. From Auckland, Sydney, Melbourne, and Perth to Western Europe.

Thai Airways, Australia ☎1300 65 19 60, New Zealand ☎09 377 02 68; www.thaiair.com. Auckland, Sydney, and Melbourne to Amsterdam, Frankfurt, and London.

Cathay Pacific, in France ☎01 41 43 75 75; in Australia ☎13 17 47. Reasonable RTW fares and flights to Paris, connecting to Australia via Hong Kong.

TRAVELING FROM SOUTH AFRICA

Good places to look for low fares are Air France (☎01 17 70 16 01; www.airfrance.com/za), British Airways (☎0860 011 747; www.british-airways.com/regional/sa), Lufthansa (☎0861 842 538; www.lufthansa.co.za), and Virgin Atlantic (☎0113 403 400; www.virgin-atlantic.co.za).

AIR COURIER FLIGHTS

If you travel light, consider courier flights. As a courier, you take only carry-on and allow the airline to use your luggage space to transport cargo. Most courier flights are round-trip only, with short fixed-length stays (usually one week) and many restrictions. Most flights leave from New York, Los Angeles, San Francisco, or Miami in the US; and from Montreal, Toronto, or Vancouver in Canada. Round-trip courier fares from the US to France can be as low as US$200. Generally, couriers must be over 21 (in some cases, 18). In summer, the most popular destinations usually require an advance reservation of about two weeks. Super-discounted flights are common for last-minute flights (three to 14 days ahead).

FROM THE UK, IRELAND, AUSTRALIA, & NEW ZEALAND

The minimum age for couriers from the **UK** is usually 18. **Brave New World Enterprises,** P.O. Box 22212, London SE5 8WB (www.courierflights.com) publishes a directory of all the companies offering courier flights in the UK (UK£10, in electronic form UK£8). **British Airways Travel Shop** (☎08702 400 747; www.batravelshops.com) arranges some flights from London to destinations in continental Europe (specials may be as low as UK£60). **Global Courier Travel** (see above) also offers flights from London and Dublin to continental Europe and often has listings from Sydney and Auckland to London, and occasionally Frankfurt.

STANDBY FLIGHTS

Companies dealing in standby flights sell vouchers rather than tickets with the promise to get you to or near your destination within a certain window of time (typically one to five days). You may receive a monetary refund if every available flight within your date range is full but you will receive only credit (if that) if you do not attempt to board an available flight. Carefully read agreements with companies offering standby flights, as tricky fine print can leave you in the lurch. To check on a company's service record in the US, call the Better Business Bureau (☎212-533-6200). One established standby company in the US is **Air-Hitch,** 481 8th Ave., #1771, New York, NY 10001, USA (☎877-247-4482 or 212-736-0505; www.airhitch.com), which offers one-way flights from the US to Paris (US$127-155) and round-trip flights from Newark to Paris (US$127-188) and Los Angeles to Paris (US$212-243).

TICKET CONSOLIDATORS

Ticket consolidators, or **"bucket shops,"** buy unsold tickets in bulk from commercial airlines and sell them at discounted rates. The best place to look is in the Sunday travel section of major papers, where many bucket shops place tiny ads. Call quickly, as availability is limited. Not all bucket shops are reliable, so insist on a receipt that gives full details of restrictions, refunds, and tickets, and pay by credit card (in spite of the 2-5% fee) so you can stop payment if you never receive tickets. For more info, see www.travel-library.com/air-travel/consolidators.html. For a list of consolidators who sell to the public, visit www.senior-center.com/air1.htm.

CHARTER FLIGHTS

Charters are flights a tour operator contracts with an airline to fly sizeable numbers of passengers during peak season. Flights may be cancelled or change their schedule as late as 48 hours before the trip without a full refund. Check-in, boarding, and baggage claim are often slow. Charter flights are, however, usually cheaper than regular flights. **Discount clubs** and **fare brokers** offer savings to members on last-minute charter and tours. **Travelers Advantage,** Trumbull, CT, USA (☎877-259-2691; www.travelersadvantage.com; US$60 annual fee includes discounts and directories) specializes in European travel and tour packages.

BY CHUNNEL FROM THE UK

Traversing 27 mi. under the sea, the Chunnel is undoubtedly the fastest, most convenient, and least scenic route from England to France.

BY TRAIN. Eurostar, Eurostar House, Waterloo Station, London SE1 8SE (UK ☎0990 186 186; US ☎800-387-6782; elsewhere call UK 020 7928 5163; www.eurostar.com; www.raileurope.com) runs frequent trains between London and the continent. Ten to twenty-eight trains per day run to Paris (3hr., €75-159), Brussels (4hr., €75-159), and Disneyland Paris. Routes include stops at Ashford in England, and Avignon, Calais, and Lille in France.

BY BUS. Both **Eurolines** and **Eurobus** provide bus-ferry combinations (see below).

BY CAR. Eurotunnel, P.O. Box 2000, Folkestone, Kent CT18 8XY (www.eurotunnel.co.uk) shuttles cars and passengers between Kent and Nord-Pas-de-Calais. Book online or via phone.

BY BUS

For British travelers, buses are the cheapest way to get to France, with return fares starting around UK£50 including ferry/chunnel transport. Often cheaper than railpasses, **international bus passes** typically allow unlimited hop-on, hop-off travel between major European cities.

> **Eurolines,** 4 Cardiff Rd., Luton L41 1PP, UK (☎08705 143 219; www.eurolines.com). Return fares from London to Paris from UK£49. 15-day (UK£113-174), 30-day (UK£153-259) and 60-day (UK£189-299) passes are available.

> **Busabout,** 258 Vauxhall Bridge Rd., London SW1V 1BS, UK (☎020 7950 1661; www.busabout.com). 5 interconnecting bus circuits covering 60 cities and towns in Europe. Consecutive day passes and Flexi Passes available. Sells two-week, consecutive-day passes (US$339, students US$309) and season passes (US$1149/1039). Flexipasses valid for 7 days out of 1 month (US$339/309) or 24 days out of 4months (US$909/809) also available.

BY BOAT

The fares below are **one-way** for **adult foot passengers** unless otherwise noted. Though standard round-trip fares are usually just twice the one-way fare, **fixed period returns** (usually within five days) are almost invariably cheaper. Ferries run

year-round unless otherwise noted. Bringing a **bike** is usually free, although you may have to pay up to UK£10 in high season. For a **camper/trailer** supplement, you will have to add UK£20-140 to the "with car" fare. A directory of ferries in this region can be found at www.seaview.co.uk/ferries.html.

GETTING AROUND FRANCE

France is blessed with a well-maintained and exceptionally complete network of roads, and traveling by car can offer greater freedom to explore the countryside and greater flexibility than trains. The costs of driving, however, can make it an expensive alternative, especially for people traveling alone or in pairs. Traveling by train is the most comfortable way to travel in France. France's network of high-speed and local trains connects all but the most minor towns.

To buy a one-way ticket for a train, bus, or plane in France, ask for *"un billet aller simple;"* for a round-trip ticket, request *"un billet aller-retour."* Round-trip fares are often cheaper than two one-ways.

 TRANSPORTATION LISTINGS: CENTER-OUT. Let's Go employs the "center-out" principle for transportation listings: for each town, we describe only how to reach towns of similar or greater importance. If you're in a big city, information on reaching neighboring small towns will be in the small towns themselves rather than in the big city.

BY PLANE

Only high-rollers get around France by plane. With most major cities linked by high-speed rail lines, taking a train can be just as fast as flying. The one exception is travel to **Corsica;** frequent air services from Nice, Marseille, and Paris to Ajaccio and Bastia compare competitively to the 10hr. ferry crossing. Expect to pay about US$150 round-trip from **Nice** to Corsica or US$200 from **Paris;** see **Corsica: Intercity Transportation,** p. 759, for details.

BY BOAT

FERRIES. Aside from accessing the many islands along the French seaboard, the only time you will take a ferry in France is to reach Corsica. Ferries are far slower than flying (the trip lasts 7-12 hr.) and not much cheaper. Expect to pay about €92.50 roundtrip per person and €30.50-91.50 per car. An additional option, high-speed hydrofoil service from Nice to Calvi and Bastia, takes about 3 hours. For details, see **Corsica: Intercity Transportation,** p. 759.

RIVERBOATS. France has over 5300 miles of navigable rivers and canals. For details on regulations and ports, see www.franceguide.com. For a list of companies renting out boats and organizing waterborne vacations, contact the **Fédération des Industries Nautiques,** Port de Javel-Haut, 75015 Paris (☎01 44 37 04 00; www.france-nautic.com).

BY TRAIN

The French national railway company, **SNCF,** operates one of the most efficient transportation systems in the world. Their **TGVs** (*trains à grande vitesse*, or high-speed trains) are among the fastest in the world. The slower but cheaper **Rapide** service stops at most major cities, and the **Express** (sometimes called **TER** for *Train Express Régionale*), which are slowest of all, stop at large and middle-sized cities. **TEE** (*Trains Europe Express*) are non-stop fast trains between European cities. **Trains de banlieue** are commuter trains to suburbs. On long trips, trains sometime split at crossroads, so make sure you're in the right carriage. Trains are not always safe. For safety tips, see p. 16. For help with planning itineraries, buying tickets, and making reservations, contact **Budget Europe Travel Services,** 2557 Meade Ct., Ann Arbor, MI 48105 (☎800-441-2387, 800-441-9413, 734-668-0529, or 734-668-0529; www.budgeteuropetravel.com).

| SNCF HOTLINE | ☎08 91 67 68 69 for timetable info and reservations. |

RESERVATIONS. The TGV requires **reservations,** which cost US$11 if made in the US and US$3.50 if made in France. Reservations are optional on local and regional trains, but it's advisable to make one during busy periods, especially if you want to avoid standing during long train rides, or sitting in the smoking section. TGV reservations can be made up to a few minutes before departure, but other services should be arranged before noon the day of a post-5pm departure and before 8pm the day before a pre-5pm departure. Most TGVs sell a limited number of **standby** tickets, which guarantee travel on the train but not necessarily a seat. Reservations (with optional seat or couchette) can be made by a travel agent, in person at the train station, or at www.raileurope.com. On especially fast or comfortable sections of the TGV, if you do not have a Eurailpass or Europass, you may need to purchase a **supplement** (US$10-50), although supplements are usually included in the price of point-to-point tickets.

COMPOSTEZ! Before boarding a train, you must validate your ticket by having it *composté* (stamped with the date and time) by one of the orange machines near the platforms. You must re-validate your ticket at any connection in your trip.

OVERNIGHT TRAINS. Night trains don't waste valuable daylight hours and defray hostel or hotel costs. Sleep upright in your seat, purchase a reclining seat, or buy a slightly more luxurious open-bunk **couchette** (about US$28 per person). These coed compartments are, to put it mildly, cozy, sleeping up to six men and women in triple-stacked bunks (1st-class couchettes have four bunks). **Sleepers** (beds) in sleeping cars offer more privacy and comfort for a bigger price tag. Singles, doubles, and sometimes triples are available. Those with limited-day railpasses should note that an overnight train that departs after 7pm uses only one travel day.

SHOULD YOU BUY A RAILPASS? Ideally, a railpass would allow you to spontaneously jump on any train to anywhere, but in practice, you still wait in line to pay for supplements and seat and couchette reservations. Worse, railpasses aren't necessarily cost-effective. There are many forms of discounts on regular rail travel in France (see **Discount Rail Tickets,** p. 45), especially for those under 25. To evaluate your options more precisely, get the prices of relevant point-to-point tickets from the SNCF website (www.sncf.com), add them, and compare with railpass prices.

MULTINATIONAL RAILPASSES

EURAILPASS. The Eurailpass is valid in most of Western Europe: Austria, Belgium, Denmark, Finland, France, Germany, Greece, Hungary, Italy, Luxembourg, the Netherlands, Norway, Portugal, the Republic of Ireland, Spain, Sweden, and Switzerland. It is not valid in the UK. Consecutive-day **Eurailpasses** are valid on any or all days for the duration of the pass. They work best if you spend a lot of time on trains every few days. **Flexipasses,** valid for any 10 or 15 days within a two-month period, are more cost-effective for those traveling long distances but less frequently. **Saverpasses** provide up to 15% discounts on 1st-class travel for travelers in groups of two to five. **Youthpasses** and **Youth Flexipasses** give discounts of up to 30% for those under 26. Usually, the cheapest option is the **Selectpass,** which allows you to travel in your choice of 3, 4, or 5 adjoining countries for any 5, 6, 8, or 10 days in a two-month period. This pass replaces the **Europass.** For more information, visit www.eurail.com.

EURAILPASSES	15 DAYS	21 DAYS	1 MONTH	2 MONTHS	3 MONTHS
1st class Eurailpass	US$572	US$740	US$918	US$1298	US$1606
Eurail Saverpass	US$486	US$630	US$780	US$1106	US$1366
Eurail Youthpass	US$401	US$518	US$644	US$910	US$1126

EURAIL FLEXIPASSES	10 DAYS IN 2 MONTHS	15 DAYS IN 2 MONTHS
1st class Eurail Flexipass	US$674	US$888
Eurail Saver Flexipass	US$574	US$756
Eurail Youth Flexipass	US$473	US$622

SELECTPASSES		5 DAYS	6 DAYS	8 DAYS	10 DAYS	15 DAYS
Selectpass:	3-country	US$356	US$394	US$470	US$542	N/A
	4-country	US$398	US$436	US$512	US$584	N/A
	5-country	US$438	US$476	US$552	US$624	US$794
Saver:	3-country	US$304	US$336	US$400	US$460	N/A
	4-country	US$340	US$372	US$436	US$496	N/A
	5-country	US$374	US$406	US$470	US$560	US$674
Youth:	3-country	US$249	US$276	US$329	US$379	N/A
	4-country	US$279	US$306	US$359	US$409	N/A
	5-country	US$307	US$334	US$387	US$437	US$556

Passholders receive a timetable for major routes and a map with details on possible ferry, bus, car rental, hotel, and Eurostar (see p. 40) discounts.

SHOPPING AROUND FOR A EURAIL PASS. Eurail passes are designed by the EU itself, and can be bought only by non-Europeans and almost exclusively from non-European distributors. These passes are sold at uniform prices set by the EU. Travel agents typically tack on a US$15 handling fee per order. Purchase a pass before January 1 if you plan to travel within six months into the year (passes must be validated within 6 months of purchase).

Purchase your Eurailpass before leaving, since only a few places in major European cities sell them (at marked-up prices). You can get a replacement for a lost pass only if you have purchased insurance on it (US$15-21). Eurailpasses are available through travel agents, student travel agencies like STA (see p. 35), and **Rail Europe,** 500 Mamaroneck Ave., Harrison, NY 10528 (US ☎888-382-7245, Canada 800-361-7245, UK 0990 84 88 48; www.raileurope.com) or **DER Travel Services,** with several posts across the US (US ☎888-337-7350; www.der.com).

OTHER MULTINATIONAL PASSES. Regional passes are good values for travels limited to one area. The **France 'n' Italy Pass** and the **France 'n' Spain Pass** offer 4-10 days of unlimited travel in two months (details vary between the two passes). The **France 'n' Italy Saverpass** and **France 'n' Spain Saverpass** offer discounts to travelers in groups of two or more; the **France 'n' Italy Youthpass** and the **France 'n' Spain Youthpass** offer discounts to travelers under 26.

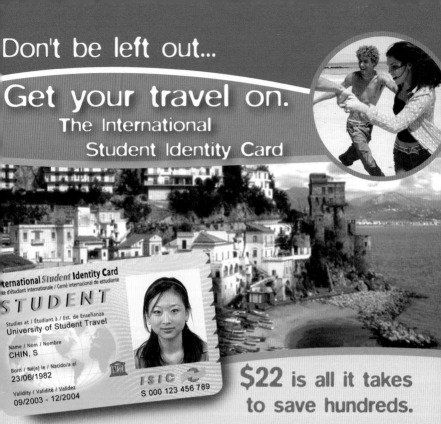

FRANCE 'N' ITALY PASS	1ST CLASS	2ND CLASS
Single Adult	US$405	US$374
Saverpass	US$347	US$304
Youthpass	N/A	US$289

FRANCE 'N' SPAIN PASS	1ST CLASS	2ND CLASS
Single Adult	US$424	US$366
Saverpass	US$360	US$311
Youthpass	N/A	US$275

InterRail Passes provide discounts on unlimited rail travel for travelers who have lived at least six months in Europe, which makes them particularly relevant to students who have studied abroad for at least six months. There are eight zones in the InterRail Pass system—France is in Zone E (along with Belgium, the Netherlands, and Luxembourg). The **Under 26 InterRail Card** gives either 21 consecutive days or one month of unlimited travel within one, two, three or all eight zones (UK£119-249, costlier for more zones). A card can be purchased for 12 days of travel in one zone (UK£119). The **Over 26 InterRail Card** provides the same services, but at UK£169-355, as does the new **Child Pass** (ages 4-11) for UK£85-178. Passholders receive **discounts** on rail travel, Eurostar journeys, and most ferries to Ireland, Scandinavia, and the rest of Europe. The pass generally does not cover **supplements** for high-speed trains. For info and ticket sales in Europe contact **Student Travel Centre,** 24 Rupert St., 1st fl., London W1V 7FN (☎020 74 37 81 01; www.student-travel-centre.com). The pass is also sold by travel agents, ticket booths at major train stations, and online (www.railpassdirect.co.uk).

DOMESTIC RAILPASSES

If you are planning to spend a significant amount of time within one country or region, a national pass may be more cost-effective than a multinational pass. Many national passes, however, are limited. Although they are valid on all rail lines of a country's rail company, many don't offer the free or discounted travel on private railways and ferries that Eurail does. Some of these passes can be bought only in Europe, some only outside of Europe: check with a railpass agent.

NATIONAL RAILPASSES. Only residents of non-EU countries are eligible for France's national railpasses, which allow four days of unlimited travel during a one-month period.

FRANCE RAILPASS	1ST CLASS	2ND CLASS
Single Adult	US$252	US$218
Saverpass	US$215	US$186
Youthpass	US$189	US$164
Seniorpass	US$228	N/A

DISCOUNTED TICKETS

For travelers under 26, **BIJ** tickets (*Billets Internationals de Jeunesse;* operated by **Wasteels**) are a great alternative to railpasses. Available for international trips within Europe as well as most ferry services, they knock 20-40% off 1st- and 2nd-class fares. Tickets are good for two months after purchase and allow stopovers along the normal direct route of the train journey. Issued for a specific international route between two points, they must be used in the direction and order of the designated route and must be bought in Europe. The equivalent for those over

26, **BIGT** tickets provide a 20-30% discount on 1st- and 2nd-class international tickets. Both types of tickets are available from European travel agents, Wasteels offices, and sometimes at the ticket counter. For more info, contact Voyages Wasteels (☎08 25 88 70 70; www.wasteels.com).

SNCF calendars designate days as **période bleue, période blanche,** and **période rouge,** depending on passenger traffic. Trips in the *période bleue* (usually noon on Monday to noon on Saturday, and Sunday before 3pm) get the largest discounts, trips in the *période blanche* (Friday noon to Saturday noon) get smaller discounts, and trips in the *période rouge* get none. You can save up to 25% if you buy a return ticket, travel on a *période bleue* day, and spend Sunday at your destination. Children under 4 travel free; those ages 4-12 usually travel at a 50% discount.

The SNCF offers a range of discounted round-trip tickets. The **Carte Enfant+** (€58) offers people traveling with children under age 12 discounts of 25-50% on train travel. The discount can apply to up to four people, either children or adults, and they don't have to be related. The **Carte 12-25** (€43, for people ages 12-25) and the **Carte Senior** (€45, for people ages 60 and over) offer discounts of 25-50% on train travel, and, in some cases, airfare and car rental. In March of 2003, the SNCF introduced the **Carte Escapades** (€99) for adults ages 26-59, which offer 25% discounts on round-trip train tickets for distances greater than 100km. The *Carte Escapade* requires that the ticket-holder spends Saturday night at her destination. All of these *cartes* are valid for a period of one year.

The SNCF recently introduced special Internet deals. **Tarif Prem's** give substantial discounts to passengers who buy their train tickets 14-60 days in advance from www.voyages-sncf.com or one of its partner sites (such as www.raileurope.com). Every Tuesday, the SNCF website selects 50 destinations throughout France with half-off fares for trips made between Wednesday and the following Tuesday.

> **FURTHER READING & RESOURCES ON TRAIN TRAVEL**
> **Info on rail travel and railpasses:** www.raileurope.com.
> **Point-to-point fares and schedules:** www.raileurope.com/us/rail/fares_schedules/index.htm. Helps you calculate whether buying a railpass would save you money.
> **SNCF:** www.sncf.com/indexe.htm is in English.
> **Wasteels:** www.voyages-wasteels.fr.
> **European Railway Server:** www.mercurio.iet.unipi.it/home.html. Links to rail servers throughout Europe.
> *Thomas Cook European Timetable,* updated monthly, covers all major and most minor train routes in Europe. In the US, order it from Forsyth Travel Library (☎800-367-7984; www.forsyth.com; US$28). In Europe, find it at any Thomas Cook Money Exchange Center, or directly from www.thomascook.com.
> *On the Rails Around Europe: A Comprehensive Guide to Travel by Train,* Melissa Shales. Thomas Cook, Ltd. US$19.

BY BUS

In France, long-distance buses are a second-class means of transportation, with less frequent service than trains. Within a given region, however, buses provide vital (often speedy) service to outlying towns and villages. Bus stations are usually adjacent to the train station, and many bus services are operated by SNCF and accept railpasses. *Let's Go* lists the local bus companies and relevant destinations for each town. Bus schedules usually indicate whether a bus runs during the *période scolaire* (school year), *période de vacances* (summer vacation), or both. Few buses run on *jours fériés* (Sundays and holidays).

BY CAR

Although a single traveler won't save by renting a car, four usually will. Sometimes a combination of train and car works well: RailEurope and other railpass vendors offer rail-and-drive packages. Fly-and-drive packages are also often available from travel agents or rental agencies.

Before setting off, know the laws of the countries in which you will be driving. Primers on European road signs and on French road signs and the French highway code can be found at www.travlang.com/signs and www.franceguide.com. **The Association for Safe International Travel (ASIRT)**, 11769 Gainsborough Rd., Potomac, MD 20854 (US ☎301-98-5252; www.asirt.org), can provide information on road conditions and safety in France. Roadway conditions throughout France can also be obtained by calling ☎01 47 05 90 01.

Tolls in France are high. *Autoroutes* (marked on signs with an A) are tolled express highways. *Routes nationales* (marked with an N) and the smaller, more scenic *routes départementales* (marked with a D) do not have tolls.

DRIVING PERMITS & CAR INSURANCE

INTERNATIONAL DRIVING PERMIT (IDP). Anybody with a valid EU-issued driving license is unconditionally entitled to drive on French roads. Others (including US citizens) are legally permitted to drive in France on the strength of their national licenses for a few months, but not all police are aware of that. It's advisable to obtain an **International Driving Permit (IDP)**, which is essentially your regular license translated into 10 languages, including French. Some car rental companies require an IDP. Even if you don't plan to drive, an IDP is a recognized form of ID and might be a good idea. You must be 18 years old to obtain the IDP. It is valid for one year, must be issued in your home country before you depart, and it is not valid without your home license. To apply, contact the national or local branch of your home country's Automobile Association.

RENTING A CAR

Travelers considering **renting** a car can do so from an international firm (e.g. Avis, Budget, or Hertz) with European offices, from a European-based company with local representatives (e.g. Europcar), or from a tour operator (e.g. Auto Europe, Europe By Car, or Kemwel Holiday Autos), which will arrange a rental from a European company, often at a good deal. Many less expensive rental cars in France will not have air conditioning or windows that roll down.

The minimum age for renting is usually 21, though some agencies will not rent to anyone under 23, and renters under 25 often must pay a surcharge of approximately $21 per day. Otherwise, most agencies require only a valid driver's license and one year of driving experience.

Reserve long before leaving for France and pay in advance. Occasionally the price and availability information from home offices do not coincide with that from local offices in France. Check with both sources to get the best price and accurate information. Local desk numbers are included in town listings; for home-country numbers, call your toll-free directory. Many websites search deals from multiple companies; try **Travel Now** (www.travelnow.com) and **Internet Travel Network** (www.itn.net). French rental agencies include:

Auto Europe: US ☎888-223-5555, UK 08001 696 414, Australia 800 2235 5555; www.autoeurope.com.

Avis: US ☎800-230-4898, Canada 800-272-5871, UK 08706 060 100, Australia toll-free 136 333, New Zealand 0800 655 111; www.avis.com.

Budget: US ☎800-404-8033, Canada 212-581-3040, international 800-472-3325; www.budgetrentacar.com.

Europe by Car: US ☎800-223-1516; www.europebycar.com.

Europcar: US and Canada ☎877-940-6900, France 01 55 66 83 00; www.europ-car.com. Unusually, rents to ages 21-24 at many sites.

Hertz: US ☎800-654-3001, Canada 800-263-0600, UK 08708 415 161; Australia 613 9698 2555; www.hertz.com.

COSTS & INSURANCE. Expect to pay at least US$200 per week, plus 19.6% tax, as the base rate for a small car rental. Automatic gearboxes cost extra and are often unavailable on cheaper cars. 4WD and air conditioning each generally cost US$7 extra per day. Many rental packages offer unlimited kilometers, while others allow 250km per day with a surcharge of approximately US$0.35 per km after that; ask your rental company which system they use before finalizing the deal. Additionally, some airlines offer fly-and-drive packages, which may provide discounted car rentals for up to a week. National chains often permit one-way rentals—dropping a rental off in a different city than it was obtained—but usually with a minimum hire period and an additional drop-off charge of several hundred dollars.

EU residents driving their own cars do not need any extra insurance coverage in France. Gold credit cards (or standard American Express cards) often cover basic insurance, though cars rented on **American Express, Visa/Mastercard Gold,** or **Platinum** credit cards might *not* carry automobile insurance. Home car insurance often covers liability overseas, but only with proof provided by a **green card** or **International Insurance Certificate,** obtained at travel agents or border crossings. Ask your insurance provider and credit card company for information before you depart. Accidents abroad, if reported, will show up on your domestic records and in your premium thereafter. If these options fail, be prepared to shell out US$10-20 per day for insurance on a rental car.

LEASING A CAR

An option only for non-EU residents, **leasing** can be cheaper than rental for periods longer than a few weeks and is often the only option for travelers aged 18-21. The cheapest leases are agreements to buy the car and then sell it back to the manufacturer at a prearranged price. The base price of a lease (US$1500 for 60 days) may not appear to differ much from a regular car rental, but it includes comprehensive insurance, unlimited mileage, and avoids taxes. Contact **Auto Europe** or **Europe by Car** (see above) at least 30 days before your departure.

BUYING A CAR

Buying a used vehicle in France and reselling it before your departure can be less expensive than renting and leasing on long trips. However, if you decide to keep your car, check with consulates about import-export laws concerning used vehicles, registration, and safety and emission standards. Camper-vans and motor homes provide the advantages of a car with the benefits of a hotel on the road.

ON THE ROAD

The French drive on the right-hand side of the road. On *autoroutes*, the speed limit is 130km/hr. (81mph); on smaller highways, 110km/hr. (68mph); in cities, 50-60km/hr. (about 35mph). Since *autoroute* toll tickets are stamped with the time of departure from the toll booth, ticket-takers at the end of your trip can calculate your speed and penalize you for excessive speeding. **Fines** range €137-762, but are reduced by 30% if paid within 24 hours of the ticketing. France has a **mandatory**

seatbelt law and prohibits children under 10 from riding in the front car seat. Child car seats are available from rental companies for an additional $25.

By French law, cars entering a road from the right have the right of way over cars already on the road, even on major thoroughfares, so be prepared for cars to turn into the road ahead without warning. Inverted-triangle road signs with exclamation marks and text *"vous n'avez pas la priorité"* or *"cédez le passage"* indicate that the rule does not apply—a practice that generally holds on major roundabouts. In another reverse of practices in most countries, a driver who flashes his highbeams wants to send the message: "I *am* going first," rather than "Go right ahead." Check out **Itinéraire** (www.iti.fr) if you plan to drive in France; enter your start and end points, your desired speed and budget, and you will receive directions as well as estimates of driving time and toll and gas costs. **Gas stations** in most towns won't accept cash after 7pm, but they will take the French *Carte Bleue* (analogous to Visa). Gas generally costs around €0.85-1.15 per liter. Diesel *(gazole)* fuel tends to be cheaper than unleaded *(essence sans plomb)*.

DRIVING PRECAUTIONS. When traveling in the summer, bring substantial amounts of water (a suggested 5L of **water** per person per day) for consumption and for the radiator. Register with the police before taking long treks to unpopulated areas. Check with the local automobile club for details. For long distance travel, bring good maps and make sure tires are in good repair. Always carry: a **compass, car manual, spare tire** and **jack, jumper cables, extra oil, flares,** a **torch (flashlight),** and **heavy blankets.** Make sure you know how to **change a tire.** If you experience a blowout in deserted areas, **stay with your car;** if you wander off, trackers are less likely to find you.

DANGERS

In general, French roads are some of the best in Europe and the world. There are a few exceptions: the roads in the Alps and on Corsica tend to be narrow and twisty, and these areas are prone to bad weather. Moreover, the French tend to drive fast, impolitely, and aggressively. They often make last-minute turns and drive under the influence. Good roads near Paris and in southern France become stressful and dangerous during the crowded high season.

BY BICYCLE

Some airlines count bikes as a second piece of luggage, but others charge an additional US$60-110 each way to transport them. Bikes must be packed in a cardboard box (available at the airport for US$10) with the pedals and front wheel detached. The SNCF rents bicycles in most train stations for a modest price, and trains almost always have room for a bike, at variable costs. Most ferries charge a nominal fee or nothing at all. Bike rental is probably a better idea; *Let's Go* lists rental places for most towns. Some hostels rent bicycles cheaply.

Riding with a frame pack strapped on your bike or back is not safe; use a **basket** or **panier.** Buy a suitable **bike helmet** (US$25-50). The most secure locks are U-shaped **Citadel** or **Kryptonite** locks (from US$30).

For those nervous about striking out on their own, **Blue Marble Travel** (Canada ☎519-624-2494, US 215-923-3788, France 01 42 36 02 34; www.bluemarble.org) organizes bike tours of France and many other countries for adults aged 20-50. Full-time graduate and professional students may get discounts; "stand-by" rates may be obtained in Europe through the Paris office. **CBT Tours,** 2506 N. Clark St.,

#150, Chicago, IL 60614, US (US ☎800-736-2453; www.cbttours.com), offers full-package 7-12 day biking, mountain biking, and hiking tours June to late August (around US$200 per day).

For further info, **Mountaineers Books**, 1001 S.W. Klickitat Way, #201, Seattle, WA 98134, US (☎206-223-6303; www.mountaineers.org), sells *Europe By Bike*, by Karen and Terry Whitehill (US$15), and country-specific biking guides.

BY MOPED & MOTORCYCLE

Motorbikes (mopeds) eliminate the negatives of costly car travel and short-ranged bicycling. They are uncomfortable for long distances, dangerous in the rain, and unpredictable on rough roads and gravel. Always wear a helmet and never ride with a backpack. Expect to pay about €15.30-23 per day for a rental. Motorcycles are more expensive and require a license, but are better for long distances. **Bosenberg Motorcycle Excursions**, Mainzer Str. 54, 55545 Bad Kreuznach, Germany (☎49 671 673 12; www.bosenberg.com), arranges tours in the Alps, Austria, France, Italy, and Switzerland and rents motorcycles April to October For **further info**, consult *Europe by Motorcycle* by Gregory Frazier (Arrowstar Publishing, US$20).

BY FOOT

Some of France's best scenery can only be reached on foot. *Let's Go* outlines day-trips and short hikes in every region, though tourist offices, locals, and fellow travelers are also good resources. France is criss-crossed by over 30,000km of sign-posted footpaths, known as **sentiers de grandes randonnées** or just **GR**. The **Fédération française de randonnée pédestre (FFRP)**, 14 rue Riquet, 75019 Paris (☎01 44 89 93 93; www.ffrp.asso.fr) publishes the valuable *Topoguide* series, which describes, maps, and lists accommodations for each GR route in French. Those hiking the GR routes join a long tradition of travelers. The GR65 route, running from Le Puy-en-Velay in the Massif Central to St-Jean-Pied-de-Port on the way to Santiago de Compostella in Spain, was trodden for centuries before hiking became popular. Thousands of people still undertake **pilgrimages** on foot. Pilgrims stay free at monasteries and special hostels along the way, with a letter from a priest certifying that they are the real deal. Check out **France on Foot** (www.franceonfoot.com) and **Hiking in France** (www.hejoly.demon.nl/countries/france.html).

BY THUMB

No one should hitchhike *(faire l'autostop)* without seriously considering the risks. Hitching puts you at risk for theft, assault, sexual harassment, and more. If you're a woman traveling alone, don't hitch, period.

France is the hardest country in Europe in which to get a lift. If you do decide to chance it, remember that hitching (or even standing) on *autoroutes* is illegal and thumbing is legal only at rest stops, tollbooths, and highway entrance ramps.

SPECIFIC CONCERNS

WOMEN TRAVELERS

Women exploring alone inevitably face additional safety concerns. Stay in hostels with single rooms or single-sex rooms that lock from the inside, or in religious organizations with exclusively female rooms. Female travelers may also want to

NATIONAL RAPE HOTLINE	**SOS Viol:** ☎0800 05 95 95 offers counseling and assistance in French. Open M-F 10am-6pm.

be cautious about using communal hostel showers. Choose centrally located accommodations and make sure they are readily accessible by a variety of means of transportation. Avoid solitary late-night treks or metro rides. When traveling, always carry extra money for a phone call or taxi.

On overnight or long train rides, pick either a women-only compartment or one that happens to be occupied by women or couples. Always ask for directions before leaving your accommodations and project confidence once out on the streets. If you get lost, approach older women or families for directions.

The less like a tourist you appear, the better. This may mean dressing conservatively, especially in rural areas—use the standard dress of local women as your guide. Provocative or inappropriate clothing may be considered offensive by locals and it may mark you as an easy target for thieves or lechers. Wearing a conspicuous **wedding band** can also forestall unwanted overtures.

The best answer to verbal harassment is one perfected by French women: a withering, icy stare. Acknowledging *dragueurs*, even with "NO!," only invites a reply. The extremely persistent may need to be dissuaded by a loud *"laissez-moi tranquille!"* (LESS-ay mwa tranhk-EEL; leave me alone) or *"au secours!"* (oh-S'KOOR; help). Consider carrying a whistle on your keychain for extra effect and don't hesitate to seek out a police officer. **In an emergency, dial ☎17 for police assistance.** *Let's Go* also lists local police authorities in the Practical Information section of cities.

TRAVELING ALONE

Lone travelers should appear confident and well-organized at all times, and should never admit to being alone. Maintaining regular contact with someone at home who knows your itinerary is also a wise idea.

For more tips, try *Traveling Solo* by Eleanor Berman (Globe Pequot Press; US$18) or subscribe to **Connecting: Solo Travel Network,** 689 Park Road, Unit 6, Gibsons, BC V0N 1V7, Canada (☎604-886-9099; www.cstn.org; membership US$35). **Travel Companion Exchange,** P.O. Box 833, Amityville, NY 11701, USA (☎631-454-0880; www.whytravelalone.com; US$48), links solo travelers with companions of similar travel habits and interests.

OLDER TRAVELERS

Senior citizens traveling abroad should be aware of specific concerns related to medication and their health. When traveling to a foreign country, always bring a sufficient supply of medication in the original pill containers, rather than in generic pill boxes, and, if possible, bring copies of your prescriptions for these medications. Packing an extra supply of your medication and an extra pair of eyeglasses in your hand luggage is also a good idea, should your checked suitcases get lost en route. Travelers with high blood pressure, anemia, or respiratory or cardiac problems should be particularly careful when travelling in high altitudes or in areas with high air pollution. If you are traveling to an area of France that may present such concerns, allow your body a few days to adjust: take it easy, eat a light diet, and cut back on the booze.

Almost all museums and sights in France offer discounts for senior citizens, and some cities also offer special rates for public transportation. Many restaurants offer special senior discounts but don't list them. Major sights are typically well equipped to deal with any special needs. The same is not true of budget accommodations, which usually have extremely steep stairs instead of elevators.

The books *No Problem! Worldwise Tips for Mature Adventurers*, by Janice Kenyon (Orca Book Publishers; US$16), and *Unbelievably Good Deals and Great Adventures That You Absolutely Can't Get Unless You're Over 50*, by Joan Rattner Heilman (NTC/Contemporary Publishing; US$15), are excellent resources for senior travelers.

ElderTreks, 597 Markham St., Toronto, ON M6G 2L7 (☎800-741-7956; www.eldertreks.com). Adventure travel programs for 50+ travelers in France.

Elderhostel, 11 Ave. de Lafayette, Boston, MA 02111 (☎877-426-8056; www.elderhostel.org). Organizes 1-4 wk. educational adventures on varied subjects for those 55+.

The Mature Traveler, P.O. Box 15791, Sacramento, CA 95852 (☎800-460-6676). Deals, discounts, and travel packages for the 50+ traveler. Subscription US$30.

Walking the World, P.O. Box 1186, Fort Collins, CO 80522 (☎800-340-9255; www.walkingtheworld.com), organizes trips for 50+ travelers to France.

BGLT TRAVELERS

France is changing its traditional attitude toward gay communities. Help-lines, bars, and meeting places have sprung up in all major cities and in a number of smaller towns as well. The **Marais,** in Paris, has a notably gay-friendly atmosphere, as do parts of Bordeaux and the French Riviera. **Montpellier** is regarded as the center of gay life in southern France. However, the French countryside and many towns (especially in the southwest, northeast, and northwest) retain their traditional perspectives. To avoid uncomfortable situations, use discretion when interacting with your significant other in public. In Paris, the **Centre Gai et Lesbien,** 3 rue Keller, has resources on health, legal, counseling, and social issues. (☎01 43 57 21 47; www.cglparis.org. Open M-Sa 4-8pm.) The monthly gay magazine **Têtu** is sold in newsstands around France and contains information on gay bars and clubs throughout France.

 FURTHER READING: BISEXUAL, GAY & LESBIAN.

Spartacus International Gay Guide 2003-2004. Bruno Gmunder Verlag. US$33.

Damron's Men's Travel Guide, Damron's Accommodations and *The Women's Traveller.* Damron Travel Guides. US$14-19. For more info, call ☎800-462-6654 or visit www.damron.com.

Ferrari Guides' Gay Travel A to Z, Ferrari Guides' Men's Travel in Your Pocket, and *Ferrari Guides' Inn Places.* Ferrari Publications (www.ferrariguides.com). US$16-20.

The Gay Vacation Guide: The Best Trips and How to Plan Them, Mark Chesnut. Kensington Publications. US$15.

Gayellow Pages USA/Canada, Frances Green (www.gayellowpages.com). Gayellow pages. US$16. Smaller regional editions available.

TRAVELERS WITH DISABILITIES

Rail is probably the most convenient form of travel for disabled visitors to France. SNCF offers wheelchair compartments on all TGV services. Ask for the *Guide du voyageur a mobilité réduit* at train stations for more details. Guide dog owners from Britain and Ireland might have trouble getting their pooches past quarantine on their return. Contact the PETS helpline at UK☎087 0241 1710 or www.defra.gov.uk for details. Other pet owners should inquire as to the specific quarantine policies of their home country and France. In Paris and other major cities, public transport has seats reserved for disabled or infirm passengers. Taxi drivers are obliged to take wheelchair-bound passengers and help them enter and exit the taxi. Hertz, Avis, and National car rental agencies have hand-controlled vehicles at some locations, which must be reserved at least 48hr. in advance.

Unfortunately, budget hotels and restaurants are generally ill-equipped for disabled visitors. Very few wheelchair-accessible bathrooms can be found in the one- to two-star range (and below). The brochure *Paris-Ile-de-France for Everyone* (available in French and English for €9 at most Parisian tourist offices) lists accessible sites, hotels, and restaurants, as well as useful travel tips.

Many museums and sights are wheelchair-accessible. Some provide guided tours in **sign language**. The following organizations provide useful info.

Mobility International USA (MIUSA), P.O. Box 10767, Eugene, OR 97440, USA (☎541-343-1284; www.miusa.org). Sells *A World of Options: A Guide to International Educational Exchange, Community Service, and Travel for Persons with Disabilities* (US$35).

Society for the Advancement of Travel for the Handicapped (SATH), 347 Fifth Ave., #610, New York, NY 10016, USA (☎212-447-7284; www.sath.org). An advocacy group that publishes free online travel info and the travel magazine *Open World* (US$18, free for members). Annual membership US$45, students and seniors US$30. Order a free copy of *Open World* online.

FURTHER READING. *Access in Paris*, by Gordon Couch (Cimino Publishing Group, US$12); *Resource Directory for the Disabled*, by Richard Neil Shrout (Facts on File; US$14); *Wheelchair Through Europe*, by Annie Mackin (Graphic Language Press;graphiclanguage@yahoo.com; US$12.95); *Global Access* (www.geocities.com/Paris/1502/disabilitylinks.html) has links for disabled travelers in France.

MINORITY TRAVELERS

Like much of Europe, France has experienced a wave of immigration from former colonies in the past few decades. North Africans compose the greatest part of the immigrants, at over a million, followed by West Africans and Vietnamese. Many of the immigrants are uneducated and face discrimination, causing poverty and crime in the predominately immigrant inner cities. In turn, there has been a surge in support for the far-right National Front party and its cry, *"La France pour les français."* Anyone who might be taken for **North African** may encounter verbal abuse and is more likely than other travelers to be stopped and questioned by the police. Racism is especially prevalent in the Southeast. The following organizations can give you advice and help in the event of an encounter with racism.

S.O.S. Racisme, 51 av. de Flandre, 75019 Paris (☎01 40 35 36 55; www.sos-racisme.org). Provides legal services and helps negotiate with police.

MRAP (Mouvement contre le racisme et pour l'amitié entre les peuples), 43 bd. Magenta, 75010 Paris (☎01 53 38 99 99; www.mrap.asso.fr). Handles immigration issues; monitors publications and propaganda for racism.

TRAVELERS WITH CHILDREN

Of course, traveling with small children requires much additional preparation and consideration both before and during your trip. If you are considering staying at a B&B, **call ahead** to ensure that it is child-friendly. If you rent a car, make certain to ask your rental company for a car seat for younger children. French law mandates that children sit in the rear. **Be sure that your child carries some sort of ID** in case there is an emergency or he gets lost.

Museums, tourist attractions, accommodations, and restaurants often offer discounts for children, usually included in the *Let's Go* listings. Children under two generally fly for 10% of the adult airfare on international flights. International fares are usually discounted 25% for children aged 2-11.

For more information, consult one of the following books:

Take Your Kids to Europe, Cynthia W. Harriman. Globe Pequot Press (US$18).

Have Kid, Will Travel: 101 Survival Strategies for Vacationing With Babies and Young Children, Claire and Lucille Tristram. Andrews McMeel Publishing (US$9).

Adventuring with Children: An Inspirational Guide to World Travel and the Outdoors, Nan Jeffrey. Avalon House Publishing (US$15).

DIETARY CONCERNS

Those with special dietary requirements may feel left behind in France. **Vegetarians** will find dining out difficult (see **Food & Drink,** p. 54) and **vegans** will find it nearly impossible. The **International Vegetarian Union** (www.ivu.org) is another valuable resource. The travel section of the Vegetarian Resource Group's website, at www.vrg.org/travel, has a comprehensive list of organizations and websites that are geared toward helping veggies traveling abroad. The website www.vegdining.com has a database of vegetarian and vegan restaurants worldwide.

Kosher food does exist in France, which has one of Western Europe's largest Jewish populations, but finding it may prove difficult, particularly in rural regions. Kosher travelers should contact synagogues in larger cities for info on restaurants. Your home synagogue or college Hillel should have lists of Jewish institutions throughout the world. **The Jewish Travel Guide,** edited by Michael Zaidner, lists synagogues, kosher restaurants, and Jewish institutions in over 100 countries and is available in Europe from Vallentine Mitchell Publishers, Crown House, 47 Chase Side, Southgate, London N14 5BP, UK (☎ 02089 202 100; fax 84 478 548), in the US at 5824 NE Hassalo St., Portland, OR 97213 (☎ 800-944-6190; fax 503-280-8832).

OTHER RESOURCES

USEFUL PUBLICATIONS

We like these books and think you might as well.

Fragile Glory: A Portrait of France and the French, Richard Bernstein. Plume, 1991 (US$15). A witty look at France by the former *New York Times* Paris bureau chief.

Portraits of France, Robert Daley. Little, Brown & Co., 1991 (US$23). An engaging, informed collection of essays on France and the French, organized by region.

Culture Shock! France: A Guide To Customs and Etiquette, Sally Adamson Taylor. Graphic Arts Center Publishing Company, 1991 (US$14). Tips and warnings.

Merde! The Real French You Were Never Taught at School, Genevieve, Michael Heath. Fireside, 1998 ($9). Lots of gutter slang and a collection of very dirty things to say.

French or Foe? Getting the Most Out of Visiting, Living and Working in France, Polly Platt. Distribooks Intl., 1998 (US$17). A popular guide to getting by in France.

A Traveller's Wine Guide to France, Christopher Fielden. Interlink Publishing Group, 1999 (US$20). Exactly what it says it is, by a well-known oenophile.

THE WORLD WIDE WEB

Below are general, all-purpose sites.

Maison de la France (www.francetourism.com), the French government's site for tourists. Tips on everything from accommodations to smoking laws. English version.

Youth Tourism (www.franceguide.com), the official site of the French Government Tourist Office. For youth planning long stays in France. Mostly in English.

France Diplomatie (www.france.diplomatie.fr/) is the site of the Department of Foreign Affairs. Info on visas and current affairs. Mostly in English.

Secretariat for Tourism (www.tourisme.gouv.fr) has a number of government documents about French tourism; links to all French tourist authorities. In French.

Tourism in France (www.tourisme.fr) has info in French and mildly amusing English.

Nomade (www.nomade.fr) is a popular French search engine.

TF1 (www.tf1.fr) is the home page of France's most popular TV station.

Météo-France (www.meteo.fr) has 2-day weather forecasts and maps. In French.

THE ART OF BUDGET TRAVEL

How to See the World: www.artoftravel.com. A compendium of great travel tips.

Travel Library: www.travel-library.com. Fantastic general info and travelogues.

Lycos: http://cityguide.lycos.com. Introductions to cities and regions throughout France.

Backpacker's Ultimate Guide: www.bugeurope.com.

Backpack Europe: www.backpackeurope.com. Helpful tips, a bulletin board, and links.

INFORMATION ON FRANCE

CIA World Factbook: www.odci.gov/cia/publications/factbook/index.html. Vital stats.

Foreign Language for Travelers: www.travlang.com. Online translating dictionary.

VisitEurope: www.visiteurope.com/France. Highlights, culture, and people of France.

Atevo Travel: www.atevo.com. Travel tips. Suggested itineraries.

World Travel Guide: www.travel-guides.com/data/fra/fra.asp. Helpful practical info.

AND OUR PERSONAL FAVORITE...

 WWW.LETSGO.COM Our newly designed website now has lots of extra information about our guides, the countries we cover, and travel in general. Trial versions of all nine City Guides are available for download on Palm OS™ PDAs. Our website also contains our newsletter, links for photos and streaming video, online ordering of our titles, info about our books, and a travel forum buzzing with stories and tips.

ESSENTIALS

ALTERNATIVES TO TOURISM

In 2002, nearly 700 million trips were made, many of which involved time in France, and this number is projected to rise to one billion by 2010. This dramatic rise in tourism has affected France, creating an interdependence between the country's economy, environment and culture, and the tourists she hosts.

We at *Let's Go* look to improve the traveler-destination interchange. We believe the philosophy of **sustainable travel** is among the most important travel tips we could impart to our readers, to help guide fellow backpackers and on-the-road philanthropists. Through a sensitivity to the local community, today's travelers can be a powerful force in preserving and restoring this fragile world.

Two rising trends in sustainable travel are ecotourism and community-based tourism. **Ecotourism** focuses on conserving natural habitats and using them to build up the economy without exploitation or overdevelopment. **Community-based tourism** aims to channel tourist euros into the local economy by emphasizing programs run by members of the host community. See **www.sustainabletravel.org** for more information.

Those looking to **volunteer** in the efforts to resolve these issues have many options. You can participate in projects from environmental protection to historical restoration, either on an infrequent basis or as the main component of your trip. Others come to France in order to **study,** and the country has numerous programs for those who just want to brush up on their French to those who are looking for a total immersion in the art of French cuisine. In addition to those who volunteer or study in France, many travelers structure their trips by the **work** that they do along the way—either odd jobs as they go, or full-time stints in cities where they plan to stay for some time. This chapter outlines some of the options available to those who crave a more in-depth perspective on France's daily life and the challenges the country faces, as wells as the opportunity to form lasting relationships with locals.

Before handing your money over to any volunteer or study abroad program, make sure you know exactly what you're getting into. It's a good idea to get the name of **previous participants** and ask them about their experience, as some programs sound much better on paper than in reality. The **questions** below are a good place to start:

–Will you be the only person in the program? If not, what are the other participants like? How old are they? How much will you be expected to interact with them?

–Is room and board included? If so, what is the arrangement? Will you be expected to share a room? A bathroom? What are the meals like? Do they fit any dietary restrictions?

–Is transportation included? Are there any additional expenses?

–How much free time will you have? Will you be able to travel around France?

–What kind of safety network is set up? Will you still be covered by your home insurance? Does the program have an emergency plan?

A NEW PHILOSOPHY OF TRAVEL

We at *Let's Go* know that the majority of travelers mean well and are not unconcerned with the state of the communities and environments they visit, but we also know that even conscientious tourists can inadvertently damage natural wonders and rich cultures. We believe the philosophy of **sustainable travel** is among the most important travel tips we could impart to our readers: by staying aware of the needs and troubles of local communities, travelers can be a powerful force in preserving and restoring this fragile world, and can potentially counteract some of the worst trends at work in the world today.

Responsible tourism can often be more a a matter of self-awareness than self-sacrifice: spending responsibly can promote the conservation of local resources more effectively than abstaining from expenditure, and sensitive, respectful interation with local cultures can have a greater positive impact than well-intentioned, self-imposed distance between locals and visitors. Information is the responsible traveler's single most powerful tool: a little conscientious research before traveling can go a long way when combined with a healthy mix of inquisitiveness and common sense while on the road. To further the cause of responsible tourism, *Let's Go* has partnered with **BEST (Business Enterprises for Sustainable Travel;** see www.sustainabletravel.org), which recognizes and promotes businesses whose operational practices follow the principles of sustainable travel. The following are some suggestions for traveling responsibly.

TIPS FOR RESPONSIBLE TRAVEL: HOW TO MAKE A DIFFERENCE

Read about your destination's history, culture, and recent news before arriving. You will not only better appreciate your travels but you will also find it easier to practice responsible travel when you are informed of issues particular to your destination.

Taking classes and watching cultural performances can be excellent ways to promote the preservation of local practices and traditions, but can also promote the corruption and commercialization of ancient practices. Where possible, inquire as to the authenticity of the material presented, the intentions of the presenters, and their relationship with both the general community and other practitioners.

Use mass transportation whenever possible. Where safe and feasible, walking and bicycling can be excellent ways to see a community firsthand.

Reduce, reuse, recycle—use electronic tickets, recycle papers and bottles wherever possible, and avoid using styrofoam containers. Refillable water bottles and rechargeable batteries both efficiently conserve expendable resources.

Take care not to buy souvenirs made from non-renewable resources, like trees from old-growth or endangered forests or items made from endangered species. Where possible, purchase souveniers that help preserve local traditions, but be careful: many seeming "local handicrafts" are manufactured in far-removed locales specifically for sale to tourists, and their purchase will do little to preserve local cultures.

Buy from local enterprises, as in developing countries many people depend on the "informal economy," but try not to purchase from businesses using non-sustainable practices, even if the businesses are locally owned.

If you are inspired by the natural environment or culture of a region, donating money to a local preservation organization can help maintain the region's integrity, as can spreading the word to friends and colleagues—travelers can not only introduce friends to particular destinations but also to causes and charities that they might choose to support when they travel to those areas.

VOLUNTEERING

Though France is considered wealthy in worldwide terms, there is no shortage of aid organizations to benefit the very real issues the region does face. Short-term volunteering stints can be found in virtually every city. More intensive volunteer services may charge participation fees which can be surprisingly hefty (although they frequently cover airfare and living expenses).

Finding the right program may require some research. Most people choose to go through a parent organization that takes care of logistics and frequently provides a group environment and support system. Talk to people who have previously participated and find out exactly what you're getting into, as living and working conditions can vary greatly. Different programs are geared toward different ages and levels of experience, so make sure that you are not taking on too much or too little. In addition to the programs listed below, **www.worldsurface.com** features photos and personal stories of volunteer experiences. **Earthwatch International, Operation Crossroads Africa, Habitat for Humanity,** and **www.volunteerabroad.com** offer fulfilling opportunities all over the world.

COMMUNITY SERVICE & DEVELOPMENT

Community-based projects are conducive to close work with disadvantaged populations of France. Due to their one-on-one nature, knowledge of French is often necessary, but these are among the most rewarding of all volunteer experiences.

Action Contre la Faim, 4 rue Niepce, 75014 Paris (☎01 43 35 88 88; fax 01 43 35 88 00; www.acf-fr.org). As an international organization combatting hunger, Action Contre la Faim can always use the help of volunteers. Among other things, volunteers play an integral role in organizing and carrying out the Race Against Hunger, a running competition to raise money for the cause.

L'Arche les Sapins, Domaine des Abels, Lignières-Sonneville, 16130 Charente (☎05 45 80 50 66; fax 05 45 80 55 88; www.archesapins.org). Small Christian community of adults with learning disabilities. Volunteers help with daily tasks and individual care. Knowledge of French required.

Fédération Familles de France, 28 pl. St-Georges, 75009 Paris (☎01 44 53 45 90; www.familles-de-france.org). Supports families in need by offering grants, providing assistance with education and résumés, and giving access to social organizations.

Fondation Claude Pompidou, 42 rue du Louvre, 75001 Paris (☎01 40 13 75 18; fax 01 40 13 75 19; www.fondationclaudepompidou.asso.fr). The Fondation Claude Pompidou is a charitable organization that aids the sick, elderly, and disabled by providing support, homecare, and companionship for them. Volunteers are generally expected to commit to a full year of service.

GENEPI, 4/14 rue Ferrus, 75014 Paris (☎01 45 88 37 00; www.genepi.asso.fr). GENEPI promotes the social rehabilitation of those in prison in France by creating relationships between students and prisoners. All volunteers are students. GENEPI has various offices throughout France.

Secours Catholique: Delegation de Paris, 13 rue St Ambroise, 74011 Paris (☎01 48 07 58 21; fax 01 58 30 70 44; www.quiaccueillequi.org). Works to support the poor, the unemployed, children with social problems, foreigners, and other marginalized groups. Its operations throughout France and internationally rely heavily upon its thousands of volunteers.

Secours Populaire Françes, 9/11 rue Froissart, 75140 Paris (☎01 44 78 21 00; www.secourspopulaire.asso.fr). Secours is a non-profit organization that provides support to poor children and families through food and clothing provisions, as well as offering sports activities and social interaction, all done with a commitment to human rights. The organization's wide range of activities and assistance programs are made possible by its thousands of volunteers.

Simon Wiesenthal Center, 64 av. Marceau, 75008 Paris (☎01 47 23 76 37; fax 01 47 20 84 01; www.wiesenthal.org). Fights anti-Semitism and Holocaust denial throughout Europe. Small, variable donation required for membership.

UNAPEI, 15 rue Coysevox, 75876 Paris (☎01 44 85 50 50; fax 01 44 85 59 60; public@unapei.org; www.apei75.org). A national non-governmental organization that aids the mentally handicapped and their families by providing transportation assistance, homecare, and friendship. Volunteers are welcome.

UNAREC, 33 rue Campagne Première, 75014 Paris (☎01 45 38 96 26; www.unarec.org). Workcamps provide assistance to communities facing various problems, often economic. Separate camps for adults and for adolescents (ages 14-16).

ENVIRONMENTAL PROTECTION

France enacted new, stiff pollution controls to protect the coastal areas of the Mediterranean after recent oil spills in 1999 and 2002. Individual volunteers continue to aid the environment where the government cannot. The following groups are dedicated largely to the preservation of France's natural landscape.

Concordia International Volunteer Programs, Heversham House, 20-22 Boundary Rd., Hove BN34ET, England (☎+1273 422 218). Concordia offers free volunteer activities (with food and lodging provided) throughout France, for those ages 18-30. Also offers archaeological restoration projects.

Jeunesse et Reconstruction, 8 et 10 rue de Trevise, 75009 Paris (☎01 47 70 15 88; fax 01 48 00 92 18; www.volontariat.org). Large searchable database of volunteer opportunities for young people, centering around environmental preservation and historical reconstruction. Open June-Sept. M-Sa 9:30am-1pm and 2-6pm.

Organisation Mondiale de Protection de la Nature, 188 rue de la Roquette, 75011 Paris (☎01 55 25 84 67; fax 01 55 25 84 74; www.wwf.fr). Offers various opportunities for environmental activism around France and the EU. €30 membership fee.

HISTORICAL RESTORATION

A continuous concern in France is the preservation and reconstruction of landmarks. Volunteers looking for a more labor-intensive experience can find various groups that assist this process, which is also a great opportunity to learn more about France's architectural history.

Archaeological Institute of America, 656 Beacon St., Boston, MA 02215, USA (☎617-353-9361; www.archaeological.org). The *Archaeological Fieldwork Opportunities Bulletin,* available on the organization's website, lists field sites throughout Europe (including France) at which you can volunteer.

Association CHAM, 5 et 7 rue Guilleminot, 75014 Paris (☎01 43 35 15 51; fax 01 43 20 46 82; www.cham.asso.fr). Organizes groups to restore medieval French landmarks. Open M-F 8:30am-12:30pm and 1:30-6pm, Sa 9am-12:30pm and 1:30-4pm.

Club du Vieux Manoir, Ancienne Abbaye du Moncel, 60700 Pontpoint (☎03 44 72 33 98; cvmclubduvieuxmanoir.free.fr). Year-long and summer work restoring castles and churches. €14 membership/insurance fee, €16 per day, including food and tent.

REMPART, 1 rue des Guillemites, 75004 Paris (☎01 42 71 96 55, www.rempart.com), Offers summer and year-long programs for the restoration of monuments. Anyone 13 or over is eligible. Membership fee €35; most projects charge €6-8 per day.

GENERAL VOLUNTEER ORGANIZATIONS

The following groups offer many volunteering opportunities of varying type and duration in France. The best way to research these programs is to visit their websites, which often contain searchable databases of current projects.

Care France, CAP 19, 13 rue de Georfes Auric, 75019 Paris (☎01 53 19 89 89; www.care.org). An international humanitarian organization providing volunteer opportunities in 6000 locations throughout France, doing such activities as combatting AIDS, urban development, and promoting education.

Council on International Educational Exchange, 7 Custom House St., 3rd floor, Portland, ME 04101, USA (☎207-553-7600; fax 207-553-7699; www.ciee.org). Large database of short-term volunteer opportunities in France, from agriculture to festivals.

Elderhostel, Inc., 11 ave. de Lafayette, Boston, MA 02111-1746, USA (☎877-426-8056; fax 877-426-2166; www.elderhostel.org). Sends volunteers age 55 and over around the world to work in construction, research, teaching, and many other projects. Costs average $100 per day plus airfare.

International Volunteer Program, 7106 Sayre Dr., Oakland, CA 94611, USA (☎415-477-3667; fax 415-477-3669; www.ivpsf.org). 6-week programs in France ranging from hospital service to elderly assistance. Fee of US$1500 includes travel expenses, room, and meals. Intermediate knowledge of French required.

Service Civil International Voluntary Service (SCI-IVS), SCI USA, 3213 W. Wheeler St., Seattle, WA 98199, USA (☎/fax 206-350-6585; www.sci-ivs.org). Arranges placement in work camps in France for those 18+. Registration fee US$65-125.

United Nations Educational, Scientific, and Cultural Organization (UNESCO), (www.unesco.org). Offers unpaid internships of 3-6 months for university graduates. For more information check the website above or write, to the attention of your country's delegation, to UNESCO PER-Staff Training Section, 1 rue Miollis, 75732 Paris.

Volunteers for Peace, 1034 Tiffany Rd., Belmont, VT 05730, USA (☎802-259-2759; fax 802-259-2922; www.vfp.org). Arranges placement in work camps in France. Membership required for registration. Annual *International Workcamp Directory* US$20. Programs average US$200-500 for 2-3 weeks.

Centre National du Volontariat, 127 rue Falguière, 75015 Paris. ☎01 40 61 01 61; fax: 01 45 67 01 61; www.globenet.org/CNV). 70 offices in France help people find the volunteer associations in which they would be the most helpful, taking into consideration their wishes, availability, and skills.

STUDYING ABROAD

For those fluent in French, direct enrollment in a French university can be more rewarding than a class filled with native English speakers and up to four times cheaper than studying through a program. On the other hand, it is easier to earn credit at home for coursework in France done with a program. Programs can also make navigating the administrative process a lot easier, and many of them include meals or planned cultural activities with other students.

Study abroad programs in France range from basic language courses to degree-granting graduate programs. Some things to consider when choosing among them are what kind of students participate in the program and what sort of accommodations are provided.

As a student at a French university, you will receive a student card *(carte d'étudiant)* upon presentation of a residency permit and a receipt for your university fees. The **Centre Régional des Oeuvres Universitaires et Scolaires (CROUS)** offers several student benefits and discounts, including cheap meals. The brochure *Le CROUS et Moi* lists addresses and info on student life. Pick up their free guidebook *Je Vais en France*, in French or English, from any French embassy.

Excellent searchable databases of study abroad programs are available at www.iiepassport.org and www.studyabroadcom. Other databases include www.studyabroaddirectory.com, www.academicintl.com, and www.internationalstudent.com. For help locating schools that are wheelchair accessible, consult **Access Abroad**, at www.umabroad.umn.edu/access.

AMERICAN PROGRAMS

American Institute for Foreign Study, College Division, River Plaza, 9 W. Broad St., Stamford, CT 06902, USA (☎800-727-2437, ext. 5163; www.aifsabroad.com). Organizes programs for high school and college study in universities in France.

Central College Abroad, Office of International Education, 812 University, Pella, IA 50219, USA (☎800-831-3629 or 641-628-5284; www.central.edu/abroad). Offers internships, as well as programs in France of various lengths. US$25 application fee.

Institute for the International Education of Students (IES), 33 N. LaSalle St., 15th fl., Chicago, IL 60602, USA (☎800-995-2300; www.IESabroad.org). Offers year-long, semester, and summer programs for college study in Dijon, Nantes, and Paris. Internship opportunities. US$50 application fee. Scholarships available.

School for International Training, College Semester Abroad, Admissions, Kipling Rd., P.O. Box 676, Brattleboro, VT 05302, USA (☎800-336-1616 or 802-257-7751; www.sit.edu). Semester- and year-long programs in France run US$10,600-13,700. Also runs the **Experiment in International Living** (☎800-345-2929; fax 802-258-3428; www.usexperiment.org), 3- to 5-week summer programs that offer high school students cross-cultural homestays, community service, ecological adventure, and language training in France, and cost US$1900-5000.

Study Abroad, 1450 Edgmont Ave., Suite 140, Chester, PA 19013, USA (☎610-499-9200; fax 610-499-9205; www.studyabroad.com), maintains a compilation of countless international exchanges and study programs, including about 175 in France.

Council on International Educational Exchange (CIEE), 633 3rd Ave., 20th fl., New York, NY 10017-6706 (☎800-407-8839; www.ciee.org/study) sponsors work, volunteer, academic, and internship programs in France.

FRENCH UNIVERSITIES

French universities are segmented into three degree levels. Programs at the first level (except the **Grandes Ecoles,** below) are two or three years long and generally focus on science, medicine, and the liberal arts. They must admit anyone holding a *baccalauréat* (French graduation certificate) or recognized equivalent to their first year of courses (British A levels or two years of college in the US). French competency or other testing may be required for non-native speakers. The more selective and more demanding **Grandes Ecoles** cover specializations from physics to photography to veterinary medicine. These have notoriously difficult entrance examinations which require a year of preparatory schooling.

French universities are far cheaper than their American equivalents; however, it can be hard to receive academic credit at home for a non-approved program. Expect to pay at least €500 per month in living expenses. EU citizens studying in France can take advantage of the three- to twelve-month **SOCRATES** program (www.socrates-france.org), which offers grants to support inter-European educational exchanges. Most UK and Irish universities will have details of the grants

available and the application procedures required. EU law dictates that educational qualifications be recognized across the Union (with the exception of some professional subjects). These organizations can supply further info on academic programs in France. For information on programs of study, requirements, and grants or scholarships, visit www.egide.asso.fr.

Agence EduFrance, 173 bd. St-Germain, 75006 Paris (☎01 53 63 35 00; www.edufrance.fr), is a one-stop resource for North Americans thinking about studying for a degree in France. Info on courses, costs, and grant opportunities.

American University of Paris, 31 av. Bosquet, 75343 Paris Cédex 07 (☎01 40 62 06 00; www.aup.fr), offers US-accredited degrees and summer programs taught in English at its Paris campus. Intensive French language courses offered. Tuition US$9000 per quarter, not including living expenses.

Université Paris-Sorbonne, 1 rue Victor Cousin, 75005 Paris Cédex 05 (☎01 40 46 25 42; www.paris4.sorbonne.fr), the grand-daddy of French universities, was founded in 1253 and is still going strong. Inscription into degree courses costs about €400 per year. Also offers 3- to 9-month-long programs for American students.

LANGUAGE SCHOOLS

Many French universities offer language courses during the summer, while independent organizations run such programs throughout the year. The American University of Paris also runs a special summer language program (see above). For more information on language courses in France, contact your national **Institut Français,** official representatives of French culture attached to French embassies around the world (contact your nearest French embassy or consulate for details). Other well-known schools include:

Alliance Française, Ecole Internationale de Langue et de Civilisation Française, 101 bd. Raspail, 75270 Paris Cédex 06 (☎01 42 84 90 00; www.alliancefr.org). Instruction at all levels, with courses in legal and business French. Courses are 1-4 months in length, costing €267 for 16 2hr. sessions and €534 for 16 4hr. sessions.

Cours de Civilisation Française de la Sorbonne, 47 rue des Ecoles, 75005 Paris (☎01 40 46 22 11; www.fle.fr/sorbonne). Courses in the French language at all levels, along with a comprehensive lecture program of French cultural studies taught by Sorbonne professors. Must be at least 18 and at *baccalauréat* level. Semester- and year-long courses during the academic year, and 4-, 6-, 8-, and 11-week summer programs.

Eurocentres, 101 N. Union St., Suite 300, Alexandria, VA 22314, USA (☎703-684-1494; www.eurocentres.com) or in Europe, Head Office, Seestr. 247, CH-8038 Zurich, Switzerland (☎14 85 50 40; fax 04 81 61 24). Language programs for beginning to advanced students with homestays in France. Schools located in **Paris, Amboise, Tours, La Rochelle, Lausanne,** and **Neuchatel.**

Language Immersion Institute, JFT 214, State University of New York at New Paltz, 75 S. Manheim Blvd., New Paltz, NY 12561-2499, USA (☎845-257-3500; fax 845-257-3569; www.newpaltz.edu/lii). 2-week summer language courses and some overseas courses in French. Program fees are around US$1000 for a 2-week course.

Institut de Langue Française, 3 av. Bertie-Albrecht, 75008 Paris (☎01 45 63 24 00; fax 01 45 63 07 09; www.inst-langue-fr.com). M: Charles de Gaulle-Etoile. Language, civilization, and literature courses. Offers 4-week up to year-long programs, 6-20hr. per week, starting at €185.

Institut Parisien de Langue et de Civilisation Française, 87 bd. de Grenelle, 75015 Paris (☎01 40 56 09 53; fax 01 43 06 46 30; www.institut-parisien.com). M: La Motte-Picquet-Grenelle. French language, fashion, culinary arts, and cinema courses. Intensive language courses for 10 (€95-117 per week), 15 (€143-177 per week), or 25 (€238-294 per week) hours per week.

CULINARY & ART SCHOOLS

One final—and pricier—study abroad option for students and amateurs of all ages is to enroll in a French culinary institute or art school. While the very best of France's trade schools are oriented toward pre-professionals, many programs allow budding chefs and closet Van Goghs to participate in semester- or year-long programs, or in some cases individual class sessions. For smaller, more intimate courses based in farms and homes, amateur cooks should check out www.cookingschools.com, which lists private schools and gastronomy tours in France.

Grande Ecole des Arts Culinaires et de l'Hôtellerie de Lyon (Lyon Culinary Arts and Hotel Management School), Château de Vivier–BP25, 69131 Lyon-Ecully Cédex (☎04 72 18 02 20; fax 04 78 43 33 51; www.each-lyon.com). Premier school affiliated with Paul Bocuse, located in France's capital city of *haute cuisine*. 8- and 16-week summer courses in French and English for amateurs (€4200-7000). Offers individual day courses ranging €62-76 (reserve in advance to dchabert@each-lyon.com).

Cordon Bleu Paris Culinary Arts Institute, 8 rue Léon Delhomme, 75015 Paris (☎01 53 68 22 50; fax 01 48 56 03 96; www.cordonbleu.edu). M: Porte de la Chapelle. The *crème de la crème* of French cooking schools. A full-year diploma course will run you about €29,500 in debt, but Gourmet Sessions are also available, ranging from half-days to 4 weeks.

Pont Aven School of Art, 5 pl. Paul Gauguin, 29930 Pont-Aven (☎02 98 09 10 45; fax 02 98 06 17 38; www.pontavensa.org). English-speaking school in Brittany offers studio courses in painting and sculpture, art history, and French language. 4- and 6-week sessions €3200-6200, including room and board.

Lacoste School of Art, P.O. Box 3146, Savannah, GA 31401, USA (☎912-525-5803; www.scad.edu/lacoste). Based in the tiny medieval town of Lacoste in Provence, this school is administered by the Savannah College of Art and Design. Summer and fall courses in architecture, painting, and historical preservation. Tuition €3850-5925; room and board €2350.

Painting School of Montmiral, rue de la Porte Neuve, 81140 Castelnau de Montmiral (☎/fax 05 63 33 13 11; www.painting-school; fpratt@painting-school.com). Teaches 2-week classes for student, amateur, teacher, and professional levels. In English or French. €1550, including accommodations and half-board.

WORKING

Many travelers structure their trips by working odd jobs along their route or getting a full-time stint in a city where they plan to stay for some time. Such jobs may be rather hard to come by, in light of France's highly competitive job market, so being fluent in French and fabulously connected couldn't hurt.

French unemployment remains stubbornly at 11%, and unqualified foreigners are unlikely to meet with much sympathy from French employers. **Non-EU citizens** will find it well-nigh impossible to get a work permit without a firm offer of a job. In order to hire a non-EU foreigner legally in France, the employer must prove that the hiree can perform a task which cannot be performed by a French person. On the bright side, many employers look favorably on English-language skills; if you're bilingual, your chances of obtaining employment can be greater. For US college students, recent graduates, and young adults, the simplest way to get legal permission to work abroad is through **Council Exchanges Work Abroad Programs.** Fees range from US$300 to US$475. Council Exchanges can help you obtain a three- to six-month work permit/visa and also provides assistance with finding jobs and housing.

LONG-TERM WORK

International placement agencies are often the easiest way to find employment abroad (including in France), especially for teaching English. **Internships,** usually for college students, are a good way to segue into working abroad, although they are often unpaid or poorly paid.

For an international internship and job database, try www.jobsabroad.com. Be wary of advertisements or companies that claim the ability to get you a job abroad for a fee—often the same listings are available online or in newspapers, or are even out of date. Some good ones include:

Council Exchanges, 52 Poland St., London W1F 7AB, UK (☎+020 7478 2000, US 888-268-6245; www.councilexchanges.org). Council Exchanges offers the simplest way to get legal permission to work abroad, charging a US$300-475 fee for arranging a three- to six-month work permit/visa. They also provide extensive information on different job and housing opportunities in France.

French-American Chamber of Commerce (FACC), International Career Development Programs, 1350 Avenue of the Americas, 6th fl., New York, NY 10019 (☎212-765-4598; fax 765-4650) has work programs, internships, and teaching opportunities.

International Association for the Exchange of Students for Technical Experience (IAESTE), 10400 Little Patuxent Pkwy., Suite 250, Columbia, MD 21044-3519, USA (☎410-997-2200; www.aipt.org). 8- to 12-week programs in France for college students who have completed 2 years of technical study. US$25 application fee.

VISA INFORMATION. **EU citizens** have the right to work and study in France without a visa, but they are required to have a **residency permit** (*carte de séjour;* see p. 11). By law, all EU citizens must be given equality of opportunity when applying to jobs not directly related to national security. In addition to a residency permit, **non-EU citizens** wishing to **study** in France for more than three months must apply for a **student visa** (US$47). To do so requires proof of admission to a French university, proof of financial independence, proof of residence (a gas or electric bill or a letter from your landlord), a medical certificate issued by a doctor approved by the French consulate, and proof of medical insurance. you must have a passport and offer of admission from a French university. Those wishing to **work** in France must have a firm offer of employment authorization from the French Ministry of Labor before applying for a **long-stay visa** (US$101) through a French consulate. International students looking for part-time work (up to 20 hours per week) can apply for a provisional work authorization upon completing their first academic year in a French university. For **au pairs, scientific researchers,** and **teaching assistants,** special rules apply; check with your local consulate.

TEACHING ENGLISH

Many private and public schools in France require teachers to have a **Teaching English as a Foreign Language (TEFL)** certificate. Even those that do not may pay certified teachers more. In almost all cases, you must have at least a bachelor's degree to be a full-fledged teacher, although oftentimes college undergraduates can get summer positions teaching or tutoring. The Fulbright Teaching Assistantship and French Teaching Assistantship program offered through the French Ministry of Education are the best options for students and recent grads with little teaching experience. Another alternative is to make contacts directly with schools. If you are going to try the latter, the best time to begin is several weeks before the start of the school year. The following organizations are extremely helpful in placing teachers in France.

Fulbright English Teaching Assistantship, US Student Programs Division, Institute of International Education, 809 United Nations Plaza, New York, NY 10017-3580, USA (☎212-883-8200; fax 212-984-5452; www.iie.org). Competitive program sends college graduates to teach in France.

French Ministry of Education Teaching Assistantship in France, Cultural Service of the French Embassy, 972 Fifth Ave., New York, NY 10021, USA (☎212-439-1400; fax 439-1455; www.frenchculture.org/education). Program for US citizens sends 1500 college students and recent grads to teach English part-time in France.

International Schools Services (ISS), 15 Roszel Rd., Box 5910, Princeton, NJ 08543, USA (☎609-452-0990; fax 609-452-2690; www.iss.edu). Hires teachers for more than 200 overseas schools, including ones in France; candidates should have experience teaching or with international affairs; 2-year commitment expected.

AU PAIR WORK

Au pairs are typically women ages 18-27 who work as live-in nannies, caring for children and doing light housework in foreign countries (including France) in exchange for full room and board and a small spending allowance or stipend. Most former au pairs speak favorably of their experience, which allowed them to get to know a region and its people without the high expenses of traveling. Drawbacks, however, often include long hours of constantly being on-duty, and the mediocre pay (wages often range from no more than US$75 to US$120 per week). Much of the au pair experience really does depend on the family you're placed with. The agencies below are a good starting point.

L'Accueil Familial des Jeunes Etrangers, 23 rue du Cherche-Midi, 75006 Paris (☎01 42 22 50 34; fax 01 45 44 60 48; accueil@afje-paris.org). Arranges summer and 18-month au pair jobs (placement fee €108). Also arranges similar jobs for non-students which require 30hr. of work per week in exchange for room, board, employment benefits, and a metro pass.

Au Pair Homestay, World Learning, Inc., 1015 15th St. NW, Suite 750, Washington, DC 20005, USA (☎800-287-2477; fax 202-408-5397).

Au Pair in Europe, P.O. Box 68056, Blakely Postal Outlet, Hamilton, Ontario, Canada L8M 3M7 (☎905-545-6305; fax 905-544-4121; www.princeent.com).

Childcare International, Ltd., Trafalgar House, Grenville Pl., London NW7 3SA (☎20890 63116; fax 8906-3461; www.childint.co.uk).

InterExchange, 161 Sixth Ave., New York, NY 10013, USA (☎212-924-0446; fax 924-0575; www.interexchange.org).

FINDING WORK ONCE THERE

Those looking for work can check help-wanted columns in French newspapers, especially *Le Monde, Le Figaro,* and the English-language *International Herald Tribune,* as well as *France-USA Contacts (FUSAC),* a free weekly circular filled with classified ads, available at Yankee hangouts. Many of these jobs are "unofficial" and therefore illegal (the penalty is deportation), but many people find them convenient because they often don't ask for presentation of a work permit. However, the best tips on jobs for foreigners come from other travelers. Be aware of your rights as an employee, and always get written confirmation of your agreements, including official job offers. Youth hostels frequently provide room and board to travelers in exchange for work.

Those seeking more permanent employment should have a **résumé** in both English and French. Type up your résumé for a prospective employer, but write the cover letter by hand. Handwriting is considered an important indicator of your character to French employers. Also, expect to be asked interview questions that might be considered inappropriate in another culture, such as your stance on ethical or political issues. The French workplace tends to be more conservative than anglo offices, so your and your employer's morals must (as far as your employer knows) correspond.

American Church, 65 quai d'Orsay, 75007 Paris (☎01 40 62 05 00; fax 01 40 62 05 11; www.americanchurchparis.org). Posts a bulletin board full of job and housing opportunities for Americans and anglophones. Open M-Sa 9am-10pm.

The Information Center, 65 quai d'Orsay, 75007 Paris (☎01 45 56 09 50). Garden level at the American Church. A clearing house of info and referrals providing immediate service to the English speaking people of Paris. The Center maintains a comprehensive database of resources available to those in need of information regarding legal matters, medical resources, housing, language courses, and more. Open Tu-Th 1:15-4pm.

Agence Nationale Pour l'Emploi (ANPE), 4 impasse d'Antin, Paris (☎01 43 59 62 63; www.anpe.fr). ANPE has lots of specific information on employment opportunities in France. Interested parties should bring a work permit and *carte de séjour.* Open M-W and F 9am-5pm, Th 9am-noon.

Centre d'Information et de Documentation Jeunesse (CIDJ), 101 quai Branly, 75015 Paris (☎01 44 49 12 00; fax 01 40 65 02 61; www.cidj.asso.fr). CIDJ is an invaluable state-run youth center that provides ample information on such work-related topics as education, résumés, employment, and careers, both in Paris and throughout France. English spoken. Jobs are posted on the bulletin boards outside. Open M-F 10am-6pm, Sa 9:30am-1pm.

European Employment Services (EURES), (☎08 00 90 97 00) facilitates employment between EU countries. For EU citizens only.

Chamber of Commerce in France, 156 bd. Haussmann, 75008 Paris (☎01 56 43 45 67; fax 01 56 43 45 60; www.amchamfrance.org). An association of American businesses in France. Keeps résumés on file for 2 months and places them at the disposal of French and American companies. Open M-Th 9:30am-1pm and 2-5pm.

SHORT-TERM WORK

Traveling for long periods of time can get expensive; many travelers try their hand at odd jobs for a few weeks to make some extra cash. Bartending, serving, and working in the tourist industry are options commonly available to travelers. Another popular option is to work several hours a day at a hostel in exchange for free or discounted room and/or board. Most often, these short-term jobs are found by word of mouth, or simply by talking to the owner of a hostel or restaurant. Due to the high turnover in the tourism industry, many places are always eager for help, even if only temporary. Youth centers *(centres de jeunesse)* often have job listings; check out our practical information sections in larger cities.

Farm work is another option; the autumn *vendanges* (grape harvest) provides plentiful opportunities for backbreaking work for a small allowance and cheap wine. Check out **WWOOF** (World-Wide Opportunities on Organic Farms; WWOOF International, P.O. Box 2675, Lewes BN7 1RB, UK; www.phdcc.com/wwoof), which maintains a list of farms seeking temporary workers in exchange for room and board. **Appellation Contrôlée,** Ulgersmaweg 26c, 9731 BT, Groningen, Holland, offers grape and other fruit picking programs in France for a placement fee of €99, or €245 with transportation (☎050 549 2434; fax 050 549 2428; www.apcon.nl).

ADVENTURE TRAVEL

For those seeking larger thrills, France will not disappoint. The country's long, challenging roads are a cyclist's dream, and the mountains to the east are frequented by climbers and hikers. Many adventure travel programs for youth incorporate language study or homestays; inquire with individual companies for specific arrangements. For detailed information on mountain climbing in France, go to the site www.cosiroc.org.

Beyond Limits (☎435-640-6435; www.byndlimits.com). Leads mountaineering and hiking trips around the Mt. Blanc range of Italy, Switzerland, and France. Flat fee of US$1795 includes 7-day trip and 15 meals.

MustGo Adventure Travel, 219 St. Vincent St., Glasgow G25QY, England (☎014 1221 9593; fax 014 1221 1377; www.mustgo.com). Arranges a number of short adventure trips in France. Giant searchable database ranks trips by physical difficulty.

Putney Student Travel, 345 Hickory Ridge Rd., Putney, VT 05346 (☎802-387-5000; fax 802-387-4276; www.goputney.org). Conducts adventure trips around France for those interested in mountaineering, skiing, and biking. Program costs range from US$6000-8000. Participants must be high school students.

Venture Europe, 2245 Stonecrop Way, Golden, CO 80401 (☎303-526-0806; fax 303-526-0885; www.aave.com). Offers a number of trips that incorporate hiking, biking, and rock climbing; geared toward teens. Program fees vary from US$2000-5000.

ALTERNATIVES TO TOURISM

FURTHER READING ON ALTERNATIVES TO TOURISM

French or Foe? Getting the Most Out of Visiting, Living and Working in France, by Polly Platt. Distribooks Intl., 1998 (US$17).

How to Get a Job in Europe, by Sanborn and Matherly. Planning Communications, 2003 ($US23).

How to Live Your Dream of Volunteering Oversees, by Collins, DeZerega, and Heckscher. Penguin Books, 2002 (US$17).

International Directory of Voluntary Work, by Whetter and Pybus. Peterson's Guides and Vacation Work, 2000 (US$16).

International Jobs, by Kocher and Segal. Perseus Books, 1999 (US$18).

Living, Studying, and Working in France, by Reilly and Kalisky. Henry Holt and Company, 1999 (US$16).

Overseas Summer Jobs 2002, by Collier and Woodworth. Peterson's Guides and Vacation-Work, 2002 (US$18).

Work Abroad: The Complete Guide to Finding a Job Overseas, by Hubbs, Griffith, and Nolting. Transitions Abroad Publishing, 2002 (US$20).

LIFE & TIMES

LAND

France's 543,965 sq. km fit into a hexagonal shape: to the southwest, the **Pyrénées mountains** form a frontier with Spain, to the east the snow-capped peaks of the **Alps** and **Jura** separate France from Italy and Switzerland, and just above the Jura, the **Rhine River** marks the divide between France and Germany. France's only artificial border is with Belgium, in the northeast corner of the country. The **English Channel** *(La Manche)* keeps Normandy's chalky cliffs at a 35km distance from England at its narrowest point. The **Atlantic Ocean** laps upon beaches of fine sand in the west and the **Mediterranean** greets the pebbly beaches of the south. The interior of France is primarily characterized by low-lying plains and river valleys, with the exception of the rugged *massif central* plateau in the southeast, a landscape of extinct volcanoes, deep gorges, and stalagmites. **Corsica,** France's Mediterranean island territory, is 170km off the French coast. Its 8681 sq. km are mostly mountainous, with high cliffs and craggy rocks on its west coast and a lagoon-spotted east coast loved by hikers from the French mainland.

FLORA, FAUNA, & THE ENVIRONMENT

France was once almost entirely covered in forest. Today, trees cover 25% of the terrain and provide a home to France's larger mammals, such as red deer, roe deer, and wild boar. Other common animals include hares, rabbits, and foxes. The Alpine chamoix and marmot, Pyrenean lynx and brown bear, and Atlantic seals are all endangered species.

The French government's relations with various environmental groups have not always been friendly. In 1985, the French secret service blew up Greenpeace's ship, the *Rainbow Warrior,* which was stationed in the South Pacific in protest to France's nuclear testing in the French Polynesian islands. France ended nuclear testing in 1996, however, and signed the **United Nations Comprehensive Test Ban Treaty** in 1998. In April 2002, President Chirac announced at the G-8 Environmental Summit that France would take an active role in leading European initiatives to protect ancient forests.

For more information on French national parks, check out www.parcsnation-aux-fr.com; for more on French environmental concerns, see the French Institute for the Environment's website: www.ifen.fr.

HISTORY

FROM GAULS TO GOTHS

In 1868, the skull of a 27,000-year-old advanced hominid was unearthed at Cro-Magnon, in **Périgord.** Ten thousand years later, his descendants left their mark on history in the graffiti-filled caves of the **Dordogne Valley,** and by 4500 BC Neolithic peoples were carving huge stone monuments at **Carnac.** These mysterious creations were admired by the Celtic **Gauls,** who arrived from the east around 600 BC. Gauls traded and co-existed peacefully with the Greek colonists who settled during the 7th century BC at Massilia (modern day **Marseille**). Rome made **Provence** a province in 125 BC and quickly conquered the rest of the South. Fierce resistance from France's northern Gauls kept the Romans out of their territory until **Julius Caesar's** victory at Alesia in 52 BC. By the time Rome itself fell in AD 476, Gaul had suffered Germanic invasions for centuries. While many of the Gothic tribes plundered and passed on, the **Franks** eventually dominated Gaul. The Frankish **Clovis** founded the Merovingian dynasty and was baptized a Christian in 507. His empire was succeeded by the grander Carolingian dynasty of **Charlemagne**. While his **Holy Roman Empire** did not actually live up to its literal name, Charlemagne did succeed in adding what are now Germany, Austria, and Switzerland to his domains. The territorial squabbles following his death in 814 were resolved with the **Treaty of Verdun,** which divided the empire among his three grandsons.

FRANCE & ENGLAND DUKE IT OUT

After the fall of the Carolingian dynasty, the noble-elected **Hugh Capet** quickly consolidated power. His descendant, **Louis VII,** set off 500 years of fighting between France and England when he made the fatal error of not signing a pre-nuptial agreement. When his ex-queen **Eleanor of Aquitaine** married into the English Plantagenêt dynasty in the 12th century, a broad swath of land stretching from the Channel to the Pyrénées became English territory. That same century, King **Philippe-Auguste** won much of northern France from England's bumbling King John. The plot thickened in the 14th century, when England's **Edward III** tried to claim the throne of France. The French **Philippe de Valois** responded by encroaching upon English-owned Aquitaine. Edward III landed his troops in Normandy, triggering the **Hundred Years' War** in 1328. The English crowned their own **Henri VI** king of France 90 years later, but salvation soon followed for France with a 17-year-old peasant girl. Leading the French army, **Joan of Arc** won a string of victories before her capture by Burgundians, who were allied with the English. While she burned at the stake in **Rouen** (p. 195) in 1430, the tide of war had already turned, and only Calais was left in English hands by 1453.

STRANGE BEDFELLOWS: RELIGIOUS DEVOTION & WAR

The Middle Ages left an impressive legacy of cathedrals, convents, and monasteries, including the haunting semi-isle of **Mont-St-Michel** (p. 226). The power of the monasteries was often as great as that of the aristocracy, if not of the monarchy. **Pope Innocent II** proclaimed the first Crusade from **Clermont** (p. 417) to wrest Jerusalem from the Saracens. Thousands flocked to take the cross, swayed by the promise of salvation and probable plunder. Though for the most part military failures, the contact with the advanced East shook Europe from her intellectual slumber. Monarchy regained its ascendancy when **Philip IV** arrested **Pope Boniface VIII** at the opening of the 14th century to prevent his imminent excommunication. Old Boniface died after the arrest, and his French successor, **Pope Clement V,** moved the pope's court from Rome to Church-owned **Avignon** (p. 504). Six more popes held mass in France. The papacy finally returned to Rome in 1377, after the **Black Death** had run its course.

In the 16th century, religious conflict between **Huguenots** (French Protestants) and **Catholics** instigated the **Wars of Religion.** The fervently Catholic queen **Catherine de Médici** orchestrated a marriage between her daughter and the Huguenot **Henri**

de Navarre in 1572. The seemingly peaceful political move turned out to be a deadly trap. Two thousand Huguenots who came to Paris to celebrate their wedding were slaughtered in the **St-Bartholomew's Day Massacre.** Henri survived, quickly converted to Catholicism, and ascended the throne as the first **Bourbon** monarch. In 1598 he issued the **Edict of Nantes,** granting tolerance for French Protestants and quelling religious warfare for almost a century.

BOURBON ON THE ROCKS

The French Bourbon monarchy reached the height of its power and extravagance in the 17th century. **Louis XIII's** capable and ruthless minister, **Cardinal Richelieu,** consolidated political power in the hands of the monarchy and created the centralized, bureaucratic administration characteristic of France to this day. Richelieu and Louis were succeeded in 1642 by another cardinal-and-king combo, **Cardinal Mazarin** and the five-year-old **Louis XIV.** By 1661, however, the 24-year-old monarch had decided he was ready to rule alone. Not known for his modesty, Louis styled himself as the **Sun King** and took the motto *"l'état, c'est moi"* ("I am the state"). He brought the nobility with him to the fabulously opulent palace of **Versailles** (p. 157), hoping that there he could keep a close watch over them and avoid any unpleasant uprisings.

Louis could not long hide the state's growing financial problems, however, and resentment toward the monarchy began to brew. When **Louis XVI** inherited the throne in 1774, the country was in desperate financial straits. Peasants blamed the soon-to-be-**Old Regime** for their mounting debts. In 1789, Louis XVI called a last-resort meeting of the **Estates General,** an assembly of delegates from the three classes of society: aristocrats, clergy, and the bourgeois-dominated **Third Estate.** The Third Estate soon broke away and proclaimed itself the National Assembly. In the tennis courts of Versailles they promised to draft a new constitution in their **Oath of the Tennis Court.** As rumors multiplied, the Parisian mob, known as the *sans-culottes* (those without breeches), took the initiative, angered by high bread prices. Their storming of the old fortress of the **Bastille** on July 14th set off a destructive orgy that stormed across the nation. Despite the Revolutionary principles of *liberté, égalité,* and *fraternité,* and the Assembly's recently authored **Declaration of the Rights of Man,** events soon turn ugly. In 1793, after the proletariat had overthrown the monarchy and officially replaced it with the **First Republic,** the radical **Jacobin** faction, led by **Maximilien Robespierre,** took over the Convention and guillotined the King and his Queen, **Marie-Antoinette.** The liberal slaughter of the **Reign of Terror** finally ended when Robespierre himself met with the guillotine blade in 1794, when power was entrusted to a five-man Directory.

THE LITTLE DICTATOR

After sweeping through northern Italy and into Austria, the young Corsican **Napoleon Bonaparte** undertook an ill-fated invasion of Egypt. Although successful on land, the destruction of his fleet at the Battle of the Nile left his disease-ridden army marooned in Cairo. Napoleon abandoned his army in Egypt to salvage his political career in France. Riding a wave of public support, he deposed the Directory and, in 1804, crowned himself **Emperor.** His **Napoleonic Code** re-established slavery and limited the legal rights of women. After crushing the Austrians, Prussians, and Russians, he left only Britain undefeated, safe in her island refuge after Horatio Nelson's 1807 victory at **Trafalgar.** In 1812, in another disastrous campaign, Napoleon's army of 700,000 captured Moscow, only to find it deserted and winter fast approaching. Barely 200,000 of his troops made it through the freezing trek home alive. A war-weary nation turned against Napoleon. In return for abdicating in 1814, he was given the Mediterranean island of **Elba,** and the monarchy was reinstated under **Louis XVIII,** brother of his headless predecessor. In a final appearance, Napoleon left Elba and landed near Cannes in 1815 and marched north as the king fled to England. The ensuing **Hundred Days' War** ended on the field of **Waterloo** in Flanders, where the **Duke of Wellington** triumphed. Napoleon was banished to **St-Helena** in the south Atlantic, where he died in 1821. Thousands still pay their respects to Napoleon's Corsican hometown of **Ajaccio** (p. 760).

REVOLUTION AGAIN...
AND AGAIN...AND AGAIN

The **Bourbon Restoration** was quick to step into the power vacuum left by Napoleon. France's reinstated monarchy soon returned to the despotism of the Old Regime. When **Charles X** restricted the press and limited the electorate to the landed classes, the people spoke up. Following the **July Revolution of 1830,** Charles, remembering the fate of his brother, abdicated quickly, and a **constitutional monarchy** was created under the head of the new Orléan regime, "bourgeois king" **Louis-Philippe.** The industrialization of France created a class of urban poor receptive to the new ideas of socialism. They provided the muscle behind the **February Revolution of 1848,** which culminated in the declaration of the **Second Republic** and the adoption of universal male suffrage. The people elected as president their famous emperor's nephew **Louis Napoleon,** who then seized power in an 1851 coup and declared himself Emperor Napoleon III. During his reign, the Second Empire, France was economically revived: her factories hummed and **Baron Haussmann** rebuilt Paris to its modern grandeur.

Across the Rhine, **Bismarck** had almost completed the unification of Germany. Tricking the French into declaring war, Bismarck's troops overran the country and captured the emperor. With German armies advancing, Parisian deputies declared the **Third Republic.** Finally capitulating just as its citizens were reduced to eating rats, France was forced to give up the Alsace-Lorraine territory and pay an exorbitant occupation indemnity. The Parisian mob revolted and declared the **Commune,** a brief-lived governmental coup which was quickly and bloodily crushed as over 10,000 *communards* died under the rifles of French troops. The Third Republic was further undermined by the **Dreyfus Affair.** In search of a scapegoat, Dreyfus, a Jewish captain in the French army, was convicted in 1894 on trumped-up charges of treason. Dreyfusard momentum became unstoppable after Emile Zola condemned the army, the government, and society for its anti-semitic prejudice in his dramatic diatribe *J'accuse;* Dreyfus was finally pardoned in 1904.

COSTLY VICTORIES:
THE TWO GREAT WARS

Germany's 1871 unification changed the balance of power in Europe. France formed the **Triple Entente** with czarist Russia and Britain, while Germany, Italy, and the Austro-Hungarian Empire formed the **Triple Alliance.** When **World War I** erupted in 1914, German armies rapidly advanced on France (again), but a stalemate soon developed as the opposing armies dug trenches along the country's length. France and her allies triumphed in 1918, after the arrival of US troops. It is still possible to visit the battle-scarred fields where Europe lost an entire generation (see **Memorials near Verdun,** p. 353). Devastated by four years of fighting on her territory and the loss of 1.3 million men, France demanded crippling reparations from Germany. These humiliations were often invoked by Hitler in his rise to power.

During the depression of the 1930s, tensions between Fascists and Socialists, bourgeois and workers, left France ill-equipped to deal with the dangers of **Hitler's** impending mobilization. The German invasion of Poland in 1939 precipitated France's declaration of war on Germany and ignited **World War II.** In May 1940, the Germans swept through Belgium, bypassing the **Maginot line,** France's main defensive position along the German border. France capitulated in June. The north fell under German occupation, while a puppet state in the south, led by WWI hero **Maréchal Pétain,** ruled from **Vichy** (p. 431). Escaped French forces operated under the command of the French government-in-exile, under **General Charles de Gaulle.** On August 25th, 1944, De Gaulle insisted that French troops lead the **liberation of Paris.** WWII monuments include the beaches of Normandy where British and American troops landed on **D-Day** (p. 217), the museum at **Caen** (p. 210), the ghost town **Oradour-sur-Glane** (p. 737) whose inhabitants were massacred by Nazi troops in 1944, **Le Natzweiler-Struthof** concentration camp (p. 382) in Alsace, and the **Resistance** headquarters in Lyon (p. 417).

FOURTH REPUBLIC & POST-COLONIAL FRANCE

The **Fourth Republic** was proclaimed in 1944 under the leadership of de Gaulle. In the next two years, his vision of a restructured society led to female suffrage and nationalized energy companies. He quit in 1946, unable to adapt to the deadlock of democratic politics. The next 14 years saw 25 governments. Meanwhile, between 1945 and 1975, France went through a period called the **Glorious Thirties,** during which the French began to embrace technology as the old-fashioned, agriculture-based country became urbanized and industrialized.

The end of the war signaled great change in residual 19th-century **colonial empire.** The 1954 liberation of **Dien Bien Phu** in Vietnam inspired the colonized peoples of France's other protectorates and colonies. **Morocco** and **Tunisia** gained independence in 1956, followed by **Mali, Senegal,** and the **Ivory Coast** in 1960. But France drew the line when Algerian nationalists moved for independence. With a population of over one million French colonists, or **pied-noirs** (literally "black footed" in French), France was reluctant to give up the colony it regarded as an extension of its own culture. De Gaulle was voted into power in 1958 to deal with the impending crisis. At a peaceful demonstration in Paris against curfew restrictions in 1961, police opened fire on the largely North African crowd, killing hundreds and dumping their bodies into the Seine. The **Algerian Revolution** erupted in 1962. Later that year, with a new **constitution** in hand, France declared itself the **Fifth Republic.** A 1962 referendum reluctantly granted independence to Algeria, the last of the French colonies.

In **May 1968,** what started as a student protest against racism, sexism, and problems in the university system rapidly grew into a full-scale revolt as 10 million state workers went on strike in support of social reform. The government responded by deploying tank and commando units into the city. The National Assembly was soon dissolved and another revolution was averted only when fresh elections returned the Gaullists to power. However, the aging General had lost his magic touch, and he resigned following a referendum defeat in 1969.

THE 80s, 90s, & TODAY

Contrary to many fears, the Fifth Republic has endured without de Gaulle, although it has undergone many changes. De Gaulle's successor, **Georges Pompidou,** had a more *laissez-faire* position toward business and a less assertive foreign policy than de Gaulle. Pompidou was followed by conservative **Valéry Giscard**

IN RECENT NEWS

EU GROWING PAINS

The public rift between France and the US over the war in Iraq made big headlines in 2003. For all its chastisement of US unilateralism in international affairs, however, France has often had a similarly dominant role within the smaller context of the European Union. In initial drafts of the EU's working constitution, France garnered a disproportionate percentage of the vote, putting it nearly on par with far more populous Germany. Now, as ten new Eastern European countries, including Poland, Hungary, and the Czech Republic, prepare to join the EU, the geographic, political, and economic center of the union will suddenly shift eastward.

Many predict that Poland, the Czech Republic, and above all Germany, the "sleeping giant" of the EU, will emerge as new leaders within the Union. France will be alone in trying to keep the locus of power from swinging too far eastward.

The nation has recently spearheaded a European effort to intervene in the violence-ridden Democratic Republic of the Congo, taking charge where the UN would not. France's new role on the international scene may serve as a welcome alternative to the somewhat *laissez-faire* attitude of its European neighbors. On the other hand, some fear that France may come to mimic what some see as the US's overly aggressive style.

d'Estaing in 1974. D'Estaing carried on de Gaulle's legacy by concentrating on economic development and strengthening French presence in international affairs. In 1981, Socialist **François Mitterrand** took over the presidency and the Socialists gained a majority in the *Assemblée Nationale*. They raised the minimum wage, added a fifth week to the annual vacation and began widespread nationalization, but the international climate could not support a socialist economy. In the face of Socialists' losses in the 1986 elections, Mitterrand appointed conservative **Jacques Chirac** as Prime Minister.

At the same time, the **far right** began to flourish under the leadership of **Jean-Marie Le Pen**. He formed the **Front National (FN)** on an anti-immigration platform with racist overtones targeting the new working class from North Africa and other former colonies. In the 1986 parliamentary elections, the FN picked up 10% of the vote by blaming unemployment on immigrants. Meanwhile, in an unprecedented power-sharing relationship known as "cohabitation," Mitterrand withdrew to control foreign affairs, allowing Chirac to assume domestic power. Chirac privatized many industries, but a large-scale transport strike and widespread terrorism hurt the right, allowing Mitterrand to win a second term in 1988. During his second term, he planned a decentralization of financial and political power. In 1995, Mitterrand chose not to run again because of his failing health, and Jacques Chirac was elected president. Denounced around the globe for conducting underground **nuclear weapons tests** in the South Pacific, and facing a 12.2% unemployment rate, Chirac faced a difficult year. In 1997, Chirac dissolved the parliament, and elections reinstated a Socialist government. Chirac was forced to accept his one-time presidential rival **Lionel Jospin**, head of the Socialist majority, as Prime Minister in 1998. The parliamentary elections in June 2002 marked the end of cohabitation between president and prime minister, as Chirac appointed conservative **Jean-Pierre Raffarin** as the next Prime Minister.

One of the most important challenges in the '80s and '90s has been the question of European integration. France supported the creation of the **European Economic Community (EEC)** in 1957. In 1991 the **Maastricht Treaty** expanded the 13-nation EEC to the **European Union (EU)**. The **Schengen agreement** of 1995 created a six-nation zone without border controls, which was extended to the entire EU (barring the UK, Ireland, and Denmark) in 1999. The **euro** was introduced as the single European legal tender in 2002. Throughout European economic integration, Franco-German cooperation has played a central role. Since the inception of the EU, however, European integration has met with significant resistance by the French, who fear a loss of French national character and autonomy.

In early 2003, France and Germany celebrated the anniversary of a postwar friendship treaty. They joined with Russia to voice opposition to the US-led **war with Iraq,** insisting on political and diplomatic means to disarm Iraq. A breach in US-France relations opened as France criticized American unilateralism and defended a multi-polar world and a powerful Europe. The US was so miffed Congress renamed *French fries* and the Pentagon withdrew from the biennial Paris Air Show. The friendship between the one-time allies seems to be redeveloping, notably at Evian's June 2003 **G-8 summit.**

The terrorist attacks of September 11, the war in Iraq, and the outbreak of SARS have all been damaging to France's economy, and in particular the airline industry. The situation was not helped by the months-long strikes that occurred in protest of Prime Minister Raffarin's **plan Fillon,** which aimed to increase the number of years public sector workers would have to pay into the state pension scheme. Beginning in April 2003, thousands of public workers went on strike, including garbage collectors, train drivers, tax officials, airport workers, teachers, electricity board workers, postal workers, and emergency doctors. The train and airline industries both lost millions of dollars. Shrugging off angry tourists with ruined vacation plans and French workers disgruntled about having to walk to work in the heat, strikers pulled through for one national major event: the *baccalauréat* exam. On the day French high schoolers were to take their graduation exams, trains throughout the country ran flawlessly.

DEMOGRAPHICS

ETHNIC MINORITIES

France's perpetually low birth rate is somewhat offset by the influx of immigrants from her former colonies over the past few decades, particularly from the West Indies and Africa. Of these, the largest number of minorities trace their roots to Algeria, which was under French rule from 1830 to 1962.

Historically, France has been relatively welcoming of immigrants, although ethnic minorities still face some hostility. The popularity of far-right nationalist **Jean-Marie Le Pen,** who edged out Socialist **Lionel Jospin** in the 2002 preliminary presidential election, is the most visible sign of negative attitudes toward immigrants. After Le Pen's success in the preliminary, however, protesters took to the streets to denounce his racism and voters turned out in droves to assure his sound defeat in the final run-off against Chirac. The French government has made efforts to combat intolerance and discrimination. Jospin's 1998 law on immigration allows foreign scientists and scholars more relaxed conditions of entry into France.

RELIGIOUS MINORITIES

Overwhelmingly Roman Catholic France has not always been the most accepting environment for religious minorities. An alarming wave of anti-Semitic violence flared up in 2002 in response to intensification of the Israel-Palestine conflict in the Middle East: synagogues in Marseille, Lyon, and Paris were firebombed, and street fighting broke out as well. But French sympathy for the Palestinians only runs so deep. One of the biggest religious flashpoints of the last ten years has been the wearing of Muslim headscarves *(hijab)* in public schools; Prime Minister Raffarin came out against the garment as the government refined the national law.

BGLT

Homophobia remains a problem, but the number of reported hate crimes based on sexual orientation or gender identity has decreased in recent years. French law prohibits discrimination based on sexual orientation in the workplace, and some French courts have allowed gender reassignment on birth registers. In 1999, France became the first traditionally Catholic country in the world to legally recognize homosexual unions, in the **Pacte Civil de Solidarité,** known by its acronym **PACS,** although gay activists still struggle to attain the same rights to adoption and reproductive technologies that married couples enjoy.

WOMEN

France has progressive legislation criminalizing sexual harassment; nevertheless, women continue to face problems in the workplace and elsewhere. The French still maintain traditional gender roles to a large extent.

REGIONAL IDENTITIES

For a country under a tremendously powerful central authority (Paris), France has a surprisingly diverse citizenry (see **One Nation Under Paris?,** p. 77). With the Celtic influences in Brittany, the Catalan influences in Aquitaine, the Italian heritage in Corsica, and the German and Flemish influences in Alsace and Picardy, respectively, France is almost a microcosm of Europe itself. A hundred years ago, half of the population of France spoke a dialect other than French, such as Breton, Basque, or Provençal. France spent much of the past century trying to eradicate these minority languages, but now, in the shadow of the homogenizing effects of the European Union, regional languages and customs are making a comeback.

In March 2003, the French Parliament passed a constitutional amendment that describes the French state as "decentralized." The French government seems to be finally recognizing the value of strong regional identities. Visitors will, too, when they shop the fairy-tale-like Christmas markets in Alsace, participate in a *corridor* at a Basque *feria,* dance at a *fest-noz* in Brittany, or soak in the beautiful rural scenery of the Normandy countryside.

CULTURE

FOOD & DRINK

Charles de Gaulle complained that no nation with 400 types of cheese could ever be united; watch a pack of ravenous Frenchwomen tearing through a *fromagerie* and you'll agree. Though *le fast-food* and *le self-service* have invaded France, many still shop daily for their ingredients, and restaurants observe the traditional order of courses. One could hardly expect less from the people who coined *haute cuisine.*

MEALS. The French ease into their food consumption for the day with a breakfast *(le petit déjeuner),* which is usually quite light, consisting largely of bread *(le pain)* or sometimes croissants plus an espresso with hot milk *(café au lait)* or a hot chocolate *(le chocolat).* The largest meal of the day is lunch *(le déjeuner),* typically eaten between noon and 2pm. Dinner *(le dîner)* begins quite late, and restaurants may not serve you if you want to dine at 6pm. A complete French meal includes an apéritif (drink), an *entrée* (appetizer), a *plat* (main course), salad, cheese, dessert, fruit, coffee, and a digestif (after-dinner drink). Though there are

ONE NATION UNDER PARIS?

Regional identities in modern France

Although the average traveler may catch a glimpse of other corners of France, Paris, that luminous center of the French solar system, can often blind us to the rest of the country. France is one of the most centralized countries in the West, both politically and culturally, and its notorious defense of its language has only reinforced the image of a unified French culture. Yet even before the recent wave of immigration, France has dealt with cultural diversity in its territory. In fact, the French State was unified by annexing several ethnically diverse territories: parts of Catalonia and the Basque Country in the South, the ever volatile island of Corsica in the Mediterranean, the rest of Southern France (which goes by the name of Occitania), the Germanic regions of Alsace and part of Lorraine, Celtic Brittany, and the Flemish northern tip of France. Until this last century, these regions were like foreign countries on French soil.

It was the Revolution that replaced the hodgepodge of these semi-autonomous provinces with *départements*, administrative sub-divisions operating under one law for all. Opponents of the Revolution saw the provinces as threats. In 1793, Bertrand Barère famously declared "Federalism and superstition speak Lower Breton; emigration and hatred of the Republic speak German [Alsatian]; the counter-revolution speaks Italian [Corsican]; and fanaticism speaks Basque." The project of unifying French language and culture was never given much support, however, until public school became mandatory in the 1880s. In many schools, children caught speaking their local tongues were punished with a *symbole*, usually a dunce cap or scarlet letter. In return, however, schools assigned readings on rural France like the enduring *Le Tour de la France par deux enfants*, a picaresque journey around France by two Alsatian boys (and the inspiration for today's famous nationwide bike race). It was only after WWII that France was fully synchronized by mass media, consumerism, and the decline of traditional peasantry. Travel around France today, and you will see the same stores, television, post offices, and phone booths everywhere, and you will rarely hear a peep of local parlance, which is spoken mostly in the home and by the elderly, when it is still spoken at all.

Yet, local identity has not, for all that, disappeared. Rather, it has made a startling comeback since the 1960s. Most conspicuously, Corsican terrorist attacks (which often involve criminal corruption as much as autonomist movements) have been making front-page news for years. There are also many quieter manifestations of local identity around France. In 1986, regional governments were elected for the first time since the Revolution, and regional languages have entered some school curricula, though not without controversy. Whereas the French State had once gone so far as to prohibit the use of non-French names on birth certificates, ethnic names such as Yann (the Breton equivalent of the French Jean or the English John) have caught on strong. In the 1980s and 1990s, French television suddenly discovered what other countries had long known, that local news was extremely popular, a rather belated realization considering that the regional newspapers like *Ouest-France* and *Les Dernières Nouvelles d'Alsace* had long outsold the national press. At the movies, every year produces several paeans to community and rural life, such as the many film adaptations of the mid-twentieth century regional novelist Marcel Pagnol (*Jean de Florette, My Mother's Castle*). And of course, tourists are treated to a parade of folkloric festivals, dance, and souvenirs.

Anyone looking for some elusive "authenticity" should be skeptical, however, for local culture ain't what it used to be. If you get a chance to attend a Breton village festival, the drunken peasant might be a Belgian professor who abandoned his career for the pastoral life. After such radical transformation as France has experienced, even the most seemingly authentic images of regional culture and country life—in fact, especially those—are little more than show. This is not to say, however, that all displays of local difference and identity are mere sham. Vestiges of regional culture combine creatively with other cultures these days, as in the regionalist rap or world music of the Celtic maestro Alan Stivell or the Southern bands The Fabulous Troubadours, Massilia Sound System, and Zebda. And of course, as any traveler will see, no two places are exactly alike. Local variations persist, and the French continue to nurture an intimate bond to community and place.

Matthew Lazen is a History and Literature lecturer at Harvard University. He is currently revising his dissertation on regional cultures in postmodern France for publication, and organizing a Harvard conference on post-War French regionalism.

countless apéritifs, the most common and most popular are *kir*, white wine mixed with sweet *cassis* (black currant liqueur), and *pastis*, a potent licorice-flavored liqueur diluted with water.

MENUS. Most restaurants offer a *menu à prix fixe* (fixed-price meal) that costs less than ordering *à la carte*. The menu may include an appetizer, *plat*, *fromage* (cheese), and dessert. The *formule* is a cheaper, two-course version. Order sparkling water *(eau pétillante* or *eau gazeuse)* or flat mineral water *(eau plate);* for a pitcher of tap water, ask for *une carafe d'eau*. Finish the meal with espresso *(un café)*, which comes in little cups with blocks of sugar. When *boisson comprise* is written on the menu, you are entitled to a free drink (usually wine) with the meal. Vegetarians will probably have the best luck at *crêperies*, ethnic restaurants, and places catering to a younger crowd.

GROCERIES. For an occasional €15 spree you can have a marvelous meal, but it's easy to assemble inexpensive meals yourself with a ration of cheese, pâté, wine, and bread. Start with bread from the *boulangerie* (bakery), and then proceed to the *charcuterie* for pâté, *saucisson* (hard salami), and *jambon* (ham), or buy a delicious freshly roasted chicken from the *boucherie* (butcher's). If you want someone else to do the work, boulangeries often sell fresh sandwiches. *Pâtisseries* will sate nearly any sweet tooth with treats ranging from candy to ice cream to pastries.

CAFÉS. Cafés in France, brooding ground of upstart poets and glooming existentialists, figure pleasantly in the daily routine. When choosing a café, remember that you pay for location. Those on a major boulevard can be more expensive than smaller establishments a few steps down a side street. Prices in cafés are two-tiered, cheaper at the counter *(comptoir)* than in the seating area *(salle)*; outdoor seating *(la terrasse)* may charge a third level. Coffee, beer, and (in the south) the anise-flavored *pastis* are the staple café drinks, while *citron pressé* (lemonade) and *diabolo menthe* (peppermint soda) are popular non-alcoholic choices. If you order *café*, you'll get espresso; for coffee with milk or cream, ask for a *café au lait* or a *café crème*. *Bière à la pression*, or draft beer, is 660ml of either pale *(blonde)* or dark *(brune)* lager; for something smaller, ask for *une demi* (330ml).

THE ELIXIR OF LIFE

Wine *(le vin)* pervades French culture, and no occasion is complete without a glass or four. Wines vary tremendously, according not only to which of the 60 grape varieties it is made from, but also the climate and soil type in which the grapes were grown. **White wine** *(vin blanc)* can be made from both white grapes *(blanc de blancs)* and red *(blanc de noirs);* in the latter case care must be taken to prevent the skins from coloring the wine. **Red wine** *(vin rouge)* and rosé are always made from red grapes.

Wine-producing regions are scattered throughout France, each with its own specialty. On the Dordogne and Garonne rivers, the famous **Bordeaux** region produces mostly reds, white Pomerol, Médoc and Graves, and sweet white Sauternes. Red Bordeaux is often called "claret" in English. **Burgundy** is especially famous for its reds, from the wines of Chablis and the Côte d'Or in the north, to the Beaujolais and Mâconnais in the south. The northeast offers **Alsatian** whites that tend to be dry and fruity, complementing spicy foods. Delicately-bouqueted whites predominate in the **Loire Valley**. In Provence, the **Côtes de Provence** around Marseille are recognized for their *rosés*, while the **Côtes du Rhône** produce the sweet white *Muscat de Beaumes-de-Venise* and celebrated reds such as the famous *Châteauneuf du Pape*. Although many areas produce sparkling wines *(vins mousseux)*, only those grown and produced in **Champagne** can legally bear its name.

Other grape-based delights include **Cognac** and **Armagnac,** which come from Charente and Gascony respectively. Technically distinguished from brandy by strict government regulations, Cognac is a double-distilled spirit and so has a higher alcohol content than the single-distilled but more flavorful Armagnac. Unlike other wines, Cognac and Armagnac are usually enjoyed as digestifs.

A budget traveler in France can be pleasantly surprised by even the least expensive *vins de tables* (table wines), which are what most French drink. When buying wine, look for the product of the region you're in. Don't feel that you have to splurge to drink well; bad wine is virtually unheard of in France, and you can buy a decent bottle of red for as little as US$5. Table wines in restaurants can be bought by the liter *(une carafe)*, the half-liter *(une demi-carafe)*, and sometimes even the quarter-liter. Many cities have wine bars where you can buy vintage wine by the glass; this is a good way to learn about wine without the prices you'd otherwise have to pay. To indulge for absolutely nothing, visit regions with vineyards, like Burgundy and Bordeaux, where wine producers frequently offer free *dégustations* (tastings).

CUSTOMS & ETIQUETTE

In Paris they simply stared when I spoke to them in French; I never did succeed in making those idiots understand their language.
—Mark Twain

BLENDING IN. A good rule of thumb in France: don't fit the local stereotype of the American tourist and the people you meet won't fit yours—that nasty, nasal Frenchman. For dress, what may look perfectly innocuous in Miami will mark you out instantly in Menton. The French are known for their conservative stylishness: go for restrained sneakers or closed-toe shoes, solid-color pants or jeans, and plain T-shirts or button-down shirts, rather than Teva sandals, baggy pants, or torn jeans. French people rarely wear shorts, even in warm climates, but if you choose to wear them, they definitely shouldn't be too short. For women, skirts or dresses are more appropriate in general. Be sure to dress respectfully in churches. Blending in is a great excuse to shop for French clothes. If you're traveling in January or August, be sure to take advantage of massive sales *(les soldes)*—prices are often slashed as much as 75%.

LES CHIENS. The French *love* their dogs. Don't be surprised to find a pampered pet in your hotel, on your train, or, yes, sitting at the dinner table next to you.

ETAGES. The French call the ground floor the *rez-de-chaussée* and start numbering with the first floor above the ground floor *(premier étage)*. The button labeled "R" and not "1" is typically the ground floor. The *sous-sol* is the basement.

HOURS. Most restaurants open at noon for lunch and close in the afternoon before reopening for dinner. Some bistros and cafés remain open during the afternoon. Small businesses, banks, and post offices close daily noon-3pm. Many establishments shut down on Sundays, and most museums are closed on Mondays.

LANGUAGE & POLITESSE. Even if your French is near-perfect, waiters and salespeople who detect the slightest accent will often immediately respond in English. If your language skills are good, continue to speak in French. More often than not, the waiter or salesperson will respect and appreciate your fortitude, and respond in French. The French put a premium on polite pleasantries, particularly in the service industry. Always say *"Bonjour Madame/Monsieur"* when you come into a business, restaurant, or hotel, and *"Au Revoir"* when you leave. If you knock into someone on the street, always say *"Pardon."* The proper way to answer the phone is *"Âllo,"* but if you use this on the street, you'll blow your cover. When meeting someone for the first time, a handshake is appropriate. However, friends and acquaintances greet each other with a kiss on each cheek (the exception is men kissing men). If you are unsure of how to appropriately greet someone, let them make the first move. Don't use first names unless the person uses your first name or is obviously younger than you are.

POCKET CHANGE. Cashiers throughout France will constantly ask you *"Avez-vous de la monnaie?"* ("Do you have the change?") as they would rather not break your €20 note for a pack of gum. If you don't have it, smile ever-so-sweetly and say *"Non, désolée."*

PUBLIC RESTROOMS. The street side public restrooms that have emerged all over France are worth the €0.30 they require. You are guaranteed a clean restroom, as these magic machines are self-cleaning after each use. Toilets in train stations, metro stops, and public gardens are tended to by *gardiens* and generally cost €0.40-0.60. Most cafés reserve restrooms for their clients only, but fast food chains usually won't notice if you use their facilities.

SAFETY & SECURITY. Personal safety in France is on par with the rest of Western Europe, with a far lower rate of violent crime than the US. It's best not to be complacent, though, especially since tourists are justifiably seen as easy victims for robbery. As big cities go, Paris is relatively safe. Certain areas of Paris can be rough at night, including Les Halles and the Bastille area. Travelers should not walk around Pigalle, Barbès-Rochechouart, Montmartre, rue St-Denis in the 2*ème*, or Belleville alone at night. In general, the northern and eastern *arrondissements* are less safe than the southern and western ones, and the Right Bank less safe than the Left. In Marseille, be especially careful of the northern section of the city, in the Quartier Belsunce. The south of France—especially the Côte d'Azur and Provence—has a reputation for being more dangerous than the north. Exercise caution and common sense—keep bags under your arm and be particularly vigilant in crowded areas. In an emergency, dial ☎ 17 for police.

SERVICE. There is no assumption in France that "the customer is always right," and complaining to managers about poor service is rarely worth your while. Your best bet in such scenarios is to take your business elsewhere. When engaged in any official process (e.g., opening a bank account, purchasing insurance, etc.), don't fret if you get shuffled from one desk to another or from one phone number to the next. Hold your ground, patiently explain your situation, and you will eventually prevail.

TABLE MANNERS. Bread is served with every meal; it is perfectly polite to use a piece to wipe your plate. Etiquette dictates keeping one's hands above the table, not in one's lap, but elbows shouldn't rest on the table.

THE ARTS

ARCHITECTURE

ANCIENT BEGINNINGS. Long before the arrival of the "civilizing" Greeks and Romans, Frenchmen were making their own impressive buildings. The prehistoric murals of **Lascaux** (p. 746) and the huge stones of **Carnac** (p. 269) testify to the presence of ancient peoples in France. No such monuments stand to the ancient Gauls, whose legacy was virtually swept away for political reasons by invading Roman conquerors. Rome's leavings are most visible in the Provence region of France, particularly in the theater at **Orange** (p. 540), and the impressive ruins of the arena and temple at **Nîmes** (p. 534). Nearby in Province are the arches of the **Pont du Gard** aqueduct (p. 540), which served up some 44 million gallons of water to Nîmes's thirsty citizens every day.

MEDIEVAL CATHEDRALS. The first distinctively "Western" style emerged in the 9th century during the **Carolingian Renaissance,** when artists under Charlemagne's patronage combined parts of the Classical legacy with elements of the northern Barbarian tradition to create a highly symbolic art form. The Carolingian church of **Germigny-des-Près** (p. 282) houses a 9th-century Byzantine mosaic in its chapel. The same religious sentiment is conveyed by French churches of the 11th and 12th centuries. Dubbed **Romanesque** and characterized by round arches and barrel-vaulting, their beauty is one of simple grandeur. These churches, like the **Basilique St-Sernin** in Toulouse (p. 601) and the **Basilique Ste-Madeleine** at Vézelay (p. 412), were designed to accommodate large crowds of worshippers and pilgrims, while the monastery of **Mont St-Michel** (p. 226) provided a secluded religious haven. The architecture that characterizes the later Middle Ages is known as the **Gothic** style. Gothic architecture utilizes a system of arches that distributes weight outward. Flying buttresses (the stone supports jutting out from the sides of cathedrals) counterbalance the pressure of the ribbed vaulting, relieving the walls of the roof's weight. As a result, the walls of Gothic churches seem to soar effortlessly sky-ward, and light streams in through enormous stained glass windows. The cathe-dral at **Laon** (p. 181) embodies the early Gothic style. In the later Middle Ages, the high Gothic style featured more elaborate ornamentation which can be seen in the cathedrals of **Amiens** (p. 190), **Chartres** (p. 162), and **Reims** (p. 323).

RENAISSANCE & NEOCLASSICAL. During the Renaissance, François I hired Ital-ian artists to improve his lodge at **Fontainebleau** and commissioned the remarkable **Château de Chambord** (p. 288). His additions to the **Louvre** (p. 143) combine flam-boyant French Gothic motifs with Italian design. As French aristocrats moved away from Paris to the surrounding countryside, they too demanded suitably lav-ish living quarters, and great châteaux began to spring up in the Loire Valley. In the 17th century, **Nicolas Fouquet,** Louis XIV's finance minister, commissioned **Le Vau, Le Brun,** and **Le Nôtre** to build for him the splendid Baroque **Château de Vaux-le-Vicomte.** Louis XIV used the same team of architect, artist, and landscaper to try to outdo Fouquet with his mansion at **Versailles** (p. 157), an exorbitantly beautiful pal-ace full of crystal, mirrors, and gold, and surrounded by formal gardens, as well as the world's largest royal residence. He moved there in 1672, bringing the seat of the French government with him. The rise of Neoclassicism, from 1804 to 1814, is exemplified by **Jacques-Germain Soufflot's** grandiose **Eglise Ste-Geneviève** (1757) in Paris, which was deconsecrated during the Revolution and rededicated as the **Pan-théon** (p. 126). It serves as the resting place of Voltaire and Rousseau.

19TH-CENTURY HAUSSMANIA. Today's Paris was remade under the direction of **Baron Georges-Eugène Haussmann** (see **Haussmania,** p. 133). From 1852 to 1870, Haussmann transformed Paris from an intimate medieval city to a modern metrop-olis under the commission of Napoleon III. He tore long, straight boulevards through the tangled clutter and narrow alleys of old Paris, creating a unified net-work of **grands boulevards.** These avenues were designed not only to increase cir-culation of goods and people, but also to make Paris a work of art, reflecting the elegance of Second Empire style. Not incidentally, the wide avenues also impeded insurrection, limiting once and for all the effectiveness of street barricades.

Engineering came onto the architectural scene in the latter part of the 19th cen-tury, as **Gustave Eiffel** and architect **Louis-Auguste Boileau** designed Le Bon Marché, the world's first department store. Eiffel's later project, the star exhibit of the Uni-versal Exhibition of 1889, was first decried by Parisians as hideous and unstable.

The **Eiffel Tower** (p. 129) is now the best-loved landmark in the country. The ornate and organic style of **art nouveau** developed in the late 19th century. The movement's characteristic ironwork can best be seen in Paris, where **Hector Guimard's** vinelike metro stops sprout from the pavement.

20TH-CENTURY MODERNISM & SUBURBAN MISERY. In the interwar period, radical French architects began to incorporate new materials in their designs. A Swiss citizen who lived and built in Paris, Charles-Edouard Jeanneret, known as **Le Corbusier**, was the architectural pioneer in reinforced concrete. A prominent member of the **International School**, Le Corbusier dominated his field from the 1930s until his death in 1965. He is famous for his mushroom-like chapel at **Ronchamp** in Alsace. The post-war years were not kind to the architecture and urban development of France's northern coast. Badly damaged during World War II, Le Havre, Dunkerque, and Calais were hurriedly rebuilt in loathsome chunks of concrete. Paris, too, capitulated to the cheap lure of cement. Large housing projects or **HLMs** (*habitations à louer modéré*) were originally intended as affordable housing, but have since become synonymous with suburban misery, racism, and the exploitation of the immigrant poor. In the '80s, Paris became the hub of Mitterand's 15-billion franc endeavor known as the *Grands Projets*, which included the construction of the **Musée d'Orsay**, the **Parc de la Villette**, the **Institut du Monde Arabe**, the **Opéra** at the Bastille, and **I. M. Pei's** glass pyramid at the **Louvre**. Skyscrapers have been exiled to the business suburb of **La Défense**, home to the **Grande Arche**, a giant, hollowed-out cube of an office building aligned with the Arc de Triomphe, the smaller arch in the Tuileries, and the Louvre. In recent news, the **ZAC project** aims to build a new university, sports complex, public garden, and metro in the 13*ème*.

FINE ARTS

MEDIEVAL MASTERPIECES. Much of France's surviving **medieval art** instructed the average 12th- and 13th-century churchgoer on religious themes. As most commoners were illiterate, brilliant stained glass and intricate stone facades, like those at **Chartres, Reims,** and **Sainte-Chapelle** in Paris, served as large reproductions of the Bible. Monastic industry brought the art of illumination to its height, as monks occupied their long days by adding ornate illustrations to manuscripts. **Chantilly** now houses the breathtaking **Très Riches Heures du Duc de Berry**, a gem-like illuminated prayer book whose realistic portrayal of peasants ushered in the Northern Renaissance. During the Middle Ages, artisans perfected the skill of weaving. The famous 11th-century **Bayeux tapestry**, which unravels a 70m long narrative of the Battle of Hastings, can still be seen in its original Norman town (p. 214). The mysterious 15th-century allegorical tapestry series, **The Lady and the Unicorn,** still charms visitors at the **Musée Cluny** in Paris.

THE RENAISSANCE IN FRANCE. Sixteenth-century France imported its styles from the painting, sculpture, and architecture of the **Italian Renaissance**. François I had viewed the new wave of art during his Italian campaigns, and when he inherited France in 1515, he decided the time had come to put France on the artistic map. He gathered a variety of Italian artists to create his château at **Fontainebleau**, and on his invitation, **Leonardo da Vinci** trekked up from Florence bearing the smiling **Mona Lisa** in tow. Da Vinci's final home and a number of his sketches for inventions can still be seen in **Amboise** (p. 290). Rosso and Francesco Primaticcio arrived in France in the 1530s to introduce the French to Italian Mannerist techniques, which were soon adopted by the **Ecole de Fontainebleau.**

BAROQUE & ROCOCO. Italy remained the arbiter of France's aesthetic taste in the 17th century, when Louis XIV imported the gilded, baubled excesses of the **Baroque** style to his own court at Versailles. The enduring masterpieces of French

Baroque, however, remain the more realist paintings of the brothers **Le Nain** and **Georges de La Tour,** who created representations of everyday life. Baroque exuberance was also subdued by the classical subjects and serene landscapes of **Nicolas Poussin,** who was fortunate enough to enjoy the support of the French **Académie Royale.** Under director **Charles Le Brun,** the Academy, founded in 1648, became the sole arbiter of taste in matters artistic, holding annual **salons,** the "official" art exhibitions held in vacant halls of the Louvre. The early 18th century brought on the even more frilly **Rococo** style. Catering to the tastes of the nobility, **Antoine Watteau** painted the *fêtes* and secret *rendez-vous* of the aristocracy, and **François Boucher** painted landscapes and rosy-cheeked shepherdesses. **Elisabeth Vigée-Lebrun** painted Europe's rich and famous. Her famous portrait of Marie Antoinette and her children is on display at Versailles. Far from the glitz of the court, **Jean-Baptiste Chardin** captured the lustre of pewter and the heavy softness of dead hares in his stunning still-life work.

NEOCLASSICAL & ROMANTIC SCHOOLS. The French Revolution inspired painters to create heroic depictions of scenes from their own time. **Jacques-Louis David's** *Death of Marat* paid gory tribute to the Revolutionary leader. Napoleon I's reign saw the emergence of **Neoclassicism** as the emperor tried to model his empire, and his purple capes, on the Roman version. Following David, and encouraged by the deep pockets of Napoleon, painters created large, dramatic pictures, often of the emperor as Romantic hero and god. But after Napoleon's fall, 19th-century France was ready to settle into respectable bourgeois ways, and few artists painted nationalistic *tableaux.* One exception was **Theodore Géricault,** whose *Raft of the Medusa* (1819) can be seen in the Louvre. The paintings of **Eugène Delacroix** were a shock to the salons of the 1820s and 1830s. His *Liberty Leading the People* (1830) and *The Death of Sardanapalus* (1827) display an extraordinary sense of color and a penchant for melodrama. Delacroix went on to do a series of "Moroccan" paintings. He soon shared this orientalist territory with another painter, **Jean-Auguste-Dominique Ingres.** Ingres's most famous painting is the nearly liquid reclining nude, *La Grande Odalisque* (1814).

REALISM & IMPRESSIONISM. If the Revolution of 1789 ushered in art with a political conscience, the Revolution of 1848 introduced an art with a social conscience. **Realists** like **Gustave Courbet** scrutinized and indeed glorified the "humble" aspects of peasant life. His *Burial at Ornans* (1850) caused a scandal when first exhibited because it used the huge canvases associated with history painting to depict a simple village scene. Fellow Realist **Jean Millet** captured the dignity of peasants, the value of their work, and the idyllic simplicity of their lives. Another group of mid-19th-century painters, particularly **Camille Corot** and **Théodore Rousseau,** transformed landscape painting: their depictions of rural subjects from direct observation pay close attention to light and atmosphere. **Edouard Manet** facilitated the transition from Courbet's Realism to what we now consider **Impressionism** by flattening the fine shading and sharp perspectives of academic art and turning his focus to texture and color. His portrait of the nude, unabashed prostitute *Olympia* and his recycling of classical poses in *Déjeuner sur l'herbe* scandalized his colleagues but held center stage at the Salon des Refusés in 1863.

By the late 1860s Manet's new aesthetic had set the stage for **Claude Monet, Camille Pissarro,** and **Pierre-Auguste Renoir,** who began to further explore Impressionist techniques. They strove to attain a sense of immediacy; colors were used to capture visual impressions as they appeared to the eye, and light became subject matter. Claude Monet's studies of haystacks and the Rouen cathedral revealed how different moments of light could transform a subject. His *Impression: Soleil Levant* (1872) inspired one mocking critic to dub the ensemble of artists "Impressionists" after their first group exhibition in 1874. The name stuck, and the Impressionist movement went on to inspire **Edgar Dégas's** ballerinas and racehorses, **Gustave Caillebotte's** rainy streets of Paris, and **Berthe Morisot's** tranquil studies of women. Monet's garden at **Giverny** (p. 163), which inspired his monumental *Water-lilies* series, remains a popular daytrip from Paris. The influence of Impressionism extended to sculpture, where **Auguste Rodin** captured barely-constrained energy in his life-sized bronzes. His *Burghers of Calais* (1886) honors the town's nobles for preparing to sacrifice their lives during the Hundred Years' War.

POST-IMPRESSIONISM. The fragmented inheritors of the Impressionist tradition share the label of **Post-Impressionism**. **Paul Cézanne** worked in Aix-en-Provence and created still-lifes, portraits, and geometric landscapes (among them his many versions of the prominent *Mont Ste-Victoire*, 1885-87), using planes of orange, gold, and green, and bold, geometric blocks of color. **Georges Seurat** took this fragmentation of shape a step further with **Pointillism**, a style in which thousands of tiny dots of paint merge to form a coherent picture in the viewer's eye. **Paul Gauguin** used large, flat blocks of color with heavily drawn outlines to paint "primitive" scenes from Brittany, Arles, Tahiti, and Martinique. He went to **Arles** (p. 519) to join his friend **Vincent Van Gogh,** a Dutch painter who had moved to the south of France in search of new light, color, and imagery. The poverty and mental illness that plagued Van Gogh throughout his short life are reflected in his work. Similarly tortured in his art and life was **Henri de Toulouse-Lautrec,** a man of noble lineage who was disabled by a bone disease and a childhood accident. Toulouse-Lautrec's vibrant posters, many of which are displayed in his hometown of **Albi** (p. 605), capture the brilliant and lascivious nightlife of 19th-century Paris. Struggling with Pointillism during a trip to **Collioure** in the Languedoc (p. 618), **Henri Matisse** abandoned the technique and began squeezing paint from the tube directly onto the canvas. This aggressive style earned the name **Fauvism** (from *fauves*, wild animals) and characterizes Matisse's mature works like *The Dance* (1931-32).

CUBISM & THE SCHOOL OF PARIS. In the 1910s, former Fauve artist **Georges Braque** and Spanish-born **Pablo Picasso** developed **cubism,** a technique of using shaded planes to reassemble familiar images and objects into an abstracted form. By converting everyday items—fruits, glasses, vases, newspapers—into these cross-cutting planes, Braque and Picasso analyzed pictorial space as an overlapping system of geometric shapes. Picasso went on to become arguably the greatest artist of the 20th century, breaking new artistic ground with his constantly innovating style. The **Musée Picasso** in Paris (p. 146) and the beautiful seaside **Musée Picasso** in Antibes (p. 572) both chronicle his career, which spanned many decades and movements. In the 1920s and 30s, Picasso was the brightest star in a group of artists who came to Paris from all over the world to practice their craft.

DADAISM, SURREALISM, & THE SCENE TODAY. The sense of loss and disillusionment that pervaded Europe after WWI prompted a group of artists to reject the bourgeois culture that had begun the war. The anarchy and nonsense of the **Dada** movement found its best expression in the works of **Marcel Duchamp,** who scrambled artistic conventions by drawing a moustache on a copy of Mona Lisa and signing a factory-made urinal (*La Fontaine*, 1917) as if it were a piece of high art. The goal of **surrealism** was to unify fantasy with the everyday world, creating "an absolute reality, a surreality," according to poet and leader of the movement, **André Breton.** Works exemplary of the period such as the bowler-hatted men of **René Magritte,** the dreamscapes of **Joan Miró,** the textures and patterns of **Max Ernst,** and the melting timepieces of **Salvador Dalí** arose from time spent in Paris. Modern 20th-century experiments in photography, installation art, video, and sculpture can be seen in the collections and temporary exhibitions of the **Centre Pompidou** and the **Fondation Cartier pour l'Art Contemporain.**

LITERATURE & PHILOSOPHY

MEDIEVAL & RENAISSANCE LITERATURE. Medieval France produced an extraordinary number of literary texts, beginning in the 12th century with popular **chansons de gestes,** stories written in verse that recount tales of 8th-century crusades and conquests. The aristocracy enjoyed more refined literature extolling knightly honor and courtly love, such as the *Lais* (narrative songs) of **Marie de France** and the romances of **Chrétien de Troyes.** Thirteenth-century readers delighted in **fabliaux,** satirical stories that celebrated the bawdy humor of the age with tales of cuckolded husbands, saucy wives, and shrewd peasants. The 14th and 15th centuries produced the feminist writings of **Christine de Pisan** and the ballads of **François Villon.** Literary texts of the Renaissance challenged medieval notions of courtly love and Christian thought. **Marguerite de Navarre** employed pilgrim stories to explore the innovative ideas of Humanism in her *Héptaméron* (1549), while **John Calvin's** humanist treatises criticized the Catholic Church and opened the road to the ill-fated Protestant Reformation in France. **François Rabelais's** fantastical *Gargantua and Pantagruel* (1562) imaginatively explored the world from giants' points of view, and **Michel de Montaigne's** *Essais* (1595) pushed the boundaries of individual intellectual thought and gave formal birth to that literary form all students dread.

RATIONALISM & THE ENLIGHTENMENT. The **Académie Française** was founded in 1635 to regulate and codify French literature and language. French philosophers reacted to the mushy musings of humanists with **Rationalism,** a school of thought that championed logic and order. In his 1637 *Discourse on Method,* **René Descartes** proved his own existence with the famously catchy deduction, "I think, therefore I am." A young **Blaise Pascal** invented the mechanical calculator and the science of probabilities, while **Jean de la Fontaine's** *Fables* and **Charles Perrault's** *Fairy Tales of Mother Goose* (1697) explored right and wrong in more didactic ways. **Molière,** the era's comic relief, used his plays to satirize the social pretensions of his age, his actors initiating the great **Comédie Française.**

As with the Enlightenment elsewhere in Europe, the French **Enlightenment** developed from the advancement of science and morality and aimed towards the promotion of reason and tolerance in an often backward, bigoted world. The ambition of **Denis Diderot's** *Encylopédie* (1752-1780) was no less than to record the entire body of human knowledge. **Voltaire's** famous satire *Candide* (1758) refuted the claim that "all is for the best in the best of all possible worlds." In his *Confessions* (1769), **Jean-Jacques Rousseau** advised readers to abandon society altogether rather than remain in a corrupt world.

ROMANTICISM & REALISM. During the 19th century the expressive ideals of **Romanticism,** which first came to prominence in Britain and Germany, found their way to analytically-minded France. **François-René de Chateaubriand** drew inspiration for his novel *Attala* (1801) from his experiences with Native Americans near the mighty Niagara Falls. The stylish **Madame de Staël** reflected upon the injustices of being a talented woman in a chauvinist world in *Delphine* (1802). Such great writers as **Henri Stendhal** (*Le Rouge et le Noir*) and **Honoré de Balzac** (*La Comédie Humaine*) helped to establish the novel as the pre-eminent literary medium, but **Victor Hugo's** *The Hunchback of Notre Dame* (1831) dominated the Romantic age. That same year, the young Aurore Dupin left her husband and childhood home of La Châtre, took the *nom de plume* of **George Sand,** and published passionate novels condemning sexist social conventions. The heroine of **Gustave Flaubert's** *Madame Bovary* (1856) spurned provincial life for romantic, adulterous daydreams in his famous realist novel. Flaubert was prosecuted for immorality in 1857 and only narrowly acquitted. Poet **Charles Baudelaire** was not so lucky; the

THE BEST EXPATRIATE LITERATURE

Ernest Hemingway. *A Moveable Feast*. The quintessential tale of a young expat in Paris. F. Scott Fitzgerald and Gertrude Stein make colorful cameo appearances.

George Orwell. *Down and Out in London and Paris*. A writer takes grimy jobs in the dark underbelly of Paris. Beautifully descriptive and funny.

W. Somerset Maugham. *The Moon and Sixpence*. A dull London businessman leaves his family to paint in Paris and Tahiti. Loosely based on the life of Paul Gauguin.

Henry James. *The American*. The New World meets the Old in this classic story of friendship, love, and betrayal in turn of the century Paris.

F. Scott Fitzgerald. *Tender is the Night*. No one captures the 1920s flapper set quite like Fitzgerald—his story of scandal and intrigue on the Riviera is a classic.

Peter Mayle. *A Year in Provence*. A staple of book clubs everywhere, a lighthearted autobiography, travelogue, and culinary guide to life in the rural town of Ménerbes.

Julian Barnes. *Flaubert's Parrot*. An elderly English doctor journeys to France to research Flaubert's life and inspiration for his short story *Un Coeur Simple*.

Adam Gopnik. *Paris to the Moon*. A *New Yorker* journalist settles down in Paris with his family. Small observations on Parisian life, lyrically woven into larger cultural themes.

same tribunal fined him 50 francs. Although he gained a reputation for obscenity during his own lifetime, today his *Flowers of Evil* (1861) is considered the most influential piece of 19th-century French poetry.

BELLE EPOQUE TO WWII. Like artistic Impressionism, literary **Symbolism** reacted against stale conventions and used new techniques to capture instants of perception. Led by **Stéphane Mallarmé, Paul Verlaine,** and the precocious **Arthur Rimbaud,** the movement was instrumental in the creation of modern poetry. **Marcel Proust's** seven-volumes *Remembrance of Things Past* (1913-1927), about *fin de siècle* high society decadence, inquired into the nature of time, memory. and love. His portrayal of homosexuality was matched by **André Gide's** novel *l'Immoraliste* and Colette's sensual descriptions of cabarets in *Le pur et l'impur*. Meanwhile, the avant-garde poet **Guillaume Apollinaire** published *Calligrammes* (1918), in which he created visual poems by using words to form pictures on the page. The anarchy of Dada art was verbally represented in the incoherent, scrambled poems of **Tristan Tzara**. In 1924, André Breton abandoned the Dada movement to argue for the artistic supremacy of the subconscious in his *Surrealist Manifesto*. **Jean-Paul Sartre** dominated France's intelligentsia in the years following World War II. His theory of **Existentialism** held that life in itself was meaningless, and existence could only take on a purpose when one commits oneself to a cause. While Sartre worked under censorship in occupied Paris, Algerian-born **Albert Camus** edited the Résistance newspaper *Combat*. He achieved fame with his debut novel *The Stranger* (1942), in which a dispassionate social misfit is condemned to death for murder.

FEMINISM & LA PRÉSENCE AFRICAINE. Existentialist and feminist **Simone de Beauvoir** attacked the myth of femininity with *The Second Sex* (1949), an essay that made waves with its famous statement, "One is not born, but becomes a woman" and inspired a whole generation of second-wave **feminism** in the 50s, 60s, and 70s. In turn, writers like **Marguerite Duras** *(The Lover)*, **Hélène Cixous** *(The Laugh of the Medusa)*, and **Luce Irigaray** *(This Sex Which Is Not One)* explored gender identity, challenged the Freudian concept of penis envy, and sparked feminist movements in France and abroad. The founding of the publishing house **Des Femmes** in the 70s ensured that French women writers would continue to have the freedom to express themselves in print. Throughout the 20th century, France's colonial exploitation has been powerfully condemned by writers from the **Antilles, Haiti, Québec**, the **Maghreb** (Algeria, Tunisia, Morocco), and **West Africa** (Senegal, Mali, Ivory Coast, Congo, and Cameroon). With the foundation of the **Négritude** movement in the 1920s by intellectuals **Aimé Césaire** (Martinique) and **Léopold Sédar Senghor** (Senegal), Francophone literature began to flourish. Their work and the subsequent founding of the press **Présence Africaine** inspired generations of Francophone intellectuals on both sides of the Atlantic. North African immigration to France in the 80s and 90s has had a profound impact on French language, culture, and politics. Many second- and third-generation Maghrebian writers in France, such as **Mehdi Charef** (*Le thé au harem d'Archi Ahmed*, 1983), have written about *beur* (slang for an Arab resident of France) culture and the difficulties of cultural assimilation.

FILM

BEGINNINGS. Not long after he and his brother Louis presented the world's first paid screening in a Paris café in 1895, **Auguste Lumière** remarked, "The cinema is a medium without a future." As if to prove how wrong this statement is, French filmmakers are forever innovating. The trick cinema of magician-turned-filmmaker **Georges Méliès** astounded audiences with "disappearing" objects, and his *Journey to the Moon* (1902) was the first motion picture to realize the story-telling possibilities of the medium. Paris was the Hollywood of early cinema, dominating production and distribution worldwide. Although WWI stunted the growth of French film, the inter-war period yielded a large number of diverse and influential films. **Luis Buñuel** and **Salvador Dalí's** *Un Chien Andalou* (1928) was a surrealist marvel of jarring associations. **Jean Renoir**, son of the Impressionist painter, directed the powerful anti-war film *La Grande Illusion* (1937), and depicted the erosion of French bourgeois society in *La Règle du Jeu* (1939). Censorship during the Occupation caused a shift from political films to escapist cinema that revelled in nostalgic themes. **Marcel Carné** and **Jacques Prévert's** epic *Enfants du Paradis* (1943-45) showcased the indomitable spirit of the French in the setting of 1840s Paris.

NEW WAVE. In the 1950s, **André Bazin** and a group of young intellectuals used their magazine **Cahiers du Cinéma** to criticize the slick insubstantial popular films of the day. Encouraged by government subsidies, they swapped the pen for the camera in 1959. **François Truffaut's** coming-of-age story *Les 400 Coups* and **Jean-Luc Godard's** gangster flick *A Bout du souffle (Breathless)* were joined the same year by **Alain Resnais's** *Hiroshima, Mon Amour*. Such films incited the **French New Wave (Nouvelle Vague)**, a movement defined by an interest in the distinction between fiction and documentary, the fragmentation of linear time, the thrill of youth, speed, cars, and noise. Three years earlier, in 1956, a star was born when **Jean Vadim** sent the incomparable **Brigitte Bardot** shimmying naked across the screen in *Et Dieu créa la femme*. Other directors associated with the New Wave are **Louis Malle** (*Les Amants*, 1958), **Eric Rohmer** (*Ma nuit chez Maud*, 1969), and **Agnès Varda** (*Cléo de 5 à 7*, 1961).

CONTEMPORARY CLASSICS & CINÉMA BEUR. The world impact of French cinema in the '60s brought international recognition of French talent, including stunning **Catherine Deneuve** (*Belle de jour*), gothic priestess **Isabelle Adjani** (*La Reine Margot*), and omnipresent **Gérard Depardieu** (*Danton, Camille Claudel*). **Edouard Molinaro's** campy *La Cage aux folles* (1975) and **Colline Serraud's** *Trois hommes et un couffin* ("Three Men and a Baby," 1985) both inspired American remakes, while **Claude Berri's** *Jean de Florette* (1986) and Polish **Krzysztof Kieslowski's** *Three Colors* trilogy, *Bleu* (1993), *Blanc* (1994), and *Rouge* (1994) have become instant classics of late 20th-century French cinema. Several recent French films (especially those that have received international attention) have explored the issue of gay identity and sexual orientation, including Belgian **Alain Berliner's** transgender tragicomedy *Ma vie en rose* (1997).

Some of the most explosive Parisian films today are the production of *cinéma beur,* the work of second-generation North Africans coming to terms with life in the housing projects of suburban Paris. Rich with graffiti art and rap music, films like **Mehdi Charef's** *Le thé au harem d'Archi Ahmed* (1986) and **Mathieu Kassovitz's** award-winning *La Haine* (1995) expose the horrors of urban racism.

MUSIC

The history of music in France dates back to the Gregorian chants of 12th-century monks and progressed through the 13th-century ballads of medieval troubadours, the Renaissance masses of **Josquin des Prez** (1440-1521), the lavish Baroque Versailles court operas of **Jean-Baptiste Lully** (1632-87), and the organ fugues of **Jean-Philippe Rameau** (1683-1764). During the terrifying reign of **Robespierre,** the people rallied to the strains of **revolutionary music,** such as **Rouget de Lisle's** *War Song of the Army of the Rhine.* Composed to rally French forces fighting the Prussians, it was so adored by volunteers from Marseille that it was dubbed **La Marseillaise** and became the national anthem in 1795.

Paris became the center of influence for 19th century European music. With the rise of the middle class in the early part of the 19th-century came the spectacle of **grand opera,** as well as the simpler **opéra comique.** These styles later merged to produce the Romantic **lyric opera,** an amalgam of soaring arias, exoticism, and tragic death best exemplified by **Georges Bizet's** *Carmen* (1875). Paris served as musical center for foreign Romantic composers as well, including **Frédéric Chopin, Franz Liszt,** and **Félix Mendelssohn.**

Music at the turn of the 20th century began a new period of intense, often abstract invention. **Claude Débussy** (1862-1918), an **Impressionist** composer, used tone color and nontraditional scales to create his *Prelude to the Afternoon of a Fawn* (1894). **Erik Satie,** to whom a funky museum is dedicated in **Honfleur** (p. 207), composed in a sarcastic, anti-sentimental spirit, in striking contrast to that of Debussy. **Ravel's** Basque origins found voice in the Spanish rhythms that pervade his most famous work, *Boléro* (1928).

The music of **Igor Stravinsky,** whose ballet *The Rite of Spring* caused a riot at its 1913 premiere at the Théâtre des Champs-Elysées, was violently dissonant and rhythmic. **Olivier Messaien** was diagnosed with synesthesia, a sensory disorder which confuses sound and vision; thus different harmonies appeared to him in different colors, making his intensely personal music texturally rich. Messaien's student, the innovative composer **Pierre Boulez,** now directs the **IRCAM** institute in the Pompidou Center in Paris.

JAZZ & CABARET. The French have been particularly receptive to jazz over the years, recognizing its artistic worth sooner than US markets. Jazz crooner **Josephine Baker** left the US for Paris in 1925, finding France to be more accepting than her segregated home. Cabaret, which grew in popularity in the 1930s, was made famous by the iconic voice of Edith Piaf in her ballads *"La Vie en Rose"* and *"Non, je ne regrette rien."* Also in the 1930s, French musicians copied the swing heard on early Louis Armstrong sides, but the 1934 Club Hot pair of violinist **Stéphane Grapelli** and stylish Belgian-Romany guitarist **Django Reinhardt** were already innovators. After WWII, a stream of American musicians came to Paris, including a young **Miles Davis,** who took the stage at a 1949 jazz festival.

THE NEXT BIG THINGS. In the late 50s and 60s, a unique French take on American rock emerged; the movement was termed, in a stroke of onomatopoetic genius, **yé-yé.** Teen idol **Johnny Hallyday** took the limelight, and youth-oriented **Salut les Copains** was the moment's rage. Contemporary musical taste is divided between the music played on the radio and the various forms of electronica that dominate dance clubs. Radio pop music includes soundtracks from French musicals like *Notre Dame de Paris* and *Romeo and Juliet,* as well as solo artists like French-Canadian **Céline Dion** and French **Lara Fabien.** France's hip-hop and rap scene includes artists like **Nique Ta Mère, MC Solaar,** and **Lunatic.** World music also dominates the airwaves, incorporating artists from North Africa (including raï musicians **Cheb Khaled, Cheb Mami,** and **Faudel),** the Middle East (**Natacha Atlas**), Latin America (**Manu Chao** and **Yuri Buenaventura**), and the West Indies (with the sounds of **reggae** and **zouk**).

SPORTS & RECREATION

There are really only two sports of any importance in France: football and cycling. The others are all just pleasant diversions.

FOOTBALL

The French take *le football* very seriously. Their national team, *Les Bleus,* has emerged from a half-century of mediocrity to perform spectacularly. They captured the 1998 **World Cup,** routing perennial favorite Brazil 3-0 in the newly-built Stade de France, outside Paris. The victory ignited celebrations from the Champs-Elysées to the Pyrénées. In the 2000 European Championship, the Blues took the trophy in an upset against Italy, and in the 2001 *Coupe des Confederations,* France completed the Triple Crown of football. The charismatic star of the French team, **Zinedine Zidane,** has attained a hero status second only to de Gaulle. The son of an Algerian immigrant, "Zizou" has helped unite a country divided by tension over immigration. Sadly, France failed to make it past the qualifying round of the 2002 *Cup Mondiale,* finishing behind even Uruguay. So shocking was the failure that President Chirac issued a message of condolence. French fans eagerly await their team's next shot at glory in the 2004 European Cup.

CYCLING

Cycling is another national obsession with an equally ardent following. France annually hosts the only cycling event anyone can name: the grueling 3-week, 3500km **Tour de France,** which celebrated its 100 year anniversary in 2003. *Malheureusement,* competitors from the host country haven't had much recent success in the competition itself, as in recent years American **Lance Armstrong** has triumphed over the rest of the field to capture five straight championships.

OTHER ACTIVITIES

Ideal for those who prefer a bit less exertion, the game of **pétanque,** once dominated by old men, has been gaining popularity among all ages. The basic premise of pétanque, like bocce or bowls, is to throw a large metal ball as close as possible to a small metal ball. It is hard to miss "pickup" games of pétanque on the beaches and dirt roads of southern France, but beware the innocent appearance; these games are often played for substantial sums of money.

Alpine and **cross-country skiing** are also popular in France, thanks to the country's several mountainous escapes. French towns such as dazzling Chamonix, Grenoble, and Albertville have all hosted the international Winter Olympics in the past.

Despite the objections of French traditionalists, sports from other continents are also gaining a foothold in France, particularly **rugby, golf,** and even the heresy that is **American football.**

HOLIDAYS & FESTIVALS

The most important national holiday is **Bastille Day**, July 14, the anniversary of the storming of the Bastille in 1789. The event is celebrated with a solemn military march up the Champs-Elysées followed by dancing, drinking, and fireworks all over the country. When Bastille Day falls on a Tuesday or Thursday, the French often also take off the Monday or Friday, a crafty practice known as *faire le pont* (making the bridge). The dates listed below are for 2004.

In addition to national holidays, there are many regional and city festivals, especially throughout the summer. *Let's Go: France* provides coverage of these major *fêtes et manifestations* throughout the guide. For more information on specific events, check out the customized search engine on the French Government Tourist Office's website (www.franceguide.com, under "Art de vivre").

DATE	NATIONAL HOLIDAY
January 1	Le Jour de l'An (also called la St-Sylvestre): New Year's
April 12	Le lundi de Pâques: Easter Monday
May 1	La Fête du Travail: Labor Day
May 8	Fête de la Victoire 1945: Celebrates the end of World War II in Europe
May 20	L'Ascension: Ascension Day
May 31	Le Lundi de Pentecôte: Whit Monday
July 14	La Fête Nationale: Bastille Day
August 15	L'Assomption: Feast of the Assumption
November 1	La Toussaint: All Saints' Day
November 11	L'Armistice 1918: Armistice Day
December 25	Noël: Christmas

PARIS

 Paris has been a center of commerce, culture, and conflict for centuries. In the midst of it all, it became the Western world's symbolic capital of romance, revolution, heroism, and hedonism. No wonder that it's the world's most heavily touristed city. From alleys that shelter the world's best bistros to broad avenues flaunting the highest of *haute couture*, from the centuries-old stone of Notre Dame's gargoyles to the futuristic motions of the Parc de la Villette, from the masterpieces of the Louvre to the installations of avant-garde galleries, Paris is both a harbor of tradition and a hotbed of innovation. You can't conquer Paris in one year or thirty, but you can get acquainted in a day, and in a week you may find you're old friends.

HIGHLIGHTS

Paris is first and foremost an international city, and second the capital of France. Wandering around the grandiose **Champs-Elysées** (p. 137), the student-filled **Latin Quarter** (p. 125), the formerly aristocratic and now supremely fun **Marais** (p. 131), and the bohemian **Montmartre** (p. 141) will give you a good feel for the city. No one can visit Paris without seeing the **Louvre** (p. 143), the **Eiffel Tower** (p. 129), and **Notre Dame** (p. 123), but don't neglect Paris's Latin past in the **Musée de Cluny** (p. 146); Gothic architecture's finest jewel, **Ste-Chapelle** (p. 124); and the mecca of Impressionism, the **Musée d'Orsay** (p. 145). Near Paris, Louis XIV's palace of **Versailles** (p. 157) is the best-known château; **Chartres** (p. 161) is the best-known cathedral.

⊞ ORIENTATION

Flowing east to west, the **Seine River** crosses the heart of Paris. The **Ile de la Cité** and neighboring **Ile St-Louis** sit at the geographical center, while the Seine splits Paris into two large expanses—the **Rive Gauche** (Left Bank) to its south and the **Rive Droite** (Right Bank) to its north. Modern Paris is divided into **20 arrondissements** (districts) that spiral clockwise around the Louvre. Each *arrondissement* is referred to by its number (e.g. 3rd, 12th), and the French equivalent of the English "th," as in 8th, is *"ème."* The proper way to pronounce this suffix is to add "iemme" to the French number, so 16*ème* is *seizième* (SEZ-yem). The exception is the 1st, for which the abbreviation is 1*er* (*premier*; PREM-yay).

◪ GETTING INTO PARIS

TO & FROM THE AIRPORTS

ROISSY-CHARLES DE GAULLE

Transatlantic flights use Charles de Gaulle. Includes a 24hr. English-speaking info center. (☎01 48 62 22 80; www.parisairports.com.)

   RER: From Roissy-CDG to Paris, take the free shuttle bus *(navette)* from Terminal 1 (every 10min.). From there, the RER B (one of the Parisian commuter rail lines) runs to central Paris. To transfer to the metro, get off at Gare du Nord, Châtelet-Les-Halles, or St-Michel. **To Roissy-CDG from Paris,** take the RER B to Roissy, which is the end of the line. Then change to the free shuttle bus if you need to get to Terminal 1 (30-35min.; RER every 15min. 5am-12:30am; €7.70, children €5.30).

Shuttle Buses: Roissybus (☎01 49 25 61 87) runs between 9 rue Scribe, near M: Opéra, and terminals 1, 2, and 9. Tickets can be purchased on the bus (45min.; to airport every 15min. 5:45am-11pm, from airport every 15min. 6am-11pm; €8.10). **Air France Buses** (recorded info in English ☎08 92 35 08 20) run daily to two sections of the city. Buy tickets on board. **Line 2** runs to and from the Arc de Triomphe (M: Charles de Gaulle-Etoile) at 1 av. Carnot, and to and from pl. de la Porte de Maillot/Palais des Congrès (M: Porte de Maillot) on bd. Gouvion St-Cyr (both lines 35min.; every 15min. 5:45am-11pm; one-way €10, children €5, round-trip €17; 15% group discount). **Line 4** runs to and from rue du Commandant Mouchette opposite the Hôtel Méridien (M: Montparnasse-Bienvenüe) and to and from Gare de Lyon (M: Gare de Lyon) at 20bis bd. Diderot (both lines to airport every 30min. 7am-9:30pm; one-way €11.50, children €5.80, round-trip €19.60; 15% group discounts). The shuttle stops at or between terminals 2A and 2F and at terminal 1 on the departures level.

ORLY

Located 18km south of the city. Charters and many continental flights use Orly. (Info in English ☎01 49 75 15 15; 6am-11:45pm.)

RER: From Orly Sud gate G or gate I, platform 1, or Orly Ouest level G, gate F, take the **Orly-Rail** shuttle bus (every 15min. 6am-11pm; €5.20, children €3.60) to the **Pont de Rungis/Aéroport d'Orly** train stop, where you can board the **RER C2** for a number of destinations in Paris. (Call RATP ☎08 36 68 41 14 for info in English. 35min., every 15min. 6am-11pm, €5.20.) The **Jetbus** (every 15min. 6am-10pm, €4.60), provides a quick connection between Orly Sud, gate H, platform 2, or Orly Ouest level 0, gate C and M: Villejuif-Louis Aragon on line 7 of the metro.

Bus: Another option is the RATP **Orlybus** (☎08 36 68 77 14), which runs to and from metro and RER stop Denfert-Rochereau, 14ème, to Orly's south terminal. (30min.; every 10-15min. 6am-11:30pm from Orly to Denfert-Rochereau, 5:35am-11pm from Denfert-Rochereau to Orly; €5.60.) You can also board the Orlybus at Dareau-St-Jacques, Glacière-Tolbiac, and Porte de Gentilly. **Air France Buses** run between Orly and **Gare Montparnasse,** near Hôtel Méridien, 6ème (M: Montparnasse-Bienvenüe), and the Invalides Air France agency, pl. des Invalides (30min.; every 15min. 6am-11pm; one-way €7.50, round-trip €12.80). Air France shuttles stop at Orly Ouest and Orly Sud's departures levels.

Orlyval: RATP also runs **Orlyval** (☎01 69 93 53 00), a combination of metro, RER, and VAL rail shuttle, and probably your fastest option. The VAL shuttle goes from Antony (a stop on the RER line B) to Orly Ouest and Sud. You can either get a ticket just for the VAL (€7), or a combination VAL-RER ticket (€8.80 and up). Buy tickets at any RATP booth in the city, or from the Orlyval agencies at Orly Ouest, Orly Sud, and Antony. **To Orly:** Be careful when taking the RER B from Paris to Orly, because it splits into 2 lines right before the Antony stop. Get on the train that says "St-Rémy-Les-Chevreuse" or just look for the track that has a lit-up sign saying "Antony-Orly." (35min. from Châtelet; every 10min. M-Sa 6am-10:30pm, Su and holidays 7am-11pm.) **From Orly:** Trains arrive at Orly Ouest 2min. after reaching Orly Sud. (32min. to Châtelet; every 10min. M-Sa 6am-10:30pm, Su 7am-11pm.)

TRAINS

Each of Paris's six train stations is a veritable community of its own. Locate the *guichets* (ticket counters), the *quais* (platforms), and the *voies* (tracks), and you will be ready to roll. Each terminal has two divisions: the *banlieue* (suburb) and the *grandes lignes* (big important trains). A telephone with direct access to the stations is to the right of the Champs-Elysées tourist office (127 av. des Champs-Elysées). Yellow *billetteries* **(ticket machines)** at every train station sell tickets. You'll need to have a MasterCard, Visa, or American Express card and know your PIN (ticket booths MC or V only).

BUSES

International buses arrive in Paris at **Gare Routière Internationale du Paris-Gallieni** (M: Gallieni), just outside Paris at 28 av. du Général de Gaulle, Bagnolet 93170. **Eurolines** (☎01 49 72 57 80, €0.34 per min.; www.eurolines.fr) sells tickets to destinations in France and neighboring countries.

⊟ GETTING AROUND PARIS

RATP helpline (☎08 92 68 41 14, daily 6am-9pm, €0.34 per min.; www.ratp.fr).

FARES & PASSES

Individual tickets for the RATP cost €1.30 each and €9.30 for a *carnet* of 10. Buses sometimes take more than one ticket, depending on the number of connections and the time of day (see **Metro**). If you're staying in Paris for several days or weeks, a **Carte Orange** can be very economical. Bring a photo ID (photo machines are found in most stations; €3.90) to the ticket counter and ask for the weekly *carte orange hebdomaire* (€13.80) or the monthly *carte orange mensuelle* (€46.10). Prices quoted here are for passes in Zones 1 and 2 (the metro and RER in Paris and suburbs), which work on all metro, bus, and RER modes of transport in these zones. If you intend to travel to the suburbs, you'll need to buy RER passes for more zones (up to 5). If you're only in town for a day or two, a cheap option is the **Carte Mobilis** (€5), which provides one day of unlimited metro, bus, and RER transportation within Zones 1 and 2. Always write the number of your *carte* on your coupon. **Paris Visite** tickets are valid for unlimited travel on bus, metro, and RER, as well as discounts on sightseeing trips, bicycle rentals, and stores like Galeries Lafayette, but the discounts you receive do not necessarily outweigh the extra cost (one day €8.40, two days €13, three days €18.30, or five days €22.90).

METRO

Metro stations are marked with an "M" or with fancy *"Métropolitain"* lettering designed by art nouveau legend Hector Guimard. The first trains start running around 5:30am, and the last ones leave the end-of-the-line stations (the *"portes de Paris"*) for the center of the city at about 12:15am. Connections to other lines are indicated by orange *correspondance* signs, exits by blue *sortie* signs. Transfers are free if made within a station; it is not always possible to reverse direction on the same line without exiting the station. **Hold on to your ticket** until you pass the point marked **Limite de Validité des Billets** on the way to the exit. Do not count on buying a metro ticket late at night; some ticket windows close by 10pm. Stay away from dangerous stations at night (Barbès-Rochechouart, Pigalle, Anvers, Châtelet-Les-Halles, Gare du Nord, Gare de l'Est). If concerned, take a taxi.

RER

The RER *(Réseau Express Régional)* is the RATP's suburban train system, which passes through central Paris. Within the city, the RER travels much faster than the metro. There are five RER lines, marked A-E, with different branches designated by a number, such as the C5 line to Versailles-Rive Gauche. The RER runs from about 5:15am to midnight, like the metro.

BUS

Although slower and often more costly than the metro, buses can act as cheap sightseeing tours and helpful introductions to the city's layout. The RATP's *Grand Plan de Paris* includes a map of the bus lines (free at metro stations). The free bus map *Autobus Paris-Plan du Réseau* is available at the tourist office and at metro information booths. Bus tickets are identical to those used on the metro, and can be purchased either in metro stations or on the bus from the driver. *Cartes oranges* and other transport passes (Paris Visite, Mobilis) are equally valid in buses and subways (see **Metro**). When you wish to leave the bus, press the red button to illuminate the *arrêt demandé* sign.

NIGHT BUSES. Most buses run daily 6:30am-8:30pm; those marked **Autobus de nuit** continue until 1am. Those named **Noctambus** run all night. Night buses (from €2.30, depending on how far you go) run from the Châtelet stop to the *portes* (end-of-the-line stations) of the city (daily every hr. on the half-hour 1:30-5:30am). Buses also run from the suburbs to Châtelet (every hr. on the hr. 1-6am). Noctambuses I through M, R, and S run along the Left Bank to the southern suburbs. Buses A through H, P, T, and V run on the Right Bank heading north. Look for bus stops marked with a bug-eyed moon sign. Ask at a major metro station for more info.

TOUR BUSES. Balabus (call the RATP ☎08 36 68 41 14 for info in English) stops at virtually every major sight in Paris (Bastille, St-Michel, Louvre, Musée d'Orsay, Concorde, Champs-Elysées, Charles de Gaulle-Etoile; whole loop 1¼hr.). The fare is the same as any standard bus (3 tickets, since it covers more than the 2-zone region), and the loop starts at the Grande Arche de La Défense or Gare de Lyon.

TAXIS

Taxis take three passengers; a fourth costs around €2.50. Companies include: **Alpha Taxis, ☎**01 45 85 85 85; **Taxis 7000, ☎**01 42 70 00 42; **Taxis G7, ☎**01 47 39 47 39.

BIKE RENTAL

Paris-Vélo, 2 rue de Fer-à-Moulin, 5è*me* (☎01 43 37 59 22). M: Censier-Daubenton. Bike rental €14 per day. Open M-Sa 10am-12:30pm and 2-7pm.

Paris à vélo, c'est sympa!, 37 bd. Bourdon, 4è*me* (☎01 48 87 60 01; www.parisvelo-sympa.com). M: Bastille. €200 or credit card deposit. 24hr. rental €16; 9am-7pm €12.50; half-day (9am-2pm or 2-7pm) €9.50. Open daily 9am-1pm and 2-6pm.

⚡ USEFUL SERVICES

TOURIST OFFICES

Bureau d'Accueil Central, 127 av. des Champs-Elysées, 8è*me* (☎08 92 68 31 12; www.paris-touristoffice.com). M: Georges V. Open high season daily 9am-8pm; low season Su 11am-7pm.

Bureau Gare de Lyon, 12è*me* (☎01 43 43 33 24). Right at M: Gare de Lyon. Open M-Sa 8am-8pm.

Bureau Tour Eiffel, Champs de Mars, 7è*me* (☎08 92 68 31 12). M: Champs de Mars. Open May-Sept. daily 11am-6pm.

GUIDED TOURS

Bateaux-Mouches (☎01 42 25 96 10, info 01 40 76 99 99; www.bateaux-mouches.fr). M: Alma-Marceau. 70min. tours in English. Departures daily every 30min. 10:15am-10:40pm (no boats 1-2pm) from the Right Bank pier near Pont d'Alma.

Mike's Bullfrog Bike Tours (☎01 56 58 10 54; www.mikesbiketours.com). Tours meet by the south leg of the Eiffel Tower. Tours daily Mar.-Nov., Dec.-Feb. by appointment. Check the website for full schedule and exact meeting point. Tickets €24, students €22; night tour €28/€26.

USEFUL PUBLICATIONS & LISTINGS

The weeklies **Pariscope** (€0.40; www.pariscope.fr) and **Officiel des Spectacles** (€0.35), both published on Wednesdays, have the most comprehensive listings of movies, plays, exhibits, festivals, clubs, and bars. *Pariscope* also includes an English-language section called **Time Out Paris**. The tourist office's free monthly **Where: Paris** highlights exhibits, concerts, walking tours, and events. The Mairie de Paris, 29 rue de Rivoli, 4ème (☎01 42 76 42 42; M: Hôtel-de-Ville), publishes the free monthly **Paris le Journal**, with articles about what's hot in the city. On Wednesday, the newspaper *Le Figaro* includes **Figaroscope**, a supplement about Paris happenings. **Free Voice**, a monthly English-language newspaper published by the American Church, and the bi-weekly **France-USA Contacts (FUSAC)**, list jobs, housing, and info for English speakers. These are available for free from English-language bookstores, restaurants, and travel agencies.

CURRENCY EXCHANGE

American Express, 11 rue Scribe, 9ème (☎01 47 14 50 00). M: Opéra or Auber. Open M-Sa 9am-6:30pm; exchange counters also open Su 10am-5pm.

Thomas Cook, 73 av. des Champs-Elysées, 8ème (☎01 45 62 89 55; fax 01 45 62 89 55). M: Georges V. Open M-Sa 9am-10:55pm, Su 8am-6pm.

LOCAL SERVICES

Dry Cleaning: Pressing Villiers, 93 rue de Rocher, 8ème (☎01 45 22 75 48). M: Villiers. Open M-F 8am-7:30pm. MC/V. **Arc en Ciel,** 62 rue Arbre Sec, 1er (☎01 42 41 39 39). M: Louvre. Open M-F 8am-1:15pm and 2:30-7pm, Sa 8:30am-1:15pm.

Gay/Lesbian Resources: ACT-UP Paris, 45 rue de Sedène, 11ème (☎01 48 06 13 89). M: Bréguet-Sabin. **Centre Gai et Lesbien,** 3 rue Keller, 11ème (☎01 43 57 21 47; fax 01 43 57 27 93). M: Ledru-Rollin or Bastille. Open M-F 4-8pm.

Disability Resources: L'Association des Paralysées de France, Délégation de Paris, 17 bd. Auguste Blanqui, 13ème (☎01 40 78 69 00; www.apf.asso.fr). M: Place d'Italie. Open M-F 9am-12:30pm and 2-5:30pm.

HEALTH & CRISIS

Emergency Numbers: Poison ☎01 40 05 48 48. In French, but some English assistance available. **Rape: SOS Viol** ☎08 00 05 95 95. Open M-F 10am-7pm. **SOS Help!** ☎01 46 21 46 46. An anonymous, confidential hotline for English speakers in crisis. Open daily (including holidays) 3-11pm.

Hospitals: Hôpital Américain de Paris, 63 bd. Hugo, Neuilly (☎01 46 41 25 25). M: Port Maillot, then bus #82 to the end of the line. **Hôpital Franco-Britannique de Paris,** 3 rue Barbès, in the Parisian suburb of Levallois-Perret (☎01 46 39 22 22). M: Anatole France. Has some English speakers, but don't count on it. **Hôpital Bichat,** 46 rue Henri Buchard, 18ème (☎01 40 25 80 80). M: Port St-Ouen. Emergency services.

24hr. Pharmacies: Every *arrondissement* has a **pharmacie de garde** which will open in emergencies; the name of the nearest one is posted on every pharmacy's door. **Pharmacie Dhéry,** in the Galerie des Champs, 84 av. des Champs-Elysées, 8ème (☎01 45 62 02 41). M: George V. 24hr. **British & American Pharmacy,** 1 rue Auber, 9ème (☎01 42 65 88 29). M: Auber or Opéra. Open M-Su 8am-8:30pm.

Birth Control: Mouvement Français pour le Planning Familial (MFPF), 10 rue Vivienne, 2ème (☎01 42 60 93 20). M: Bourse. Open for calls M-F 9:30am-5:30pm. On F, the clinic is held at 94 bd. Massanna, on the 1st floor of the Tour Mantoue, door code 38145, 13ème (☎01 45 84 28 25); call ahead F 10am-4pm. M: Porte d'Ivry.

Paris Overview

○ SIGHTS

1 Cimetière Montmartre
2 Basilique du Sacré-Coeur
3 Parc de la Villette
4 Parc des Buttes-Chaumont
5 Jardins du Trocadéro
6 Palais de Chaillot
7 Cimetière de Passy
8 American Embassy
9 British Embassy
10 Petit Palais
11 Grand Palais
12 Arc de Triomphe
13 Madeleine
14 Gare St-Lazare
15 Parc Monceau
16 Palais de la Découverte
17 Opéra Garnier
18 Galeries Lafayette
19 Au Printemps
20 Gare du Nord
21 Gare de l'Est
22 Opéra Bastille
23 Palais Omnisports de Paris-Bercy
24 Ministère des Finances
25 Gare de Lyon
26 Parc Montsouris
27 Cité Universitaire
28 Cimetière Montparnasse
29 Gare Montparnasse

30 Bureau des Objets Trouvés (Lost and Found)
31 Louvre
32 Palais Royale
33 Forum des Halles
34 Musée de l'Orangerie
35 Central Post Office
36 Bourse
37 Bibliothèque Nationale
38 Ecole des Arts et Métiers
39 Archives Nationales
40 Musée Carnavalet
41 Musée Picasso
42 Centre George Pompidou
43 place des Vosges
44 Musée Victor Hugo
45 Notre Dame
46 Mémorial de la Déportation
47 Université de Paris (Sorbonne)

48 Ecole Normal Supérieure
49 Musée de Cluny
50 Museum Nationale d'Histoire Naturelle
51 Panthéon
52 Eglise St-Etienne du Mont
53 La Mosquée
54 Jardin des Plantes
55 Jardins du Luxembourg
56 Eglise St-Sulpice
57 Théâtre Nationale de l'Odéon
58 Eiffel Tower
59 Champs de Mars

60 Ecole Militaire
61 UNESCO
62 Hôtel des Invalides
63 Assemblée Nationale
64 Musée d'Orsay
65 Cimetière de l'Est du Pere Lachaise

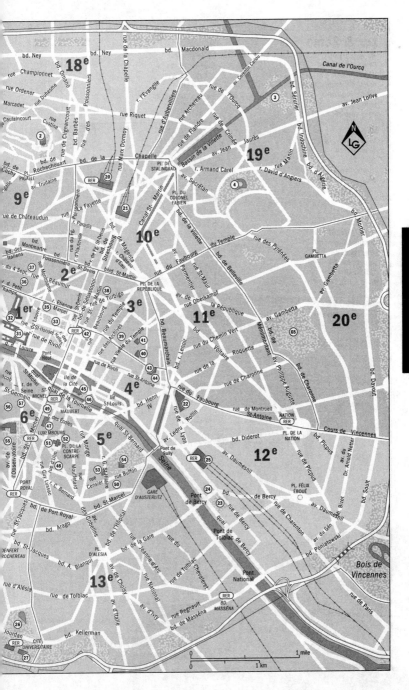

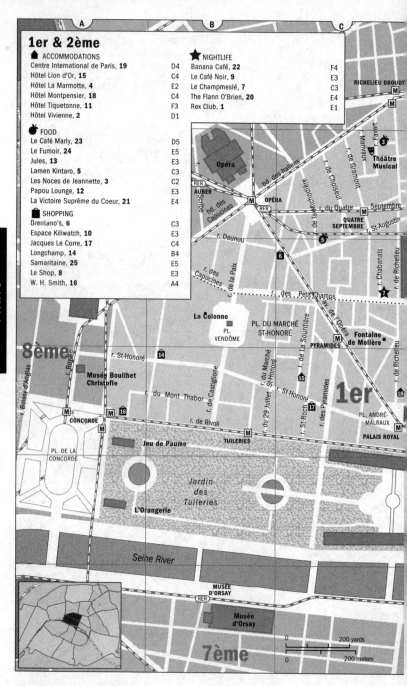

1er & 2ème

ACCOMMODATIONS

Centre International de Paris, **19**	D4
Hôtel Lion d'Or, **15**	C4
Hôtel La Marmotte, **4**	E2
Hôtel Montpensier, **18**	C4
Hôtel Tiquetonne, **11**	F3
Hôtel Vivienne, **2**	D1

FOOD

Le Café Marly, **23**	D5
Le Fumoir, **24**	E5
Jules, **13**	E3
Lamen Kintaro, **5**	C3
Les Noces de Jeannette, **3**	C2
Papou Lounge, **12**	E3
La Victoire Suprême du Coeur, **21**	E4

SHOPPING

Brentano's, **6**	C3
Espace Kiliwatch, **10**	E3
Jacques Le Corre, **17**	C4
Longchamp, **14**	B4
Samaritaine, **25**	E5
Le Shop, **8**	E3
W. H. Smith, **16**	A4

★ NIGHTLIFE

Banana Café, **22**	F4
Le Café Noir, **9**	E3
Le Champmeslé, **7**	C3
The Flann O'Brien, **20**	E4
Rex Club, **1**	E1

RICHELIEU DROUOT

Opéra

bd. des Italiens

Théâtre Musical

r. de Gramont

r. de Choiseul

r. Marsoulan

r. Favart

RER AUBER

bd. des Capucines

OPÉRA

RER

QUATRE SEPTEMBRE

r. du Quatre Septembre

St-Augustin

r. de la Michodière

r. Daunou

r. Chabanais

r. de Richelieu

r. des Capucines

r. de la Paix

r. des Petits Champs

av. de l'Opéra

La Colonne

PL. VENDÔME

PL. DU MARCHÉ ST-HONORÉ

Fontaine de Mollière

PYRAMIDES

PL. DE La Sourdière

8ème

r. Royale

r. St-Honoré

Musée Bouilhet Christofle

r. du Mont-Thabor

r. de Castiglione

r. du Marché St-Honoré

r. St-Honoré

r. de Rivoli

r. du 29 Juillet

r. St-Roch

r. des Pyramides

1er

PL. ANDRÉ-MALRAUX

PALAIS ROYAL

r. de Richelieu

CONCORDE

Jeu de Paume

TUILERIES

PL. DE LA CONCORDE

r. Boissy d'Anglas

Jardin des Tuileries

L'Orangerie

Seine River

MUSÉE D'ORSAY

RER

Musée d'Orsay

7ème

0	200 yards
0	200 meters

PARIS

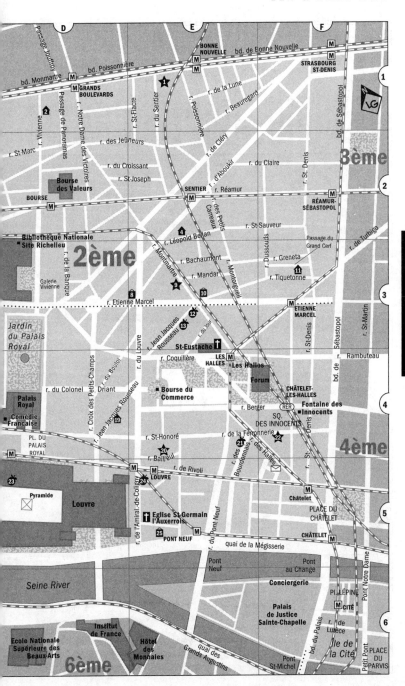

PARIS

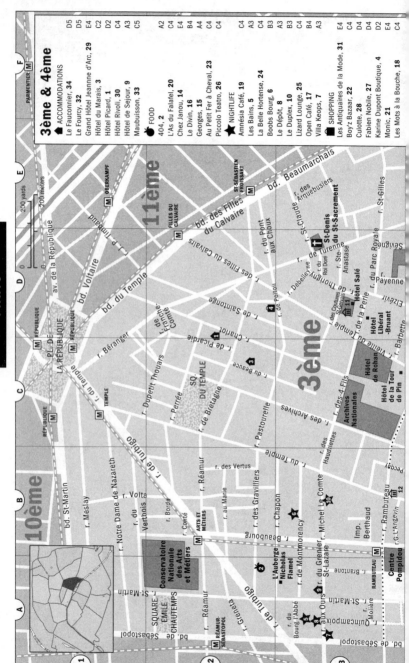

3ème & 4ème

▲ ACCOMMODATIONS

Le Fauconnier, 34	D5
Le Fourcy, 32	D5
Grand Hôtel Jeanne d'Arc, 29	E4
Hôtel du Marais, 3	C2
Hôtel Picard, 1	D2
Hôtel Rivoli, 30	C4
Hôtel de Séjour, 9	A3
Maubuisson, 33	C5

🍴 FOOD

404, 2	A2
L'As du Falafel, 20	C4
Chez Janou, 14	E4
Le Divin, 16	B4
Georges, 15	A4
Au Petit Fer à Cheval, 23	C4
Piccolo Teatro, 26	C4

★ NIGHTLIFE

Amnésia Café, 19	C4
Les Bains, 5	A3
La Belle Hortense, 24	C4
Boobs Bourg, 6	B3
Le Dépôt, 8	A3
Le Duplex, 10	B3
Lizard Lounge, 25	C4
Open Café, 17	C4
Villa Keops, 7	A3

■ SHOPPING

Les Antiquaires de la Mode, 31	E4
Boy'z Bazaar, 22	C4
Culotte, 28	D4
Fabien Nobile, 27	D4
Karine Dupont Boutique, 4	D2
Monic, 21	E4
Les Mots à la Bouche, 18	C4

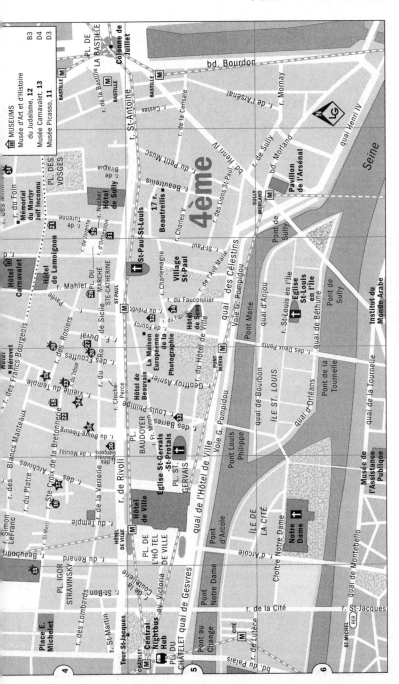

🏛 MUSEUMS
Musée d'Art et d'Histoire
du Judaïsme, **12** B3
Musée Carnavalet, **13** D4
Musée Picasso, **11** D3

PARIS

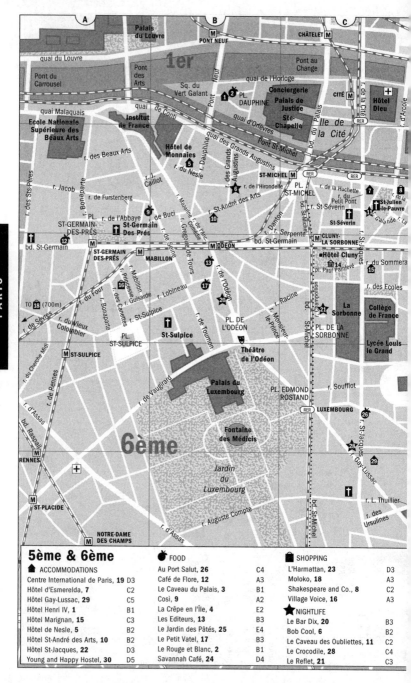

5ème & 6ème

🏠 ACCOMMODATIONS

Centre International de Paris, **19**	D3
Hôtel d'Esmerelda, **7**	C2
Hôtel Gay-Lussac, **29**	C5
Hôtel Henri IV, **1**	B1
Hôtel Marignan, **15**	C3
Hôtel de Nesle, **5**	B2
Hôtel St-André des Arts, **10**	B2
Hôtel St-Jacques, **22**	D3
Young and Happy Hostel, **30**	D5

🍴 FOOD

Au Port Salut, **26**	C4
Café de Flore, **12**	A3
Le Caveau du Palais, **3**	B1
Così, **9**	A2
La Crêpe en l'Île, **4**	E2
Les Editeurs, **13**	B3
Le Jardin des Pâtés, **25**	E4
Le Petit Vatel, **17**	B3
Le Rouge et Blanc, **2**	B1
Savannah Café, **24**	D4

🛍 SHOPPING

L'Harmattan, **23**	D3
Moloko, **18**	A3
Shakespeare and Co., **8**	C2
Village Voice, **16**	A3

⭐ NIGHTLIFE

Le Bar Dix, **20**	B3
Bob Cool, **6**	B2
Le Caveau des Oubliettes, **11**	C2
Le Crocodile, **28**	C4
Le Reflet, **21**	C3

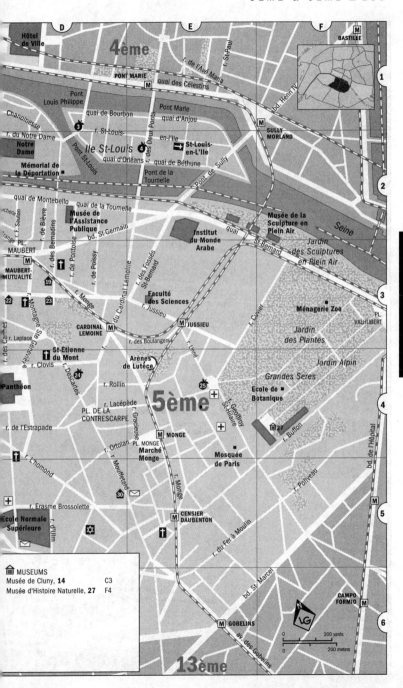

PARIS

MUSEUMS
Musée de Cluny, **14**   C3
Musée d'Histoire Naturelle, **27**   F4

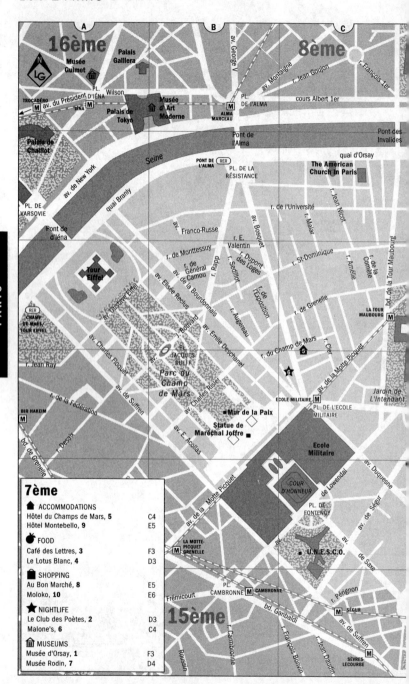

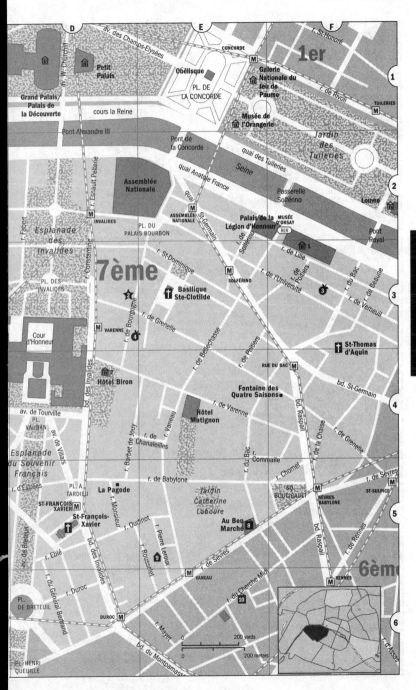

PARIS

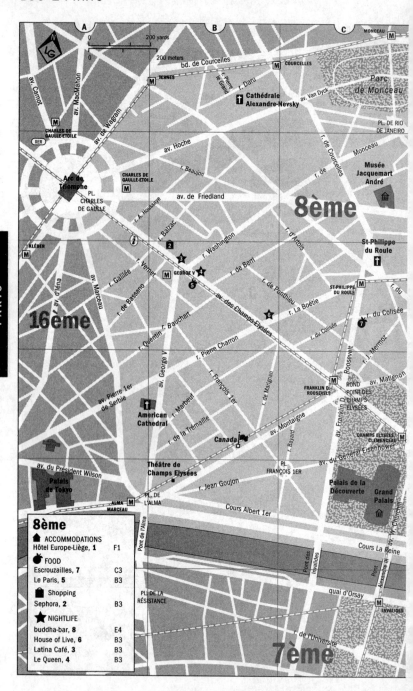

8ème

⌂ ACCOMMODATIONS
Hôtel Europe-Liège, **1**   F1

🍎 FOOD
Escrouzailles, **7**   C3
Le Paris, **5**   B3

🛍 Shopping
Sephora, **2**   B3

★ NIGHTLIFE
buddha-bar, **8**   E4
House of Live, **6**   B3
Latina Café, **3**   B3
Le Queen, **4**   B3

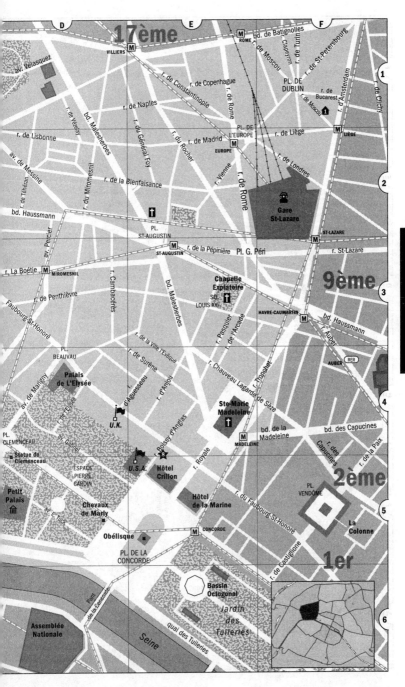

PARIS

PARIS

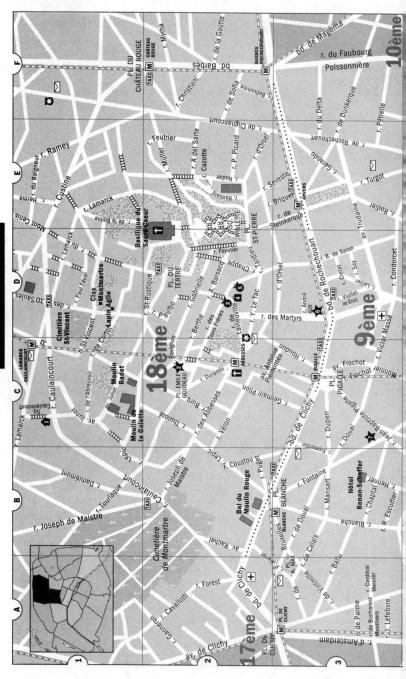

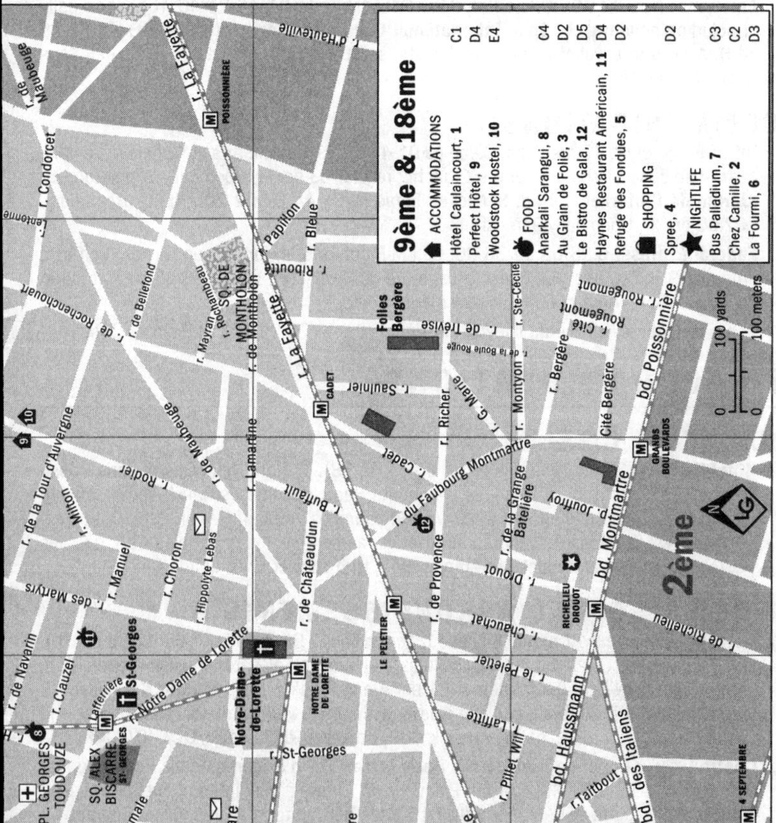

PARIS

9ème & 18ème

ACCOMMODATIONS
Hôtel Caulaincourt, 1 — C1
Perfect Hôtel, 9 — D4
Woodstock Hostel, 10 — E4

FOOD
Anarkali Sarangui, 8 — C4
Au Grain de Folie, 3 — D2
Le Bistro de Gala, 12 — D5
Haynes Restaurant Américain, 11 — D4
Refuge des Fondues, 5 — D2

SHOPPING
Spree, 4 — D2

★ **NIGHTLIFE**
Bus Palladium, 7 — C3
Chez Camille, 2 — C2
La Fourmi, 6 — D3

Emotional Health: SOS Crisis Help Line Friendship: (☎01 46 21 46 46). Open daily (including holidays) 3-11pm. **International Counseling Service (ICS)** (☎01 45 50 26 49). Access to psychologists, psychiatrists, social workers, and clergy. Open M-F 8am-8pm, Sa 8am-4pm.

COMMUNICATIONS

Internet: Artefak, 42 rue Volta, 3ème (☎01 44 59 39 58). M: Arts et Metiers or Temple. Early-bird specials (before 1pm), €2 per hr.; regular €3 per hr. Open daily 10pm-2am. **Le Jardin de l'Internet,** 79 bd. St-Michel, 5ème (☎01 44 07 22 20). RER: Luxembourg. €2.50 per hr. Open daily 9am-11pm.

Federal Express, ☎08 00 12 38 00. Call M-F before 5pm for pick-up. Or, drop-off at 2 rue du 29 Juillet, between Concorde and rue du Rivoli, 1er. Open M-Sa 9am-7pm; drop off by 4:45pm. **Also** at 63 bd. Haussmann, 8ème.

Poste du Louvre: 52 rue du Louvre, 1er (info ☎01 40 28 20 40). M: Louvre. 24hr.

ᙁ ACCOMMODATIONS

ILE DE LA CITÉ

▓ **Hôtel Henri IV,** 25 pl. Dauphine (☎01 43 54 44 53). M: Pont Neuf. One of Paris's best-located and least expensive hotels, named for Henri IV's presses, which once occupied the 400-year-old building. Big windows and charming views of tree-lined pl. Dauphine. Showers €2.50. Reserve 1 month in advance, earlier in summer. Singles €23; doubles €30, with shower and toilet €54; triples €41, with shower €48; quads €48. ❷

FIRST & SECOND ARRONDISSEMENTS

▓ **Hôtel Montpensier,** 12 rue de Richelieu, 1er (☎01 42 96 28 50; fax 01 42 86 02 70). M: Palais-Royal. Clean rooms, lofty ceilings, bright décor, elevator. English spoken. TV in rooms with shower or bath. Internet €1 per 4min. Breakfast €7. Shower €4. Reserve 2 months ahead in high season. Singles and doubles with toilet €57, with toilet and shower €76, with toilet, bath, and sink €89. Extra bed €12. AmEx/DC/MC/V. ❺

▓ **Centre International de Paris (BVJ): Paris Louvre,** 20 rue Jean-Jacques Rousseau, 1er (☎01 53 00 90 90). M: Louvre or Palais-Royal. Draws a very international crowd. 200 beds. Bright, dorm-style rooms with 2-10 beds per room. English spoken. Internet €1 per 10min. Breakfast and showers included. Lockers €2. Reception 24hr. Weekend reservations up to 1 week in advance; reserve by phone only. Rooms held for only 5-10min. after your expected check-in time; call if you'll be late. Doubles €28 per person; other rooms €25 per person. ❷

Hôtel Tiquetonne, 6 rue Tiquetonne, 2ème (☎01 42 36 94 58; fax 01 42 36 02 94). M: Etienne-Marcel. This affordable 7-story hotel is a study in faux finishes: from fake-marble corridors to "I-can't-believe-it's-not-wood" doors. But the (friendly) giant German Shepherd is real. Elevator. Breakfast €5. Hall showers €5. Closed Aug. and 1 week at Christmas. Reserve 2 weeks in advance. Singles €28, with toilet €38; doubles with shower and toilet €46. AmEx/MC/V. ❸

Hôtel Vivienne, 40 rue Vivienne, 2ème (☎01 42 33 13 26; paris@hotel-vivienne.com). M: Grands Boulevards. Hardwood floors in its reception area and spacious rooms with armoires add a touch of refinement. Some rooms with balconies. Elevator. Breakfast €6. Singles with shower €50, with shower and toilet €78; doubles €65/€80, third person under age 10 free, over 10 add 30%. MC/V. ❹

Hôtel Lion d'Or, 5 rue de la Sourdière, 1er (☎01 42 60 79 04; fax 01 42 60 09 14). M: Tuileries or Pyramides. Clean and carpeted, in a quiet area. Phone and TV in most rooms. Friendly staff. Breakfast €6.10. 20 rooms; reserve 1 month in advance in high

UNDER €15 ❶		€26-35 ❸, CONT'D	
Aub. de Jeun. "Jules Ferry" (114)	11ème	Hôtel Rivoli (112)	4ème
€15-25 ❷		🏨 Hôtel du Séjour (111)	3ème
Aloha Hostel (115)	15ème	Hôtel St-André des Arts (112)	6ème
🏨 Cambrai Hôtel (113)	10ème	Hôtel St-Jacques (112)	5ème
Ctr. Int'l CISP "Ravel" (114)	12ème	Hôtel Tiquetonne (110)	2ème
Ctr. Int'l (BVJ) Quartier Latin (113)	5ème	Nièvre-Hôtel (114)	12ème
🏨 Ctr. Int'l (BVJ) Paris Louvre (110)	1er	🏨 Perfect Hôtel (113)	9ème
🏨 Hôtel des Jeunes (MIJE) (111)	4ème	**€36-55 ❹**	
Hôtel Gay-Lussac (113)	5ème	Eden Hôtel (115)	20ème
🏨 Hôtel Henri IV (110)	Ile de la Cité	FIAP Jean-Monnet (115)	14ème
Hôtel du Marais (112)	3ème	🏨 Hôtel de Blois (114)	14ème
Hôtel Palace (113)	10ème	Hôtel Marignan (112)	5ème
🏨 Hôtel Printania (114)	12ème	🏨 Hôtel de Nesle (112)	6ème
🏨 Ouest Hôtel (114)	14ème	Hôtel Ribera (115)	16ème
Three Ducks Hostel (115)	15ème	Hôtel Vivienne (110)	2ème
🏨 Young & Happy Hostel (112)	5ème	Rhin et Danube (115)	19ème
Woodstock Hostel (114)	9ème	**ABOVE €55 ❺**	
€26-35 ❸		Grand Hôtel Jeanne d'Arc (112)	4ème
🏨 Hôtel Caulaincourt (115)	18ème	🏨 Hôtel Boileau (115)	16ème
Hôtel d'Esmeralda (113)	5ème	🏨 Hôtel du Champs de Mars (113)	7ème
Hôtel La Marmotte (111)	2ème	Hôtel Europe-Liège (113)	8ème
Hôtel Montebello (113)	7ème	Hôtel Lion d'Or (110)	1er
Hôtel Picard (112)	3ème	🏨 Hôtel Montpensier (110)	1er
🏨 Hôtel Printemps (115)	15ème	🏨 Modern Hôtel (114)	11ème

PARIS

season. 5% discount for stays of more than 3 nights. Singles with shower, toilet, and double bed €58-74, with bath €68-80; doubles €74-85/€80-95; triples €84-95/€90-105. Extra bed €10. AmEx/MC/V. ❺

Hôtel La Marmotte, 6 rue Léopold Bellan, 2ème (☎01 40 26 26 51; fax 01 21 42 96 20). M: Sentier. Quiet rooms with TV, phone, and safe-box. Over a bar. Breakfast €4. Shower €3. Reserve 2 weeks in advance. Singles and 1-bed doubles €28-35, with shower €42-54; 2-bed doubles €60. Extra bed €12. ❸

THIRD & FOURTH ARRONDISSEMENTS

🏨 **Hôtel du Séjour,** 36 rue du Grenier St-Lazare, 3ème (☎/fax 01 48 87 40 36). M: Etienne-Marcel or Rambuteau. Located just one block from Les Halles and the Centre Pompidou, this family-run hotel offers clean, bright rooms and a warm welcome in a convenient location. Reserve at least one week in advance. 20 rooms. Showers €4. Reception daily 7am-10:30pm. Singles €31; doubles €43, with shower and toilet €55, third person €23. ❸

🏨 **Hôtel des Jeunes (MIJE)** (☎01 42 74 23 45; www.mije.com). This umbrella organization books beds in the Le Fourcy, Le Fauconnier, and Maubuisson (see below), 3 small hostels located on cobblestone streets in beautiful old Marais residences. No smoking. English spoken. Restaurant. Internet €0.15 per min. Public phones and free lockers (with €1 deposit). Ages 18-30 only. 7-day max. stay. Reception daily 7am-1am. Lockout noon-3pm. Curfew 1am. Quiet after 10pm. Breakfast, shower, and sheets included. Arrive before noon the first day of reservation (call in advance if late). Groups of 10 or more may reserve a year in advance. Individuals should reserve at least 1 week in advance. 5-bed (or more) dorms €24-26; singles €40-47; doubles €30-36; triples €26-31; quads €25-27. ❷

Le Fourcy, 6 rue de Fourcy, 4ème. M: St-Paul or Pont Marie. Surrounds a large courtyard ideal for meeting travelers or picnicking. Rooms on the social courtyard can be noisy. Elevator.

Le Fauconnier, 11 rue du Fauconnier, 4ème. M: St-Paul or Pont Marie. From M: St-Paul, take rue du Prevôt, turn left onto rue Charlemagne, and turn right onto rue du Fauconnier. Ivy-covered building steps away from the Seine and Ile St-Louis.

Maubuisson, 12 rue des Barres, 4ème. M: Hôtel-de-Ville or Pont Marie. A half-timbered former girls' convent on a silent street by the St-Gervais monastery. Elevator.

Grand Hôtel Jeanne d'Arc, 3 rue de Jarente, 4ème (☎01 48 87 62 11; www.hotel-jeannedarc.com). M: St-Paul or Bastille. Bright hotel on a quiet side street with a pleasant lounge and breakfast area. Recently renovated rooms with shower, toilet, and TV. 2 are wheelchair-accessible. Elevator. Breakfast €5.80. Reserve 2-3 months in advance. Singles €55-64; doubles €67-92; triples €107; quads €122. Extra bed €12. MC/V. ❺

Hôtel Picard, 26 rue de Picardie, 3ème (☎01 48 87 53 82; fax 01 48 87 02 56). M: République. Follow bd. du Temple and turn right onto rue Charlot. Take the first right onto rue de Franche Comte, which becomes rue de Picardie. In a superb location with a friendly, helpful staff. TVs in rooms with showers. Elevator. Breakfast €4.50. Hall showers €3. Reserve 2 weeks ahead Apr.-Sept. Singles €33, with shower €41, with shower and toilet €51; doubles €40-43, with shower €52, with bath €63; triples €59-82. 5% discount if you flash your *Let's Go.* Wheelchair-accessible. MC/V. ❸

Hôtel du Marais, 16 rue de Beauce, 3ème (☎01 42 72 30 26; hotelmarais@voila.fr). M: Temple or Filles-de-Calvaire. This small hotel offers simple but spotless rooms in a great location near an open-air market. Take the stairs above the café owned by the same friendly man. Curfew 2am. Showers €3. Singles with sink €25; doubles €33. ❷

Hôtel Rivoli, 44 rue de Rivoli/2 rue des Mauvais Garçons, 4ème (☎01 42 72 08 41). M: Hôtel-de-Ville. Walk against traffic on rue de Rivoli; the hotel will be on your left. Small with basic rooms, but extremely well-situated. No entrance 2-7am. Reserve 1 month in advance. Singles €27, with shower €35; doubles €35, with shower €39, with bath and toilet €49; triple €54. Extra bed €9. ❸

FIFTH & SIXTH ARRONDISSEMENTS

▓ **Young and Happy (Y&H) Hostel,** 80 rue Mouffetard, 5ème (☎01 45 35 09 53; www.youngandhappy.fr). M: Monge. A funky, lively hostel located on rue Mouffetard, the emblematic street of the hopping student quarter. Laid-back staff, clean rooms, and commission-free currency exchange. Kitchen and Internet access (€1 per 10min.). English spoken. Breakfast included. Sheets €2.50. Towels €1. Laundry nearby. Lockout 11am-4pm. Curfew 2am. 25 rooms, a few with showers and toilets. Dorms from €20 per person; doubles from €46; Jan.-Mar. prices €2 less per night. ❷

▓ **Hôtel de Nesle,** 7 rue du Nesle, 6ème (☎01 43 54 62 41; www.hoteldenesle.com). M: Odéon. Fantastic, friendly, and absolutely sparkling. Garden with terrace and duck pond, laundry room. Extra bed €12. Reserve by telephone, confirm 2 days in advance with arrival time. Singles €50-69; doubles €69-99. AmEx/MC/V. ❹

Hôtel St-André des Arts, 66 rue St-André-des-Arts, 6ème (☎01 43 26 96 16; hsaintand@minitel.net). M: Odéon. Stone walls, high ceilings and exposed beams lend a country inn feeling. New bathrooms and friendly owner. Breakfast included. Singles €63; doubles €80-85; triples €100; quads €110. MC/V. ❸

Hôtel St-Jacques, 35 rue des Ecoles, 5ème (☎01 44 07 45 45; hotelstjacques@wanadoo.fr). M: Maubert-Mutualité; RER: Cluny-La Sorbonne. Cary Grant filmed *Charade* here. Spacious, faux-elegant rooms with balconies, renovated bathrooms, and TV. English spoken. Elevator. Internet access. Breakfast €7. Singles €49, with toilet and shower €75; doubles with toilet and shower €85, with bath €112. AmEx/MC/V. ❸

Hôtel Marignan, 13 rue du Sommerard, 5ème (☎01 43 54 63 81; www.hotel-marignan.com). M: Maubert-Mutualité. Clean, freshly decorated rooms for up to 5; the privacy of a hotel and the welcoming atmosphere of a hostel. Free laundry and kitchen access. TV in room on request. Hall showers open until 11pm. Internet access. Breakfast €3. Reserve 2 months in advance with credit card or check deposit. Singles €42-45; doubles €60, with shower and toilet €80-86; triples €90-110; quads €100-130. 15% discount mid-Sept. to Mar. AmEx/MC/V for stays longer than 5 nights. ❹

Hôtel d'Esmeralda, 4 rue St-Julien-le-Pauvre, 5ème (☎01 43 54 19 20; fax 01 40 51 00 68). M: St-Michel. Clean rooms feel professorial and ancient, with antique wallpaper, ceiling beams, and red velvet. Great location. Breakfast €6. Singles €35, with shower and toilet €65; doubles €90; triples €110; quads €120. ❸

Centre International de Paris (BVJ): Paris Quartier Latin, 44 rue des Bernardins, 5ème (☎01 43 29 34 80; fax 01 53 00 90 91). M: Maubert-Mutualité. Boisterous, generic hostel with large cafeteria. English spoken. Internet €1 per 10min. Breakfast included. Microwave, TV, and message service. Showers in rooms. Lockers €2. Reception 24hr. Reserve at least 1 week in advance and confirm, or arrive at 9am to check for availability. 97 beds. 5- and 6-person dorms €25; singles €30; doubles €54; triples €81. ❷

Hôtel Gay-Lussac, 29 rue Gay-Lussac, 5ème (☎01 43 54 23 96; fax 01 40 51 79 49). M: Luxembourg. Friendly owner and clean, stately old rooms, some with fireplaces. It can get a bit noisy from neighborhood traffic, but the peaceful shade of the Luxembourg gardens is just a few blocks away. Elevator. Discounts during the winter. Reserve by fax at least 2 weeks in advance (1 month in the summer). Breakfast included. Singles €38, with toilet €50, with shower and toilet €64; doubles with toilet €65, with shower and toilet €74; triples with shower €83, with shower and toilet €74; quads €100. ❷

SEVENTH & EIGHTH ARRONDISSEMENTS

▨ **Hôtel du Champs de Mars,** 7 rue du Champ de Mars, 7ème (☎01 45 51 52 30; www.hotel-du-champs-de-mars.com). M: Ecole Militaire. Rooms, each named after a particular flower, have phone and satellite TV. Homemade breakfast €6.50. Reserve 1 month ahead and confirm by fax or email with a credit card number. Small elevator. Singles and doubles with shower €68-74; triples with bath €94. MC/V. ❺

Hôtel Montebello, 18 rue Pierre Leroux, 7ème (☎01 47 34 41 18; fax 01 47 34 46 71). Amazing prices for this upscale neighborhood. Behind the unremarkable façade are clean, cheery rooms with full baths. Reserve at least 2 weeks in advance. Breakfast 7:30-9:30am, €3.50. 1 person €37; 2 people €42-45. ❸

Hôtel Europe-Liège, 8 rue de Moscou, 8ème (☎01 42 94 01 51; fax 01 43 87 42 18). M: Liège. Very quiet and reasonably priced for the 8ème, with clean, fresh rooms, a friendly staff, and a lovely courtyard. Reserve 15 days in advance. All rooms have TV, hair dryer, phone, and shower or bath. 2 wheelchair-accessible rooms on the ground floor. Breakfast €7. Singles €68; doubles €84. AmEx/MC/V. ❺

NINTH & TENTH ARRONDISSEMENTS

▨ **Perfect Hôtel,** 39 rue Rodier, 9ème (☎01 42 81 18 86 or 01 42 81 26 19; perfecthotel@hotmail.com). This hotel almost lives up to its name, with hotel-quality rooms at hostel prices, some with balconies; the upper floors have a beautiful view. Phones, communal refrigerator and kitchen access, free coffee, beer vending machine (€1.50), and an attentive, English-speaking staff. Elevator. Breakfast free for *Let's Go* users. Singles €30, with shower and toilet €50; doubles €36/€50; triples €53/€65. MC/V. ❸

▨ **Cambrai Hôtel,** 129bis bd. de Magenta, 10ème (☎01 48 78 32 13; www.hotel-cambrai.com). M: Gare du Nord. Clean rooms with high ceilings and TVs. Breakfast €5. Showers €3. Singles €30, with toilet €35, with shower €41, with full bath €48; doubles with shower €46, with full bath €54, with twin beds and full bath €60; triples €80; 4-person family suite €90; 5-person family suite €110 (wheelchair-accessible). AmEx/MC/V. ❷

Hôtel Palace, 9 rue Bouchardon, 10ème (☎01 42 06 59 32; hotel.palace@club-internet.fr). M: Strasbourg-St-Denis. Walk against traffic on bd. St-Denis until the small arch; follow rue René Boulanger on the left, then turn left on rue Bouchardon. A clean, centrally located hotel with hostel rates, near laundromat and supermarket. Breakfast €3.50. Shower €3.50. Reserve 2 weeks ahead. Singles €17-21, with shower €31; doubles €26/€36; triples €48; quads €58; quints €68. AmEx/MC/V. ❷

Woodstock Hostel, 48 rue Rodier, 9ème (☎01 48 78 87 76; www.woodstock.fr). M: Anvers. Ubiquitous incense, reggae music, tie-dye, and a Beatles-decorated VW Bug hanging from the ceiling. Communal kitchen, safe deposit box, Internet €1 per 10min., and fax. English spoken. Breakfast included. Sheets €2.50, towels €1. Free, clean showers on every floor. Reserve ahead. Max. stay 1 week. Curfew 2am. Lockout 11am-4pm. 4- to 8-person dorms €20; doubles €23; max. 8 people per room. ❷

ELEVENTH & TWELFTH ARRONDISSEMENTS

▨ **Modern Hôtel,** 121 rue de Chemin-Vert, 11ème (☎01 47 00 54 05; www.modern-hotel.fr). M: Père Lachaise. Newly renovated, with modern furnishings and spotless marble bathrooms. All rooms have a hair dryer, modem connection, and safe-deposit box. 6 floors of rooms but no elevator (ask for a low floor). Breakfast €5. Singles €60; doubles €70-75; triples €85; quads €95. Extra bed €15. AmEx/DC/MC/V. ❺

▨ **Hôtel Printania,** 91 av. du Dr. Netter, 12ème (☎01 43 07 65 13; fax 01 43 43 56 54). M: Porte de Vincennes. Mini-fridges, large soundproof windows, and faux-marble floors. Breakfast €4.60. Credit card deposit in high season. Reserve at least 2 weeks in advance; confirm reservations by fax. Doubles with sink and *bidet* €39, with shower and bath €48, with TV €54; triples with shower, bath, and TV €61. AmEx/MC/V. ❷

Auberge de Jeunesse "Jules Ferry" (HI), 8 bd. Jules Ferry, 11ème (☎01 43 57 55 60; auberge@easynet.fr). M: République. 100 bunks in a wonderful location. Party atmosphere. Clean rooms with sinks, mirrors, and tiled floors. Doubles with big beds. Breakfast and showers included. Lockers €1.60. Sheets free. Laundry €3.10 wash, €1.60 dry. 1-week max. stay. Internet €0.15 per min. Lockout 10am-2pm. Reception and dining room 24hr. No reservations; arrive by 8am. If they are full, they will try to book you in a nearby hostel. 4- to 6-bed dorms €19.50 per person; doubles €39. MC/V. ❶

Nièvre-Hôtel, 18 rue d'Austerlitz, 12ème (☎01 43 43 81 51). M: Gare de Lyon or Quai de la Rapée. Centrally located but quiet, this recently redone hotel has a friendly atmosphere and rooms with high ceilings and spotless baths. Breakfast €4. Singles €31; doubles €37, with shower €46, with toilet €54. MC/V. ❸

Centre International du Séjour de Paris: CISP "Ravel," 6 av. Maurice Ravel, 12ème (☎01 44 75 60 00; www.cisp.asso.fr). M: Porte de Vincennes. Large, clean rooms, auditorium, outdoor public pool (€3.40), and ubiquitous art. Cafeteria open daily 7:30-9:30am, noon-1:30pm, and 7-8:30pm. Restaurant open noon-1:30pm. Internet €1.50 per 10min. Breakfast, sheets, and towels included. 5-day max. stay (can renew at the end). Reception daily 6:30am-1:30am; the night guard can let you in after 1:30am. Reserve at least a month ahead. 8-bed dorm with hall bath €15.50; 2-to 4-bed dorms €19.50; singles with bath €30; doubles with bath €48. AmEx/MC/V. ❷

THIRTEENTH & FOURTEENTH ARRONDISSEMENTS

▨ **Hôtel de Blois,** 5 rue des Plantes, 14ème (☎01 45 40 99 48; fax 01 45 40 45 62). M: Mouton-Duvernet. 25 rooms with glossy wallpaper, ornate ceiling carvings, velvet chairs, TV, phone, hair dryer, and big, clean bath. Breakfast €5. Reserve 10 days ahead. Singles €39, with shower €43, with shower and toilet €45, with bath and toilet €51; doubles €41/€45/€47/€56; triples €61. Free hall showers. AmEx/MC/V. ❹

▨ **Ouest Hôtel,** 27 rue de Gergovie, 13ème (☎01 45 42 64 99; fax 01 45 42 46 65). M: Pernety. A clean hotel with modest furnishings, outstanding rates, friendly staff, and *brasserie*-style walls in the lobby. Charming dining room. Breakfast €5. Hall shower €5 (sometimes long waits). Singles with small bed €22, with larger bed €28; 1-bed doubles €28, with shower €37; 2-bed doubles €34/€39. MC/V. ❷

FIAP Jean-Monnet, 30 rue Cabanis, 14ème (☎01 43 13 17 00, reservations ☎01 43 13 17 17; www.fiap.asso.fr). M: Glacière. 500-bed student center offers spotless rooms with phone, toilet, and shower. Game and TV rooms, laundry, sunlit piano bar, restaurant, outdoor terrace, and disco. Breakfast included; add €1.60 for buffet. Curfew 2am. Reserve 2-4 weeks ahead. Specify if you want a dorm bed or you will be booked for a single. €15 non-cash deposit per person per night. Wheelchair-accessible. Check-in after 2:30pm. Checkout 9am. 3-month max. stay. 6-bed rooms €22 per person; singles €49.50; doubles €64; quads €110. MC/V. ❹

FIFTEENTH & SIXTEENTH ARRONDISSEMENTS

▨ **Hôtel Printemps,** 31 rue du Commerce, 15ème (☎01 45 79 83 36; hotel.printemps.15e@wanadoo.fr). M: La Motte-Picquet-Grenelle. 53 pleasant, clean rooms in a busy neighborhood. Breakfast €4. Hall showers €3. Reserve 3-4 weeks ahead. Singles and doubles with sink €30, with shower €39, with shower and toilet €43. MC/V. ❸

▨ **Hôtel Boileau,** 81 rue Boileau, 16ème (☎01 42 88 83 74; www.cofrase.com/boileau). M: Exelmans. Marble busts, Oriental rugs, vintage cashboxes, a sunny breakfast room, and an equally sunny staff. Cable TV, Internet, and clean rooms to boot. Breakfast €6. Singles €69; doubles €77-86; triples €109. AmEx/MC/V. ❺

Three Ducks Hostel, 6 pl. Etienne Pernet, 15ème (☎01 48 42 04 05; www.3ducks.fr). M: Félix Faure. With palm trees in the courtyard and beach-style shower shacks, this hostel is aimed at anglo fun-seekers. Enjoy the in-house bar (residents only) until the 2am curfew. Kitchen, lockers, and small 2- to 8-bed dorm rooms. Laundry and groceries nearby. Internet access in lobby. Shower and breakfast included. Reception daily 8am-2am. Lockout daily 11am-5pm. 1-week max. stay. Sheets €2.30; towels €0.80. Reserve with credit card a week ahead. Mar.-Oct. dorm beds €22; doubles €50. Nov.-Feb. special low season rates; call for details. MC/V. ❷

Aloha Hostel, 1 rue Borromée, 15ème (☎01 42 73 03 03; www.friends@aloha.fr). M: Volontaires. Lively mix of international backpackers. Music in the café. No outside alcohol on premises. Breakfast included. Safety deposit boxes and security cameras. Sheets €3, towels €3—but you get to keep them. Reception daily 8am-2am. Lockout 11am-5pm. Curfew 2am. Reserve a week ahead. Apr. to mid-Sept. dorms €21; doubles €25. Mid-Sept. to Nov. dorms €17; doubles 22. Apr.-June dorms €21; doubles €25. ❷

Hôtel Ribera, 66 rue La Fontaine, 16ème (☎01 42 88 29 50; fax 01 42 24 91 33). M: Jasmin. Cheerful, colorful rooms with safe and TV. Excellent location. Pull-out beds in doubles perfect for a small child. Breakfast €5. Rooms €43-54. 10% discount mid-July to mid-Aug. AmEx/MC/V. ❹

OUTER ARRONDISSEMENTS

▨ **Hôtel Caulaincourt,** 2 sq. Caulaincourt, 18ème (☎01 46 06 46 06; bienvenue@caulaincourt.com). M: Lamarck-Caulaincourt. Half hotel, half hostel, this friendly establishment is located in a pleasant, quiet area of Montmartre. TV and phone in every room. Breakfast €5.50. Reserve up to 1 month in advance. Singles €33, with shower €42, with shower and toilet €50; doubles €44-74; triples with shower €60-75. MC/V. ❸

Eden Hôtel, 7 rue Jean-Baptiste Dumay, 18ème (☎01 46 36 64 22; fax 01 46 36 01 11). M: Pyrénées. An oasis of hospitality, with good value for its 2 stars. Clean rooms with TVs and toilets. Elevator. Breakfast €4.50. Bath or shower €4. Reserve rooms by fax 1 week in advance. Singles €36, with shower €49; doubles with shower €51-54, 1 double with bath €54. Extra bed €10. MC/V. ❹

Rhin et Danube, 3 pl. Rhin et Danube, 19ème (☎01 42 45 10 13; fax 01 42 06 88 82). M: Danube; or bus #75 from M: Châtelet (30min). Over a quaint *place,* spacious rooms have kitchen, fridge, dishes, coffee maker, hair dryer, shower, toilet, phone, and satellite TV. Singles €46; doubles €61; triples €73; quads €83; quints €92. MC/V. ❹

🔲 FOOD & DRINK

AMERICAN
🍴 Haynes Restaurant (119)   9ème ❸

BASQUE
🍴 Le Caveau du Palais (117)   Ile de la Cité ❹

BISTRO
Le Rouge et Blanc (117)   Ile de la Cité ❹
Les Noces de Jeannette (117)   2ème ❺
Le Divin (118)   4ème ❹
Le Petit Vatel (119)   6ème ❷
Le Bistro de Gala (119)   9ème ❺
Cantine d'Antoine et Lili (120)   10ème ❶
🍴 Chez Paul (120)   11ème ❸
Le Zéphyr (122)   20ème ❹

BRUNCH
Le Fumoir (117)   1er ❸
Café des Lettres (119)   7ème ❷
🍴 Café du Commerce (120)   13ème ❸
Phinéas (121)   14ème ❷
L'Endroit (122)   17ème ❷
🍴 The James Joyce Pub (121)   17ème ❸
🍴 Café Flèche d'Or (122)   20ème ❷

CAMBODIAN, THAI & VIETNAMESE
🍴 Le Lotus Blanc (119)   7ème ❸
Tricotin (120)   13ème ❶
🍴 Thai Phetburi (121)   15ème ❷
Lao Siam (122)   19ème ❷

CRÊPERIE
La Crêpe en l'Ile (117)   Ile St-Louis ❷

HISTORIC
Café de Flore (119)   6ème ❸

ICE CREAM
🍴 Octave (123)   5ème ❶

INDIAN
Anarkali Sarangui (120)   9ème ❸

IRISH
🍴 The James Joyce Pub (121)   17ème ❸

JAPANESE
Lamen Kintaro (118)   2ème ❷

KOSHER
L'As du Falafel (118)   4ème ❶

LATE NIGHT FOOD (1AM OR LATER)
Le Fumoir (117)   1er ❸
Le Café Marly (118)   1er ❷
🍴 Au Petit Fer à Cheval (118)   4ème ❷
Les Editeurs (119)   6ème ❷
Café de Flore (119)   6ème ❸
Le Paris (119)   8ème ❷

LATE NIGHT FOOD, CONT'D
🍴 Cantine d'Antoine et Lili (120)   10ème ❶
Café de l'Industrie (120)   11ème ❷
Chez Papa (120)   14ème ❸
L'Endroit (122)   17ème ❷
Refuge des Fondues (122)   18ème ❸

MIDDLE EASTERN & TURKISH
L'As du Falafel (118)   4ème ❶
Le Cheval de Troie (120)   12ème ❸
🍴 Comptoir Méditerranée (118)   5ème ❷
🍴 Savannah Café (118)   5ème ❹
Byblos Café (121)   16ème ❷

NORTH AFRICAN
404 (118)   3ème ❸
🍴 Café Flèche d'Or (122)   20ème ❷

PROVENÇAL
Le Divin (118)   4ème ❹
🍴 Le Patio Provençal (121)   17ème ❸

SANDWICHERIE/DELI
Così (119)   6ème ❶

SCANDINAVIAN
Café des Lettres (119)   7ème ❷

TRADITIONAL & MODERN FRENCH
🍴 Jules (117)   1er ❹
🍴 Papou Lounge (117)   1er ❸
🍴 Au Petit Fer à Cheval (118)   4ème ❷
🍴 Au Port Salut (118)   5ème ❸
Escrouzailles (119)   8ème ❸
Le Bistro de Gala (119)   9ème ❺
La Connivence (120)   12ème ❷
🍴 Café du Commerce (120)   13ème ❷
Phinéas (121)   14ème ❷
Chez Papa (120)   14ème ❷
Aux Artistes (121)   15ème ❷
🍴 Le Tire Bouchon (121)   15ème ❹
Refuge des Fondues (122)   18ème ❸
🍴 Café Flèche d'Or (122)   20ème ❷

TRENDY/INTELLIGENTSIA
Le Café Marly (118)   1er ❹
Le Fumoir (117)   1er ❸
🍴 Chez Janou (118)   3ème ❸
Georges (118)   4ème ❸
Café de Flore (119)   6ème ❸
Les Editeurs (119)   6ème ❷
🍴 Chez Paul (120)   11ème ❸
Café de l'Industrie (120)   11ème ❷
Aux Artistes (121)   15ème ❸
🍴 La Rotunde de la Muette (121)   16ème ❷
L'Endroit (122)   17ème ❷
🍴 Café Flèche d'Or (122)   20ème ❷

VEGETARIAN & VEGAN/DETOX		Le Petit Vatel (119)	6ème ❷
▨ La Victoire Suprême		▨ Le Lotus Blanc (119)	7ème ❸
du Coeur (117)	1er ❷	Escrouzailles (119)	8ème ❸
Piccolo Teatro (118)	4ème ❷	Phinéas (121)	14ème ❷
Le Jardin des Pâtés (119)	5ème ❸	Au Grain de Folie (121)	18ème ❷

SEINE ISLANDS

▨ **Le Caveau du Palais,** 19 pl. Dauphine, Ile de la Cité (☎01 43 26 04 28). M: Cité. Chic, intimate restaurant serves hearty Basque specialties from an old-style brick oven, including steak (€16-25) and fish (€20-25), on the sidewalk or in an intimate dining area. Reservations encouraged. Open daily noon-3pm and 7-10:30pm. MC/V. ❹

Le Rouge et Blanc, 26 pl. Dauphine, Ile de la Cité (☎01 43 29 52 34). M: Cité. This simple, Provençal bar and bistro is the creation of proprietor Rigis Tillet, a friendly young man proud of his southern roots. *Menus* €17 and €22; à la carte *plats* €14-20. On sunny days, tables are set out along the sidewalk. Open M-Sa 11am-3pm and 7-10:30pm. Closed when it rains. MC/V. ❹

La Crêpe en l'Ile, 13 rue des Deux Ponts, Ile St-Louis (☎01 43 26 28 68). M: Pont Marie. A *crêperie* just off of the main drag and a bit less crowded than its island siblings. Incredible selection of unique and flavorful teas enhances the friendly atmosphere. Prices €2.50-€7.20; 3-course *menu* €8.40. Open daily in high season 11:30am-midnight; low season 11:30am-11pm. ❷

FIRST & SECOND ARRONDISSEMENTS

Cheap crêpe, sandwich, and pizza stands abound in the **Les Halles** area. You'll find classier but usually affordable options around **rue Jean-Jacques Rousseau** in the 1er and **rue Tiquetonne** in the 2ème.

▨ **Papou Lounge,** 74 rue Jean-Jacques Rousseau, 1er (☎01 44 76 00 03). M: Les Halles. Papou's cuisine is both flavorful (*rumsteak* €13) and inventive (tuna tartar with strawberries €13.50). With world music, black-and-white tile floors, and photographs of tribal warriors, your other senses will be happy, too. Lunch special €10. Beer €3.30. Open daily 10am-2am; food served noon-4:30pm and 7pm-midnight. MC/V. ❸

▨ **Jules,** 62 rue Jean-Jacques Rousseau, 1er (☎01 40 28 99 04). M: Les Halles. Follow directions for Papou Lounge, above. Named after award-winning chef and owner Eric Teyant's son, this restaurant feels like home, with a mantelpiece and blinds on the windows. Subtle blend of modern and traditional French cooking; selections change by season. 4-course *menus* (€21-29) include terrific cheese course. Open M-Sa noon-2:30pm and 7-10:30pm. AmEx/MC/V. ❹

▨ **La Victoire Suprême du Coeur,** 41 rue des Bourdonnais, 1er (☎01 40 41 93 95). M: Châtelet. Run by devotees of guru Sri Chinmoy, who consider both body and soul when creating dishes like *escalope de seitan à la sauce champignon* (€8.50). All vegetarian, all tasty. Meals marked with a "V" can be made vegan. 2-course lunch *menu* €10.80. Open M-F 11:45am-3pm and 6:40-10pm, Sa noon-3pm and 6:40-10pm. MC/V. ❷

Le Fumoir, 6 rue de l'Amiral Coligny, 1er (☎01 42 92 05 05). M: Louvre. Conveniently close to the Louvre. Decidedly untouristy types drink their chosen beverage in deep leather sofas. Part bar, part tea house in feel. Serves one of the best brunches in Paris (€20) Su noon-3pm. Coffee €2.50. Open daily 11am-2am. AmEx/MC/V. ❸

Les Noces de Jeannette, 14 rue Favart, and 9 rue d'Amboise, 2ème (☎01 42 96 36 89). M: Richelieu-Drouot. Jeanette's elegance and diverse clientele will impress your date. *Menu du Bistro* (€27.50) includes large salad entrées, roasted fish, duck, and grilled meat *plats,* desserts to make you faint with delight, and *kir.* Reservations recommended. Open daily noon-1:30pm and 7-9:30pm. ❺

PARIS

Le Café Marly, Cour Napoleon, 1er (☎01 49 26 06 60). M: Palais-Royal. One of Paris's classiest cafés. Located in the Richelieu wing of the Louvre, with a terrace facing the famed I. M. Pei pyramids and others overlooking the Louvre's Cour Napoleon. Main dishes €16-28, omelettes €10. Open daily 8am-2am. AmEx/DC/MC/V. ❹

Lamen Kintaro, 24 rue St-Augustin 2ème (☎01 47 42 13 14). M: Opéra. Delicious and popular Japanese restaurant, serving great noodle bowls (€7.80) and an array of menu combinations (€8-13). Sapporo €4.30. Open M-Sa 11:30am-10pm. MC/V. ❷

THIRD & FOURTH ARRONDISSEMENTS

◪ **Chez Janou,** 2 rue Roger Verlomme, 3ème (☎01 42 72 28 41). M: Chemin-Vert. Tucked into a relatively quiet corner of the 3ème, this hip and friendly restaurant is lauded for its reasonably priced gourmet food. Delightful main courses, such as *thon à la provençale* (€14), and desserts (€6). Open daily noon-3pm and 8pm-midnight. ❸

◪ **Au Petit Fer à Cheval,** 30 rue Vieille-du-Temple, 4ème (☎01 42 72 47 47). M: Hôtel-de-Ville or St-Paul. An oasis of chèvre, *kir*, and *Gauloises*, and a loyal local crowd. Invisible from the front, a few tables huddle behind the bar, where you can order *filet mignon de veau* (€15) or any of the excellent house salads (€3.50-10). Dessert €4-7. Open daily 10am-2am; food served noon-1:15am. MC/V. ❸

◪ **L'As du Falafel,** 34 rue des Rosiers, 4ème (☎01 48 87 63 60). M: St-Paul. Lenny Kravitz rightly credited this kosher falafel stand and restaurant with "the best falafel in the world." Go his way. Falafel special €5. Thimble-sized (but damn good) glass of lemonade €3.50. Open Su-F 11:30am-11:30pm. MC/V. ❶

Piccolo Teatro, 6 rue des Ecouffes (☎01 42 72 17 79). M: St-Paul. A romantic vegetarian hideout. Weekday lunch *menus* €8.20, €9.90, or €13.30. Appetizers €3.60-7.10. *Plats* €7.70-12.50. Open Tu-Sa noon-3pm and 7-11:30pm. AmEx/MC/V. ❷

404, 69 rue des Gravilliers, 3ème (☎ 01 42 74 57 81). M: Arts et Métiers. Metal hanging lights and rich red curtains create an almost mystical world behind the plain stone façade of this classy North African restaurant. Mouth-watering couscous €13-23, *tagines* €13-19. Lunch *menu* €17. Open daily noon-2:30pm and 8pm-midnight. AmEx/MC/V. ❸

Georges, on the 6th fl. of the Centre Pompidou (☎01 44 78 47 99); entrance through the center and also from an elevator just to the left of the Pompidou's main entrance on rue Beaubourg. Ultra-sleek, Zen-cool, in-the-spotlight café; especially the terrace. Come for a glass of wine (€8), a small snack (fresh fruit salad €9.50), or a pricey *plat* (filet of lamb €28), or just to take a peek at the menu—supposedly designed by Dior menswear creator Hedi Slimane. Open M and W-Su noon-2am. ❺

Le Divin, 41 rue Ste-Croix-de-la-Bretonnerie (☎01 42 77 10 20). M: Hôtel-de-Ville. Go south, where sun and cheer (in the form of friendly service and nude paintings) complement fab Provençal fare. Vegetarian options available. *Menus* €16 and €21. Open Tu-Su 7-11:30pm. MC/V. ❹

FIFTH & SIXTH ARRONDISSEMENTS

◪ **Savannah Café,** 27 rue Descartes (☎01 43 29 45 77). M: Cardinal Lemoine. Decorated with eclectic knick-knacks, this cheerful yellow restaurant prides itself on its Lebanese food. Try the perfectly composed starter sampler (€14). Appetizers €7-12.50, *formule* €23. Open M-Sa 7-11pm. MC/V. ❹ Around the corner is its little sister, the **Comptoir Méditerranée,** 42 rue du Cardinal Lemoine (☎01 43 25 29 08), with takeout and lower prices. Open M-Sa 11am-10pm. ❷

◪ **Au Port Salut,** 163bis rue St-Jacques (☎01 46 33 63 21). M: Luxembourg. This old stone building (once a cabaret of the same name) houses 3 floors of traditional French gastronomic joy. Fabulous 3-course *menus* that change with the season €12.40 and €21.90. Salads €8.90-9.30. Open Tu-Sa noon-2:30pm and 7-11:30pm. MC/V. ❸

Le Petit Vatel, 5 rue Lobineau (☎01 43 54 28 49). M: Mabillon. This home-run bistro serves up a fresh menu of French Mediterranean specialties like *catalan pamboli* (bread with puréed tomatoes, ham, and cheese), all a reasonable €10. Non-smoking. €11 lunch *menu*. Vegetarian options. Open Tu-Sa noon-2:30pm and 7-10:30pm. ❸

Les Editeurs, 4 carrefour d'Odéon (☎01 43 26 67 76). The newest and classiest café on the block, Les Editeurs pays homage to St-Germain's literary pedigree with books overflowing its plush red and gold dining rooms, and outlets for struggling, laptop-toting young writers. Jazz music and a piano upstairs. Coffee €2.50, *pressions* €4.50, cocktails €9. *Croque-monsieur* €9.50. Happy hour daily 6-8pm; cocktails €6-8, and delicious complementary olives! Open daily 8am-2am. AmEx/MC/V. ❷

Café de Flore, 172 bd. St-Germain (☎01 45 48 55 26). M: St-Germain-des-Prés. Sartre composed *Being and Nothingness* here; Apollinaire, Camus, Artaud, Picasso, Breton, and Thurber sipped brew; and in its current feud with Les Deux Magots, Flore reportedly snags more local intellectuals—possibly by offering a respected literary prize. Espresso €4. Pastries €6.10-10.40. Open daily 7:30am-1:30am. AmEx/MC/V. ❸

Le Jardin des Pâtés, 4 rue Lacépède (☎01 43 31 50 71). M: Jussieu. As calming and pleasant as the Jardin des Plantes around the corner. Organic menu is heavy on pâté (€7-12.50), pasta, and vegetables. Open daily noon-2:30pm and 7-11pm. MC/V. ❸

Cosi, 54 rue de Seine (☎01 46 33 35 36). M: Mabillon. Named for the Mozart opera, this hip *sandwicherie* sells enormous, tasty, inexpensive sandwiches on fresh, brick-oven bread. Sandwiches €5.20-7.60, dessert €2.80-3.40. Open daily noon-11pm. ❷

SEVENTH & EIGHTH ARRONDISSEMENTS

▨ **Le Lotus Blanc,** 45 rue de Bourgogne, 7ème (☎01 45 55 18 89). M: Varenne. Chef Pham-Nam Nghia has been creating Vietnamese specialties for over 25 years. Lunch and all-day *menus* €9-29. Vegetarians and vegans will appreciate the great veggie *menu* (€6.50-12.50). Reservations encouraged. Open M-Sa noon-2:30pm and 7-10:30pm. Closed 2 weeks in Aug. AmEx/MC/V. ❸

Escrouzailles, 36 rue du Colisée, 8ème (☎01 45 62 94 00). M: Franklin D. Roosevelt. Several comfortable dining rooms. Perhaps the best place to enjoy fine yet relaxed dining after a day wandering the Champs-Elysées. Plenty of vegetarian options. Appetizers €8, *plats* €12, dessert €6. Open M-Sa noon-2:30pm and 7:30-10:30pm. MC/V. ❸

Café des Lettres, 53 rue de Verneuil, 7ème (☎01 42 22 52 17). M: Solférino. This Scandinavian café offers unique tastes in a fantastic atmosphere. Patrons enjoy platters of smoked salmon and *blindis* (€16) and other Danish seafood dishes (€12.50-19.50). Su features a Scandinavian-style brunch buffet (€25); reservations recommended. Coffee €2.50, beer €5-6. Open M noon-3pm, Tu-F noon-11pm, Sa noon-7pm. ❷

Le Paris, 93 av. des Champs-Elysées, 8ème (☎01 47 23 54 37). M: George V. Rivalled in snobbery only by Fouquet's, Le Paris has some selling points, such as the unique décor: a deep purple and turquoise *mélange*, with plasma screens playing Anime above the bar. At night, it turns into a bar with a live DJ. Coffee €3.50, tea €5.50, glass of wine €5.50-7. Sandwiches €10-12.50, soup €7. Open daily 8am-6am. ❷

NINTH & TENTH ARRONDISSEMENTS

▨ **Haynes Restaurant Américain,** 3 rue Clauzel (☎01 48 78 40 63). M: St-Georges. The first African-American owned restaurant in Paris (it opened in 1949) and a center for expatriates, Haynes is famous for its "original American Soul Food." Very generous portions, most under €16. Vocal jazz concerts F nights; funk and groove Sa nights (€6 cover). Open Tu-Sa 7pm-12:30am. AmEx/MC/V. ❸

Le Bistro de Gala, 45 rue du Faubourg-Montmartre (☎01 40 22 90 50). M: Grands Boulevards. The commercial noise and neon lights of Faubourg-Montmartre fade away in this spacious but still intimate bistro lined with film posters. This is the reputed hangout of Paris's theater elite. The price of the *menu* is predictably high (€26-36), but worth it. Reservations strongly recommended. Open M-F noon-2:30pm and 7-11:30pm, Sa 7-11:30pm. AmEx/MC/V. ❺

Cantine d'Antoine et Lili, 95 quai de Valmy (☎01 40 37 34 86). M: Gare de l'Est. This canal-side café-bistro is one third of the Antoine and Lili operation, which also includes a neighboring furniture store and a clothing boutique. The tasty food consists mostly of light café fare: pasta salads €6, salads €6.50. Prices lower for takeout. Open Su-Tu 11am-8pm, W-Sa 11am-1am. AmEx/MC/V. ❶

Anarkali Sarangui, 4 pl. Gustave Toudouze, 8ème (☎01 48 78 39 84). M: St-Georges. This North Indian restaurant has a pleasant outdoor seating area and a classy and comfortable interior. Tandoori and curries €7.50-12.50, vegetarian dinner *menu* €22. Open M 7-11:30pm, Tu-Su noon-2:30pm and 7-11:30pm. MC/V. ❸

ELEVENTH & TWELFTH ARRONDISSEMENTS

▧ **Chez Paul,** 13 rue de Charonne, 11ème (☎01 47 00 34 57). M: Bastille. Downstairs has a classic bistro feel; upstairs has a cozy, romantic atmosphere. Paul's fun staff serves dishes to make your palate sing. Extensive appetizer list; great *steak au poivre* with *au gratin* potatoes (€13). Reservations are a must during peak hours. Open daily noon-2:30pm and 7pm-2am; food served until 12:30am. AmEx/MC/V. ❸

Café de l'Industrie, 16 rue St-Sabin, 11ème (☎01 47 00 13 53). M: Breguet-Sabin. This happening café could double as a museum of French colonial history, with its photos of colonized peoples, palm trees, and weapons on the walls. With the recent acquisition of a neighbor across the way, l'Industrie may be the only restaurant in Paris to straddle a street. Both serve the same quality food, including a €9 lunch *menu*. Coffee €2, *vin chaud* €4. Salads €7-7.50. After 10pm, add €0.61. Open Su-F 10am-2am; lunch served noon-2pm. ❷

La Connivence, 1 rue de Cotte, 12ème (☎01 46 28 49 01). M: Ledru-Rollin. An elegant and intimate restaurant with deep orange walls and mint-green tablecloths. Choose from main courses such as veal cooked in white chocolate sauce (€13.50) and desserts like *crêpes suzettes* (€5.80). Lunch *menus* €13-16, dinner *menus* €17-22, wine €14-38 per bottle, cocktails €3-6. Open M-Sa noon-2:40pm and 7:40-11pm. MC/V. ❹

Le Cheval de Troie, 71 rue de Charenton, 12ème (☎01 43 44 24 44). M: Bastille. Savory Turkish food in an appealing setting. Lunch *formule* €10.30. *Çoban salatası* with fresh cucumbers, tomatoes, and feta €4.70; *Imambayıldı* (stuffed eggplant) €5.50; *balli yogurt* (the house yogurt with honey and almonds) €3.90. Dinner *menu* €16. Open M-Sa noon-2:30pm and 7-11:30pm. MC/V. ❸

THIRTEENTH & FOURTEENTH ARRONDISSEMENTS

▧ **Café du Commerce,** 39 rue des Cinq Diamants, 13ème (☎01 53 62 91 04). M: Place d'Italie. This funky and relaxed establishment serves traditional food with a twist. Dinner (€15.50) and lunch (€10.50) *menus* both feature options like *boudin antillais* (spiced bloodwurst), and *fromage blanc aux kiwis*. Reservations recommended for dinner. Open daily noon-3pm and 7pm-2am, Sa-Su brunch noon-4pm. AmEx/MC/V. ❸

Tricotin, 15 av. de Choisy, 13ème (☎01 45 84 74 44). M: Porte de Choisy. This Asian eatery, one of the best in Chinatown, serves delicious food from Cambodia, Thailand, and Vietnam in two incredibly noisy but appealing cafeteria-style rooms. The *vapeur* foods are specialties here—see if you can eat just one order of steamed shrimp ravioli (€3.40). Open daily 9:30am-11:30pm. MC/V. ❶

Chez Papa, 6 rue Gassendi (☎01 43 22 41 19). M: Denfert-Rochereau. Chez Papa's massive traditional *salade boyarde* is chock full of lettuce, potatoes, ham, cantal, and *bleu de brebis* (€6.40). Hearty *menu* (€9.20) served M-F until 4pm. **Also** in the 8ème

(29 rue de l'Arcade; ☎01 42 65 43 68), 10ème (206 rue Lafayette; ☎01 42 09 53 87), and 15ème (101 rue de la Croix Nivert; ☎01 48 28 31 88). Open daily 10am-1am. AmEx/MC/V. ❷

Phinéas, 99 rue de l'Ouest, 14ème (☎01 45 41 33 50). M: Pernety. Wild ferns, hand-painted stained-glass windows, and an oversized crown cover the pink walls of this restaurant's two dining rooms, while in an open kitchen the chef makes *tartes salées* (€6.50-8) and *tartes sucrées* (€6-6.50). Vegetarian options. Su brunch 11am-3pm. Open Tu-Sa 9am-noon for takeout, noon-11:30pm for dine-in. AmEx/MC/V. ❷

FIFTEENTH & SIXTEENTH ARRONDISSEMENTS

▨ **Thai Phetburi,** 31 bd. de Grenelle, 15ème (☎01 41 58 14 88; www.phetburi-paris.com). M: Bir-Hakeim. Award-winning food, friendly service, low prices, and a relaxing atmosphere. The *tom yam koung* (shrimp soup flavoured with lemongrass; €7) and the *lab kai* (chicken in thai grass; €8.80) are favorites. Open M-Sa noon-2:30pm and 7-10:30pm. AmEx/MC/V. ❷

▨ **La Rotunde de la Muette,** 12 Chaussée de la Muette, 16ème (☎01 45 24 45 45). M: La Muette. Located in a beautiful fin-de-siècle building overlooking the tree-lined Chaussée de la Muette. Indoors, the stylish red and yellow lamps, hip music, and plush Burgundy seats take a sleek spin on the patio's classic feel—but the outdoor seating is best. Sandwiches €5-9.60, salads €4-9.20. AmEx/MC/V. ❷

Byblos Café, 6 rue Guichard, 16ème (☎01 42 30 99 99). M: La Muette. This airy Lebanese restaurant serves cold *mezzes* are good for pita-dipping; taboule, moutabal, moussaka, and a few hummus dishes, all €5.80-8. *Menu* €15. Vegetarian options available. Open daily 11am-3pm and 5-11pm. AmEx/MC/V. ❸

Aux Artistes, 63 rue Falguière, 15ème (☎01 43 22 05 39). M: Pasteur. One of the 15ème's coolest spots, this lively café draws a mix of professionals, students, and artists. Modigliani was supposedly a regular. The chaotic décor and friendly waitstaff will charm you. Lunch *menu* €9.20, dinner *menu* €12.50. Open M-F noon-2:30pm and 7:30pm-midnight, Sa 7:30pm-midnight. ❸

Le Tire Bouchon, 62 rue des Entrepreneurs, 15ème (☎01 40 59 09 27). M: Charles Michels. Run by a charming couple, Tire Bouchon serves classic French cuisine with a creative touch. For dessert, a number of inventive departures from the standard mousse or caramel are offered, including a carrot, cumin, and orange cake (€6.50). *Menu* (M-Th nights) €20, starters €7, main dishes €18.50. Open M and Sa 7:30-11pm, Tu-F noon-2:30pm and 7:30-11pm. MC/V. ❹

SEVENTEENTH & EIGHTEENTH ARRONDISSEMENTS

▨ **Le Patio Provençal,** 116 rue des Dames, 17ème (☎01 42 93 73 73). M: Villiers. Quality rustic restaurant serves staples of southern French fare, such as *filet de rascasse* (€14.50). Glass of wine €2. 3-course *formule* €24. Super-busy, making service a bit slow and reservations a must. Open M-F noon-2:30pm and 7-11pm. MC/V. ❹

▨ **The James Joyce Pub,** 71 bd. Gouvion St-Cyr, 17ème (☎01 44 09 70 32; www.kittyosheas.com). M: Porte Maillot (exit at Palais de Congrès). Upstairs from the pub is a restaurant with stained-glass windows depicting scenes from Joyce's novels. Spectacular Su brunch (noon-3pm) is a full Irish fry (€13.90). An informal tourist office for anglophone expats. Televised sporting events. Pub open M-Th 9pm-1:30am, F-Su 10am-2am; restaurant M-Sa noon-3pm and 7:30-10:30pm, Su noon-5pm. AmEx/MC/V. ❸

Au Grain de Folie, 24 rue Lavieuville (☎01 42 58 15 57). M: Abbesses. A small, unassuming hide-out on a quiet side street. The friendly staff serves delightful vegetarian and vegan treats at great prices. Try the *grain de folie* plate (€11), which includes grilled goat cheese, lentils, grains, grilled vegetables, and fresh salad. Delicious desserts (including frozen bananas doused in chocolate; €5). Open M-Sa 12:30-2:30pm and 7:30-11pm, Su 12:30-11pm. ❷

PARIS

Refuge des Fondues, 17 rue des Trois Frères, 18ème (☎01 42 55 22 65). M: Abbesses. 2 main dishes: *fondue bourguignonne* (meat fondue) and *fondue savoyarde* (cheese fondue). The wine is served in baby bottles with rubber nipples; leave your Freudian hangups at home. *Menu* with apéritif, wine, appetizer, fondue, and dessert €15. Reserve a table or go early. Open daily 6:30pm-2am (no new diners after 12:30am). Closed Aug. ❸

L'Endroit, 67 pl. du Dr. Félix Lobligeois, 17ème (☎01 42 29 50 00). M: Rome. Look for the blue exterior. As cool by day as it is at night, L'Endroit is "the place" to go in the 17ème. 4-course Su brunch (noon-3:30pm; €16) heads a long menu packed with things like melon and *jambon* (€10.80), salads (€10.70), and toasted sandwiches (€9.90). Open daily noon-2am. MC/V. ❸

NINETEENTH & TWENTIETH ARRONDISSEMENTS

⬛ **Café Flèche d'Or,** 102 rue de Bagnolet, 20ème (☎01 43 72 04 23; www.flechedor.com). M: Alexandre Dumas. In a defunct train station, this bar/café/performance space serves North African, French, Caribbean, and South American cuisine with nightly jazz, ska, folk, salsa, and samba (cover €5-6). Political cafés first Sa morning of the month; political debates every other Su morning. Dinner *menus* €12-15, Su brunch *menu* €11. Open daily 10am-2am; dinner 8pm-1am. MC/V over €15.25. ❸

Lao Siam, 49 rue de Belleville, 19ème (☎01 40 40 09 68). M: Belleville. Every bite is worth writing about. A unique dried calamari salad (€8.40) makes for a light preamble to the *poulet royal au curry* (€8.40) or *boef piquant au basilic* (€7.60). Finish it off with a *citron presse* (€2.30) and fan order of kumquats (€2.80) and you'll forget that you came so far out of your way. Open daily noon-3pm and 6:30-11:30pm. MC/V. ❷

Le Zéphyr, 1 rue Jourdain, 20ème (☎01 46 36 65 81). M: Jourdain. Parisian bistro with unique dishes and 1930s décor. 4-course dinner *menu* €26. Lunch *menu* €12.50. Reservations recommended. Open M-F noon-2pm and 8-11pm, Sa 8-11pm. MC/V. ❹

SALONS DE THÉ

Parisian *salons de thé* (tea rooms) fall into three categories: stately salons straight out of the last century piled high with macaroons, Seattle-inspired joints for pseudo-intellectuals, and cafés that simply want to signal they also serve tea.

Angelina's, 226 rue de Rivoli, 1er (☎01 42 60 82 00). M: Concorde or Tuileries. Audrey Hepburn's old favorite. Little has changed here since its 1903 opening, including the frescoes, mirrored walls, and marble tables. *Chocolat africain* (hot chocolate; €6.20) and *Mont Blanc* (meringue with chestnut nougat; €6) are the dangerous house specialties. Tea €6. Open daily 9am-7pm. AmEx/MC/V. ❷

Mariage Frères, 30 rue du Bourg-Tibourg, 4ème (☎01 42 72 28 11). M: Hôtel-de-Ville. Started by two brothers who found British tea shoddy, this *salon* offers 500 varieties of tea (€7-15), from Russian to Vietnamese. The white-suited waiters and sophisticated clientele make this a classic French institution. Tea *menu* of sandwich, pastry, and tea and the classic brunch *menu* of brioche, eggs, tea, cakes are both excellent (each €25). Reserve for brunch. Open daily 10:30am-7:30pm; lunch M-Sa noon-3pm; afternoon tea 3-6:30pm; Su brunch 12:30-6:30pm. AmEx/MC/V. ❺

MARKETS

Marché rue Montorgueil, 2ème. M: Etienne-Marcel. A center of food commerce and gastronomy since the 13th century, the marble Mount Pride Market is comprised of wine, cheese, meat, and produce shops. Open Tu-Su 8am-7:30pm.

Marché Monge, 5ème. M: Monge. In pl. Monge right at the exit from the metro. A bustling, easy-to-navigate market, with everything available for purchase—from cheese to jewelry. The popular prepared foods are perfect for a lunch picnic at the Arènes de Lutèce. Open W, F, and Su 8am-1:30pm.

Marché Mouffetard, 5ème. M: Monge. Walk through pl. Monge and follow rue Ortolan to rue Mouffetard. Cheese, meat, fish, produce, and housewares sold here. The bakeries are reputed to be some of the best of all the markets. Don't miss the ice cream at Octave near the far end of the market (see **Specialty Shops**). Open Tu-Su 8am-1:30pm.

SPECIALTY SHOPS

Fauchon, 26 pl. de la Madeleine, 8ème (☎01 47 42 60 11). M: Madeleine. Paris's favorite gourmet food shop (complete with gourmet prices), this *traiteur/pâtisserie/ épicerie/charcuterie* has it all. Go home with a prettily packaged tin of *madeleines*, or browse their wine cellar, one of the finest in Paris. Open M-Sa 10am-7pm. MC/V.

Octave, 138 rue Mouffetard, 5éme (☎01 45 35 20 56). M: Censier-Daubenton. If heaven ever froze over, it would be served in a cone at Octave. The best ice cream you will ever eat. With no preservatives or coloring, all you taste in each lovely scoop is fresh melon, rich chocolate, soothing cinnamon, or one of their many other *parfums*. One scoop €2, two scoops €3. Open Tu-Su 10am-11:30pm, M 2-7:30pm.

Nicolas, locations throughout Paris. The best place to buy wine. The English-speaking staff will even pack it in travel boxes. Most branches open M-F 10am-8pm. AmEx/MC/V.

Poujauran, 20 rue Jean-Nicot, 7ème (☎01 47 05 80 88). M: La Tour-Maubourg. A taster's delight, selling a wide range of *petit pains*, alongside their bigger brothers. Try bread studded with olives, herbs, figs, or sesame seeds, or dive right into dessert with one of several kinds of tarts and cookies. 2 *petit pains* average €1.50. Open Tu-Sa 8:30am-8:30pm.

La Maison du Chocolat, 8 bd. de la Madeleine, 9ème (☎01 47 42 86 52). M: Madeleine. A whole range of exquisite chocolates, from milk to dark, and a mysterious distilled chocolate essence drink. Box of 2 chocolates €3.30. Also at **other locations,** including 19 rue de Sèvres, 6ème (☎01 45 44 20 40). Open M-Sa 10am-7pm. MC/V.

Gérard Mulot, 76 rue de Seine, 6ème (☎01 43 26 85 11). M: Odéon or St-Sulpice. Outrageous selection of painstakingly crafted pastries, from flan to marzipan with virtually any kind of fruit. The *macaron* is heaven on earth (€4.20). Tarts from €2.50; éclairs €2; *mousse chocolat noisettes* €6.10. Open Tu and Th-Su 7am-8pm.

◉ SIGHTS

ILE DE LA CITÉ

NOTRE DAME

Once the site of a Roman temple to Jupiter, the ground upon which Notre Dame stands housed three churches before Maurice de Sully, the bishop of Paris under King Philip II, began construction of the Catholic cathedral in 1163. He aimed to create an edifice filled with air and light. This style that would later be dubbed **Gothic.** He died before his plan was completed; it was up to later centuries to rework the cathedral into today's masterpiece, finished in 1361. Royals used Notre Dame for weddings, most notably that of **Henri of Navarre** to Marguerite de Valois.

In addition to its royal functions, the cathedral was also the setting for **Joan of Arc's** trial for heresy in 1455. During the Revolution, secularists renamed the cathedral Le Temple de la Raison (The Temple of Reason) and defaced its Gothic arches with plaster façades of virtuous Neoclassical design. Re-consecrated after the Revolution, the church was the site of **Napoleon's** papal coronation in 1804, but the building fell into disrepair and was used to shelter livestock before **Victor Hugo's** 1831 novel *Notre-Dame de Paris (The Hunchback of Notre Dame)* revived the cathedral's popularity and inspired Napoleon III and Haussmann to invest time and money in its restoration. Modifications by **Eugène Viollet-le-Duc** invigorated the cathedral and made Notre Dame once again a valued symbol of civic unity: in 1870 and again in 1940 thousands of Parisians attended masses to pray for deliverance from the invading Germans. On August 26, 1944, **Charles de Gaulle** braved Nazi sniper fire to give thanks here for the imminent liberation of Paris. All these upheavals (not to mention hordes of tourists) seem to have left the cathedral unmarked; e.e. cummings even once remarked, "the Cathedral of Notre Dame does not budge an inch for all the idiocies of this world."

EXTERIOR. Notre Dame is still is in the throes of a massive cleaning project, though its newly glittering **West Façade** is now scaffolding-free. The oldest work is above the **Porte de Ste-Anne** (right), dating from 1165 to 1175. Not content with decapitating Louis XVI, the Revolutionaries attacked the Kings of Judah above the doors, which they incorrectly thought were his ancestors. The heads are now exhibited in the Musée de Cluny (p. 146).

TOWERS. The soot-smeared towers of Notre Dame were an imposing shadow on the Paris skyline for years, but two years of sandblasting has brightened the exterior, revealing the rosary windows and rows of saints. The claustrophobia-inducing staircase emerges onto a spectacular perch, where rows of gargoyles survey the city. In the south tower, a tiny door opens onto the 13-ton bell that even Quasimodo couldn't ring: it requires the force of eight people to move.

INTERIOR. From the inside, the cathedral seems to be constructed of soaring, weightless walls, thanks to the spidery **flying buttresses** that create room for delicate stained-glass walls by supporting the vaults of the ceiling from outside. The transept's **rose windows,** nearly 85% 13th-century glass, are the most spectacular feature. The **treasury,** south of the choir, contains an assortment of gilded artifacts. The famous Crown of Thorns, which is supposed to have been worn by Christ, was moved to Notre Dame at the end of the 18th century. The relic is presented only on Fridays during Lent (5-6pm). Far below the cathedral towers, the **Crypte Archéologique,** pl. du Parvis du Notre Dame, houses artifacts unearthed in the construction of a parking garage. (*M: Cité. ☎01 53 40 60 87, crypt 01 43 29 83 51. Cathedral open daily 8am-6:45pm. Towers open July-Aug. 9am-7:30pm; Apr.-June and Sept. 9:30am-7:30pm; Jan.-Mar. and Oct.-Dec. 10am-5:30pm. €6.10, ages 18-25 €4.10. Tours begin at the booth to the right as you enter. In English W-Th noon, Sa 2:30pm; in French M-F noon, Sa 2:30pm. Free. Confession can be heard in English. Roman Catholic Mass M-F 8, 9am, noon, 6:15pm; Sa 8, 8:45, 10, 11:30am, 12:45, 6:30pm; Vespers sung 5:30pm in the choir. Treasury open M-Sa 9:30am-12:30pm and 1:30-5:30pm, Su 1:30-5:30pm; last ticket at 5pm. €2.50, students and ages 12-17 €2, 6-12 €1, under 6 free. High Mass with Gregorian chant Su 10am, with music at 11:30am, 12:45, 6:30pm. Before Vespers, one of the cathedral organists gives a free recital starting at 4:30pm. Crypt open daily 10am-5:30pm; last ticket sold 30min. before closing. €3.90, over 60 €2.80, under 27 €2.20, under 13 free.*)*

PALAIS DE LA CITÉ

■**STE-CHAPELLE.** Ste-Chapelle remains the foremost example of flamboyant Gothic architecture and medieval stained glass. The chapel was constructed in 1241 to house the most precious of King Louis IX's possessions: the Crown of Thorns from Christ's Passion (now in Notre Dame). The simpler Lower Chapel has portraits of saints beneath the blue vaulted ceiling, but the real star is the breathtaking Upper Chapel. On sunny days, light pours through its walls of stained glass, illuminating frescoes of saints and martyrs. Read from bottom to top, left to right, the 1136 windows narrate the Bible from Genesis to the Apocalypse. (*4 bd. du Palais. M: Cité. Within Palais de la Cité. ☎01 53 73 78 51; www.monum.fr. Open Apr.-Sept. daily 9:30am-6pm. Last admission 30min. before closing. Admission €6.10, seniors and ages 18-25 €4.10, under 18 free. Twin ticket with Conciergerie €9, seniors and ages 18-25 €6, under 18 free. Occasional candlelit, classical music concerts €16-30, held in the Upper Chapel mid-Mar. to Oct. Check at FNAC (www.fnac.fr) or inquire at the information booth to the left of the ticket-taker for details.*)*

CONCIERGERIE. This dark monument to the Revolution stands over the Seine. Originally an administrative building, then a royal prison, it was taken over by the Revolutionary Tribunal after 1793. Rows of cells come complete with preserved props and plastic people. Plaques explain how the rich and famous could buy themselves private rooms with tables for writing while the poor slept on straw in pestilential cells. Among the 2700 people awaiting execution between 1792 and 1794 were Robespierre and Marie Antoinette. *(1 quai de l'Horloge, entrance on bd. du Palais, to the right of Palais de Justice. M: Cité. ☎01 53 73 78 50; www.monum.fr. Open daily Apr.-Sept. 9:30am-6:30pm; Oct.-Mar. 10am-5pm. Last ticket 30min. before closing. €6.10, students €4.10. Includes tour in French, 11am and 3pm. For tours in English, call in advance.)*

PALAIS DE JUSTICE. Built after the great fire of 1776, the Palais is now home to the district courts of France. A wide set of stone steps at the main entrance leads to three doorways marked *"Liberté," "Egalité,"* or *"Fraternité."* All trials are open to the public: choose a door and make your way through the green gates that stand beyond *"Egalité."* Climb the stairs to the second floor and go immediately left (look for signs for "Cour d'Appel") and guards will let you into a viewing gallery. *(Within Palais de la Cité, 4 bd. du Palais; use the entrance for Ste-Chapelle. M: Cité. ☎01 44 32 51 51. Courtrooms open M-F 9am-noon and 1:30-6pm. Free.)*

MÉMORIAL DE LA DÉPORTATION. This haunting memorial commemorates the 200,000 French victims of Nazi concentration camps. Inside, the focal point is a tunnel lined with 200,000 quartz pebbles, reflecting the Jewish custom of placing stones on graves of the deceased. To the sides are empty cells and carvings of concentration camp names. *(M: Cité. At the very tip of the island on pl. de l'Ile de France, a 5min. walk from the back of the cathedral, and down a narrow flight of steps. Open daily Apr.-Sept. 10am-noon and 1-7pm; Oct.-Mar. 10am-noon and 1-5pm. Free.)*

PONT NEUF. Leave Ile de la Cité by the oldest bridge in Paris, Pont Neuf (New Bridge), located just behind pl. Dauphine. Before the Champs-Elysées, it was Paris's most popular thoroughfare, attracting peddlers, performance artists, and thieves.

ILE ST-LOUIS

QUAI DE BOURBON. Sculptor **Camille Claudel** lived and worked at **no. 19** from 1899 until her brother, the poet Paul Claudel, had her committed in 1913. The protegé and lover of sculptor Auguste Rodin, Claudel's most striking work is displayed in the Musée Rodin (p. 145). At the intersection of the quai and rue des Deux Ponts sits the café **Au Franc-Pinot**, whose wrought-iron façade is almost as old as the island itself. Closed in 1716 when authorities discovered a stash of anti-government tracts, the café-cabaret reemerged as a center for treason during the Revolution: Cécile Renault, daughter of the proprietor, mounted an unsuccessful attempt on Robespierre's life in 1794 and was guillotined the following year. Today the Pinot houses a mediocre jazz club.

EGLISE ST-LOUIS-EN-L'ILE. Louis Le Vau's 17th-century Rococo interior is lit by a surprising number of windows. The third chapel has a splendid gilded wood relief, *The Death of the Virgin.* *(19bis rue St-Louis-en-l'Ile. ☎01 46 34 11 60. Open Tu-Su 9am-noon and 3-7pm. Check with FNAC (www.fnac.com) or call the church for concert details; ticket prices vary, around €20 general admission and €15 for students.)*

RIVE GAUCHE

The animated **boulevard St-Michel** runs through the **Latin Quarter,** which encompasses area around the **Sorbonne** and the **Ecole des Beaux-Arts** (School of Fine Arts). The equally lively **rue Mouffetard** is quintessential Latin Quarter. The area around **boulevard St-Germain,** which crosses bd. St-Michel just south of pl. St-Michel, is known as **St-Germain des Prés.** To the west, the gold-domed **Invalides** and the stern Neoclassical **Ecole Militaire,** which faces the **Eiffel Tower** across the **Champ-de-Mars,** recall the military past of the 7*ème* and northern 15*ème,* now a family neighborhood full of traveling businesspeople. South of the Latin Quarter, **Montparnasse** lolls in its tower's shadow. The glam **boulevard Montparnasse** belies the surrounding residential districts. The 13*ème* is a new hot spot, centered on **place d'Italie.**

FIFTH ARRONDISSEMENT

PLACE ST-MICHEL. The busiest spot in the Latin Quarter, pl. St-Michel is where the Paris Commune in 1871 and the student uprising of 1968 took off. The majestic 1860 fountain features bronze dragons, an angelic St-Michel, and a WWII memorial commemorating the citizens who fell here defending their *quartier* in August 1944. Today this end of bd. St-Michel is dotted with several branches of Gibert Jeune and scores of antiquarian booksellers and university presses.

The nearby **Eglise St-Julien-le-Pauvre** (a right off bd. St-Michel and another right onto rue St-Julien-le-Pauvre) is one of the oldest churches in Paris, dating back to 1170. Across bd. St-Jacques is another architectural behemoth, the huge, bizarre **Eglise St-Séverin.** Spiraling columns and modern stained glass ornament the Gothic interior. At the intersection of bd. St-Germain and bd. St-Michel, the **Musée de Cluny's** collection of medieval art, tapestries, and illuminated manuscripts has something to suit just about everyone (see **Museums,** p. 146). Off the major tourist and student thoroughfare **boulevard St-Michel** (or *"Boul' Mich'"*), many of the traditional bistros of the quarter hold their ground on charming nearby streets like **rue Soufflot** and **rue des Fossés St-Jacques.**

LA SORBONNE. Founded in 1253 by Robert de Sorbon as a dormitory for 16 poor theology students, the Sorbonne is one of Europe's oldest universities. Soon after its founding, it became the administrative base for the University of Paris and the site of France's first printing house, opened in 1469. As it grew in power and size, the Sorbonne was often at odds with the authority of the French throne, even siding with England during the Hundred Years' War. Today, the university is safely in the folds of governmental administration, officially known as *Paris IV,* the fourth of the University of Paris's 13 campuses. Its main building, **Ste-Ursule de la Sorbonne,** which is closed to the public, was commissioned in 1642 by Cardinal Richelieu, and is located on rue des Ecoles. Security has been drastically tightened following September 11, but visitors can still stroll through the **Chapelle de la Sorbonne** (entrance off of the pl. de la Sorbonne), an impressive space which houses temporary exhibitions on the arts and letters. The **place de la Sorbonne** is sprinkled with a flavorful assortment of cafés, bookstores, and—during term-time—students. *(45-7 rue des Ecoles. M: Cluny-La Sorbonne or RER: Luxembourg.)*

COLLÈGE DE FRANCE. Created by François I in 1530 to contest the university's authority, the Collège de France stands behind the Sorbonne with the humanist motto "Doce Omnia" ("Teaches Everything") in mosaics on the interior courtyard. The outstanding courses at the Collège, given by such luminaries as Henri Bergson, Pierre Boulez, Paul Valéry, and Milan Kundera, are free and open to all. *(11 pl. Marcelin-Berthelot. M: Maubert-Mutualité. Courses run Sept.-May. Info ☎ 01 44 27 12 11; www.college-de-france.fr. Closed Aug.)*

THE PANTHÉON. The Panthéon is one of Paris's most beautiful buildings, an extravagant landmark in a city known for its extravagance. In 507, King Clovis converted to Christianity and had a basilica designed to accommodate his tomb and that of his wife, Clotilde. Five years later, the basilica became the resting place of **Ste-Geneviève,** who was believed to have protected Paris from the attacking Huns with her prayers. Louis XV, wanting to build a prestigious monument to the saint, entrusted its design to the architect Jacques-Germain Soufflot in 1755. Louis laid the first stone himself in 1764. After Soufflot's death, the neoclassical basilica was continued by architect Jean-Baptiste Rondelet and completed in 1790. The Revolution converted the church into a mausoleum of heroes on April 4, 1791, in an attempt to find a place for proletariat poet Mirabeau's body. In 1806, Napoleon reserved the crypt for those who had given "great service to the State." Some of France's most distinguished citizens are now buried in its crypt, including Marie and Pierre Curie, Jean Jaurès, Louis Braille, Voltaire, Jean-Jacques Rousseau, Emile Zola, and Victor Hugo. Two million mourners followed Hugo's coffin here for its burial in 1885. Fans of *Le Petit Prince* may want to pay homage at the memorial to Antoine de St-Exupéry in the main rotunda.

The Panthéon's other main attraction is **Foucault's Pendulum.** The plane of oscillation of the pendulum stays fixed as the Earth rotates around it. The pendulum's rotation is confirmation of the rotation of the Earth for nonbelievers, such as Louis Napoleon III. (*Pl. du Panthéon. M: Cardinal Lemoine. ☎01 44 32 18 00. Open daily 10am-6pm; last admission 5:15pm. €7, students €4.50, under 18 and the first Su of every month Oct.-Mar. free. Guided tours in French daily at 2:30 and 4pm.*)

PLACE DE LA CONTRESCARPE. South on rue Descartes, past the prestigious Lycée Henri IV, pl. de la Contrescarpe is the geographical center of the 5ème. Lovely outdoor restaurants and cafés cluster around a fountain. From here, it's only a 5min. walk to St-Germain, the Panthéon, or the Jardin des Plantes.

RUE MOUFFETARD. South of pl. de la Contrescarpe, **rue Mouffetard** is home to one of the liveliest street markets in Paris, and is generally crowded with a friendly mix of Parisians and visitors. This most storied of Latin Quarter streets went through various incarnations before ending up as the snaking alley of charming boutiques and restaurants that you see today. Poet Paul Verlaine died at 39 rue Descartes in 1844. Hemingway lived down the Mouff' at 74 rue du Cardinal Lemoine. Perfect for an afternoon stroll or Latin Quarter people-watching is the winding stretch up rue Mouffetard, past pl. de la Contrescarpe, and onto **rue Descartes** and **rue de la Montagne Ste-Geneviève.** (*M: Cardinal Lemoine, Place Monge, or Censier Daubenton.*)

JARDIN DES PLANTES. The Jardin des Plantes has 45,000 sq. m of carefully tended flowers and lush greenery. Opened in 1640 by Louis XIII's doctor, the gardens originally grew medicinal plants to promote His Majesty's health. The **Ecole de Botanique** is a landscaped botanical garden tended by students, horticulturists, and amateur botanists. The **Roserie** contains luscious, fragrant displays of roses from all over the world (in full bloom in mid-June). The botanical boxes of the **Grandes Serres** span two climates. The gardens also include the tremendous **Musée d'Histoire Naturelle** and the **Ménagerie Zoo.** Although no match for the Parc Zoologique in the Bois de Vincennes, the zoo will brighten anyone's day with its 240 mammals, 500 birds, and 130 reptiles. (*M: Gare d'Austerlitz, Jussieu, or Censier-Daubenton. ☎01 40 79 37 94. Jardin des Plantes, Ecole de Botanique, Jardin Alpin, and Roserie open daily summer 7:30am-8pm; winter 7:30am-5:30pm. Free. Grandes Serres, 57 rue Cuvier. Open Apr.-Oct. M and W-F 1-5pm, Sa-Su 1-6pm; Nov.-Mar. M and W-Su 1-5pm. €2.30, students €1.50. Ménagerie Zoo, 3 quai St-Bernard and 57 rue Cuvier. Open daily Apr.-Sept. 10am-6pm, Oct.-Mar. 10am-5:30pm. Last ticket 30min. before closing. €4.60, students €3.10.*)

MOSQUÉE DE PARIS. The Institut Musulman houses the beautiful Persian gardens, elaborate minaret, and shady porticoes of the Mosquée de Paris, constructed in 1920 by French architects to honor the role played by the countries of North Africa in WWI. The cedar doors open onto an oasis of blue and white where Muslims come to meet around the fountains and pray in the carpeted prayer rooms (visible from the courtyard but closed to the public). Frenzied tourists can relax in the steam baths at the exquisite *hammam* (Turkish bath) or sip mint tea at the equally soothing café. *(M: Jussieu. ☎01 48 35 78 17. Open daily June-Aug. 10am-noon and 2-6:30pm, Sept.-May until 5:30pm. Guided tour €3, students €2. Hammam open for men Tu 2-9pm, Su 10am-9pm; women M, W-Th, and Sa 10am-9pm, F 2-9pm; €15. 10min. massage €10, 30min. massage €30, bikini wax €11. MC/V.)*

SHAKESPEARE & CO. BOOKSTORE. A legend among Parisian anglophones, this shop seeks to reproduce the atmosphere of Sylvia Beach's establishment of the same name at 8 rue Dupuytren (later at 12 rue de l'Odéon), which was a gathering place for expatriates in the 20s. The original shop closed in 1941, and George Whitman, alleged grandson of the poet Walt Whitman, opened his rag-tag bookstore, which has itself become a cultish landmark, in 1951. Frequented by Allen Ginsberg and Lawrence Ferlinghetti, Shakespeare hosts poetry readings, Sunday evening tea parties, a literary festival, and other funky events. *(M: St-Michel. 37 rue de la Bucherie. Open daily noon-midnight.)*

INSTITUT DU MONDE ARABE. The Institut du Monde Arabe (IMA) was built to look like a ship to represent those on which Algerian, Moroccan, and Tunisian immigrants sailed to France. It houses permanent and rotating exhibitions on Maghrébin, Near Eastern, and Middle Eastern Arab cultures as well as a library, research facilities, lecture series, film festivals, and a rooftop terrace with gorgeous views of the Seine, Montmartre, and Ile de la Cité. *(M: Jussieu. 1 rue des Fossés St-Bernard. ☎01 40 51 38 38. Walk down rue Jussieu away from the Jardin des Plantes and make your first right onto rue des Fossés St-Bernard. Museum open Tu-Su 10am-6pm. €4, reduced rate €3, under 12 free. Library open July-Aug. Tu-Sa 1-6pm; Sept.-June Tu-Sa 1-8pm. Free.)*

SIXTH ARRONDISSEMENT

JARDIN DU LUXEMBOURG. Parisians flock to these formal gardens to sunbathe or read. A residential area in Roman Paris, the site of a medieval monastery, and later the home of naughty 17th-century French royalty, the gardens were liberated during the Revolution and are now free to all. *(M: Odéon or RER: Luxembourg. Open daily dawn-dusk. The main entrance is on bd. St-Michel. Guided tours in French Apr.-Oct. first W of every month at 9:30am; depart from pl. André Honorat behind the observatory.)*

PALAIS DU LUXEMBOURG. The Palais du Luxembourg in the park now serves as the home of the French Senate. It was built in 1615 for Marie de Médici, and went on to house a number of France's most elite nobility. In later years, it incarcerated those same nobles. One of the palace-jail's most famous residents was the future Empress Josephine and her first husband Beauharnais. During the Nazi occupation, the palace was the headquarters of the *Luftwaffe*. *(www.monum.fr. Infrequent tours May-Sept. Call ☎01 44 54 19 49 to reserve a spot.)*

EGLISE ST-SULPICE. The balconied, neoclassical façade of the huge Eglise St-Sulpice dominates the enormous square of the same name. Designed by Servadoni in 1733, the church remains unfinished. St-Sulpice's claims to fame are a set of fierce, gestural Delacroix frescoes in the first chapel on the right, a *Virgin and Child* by Jean-Baptiste Pigalle in a rear chapel, and an enormous organ. *(M: St-Sulpice or Mabillon. 2 blocks west of the theater. ☎01 46 33 21 78 or 01 42 34 59 60. Open daily 7:30am-7:30pm. Guided tour in French daily 3pm.)*

BOULEVARD ST-GERMAIN. Most famous as the ex-literati hangout of existentialists (who frequented the Café de Flore) and surrealists like André Breton (who preferred the neighboring Les Deux Magots), bd. St-Germain is stuck somewhere between nostalgia for its intellectual café-culture past and an unabashed delight with all things fashionable and cutting edge. The long boulevard is home to scores of cafés both new and old, where expensive cups of coffee can be sipped while watching all manner of stylish Parisians go by. The boulevard and its many sidestreets, particularly around rue de Rennes, have become a serious shopping neighborhood in recent years, filled with high-end designer boutiques, from Louis Vuitton to Emporio Armani.

EGLISE DE ST-GERMAIN-DES-PRÉS. The Eglise de St-Germain-des-Prés is the oldest standing church in Paris, completed in 558. Its only ornate decorations are the pink and white hollyhocks growing to the side. King Childebert I commissioned a church on this site to hold relics he had looted from the Holy Land. The rest of the church's history reads like an architectural Book of Job. It was sacked by the Normans and rebuilt three times. During the Revolution, 15 tons of gunpowder that had been stored in the abbey exploded, devastating much of the church. Baron Haussmann destroyed the last remains of the deteriorating abbey walls and gates when he extended rue de Rennes to the front of the church to create pl. St-Germain-des-Prés. Completely redone in the 19th century, the magnificent interior is painted in shades of maroon, deep green, and gold with enough regal grandeur to counteract the building's modest exterior; especially striking are the royal-blue and gold-starred ceiling, frescoes depicting the life of Jesus, and decorative mosaics along the archways. The information window at the church's entrance has a schedule of the church's frequent concerts. *(M: St-Germain-des-Prés. 3 pl. St-Germain-des-Prés. ☎ 01 55 42 81 33. Open daily 8am-8pm. Info office open M 2:30-6:45pm, Tu-Sa 10:30am-noon and 2:30-6:45pm. Mass in Spanish Su 5pm.)*

ODÉON. **Cour du Commerce St-André** is one of the most picturesque walking areas in the *6ème*, with cobblestone streets, centuries-old cafés (including **Le Procope**), and outdoor seating. Beyond the arch stands the **Relais Odéon,** a Belle Epoque bistro whose stylishly painted exterior is a fine example of art nouveau. Just to the south of bd. St-Germain-des-Prés, the **Carrefour d'Odéon,** is a favorite Parisian hangout filled with bistros, cafés, and more outdoor seating. The **Comptoir du Relais** still holds court here, while newcomer cafés strut their flashy selves across the street.

PONT DES ARTS. The wooden footbridge across from the Institut, at the very heart of France's prestigious Academy of Arts and Letters and thus appropriately called the Pont des Arts, is celebrated for its delicate ironwork and beautiful views of the Seine.

SEVENTH ARRONDISSEMENT

EIFFEL TOWER. Gustave Eiffel, its designer, wrote: "France is the only country in the world with a 300m flagpole." Designed in 1889 as the tallest structure in the world, the Eiffel Tower was conceived as a monument to engineering that would surpass the Egyptian pyramids in size and notoriety. Before construction had begun, shockwaves of dismay reverberated through the city. Critics dubbed it a "metal asparagus" and a Parisian tower of Babel. Writer Guy de Maupassant ate lunch every day at its ground-floor restaurant—the only place in Paris, he claimed, from which he couldn't see the offensive thing.

Nonetheless, when it was inaugurated in March 1889 as the centerpiece of the Universal Exposition, the Eiffel Tower, then considered an impressive wonder of design and engineering, earned the immediate love of the citizenry of Paris; nearly 2 million people ascended during the event alone. As the icon most symbolic of Paris, Eiffel's wonder still takes the heat from some (tourists and residents alike) who see the tower as Maupassant did: an "excruciating nightmare" overrun with tourists and their trinkets. *(M: Bir-Hakeim or Trocadéro. ☎ 01 44 11 23 23; www.tour-eiffel.fr. Open daily mid-June to Aug. 9am-midnight; Sept.-Dec. 9:30am-11pm (stairs 9:30am-6pm); Jan. to mid-June 9:30am-11pm (stairs 9:30am-6:30pm). Elevator to 1st fl. €3.70, under 12 €2.10; 2nd fl. €7/€3.80; 3rd fl. €10.20/€5.30. Stairs to 1st and 2nd fl. €3. Under 3 free. Last access to top 30min. before closing.)*

CHAMPS DE MARS. The Champs de Mars, a tree-lined expanse stretching from the Ecole Militaire to the Eiffel Tower, is named, appropriately enough, after the god of war. Close to the 7ème's monuments and museums, the field was a drill ground for the Ecole Militaire in the days of Napoleon. It also witnessed civilian massacres and political demonstrations during the Revolution. Today, Mars would be ashamed by the flower-strewn lawns filled with tourists and children, not to mention the new glass monument to international peace.

INVALIDES. The gold-leaf dome of the Hôtel des Invalides shines at the center of the 7ème, at the other end of the grassy **Esplanade des Invalides** from the gilded lampposts of **Pont Alexandre III.** The Invalides museum complex houses the **Musée de l'Armée, Musée des Plans-Reliefs, Musée de l'Ordre de la Libération,** and **Napoleon's tomb,** in the **Eglise St-Louis.** Enter from either pl. des Invalides or pl. Vauban and av. de Tourville. *(M: Invalides. 2 av. de Tourville or main entrance at 127 rue de Grenelle.)*

LA PAGODE. A pseudo-Japanese pagoda built in 1895 by the Bon Marché department store magnate M. Morin as a gift to his wife, La Pagode is an artifact of the 19th-century Orientalist craze in France. When Mme. Morin left her husband on the eve of WWI, the building became the scene of Sino-Japanese *soirées.* In 1931, La Pagode opened its doors to the public, becoming a cinema and swank café where silent screen stars like Gloria Swanson were known to raise a glass. The theater closed during the Nazi occupation, despite its friendliness toward German patrons. It reopened under a private owner in November 2000. *(M: St-François-Xavier. 57bis rue de Babylone. ☎ 01 45 55 48 48. Café open daily between show times. Coffee €2.50. MC/V.)*

THIRTEENTH ARRONDISSEMENT

CHINATOWN. Paris's Chinatown lies in the area bounded by rue de Tolbiac, bd. Masséna, av. de Choisy, and av. d'Ivry. It is home to large Chinese, Vietnamese, and Cambodian communities, and a host of Asian restaurants and markets like Tang Frères. The shop windows on av. de Choisy and av. d'Ivry are filled with beautiful embroidered dresses, elegant chopstick sets, ceramic Buddha statuettes, fresh vegetables, and Asian *à la vapeur* specialties.

BIBLIOTHÈQUE NATIONALE DE FRANCE: SITE FRANÇOIS MITTERRAND. This library is the last and most expensive of Mitterrand's *grand projets.* Replacing the old Bibliothèque Nationale in the 2ème (still open to scholars), the new, extensive library is open to the public (except the research rooms, which require special permission). The four L-shaped towers of Dominique Perrault's controversial design are meant to look like open books from above. Inside, the uber-modern building features grand reading rooms and multiple galleries displaying exhibits on photography and the history of sound. *(M: Quai de la Gare or Bibliothèque François Mitterrand. Quai F. Mauriac. ☎ 01 53 79 59 79; www.bnf.fr. Open mid-Sept. to mid-Aug. Su noon-7pm, Tu-Sa 10am-8pm. Open to those over 16. Admission €3; some special exhibits and lectures will charge an additional entrance fee. Annual membership €30. MC/V.)*

FOURTEENTH ARRONDISSEMENT

BOULEVARD MONTPARNASSE. In the early 20th century, Montparnasse became a center for avant-garde artists like Modigliani, Utrillo, Chagall, and Montmartre transplant Léger. Exiles Lenin and Trotsky talked strategy over cognac in the cafés such as **Le Dôme, Le Sélect,** and **La Coupole.** After WWI, Montparnasse attracted American expatriates and artistic rebels like Calder, Hemingway, and Henry Miller, in a bohemian golden age that ended with the Spanish Civil War and WWII. Now heavily commercialized, Montparnasse is crowded with chain restaurants and tourists. Classic restaurants still hold their own, however (the best is the pricey **La Coupole**), and provide a wonderful place to sip a café express and read Apollinaire.

CATACOMBS. A series of tunnels 20m below ground and 1.7km in length, the Catacombs were originally excavated to provide stone for building the city. By the 1770s, much of the Left Bank was in danger of caving in and digging promptly stopped. The former quarry was then used as a mass grave, relieving Paris's foul and overcrowded cemeteries. During WWII, the Resistance set up headquarters there. Their underground city had street names on walls lined with femurs and craniums. Be prepared to climb 85 steep steps if you visit. *(M: Denfert-Rochereau. 1 pl. Denfert-Rochereau. ☎01 43 22 47 63. Open Tu 11am-4pm, W-Sa 9am-4pm. €5, seniors €3.30, ages 14-26 €2.50, under 14 free. Tour 45min.)*

FIFTEENTH ARRONDISSEMENT

LE PARC ANDRÉ CITROËN. The futuristic-looking Parc André Citroën was created by landscapers Alain Provost and Gilles Clément in the 1970s. Rides in the hot-air balloon that launches from the central garden offer spectacular aerial views of the park and of Paris. Located alongside the Seine, the six gardens contain a variety of fountains, huge glass greenhouses, and a wild garden whose plant life changes from one year to the next. In the summer months, the grass is crowded with sunbathers and picnickers of all ages. *(2 rue de la Montagne de la Fage. ☎01 44 26 20 00; www.volenballon.com. M: Javel-André Citroën or Balard. Open M-F 7:30am-9:30pm, Sa-Su 9am-9:30pm. Tours of the park in English; June-Sept. Sa 10:30am; €5.80; call ☎01 40 71 75 60 for more info. Balloon rides €12, ages 12-17 €10, ages 3-11 €6, under 3 free.)*

RIVE DROITE

The *Rive Droite* has long been considered the more fashionable side of the Seine. The **Louvre** and **rue de Rivoli** dominate the sight- and tourist-packed 1*er* and the more business-oriented 2*ème*. The crooked streets of the **Marais**, in the 3*ème* and 4*ème*, escaped Baron Haussmann's redesign of Paris and now support many diverse communities, cafés, and shops. From **place de la Concorde**, at the western end of the 1*er*, **avenue des Champs-Elysées** bisects the 8*ème* as it sweeps up toward the **Arc de Triomphe** at **Charles de Gaulle-Etoile.** South of the Etoile, old and new money fills the exclusive 16*ème*, bordered to the west by the **Bois de Boulogne** park and to the east by the Seine and the upscale **Trocadéro**, which faces the Eiffel Tower across the river. Back toward central Paris, the 9*ème*, just north of the 2*ème*, is defined by the sumptuous **Opéra.** East of the 9*ème*, the 10*ème* hosts cheap lodgings and the **Gare du Nord** and **Gare**

As the saying goes, if you can't stand the heat, then get the hell out of town. Among those who heed this mantra are the citizens of Paris, who, come August, flee their beloved city for the shores of Normandy and the Côte d'Azur. But in the summer of 2002, the city figured out how to bring the beach to Paris. Bertrand Delanoe, the city's mayor, decided to transform 2km of Seine riverfront into "Paris Plage." The result was five patches of "beach"—one of sand, two of grass, and two of pebbles— that stretched from **quai Tuileries** to **quai Henri IV.** Equipped with lounge chairs, parasols, palm trees, and even a volleyball court, the beach drew hordes of sun-hungry citizens. The city has also temporarily closed the road next to the *plage* to car traffic so that visitors can enjoy the sand and sunshine by in-line skating and bicycle-riding along the edge of the beach.

True, the *plage*, for which the city shelled out €1.5 million, has fallen short of paradise. Pollution by Parisians past makes the Seine unfit for swimming. More tragically, perhaps, the city discourages one of Europe's age-old customs: nude sunbathing.

Despite these setbacks, the *plage* was a resounding success, returning for a month in 2003, drawing crowds eager to, if not beat the summer heat, then at least get a tan for their trouble. Just not a seamless one.

de l'Est. The 10*ème*, 3*ème*, and 11*ème*, which claims the newest hip nightlife in Paris (in **Bastille**), meet at **place de la République.** South of Bastille, the 12*ème* surrounds the **Gare de Lyon,** petering out at the **Bois de Vincennes.** East of Bastille, the party atmosphere gives way to the quieter, more residential 20*ème* and 19*ème*, while the 18*ème* is home to the quaint and heavily touristed **Montmartre,** which is capped by the **Sacré-Cœur.** To the east, the 17*ème* begins in the red-light district of **Pigalle** and bd. de Clichy, and grows more elegant toward the Etoile, the **Opéra Garnier,** and the 16*ème*. Farther west along the *grande axe* defined by the Champs-Elysées, the skyscrapers of **La Défense,** Paris's newest quarter, loom across the Seine from Bois de Boulogne.

FIRST ARRONDISSEMENT

JARDIN DES TUILERIES. Sweeping down from the Louvre to pl. de la Concorde, the Jardin des Tuileries celebrates the victory of geometry over nature. Missing the public promenades of her native Italy, Catherine de Médici had the gardens built in 1564. In 1649, André Le Nôtre (gardener for Louis XIV and designer of the gardens at Versailles) imposed straight lines and sculpted trees on the grounds. The elevated terrace by the Seine offers remarkable views of the **Arc de Triomphe du Carrousel** and the glass pyramid of the Louvre's Cour Napoléon. Sculptures by Rodin and others stand amid the garden's cafés and courts. In the summer, the rue de Rivoli terrace becomes an amusement park with children's rides, food stands, and a huge ferris wheel. The **Galerie National du Jeu de Paume** and the **Musée de l'Orangerie** flank the pathway at the Concorde end of the Tuileries. (*M: Tuileries.* ☎*01 40 20 90 43. Open daily Apr.-Sept. 7am-9pm; Oct.-Mar. 7:30am-7:30pm. Tours in English from the Arc de Triomphe du Carrousel. Free; call for details. Amusement park open late June to mid-Aug. Rides €2-15.*)

PLACE VENDÔME. Stately pl. Vendôme, three blocks north of the Tuileries, was begun in 1687 by Louis XIV. Designed by Jules Hardouin-Mansart, the square was built to house embassies, but bankers created lavish private homes behind the elegant façades. Today, the smell of money is still in the air: bankers, perfumers, and jewelers, including Cartier (at no. 7), line the square.

PALAIS-ROYAL. One block north of the Louvre along rue St-Honoré lies the once regal and racy Palais-Royal, constructed in the 17th century as Cardinal Richelieu's Palais Cardinal. After the Cardinal's death in 1642, Anne d'Autriche moved in, with her son, young Louis XIV. In the central courtyard, the controversial **colonnes de Buren,** a set of black-and-white-striped pillars, were installed by artist Daniel Buren in 1986. (*Fountain open daily June-Aug. 7am-11pm; Sept. 7am-9:30pm; Oct.-Mar. 7am-8:30pm; Apr.-May 7am-10:15pm. Free.*)

EGLISE DE ST-EUSTACHE. There is a reason why Richelieu, Molière, and Mme. de Pompadour were all baptized in the Eglise de St-Eustache, why Louis XIV received communion in its sanctuary, and why Mozart chose to have his mother's funeral here. This church is a magnificent blend of history and beauty, honoring Eustache (Eustatius), a Roman general who adopted Christianity upon seeing the sign of a cross between the antlers of a deer. As punishment for converting, the Romans locked him into a brass bull and placed it over a fire. The chapels contain paintings by Rubens, as well as the British artist Raymond Mason's bizarre relief *Departure of the Fruits and Vegetables from the Heart of Paris,* commemorating the closing of the market at Les Halles. (*M: Les Halles. Above rue Rambuteau.* ☎*01 42 36 31 05. Open M-F 9am-7:30pm, Su 9:15am-7:30pm. High mass with choir and organ Su 11am and 6pm. Free organ recital Su 5:30-6pm. Hours and masses vary in Aug.; call in advance.*)

LES HALLES. The metro station Les Halles exits directly into the underground mall. The escalators lead up to the gardens. A sprawling market since 1135, Les Halles received a much-needed face-lift in the 1850s with the construction of large

How Paris cleaned up its act

Like a clock that has lost an hour, eleven straight boulevards radiate outward from pl. Charles de Gaulle. A view through the arc at the foot of the Louvre aligns with the Obelisk in pl. de la Concorde, the Arc de Triomphe, and the modern arch at La Défense. Café-lined streets seem as organic to Paris as its wide tree-lined boulevards and the murky snaking of the Seine. Yet none of this is an accident. And, despite modern notions that Paris is a city to which pleasure—be it amorous, gastronomic, artistic, or commercial—comes naturally, the city's charm is as calculated as the strategic application of paint to a courtesan's lips, and the city wasn't always so beautiful.

Social commentator Maxime Du Camp observed in the mid-19th century: "Paris, as we find it in the period following the Revolution of 1848, was uninhabitable. Its population…was suffocating in the narrow, tangled, putrid alleyways in which it was forcibly confined." Sewers were not used in Paris until 1848, and waste and trash rotted in the Seine. Streets followed a maddening 12th-century design; in some *quartiers*, winding thoroughfares were no wider than 3.5m. Toadstool-like rocks lined the streets, allowing pedestrians to jump to safety as carriages sped by. In the hands of the Seine prefect, Baron Georges-Eugène Haussmann, bureaucrat and architect under Louis Napoleon, nephew of the Corsican emperor, the medieval layout of the city was demolished and replaced with a new urban vision guided by the second emperor's technological, sanitary, and political agenda.

Haussmann replaced the tangle of medieval streets with his sewers, trains, and grand boulevards. The prefect's vision bisected Paris along two central, perpendicular axes: rue de Rivoli and bd. de Sébastopol (which extended across the Seine to bd. St-Michel). Haussmann, proclaiming the necessity of unifying Paris and promoting trade among the different *arrondissements*, saw the old streets as antiquated impediments to modern commercial and political progress. His wide boulevards swept through whole neighborhoods of cramped row houses and little passageways; incidentally, he displaced 350,000 of Paris's poorest residents.

The widespread rage at Haussmann's plans reinforced the emperor's desire to use the city's layout to reinforce his authority. The old, narrow streets had been ideal for civilian insurrection in preceding revolutions; rebels built barricades across street entrances and blocked off whole areas of the city from the government's military. Haussmann believed that creating *grands boulevards* and carefully mapping the city could bring to an end the use of barricades and prevent future uprisings. However, he was gravely mistaken. During the 1871 revolt of the Paris Commune, which saw the deposition of Louis Napoleon and the rise of the Third Republic, the *grands boulevards* proved ideal for the construction of higher and stronger barricades.

Despite the underlying political agenda of Haussmannization, many of the prefect's changes were for the better. Haussmann transformed the open-air dump and grave (for the offal of local butchers and the bodies of prisoners) at Montfauçon with the whimsical waterfalls, cliffs, and grottos of Park Buttes-Chaumont. Paris became eminently navigable, and to this day a glance down one of Paris's many *grands boulevards* will offer the *flâneur* an unexpected lesson in the layout of Paris. Stroll down bd. Haussmann, the street bearing this architect's name. En route to the ornate Opéra Garnier, one glimpses the Church of the Madeleine and Gare St-Lazare; The layout silently links these monuments to religion, art, and industry. The façades of the *grands magasins* (department stores) Printemps and Galeries Lafayette respectively resemble a temple and a theater, again suggesting something of the religious and the panoptic in the art of strolling and shopping along Paris's grand streets.

It is hard to imagine Paris as a sewerless, alley-ridden metropolis; but the Paris of today seems perhaps all the more beautiful if we do so.

Charlotte Houghteling *has worked on Let's Go's Middle East, Egypt, and Israel titles. She wrote her senior thesis on the development of department stores during the Second Empire and will complete her M.Phil at Cambridge on the consumer society of Revolutionary Paris.*

Sarah Houghteling *was a researcher-writer for Let's Go: France 1999. She taught at the American School in Paris for a year. Now a graduate student in creative writing at the University of Michigan, she is currently in Paris researching Nazi art theft during World War II.*

iron-and-glass pavilions to shelter the vendors' stalls. In 1970, when authorities moved the old market to a suburb, planners destroyed the pavilions to build a subterranean transfer-point between the metro and the new commuter rail and a subterranean shopping mall, the **Forum des Halles,** with over 200 boutiques and three movie theaters. Watch out for pickpockets.

SECOND ARRONDISSEMENT

GALLERIES AND PASSAGES. In the early 19th century, speculators built **passageways** designed to attract window shoppers using sheets of glass held in place by lightweight iron rods, a startling new design.

The most beautiful remaining passage, the **Grand Cerf,** 10 rue Dussoubs to 145 rue St-Denis, is worth visiting for its stained-glass portal windows and exquisite ironwork. The Grand Cerf has the highest glass-and-iron arches in Paris. Returning to rue Etienne Marcel, walk 10min. until you reach rue Montmartre on your right. Follow rue Montmartre onto bd. Montmartre. Between bd. Montmartre and rue St-Marc is the oldest of the galleries, **Passage des Panoramas,** 10 rue St-Marc and 11 bd. Montmartre. Built in 1799, it contains a 19th-century glass-and-tile roof and a collection of ethnic restaurants. A chocolate shop (François Marquis), a printer (at no. 8), and an engraver (at no. 47) have all managed to stay open since the 1830s. Across bd. Montmartre, mirroring the Passage des Panoramas, **Passages Jouffry** and **Verdeau** are filled with charming toy shops, bookstores, and gift shops. From bd. Montmartre, make a left onto rue Vivienne. On your left just before you reach the Palais-Royal are the most fashionable *galeries* of the 1820s. Inlaid marble mosaics swirl along the floor, and stucco friezes grace the entrance of **Galerie Vivienne,** 4 rue des Petits Champs to 6 rue Vivienne. Built in 1823, Vivienne today boasts the boutique of bad boy Jean-Paul Gaultier.

BIBLIOTHÈQUE NATIONALE: SITE RICHELIEU. With 12 million volumes, including Gutenberg Bibles and first editions from the 15th century, the Bibliothèque Nationale, of which Richelieu is a branch, is possibly the largest library in Continental Europe. Since 1642, every book published in France has been legally required to enter the national archives. At one point, books considered a little too titillating for public consumption descended into a room named "Hell." In the late 1980s, the French government built the mammoth **Bibliothèque de France** in the 13*ème* (p. 130), where the collections from the Richelieu branch were relocated between 1996 and 1998. Richelieu still holds collections of stamps, money, photography, medals, and maps, as well as original manuscripts written on everything from papyrus to parchment. Scholars must pass through a strict screening process to gain access to the main reading room. For the general public, the **Galerie Mazarin** and **Galerie Mansart** host excellent temporary exhibits of books, prints, and lithographs. Upstairs, the **Cabinet des Médailles** displays coins, medallions, and confiscated *objets d'art* from the Revolution. *(M: Bourse. 58 rue de Richelieu. Just north of the Galeries Vivienne and Colbert, across rue Vivienne. Info ☎01 53 79 59 59, galleries 01 47 03 81 10, cabinet 01 47 03 83 30; www.bnf.fr. Library open M-Sa 9am-7pm. Books available only to researchers who prove they need access to the collection. Tours of the former reading room (through a window), La Salle Labrouste, first Tu of the month 2:30pm in English and French; €6.90; ☎01 53 79 86 87. Galleries open Sa 10am-7pm, Su noon-7pm, only when there are exhibits. €5, students €4. Cabinet des Médailles open M-F 1-6pm, Sa 1-5pm. Free.)*

THIRD ARRONDISSEMENT

RUE VIEILLE-DU-TEMPLE. This street is lined with stately residences including the 18th-century **Hôtel de la Tour du Pin** (no. 75) and the more famous **Hôtel de Rohan** (no. 87). Built for Armand-Gaston de Rohan, Bishop of Strasbourg and alleged love-child of Louis XIV, the *hôtel* has housed many of his descendants. Frequent temporary exhibits allow access to the interior *Cabinet des Singes* and its original decorations. The Hôtel also boasts an impressive courtyard and rose garden. Equally engaging are the numerous art galleries that have taken root on the street. At the corner of rue des Francs-Bourgeois and rue Vieille-du-Temple, the flamboyant Gothic **Hôtel Hérouët** and its turrets were built in 1528 for Louis XII's treasurer, Hérouët. *(M: Hôtel-de-Ville or St-Paul. Info on guided tours ☎ 01 40 27 63 94.)*

ARCHIVES NATIONALES. In the 18th-century Hôtel de Soubise, the **Musée de l'Histoire de France** exhibits the most famous documents of the National Archives, including the Treaty of Westphalia, the Edict of Nantes, the Declaration of the Rights of Man, Marie-Antoinette's last letter, Louis XVI's diary, letters between Benjamin Franklin and George Washington, and Napoleon's will. Documents are displayed only in temporary exhibits. *(M: Rambuteau. 60 rue des Francs-Bourgeois. ☎ 01 40 27 60 96. Open M-F 10am-12:30pm and 2-5:30pm, Sa-Su 2-5:30pm.)*

MÉMORIAL DU MARTYR JUIF INCONNU. The Memorial to the Unknown Jewish Martyr is the child of a 1956 committee that included de Gaulle, Churchill, and Ben-Gurion; it commemorates European Jews who died at the hands of the Nazis and their French collaborators. Usually located in the 4*ème*, the memorial was under renovation in 2003; the address below is temporary. *(M: St-Paul. 37 rue de Turenne. ☎ 01 42 77 44 72; fax 01 48 87 12 50. Exposition open M-Th 10am-1pm and 2-5:30pm, F 10am-1pm and 2-5pm. Archives open M-W 11am-5:30pm, Th 11am-8pm.)*

FOURTH ARRONDISSEMENT

RUE DES ROSIERS. At the heart of the Jewish community of the Marais, rue des Rosiers is packed with kosher shops, butchers, bakeries, and falafel counters. Until the 13th century, Paris's Jewish community was concentrated in front of Notre Dame. When Philippe-Auguste expelled the Jewish population from the city limits, many families moved to the Marais, just outside the walls. Since then, this quarter has taken in the influx of Russian Jews in the 19th century and new waves of North African Sephardim fleeing Algeria in the 1960s. During WWII, many who had fled to France to escape the pogroms of Eastern Europe were murdered by the Nazis. Assisted by French police, Nazi soldiers stormed the Marais and hauled Jewish families to the Vélodrome d'Hiver, an indoor cycling stadium, where they awaited deportation to work camps like Drancy, in a northeastern suburb of Paris, or to camps farther east in Poland and Germany. Today, the Jewish community thrives, with two synagogues, at 25 rue des Rosiers and 10 rue Pavée, both designed by art nouveau architect Hector Guimard. The mix of Mediterranean and Eastern European Jewish cultures gives the area a unique flavor, with kugel and falafel served side by side. *(M: St-Paul.)*

RUE VIEILLE-DU-TEMPLE & RUE STE-CROIX DE LA BRETTONERIE. The epicenter of Paris's thriving gay community, the intersection of rue Vieille-du-Temple and rue Ste-Croix de la Brettonerie boasts stylish men and beautiful boys in tight pants out to cruise and be cruised. Although many establishments fly the rainbow flag, gay and straight go together: chic women wander through trendy boutiques while intellectuals of all orientations sip merlot at **La Belle Hortense,** a bookish oasis in this on-the-move and in-the-scene enclave. Day or night, come play where the boys are—if you can stand the heat. *(M: St-Paul or Hôtel-de-Ville.)*

HÔTEL DE VILLE. Paris's grandiose city hall dominates a large square with fountains and Belle Epoque lampposts. The present edifice is a 19th-century creation built to replace the original medieval structure, a meeting hall for the cartel that controlled traffic on the Seine. Municipal executions took place on pl. Hôtel-de-

Ville: in 1610, Henri IV's assassin Ravaillac was drawn and quartered here. On May 24, 1871, the *communards* doused the building with petrol and set it on fire. The blaze, which lasted eight days, spared only the frame. The Third Republic built a virtually identical structure on the ruins. Poised on a marshy embankment *(grève)* of the Seine, the medieval square served as a meeting ground for angry workers, giving France the useful phrase *en grève* (on strike). Strikers and riot police still gather here. Less frequently, the square hosts concerts, TV broadcasts, and light shows. *(29 rue de Rivoli. M: Hôtel-de-Ville.* ☎*01 42 76 43 43. Open M-F 9am-6:30pm when there is an exhibit, until 6pm otherwise. Tours given by individual lecturers available for groups with advance reservations; the Hôtel provides a list of lecturers, their dates, and phone numbers. Some lecturers offer English tours.)*

TOUR ST-JACQUES. The Tour St-Jacques stands alone in the center of its own park. This flamboyant Gothic tower is the only remnant of the 16th-century Eglise St-Jacques-la-Boucherie. The 52m tower's meteorological station and the statue of Pascal at its base commemorate Pascal's experiments on the weight of air, performed here in 1648. The tower was closed for renovations in 2003 and is scheduled to reopen in 2004. *(39-41 rue de Rivoli. M: Hôtel-de-Ville. Two blocks west of the Hôtel-de-Ville.)*

HÔTEL DE SENS. The Hôtel de Sens is one of the city's few surviving examples of medieval residential architecture. Built in 1474 for Tristan de Salazar, the Archbishop of Sens, its military features reflect the violence of those times. The turrets were designed to guard the streets outside; the square tower served as a dungeon. An enormous Gothic arch entrance is carved with chutes for pouring boiling water on invaders. The former residence of Queen Margot, Henri IV's first wife, the Hôtel de Sens has witnessed some of Paris's most daring romantic escapades. In 1606, the 55-year-old queen drove up to her beautiful courtyard to find her two lovers-of-the-month arguing. One opened the lady's carriage door, and the other shot him dead. Unfazed, the queen ordered the perpetrator's execution. The *hôtel* now houses the **Bibliothèque Forney.** *(M: Pont Marie. 1 rue du Figuier. Courtyard open to the public. Library open Tu-F 1:30-8:30pm, Sa 10am-8:30pm; closed early to mid-July.)*

EGLISE ST-PAUL-ST-LOUIS. The Eglise St-Paul-St-Louis dominates rue St-Antoine, its large dome, characteristic of Jesuit architecture, is visible from afar. Its first stone was placed by Louis XIII in 1627. Paintings inside the dome depict four French kings: Clovis, Charlemagne, Robert the Pious, and St-Louis. Before being destroyed during the Revolution, the embalmed hearts of Louis XIII and Louis XIV were kept in vermeil boxes guarded by gilded silver angels. The church's Baroque interior is graced with three 17th-century paintings of the life of St-Louis, as well as Eugène Delacroix's dramatic *Christ in the Garden of Olives* (1826). The holy-water vessels were gifts from Victor Hugo. *(M: St-Paul. 99 rue St-Antoine.* ☎*01 49 24 11 43. Open M-Sa 8am-9pm, Su 9am-8:30pm. Free tours at 3pm, every 2nd Su of the month. Mass M 7pm; Tu, W, and F 9am and 7pm; Th 9am, 7, 10pm; Sa 9am and 6pm; Su 9:30, 11:15am, 7pm.)*

PLACE DES VOSGES. The magnificent pl. des Vosges, at the end of rue des Francs-Bourgeois, is Paris's oldest public square and one of its most charming spots for a picnic or afternoon siesta. The central park, lined with immaculately manicured trees centered around a splendid fountain, is surrounded by 17th-century Renaissance townhouses. Kings built several mansions on this site, including the Palais de Tournelles, which Catherine de Médici ordered destroyed after her husband Henri II died there in a jousting tournament in 1563. Henri IV subsequently ordered it rebuilt.

Each of the 36 buildings lining the square has arcades on street level, two stories of pink brick, and a slate-covered roof. The largest townhouse, forming the square's main entrance, was the king's pavilion. Originally intended for merchants, pl. Royale attracted elites like Mme. de Sevigné and Cardinal Richelieu. Molière, Racine, and

Voltaire filled the grand parlors with their *bon mots,* and Mozart played a concert here at the age of seven. Even when the city's nobility moved across the river to the Faubourg St-Germain, pl. Royale remained among the most elegant spots in Paris. During the Revolution, however, the 1639 Louis XIII statue in the center of the park was destroyed (the statue there now is a copy), and the park was renamed pl. des Vosges after the first department in France to pay its taxes. **Victor Hugo** lived at no. 6, which is now a museum of his life and work. *(M: Chemin Vert or St-Paul.)*

HÔTEL DE SULLY. Built in 1624, the Hôtel de Sully was eventually acquired by the Duc de Sully, the minister under Henri IV. Often cuckolded by his young wife, Sully would tease when giving her money, *"Voici tant pour la maison, tant pour vous, et tant pour vos amants."* ("Here's some for the house, some for you, and some for your lovers.") The small inner courtyard of the hotel offers the fatigued tourist several stone benches and an elegant formal garden. The *hôtel* occasionally hosts small exhibits. *(M: St-Paul. 62 rue St-Antoine. ☎01 44 61 20 00. Open M-Th 9am-12:45pm and 2-6pm, F 9am-12:45pm and 2-5pm.)*

EIGHTH ARRONDISSEMENT

ARC DE TRIOMPHE. The world's largest triumphal arch, looming gloriously above the Champs-Elysées at pl. Charles de Gaulle-Etoile, was first designed as a huge, bejeweled elephant by architect Ribart. Fortunately for France, construction did not begin until 1805, when Napoleon envisioned a more appropriate monument to welcome troops. Construction stalled during Napoleon's exile, but Louis XVIII ordered it completed in 1823 to commemorate the war in Spain, though still allowing the names of Napoleon's generals and battles to be engraved inside.

In 1871, the victorious Prussians marched through in 1871; mortified Parisians later purified the ground with fire. On July 14, 1919, the Arc provided the backdrop for an Allied celebration parade headed by Maréchal Foch. During WWII, Frenchmen were reduced to tears as the Nazis goose-stepped through their beloved arch. After the torturous years of German occupation, a sympathetic Allied army made sure a French general would be the first to drive under the famous edifice.

The **Tomb of the Unknown Soldier** has been under the Arc since November 11, 1920. Its marker bears the inscription, "Here lies a French soldier who died for his country, 1914-1918." It represents the 1½ million men who died during WWI. Inside the Arc, 205 winding steps (and an elevator) lead up to the *entresol* between the Arc's two supports; a museum is 29 steps farther up. The observation deck above provides a brilliant view of the Champs-Elysées, tree-lined av. Foch, and the "Axe Historique"—from the Arc de Triomphe du Carrousel and the Louvre Pyramid at one end to the Grande Arche de la Défense at the other. *(M: Charles de Gaulle-Etoile. ☎01 44 09 89 84. Open daily Apr.-Sept. 10am-11pm; Oct.-Mar. 10am-10:30pm. Last entry 30min. before closing. €7, ages 18-25 €4.50, under 17 free.)*

AVENUE DES CHAMPS-ELYSÉES. The av. des Champs-Elysées is the most famous of the 12 symmetrical avenues radiating from the huge rotary of pl. Charles de Gaulle-Etoile. Although it has been a fashionable avenue since Marie de Médici ploughed its first incarnation, the Cours-la-Reine, through fields and marshland in 1616, it remained unkempt until the early 19th century, when the city built sidewalks and installed gas lighting. From that point on, the Champs flourished, and elegant houses, restaurants, and bars sprang up. No. 25, is a true *hôtel particulier* from the Second Empire—here the Marquise de Paiva, famous adventuress, courtesan, and spy, entertained luminaries of the era. In recent years, the Champs has become thoroughly commercialized, and its glamour has faded, though Jacques Chirac has made a concerted effort to resurrect the avenue, widening the sidewalks, planting more trees, and building underground parking lots. Today, the ave-

THE LOCAL STORY

COUTURE CULTURE

Every year, in January and July, the stars collide (literally): models, designers, actresses, and heireses descend on Paris for the *haute couture* fashion shows. Journalists and groupies follow in their wake—and the world, or at least the part of it that cares about fashion, watches.

Haute couture (high fashion) is a strictly defined business, subject to regulations of the French Department of Industry. Only 18 houses qualify as *haute couturiers* today, employing 4500 designers and craftspeople. Every *haute* garment is made by hand and fitted precisely to the body of the model or client. Due to the astronomical price tags—dresses can cost up to US$100,000—there are only 1500 *couture* clients in the world (there were 15,000 in 1947). Many of the designs are totally unwearable, made only for the runway spectacle. *Couture* houses gain most profit from the less expensive **prêt-a-porter** (ready-to-wear) lines and from overpriced fragrances and cosmetics.

Some have claimed that due to dwindling profits and supposedly lessening creativity, *haute couture* will soon die out. But it continues to be defended by designers and scholars, who see it as the space where fashion forgets practicality and becomes art, and by the government, which sees it as a part of French cultural heritage—and to influence, however indirectly, what the world wears.

nue is an intriguing mixture of old and new, as tourists tramp through enormous superstores and dance until dawn in glitzy nightclubs amid pockets of greenery and remnants of timeless grandeur. The tree-lined streets merge with park space just past av. Franklin D. Roosevelt. Avenue Montaigne, lined with Paris's finest houses of *haute couture*, runs southwest. An enormous **tourist office** is at no. 127.

GRAND & PETIT PALAIS. At the foot of the Champs-Elysées, the Grand and Petit Palais face one another on av. Winston Churchill. Built for the 1900 World's Fair, they exemplify the ornate art nouveau architecture. While the Petit Palais (**closed for renovations** until winter 2004-05) houses an eclectic mix of artwork, its big brother has been turned into a space for temporary exhibitions on architecture, painting, sculpture, and French history. The Grand Palais also houses the **Palais de la Découverte**, a science museum/playground for children (see **Museums**, p. 147). The Palais is most beautiful at night, when its statues are backlit and the glass dome glows green from within.

PLACE DE LA CONCORDE. Paris's largest and most infamous public square forms the eastern terminus of the Champs-Elysées. With your back to av. Gabriel, the Tuileries Gardens are to your left; the gold-domed Invalides and the columns of the Assemblée Nationale are straight ahead, across the river; and the Madeleine is behind. Constructed from 1757 to 1777 to house a monument to Louis XV, it later became pl. de la Révolution, the site of the guillotine that severed 1343 necks from their blue-blooded bodies. On Sunday, January 21, 1793, Louis XVI was beheaded by guillotine on a site near where the Brest statue now stands. The celebrity heads of Marie-Antoinette, Lavoisier, Danton, Robespierre, and others rolled into baskets here and were held up to cheering crowds. After the Reign of Terror, the square was optimistically renamed pl. de la Concorde (Square of Harmony), though the noise pollution of the cars zooming through is somewhat less than harmonious.

In the center of the *place* is the **Obélisque de Luxor.** Transplanted to Paris in 1836, Paris's oldest monument dates back to the 13th century BC. At night the obelisk, fountains, and cast-iron lamps are illuminated, creating a romantic glow. Flanking the Champs-Elysées at pl. de la Concorde stand replicas of Guillaume Coustou's **Chevaux de Marly,** also known as *Africans Mastering the Numidian Horses*. The originals are now in the Louvre.

MADELEINE. Mirrored by the Assemblée Nationale across the Seine, the Madeleine was begun in 1764 by Louis XV and modeled after a Greek temple. Construction was halted during the Revolution, but was completed in 1842. The structure stands alone amongst a medley of Parisian churches, distinguished by four ceiling domes that light the interior, 52 exterior Corinthian columns, and a curious altarpiece. A sculpture of the ascension of Mary Magdalene, the church's namesake, adorns the altar. A colorful flower market thrives alongside the church. *(M: Madeleine. ☎ 01 44 51 69 00. Open daily 7:30am-7pm. Regular organ and chamber concerts; contact the church for a schedule and Virgin or FNAC for tickets.)*

CHAPELLE EXPIATOIRE. The Chapelle Expiatoire is the pl. Louis XVI's monument to Marie Antoinette and Louis XVI. Louis XVIII had his brother's and sister-in-law's remains removed to St-Denis in 1815, but the Revolution's Most Wanted still lie here. Marat's assassin Charlotte Corday and Louis XVI's cousin Philippe-Egalité are buried on either side of the staircase. *(M: Madeleine. 29 rue Pasquier, pl. Louis XVI, below bd. Haussmann. ☎ 01 44 32 18 00. Open Th-Sa 1-5pm. €2.50, under 18 free.)*

PARC MONCEAU. This expansive urban oasis, guarded by gold-tipped, wrought-iron gates, borders the elegant bd. de Courcelles. An array of architectural follies—a pyramid, a covered bridge, an East Asian pagoda, Dutch windmills, Roman ruins, and roller rink—make this formal garden and kids' romping ground a Kodak commercial waiting to happen. *(M: Monceau or Courcelles. Open daily Apr.-Oct. 7am-10pm; Nov.-Mar. 7am-8pm. Last entrance 15min. before closing.)*

CATHÉDRALE ALEXANDRE-NEVSKI. Built in 1860, the onion-domed Eglise Russe, also known as Cathédrale Alexandre-Nevski, is a Russian Orthodox church. The spectacular and recently restored domes were intricately painted by artists from St-Petersburg in gold, deep reds, blues, and greens. The cathedral is the modern center of Russian culture in Paris. *(M: Ternes. 12 rue Daru. ☎ 01 42 27 37 34. Open Tu, F, Su 3-5pm. Services in French and Russian Su 10am, Sa 6-8 pm.)*

NINTH ARRONDISSEMENT

▧ OPÉRA GARNIER. The stunning exterior of the Opéra Garnier, with its restored multi-colored marble façade and sculpted goddesses, is one of the most breathtaking sights in all of Paris. Designed by Charles Garnier under Napoleon III, the Opéra is perhaps most famous for being home to the Phantom of the Opera. *(M: Opéra. General info and reservations ☎ 08 36 69 78 68, tour info 01 40 01 22 63; www.opera-de-paris.fr. Concert hall and museum open daily mid-July to Aug. 10am-6pm, last entry 5:30pm; Sept. to mid-July 10am-5pm, last entry 4:30pm. €6; ages 10-16, students and over 60 €3. English tours daily at noon and 2pm. €10; students, ages 10-16, and over 60 €8; under 10 €4.)*

EGLISE NOTRE-DAME-DE-LORETTE. Built in 1836 to "the glory of the Virgin Mary," this neoclassical church is filled with statues of saints and frescoes depicting the life of Mary. **Rue Notre-Dame-de-Lorette,** however, somewhat less saintly than its namesake, was the debauched hangout of Emile Zola's Nana and a thoroughfare of ill repute in the late 1960s. *(Pl. Kossuth. M: Notre-Dame-de-Lorette.)*

PIGALLE. Farther north, at the border of the 18*ème*, the salacious, voracious, and generally naughty area of Pigalle stretches along trash-covered bd. de Clichy from pl. Pigalle to pl. Blanche, home to famous cabarets-*cum*-nightclubs (Folies Bergère, Moulin Rouge, Folies Pigalle) and well-endowed newcomers with names like "Le Coq Hardy" and "Dirty Dick." The areas north of bd. Clichy and south of pl. Blanche are comparatively calmer, but visitors should **exercise caution.** *(M: Pigalle.)*

TENTH ARRONDISSEMENT

CANAL ST-MARTIN. The most pleasant area of the 10*ème* is unquestionably the tree-lined Canal St-Martin. The 4.5km canal has several locks, which can be observed on one of the Canauxrama trips. The canal was built in 1825 as a shortcut for river traffic on the Seine (to which it no longer connects), and it also served as a defense against the upstart eastern *arrondissements*. This currently residential area is being rediscovered by Parisians and tourists alike, who stroll the tree-lined sides of the canal to check out the new upscale shops and restaurants and the antique market that takes place on Sundays along the quai de Valmy. *(M: République or Goncourt will take you to the more beautiful end of the canal.)*

ELEVENTH ARRONDISSEMENT

THE BASTILLE PRISON. Originally commissioned by Charles V to safeguard the eastern entrance to Paris, Bastille was later made into a state prison by Louis XIII, though it was hardly the hell-hole the Revolutionaries who tore it down imagined. Titled inmates were allowed to furnish their suites and bring their own servants.

Revolutionaries stormed the Bastille for munitions in 1789. Surrounded by armed rabble, too short on food to entertain a siege, and unsure of the loyalty of the Swiss mercenaries who defended the prison, the Bastille's governor surrendered. Defarge & Co. demolished it the next day. Today, the **July Column,** at one corner of pl. de la Bastille, commemorates the site where the prison once stood. Since the late 19th century, July 14 has been the official state holiday of the French Republic, and is usually a time of glorious firework displays and equally glorious alcohol consumption. *(M: Bastille.)*

TWELFTH ARRONDISSEMENT

OPÉRA BASTILLE. One of Mitterrand's *Grands Projets*, the Opéra opened in 1989 to protests over its unattractive design. On the impressive tour you'll see a different side of the largest theater in the world. The immense auditorium seats 2703 people, but 95% of the building is taken up by exact replicas of the stage for rehearsals and workshops. *(M: Bastille. 130 rue de Lyon. ☎ 01 40 01 19 70; www.opera-de-paris.fr. 1hr. tour almost every day, usually at 1 or 5pm; call ahead. Tours in French, but groups of ten or more can arrange for English. €10, over 60 €8, students and under 26 €5.)*

VIADUC DES ARTS AND PROMENADE PLANTÉE. The *ateliers* in the **Viaduc des Arts** house artisans who make everything from *haute couture* fabric to hand-painted porcelain. Restorers of all types fill the arches of the old railway viaduct; they can make an oil painting, 12th-century book, or childhood dollhouse look as good as new. Interspersed among the stores are gallery spaces that are rented by new artists each month. High above the avenue, on the "roof" of the viaduct, runs the rose-filled **Promenade Plantée,** Paris's skinniest park. *(M: Bastille. 9-129 av. Daumesnil. Entrances to the Promenade at Ledru Rollin, Hector Malot, and bd. Diderot. Open M-F 8am, Sa-Su 9am; closing hours vary, around 5:30pm in winter and 9:30pm in summer.)*

SIXTEENTH ARRONDISSEMENT

PLACE D'IÉNA. Pl. d'Iéna, next to the rotunda of the **Conseil Economique,** is in front of a sweep of popular museums, including the round façade of the **Musée Guimet,** the **Musée de la Mode et du Costume,** and the **Palais de Tokyo,** just down the street. Henri Bouchard's impressive façade for the **Eglise St-Pierre de Chaillot** lies between rue de Chaillot and av. Pierre I de Serbie, 5min. away. *(M: Iéna. Open M-Sa 9:30am-12:30pm and 3-7pm, Su 9:30am-12:30pm.)*

PLACE DU TROCADÉRO. In the 1820s, the Duc d'Angoulême built a memorial to his victory in Spain at Trocadéro. Jacques Carlu's modern design for the 1937 World Exposition (which beat out Le Corbusier's plan) for the **Palais de Chaillot** features two white stone wings cradling an austere, Art Deco courtyard that extends from the *place* over spectacular cannon-shaped fountains. Surveyed by Henri Bouchard's 7.5m bronze **Apollo** and eight other figures, the terrace attracts tourists, vendors, skateboarders, and in-line skaters and offers brilliant panoramic views of the Eiffel Tower and Champs de Mars, particularly at night. Be aware of possible pickpockets and of traffic as you gaze upward.

PASSY AND AUTEUIL. Located southwest of Trocadéro, **Passy** and **Auteuil,** famous for their avant-garde architecture, once attracted such visitors as Molière, Racine, and Proust with their restorative waters. Now, the ex-hamlets are a pricey shopping district, best known as the site where *Last Tango in Paris* was filmed. The intersection of **rue Passy, rue Mozart,** and **avenue Paul Doumer,** near M: La Muette, is the glitziest spot. The narrow, winding streets named after famous composers, writers, and artists recall 18th-century *salon* culture. **No. 59 rue d'Auteuil** was the site of Mme. Helvetius's house, where the so-called "Notre Dame d'Auteuil" hosted her notorious *salons*.

SEVENTEENTH ARRONDISSEMENT

VILLAGE BATIGNOLLES. In the eastern half of the 17*ème*, **rue des Batignolles** is considered the center of the Village Batignolles, a quiet, old-fashioned village of shops and residences starting at bd. des Batignolles to the south and extending up to **place du Dr. Félix Lobligeois.** Just north of the *place*, the craggy waterfalls and duck-ponds of the romantic park, **square des Batignolles,** recall its more famous neighbor to the south, the English-style **Parc Monceau** (p. 139); it was from the park's western end that Monet painted the train tracks running from the southern Gare St-Lazare. To the west, restaurants and cafés line **rue des Dames,** while shops stand on **rue de Lévis** (M: Villiers). On the other side of rue des Batignolles, at **rue Lemercier** between rue Clairaut and rue des Moines (M: Brochant), is a daily covered market filled with meat, cheese, flowers, produce, and old women who have shopped here since WWII. **La Cité des Fleurs,** 59-61 rue de la Jonquière (at the intersection with rue des Epinettes), is a row of exquisite private homes and gardens that look like they were lifted out of a Balzac novel. Designed in 1847, this prototypical condominium required each owner to plant at least three trees in the gardens.

EIGHTEENTH ARRONDISSEMENT

MOUNTING MONTMARTRE. Montmartre is Paris's northernmost area, with a distinctly artsy and bohemian character. The standard approach up this hill is from the south, via M: Anvers or M: Abbesses, although other directions provide interesting, less-crowded paths up. The glass-covered **funicular** from the base of rue Tardieu provides a less difficult ascent. From M: Anvers, walk up rue Steinkerque and take a left onto rue Tardieu. *(Funicular runs cars up and down the hill every 2min. Open daily 6am-12:30am. €1.30 or metro ticket.)*

BASILIQUE DU SACRÉ-COEUR. In 1873, the Assemblée Nationale selected the birthplace of the Commune as the location for Sacré-Coeur, "in witness of repentance and as a symbol of hope," although politician Eugène Spuller called it "a monument to civil war." The Catholic establishment hoped that Sacré-Coeur would "expiate the sins" of France after the bloody civil war in which thousands of *communards* (leftists who declared a new populist government) were massacred by government troops. After a massive fund-raising effort, the basilica was completed in 1914 and consecrated in 1919. Its hybrid style of onion domes, arches, and white color set it apart from the smoky grunge of most Parisian buildings. Most striking inside the basilica are the **mosaics,** especially the depiction of Christ on the ceiling and the mural of the Passion at the back of the altar. The narrow climb up the dome offers the highest vantage point in Paris and a view that stretches as far as 50km on clear days. Farther down, the **crypt** contains a relic that many believe to be a piece of the heart of Christ. While the views up the grassy slopes to the basilica are among the most beautiful in Paris, the streets beneath the winding pedestrian pathways leading up to the basilica are over-touristed; to circumvent the onslaught, walk up rue des Trois Frères instead. *(M: Anvers, Abbesses, or Château-Rouge. 35 rue du Chevalier de la Barre. ☎ 01 53 41 89 00. Open daily 7am-10:30pm. Wheelchair-accessible. Free. Dome and crypt open daily 9am-6:45pm. €5.)*

RUES DES ABBESSES & LEPIC. Great restaurants, trendy cafés, and *boulangeries* crowd around rue des Abbesses and rue Lepic. Tall iron gates hide the beautiful gardens of 18th-century townhouses. Walking down rue Lepic will carry you past the **Moulin Radet,** one of the last remaining windmills on Montmartre. Farther down is the site of the **Moulin de la Galette,** depicted by Renoir during one of the frequent dances held there, and one of van Gogh's former homes at 54 rue Lepic.

CIMETIÈRE MONTMARTRE. Parallel to rue Lepic, rue Caulaincourt leads downhill to the secluded Cimetière Montmartre, where writers Dumas and Stendhal, painter Dégas, physicists Ampère and Foucault, composer Berlioz, filmmaker Truffaut, and dancer Nijinksy are buried. In 1871, the cemetery held the mass graves from the siege of the Commune. *(M: Place de Clichy or Blanche. 20 av. Rachel. ☎ 01 53 42 36 30. Open M-F 8am-6pm, Sa 8:30am-6pm, Su 9am-6pm; winter closes 5:30pm.)*

BAL DU MOULIN ROUGE. Along bd. de Clichy and bd. de Rochechouart are many of the cabarets and nightclubs of the Belle Epoque, including the notorious cabaret Bal du Moulin Rouge, immortalized by Toulouse-Lautrec's paintings, Offenbach's music, and, most recently, Baz Luhrmann's Hollywood blockbuster. At the turn of the century, Paris's bourgeoisie came to the Moulin Rouge to play at being bohemian. After WWI, Parisian bohemians relocated to the Left Bank and the area around pl. Pigalle became a world-renowned red-light district (see p. 139). Today, the crowd consists of tourists out for an evening of sequins, tassels, and skin. The revues are still risqué, but the price of admission is prohibitively expensive—a show and dinner cost €130. You can be risky yourself and buy a ticket (€63) for a spot at the bar, which includes two drinks but no guarantee that you'll have somewhere to sit. *(M: Blanche. 82 bd. de Clichy. ☎ 01 53 09 82 82; www.moulin-rouge.com. Shows 7, 9, 11pm.)*

NINETEENTH ARRONDISSEMENT

PARC DES BUTTES-CHAUMONT. Parc des Buttes-Chaumont is a mix of manmade topography and transplanted vegetation, commissioned by Napoleon III in 1860 out of a longing for London's Hyde Park, where he spent much of his time in exile. Since the 13th century, the *quartier* had been host to a *gibbet* (an iron cage filled with the rotting corpses of criminals), a dumping-ground for dead horses, a breeding-ground for worms, and a gypsum quarry (the source of "plaster of Paris"). Making a park out of the existing mess took four years and 1000 workers. Designer Adolphe Alphand had all of the soil replaced and the quarried remains built up with new rock to create enormous fake cliffs surrounding a lake. Today's visitors walk the winding paths and enjoy a great view of the *quartier* from the cave-filled cliffs topped with a Roman temple. Watch out for the ominously named **Pont des Suicides** (Suicide Bridge). *(M: Buttes-Chaumont or Botzaris. Open daily 7am-11pm.)*

PARC DE LA VILLETTE. Cut in the middle by the **Canal de l'Ourcq** and the **Canal St-Denis,** the **Parc de la Villette** separates the Cité des Sciences from the Cité de la Musique, a Bernard-Tschumi-designed 20th-century urban park that feels like a step into the future. Constructed in 1867 as the La Villette beef building, the steel-and-glass **Grande Halle** (☎ 01 40 03 75 03) now hosts frequent plays, concerts, temporary exhibitions, and films. Unifying the park is a set of red cubical structures that form a grid of squares, known as **Folies.** The **Promenade des Jardins** links several thematic gardens, such as the **Mirror Garden,** which uses an array of mirrors to create optical illusions, the **Garden of Childhood Fears,** which winds through a wooded grove resonant with spooky sounds, and the roller coaster **Dragon Garden.** The promenade ends at Jardin des Dunes and the Jardins des Vents, a playground for kids ages 12 and under accompanied by parents. *(Promenade open 24hr. Free.)*

TWENTIETH ARRONDISSEMENT

CIMETIÈRE PÈRE LACHAISE. The cemetery is a 19th-century neighborhood-of-the-dead laid out in streets, with winding paths and elaborate sarcophagi. Balzac, Colette, David, Delacroix, La Fontaine, Haussmann, Molière, Proust, Chopin, Jim Morrison, Gertrude Stein, and Oscar Wilde are buried here. Many of the tombs remind visitors of the dead's worldly accomplishments: a reproduction of his *Raft of the Medusa* adorns the tomb of French Romantic painter **Géricault;** the muse Calliope sits on **Chopin's** tomb. **Oscar Wilde's** grave is marked by a striking larger-than-life Egyptian figure. **Haussmann** originally wanted to destroy the cemetery as part of his urban-renewal project. He now occupies a mausoleum here. Plaques here commemorate dancer **Isadora Duncan,** author **Richard Wright,** opera diva **Maria Callas,** and artist **Max Ernst.** The most visited grave is that of **Jim Morrison,** the former lead singer of The Doors. His graffiti-covered bust was removed from the tomb, allowing his fans to fill the rest of the memorial with their messages. In summer, dozens of young people bring flowers, joints, beer, poetry, and Doors paraphernalia to his tomb. At least one guard polices the spot at all times.

The **Mur des Fédérés** (Wall of the Federals) has become a site of pilgrimage for left-wing sympathizers. In May 1871, a group of *communards* murdered the Archbishop of Paris. They dragged his mutilated corpse to their stronghold in Père Lachaise and tossed it in a ditch. Four days later, the victorious Versaillais found the body. In retaliation, they lined up 147 Fédérés against the eastern wall of the cemetery, shot them, and buried them on the spot. Near the wall, a number of moving monuments commemorate the Resistance fighters of WWII and Nazi concentration camp victims. *(M: Père Lachaise. 16 rue du Repos. ☎01 55 25 82 10. Open Mar.-Oct. M-F 8am-6pm, Sa 8:30am-6pm, Su and holidays 9am-6pm; Nov.-Feb. M-F 8am-5:30pm, Sa 8:30am-5:30pm, Su and holidays 9am-5:30pm. Last entrance 15min. before closing. Free. Free maps supposedly available at guard booths by main entrances, but they're usually out; it is worth the €2 to buy a detailed map from a nearby tabac before entering. 2hr. guided tour June-Sept. in English Sa 3pm; in French Sa 2:30pm, occasionally Tu 2:30pm and Su 3pm, as well as numerous "theme" tours. €6, students €4. Tours meet at the bd. de Ménilmontant entrance; call ☎01 40 71 75 60 for info.)*

🏛 MUSEUMS

Listed below are some of Paris's best museums. The **Carte Musées et Monuments** offers admission to 70 museums in the area. It will save you money if you visit three or more museums per day; it also allows you to move to the front of most lines. It's sold at major museums and in most metro stations. A pass for one day is €22; for three consecutive days €38; for five consecutive days €52. For more information, call **Association InterMusées,** 4 rue Brantôme, *3ème* (☎01 44 61 96 60; www.intermusees.com). Most museums are closed on Mondays; the Louvre is closed on Tuesdays.

MAJOR MUSEUMS

▧ MUSÉE DU LOUVRE. Construction of the Louvre, begun in 1190, is still not finished. Under King Philippe-Auguste, the structure was a fortress attached to the city walls, designed to defend Paris while he was away on a crusade. In the 14th century, Charles V built a second city wall beyond what is now the Jardin des Tuileries (p. 132), thus rendering the Louvre useless. Not one to let a good castle go to waste, Charles converted the fortress into a residential château. In 1528, François I returned to the Louvre in an attempt to flatter the Parisian bourgeoisie. He razed Charles's palace and commissioned Pierre Lescot to build a new royal palace in the open style of the Renaissance. The old foundations are displayed in an exhibit entitled Medieval Louvre, on the ground floor of the Sully wing. Henry II's widow, Catherine de Médici, had the Tuileries Palace built looking onto an Italian-style garden. Henri IV completed the Tuileries and embarked on what he called the Grand Design—a project to link the Louvre and the Tuileries with the two large wings you see today in a "royal city." He only built a fraction of the project before his death in 1610. Louis XIV moved into the Louvre in 1650, hiring a trio of architects—Le Vau, Le Brun, and Perrault—to transform it into the grandest palace in Europe, but he later abandoned it in favor of Versailles.

In 1725, after years of relative abandonment, the Academy of Painting inaugurated annual salons in the halls to show the work of its members. In 1793, the exhibit was made permanent, creating the Musée du Louvre. Napoleon filled the Louvre with plundered art, most of which had to be returned. He happily continued Henri IV's Grand Design, extending the Louvre's two wings to the Tuileries palace and remodeling the façades of the older buildings. Mitterrand's *Grands Projets* campaign transformed the Louvre into an accessible, well-organized museum. Architect I. M. Pei came up with the idea of moving the museum's entrance to the center of the Cour Napoléon, on an underground level surmounted by his stunning and controversial **glass pyramid.**

Renaissance works include Leonardo da Vinci's *Mona Lisa (La Joconde)* and canvases by Raphaël and Titian, while among the French paintings are David's *Oath of the Horatii,* Ingres's sensual *Odalisque,* Géricault's gruesome *Raft of the Medusa,* and Delacroix's patriotic *Liberty Leading the People.* Sculptures include Michelangelo's *Slaves,* as well as an incredible collection of antiquities; be sure to see the *Venus de Milo* and the *Winged Victory of Samothrace.* The underground complex beneath the Pyramid also houses temporary exhibits. Visitors can either enter through the pyramid or directly from the metro into the new Carrousel du Louvre mall—follow the signs; if you have a *Carte Musée et Monuments,* you can enter directly from the Richelieu entrance, in the passage connecting the Cour Napoléon to the rue de Rivoli. Otherwise, you can buy full-price tickets from machines underneath the pyramid; reduced-rate tickets must be bought from ticket offices. The Louvre is less crowded on weekday afternoons and on Monday and Wednesday evenings, when it stays open until 9:45pm. The museum is enormous; you'll only be able to cover a fraction of it in any one visit. Pick up an updated **map** at the info desk below the pyramid. *(M: Palais-Royal/Musée du Louvre. 1er. ☎01 40 20 51 51; www.louvre.fr. Open M and W 9am-9:30pm, Th-Su 9am-5:30pm. Closed Tu. Last entry 45min. before closing, but people are asked to leave 15-30min. before closing. Admission M and W-Sa 9am-3pm €7.50, M and W-Sa 3pm-close and Su €5, under 18 and first Su of the month free. Prices include both the permanent and most temporary collections. Temporary exhibits in the Cour Napoléon open at 9am. Sign up for the English tours at information desk; M and W-Sa at 11am, 2, 3:45pm; €3. Bookstore and cafés open same hours as the museum on M and W, Th-Su close at 7pm.)*

■ **CENTRE POMPIDOU.** Often called the Beaubourg, the **Centre National d'Art et de Culture Georges Pompidou** fulfills former French President Pompidou's desire for Paris to have a cultural center embracing music, cinema, books, and the graphic arts. The Centre has inspired architectural controversy ever since its inauguration in 1977. Richard Rogers and Renzo Piano's building-turned-inside-out bares its circulatory system to all. Piping and ventilation ducts in various colors run up, down, and sideways along the outside (blue for air, green for water, yellow for electricity, red for heating). It attracts more visitors per year than any other museum or monument in France—eight million annually compared to the Louvre's three million. The **Musée National d'Art Moderne,** the Pompidou's main attraction, houses a rich selection of 20th-century art, from the Fauvists and cubists to Pop and Conceptual Art. *(M: Rambuteau or Hôtel-de-Ville; RER: Châtelet-Les-Halles. Place Georges-Pompidou, 4ème.* ☎*01 44 78 12 33, wheelchair info 01 44 78 49 54; www.centrepompidou.fr. Centre open M and W-Su 11am-10pm; museum open M and W-Su 11am-9pm, last ticket sales 8pm; library open M and W-F noon-10pm, Sa-Su 11am-10pm. Library and Forum free. Prices differ depending on how much of the center you want to see: permanent collection €5.50, students and over 60 €3.50, under 18 free, first Su of month free for all visitors; current exhibition €6.50, students and over 60 €4.50, under 13 free; permanent collection, current exposition, and Atelier Brancus €10, students and over 60 €8. Audio guides €4.50. 160-page visitor's guide €12.)*

■ **MUSÉE D'ORSAY.** If only the *Académiciens* who turned the Impressionists away from the Louvre could see the Musée d'Orsay today. Hundreds come daily to see these famous rejects. Paintings, sculpture, decorative arts, architecture, photography, and cinema are presented in this former railway station, with works spanning the period from 1848 until WWI.

The best plan of attack for the museum is (counter-intuitively) to visit the ground floor, the top floor, and then the mezzanine. This is clearly indicated both by signs and maps. The central atrium is dedicated to **sculpture** and highlights the likes of Jean-Baptiste Carpeaux. Galleries around the atrium display 19th-century works of the **Neoclassical, Romantic, Barbizon,** and **Realist** schools; important canvases include Manet's *Olympia,* Ingres's *La Source,* Delacroix's *La Chasse aux lions,* and Courbet's *Un Enterrement à Ornans.* The top floor is dedicated to the **Impressionists,** with important works by virtually all of the school of light's movers and shakers; famous works include Monet's *Gare St-Lazare* and Manet's *Déjeuner sur l'herbe.* The **Post-Impressionist** collection includes van Gogh's *Portrait of the Artist* (1889) and still-lifes and landscapes by Cézanne. The small mezzanine, meanwhile, is dedicated to **Rodin,** and is dominated by his huge *La Porte de l'Enfer.* The museum is least crowded on Sunday mornings and Thursday evenings. *(M: Solférino; RER: Musée d'Orsay. 62 rue de Lille, 7ème.* ☎*01 40 49 48 14; www.musee-orsay.fr. Open late June to late Sept. Tu-W and F-Su 9am-6pm, Th 9am-9:45pm; late Sept. to late June Tu-W and F-Su 10am-6pm, Th 10am-9:45pm. Closed M. Last ticket sales 45min. before closing. €7, ages 18-25 and all on Su €5, under 18 free. All free first Su of every month. Tours in English Tu-Sa 11:30am, 2:30pm; 1½hr.; €5.50. Bookstore and boutique open Tu-W and F-Su 9am-6:30pm, Th 9am-9:30pm. Wheelchair- accessible. MC/V.)*

■ **MUSÉE RODIN.** The elegant 18th-century **Hôtel Biron,** where Auguste Rodin lived and worked at the end of his life, now houses many of his better-known sculptures (e.g. *La Main de Dieu* and *Le Baiser*) in one of Paris's best museums. He was among the country's most controversial artists, classified by some as Impressionism's sculptor and by others as the father of modern sculpture. Many sculptures rest on beautiful antiques, and the walls are adorned with paintings and photographs by artists like Renoir, Van Gogh, Meunier, and Steichen. The museum also has several works by **Camille Claudel,** Rodin's muse, collaborator, and lover. The *hôtel's* expansive garden displays Rodin's work amongst rose trees and fountains, including the collection's star: *Le Penseur (The Thinker).* On the other side of the garden stands one version of Rodin's largest sculpture, *La Porte de l'Enfer (The Gates of Hell,* 1880-1917), the final version of which sits in the Musée d'Orsay. *(M: Varenne. 77 rue de Varenne, 7ème.* ☎*01 44 18 61 10; www.musee-rodin.fr. Open Tu-Su Apr.-Sept. 9:30am-5:45pm; Oct.-Mar. 9:30am-4:45pm. Last admission 30min. before closing. €5; seniors, ages 18-25, and all on Su €3. Park open Tu-Su Apr.-Sept. 9:30am-6:45pm; Oct.-Mar. 9:30am-5pm. Admission to park alone €1. Audio tour €4. Temporary exhibits housed in the chapel. Persons who are blind or vision-impaired may obtain advance permission to touch the sculptures. Ground floor and gardens wheelchair-accessible.)*

■ **LA VILLETTE.** Dedicated to bringing science to young people, the ■**Explora science museum** is in La Villette, a park-museum complex dedicated, in Mitterrand's words, to "intelligent leisure." Kids will love the fabulous exhibits in this architecturally impressive building. The museum features a **planetarium**, a **3-D cinema**, a modest **aquarium**, and the **Médiathèque**. *(M: Porte de Pantin. ☎01 40 03 75 03. Museum open Su 10am-7pm, Tu-Sa 10am-6pm. €7.50, under 25 or those accompanying children €5.50, under 7 free. Planetarium €2.50, under 7 free. Médiathèque open Su and W-Sa noon-6:45pm, Tu noon-7:45pm. Free. Cité des Enfants programs about every 2hr. Tu-Su; 1½hr. €5.)*

At the opposite end of La Villette from the Cité des Sciences is the **Cité de la Musique.** Designed by Franck Hammoutène and completed in 1990, the complex of buildings is visually stunning, full of curves and glass ceilings. The highlight is the **Musée de la Musique,** a collection of paintings, sculptures, and 900 musical instruments explained in an audio guide. The building's two performance spaces—the **Salle des Concerts** and the **Amphithéâtre**—host an eclectic range of shows and concerts year-round. The Cité also has a **music information center** and the **Médiathèque Pédagogique.** *(☎01 44 84 44 84, info 01 44 84 45 45, médiathèque 01 44 84 46 77; www.cite-musique.fr. Info center open Tu-Su noon-6pm. Musée de la Musique open Su 10am-6pm, Tu-Sa noon-6pm. €6.10, students €4.60, children 6-18 €2.30, under 6 free; €2.30 more for temporary exhibits. Guided tours in French; call the info office for times. €10, reduced €7.60, under 18 €4.60. Médiathèque open Tu-Su noon-6pm. Free.)*

■ **MUSÉE PICASSO.** When Picasso died in 1973, his family paid the French inheritance tax in artwork. The French government put this collection, which includes work from his cubist, surrealist, and neoclassical years, on display in 1985 in the 17th-century Hôtel Salé. *(M: Chemin-Vert. 5 rue de Thorigny, 3ème. ☎01 42 71 63 15, 01 42 71 70 84, or 01 42 71 25 21. Open Apr.-Sept. M and W-Su 9:30am-6pm; Oct.-Mar. 9:30am-5:30pm; last entrance 30min. before closing. €5.50, Su and ages 18-25 €4, under 18 free.)*

■ **MUSÉE DE LA MODE ET DU COSTUME.** The small museum has appealing rotating exhibits of 30,000 outfits and 70,000 accessories from the past three centuries. *(In the Palais Galliera, 10 av. Pierre 1er de Serbie, in pl. de Tokyo. M: Iéna. The museum entrance is in the center of the Palais and can be reached from the pl. de Rochambeau side. ☎01 56 52 86 00. Open Tu-Su 10am-6pm; last entrance 5:30pm. €7, students and seniors €5.50, children €3.50. Audio tour in French free.)*

MUSÉE DE CLUNY. The **Musée National du Moyen Age** is one of the world's finest collections of medieval art, jewelry, sculpture, and tapestries. In the 15th century, this *hôtel* was the home of the monastic Order of Cluny, led by the powerful Amboise family. In 1843, the state converted the *hôtel* into the medieval museum; excavations after WWII unearthed Roman baths below. The collection includes art from Paris's most important medieval structures: Ste-Chapelle, Notre Dame, and St-Denis. Its highlight is the stunning series of allegorical tapestries, *The Lady and the Unicorn. (M: Cluny-Sorbonne. 6 pl. Paul Painlevé, 5ème. ☎01 53 73 78 00. Open M and W-Sa 9:15am-5:45pm; last ticket sold at 5:15pm. €6.70; students, under 25, over 60, and Su €5.20; under 18 free. Garden open 8 or 9am to 5:30pm in winter and 9:30pm in summer; free. Call for information on weekly concerts ☎01 53 73 78 16; prices and schedule vary.)*

PALAIS DE TOKYO. Part of the magnificent Palais houses the **Musée d'Art Moderne de la Ville de Paris,** one of the world's foremost collections of 20th-century art. Two works stand out: Matisse's *La Danse Inachevée* and Dufy's epic of electricity, *La Fée Électricité. (M: Iéna. 11 av. du Président Wilson, 16ème. ☎01 53 67 40 00. Open Tu-F 10am-5:30pm, Sa-Su 10am-6:45pm. Admission to permanent exhibits free; special exhibits admission varies, expect approximately €5, students €2.20-3. Wheelchair-accessible.)*

On the other side, the **site création contemporaine** displays several exhibits a year, all guaranteed to challenge standard conceptions of art. Showing off exciting, controversial international work, the large, open space of the *site* accommodates massive abstract sculpture, video displays, and other creative forms of media. *(Open Tu-Su noon-midnight. Admission varies with exhibit, expect approximately €5, with reduced student/youth/senior prices. Free admission for art students.)*

PALAIS DE LA DÉCOUVERTE. Kids tear around the Palais's interactive science exhibits, pressing buttons to start comets on celestial trajectories, spinning on seats to investigate angular motion, and seeing all kinds of creepy-crawlies. The **planetarium** has 4 shows per day. *(In the Grand Palais, entrance on av. Franklin D. Roosevelt. ☎01 56 43 20 20, planetarium 01 40 74 81 73; www.palais-decouverte.fr. M: Franklin D. Roosevelt or Champs-Elysées-Clemenceau. Open Tu-Sa 9:30am-6pm, Su 10am-7pm. €5.60; students, seniors and under 18 €3.70; under 5 free. Planetarium entrance €3.10. Family entrance €12.20 for 2 adults and 2 children over 5. AmEx/MC/V.)*

MUSÉE JACQUEMART-ANDRÉ. The fantastically ornate former home of Nélie Jacquemart and her husband contains a collection of Renaissance artwork worthy of the most prestigious museums in Paris, including *Madonna and Child* by Botticelli and *St-George and the Dragon* by Ucello. *(M: Miromesnil. 158 bd. Haussmann, 8ème. ☎01 45 62 11 59. Open daily 10am-6pm; last entrance at 5:30pm. Admission €8, students and ages 7-17 €6, under 7 free. English headsets free with admission.)*

MUSÉE CARNAVALET. Housed in Mme. de Sévigné's 16th-century *hôtel particulier*, this amazing museum traces Paris's history, with exhibits from prehistory and the Roman conquest to 18th-century extravagance and Revolution, 19th-century Haussmannization, and Mitterrand's *Grands Projets. (M: Chemin-Vert. 23 rue de Sévigné, 3ème. ☎01 44 59 58 58; www.paris.fr/musees/musee_carnavalet. Open Tu-Su 10am-5:40pm; last entrance 5:15pm. Admission free. Special exhibits €5.50, students and elderly €4, ages 13-18 €2.50, under 12 free.)*

MUSÉE D'HISTOIRE NATURELLE. Three museums in one. The new-fangled **Grande Galerie de l'Evolution** tells the story of evolution via a Genesis-like parade of naturalistic stuffed animals. Next door, the **Musée de Minéralogie** contains some lovely jewels. The **Gallery of Comparative Anatomy and Paleontology**, at the other end of the garden, whose exterior looks like a Victorian house of horrors, is filled with a ghastly collection of fibias, rib-cages, and vertebrae formed into historic and prehistoric animals. *(M: Gare d'Austerlitz. 57 rue Cuvier, in the Jardin des Plantes, 5ème. ☎01 40 79 30 00; www.mnhn.fr. Grande Galerie de l'Evolution open M and W-Su 10am-6pm, Th 10am-10pm. €6.10, students €4.60. Musée de Minéralogie open M and W-Su 10am-6pm. €4.60, students €3.10. Galeries d'Anatomie Comparée et de Paléontologie open Nov.-Mar. M and W-Su 10am-5pm, Apr.-Oct. also Sa-Su 5-6pm. €4.60, students €3.10.)*

MUSÉE MARMOTTAN MONET. Owing to generous donations by Monet's family, the Empire-style house has been transformed into a shrine to Impressionism. The top floor is dedicated to paintings by Berthe Morisot, the First Lady of Impressionism, but most visitors come for the Monet's famed water lilies in the basement. *(M: La Muette. 2 rue Louis-Boilly, 16ème. ☎01 44 96 50 33. Open Tu-Su 10am-6pm. €6.50, students €4, under 8 free Wheelchair-accessible.)*

MUSÉE D'ART ET D'HISTOIRE DU JUDAISME. Recently renovated and housed in the grand **Hôtel de St-Aignan,** once a tenement populated by Jews fleeing Eastern Europe, this museum displays a history of Jews in Europe, France, and North Africa. The collection includes an ornate 15th-century Italian ark, letters written to wrongly accused French general Dreyfus, a small collection of Chagall and Modigliani paintings, Lissitzky lithographs, and modern art collections looted from Jewish homes by the Nazis. *(M: Hôtel de Ville or Rambuteau. 71 rue du Temple, 3ème. ☎01 53 01 86 60; www.mahj.org. Open M-F 11am-6pm, Su 10am-6pm; last entrance at 5:15pm. €6.10, students and ages 18-26 €3.80, under 18 free; includes an excellent English audio guide. Wheelchair-accessible.)*

GALLERIES

Paris has dozens of galleries displaying the work of both established and up-and-coming international artists. The highest concentration of hip contemporary art galleries is in the **Marais** (along rue de Perche, rue Debellyme, rue Vieille-du-Temple, rue Quincampoix, rue des Coutures St-Gervais, rue de Poitou, and rue Beaubourg) and in the 6ème's **St-Germain-des-Prés** area. Cutting-edge paintings, sculptures, and photography peek out of store-front windows. The **Champs-Elysées** area in the 8ème, on the other hand, is loaded with Old Masters. Galleries near M: Franklin D. Roosevelt on the Champs-Elysées, av. Matignon, rue du Faubourg St-Honoré, and rue de Miromesnil focus on Impressionism and post-Impressionism. The 13ème also has a coterie of new galleries along **rue Louise-Weiss** (M: Chevarelet) and the perpendicular **rue Duchefdelaville**. The *Portes Ouvertes* festival (May-June; check *Pariscope* for information) allows visitors to witness artists in action in their studios. Almost all galleries close on Mondays, in August, and at lunchtime.

🎵 ENTERTAINMENT

FREE CONCERTS

For listings of free concerts, check *Paris Selection*, free at tourist offices. Free concerts are extremely popular, so plan to arrive early. The **American Church in Paris**, 65 quai d'Orsay, 7ème, sponsors free concerts. (☎01 40 62 05 00; concerts Sept.-May Su 6pm; M: Invalides or Alma Marceau.) **Eglise St-Germain-des-Prés** also has free concerts; check the information booth just inside the door for times. **Eglise St-Merri**, 78 rue St-Martin, 4ème, is also known for its free concerts (Sept.-July Sa 9pm, Su 4pm; M: Hôtel-de-Ville); contact Accueil Musical St-Merri, 76 rue de la Verrerie, 4ème. (☎01 42 71 40 75 or 01 42 71 93 93; M: Châtelet.) Concerts take place W-Su in the **Jardin du Luxembourg's** band shell, 6ème (☎01 42 34 20 23); show up early to get a seat. Occasional free concerts are in the **Musée d'Orsay**, 1 rue Bellechasse, 7ème. (☎01 40 49 49 66; M: Solférino.)

OPERA

Opéra de la Bastille, pl. de la Bastille, 12ème (☎08 92 69 78 68; www.opera-de-paris.fr). M: Bastille. Opera and ballet with a modern spin. Because of acoustical problems, it's not the place to go all-out for front row seats. Subtitles in French. Call, write, or stop by for a free brochure of the season's events. Tickets can be purchased by Internet, mail, fax, phone (M-Sa 9am-7pm), or in person (M-Sa 11am-6:30pm). Rush tickets for students under 25 and those over 65 15min. before show. For wheelchair access, call 2 weeks ahead (☎01 40 01 18 08). Tickets €60-105. MC/V.

Opéra Garnier, pl. de l'Opéra, 9ème (☎08 92 89 90 90; www.opera-de-paris.fr). M: Opéra. Hosts symphonies, chamber music, and Ballet de l'Opéra de Paris. Tickets available 2 weeks before shows. Box office open M-Sa 11am-6pm. Last-minute discount tickets available 1hr. before showtime. For wheelchair access, call 2 weeks ahead (☎01 40 01 18 08). Tickets usually €19-64. AmEx/MC/V.

Opéra Comique, 5 rue Favart, 2ème (☎01 42 44 45 46; www.opera-comique.com). M: Richelieu-Drouot. Operas on a lighter scale—from Rossini to Offenbach. The 2003-2004 season includes *L'Amour masqué* and *Rita (ou Le mari battu)*. Box office open M-Sa 11am-7pm. Tickets €29-112. Student rush tickets available 15min. before show.

CABARET

Au Lapin Agile, 22 rue des Saules, 18ème (☎01 46 06 85 87). M: Lamarck-Coulaincourt. Picasso, Verlaine, Renoir, and Apollinaire hung out here during Montmartre's heyday; now a mainly tourist audience crowds in for comical poems and songs. Originally called the

Cabaret des Assassins, it came to be known as *le lapin à Gill* (Gill's Rabbit) in 1875, when the artist André Gill painted a rabbit on the façade. The name eventually morphed into *le lapin agile* (the nimble rabbit). The *chansonnier* inspired Steve Martin's 1996 hit play *Picasso at the Lapin Agile.* Shows Tu-Su at 9pm-2am. Admission and first drink €25, Su-F students €18. Subsequent drinks €6-7.

THEATER

Much of Parisian theater is highly accessible for non-French speakers, thanks in part to its dependence on the classics and in part to its love of a grand spectacle. Most theaters have shows Sept.-June Tu-Su. *Pariscope* (€0.40 at any newsstand) and *l'Officiel des Spectacles* (€0.35) provide listings and information on one of the best ways to see theater in Paris; **half-price previews.**

La Comédie Française, 2 rue de Richelieu, 1er (☎01 44 58 15 15; www.comedie-francaise.fr). M: Palais-Royal. Founded by Molière, now the granddaddy of all French theaters. Expect wildly gesticulated slapstick farce; you don't need to speak French to understand the jokes. Performances take place in the 896-seat Salle Richelieu. Box office open daily 11am-6pm. Tickets €4.50-30, under 27 €4.50-7.50 (no category A seating available). Rush tickets for students (€9) available 1hr. before show. Handicapped patrons and their guests are asked to make reservations in advance (tickets €11). The *comédiens français* also mount the same sort of plays in the low season.

Théâtre du Vieux Colombier, 21 rue des Vieux Colombiers, 6ème (☎01 44 39 87 00 or 01 44 39 87 01). M: St-Sulpice or Sèvres-Babylone. Tickets €25, over 60 €17.50; student rush tickets (€9-13) sold 45min. before performances. AmEx/MC/V.

Bouffes du Nord, 37bis bd. de la Chapelle, 10ème (☎01 46 07 34 50; www.bouffes-dunord.com). M: La Chapelle. This experimental theater headed by British directors Peter Brook and Stephen Lissner produces cutting-edge performances with some productions in English. Closed Aug. Box office open M-Sa 11am-6pm. Concerts €18.50, under 26 and over 60 €12; plays €14-24.50. Wheelchair-accessible if you call in advance.

La Cartoucherie, route du Champ de manoeuvre, 12ème. M: Château de Vincennes; a free shuttle departs every 15min. beginning 1hr. before performance, from the station. This 19th-century weapons factory has housed cutting-edge, socially conscious, and refreshingly democratic theater since 1970. Internationally renowned, it is home to 5 collectives, 2 studios, and 7 performance spaces. Most shows €15-20. For more information, visit www.la-tempete.fr/theatre/cartoucherie.html, or check *Pariscope.*

JAZZ

▨ **Au Duc des Lombards,** 42 rue des Lombards, 1er (☎01 42 33 22 88; www.jazzvalley.com/duc). M: Châtelet. Murals of Ellington and Coltrane cover the exterior of this premier jazz joint. Still the best in French jazz, with occasional American soloists, and hot items in world music. Three sets each night—you pay less cover if you only catch the last set. Cover €12-23, music students €8-19. Beer €5-8, cocktails €9. Music 9:30pm-1:30am. Open M-Sa 8pm-2am. MC/V.

Le Baiser Salé, 58 rue des Lombards, 1er (☎01 42 33 37 71). M: Châtelet. Cuban, African, and Antillean music featured together with modern jazz and funk in a welcoming, mellow space. Month-long African music festival (month varies). Concerts start at 10pm, music until 3am (typically 3 sets). Cover €6-18, depending on performers; mainly new talent. Free M jam sessions at 9:30pm with 1 drink min. Beer €4.80, cocktails €9. Happy hour 5-7:15pm. Bar and club open daily 5pm-6am. AmEx/MC/V.

Aux Trois Mailletz, 56 rue Galande, 5ème (☎01 43 54 00 79, before 5pm 01 43 25 96 86). M: St-Michel. What you'd expect a cool jazz club to look like. The basement houses a crowded café featuring world music and jazz vocals. The upper floor is packed with a mix of well-dressed students and well-dressed forty-somethings. Club cover €12.20-18.30 on weekends; bar free. Grog €9 at bar, cocktails €12.50 at bar. Bar open daily 5pm-dawn; *cave* 10pm-dawn.

CINEMA

There are scores of cinemas throughout Paris, particularly in the *Quartier Latin* and on the Champs-Elysées. Many theaters in Paris specialize in programs featuring classic European film, current independent film, Asian and American classics, and Hollywood blockbusters. Most listed offer movies in their original version (*version originale*, or V.O.), without subtitles. Two big theater chains—**Gaumont** and **UGC**—offer *cartes privilèges* discounts for five visits or more. Paris's cinemas offer student, senior, and family discounts. On Mondays and Wednesdays, prices drop by about €1.50. Check *Pariscope* or *l'Officiel des Spectacles* (€0.35, at newsstands) for film schedules, prices, and reviews.

Musée du Louvre, 1er (info ☎01 40 20 53 17, schedules and reservations 01 40 20 52 99; www.louvre.fr). M: Louvre. Art films, films on art. Open Sept.-June. Free.

Les Trois Luxembourg, 67 rue Monsieur-le-Prince, 6ème (☎01 46 33 97 77). M: Cluny. Independent, classic, and foreign films, all in V.O. €6.40, students and seniors €5.

Action Christine, 4 rue Christine, 6ème (☎01 43 29 11 30). M: Odéon. Off rue Dauphine. International selection of art and classic films from the 40s and 50s. Many famous Hollywood pics. Always V.O. €7; early show (usually 6 or 7pm), M, and students €5.50. 1-year pass for 10 movies €40.

La Pagode, 57bis rue de Babylone, 7ème (☎01 45 55 48 48). M: St-François-Xavier. A pseudo-Japanese pagoda built in 1895 and reopened as a cinema in 2000, La Pagode screens foreign and independent films. Stop in at the café between shows. Tickets €7.30; over 60, under 21, students, and M and W €5.80. MC/V.

Cinémathèque Française, pl. du Trocadéro, 16ème (☎01 45 53 21 86, recorded info 01 47 04 24 24 lists all shows; www.cinemathequefrancaise.com). M: Trocadéro. At the Musée du Cinéma in the Palais de Chaillot; enter through the Jardins du Trocadéro. **Also** 42 bd. Bonne Nouvelle, 10ème. M: Bonne Nouvelle. A must for film buffs. 2-3 classics, near-classics, or soon-to-be classics per day. Foreign films usually in V.O. Buy tickets 20min. early. Open W-Su 5-9:45pm. €4.70, students €3.

ⓘ NIGHTLIFE

Those on the prowl for dancing may be frustrated by Paris's rather closed-off club scene, but *Let's Go* has tried to list clubs that admit non-models. As far as gay nightlife goes, the Marais is the place to see and be seen.

FIRST & SECOND ARRONDISSEMENTS

⬛ **Banana Café,** 13-15 rue de la Ferronnerie, 1er (☎01 42 33 35 31). M: Châtelet. This *très branché* (way cool) evening arena is the most popular gay bar in the entire 1er, and draws a fairly mixed group most nights; head downstairs for an exclusively male crowd. Legendary theme nights. "Go-Go Boys" perform W-Sa midnight-dawn. During Happy hour (6-9pm) drinks are 2-for-1, except cocktails. Beer M-F €5.20, Sa-Su €6.80. Open daily 4pm-dawn. AmEx/MC/V.

Le Champmeslé, 4 rue Chabanais, 1er (☎01 42 96 85 20; lachampmesle.no-ip.com). M: Pyramides or Quatre Septembre. This welcoming lesbian bar is Paris's oldest and most famous. Mixed crowd in the front, but women-only in back. Beer €4. Cocktails (€8) garnished with a glow stick. Popular cabaret show Th 10pm (first drink is €8). Monthly art exhibits. Open M-Sa 2pm-2am. MC/V.

PARIS

Le Café Noir, 65 rue Montmartre, 2ème (☎01 40 39 07 36). M: Sentier. Plastic creatures hanging from the ceiling, crazy tiling on the floor, and bartenders leaping onto the bar to perform comedy. A true mix of locals and anglophones. Beer €2-3. Open M-F 8am-2am and Sa 2pm-2am. AmEx/MC/V.

The Flann O'Brien, 6 rue Bailleul, 1er (☎01 42 60 13 58). M: Louvre-Rivoli. Arguably the best Irish bar in Paris, Flann is often packed, especially on live music nights (F-Su). Go for the Guinness and stay for the reportedly good "craic" downstairs (that's Irish for good fun). Demi €4, full pint €6. Open daily 6pm-5am.

DANCE CLUBS

Rex Club, 5 bd. Poissonnière, 2ème (☎01 42 36 10 96). M: Bonne-Nouvelle. A non-selective club which presents the most selective of DJ line-ups. Very young clubbers crowd this casual venue to hear cutting-edge techno, jungle, and house fusion from international DJs on one of the best sound systems in Paris. Large dance floor and lots of seats as well. Shots €4-5, beer €5-7. Cover €8-13. Open Th-Sa 11:30pm-6am.

THIRD & FOURTH ARRONDISSEMENTS

◪ **L'Apparemment Café,** 18 rue des Coutures St-Gervais, 3ème. M: St-Paul. Beautiful lounge with games and a young crowd. Late-night meals €10-13, served until closing.

◪ **Chez Richard,** 37 rue Vieille-du-Temple, 4ème (☎01 42 74 31 65). M: Hôtel-de-Ville. Inside a courtyard off rue Vieille-du-Temple, this bar's stone interior, hidden balcony, yellow lighting, slowly spinning ceiling fan, and shadow-casting palm leaves are reminiscent of Casablanca. A hot spot to people-watch on weekends, but during the week it's ideal for chilling, with hip bartenders and smooth beats. Happy hour 6-8pm for cocktails. Beer €4-6, cocktails €9. Food €6-12. Open daily 6pm-2am. AmEx/MC/V.

◪ **Lizard Lounge,** 18 rue du Bourg-Tibourg, 4ème (☎01 42 72 81 34). M: Hôtel-de-Ville. A happening, split-level space for college-age Americans and French. Underground cellar has DJs every night from 10pm. Happy hour upstairs 6-8pm, throughout the bar 8-10pm. Pint of lager €6.20, "Lizard Juice" €7.50. Open daily noon-2am. Serves food noon-3pm and 7-10:30pm, Sa-Su brunch noon-4pm. MC/V.

Villa Keops, 58 bd. Sébastopol, 3ème (☎01 40 27 99 92). M: Etienne-Marcel. Stylish, candlelit couch bar where the boy-toy waiters are as beautiful as the designer drinks. Divine Rose du Nile €8.50, caramelized vodka €7.50. Happy hour 8-10pm. Open M-Th noon-2am, F-Sa noon-4am, Su 4pm-3am. AmEx/MC/V.

La Belle Hortense, 31 rue Vieille-du-Temple (☎01 48 04 71 60). M: St-Paul. A breath of fresh intellectual air for those worn out by the *hyper-chic* scene along the rest of the rue. Varied wine selection from €3 per glass, €20-36 per bottle. Coffee €1.30-2. Walls of books (literature, art, philosophy). Frequent exhibits, readings, lectures, signatures, and discussions in the small back room. Open daily 5pm-2am. MC/V.

Boobs Bourg, 26 rue de Montmorency, 3ème (☎01 42 74 04 82). M: Rambuteau. This is where the well-spiked, stylishly punk girls go to find each other. Always lively at night, occasional daytime lectures and discussions. Boys welcome if accompanied by women. Beer on tap €3.80, mixed drinks €7. Open Tu-Su 5:30pm-2am. MC/V.

Amnésia Café, 42 rue Vieille-du-Temple, 3ème (☎01 42 72 16 94). M: Hôtel-de-Ville. A largely gay crowd comes to lounge on plush sofas in Amnésia's classy wood-paneled interior. This is one of the top see-and-be-seen spots in the Marais, especially on Sa nights. Espresso €2, kir €4. Open daily 10:30am-2am. MC/V.

Le Duplex, 25 rue Michel Le Comte, 3ème (☎01 42 72 80 86) M: Rambuteau. A great place to make friends instead of trouble. The small and intimate atmosphere features a computer where patrons can snap photos to remember their evening. Not an exclusively male bar, but few women hang out here. Beer €2.60 until 10pm, €3.50 after. Cocktails €7.30. Open Su-Th 8pm-2am, F-Sa 8pm-4am.

Open Café, 17 rue des Archives (☎01 42 72 26 18). M: Hôtel-de-Ville. The most popular of the Marais gay bars. Women welcome, but most patrons are men. Bring your sassiest attitude and wear your tightest pants. Beer €3.30, cocktails €6.90. Open daily 11am-2am. Happy hour 6-9pm. AmEx/MC/V.

DANCE CLUBS

Les Bains, 7 rue du Bourg l'Abbé, 3ème (☎01 48 87 01 80). M: Etienne-Marcel or Réaumur-Sébastopol. Ultra-selective, super-crowded, and expensive. It used to be a public bath, visited at least once by Marcel Proust, and, since becoming a club, by Madonna and Mick Jagger. Models on the floor; mirrored bar upstairs. Funky house and garage grunge; W is hip hop. Cover (includes first drink) Su-Th €16, F-Sa €19. Drinks €11. Clubbing daily 11pm-6am. AmEx/MC/V.

Le Dépôt, 10 rue aux Ours, 3ème (☎01 44 54 96 96; www.ledepot.com). M: Etienne-Marcel. A veritable pleasure complex for gay men. Dance for inspiration, but don't waste time on small talk; just take your newest conquest to one of the rooms in the downstairs labyrinth. Women welcome after 11pm on the upstairs dance floor. The post-Su-brunch Gay Tea Dance is especially popular. Disco M, House/Techno W, Queer Mother Night Th, visiting DJ F, House Sa (called "*Putas* at Work"). Cover includes first drink; M-Th €7.50, F €10, Sa €12, Su €10. Open daily 2pm-8am. V.

FIFTH & SIXTH ARRONDISSEMENTS

■ **Le Caveau des Oubliettes,** 52 rue Galande, 5ème (☎01 46 34 23 09). M: St-Michel. Three scenes in one, all with a mellow, funky atmosphere: the bar upstairs (called "La Guillotine") has sod carpeting, ferns, and a real-life guillotine; downstairs in the cellar, there's an outstanding jazz club; and beneath the club, you can romp around the narrow tunnels of the "*caveau des oubliettes*" (cave of the forgotten ones), a prison where criminals were locked up and (obviously) forgotten. Free *soirée boeuf* (jam session) Su-Th 10:30pm-1:30am; F-Sa concerts €7.50. Beer €3.70-4.10. Rum drinks €3.80. Happy hour 5-9pm. Open daily 5pm-2am.

■ **Le Reflet,** 6 rue Champollion, 5ème (☎01 43 29 97 27). M: Cluny-La Sorbonne. Small, low-key, and crowded with students and younger working folk who stop by for a post-cinematic drink. Beer €1.90-2.70 at the bar, *kir* €2, cocktails €5. Also serves food; salads €7-9. Open M-Sa 10am-2am, Su noon-2am. MC/V.

■ **Le Bar Dix,** 10 rue de l'Odéon, 6ème (☎01 43 26 66 83). M: Odéon. A classic student hangout where you might overhear existentialist discussions in the downstairs cellar. After a few glasses of sangría (€3), you might join in. A great jukebox plays everything from Edith Piaf to Aretha Franklin. Open daily 5:30pm-2am.

Bob Cool, 15 rue des Grands Augustins, 6ème (☎01 46 33 33 77). M: Odéon. Laid-back clientele, friendly vibe, and a reputation among those in the know for being one of the best bars in Paris. The music is at the discretion of the bartender and veers between salsa and Corrs. Ask for "sweeties" with your drinks and you'll be pleasantly surprised. Mexican *mezcal* €8.50. Open daily 5pm-2am.

Le Crocodile, 6 rue Royer-Collard, 6ème (☎01 43 54 32 37). M: Cluny-La Sorbonne. A lively crowd of 20-somethings packs into this unassuming bar on a quiet side street. 238 tasty cocktails (€8, before midnight M-Th €6) to choose from. Open M-Sa 10:30pm-4am.

SEVENTH & EIGHTH ARRONDISSEMENTS

■ **Le Club des Poètes,** 30 rue de Bourgogne, 7ème (☎01 47 05 06 03; www.poesie.net). M: Varenne. A restaurant by day, Le Club is transformed at 10pm each night when a troupe of readers, including Jean-Pierre Rosnay's family, bewitch the audience with poetry. Lunch *menu* €15. Drinks €9, students €5-7. Open M-Sa noon-2:30pm and 8pm-1am; food served until 10pm. AmEx/MC/V.

House of Live, 124 rue La Boétie, 8ème (☎01 42 25 18 06) M: Franklin D. Roosevelt. Formerly the Chesterfield Café. This friendly and happening American bar has first-class live music, usually free, scheduled most nights of the week. Snack bar has good ol' Yankee fare: hamburgers €11, brownies €5.50, key lime pie €5.90. Beer €6, cocktails €6.80, coffee €2-4. No cover Su-Th. Open daily 9am-5am. AmEx/MC/V.

buddha-bar, 8 rue Boissy d'Anglas, 8ème (☎01 53 05 90 00). M: Madeleine or Concorde. An elegant bar and restaurant that combines candlelight and music to create an evening so close to perfect, you won't notice the difference. The giant buddha keeps watch over those really important (and often really famous) people eating on the ground floor; the upstairs has a more relaxed atmosphere. Mixed drinks and martinis €12; the mysterious Delight (€12.50) is indeed that. Weekday lunch *menu* (€32) includes wine and coffee. Open M-F noon-3pm and daily 6pm-2am.

Malone's, 64 av. Bosquet (☎01 45 51 08 99). M: Ecole Militaire. Chic mahogany décor and warm candlelight create a surprisingly easy-going atmosphere, enhanced by the friendly waitstaff. Cocktails (try the grasshopper) €8; beer €5. Tasty snacks like *croques* served until closing (€4.90-5.90). Open M-Sa 5pm-2am, Su 5pm-1am. MC/V.

DANCE CLUBS

▓ **Latina Café,** 114 av. des Champs-Elysées (☎01 42 89 98 89). M: George V. Drawing one of the largest nightclub crowds on the Champs, Latina Café plays energetic world music, including salsa, Cuban, and hip hop. Drinks €9-11. Women get in free Su-Th, men €7 cover which includes a drink. €16 cover F-Sa includes first two drinks. Café open daily 7:30pm-2am, club open daily 11:30am-6:30am.

Le Queen, 102 av. des Champs-Elysées (☎01 53 89 08 90). M: George V. Where drag queens, superstars, models, moguls, and go-go boys get down to the mainstream rhythms of a 10,000 gigawatt sound system. Her majesty is one of the cheapest and most fashionable gay clubs in town, but caters to a mix of tastes; girls are welcome. M disco, Th-Sa house, Su 80s. Cover Su-Th €12, includes one drink; F-Sa €18. All drinks €9. Open daily midnight to dawn. AmEx/MC/V.

NINTH TO THIRTEENTH ARRONDISSEMENTS

▓ **Boteco,** 131 rue Oberkampf, 11ème (☎01 43 57 15 47). M: Parmentier. A popular Brazilian bar-restaurant with trendy waitstaff, jungle décor, and avant-garde art. Flip-up benches transform the small space into a spontaneous late-night dance floor. Munch on free homemade thick-cut potato chips while you sip a delicious Boteco (€6.50) made with Brazilian cachaca, pineapple juice, and vanilla extract. Open daily 9am-2am.

La Folie en Tête, 33 rue de la Butte-aux-Cailles, 13ème (☎01 45 80 65 99). M: Corvisart. *The* artsy axis mundi of the 13ème. Exotic instruments line the walls. Crowded concerts on Sa nights, usually Afro-Caribbean music (€8); no concerts July-Aug. Beer €2.40; Ti punch €4.50. Happy hour 6-8pm (*kir* €1.50). Open M-Sa 6pm-2am. MC/V.

Bateau El Alamein, Port de la Gare, 13ème (☎01 45 86 41 60). M: Quai-de-la-Gare. This docked boat is like a floating Eden, with everything from orange trees to morning glories blooming on its pleasant deck. The stage downstairs features local performers nightly, but call ahead to be sure. Entrance €5-8. Popular drinks include a mean mojito and the TGV (tequila, gin, vodka), both €8. Open daily 7pm-2am.

DANCE CLUBS

Batofar, facing 11 quai François-Mauriac, 13ème (☎01 56 29 10 33). M: Quai-de-la-Gare. Facing the river, walk right along the quai—Batofar has the red lights. This barge/bar/club has made it big with the electronic music crowd, but maintains a friendly vibe. Open Tu-Th 9pm-3am, F-Sa until 4am; hours change for special film and DJ events. Cover €6.50-9.50 usually includes first drink. "Electronic brunch" on Sunday afternoon. MC/V.

THE INSIDER'S CITY

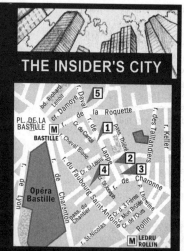

BAR STORMING

The 11ème may have been the site of the Revolution's send-off party, but the only places being stormed in the Bastille nowadays are its nightspots. The 11ème has been called the next Montmartre, the next Montparnasse, and the next Latin Quarter. But the next bar is your only concern; here are a few to get you started:

1 **Bar des Familles.** Small and low-key, though still not the place to take your parents. (☎01 43 14 64 77. Open daily 6pm-2am.)

2 **Bar Bat.** This one draws a young and lively crowd, good for kicking the revelry up a notch. (☎01 43 14 26 06. Open daily 5pm-2am.)

3 **Le Bar Sans Nom.** The jazz will go along with your buzz. (☎01 48 05 59 36. Open M-Sa 7pm-2am.)

4 **Sanz Sans.** Popular and upbeat, with a screen that projects scenes from the bar. (☎01 44 75 78 78. Open daily 9:30pm-1am.)

5 **Wax.** A Parisian miracle: a club that is free and fun. Set in a concrete bunker. House music only. (☎01 48 05 88 33. Open daily 6pm-2am; summer closed Su.)

Bus Palladium, 6 rue Fontaine, 9ème (☎01 53 21 07 33). M: Pigalle, Blanche, or St-Georges. Getting past the bouncers can be tough—try to look hot. A trendy, beautiful crowd rocks this club, which still sports vintage posters and faded gilded décor. Cover €16. Tu free cover and drinks for ladies. Drinks €13. Open Tu-Sa 11pm-6am. AmEx/V.

FOURTEENTH TO TWENTIETH ARRONDISSEMENTS

L'Entrepôt, 7-9 rue Francis de Pressensé, 14ème (☎01 45 40 07 50, film schedule 08 36 68 05 87, restaurant reservations 01 45 40 07 50; www.lentrepot.fr). M: Pernety. Proving that intellectualism and good times go together, this establishment offers a 3-screen cinema, a fancy ivy-decked restaurant with garden patio, and an art gallery and a trendy bar that features live jazz, Latin, and world music. Poetry readings (Tu 7pm) and jazz (Th 7pm). Ciné-Philo, a screening, lecture, and discussion café, is held 2 Sa per month at 2pm; check the monthly schedule in the main foyer. Concerts F-Sa; usually around €5. Beer €2.50. Su brunch 11:30am-4:30pm (€15). Open M-Sa 9am-midnight (though usually stays open later), Su 11:30am-midnight; food served noon-3pm and 7:30-11:30pm.

L'Endroit, 67 pl. du Dr. Félix Lobligeois, 17ème (☎01 42 29 50 00). M: Rome. Hip, young 17èmers come for the snazzy bar and idyllic location. Beer €4.50-5.10, wine €3.50-4, cocktails €6. Try the Pearl Harbor (vodka, melon liquor, and pineapple nectar) or down the mysterious and fruity "Bitch." Open daily noon-2am. MC/V.

Chez Camille, 8 rue Ravignan, 18ème (☎01 46 06 05 78). M: Abbesses. Small, trendy, bright yellow bar on the safe upper slopes of Montmartre, with funky charm and a pretty terrace looking down the *butte* to the Invalides dome (especially dramatic at night). Cheap coffee (€1.20) and tea (€2.80). Beer €2.20-3.30, wine from €2.80, cocktails €6.50. Open M 11am-2pm, Tu-Sa 9am-2am, Su 9am-8pm.

La Fourmi, 74 rue des Martyrs, 18ème (☎01 42 64 70 35). M: Pigalle. An artsy atmosphere with a large zinc bar and industrial-chic décor. A hyper-hip, energetic, and scrappy young crowd. Beer €2.30-3.20, wine €2.50-2.60, cocktails €5.40-10. Open M-Th 8:30am-2am, F-Sa 8:30am-4am, Su 10am-2am. V.

🗖 SHOPPING

Like its food, nightlife, and conversation, Paris's fashion is an art. From the wild clubwear near rue Etienne-Marcel to the unique boutiques of the Marais to the upscale designer shops of St-Germain-des-Prés, everything Paris touches turns to gold. The great *soldes* (sales) of the year begin after New Year's and at the very end of June, with the best prices at the beginning of February and the end of July. If at any time of year you see the word *braderie* (clearance sale) in a store window, march in without hesitation. The following listings are by *arrondissement* and by type of store.

CLOTHING

▨ Le Shop, 3 rue d'Argout, 2*ème* (☎01 40 28 95 94). M: Etienne-Marcel. Whatever you buy here, you'll be the only one with it back home. Sleek Asian-inspired club-wear plus a live DJ. Shirts and pants from €50. Open M 1-7pm, Tu-Sa 11am-7pm. AmEx/MC/V.

▨ Espace Kiliwatch, 64 rue Tiquetonne, 2*ème* (☎01 42 21 17 37). M: Etienne-Marcel. One of the most popular, fun shops in Paris. Pre-owned *(fripe)* shirts from €19, pants from €30. Pricier clothes, books, furnishings, and other funky stuff for sale. MC/V.

▨ Culotte, 7 rue Malher, 4*ème* (☎01 42 71 58 89). M: St-Paul. Japanese designs ranging from ripped printed tees to 40s-style dresses, all handmade. Funky vintage jewelry. Most items under €100. Open Su 1-7pm, Tu-Sa 11am-7pm. AmEx/MC/V.

Boy'z Bazaar, 5 rue Ste-Croix-de-la-Bretonnerie, 4*ème* (☎01 42 71 94 00). M: Hôtel-de-Ville. A large selection of all that's elegant and trendy in casual menswear from Energie to Paul Smith. Jeans €100-200. T-shirts €40-50. Athletic-wear branch down the street at no. 38. Open M-Th noon-9pm, F-Sa noon-midnight, Su 2-8pm. AmEx/MC/V.

Fabien Nobile, 7 rue Ferdinand Duval, 4*ème* (☎01 42 78 51 12). M: St-Paul. With brands like Be Ice Be, Desize, Phard, and Free, this campy boutique is the place to expand your *club couture.* Open daily noon-8pm, Th until 9pm.

Les Antiquaires de la Mode, 11 rue d'Ormesson, 4*ème* (☎01 42 78 05 45). M: St-Paul. Eric and Jaques, the friendly "antique dealers of fashion" who run this vintage-trendy boutique, offer reincarnated Jackie O.-style dresses (€100), Chanel suits (€150), and the latest line of Playboy Bunny handbags (€60-70). Open Su and Th-Sa 2-7:30pm. MC/V.

Moloko, 53 rue du Cherche-Midi, 6*ème* (☎01 45 48 46 79). M: Sèvres-Babylone, St-Sulpice, or Rennes. Simple, Asian-inspired women's clothing with creative twists: surprising colors, shapes, and unique closures. Dresses from €120. Other boutiques in the 4*ème* and Forum des Halles. Open Tu-Sa 11am-1pm and 2-7pm; closed Aug. MC/V.

Incognito, 41 rue de la Roquette, 12*ème* (☎01 40 21 86 55). M: Bastille. With provocative dresses (€125), scintillating shear tops (€40), and super-tight jeans (from €60), this boutique lets you look hot and pay little. Open daily 11am-8pm. AmEx/MC/V.

Spree, 16 rue de Lavieuville, 18*ème* (☎01 42 23 41 40). M: Abbesses. A colorful mix of fabrics and styles, Spree carries some of the cutest and most original girl's wear in Paris. Skirts around €70, screen-printed t-shirts €30. Open Tu-Sa 11am-7pm.

SHOES & ACCESSORIES

▨ Jacques Le Corre, 193 rue St-Honoré, 1*er* (☎01 42 96 97 40). Stunning high-end women's shoes, handbags, and hats. Only 4 pairs of each model are made, and they're only sold here and at a sister NYC boutique (at higher prices). Shoes €350, hats €140, handbags €300 (about half-price June-July). Open M-Sa 10am-7pm. AmEx/MC/V.

Longchamp, 404 rue St-Honoré, 1*er* (☎01 43 16 00 18). The classic leather-strapped canvas totes that fold up into painfully cute and glaringly useless little bundles. Basic bags from €45. Open M-Sa 10am-7pm. AmEx/MC/V.

▨ Karine Dupont Boutique, 22 rue de Poitou, 3*ème* (☎01 40 27 84 94). M: St-Sébastien Froissart. From unassuming, waterproof tent material, Karine Dupont makes ingenious bags in every shape imaginable. Most bags €40-80. Open M-Sa noon-7:30pm. MC/V.

Monic, 5 rue des Francs-Bourgeois, 4*ème* (☎01 42 72 39 15). M: Chemin Vert or St-Paul. Jewelry of all types abounds at this fantastic boutique. Pieces mostly under €50. Open Su-M 2:30-7pm, Tu-Sa 10am-7pm. AmEx/MC/V.

PARIS

Sephora, 70-72 av. des Champs-Elysées, 8ème (☎01 53 93 22 50). M: Charles de Gaulle-Etoile. An enormous array of cosmetic products that will awaken your secret (or not-so-secret) vanity. The welcoming carpeted corridor is lined with almost every *eau-de-toilette* on the market, both for men and women. Prices run the gamut from reasonable to absurd. Open daily 10am-midnight. AmEx/MC/V.

Total Eclipse, 40 rue de la Roquette, 12ème (☎01 48 07 88 04). M: Bastille. It's time to accessorize. Purchase you-can't-find-me-anywhere-else jewelry in bright colors (from €20), one-of-a-kind necklaces (€56), and a "where-did-you-get-that" bracelet (€30-50). Then shove them in your trendy new bag (€20-160). Open M-Sa 11am-7:30pm. AmEx/MC/V.

DEPARTMENT STORES

Au Printemps, 64 bd. Haussmann, 9ème (☎01 42 82 50 00). M: Chaussée d'Antin-Lafayette or Havre-Caumartin. **Also** at 30 pl. d'Italie, 13ème (☎01 40 78 17 17), M: Place d'Italie; and 21-25 cours de Vincennes, 20ème (☎01 43 71 12 41), M: Porte de Vincennes. One of the two biggies in the Parisian department store scene. Haussmann open M-W and F-Sa 9:35am-7pm, Th 9:35am-10pm. Other locations open M-Sa 10am-8pm. AmEx/MC/V.

Galeries Lafayette, 40 bd. Haussmann, 9ème (☎01 42 82 34 56). M: Chaussée d'Antin. **Also** 22 rue du Départ, 14ème (☎01 45 38 52 87), M: Montparnasse. The equivalent of Paris's population visits here each month. Haussmann open M-W and F-Sa 9:30am-7:30pm, Th 9:30-9pm; Montparnasse M-Sa 9:45am-7:30pm. AmEx/MC/V.

Samaritaine, 67 rue de Rivoli, on the quai du Louvre, 1er (☎01 40 41 20 20). M: Pont Neuf, Châtelet-Les Halles, or Louvre-Rivoli. 4 large, historic Art Deco buildings between rue de Rivoli and the Seine, connected by tunnels and bridges. Not as chic as the other department stores, but a calmer, pleasant shopping experience. The rooftop observation deck provides one of the best views of the city; take the elevator to the 9th floor and climb the short, spiral staircase. Open M-W and F-Sa 9:30am-7pm, Th 9:30am-10pm. AmEx/MC/V.

Au Bon Marché, 22 rue de Sèvres, 7ème (☎01 44 39 80 00). M: Sèvres-Babylone. Paris's oldest department store. Across the street is *La Grande Epicerie de Paris,* Bon Marché's celebrated (and reasonably priced) gourmet food annex. Open M-W and F 9:30am-7pm, Th 10am-9pm, Sa 9:30am-8pm. AmEx/MC/V.

OUTLET STORES

Stock is French for outlet store, with big-name clothes for less—often because they are from last season or have small imperfections. Many are on rue d'Alésia in the 14ème (M: Alésia), including **Cacharel Stock,** no. 114 (☎01 45 42 53 04; open M-Sa 10am-7pm; AmEx/MC/V); **Stock Chevignon,** no. 122 (☎01 45 43 40 25; open M-Sa 10am-7pm; AmEx/MC/V); **S.R. Store** (Sonia Rykiel) at nos. 110-112 and no. 64 (☎01 43 95 06 13; open Tu 11am-7pm, W-Sa 10am-7pm; MC/V); **Stock Patrick Gerard,** no. 113 (☎01 40 44 07 40). A large **Stock Kookaï** bustles at 82 rue Réamur, 2ème (☎01 45 08 93 69; open M 11:30am-7:30pm, Tu-Sa 10:30am-7pm); **Apara Stock** sits at 16 rue Etienne Marcel (☎01 40 26 70 04); and **Haut-de-Gomme Stock,** with names like Armani, Khanh, and Dolce & Gabbana, has two locations: 9 rue Scribe, 9ème (☎01 40 07 10 20; open M-Sa 10am-7pm; M: Opéra) and 190 rue de Rivoli, 1er (☎01 42 96 97 47; open daily 11am-7pm; M: Louvre-Rivoli).

BOOKS

Paris overflows with high-quality bookstores. The 5ème and 6ème are particularly bookish: interesting shops line every large street in the Latin Quarter, not to mention the endless stalls *(bouquinistes)* along the quais of the Seine. Some specialty bookshops serve as community centers, too. English bookshops like **Shakespeare & Co.** (below) and **The Village Voice,** 6 rue Princesse, 6ème, have bulletin boards for posting events and housing notices. (Village Voice ☎01 46 33 36 47. M: Mabillon. Open M 2-8pm, Tu-Sa 10am-8pm, Su 2-7pm; Aug. closed Su.) **Les Mots à la Bouche,** 6 rue Ste-Croix de la Bretonnerie, *4ème*, carries literature, essays, and art relating to homosexuality, and has info for gays and lesbians. (☎01 42 78 88 30; www.motsbouche.com. M: Hôtel-de-Ville. Open M-Sa 11am-11pm and Su 2-8pm.) **L'Harmattan,** 21bis rue des Ecoles, *5ème*, can direct you to Caribbean, Maghrébin, and West African resources. (☎01 46 34 13 71. M: Cluny la Sorbonne. Open M-Sa 10am-12:30pm and 1:30-7pm. MC/V.)

The large, English-language **W.H. Smith**, 248 rue de Rivoli, 1*er*, has many scholarly works and magazines. Sunday *New York Times* available Monday after 2pm. (☎01 44 77 88 99. M: Concorde. Open M-Sa 9am-7:30pm, Su 1-7:30pm. AmEx/MC/ V.) **Brentano's,** 37 av. de l'Opéra, *2ème*, is an American and French bookstore with an extensive selection of English literature. (☎01 42 61 52 50. M: Opéra. Open M-Sa 10am-7:30pm. AmEx/MC/V.) Shakespeare & Co., 37 rue de la Bûcherie, *5ème*, across the Seine from Notre Dame, is run by *bon vivant* George Whitman. Walt's grandson sells a quirky and wide selection of new and used books, including bargains (€2.50) in bins outside the shop. (M: St-Michel. Open daily noon-midnight.)

MARCHÉ AUX PUCES DE ST-OUEN

The granddaddy of all flea markets, the Puces de St-Ouen began in the Middle Ages, when merchants resold the cast-off clothing of aristocrats (crawling with its namesake insects) to peasant-folk. Today it's an overwhelming smorgasbord of stuff. It opens early and shuts down late, and serious hunters should allow themselves the better part of a day in order to cover significant ground, although the market tends to be least crowded before noon. (*Located in St-Ouen, a town just north of the 18ème. M: Porte-de-Clignancourt. Open Sa-M 7am-7:30pm; most vendors only open M 9am-6pm; many of the official stalls close early, but renegade vendors may open at 5am and close at 9pm.*)

▨ OFFICIAL MARKET. If the renegade bazaar turns you off, continue down rue Fabre to the official market, on rue des Rosiers and rue Jules Vallès. Here you can browse leisurely in a much less crowded setting. The whole enterprise is officially divided into a number of sub-markets, each specializing in a certain type of item, but they generally all have the same eclectic collection of unusual antiques.

RENEGADE MARKET. The 10min. walk along av. de la Porte de Clignancourt is jammed with tiny unofficial stalls. Vendors sell flimsy clothes, African masks, and teenage jewelry. It's a tourist trap and pickpockets know it, so be vigilant.

NEAR PARIS

VERSAILLES

By sheer force of ego, the Sun King converted a simple hunting lodge into the world's most famous palace. The sprawling château and bombastic gardens stand as a testament to the despotic playboy-king, Louis XIV, who lived, entertained, and governed here on the grandest of scales. A century later, young King Louis XVI and his bride Marie-Antoinette would discover that the dream of ridiculous luxury at the expense of near-universal poverty could not last forever.

A child during the aristocratic insurgency called the Fronde, Louis XIV is said to have entered his father's bedchamber one night only to find (and frighten away) an assassin. Fearing conspiracy, Louis as king chose to move the center of royal power out of Paris and away from potential aristocratic insubordination. In 1661, the Sun King renovated his small hunting lodge in Versailles. Naturally, the nobility followed him there, but on Louis's terms.

HISTORY OF VERSAILLES

No one knows just how much it cost to build Versailles; Louis XIV burned the accounts to keep the price a mystery. At the same time, life there was less luxurious than one might imagine: courtiers wore rented swords and urinated behind statues; wine froze in the drafty dining rooms; dressmakers invented the color *puce* (literally, "flea") to camouflage the insects crawling on noblewomen.

Louis XIV was succeeded by his great-grandson Louis XV in 1722. His most memorable act was to commission the Opéra, in the North Wing, for the marriage of Marie-Antoinette and the future Louis XVI. The newlyweds inherited the throne and Versailles when Louis XV died of smallpox in 1774. On October 5, 1789, 15,000 Parisian fishwives and National Guardsmen marched out to the palace and hauled the royal family back to Paris, where they were guillotined in 1793.

In the 19th century, King Louis-Philippe established a museum to preserve the château, against the wishes of many French, who wanted Versailles demolished like the Bastille. In 1871, the château took the limelight again, when Wilhelm of Prussia became Kaiser Wilhelm I of Germany in the Hall of Mirrors. That same year, as headquarters of the Thiers regime, Versailles sent an army against the Parisian Commune. The *Versaillais* pierced the city walls and crushed the *communards*. On June 28, 1919, at the end of WWI, France forced Germany to sign the ruinous Treaty of Versailles in the Hall of Mirrors.

🔲 🔢 TRANSPORTATION & PRACTICAL INFORMATION

Trains: The **RER** runs from M: Invalides or any stop on RER Line C5 to the Versailles Rive Gauche station (30-40min., every 15min, round-trip €4.90). From the Invalides or other RER Line C stop, take trains with labels beginning with "V." Buy your RER ticket before going through the turnstile to the platform; although a metro ticket will get you through these turnstiles, it will not get you through RER turnstiles at Versailles and could get you fined by the *contrôleurs*. From the RER Versailles train station, turn right down av. de Général de Gaulle, walk 200m, and turn left at the first big intersection on av. de Paris; the entrance to the château is straight ahead.

Tourist Office: Office de Tourisme de Versailles, 2bis av. de Paris (☎01 39 24 88 88; www.versailles-tourisme.fr). From the RER Versailles train station, follow directions to the château; the office will be on your left on av. de Paris before you reach the courtyard of the château. A great place to get an explanation of your options in Versailles from a human being before reaching the tourist mayhem in the palace. The office sells tickets for château events like the Fêtes de Nuit, and provides brochures on accommodations, restaurants, and events in town. Open daily summer 9am-7pm; winter 9am-6pm.

Tours: ☎01 30 83 76 79; www.chateauversailles.com. Open Tu-Su May-Sept. 9am-6:30pm; Oct.-Apr. 9am-5:30pm. Last admission 30min. before closing. Admission to palace and **self-guided tour, Entrance A:** €7.50, over 60 and after 3:30pm €5.30, under 18 free. Supplement for **audio tour, Entrance C:** 1hr.; €4, under 7 free. Supplement for **guided tour, Entrance D:** 1hr. tour of Chambres du Roi €4, under 18 €2.70; 1½hr. tour of the apartments of Louis XV and the opéra €6, ages 7-17 €4.20. **Full-day tour** "A Day at Versailles" (two 1½hr. segments, in the morning and afternoon) €17.90. Sign-language tours available; make reservations with the Bureau d'Action Culturelle (☎01 30 83 77 88).

🔲 SIGHTS

Arrive early in the morning to avoid the crowds, which are worse on Sundays from May to September and in late June. Pick up a map at one of the entrances or the info desk in the center of the courtyard. There are half a dozen entrances. Most visitors enter at **Entrance A**, on the right-hand side in the north wing, or **Entrance C**, in the archway to the left (either ticket allows free entrance to the other; native speakers of Russian, Chinese, Japanese, Spanish, or Italian start at C). **Entrance B** is for groups; **Entrance D** is where tours with a live guide begin, and **Entrance H** is for those in wheelchairs. **General admission** allows entrance to the *grands appartements*, the War and Peace Drawing Rooms, the *Galerie des Glaces* (Hall of Mirrors), and Marie-Antoinette's public apartment. Head for Entrance C to purchase an **audio guide**. From Entrance D, at the left-hand corner as you approach the palace, you can choose between four excellent **tours** of different parts of the château. The best is the 1½hr. tour of the Louis XV apartments and opéra.

SELF-GUIDED TOUR

Begin at **Entrance A.** Start in the **Musée de l'Histoire de France,** created in 1837 by Louis-Philippe. Along its walls are portraits of those who shaped the course of French history. The 21 rooms (arranged in chronological order) seek to construct a historical context for the château.

Up the staircase to the right is the dual-level **royal chapel,** designed by architect Hardouin-Mansart. Back toward the staircase and to the left is a series of gilded **drawing rooms** in the **State Apartments** that are dedicated to Hercules, Mars, and the ever-present Apollo (the Sun King identified with the sun god). The ornate **Salon d'Apollo** was Louis XIV's throne room. Framed by the **War and Peace Drawing Rooms** is the **Hall of Mirrors,** which was originally a terrace until Mansart added a series of mirrored panels and windows to double the light in the room and reflect the gardens outside. In their time, these mirrors were at the boundaries of 17th-century technology. Le Brun's ceiling paintings (1679-1686) tell the story of Louis XIV, culminating with *The King Governs Alone*.

The **Queen's Bedchamber,** where royal births were public events, is now furnished as it was on October 6, 1789, when Marie-Antoinette left the palace for the last time. A version of the David painting of Napoleon's self-coronation dominates the **Salle du Sacré** (also known as the Coronation Room). The **Hall of Battles** installed by Louis-Philippe is a monument to 14 centuries of the French military.

GARDENS

Open daily sunrise-sundown. Apr.-Oct. M-F €3, under 18 and after 6pm free. Fountains turned on for special displays like the Grandes Eaux Musicales, Apr.-Oct. Sa-Su 11am-noon and 3:30-5:30pm. €6. Though the most convenient place for bike rentals is across from the base of the canal, there are 2 other locations: one to the north of the Parterre Nord by the Grille de la Reine, and another by the Trianons at Porte St-Antoine. ☎01 39 66 97 66. Open Feb.-Nov. M-F 1pm-closing and Sa-Su 10am-closing. 1hr. €5, 30min. €3.30. Rent boats for 4 at the boathouse to the right side of the base of the canal. ☎01 39 66 97 66. Open Tu-F noon-5:30pm, Sa-Su 11am-6pm. €11 per hr., €8 per 30min.; €7.70 refundable deposit. Horse-drawn carriages run Tu-Su, departing from near the main terrace. ☎01 30 97 04 40.

Numerous artists—Le Brun, Mansart, Coysevox—executed statues and fountains, but master gardener André Le Nôtre provided the overall plan for Versailles's gardens. Louis XIV wrote the first guide to the gardens himself, entitled the *Manner of Presenting the Gardens at Versailles*. Tours should begin, as the Sun King commanded, on the terrace.

To the left of the terrace, the **Parterre Sud** graces the area in front of Mansart's **Orangerie,** once home to 2000 orange trees. In the center of the terrace lies the **Parterre d'Eau;** the **Bassin de Latone** fountain below features Latona, mother of Diana and Apollo, shielding her children as Jupiter turns villains into frogs. Past the fountain is one of the garden's gems: the flower-lined sanctuary of the **Jardin du Roi,** accessible only from the easternmost side facing the **Bassin du Miroir.** Near the south gate of the grove is the magnificent **Bassin de Bacchus,** one of four seasonal fountains depicting the god of wine. Working your way north toward the center of the garden, you can see where the king used to take light meals amid the exquisite **Bosquet de la Colonnade's** 32 violet-and-blue marble columns, sculptures, and basins, just east of the Jardin du Roi. The north gate to the Colonnade exits onto the 330m-long **Tapis Vert** (Green Carpet), the central mall linking the château to the garden's conspicuously central fountain, the **Bassin d'Apollon,** whose charioted Apollo rises, youthful and god-like, out of the water to enlighten the world.

On the north side of the garden is Marsy's incredible **Bosquet de l'Encelade.** When the fountains are turned on, a 25m-high jet bursts from Titan's enormous mouth, which is plated with shimmering gold and half-buried under a pile of rocks. Flora reclines on a bed of flowers in the **Bassin de Flore,** while a gilded Ceres luxuriates in sheaves of wheat in the **Bassin de Cérès.** The **Parterre Nord,** full of flowers, lawns, and trees, overlooks some of the garden's most spectacular fountains. The **Allée d'Eau,** a fountain-lined walkway, provides the best view of the **Bassin des Nymphes de Diane.** The path slopes toward the sculpted **Bassin du Dragon,** where a dying beast slain by Apollo spurts water 27m into the air. Ninety-nine jets of water from urns and seahorns surround Neptune in the **Bassin de Neptune,** the gardens' largest fountain.

Beyond the classical gardens stretch wilder woods, meadows, and farmland which are perfect for a more rustic picnic away from the manicured perfection of Versailles. Stroll along the **Grand Canal,** a rectangular pond beyond the Bassin d'Apollon measuring 1535m long.

TRIANONS & MARIE-ANTOINETTE'S HAMLET

*Shuttle trams from the palace to the Trianons and the Hameau leave from behind the palace facing the canals; head right. Round-trip €5, ages 3-12 €3. The walk takes 15min. Both Trianons open Nov.-Mar. Tu-Sa noon-5:30pm; Apr.-Oct. noon-6:30pm; last entrance 30min. before closing. **Admission** to the Trianons €5, after 3:30pm €3, under 18 free.*

The Trianons and Hameau provide a racier counterpoint to the château: here kings trysted with lovers, and Marie-Antoinette lived like the peasant she wasn't.

PETIT TRIANON. On the right down the wooded path from the château is the **Petit Trianon,** built between 1762 and 1768 for Louis XV and his mistress Madame de Pompadour. Marie-Antoinette took control of the Petit Trianon in 1774, and it soon earned the nickname "Little Vienna." In 1867, the Empress Eugénie, who worshipped Marie-Antoinette, turned it into a museum.

Exit the Petit Trianon, turn left, and follow the marked path to the libidinous **Temple of Love,** a domed rotunda with 12 white marble columns and swans. Marie-Antoinette held many intimate nighttime parties in the small space, during which thousands of torches would be illuminated in the surrounding ditch. The Queen was perhaps at her happiest and most ludicrous when at the **Hameau,** her own pseudo-peasant "hamlet" down the path from the Temple of Love. Inspired by Rousseau's theories on the goodness of nature by the *hameau* at **Chantilly,** the queen fashionably aspired for a more simple life. She commissioned Richard Mique to build a compound of 12 buildings (including a mill, dairy, and gardener's house, all surrounding a quaint artificial lake), in which she could play at country life. The result is something of a cross between English Romanticism and Euro-Disney. At the center is the **Queen's Cottage,** which contained ornate furniture, marble fireplaces, and walk-in closets for linens, silverware, and footmen.

GRAND TRIANON. The single-story, stone-and-pink-marble Grand Trianon was intended as a château-away-from-château for Louis XIV. Here the king could be reached only by boat along the **Grand Canal.** The palace consists of two wings joined together by a central porch. **Formal gardens** are located behind the colonnaded porch. The mini-château was stripped of its furniture during the Revolution but was later restored and inhabited by Napoleon and his second wife.

CHARTRES

Were it not for a piece of fabric, the cathedral of Chartres and the town that surrounds it might be only a sleepy hamlet. Because of this sacred relic—the cloth that the Virgin Mary supposedly wore when she gave birth to Jesus—Chartres became a major medieval pilgrimage center. The spectacular cathedral that towers above the surrounding rooftops is not the only reason to take the train ride here: the *vieille ville* (old town) is also a masterpiece of medieval architecture.

⌨ TRANSPORTATION & PRACTICAL INFORMATION

Trains: Chartres is accessible by frequent trains from **Gare Montparnasse, Grandes Lignes.** At least 1 train per hr. during the summer; call ahead for winter schedule. Trains take 50-75min.; round-trip €23.60, under 26 and groups of 2-4 €17.80, over 60 €17.60. To reach the cathedral from the train station, walk straight along rue Jehan de Beauce to pl. de Châtelet and turn left into the *place,* right onto rue Ste-Même, and left onto rue Jean Moulin (or just head toward the massive spires).

Tourist Office: (☎02 37 18 26 26; info@otchartres.fr), in front of the cathedral's main entrance at pl. de la Cathédrale. Helps **find accommodations** (€1.50) and supplies visitors with a very helpful map guide with a walking tour and a list of restaurants, hotels, and additional sights. The *Petit Train Chart'train* runs late Mar. to early Nov. with 35min. narrated tours (in French only) of the old city. (☎02 37 21 87 60. Tours leave the tourist office every hr. starting at 10:30am. €5.50, under 12 €3.) Open Apr.-Sept. M-Sa 9am-7pm, Su and holidays 9:30am-5:30pm; Oct.-Mar. M-Sa 10am-6pm, Su and holidays 10am-1pm and 2:30-4:30pm. Closed Jan. 1, Nov. 1 and 11, and Dec. 25.

◉ SIGHTS

☎02 37 21 75 02; www.cathedrale-chartres.com. Open daily Easter to Oct. 8am-8pm; Nov. to Easter 8:30am-7pm. No casual visits during mass. **Masses** M-F 11:45am and 6:15pm; Sa 11:45am and 6pm; Su 9:15am (Latin), 11am, 6pm (in the crypt). Call the tourist office for info on concerts in the cathedral, the annual student pilgrimage in late May, and other pilgrimages and festivals throughout the year. **North Tower** open May-Aug. M-Sa 9:30am-noon and 2-5:30pm, Su 2-5:30pm; Sept.-Apr. M-Sa 9:30am-noon and 2-4:30pm, Su 2-4:30pm; Tower closed Jan. 1 and 5 and Dec. 25. **Tower admission** €4, ages 18-25 €2.50, under 18 and some Su free. English audio guides available at the gift shop (€2.90, €3.80, or €5.70, depending on tour) and require ID deposit. **Tours in English of the cathedral by Malcolm Miller** begin outside the gift shop in the cathedral and last 1¼hr. Easter to early Nov. M-Sa noon and 2:45pm, call ☎02 37 28 15 58 for tour availability during winter months. €8, students €5. **Tours in French of the crypt** leave from the inside of the cathedral. ☎02 37 21 75 02. Tours 30min. Apr.-Oct. M-Sa 11am, 2:15, 3:30, 4:30pm; Nov.-Mar. 11am and 4:15pm; additional 5:15pm tour late June to late Sept.; no 11am tours anytime during the year on Su. €2.50, students €1.70, under 7 free.

The Cathédrale de Chartres, which escaped major damage during the Revolution and WWII, is the best-preserved medieval church in Europe. A patchwork masterpiece of Romanesque and Gothic design, the cathedral was constructed by generations of unknown masons, architects, and artisans who labored for centuries.

SANCTA CAMISIA. The year after he became emperor in AD 875, Charlemagne's grandson, Charles the Bald, donated the Sancta Camisia, believed to have been worn by the Virgin Mary when she gave birth to Christ. It cannot be seen until the Treasury reopens. A church existed on the site, but the emperor's bequest required a new cathedral to accommodate the many pilgrims. The sick were nursed in the crypt below. In 911, the powers of the relic supposedly saved the city; just as he started to besiege Chartres, the Viking leader Rollon converted to Christianity.

STAINED GLASS. At a time when most people were illiterate, the cathedral served as an educational beacon, depicting the stories of the Bible in the 13th-century stained glass, including the famous Blue Virgin, Tree of Jesse, and Passion and Resurrection of Christ windows. These were preserved through WWI and WWII by town authorities who shipped the glass to the Dordogne.

LABYRINTH. A winding labyrinth is carved into the floor in the rear of the nave. Designed in the 13th century, the labyrinth was laid out for pilgrims as a substitute for a journey to the Holy Land. By following this symbolic journey on their hands and knees, the devout would act out a voyage to heavenly Jerusalem.

TOUR JEHAN-DE-BEAUCE. The adventurous can climb the cathedral's north tower for a stellar view of the cathedral roof, the flying buttresses, and the city below. The tower, a wonderful example of flamboyant Gothic style, provides a striking counterpart to its more sedate partner, the Romanesque **octagonal steeple** (the tallest in its style still standing), built just before the 1194 fire.

CRYPT. Parts of Chartres's crypt, such as a well down which Vikings tossed the bodies of their victims, date from the 9th century. You can enter the 110m-long subterranean crypt only on a tour that leaves from La Crypte, the store opposite the cathedral's south entrance. *(Tour in French. English info sheets available.)*

ELSEWHERE IN THE CATHEDRAL. Inside the church, the Renaissance choir screen, begun by Jehan de Beauce in 1514, depicts various events from the life of the Virgin Mary. The lovely, candlelit shrine to *Notre Dame de Pilier* is near the Sancta Camisia. Both are worth a visit.

The only English-language **tours** of the cathedral are given by veteran tour guide **Malcolm Miller,** an authority on Gothic architecture. His presentations on the cathedral's history and symbolism are witty and enjoyable for all ages. If you can, take both his morning and afternoon tour—no two are alike.

GIVERNY

Drawn to the verdant hills, haystacks, and lily pads of this stretch of the Epte River, French painter Claude Monet and his eight children settled in Giverny in 1883. By 1887, John Singer Sargent, Paul Cézanne, and Mary Cassatt had placed their easels beside Monet's and turned the village into a major artists' colony. Today, the town remains as it was back then (the cobblestone street that was the setting for Monet's *Wedding March* is instantly recognizable), save for the tourists, who come in droves.

▐ TRANSPORTATION

The **SNCF** runs several **trains** sporadically from Paris's Gare St-Lazare to Vernon, the nearest station to the town of Giverny. To get to the train in Paris, take the metro (M: St-Lazare), and take the rue d'Amsterdam exit, then walk straight into the right-hand entrance of the Gare. From there, go to the Grandes Lignes reservation room. €21 round-trip, couples €31.60.

Take the bus (☎02 32 71 06 39) from Vernon to Giverny (10min.; Tu-Su 4 per day 15min. after the train arrives in Vernon; return only 3 per day, schedule for return inside the info office in the train station; €2, round-trip €4), or rent a **bike** from the Café du Chemin de Fer right across from the Vernon station (☎02 32 51 01 72. €12 per day, plus deposit of driver's license or other identification. MC/V.) Coordinate train and bus schedules before your trip to avoid 3hr. delays.

◉ SIGHTS

FONDATION CLAUDE MONET. Today, Monet's serenely beautiful house and gardens are maintained by the Fondation Claude Monet. From April to July, the gardens overflow with wild roses, hollyhocks, poppies, and the scent of honeysuckle. The water lilies, the Japanese bridge, and the weeping willows of the Orientalist Water Gardens look like—well, like *Monets*. The only way to avoid the rush is to go early in the morning and, if possible, early in the season. In Monet's thatched-roof home, big windows, solid furniture, and pale blue walls complement his collection of 18th- and 19th-century Japanese prints. *(84 rue Claude Monet. ☎02 32 51 28 21; www.fondation-monet.com. Open Apr.-Oct. Tu-Su 9:30am-6:30pm. €5.50, students and ages 12-18 €4, ages 7-12 €3. Gardens €4.)*

MUSÉE D'ART AMÉRICAIN. Near the Claude Monet Foundation, the incongruously modern but respectfully hidden Musée d'Art Américain houses a small number of works by American expatriates to France (and specifically Giverny), such as Theodore Butler and John Leslie Breck, who came to Giverny to learn the Impressionist style. *(99 rue Claude Monet. ☎02 32 51 94 65; www.maag.org. Open Apr.-Oct. Tu-Su 9:30am-6:30pm. €5.50; students, seniors, and teachers €4; ages 12-18 €3. Free the first Su of each month. Audio guides €1.)*

VAUX-LE-VICOMTE

Nicolas Fouquet, Louis XIV's Minister of Finance, assembled architect Le Vau, artist Le Brun, and landscaper Le Nôtre to build Vaux in 1641. On August 17, 1661, upon the completion of what was then France's most beautiful château, Fouquet threw an extravagant 6000-guest party in honor of Louis XIV. Young Louis XIV, supposedly furious at having been upstaged, ordered Fouquet arrested soon after. In a trial for embezzlement of state funds that lasted three years, the judges voted narrowly for banishment over death. Louis XIV overturned the judgment in favor of life imprisonment—the only time in French history that the head of state overruled the court's decision in favor of a more severe sentence. Fouquet remained imprisoned at Pignerol, in the French Alps, until his death in 1680. Many, including Alexandre Dumas, who fictionalized the story in *Le Vicomte de Bragelonne*, believe Fouquet to be the legendary man in the iron mask.

■ ? TRANSPORTATION & PRACTICAL INFORMATION

Driving: The château is 50km from Paris. Take Autoroute A4 or A6 from Paris and exit at Troyes-Nancy by N104. Head toward Meaux on N36 and follow the signs.

Train: Take the **RER** to Melun from Châtelet-Les Halles or Gare de Lyon (45min., round-trip €13.40). Then take a taxi (at least €15) to the château (be sure to ask the driver to meet you back at the château at a certain time, or pay €0.20 for the staff at the exit to phone for you). You can walk, but it's a perilous 2hr. trek on the highway. Follow av. de Thiers to highway 36, direction "Meaux," and follow signs to Vaux-Le-Vicomte.

Tour Groups: Several tourist groups run trips to the château with varying frequencies and prices; call ahead. Services with regularly scheduled trips are **ParisVision** (☎01 42 60 30 01; www.parisvision.com) and **Cityrama** (☎01 44 55 61 00; www.cityrama.fr).

Tourist Office: 2 av. Gallieni (☎01 64 37 11 31). By Melun's train station. Information on accommodations and free maps. Open Tu-Sa 10am-noon and 2-6pm.

◉ SIGHTS

CHÂTEAU & GARDENS

☎01 64 14 41 90; www.vaux-le-vicomte.com. Open late Mar. to mid-Nov. daily 10am-6pm; visits by appointment for groups of 20 or more the rest of the year. **Admission** to château, gardens, and carriage museum €12; students, seniors, and ages 6-16 €9.50; under 6 free. On Sa evenings from May to early Oct., and F in July and Aug., the château is open for visites aux chandelles (candlelight visits) 8pm-midnight. €15; ages 6-16, students, and seniors €13. Fountains on Apr.-Oct., 2nd and last Sa of each month 3-6pm. Château audiotour includes good historical presentation in English; €2.50. Club cars station to the right of the garden from the entrance; €13 for 45min. ride; €125 deposit. First floor only of the château is wheelchair-accessible. MC/V.

CHÂTEAU. The château seems rather plain when viewed from the front, but inside is a kind of baroque celebration. The building is covered with ornate scripted "F"s and squirrels (Fouquet's symbol) and the family motto *"Quo non ascendit"* ("what heights might he not reach"); the tower with three battlements has his second wife's crest engraved on it. **Madame Fouquet's Closet** once had walls lined with small mirrors, the decorative forerunner of Versailles's Hall of Mirrors. Over the fireplace of the **Square Room** hangs Le Brun's portrait of Fouquet. Le Brun's **Room of the Muses** is one of his most famous decorative schemes. The artist had planned to crown the cavernous, Neoclassical **Oval Room** (or **Grand Salon**) with a fresco entitled *The Palace of the Sun*, but Fouquet's arrest halted all decorating activity, and only a single eagle and a patch of sky were completed. The tapestries once bore Fouquet's menacing squirrels, but Colbert seized them and replaced the rodents with his own adders. The ornate **King's Bedchamber** boasts an orgy of cherubs and lions fluttering around the centerpiece, Le Brun's *Time Bearing Truth Heavenward.*

GARDENS. At Vaux, Le Nôtre gave birth to the classical French garden, with trimmed shrubs, shaved lawns, sculpted bushes, and strategically placed pools. Vaux's multilevel terraces, fountained walkways, and fantastical *parterres* (low-cut hedges and crushed stone in arabesque patterns) are still the most exquisite example of 17th-century French gardens. The collaboration of Le Nôtre with Le Vau and Le Brun ensured that the same patterns and motifs were repeated with astonishing harmony in the gardens, château, and tapestries inside. Vaux owes its most impressive *trompe l'oeil* effect to Le Nôtre's whimsical and adroit use of the laws of perspective. From the back steps of the château, it looks as if the grottoes at the far end of the garden appear directly behind the large pool of water, but as you approach the other end, the grottoes seem to recede, revealing a sunken canal known as **La Poêle** (the Frying Pan), which is invisible from the château. The **Round Pool** and its surrounding 17th-century statues mark an important intersection; to the left, down the east walkway, are the **Water Gates**, the backdrop for Molière's performance of *Les Fâcheux.* The **Water Mirror**, farther down the central walkway, was designed to reflect the château perfectly, but you may have some trouble positioning yourself to enjoy the effect. A climb to the **Farnese Hercules** provides the best vista of the grounds. The tremendous Hercules sculpture at the top was at the center of Fouquet's trial. In a country that believed in the divine right of kings, Fouquet had to justify why he had likened himself to Hercules, the only mortal to become a god. The old stables, **Les Equipages,** also house a fantastic **carriage museum.** The best way to see Vaux's gardens is during the 🕯**visites aux chandelles,** when the château and grounds are lit up by thousands of candles, and classical music plays through the gardens in imitation of Fouquet's legendary party; arrive around dusk to see the grounds in all their glory.

CHANTILLY

The château itself is much less famous than the *crème chantilly* (whipped cream) that was invented here, which means it won't be overrun with tour buses and souvenir salesmen. The 14th- to 19th-century Château de Chantilly is a whimsically baroque amalgam of Gothic extravagance, Renaissance geometry, and flashy Victorian ornamentalism. The triangular-shaped château (a dolled-up hunting lodge) is surrounded by a moat, lakes, canals, and the simple, elegant Le Nôtre gardens (no Versailles fireworks here). With the architecturally masterful Grandes Ecuries (stables) and world-class **Musée Condé,** it's a wonder that this château has stayed a hidden treasure for so long.

🚉 TRANSPORTATION & PRACTICAL INFORMATION

Trains: Take the **train** from the Gare du Nord (Grandes Lignes) to Chantilly Gouvieux (35min., approximately every hr. 5am-midnight, round-trip €11.40). Free and frequent **navettes** (shuttles) to the château (dir: Senlis); catch one just to the left as you exit the train station. Otherwise, the château is a 30min. walk from the station—your only option Su when the shuttle is not running.

Tourist Office: 60 av. du Maréchal Joffre (☎03 44 67 37 37; www.chantilly-tourisme.com). From the train station, go straight up rue des Otages. Offers brochures, maps, and a schedule of the free shuttle buses running to and from the château. The tourist office can also call a taxi (€6). Mind-numbing hours of operation: May-Sept. M-Th

9am-12:30pm and 1:30-6pm, F 9am-12:30pm and 1:30-5pm, Sa 10am-12:30pm and 1:30-5pm, Su 10am-1:30pm; Oct.-Apr. M-Th 9am-12:30pm and 2-6pm, F 9am-12:30pm and 2-5pm, Sa 10am-12:30pm and 2-5pm. To continue to the stables and château, leave the office and turn left onto av. Maréchal Joffre, and then right onto rue de Connetable, or take a more scenic route straight through the forest.

◎ SIGHTS

CHÂTEAU, GARDENS, & MUSÉE CONDÉ

☎ 03 44 62 62 62; www.institut-de-france.fr/patrimoine/chantilly/chantilly.htm. Open M and W-Su Mar-Oct. 10am-6pm; Nov.-Feb. 10:30am-12:45pm and 2-5pm. (last entrance 1hr. before closing). **Admission** to **gardens** €3, students and children €2; to **gardens and château** €7, students €6, children €2.80. Various **ticket packages** available: gardens and boat or train ride €8.50, students €7.50, children €5; gardens, château, and boat or train ride €13/€11/€7; gardens, train and boat ride €13/€11/€7; gardens, château, boat and train ride €15/€13/€9. Miniature trains offer 30min. tours of the gardens and grounds in French and English. Frequent free 45min. **tours** in French of the château's appartements. AmEx/MC/V.

Maps of the **gardens** (€1 at the information office) offer a suggested walking tour of the grounds, but wandering is just as effective. A bike can help you explore the château's 115 hectares of parks and grounds. Directly in front of the château lies the gardens' central expanse, which is designed in the French formal style, with neat rows of carefully pruned trees, calm statues in serene repose, and geometric pools. To the left, hidden within a forest, a garden in the English Romantic style attempts to re-create untamed nature. Here, paths meander around pools where lone swans glide elegantly. Windows carved into the foliage allow you to see fountains in the formal garden as you stroll past. To the right the gardens hide a huge village **hameau** (hamlet), the somewhat less corny inspiration for Marie-Antoinette's hamlet at Versailles. Farther in, a statue of Cupid reigns over the "Island of Love." A 2003 addition is the kangaroo enclosure. These 15 or so wallabies represent the park's first hop toward recreating the *ménagerie* that existed during the château's heyday.

Chantilly's biggest attraction lies inside the château: the spectacular **Musée Condé** houses the Duc d'Aumale's private collection of pre-modern paintings, and is one of only two museums in France to boast three Raphaëls (the other is the Louvre). The skylit picture galleries contain 800 paintings, 3000 drawings, and hundreds of engravings, sculptures, and tapestries, among them works by Titian, Corot, Botticelli, Delacroix, and Ingres. Bronze basset hounds, deer antlers, and huge Gobelin tapestries depicting hunting scenes all confirm the château's ribald and gamey past. Following the Duke's will, the paintings and furniture are arranged as they were over a century ago, in the distinctively 19th-century frame-to-frame ("academic") style.

The absolute gem of the building, however, is the tiny **santuario.** This hidden gallery contains what the Duke himself considered the finest works in his collection: this includes such highlights as illuminated manuscripts by Jean Fouquet, a painting by Fra Filippo Lippi, and two Raphaëls. The museum's two most valuable pieces, a Gutenberg Bible and the illuminated manuscripts of the *Très Riches Heures* (1410), are too fragile to be kept in public view, but a near-perfect facsimile of the latter can be seen by the entrance. The illustrious **library** (second only to the Bibliothèque Nationale in prestige) is filled with enough centuries-old books to make any bibliophile drool. The rest of the château's **appartements** can be visited only by taking a free guided tour in French.

GRANDES ECURIES

☎ 03 44 57 13 13 or 03 44 57 40 40, reservations 03 44 57 91 79; www.musee-vivant-du-cheval.fr. Open Apr.-Oct. M and W-F 10:30am-5:30pm, Sa-Su 10:30am-6pm; Nov.-Mar. M and W-F 2-5pm, Sa-Su 10:30am-5:30pm. **Museum** €8; children, students, and seniors €7.50. **Equestrian show** first Su of each month, 3:30pm. €17, children €16. **Hippodrome** matches daily in June 11am, 12:30, 2, 3:15, 4:30pm. ☎ 03 44 57 13 13. Open Apr.-Oct. M and W-F 10:30am-6:30pm, Sa-Su 10:30am-7pm; May-Aug. also open Tu 10:30am-5:30pm. Call for schedule of horse shows.

The other great draw to the château is the Grandes Ecuries (stables), whose immense marble corridors, courtyards, and façades are masterpieces of 18th-century French architecture. Originally commissioned by Louis-Henri Bourbon, who hoped to live here when he was reborn as a horse, the Ecuries feature extravagant fountains, domed rotundas, and sculptured patios. From 1719 to the Revolution, the stables housed 240 horses and hundreds of hunting dogs, and now are home to the **Musée Vivant du Cheval,** an extensive collection (supposedly the largest in the world) of all things equine (beware the rather graphic horse biology exhibit near the end of the museum tour). In addition to the stables' 30 live horses, donkeys, and ponies, on display are saddles, horseshoes, international merry-go-rounds, and a horse statue featured in a James Bond film. On the first Sunday of every month and Christmas, equestrian shows, such as "Horses, Dream, and Poetry" and "Horse Gospel" are a fanciful highlight. The Hippodrome (or racetrack) on the premises is the Kentucky Derby of France: two of France's premier horse races are held here in June. In mid-September, polo at the Hippodrome is free to the public.

DISNEYLAND PARIS

When Euro-Disney opened in 1992, Mickey Mouse, Cinderella, and Snow White were met by the jeers of French intellectuals and the popular press, who called the Disney theme park a "cultural Chernobyl." Resistance seems to have subsided since Walt & Co. renamed it Disneyland Paris and started serving wine. Despite its dimensions, this Disney park is the most technologically advanced yet; the special effects on some rides are incredible.

Everything in Disneyland Paris is in English and French. The detailed guide called the *Park Guide Book* (free at Disney City Hall to the left of the entrance) has a map and information on everything from restaurants and attractions to bathrooms and first aid. The *Guests' Special Services Guide* has info on wheelchair accessibility. For more info on Disneyland Paris, call ☎ 01 60 30 60 81 (from the US) or ☎ 01 60 30 63 53 from all other countries, or visit www.disneylandparis.com.

Instead of selling tickets, Disneyland Paris issues **passeports,** which is valid for one day and allow entry to either Disneyland Park or Walt Disney Studios. For an extra €10, you can visit both theme parks. (Apr.-Nov. €39/€29; Nov.-Jan. €38, ages 3-11 €29; Jan.-Apr. €29/€25. 2- and 3-day *passeports* also available.) They can be bought at the ground floor of the Disneyland Hotel. *Passeports* are also sold at the Paris tourist office on the Champs-Elysées, FNAC, Virgin Megastores, the Galeries Lafayette, any Disney store, many hotels in Paris, or at any of the major stations on RER line A, such as Châtelet-Les Halles, Gare de Lyon, or Charles de Gaulle-Etoile. Any of these options beats buying tickets at the park, as ticket lines can be very long. ▓**Fastpasses** allow guests to make reservations to ride attractions, shaving 45min. off of the wait to ride a roller coaster. Inquire at the Fastpass counters outside of each attraction. The park is open Apr.-Sept. daily 9am-11pm; Oct.-Apr. M-F 10am-9pm, Sa-Su 10am-10pm. Hours are subject to change, especially during winter; call ahead for details.

To get to Disneyland Paris, take **RER** A4 from either M: Gare de Lyon or Châtelet-Les Halles (dir. Marne-la-Vallée) to the last stop, M: Marne-la-Vallée-Chessy. Before boarding the train, check the boards hanging above the platform to make sure there's a light next to the Marne-la-Vallée stop and not the Boissy-Saint-Leger stop (40min., every 30min., round-trip €11). The last train to Paris leaves Disney at 12:22am, but the metro closes at midnight, so you'll have to catch an earlier train to make it to the metro in time. **TGV** service from de Gaulle reaches the park in a mere 15min., making Disneyland Paris easily accessible for travelers with Eurail passes. Certain **Eurostar** trains now run directly between Waterloo Station in London and Disneyland. (☎ 08 36 35 35 39. Departure usually around 9:15am returning at 7:30pm. €135-375. Reserve far in advance.) By **car,** take the A4 highway from Paris and get off at Exit 14, marked "Parc Disneyland Paris," about 30min. from the city. (Parking €8 per day; 11,000 spaces in all.) Disneyland Paris **buses** run between the terminals of both Orly and de Gaulle and the bus station near the Marne-la-Vallée RER. (40min.; every 45-60min. 8:30am-7:30pm, 8:30am-9:30pm at CDG on F and Su; round-trip €14, ages 3-11 €11.50.)

FLANDERS & PAS DE CALAIS

 Flanders (on the Belgian border), Picardy (farther inland), and the coastal Pas de Calais remain the final frontiers of unadulterated France. Although every day thousands of tourists travel to and from Britain through the channel ports (the *Côte d'Opale*), including lively **Calais** (p. 184) and genial **Boulogne-sur-Mer** (p. 183), few take the time to explore the lovely, ancient towns away from the coast, which therefore preserve a charming local flavor.

The windmills and gabled homes of once-Flemish Flanders possess gingerbread charm. Chalk cliffs loom along the Brit-accented coast, and cows and sheep graze near collapsed bunkers from the wars. In Picardy, seas of wheat extend in all directions, interrupted in spring and summer by red poppies. When fleeing the ferry ports, don't overlook the area's hidden gems. **Lille** (p. 169), a large, lively, but untouristed metropolis, has a heavy Flemish flavor and world-class art collections. Smaller but more picturesque are the cities of **Amiens** (p. 188), known for its cathedral and floating gardens, and **Arras** (p. 177), with beautiful gabled houses, mossy chalk tunnels, intriguing Flemish culture, and WWI monuments. Less hectic are flower-lined **Montreuil-sur-Mer** (p. 186) and the fine cathedral of **Laon** (p. 179).

Even after five decades of peace, the memory of two world wars is never far from the minds of the inhabitants of northern France. Nearly every town bears scars from the merciless bombing of World War II, and German-built concrete observation towers still peer over the dunes. Regiments of tombstones stand as reminders of the terrible toll exacted at Arras, Cambrai, and the Somme.

Belgian-influenced Flanders is known for its abundance of beer and *moules* (mussels) swathed in an astounding variety of sauces. Other specialties include plums preserved in vinegar and *jenever*, a type of gin particular to the region.

FLANDERS

LILLE

With its candy-colored Flemish façades crowding broad *avenues* and picturesque *places*, Lille (pop. 175,000), the hometown of Charles de Gaulle, is the most distinctly foreign-feeling city outside Strasbourg. With 100,000 students in the area and 25% of the population under 25, France's 4th-largest metropolis has the best nightlife in the north.

▐ TRANSPORTATION

Flights: Aéroport de Lille-Lesquin (☎03 20 49 68 68). Cariane Nord **shuttles** leave from rue le Corbusier at Gare Lille Europe (☎03 20 90 79 79; 5-6 per day according to flight times, €4.60). Manual luggage storage available.

Trains: Lille has two stations:

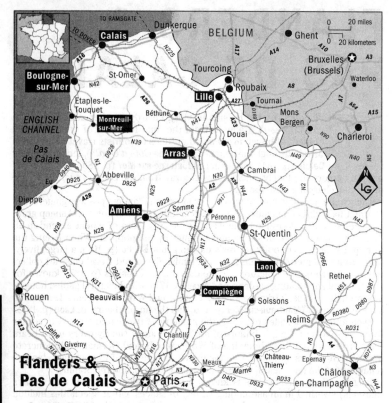

TO RAMSGATE
TO DOVER
BELGIUM
Dunkerque
Calais
Ghent
N25
A17
A14
A10
A3
Bruxelles
(Brussels)
St-Omer
Tourcoing
Waterloo
Boulogne-sur-Mer
N42
A26
Roubaix
A8
Lille
A27
Tournai
Étaples-le-Touquet
Béthune
N41
A23
Mons
Bergen
A7
A54
A15
Montreuil-sur-Mer
ENGLISH CHANNEL
Douai
N90
Charleroi
Pas de Calais
N39
Arras
N1
Cambrai
N49
N40
N5
Abbeville
D925
D928
D925
N25
A2
A28 N44
N43
N2
Eu
D940
D929
D917
Dieppe
A28
Somme
Amiens
Péronne
N29
N43
N28
N29
St-Quentin
A16
N17
D934
N32
Laon
D966
N31
D962
Noyon
Rouen
Beauvais
Compiègne
N31
Soissons
Rethel
N51
D987
RD380
D980
Seine
A1
Reims
RD31
N14
N2
N5
A4
Giverny
D1
N44
Chantilly
RD33
Flanders & Pas de Calais
Paris
A4
Meaux
Marne
N3
Château-Thierry
Épernay
Châlons-en-Champagne
D407
D933
N3
0   20 miles
0   20 kilometers

Gare Lille Flandres, pl. de la Gare, is more central and connects to more of the surrounding area. **Currency exchange** open M-Sa 8am-8pm, Su 10am-6pm. Info desk open M-Sa 9am-7pm. Ticket office open M-F 5:20am-9pm, Sa 5:55am-9pm, Su 7:20am-10:45pm. Manual luggage storage available. To: **Arras** (40min., 18 per day, €8.60); **Brussels,** Belgium (1½hr., 20 per day, €20.40); **Paris** (1hr., 21 per day, €33.70).

Gare Lille Europe, av. le Corbusier (☎08 36 35 35 35). M: Gare Lille Europe. Info office open daily 5:30am-10:45pm. Station open daily 5:30am-12:15am. **Eurostar** runs to **London** and **Brussels.** **TGVs** run to the south of France and **Paris** (1hr., 4 per day, €33.70).

Bus Station: Eurolines, office at 23 Parvis St-Maurice (☎03 20 78 18 88), sends buses from Gare Lille Europe to **London** (round-trip €52), **Brussels** (round-trip €15), **Amsterdam** (round-trip €45), and other Continental cities. Office open mid-Sept. to mid-June M-F 9:30am-12:30pm and 1:30-6pm, Sa 1-6pm; mid-June to mid-Sept. M-Sa until 7pm. MC/V.

Public Transportation: The **Transpole** central **bus terminal** is next to the train station. **Metro (M)** and **trams** serve the town and periphery daily 5:12am-12:12am. Tickets €1.15, *carnet* of 10 €10, daypass €3.40. Info at the tourist office or below Gare Flandres (☎08 20 42 40 40). Kiosks open M-F 7am-7pm, Sa 9am-1pm and 2-5pm.

Taxis: Taxi Union (☎03 20 06 06 06) or **Taxi Gare** (☎03 20 06 64 00). Both 24hr.

Bike Rental: Peugeot Cycles, 64 rue Léon Gambetta (☎03 20 54 83 39). €8 per day. €160 deposit. Open Tu-Sa 9am-12:30pm and 2-7pm. MC/V.

▦ ⊉ ORIENTATION & PRACTICAL INFORMATION

Lille is easy to navigate—it even has a metro—but use a map when tackling *vieille Lille*, a maze of narrow streets from the tourist office to the cathedral. The newer part of town, with wide boulevards and 19th-century buildings, culminates in the **Marché de Wazemmes.** The city's largest shopping district is in the primarily pedestrian district off **place du Théâtre.** Lille is a big city, and can be unsafe. In general, be cautious outside the pedestrian city center, especially near the train station, the Marché de Wazemmes, the sidestreets between the Gare Lille Flandres and bd. Carnot, rue Molinel, and in the areas east of the city.

Tourist Office: pl. Rihour (☎03 20 21 94 21; fax 03 20 21 94 20), located inside the Palais Rihour. M: Rihour. From Gare Lille Flandres, head straight down rue Faidherbe for 2 blocks and turn left through pl. du Théâtre and pl. de Gaulle. Beyond pl. de Gaulle, there's a huge war monument; the tourist office is in the palace behind it. Free maps, free **accommodations service,** and a host of useful pamphlets and brochures, including the essential mass transit guide, a detailed city guide (€1) in English and French, a free student guide, *L'Indic*, and a comprehensive guide to the nightlife of the city (both in French). English-speaking staff. Several city tours, in French and English, from €6 to €9, including one of *vieux Lille* and a night tour with a beer tasting. **Currency exchange,** though the post office has a better rate. The **Lille Metropole City Pass** (€15) gives one day of unlimited transportation in Lille, as well as covering entrance into museums and monuments, a panoramic tour, and additional discounts valid in Lille for up to one week (two-day pass €25, three-day pass €30). Office open M-Sa 9:30am-6:30pm, Su 10am-noon and 2-5pm.

Budget Travel: Wasteels, 25 pl. des Reignaux (☎08 25 88 70 41). Open M-Th 9am-noon and 2-6pm, F 9am-1pm and 2-6pm, Sa 9am-noon.

Youth Information: Centre Régional Information Jeunesse (CRIJ), 2 rue Nicolas Leblanc, has information about seasonal work and long-term lodging, plus Internet (€1.80 per hr.) Summer hours vary, but generally open Tu and Th 10am-8pm, W and F 10am-6pm, Sa 10am-12:30pm. CROUS, 74 rue de Cambrai (☎03 20 88 66 33), has an extremely helpful staff dedicated to helping students find lodging, jobs, and study opportunities. Open M-Th 9am-noon and 1-4:30pm, F 1-4pm.

English Bookstore: V.O., 36 rue de Tournai (☎03 20 14 33 96), is an international bookstore with a section of books in English. Open Tu-Sa noon-8pm.

Laundromat: 57 rue du Molinel. Open daily 7am-7pm. Also **Lavarama,** 2 rue Ovigneuz. Open daily 7am-8pm.

Police: pl. Salengro (☎03 20 49 56 66), in the Hôtel de Ville.

Hospital: 2 av. Oscar Lambret (☎03 20 44 59 62). M: CHR-Oscar Lambret.

24hr. Pharmacy: for the **pharmacie de garde,** call ☎03 20 16 96 96.

Internet: Apart from the inexpensive **CRIJ** (see **Youth Information**), there's also **NetK,** 13 rue de la Clef. €2-4 per hr. Open M-Sa 10am-11pm, Su 3-9pm. **Cybertime,** 4 rue St-Pierre St-Paul off rue Gambetta. €3 per hr. Open Tu-Su 10am-11pm. **Agence France Télécom,** pl. Général de Gaulle (☎03 20 57 40 00), facing the Vieille Bourse. €0.15 per min., students half-price. Open M 2-7pm, Tu-Sa 9am-7pm.

Post Office: 8 pl. de la République (☎03 28 36 10 20). M: République. **Currency exchange** with good rates. Open M-F 8am-7pm, Sa 8am-noon. **Poste Restante:** 59035 Lille Cédex. **Branches:** on bd. Carnot, near pl. du Théâtre. Open M-F 8am-6:30pm and Sa 8am-noon. On the corner of rue Nationale and rue J. Roisin. Open M 10am-6:30pm, Tu-F 9am-6:30pm, Sa 10am-12:45pm and 1:45-4pm. 125 rue Gambetta. Open Tu-F 9:30am-12:30pm and 1:45-6:15pm, Sa 10am-4pm. **Postal code:** 59000.

ACCOMMODATIONS & CAMPING

One- and two-star hotels in the €22-35 range cluster around **Gare Lille Flandres;** more expensive accommodations dot **place du Théâtre** and **place de Gaulle.**

Auberge de Jeunesse (HI), 12 rue Malpart (☎03 20 57 08 94; fax 03 20 63 98 93; lille@fuaj.org). M: Mairie de Lille. Friendly reception, international atmosphere, and spacious quarters. Some rooms have showers, though others have co-ed hall bathrooms. Bar open 7:30pm-1am. Breakfast included. Sheets €2.80. Kitchen. Laundry. Luggage storage €2 per day. Checkout 10am. Curfew 1am. Reception daily 7-11am and 3pm-1am. Open late Jan. to mid-Dec. 3- to 6-bed dorms €13 per person, €2.90 extra per night for **non-members;** deposit of €10 required for key. MC/V. ❶

Hôtel de France, 10 rue de Béthune (☎03 20 57 14 78; fax 03 20 57 06 01). The least expensive option in the ritzy pedestrian district, Hôtel de France offers spacious, TV-equipped rooms, some brand-new, others a little worn. Breakfast €4.50. Reception daily 7am-11pm. Singles €29.50, with shower €39.50-54.50; doubles €34/€39-61; triples with shower €47.40-65.40. Extra bed €4.60. AmEx/MC/V. ❸

Hôtel Faidherbe, 42 pl. de la Gare (☎03 20 06 27 93; fax 03 20 55 95 38). M: Gare Lille Flandres. Convenience with an institutional feel, complete with linoleum-floored rooms and a payphone in the hall. Near the train station. Breakfast €4.30. Reception 24hr. Singles and doubles €27.50, with shower €36.60-42.70; triples €50.30. Extra person €7.60. 10% discount with *Let's Go* guide. AmEx/MC/V. ❸

Le Grand Hôtel, 51 rue Faidherbe (☎03 20 06 31 57; www.legrandhotel.com). Between Gare Lille Flandres and pl. du Théâtre, this high-end option offers large, luxurious rooms, with full bath, TV, and tasteful décor. Breakfast €6. Reception daily 7am-11pm. Singles €60; doubles €65-68; triples €76. AmEx/MC/V. ❺

Hôtel Coq Hardi, 34 pl. de la Gare (☎03 20 06 05 89; fax 03 20 74 11 95). M: Gare Lille Flandres. The cheapest rooms are clean and somewhat worn; the larger €35 rooms are a better value. Convenient location. Breakfast €4. Reception daily 7am-11pm. Singles €22, with shower €33; doubles €27/€35-40. Extra person €8. MC/V. ❷

Camping Les Ramiers, 1 chemin des Ramiers (☎03 20 23 13 42), in Bondues. To get there, take either bus #35 (dir: Halluin Colbras) or #36 (dir: Comines Mairie) to Bondues Centre, then follow rue Césair Loridan for 1km (25min.). Fences and garden plots divide private sites. Showers €1. Reception daily July-Aug. 8am-7:30pm; Sept.-May 9am-7:30pm. Open mid-Apr. to Nov. €2.50 per site, €1.60 per person, €0.80 per car. Electricity €2.

FOOD

Lille is known for *maroilles* cheese, *genièvre* (juniper berry liqueur), and—this being Flanders—mussels. Find the cheese in any local market or *épicerie* around the central *places*, the liqueur in a *brasserie* on rue Gambetta, and the mussels, well, everywhere. Decently priced restaurants and cafés fill the fashionable pedestrian area around **rue de Béthune.** The highest-value food is south of bd. de la Liberté, near rue Solférino, rue Masséna, and the Halles Centrales. Bustling, crowded **rue Léon Gambetta** boasts a slew of cheap kebab joints, and leads to the enormous **Marché de Wazemmes,** pl. de la Nouvelle Aventure.

Markets open both indoors (open M-Th 7am-1pm, F-Sa 7am-8pm, Su 7am-3pm) and out. (Open Su, Tu, and Th 7am-3pm.) **EuraLille,** the big shopping center next to the Eurostar station, has an enormous **Carrefour** supermarket. (Open M-Sa 9am-10pm.) There is a **Monoprix** grocery is at 31 rue du Molinel near Gare Lille Flandres. (Open M-Sa 8:30am-8:30pm.)

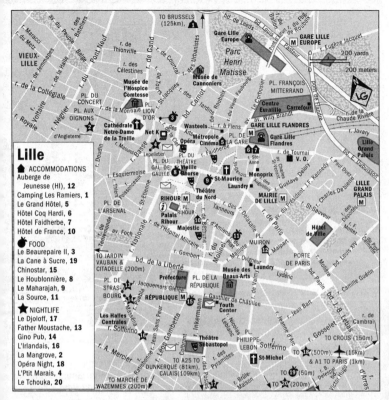

Lille

⬆ ACCOMMODATIONS
Auberge de
Jeunesse (HI), 12
Camping Les Ramiers, 1
Le Grand Hôtel, 5
Hôtel Coq Hardi, 6
Hôtel Faidherbe, 7
Hôtel de France, 10

🍎 FOOD
Le Beaurepaire II, 3
La Cane à Sucre, 19
Chinostar, 15
Le Houblonnière, 8
Le Maharajah, 9
La Source, 11

⭐ NIGHTLIFE
Le Djoloff, 17
Father Moustache, 13
Gino Pub, 14
L'Irlandais, 16
La Mangrove, 2
Opéra Night, 18
L'Ptit Marais, 4
Le Tchouka, 20

🔲 **Le Maharajah,** 4 rue du Sec Arembault (☎03 20 57 67 77), in the pedestrian district. Scrumptious Indian food in an ornate, atmospheric dining area. Vegetarian plates €12-12.50. Open M-Th noon-1:30pm and 7-10pm, F-Sa until 10:30pm. AmEx/MC/V. ❸

🔲 **La Cane à Sucre,** 68 bd. Victor Hugo (☎03 20 52 29 00), on the corner of rue Jeanne d'Arc. Vibrant Afro-Caribbean specialties, from *volaille* in coconut sauce (€9) and *poulet à la mangue* (mango chicken, €10) to banana *flambé* for dessert (€4). Open M-F 11:45am-1:30pm and 8-10:30pm, Sa until 1am. MC/V. ❷

La Source, 13 rue du Plat (☎03 20 57 53 07). Downstairs a friendly natural food store carries vegetarian specialties; upstairs a charming restaurant serves vegetarian and other organic *menus* (€7.50-11). Store open M-Sa 7am-7pm, F until 9pm. Restaurant open M-Th and Sa noon-2pm, F also 7-9pm. MC/V. ❷

Le Houblonnière, 42 pl. du Gal. de Gaulle (☎03 20 74 54 34). With primo terrace space, this eatery's regional specialties include *moules marinière* (€12) and *Le Welsh,* a cheddar fondue cooked with beer (€10). Be adventurous and order the *andouillettes au Cambrai,* intense sausages in sauce made from the local Cambrai cheese (€10). Open Su-Th noon-2:30pm and 7-10:30pm, F-Sa until 11pm. AmEx/MC/V. ❸

Le Beaurepaire II, 6 pl. Lion d'Or (☎03 20 74 20 36). This cozy brick-and-wood *crêperie,* nestled in a lively pedestrian area, makes a superb mealstop. Filling *galettes* (€2.20-8.30), crêpes (€2.20-5.80), and meal-sized salads (€4-5.80) hit the spot. Open M-Sa noon-2pm and 7:30-11pm. MC/V after €10. ❶

START: Musée de l'Hospice Comtesse

FINISH: Marché de Wazemmes

DISTANCE: 5km/3.1 mi.

DURATION: 2-3hr.

WHEN TO GO: Start in the early afternoon.

1 MUSÉE DE L'HOSPICE COMTESSE. This dark and atmospheric museum is less visited than most, but the former hospital and orphanage houses an intriguing collection of statues and well-kept period rooms. (Open M 2-6pm, W-Su 10am-12:30pm and 2-6pm. €2.30, students €1.50, under 12 free.)

2 LE BEAUREPAIRE. Take a quick crêpe or galette break at this tiny cave-like eatery, nestled snuggly in the middle of the cobblestone maze of old Lille. (6 pl. Lion d'Or. Open M-Sa noon-2pm and 7:30-11pm.)

3 RUE DE LA CLEF. This quintessential vieille ville street is a charming cobbled walk filled with offbeat boutiques and tiny cafés for shoppers and people-watchers.

4 PLACE DU THÉÂTRE. The theater is at the center of it all, flanked by dazzling Flemish façades and scads of restaurants, cafés, pubs, shops. Take a moment to walk through the impossibly ornate **Vieille Bourse,** a former st exchange, and see if there's anything you'd like to see at the **Théâtre du Nord.**

5 RUE DE BÉTHUNE. Pass by the elaborate pl. Rihour, and then move down along the br prettiness of this bustling counterpart to the quiet rue de la Clef. The most popular boutiques, emas, and terraced restaurants crowd this lively center. If the crêpes didn't fill you up ear stop at **Le Maharajah,** just above rue Béthune, at 4 rue du Sec Arembault. (Open M-Th n 1:30pm and 7-10pm, F-Sa until 10:30pm.)

6 MUSÉE DES BEAUX-ARTS. One of the most extensive collections in France, this grand well-designed museum houses a host of 15th- to 20th-century masters under its vaulted ceilin See what this month's featured temporary exhibit is, but don't miss Monet's Parliament de dres in the Impressionist wing. (Pl. de la République. Open M 2-6pm, W-Th and Sa-Su 10 6pm, F 10am-7pm. €4.60, students €3. Most tours €7.70. Audio guides in English €4.50.)

7 RUE LÉON GAMBETTA. The more modern section of town begins with this broad avenue its rows of restaurants, cafés, and boulangeries. Stop at one of the many pâtisseries for a q ice cream break.

8 MARCHÉ DE WAZEMMES. The tour ends with local produce and charcuterie indoors a swirling flea market crowding the outdoor place. Spend an hour looking through the endless r of clothing, regional products, and everything else under the sun, then buy some fresh peac or plums to munch on during the walk back uptown.

Chinostar, 37 rue Léon Gambetta (☎03 20 57 62 44), doesn't look like much from the outside, but the interior is cavernous and pretty and the food low-priced. €5.40 buys a starter, entrée, rice, and dessert. Open daily noon-2pm and 7-11pm. MC/V. ❶

👁 SIGHTS

🏛 MUSÉE DES BEAUX-ARTS. In a 19th-century mansion surrounded by the lovely gardens of the pl. de la République is the second-largest art collection in France, including an encyclopedic display of 15th- to 20th-century French and Flemish masters. The hallway of Impressionists is particularly dazzling. Guides to each room in English, French, and German. *(Pl. de la République. M: République. ☎03 20 06 78 00. Open M 2-6pm, W-Th and Sa-Su 10am-6pm, F 10am-7pm. Schedule of tours, in French, at the museum. Most tours €7.70. Audio guides in English €4.50. €4.60, students €3.)*

🏛 LA PISCINE. The creative exhibits at this fantastic new museum are both unexpected and exhilarating. The heart of the museum is a glittering renovated indoor pool flanked by 19th- and 20th-century statues and bright former shower-rooms of paintings. As water trickles and lights dance across the ceiling, look through the fabulous *portique* framing the far end of the pool. *(23 rue de L'Espérance. Take M: Gare Jean Lebas and follow large av. Jean Lebas straight ahead; take a right on rue des Champs, then a left on rue de l'Esperance. The museum is on the right. ☎03 20 69 23 60. Open Tu-Th 11am-6pm, F 11am-8pm, Sa-Su 1-6pm. €3, students €2.)*

MUSÉE D'ART MODERNE. Fascinating for fans of cubism and postmodernism, this museum displays works by well-known masters like Braque, Picasso, and Miró. Temporary exhibits are quite impressive. *(1 allée du Musée, in Villeneuve d'Ascq. Take metro, dir: 4 Cantons, to Pont du Bois, then bus #41, dir: Villeneuve d'Ascq, to Parc Urbain-Musée. ☎03 20 19 68 68. Open Su-M and W-Sa 10am-6pm. Tours in French Su 11am; €2.50. Museum €3.70, under 25 €1.50, under 12 free; first Su of every month 10am-2pm free.)*

VIEILLE BOURSE. The old stock exchange epitomizes the Flemish Renaissance. Encircled by garland-like moldings, it resembles a huge wedding cake. *(Pl. du Gal. de Gaulle. Markets open Tu-Su 9:30am-7:30pm.)*

OTHER SIGHTS. The **Citadel** on the city's north side was redesigned in the 17th century by military genius Vauban. *(Open with tour in French May-Aug. Su 3-5pm. €7.)* The **Jardin Vauban** has fields for Frisbee-playing, a carousel, and carnival games. The dim, creaky **Musée de l'Hospice** has served as a hospital, hospice, and orphanage. Today its curiosities include *enseigne de la fille mal gardée,* a rather primitive sculpture of a suspiciously young woman holding out a baby, designed as a moralistic lesson for children. The downstairs chapel is directly across the hall from the massive former sick ward; on Sunday, the doors were opened and patients watched the services from their beds. *(32 rue de la Monnaie. ☎03 28 36 84 00. Open M 2-6pm, W-Su 10am-12:30pm and 2-6pm. €2.30, students €1.50, under 12 free.)*

📷📀 NIGHTLIFE & FESTIVALS

Lille is a huge party town, liveliest during the school year. Around les Halles Centrales, college students pack the pubs on **rue Solférino** and **rue Masséna.** Across town, the *vieille ville* offers a more sophisticated, though touristed, scene.

🍺 L'Irlandais, 160-162 rue Solférino (☎03 20 57 04 74). Fairly typical Irish setting, but separates itself from the pack with its friendly crowd. Don't be shy: grab a young lad or lass by the arm and join in the jig. Beer €2.50. Open daily 4pm-2am. MC/V.

FROM THE ROAD

MA VIE EN CLOTHES

Fannypack-sporting Yanks at McDonald's are good for a chuckle now and then, but foreigners in France haven't completely cornered the market on inexplicable fashion desicions:

Men: To emulate the stylish 20-something young man on the go, find yourself a pair of three-quarter-length shorts. Think 13-year-old skateboarder circa 1992. The more mature 30-and-over set adds a few inches: calf-hugging clamdiggers are mysteriously popular. For the nice young small-town father, the look is a little misleading: cut-off Levi's clipped high enough to raise eyebrows at a Fire Island beach party can be seen in every town square from Montreuil to Pontarlier.

Women: On a hot day, turn to the skort. While the boys are off flaunting their Daisy Dukes with reckless abandon, a few fashion-forward individuals sport various updates on the baffling skirt/short hybrid. The one-shoulder shirt is the height of summer fashion for the younger set. Make sure to take frequent stock of your perilously secured assets while going wild.

Everyone: During the summer sale season (where it pays to hold out through the *première démarqué* and *deuxième démarquée* in anticipation of the hallowed *dernière* discount), don't be shocked by the anatomical detail on display in the windows of even the most family-friendly boutiques.

–Robert Hodgson

Le Tchouka, 80bis rue B. Delespaul (☎03 20 14 37 50), is a gay bar/club, but is usually filled with as many women as men. After other places have shut down, seemingly half the city heads here to dance under 20 disco balls and sing along to the French music. €4 shooters are creative, €3 beer a bargain. Open Th-Sa 10:30pm-5am. MC/V.

Le Djoloff, 37 rue des Postes (☎03 20 30 84 23). Bamboo, wall hangings, and colorfully painted boats distinguish this Caribbean bar. Try the *ventilateur,* a cocktail with rum, ginger, curaçao, and a secret ingredient (€6). Open daily 5:30pm-2am. MC/V.

Gino Pub, 21 rue Masséna (☎03 20 54 45 55), is a rowdy place with a raucous college clientele. Enjoy pheromone cocktails, billiards, and cheap €1.50 beer. Open M-Sa noon-2am, Su 5pm-2am. MC/V.

L'Ptit Marais, 45 rue Lepelletier, is a friendly lesbian bar, but a good number of men also frequent this laid-back spot. Sangría €4. Beer €2-3. Cocktails €5.50. Open Tu 2:30pm-10pm, W 2:30pm-1am, Th-F 2:30pm-2am, Sa 3pm-2am. MC/V after €7.50.

Opéra Night, 84 rue de Trevise (☎03 20 88 37 25). This favorite among clubbers blasts "house-happy techno" to a 20- to 30-something clientele. Theme nights from "student dance party" to "gay tea dance." On a deserted street; be cautious. Cover €10, includes one drink. Open Tu-Su from 10pm. MC/V.

La Mangrove, 36 rue d'Angleterre (☎03 20 51 88 89). This *rhumerie* offers a bouncing dance floor, salsa nights, DJs Th-Sa from 10pm, and a friendly welcome. Beer from €2.20. Open M-Th 5pm-3am, F-Sa 3pm-3am, Su 6pm-3am. MC/V after €10.

Father Moustache, 19 rue Masséna (☎06 11 26 16 15), is a romantic place with dim lights, wood décor, and a dance floor downstairs. Beer €2-4. Cocktails €6. Open daily 7pm-3am. MC/V.

Many neighborhood and one-time festivals and events come to cosmopolitan Lille; the tourist office provides a detailed guide. Every year, the **Marché aux Fleurs** carpets the center of town at the end of April, while the huge flea market **La Braderie** sets up shop in the city's central squares on the first weekend of September. For a dose of culture, **Théatre du Nord,** on pl. Général de Gaulle, performs September to June. (☎03 20 14 24 24; www.theatredunord.fr. Schedule available at tourist office; prices vary.) Or, visit the **Orchestre Nationale de Lille,** 30 pl. Mendes France. (☎03 20 12 82 40; www.onlille.com. Tickets €25, students €9.) The tourist office has information on **film festivals,** held at **Le Métropole,** rue des Ponts de Comines (☎08 36 68 00 73), and the **Majestic,** 54 rue de Béthune (☎03 28 52 40 40).

ARRAS

The official symbol of Arras (pop. 80,000) is the noble lion, but for centuries it hasn't been able to escape the "Arras"/"A *rats*" connection made by friends and enemies alike. The dignified gabled townhouses and Flemish arcades of Artois's capital do have a bit of the king of the jungle in them, but there's definitely a hint of the scrappy, little survivor in its battle-plagued history. Go for the well-preserved war monuments (including the towering Canadian site at Vimy), but also enjoy the small-town bustle and gingerbread appeal.

▊▊ TRANSPORTATION & PRACTICAL INFORMATION. Trains (info desk open M-F 8am-7pm, Sa 8am-6pm) leave pl. Mal. Foch to: Amiens (1hr., 12 per day, €9.60); Lille (45min., 20 per day, €8.60); Lyon (3hr., 2 per day, €71); Paris (50min., 12 per day, €27.20). The new **bus station** is right of the train station (open M-F 7:30am-12:30pm and 1:30-6:30pm, Sa 9am-1pm), but many regional lines still run from the old one; make sure to check which station is correct. To reach the old station from the train station, turn left onto rue du Dr. Brassart. At the end of the road, turn right; the bus station is ahead to the left. **Local transportation** is operated by **STCRA** (☎03 21 58 08 58; tickets €1.10). **Arras Taxis** wait at the train station. (☎03 21 23 69 69. 24hr.) **Avis Car Rental** is near the train station on 4 rue Gambetta. (☎03 21 51 69 03. Open M-F 8am-noon and 2-6pm, Sa 9am-noon and 4-6pm. MC/V.)

To get to the **tourist office**, pl. des Héros, from the station, walk across pl. Foch onto rue Gambetta. Continue for five blocks, then turn right on rue Desiré Delansorne. The tourist office is across pl. des Héros in the Hôtel de Ville. The bilingual staff offers a free map, brochures in English and French, a book of local walking trails, and **Internet** access with a *télécarte* €0.12-0.18 per 3min. (☎03 21 51 26 95; www.ot-arras.fr. Open May-Sept. M-Sa 9am-6:30pm, Su 10am-1pm and 2:30-6:30pm; Oct.-Apr. M-Sa 9am-noon and 2-6pm, Su 10am-12:30pm and 3-6:30pm.) The town's other main square, **Grand'Place**, is on the opposite side of pl. des Héros. **Crédit Agricole**, 9 Grand'Place, has the best rates of **currency exchange**, 24hr. exchange machines, and **ATMs**. (☎03 21 50 41 80. Open M 2-6pm, Tu-F 8:45pm-12:30pm and 2-6pm, Sa 8:45am-12:45pm.) Free **Internet** and information on lodging, jobs and study opportunities are at the **Centre d'Information Jeunesse**, 17 bd. de Strasbourg. (☎03 21 23 35 64. Open M-Th 1:30-6pm, F 1:30-5pm; some mornings 10am-noon.) Other services include: **laundromat** Superlav, 17 pl. d'Ipswich, next to the Eglise St-Jean-Baptiste (open daily 7am-8pm); **police** in the Hôtel de Ville (☎03 21 23 70 70 or ☎03 21 50 51 60 after 6pm); a **hospital** at 57 av. Winston Churchill (☎03 21 24 40 00); and a **post office**, 13 rue Gambetta, which **exchanges currency**. (☎03 21 22 94 94. Open M-F 8am-7pm, Sa 8am-12:30pm.) **Postal code:** 62000.

▊▊ ACCOMMODATIONS & FOOD. Cheerful **Le Passe Temps ❷**, 1 pl. Maréchal Foch, across from the station, rents clean, spacious quarters above a friendly bar, with a hall shower available. (☎03 21 50 04 04. Breakfast €6.10. Reception daily 7am-11pm. Singles €24, with private shower €32; doubles €26/€35. MC/V.) The **Auberge de Jeunesse (HI) ❶**, 59 Grand'Place, is a busy, average hostel with tiny 3- to 10-bed rooms in the middle of the *Grand'* action (☎03 21 22 70 02; fax 03 21 07 46 15. Breakfast €3.30. No door locks and iffy shower locks; safes €0.15. Sheets €2.80. Kitchen. Reception daily 7:30am-noon and 5-11pm. Lockout noon-5pm. Curfew 11pm. June-Aug. reserve ahead. Open Feb.-Nov. Bunks €8.40. MC/V. **Members only.**) A few doors down, the **Hostel les Trois Luppars ❹**, 47 Grand'Place, is in the oldest house in Arras. Large, understated rooms overlook a charming courtyard. All rooms have shower or bath, toilet, TV, and safe. (☎03 21 60 02 03; fax 03 21 24 24 80. Breakfast €7. Sauna €5 for 30min. Reception daily 6:30am-9pm. Singles €44-60; doubles €60-65; triples €65; quads €70. AmEx/MC/V.) In the shadow of the massive town hall belfry, **Le Beffroi ❸**, 28 pl. de la Vacquerie, does not have the most creative name, but its sizeable rooms and quiet, central location don't disappoint. (☎03 21 23 13 78; fax 03 21 23 13 78. Breakfast €6. Hall showers. Reception daily 7am-10pm. Singles €30, with private shower €36; doubles €34/€40. MC/V.) The local **campsite ❶**, 138 rue du Temple, is basically a parking lot with a few grassy plots. From the station, turn left onto rue du Dr. Brassart, then left on av. du Mal. Leclerc. Cross the bridge; after 10min., rue du Temple will be on the left. (☎03 21 71 55 06. Reception 8:30am-10pm. Open Apr.-Sept. €2.30 per person, €1.40 per child; €1.30 per car; €1.40 per tent. Electricity €2.30.)

There is a huge **Monoprix** supermarket across from the post office at 28 rue Gambetta (open M-Sa 8:30am-8pm), an open-air **market** in **place des Héros** (open W and Sa 8am-1pm), and bakeries and specialty shops in the pedestrian shopping area between the post office and the Hôtel de Ville. Inexpensive cafés skirt pl. des Héros and the pedestrian area, elegant restaurants ornament the **Grand'Place,** and cheap *friteries* line the alley between the *places*. The tasty, inexpensive ▨**La Cave de l'Ecu ❷**, 54 Grand'Place, serves huge salads (€7.50-12.80), filling crêpes and *galettes* (€3-9.50), and free-range chicken (€9-13.50) in a beautiful brick cellar. (☎03 21 50 00 39. Open daily noon-2:30pm and 7-10pm. MC/V.) For a hearty bit of local finery, pull up a chair at **La Clef des Sens ❹**, 60-62 pl. des Héros. *Menus* range from two-courses (€20) to a four-course version (€31) with fresh *foie gras aux pommes et cidre. Andouillettes d'Arras* run €13.50. (☎03 21 51 00 50. Open Tu-Su noon-3pm and 7-11pm. MC/V.) The mouth-watering aroma of *Les Best Ribs in Town* wafts all the way across the *place* from **Le Saint-Germain ❷**, 14 Grand'Place, where France and America shake greasy hands. Gorge on a plateful of ribs (€11, take-out €9) or the all-you-can-eat *mousse au chocolat* or *crème caramel* (€6). (☎03 21 51 45 45. Open daily noon-2:30pm and 7-10pm. AmEx/MC/V.)

◪ **SIGHTS.** Arras's two great squares are framed by rows of nearly identical houses; interesting sights cluster in the small, lively **place des Héros.** Amid shops, bars, and cafés, the ornate **Hôtel de Ville** is a faithful copy of the 15th-century original that reigned over pl. des Héros until its destruction in WWI. The best view of Arras is from its 75m **belfry.** (Open M-Sa 10-11:45am and 2-5:45pm, Su 10am-12:15pm and 2-6:15pm. €2.40, students €1.60.) Beneath the town hall, eerie, labyrinthine, underground tunnels, named **Les Boves,** were bored into the soft chalk in the 10th century and used at various times as chalk mines, wine cellars, and headquarters for the British army during WWI. The tourist office leads fascinating bilingual tours. (☎03 21 51 26 95. €3.90, children and students €2.40.) A few blocks behind the Hôtel de Ville stands the **Abbaye St-Vaast,** built in 667 on the hill where St-Vaast used to pray. Its traditional Gothic floor plan includes massive Corinthian columns. (Open daily Mar.-Nov. 2:15-6:30pm; Dec.-Feb. 2:15-6pm.) Inside the abbey, the **Musée des Beaux-Arts** displays some dull artifacts and paintings, and a surprisingly extensive sculpture collection. Look for (or away from) a gruesome skeletal sculpture of Guillaume Lefrançois and his worm-infested entrails. (☎03 21 71 26 43. Open Su-M, W, and F-Sa 9:30am-noon and 2-5:30pm, Th 9:30am-5:30pm. €4, students €2, first Su of each month free.) On the outskirts of the *vieille ville,* a number of military monuments and memorials dot the area around the **Citadel** (map at the tourist office).

▨ ▧ **NIGHTLIFE & ENTERTAINMENT.** Young blood courses into bars and cafés on **place des Héros, Grand'Place,** and the surrounding pedestrian roads. ▨**The Ould Shebeen,** 6 rue Faidherbe, is an authentic Irish pub with a lively atmosphere and raucous, bilingual "Quiz Nights" every Th. (☎03 21 71 87 97. Guinness from €3.70. Open M 8pm-1am, Tu-Sa 4pm-1am, Su 6pm-midnight. MC/V.) **Le Couleur Café,** 35 pl. des Héros, draws the college set with tropical décor and a DJ playing house and drum'n'bass. (☎03 21 71 08 70. Beer from €2.10. Open Su-M 2pm-1am, Tu-Th 10:30am-1am, F-Sa 10:30am-2am. AmEx/MC/V.) **Dan Foley's Irish Pub,** 7 pl. des Héros, fills with chic youngsters for karaoke Tuesdays. (☎03 21 71 46 08. Beer from €2.20. Open M-Th noon-1am, F noon-2am, Sa 3pm-2am, Su 3pm-1am. AmEx/ MC/V.)

Cosmopolitan **Noroit,** 6-9 rue des Capucins, hosts foreign films, concerts, and plays each month. (☎03 21 71 30 12. Office open M-F 8:30am-noon and 1:30-5:30pm. Closed mid-July to Aug.) Nope, you didn't take the wrong train to the shores of the Riviera; that's just **Arras on the Beach.** In July the town dumps a few tons of sand in Grand'Place; wild beach parties and volleyball tournaments ensue.

▓ DAYTRIP FROM ARRAS: VIMY MEMORIAL

The Vimy Memorial is located just 3km from the town of Vimy, which is about 15min. by **car** *from the town of Arras. Catch a taxi in Arras (€18-24). A* **bus** *goes from Arras to the Vert Tilleul stop in Thelus (€1.60), but from there the walk along the highway to Vimy is a dangerous 50min.*

The Vimy Memorial, 12km northeast of Arras along N17, honors the more than 66,000 Canadian soldiers who were killed during WWI and commemorates the Canadians' impressive success in overtaking the strategic Vimy Ridge in April 1917, after numerous other forces had failed to dislodge the Germans. Their success solidified the newly independent nation's fledgling identity. The two pylons of the monument are covered with the names of 11,000 soldiers thought to have been killed in the battle. Sculpted figures surround the edifice: the most poignant is a sorrowful woman, *Canada Weeping for Her Children*, carved from a single 30 ton limestone block.

The surrounding park, criss-crossed by German and Canadian trenches, is morbidly beautiful; hills and craters carved out by shells and mines are now covered in grass and sheep. Explore the trenches, but **stay on the marked paths,** as there are still active mines in the fenced-off areas.

An underground tour of the crumbling tunnels starts at the kiosk near the trenches. Little details suggest the realities of life on the front lines: the registration room, the commander's desk, a maple leaf chiseled in the wall by an anonymous soldier, and a protruding shell that didn't make it all the way into the tunnels. A small museum near the monument recounts the battle and Canada's place in the war. (Museum ☎03 21 58 19 34, tunnels ☎03 21 48 98 97. Tours May-Nov. 10am-6pm every 30min. in English and French; last tour leaves at 5:15pm; free. Memorial open daily sunrise to sunset. Museum open daily in summer 10am-6pm; in winter 10am-5pm.)

LAON

The cathedral of Laon, one of France's Gothic masterpieces, presides over the surrounding farmland from its hilltop throne. The birthplace of both Charlemagne's mother and the great folk hero Roland, Laon (pronounced "Laahn;" pop. 28,000) was the capital of the mighty Carolingian Empire in the 9th and 10th centuries. While residence in the fortified *haute ville* was once limited to kings and nobles, there's no royalty here today. The skyscraping *quartier* offers a few charming and windy streets and some glorious views of the surrounding countryside, but there's nothing here to merit more than a few days' exploration.

▐▓ TRANSPORTATION & PRACTICAL INFORMATION. Laon's *haute ville* is built around one main street whose name is rue du Cloître by the cathedral and rue de Bourg by the Hôtel de Ville. **Trains** leave pl. des Droits de l'Homme (☎03 23

79 10 79). Ticket office open M-F 4:55am-9:15pm, Sa 6am-8:35pm, Su 6:45am-9:20pm. To: Amiens (1½hr., 7 per day, €14); Paris (1¼hr., 12 per day, €17.40); Reims (50min., 9 per day, €7.70). SNCF **buses** leave from the same station. Call a **taxi** at ☎03 23 79 00 79. The **POMA car** runs every 2min. from the station to the *haute ville* and tourist office, providing breathtaking views of the *basse ville* from above. (☎03 23 79 07 59. Open July-Aug. M-Sa 7am-8pm, Su 2:30-7pm; Sept.-June closed Su. Round-trip €1.)

Exit straight from the POMA station in the *haute ville*, cross the parking lot, and turn left across pl. du Général Leclerc onto rue Sérurier. Follow it to the cathedral; the **tourist office** occupies the squat 12th-century stone structure on the right (this unlikely building was France's first hospital). The path on foot from the base is straightforward but is at least a 30-40min. hike and quite steep. From the train station, walk toward the hill, past the rotary, onto av. Carnot, and up the endless steps. At the top, circumvent the POMA tracks, and take the pedestrian path to your left that heads uphill and to the right. Head toward the cathedral tower. The English-speaking tourist office, ask for a free map and *Le Bon P'Laon*, a free practical guide (in French) that also gets various discounts around town. They give tours of the medieval city and cathedral in French, with a cell-phone audio tour available in English. (☎03 23 20 28 62; www.ville-laon.fr. Cathedral tours mid-July to mid-Sept. daily 4pm; mid-Sept. to Oct. and Apr. to mid-July weekends only. City tours mid-July to mid-Sept. daily 3pm; mid-Sept. to Oct. and Apr. to mid-July weekends only. Tours €3, students €2.50, under 12 free. Office open July-Aug. M-Sa 9:30am-6pm, Su 10am-6pm; Sept.-Oct. and Apr.-June M-Sa 9:30am-12:30pm and 2-6pm, Su 1-6pm; Nov.-Mar. M-Sa 9:30am-12:30pm and 2-6pm, Su 1-5pm.) Other services include: **banks** with **ATMs** and **currency exchange** around the train station in the *basse ville* and pl. du Gal. Leclerc on the hilltop; a **laundromat** on bd. Pierre Brossolette in the *basse ville*, right of the train station (open daily 8am-7pm); **police** at 3 bd. de Gras Boncourt (☎03 23 27 79 79; call here for the **pharmacie de garde**); a **hospital** at 33 rue Marcellin-Berthelot (☎03 23 24 33 33); and free **Internet** at the **Centre Information Jeunesse**, 56 bd. Gras Brancourt, in the *basse ville*, which also provides information on lodging, work, and study opportunities. (☎03 23 23 70 09. Open M-F 9am-1pm and 1:30-5:30pm.) There is a **post office** next to the station on pl. des Droits de l'Homme, with **currency exchange.** (☎03 23 21 55 78. Open M-F 8am-7pm, Sa 8am-noon.) A branch office is located at 6 rue du Bourg in the *haute ville* (☎03 23 28 61 20. Open M-F 8am-6pm, Sa 8am-noon.) **Postal code:** 02000.

⚄⚃ ACCOMMODATIONS & FOOD. Popular with backpackers, the ⚄**Hôtel Welcome ❷**, 2 av. Carnot in the *basse ville*, lets attractive, newly renovated rooms at bargain prices. (☎03 23 23 06 11; fax 03 23 79 33 93; hotel-welcome.laon@wanadoo.fr. Breakfast €4. Washing machine and microwave access. Reception 24hr. Singles €23, with shower €25; doubles €24/€27; triples without shower €27; quads without shower €29. All showerless rooms have hall shower access. MC/V.) Château-like **Les Chevaliers ❸**, 3-5 rue Sérurier, rents handsome dark rooms a block from the cathedral. (☎03 23 27 17 50; fax 03 23 79 12 07. Breakfast included. Reception 6:30am-8:30pm. Singles €30, with shower €40-48; doubles €40/€50-60; triples with shower €60-80; quads with shower €70. Extra bed €10.70. MC/V.) **Hôtel de la Paix ❷**, 52 rue Saint Jean, is in the *haute ville*. Dark, winding stairs above a bar lead to surprisingly big, bright, clean rooms. (☎03 23 79 06 34; fax 03 23 79 06 34. Reception daily 7am-midnight. Reserve ahead; there are only a few rooms. Singles €21, with shower €24; doubles €24/€27.50; triples €31.50. Hall showers available. MC/V.) **Hôtel de la Bannière de France ❹**, 11 rue Franklin Roosevelt, offers rooms that range in size from big to large to humongous. With all the fixings (TV, toilet, shower), and a swanky restaurant downstairs, this is the *haute ville's* classy splurge. (☎03 23 23 21 44; www.hoteldelabanniere-de-france.com. Breakfast €7. Reception daily 6:30am-11pm. Singles €42-53; doubles €52-62; triples €72; quads €77; quints €85. AmEx/MC/V.) Rural **Camping Municipale ❶**, allée de la Chênaie, about 3km from the train station, is mostly full of caravans but has some private areas for tents. (☎03 23 20 25 56. Reception daily 8am-10pm. Open May-Sept. €3.10 per person; €2.10 per site; €1.60 per car. Electricity €2.70.)

The ever-reliable **Monoprix** supermarket is on rue de Bourg (open M-F 8:30am-7pm, Sa 9am-noon and 2-7pm. MC/V). Local **markets** happen Th in pl. Victor Hugo and W in pl. de l'Hôtel de Ville. Full of bakeries, restaurants, and sandwich shops, **rue Châtelaine** and **rue du Bourg**, both leading from pl. du Général Leclerc, are the only places in the *haute ville* to find food. 🍴**La Bonne Heure ❷**, 53 rue Châtelaine, is the best find in Laon; you'll even forgive the overly enthusiastic regional décor. The friendly owner cooks with local ingredients and has invented a crust for his specialty *tourtinette* (€6.50-7), a pizza-like food topped with ingredients like leeks, ham, smoked trout, lemon, tomatoes, mozzarella, and escargot. Be sure to try the *montagne couronnée* (€4), a chocolate-covered wafer filled with berries and dessert cheese; it honors Laon's nickname, "the crowned mountain." (☎03 23 20 57 09. Open Tu-Su 9am-9pm, most food only served noon-2pm and 7-9pm. MC/V.) Nestled in the center of town, *crêperie* **Le St-Jean ❶**, 23 rue St-Jean, serves tasty and inexpensive *galettes* (€2-8) and crêpes (€1.90-4.80) in a *brasserie atmosphere*. (☎03 23 23 05 53. Open M-Th 10:30am-12:30pm and 5-11pm, F-Sa 10:30am-1am. MC/V.) **Les Chenizelles ❸**, 1 rue du Bourg, is a hearty *brasserie* on pl. du Général Leclerc with a snazzy, see-it-all terrace and a solid regional menu. *Tête de veau* (calf's head) runs €12.50, and 3-course *menus* €13.50. (☎03 23 23 02 34. Open Tu-F 9am-1am, Sa 10am-1am, Su 10am-6pm. MC/V.) For something on the gourmet side, **Restaurant de la Bannière de la France ❹**, 11 rue Franklin Roosevelt, offers a pretty meal with a somewhat hefty dessert bill. Specialties include *foie gras tiède* and *œufs cocotte aux crevettes et champignons*. (☎03 23 23 21 44. Open daily noon-2pm and 7-9:30pm. *Menus* €15, €20, €28, and €38. MC/V.)

🄶 **SIGHTS.** A maze of narrow, twisting alleys and medieval walls surrounds Laon's main attraction, the **Cathédrale de Notre-Dame**, one of the earliest and finest examples of Gothic architecture in France. The striking white interior contrasts with a simple, sumptuous rose window. According to one amusing legend, the Virgin Mary herself showed up here in the 13th century to thank "Jo the Juggler" for a particularly impressive exhibition of in-church flame-juggling, before a perturbed local clergy. (☎03 23 25 14 18. Open daily 9am-6:30pm. Tours available through the tourist office.) The **ramparts** encircling the *haute ville* offer a panoramic view of the *basse ville* and the surrounding countryside, and their far southwestern tip (20min. from pl. du Général Leclerc), near the **Abbaye St-Vincent,** is home to a fascinating old *Morgot* gun station and a series of trails that wind down to the lower village. Nearby is the crumbling, cool **Eglise St-Martin,** at the end of rue St-Martin, a worthy walk-by for its aged façade. Behind a lush courtyard at 32 rue Georges Ermant are the tiny **Musée de Laon** and the 13th-century **Chapelle des Templiers.** The chapel's claim to fame, the carved 14th-century corpse of one Guillaume de Harcigny, physician to Charles VI, is on loan to the Louvre in Paris for a Mar.-July 2004 exhibit on the famously mad king. The museum's fairly ho-hum collection of paintings and Greek and Egyptian antiquities doesn't merit a detour. (☎03 23 20 19 87. Both open June-Sept. Tu-Su 11am-6pm; Oct.-May Tu-Su 2-6pm. Museum €3.20, students €2.50.)

🄽🄾 **NIGHTLIFE & FESTIVALS.** At night, a somewhat sedate pub scene emerges in the *haute ville* on pl. du Gal. Leclerc and rue St-Jean. Hit up **Le Lutin Bleu,** 22 pl. St-Julien, down the street, for Belgian beer (€2.80-4) and a bouncy musical vibe that jumps from reggae to rock to salsa in a single night. (Open M-F 7:30am-1am, Sa 3pm-1am. Discount drink with *Le Bon P'Laon*, see **Practical Information.** Happy hour M-F 6-7pm.) Lively **Le Gibus,** 14 pl. St-Julien, offers concerts and Th night DJs. (☎ 03 23 20 45 47. Beer from €2.50. Open during the school year daily 7:30am-12:45am, school vacation daily 2pm-12:45am. MC/V.) In the *basse ville,* seedy pubs flank the train station.

The **Festival de Laon** presents mainly modern classical music. (☎ 03 23 20 87 50. Oct. to early Nov. Tickets €16-28; students and over 65 €10-28. Tickets at tourist office June-Sept. and over the phone in Sept.) Free **summer concerts** of all kinds invade the pl. de l'Hôtel de Ville June-Aug. On the 3rd weekend of May, **Les Euromédiévals** bring jousts, falconry, street performers, and medieval food to the cathedral area. (☎ 03 23 22 30 30. Free.) The **Festival International du Cinéma Jeune Public,** the first week of April, is an international film and animation festival aimed at kids. (In the Maison des Arts et Loisirs. ☎ 03 23 79 39 37.) In June, **Jazzitudes** hits a number of venues in Laon. (Info at www.jazztitudeslaon.free.fr. Tickets €4-18.)

▨ DAYTRIPS FROM LAON

South of Laon and reachable by car, the scenic **Chemin des Dames**—named for the Princesses Adelaïde and Victoire *(les Dames de France),* who passed over it in the 18th century. Of great military importance since Roman times, the route follows a 200m ridge whose value as a natural barrier was first noticed by Caesar when he conquered Northern Gaul in 57 BC. The Chemin was the scene of Napoleon's last battle before Waterloo and later the site of crucial German-held strategic depot during WWI. The route is peppered with monuments to this turbulent history, including the ▨**Caverne des Dragons,** a former quarry used by the Germans as a barracks, hospital, and chapel during WWI. At the height of the war, both Germans and French used the dark, dreary tunnels as sleeping quarters, but refused to fight each other except when they emerged into the light. Particularly moving are the sculptures and graffiti on display, produced by soldiers during the fighting. (☎ 03 23 25 14 18. Open July-Aug. daily 10am-7pm; May-June and Sept. daily 10am-6pm; Oct.-Dec. and Feb.-Apr. Tu-Sa 10am-6pm, Su 10am-7pm. €5, students €2.50. 1½hr. tours in French every 30min.; Sept.-June daily 10am-4:30pm; July-Aug. M-Sa 10am-5:30pm. Free.) For more information on getting to the Chemin des Dames and the Caverne des Dragons, check with the tourist office.

CHANNEL PORTS (CÔTE D'OPALE)

They're big, they're bad, they're ugly. The sprawling ports that greet travelers from Britain and beyond were fought over for centuries, though this might baffle modern visitors confronted with the soggy weather, schlocky boutiques, and cafés promising genuine steak and kidney pie that suggest the ports combine the worst of both sides of the water. This distinctly Anglicized area of France has a charm and character that is missing from the southern country. Lively beaches spruce up a bustling coastal atmosphere such that summertime along the Channel can merit a few days exploration. Outside of prime Coppertone season, however, don't go out of the way to get here.

BOATS TO BRITAIN. Both towns offer frequent service to the UK; Calais is by far more heavily trafficked (though not necessarily the better visit). **Eurostar trains** zip under the tunnel from London and Ashford, stopping outside Calais on their way to Lille, Brussels, and Paris. **Le Shuttle** carries cars between Ashford and Calais. **Ferries** from Calais cross to Dover, while Boulogne services Dunkerque and Ramsgate. For details on operators, schedules, and fares, see **Getting There: By Boat** (p. 40) and **Getting There: By Channel Tunnel** (p. 40).

BOULOGNE-SUR-MER

With a refreshing sea breeze and bright floral displays, Boulogne (pop. 46,000) is by far the most attractive of the channel ports. The busy harbor is the heart of town, the *vieille ville* a charming surprise, and the aquarium an entertaining diversion. Without sun-kissed beach weather, though, Boulogne is less of a treat.

⊑ TRANSPORTATION. Trains leave Gare Boulogne-Ville, bd. Voltaire (☎ 08 36 35 35 35), to: Calais (30min., 13 per day, €6); Lille (2½hr., 11 per day, €17.80); Paris (2-3hr., 11 per day, €38.90). Info office open M-Sa 8:15am-7pm. **BCD buses** leave pl. Dalton for Calais (30min., 4 per day, €6.20) and Dunkerque (1¼hr., 4 per day, €10.50). **TCRB,** with a station at 14 rue de la Lampe (☎ 03 21 83 51 51), sends **local bus #10** from the train station and pl. de France to the *haute ville* (€1); most buses go through pl. de France (prices €0.70-€1.15). **Taxis** (☎ 03 21 91 25 00 or 06 80 95 14 78) wait at the station.

▆▐ ORIENTATION & PRACTICAL INFORMATION. The river Liane separates the ferry terminal from everything else. The train station posts a large map on its doors. To reach the central **place de France** from Gare Boulogne-Ville, turn left on bd. Voltaire, then right onto bd. Diderot before the bridge. Follow Diderot to the *place.* The tourist office is on Diderot, past pl. de France and the roundabout. On the other side of pl. de France, **Pont Marquet** leads to the **ferry port.** The streets between **place Frédéric Sauvage** and **place Dalton** form the town center, while the *vieille ville* is at the top of the hill.

The English-speaking **tourist office,** 24 quai Gambetta, has bus info, **reservations service,** and a free map. (☎ 03 21 10 88 10; www.tourisme-boulognesurmer.com. Port **tours** in French Sa at 10am, check office for dates; €5.50, students €4, under 12 free. Open July-Aug. M-Sa 9am-7pm, Su 10am-1pm and 3-6pm; Sept.-June M-Sa 9:15am-12:30pm and 1:30-6:15pm, Su 10am-1pm and 3-6pm.) **Crédit Agricole,** 26 rue Nationale, has a 24hr. **currency exchange** machine, plus an **ATM.** Other services include: **laundromats** at 62 rue de Lille in the *haute ville* (open daily 7am-8pm) and 6 pl. Navarin (open daily 8am-8pm); **Internet** at Antares, 147 rue Nationale (€4 per hr.; open Tu-Sa 10am-noon and 1-7pm) and at the Youth Hostel (see **Accommodations**); **police** at 9 rue Perrochel (☎ 03 21 99 48 48; call for the **pharmacie de garde**); a **hospital** on allée Jacques Monod (☎ 03 21 99 33 33); and a **post office** on pl. Frédéric Sauvage. (☎ 03 21 99 09 03. Open M-F 8am-7pm, Sa 8am-12:30pm.) **Postal code:** 62200.

▌ ACCOMMODATIONS. Many hotels in the €17-25 range are near the ferry terminal; the tourist office has a list. The ▨**Hôtel Au Sleeping ❷,** 18 bd. Daunou, above a *brasserie* and minutes from the train station, has spotless, newly renovated, lovingly decorated rooms, with shower, TV, and coffee-maker. (☎ 03 21 80 62 79; fax 03 21 80 62 79. Breakfast €5. Reception daily 7am-10pm. Reserve ahead June-Aug. Singles and doubles €27-34; triples €39. Sept.-June prices about €3 lower. MC/V). The **Auberge de Jeunesse (HI) ❶,** 56 pl. Rouget de Lisle, across from the train station, feels like a pine cabin and gets crowded during the summer. 2- to 4-bed rooms, each with lockless bathroom, are a mixed blessing. Lively bar packed with backpackers. (☎ 03 21 99 15 30; fax 03 21 80 45 62. Internet €2 per 40min. Breakfast included. Late-night snack until 1am. Sheets included. Wheelchair-accessible. Reception M-F 8am-11pm, Sa-Su 8-11am and 5-11pm. 24hr. code access. Check-in

FLANDERS &
PAS DE CALAIS

5pm. Checkout 11am. 2- to 4-bed dorms €15. **Non-members** €2.90 extra per night for first 6 nights. MC/V.) The central **Hôtel de Londres ❹**, 22 pl. de France, behind the post office, is pricey but slightly luxurious, with polished hardwood floors and all the amenities. (☎ 03 21 31 35 63; fax 03 21 83 50 07. Breakfast €5.40. 24hr. reception. Small singles €30; larger singles and doubles €38.50-45.50; family quads with 2 rooms €59.50. Extra bed €7.60. MC/V.)

■ ■ **FOOD & ENTERTAINMENT.** Scads of restaurants, cafés, and bakeries cluster in the center of town; an excellent **market** is on pl. Dalton (open W and Sa 6am-1pm); **daily fish markets** surface along pl. Gambetta. A **Champion** supermarket, rue Daunou near bd. de la Liane, in the Centre Commercial de la Liane mall, is up the road from the hostel. (Open M-Sa 8:30am-8pm.) **Rue de Lille,** with its cobbled *haute ville* charm, is the finest place to dine, though the ambiance is costly. **Le Restaurant de la Haute Ville ❸**, 60 rue de Lille, serves a 3-course *menu végétarien* (€12) and tasty mussel soup (€8) in a timbered, flower-strewn courtyard. (☎ 03 21 80 54 10. Open July-Aug. Tu-Su 11:30am-10pm, closed M night; Sept.-June Tu-Sa noon-2pm and 7-10pm, Su noon-2pm. MC/V.) Grab a delicious, cheaper bite down the road at **La Scala ❶**, 16 pl. G. de Bouillon, an Italian eatery with €4.30 pizza and pricier pastas. (☎ 03 21 80 49 49. Open daily noon-2pm and 6-10pm. MC/V.) **Le Doyen ❸**, 11 rue du Doyen, offers seafood-themed regional dishes in a cozy, candlelit dining room. (☎ 03 21 30 13 08. Open M-Sa noon-2pm and 7-9:30pm. MC/V.)

Neon-lit bars fill the pedestrian *centre ville*, particularly **place Dalton** or its offshoot **rue du Doyen,** which fits an American, an Irish, an African, and a Cuban pub along its 35m length. Drink a glass of Belgian beer (€3) at the **Pub "J.F. Kennedy,"** 20 rue du Doyen. (☎ 03 21 83 97 05. Mussels €9.50. Beer €2.10. Open M-F 11am-10pm, Sa-Su 11am-11pm; food served 11am-3pm and 7pm to close. MC/V.)

■ **SIGHTS.** Boulogne capitalizes on its main source of commerce and nutrition at the huge aquarium ■**Le Grand Nausicaä**, bd. Ste-Beuve. (☎ 03 21 30 98 98; www.nausicaa.fr. Audio guides in English, French, and German €3. Open daily July-Aug. 9:30am-8pm; Sept.-June 9:30am-6:30pm. €12.50, students €9.50, ages 5-16 €9.) Next door is the **beach**, where Le Yacht Club Boulonnaise, 234 bd. Ste-Beuve, rents **windsurfers** and **catamarans**. (☎ 03 21 31 80 67. Windsurfers €9 per hr., €15 for 1hr. lesson. Catamarans €21/€23. Open July-Aug. M-F 10am-5pm, Sa-Su 1-5pm; Sept.-Oct. and Mar.-June daily 10am-noon and 2-5pm.)

Boulogne's *vieille ville* was built by the Romans. Its ramparts have exhilarating views. Dominating the east corner of the battlements is the massive **Château-Musée,** rue de Bernet, whose collection is more striking for its size and variety than for any individual works, which include a bare-faced Egyptian mummy and Napoleon's second-oldest hat. The armory adjoining the old prison is a treat. (☎ 03 21 10 02 20, tours ☎ 03 21 80 56 78. Tours in French €5.50, students €3.50. Open M and W-Sa 10am-noon and 2-5pm, Su 10am-12:30pm and 2:30-5:30pm. €3.50, students €2.50, under 12 free, Oct.-May first Su of the month free.) A block over, on rue de Lille, the domed 19th-century **Basilique de Notre-Dame** sits above 12th-century crypts; look for the Italian mosaics on the high altar. (☎ 03 21 99 75 98. Basilica open Apr. to mid-Sept. daily 9am-noon and 2-6pm; mid-Sept. to Mar. 10am-noon and 2-5pm. Crypt open Tu-Su 2-5pm. €2, children €1.)

CALAIS

With an electric neon *centre-ville* leading out to the crowded *plage*, Calais (pop. 80,000) contents itself with being brash and lively. This English-accented swath of shoreline (the Chunnel is right next door) is an interesting, if loud, port city. Outside the summer months, though, Calais loses much of its charm.

🖭🎵 TRANSPORTATION & PRACTICAL INFORMATION. Free buses connect the ferry terminal, pl. d'Armes, and station (every 30min. 4:45am-9:15pm). Avoid the area around the harbor at night. **Eurostar** stops outside town at the new Gare Calais-Fréthun, but most **SNCF trains** stop in town at the Gare Calais-Ville, bd. Jacquard. Ticket office open M-Sa 6:30am-8:30pm, Su 8:30-9:30am and 1:30-8:30pm. They go to Boulogne (45min., 11 per day, €6.60); Dunkerque (1hr., 2 per day, €7.20); Lille (1¼hr., 16 per day, €14); Paris (3¼hr., 6 per day, €39.50). **BCD buses** (☎ 03 21 83 51 51) stop at the station en route to Boulogne (30min.; Su-F 5 per day, Sa 2 per day; €6.70) and Dunkerque (40min.; M-F 6 per day, Sa 3 per day; €7.30). **OpaleBus,** 22 rue Caillette (☎ 03 21 00 75 75), operates **local buses.** Line #3 (dir: Blériot/VVF) runs from the station to the beach, hostel, and campground (M-Sa 7:15am-7:20pm, Su 10:30am-7:15pm; €0.90). For a **taxi,** call ☎ 03 21 97 13 14.

The **tourist office,** 12 bd. Clemenceau, is near the station; cross the street, turn left, cross the bridge onto bd. Clemenceau, and it's on the right. English-speaking staff, free map, and free **accommodations booking.** (☎ 03 21 96 62 40; www.ot-calais.fr. Open Easter-Aug. M-Sa 9am-7pm, Su 10am-1pm; Sept.-Easter M-Sa 9am-1pm and 2-6:30pm.) **Exchange currency** at the ferry or Hovercraft terminals (both 24hr.) or more cheaply at the post office or **banks** (clustered along rue Royale). Other services include: **police** on pl. de Lorraine (☎ 03 21 19 13 17; call here for the **pharmacie de garde,** or look in the tourist office window), a **hospital** at 11 quai du Commerce (☎ 03 21 46 33 33), **laundromat** Lavorama, 48 pl. d'Armes (open daily 7am-9pm), **Internet** at Dixie Bar, 10 pl. d'Armes (☎ 03 21 34 71 56. Free with purchase of drink or food; open daily June-Aug. 11am-2am, Sept.-May 11am-1am) or at the **Hôtel Royal's** café (€3 per hr.; open daily 11am-10pm). The **post office** is on pl. d'Alsace (☎ 03 21 85 52 72. Open M-F 8:30am-6pm, Sa 8:30-noon); there's a **branch** on pl. du Rheims, off pl. d'Armes. (Open M-F 8:30am-6pm, Sa 9am-noon.) **Postal code:** 62100.

🖭🎵 ACCOMMODATIONS & FOOD. The few budget hotels fill quickly in the summer; call 10-14 days in advance. The tourist office provides a list of hotels. Better than any hotel is the modern, recently renovated ☒**Centre Européen de Séjour/ Auberge de Jeunesse (HI) ❶,** av. Maréchal Delattre de Tassigny, one block from the beach. From the station, turn left and follow the main road through various name changes past pl. d'Armes. From the ferry, take a shuttle bus to pl. d'Armes. Cross the bridge and take a left at the roundabout onto bd. de Gaulle, then go right on tiny rue Alice Marie; the white hostel is the third building on the left. Or take bus #3 to Pluviose. A fabulous location is complemented by sparkling new doubles and singles that share a bathroom with one neighboring room. Pool table, bar, library, and an attentive staff. (☎ 03 21 34 70 20; fax 03 21 96 87 80. Breakfast and sheets included. Cafeteria open M-F 7-9am, noon-1pm, and 5-7pm; Sa 7-9am and noon-1pm. Wheelchair-accessible. Reception 24hr. Checkout 11am. Bunks €14.50 first night, €12.20 every extra night; singles €19. **Non-members** €1.50 extra per night. MC/V.) Two hotels, under the same friendly management, offer mid-range prices for quality rooms. Homey **Hôtel Bristol ❷,** 13-15 rue du Duc de Guise, off the main road, has newly renovated, quiet, pretty rooms and the reception for both establishments. (☎/fax 03 21 34 53 24. Free Internet. Breakfast €5. Hall shower for showerless rooms. Reception 24hr. Reservations suggested. Singles €25, with private shower €31; doubles €28/€36. MC/V.) The quainter **Hôtel Tudor ❸,** 6 rue Marie Tudor, off rue Duc de Guise, has larger, fancier rooms, all with shower and TV. (☎ 03 21 34 53 24. Singles and doubles with shower €31-36; triples, quads, and quints €48-70. Reservations suggested. MC/V.) **Camping Municipal de Calais ❶,** av. Raymond Poincoiré, has cramped sites with little privacy, but hey, it's on the beach. (☎ 03 21 34 73 25. Reception July-Aug. daily 7:30am-12:15pm and 2:30-7:15pm; Sept.-June M-F 8am-noon and 2-5pm, Sa 9am-noon, Su 10am-noon. 1 person €3.30, children €2.70; €2.20 per site. Electricity €1.80.)

Calais cuisine is understandably seafood-centric; English-style fried fish is a local favorite. Any bakery will have the *gâteau Calais*, with a crumbly cookie base and *crème de café* smothered in icing. Morning **markets** are held on pl. Crèvecoeur (Th and Sa) and pl. d'Armes (W and Sa). Otherwise, look for bakeries on **boulevard Gambetta, boulevard Jacquard,** and **rue des Thermes,** or one of two supermarkets: **Match,** 50 pl. d'Armes (open M-Sa 9am-7:30pm; July-Aug. Su 9am-noon) and **Prisunic,** 17 bd. Jacquard. (Open M-Sa 8:30am-7:30pm, Su 10am-7pm.) The hostel and campsite cafeterias are inexpensive options, while restaurants and *brasseries* line **rue Royale** and **boulevard Jacquard.** Ice cream stands line the shore. █**Histoire Ancienne** ❸, 20 rue Royale, is the nicest dining option for miles. A deep, tiled *salle à manger* is pretty and welcoming, while the tasty regional dishes such as grilled salmon (€10.50) and a *toques d'Opale menu* (€22), are prepared with great care. (☎03 21 34 11 20; fax 03 21 96 19 58. Open M 7-10pm, Tu-Su noon-2pm and 7-10pm. Closed for 3 weeks in Aug. MC/V.) A fine, inexpensive option is the cheery brick décor of **Tonnerre de Brest** ❶, 16 pl. d'Armes. A massive, mouth-watering selection of crêpes and *galettes* ranges from €2.20 to 8.50. (☎03 21 96 95 35. Open Su-Tu and Th-Sa 11:30am-2pm and 6-10:30pm. MC/V.)

■■ **SIGHTS & NIGHTLIFE.** One's first steps in Calais should be to the **beach;** follow rue Royale to rue de Mer until the end, then walk along the shore away from the harbor. The off-shore sights are less impressive, except for Rodin's evocative sculpture, **The Burghers of Calais,** by the station, framed by the dazzlingly flowered lawn of the Hôtel de Ville. The statue depicts six leading burghers who, during the Hundred Years' War, offered the keys to Calais and offered their lives to England's King Edward III in exchange for those of the starving townspeople. Edward's French wife Philippa pleaded for mercy, and they were spared. The best view in town is from atop **Le Phare de Calais,** pl. Henri Barbuisse, the 58m lighthouse with a draining 271-step climb. (☎03 21 34 33 34. Open June-Sept. M-F 2-6:30pm, Sa-Su 10am-noon and 2-6:30pm; Oct.-May W 2-5:30pm, Sa-Su 10am-noon and 2-5:30pm. €2.50, ages 5-15 €1.50.) The noticeably dank **Musée de la Deuxième Guerre Mondiale,** in the slightly seedy Parc St-Pierre, is an old German naval bunker from WWII that has been converted into a photographic retelling of the war's history. (☎03 21 34 21 57. Open May-Aug. daily 10am-6pm; Apr. and Sept. daily 11am-5:30pm; Oct. to mid-Nov. Su-M and W-Sa noon-5pm; mid-Feb. to Mar. Su-M and W-Sa 11am-5pm. Free audio guide in English, French, and German. €6, students €5.)

Pendant les soirs, a lively bit of pub life picks up all along rue Royale, especially where it meets rue R. Poincaré. **Le Coco Mambo,** 26 rue de la Mer, is a Cuban-flavored bar with a small terrace and a cozy back corner. (☎06 08 04 81 52. Beer from €2.70. Open July-Aug. daily 2pm-2am; Sept.-June Su-Th 2pm-1am. MC/V.)

MONTREUIL-SUR-MER

Though its name is misleading (not a drop of salt water has been seen here since the 13th century, when the ocean began to recede considerably), tiny Montreuil (pop. 2400) could hardly be more idyllic if it actually were on the ocean. Its unmanicured *vieille ville* and the rough, peaceful hills beyond have a simple, authentic appeal, in part because the tourist hordes have not yet discovered them. Montreuil was the setting for a large section of Victor Hugo's *Les Misérables.*

■■ **TRANSPORTATION & PRACTICAL INFORMATION.** The **train station** lies just outside the walls of the citadel. (☎03 21 06 05 09. Office open M-Sa 5am-7:30pm, Su 9am-7:30pm.) **Trains** go to: Arras (1½hr., 4 per day, €11.80); Boulogne (40min., 6 per day, €6.20); Calais (1hr., 3-4 per day, €11); Lille (2hr., 4 per day, €15.90); Paris (3hr., 3 per day, €26.20) via Etaples and Arras. Rent a **bike** at ETS

Vignaux, 73 rue Pierre Ledent. (☎03 21 06 00 29. €15.30 per day, €150 deposit. Open Tu-F 9am-noon and 2-7pm, Sa 9am-noon and 2-6pm. MC/V.)

To reach the **tourist office,** 21 rue Carnot, climb the stairs across from the station, turn right on av. du 11 Novembre, then right at the sign for "Auberge de Jeunesse." Follow rue des Bouchers to its end, then take a left onto the footpath at the shrine of Notre-Dame; the office is straight ahead. The English-speaking staff distributes a map and bilingual brochures. (☎03 21 06 04 27; otmontreuilsurmer@nordnet.fr. Open Apr.-Oct. M-Sa 9:30am-12:30pm and 2-6pm, Su 10am-12:30pm and 3-5pm; Nov.-Mar. closed Su 3-5pm.) Other services include: **currency exchange** and an **ATM** at BNP, 70 rue Pierre Ledent, off pl. Darnétal (☎08 20 35 63 28; open Tu-W 8:30am-noon and 1:30-5:30pm, Th 8:30am-noon, F 1:30-5:30pm, Sa 8:45am-12:30pm), **police** at pl. Gambetta (☎03 21 81 08 48; call here for the **pharmacie de garde**), a **hospital** in Rang du Fliers (☎03 21 89 45 45), **Internet** at Télé Bureau Services, 64 Grand'rue, near the train tracks (☎03 21 90 06 00; €2.50 for 30min., €4 per hr.; open M-F 9am-noon and 2-7pm, Sa 9am-noon), and a **post office** on pl. Gambetta. (☎03 21 06 70 00. Open M-F 8:30am-noon and 1:30-5pm, Sa 8:30-noon.) **Postal code:** 62170.

⚏☐ ACCOMMODATIONS & FOOD. Th excellent ⚏**Renards ❸,** 4 av. du 11 Novembre, rents huge, old-fashioned *chambres d'hôte* at the top of the stairs from the train station, with fireplaces, old furniture, and a charming back garden. (☎03 21 86 85 72. Breakfast included. Singles with sink and shared bath €30, with private bath €35; doubles €35/€40. Extra bed €12.50. No credit cards.) The **Auberge de Jeunesse "La Hulotte" (HI) ❶,** inside the citadel on rue Carnot, is under construction, but still offers 12 beds with summer camp-style accommodations and sweeping views. (☎03 21 06 10 83. Kitchen. Reception daily 2-6pm. Open Mar.-Oct. Bunks €7.) The **Hôtel le Vauban ❹,** 32 pl. de Gaulle, has sun-drenched, yellow-and-blue rooms with TV and mini-bar in a petal-pink building on the central *place.* (☎03 21 06 04 95; fax 03 31 06 04 00. Breakfast €6. Reception 8am-8pm. Singles €32, much bigger and with shower €40; doubles €32/€47; triples with shower €55; quads with shower €62. AmEx/MC/V.) The beautiful, forested **campground ❶,** 744 rte. d'Etaples, is on the banks of the river, near a pool, restaurant, and tennis courts. (☎03 21 06 07 28. Reception daily 9am-noon and 2-6pm. 1 or 2 people with car or tent €6.50; extra person €1.80. Electricity €2.80.)

Many restaurants and a **Shopi** (open Tu-Sa 8:30am-8pm, Su 9am-12:45pm) are located at **place de Gaulle;** bakeries are on the adjacent streets. ⚏**La Crêperie**

THE LOCAL STORY

PUTTING ON *LES MIS*

Dominique Martens is the writer/director behind Montreuil-sur-Mer's 250-person restaging of Victor Hugo's Les Misérables, which is set partly in Montreuil.

Q: Could you describe what makes the production special?
A: To my knowledge, [this] is the only adaptation that uses exclusively the words of Victor Hugo, both the words that he wrote in his novel, and also the letters that he wrote when he visited Montreuil-sur-Mer. Spectators can be dazzled by the costumes, the lights, the music, but above all by the quality of the text and the outdoor staging, which is quite original.

Q: How long have you been involved with this production?
A: This is the eighth year that the people of Montreuil have recreated [Hugo's book].

Q: Has anything unexpected or particularly wild ever happened during one of the shows? Any grand disasters or funny stories?
A: No, no—[eyes grow wide] not yet! No, we've avoided any pitfalls so far....It's been a grand success, really, with tickets sold out almost every night. [Relaxing] No problems so far.

Q: Finally, we know that Victor Hugo's book gets rather violent toward the end; do we have your word that no revolutionaries or beggar children were harmed during the making of this production?
A: [Chuckling] No, no, I promise.

Montreuil ❶, 3 rue du Clape en Bas, serves velvety crêpes (€1.50-8) in a jovial atmosphere and closes off its tiny cobbled street for free rock, jazz, and blues shows. (Shows July-Aug. Th 9:30pm, Su 5pm. Open July to Aug. daily 4pm-midnight). If you like *coq*, you'll love ▓**Le Cocquempot ❹**, 2 pl. de la Poissonnerie, off pl. Darnétal, in a grand, old house with a classy, elegant dining room. The famous chicken dish *coq du Cocquempot à la Bière* is part of the €21.50 *menu*. (☎03 21 81 05 61. *Menus* €15-36.50. Open July-Aug. Su-W and F-Sa noon-1:30pm and 7-9pm; Sept.-June closed W. MC/V.). Less ritzy, but equally tasty, is **La Taverne de l'Ecu de France ❷**, 5 porte de France, offering everything from snack sandwiches (€4-5) to a €14 regional specialty *menu*. (☎03 21 06 01 89. Open July-Aug. daily 12:30-3pm and 7-9:30pm; Sept.-June closed Tu-W. MC/V.)

▓▓ **SIGHTS & ENTERTAINMENT.** The 3km-long **ramparts** look over forested valleys and ancient ruins. The crumbling 16th-century **citadel** in the *haute ville* occupies the site of the old royal castle. (Open July-Aug. Su-M and W-Sa 10am-noon and 2-6pm; Sept.-June 10am-noon and 2-5pm. €2.50, children €1.30.) Pretty tumbledown cottages line the **rue du Clape en Bas** and the **Cavée St-Firmin;** the latter has actually been featured in several films, including the first version of *Les Misérables*. Club Canoë Kayak, 4 rue Moulin des Orphelins, across the canal from the train station, runs **canoe** and **kayak excursions** on the river Canche. (☎03 21 06 20 16. Open daily 9am-noon and 2-5pm. Sessions from €10, different difficulty levels available. Call ahead for reservations.) What nightlife there is can be found on **rue d'Herambault** and the streets around **place de Gaulle.** In late July and early August, the Citadel stages an impressive *son-et-lumière* version of *Les Misérables* with 250-300 actors, featuring dance, song, and pyrotechnics. (Contact tourist office for info. €14, children €9.50. See **The Local Story**, p. 187.) A theater festival, **Les Malins Plaisirs,** comes to town every summer. (Tourist office has dates, or call ☎03 21 98 12 26. €14-18, under 25 €9-14.) August 15 brings the **Day of the Street Painters,** an exuberant, artsy celebration in the town's winding *haute ville*.

PAS DE CALAIS

AMIENS

Amiens (pop. 136,000), capital of Picardy and adopted hometown of Jules Verne, captures the imagination more than its low profile would suggest. A lively student center with peppy nightlife, it also boasts France's largest Gothic cathedral and a canal-lined pedestrian *quartier* known as "Little Venice." Nature-lovers can enjoy the tranquil *hortillonages*, floating gardens cultivated since Roman times.

▐ TRANSPORTATION

Trains: Gare du Nord, pl. Alphonse Fiquet. To: **Boulogne-sur-Mer** (1¼hr., 13 per day, €15.70); **Calais** (2hr., 10 per day, €19.70); **Lille** (1¼hr., 14 per day, €20.40); **Paris** (1¼hr., 20 per day, €16.50); **Rouen** (1½hr., 3 per day, €15.50). Office open M-F 5am-9:15pm, Sa 5:10am-8:30pm, Su 6am-10:30pm. Info office open M-Sa 9am-6pm.

Buses: (☎03 22 92 27 03). Depart from under the shopping center to the right of the station for **Beauvais** (1-1½hr., 5 per day, €7) and other regional destinations.

Local Transportation: SEMTA, 10 pl. Alphonse Figuet (☎03 22 71 40 00). Office open M-F 7am-7pm, Sa 8am-5:30pm. Buses run 6am-9pm. Tickets €1.10. All buses stop at the train station; buy tickets on board or at the office.

Bike Rental: Buscyclette, near train station (☎03 22 72 55 13). €1 per hr., €3.30 per half-day, €5 per day. €100 deposit. Open M-Sa 6:30am-8:30pm, Su 9am-7pm.

Car Rental: Hertz, 5 bd. Alsace-Lorraine (☎03 22 91 26 24), across from the train station. Open M-F 8am-noon and 2-6:30pm, Sa 9am-noon and 4-6pm. MC/V.

Taxis: ☎03 22 91 30 03 or 03 22 98 08 97. 24hr.

▲ PRACTICAL INFORMATION

Tourist Office: 6bis rue Dusevel (☎03 22 71 60 50; www.amiens.com/tourisme). Turn right out of the the station parking lot, then left onto rue Gloriette. After the cathedral, turn left onto rue Dusevel. The energetic, English-speaking staff organizes tours, takes care of **hotel reservations** (€3 in person), provides free French and English brochures, and has an excellent free town map. Open Apr.-Sept. M-Sa 9:30am-7pm, Su 10am-noon and 2-5pm; Oct.-Mar. M-Sa 9:30am-6pm, Su 10am-noon and 2-5pm. Cathedral tours daily 11am and 4:30pm; city tours daily 2:30pm. Call ahead for a bilingual guide. €5.50, students €4, under 12 €3. Special themed tours available throughout the year.

Youth Center: CROUS, 25 rue St-Leu (☎03 22 97 37 31; www.cr-picardie.fr), offers info and assistance on lodging, work, and study opportunities in the area. They also have a helpful practical guide to life in Amiens. Open M-F 8:30am-5pm.

Laundromats: Net Express, 10 rue André. (☎03 22 72 33 33. Open daily 7am-8pm.) Also at 13bis rue des Majots (open daily 8am-10pm), and 165 av. du Gal. Foy. (Near the hostel. Open daily 8am-7pm.)

Money: Banks with **ATMs** and **currency exchange** cluster around the station, around the cathedral, and all over the pedestrian district.

Police: 2 rue des Chaudronniers (☎03 22 71 53 00).

Hospital: Hôpital Nord, pl. Victor Pauchet (☎03 22 66 80 00); take bus #10 (dir: Collège César Frank).

24hr. Pharmacy: for the **pharmacie de garde,** call ☎03 22 44 72 60 or check the tourist office window.

Internet: surf for free at the **Centre d'Information Jeunesse,** 56 rue du Vivier (☎03 22 91 21 31; www.jeunes-en-picardie.org). Open M-Th 9am-12:30pm and 1:30-6pm, F closes at 5pm.) **Branch** at 4 rue Henri IV near the cathedral. (Open Tu-F 1-7pm, Sa 1-6pm.) **Neurogames,** 17 rue Vergeaux (☎03 22 72 68 79). €3.50 per hr. Open M-Sa 10am-midnight. **Microgames,** 27 rue des Otages (☎03 22 80 16 53). €3.50 per hr. Open M-Sa 10am-8pm.

Post Office: 7 rue des Vergeaux (☎03 22 44 60 00), located just down the block from the Hôtel de Ville. Open M-F 8am-7pm, Sa 8am-12:30pm. **Branch offices** located at 37 pl. Alphonse Fiquet (open M-F 8am-7pm, Sa 8am-noon), as well as at 6 pl. Parmentier. (Open M-F 9am-noon and 2-6pm, Sa 9am-noon.) **Poste Restante:** 80050. **Postal code:** 80000.

▲ ACCOMMODATIONS

Hotels with €25-30 rooms cluster around the train station; options in the center of town tend to be pricier.

▨ **CRJS (HI),** 24 sq. des 4 Chênes (☎03 22 33 27 30; www.osam.asso.fr). The 35min. walk is tiring; instead, take a bus to Foy (2-3 per hr., fewer on weekends), then walk 75m to the giant square just ahead. The hostel itself is safe, but be careful in this area at night. Spotless, newly opened complex offers modern, attractive rooms with 1-4 beds, private bathrooms, and a Match supermarket just outside the door. The staff organizes activities, offers meals in a shiny dining area, and boasts a fleet of washing machines. Breakfast €3.10. Other meals €6.10. Reception 24hr. 2- to 4-bed rooms €13; singles €15. Sheets included. **Non-members** €2 extra per night. MC/V. ●

■ **Hôtel Victor Hugo,** 2 rue l'Oratoire (☎03 22 91 57 91; fax 03 22 92 74 02). The spacious rooms at this two-star hotel are beautifully maintained; all have shower or bath, toilet, and TV. A quiet, central location and a friendly owner make it a snap-it-up bargain. Breakfast €5. Reception 24hr. Reserve well in advance. Singles and doubles €36-41; triples and quads €42-51. Extra bed €10. MC/V. ❸

Hôtel Puvis de Chavannes, 6 rue Puvis de Chavannes (☎03 22 91 82 96; fax 03 22 72 95 35). On a quiet street 3min. from the pedestrian district (15min. from the station), the rooms are clean and newly renovated. Breakfast €4.20. Shower €1.60. Reception M-Sa 7:20am-9:30pm, Su 7:20-11am and 8-9:30pm. Singles and doubles €21-25, with private shower €28.90; triples with shower €41. Extra bed €9. MC/V. ❷

Hôtel le Prieuré, 6 rue Porion (☎03 22 71 16 71), combines old-fashioned luxury and modern amenities. Big, classy rooms overlook a quiet courtyard under the shadow of the cathedral. Breakfast €6. Reception M-Sa 7pm-9pm, Su 7am-6pm. Singles €36-65 (most €49); doubles €52-68; triples €60. MC/V. ❹

Hôtel Spatial, 15 rue Alexandre Fatton (☎03 22 91 53 23; fax 03 22 92 27 87). Right between the train station and the cathedral, this convenient option offers clean, average-looking rooms with TV. Breakfast €5. Hall showers available. Reception daily 7:30am-9:30pm. Singles €25.50, with shower €32-42; doubles €28.50/€36-48; triples €38.50/€49-51; quads with bath €56. Extra bed €7. AmEx/MC/V. ❷

🍴 FOOD

The place to be for a good meal and the best views in town, **quai Bélu** (in the *St-Leu* quarter of Little Venice) is tightly-packed with canal-front cafés and restaurants. Cheaper grub and scads of kebab stands cluster around the station and the cathedral; *brasseries* surround the ancient **Forum** in the pedestrian district. A **Match** supermarket is in the mall, right of the station (open M-Sa 9am-8pm); another faces the hostel on sq. des 4 Chênes. (Open M-Sa 8:30am-7:30pm.) Amiens's main **market** in pl. Parmentier sells vegetables from the *hortillonnages* on Sa (see **Sights**). Smaller markets are on pl. Beffroi. (Open W and Sa.)

■ **La Soupe à Cailloux,** 12-16 rue des Bondes (☎03 22 91 92 70), on the beautiful pl. du Don. Look for the *suggestions du jour* (€6.10-13) at this congenial restaurant or go ahead and order the *lapin au cidre* (€12), the *salade spéciale* (with apple, avocado, and Roquefort; €8.60), or one of the many vegetarian options (€6-15). Open June-Aug. daily noon-2pm and 7-10pm; Sept.-May closed M. AmEx/MC/V. ❷

■ **Restaurant Tante Jeanne,** 1 rue de la Dodane (☎03 22 72 30 30). Waterfront restaurant in St-Leu serves the regional specialty *ficelles picardie* (thin crêpe), and a fantastic *galette chèvrette* (with chèvre, greens, nuts, and raisins), each for €6.50. Read about the sweet, loving *"Tante Jeanne"* while her glowering photograph stares menacingly up at you from the cover of your menu. Open daily noon-2pm and 7-10:30pm. MC/V. ❶

Joséphine, 20 rue Sire Firmin Leroux (☎03 22 91 47 38). A homey, cozy restaurant with 2- to 4-course *menus* featuring traditional goodies from *agneau filet* to *ratatouille*. *Menus* €12-33. Open daily noon-2pm, M and W-Sa also 7-10pm. MC/V. ❸

Greenwish, 18 rue Sire Firmin Leroux (☎03 22 80 19 69). Huge array of sandwiches, salads, and paninis, all €2-4.50. Open M-F 9am-5pm. MC/V. ❶

👁 SIGHTS

CATHÉDRALE DE NOTRE-DAME. The largest Gothic cathedral in the world was built for the less than space-intensive task of holding John the Baptist's head, brought home from the unsuccessful Fourth Crusade. The small Weeping Angel behind the choir was made famous during WWI when Allied troops mailed home thousands of postcards of it. The front portals are lit up nightly mid-June to mid-Sept. to display their dazzling original colors. (☎ *03 22 71 60 56. Nightly illuminations June 10:45pm, July 10:30pm, Aug. 10pm, Sept. 9:45pm, Dec.-Jan. 8pm. Free. Open daily Easter-Oct. 8:30am-6:45pm; Nov.-Feb. 8:30am-noon and 2-5pm; Mar. until 6pm. French tours daily mid-June to mid-Sept. 11am and 4:30pm; mid-Sept. to mid-June Su 3pm. €5.)*

▓ **QUARTIER ST-LEU.** Just north of the Somme is the oldest, most attractive part of Amiens. Its narrow, cobbled streets and flower-strewn squares are built along a system of waterways and canals; locals call it "Little Venice of the North." Nearby are the **hortillonages,** market gardens spread into the marshland. Walk along the flower-strewn towpath starting from **Parc St-Pierre,** or tour the waterways on a traditional *barque à cornets.* *(Tours ☎ 03 22 92 12 18. Boat tours in French leave from 54 bd. Beauvillé Apr.-Oct. daily 2-6pm. €4.80, ages 11-16 €4, ages 3-10 €2.40. MC/V.)* There are a daily antique market and countless small art studios on passage Bélu.

MUSÉE DE PICARDIE. This museum houses a distinguished collection of mostly French paintings and sculptures. The sparkling white marble of the 19th-century figures is particularly dazzling; don't miss the Picasso and Balthus works on the second floor. *(48 rue de la République. ☎ 03 22 97 14 00. Open Tu-Su 10am-12:30pm and 2-6pm, summer hours change with temporary exhibitions. €4, students and ages 6-18 €2.50. Special group rates. Ask for guides and brochures in English. Wheelchair-accessible.)*

MAISON JULES VERNE. One would expect a little more pizzazz from this understated homage to a writer of such fantastical imagination. The *20,000 Leagues Under the Sea* author wrote most of his illustrious work in the study of this unassuming *maison.* The ground floor might thrill obsessed fans, but the models and posters on display do little to evoke the man's famed art. *(2 rue Charles Dubois. ☎ 03 22 45 37 84. Open Apr.-Sept. Tu-F 10am-noon and 2-6pm, Sa-Su 2-6pm; Oct.-Mar. closed mornings. Entrance only by tour, 45min. in French or English. Last tour 1hr. before closing. €3, students €1.50.)*

▨ ♫ NIGHTLIFE & ENTERTAINMENT

Pierre Choderlos de Laclos, author of *Les Liaisons Dangereuses,* was born in Amiens. More dangerous liaisons can be made in the city's canal-crossed older neighborhood. The gas-lit, cobbled **place du Don** and **rue Belu,** in the Quartier St-Leu, teem with French students. Kitschy **Le Living,** 3 rue des Bondes, just off pl. du Don, is packed with a fun-loving young clientele. (☎ 03 22 92 50 30. Happy hour 6-8pm with beer €2.50. Open daily 4pm-3am. AmEx/MC/V.) Across the street, **Le Zeppelin II,** 2 rue des Bondes, across the street from Le Living,) is a party- and trip-hop-filled stairway to heaven. (☎ 03 22 92 38 16. Beer from €3. Open M 9pm-3am, Tu-Su 8pm-3am. MC/V.) Dark, sexy bar and dance hall **Baroque Café,** 7 quai Bélu, is filled with a sleek, seductive crowd. (☎ 06 70 64 50 45. No cover. Cocktails €5.30. Open Su-M 3pm-1am, Tu-Sa 3pm-3am. MC/V.) **Le Forum,** espace piétons Gambetta, on the Forum in the pedestrian district, is a mellow pubbing alternative. (☎ 03 22 92 44 45. Beer from €2.70. Open Su 2pm-1am, M-Sa 7:30am-1am. MC/V.)

The adorable **Théâtre de Marionnettes,** 31 rue Edouard David, off rue Vanmarcke, stages elaborate shows in the "Chés Cabotans d'Amiens" theater, with various exhibitions of the stringed puppets during the day. (☎ 03 22 22 30 90. Check www.ches-cabotans-damiens.com for schedules, exhibition times, and prices. Shows Tu-Su 6pm.)

The November **Festival du Jazz** brings noted musicians from all over the world. (Contact the tourist office for schedules and venues for this year.) On the 3rd weekend in June, the **Fête dans la Ville** fills the streets with concerts, street festivals, jugglers, and circus performers. It's no Cannes—and this isn't the Riviera—but an international jury and an engaging slate of dramas and documentaries comes out for the November **Festival International du Film.**

COMPIÈGNE

Royalty dating back to Merovingian times fled to the cool woodlands and delicate beauty of this hamlet on the forested southern border of Picardy. The grand Château de Compiègne has played summer home to scads of Louis's, Napoleon I, and Napoleon III. More somberly it is the site of Joan of Arc's final capture by the Burgundian army, who delivered her to her English enemies. Today, Compiègne (pop. 40,000) is a picturesque retreat favored by Parisians, its royal pedigree shamelessly apparent in its ornate central square and acres of imperial gardens.

█ ▌ TRANSPORTATION & PRACTICAL INFORMATION

Trains leave from pl. de la Gare (☎03 44 83 89 65), across the river from the rest of the town, to Paris (45-60min., 27 per day, €11.40) and Lille (2-3hr., 8 per day, €24). Ticket windows open M-Sa 4:45am-9:10pm, Su 6:25am-10:10pm. **Regional buses** run from the station to surrounding towns daily. **Local TUC buses** run throughout town daily 6am-8pm, some until 10pm. (Schedules and maps at the tourist office. €0.80 per ride; buy tickets on board.) **Taxis** can be reached at ☎03 44 83 24 24 or 06 07 79 48 87. The local **bike rental** company delivers to hotels. (☎06 17 39 16 87. €9-15 per day, depending on type. €150 deposit.)

The **tourist office** is in the Hôtel de Ville (☎03 44 40 01 00; otsi@mairie-compiegne.fr). Cross the station parking lot, turn right, cross the bridge, and follow rue Solférino to pl. de l'Hôtel de Ville. (5min.) A helpful, English-speaking staff provides a list of hotels and restaurants, free maps and brochures (most in English), and information on hiking and biking trails in the Compiègne forest (in French). (Open Easter-Oct. M-Sa 9:15am-12:30pm and 1:45-6:15pm, Su 10am-1pm and 2:30-5pm; Nov.-Dec. closed Su; Jan.-Easter closed Su-M.) Other services include: **banks** with **ATMs** and **currency exchange** along rue Solférino and around the Hôtel de Ville, a **laundromat** at 15 rue de Paris (open daily 7am-10pm), **police** at 2 av. Thiers (☎03 44 40 00 45; call for the **pharmacie de garde,** or check the tourist office window), a **hospital** at 8 av. H. Adnot (☎03 44 23 60 00), **Internet** on the second floor of El Latino Restaurant, 29 rue Fournier Sarlovèze (€2 per hr; open Su-M and W 11am-9:30pm, Th-F 11am-1am, Sa 2pm-1am) or Microcom, pl. du Marché aux Herbes (€4 per hr.; open M-Sa 9am-12:30pm and 2-5pm), and a **post office** at 42 rue de Paris. (☎03 44 36 31 80. Open M-F 8:30am-6:30pm, Sa 8:30am-12:30pm.) A **branch** is at pl. du Marché aux Herbes. (☎03 44 40 21 50. Open Tu and Th-F 10:30am-6pm, W 9:30am-6pm, Sa 9am-12:30pm and 2-5pm.) **Postal code:** 60200.

▐ ◖ ACCOMMODATIONS & FOOD

There is no hostel in Compiègne. Hotels cluster around the train station; just across the river is a slew of more expensive establishments. The rooms in convenient, enormous **Hôtel de Flandre ❸,** 16 quai de la République, off pl. de la Gare, are spacious, comfortable, and TV-equipped. (☎03 44 83 24 06 or 03 44 83 24 40; fax 03 44 90 02 75. Breakfast €7. Reception daily 7am-12:30am. Singles €27, with shower or bath €41-44; doubles €30/€49-52. DC/MC/V.) Above a Chinese restaurant and next to a laundromat, it doesn't get much more convenient for the budget traveler than **Hôtel St-Antoine ❷,** 17-19 rue de Paris, 3-5min. from the Hôtel de Ville. Rooms are a bit worn but clean and cheap. (☎03 44 23 22 27. Reception daily 7am-10pm. Singles €15.30, with shower €18.30, with shower and TV €21; doubles €20/€23/

€26. Hall toilets. No shower available for showerless rooms. MC/V.) The **Hôtel Sunset ❷**, 4 rue Solférino, over the bridge from the train station, and 2min. from the Hôtel de Ville, rents clean rooms with a shower, TV, and toilet at a fantastic price. (☎03 44 20 47 47. Breakfast €5. Reception M-Sa 6pm-9pm, otherwise go next door to *Opticien KRYS*. Singles €25; doubles €30-34. MC/V.)

Food, like everything else in Compiègne, is concentrated heavily around **place de l'Hôtel de Ville** and along both sides of the **river Oise** near the train station. Restaurants also cluster in the pedestrian district between **rue Solférino** and **place du Marché aux Herbes**. For the do-it-yourself type, there's a **Monoprix** at 33 rue Solférino. (Open M-Sa 8:30pm-8pm, F until 8:30pm. MC/V after €15). The oddly named **L'Histoire de... ❷**, 9 rue des Lombards, is a charming little eatery with a varied but uniformly delicious selection, from voluminous salads and tasty *tartines* to *chile con carne*. (☎03 44 40 13 62. *Menus* from €10, salads from €8. Open daily noon-2pm and 7-10pm. MC/V.) At **La Rotisserie du Chat qui Tourne ❸**, 17 rue Eugène Floquet, attached to the Hôtel de France, traditional *onglet de veau au bleu* shares menu space with a series of vegetarian specialties, from roasted vegetable dishes to *pesto et parmesan* zucchini with pasta. (☎03 44 40 02 74. Two-course *menus* from €13, 3-course €20, with wine and a 4th course €32. Open Sept.-June M-Sa noon-2pm and 7-10pm, Su noon-2pm; July-Aug. closed M. AmEx/MC/V.) Nonvegetarians, put those pointy teeth to work at **Bistrot du Boucher ❷**, 39 rue Vivenel. €12.80 *plats* include veal, steak, duck, and poultry. (☎03 44 36 43 60. Open daily noon-1:45pm and 7:30-10pm. Four-course *menu* with wine €24. MC/V.)

🅖 SIGHTS

CHÂTEAU DE COMPIÈGNE. The most famous landmark in town, this palace, reconstructed by the monarchy in the 18th century, became a favorite retreat of Napoleon I and even more so Napoleon III. A tour of the *grands appartements* brings you to the sumptuously restored living quarters of various rulers. Even the cattle-herding tactics of the guides can't obscure some incredible sights. Look for the marble table upon which a sulking, punished young noble carved his initials in 1868, and the leopard-carpeted *salle* in which Napoleon first met his wife Marie-Louise. In addition to the preserved gilded chambers and halls, the large complex houses a fascinating **Musée de la Voiture**, which showcases classic cars, bicycles, and motorcycles, as well as various exhibits dedicated to the First and Second Empires. *(Pl. du Général de Gaulle. ☎03 44 48 47 02; fax 03 44 38 47 01; chateau.compiegne@culture.gouv.fr. Open Su-M and W-Sa 10am-6pm, last admission 5:15pm. 1hr. tours in French leave every 20-30min.; call ahead for English. Free with the price of admission. €5.50, ages 18-25 €4, 1st Su of each month and under 18 free. Wheelchair-accessible.)*

▨ PARC DU CHÂTEAU. Behind the palace, and, mercifully, too expansive to be crowded by tourists, this massive park includes miles of breathtaking royal gardens designed by Berthault under Napoleon. With tree-lined paths, floral *jardins*, wide-open spaces, and shady nooks, the only downside to this park is a giddy overload of space. *(Open daily 8am-7pm, entrance to the right of the Château.)*

▨ HARAS NATIONAL. This national stable along rue de la Procession houses over 50 stallions of all breeds in what was once the palace stables, quite befitting a town that was once a famous hunting retreat. Open to visitors free of charge (except during the parts of the summer when the stallions are, ahem, doing their work...), the Haras also offers a guided tour every Sa at 3pm. *(☎03 44 38 54 40. Open daily 9am-noon and 2-5pm. Tours in French leave from the château. €5.50.)*

OTHER SIGHTS. The squint-inducing but delightful **Musée de la Figurine**, 28 pl. de l'Hôtel de Ville next to the tourist office, displays over 5000 historic and military figurines from its unique collection. Hand-painted battalions of ½-inch soldiers shine with detail, while 8-inch giants sport tailored cloaks and hats. (☎ 03 44 40 72 55. Open Mar.-Oct. Tu-Sa 9am-noon and 2-6pm, Su 2-6pm; Nov.-Feb. closes at 5pm. €2, ages 18-25 €1, under 18 free. 1st Su of each month free. Wheelchair-accessible.) The 13th-century **Eglise St-Jacques**, pl. St-Jacques, is where Joan of Arc came to pray the morning she was captured in 1430.

🎵 🌸 ENTERTAINMENT & FESTIVALS

The **Théâtre Impérial,** 3 rue Othenin, provides opera, ballet, and drama to the sophisticated masses. Originally planned to have an 1871 debut, the grand building, with its amazing acoustics, was finally finished…in late 1991. (☎ 08 25 00 06 74; www.theatre-imperial.com. Info office open Sept.-June M-F 8:30am-12:30pm and 2-6pm, Sa 8:45am-12:30pm and 2-5pm; July-Aug. closed Sa-Su. MC/V.) In mid-May, the **Concours Complet International** takes place in the Hippodrome above the Parc du Château. This equestrian competition, one of the biggest in the world, is free to watch and reaffirms the charming horsiness of the town. Also in mid-May, the annual **Foire aux Vins** brings free wine tastings and exhibits to the pl. St-Jacques. (Call ☎ 03 44 86 69 45 for details.) Around Easter, an international exhibition of decorated Easter eggs, the **Salon des Œufs Décorés,** hits the Salle Tainturier, rue de Clamart. (Call the tourist office for details. €6, under 12 free.) At night, bars and pubs liven up the pedestrian district and the streets around pl. de l'Hôtel de Ville.

🥾 HIKING

The misty trails of the **Forêt de Compiègne** provide a 15,000-hectare maze of peaceful hikes and winding bike routes, all eventually leading back to the château. Ask at the tourist office for a detailed map of these well-marked paths. Many lengths and levels of difficulty are available; the most rewarding route, a 7½-mile stroll through the center of the forest, culminates in dazzling **Le Château de Pierrefonds,** in the tiny village of the same name. Bought by Napoleon I and marvelously restored by Viollet le Duc under Napoleon III, the medieval-style château is a breathtaking reminder that, even in the 19th century, "authentic restoration" was a popular and successful endeavor. Walk the ramparts, view the gallery, and visit the cavernous knight's hall. (☎ 03 44 42 72 72. Château open May-Aug. daily 10am-6pm; Sept.-Oct. and Mar.-Apr. M-Sa 10am-12:30pm and 2-6pm, Su 10am-6pm; Nov.-Feb. M-F 10am-12:30pm and 2-5pm, Sa 10am-12:30pm and 2-6pm, Su 10am-5:30pm. Last admission 45min. before closing. €6, students 18-25 €4, under 18 free.) Another route passes by the **Wagon de l'Armistice,** with a museum that recounts the famous history of the railway car in which the German army conceded defeat in WWI and the French were forced by Hitler to do likewise in 1940. (☎ 03 44 85 14 18. Museum open daily Apr. to mid-Oct. 9am-12:30pm and 2-6pm; mid-Oct. to Mar. 9am-noon and 2-5:30pm. €3, ages 7-14 €1.50, under 7 free.)

NORMANDY (NORMANDIE)

In AD 911, Rollo, the leader of a band of Vikings who had settled around Rouen, accepted the title Duke of Normandy from King Louis the Simple. Over the centuries, Norman power grew beyond his wildest dreams. The most famous Norman achievement was the successful 1066 invasion of England, celebrated in a magnificent tapestry that still hangs in **Bayeux** (p. 214). The tables turned when Normandy was occupied in 1346 by English King Edward III, but by 1450, Normandy was re-incorporated into France. The English didn't attempt another invasion until June 6, 1944, when they returned with North American allies to wrest Normandy from the Germans.

In the intervening centuries, Normandy exchanged its warlike reputation for a quiet agricultural role. Far removed from the border wars which raged between France and its neighbors, Normandy's towns and villages remained virtually unchanged from the Middle Ages—an architectural heritage mostly destroyed during the heavy fighting following the D-Day landings.

Normandy's towns and cities range from seaside resorts to bleak coastal transportation hubs (**Le Havre**, p. 202; and **Cherbourg**, p. 221). **Caen** (p. 210), a chic university town, has the best WWII museum in Normandy. An equally powerful memorial to the war are the **D-Day beaches** (p. 217), where the Allies landed in 1944. The gem of the High Normandy coast, **Etretat** (p. 204) provides soaring chalk cliffs for beach-goers and wealthy vacationers. Also with terrific ocean views, **Granville's** (p. 223) old-world *haute ville* won't disappoint, nor will the spectacle of **Mont-St-Michel** (p. 226), an abbey on an ancient fortified island **Honfleur's** (p. 206) unforgettable Satie museum continually amazes travelers unfamiliar with the artist's work. History lovers won't want to miss **Rouen's** (p. 195) expansive tributes to Joan of Arc, the beautiful 13th-century cathedral of **Coutances** (p. 225), or **Fécamp's** (p. 205) Bénédictine palace, with its famous healing liqueur. The twin resort towns of **Deauville** and **Trouville** (p. 208) empty wallets at their casinos.

Norman cuisine maximizes the potential of fermented apples; *cidre, calvados* (apple brandy) and *pommeau* (the regional apéritif of choice), are the region's most beloved alcoholic offerings. Normandy's diverse cheese selection is dominated by the pungent Camembert, which is best when it's soft. The region's fresh fish markets are unbeatable; local favorites include oysters, mussels, and lobster.

ROUEN

However sharply Gustave Flaubert criticized his hometown through the eyes of his famous discontented housewife in *Madame Bovary*, Rouen (pop. 108,000) is no petty provincial hamlet. It will go down in history as the site where Joan of Arc was burned at the stake in 1431 and innumerable cathedrals and tributes to Mlle. Joan are still the primary attractions, but Rouen's vibrant urban energy sets it apart from its neighbors. Its charming streets weave among loud, snarling thoroughfares in an often uneasy juxtaposition of old and new. Post-World War II reconstruction didn't exactly beautify Rouen, yet it hasn't marred the architectural and historical appeal at its heart. Of late, a hip, young population has inherited the *vieille ville*—Madame B. would be jealous.

ENGLISH CHANNEL

Normandy

▐ TRANSPORTATION

Trains: rue Jeanne d'Arc, on pl. Bernard Tissot. Info office open M-Sa 7:45am-7pm. To: **Caen** (2hr., 7 per day, €18.80); **Le Havre** (1hr., 15 per day, €11.60); **Lille** (3hr., 5 per day, €26.10); **Paris** (1½hr., every hr., €16.90). Ask about student discounts on fares. Daytime luggage storage.

Buses: SATAR and **CNA,** both at rue Jeanne d'Arc, in front of the Théâtre des Arts (☎08 25 07 60 27). Info office open M-F 8am-6:30pm. Most buses depart from quai du Havre or quai de la Bourse. To **Le Havre** (2½hr., 8 per day, €12.80), and various small towns in the **Seine Valley.**

Public Transportation: Métrobus, with SATAR and CNA (see above; ☎02 35 52 52 52). Office open M-Sa 7am-7pm. Most buses run 6am-8pm, some night lines until midnight. Subway 5am-11pm. 1hr. ticket €1.30, *carnet* of 10 €10. Day pass €3.50, 2-day €5.

Taxis: 67 rue Jean Lecanuet (☎02 35 88 50 50). Stands at the train and bus stations, as well as the Palais de Justice on rue Jeanne d'Arc. 24hr.

◆ ▐ ORIENTATION & PRACTICAL INFORMATION

To get to the city center from the station, exit straight out and follow **rue Jeanne d'Arc** several blocks. A left onto the cobblestoned rue du Gros Horloge leads to

place de la Cathédrale and the tourist office; a right leads to **place du Vieux Marché.** Farther along, almost to the Seine, the *gare routière* is on the right.

Tourist Office: 25 pl. de la Cathédrale (☎02 32 08 32 40; fax 02 32 08 32 44). Free map (available in English). Commission-free **currency exchange.** The student guide *Le Viking* clues travelers in to all the local favorites. Open May-Sept. M-Sa 9am-7pm, Su 9:30am-12:30pm and 2-6pm; Oct.-Mar. M-Sa 9am-6pm, Su 10am-1pm.

Work Opportunities: Centre Rouen Information Jeunesse (CRIJ), 84 rue Beauvoisine (☎02 32 10 49 49; www.crij-haute-normandie.org), helps find work—primarily as *animateurs* or at hotels—and has info on activities. Free **Internet.** Open M-F 10am-6pm.

Bank: Crédit Lyonnais, 48 rue Jeanne d'Arc (☎08 20 82 43 00). Open M 10am-12:30pm and 1:45-5pm, Tu-F 9am-12:30pm and 1:45-5:45pm, Sa 9am-12:30pm and 1:45-4pm. There are **ATMs** throughout Rouen, including one across the street from the train station, and one across from Eglise Ste-Jeanne d'Arc at the Vieux Marché.

English Bookstore: ABC Bookshop, 11 rue des Faulx, behind Eglise St-Ouen (☎02 35 71 08 67). Displays ads for au pairs and tutors for hire. Open Jan.-June and Aug.-Dec. Tu-Sa 10am-6pm; July Tu-Sa 10am-3pm. Usually closed late July to mid-Aug. MC/V.

Laundromat: 87 rue Beauvoisine. Open daily 8am-8pm. Also at rue Cauchoise near pl. du Vieux Marché. Open daily 7am-9pm.

Police: 7-9 rue B. de Barneville (☎02 32 81 25 00), on the southern side of the Seine.

Hospital: 1 rue de Germont (☎02 32 88 89 90), near pl. St-Vivien.

Pharmacy: Grande Pharmacie du Centre, pl. de la Cathédrale (☎02 32 08 04 30, info 02 32 88 89 95), beside tourist office. Open M 10am-7:30pm, Tu-F 9am-7:30pm, Sa 9am-7pm. Rouen has many pharmacies, a number of which provide service at night (8pm-9am) and on holidays. Call for more info.

Internet: Free at CRIJ (see **Work Opportunities**). **Place Net,** 37 rue de la République (☎02 32 76 02 22), near the Eglise St-Maclou. €4 per hr. Open M-Sa 11am-midnight, Su 2-10pm. **Le Cœur Net,** 54 rue Cauchoise (☎02 35 15 45 42; www.coeur-net.fr.st), near pl. du Vieux Marché. €4 per hr. Open M-Sa 10am-1am, Su 2-10pm.

Post Office: 45bis rue Jeanne d'Arc (☎02 35 15 66 73). **Currency exchange.** Open M-F 9:30am-6:30pm, Sa 9am-noon. Branch at 122 rue Jeanne d'Arc, just left of the train station. Open M-F 8am-7pm, Sa 8:30am-noon. **Postal code:** 76000.

⛰ ACCOMMODATIONS & CAMPING

▨ **Hôtel Normandya,** 32 rue du Cordier (☎02 35 71 46 15). An inexpressibly friendly couple runs this charming hotel in a 300-year-old building. A few of the rooms are without windows, but most are comfortable and nicely decorated. Reception 8am-8pm. Singles €20, €25 with shower; add €2 for a second person. No credit cards. ❷

Hôtel Beauséjour, 9 rue Pouchet (☎02 35 71 93 47; fax 02 35 98 01 24), right from the station. Cheery rooms with comfy beds overlook the small street or pretty courtyard. Access to hotel bar and sitting room. Breakfast €4.50. Reception 6am-11pm. Singles €35; doubles €39.50; twins €41; triples €45; quads €55; all with shower. MC/V. ❸

Hôtel Solférino, 51 rue Jean Lecanuet (☎02 35 71 10 07). Spare, comfy rooms have all the essentials, some with TV, located near the center of town. Singles €22, with shower €26; doubles €25/€30. Rooms with bath also available. MC/V. ❷

Hôtel des Arcades, 52 rue de Carmes (☎02 35 70 10 30; fax 02 35 70 08 91). Bright, clean, centrally located. Breakfast €5.50. Reception M-F 7am-8pm, Sa-Su 7:30am-8pm. Singles and doubles €27, with shower €36; twins €33/€42. AmEx/MC/V. ❷

Hôtel de la Cathédrale, 12 rue St-Romain (☎02 35 71 57 95; www.hotel-de-la-cathedrale.fr). Attractive, spacious rooms, some with chandeliers. Features a bar, elevator,

Internet, parking, and tea room (11am-8pm). Buffet breakfast €7.50. Singles €47, with shower €56; doubles €56/€64. MC/V. ❹

Camping Municipal de Déville, rue Jules Ferry in Déville-les-Rouen (☎02 35 74 07 59), 4km from Rouen. Take the metro from the train station (dir: Technopole or Georges Braque) to Théâtre des Arts, transfer to Metrobus line TEOR (T2; dir: Mairie), and get off at Mairie de Deville-les-Rouen. Continue down the street one block and turn left on rue Jules Ferry. More gravel for caravans than greenery for tents, but space is never a problem. Showers free. Open Apr.-Oct. for tents, year-round for caravans. Reception open M-F 8am-1pm and 2-8pm; Sa-Su 9am-noon and 2-8pm. Gates close at 10pm. €4 per person, €1.60 per tent, €2.80 per caravan. Electricity €2. ❶

🍴 FOOD

Outdoor cafés and brasseries crowd around **place du Vieux Marché,** which hosts a **market** with fresh flowers, fish, fruit, and cheese Tu-Su 6am-1:30pm. There are also plenty of eateries near the **Gros Horloge** and the **Cathédrale de Notre Dame,** as well as a **Monoprix** supermarket at 73-83 rue du Gros Horloge (open M-Sa 8:30am-9pm), and a **Marché U** on pl. du Vieux Marché. (Open M-Sa 8:30am-8pm.) With a patio overlooking the Cathédrale de Notre Dame, the welcoming **Saint Romain Café Crêperie** ❶, 52 rue St-Romain, is surprisingly cheap. (☎02 35 88 90 36. Lunch €3-4, dinner with salad €7. Open Tu-W noon-2pm, Th-Sa noon-2pm and 7pm-10pm. MC/V.) Cozy bistro **Le P'tit Zinc** ❸, pl. du Vieux Marché, has a prime view of the Eglise Ste-Jeanne d'Arc. (☎02 35 89 39 69. Dinners €12-19. Open M-Sa noon-2pm and 8-10pm. MC/V.) **Restaurant Punjab** ❸, 3 rue des Bons Enfants, just off rue Jeanne d'Arc, provides a taste of India in a central location. Dinner (from €10) includes many vegetarian selections as well as a full bar and wine list. (☎02 35 88 63 48. Lunch *menus* €8-10, dinner *menus* €16-21. Open daily 11:30am-2:30pm and 6:30-11:30pm. MC/V.) Those with exceptionally full wallets gorge at **La Couronne** ❺, 31 pl. du Vieux Marché, the oldest *auberge* in France. Built in 1345, it is now frequented by a slightly older crowd. A variety of *prix fixe menus* (€27-42; individual entrées €15-23) feature the most decadent French dishes, such as foie gras, soufflé, and *"le véritable canard."* (☎02 35 71 40 90. Open daily noon-2pm and 7-10pm. AmEx/MC/V.) Vegetarian and organic foods store **Gourmand'grain** ❷, 3 rue du Petit Salut, off pl. de la Cathédrale and beside the tourist office, doubles as a lunch counter in the afternoons. Their modest selection of take-away items is tasty and healthy. (☎02 35 98 15 74. *Plat du jour* €6.90. Restaurant open Tu-Sa noon-2pm; store open Tu-Sa 10am-7pm. MC/V.)

👁 SIGHTS

Sights in Rouen fall into three basic categories: museums, churches, and museums and churches related to Joan of Arc. The real show-stoppers are the cathedral, the Musée des Beaux-Arts, and Flaubert's former house. Sorry, Joan.

▣ CATHÉDRALE DE NOTRE-DAME. This undeniably impressive cathedral, among the most important in France, incorporates nearly every intermediate style of Gothic architecture. It gained artistic fame when Monet chose to use it (justifiably) for his celebrated studies of light. Of the stained-glass windows that survived the bombings of World War II, those depicting the beheading of St. John the Baptist and the legend of St-Julien in the **Chapelle St-Jean de la Nef** are the best. To the left of Notre-Dame stands the 12th-century **Tour St-Romanus,** to the right the 17th-century **Tour de Beurre (Tower of Butter),** which was funded by cholesterol-loving parishioners who chose to pay a dispensation rather than go without butter during Lent. The cathedral, whose central spire is the tallest in France (151m), is illumi-

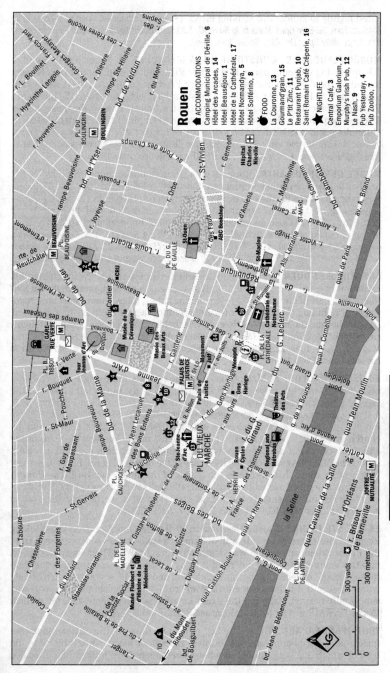

Rouen

▲ **ACCOMMODATIONS**
Camping Municipal de Déville, **6**
Hôtel des Arcades, **14**
Hôtel Beauséjour, **1**
Hôtel de la Cathédrale, **17**
Hôtel Normandya, **5**
Hôtel Solférino, **8**

✚ Hôpital Charles Nicolle

◆ **FOOD**
La Couronne, **13**
Gourmand'grain, **15**
Le P'tit Zinc, **11**
Restaurant Punjab, **10**
Saint Romain Café Créperie, **16**

★ **NIGHTLIFE**
Central Café, **3**
Emporium Galorium, **2**
Murphy's Irish Pub, **12**
Le Nash, **9**
Pub Yesterday, **4**
Pub Zooloo, **7**

NORMANDY

nated nightly in summer to striking effect. (*Pl. de la Cathédrale. Open M 2-7pm, Tu-Sa 7:45am-7pm, Su 8am-6pm. Mass held Su 8:30, 10:15am, noon; Tu-Sa 8, 10am. Tours in French June-Sept. daily 3pm; Oct.-May Sa-Su 3pm. Free.*)

MUSÉE FLAUBERT ET D'HISTOIRE DE LA MÉDECINE. Cute but hardly cuddly, this intriguing museum packs in a formidable amount of paraphernalia loosely hinged on the disparate themes of Gustave Flaubert (who was raised on the premises) and the history of medicine. A must for Flaubert obsessives (the museum's Flaubertalia includes the parrot that inspired *Un Cœur Simple*), the museum also displays Napoleon's death mask and bizarre examples of the ancient "arts" of phrenology and taxidermy. (*51 rue de Lecat, next to the Préfecture. Follow rue de Crosne from pl. du Vieux Marché.* ☎02 35 15 59 95. *Open Tu 10am-6pm, W-Sa 10am-noon and 2-6pm. Free English brochure. €2.20, ages 18-25 €1.50, students and under 18 free.*)

MUSÉE DES BEAUX ARTS. Rouen's gem, though not as impressive as its big brother in Paris, nevertheless houses a thorough collection of 16th- and 17th-century religious art, with the occasional masterpiece sprinkled in (including Caravaggio's *Flagellation of Christ* and Monet's stunning depiction of the Notre Dame Cathedral). There is also an extensive collection of Impressionist art and a smattering of cubist and Abstractionist pieces. (*26bis rue Jean Lecanuet, down rue Jeanne d'Arc from the train station.* ☎02 35 71 28 40. *Open Su-M and W-Sa 10am-6pm. Some exhibits closed 1-2pm. €3, ages 18-25 and groups €2, under 18 free. Special exhibitions cost more.*)

ABBATIALE ST-OUEN. Although not as architecturally rich as Notre Dame, this cathedral is equally impressive, if only because it is so neck-strainingly gargantuan. Once part of an 8th-century Benedictine abbey, it has undergone many renovations, including the addition of a 19th-century façade. Perfect for reading or lying in the sun, the **Jardins de l'Hôtel de Ville**, behind St-Ouen, are possibly Rouen's single most beautiful place. (*Next to the Hôtel de Ville, at pl. du Général de Gaulle. Open mid-Mar. to Oct. Tu-Sa 10am-12:15pm and 2-6pm, opens Su at 9am; Nov to mid-Dec. and mid-Jan. to mid-Mar. Tu and Sa-Su 10am-noon and 2-5pm.*)

EGLISE ST-MACLOU. St-Maclou merits a look for its imposing Gothic façade. Look for *les enfants pisseurs*, two urinating cherubs in the left corner of the façade. (*3 rue de Général Sarrail. Open to tourists M-Sa 10am-noon and 2-5:30pm, Su 3-5:30pm. Concerts July and Aug. Tickets available 30min. before concert at the church. For more info, pick up a brochure at the church or call* ☎02 35 70 84 90. *€8, students €5.*) Beyond the church to the left, a poorly marked passage at 186 rue de Martainville leads to the **Aître St-Maclou.** This cloister served as the church's slaughterhouse and cemetery during the Middle Ages, including the years of the deadly plagues, hence the grisly 15th-century frieze that decorates the beams of the inner courtyard. The *Rouennais* once entombed a live black cat inside the walls to exorcise spirits. The shriveled feline is still suspended behind a glass panel for all to see. (*Pl. Barthélémy, behind the cathedral. Open M-Sa 10am-noon and 2-5:30pm, Su 3-5:30pm.*)

EGLISE STE-JEANNE D'ARC. Designed in 1979 to resemble an overturned Viking longboat, this church's outside wall of luminous stained glass was recovered from the Eglise St-Vincent, which was destroyed during WWII. The massive intrusion into the Vieux Marché has a certain kitschy charm, but a trip through the interior—a cross between a spaceship's cathedral and a bad disco movie—isn't really worth it, even if it is free. Outside, a 6½m cross marks the spot where Joan was supposedly burned, although the exact location is much contested. (*Pl. de Vieux Marché. Open M-Th and Sa 10am-12:30pm and 2-6pm, F and Su 2-6pm.*)

TOUR JEANNE D'ARC. This is the last remaining tower of the château that confined Joan of Arc before she was burned. Each floor has a minor attraction, the best of which is a scale model of what Rouen might have looked like in Joan's time, though the tower may leave you feeling a bit burned unless you're looking for the extra exercise. (*To the left of the station on rue du Donjon. Due to renovations, the entrance is on rue Bouvreuil. Open Su-M and W-Sa 10am-noon and 2-5:30pm. Closes at 5pm from late Dec. to late Mar. €1.50, students and under 18 free.*)

OTHER SIGHTS. Built into a bridge across rue du Gros Horloge, the ornately gilded **Gros Horloge** (Big Clock) dings and dongs to its own schedule. Walk underneath to glimpse the friezes of the Lamb of God. When the renovations of the belfry are completed, visitors will be able to climb it for a view of the 14th-century clockwork and the rooftops of Rouen. Under the war-marked Palais de Justice stands the **Monument Juif** (Jewish Monument), uncovered in the 1970s. The building, with Hebrew writing on the walls, might date as far back as 1100 AD, though whether it was a synagogue, Talmudic school, or private home is unknown. (*Entrance with two-day advance notice only. Call tourist office to arrange a tour in French.*)

■ NIGHTLIFE

Rouen has more options for the civilized pubber than for the would-be clubber. **Central Café**, 138 rue Beauvoisine, feels hip with its young, well-dressed crowd and mellow mix of house and trance. There is no dancing to speak of, but it's a nice soundtrack to a late-night apéritif. (☎02 35 07 71 97. Open daily 6pm-2am.) One of the better bars is zebra-pillowed **Le Nash**, 97 rue Ecuyère, just off rue des Bons Enfants, whose porch encourages open-air interaction. (☎02 35 98 25 24. Beer €3. Open M-Sa 11am-2am.) For a jumpin' drinking scene, check out **Murphy's Irish Pub**, 12 pl. du Vieux Marché, where a bustling crowd spills onto the sidewalk. (☎02 35 71 17 33. Open daily 4pm-2am. MC/V.) The out-of-the-way **Pub Yesterday**, 3 rue Moulinet, parallel to rue Jeanne d'Arc near the train station, is a laid-back, friendly place to have a conversation over Guinness (€3) at the bar. (☎02 35 70 43 98. Whiskey €5. Open M-Sa 5pm-2am.) Smoky **Emporium Galorium**, 151 rue Beauvoisine, hosts perhaps the loudest and most raucous of Rouen's weekend bar scenes. (☎02 35 71 76 95. Beers and mixed drinks from €4. Open M-Sa 7pm-2am.) A safari theme defines **Pub Zooloo**, 79 rue Cauchoise, where packed tables full of talkative locals can be found outside or in the smoke-filled, well-lit back room. Cheap half-liters of the beer of the month (€4), hailing from places like Germany, Holland, and England, make it worth the stop. (Open M-Sa 10am-2am.)

NEAR ROUEN: SEINE VALLEY

The lazy Seine trails natural and historic gems behind it on its path through rolling farmland to the sea. You can theme-trek along it on an Impressionist route, an Emma Bovary route, a route of major castles and mansions, or the best-known route of them all, the Route des Abbayes. The first you'll encounter out of Rouen is the still-functioning **Abbaye St-Martin de Boscherville,** but the star of the bunch is the **Abbaye de Jumièges,** founded by St-Philibert in 654. A legend since Merovingian times, the abbey became a stone quarry during the Revolution but was bought and restored by the state in 1947. Now it's a splendid ruin, set in lush grounds that incorporate a 17th-century French garden. (☎02 35 37 24 02. Open mid-Apr. to mid-Sept. daily 9:30am-7pm; mid-Sept. to mid-Apr. 9:30am-1pm and 2:30-5:30pm. Tours available in French every hr. €4, students €2.50, under 18 free.) The **Parc Naturel Régional de Brotonne** sprawls across the Seine midway to Le Havre; before you hit the concrete jungle, get in some green time on this network of trails (inquire at the Rouen tourist office). The town of **Caudebec-en-Caux,** easily accessible by bus from Rouen or Le Havre, makes an excellent base from which to explore the park. A bit farther on toward the sea, the town of **Villequiers,** the site of the tragic drowning of

Victor Hugo's daughter Léopoldine and her husband, Charles Vacquerie, now houses the **Musée Victor Hugo,** rue Ernest Binet. (☎ 02 35 56 78 31. Open M and W-Sa 10am-12:30pm and 2-6pm, Su 2-6:30pm. €3.) The museum holds memorabilia from the Hugo and Vacquerie families, as well as drawings and first editions by Hugo himself—not an essential stop, but one to make if you're in the area. Cap off your tour of the valley with a peek at the enormous **Pont de Normandie,** the stark, futuristic bridge over the Seine just above Le Havre.

The best way to explore the valley is by car. If you go by bus, allow a whole day for exploration. Bus schedules change frequently. You can pick up a schedule at the Metrobus station or call the **CNA buses** directly. (☎ 08 25 07 60 27.) Line #30A runs from Rouen's bus station to several of the abbeys, stopping in some seasons at Jumièges (45 min., €5.50). Change buses at Caudebec-en-Caux to reach Villequiers and the Musée Victor Hugo. Biking is feasible as well, though distances are great. For any trip into the valley, the Rouen tourist office is the best place to start.

LE HAVRE

Founded in 1517 by François I, Le Havre (pop. 200,000) may be the largest transatlantic port in France, but it has little else to recommend it. In the 1930s, Jean-Paul Sartre served as a teaching assistant in Le Havre, which he renamed Bouville (Mudtown) in his first novel, *Nausea.* Le Havre's solution to the devastation of WWII was to call in architect Auguste Perret, who spewed reinforced concrete everywhere, compounding the unsightliness of the already utilitarian harbor. The town is trying desperately to improve its image with a good museum and tree-lined boulevards, but it is still best as a stopover. Get in, get out, and nobody gets hurt.

▐ TRANSPORTATION

Trains: cours de la République (☎ 08 36 35 35). Info office open M-Sa 9:30am-6:15pm. To: **Fécamp** via Etretat (1hr., 9 per day, €6.70); **Paris** (2hr., 8 per day, €23.70); **Rouen** (50min., 13 per day, €11.60).

Buses: bd. de Strasbourg (☎ 02 35 26 67 23). Connected to the train station (exit from the platforms to your left). Info office open M-Sa 7am-7pm. CNA runs to **Rouen** (3hr.; M-Sa 7 per day, 2 on Su; €13.40). Bus Verts (☎ 08 01 21 42 14) goes to **Caen** (1½hr., 5 per day, €19) and **Honfleur** (30min., 4 per day, €5.60). See p. 210 for Caen-Le Havre express info. **Autocars Gris** (☎ 02 35 28 19 88) runs to **Fécamp** via Etretat (45min.-1¾hr.; 10 per day; €7.20, 50% reduction on same-day return).

Ferries: P&O European Ferries, av. Lucien Corbeaux (☎ 08 03 01 30 13 or 08 25 01 30 13; www.poportsmouth.com), leave from Terminal de la Citadelle (☎ 02 35 19 78 78) for **Portsmouth** (see **Getting There: By Boat,** p. 40, for details). Ticket and info office open M-F 8:30am-7pm, Sa 9am-5pm; terminal closes at 11pm.

Taxis: Radio-Taxis wait at the train station (☎ 02 35 25 81 81). 24hr.

✈ 🛈 ORIENTATION & PRACTICAL INFORMATION

Be cautious when alone at night, especially around the train station and harbor.

Tourist Office: 186 bd. Clemenceau (☎ 02 32 74 04 04; www.lehavretourism.com). From the station, exit left, take a right on bd. de Strasbourg, follow it across town as it changes to av. Foch and eventually hits the beach, and turn left onto bd. Clemenceau. (20min.) From the ferry terminal, walk left down quai de Southampton, then right up bd. Clemenceau. Info on outdoor activities, a list of hotels and restaurants, a small guide to regional nightlife *(Bazart),* and a free map. Open May-Sept. M-Sa 9am-7pm, Su 10am-12:30pm and 2:30-6pm; Oct.-Apr. M-Sa 9am-6:30pm, Su 10am-1pm.

Money: ATMs are throughout the city center. The cluster closest to the train station is at the far end of bd. de Strasbourg, near the Hôtel de Ville.

Laundromat: 54 rue Edward Lang. Open daily 7am-8pm.

Pharmacy: Pharmacie de la Gare, 35 cours de la République (☎02 35 25 18 74), from the train station, across the street and to the right. Open M-F 9am-9pm, Sa 9am-noon.

Hospital: 55bis rue Gustave Flaubert (☎02 32 73 32 32).

Police: 16 rue de la Victoire (☎02 32 74 37 00).

Internet: Cybermetro, cours de la République (☎02 35 25 40 34), across from the train station. €2.30 for 15min., €3.10 for 30min., €4.60 per hr. Open daily 10am-10pm. The **library,** 17 rue Jules Lecesne (☎02 32 74 07 40), by appointment, but you can use a computer when others don't show up. Open July-Aug. Tu-W and F-Sa 10am-5pm, Th noon-5pm; Sept.-June Tu and F 10am-7pm, W and Sa 10am-6pm, Th noon-6pm.

Post Office: 62 rue Jules Siegfried (☎02 32 92 59 00). **Cyberposte.** Open M-F 8am-7pm, Sa 8am-noon. **Postal code:** 76600.

ACCOMMODATIONS

One-star hotels, offering mostly singles, line the cours de la République across from the train station. Affordable two-star establishments line bd. de Strasbourg. A good bet is **Hôtel Britania ❸,** 5 cours de la République, 10min. from the city center. It isn't the lap of luxury, but its rooms are comfortable, with shower and TV, and some with small balconies—not that the views are anything spectacular. (☎02 35 25 42 51. Breakfast €5. Reception 6am-8pm. Singles €26, with toilet €30, with bath €32; doubles €29/€33/€35; triples €35, with toilet €38. V.) **Hôtel le Monaco ❷,** 16 rue de Paris, near the ferry terminal, has spacious rooms in a classy, countryside décor above a popular brasserie, that serves 3-course *menus* for €20-33. (☎02 35 42 21 01. Breakfast €4.60. Reception 6:30am-11pm. Singles €22.90, with shower €31.30-33.60; doubles €26.70, with bath or shower €35.60-41.20; triples €36.60-47.30; quads €54.90. AmEx/MC/V.) Offering a more upscale feel, **Hôtel Celtic ❹,** 106 rue Voltaire, sits across the street from Le Volcan. From the station, follow bd. de Strasbourg to the Hôtel de Ville, turn left down rue de Paris, and the hotel appears on the right. The comfortable rooms come at reasonable prices, all with shower, and most with toilet and TV. (☎02 35 42 39 77; www.hotel-celtic.com. Reception 8am-11pm. Breakfast €5.30. Singles €31.30-42.70; doubles €31.30-47.30. AmEx/MC/V.)

FOOD

For grocery needs, **Super U,** bd. François I, is almost a full turn around the block behind the tourist office (open M-Sa 7am-8pm), a **Marché Plus** is near the Volcan on rue de Paris (open M-Sa 7am-9pm, Su 8:30am-12:30pm), and **Epicerie,** 150 bd. de Strasbourg, near the train station. (Open daily 8am-2am.) The freshest food is at the morning **market** at pl. Thiers, by the Hôtel de Ville (M, W, F), or the all-day market on cours République (Tu, Th, Sa). A list of all markets is available from the tourist office. Le Havre has no shortage of cheap eateries, but don't set your sights too high. Restaurants crowd **rue Victor Hugo** near the Hôtel de Ville, while the streets between **rue de Paris** and **quai Lamblardie** host a range of neighborhood favorites frequented by locals. For a bite (slightly) off the beaten path, **La Taverne Paillette ❸,** 22 rue Georges Braque, has a wide selection of fresh fish entrées (€12-17), the standard *carte* of hot and cold entrées (€8-14), a *prix fixe menu* (€25.20), and a lunchtime express *menu* (€16). Take av. Foch towards the beach, turn right just before sq. St-Roch, and continue to the end of this small unmarked street to find this quieter alternative to Le Havre's bustling *brasseries*. (☎02 35 41 31 50. Open daily noon-midnight.) If in town on an afternoon, swing into the **Côté Jardin ❷**, 9 pl. de l'Hôtel de la Ville, next to the gardens in the center of town. This cozy *salon de thé* serves designer salads (€8.60), pastries (€2.50-4), and a *plat du jour* (€8), in addition to a full slate of coffee, beer, and wine. (☎02 35 43 43 04. Open M-Sa 11:30am-7pm. MC/V.)

🍴 🏠 SIGHTS & ENTERTAINMENT

The **Musée des Beaux Arts André Malraux,** 2 bd. Clémenceau, displays a small but delightful collection of pre-Impressionist works, Monet, Manet, Gauguin, and a host of local artists. Boudin has painted every cow in Normandy; most of these paintings seem to be on display on the 2nd floor. (☎02 35 19 62 62. Open M and W-F 11am-6pm, Sa-Su 11am-7pm. €3.80, under 18 free.) The quiet shade of the weeping willows in the **Jardin Sarraute,** off av. Foch, provides a refreshing contrast to the overall griminess of the town, as do the ivy-covered walkways and sparkling fountains on **place de l'Hôtel de Ville.**

Visible from practically everywhere in town, the **Eglise St-Joseph** is yet another testament to the architect Perret's vision of the wonders of concrete. Despite the tiny cross at the top, it looks more like an Erector-set version of a rocket ship than anything a major religion would construct. If St-Joseph isn't enough to disillusion you about the beauty of French architecture, the center of the city flaunts the Maison de la Culture du Havre, popularly known as **Le Volcan,** which resembles a decapitated toilet more than any kind of architecture. Nevertheless, it is home to a state-of-the-art theater for renowned orchestras and plays, as well as a cinema that screens new releases and classics. (☎02 35 19 10 10. Closed July 20-Aug.)

The fresh-off-the-ferry crowds head to a number of night spots for evening entertainment. **Havana Café,** 173 rue Victor Hugo (away from the beach), exudes a Cuban vibe with €5 cocktails and Thursday night karaoke. (☎02 35 42 35 77. Open Tu-Sa 6pm-2am. MC/V.) If in search of a DJ, try **Le Plazza,** 159 bd. de Strasbourg, near the station. The unassuming exterior belies a hip décor and the latest selection of lounge, house, and other club favorites. (☎02 35 43 04 28; www.leplazza.com. Beer €3; cocktails €6. No cover. Open Tu-Sa 6pm-2am.)

HIGH NORMANDY COAST

ETRETAT

Northeast along the coast from Le Havre is Etretat (pop. 1,640). Once there, head straight for the water. The stunning view from the two soaring chalk cliffs and from bluffs overlooking the water makes this perhaps the most breathtaking spot along the Channel coast. Guy de Maupassant likened the arching western cliff, the **Falaise d'Aval,** to an elephant dipping its trunk into the sea. Perched atop the eastern cliff, the **Falaise d'Amont,** is the tiny **Chapelle Notre Dame de la Garde,** constructed by the Jesuits in 1854. Behind it sits the miniscule **Musée Nungesser et Coli** and a modern wishbone of a monument dedicated to the first aviators to attempt a trans-Atlantic flight. Their plane was lost off the coast of Etretat in 1927. (☎02 35 27 07 47. Open mid-June to mid-Sept. Su-M and W-Sa 10:30am-noon and 2-5pm; mid-Sept. to mid-June Sa-Su only. €0.90, children €0.60.) The town itself is just a handful of crooked streets, strewn with eateries and small shops, that wend between the main avenue, Georges V, and the beach. Hidden just outside the town center are the former house and gardens of crime novelist Maurice Leblanc, who created Arsène Lupin, the original "gentleman burglar." Solve a murder mystery at

Le Clos Lupin, 15 rue de Maupassant—with the help of headphones, you can foil Lupin in the rooms of the antique home. (☎ 02 35 10 59 53. Open Apr.-Sept. daily 10am-7pm; Oct.-Mar. F-Su 11am-6pm. €5.60. Available in French or English.)

The **tourist office,** behind the bus stop, provides free maps, **bike** rental information, and a **tour.** (☎ 02 35 27 05 21; fax 02 35 28 87 20. Open mid-June to mid-Sept. daily 10am-7:30pm; mid-Sept. to Nov. and Apr. to mid-June daily 10am-noon and 2-6pm; Dec.-Mar. Sa-Su only.) Les Autos Cars Gris (☎ 02 35 27 04 25) runs **buses** to Fécamp (35min., 9 per day, €4.50) and Le Havre (1hr., 10 per day, €6.10). Taxis wait at the bus stop (☎ 02 12 16 48 27).

There are plenty of hotels, but no truly budget ones: the closer to the beachfront, the higher the rates. Reservations are crucial in summertime. **Hôtel l'Angleterre ❹,** 35 av. Georges V, and the posh **Hôtel de la Poste ❸,** 6 av. Georges V, off the tourist office, may not be cheap, but they're the best options. Both feature immaculate, luxurious rooms with shower, toilet, and TV. (La Poste ☎ 02 35 27 01 34; fax 02 35 27 76 28. Angleterre ☎ 02 35 28 84 97. Shared reception 8am-8pm at the Hôtel de la Poste. Buffet breakfast €7. Angleterre singles and doubles €40; triples or quads €60. Poste singles €29; doubles €40. Lower prices Sept.-Easter. MC/V.) The small **town campsite ❶,** a 10min. walk down rue Guy de Maupassant from the tourist office, is dirt-cheap. (Some buses from Le Havre and Etretat stop opposite: look for Camping le Grandval. (☎ 02 35 27 07 67. Reception open daily 9am-noon and 3-7pm. Gates 7:30am-10pm. Open April-Sept. €2.50 per person, €2.50 per tent, €3 per caravan. Electricity €3.50-4.20. Laundry available.)

FÉCAMP

Without quite the natural beauty of Etretat or the subtle charm of Honfleur, Fécamp (pop. 22,000), makes a good daytrip from Le Havre or Rouen. Fécamp first found fame as a pilgrimage site in the 6th century, when some drops of *précieux-sang* (Christ's blood) allegedly washed ashore in a fig-tree trunk. The holy plasma is still kept at the **Eglise Abbatiale de la Trinité,** rue des Forts. Most visitors now are after a much less sacrosanct liquid—Bénédictine. Distilled from 27 local plants and Asian spices, the drink is now made in the magnificent **Palais Bénédictine,** 110 rue Alexandre Le Grand, which justifiably remains the town's greatest draw. The museum has an excellent collection of medieval and Renaissance artifacts and contemporary art, and provides a free shot of the famous liqueur. (☎ 02 35 10 26 10; www.benedictine.fr. Open daily Apr.-Jun. and Sept.

THE LOCAL LEGEND

HOLY SPIRITS

One way or another, most local stories are liable to come down to one basic theme: liquor. So it is quite fitting that Fécamp's most famous story begins and ends with its own home-brewed libation, *bénédictine.*

Between the 16th and 18th centuries, Fécamp's Benedictine monks created a mysterious concoction of 27 local plants and Asian spices for use as a healing agent. The liquor quickly became a favorite indulgence of Francois I, though the recipe was almost lost during the tumoil of the French revolution. It wasn't until 1888 that a local wine merchant, the felicitously-named Alexandre Le Grand, rediscovered the recipe, and built an ornate palace to distill the spirit, which he named named after the monks who invented it.

With origins both religious and regal and all the massive hype that surrounds the formidable-sounding brew, one may hesitate to try it. Fear not. The drink is actually quite sweet, even when taken straight. Vanilla, cinnamon, and juniper berry are its most distinct flavors. Even the names of the cocktails which incorporate it, such as "Rainbow" and "Sunny Day," reflect its mildness.

All told, it takes two years to brew *bénédictine,* but it's worth the wait, as those well-healed monks of four centuries ago would surely agree.

10am-noon and 2-5:30pm; July-Aug. 10am-6pm; Oct.-Dec. 10:30-11:45am and 2-5pm; Feb.-Mar. daily 10:30am-12pm, 2-5:30pm. Last admission 1hr. before closing. €5, under 18 €2.50.)

Fécamp's pricey lodgings don't come cheaper than **Hôtel Vent d'Ouest ❹**, 3 av. Gambetta, opposite the bus stop, up the steps from the train station. Each of the bright clean rooms comes with shower, toilet, and TV; most have a phone. (☎ 02 35 28 04 04; fax 02 35 28 75 96. Breakfast €5. Reception 8am-10pm. June-Aug. singles €34, doubles €40.50; Sept.-May singles €27.50, doubles €34. AmEx/MC/V.) The picturesque **◢Camping Municipal de Reneville ❶**, chemin de Nesmond, affords a spectacular cliff view of the ocean. From the train station or bus stop, turn right onto av. Gambetta, which becomes quai Berigny. Turn left onto rue du Président Coty, right onto rue Caron, left onto rue d'Yport, and right onto chemin de Nesmond. (☎ 02 35 26 20 97. Office open 8:30-11:30am and 2-6pm. Gates closed 10pm-7am. Tent with two people €6.30; caravan €8.20. €2.15 per additional person. Electricity €2. Daily tax €0.15. Showers free.) For supplies, there's a **Marché-Plus** supermarket at 83 quai Berigny. (Open M-Sa 7am-9pm, Su 9am-1pm.)

Fécamp's main bus stop is in the town center, behind Eglise St-Etienne, across the street from the train station and up the steps. To reach the **tourist office**, 113 rue Alexandre Le Grand, turn right onto av. Gambetta, which becomes quai Berigny. Turn left onto rue du Domaine, and then right again onto rue Le Grand. Staff books rooms for €1.60 and dispenses maps. (☎ 02 35 28 51 01; fax 02 35 27 07 77. Open July-Aug. daily 9am-6pm; May-June and Sept. daily 10am-7:30pm; Oct.-Mar. M-F 9am-noon and 2-6pm.) Fécamp is accessible by **train** from Bréauté-Beuzeville with connections to Le Havre (45min., 5 per day, €6.80); Paris (2½hr., 6 per day, €24); and Rouen (1¼hr., 6 per day, €11). Get there by **bus** on Les Autos Cars Gris, 55 chemin de Nid Verdier, pl. St-Etienne. (☎ 02 35 27 04 25. Open M-Tu and Th-F 8:30-11:45am and 1:30-5:45pm, W 8:30-11:45am and 1:30-5pm, Sa 8:30am-12:30pm.) The stop is across from the church on av. Gambetta. Buses run from Le Havre ("rapidbus" 45min., 7 per day; regular bus 1¼hr., 17 per day; €7.15. Buy tickets on board). There is a **taxi** stand (☎ 02 35 28 17 50) on pl. St-Etienne at the top of av. Gambetta.

CÔTE FLEURIE

Doubling as resort towns and thalassotherapy centers (seaside health spas), the smaller villages along the northeastern coast of Lower Normandy, known as the Côte Fleurie, have served as weekend retreats for Paris's elite since the mid-19th century. Today, they cater to a more international crowd, which means that they won't turn up their noses at your French, but they might take exception to your attire. The Côte's reputation as the "Norman Riviera" stems largely from its fixation on wealth and style. Some of the smaller beach towns between Le Havre and Caen aren't always of enough interest to justify the cost. Caen's hotels or hostels can make good budget bases. Bus Verts (see **Practical Information**) provides regular connections between coastal towns, Caen, and Bayeux. Travelers doing a lot of touring will find *Carte Liberté* bus passes to be very useful (p. 210).

HONFLEUR

Miraculously unharmed by World War II, Honfleur (pop. 6000) stands out among the pretty, well-preserved towns in northwestern France for its culture and architecture. The narrow, multicolored houses surrounding the old port look the same as they have for centuries. The beautiful wilds around the town have attracted a close-knit community of artists, whose works can be seen in the many local galleries. Large numbers of middle-aged and older tourists flock to Honfleur in the sunny months and mill around the waterfront *Vieux Bassin*.

7 PRACTICAL INFORMATION. Bus Verts (☎08 10 21 42 14), located at the end of quai Lepaulmier, near Bassin de l'Est, go to Caen (1½hr., 15 per day, €13.50) and Le Havre (30min., 12 per day, €6.40) by lines #20 and #50. To get to the **tourist office**, 33 pl. Arthur Boudin, turn right out of the bus station and follow rue des Vases along the Avant Port. A large sign hangs outside the tourist office, which is in the stone section of the library. The *guide pratique* has a good town map that lays out four walking tours (2½-7km) in the town and its forests, and lists all of the town's business establishments, restaurants, and hotels. (☎02 31 89 23 30; fax 02 31 89 31 82. Open July-Aug. daily 10am-7pm; Oct.-Easter M-Sa 9:30am-noon and 2-6pm; Easter-June and Sept. daily 9:30am-12:30pm and 2-6:30pm.)

☎☐ ACCOMMODATIONS & FOOD. The hotels here have more stars than most constellations. **Les Cascades ❹**, 17 pl. Thiers, on cours des Fossés, offers comparatively inexpensive rooms in an ideal location next to the port. From the tourist office, cross the street at the roundabout; cours des Fossés is at the right. Huge begonia-filled boxes adorn the windows of comfortable rooms, some with skylights and half-timbered walls. (☎02 31 89 05 83. Breakfast €5.50. Open Feb.-Nov. 8am-9pm. Rooms for 1-2 people €32-53, all with shower. AmEx/DC/MC/V.) The seaside **Camping du Phare ❶**, 300m from the town center at the end of rue Haute, is conveniently located near the beach, minutes from the town center. From the tourist office, cross the street at the roundabout, turn left onto cours des Fossés, right on Quai St-Etienne, and then left after passing the Vieux Bassin; follow Quai de la Quarantaine until it forks; the right fork is rue Haute, which ends at the campsite. It gets crowded in summer, so arrive early to get a shady spot. (☎02 31 89 10 26. Reception July-Aug. 8am-10pm; low season hours vary. Car curfew 10pm. Open Apr.-Sept. and July-Aug. €4.75 per person; Apr.-June and Sept. €4.10; Apr.-Sept. €5.40 per tent and car. Electricity €4-5.80. Shower €1.20.)

A number of relatively pricey and indistinguishable restaurants and *brasseries* along the Ste-Catherine side of the *Vieux Bassin* provide a taste of local seafood (most fixed *menus* range €13-25). Less expensive food is available from storefronts on the quai Ste-Catherine and on quieter streets off the main pedestrian thoroughfare. For groceries, drop by the **Champion** supermarket, pl. Sorel. (Open July-Aug. M-F 8:30am-1pm and 2:30-7:30pm, Sa 8:30am-7:30pm, Su 9am-1pm; Sept.-June hours slightly shorter.) A **market** goes up in pl. Ste-Catherine, in front of the church (Sa morning), while pl. St-Léonard has an organic **Marché Bio** (W morning). Be sure to pick up some *pain Breton*. One hundred flavors of homemade ice cream make **Pom'Cannelle**, 60 quai Ste-Catherine, worth the price. (☎02 31 89 55 25. 1 scoop €2, 2 scoops €3. Open Su-Th 11am-7pm, F-Sa 11am-11pm.)

◖ SIGHTS. Honfleur's tucked-away streets hide lesser-known architectural delights, small antique shops, and specialized boutiques. The *Pass Musées* gives access to Honfleur's four museums and bell tower. (€8.50, students and children €5.50, under 10 free.) Worth the trip to Honfleur alone is the ▓**Maisons Satie,** 67 bd. Charles V, the 1866 birthplace and museum of composer, musician, artist, and author Erik Satie, whom you may not have heard of before coming to Honfleur but won't soon forget afterwards. Breathtaking, fanciful, and psychedelic, this maze of rooms is a merry jaunt through the mind of an artist. Expect starry ceilings, indoor rainshowers, and a whimsical *laboratoire des émotions*. (☎02 31 89 11 11. Open Su-M and W-Sa May-Sept. 10am-7pm; Oct.-Dec. and mid-Feb. to Apr. 11am-6pm. €5, students and seniors €3.50, under 10 free. Taped tour in French and English.)

Part of the ramparts that once surrounded the village, the **Porte de Caen** at the end of quai Ste-Catherine is the only gate left through which the king rode into the fortified town. A block away from the *bassin* is the splendidly carved 15th-century

Eglise Ste-Catherine, the largest wooden church in France, built hurriedly by pious sailors after the first one burned down in 1450. It resembles a cross between an ornamented market hall and a half-timbered barn. (Open daily July-Aug. 8am-8pm; Sept.-June 8:30am-noon and 2-6pm.) Climb the **bell tower** across the street. (Open mid-Mar. to Sept. daily 10am-noon and 2-6pm; Oct. to mid-Nov. M-F 2:30-5pm and Sa-Su 10am-noon and 2:30-5pm. Included with Musée Eugène Boudin; see below.)

The **Musée d'Ethnographie et d'Art Populaire,** quai St-Etienne, consists of two 15th-century houses decorated in the style of Honfleur's glory days. A walk through a prison and a soldiers' quarters gives a glimpse into the lives of the town's past inhabitants. The almost-adjacent **Musée de la Marine,** in the former Eglise St-Etienne, is a tiny, informative museum that recounts Honfleur's affair with the sea. (☎02 31 89 14 12. Both open July-Aug. daily 10am-1pm and 2-6:30pm; Apr.-June and Sept. Tu-Su 10am-noon and 2-6pm; mid-Feb. to Mar. and Oct. to mid-Nov. Tu-F 2-5:30pm, Sa-Su 10am-noon and 2-5:30pm. Closed mid-Nov. to mid-Feb. €3 for each, €4 combined; students and children €1.70/€2.50.)

Paintings of Honfleur by Eugène Boudin and his circle became popular in the 19th century. Many consider them the precursors of Impressionism. At the **Musée Eugène Boudin,** pl. Erik Satie, off rue de l'Homme de Bois, is a small but diverse collection of their works that includes some fine pieces of early 20th-century work, not to mention a nice view of the Pont de Normandie from the top floor. (☎02 31 89 54 00. Open mid-Mar. to Sept. Su-M and W-Sa 10am-noon and 2-6pm; Oct. to mid-Mar. M and W-F 2:30-5pm, Sa-Su 10am-noon and 2:30-5pm. €5, students and children €3.50, under 10 free.) The shaded **public gardens** on the bd. Charles V, beside the port, make the perfect spot for a picnic, with flower beds, swingsets, a wading pool, and a waterfall. With its brightly colored houses and cramped streets, Honfleur can't help but seem like it was planned by Disney animators. From the lookout point atop **Mont-Joli,** Honfleur looks like a toy city complete with the space-age Pont de Normandie. To get to the lookout point, follow rue du Puits from pl. Ste-Catherine to the steep, winding rampe du Mont-Joli (about 1½ km).

DEAUVILLE & TROUVILLE

Deauville and Trouville, with their twin boardwalks, beaches, and casinos, split at the Pont de Belges, a small bridge across the river Touques shared by the two towns. The wending, crooked streets of **Trouville** (pop. 5500) contrast with the expansive geometric, fountain-speckled layout of *haute*-style **Deauville** (pop. 4518), but little else differentiates them. The playground of the *nouveau riche*, these seaside resorts offer the common traveler little more than a sore wallet.

⚏ TRANSPORTATION. Trains go to Caen (1hr., 5 per day, €10.40); Paris (2hr., 5-6 per day, €23.70); Rouen (2½-3hr., 3 per day, €16.40). **Bus Verts** (☎08 01 21 42 14) go to Caen (70min., €8.80); Honfleur (20min., €3.20); Le Havre via Honfleur (1hr., €9.60). Agence Fournier, pl. du Maréchal Foch in Trouville, runs **shuttles** between the two towns (☎02 31 88 16 73; €1.60). The Bac de Deauville/Trouville, pl. du Maréchal Foch in Trouville, **ferries** across the canal from Deauville to Trouville's Monoprix when the tide is high enough. (Mid-Mar. to Sept. daily 8:30am-6:45pm, €0.90.) For a **taxi,** call ☎02 31 88 35 33 or 08 00 51 41 41.

⚏ ⚏ ORIENTATION & PRACTICAL INFORMATION. To get to **Trouville** from the train station, turn right and cross Pont des Belges onto bd. Fernand Moureaux. Turn left to get to the **tourist office,** 32 quai Fernand Moureaux. The staff distributes vacationing guides, which include listings of Trouville's lodgings and dining establishments. Also available are two walking tours (map €0.50) and a town map. (☎02 31 14 60 70; www.trouvillesurmer.org. Open July-Aug. M-Sa 9:30am-7pm, Su

10am-4pm; Apr.-June and Sept.-Oct. M-Sa 9:30am-noon and 2-6:30pm, Su 10am-1pm; Nov.-Mar. M-Sa 9:30am-noon and 2-6pm, Su 10am-1pm.)

To get to **Deauville**, turn left from the station; at the second roundabout take a right onto rue Désiré le Hoc and follow it through pl. Morny to the **tourist office** on pl. de la Mairie. (10min.) Info on prestigious film and music festivals, frequent horse races, and polo games. (☎ 02 31 14 40 00; www.deauville.org. Open July to early Sept. M-Sa 9am-7pm, Su 10am-1pm and 3-6pm; mid-Sept. to Apr. M-Sa 9am-12:30pm and 2-6:30pm, Su 10am-1pm and 2-5pm; May-June M-Tu and Th 9am-12:30pm and 2-6:30pm, W 10am-12:30pm and 2-6:30pm, F-Sa 9am-6:30pm, Su 10am-1pm and 2-5pm.) Rent **bikes** at La Deauvillaise, 11 quai de la Marine. (☎ 02 31 88 56 33. €4.50 per hr., €14 per day, €40 per week. Open July-Aug. daily 9am-6:30pm; Sept.-June Tu-Su 9am-12:30pm and 2-6:30pm.)

ⓘ⌂ ACCOMMODATIONS & FOOD. You'll have to stay in Trouville if you want to sleep without pawning your pack. Even then, rooms don't let for much less than €35. At **Hôtel les Sablettes ❸**, 13-15 rue Paul Besson, left off av. Victor Hugo after turning onto it from bd. Fernand Moureaux, an exceptionally friendly couple rents immaculate rooms with toilet and TV. (☎ 02 31 88 10 66; www.trouville-hotel.com. Breakfast €6. Singles €32; singles and doubles with shower €42-53, with bath €60; triples with shower €64. €4-5 less in the low season. MC/V.) Equally close to the beach and the boulevard, **Au Ch'ti-mi ❸**, 28 rue Victor Hugo, has well-decorated rooms over a little bar, each with a shower. (☎ 02 31 88 49 22. Breakfast €4.60. Reception at bar. Doubles with shower €38; triple with shower and toilet €53.50.) **Camping Le Chant des Oiseaux ❶**, 11 rte. d'Honfleur, is a well-maintained site 2km from town on cliffs overlooking the sea. From bd. Fernand Moureaux, follow rue Victor Hugo through many name changes until it becomes rue du Général Leclerc, past the Musée Montebello. When the road forks, go right, up the steep incline and past the giant crucifix. When this route merges with the main road, continue for 5min. and the site will be on the left. (☎ 02 31 88 06 42; fax 02 31 98 16 09. Open Apr.-Oct. Reception July-Aug. 8am-10pm; in low season, someone is almost always in the office or nearby. €4.30 per person, ages 2-7 €2.70; €5 per tent; €2.70 per car. Electricity €5.40-6.30. July-Aug. shower €0.50.)

In Trouville, a **Monoprix** supermarket is on the corner of bd. Fernand Moureaux and rue Victor Hugo (open July-Aug. M-Sa 9am-8pm, Su 9:30am-1pm; Sept.-June daily 9am-12:30pm and 2-7:30pm), a **market** on pl. Mal. Foch (W and Su morning), and a **poissonnerie** along the waterfront of bd. Moureaux. Many of the beachfront restaurants face the setting sun; locals flock to their terraces to dine in the last light of day. Reasonably priced seafood restaurants, pizzerias, and *crêperies* line the pedestrian **rue des Bains** and **boulevard Fernand Moureaux.** One of the best may be the traditional **Tivoli Bistro ❹**, 27 rue Charles Mozin in Trouville. (☎ 02 31 98 43 44. *Menus* €14-24, *plat du jour* €12, other entrées €11-22. Open Su-Tu and F-Sa 12:15-2pm and 7:15-10pm, W 12:15-2pm. MC/V.) In Deauville, **Mamy Crêpes ❶**, 57 rue Désiré le Hoc, just before the tourist office, serves cheap, delicious sandwiches, including a few vegetarian options (€2.70-4) and €2 dessert crêpes and flan. (☎ 02 31 14 96 44. Open M, W, Th 9am-10pm, F-Su 9am-11pm. MC/V.)

◎♫ SIGHTS & ENTERTAINMENT. The pride of each town are their boardwalk promenades along the beach. In Trouville, a stroll along them affords a view of the spectacular houses that inspired realist novelist Gustave Flaubert; Deauville's planks are lined with names of movie stars. The **Natur'Aquarium de Trouville,** on the boardwalk, will delight the prepubescent set, with everything from finches to tarantulas. (☎ 02 31 88 46 04. Open daily July-Aug. 10am-7:30pm; Sept.-Oct. 10am-noon and 2-7pm; Nov.-Easter 2-6:30pm; Easter-June 10am-noon and 2-7pm. €6.50, students and seniors €5.50, ages 6-14 €4.50, ages 3-6 €3.50.)

The **Casino Barrière de Trouville**, pl. du Mal. Foch (☎ 02 31 87 75 00), has an adjoining nightclub and cinema and is more laid-back than the **Casino de Deauville** (☎ 02 31 14 31 14). **Café Trouville**, a series of café-side concerts (July-Aug. 4-5 per week), can be enjoyed from the terrace of a café or for free from the sidewalk. The wine-bar/café **La Maison**, 66 rue des Bains in Trouville, off bd. Fernand Moureaux, provides a relaxed, sophisticated evening. Grass mats and wrought-iron furniture give a dreamy, Spanish flavor to the terrace. (☎ 02 31 81 43 10. Open daily 11am-1am or 2am.) Deauville's **Le Zoo**, 53 rue Désiré le Hoc, just before the tourist office, is equally sophisticated, but at a price (*cocktail du jour* €7.20). If you can make that one drink last, the relaxed atmosphere that suffuses the indoor lounge and street-side tables is worth it. (☎ 02 31 81 02 61; www.lezoo.fr. Open W-Su noon-2am.)

Residents of Deauville satisfy their love of the equestrian at two hippodromes: **Clairefontaine**, dedicated to racing, and **La Touques**, where the polo games are held. Deauville also hosts several festivals, including **Swing'In Deauville** (3rd week of July) and the **American Film Festival** (Sept.).

CAEN

At the end of World War II, three quarters of Caen (pop. 120,000) was destroyed and two thirds of its citizens were left homeless. The ancient city has been skillfully restored to its pre-war beauty and is now a combination historical monument/sizzling university town. It makes an ideal base from which to explore the D-Day beaches, but it is also decidedly younger in tenor than many of its neighbors along the Côte Fleurie, packed with lively bars and outdoor *brasseries*.

▐ TRANSPORTATION

Trains: pl. de la Gare. Info office open M-Sa 8am-6pm, Su 9:15am-6:45pm. Some lockers available at the station. To: **Cherbourg** (1½hr.; 10 per day, 5 on Su; €16.10); **Paris** (2½hr., 12 per day, €25.40); **Rennes** (3hr., 3 per day, €26.40); **Rouen** (2hr., 5 per day, €18.80); **Tours** (3½hr., 2 per day, €26.70).

Buses: Bus Verts, (☎ 08 10 21 42 14), to the left of the train station and at pl. Courtonne in the center of town, covers the region. Office open M-F 7:30am-7pm, Sa 8:30am-7pm, Su 9am-2:30pm. See p. 217 for coverage of the D-Day beaches. To **Bayeux** (1hr.; M-Sa 2-3 per day; €5.60, students €4.55) and **Le Havre** (2-3hr.; M-Sa 6 per day, Su 5 per day; €16, students €13). Also **Caen-Le Havre** express (1½hr., 2 per day, €19) stops in **Honfleur** (1hr. from Caen, 2 per day, €13.50). Full-day **Carte Liberté** €17.50, 3 days €27, 7 days €43; accepted on local bus Twisto.

Ferries: Brittany Ferries go to **Portsmouth, England** from Ouistreham, 13km north of Caen. See **Getting There: By Boat**, p. 40. Bus Verts #1 links Ouistreham to Caen's center and train station (40min., 8 per day, €3.20).

Public Transportation: Twisto, 15 rue de Geôle (☎ 02 31 15 55 55), at Château, pl. St-Pierre. Kiosks at Théâtre (at square where bd. Maréchal Leclerc terminates), St-Pierre (top of bd. Maréchal Leclerc), SNCF (pl. de la Gare). Tickets €1, *carnet* of 10 €8.50, day pass €2.70. Open M-F 7:15am-6:45pm, Sa 10am-4:45pm; hours vary seasonally.

Taxis: Abbeilles Taxis Caen, 19 pl. de la Gare (☎ 02 31 52 17 89). 24hr. **late-night taxi kiosk** at bd. Maréchal Leclerc near rue St-Jean (10pm-3am).

◼✦ ▐ ORIENTATION & PRACTICAL INFORMATION

Caen's train station and youth hostel are located quite far from the town center; it's most convenient to take the bus. The two lines of the city's tram system, A and B, leave from the train station and cut through the city center; take either line to

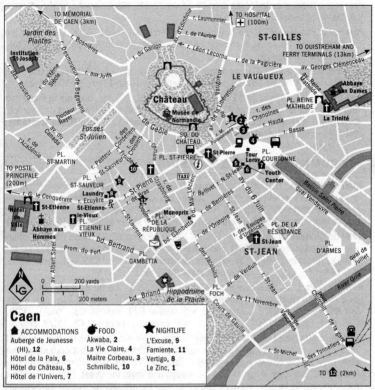

Caen

♠ ACCOMMODATIONS
Auberge de Jeunesse (HI), **12**
Hôtel de la Paix, **6**
Hôtel du Château, **5**
Hôtel de l'Univers, **7**

🍅 FOOD
Akwaba, **2**
La Vie Claire, **4**
Maitre Corbeau, **3**
Schmiblic, **10**

★ NIGHTLIFE
L'Excuse, **9**
Farniente, **11**
Vertigo, **8**
Le Zinc, **1**

NORMANDY

stop St-Pierre. From the station, **avenue du 6 Juin** and **rue St-Jean** run parallel to each other toward the city center and to the lively commercial districts between **rue St-Pierre** and **rue de l'Oratoir**.

Tourist Office: pl. St-Pierre (☎02 31 27 14 14; www.ville-caen.fr), on rue St-Jean by the Eglise St-Pierre. **Hotel booking** €1.50. Free map and multilingual visitor's guide, *Le Mois à Caen,* lists concerts and events. **City tours** July-Sept. (in French; 1hr., €4). Theatrical performances at night in French mid-July to Aug. (2hr.; €10.80, students and children over 5 €7.80; reservations required.) Office open July-Aug. M-Sa 9:30am-7pm, Su 10am-1pm and 2-5pm; Sept.-June M-Sa 9am-1pm and 2-6pm, Su 10am-1pm.

Money: Currency exchange at the post office and most banks. **Crédit Agricole** has a booth on bd. Maréchal Leclerc, at the intersection with rue St-Jean. Open M 10am-12:30pm and 2-6pm, Tu-F 9am-12:30pm and 2-6pm, Sa 9am-12:30pm and 2-5pm.

Youth Center: Centre Information Jeunesse (CIJ), 16 rue Neuve-St-Jean (☎02 31 27 80 80; crij.bn@wanadoo.fr), off av. du 6 Juin next to the Hôtel de la Paix. Info on events, jobs, lodging, and work opportunities. The EU Information booth offers free **Internet:** Open M 1-6pm, Tu-Th 10am-6pm, F 10am-5pm.

Laundromat: rue de Geôle (☎06 60 55 75 60). Open daily 7am-9pm. Also at 16 rue Ecuyère (☎06 80 96 08 26). Open daily 7am-8pm.

Hospital: Centre Hospitalier Universitaire, av. Côte de Nacre (☎02 31 06 31 06).

Police: rue Thiboud de la Fresnaye (☎02 31 29 22 22). Kiosk near the tourist office on rue Maréchal Leclerc.

Pharmacy: Pharmacie Danjou Rousselot, 5 pl. Malherbe (☎02 31 30 78 00), at the intersection of rue Ecuyère and rue St-Pierre. Open M 9am-7:30pm, Tu-F 8:30am-7:30pm, Sa 9am-7:30pm.

Internet: Free access at **CIJ** (see **Youth Center**). 30 computers at **Espace Micro**, 1 rue Basse (☎02 31 53 68 68). €4 per hour. Open M-Sa 10am-11pm, Su 10am-1pm.

Post Office: pl. Gambetta (☎02 31 39 35 78). From pl. St-Pierre, take rue St-Pierre and turn left on rue St-Laurent; post office will be at the bottom of the street on your left. **Currency exchange.** Open M-F 7:30am-7pm, Sa 8am-12:30pm. **Poste Restante:** 14016 Gambetta. **Postal code:** 14000.

ACCOMMODATIONS & CAMPING

Hôtel de l'Univers, 12 quai Vendeuvre, (☎02 31 85 46 41). From the station, follow av. du 6 Juin to its end and turn right; or take the bus. Cheap two-star hotel, a stone's throw from the château. TV, telephone, shower. Breakfast €5.50. Single with shower €28; double with shower €33, with WC €38-40; double or single with bath €45. AmEx/V. ❸

Hôtel du Château, 5 av. du 6 Juin (☎02 31 86 15 37; fax 02 31 86 58 08). Exceptionally large, bright rooms with TV and tasteful furniture on a pedestrian street near the château. Breakfast €6. Reception 24hr. Singles and doubles €35, with shower €45, with bath €55. Extra bed €10. Prices lower Oct.-Easter. MC/V. ❹

Hôtel de la Paix, 14 rue Neuve-St-Jean (☎02 31 86 18 99; fax 02 31 38 20 74), off av. du 6 Juin, in a great spot. Run-down rooms have clean bathrooms and firm beds. Breakfast €5. Reception 24hr. Singles €26, with shower €29, with WC €32; doubles €29/€35/€37; triples €37/€43/€45; quads with bath €53. Extra bed €5. MC/V. ❸

Auberge de Jeunesse (HI), Foyer Robert Reme, 68bis rue Eustache-Restout (☎02 31 52 19 96; fax 02 31 84 29 49). Turn right from the station, then left onto rue de Falaise. Look for the bus stop on your right. Take bus #5 (dir: Fleury Cimitière) to Lycée Fresnel. On foot, take a right out of the station and cross the street. Follow it until the road (now rue de Falaise) curves to the left and up the hill until you see bd. Leroy on the left; turn right onto bd. Mal. Lyautey and continue for 10min. Turn left onto rue Eustasche-Restout and continue 10min. The road turns right after a large school; the hostel will be on your right. The hostel has clean four-person, single-sex dorms with shower and stove, but is far from the center of town (3km). Breakfast €2.50; sheets €2.50. Reception 5-9pm. Hostel open June-Sept. Beds €9. **HI members only.** ❶

FOOD

Brasseries vie with Chinese eateries and African restaurants in the **quartier Vaugueux** near the château and between the Eglise St-Pierre and the Eglise St-Jean. **Markets** are held at pl. St-Sauveur (F), on pl. Courtonne (Su), and at quai Vendeuvre. Smaller markets abound on Grace de Dieu and rue de Bayeux (Tu), bd. Leroy (W and Sa), and La Guernière and Le Chemin Vert (F). All open 8am-1pm. There's a **Monoprix** at 45 bd. Maréchal Leclerc (open M-Sa 9am-8:30pm), and a small **7-11** market at 1167 rue de Caen near the hostel. (Open Tu-Sa 9:15am-1pm and 3-11pm.)

Locals flock to ▨**Maître Corbeau** ❸, 8 rue Buquet, to feast on *fondue normande* (made with camembert, calvados, and crème fraîche; €11.60 per person) amidst giant sunflowers and stuffed cows. Reserve 2-3 days in advance. (☎02 31 93 93 00. Open M and Sa 7-10:30pm, Tu-F noon-1:30pm and 7-10:30pm. Closed last week in Aug. and 1st week in Sept.) For a delicious lunch, try ▨**La Vie Claire** ❷, (see **Hidden Deal**). A charming traditional African restaurant in the hip Vaugueux section of town, to the left of the château, **Akwaba ❸**, 3 rue de Vaugueux, serves exotically spiced chicken and lamb dishes. (☎02 31 93 90 80. *Menu* €11.50; individual entrées €8.70-13.40. Open M-Sa noon-2pm and 7-11pm. MC/V.) The gigantic made-to-order sandwiches (€2.30-4.50) at **Schmilblic ❶**, 53 rue Froide, off rue St-Pierre, are incredibly popular with the local population of starving college students. (Dessert crepes €0.90-2.30. Open M-W 10:30am-8pm, Th-F 10:30am-9:30pm.)

👁 SIGHTS

Some of Caen's sights are discounted with the purchase of a full-price ticket to other sights or museums in the area. The tourist office has details.

▨ MÉMORIAL DE CAEN. Hands-down the best of Normandy's WWII museums, the Mémorial de Caen starts with a bang: a spiraling walkway takes visitors through the "Failure of Peace" between the world wars, and shows how such 20th century trends as the spread of communism, the rise of Fascism, and the consolidation of imperial empires contributed to World War II. The extremely engaging exhibit is presented through vintage footage and high-tech audiovisuals. Allow at least two hours to explore the museum. Unfortunately, later exhibits of light artillery from the war, eliciting the "oohs" of receptive young children, contradicts the spirit of the museum. *(Take bus #2 to Mémorial. ☎02 31 06 06 44; www.memorial-caen.fr. Open mid-July to late Aug. 9am-8pm; early Feb. to mid July and late Aug. to Oct. 9am-7pm; mid-Jan. to early Feb. and Nov.-Dec. 9am-6pm. Closed first two weeks in Jan. Last entry 1¼hr. before closing. €17; students, seniors, and ages 10-18 €15; may be lower Oct.-Mar.)*

ABBEYS & CHURCHES. Caen, the seat of William the Conqueror's duchy, owes its first-class Romanesque architecture chiefly to William's guilty conscience: William married his distant cousin Mathilda despite the pope's explicit interdiction. To get back on the road to Heaven, the two built several ecclesiastical structures, most notably Caen's twin abbeys. Begun in 1066 the **Abbaye-aux-Hommes**, off rue Guillaume le Conquérant, now functions as the Hôtel de Ville. *(☎02 31 30 42 81.)* The adjacent **Eglise St-Etienne** contains William's tomb, an enormous organ, and a small collection of photographs taken in Caen during and after the bombings. Many of the city's displaced citizens took shelter in the abbey: photographs show upper-class women primping in the mirror by candlelight between the church's columns. *(Open daily 9:15am-noon and 2-6pm. 1¼hr. tours of church in French at 9:30am, 2:30, 4pm; of Hôtel de Ville at 11am. €2,*

THE HIDDEN DEAL

A VEGETARIAN OASIS

Small and unassuming, **La Vie Claire ❷**, 3 rue Basse, is hidden in plain sight, wedged behind an organic foods store in the center of town, removed from the busy college-town environs. For a quick sit-down lunch, the quality of the restaurant's selections is hard to match anywhere in Caen.

Everything on the shockingly inexpensive *prix fixe* lunch menu (€8.50 or €12.50 with both starter and dessert) is generously portioned. All the dishes are vegetarian, and the small menu changes daily to ensure that the food is always fresh. Entrees may include delicious vegetable, egg, or seasoned tofu options, served with tasty homebaked bread. The more carnivorous may spot the occasional fish selection to complement the seaside décor. For dessert, the apple cake is a must.

Family-run, the original La Vie Claire opened in 1986 as an alternative to the lifeless, ubiquitous *brasseries* that populate the city, and it has resided in its current location since 1991. The coziness of its inviting dining room, seating only 32 guests, completes the extremely welcoming atmosphere and makes this restaurant a worthwhile stop for all of Caen's visitors, vegetarian or otherwise.

(3 rue Basse. ☎02 31 93 66 72. Open for lunch Tu-Sa noon-2pm; organic foods store and bakery open Tu-Sa 9am-7pm. MC/V.)

students €1, under 18 free.) Across the street from the abbey's gardens the remains of the Eglise St-Etienne-le-Vieux, reminder passers-by of the destruction of the bombings. The smaller Eglise de la Trinité of the Abbaye-aux-Dames, off rue des Chanoines, houses Mathilda's tomb. (*Open M-Sa 8am-5:30pm, Su 9:30am-12:30pm. Free 1hr. tours in French at 2:30 and 4pm.*)

CHÂTEAU. Between the two abbeys sprawl the ruins of William's enormous **château**, begun in 1060. A pre-sunset stroll around the château walls is amazing. (*Open daily May-Sept. 6am-1am; Oct.-Apr. 6am-7:30pm. Free. Tours may be available.*) The small **Jardin des Simples** holds a collection of plants used in the Middle Ages. (*Same hours as château.*) The **Musée de Normandie** traces the origins of Norman craftsmanship and farming. (*☎02 31 30 47 60. Open Su-M and W-Sa 9:30am-6pm. €2, students €1, under 18 free.*) To reach the sheltered, romantic **Jardin des Plantes** on pl. Blot, turn left on rue Bosnières from rue de Geôle. (*Open daily June-Aug. 8am-sunset; Sept.-May 8am-5:30pm.*)

🎵 ENTERTAINMENT

Numerous bars and clubs on **rue de Bras, rue des Croisiers, quai Vendeuvre,** and **rue St-Pierre** are packed with well-attended bars and clubs. Crowds of university students wait for the night to heat up at **Vertigo,** 14 rue Ecuyère, just past the intersection with rue St-Pierre, gathering around outdoor tables, . Happy hour 7-9pm. (*☎02 31 85 43 12. Cocktails €3, beer €2-3. Open July-Sept. M-W noon-1am, Th-Sa noon-2am; Oct.-June M-Sa noon-1am.*) The hipper-than-thou bar and lounge, **Farniente,** 13 rue Paul Doumer, draws the young and chic who warm up for the clubs by grinding to Latin music and throwing back tequila. (*☎02 31 86 30 00. Star DJs Th-Sa. Open W 6pm-1am, Th-Sa 6pm-2am. MC/V.*) Glance at the funky modern artwork on your way to the dance floor at **L'Excuse,** 20 rue Vauquelin, where they work it to everything from house to Arab-inspired techno. (*☎02 31 38 80 89. Beer and liquor €4. Cover €5, includes 1 drink ticket. Open June-Aug. Th-Sa 11pm-4am, Sept.-May Th-Sa 10pm-4am. Doors close 2am. MC/V.*) Steamy **Le Zinc,** 12 rue du Vaugueux, supplies a lively crowd with heart-pounding house. (*☎02 31 93 20 30. Beer €3, liquor €5. Open Tu-Th 6pm-2am and F-Sa 6pm-4am.*)

Caen hosts a popular Latin festival of music and dance, **Cap Latino,** during the first weekend of June. It takes place inside the walls of the château and tends to bring down the house. (For info, see www.shilpa.com.fr.)

BAYEUX

Bayeux (pop. 15,000), unharmed by Nazi occupation and Allied liberation, retains its original architecture and resplendent cathedral. Its pleasant pedestrian byways and old-world atmosphere cater to a middle-aged crowd. Bayeux's real jewel is its 900-year-old tapestry, which narrates William the Conqueror's victory over England in 1066. Bayeux is also a beautiful base for D-Day beach exploration.

🛈 PRACTICAL INFORMATION

Trains: pl. de la Gare (*☎02 31 92 80 50*). Ticket counters open M-F 6am-8pm, Sa-Su 8am-8pm. To: **Caen** (20min., 15 per day, €5.20); **Cherbourg** (1hr., 12 per day, €12.70); **Paris** (2½hr., 12 per day, €27.10).

Buses: Bus Verts, pl. de la Gare (*☎02 31 92 02 92*). Open M-F 9:15am-noon and 1:30-6pm. Buses head west to small towns and east to **Caen** (1hr., M-Sa 2-3 per day, €5.60). See p. 217 for coverage of the D-Day beaches. Buy tickets from the driver or at the office. **Bybus,** pl. de la Gare (*☎02 31 92 02 92*). In-town bus circuit runs about 9am-6pm. €0.85, 9-11:30am and 2-4pm €0.65.

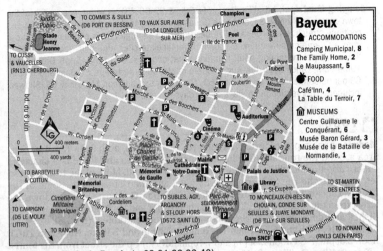

Bayeux

⌂ ACCOMMODATIONS

Camping Municipal, 8
The Family Home, 2
Le Maupassant, 5

◆ FOOD

Café'Inn, 4
La Table du Terroir, 7

🏛 MUSEUMS

Centre Guillaume le
  Conquérant, 6
Musée Baron Gérard, 3
Musée de la Bataille de
  Normandie, 1

Taxis: Les Taxis du Bessin (☎02 31 92 92 40).

Bike Rental: Available at the hostel. €10 per day with a €20 deposit.

Tourist Office: Pont St-Jean (☎02 31 51 28 28; www.bayeux-tourism.com). From the station, turn left onto bd. Sadi-Carnot, then bear right at the roundabout. In the *centre ville*, continue up rue Larcher and turn right on rue St-Martin. The office will be on your left, at the edge of the pedestrian zone. The staff offers a regional brochure, **Internet** (€5 for 30min.), and **accommodation booking** anywhere in Calvados (€1.50). Open June-Aug. M-Sa 9am-7pm, Su 9am-1pm and 2-6pm; Apr.-May and Sept.-Oct. daily 9:30am-12:30pm and 2-6pm; Nov.-Mar. M-Sa 9:30am-12:30pm and 2-5:30pm.

Laundromat: 10 rue Maréchal Foch. Open daily 7am-9pm.

Police: 49 av. Conseil (☎02 31 92 94 00).

Hospital: 13 rue de Nesmond (☎02 31 51 51 51), next to the tapestry center.

Post Office: rue Larcher (☎02 31 51 24 90). **Currency exchange** and **Cyberposte.** Open M-F 8am-6:30pm, Sa 8am-noon. **Postal code:** 14400.

🏠 ACCOMMODATIONS & CAMPING

The demand for lodging often outstrips supply, especially in summer. Plan with military precision to get a room around June 6, the anniversary of D-Day.

The Family Home/Auberge de Jeunesse (HI), 39 rue Général de Dais (☎02 31 92 15 22; fax 02 31 92 55 72), in the center of town. Well-equipped accommodations in one- to seven-person rooms branching off a courtyard. Communal laundry, kitchen, TV, and dining room make meeting other guests a cinch. Huge breakfast included; fantastic dinner fare at night (€10). Reception hours are inconsistent, but someone is always around during the day. So popular in the summer that guests may be displaced after one night. Beds €16, without HI membership €18; single room €28. Help clean the kitchen and they promise lunch and a free bed for the night; understandably, however, it's a popular option and shouldn't be counted on. ❷

Le Maupassant, 19 rue St-Martin (☎02 31 92 28 53). Clean rooms over a *brasserie* and pedestrian traffic-heavy street, in the center. Breakfast €5.40. Reception 8am-10pm. Singles €26; doubles with shower or toilet €33.60; quads with bath €61. ❸

NORMANDY

Camping Municipal, bd. d'Eindhoven (☎02 31 92 08 43), is within easy reach of the town center and the N13. Follow rue Genas Duhomme to the right off rue St-Martin and continue straight on av. de la Vallée des Prés. The campground is on your right, across from a Champion supermarket. (10min.) Immaculate sites and shiny facilities next to the municipal swimming pool. Laundry, great showers. Open May-Sept. Gates close 10pm-7am. Office open July-Aug. 7am-9pm; May-June and Sept. 8-10am and 5-7pm. €3 per person, children under 7 €1.60, €3.60 per tent and car. Electricity €3. Showers included. 10% reduction on stays of five days or more. ❶

🟥 FOOD

Markets open on pl. St-Patrice (Sa) and rue St-Jean (W), both from 7am-1pm. The area around the tourist office has small grocery stores and there is a **Champion** supermarket on bd. d'Eindhoven, near the campground. Most of the town's eateries populate the rue St-Martin, rue St-Jean, and their sidestreets. Some of the heartiest meals in the city are at **La Table du Terroir ❹**, 42 rue St-Jean, down the street from the tourist office. The jovial chef/owner and his family serve local meat dishes and delicious desserts at communal wooden tables. (☎02 31 92 05 53. *Menus* €16, €20, and €26. Open Tu-Sa noon-2:30pm and 7-10pm; Nov.-Mar. Tu-Th noon-2:30pm, F-Sa noon-2:30pm and 7-10pm. MC/V.) Up the street from the tourist office, **Café'Inn ❶**, 67 rue St-Martin, offers reasonably priced salads (€4.50), sandwiches (€3), and omelettes (around €4) that make a delicious, light option for lunch. (☎02 31 21 11 37. *Prix fixe* lunch menu €8, homemade pastries €2-4.50. Open M-Sa 9am-7pm. MC/V.)

🔵 SIGHTS

▥ TAPISSERIE DE BAYEUX. The exquisite tapestry, most remarkable for its strikingly modern narrative technique, illustrates in vibrant detail the events leading up to the Battle of Hastings. In 1066, William the Bastard earned himself a more sociable nickname by crossing the Channel with a large cavalry to defeat his cousin Harold, who, according to the Norman version of the tale, had stolen the English throne from William. After a grueling 14-hour battle in which Harold was dramatically killed by an archer, William triumphed in this last successful invasion of England. A mere 50cm wide but 70m long, the tapestry, now over 900 years old, hangs in all its glory at the **Centre Guillaume le Conquérant,** rue des Nesmond. Take note of the horses, the soldiers flailing in quicksand at Mont-St-Michel (frames 16-17), Halley's comet (32-33), poor Harold with the fatal arrow in his eye (57), and the irreverent, sometimes humorous images that line the bottom of the tapestry. An elaborate exhibit, including an annotated reprint of the tapestry, precedes the viewing of the masterpiece itself, providing historical background and an exegesis of one of the great pieces of world art. The thorough audio guide provided for the actual viewing of the tapestry makes the film skippable. Everything is translated into English. (☎02 31 51 25 50. Open May-Aug. daily 9am-7pm; mid-Mar. to Apr. and Sept. to mid-Oct. 9am-6:30pm; mid-Oct. to mid-Mar. 9:30am-12:30pm and 2-6pm. Last entrance 45min. before closing. €7.40, students €3, under 10 free; includes Musée Baron Gérard.)

CATHÉDRALE NOTRE-DAME. Nearby is the original home of the tapestry, the **Cathédrale Notre-Dame.** Above the transept are Gothic arches with dizzyingly intricate carvings, while the 11th-century crypt beneath displays chipping 15th-century frescoes. To the left of the entrance is the *salle capitulaire*, which contains France's only *chemin de Jerusalem*, a tile labyrinth on the floor that retraces Jesus's *via crucis*, the route he followed on the way to Calvary. (Open July-Aug. M-Sa

8am-7pm, Su 9am-7pm; Sept.-June M-Sa 8:30am-noon and 2:30-7pm, Su 9am-12:15pm and 2:30-7pm. Informal tours of the cathedral July-Aug. Tu-F approximately 10am-noon and 3-7pm. Tours of the salle capitulaire July-Aug. M-F 1, 3, 5pm.)

MUSÉE BARON GÉRARD. Next to the cathedral, the **Musée Baron Gérard,** on pl. de la Liberté, houses a large collection of porcelain, in addition to tapestries, 16th- and 17th-century paintings, and the delicate lace that is characteristic of Bayeux. The enormous tree at its entrance was planted in 1793 to commemorate the French Revolution. (☎ 02 31 51 60 50. *Open daily June to mid-Sept. 9am-7pm; mid-Sept. to May 10am-12:30pm and 2-6pm. €7.40, students €3, under 10 free.)*

LOCAL D-DAY SIGHTS. The events of the D-Day landing and the subsequent 76-day battle are recounted in the **Musée de la Bataille de Normandie,** bd. Fabian Ware, through photos, weapons, and innumerable uniform-clad mannequins. The exhibit is a little sterile, but there are interesting newspaper clippings. Do not attempt to cover the entire exhibit—there's just too much small type. (☎ 02 31 51 46 90; www.maire-bayeux.fr. *Open May to mid-Sept. daily 9:30am-6:30pm, last entrance 5:30pm; mid-Sept. to Apr. 10am-12:30pm and 2-6pm, last entrances noon and 5pm. 30min. film in English approx. every 2hr. Closed last two weeks in Jan. €5.70, seniors and military €5.50, students €2.60, under 10 free.)* The striking though simple **British Cemetery** across the street provides a more moving wartime record.

D-DAY BEACHES

By 1944, the German forces along the northern coasts of France had been waiting for an Allied invasion for four years, ever since they had taken over the Republic. Normandy was slightly less prepared for a full-scale invasion than heavily-fortified Calais, but German General Erwin Rommel's troops still made it a treacherous landing zone. Preparations for the daring attack began in 1943, when the Allied leaders concluded that the only way to defeat Hitler was to recapture his "Fortress Europe" from the sea. Allied counterintelligence flooded the radio waves with false attack plans and inflated dummy tanks near Norway to keep secret "Operation Overlord," the planned landing on the Normandy coast between the Cotentin Peninsula and the Orne. In the pre-dawn hours of **June 6, 1944,** 16,000 British and US paratroopers tumbled from the sky; a few hours later, 135,000 troops and

NORMANDY

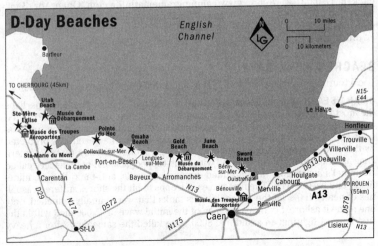

20,000 vehicles landed on the beaches code-named Utah and Omaha (American), Gold and Sword (British), and Juno (Canadian). The losses incurred during the D-Day landings were devastating on both sides but were a crucial precursor to great successes later for the Allies. The Battle of Normandy raged for two-and-a-half months, finally ending on August 21. Three days later, free French forces liberated Paris. Less than a year later, Allied forces took Berlin, and Germany surrendered.

The **Voie de la Liberté** (Liberty Highway) follows the US army's advance from Utah Beach to Bastogne in Belgium. For a complete description of the sites and museums that commemorate the battle, pick up *The D-Day Landings and the Battle of Normandy*, a brochure available from most tourist offices in the area. Every year on June 6, veterans return to pay their respects at memorial services.

E TRANSPORTATION. While the D-Day beaches may be easier to approach today than in 1944, it is still no easy task to get from one to another without a car. Even with a car, it would be difficult to see all the sites in a single day. For a one-day tour of the beaches, the best idea is to focus on either Utah or Omaha beach and fan out from there. **Bus Verts** (☎08 10 21 42 14) is by far the best way to see the most in one day without a car (see **Hidden Deal**). Line **#70** (M-Sa 5 per day, 3 on Su) runs from Bayeux to Pointe du Hoc and the American Cemetery. Line **#75** goes to Arromanches and Ouistreham (3 per day).

Normandy Sightseeing Tours, formerly **Bus Fly,** rue des Cuisiniers in Bayeux, runs **tours** with fluent English-speaking guides. Tours are also given in German, Spanish, Italian, Japanese, and Chinese. (☎02 31 22 00 08 or 02 31 51 70 52; www.normandywebguide.com. 4hr. tour €35, students €30; 8hr. tour €70. Pick-up 8:30am and 1:30pm from your hotel or hostel. Reservations required.) **Victory Tours** leads tours in English from behind the Bayeux tourist office. (☎02 31 51 98 14; www.victory-tours.com or www.lignerolles.homestead.com. 4hr. tour 12:30pm, €31. 8hr. tour 9:15am, €54. Reservations required.) **Normandy Tours,** 26 pl. de la Gare, based in Bayeux's Hôtel de la Gare, runs flexible tours with less commentary, in English and French. (☎02 31 92 10 70; fax 02 31 51 95 99. 4hr. tour at 8:30am and 1pm. €31.) All three companies include admission to the museum in Arromanches.

Ħ ACCOMMODATIONS. Camping Reine Mathilde, in Etreham, near Port-en-Bessin, is 5km from the sea and Omaha Beach, 10km from Bayeux, and always packed. (☎02 31 21 76 55; www.campingreinemathilde.com. Open Apr.-Sept. Reception daily 8:30am-12:30pm and 2:30-7:30pm. €4.75-5.30 per person, children under age 7 €2.10-2.20, €4.50-5 per tent and car. Electricity €3.75.) Bayeux's tourist office can help you find *chambres d'hôte* and campgrounds.

BEACHES NEAR BAYEUX

Local tourist offices have a list of D-Day sights that offer discounted admission.

OMAHA BEACH. Omaha Beach, often referred to as "bloody Omaha," is perhaps the most famous of the beaches. Nothing went right here on D-Day: scouts failed to detect a German presence, and aerial and naval bombardment of the fortifications were entirely ineffective due to foggy conditions. The beach was protected by three veteran battalions (instead of the single motley division that the Americans had expected); it was covered with mine-topped jack-and-pole devices called "Rommel's asparagus;" and it ended in concrete walls, anti-tank ditches, minefields, and barbed wire. The first waves of troops to hit the shores suffered casualties of nearly 100%. Of the 32 amphibious tanks that were initially launched, only one made it ashore. Six thousand men of the initial wave of 35,000 died within the first hour of fighting; an additional 8000 were killed the same day. After a heavy rain, pieces of 57-year-old German barbed wire can still be found peeking out of the sand near the grass at the back of the beach.

■ **AMERICAN CEMETERY.** Overlooking Omaha beach, 9387 American graves stretch across a 172-acre coastal reserve. The **American Cemetery** in Colleville-sur-Mer contains rows of white crosses and stars of David, among them the graves of a father and son and 38 pairs of brothers. A simple marble chapel and a 7m bronze statue, *The Spirit of American Youth Rising from the Waves*, face the soldiers' graves. The Garden of the Missing, behind the memorial lists the names of 1557 individuals whose remains were never recovered. A walk through the neat rows of white headstones is one of the most moving reminders of the sacrifices of June 6. The cemetery contains only a fraction of those killed here. *(☎02 33 89 24 90; www.abmc.gov. Open daily 9am-5pm. The American staff at the office can help locate specific graves.)* Not far from Omaha Beach, in La Cambe, is the **German Military Cemetery.** It contains the often overlooked graves of 21,300 German casualties of World War II, as well as a Peace Garden of maple trees. *(☎02 31 22 70 76; www.volksbund.de. Open Apr.-Oct. daily 8am-7pm; Nov.-Mar. 8am-5:30pm.)*

■ **UTAH BEACH.** The Americans spearheaded the western flank of the invasion at **Utah Beach,** near Ste-Marie du Mont. Utah was one of the more successful operations of the day. All objectives were completed on schedule, with fewer casualties than expected, a feat honored by the **American Commemorative Monument** and the **Musée du Débarquement,** whose films and models show how 836,000 soldiers, 220,000 vehicles, and 725,000 tons of equipment came ashore. *(☎02 33 71 53 35; www.utah-beach.org. Open June-Sept. daily 9:30am-7pm; Apr.-May and Oct. daily 10am-12:30pm and 2-6pm; Nov.-Feb. weekends and public holidays 10am-12:30pm and 2-5:30pm. €4.50, ages 6-16 €2.)* Nearby **Ste-Mère-Eglise,** on the road to a German depot in Carentan and to the strategic German-held port of Cherbourg, was one of the most important targets of the invasion. Many paratroopers were misdropped, falling directly into the town. Visible targets for German artillery and encumbered by heavy equipment, 16% were killed before they hit the ground. Even so, a badly outnumbered group of them broke through heavy German defenses after six hours of fighting. The parachute-shaped **Musée des Troupes Aéroportées,** 14 rue Eisenhower, houses one of the planes that dropped them. *(☎02 33 41 41 35; www.airborne-museum.org. Open daily Apr.-Sept. 9am-6:45pm; Feb.-Mar. and Oct.-Nov. 9:30am-noon and 2-6pm; closed Dec.-Jan. €4.60, ages 6-14 €1.80.)* Ste-Mère-Eglise is accessible

THE HIDDEN DEAL

BUS VERTS

Many, if not most, who venture to Normandy come to see the D-Day beaches. Yet owing to the scattered nature of the most popular and poignant sites, the beaches aren't easy to visit without a car.

Fortunately, **Bus Verts's** special **"D-Day line"** is a perfect, inexpensive way to see the beaches (June Sa-Su, July-Aug. daily; €17). Buses leave Caen at 9:30am and head to Arromanches, site of **Gold Beach,** where the British built Port Winston under fire and in rough weather. Today it's a beautiful beach to which families bring their children, but the relics of the port still remain in an impressive, broken semi-circle. After a 3hr. stay in Arromanches, the bus takes off for a 20min. stopover at **Longues-sur-Mer,** where German bunkers remain in the earth, surrounded by miles of scenic pastureland. The bus continues to the **American Cemetery** (1hr.) with a panoramic view of **Omaha Beach,** perhaps the most moving experience of the day. The final stop is **Pointe du Hoc** (45min.), where the pockmarked land makes one imagine what it must have been like for the American Rangers who had to scale the cliff sixty years ago. You'll return to Caen just past 6pm, satisfied and tired.

(☎08 10 21 42 14; www.busverts14.fr. From Bayeux, take bus #75 to Arromanches and meet up with the D-Day line for a 1:20pm departure to Longues-sur-Mer.)

by STN **bus** (☎ 02 33 77 44 88) from Carentan (15min.; 1 per day 12:50pm, return 6:35pm; €2.90). Call the Carentan **tourist office** (☎ 02 33 42 74 01) for more info. To get to Carentan, take the train from Bayeux (30min., 10 per day, €6.70). Utah Beach and the Musée du Débarquement are only accessible by car from Ste-Mère-Eglise.

■ **POINTE DU HOC.** The most difficult landing was that of the First US Infantry Division at **Pointe du Hoc.** Not only did it stand above 30m cliffs that had to be scaled with ropes and hooks, but it was also the most heavily fortified of all the coastline strongholds. Nevertheless, 225 specially trained US Rangers climbed the bluff, neutralized a key German position, and single-handedly defended it for two days. Only 90 survived. German losses were even heavier: only 40 prisoners were left among the 2000 stationed there. The Pointe is considered to be a military cemetery because so many casualties remain there, crushed beneath collapsed sections of the 5m-thick concrete bunkers. Dozens of unfilled bomb craters from the initial strike still roll across the acreage amidst both collapsed and surviving bunkers, many of which can be climbed through.

GOLD BEACH. At **Arromanches,** a small town at the center of **Gold Beach,** the British used retired ships and 600,000 tons of concrete they had towed across the Channel to build **Port Winston,** the floating harbor that was to supply the Allied forces until Cherbourg was liberated months later. Sixty years later, the hulking ruins of a port built in six days and designed to last only 18 months remain in a broken semicircle just off the coast. The **Musée du Débarquement,** pl. du 6 Juin on the beach, uses models and newsreel footage to show how the port was assembled under fire. (☎ 02 31 22 34 31; www.normandy1944.com. Open daily May-Aug. 9am-7pm; Sept. 9am-6pm; Oct. and Mar. 9:30am-12:30pm and 1:30-5:30pm; Apr. 9am-12:30pm and 1:30-6pm; Nov.-Dec. and Feb. 10am-12:30pm and 1:30-5pm. Opens at 10am on Sunday, except June-Aug. Closed late Dec. to late Jan. €6, students and children €4.) The **Arromanches 360° Cinéma** shows a well-made 18-minute film, Le Prix de la Liberté (The Price of Freedom), on its circular screen. The movie combines battle footage with peaceful images of pre-war Normandy. To reach the cinema from the museum, turn left on rue de la Batterie and follow the steps to the top of the cliff. (☎ 02 31 22 30 30; www.arromanches360.com. Open daily June-Aug. 9:40am-6:40pm; mid-to late May and early Sept. 10:10am-6:10pm; mid-Sept. to Oct. 10:10am-5:40pm; Mar. to mid-May and Nov. 10:10am-5:10pm; Dec. and Feb. 10:10am-4:40pm. Closed Jan. Movies at 10 and 40min. past the hour. €3.70, students and under 18 €3.30.)

BATTERIES DE LONGUES. Six kilometers west of Arromanches in tiny **Longues-sur-Mer,** the **Batteries de Longues** are an ominous reminder of the German presence. Visitors can climb through these four bunkers, constructed in 1944, which still hold their original artillery. One contains the only cannon in the region still loaded with its original ammunition. The D-Day naval bombardment destroyed the town 1km inland, but left the bunkers mostly intact. On June 7, German and Polish troops stationed here surrendered to British troops almost instantaneously. (☎ 02 31 06 06 45; fax 02 31 06 01 66. Tours in French and English through the Caen Memorial June-Mar. daily 10am-5:30pm; Apr.-May W-Su only. €4, €3.50 with ticket stub from almost any other area museum. Open daily June-Aug. 10am-7pm; Sept.-May 10am-6pm.)

BEACHES NEAR CAEN

These eastern beaches were the landing sites for the Canadian and British armies. German defenders fired on them from expensive stone vacation houses along the beach. The beaches have changed considerably since 1944. The bunkers of Juno, Sword, and Gold Beaches have been replaced by resorts, and the somber taboos against recreation which characterize the American sites are not maintained here.

JUNO BEACH. The Canadians fought at **Juno Beach.** The last Canadian amphibious attack, in Sicily in 1942, had resulted in 75% casualties and ultimate failure. Bent on revenge at Juno, the Canadian soldiers pushed their attacks through without air or naval support, despite terrible losses. Opened in June 2003, the **Centre Juno Beach,** Voie des Français Libres, is devoted to the story of Canadian soldiers during the war, as well as some exhibits on present-day Canada. The **Canadian Cemetery** is located at **Bény-sur-Mer-Reviers;** take Bus Verts #4 from Caen. (☎ 02 31 37 32 17; www.junobeach.org. Open daily Apr.-Sept. 9am-7pm; Oct.-Mar. 10am-1pm and 2-6pm; closed Jan. €6.50, students €5.) The British anchored the easternmost flank of the invasion with their landing at **Sword Beach.** This enormously successful mission was accomplished with the help of the quirky "Hobart's Funnies," tanks outlandishly fitted with bridge-building, mine-sweeping, and ditch-digging apparatus.

BENOUVILLE. It was here that British paratroopers captured Pegasus Bridge within 10min. of landing and held it until Scottish reinforcements arrived. The **Musée des Troupes Aéroportées,** also known as the **Mémorial Pegasus,** at the Pegasus Bridge between Benouville and Ranville, recounts the Parachute Brigades' operations. Take Bus Verts #1 from Caen to Mairie in Benouville. Continue down the road, take a right at the roundabout, and cross the bridge. (☎ 02 31 44 62 54; www.normandie1944.com. Open daily May-Sept. 9:30am-6:30pm; Oct.-Nov. and Feb.-Apr. 10am-1pm and 2-5pm. €5, students and children €3.50.) One of the largest of the 16 British cemeteries is 1½km away in **Ranville.** The only French troops involved in the D-Day landings came ashore at **Ouistreham,** at the mouth of the Orne River. They and Normandy's resilient citizens are memorialized in **le Grand Bunker: Musée du Mur de l'Atlantique** (€6, children 6-12 €4) and in the **N°4 Commando Museum,** pl. Alfred Thomas. (☎ 02 31 96 63 10. Open Feb. to mid-Nov. daily 10:30am-6pm. €4, students and children €2.50, under 10 free.) The museums and the Ouistreham **tourist office** lie in a row: take Bus Verts #1 from Caen and get off at Centre in Ouistreham; turn right down rue Général Leclerc, turn left on av. de la Mer and follow it to the beach. The tourist office will be directly ahead, N°4 Commando Museum is on the left, and the Grand Bunker will be down the street to the right.

CHERBOURG

Strategically located at the tip of the Cotentin peninsula, Cherbourg (pop. 44,000) was the Allies' "Gateway to France," their major supply port following the

THE LOCAL STORY

ROBERT HALLIDAY, D-DAY VETERAN

Mr. Halliday served as a parachutist in the 12th Yorks Battalion, 6th British airborne Division, nicknamed the Red Berets. His division was one of the first to arrive in Normandy on the early morning of June 6, 1944.

Q: How often do you come back to the battle site?
A: We [the Red Berets] come over every year. We gradually get fewer and fewer, because the men are now in their eighties. It gets sadder every year.

Q: What was your experience at Normandy?
A: The American aircraft we jumped out of was hit, and as soon as we left, the plane crashed. The outcome of the crew we don't know; that sort of thing happened all the time.

Q: How do you think the tributes to the D-Day vets personally affect you?
A: The nicest thing was someone who spoke to me the year before last. He was French. He had our insignias on his jacket, and he showed me an original photo of the beaches he had given his son.

Q: Do you think films teach real lessons about WWII?
A: Hollywood films today fabricate stories about D-Day, with big handsome guys doing impossible things. It was blokes like us, who had next to nothing, on a few shillings a week, all volunteers. I was 17 when I joined the army.

D-Day offensive of 1944. Today, the town's numerous ferry lines shuttle tourists from France to England and Ireland. Cherbourg is short on both sights and charm, but for those on layover between ports, there's just enough to keep one busy.

⑦ PRACTICAL INFORMATION. Ferries leave from the *gare maritime*, northeast of the town center, along bd. Maritime (open daily 5:30am-11:30pm). **Irish Ferries** goes to Rosslare about every other day. **P&O European Ferries** goes to Portsmouth, and **Brittany Ferries** to Poole (see **Getting There: By Boat,** p. 40). It is essential to both reserve ahead and check the most up-to-date ferry schedules. To reach the **train station** (open daily 5:30am-7:30am), take bd. Felix Amiot, go left at the roundabout onto av. Aristide Briand, which becomes av. Carnot. Turn right at the end of the canal onto av. Millet; the station will be ahead on the left. (25min.) **Trains** run to Bayeux via Lison (1hr., 8 per day in the afternoon, €12.80); Caen (1½hr., 10 per day, €15.70); Paris (3hr., 7 per day, €34.20); Rennes via Lison (3½hr., 3 per day, €27.10); Rouen (4½hr., 4 per day, €29.10). STN (☎02 33 88 51 00) sends **buses** around the region; the bus station is across the street from the train station. (Open M-F 8am-noon and 2-6pm.) The hostel rents **bikes** in the summer, and **taxis** wait at the train station and at the top of quai Alexandre III by the tourist office and the bridge (☎02 33 53 36 38).

To get to the **tourist office**, 2 quai Alexandre III, and the center of town, turn right from the terminal onto bd. Felix Amiot. At the roundabout, go straight and continue around the bend to the left. Turn right over the first bridge; the tourist office is on the left. (20min.) The staff leads hikes and **tours** in summer, and provides a free **accommodations service.** (☎02 33 93 52 02; www.ot-cherbourg-cotentin.fr. Open 9am-12:30pm and 2-6pm.) An **annex** is open at the *gare maritime.* (☎02 33 44 39 92. Open June-July daily 7am-noon and 2-8pm; Sept.-May closes at 6pm.) **Currency exchange** is available at the ferry terminal or at banks around **place Gréville.** Other services include: a **laundromat** on rue au Blé, a **pharmacy,** La Croix Blanche, at pl. de la Révolution, at the intersection of rue au Blé and rue Tour Carrée (open M 2-7:15pm, Tu-Sa 9am-12:15pm and 2-7:15pm), **Internet** at the Forum Espace Culture, pl. Centrale, a large bookstore off rue au Blé (☎02 33 78 19 30; open M 2-7pm, Tu-Sa 10am-7pm; €1.50 per 10 min., €3.25 per 30min.), and a **post office** on rue de l'Ancien Quai, at pl. Divette. A **branch** office is on av. Carnot near the ferry terminal. (☎02 33 08 87 00. Open M-F 8am-7pm, Sa 8am-noon.) **Postal code:** 50100.

⌐⌐ ACCOMMODATIONS & FOOD. The tourist office has lists of *chambres d'hôte* (around €23) and campsites. The cheapest option is the ▨**Auberge de Jeunesse (HI) ❶,** 57 rue de l'Abbaye, one of the best hostels in Normandy. From the tourist office, turn left onto quai de Caligny, then left on rue de Port, which becomes rue Tour Carrée and rue de la Paix. Bear left onto rue de l'Union, which feeds into rue de l'Abbay. (10min.) From the station, take bus #3 or 5 to Arsenal (last bus around 7:30pm); the hostel is across the street from the bus stop. Across town from the train station, it may not be the best option for those planning an in-and-out stay. The hostel has 100 beds in spotless two- to five-person rooms, each with a sink, shower, TV, and lockers (bring your own lock). A kitchen and bar are also on the premises. (☎02 33 78 15 15; cherbourg@fuaj.org. Breakfast included. Bike rental available, approx €8 per half-day, €12.50 per day. Reception 9am-3pm and 6-11pm. Lockout 1-6pm; guests can enter after 1pm if they've already checked in. No curfew. Bunks €15.50, for two nights €28.20; €18.40/€34 for non-HI members.) **Hôtel de la Gare ❸,** 10 pl. Jean Jaurès, lets large, colorful, well-tended rooms that make the perfect stopover for an early morning train. (☎02 33 43 06 81; fax 02 33 43 12 20. Bacon-and-egg breakfast €5.50. Reception 24hr. Singles and doubles with shower €28-31, with toilet €36-39; triples and quads €48-57. MC/V.)

There is a huge **market** on pl. du Théâtre (Tu morning and Th until 3pm), a **Carrefour** supermarket, quai de l'Entrepôt, next to the station (open M-Sa 8:30am-9pm), and a **Proxi**, rue de l'Union, near the hostel. (Open daily 8:30am-1pm and 3-7:30pm.) Bars and inexpensive ethnic restaurants line **rue de la Paix. Crêperie Ty-Billic ❷**, 73 rue au Blé, is a tourist-free haven. Two galettes, two crêpes, and one cider run €10-13.50. (☎ 02 33 01 11 90. Open daily noon-2pm and 7-11pm. MC/V.) For a more upscale meal, **L'Antidote ❸**, 41 rue au Blé, offers a varied selection of *prix fixe menus* (lunch €12, dinner €20 and €28.50) and a wide selection of wines. Reserve ahead. (☎ 02 33 79 01 28. Open 10am-1am, kitchen closes at 11pm. MC/V.)

◨♫ SIGHTS & ENTERTAINMENT. Cherbourg's newest attraction is **La Cité de la Mer.** At the Gare Maritime Transatlantique, across the bridge from the tourist office, the vast complex is dedicated to the underwater exploits of men and animals. The highlight of the visit is a full audio-guided walking tour (in French or English) of Le Redoutable, a nuclear submarine (ages 6 and over only). Convenient to the ferry terminal and equipped with a post office, restaurant, and bar, La Cité de la Mer is the best way to pass an afternoon in Cherbourg. *(☎ 08 25 00 25 50; www.citedelamer.com. Open June to mid-Sept. 9:30am-7pm; mid-Sept. to May 10am-6pm. May-Sept. €13, ages 8-17 €9.50; Oct.-Apr. €11.50/€8.50; year-round under 7 free.)*

Founded by Mathilde, granddaughter of William the Conqueror and mother of England's King Henry I, the 12th-century semi-ruined **Abbaye du Vœu** and its gardens lie at the western edge of town, past the hostel. (Free. Occasional guided tours of abbey at 2:30pm.) With intricate lacework and dark, angular windows, the **Basilique de la Trinité**, pl. Napoléon, off quai de Caligny, blends centuries of architectural styles. Sixteenth-century carvings above the nave include a grotesque skeleton on the left, who reminds that "death comes for us all."

The streets around **place Central** are filled with bars and late-night eateries. Multilingual crowds congregate nightly at **Art's Café**, 69 rue au Blé. (☎ 02 33 53 55 11. Live DJ F-Sa. Beer €2, mixed drinks €4.20. Open M-Sa 11am-1am.) Mellow **Le Solier**, 52 Grande Rue, caters to a jovial, slightly older crowd of locals and plays a good mix of Celtic music and blues. (☎ 02 33 94 76 63; www.multimedia.com/lesolier. Pint of Guinness €5.90. Open M-Sa June-Sept. 6pm-2am; Oct.-May 6pm-1am.) The second week of October, Cherbourg hosts the **Festival des Cinémas d'Irlande et de Grande Bretagne,** celebrating films from across the Channel.

GRANVILLE

In 1439, the expatriate Lord Jean d'Argouges sold his great-grandmother's dowry, the rocky peninsula of Granville, to the English. It quickly became a fortified city from which the English spent 30 years trying to take Mont-St-Michel. The exceptional seaside charms of Granville (pop. 13,700) include a beautiful beach that changes dramatically with the tide and a walled-in *haute ville*. It is a popular base for trips to Mont-St-Michel and the Chausey Islands, but its distance from Paris keeps it less crowded and less expensive than might be expected.

◨▨ ORIENTATION & PRACTICAL INFORMATION. To reach the city center from the train station, follow av. Maréchal Leclerc, which becomes rue Couraye. The easiest access to the *haute ville* is the stairwell in front of the casino. The **train station,** pl. Pierre Semard, off av. Mal. Leclerc, has service to: Bayeux (2hr., 4 per day, €14.20); Cherbourg (3hr., 3 per day, €17.90) via Lison; Paris (3hr., 4 per day, €31.30). The info office is open M-Sa 9:10am-noon and 2-6:30pm, Su 10:10am-noon and 1:45-7:30pm. **SNCF buses** go to Coutances (30min., 3 per day, €6.60). **Emeraude Lines** (☎ 02 33 50 16 36), at the *gare maritime*, sails to the Chausey Islands (1hr.; 1-2 per day; €16.80, ages 3-14 €10.30); Guernsey (2hr.; 3 per week;

NORMANDY

€56, ages 16-23 €38, ages 4-15 €34); and Jersey (1¼hr.; 3 per week; €46, ages 16-23 €34, ages 4-15 €26). Ask about family rates. **Compagnie Corsaire** also sails to the Chauseys. Schedules change frequently. (☎02 33 50 16 36; www.compagniecorsaire.com. Round-trip €16.90, children €10.50.) Access the **Internet** at the post office or at the back of the bar La Citrouille, 8 rue St-Sauveur. (☎02 33 51 35 51. €1 per 15min., €3.50 per hr. Open M 5pm-1am, Tu-Sa 8:30am-1am.)

The **tourist office**, 4 cours Jonville, is around the corner on your right as soon as you reach the main *place*. They offer **tours** of the city and the *Calendrier des manifestations*, a list of summer events in town. (☎02 33 91 30 03; www.ville-granville.fr. Office open July-Aug. M-Sa 9am-1pm and 2-6:30pm, Su 10am-1pm; Sept.-June M-F 9am-noon and 2-6pm, Sa 9am-12:30pm and 2-6pm. Tours in French July-Aug. Tu and F at 2pm, €2.) Other services include: **ATMs** on av. Maréchal Leclerc, a **laundromat**, 10 rue St-Sauvier (open daily 7am-9pm), **police** at rue du Port (☎02 33 91 27 50), and a **hospital** at rue des Menneries (☎02 33 91 50 00). The **post office**, 8 cours Jonville, has **currency exchange**. (☎02 33 91 12 30. Open M-F 8am-12:30pm and 2:30-6:30pm, Sa 8:30am-noon.) **Postal code:** 50400.

⌂ ACCOMMODATIONS. Hotels and the hostel are packed in summer. To get to the **Auberge de Jeunesse (HI) ❶**, bd. des Amiraux Granvillais, from the train station, turn right onto av. Maréchal Leclerc and follow it downhill. Just before the town center, turn left onto rue St-Sauveur; head right when the road forks and look for "Centre Nautisme" signs straight ahead. To get to the reception, follow sign that says *accueil visiteurs*. Part of a huge sailing center, it runs week-long camps July-Aug. Dorms are comfortable and newly redone. (☎02 33 91 22 62; fax 02 33 50 51 99. Breakfast €2.40, for non-HI members €3.70. Meals €8.90/€11.20. Sheets €3.70/€4.70. Office open for checkout 8:30-10am and for check-in 3-6pm. Code for late entry. Singles €18.40/€20.50; 2-bed dorms €15.20/€17 per person; 4-bed dorms €10.30/€11.70 per person. MC/V.)

To reach **▧Hôtel Michelet ❷**, 5 rue Jules Michelet, from the tourist office, head straight across pl. de Gaulle onto rue P. Poirier. When rue Poirier ends, take a right onto rue Georges Clemenceau (becomes av. de la Libération), then a sharp left up the hill onto rue Jules Michelet. The comfortable, unbelievably spacious, modern rooms, some with balconies, are in a calm location near the beach. (☎02 33 50 06 55; fax 02 33 50 12 25. Breakfast €5. Reception 7:30am-10pm. Doubles €22; with toilet €29; with shower, toilet, and TV €38; with bath, toilet, and TV €47. AmEx/MC/V.) Run by accommodating owners, **Hôtel Terminus ❷**, 5 pl. Pierre Semard, right across from the train station, feels like a Victorian dollhouse. All rooms have toilet and TV. (☎02 33 50 02 05. Breakfast €4.50. Singles €20, with shower €26; doubles €26, with shower €32, with bath €33; triples €34-41; quads €39-46.)

◖ FOOD. There are **markets** on cours Jonville (Sa all day) and on pl. du 11 Novembre 1918 (W mornings). For groceries, head to **Marché Plus**, 107 rue de Couraye. (Open M-Sa 7am-9pm, Su 9am-1pm.) Skip the pricey restaurants in town for one of the small *crêperies* of the *haute ville* near the Eglise de Notre-Dame. Try the large savory dishes (€4-7) and desserts (€2-5) at **▧La Gourmandise ❷**, 37 rue St-Jean. (☎02 33 50 65 16. Open M-Sa noon-3pm and 7-11pm. Open Su in July. AmEx/MC/V). The terrific Turkish cuisine, authentic décor, and cozy vibe at **La Porte de Byzance ❷**, 2 av. de la Libération, set it apart from the other *salons de thé*. (☎02 33 51 49 22. Starters €3.50, *plats* €8-9. Open daily 11:30am-midnight. MC/V.) Near the hostel, **Monte Pego ❷**, 13 rue St-Sauveur, serves delicious pastas, pizzas, and salads for €6.70-9. (☎02 33 90 74 44. Open July-Aug. daily noon-2:30pm and 7-10:30pm; Sept.-June closed Su-M. MC/V.) Kebab vendors and ice cream stands cluster near the beach.

🎥 🎵 **SIGHTS & ENTERTAINMENT.** Granville's old English walled city, known as the *haute ville*, is its most charming attraction. It stretches from the casino to the **Eglise de Notre-Dame** (where classical concerts are held on summer weekends). A walk around the outer walls of the *haute ville* affords an incredible view of the surrounding shoreline. Stretching northward from the *vieille ville* is Granville's most popular **beach,** but you'll also find quiet stretches of sand past the port on the opposite side of the point. Anchored at the edge of the *haute ville*, at the pl. de l'Isthme, is the **Musée Richard Anacréon,** the area's only 20th-century art museum. It focuses on the first half of the century, and on Fauvism in particular. Temporary exhibitions supplement the permanent collection during the summer. (☎02 33 51 02 94. Open July-Sept. Su-M and W-Sa 11am-6pm; Oct.-June W-Su 2-6pm. €2.50; students and children July-Sept. €1.30, Oct.-June €1.60.)

A coastal path leads from the beach promenade to the stairs at the clifftop **Musée Christian Dior,** in the childhood home of Granville's most famous son. The museum offers a showcase of the extravagant creations of the house of Dior, with themed exhibits that change each year. The villa's immaculate gardens were designed from 1905 to 1930 by Dior and his mother. (☎02 33 61 48 21. Open mid-May to Sept. 10am-12:30pm and 2-6:30pm. Gardens 9am-8pm. €5, students and over 60 €4.)

From May to September, boats leave daily for the **Chausey Islands,** a sparsely inhabited archipelago of 52 to 365 islets, depending on the tide (for ferry info, see **Practical Information**). Visitors revel in the idyllic natural beauty of the islands.

Nightlife is limited and pleasantly low-key. The best bet in town is the laidback **La Citrouille,** 8 rue St-Sauveur, which features occasional live jazz in the evenings, a dartboard for the best sort of drunken wagering, and cheap Internet access. (☎02 33 51 35 51. Beer on tap €2.50. Open M 5pm-1am, Tu-Sa 8:30am-1am.) The **Bar les Amiraux,** bd. des Amiraux, across from the hostel, pulls in relaxed, mid-summer crowds fresh off the beach in search of €2 brews. (☎02 33 50 12 83. Open daily noon-2am.) Granville hosts **Carnaval** every year on the Sunday before Mardi Gras and the **Fête de la Mer** at the end of July. In keeping with its large number of antique shops, Granville hosts a **Salon des Antiquitaires** in mid-August.

🧭 DAYTRIP FROM GRANVILLE: COUTANCES

The STN bus office (☎02 33 45 00 50) runs buses to Granville (30min., 3 per day, €6.60). To reach the cathedral from the bus station, walk straight ahead to the roundabout and turn right onto rue de la Croute, then turn at the first left onto rue de la Mission. Take the second right onto rue Maréchal Foch, then take the first left.

Miraculously unscathed by World War II, the 13th-century cathedral of Coutances (pop. 11,000) is second in beauty perhaps only to Chartres. Flanked by the churches of St-Pierre and St-Nicolas, the **cathedral** forms the centerpoint of the town's three-spired skyline, visible for miles. The cathedral's impressive lantern-tower, a three-tiered structure that catapults upward from the choir, fills it with light. Tours organized by the tourist office guide visitors through its illuminated galleries. (Open daily 9am-7pm. Tours at the end of May, June, and Sept. in French Su-F 2:30pm; July-Aug. 3 per day in French M-F 10:30am, 2:30, 4pm; in English Tu and Th 2:30pm. Tours €5.50, ages 10-18 and students €4.)

The ingeniously designed flowerbeds in the **Jardin des Plantes,** near the tourist office, are among the oldest in France. The garden features an arrangement in the shape of a ship and illuminated flowers on summer nights. (Open daily July-Aug. 9am-11:30pm; Apr.-June and Sept. 9am-8pm; Oct.-Mar. 9am-5pm.) To reach the **tourist office,** pl. Georges Leclerc, from the front of the cathedral, turn left, then right behind the Hôtel de Ville. (☎02 33 19 08 10; fax 02 33 19 08 19; tourisme-cou-

NORMANDY

tances@wanadoo.fr. Open July-Aug. M-Sa 10am-12:30pm and 1:30-7pm, Su 2-6pm; mid-Sept. to June M-Sa 10am-12:30pm and 2-6pm; Oct.-Apr. closes Su at 5pm.)

There are many treasures to be found within 4-5km of town; the brochure *Monuments et Lieux de Visite* (available in English at the tourist office) covers a number of châteaux, manors, museums, and abbeys within walking distance. The **Château de Gratot**, an easy 50min. walk from Coutances, offers a look at the typical renovations old châteaux undergo. (☎02 33 45 18 49. Open daily 10am-7pm. €3, ages 10-18 €2.) On the week of Ascension Thursday (May 23-30, 2004), Coutances celebrates **Jazz sous les Pommiers**, a week of more than 30 concerts in the streets and bars. (☎02 33 76 78 61; www.jazzsouslespommiers.com.)

MONT-ST-MICHEL

Visitors are stunned when they turn around the last bend in the road and Mont-St-Michel rises into sight. It's little wonder that the English spent such effort trying to capture the incomparable Mont (pop. 42). To this day both Normandy and Brittany claim it within their borders. A trip into the abbey, with or without a tour, is an indispensable part of the experience, but no less enthralling are the views of soaring spires and stunning marshland from the crags and coils around its outer walls.

▐ TRANSPORTATION

Trains: In Pontorson (☎02 33 60 00 35). Open M-Sa 9:15am-noon and 2:45-7:10pm, Su 1:10-7:15pm. To: **Dinan** (1hr., 2-3 per day, €7.10); **Granville** (1hr.; M-F 3 per day, Sa-Su 2 per day; €7.30) via Folligny; **Paris** (3½hr., 3 per day, €37 plus TGV supplement) via Caen; and **St-Malo** (90min., 2-3 per day, €6.60) via Dol.

Buses: Courriers Bretons, 104 rue Couesnon (☎02 99 12 70 70) in Pontorson. Buses leave Mont-St-Michel from its entrance at Porte de l'Avancée, and leave Pontorson from outside the train station and the Courriers Bretons office. Buy tickets on board. Mont and Pontorson buses run M-Sa about 12 per day, 6 on Su, last bus back from the Mont 8pm; €1.70. The same company also runs to **Rennes** (1½hr.; June-Sept. M-Sa 5 per day, Su 3 per day; Sept.-June M-Sa 6 per day, 1 on Su; €11) and **St-Malo** (1½hr.; July-Aug. 3-4 per day, Sept.-June 1-2 per day; €9). Office open M-F 10am-noon and 4-7pm.

Bike Rental: Couesnon Motoculture, 1bis rue du Couesnon (☎02 33 60 11 40), in Pontorson. €7 per half-day, €12 per day, €23 for 2 days, €32 for 3 days. Passport deposit. Open Tu-Sa 8:30am-noon and 2-7pm. Closes at 6:30pm on Sa. MC/V.

◀▐ ORIENTATION & PRACTICAL INFORMATION

Mont-St-Michel is on the outer edge of both Brittany and Normandy. **Pontorson,** 9km due south down D976, has the closest train station, supermarket, and affordable hotels. The tourist office is just inside the Porte de l'Avancée, the only entrance to the Mont. **Grande Rue** is the town's main thoroughfare. There's no public transportation off the Mont late at night. Biking from Pontorson takes about one hour on terrain that is relatively flat but not always bike-friendly. The path next to the Couesnon River may be the best route.

Tourist office at Mont-St-Michel: (☎02 33 60 14 30; www.ot-montstmichel.com). Busy but helpful multilingual staff has info on sites and nearby lodging. A free *horaire des marées* (tidetable) will inform you whether your view from the Mont will be of ocean or sandy marsh. Hours vary in the low season. Open July-Aug. M-Sa 9am-7pm, Su 9am-1pm and 2-7pm; Apr.-June and Sept. M-Sa 9am-12:30pm and 2-6:30pm, Su 9am-noon and 2-6pm; Nov.-Feb. M-Sa 9am-noon and 2-5:30pm, Su 10am-noon and 2-5pm; Mar. and Oct. M-Sa 9am-noon and 2-5:30pm, Su 10am-noon and 2-5pm.

Tourist office in Pontorson: pl. de l'Eglise (☎02 33 60 20 65; mont.st.michel.pontorson@wanadoo.fr), has maps and info on walking tours and on the Mont. **Internet** €4.50 per 30min., €8 per hr. Open July-Aug. M-F 9am-12:30pm and 2-6:30pm, Sa 10am-12:30pm and 3-6:30pm, Su 10am-12:30pm; Sept.-June M-F 9am-noon and 2-6pm, Sa 10am-noon and 3-6pm.

Laundromat: on the rue St-Michel next to the Champion supermarket (see **Food**). From the train station, take a right on rue Dr. Bailleul, following the road as it becomes bd. Général de Gaulle. At the roundabout, take the road to your right (the D976) to Mont-St-Michel, and the laundromat will be just ahead on the right. Open daily 7am-9pm.

Police: entrance just to the left of the Porte de l'Avancée before you enter (☎02 33 60 14 42). Open daily 11am-1pm and 5:30-7:30pm.

Hospital: Emergency services are in Avranches. A small **clinic** on the Mont, across from the post office.

Internet: At the Pontorson tourist office (see listing).

Post Office: Grande Rue (☎02 33 89 65 00), about 100m to the right of Porte de l'Avancée. **Currency exchange** at tolerable rates. Open June-Aug. M-F 9am-5:30pm, Sa 9am-4pm; Mar.-May and Sept.-Oct. M-F 9am-noon and 2-5pm, Sa 9am-noon; Nov.-Feb. 9am-noon and 1:30-4:30pm. **Postal code:** 50116.

ACCOMMODATIONS

Forget about staying on the Mont unless St-Michel himself is bankrolling your visit. More affordable lodging is available in Pontorson. Some choose to daytrip to the Mont from St-Malo. There are also a number of campsites and *chambres d'hôte* near Beauvoir. Reserve ahead, since prices climb faster than the spring tide.

Centre Duguesclin (HI), rue Général Patton, Pontorson (☎/fax 02 33 60 18 65; aj@ville-pontorson.fr). From the station, turn right onto the main road, then left onto rue Couesnon. Take the third right onto rue St-Michel. When you see the tourist office on your left, cut diagonally across the square, following signs toward the church. Bear left in front of the church onto rue Hédou. Follow that to the end, then turn right on rue Gal. Patton. The hostel is on your left. (10min.) Clean 3-, 4-, and 6-person dorms in a 1910 stone house with communal lounge, kitchen, and dining area. Breakfast €3.20. Sheets €2.70. Reception July-Aug. 8am-9pm; Sept.-June 8am-noon and 5-9pm. Lockout Sept.-June noon-5pm. Call at least 1 week ahead, 1 month in the summer, as many groups stay here. Dorms €8 for members, €8.40 for non-members. ❶

Hôtel le Grillon, 37 rue du Couesnon, on the right after rue St-Michel, Pontorson (☎02 33 60 17 80). Pleasant owners rent 5 quiet, shiny rooms behind a cheery *crêperie*, all with shower. Breakfast €5. Reception Su-W and F-Sa 7am-11pm; closed W afternoon. Reserve 1-2 weeks ahead July-Aug. Doubles €29, with toilet €32. Extra bed €5. MC/V. ❸

Hôtel de Guesclin, Grande Rue, Mont-St-Michel (☎02 33 60 14 10) halfway up the Grande Rue on the right-hand side. Ten comfortable rooms are one of the best bets for staying on the Mont itself. Half-board available at the restaurant downstairs. Breakfast €7. Open Apr.-Nov. Doubles with shower, toilet, TV, and telephone €55-75. MC/V. ❺

Hôtel de l'Arrivée, 17 rue de Dr. Tizon, Pontorson (☎/fax 02 03 60 01 57), over a bar across the street from the station, on the other side of the Courriers Bretons office. This no-frills hotel is a good choice for its low prices and proximity to the bus and train stations. Breakfast €5. Reception 8am-10pm. Singles and doubles €15.40-19.90, with shower €21-26.90, with shower and toilet €35; triples with shower €38; quads with shower and toilet €65. Extra bed €5. Prices drop slightly in winter. MC/V. ❷

Hôtel de France et Vauban, 50 bd. Clemenceau, Pontorson (☎02 33 60 03 84; www.hotel-france-vauban.com), across the street from the station on the left. Pleasant, sparkling bedrooms (all with shower or bath) provide a quiet night's rest. Reception

THE LOCAL STORY

FRÈRE TOBIE, BROTHER OF JERUSALEM

Frère Tobie, age 25, is a native Breton and monk at Mont-St-Michel. He is a serious-looking young man and wears a monk's full-length dark blue robe and sandals. Attached to his belt, with his prayer beads, is a mobile phone.

Q: What is it like to live here?

A: Life on the Mont is entirely different than elsewhere, because this is not just a monastery but also a tourist site, a place of pilgrimage, and an ancient monument. Life varies each day, but for us essentially this is a place of sanctuary, although almost three million people visit each year. Living in the midst of the sea, we have to pay attention to the tides, because they dictate when we can venture off the island. At night and in the early morning the Mont is completely deserted. When you look out on the bay, with 500km of sand, it is a great desert.

Q: What is the monastic community like here?

A: We have two communities who live in parallel and have liturgies together. We have four monks and seven nuns. We hope to become more numerous over time, with more brothers and sisters from other communities. The community is here indefinitely; our superior can send us elsewhere, because we pledged obedience.

Q: What is a normal day for you?

A: Our day begins at 6am. At 6:30

(Continued on next page)

8am-10pm, in the Restaurant l'Orson Bridge Café. Breakfast €6. Doubles €32, with toilet €39-49; triples €38-62; quads with toilet €65. Mention *Let's Go* for a 10% discount during the low season. MC/V. ❸

CAMPING

Camping Haliotis at Pontorson, chemin des Soupirs (☎/fax 02 33 68 11 59; www.camping-haliotis-mont-saint-michel.com). Follow hostel directions to rue Hédou, then take a left on rue Général Patton and the first right onto chemin des Soupirs. The campsite will be 300m ahead on the left. Hedges and cornfields hide this well-kept and newly renovated 3-star site from the road and the nearby Couesnon river. Clean, extensive central bathrooms and showers as well as newly-built heated pool, bar, and restaurant on site. Open Apr.-Sept. Reception 7:30am-10pm. €4.20 per person, €2 per child; €3.50 per tent and car. Electricity €2.50. Wheelchair-accessible. ❶

Camping du Mont-St-Michel, 1¾km from the Mont at the junction of D275 and N776 (☎02 33 60 22 10; www.le-mont-saint-michel.com). More like a small town, with 350 spots and many dependent businesses. They also **rent bikes** (€4.80 per hr., €16 per day). Open mid-Feb. to mid-Nov. €6.50 per site, €3 per person. Electricity included. ❶

Camping St-Michel, rte. du Mont-St-Michel (☎02 33 70 96 90), is by the bay in Courtils, 9km from the Mont (9km). This 3-star site was named the most garden-like campsite in the *département*. Flowers surround the heated swimming pool, common room, grocery store, breakfast room, and snack bar. They **rent bikes** (€5 per half-day, €8 per day). Open mid-Mar. to mid-Oct. July-Aug. $4 per person, €1.60 per child under 7, €3.50 per car and tent. Prices slightly reduced in low season. ❶

FOOD

If you dare invest in more than a postcard on the Mont, look for local specialties such as *agneau du pré salé* (lamb raised on the surrounding salt marshes) and *omelette poulard* (a fluffy soufflé-like dish; about €10-14). **Chapeau Rouge ❸,** Grande Rue, serves these delicacies at lower prices than most, in a homey wood-furnished dining room. (☎02 33 60 14 29. Lamb €9.50, 3-course *menus* €11.50-25. Open daily 11:30am-2:30pm and 7-9pm. Sometimes closed at night.) You could be lured to a sticky end at **La Sirène ❷,** Grande Rue, past the post office, by a bursting chocolate-banana crêpe (€4.80), topped with a *mont* of chocolate sauce. (☎02 33 60 08 60. *Menu*

€9.20. Open daily 10am-6pm. MC/V.) For a splurge, get your eggs from **La Mère Poulard ❹**, Grande Rue, Mont-St-Michel, just on your left as you walk through the gates. The exorbitant prices (*menus* €25-65), are partly for the experience of watching cooks in traditional garb craft omelettes in copper pots over a wood fire. (☎02 33 89 68 68; www.mere-poulard.fr. Open 11:30am-10pm. AmEx/MC/V.) If you plan to picnic, arrive prepared, as there are no grocery stores within the walls. Pontorson has a **market** (W morning) on rue Couesnon and at pl. de la Mairie, and a **Champion** supermarket, rue St-Michel, just outside Pontorson. (☎02 33 60 37 38. Open July-Aug. M-Sa 9am-7:30pm; Sept.-June reduced hours.)

🗿 SIGHTS

Mont-St-Michel's **Grande Rue** is jam-packed with restaurants and souvenir shops. For more detailed information on Mont architecture, pick up one of the many guidebooks (€5-40), although brochures and tours are offered for free within the abbey walls. None of the "museums" on Grande Rue are worth the money or time. The sand around the bay should be explored with caution, if at all: the broad expanses are riddled with quicksand, and the bay's tides, changing every six hours or so, are the highest in France. During the bi-monthly spring tides, the *mascaret* (initial wave) rushes in at 2m per second, flooding the beaches along the causeway. To see this event, you must be within the abbey two hours ahead of time. Grande Rue has countless little stairwells jutting off of it, some alarmingly vertiginous. Many take the curious on a near-total circuit around the base of the abbey's walls.

HISTORY. Legend holds that the Baie de St-Michel was created by a giant tidal wave that created three islands: Tombelaine, Mont Dol, and Mont Tomba (meaning "mound" or "tomb"). So appealing was Tomba, the last island, that heaven wanted a piece of it. In 708 AD, the Archangel Michael supposedly appeared to St-Aubert, Bishop of Avranches, and instructed him to build a place of worship on the barren island. Construction did not begin, however, until Richard I, the third duke of Normandy, sent Benedictine monks to the Mont in 966. Four crypts were built, one in each cardinal direction, to support the base of a church on Tomba's 80m high point. These became the monastery's very first chapels, beginning with Notre-Dame-sous-Terre, completed later in the 10th century. The Mont soon became as important a destination for Christian pilgrims to visit as Rome and Jerusalem.

(Continued from previous page)

we have a half-hour of silent prayer, and then *laudes*, the first services of the day. After breakfast we have *lectio divino*, a reading from the Bible. At noon we have daily mass—in the abbey in summer, and the crypt in winter. We eat lunch in silence. In the afternoon we work. At 6:30pm, we have the adoration of the sacrament for an hour and vespers, in which the public can participate. Later we eat dinner, also in silence, and then *complies*, our final service.

Q: What kind of work do you do?
A: Our vocation is being monks in the town, among people. Here at Mont-St-Michel, we divide our daily tasks: we have one brother who cooks, one who cleans and gardens, our superior who coordinates masses. I am the webmaster, so I develop Internet sites.

Q: Why did you pick monastic life?
A: The monastic life is chosen in response to a call from God. This is our answer. This call from God isn't an apparition, but a verification of spirituality. In the community, we have many possible routes: one brother converted after spending 20 years as a communist, because he had a strong personal experience. There are also those from Christian families who joined after finishing high school.

Q: How do you feel about tourists here?
A: For us, it's not difficult, because we need to interact with people. When they arrive at the top of the Mont, they are panting and out of breath. Tired, they are perhaps more able to receive the Mont's message and the calm of the environs. We have a mission here, and it allows this place to touch the hearts of those who come.

In the 14th and 15th centuries, Mont-St-Michel was fortified against a 30-year English attack with ramparts designed by Abbot Jolivet. The Benedictines continued their work of copying and illuminating the *Manuscrits du Mont-St-Michel*, the remains of which are now on display in nearby Avranches (p. 226). In 1789, the Revolutionary government turned the island into a prison, first jailing 600 monks, followed by Robespierre and 14,000 others who ranged from royalists to ordinary criminals. The prison was closed in 1863, and in 1874 Mont-St-Michel was classified as a national monument. In 1897, the church was topped with a neo-Gothic spire identical to the one atop Ste-Chapelle in Paris, and a copper and gold leaf statue of St-Michel. Around that time a new dike made the island a peninsula, facilitating tourist access. Today the abbey is again home to a small community of monks—not Benedictines, but instead the *moines* (monks) and *moniales* (nuns) of the Brothers and Sisters of Jerusalem.

ABBEY & CRYPTS. The twisting road and ramparts end at the abbey entrance, but the steps continue to the **west terrace,** the entrance to the **abbey church** and departure point for five free 1hr. English tours daily in summer. (French tours every 30min. Mass daily 12:15pm; entry to the abbey church for the service only free noon-12:15pm.) The **church,** the most ornate portion of the abbey, spans an impressive 80m in length, thanks to ingenious planning over 1000 years ago. The interior's hodgepodge of architectural styles is the result of reconstruction following the collapse of half of the nave in 1103, the Romanesque choir in 1421, and 13 separate fires over the past 1000 years. The adjacent **cloister,** lined with small columns around an empty space, is the center of **La Merveille** ("the Marvel"), the 13th-century Gothic monastery. Beneath the church and the cloister are the Mont's frigid **crypts,** which can only be seen on 2hr. tours. The descent passes through the **refectory,** where the monks took their meals in silence as St. Benedict's rules were read. The **Chapelle St-Etienne,** below, was the chapel of the dead. Prisoners held on the Mont's **treadmill** during the Revolution walked on the wheel for hours, their labor powering an elaborate pulley system that carried supplies up the side of the Mont. Many actually volunteered for the grueling task, since it meant they got more food to keep them strong. The **crypte des gros piliers,** directly under the choir, was built at the same time; its pillars, 6m in circumference, were described by Victor Hugo as a forest of palm trees. The narrow abbey gardens, clinging to the side of the rock, surround the compound's exit. (☎02 33 89 80 00. Open May-Aug. 9am-7pm; Sept.-Apr. 9:30am-6pm. Last entrance 1hr. before closing. Closed Jan. 1, May 1, Nov. 1 and 11, and Dec. 25. €7, ages 18-25 €4.50; Oct.-Mar. first Su of the month free. A 2hr. conference tour with a guide (only in French) leaves once a day at 2pm (July-Aug. 4 times per day) and costs €4, ages 12-25 €3. Audio tour €4, or €5.50 for two sets of headphones.)

SPECTACLES. At night, the lit Mont is best seen either from the causeway entrance or from across the bay in Avranches. (Illumination nightly, 9-10pm in the summertime.) At night a separate entrance opens into the abbey, from which there is an unforgettable view of the heavens in pitch-black skies (though there is no public transportation off the Mont at night). (☎02 33 89 80 00. Mid-July to Aug. only. Call ahead to reserve. M-Sa 9pm-12:30am, last entrance 11:30pm. From 6-9pm in the gardens there is a musical performance. Admission same as above.) The **St-Michel d'Automne** festival, held on the Sunday before Michaelmas (September 14 in 2004), is a religious folk festival featuring costumed men and women parading through the streets.

BRITTANY
(BRETAGNE)

 Brittany's millennia-old Celtic heritage has withstood Paris's many efforts to Frenchify the province. The traditional costume of Breton women—a black dress and an elaborate white lace *coiffe* (headdress)—still appears in folk festivals and some markets, and lilting *Brezhoneg* is spoken energetically at pubs in the western part of the province, such as major port city **Brest** (p. 255) and **Quimper** (p. 261), a center of Breton culture. Historically important **Nantes** (p. 269), though quite far south, remains Breton in spirit. Once home to Gauls, Romans, and, finally, Britons fleeing from Anglo-Saxon invaders, Brittany's breathtaking landscape bears the imprint of its many settlers. In addition to the Neolithic stones of **Carnac** (p. 269), Brittany is home to the mysterious woodlands and moors of **Brocéliande Forest** (p. 238) where Arthur once roamed, a thousand-year-old fortress in **Fougères** (p. 238), a ruined abbey at **Paimpol** (p. 248), and a number of charming medieval villages (**Dinan,** p. 246; **Morlaix**, p. 250; and **St-Malo,** p. 239).

Despite heavy tourism, Brittany has largely retained its natural splendor, from the woodland streams of **Pont-Aven** (p. 265) that inspired a school of painters. This natural beauty is especially apparent on the misty isles off the coast: outdoorsmen and nature-lovers adore the flower-strewn island of **Ile d'Ouessant** (p. 259), the misty heather fields of **Belle-Ile** (p. 267), and the quiet, rocky beaches of **Ile de Batz** (p. 253). Excursions from Morlaix and rugged of **Quiberon** (p. 265) satisfy serious hikers and bikers. With sunny beaches and roaring college towns complementing this scenery, Brittany is a wildly popular vacation destination. St-Malo's stunning beaches are favorites of the beach-bum set, while those seeking great nightlife can't go wrong in student-populated **Rennes** (p. 231). During the low season, some coastal resorts such as St-Malo and Quiberon close down, but the churches, beaches, and cliffs become more eerily romantic.

Brittany's trademark buckwheat *galettes* envelop eggs, mushrooms, seafood, or ham; dessert crêpes feature chocolate, fruit, or jam. The freshest of *huîtres* (oysters) come from this area, as well as seafood of all kinds. A traditional Breton meal may be complemented by either cider or *muscadet*, the regional wine specialty.

RENNES

It would be easy to compare the sophistication of Rennes (pop. 210,000) to Paris, but such comparisons wouldn't do it proper justice. The throbbing heart of Brittany, Rennes has a well-earned reputation as the party mecca of northwest France, though it should not be dismissed as strictly a hedonists' haven. The cobblestoned *vieille ville*, filled with half-timbered houses, is as charming as any of France's small medieval towns. Rennes may not be Paris, but then again, you may not care.

▐ TRANSPORTATION

Trains: pl. de la Gare (☎02 99 29 11 92). Info and ticket office open M-Sa 8:45am-7:45pm, Su and holidays 11am-7:45pm. To: **Brest** (2-2½hr.; at least 1 per hr., all TGV; €27); **Caen** (3hr., 8 per day, €27.30); **Nantes** (1¼-2hr., 7 per day, €18.50); **Paris**

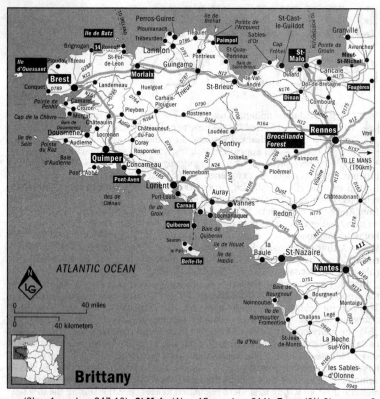

Brittany

(2hr., 1 per hr., €47.10); **St-Malo** (1hr., 15 per day, €11); **Tours** (2½-3hr., every 2-3hr., €29.50) via **Le Mans.**

Buses: 16 pl. de la Gare (☎02 99 30 87 80), to the right of the train station's north entrance. **Cars 35** (☎02 99 26 11 11) services **Dinan** (1¼hr.; M-Sa 6-7 per day, Su 3 per day; €8.70); **Fougères** (1hr.; M-F 10 per day, Sa 3 per day, Su 2 per day; €8.50); Paimpont, site of **Brocéliande Forest** (1¼hr.; M-F 3-4 per day, Sa 2 per day; €2.80); **St-Malo** (3hr.; M-Tu and Th-Sa 1 per day, W 2 per day, Su no service; €10). **Cariane Atlantique** (☎02 40 20 46 99, 08 25 08 71 56 in Nantes) goes to **Nantes** (2hr.; M 3 per day, Tu-Th and Sa 2 per day, F 4 per day; €15.70). **Anjou Bus** (☎02 41 69 10 00) goes to **Angers** (2½-3hr.; 3-4 per day; €15.90, express €19.80). **Les Courriers Bretons** (☎02 99 19 70 70) serves **Mont-St-Michel** (2½hr., 1-2 per day, €11.30).

Public Transportation: Star, 12 rue du Pré Botté (☎02 99 79 37 37). Office open M-Sa 7am-7pm. **Buses** daily 5am-8pm; lines through areas with busy nightlife run as late as midnight. Buy tickets on the bus, from the bus office, or at newsstands. A **metro** line runs through the heart of Rennes and accepts the same ticket. Dir: Kennedy runs from the train station to pl. de la République; dir: Poterie the other way (€1, *carnet* of 10 €8.40, 1-day pass €3).

Taxis: 4 rue Georges Dottin (☎02 99 30 79 79), at the train station. 24hr.

Bike Rental: Guedard, 13 bd. Beaumont (☎02 99 30 43 78) . €12 per day. Open M 2-7pm, Tu-Th 9am-12:30pm and 2-7pm, F 10am-7pm, Sa 9am-6:30pm. MC/V.

◢◣ 🛈 ORIENTATION & PRACTICAL INFORMATION

The **Vilaine river** separates the station in the south from most of the city's historic sights in the north. **Avenue Jean Janvier**, at the north exit of the station, runs through the town center; to reach the old city, take it across the river and turn left.

Tourist Office: 11 rue St-Yves (☎02 99 67 11 11; fax 02 99 67 11 10). From the station, take av. Jean Janvier to quai Chateaubriand. Turn left and walk along the river and through pl. de la République. Turn right on rue George Dottin, then right again on rue St-Yves. The office is on the right, just past the church on the corner. Free maps, directions, and lists of hotels, restaurants, and shops. **Accommodations service** (€1). Call in advance to reserve tours of the Parliament, the *vieille ville*, the Jardin du Thabor, or themed visits of historical houses (July-Aug. daily; Sept.-June 1-3 times per week; €6.10, students €3.10). Open Apr.-Sept. M-Sa 9am-7pm, Su and holidays 11am-6pm; Oct.-Mar. M-Sa 9am-6pm, Su and holidays 11am-6pm.

Hiking and Biking Information: France Randonnée, 4 rue Ronsard (☎02 99 26 13 56). Info on **GR trails.** Open M-F 10am-6pm, Sa 10am-1pm.

Consulates: US, 30 quai Duguay-Trouin (☎02 23 44 09 60; fax 02 99 35 00 92).

Youth Center: Centre Information Jeunesse Bretagne (CIJB), Champ du Mars, 6 cours des Alliés (☎02 99 31 47 48; www.crij-bretagne.com), has info on summer jobs. Free Internet (June-Aug. Tu-F 1-6pm; Sept.-May M and Th 1-9pm, W and F 1-6pm, Sa 2-6pm). Open Tu-F 10am-6pm, but hours change frequently.

English Bookstore: Comédie des Langues, 25 rue St-Malo (☎02 99 36 72 95; www.comediedeslangues.fr). Carries books in a variety of foreign languages; features a well-chosen selection of English fiction. Open M-Sa 9:30am-7pm.

Laundromat: 25 rue de Penhoet. Open daily 7am-8pm.

Police: 22 bd. de la Tour d'Auvergne (☎02 99 65 00 22).

Hospital: The most central of Rennes's hospitals is on Pontchailloux, past rue St-Malo.

Internet: Free at the Youth Center **(CIJB),** above. **Neurogame,** 2 rue de Dinan (☎02 99 65 53 85). €3 per hr., €1 minimum. Open M-Th 2pm-1am, F-Sa 2pm-3am. **Next Generation Cybercafé,** 36 rue d'Antrain (☎02 99 27 09 72), just past pl. du Maréchal Foch. €1 per 15min., €3.50 per hr. Open M-Sa 11am-8pm. **Online Station,** 5 quai d'Ille et Rance (☎02 99 14 23 93). €2 per hr. Open M-Sa noon-midnight, Su 2-11pm. **Cybernet Online,** 22 rue St-Georges (☎02 99 36 37 41). €0.80 per 5min., €3.80 per 30min, €6 per hr. Open daily 10:30am-10pm. Closed most of Aug.

Post Office: 27 bd. du Colombier (☎02 99 01 22 11), 1 block left of the train station exit. **Postal code:** 35032. **Branch** office, pl. de la République (☎02 99 78 43 35). From the station, walk up av. Jean Janvier and turn left onto the quai three blocks over. **Currency exchange** with 2.5% commission. **Western Union** at branch. Both open M-F 8am-7pm, Sa 8am-noon. **Postal code:** 35000.

🏠 ACCOMMODATIONS & CAMPING

Reserve ahead, especially for the first week of July, during the *Tombées de la Nuit* festival. Several moderately priced hotels are between quai Richemont and the train station. Most budget hotels, unfortunately, are not central.

▨ Au Rocher de Cancale, 10 rue St-Michel (☎02 99 79 20 83). This ancient half-timbered building houses charming, stylish rooms with shower and toilet, in the heart of the old quarter. Restaurant downstairs (*menus* €13-23). Breakfast €5.50. Reservations recommended, especially July-Aug. Doubles €34; triples €43. MC/V. ❸

Auberge de Jeunesse (HI), 10-12 rue St-Martin (☎02 99 33 22 33; rennes@fuaj.org). Simple beds on clean, color-coded floors. Kitchen, common room, cafeteria, and **Inter-**

net with *télécarte*. Discount bus fares to Mont-St-Michel and St-Malo. Breakfast included. Showers in all rooms; lockers in most. Bottom sheet and blanket provided, top sheet €2.80. Laundry. Wheelchair-accessible. Reception daily 7am-11pm. Doubles, triples, and quads €12.70 per person. MC/V. ❶

Hôtel Maréchal Joffre, 6 rue Maréchal Joffre (☎02 99 79 37 74; fax 02 99 78 38 51). Small, cheerful rooms with a little wear and tear. No front door lock. Breakfast €5. Reception 24hr. Closed last week of July and 1st week of Aug. Singles €22, with shower and toilet €31; doubles €22/€35.50; triples with shower, toilet, and TV €41. MC/V. ❷

Hôtel d'Angleterre, 19 rue Maréchal Joffre. (☎02 99 79 38 61; fax 02 99 79 43 85). One-star establishment with street or courtyard views, equidistant from the station and the center of town. Breakfast €5. Reception M-Sa 7am-10:30pm, Su 7am-noon and 6-10:30pm. Singles €23, with shower €32, with shower and toilet €36, with bath and toilet €37; doubles with shower €32-39, with toilet €36-43, with bath €37-44; triples €41/€35/€36. MC/V. ❷

Hôtel Venezia, 27 rue Dupont des Loges (☎02 99 30 36 56; fax 02 99 30 78 78). On an island in the Vilaine River. Unremarkable but comfortable rooms have spectacular views of the canal. Breakfast €5. Reservations recommended. Singles €25, with shower, toilet, and TV €29; doubles €30/€38. Extra bed €8. MC/V. ❷

Camping: Municipal des Gayeulles, in Parc des Gayeulles (☎02 99 36 91 22; www.ville-rennes.fr/camping). Take bus #3 (dir: St-Laurent) from pl. du Colombier (left of the train station) or pl. de la République to Piscine/Gayuelles (last bus midnight; M-Sa every 10min., Su every 40min.). Follow the path around the swimming pool on the right, with the deer park on the left, until reaching a paved road. Turn left and follow signs to the campground, deep within the Parc des Gayeulles (see **Excursions**). Reception daily mid-June to mid-Sept. 7:30am-1pm and 2-8pm; mid-Sept. to mid-June 9am-12:30pm and 4:30-8pm. Mid-June to mid-Sept. gates closed 11pm-7am; low season 10pm-7am. Laundry €2.30. €3.10 per person, €1.50 per child under 10. €1.50 per car. Electricity €2.60. Nov.-Mar. prices 10% lower. MC/V. ❶

🍴 FOOD

Cajun, African, Afghani, and Indian restaurants sit cheek by jowl on **rue St-Malo.** Inside the *vieille ville* there are more traditional *brasseries* and cheap kebab stands, though in general, the best food is on the outskirts of the city center. A huge **market** livens pl. des Lices. (Sa 6am-1pm.) Local **supermarkets** include **Champion** on the rue d'Isly near the train station (open M-Sa 9am-8pm), and **Marché Plus** at pl. Hoche (open M-Sa 7am-9pm, Su 9am-noon); there's another in the apartment complex on the left side of rue de St-Malo on the way from rue de l'Hôtel Dieu to the youth hostel. (Open M-Sa 9am-8pm.)

🍴 **Café Breton,** 14 rue Nantaise (☎02 99 30 74 95). As its name implies, this restaurant features an ever-changing menu of Breton cuisine in an upscale atmosphere reminiscent of a country kitchen. *Plats* €9.50-12; desserts €3.50-4. Open M and Sa noon-4pm, Tu-F noon-3pm and 7-11pm. ❸

Léon le Cochon, 1 rue Maréchal Joffre (☎02 99 79 37 54). Enticing local dishes and dried chili-pepper decorations fuse modern and traditional at this elegant restaurant. *Plats* €10-14. Open M-F noon-2:30pm and 8-11pm, Sa until 11:30pm, Su 8-11:30pm. July-Aug. Closed Su. MC/V. ❸

Le St-Germain des Champs (Restaurant Végétarien-Biologique), 12 rue du Vau St-Germain (☎02 99 79 25 52). This restaurant's chef-owners happily welcome guests to their popular organic kitchen and bamboo-accented dining room. Sandwiches €4, lunch *menu* €15, dinner *menu* €18. Open M-Sa noon-2:30pm and F-Sa 7-10pm. Closed Aug. MC/V. ❸

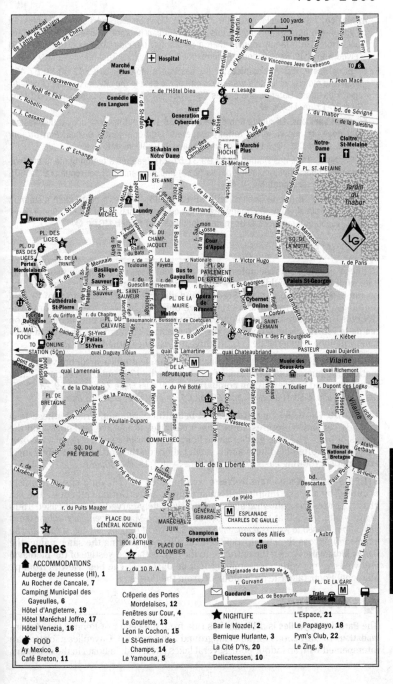

Rennes

ACCOMMODATIONS
Auberge de Jeunesse (HI), 1
Au Rocher de Cancale, 7
Camping Municipal des
  Gayeulles, 6
Hôtel d'Angleterre, 19
Hôtel Maréchal Joffre, 17
Hôtel Venezia, 16

FOOD
Ay Mexico, 8
Café Breton, 11
Crêperie des Portes
  Mordelaises, 12
Fenêtres sur Cour, 4
La Goulette, 13
Léon le Cochon, 15
Le St-Germain des
  Champs, 14
Le Yamouna, 5

NIGHTLIFE
Bar le Nozdei, 2
Bernique Hurlante, 3
La Cité D'Ys, 20
Delicatessen, 10
L'Espace, 21
Le Papagayo, 18
Pym's Club, 22
Le Zing, 9

BRITTANY

Ay Mexico, 7 rue de Juillet (☎02 99 31 67 02). Don't be shocked if someone whips out a guitar and bursts into song at this rowdy Mexican hotspot, whose controlled chaos feels more like a family reunion than a restaurant. Delicious standard fare (€11-13) served with style. Reservations recommended. Open nightly 7pm-midnight. MC/V. ❸

Crêperie des Portes Mordelaises, 6 rue des Portes Mordelaises (☎02 99 30 57 40). Below the old city walls, this *crêperie* is one of the best in the city, as queues of college-aged kids attest. *Galettes* and crêpes €3-7. Open M-Sa 11:30am-2pm and 6:30-11pm, Su 6:30-11pm. MC/V. ❶

Fenêtres sur Cour, 18 rue de Robien (☎02 99 36 13 26). Charming brick-walled restaurant near the hostel serves artfully prepared traditional bistro dishes. *Plat du jour* €7.50, *menu* €20. Open Tu-Sa noon-2pm and 7-10:30pm. MC/V. ❸

La Goulette, 3 rue des Dames (☎02 99 31 57 23), features a tempting menu of Mediterranean specialties, including *paëlla* (€12) and all manner of couscous (€9-12.50). Open nightly for dinner. MC/V. ❸

Le Yamouna, 16 rue de Robien (☎02 99 63 40 95). Rennes's best Indian restaurant has a traditional menu with many vegetarian options. Lunch *menu* €8.50, dinner *menu* €17, vegetarian *menu* €14. Open daily for lunch and dinner. MC/V. ❹

◉ SIGHTS

Rennes's *vieille ville* resembles the prototypical Western European medieval village. Half-timbered buildings, now filled with bars and pubs, pepper the old city, on **rue St-Georges** and in **place Ste-Anne** and **place St-Michel.** For a tour of the old buildings, turn left from the tourist office onto rue St-Yves, then right onto rue Georges Dottin, passing the buildings on rue du Chapitre. Pass the old buildings on **rue de la Psalette,** which becomes **rue St-Guillaume.** Turn left onto rue de la Monnaie, which becomes rue de la Cathédrale, to visit the Cathédrale St-Pierre.

MUSÉE DES BEAUX-ARTS. This eclectic museum features a small but varied collection. The jarring juxtapositions of pieces from the 17th and 20th centuries allow for unexpected and rewarding comparisons. *(20 quai Emile Zola. ☎02 99 28 55 85. Open Su-M and W-Sa 10am-noon and 2-6pm. €4, students €2, under 18 free.)*

JARDIN DU THABOR. One of the most beautiful gardens in France, these lush grounds contain sculptures, fountains, a carousel, a massive bird cage, and the "caves of hell." The rose garden alone holds 1700 varieties of the *fleur d'amour*. Concerts are often held here and a small gallery on the north side exhibits local artwork on a rotating basis. *(Open daily June-Sept. 7:15am-9:30pm.)*

OTHER SIGHTS. Cathédrale St-Pierre was founded in 1787 on a site previously occupied by a pagan temple, a Roman church, and a Gothic cathedral. The 5th chapel houses the cathedral's treasure: a delicately-carved, glass-encased 16th-century altarpiece that traces the life of the Virgin Mary. *(Open daily 9:30am-noon and 3-6pm. Closed to visitors during high mass Su 10:30-11:30am, July-Aug. also M and Su afternoon.)* Across the street, tucked in an alleyway bearing the same name, the **Portes Mordelaises,** once the entrance to the city, is the last vestige of the medieval city walls, along with the crumbling **Tour de Duchesne.** The best view is from pl. Maréchal Foch; take rue de la Monnaie from the Portes.

◪ EXCURSIONS

The **Parc des Gayeulles** is a 15min. bus ride from the center of Rennes (see **Accommodations** for directions to the campground and bus info). Gayeulles's forests are interspersed with an indoor pool, several lakes (with paddle-boats in the summer),

BRITTANY

sports fields, tennis courts, mini-golf, and a campground. Many walking paths and bike paths cut through the park. (Cyclers should check the maps posted in the park to be sure they're cycling legally.) The park is also home to a working farm and animal reserve. The farm, an instructional facility where local youngsters are taught about gardening, milking cows, and feeding horses, is open to children staying at the campground when accompanied by a parent. (☎02 99 36 71 73. Open July-Aug. M-F 9am-5:30pm; Sept.-June Tu and Th-F 4:30-6pm. Free.)

▣ NIGHTLIFE

After the sun sets (as late as 10:30pm in the summer), the city's population seems to double, and the partiers don't disappear until the sun rises. Much of the action centers around **place Ste-Anne, place St-Michel,** and the radiating streets, but don't just stop there—hot nightspots pervade the city, including a few great bars and *discothèques* to the south of the Vilaine. Two good places to begin nighttime revels are Bernique Hurlante and Bar le Nordzei, listed below.

BARS

▣ **Le Zing,** 5 pl. des Lices (☎02 99 79 64 60). 2 floors and 8 rooms fill with the young and the beautiful, who appear even more alluring under the flattering amber lights. DJ spins on the first floor. Beer €3 before midnight, €3.50 after. Cocktails €7.50. Open from 2pm; filled from around midnight until the crowd heads for the discos at 2am. MC/V.

Bernique Hurlante, 40 rue de St-Malo (☎02 99 38 70 09), welcomes a diverse crowd to its intimate, book-lined bar. Beer €2.20; punch €3.50. Open daily 4pm-1am.

Bar le Nordzei, 39 rue de Dinan (☎02 99 30 61 64), is a little out of the way but hosts live music the first Tu of the month. Beer €2.30. Open daily 11am-1am.

La Cité D'Ys, 31 rue Vasselot (☎02 99 78 24 84), is so staunchly Breton that regulars won't even speak French. 2 floors, adorned with Celtic knots and crosses, are linked by a twisting spiral staircase. Fabulous variety of traditional music nightly. Coreff €2.40. Open M-Sa 11am-1am.

Le Papagayo, 10 rue Maréchal Joffre (☎02 99 79 65 13). An unassuming *tapas* bar by day, this place becomes a party after dark—especially on tequila nights (tequila €1.50), when salsa music blares. Open M-Sa 8am-1am. MC/V.

CLUBS

▣ **Delicatessen,** 7 allée Rallier du Baty (☎02 99 78 23 41), one of Rennes's hottest clubs, around the corner from pl. St-Michel in a former prison, has swapped jailhouse rock for dance cages and electronic beats. Open Tu-Sa midnight-5am. Beer €5, after 2am €8. Cover after 1:30am Th-Sa €10, F-Sa €14.

Pym's Club, 27 pl. du Colombier (☎02 99 67 30 00). Look for the signs for Colombier, not Colombes, from pl. Maréchal Juin. Walk up the stairs to the platform. The club is located below a cinema. The poshest of Rennes's *discothèques;* Pym's 3 rooms and techno, house, and 80s hits draw a young crowd hellbent on having a raucous good time. One room, Le Salon, is exclusively for those 28 and under. Pym's is in an otherwise dark area, so it is wise to travel in a group when going to the club. Cover F-Sa €13, students before 1am €8, students after 1am €10; Su-Th €10, students €8. Open daily 11pm-5am; music stops at 4am.

L'Espace, 45 bd. La Tour d'Auvergne (☎02 99 30 21 95). From 2am on, a lively crowd fills the stage and dance floor of L'Espace, gyrating to the thumping house music blaring from the speakers. As with Pym's, L'Espace is located amid darkened storefronts on a poorly lit street; travel in a group for safety. Open Su-W midnight-4am, Th 11pm-4am, F-Sa 11pm-6am. Cover Su-F €9, Sa €10. For students €7; Su-Th before 1am free; Sa before 2am €8, after 2am €9.

🎵 📷 THEATRE & FESTIVALS

Contact Hebdo Le Guide-Loisirs, available at the tourist office, lists theater, dance, and classical music performances. For information on **Orchestre de Bretagne** concerts call ☎02 99 27 52 83.

The best-known of Rennes's summer festivals, **Les Tombées de la Nuit,** is a week-long riot of music, theater, mime, and dance (complete with a 14hr. traditional Breton dancefest) in early July (www.tdn.rennes.fr). The **Festival Transmusicales** fills the city in December, exhibiting local artists and international bands (www.transmusicales.com). March brings the **Festival Mythos,** a celebration of *contes* (tales), the spoken word, and oral tradition. April features the **Festival du Cinéma.** The tourist office has more information on all of the above.

🏃 DAYTRIPS FROM RENNES

BROCÉLIANDE FOREST

Brocéliande, 1hr. from Rennes, is enshrouded in legend, deeply tied to King Arthur and his knights. A 75km road through the forest passes Merlin's Tomb, the Fountain of Youth, the Valley of No Return, and the field where Lancelot confessed his forbidden love for Guenevere and stole the kiss that would ruin Camelot. Many of the forest's supposedly Arthurian structures are probably the remnants of stone-age megaliths (*à la* Stonehenge) dating from 3000 to 2000 BC; the stones are so worn that there's almost nothing there anymore. They're also fenced in and heavily touristed by myth-seekers. Magic emanates from the misty forests and moors, where some trees have lived 6000 years.

To get a real sense of the forest, visitors might want to camp or stay in a nearby *gîte.* The tourist office has a complete list. **Rent bikes** at Le Bar Brecilien, 1 rue Général Charles de Gaulle, behind the tourist office. Their selection is small and the bikes a little worn, but they can handle the paved roads and flat terrain of Brocéliande. (☎02 99 07 81 13. €3 per hr., €9 per half-day, €14 per day. Open July-Aug. daily 8am-8pm; Sept.-June closed M.)

Those in a hurry should try the 9km route (2-3hr.) to **Merlin's Tomb** and the **Fountain of Youth,** north of Paimpont. Those with an entire day to spend can continue to the alluring **Valley of No Return.** Lesser-known treasures lie in the small paths that veer off the pavement toward sun-splattered clearings or vast lakes.

TIV **buses** depart from Rennes (1hr.; M-F 3-4 per day, Sa 2 per day; €2.80) and stop in the village of **Paimpont,** in the middle of the forest. From the bus stop, turn around and walk back 200m in the direction from which the bus came. Before the road crosses the water, there is a sign for the "Syndicat d'Initiative" on the left. Turn left and proceed toward the old abbey ahead, now a Presbyterian church and town hall. The **tourist office** next to the abbey has info on bike and car routes and local accommodations, as well as maps of the forest. (☎02 99 07 84 23. Basic map free; hiking routes €4; complete road map recommended for serious hikers €8. 4hr. tours in French M-Tu, Th-F, and Su 2pm; W and Sa 10am-12:30pm and 2-6:30pm. €4.50-7 per person; reserve a spot by phone. July-Aug. guided car tours to major forest sites. Open Feb.-Dec. M-F 10am-noon and 2-5pm, Sa-Su until 6pm.)

FOUGÈRES

Atop a hill overlooking the pristine Nançon Valley, picturesque Fougères has been a center for feudal lords and a haven for artists. Today, it is a modern town with a perfectly preserved historic center and a breathtaking château. To reach the château from pl. Aristide Briand, turn left onto rue Porte Roger (near the tourist office) and head to the right of the fountain onto rue de la Pinterie, the main artery of the medieval city. Proceed downhill until the château appears ahead. Proceed directly to the castle, or make a detour into the garden immediately to the left.

Fougères's awe-inspiring ◾château sits on a promontory flanked by rock walls and the Nançon river. Its construction began around AD 1000 as part of a plan to reinforce the entire Breton duchy. The château fell into disrepair centuries later, but a number of architectural ingenuities remain standing. The behemoth **Tour Mélusine**, built by the Lusignans of Poitou to honor their half-human, half-snake ancestor, it stands 30m high, with 3m-thick walls and a dungeon to boot—peek through the trap door to check it out. (☎ 02 99 99 79 59. Open daily mid-June to mid-Sept. 9am-7pm; mid-Sept. to Oct. and Apr. to mid-June 9am-noon and 2-6pm; Nov.-Dec. and Feb.-Mar. 10am-noon and 2-5pm. French tours July-Aug., on the hr., 10-11am and 2-5pm. English tours leave 5min. later. €4.50, students €3.50, ages 10-16 €2, under 10 free. Low season prices lower. Clocktower €2.) Look for signs to the **Jardin Public**, which has breathtaking panoramic views of the château and surrounding countryside. The **Musée Emmanuel de la Villéon**, 51 rue Nationale, features over 100 paintings by one of the last Impressionists, including a few worthwhile gems. (Open mid-June to mid-Sept. daily 10am-12:30pm and 2-6pm. Admission free.) In summer the tourist office offers **Promenades Nocturnes**, historical tours of the city and château by night. (Mid-July to mid-Aug. Th-F at 8:30pm. €4, students €2. Departs from the tourist office.)

TIV buses (☎ 02 99 99 02 37) run from Rennes (1hr.; M-F 10 per day, Sa 4 per day, Su 2 per day; €8.50). Get off at Fougères Jean Jaurès for the historic center of the city; there's also a stop at the château. The main **bus terminal** (☎ 02 99 99 08 77) is at pl. de la République. From Fougères Jean Jaurès, walk downhill on bd. Jean Jaurès for 7min. until you reach the fountain in the center of the traffic circle. The terminal is on the left side of the fountain. (Office open M-Sa 9:30am-noon and 2-7pm.) **Les Courriers Bretons** (☎ 02 99 19 70 70; www.lescourriersbretons.fr) run from St-Malo (2¼hr., 2 per day, €12.50) via Pontorson (1hr., 2 per day, €7). To get to the **tourist office**, 2 rue Nationale, walk uphill on bd. Jean-Jaurès; at the traffic circle, continue straight uphill to the end of rue de Paris; pl. Aristide Briand will be on the right. Walk to the end of the *place* and turn left at the Marché Plus; the tourist office is ahead to the left of the Théâtre. (☎ 02 99 94 12 20; www.ot-fougeres.fr. Open July-Aug. M-Sa 9am-7pm, Su 10am-noon and 2-4pm; Sept.-June M-Sa 9:30am-12:30pm and 2-6pm, Su 1:30-5:30pm.)

ST-MALO

Scenic St-Malo (pop. 52,000) combines all the best qualities of France's northern cities. It has the most beautiful beaches outside of the Côte d'Azur, without the Côte d'Azur's pretension, as well as a charming walled *vieille ville*, and with countless *crêperies*, boutiques, and cafés.

▄ TRANSPORTATION

Trains: pl. de la Grande Hermine (☎ 02 99 40 70 20). Info office open daily 9:30am-7pm. Trains run, all via **Dol**, to: **Caen** (3½hr., 8 per day, €22.80); **Dinan** (1hr., 5 per day, €7.30); **Paris** (5hr., 3 per day, €49.60); **Pontorson** (45min., 5 per day, €6.50); **Rennes** (1hr., 8-12 per day, €10.70).

Buses: At espl. St-Vincent. Offices beside tourist office, pick-up across the street. **Tourisme Verney** (☎ 02 99 82 26 26) runs to: **Cancale** (30min., 3 per day, €3.40); **Dinard** (30min., 11 per day, €3.30); **Rennes** (1½hr.; M-F 4 per day, Sa 2 per day, Su 1 per day; €9.40). Purchase tickets on the bus. Office open July-Aug. M-Sa 8:30am-12:30pm and 1:30-7pm; Sept.-June M-F 8:30am-noon and 2-6:30pm, Sa 8:30am-noon. **Courriers Bretons** (☎02 99 19 70 80; www.lescouriersbretons.fr) goes to: **Cancale** (45min., 4 per day, €3.70) and **Mont-St-Michel** (1½hr.; M-Sa 4 per day, Su 3 per day; €9). Buses also stop at the hostel.

Tours in summer to **Fréhel** or **Dinan** (both 5hr., €15); **Ile de Bréhat** (full-day, €26); and **Mt-St-Michel** (half-day W and Th 1:45-6:15pm; full-day Tu and Sa 9:30am-6:15pm; €20.50; ages 4-11 €11; students, under 18, and over 60 at 10% discount.) Office open July-Aug. M-F 8:30am-6:30pm; Sept.-June 8:30am-12:15pm and 2-6:15pm.

Ferries: Gare Maritime de la Bourse. **Brittany Ferries** (☎02 99 40 64 41; www.brittany-ferries.fr) serves **Portsmouth** (9hr.; 1 per day in summer, less frequently in winter; €45). See **Getting There: By Boat,** p. 40, for details. **Condor Ferries** (☎02 99 20 03 00; www.condorferries.co.uk) travels to **Jersey** (70min.) and **Guernsey** (1¾hr.; 4 per day; round-trip €46, ages 4-15 €24, car €20). **Emeraude Lines** (☎02 33 18 01 80; fax 02 99 18 15 00; www.emeraudelines.com) runs to **Jersey** (70min., 3 per day, round-trip €45), **Guernsey** via Jersey (2hr., round-trip €55), and **Sark** via Jersey (2¼hr., round-trip €45) and has all-inclusive vacation packages. Reduced fares for ages 23 and under. Bikes €8-10 round-trip; call for car prices (around €55).

Public Transportation: St-Malo Bus (☎02 99 56 06 06), in the bus office pavilion. Buses run July-Aug. daily 8am-midnight; Sept.-June 8am-7pm. The tourist office and the hostel have free copies of the master map and schedule. Tickets €1.10 (valid 1hr.), carnet of 10 €7.80, 24hr. pass €3.20.

Taxis: Taxi Malovins (☎02 99 81 30 30) or **Taxi Daniel** (☎06 60 21 59 95). Stands at St-Vincent and the train station.

Bike Rental: Les Vélos Bleus, 47 quai du Duguay-Trouin (☎02 99 40 31 63), also has mountain bikes. €8-10 per half-day, €11-13 per day, €46-75 per week. €100-150 or passport deposit. Open Mar.-Nov. daily 9am-noon and 2-6pm. No credit cards.

Windsurfer Rental: Surf School St-Malo, 2 av. de la Hoguette (☎02 99 40 07 47). Along Grande plage, located about 1km away from the walled city (look for the sign). Rental €25.20 per hr., €40.40 per half-day. Lessons €30 per hr. Open daily 9am-noon and 2-6pm.

■✦❷ ORIENTATION & PRACTICAL INFORMATION

The small walled city *(intra-muros)* is the westernmost point of St-Malo and the heart of the shopping and restaurant district. The train station is closer to the uninteresting town center. The area from four blocks to the west of the train station down to the old city is prime beach territory.

Tourist Office: espl. St-Vincent (☎02 99 56 64 48; www.saint-malo-tourisme.com), near the entrance to the old city. From the train station, cross bd. de la République and follow espl. St-Vincent. (10min.) Or take bus #1, 2, 3, 4, or 6 (every 20min., €1.10) from bd. de la République to St-Vincent. From the *gare maritime,* turn left onto quai St-Louis. Free map (more detailed map €1) and list of accommodations. Open July-Aug. M-Sa 9am-7:30pm, Su 10am-6pm; June and Sept. M-Sa 9am-12:30pm and 1:30-7pm, Su 10am-12:30pm and 2:30-6pm; Oct.-Easter M-Sa 9am-12:30pm and 1:30-6pm; Easter-June M-Sa 9am-12:30pm and 1:30-7pm, Su 10am-12:30pm and 2:30-6pm.

Money: Exchange currency at **Banque de France,** rue d'Asfeld at the southeast corner of the walled city. Exchange desk open M-F 9am-noon.

Laundromat: 25 bd. de la Tour d'Auvergne. Open daily 7am-9pm.

Police: 5 av. Louis Martin (☎02 23 18 18 18).

Hospital: Centre Hospitalier Broussais, 1 rue de la Marne (☎02 99 21 21 21).

Pharmacy: Pharmacie Metel-Berhault (☎02 99 40 98 08). One of several *intra-muros;* others near the station. Open M-Sa 9am-noon and 2-7:30pm. MC/V.

Internet: Cyber L@n, 68 chausseé du Sillon (☎02 99 56 07 78). €2.50 per 30min., €4 per hr. Open M-Sa noon-1am and Su 3pm-1am. **Cyber'Com,** 26 bd. des Talards (☎02 99 56 05 83), on the left and across the street from the train station. €3.60 per hr. Open M 2-6pm, Tu-W 9am-noon and 2-6pm, Th 1-8pm, F 2-6pm, Sa 9am-noon and 2-5:30pm.

Post Office: 1 bd. de la Tour d'Auvergne (☎02 99 20 51 70), at the intersection with bd. de la République. Open M-F 8am-7pm, Sa 8am-noon. **Poste Restante:** 35401. **Postal code:** 35400. **Branch office,** pl. des Frères Lamennais (☎02 99 40 89 90). Open M-F 8:45am-12:15pm and 1:30-5:45pm, Sa 8:45am-noon. **Postal code:** 35402.

ACCOMMODATIONS & CAMPING

Reserve up to six months in advance to stay in the *vieille ville* in July and August. The extremely popular hostel doesn't take phone reservations; book by fax or letter—and well in advance—to stay there in summer. Aside from camping and the hostel, the best budget options are far and away Hôtel l'Avenir and Hôtel Neptune; beware of similarly outfitted options next to the train station, which run €10-15 higher and offer nothing special other than a sore wallet.

▨ **Les Chiens du Guet,** 4 pl. du Guet (☎02 99 40 87 29; fax 02 99 56 08 75). Any closer to the beach and you'd be swimming in your sleep. Overlooking the plage de Bon Secours, this charming hotel features bright rooms, elegant furnishings, and the lowest prices *intra-muros,* overseen by a charming Swiss proprietress. Breakfast €5. Closed mid-Nov. to Jan. Reserve 2-4 weeks in advance June-Aug. July-Aug. doubles €31, with shower €39, with shower and toilet €45; triples €34, with shower and toilet €56; quads €66. Low season prices reduced €5-6. AmEx/MC/V. ❸

Auberge de Jeunesse/Centre Patrick Varangot/Centre de Rencontres Internationales (HI), 37 av. du Révérend Père Umbricht (☎02 99 40 29 80; info@centrevarangot.com). From the train station, take bus #5 (dir: Paramé or Davier) or bus #1 (dir: Rothéneuf) to Auberge de Jeunesse (last bus 7:30pm). You can also take bus #1 (July to late Aug., 1 per hr. 8am-11:30pm) from St-Vincent or the tourist office. By foot, follow bd. de la République to the right from the station; turn right onto av. Ernest Renan. When it ends, turn left onto av. de Moka. Turn right on av. Pasteur, which becomes av. du Rév. Père Umbricht, and keep right at the sign say-

THE LOCAL LEGEND

BAD TIME TO BE AN ERMINE

One look at Brittany's curious black-and-white flag may conjure jokes of a bad copy of the Stars and Stripes. After all, it has bars (if only nine), and in the upper left-hand corner—not stars, and not nearly fifty, but something close enough. Designed in 1925 by Morvan Marchal, the flag is meant to be a symbol of unity for Brittany, no stranger to good old-fashioned identity crises. The five black bands represent the major cities of *Haute Bretagne* (Dol, Nantes, Rennes, St-Malo, and St-Brieuc), who speak a French dialect; and the four white bands are for the major cities of *Basse Bretagne* (Quimper, Tréguier, St-Pol de Léon, and Vannes), which speak the old tongue.

But what *are* those things in the corner? They represent the caped ermine, symbol of the king of Brittany. Legend has it that the first king encountered an ermine during a hunt and, taken by its beauty, pursued it to the edge of a bog. The animal ended the chase by pausing and turning to face the stunned king. The animal then proudly declared that it would rather die than soil its coat. Such gallantry left its impression on the king, who rewarded the ermine not by sparing its life (which, arguably, it would have preferred), but by insisting that its still unsoiled hide be placed before him at every meal.

ing "Auberge de Jeunesse." (30min.) The professional staff runs an enormous establishment popular with school groups and backpackers. Clean 2- to 6-person rooms with new furniture, sinks, and bathrooms. Tennis and basketball courts on premises. 3 blocks from the beach. Kitchen with individual refrigerators (€1.50). Laundry. After 10pm, guard in the neighboring Foyer des Jeunes Travailleurs can let you in. M-F meals €6.40. Reception 24hr. 4- to 6-person rooms with sink €12.60; 2- to 3-person rooms with shower €13; 2- to 5-person rooms with bunk beds, toilet, and shower €14.10; 2- to 3-person rooms with toilet and shower €15.30. Oct.-Apr. prices are €0.80 lower. Wheelchair-accessible. ❶

Hôtel Avenir, 31 bd. de la Tour d'Auvergne (☎02 99 56 13 33). Friendly owner provides simple, spotless rooms over a modest bar. Some second-story rooms over street may lack privacy. Breakfast €4. Doubles €20-21.50, with shower €24.50-26; triple with shower and toilet €45. No credit cards. ❷

Hôtel le Neptune, 21 rue de l'Industrie (☎02 99 56 82 15), on an empty street 5min. from both station and *intra-muros*, one block from the beach. Unremarkable hotel near the old and new parts of the city, recently renovated. Breakfast €5. Reception 8am-midnight. Singles and doubles with shower €28, with shower and toilet €31, with bath €33. Extra bed €8. MC/V. ❷

Camping Municipal La Cité d'Alet, at the western tip of St-Servan (☎02 99 81 60 91; www.ville-st-malo.fr/campings). Buses #1 and 6 run to Alet about twice per day (otherwise, take a bus to St-Servan and head northwest to Alet). From the bus stop, head uphill and bear left at the ruined 4th- to 10th-century Cathédrale St-Pierre onto allée Gaston Buy; the campground is 50m away. 350 spots in a quiet, scenic location. Reception daily July-Aug. 8am-9pm; Sept.-June 11am-noon and 2-7:30pm. Gates closed 11pm-7am. €5 per person, ages 2-7 €2.30. 2 people and tent €10, 2 people and caravan with electricity €14. ❶

🍴 FOOD

Skip the generic, overpriced restaurants huddled just within the entrances to the *intra-muros*. **Outdoor markets** (8am-12:30pm) are on pl. Bouvet in St-Servan, at the Marché aux Légumes *intra-muros* (Tu and F) and on pl. du Prieuré in Paramé (W and Sa). There is an underground **Marché Plus,** 9 rue St-Vincent, near the entrance to the city walls at Porte St-Vincent (open M-Sa 7am-9pm and Su 9am-1pm), and a **Champion** supermarket on av. Pasteur near the hostel. (Open M-F 8:30am-1pm and 3-7:30pm, Sa 8:30am-7:30pm, Su 9:30am-noon. Longer hours July-Aug.) Try the classy country interior of **La Brigantine ❷,** 13 rue de Dinan, where the savory *galettes* (€3-7) are stuffed to bursting and the sweet crêpes (€2-5) show off in-house recipes. (☎02 99 56 82 82. Open M and Th-F noon-3pm and 6-11pm, Sa-Su noon-11pm. MC/V.) The freshest market fare is given the traditional French bistro treatment at **Le Bistro de Jean ❹,** 6 rue de la Corne de Cerf, where the menu changes daily and there's always something interesting. (☎02 99 40 98 68. Starters €6.50-12; *plats* €15-18; desserts €6. Open for lunch and dinner M-Sa; closed W and Sa afternoon.) Sweet-toothed travelers will love the exotic flavors of homemade gelato at **Le Sanchez,** pl. du Pilori. (☎02 99 56 67 17. One scoop €1.60, two €2.50; truly decadent "Super Sanchez" a bargain at €4. Open daily about 11am-11pm.)

👁 SIGHTS

It's hard to go wrong with the beaches in St-Malo. On the western side of the *intra-muros*, best accessed by stairwells that lead down from the walls, the **plage de Bon Secours** is secluded (by St-Malo standards, at least) and features the curious **Piscine de Bon-Secours,** three cement walls that hold in a pool's worth of

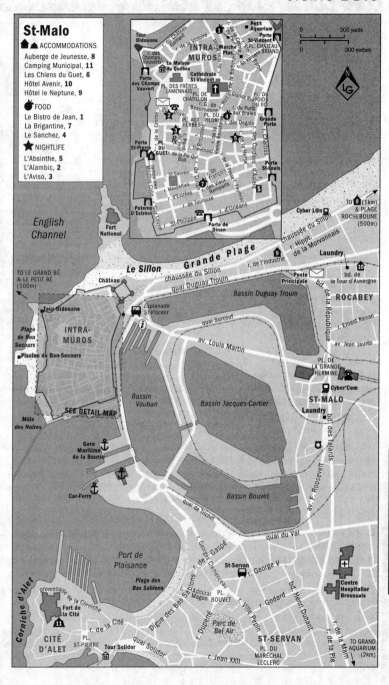

St-Malo

♦▲ ACCOMMODATIONS

Auberge de Jeunesse, **8**
Camping Municipal, **11**
Les Chiens du Guet, **6**
Hôtel Avenir, **10**
Hôtel le Neptune, **9**

🍎 FOOD

Le Bistro de Jean, **1**
La Brigantine, **7**
Le Sanchez, **4**

★ NIGHTLIFE

L'Absinthe, **5**
L'Alambic, **2**
L'Aviso, **3**

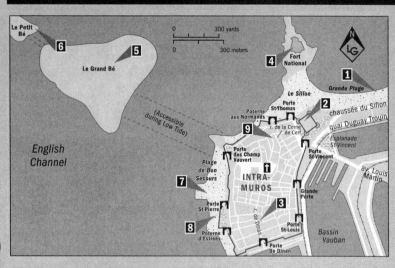

The most important tool for any excursion around sandy St-Malo is a good knowledge of the tides, which change every six hours. For this, pick up a tide chart at the tourist office. Go at the wrong time and half of the best sites will be guarded by a hundred meters of rollicking ocean.

START: Grande plage
FINISH: rue de la Corne de Cerf
DISTANCE: 4.2km/2.6 mi.
DURATION: 4-5hr.

◼ GRANDE PLAGE. St-Malo's bread-and-butter, Grande plage should be visited a couple hours or so after high tide, as the waves begin to recede. Take off your shoes and (France being France) perhaps more than that.

◼ CHÂTEAU. Farther down the stretch of sand of the Grande plage, the old château is now home to a modest museum.

◼ LA BRIGANTINE. The best Breton lunch in town is found at this *crêperie* in the *intra-muros*. (13 rue de Dinan. Open M and Th-F noon-3pm and 6-11pm, Sa-Su noon-11pm.)

◼ FORT NATIONAL. Once sated, double back toward this fort, which by now should be left bare by the tides and ready for a not-quite-nautical assault. (Open June-Sept. daily; Easter-May Sa-Su only. Hours vary with tides. €4, ages 6-15 €2.)

◼ LE GRAND BÉ. The newly exposed footpaths wend to this burial site of Chateaubriand.

◼ LE PETIT BÉ. This isolated gravesite, located a little farther on, completes the circuit of St-Malo's walkable islands.

◼ PLAGE DE BON SECOURS. Even if the tide's still out, you can soothe your sun-soaked skin in the quirkily innovative **Piscine be Bon-Secours,** a 10 ft. deep pool filled by the sea.

◼ RAMPARTS. Let the sun act as a hairdryer during a much-needed stroll around the city's impressive protection against invaders.

◼ LE BISTRO DE JEAN. Such a long day of dodging merciless tides and topless sunbathers will leave anyone hungry. This bistro is an excellent place to have a just dessert and a fine vintage wine. (6 rue de la Corne de Cerf. Open M-Sa for lunch and dinner, closed W and Sa afternoon.)

WALKING TOUR

warm salt water even when the tide recedes. To the east is the **Grande plage,** which is larger and slightly more crowded than most. Farther up the coast is the couple-filled **plage Rochebonne.**

The best view of St-Malo is from its **ramparts.** All entrances to the city have stairways leading up to the old walls. From the northern side of the city, you can see a series of small islands drifting out into the sea. The three largest, Fort National, Le Grand Bé, and Le Petit Bé, can be reached at low tide over a pebbly path strewn with stranded mollusks. **Fort National** (look for the French flag) was built in 1689 by the military's master architect, Vauban, to protect St-Malo from the English. It's not really worth paying for a tour of the empty, stony fortresses, except for the fabulous view of the bay and the city from the top. (☎02 99 69 03 17 or 02 99 85 34 44. Open June-Sept. daily; Easter-May Sa-Su only. Hours depend on the tides; call the tourist office for a schedule. Tours in French every 20min.; written explanations in English. €4, ages 6-15 €2.) The other two islands, west of the Fort and near the Piscine de Bon-Secours, are worth a visit for their strange rocky seclusion. **Le Grand Bé** holds the grave of native son **Chateaubriand** (1768-1848), who asked to be buried amid the wind and waves that inspired his books. "Bé" means "tomb" in Breton, and those who prefer theirs dry ought to heed the posted warnings not to set out for any of the islands if the tide is within 10m of the causeway.

The **Grand Aquarium** (not to be confused with the smaller aquarium *intra-muros*) displays an impressive marine bestiary hailing from Atlantic to Amazonian climes. The Nautibus gives visitors an up-close look, and the giant wraparound CineMerScope gets visitors close enough to the sharks to separate the real marine biologists from the chaff. Take bus #5 (dir: Moinerie or Grassinais) from the station, the tourist office, or the hostel; in summer special A line (€1.10) goes straight there from the tourist office. (☎02 99 21 19 00; www.aquarium-st-malo.com. Open daily July-Aug. 9:30am-8pm or 10pm; Apr.-June and Sept. 10am-7pm; Oct.-Mar. 10am-6pm. Closed Nov. 17-28 and Jan. 6-24. Last entry 1hr. before closing. €12, ages 4-17 €9.)

St-Malo native and Canada explorer Jacques Cartier is buried in the 12th-century **Cathédrale St-Vincent,** which has been carefully restored following heavy damage in WWII. Purists may disdain them, but the 20th-century altar and iridescent stained glass have an undeniable psychedelic allure. (*Open June-Aug. M-Sa 9:45am-6pm, Su 9:30am-6pm; Sept.-May closed noon-2pm.*) During July and August, the cathedral presents a series of classical and choral music concerts through the **Festival de Musique Sacrée.** (☎02 99 56 05 38, reservations ☎06 08 31 99 93.)

🎵 ENTERTAINMENT

🌟**L'Absinthe,** 1 rue de l'Orme, attracts a wildly varied clientèle to an equally varied interior, with everything from tatami-style tables to plush velvet couches. (☎02 99 40 85 40. Frozen margaritas €1.50 and €3.10. Open daily 3pm-2am; noon-1am in winter. Closed Su night low season.) **L'Alambic,** 8 rue du Boyer, looks like a brewery with its brass lamps, stone walls, and timbered ceilings, and draws a young crowd every night. (☎02 99 40 86 41. Open daily 10am-2am.) **L'Aviso,** 12 rue Point du Jour, sells 300 types of beer (starting at €2.60) and 12 whiskeys in a unique, hip take on the neighborhood corner bar. (☎02 99 40 99 08. Open daily 5pm-2:45am.)

St-Malo draws big crowds to its festivals. Travel and adventure writers come to the city in mid-May for **Etonnants Voyageurs,** the pre-eminent international literary festival in France. The **Festival des Folklores du Monde** attracts international folk musicians and dancers the first week of July. The **Route du Rock** draws 20 bands to the city during the second weekend of August. The **Quai des Bulles,** held the last weekend in October, lets you meet the creators of your favorite comic strips. The newly begun **Festival des Films de l'Eté** brings in 20 films, many of them French. (Late June; check www.festivaldesfilmsdelete.com for more information.)

DINAN

Dinan (pop. 10,000) leads two lives. Its *vieille ville*, imposingly lodged 66m above the river Rance, has all the charms of a well-preserved Breton medieval town, with cobblestone streets, traditional artisans and *crêperies*. But follow the steep slope down to the river and Dinan is a lush valley dotted with peaceful restaurants. Together, these two faces add up to one of Brittany's more appealing destinations.

▐ TRANSPORTATION

Trains: pl. du 11 Novembre 1918 (☎02 96 39 22 39). Office open M-Th 6am-7pm, F-Sa 7:10am-7pm, Su 9am-8pm. To: **Morlaix** (1½hr., 2-3 per day, €19.10) via St-Brieuc; **Paris** (3hr., 8 per day, €49.60); **Rennes** (1hr., 8 per day, €11.60); **St-Malo** (1hr., 7 per day, €7.30) via Dol.

Buses: CAT/TV buses (☎02 96 39 21 05) leave from the train station and pl. Duclos. Office open M-F 8am-noon and 2-6pm. To **St-Malo** (45min.; M-Sa 5 per day, Su 3 per day; €5.30). July-Aug. leads **tours** of **Mont-St-Michel** (1-2 per week, €18). **TAE** buses/**Cars 35** (☎02 99 26 16 00), leave from the station to **Dinard** (30min., 7 per day, €1.80) and **Rennes** (70min., 7 per day, €8.20).

Taxis: ☎02 98 39 06 00.

Bike Rental: Cycles Scardin, 30 rue Carnot (☎02 96 39 21 94). Bikes €12.20-14 per day, €73.20-84 per week. €150 deposit. Open Tu-Sa 9am-noon and 2-7pm. MC/V.

Canoe and Kayak Rental: Club de Canoë, 12 rue du Quai Talard (☎02 96 39 01 50), at Port de Dinan. Canoes €16 per half-day, €23 per day. Kayaks €13/€19. Passport deposit. Open Sa-Su in June; July-Aug. daily 10am-noon and 2-5:30pm.

✦ ▐ ORIENTATION & PRACTICAL INFORMATION

The road downhill from the Jerzual gate leads to the valley. To get to the **tourist office,** rue du Château, from the station, bear left across pl. du 11 Novembre 1918 onto rue Carnot, then right onto rue Thiers, which brings you to pl. Duclos. Turn left to go inside the old city walls, and bear right onto rue du Marchix, which becomes rue de la Ferronnerie. Pass the parking lots on pl. du Champ and pl. Duguesclin to your left; the tourist office is ahead on the right. The staff provides free walking tour map of city, a historical guide with circuits in the city and region (€2), a "Keys to the City" pass (€6) that gives access to Dinan's major sights, a **reservations service** (€2), and walking **tours** of the ramparts and the *intra-muros*. (☎02 96 87 69 76; www.dinan-tourisme.com. Open mid-June to mid-Sept. M-Sa 9am-7pm, Su 10am-12:30pm and 2:30-6pm; mid-Sept. to mid-June M-Sa 9am-12:30pm and 2-6pm. Tours Apr.-Sept. daily €5, children €2.50; in English July-Aug. Other services include: a **laundromat,** 19 rue de Brest, off rue Thiers on rue des Rouairies, which becomes rue de Brest (open M 2-7pm, Tu and Th 8:30am-noon and 2-7pm, W and F-Sa 8:30am-7pm), **police,** 16 pl. du Guesclin (☎02 96 39 03 02), near the château, a **hospital,** rue Chateaubriand (☎02 96 85 72 85), in Léhon, **Internet** at Aerospace Cybercafé, 9 rue de la Chaux, off rue de l'Horloge. (☎02 96 87 04 87. €1.50 per 15min. Open Tu-Sa 10am-12:30pm and 1:30-7pm.) The **post office,** pl. Duclos, has currency exchange. (☎02 96 85 83 50. Open M-F 8am-6:30pm, Sa 8am-noon.) **Postal code:** 22100.

▐ ACCOMMODATIONS & CAMPING

The best place to **camp** is at the hostel in a shaded field behind the main building (€4). The tourist office lists other, more urban sites.

Auberge de Jeunesse Moulin du Méen (HI), (☎02 96 39 10 83; dinan@fuaj.org), slightly outside town in Vallée de la Fontaine-des-Eaux. Turn left from the train station, turn left across tracks, then turn right and follow tracks and signs downhill for 1km. Turn right and continue through wooded lanes (be careful, as there is no sidewalk) for ½km until you reach the hostel on the right. (30min.) Beautiful old stone house by a brook. Small, clean 2- to 8-bed rooms. Summer photo workshops and equestrian activities. Breakfast €3.20, dinner €8. Kitchen access. Lockers. Sheets €2.70. Laundry. Reception 8am-noon and 5-8pm. Curfew 11pm. Beds €8.50. ❶

Hôtel de la Tour de l'Horloge, 5 rue de la Chaux (☎02 96 39 96 92; perso.wanadoo.fr/hotel-latourdelhorlage). Exceptionally spacious and colorful rooms in the shadow of the Tour de l'Horloge, all with bath and toilet. Breakfast €6. Doubles with either large bed or two single beds €42-77. AmEx/MC/V. ❹

Hôtel du Théâtre, 2 rue Ste-Claire (☎02 96 39 06 91), above quiet bar of same name, has bright rooms, some with large windows, in the heart of the *vieille ville*. Cheaper top-floor rooms are a bit cramped. Breakfast €4. One single with sink €14.50; doubles €20.50-22, with shower and toilet €27-36. No credit cards. ❶

Hôtel de la Gare, pl. de la Gare (☎02 96 39 04 57; fax 02 96 39 02 29), across from the station, 10min. from the historic quarter. Friendly owners rent simple, bright, clean rooms over a corner bar. Breakfast €4.60. Shower €1.60. Singles €22; doubles €24, with shower and TV €27; triples or quads with shower, TV, and toilet €40. MC/V. ❷

🄵 FOOD

Simple bars and *brasseries* line the streets linking rue de la Ferronnerie with pl. des Merciers, especially on narrow **rue de la Cordonnerie. Monoprix** supermarket is on rue du Marchix. (Open M-Sa 9am-7:30pm.) There is also a **Marché Plus,** 28 pl. Duclos, near the post office. (☎02 96 87 50 51. Open M-Sa 7am-9pm, Su 9am-1pm.) Buy a picnic of fruit and crêpes at the outdoor **market** on pl. du Champ and pl. du Guesclin in the *vieille ville*. (Open Th 8am-noon.) Small restaurants cluster in the cobbled streets outside the ramparts and along the port. Within the walls of the old town, you'll need to beat the *crêperies* off with a stick. The **Crêperie des Artisans ❶,** 6 rue Petit Fort, on the charming street that leads down to the river, has a rustic atmosphere. (☎02 96 39 44 10. Crêpes €4-7. Open July-Aug. daily; Apr.-Oct. Tu-Su. Hours vary.) Right around the corner from the Tour de l'Horloge, **Taj Mahal ❸,** 9 rue Ste-Claire, serves authentic Indian delights, including plenty of vegetarian options. (☎02 96 85 45 30. *Menus* €16-20, *plats* €8-12. Open daily for lunch and dinner. MC/V.)

🄶 SIGHTS

The city walls, and the churches and houses within, are a sight unto themselves.

The **⬛Maison d'Artiste de la Grande Vigne,** 103 rue du Quai, past the port, is the former home of painter Yvonne Jean-Haffen (1895-1993). Reaching it entails a long but pleasant walk from the town through Jerzual gate, down the steep rue du Petit Fort, and left along the rue du Quai, which takes you down into the city's picturesque valley. The house is a work of art: Jean-Haffen's paintings adorn the walls, and the garden outside is an artist's dream. (☎02 96 87 90 80 or 02 96 39 22 43. Open daily May 2-6pm; June-Sept. 2-6:30pm. €2.50, students and ages 12-18 €1.60.)

On the ramparts, the 13th-century **Porte du Guichet** is the entrance to the **Château de Dinan.** Its former keep in the Tour de la Duchesse Anne houses a small museum of local art and history. A great view of the town greet those who make it up the 150 steps of the 34m tower. On the same ticket is the 15th-century **Tour de Coëtquen,** next to the keep. Along with the occasional temporary exhibit, its dank,

BRITTANY

drafty basement possesses a fine collection of funerary ornaments. (*Open June-Sept. daily 10am-6:30pm, last entrance 6pm; Oct. to mid-Nov. and mid-Mar. to May Su-M and W-Sa 10am-noon and 2-6pm; mid-Nov. to Dec. and early Feb. to mid-Mar. Su-M and W-Sa 1:30-5:30pm. €3.90, ages 12-18 €1.50.*) The **Jardin du Val Cocherel**, on the ramparts far from the château, begins hilly, twisting, and dense, but gives way to huge bird cages, a rose garden, a checkerboard for life-sized chessmen, a small zoo, and a children's library. (*Garden open daily 8am-7:30pm. Library open daily 10am-noon and 1:30-6:30pm.*)

The **Basilique St-Sauveur** was built by a local man grateful to have been spared in the Crusades. The Romanesque façade, including the lion and bull above the doorway and the four statues in the side arches, dates to AD 1120. Within is the heart of the unfortunate Bertrand du Guesclin, perhaps the only Frenchman to have five tombs, for various body parts.

The **Eglise St-Malo**, on Grande Rue, contains a remarkable 19th-century organ with blue and gold pipes and a massive Baroque altar. The 30m 15th-century **Tour de l'Horloge**, on rue de l'Horloge, commands a brilliant view of Dinan's jumbled streets and the countryside. On the way up, you'll pass through the stone rooms that once held the town archives, now a museum of Arthurian legend and lore. (☎ 02 96 87 02 26. *Open June-Sept. daily 10am-6:30pm. €2.50, ages 12-17 €1.60.*)

🎵🎭 ENTERTAINMENT & NIGHTLIFE

L'Absinthe, 15 place St-Sauveur, feels like an old-fashioned speakeasy, except for the sunny, inviting porch on its doorstep. The soft jazz music and piano give it an air of sophistication. (☎ 02 96 87 39 28. Beer €2. Open M-Sa 9am-10pm.)

Every two years (next in 2004), Dinan hosts the two-day **Fête des Remparts** during the second half of July, when the whole town dons medieval garb for jousting tournaments, markets, and merrymaking. (☎ 02 96 87 94 94; http://perso.wanadoo.fr/fete-remparts.dinan. €15 per day for access to all activities, those under 12 or in medieval garb free. Daily 11am-9pm.)

PAIMPOL

Anchored on the border of the Côte de Granite Rose and the Côte de Goëlo, Paimpol (pronounced "PAM-pol;" pop. 8200) is a pretty little fishing village. While its traditional ties are to the rod and reel, a string of snazzy bars, restaurants, and yachts brings a lively modern flair. Paimpol itself has few sights, but it provides easy access to the surrounding islands, cliffs, beaches, hiking trails, and the picturesque ruins of Abbaye de Beauport.

🚊🛈 TRANSPORTATION & PRACTICAL INFORMATION

Trains leave from av. du Gal. de Gaulle to **Pontrieux** (18min., 4 per day, €2.70). At Guingamp (☎ 02 96 20 81 22), there are connections to **Morlaix** (1¼hr., 4 per day, €12). (Office open M-Sa 6:40-7:10am and 8am-7pm, Su and holidays 9am-7pm.) CAT **buses** (☎ 02 96 22 67 72) run from the train station to **Pointe de l'Arcouest** (15min.; M-Sa 7 per day, Su 5 per day; €1.80.) The same bus system runs throughout the Côtes d'Armor and to the campground. Buy tickets on the bus. **Bikes** can be rented at **Cycles du Vieux Clocher,** pl. de Verdun. (☎ 02 96 20 83 58. €6 per half-day, €11 per day. Open M-Sa 8:30am-12:30pm and 2-7:30pm, Su 8am-noon.Visa.)

To reach the port and the **tourist office** on place de la République, turn right onto av. du Général de Gaulle and follow it to the roundabout, then bear left. The tourist office will be on the left, opposite the Marché Plus; the port will be to the right. The jolly tourist office staff provides a map of the hiking trails leading from Paimpol to the Pointe de l'Arcouest. Pick up *La Presse d'Armor*, a local publication with a schedule of events (€1), at a newsstand. (☎02 96 20 83 16; www.paimpol-goelo.com. Open June-Sept. M-Sa 9:30am-7:30pm, Su 10am-6pm; Oct.-May M-Sa 9:30am-12:30pm and 1:30-6:30pm.) Other services include: **currency exchange** at the Société Générale, 6 pl. de la République (☎02 96 20 81 34), **police** at rue Raymond Pellier (☎02 96 20 80 17), a **hospital** at chemin de Malabry (☎02 96 55 60 00), off the right side of the port, and **Internet** at Cybercommune, Centre Dunant, near the church. (☎02 96 20 74 74. €0.09 per min., €5.40 per hr. Open M-F 3-8pm, Tu-W also 9am-12:30pm.) Do **laundry** or rent sheets at Au Lavoir Pampolais, 23 rue du 18 Juin, near the station. (☎02 96 20 96 41. Open daily 8am-8pm. Also near the port on rue de Labenne. Open daily 7am-10pm.) The **post office,** av. du Général de Gaulle, has **currency exchange.** (☎02 96 20 82 40. Open M and W-F 8am-noon and 1:30-5:30pm, Tu 8am-12:30pm and 1:30-5:30pm, Sa 8am-12:30pm.) **Postal code:** 22500.

▐▌ ACCOMMODATIONS

Relatively identical options crowd the port area. The cheapest stay in the center of town is also one of the nicest: **Hôtel Le Goëlo ❸**, quai Duguay Trouin, with modern, comfortable rooms, some overlooking the port. From the tourist office, walk toward the water and take the first right; the hotel is just ahead. (☎02 96 20 82 74. Breakfast €4.60. Singles €25, with shower and toilet €31; doubles with shower and/or toilet €34-42; triples with toilet and bath or shower €54. MC/V.) Another good bet is **Hôtel Berthelot ❸**, 1 rue du Port. From the tourist office, walk straight toward the port and turn left after three blocks onto rue du Port. A blue "H" marks the hotel's entrance on the right. The hotel employs a friendly reception staff and offers large, comfy rooms with big windows. (☎02 96 20 88 66. Breakfast €4.40. Singles and doubles €26, with toilet €28, with bath €37, with TV €39. MC/V.) **Le Terre-Neuvas ❸**, quai Duguay-Trouin, on the waterfront, over the restaurant of the same name (see **Food**), has small, welcoming rooms, some with harbor views. (☎02 96 55 14 14; fax 02 96 20 47 66. Breakfast €5. Call ahead in summer. Doubles with shower and toilet €31, with harbor view €37; triples €39/€45. MC/V.)

   The **Auberge de Jeunesse (HI) ❶**, Château de Kéraoul (☎02 96 20 83 60), 20min. uphill on the western edge of town, will be closed until 2005 for massive renovations. The popular seaside **Camping Municipal de Cruckin ❶**, off the plage de Cruckin, is by the Abbaye de Beauport. From the station, turn right onto av. du Gal. de Gaulle and take the third exit at the roundabout onto rue du Gal. Leclerc. Follow the street as it twists through four name changes and take rue de Cruckin from rue du Commandant le Conniat. The entrance is 150m down the hill on the right. (25min.) Wheelchair-accessible. (☎02 96 20 78 47. Reception M-Sa 8am-noon and 4:30-8pm; Su 9-11am and 6:30-7:30pm. Gates closed 10pm-7am. Open Apr.-Sept. One person and tent €7.50; 2 to 3 people and tent €12.20. Extra person €2.90. Electricity €2.40-2.90. Prices slightly lower Apr.-June and Sept.)

▐▌ FOOD

Picnickers can find supplies at both the Tuesday morning **market,** held in squares throughout the town, and the **Marché Plus,** rue St-Vincent, located directly across from the tourist office. (Open M-Sa 7am-9pm and Su 10am-noon.) For sit-down fare, those who don't like seafood may be at a loss in Paimpol. **La Braise ❹**, 20 rue des 8 Patriots, exudes a homey kitchen feel in its upstairs dining room while serving high-quality grilled seafood and meat dishes, including Breton duck. (☎02 96 55 11 41. *Menus* €16 and €22. Open daily noon-2pm and 7-10pm. MC/V.) Portside **Le Terre-Neuvas ❷**, quai Duguay-Trouin, serves elegant food at backpacker prices. The specialties of the house are *moules frites* (€7.50, with appetizer and dessert €13). In July and August, five *grandes assiettes gourmandes* are served with

BRITTANY

grilled and seasoned bread, the catch of the day, salad, vegetables, and a side dish for only €9-12. (☎02 96 55 14 14. Open July-Aug. daily noon-2pm and 7-10pm; Sept.-June closed M. MC/V.)

🗗 SIGHTS

Hidden from the road by vegetation, the ruins of the ⬛**Abbaye de Beauport,** chemin de l'Abbaye, look dreamily out to sea. Built in 1202, the abbey, east of Paimpol, has been revamped for its 800th anniversary. The now-roofless church sprouts flowers from its flying buttresses, and birds flutter where rafters used to be. The crumbling building gives the sense of an undiscovered ruin. Arrive early to catch the abbey in the beauty of the morning sun and to avoid crowds. The book-guided self-tour (in French, English, or German) gives a complete account of the many other portions of the abbey, from the intact cellars to the picturesque garden. To get there, follow directions to the campground, but continue past rue de Cruckin to the next major left turn; the abbey is at the end of the lane. (☎02 96 55 18 58; www.abbaye-beauport.com. Open daily mid-June to mid-Sept. 10am-7pm; mid-Sept. to mid-June 10am-noon and 2-5pm. English tours July-Aug. daily 11am; 3-4 tours in French per day. €5, students and seniors €4.50, ages 11-18 €3.50, ages 5-10 €2.50.)

🗗 🗗 NIGHTLIFE & FESTIVALS

The port is boxed in by bars and restaurants, where it's overrun by private yachts. The sidestreets that trickle away from the waterfront have the real gems. As the sun sets, the crowds head across the port to bars along quai de Kernoa. Just around the corner from Hôtel Berthelot, ⬛**Le Corto Maltese,** 11 rue du Quai, earns its popularity among locals with its good music, laid-back atmosphere, interesting selection of various Dutch and Irish beers on tap, and two old-school pinball machines in the back. (☎02 96 22 05 76. Beer under €3. Open daily 5pm-2am.) The heavy oak door of **Le Pub,** 3 rue Islandais, can't contain the revelry into the early hours. Occasional live music spices up the atmosphere. (☎02 96 20 82 31. Open June-Sept. daily 7pm-3am; Oct.-May Th-Sa 7pm-3am, Su 10pm-3am.) **Le Cargo,** 15 rue des 8 Patriotes, sits streetside with unusual aplomb, unafraid to wear plaid with its chunky wooden tables. (☎02 96 20 72 46. Open Su-Th 12:30pm-1am, F-Sa 12:30pm-2am.) For a true Breton dockside pub atmosphere, the **Tavarn An Tri Martolod** (Tavern of the Three Sailors), 11 quai de Kernoa, cannot be topped. (☎02 96 20 75 15. Beer €2. Open July-Aug. Su-Th 11am-1am, F-Sa 11am-2am; Sept.-June Su-M and W-Sa 11am-1am.)

The August **Festival du Chant de Marin** draws sailor-musicians from around the world for three days of dancing, boating, and general merriment (☎02 96 55 12 77).

MORLAIX

Morlaix (pop. 17,000) traces its origins back to Gallo-Roman times, when Armorican Celts built a fort here called "Mons Relaxus" (Mount of Rest). Ironically, the town did not see much rest during its tumultuous history: it was continually invaded during the Middle Ages by the Duchy of Brittany, the French crown, and the British, all of whom sought to control Morlaix's enviably located port. The city got its modern name after British invaders successfully captured the port, and the town's angry citizens surprised them in their drunken excess with cries of "S'ils te mordent, mords-les!" ("If they bite you, bite them back!"). History looms large over Morlaix in the form of the impressive two-tier viaduct above the city, but the fast-paced town refuses to live in its shadow. Although small and pleasantly untouristed, Morlaix has the busy cafés, crêperies, and bars of a big city.

▛ TRANSPORTATION

Train Station: rue Armand Rousseau (☎08 36 35 35 35). Info office open M 4:30am-10:30pm, Tu-Sa 5am-10:20pm, Su 8am-midnight. To: **Brest** (45min., 8-10 per day, €8.40); **Paimpol** (1¼hr., 5 per day, €12.20); **Quimper** via **Landerneau** (2hr., 5-7 per day, €15.40); **Roscoff** (30min., 2 per day, €4.70).

Buses: SNCF also leaves from the train station for **Roscoff** (30-45min., 4 per day, €4.60). **CAT** (☎02 98 72 01 41) runs to: **Quimper** (2hr., 3-5 per week, €10); **Roscoff** (30-45min.; M-Sa 3-4 per day, Su 1 per day; €7.20). Buses also run from the Morlaisiennes stop, in front of the Monoprix on rue d'Aiguillon, or at the station.

Public Transportation: TIM, pl. Cornic (☎02 98 88 82 82). Tickets €.90, *carnet* of 10 €8.40. Buses run 7:30am-7pm.

Taxis: Radio Taxis (☎02 98 15 12 73) are usually at pl. des Otages and the station.

◢▗ ORIENTATION & PRACTICAL INFORMATION

All roads run downhill from the station to the city center. There are three ways to get there. Most direct route is to go down **rue Courte,** also known as the Cent Marches, which is actually a long, winding stairwell. From the station, walk straight on **rue Gambetta** for 100m and turn left onto the stairs, which lead directly to the central **place Emile Souvestre.** The **rue Gambetta** (walk straight from the station; it eventually curves back toward the opposite direction it begins in) and the steep **rue Longue** (the next road to the left after rue Courte) wind up in the same place. To get from the station to the **tourist office,** follow the directions above to pl. Emile Souvestre. Turn left and you will shortly be in **place des Otages.** The tourist office is the free-standing brown building across the *place,* in front of the viaduct.

Tourist Office: pl. des Otages (☎02 98 62 14 94; officetourisme.morlaix@wanadoo.fr). Pick up maps and a complete city guide. Tours of the city in French July-Aug. Th at 2:30pm. Open July-Aug. M-Sa 10am-noon and 2-7pm, Su 10:30am-12:30pm; Sept.-June Tu-Sa 10am-noon and 2-6pm.

Laundromat: 4 rue de Lavoirs or pl. Charles de Gaulle. Both open daily 8am-8:30pm.

Police: 17 pl. Charles de Gaulle (☎02 98 88 17 17).

Hospital: Hôpital Général, 15 rue Kersaint Gilly (☎02 98 62 61 60).

Internet: Cyber @rena, rue Basse, past pl. Allende. €4.50 per hr. Open M-Th 11am-midnight, F-Sa 11am-1am, Su 2pm-1am. **Le Millenium Café,** 9 rue Gambetta (☎02 98 63 99 78), just off pl. Emile Souvestre at the bottom of rue Courte. €2.30 per 30min., €3.80 per hr. Open Tu-F 8am-8pm, Sa 1pm-1am.

Post Office: 15 rue de Brest (☎02 98 88 93 22), off pl. Emile Souvestre. **Currency exchange** and **Cyberposte.** Open M-F 8:30am-6:30pm, Sa 8:30am-noon. **Postal code:** 29600.

▛ ACCOMMODATIONS

Morlaix no longer has a hostel and budget options are in short supply. Ask the tourist office about local *gîtes d'étape* (around €8) or *chambres d'hôte* (€15-30).

Hôtel Le Roy d'Ys, 8 pl. des Jacobins (☎02 98 63 30 55). Historic building near the town center. Follow directions to pl. Emile Souvestre; head straight on rue Carnot, which is to the right; follow to the end and turn right on rue au Fils to pl. des Jacobins. Brightly decorated, spacious rooms fitted with stained glass, above a bar frequented by locals, some overlooking the *place.* Doubles with shower and/or toilet €30.60. MC/V. ❸

BRITTANY

THE HIDDEN DEAL

CHAMBRES D'HÔTE

Found amid fragrant lavender fields, within majestic châteaux, or even nestled neatly in the heart of a city, France's *chambres d'hôte*, or bed and breakfasts, provide an opportunity to stay with local families. Organized through the **Gîtes de France**, *chambres d'hôte*, or *ferme auberges* if they are located on a working farm, provide a more intimate option than most hotels.

Although often off the beaten path, many of the slightly more expensive *chambres* and *fermes* offer *tables d'hôte* as well, where guests are served a full French-style dinner with the hosts and other guests, from apéritif to *fromage*. If the tranquil location and the home-cooked meals are not enough of a draw, *chambres d'hôte* offer visitors the opportunity to better understand the people and culture of a specific region. Guests are encouraged to meet the hosts and other guests. A communal dinner can easily slip into a long conversation about local politics, family, or local delicacies. Many hosts serve regional cuisine, such as home-made jam and honey from the beekeeper down the road. Tourist offices usually have extensive listings of the various *chambres d'hôte* and *tables d'hôte* in the region. For those seeking a first-hand taste of French culture and daily life, these unique lodging opportunities are the ideal way to live *la vie française*.

Hôtel de la Gare, 25 pl. St-Martin (☎02 98 88 03 29; fax 02 98 63 97 80), on rue Gambetta south of the train station, across the street from the top of rue Courte. In a quiet location with quick access to the center of town via the Cent Marches, this hotel has large, clean rooms with futon-like mattresses, and spare but pretty furniture. All rooms with shower and TV. Breakfast €6. Reception M-F 7am-10pm, Sa 8am-10pm, Su 10am-10pm. Singles €35, with toilet €38; doubles €38/€42. MC/V. ❸

Camping à la Ferme, in Croas-Men (☎/fax 02 98 79 11 50; croasmen@wanadoo.fr), is worth the 7km walk. From the center of town, follow signs first to Plouigneau, then to Garlan. The campsite will be past Garlan on the left. The owners, third-generation farmers, want campers to love the farm as much as they do. To this end, they offer breakfast in the 1840s farmhouse, a petting farm, tractor rides for kids, and fresh yogurt and cider for a modest price. Reception 8am-10pm; gates open 24hr. Open Apr.-Oct. €4 per site, €2.50 per person, children under 7 €2. Electricity €2.50. Pets €0.80. ❶

☕ FOOD

An all-day food and crafts **market** stretches from pl. des Otages to pl. Allende (Sa). A **Marché Plus** supermarket is on rue de Paris. (Open M-Sa 7am-9pm, Su 9am-noon.) Comforting **Ar Bilig ❷,** 6 rue au Fil, stands out in a city stuffed to the gills with indistinguishable *crêperies*. A warm, friendly couple prepares a generous *menu* of a *galette* and two sweet crêpes for €8. (☎02 98 88 50 51. Open July-Aug. daily 11:30am-3pm and 6:30-10pm, closed Su for lunch. Sept.-June Tu-Sa 11:30am-2pm and 6:30-9pm. MC/V.) The restaurant **La Marée Bleue ❹,** 3 rampe St-Melaine, just off pl. des Otages near the tourist office, serves the swankiest meals in town, featuring a delectable variety of fresh fish, in a friendly environment. (☎02 98 63 24 21. *Menus* €19, €28, and €36. Open Tu-Sa noon-1:30pm and 7-9:30pm, Su 7-9:30pm. MC/V.)

👁️ 🎵 SIGHTS & ENTERTAINMENT

The **Circuit des Venelles,** an organized walking tour through medieval Morlaix, is the best way to see the city's ancient attractions. The steep, sometimes stairwayed alleys *(venelles)* were the city's main thoroughfares in medieval times. They lead past all of Morlaix's main sights, including the churches, wooden architecture, and views. The tourist office has a map of the circuit, as well as theatrical tours of the *venelles* in summer.

The **viaduct,** 58m high and 285m long, is Morlaix's most visible sight. Though the airy walkway is now closed to the public, sightseers can still get a good view of steep, near-vertical Morlaix from its gates. **La Maison de la Duchesse Anne,** across pl. Allende on rue du Mur, commemorates the Queen's 1505 visit to the city. The house is a prime example of a Morlaisienne *maison à pondalez,* or lantern house. (☎ 02 98 88 23 26. Open M-Sa 11am-6pm. €1.60, ages 10-18 €0.80, under 10 free.) The collection at the **Musée des Jacobins,** in the 13th-century Jacobin church on pl. des Jacobins, mixes traditional Bretonalia like carved *lits-clos* (cabinet-like beds) with temporary art exhibits and a collection of paintings all themed around Brittany. (☎ 02 98 88 68 88. Open July-Aug. daily 10am-12:30pm and 2-6:30pm; Easter-June and Sept.-Oct. Su-M and W-F 10am-noon and 2-6pm, Sa 2-6pm; Nov.-Easter Su-M and W-Sa 10am-noon and 2-5pm, Su 2-6pm. €4, students €2, under 12 free. Families €6.10. Joint ticket with **Maison** €5.30, students €3.10.)

The **⊠Ty Coz,** 10 venelle au Beurre, overlooking the pl. Allende, seems straight out of an Arthurian legend; there's Breton music, Breton beer, and thick cross-sections of trees for tables. The porch overlooking the *place* is perfect for a late afternoon drink in the sun. (☎ 02 98 88 07 65. Coreff beer €2. Open M-W and F-Sa 11am-1am, Su 6pm-1am.) After the sun goes down, things heat up at **Café de L'Aurore,** 17 rue Traverse, on the other side of the square. Folks of all ages crowd the sidewalk until late at night. (☎ 02 98 88 03 05. Beer €2. Open M-F 8am-1am, Sa 7am-1am.)

NEAR MORLAIX

ROSCOFF & ILE DE BATZ

Fifteen minutes off the coast of Roscoff (pop. 3700), tiny, wind-battered Ile de Batz has unmistakable appeal. Thanks to unusual meteorological phenomena, Batz experiences quite temperate weather. Even when clouds build over Roscoff, the skies over Batz stay deep blue and cloud-free.

▉ ▐ ORIENTATION & PRACTICAL INFORMATION. SNCF **trains** and **buses** (☎ 02 98 69 70 20) go from the station to Morlaix (30-45min., 7-11 per day, €7) with connections to Brest and Paris. The train station provides free long-term parking. CAT **buses** (☎ 02 98 90 68 40) go to Morlaix (30-45min.; M-Sa 3-4 per day, Su 1 per day; €4.60) and Quimper (2hr., 2 per day, €15.30). **Brittany Ferries** (☎ 02 98 29 28 00; www.brittany-ferries.fr) sends boats to Plymouth, England and west to Cork, Ireland, and **Irish Ferries** (☎ 02 98 61 17 17; shamrock@wanadoo.fr) serves Rosslare, Ireland (see **Getting There: By boat,** p. 40). Both offer Eurail discounts of up to 50%. To reach Roscoff's port, turn right from the bus station onto rue Ropartz (unmarked) and follow the bus signs to the *centre ville* (bear left). **Ferry** companies **Armein** (☎ 02 98 61 77 75) and **CFTM** (☎ 02 98 61 78 87) connect Roscoff and Batz in 10-15min. Boats leave from the port during high tide and from the long walkway extending into the harbor at low tide. (Late June to early Sept. every 30min.; mid-Sept. to late June 8-9 per day. Round-trip €6, ages 4-12 €3.50, under 4 free.)

The **tourist office,** 46 rue Gambetta, set back from the port, has transportation schedules, walking tours, maps, info on *chambres d'hôte,* and a shiny visitor's guide. (☎ 02 98 61 12 13; fax 02 98 69 75 75. Open July-Aug. M-Sa 9am-12:30pm and 2-7pm, Su 10am-12:30pm; Sept.-June M-Sa 9am-noon and 2-6pm.) The Ile de Batz **tourist office** is in the town hall *(mairie).* Turn left out of the port and follow the signs. (Open Sept.-June daily 9am-noon and 2-5pm, though hours sometimes fluctuate. Annex at port open July-Aug. M-Sa 9am-1pm and 2-5pm.) There are a number of bike rental places in convenient locations on the island, including **Vélos et Nature,** to the right of the hotel at the ferry dock. Maps and guided tours are also available. Look for the sign "Location de Vélos." (☎ 02 98 61 75 75. Bikes €3 per hr., €7 per half-day, €9 per day.) There is a **laundromat** in Roscoff at 23 rue Jules Ferry. (open daily 9am-8pm) and one on the island, in a private home 50m to the right of the 8 à Huit supermarket. (Open daily 8am-9pm.) The Roscoff **post office,** 17 rue Gambetta, offers **currency exchange.** (☎ 02 98 69 71 28. Open July-Aug. M-F 9am-12:30pm and 1:30-5:30pm, Sa 9am-12:15pm; Sept.-June M-F 9am-noon and 2-5:30pm, Sa 9am-12:15pm.) **Postal code:** 29680. The Ile de Batz **post office** is up the hill in the center of town; look for the signs. (☎ 02 98 99 73 90. Open M-F 9:30am-noon and 1:30-4:30pm, Sa 9:30am-noon.) **Postal code:** 29253.

▓▓ ACCOMMODATIONS, CAMPING, & FOOD. Roscoff has few budget hotels. Backpackers might prefer the **Auberge de Jeunesse Marine ❶** on Ile de Batz. Be sure to call ahead, especially in summer, as it fills up quickly. To reach the hostel the from the port, take the road that goes sharply uphill immediately to the left of the hotel. Signs clearly mark the path to the hostel. (5min.) Perched on a hill, the five-building hostel has amazing views of Roscoff and access to a private beach. In July and August, the hostel doubles as a sailing school—call ahead to enroll in a course. (☎ 02 98 61 77 69; fax 02 98 61 78 85. Breakfast €3.20. Dinner €3.50. Sheets €3.20. Reception hours vary, but there is usually someone around. Open Apr.-Oct. Beds €7.60, bunk cots in big tent €6, camping €5.20.) The *chambres d'hôte* **Ty Va Zadou ❸,** which overlook the port on Ile de Batz, are more expensive but a good value. From the ferry, head left toward town. The stone house with light blue shutters is at the top of a hill, on the right fork just before the church. The four guest rooms are carefully color-coordinated and decorated with lovely dark wood furniture. (☎ 02 98 61 76 91. Breakfast included. All rooms with bath. Open Mar. to mid-Nov. Reserve at least a month in advance June-Aug. Singles €35; doubles €50; 2-room family suite €65-75.) In Roscoff, the **Hôtel d'Angleterre ❸,** 28 rue Albert de Mun, is in an old mansion that retains original Breton furniture and stained-glass windows in the restaurant downstairs. An adjacent sunroom looks onto the enormous backyard garden. (☎ 02 98 69 70 42; fax 02 98 69 75 16. Breakfast €5.80. Singles and doubles €30, with toilet €37, with bath €48. Apr.-May and Sept.-Oct. prices €3-5 lower. Open Apr.-Sept. AmEx/MC/V.)

The grassy, wind-scoured **Terrain d'Hébergement de Plein Air ❶,** on the beach near the lighthouse, is the only legal campground on the island. (☎ 02 98 61 75 70. €1 per person, €0.50 per child, €1 per tent.) Campers might do even better, however, at **▓Camping de Kérestat Peoc'h ❶,** rue de Pontigou, located on the estate of a 15th-century manor 25min. from Roscoff by foot. With a 19th-century mini-labyrinth, a tower built under Louis XIV, remnants of Gallo-Roman walls, and flower-tufted wilds stretching to the sea, this campground is almost reason enough to visit Roscoff. From the train station, turn left onto rue Brizeux, and head left when it ends on rue Albert de Mun and rue Laennec, which becomes rue du Pontigou. Continue down this road, straight through the car-ferry roundabout (bearing slightly right); the campsite is at the end of the first lane on the right. The estate and its tennis courts are open to campers. (☎/fax 02 98 69 71 92; perso.wanadoo.fr/kerestat. Reception 10am-noon and 5-8pm. Open mid-July to mid-Aug. €4 per person, €7 per tent, €2 per car, under 10 €2, caravans €15. 10-30% discount if reserved in advance. Hot water included. Electricity €3.)

In Roscoff, restaurants serving seafood *menus* (€12.20-15.30) line the port. There is a **market** (W morning) on quai Auxerre, and a **Casino** supermarket, between the town and Camping de Kérestat before the roundabout on the right-hand side. **Le Surcouf ❸,** 14 rue Admiral Réveillère, dishes up fresh fish from €12 (pan-fried sole €17), with a €22 *menu.* (☎ 02 98 69 71 89. Open Su-M and Th-Sa for lunch and dinner. MC/V.) One of the more distinctive *crêperies* in Roscoff is **Ti Saozon ❶,** 30 rue Gambetta, just past the tourist office, where flavorful *galettes* (€4-6) are served in an intimate dining room. (☎02 98 69 70 89. Open M-Sa for dinner.) A **8 à Huit** supermarket is located at the highest point on the Ile de Batz. (☎02 98 61 78 79. Open July-Aug. M-Sa 9am-1pm and 2:30-8pm, Su 9am-12:30pm; Sept.-June Tu-Sa 9am-12:30pm and 2:30-7:30pm, Su 10am-12:30pm.)

◙ ◪ SIGHTS & HIKES. The best way to see the Ile de Batz is to take the *sentier côtier*, 14km of easy-to-follow trails line the coast. They run past the *côte sauvage* on the west side of the island, along small, white sandy beaches, over massive rocks, and beside inland lakes. The 4hr. hike is easy. Find the trails from any point on the island by heading toward water or by following signs from the port. The trails are technically private property, but many still use them.

West of the town center, a **lighthouse** gives great views of the island and Roscoff. (Open July-Aug. daily 1-5:30pm; June to mid-Sept. Su-Tu and Th-Sa 2-5pm. €1.70, children €1.) At the southeast tip of the island rests a tranquil **botanical garden.** (☎02 98 61 75 65. Open July-Aug. daily 1-6pm; Apr.-June and Sept. Su-M and W-Sa 2-6pm; Oct. Sa-Su 2-6pm. Guided visits Su at 3pm. €4, students and seniors €3.50, children €2.) Slightly inland, west of the garden, stand the ruins of the 12th-century **Chapelle Ste-Anne,** first the site of a Viking structure in AD 878. During the **Fête de Ste-Anne,** on the last Saturday in July, everyone on the island comes out to light a massive bonfire on the dunes as part of this, the largest celebration of the year.

The most popular sight in Roscoff is **Le Jardin Exotique,** featuring a large collection of tropical flora and a panoramic view of the bay of Morlaix. From the tourist office, walk to the dock and turn right. Follow quai d'Auxerre, bear right onto rue Jeanne d'Arc, and take a soft right onto rue Plymouth; when it ends, turn right onto Voie de Port en Eau Profonde. The *jardin* comes up on the left. (☎02 98 61 29 19; www.jardinexotiqueroscoff.com. Open daily June-Sept. 10am-7pm; Apr.-May and Oct. 10:30am-12:30pm and 2-6pm; Mar. and Nov. 2-5pm.) The 16th-century **Eglise Notre-Dame de Kroaz-Batz** is reminiscent of an overgrown sand castle with turreted spires, two-tiered belfry, and massive, golden Baroque choir. (Open daily 9am-noon and 2-7pm.) On the far right side of the port is the **Pointe St-Barbe,** a tall rock outcropping wrapped in spiraling stone steps and crowned with a white chapel, which provides a wonderful panoramic view of the coast, the port, and the Ile de Batz. Take one of the 1½-3hr., 6-12km, walking tours around the environs of Roscoff, explained in the free *Circuits Pedestre* brochure.

BREST

Brest (pop. 156,000) became a somber wasteland in 1944 when Allied bombers drove out the occupying German flotilla. Despite efforts to rebuild, the city still feels large and impersonal. Although it is known as one of the dreariest places in Brittany, signs of life have begun to emerge, albeit slowly. Brest features a number of pleasant cafés and a summer concert series, as well as one of the largest aquariums around. It is also the ideal jumping-off point for nearby gem Ile d'Ouessant.

▮ TRANSPORTATION

Trains: pl. du 19ème Régiment d'Infanterie (☎02 98 31 51 72). Info office open M-F 8:30am-7:30pm, Sa 8:30am-7pm, Su 9:30am-7pm. To: **Morlaix** (€8.40); **Nantes** (€34.40); **Paris** (€60.20); **Quimper** (30min., 5 per day, €13.10); **Rennes** (1½hr., 15 per day, €26.10).

Buses: Buses leave from next to the train station (☎02 98 44 46 73). Open July-Aug. M-F 7am-12:30pm and 1-7pm, Sa 7:15-11am and 1-6:30pm, Su 8:45-10:15am, 1-2pm, and 5:15-7:45pm; Sept.-June M-F 7am-12:30pm and 1-7pm, Sa 8am-1:15pm and

2:30-6:30pm, Su 6-7pm. Buses run to: **Crozon** and **Camaret** (1½hr.; M-Sa 2 per day, Su 1 per day; €9.60); **Quimper** (1¼hr.; 4 per day, 1 on Su; €13.10); **Roscoff** (30-45min., 7-11 per day, €9.10).

Ferries: For ferry lines serving Brest, see **Ile d'Ouessant** (p. 259).

Local Transportation: Bibus, 33 av. Georges Clemenceau (☎02 98 80 30 30; www.bibus.fr). Buses run daily 6am-8pm with erratic service on a specially designated route until about 10pm, F-Sa until midnight. Service is infrequent, particularly in the summer months, so plan ahead. Ask at the tourist office or the Bibus *point d'accueil* at the Hôtel de Ville (M-F 8:15am-12:15pm and 1:15-6:45pm, Sa 9am-noon and 1:30-6pm) for a bus map and book-sized schedule. Buy tickets on the bus: €1, *carnet* of 10 €8, full-day €3, students for 1 week €8.

Taxis: Allô Taxis, 234 rue Jean Jaurès (☎02 98 80 68 06).

■✴ ❼ ORIENTATION & PRACTICAL INFORMATION

To the right of the train station, av. Georges Clemenceau leads to the central **place de la Liberté,** the main terminal for the city's internal bus system. **Rue Jean Jaurès,** north of the *place*, is prime shopping territory, but be careful at night. **Rue de Siam,** south of the *place*, overlooking the water, is the most vibrant street in the city. A handful of good restaurants and bars cluster at **Port du Commerce. The tourist office,** 8 av. Georges Clemenceau, on pl. de la Liberté near the Hôtel de Ville, provides free maps, a **reservations service,** tickets for the ferry to Ile d'Ouessant, and info on food, sights, and tours. (☎02 98 44 24 96; fax 02 98 44 53 73. Open July-Aug. M-Sa 9:30am-7pm, Su 10am-noon; Sept.-June M-Sa 10am-12:30pm and 2-6pm.) The **Bureau Information Jeunesse Brest,** 4 rue Morvan, off pl. de la Liberté, has free **Internet** and info on jobs. (☎02 98 43 01 08; bij@wanadoo.fr. Open M and F 1:30-6pm, Tu and Th 1:30-6pm and 8-10pm, W and Sa 9:30am-noon and 1:30-6pm.) Other services include: a **laundromat** at Point Blue, 7 rue de Siam (open daily 8am-9:30pm), **police** at 15 rue Colbert (☎02 98 43 77 77), a **hospital** at rue de la Cavale Blanche (☎02 98 22 33 33), and **Internet** at @cces.cibles, 31 av. Clemenceau. (☎02 98 46 76 10. €3 per hr. Open M-Sa 11am-1pm, Su 2-11pm. The **post office,** rue de Siam, on pl. Général Leclerc, has **currency exchange.** (☎02 98 33 73 07. Open M-F 8am-7pm, Sa 8am-noon.) **Poste Restante:** 29279. **Postal code:** 29200.

⬛ ACCOMMODATIONS & CAMPING

Reserve 2-3 weeks ahead in July and August.

❄ Auberge de Jeunesse (HI), 5 rue de Kerbriant (☎02 98 41 90 41; fax 02 98 41 82 66), about 4km from the train station, near Océanopolis, next to the artificial beach in Le Moulin Blanc. Take bus #7 to its terminus at Port de Plaisance (M-Sa 6:45am-7:30pm, Su 2-5:45pm; €1). With your back to the bus stop, go left toward the beach, take a left onto rue Moulin Blanc, and follow signs to the hostel; look for one reading *ostaleri ar yaouankiz*. Looks like an IKEA ad set in the tropics. Ping-pong, foosball, and TV room. Kitchen. Breakfast included. Dinner €8. Sheets €3.80. Reception M-F 7-9am and 5-8pm, Sa-Su 7-10am and 6-8pm. Lockout 10am-5pm. Curfew July-Aug. midnight; Sept.-June 11pm; ask for a key if you'll be late. Beds €12.10. ❶

Hôtel Astoria, 9 rue Traverse (☎02 98 80 19 10; www.hotel-astoria-brest.com). Central, quiet, and spotless. Modern rooms with TV. Helpful staff. Breakfast €6. Reception M-Sa 7am-11pm, Su 8am-noon and 6-11pm. Call ahead, especially July-Aug. Singles and doubles €25, with shower €40-45, with bath €50; triples €50. AmEx/MC/V. ❸

Kelig Hôtel, 12 rue de Lyon (☎02 98 80 47 21; lucas.pascale@wanadoo.fr). Clean, spacious rooms with TV run by friendly folks. Located just 5min. from rue de Siam. Breakfast €6. Reception M-F 7am-9:30pm, Sa 8am-12:30pm and 5-9:30pm, Su 8am-

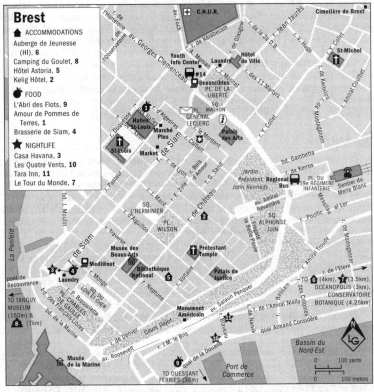

Brest

🏠 ACCOMMODATIONS

Auberge de Jeunesse (HI), **6**
Camping du Goulet, **8**
Hôtel Astoria, **5**
Kelig Hôtel, **2**

🍴 FOOD

L'Abri des Flots, **9**
Amour de Pommes de Terres, **1**
Brasserie de Siam, **4**

⭐ NIGHTLIFE

Casa Havana, **3**
Les Quatre Vents, **10**
Tara Inn, **11**
Le Tour du Monde, **7**

12:30pm. Singles with shower €24, with shower and toilet €30-36, with bath and toilet €37; doubles €27/€34-39/€40; triple with shower and toilet €44, with bath €47. AmEx/MC/V. ❷

Camping du Goulet, (☎/fax 02 98 45 86 84), 7km from downtown in Ste-Anne du Portzic; take bus #14 (dir: Plouzané) to Le Cosquer. (15min.) At night take bus B, route A (dir: Plouzané). Follow signs 100m down the side road to this large, often crowded site. Clean facilities, manicured hedges, and hot showers. Laundry. Reception M-F 10am-noon and 2:30-7pm, Sa 9am-noon, longer hours July-Aug. €3.40 per person, under 7 €2; €3.90 per tent; €1.20 per car. Electricity €1.70-2.50. ❶

🍴 FOOD

Markets are held every day in various locations, including the traditional and organic market on rue du Moulin à Poudre (Tu 4-8pm and Sa mornings) and the enormous market in the area around St-Louis (Su morning), and a slightly pricey **indoor market** at Les Halles St-Louis, a block from rue de Siam. (Daily 7am-1pm and 4-7:30pm.) Bakeries, *pâtisseries*, and vegetable stores can be found on and around rue de Siam; more filling meals are found at the end near the port. A **Marché Plus** is just off rue de Siam on rue Pasteur (Open M-Sa 9am-9pm, Su morning). **Amour de Pommes de Terre ❷**, 23 rue des Halles, just behind the indoor market, is an inventive spuds-only establishment. Oddly, there are almost no vegetarian

BRITTANY

options. (☎02 98 43 48 51. *Menus* €9.50-18. Open daily for lunch and dinner.) **L'Abri des Flots ❸**, 8 quai de la Douane, at the Port de Commerce, will satisfy all with its jovial ambiance, huge portions, and relatively low prices. They serve *galettes* and crêpes (€1.60-5.50) but are known for their seafood couscous. (☎02 98 44 07 31. Seafood meals €10-18. Open daily noon-2pm and 7pm-midnight.) At the end of rue de Siam near the port, **Brasserie de Siam ❸**, 12 rue de Siam, serves up a variety of seafood dishes as well as *brasserie* standards in a sleek, modern setting whose bold use of primary colors might have come from one of Keith Haring's milder dreams. The day's catch is cooked up for €10-16; ubiquitous *moules frites* for €8.50-9.90. (☎02 98 46 05 52. Open daily noon-midnight. V.)

🧭 SIGHTS

Brest's **château** was the only major building to survive the bombings of World War II. In over 1700 strife-laden years, the world's oldest active military institution has withstood Roman, Breton, English, French, and German attacks. You can only enter the château through the **Musée de la Marine**, which occupies most of the sprawling fortress. The museum itself occurs rather spontaneously at points throughout the château, featuring worthwhile small exhibits on points of nautical interest. (☎02 98 22 12 39. Open Apr.-Sept. daily 10am-6:30pm; Oct.-Mar. Su-M and W-Sa 10am-noon and 2-6pm. Last entrance 1hr. before closing. €4.60, students €3, ages 6-18 €2.30, under 6 free.) The rose-tinted **Monument Américain**, on rue de Denver, overlooks the Port du Commerce, a reminder of the Americans' landing in 1917. Locals joke that you need a passport to visit this American-built monument to the US, guarded by American officers on American-owned soil.

Océanopolis, port de Plaisance, emphasizes Brittany's marine life (much of it in tidal tanks) as well as the Iroise Sea (which surrounds the Ile d'Ouessant). A polar pavilion with a 3-D theater that opens onto the penguin playland, and a tropical pavilion, complete with a coral reef, are some of the highlights here. Océanopolis is huge and can have massive lines; don't expect to spend less than a day there. To get there, take bus #7 (dir: Port de Plaisance) from the Liberty terminal (M-Sa every 30min. until 7:30pm; €1) to Océanopolis. (Aquarium ☎02 98 34 40 40; www.oceanopolis.com. Open Apr.-Aug. daily 9am-6pm; Sept.-Mar. Tu-Sa 10am-5pm, Su 10am-6pm. €14.50, ages 4-17 €10, under 4 free.) The beautiful **Conservatoire Botanique de Brest**, 5min. away, stretches through 3km of exotic plant life, bamboo groves, and trickling brooks.

📻 NIGHTLIFE

Nightlife centers around the Port de Commerce, the pont de Recouvrance at the end of rue de Siam, and the streets near pl. de la Liberté. You may want to avoid the neighborhoods on the other side of pl. de la Liberté after dark. On Thursdays, the popular **Jeudis du Port** concerts dominate the Port with the sounds of Breton music, rock, and jazz. (Port du Commerce. Open mid-July to late Aug. 7:30pm-midnight.) The aggressively Celtic-themed **Tara Inn**, 1 rue de Blaveau, near the Port du Commerce, attracts live traditional Irish music every Tu night, and the last Su of the month, at 10pm. Features an unusually large selection of beer on tap. (€2-3. ☎02 98 80 36 07. Open M-F 11am-1am, Sa-Su 3pm-1am. MC/V.) The sea-themed **Le Tour du Monde**, port du Moulin Blanc, near the aquarium and hostel, is owned by a famous navigator and draws crowds with cheap beer, mussels, and port views. (☎02 98 41 93 65. Beer around €2. Open daily 11am-1am.) Locals pack nearby **Les Quatres Vents**, 28 quai de la Douane, rocking the boatside bar from 10pm to 1am. (☎02 98 44 42 84. Beer €2-3. Open M-Sa 9am-1am, Su 2pm-1am.) The young, fresh crowd in **Casa Havana**, 2 rue de Siam, munches *tapas* and other Mediterranean treats (€2.80-6) amid tropical plants and Latin music. (☎02 98 80 42 87. Cocktails €4, beer €2.50. Restaurant open M-Sa noon-2pm; *tapas* served all day except Su. Bar open 11am-1am. MC/V.)

ILE D'OUESSANT

The westernmost point in France, windswept Ouessant (*Enez Eussa* in Breton; pop. 951) is a peaceful oasis for hikers and naturalists, an hour's boat ride from the nearest point of the mainland. Ouessant's mysterious jagged rock formations rise up from rugged grounds covered in wildflowers and grazing sheep.

■ TRANSPORTATION. Two **ferry** companies offer service to Ouessant. Buy tickets at the port or at the Brest tourist office, and reserve in advance in summer. If traveling from Brest, the best and easiest route is to use **Penn Ar Bed,** which sails year-round between Ouessant and Brest via Le Conquet and Molène. (2½hr.) It also serves the islands of Molène and Sein. (☎02 98 80 80 80; www.penn-ar-bed.fr. July-Aug. 4-6 per day; Sept.-June 1-2 per day. Brest-Ouessant round-trip €29.50, students €26, children €17.70; Le Conquet-Ouessant €25.50, students €21.70, children €15.30. Reservations required.) **Finist'mer** runs "fast ferries" from Ouessant to Camaret (1hr.) and Ouessant to Le Conquet. (30min.) (☎02 98 89 16 61; www.finist-mer.fr. Camaret 1 per day. Le Conquet July-Aug. 4-6 per day; Apr.-June and Sept. 2-3 per day. Round-trip €30, students and over 60 €25, ages 4-16 €17.50.) To get to Le Conquet, take the Cars de St-Mathieu **bus** (☎02 98 89 12 02) from Brest (40min., €4.30), though it's difficult to impossible to coordinate the bus schedule with Finist'mer departures. It's therefore a better idea to use Penn Ar Bed from Brest. Both ferry companies charge €6 one-way for bikes.

Boats dock at Port du Stiff, 3.5km from Lampaul, the main town on the Ile d'Ouessant. Jean Avril **buses** (☎02 98 48 85 65) await the boats' arrival at the port and take you into town in a few air-conditioned minutes (€1.50). On foot it's a 45min. stroll. Four companies **rent bikes** for identical prices at the port and in Lampaul (€10 per day, €11 for a beach bike, €14 for a mountain bike; €7/€8/€10 per half-day, €37/€39/€50 per week. Most accept MC/V.)

■ ■ ORIENTATION & PRACTICAL INFORMATION. Lampaul's **tourist office,** near the church in the town center, sells a pedestrian guide (€2.30) with four routes that cover the entire coastline in 1½-3hr. hikes. The island's bike paths are marked on a separate map since cycling is forbidden on the foot paths. (☎02 98 48 85 83; www.ot-ouessant.fr. Office open M-Sa 10am-noon and 1:30-6pm, Su 10am-noon.) **Police** (☎02 98 48 81 61) only operate on the island July-Aug. The **post office** is to the left of the church and 30m downhill. (☎02 98 48 81 77. Open mid-June to mid-Sept. M-F 9:15am-12:30pm and 2-5:15pm, Sa 9am-12:15pm; mid-Sept. to mid-June M-F 9:30am-noon and 2-5pm, Sa 9am-noon.) **Postal code:** 29242.

■ ■ ACCOMMODATIONS & FOOD. Tiny Lampaul is home to all the island's food and lodging. Reserve ahead in the summer. The cheerful and spotless **Auberge de Jeunesse d'Ouessant ❶** is 5min. from the tourist office and the center of Lampaul. Take the stairs to the right of the SPAR supermarket across from the church and turn right onto the first road the stairs bring you to (not at the top of the stairs). Follow it as it bears left; the hostel is ahead on the right. There are 48 beds in sunny, clean 2- to 6-person rooms, a communal kitchen, and a dining area with views of the water. (☎02 98 48 84 53 or 06 81 23 72 95; fax 02 98 48 87 42. Breakfast included. Reception closed midday. Sheets €3.60. Dorms €13, students and under 25 €11.30. *Demi-pension* €22.50/€20, full *pension* €32/€28.90.) The lovely hotel **Le Roc'h Ar Mor ❹** has spacious blue and yellow bedrooms and bathrooms in a prime seaside location just beyond the center of Lampaul. An appealing seafood restaurant is downstairs (*menus* €15, €17, €46). Room prices vary depending on view; all have bath, shower, toilet, telephone, and TV. (☎02 98 48 80 19; www.roc-harmor.com. Breakfast €7.60, children €5.80. Singles and doubles €48-75; triples €58-75; quads €70. Discounts Oct.-Dec. Extra bed €8. Wheelchair-accessible. MC/V.) **Le Fromveur** ❸ has simpler rooms with plain pastel décor in the dead center of Lampaul, over a popular restaurant (*menus* €13-26) that serves up local catches. (☎02 98 48 81 30. Breakfast €5.50. Singles and doubles with TV, toilet, and shower €40; triples and quads €70. MC/V.) The **Centre d'Etude du Milieu Ouessantin** ❶, an environmental studies and ornithological center, doubles as a hostel. From Lampaul's tourist office, bear right onto the road just past the supermarket and follow the signs for the Musée des Phares. It is the last major building before you reach the lighthouse—it's unmarked but its modern architecture makes in unmistakable. (30min.) The beds and facilities aren't as spiffy as those at the Auberge, but it's just down the road from the lighthouse and the spectacular coast. (☎02 98 48 82 65; fax 02 98 48 87 39. Reception M-F 8am-5pm. Sheets €3.10. Reservations are required and should be made early, especially for July. 4- to 5-person dorms €9.20 per person, students €8.40, under 15 €8.20. Price drops on a sliding scale, €0.50 per night, for 2nd to 6th nights.) **Camping Municipal** ❶, located just 2km from the port along the main road, is on the left about 300m before the church in Lampaul. The bus from the port makes a stop here; ask the driver. (☎02 98 48 84 65. Laundry €4.70. Showers €1.60. Reception July-Aug. daily 7am-10pm; call ahead in the low season. Open Apr.-Sept. €2.70 per person, under 7 €1.30; €2.70 per tent, bed in communal tent €3.20.)

A **SPAR** supermarket is next door to the tourist office (open M-Sa 8:30am-7:30pm, Su 9:30am-12:30pm), and a **8 à Huit** supermarket lies just downhill (open Tu 8:30am-12:30pm, W-Sa 8:30am-7:30pm, Su 9:30am-12:30pm); together they have the island's only cash machines. There is also a small market, **Le Marché des Iles**, 50m from the campground. (☎02 98 48 88 08. Open M-Sa 8:30am-7:30pm, Su 8:30am-12:30pm.) For food more filling than a picnic lunch, head to **Ty Korn** ❸ (☎02 98 48 87 33) in Lampaul. They offer a variety of marine delights. (*Menus* for €16 and €24. Open Tu-Sa noon-1:30pm and 7-9:30pm, Su noon-1:30pm. MC/V.)

◪ **SIGHTS.** Biking is forbidden on footpaths and, for safety reasons, along the coast. There are bike trails, however, and the island's roads, well paved and almost devoid of cars, are ideal for biking and lead to all the major sights. A good hiking companion is the tourist office's booklet of coastline paths (€2.30), which contains details of all of the ruins and rocks along each route. A free basic map is also available. The terrain is relatively flat, and if you lose your way it is always easy to mark your position by the large lighthouses. If you only have time to choose one path, take the 12km northwest trail to the **Pointe de Pern**, whose breathtaking rock formations rising from the ocean are the westernmost point in continental Europe. Ouessant's two museums lie on this trail. A joint ticket for the two is available for €6, ages 8-14 €3.90. The **Musée des Phares et Balises**, in du Créac'h, once Europe's most powerful lighthouse, is devoted to the history of lighthouses and maritime signaling. (☎02 98 48 80 70. Open May-Sept. daily 10:30am-6:30pm; Oct.-Mar. Tu-Su 2-4pm; Apr. Tu-Su 2-6:30pm. €3.90, ages 8-14 €2.30, under 8 free.) The **Ecomusée and Maison du Niou**, 1km northwest of Lampaul, has a display of traditional local women's clothing and a replica of a traditional *ouessantine* home. (☎02 98 48 86 37. Hours same as Musée des Phares. €3.10, ages 8-14 €1.90.)

In late August, Ouessant hosts the **Salon International du Livre Insulaire**, a half-week of literary conferences, exhibitions, and meetings with writers. (Info ☎02 98 90 33 32; perso.club-internet/jacbayle/livres/salon.html.)

QUIMPER

Its central waterway criss-crossed by flower-lined pedestrian footbridges, Quimper (pronounced "kem-PAIR," pop. 63,000) has a quaint, cobblestoned charm, a fierce pride in its deep-rooted Breton heritage (one local school teaches exclusively in Breton), and its *faïencerie* (local stoneware), still hand-painted just as it was 300 years ago.

⌷ TRANSPORTATION

Trains: av. de la Gare (☎08 36 35 35 35). Open M-Sa 8:15am-7pm. To: **Quiberon** (1hr., €16); **Brest** (1½hr., 4 per day, €13.10); **Nantes** (2¾hr., 4 per day, €26.20); **Paris** (4¾hr., 8 TGV per day, €60.10); **Rennes** (2¼hr.; 10 per day, 4 TGV; €27.30).

Buses: next to the train station (☎02 98 90 88 89). To: **Brest** (1¼hr.; M-Sa 4 per day, 2 on Su; €13.10); **Pointe du Raz** (1½hr., 2-4 per day, €7.70); **Pont-Aven** (1¼hr.; M-Sa 3 per day, 2 on Su; €5.80); **Roscoff** (2hr., July-Aug. 1 per day, €22.30).

Local Transportation: QUB (Quartabus), 2 quai Odet (☎02 98 95 26 27). **Buses** run 6am-7:30pm. Tickets €1; day pass €2.90; *carnet* of 6 €5.20; *carnet* of 10 €8. Bus #1 serves the hostel and campground. The office has schedules and a map of the bus lines. Open M-F 8am-12:15pm and 1:30-6:30pm, Sa 9am-noon and 2-6pm.

Taxis: (☎02 98 90 21 21), in front of the train station.

Car Rental: Hertz (☎02 98 53 12 34, reservations 08 03 86 18 61), across the street from the train station. Open M-F 8am-noon and 2-7pm, Sa 8am-noon and 2-6pm.

Bike Rental: MBK s.a. Lennez, 13 rue Aristide Briand (☎02 98 90 14 81), off av. de la Gare. Bikes €7.70 per half-day, €12.20 per day. Passport or check deposit. Open Tu-F 9am-noon and 2-7pm, Sa 9am-noon and 2-6:30pm. MC/V. **Torch'VTT,** 58 rue de la Providence (☎02 98 53 84 41). €14 per day. €450 deposit. Open Tu-Sa 9:30am-12:30pm and 2:30-7pm.

◪ ⸮ ORIENTATION & PRACTICAL INFORMATION

In the heart of the Cornouaille region, Quimper is separated from the sea to its south and west by rich farmland. To reach the center of town from the train station, go right onto av. de la Gare, which becomes bd. Dupleix. Keeping the river on your right, follow it to pl. de la Résistance. The tourist office will be on your left; the *vieille ville* will be across the river to your right. (10min.)

Tourist Office: 7 rue de la Déesse (☎02 98 53 04 05; www.quimper-tourisme.com). Free, detailed map. **Tours** of city in English (1½hr., July-Aug. 1 per week; call to reserve). Office open July-Aug. M-Sa 9am-7pm, Su 10am-1pm and 3-5:45pm; Apr.-May M-Sa 9:30am-12:30pm and 1:30-6:30pm; June and Sept. M-Sa 9:30am-12:30pm and 1:30-6:30pm, Su 10am-12:45pm; Oct.-Mar. M-Sa 9am-12:30pm and 1:30-6pm.

English Bookstore: Librairie de Mousterlin, 19 rue de Frout (☎02 98 64 37 94). Open M-Sa 3-7pm.

Youth Center: Bureau Information Jeunesse, pl. Louis Armand, next to the train station. Open M and F 1:30-5:30pm, Tu-Th 10am-noon and 1:30-5:30pm, Sa 10am-4pm.

Laundromats: Point Laverie, 47 rue de Pont l'Abbé, about 5min. from the hostel. Open daily 8am-10pm. **Laverie de la Gare,** 2 av. de la Gare. Open daily 8am-8pm.

Police: 3 rue T. Le Hars (☎02 98 90 15 41).

Hospital: Centre Hospitalier Laënnec, 14bis av. Yves-Thépot (☎02 98 52 60 60).

Internet: CyberCopy, 3 bd. Amiral de Kerguelen (☎02 98 64 33 99). €2.30 for 15min., €3.10 for 30min., €4.50 per hr. Open M 1-7pm, Tu-F 9am-7pm, Sa 9am-3pm.

Post Office: 37 bd. A. de Kerguelen (☎02 98 64 28 28). **Currency exchange.** Open M-F 8am-6:30pm, Sa 8am-noon. **Branches** on chemin des Justices, 2min. from hostel, and on rue Châpeau Rouge. **Poste Restante:** 29109. **Postal code:** 29000.

ACCOMMODATIONS & CAMPING

Ask at the tourist office about *chambres d'hôte*. For July and August, it's a good idea to make reservations in writing as early as possible.

Centre Hébergement de Quimper (HI), 6 av. des Oiseaux (☎02 98 64 97 97; quimper@fuaj.org). Cross the river from pl. de la Résistance and go left on quai de l'Odet. Turn right onto rue de pont l'Abbé and continue through the large roundabout; the hostel will be on your left. (20-25min.) Or, take bus #1 from pl. de la Résistance (dir: Kermoysan) to Chaptal (last bus 7:30pm). Clean, if somewhat run-down, facilities, with TV, foosball, and a communal kitchen. Breakfast €3.30. Sleepbag €2.70, sheets €3. Reception daily 8-11am and 5-11pm; call if arriving later. Bunks in 8- to 14-bed dorms €8.40; two singles available for €10. **Members only. ❶**

Hôtel de la Gare, 17 av. de la Gare (☎02 98 90 00 81; fax 02 98 53 21 81). Modern, freshly redone rooms face the inner courtyard and parking lot, away from the traffic of the street. All rooms have shower, toilet, TV, and kitchenette. Breakfast €5.50. Singles €38; doubles €53; triples €58. MC/V. ❸

Hôtel le Derby, 13 av. de la Gare (☎02 98 52 06 91; fax 02 98 53 39 04). Cheerful, tastefully decorated rooms with shower and toilet, over a bar. Breakfast €5.40. Singles €25; doubles €35. Extra bed €4. May-Sept. prices increase €3. ❷

Camping Municipal, av. des Oiseaux (☎/fax 02 98 55 61 09), next to the hostel. A forested area with shady trees, not entirely removed from city life. Reception M 1-7pm; Tu, Th, Sa 8-11am and 3-8pm; W 9am-noon; F 9-11am and 3-8pm; Su 9-11am. €3 per person, under 7 €1.50; €1.10 per car; €0.70 per tent. Electricity €2.70. ❶

FOOD

The lively **covered market** at **Les Halles,** off rue Kéréon on rue St-François, good bargains on produce, seafood, meats, and cheeses (as well as fabulous crêpes), but the earlier you get there the better. (M-Sa 7am-8pm, Su 9am-1pm.) An **open market** is held twice per week. (W in Les Halles, Sa outside Les Halles and in pl. des Ursulines. Both open June-Aug. 9am-6pm; Sept.-May 9am-1pm.) A **Casino** supermarket is on av. de la Gare. (Open M-Sa 8:30am-7:30pm, Su 9:30am-1pm and 5-7:30pm.) There is a **Shopi** grocery downstairs at 20 rue Astor. (Open M-Sa 8:30am-7:30pm, Su 9:30am-12:30pm.) On a quiet street just around the corner from the cathedral, the classy, modern bistro **Le Saint Co. ❸,** 20 rue Frout, offers a tasty variety of steak *plats*, as well as creative and filling salads and mussels. (☎02 98 95 11 47. Steak €12-14, salads €3-7, mussels €7-8. *Menu* €16-20. Open daily July-Aug. 11:30am-midnight; Sept.-June noon-2pm and 7:30pm-midnight. Kitchen closes at 9pm. MC/V.)

Quimper also has a surprising surfeit of quality ethnic food restaurants. One of the best is **Gandhi ❸,** 13 bd. de Kerguelen, near the train station. Despite its slightly tacky homage to its namesake peace-loving Indian hero, Gandhi still serves up delicious authentic cuisine, including plenty of vegetarian options. (☎02 98 64 29 50. *Plats* €7.70-13, *menu* €17. Open daily noon-2:30pm and 7-11pm. V.) For your pick of the aquarium, head a little farther afield to **Au P'tit Rafiot ❹,** 7 rue de Pont-l'Abbé, which serves enormous helpings of such marine favorites as *bouillabaisse* and *cassoulet marin* for around €20. (☎02 98 53 77 27. Open W-Su noon-1:30pm and 7:30-10pm.)

Quimper

FOOD
Gandhi, 4
Au P'tit Rafiot, 6
Le Saint Co., 3

ACCOMMODATIONS
Camping Municipal, 7
Centre Hébergement
de Quimper (HI), 5
Hôtel le Derby, 10
Hôtel de la Gare, 11

NIGHTLIFE
Café XXI, 2
Le Café des Arts, 9
Molly Malone's, 1
St. Andrew's Pub, 8

SIGHTS

The unmistakable, magnificent dual spires of the **Cathédrale St-Corentin,** built between the 13th and 15th centuries, mark the entrance to the old quarter from quai St-Corentin. Quimper's patron is one of dozens of Breton saints not officially recognized by the Church. (Open M-Sa 8:30am-noon and 1:30-6:30pm, Su 8:30am-noon, except during mass, and 2-6:30pm.) **Mont Frugy,** next to the tourist office, offers an amazing view of the cathedral spires and some relief from the bustle of the city center. It's an easy hike, with numerous wooded walking trails.

The **Musée des Beaux-Arts,** 40 pl. St-Corentin, has a fascinating exhibit on poet and artist Max Jacob, a Quimper native killed in the Holocaust. It includes portraits by several of his friends, including Picasso. The first room on the left holds a dozen paintings that render Breton folklore with surprising vitality. (☎02 98 95 45 20; musee-beauxarts.quimper.fr. Open July-Aug. daily 10am-7pm; Sept.-June Su-M and W-Sa 10am-noon and 2-6pm. Tours daily July-Aug.; call for info. €4, ages 13-26 and over 60 €2.50, under 12 free.) The **Musée Départemental Breton,** 1 rue du Roi Gradlon, through the cathedral garden, offers unusually stylish exhibits on local history, archaeology, and ethnography, including an elaborate display of traditional Breton clothing and innovative temporary exhibits. (☎02 98 95 21 60. Open June-Sept. daily 9am-6pm; Oct.-May Tu-Sa 9am-noon and 2-5pm, Su 2-5pm. €4, students €2.50, under 18 and Su free. July-Aug. tours in French, at least 1 per day; call

BRITTANY

NO WORK, ALL PLAY

QUIMPER LETS ITS HAIR DOWN

Even on an ordinary day, Quimper is one of Brittany's best cities, but during its famous festival it's a spectacle unrivaled in France. For 80 years, Quimper has celebrated its Breton heritage with the **Festival de Cornouaille** held during the second half of July. Lasting nine days, it features everything from traditional folk music and dance to cooking demonstrations of regional cuisine and plays and concerts. Although the ostensible purpose is to show off Brittany's unique mixture of Celtic and French culture, the festival has grown through the years to an impressive international scale. Performers arrive from as far away as Russia and the UK. In terms of size and sheer spectacle it is easily the rival of Edinburgh's famous August revels. In addition to countless performances by local dance troupes and musical acts, the 80th anniversary blow-out in 2003 featured the National Ensemble of Grozny and the Scottish band Simple Minds. The local Breton tradition is the heart of the festival, but the international presence may account for its enduring popularity.

As early as June, the tourist office has plentiful information, including a thick booklet with a schedule of dates and times for all performances. Some events are free; others cost €15-25. For more information, visit www.festival-cornouaille.com.

for details and reservations; €1.50.) The **Musée de la Faïence,** 14 rue J-B Bousquet, displays Quimper's beautiful characteristic earthenware, as well as temporary exhibits. (☎02 98 90 12 72. Open mid-Apr. to mid-Oct. M-Sa 10am-6pm. €4, ages 18-25 €3.20, under 17 €2.30.) **Faïenceries de Quimper H. B. Henriot,** rue Haute, lets visitors to tour the studio and watch potters. (☎02 98 90 09 36; www.hb-henriot.com. Open M-F 9-11:15am and 1:30-4:45pm; June closed F. Tours every 30-60min. English text available with French tour. €3, ages 7-17 €1.50, under 7 free.)

◪ NIGHTLIFE

The best Irish pub in Brittany may well be ▉**Molly Malone's,** pl. St-Mathieu, on rue Falkirk. Its long bar runs toward a large, dimly-lit room filled with friendly chatter and Irish music. (☎02 98 53 40 42. Beamish stout €3.10, pint €5.40. Open daily 11am-1am.) The 21st century meets the 11th in glittering **Café XXI,** 38 pl. St-Corentin, across from the cathedral and next to the Musée des Beaux-Arts. This popular daytime people-watching venue doubles as a glam nightspot, serving its "XXI" specialty (white rum, curaçao, and fresh citrus juice; €5.40) to a chic, sophisticated clientele. (☎02 98 95 92 34. Open daily 8:15am-1am; *brasserie* noon-3pm. MC/V.) Quimper has no shortage of typically large European cafés, some around the cathedral, but the best is cavernous **Le Café des Arts,** 4 rue Ste-Catherine, down the street from the tourist office, which occupies nearly an entire block of its own. (☎02 98 90 32 06. Beer €2. Open M-F 11:30am-1am, Sa-Su 3:30pm-1am. MC/V.) **St. Andrew's Pub,** 11 pl. Styvel, is just across the river from rue de Pont l'Abbé. Its breezy terrace is the perfect setting for a relaxed drink served by friendly managers. (☎02 98 53 34 49. Drinks €2-3. Open daily 11am-1am.)

◪ FESTIVALS

Catch some Breton culture at the **Festival de Cornouaille** Quimper's annual summer gala (see **No Work, All Play: Quimper Lets its Hair Down,** at left). The festival is held every year in the attractive cathedral gardens, right next to the Odet, which fill with Breton dancers in traditional costume, accompanied by lively music from the *biniou* (bagpipes) and the reed instrument *bombarde,* similar to an oboe. (Late June to early Sept. Th 9pm, €3.10.) Quimper holds its increasingly popular **Semaines Musicales** during early to mid-August every year. Various quality orchestras and choirs perform nightly in the Théâtre Municipal and the cathedral.

DAYTRIPS FROM QUIMPER

PONT-AVEN

Pont-Aven is connected by Caoudal **buses** *(☎02 98 56 96 72) to* **Quimper** *(1¼hr.; 3 per day; €5.80, round-trip €9) and nearby towns (line 14A).*

The first to paint Pont-Aven (pop. 3000) was Paul Gauguin (1848-1903), who, fed up with mainstream Impressionism, came here in 1886 and inspired movement that emphasized pure color, absence of perspective, and simplified figures. Pont-Aven's pride and joy are the museums celebrating its art—it is likely that Pont-Aven has more art galleries per capita than anywhere else in the world. Its beating heart, however, are the surrounding acres of woodland that inspired those paintings. The tourist office provides maps detailing a number of short hikes, many of them passing through places where artists once congregated. From the town center, you can follow the **Promenade Xavier Graal,** a series of bridges hovering over the swift river Aven on their way to the **Chaos de Pont-Aven,** a set of flat rocks around which the river swirls. A path through the tranquil **Bois d'Amour** (Lover's Wood) meanders along the Aven beneath the rich, dappled load of gnarled old trunks. The most enticing part of the walk in the woods is closest to town and runs next to the river. Above the woods, amid thriving farmland, is the **Chapelle de Trémalo,** the most obvious migration point of any walk through Pont-Aven's woods. The 16th-century church itself is quite simple but nonetheless an isolated treat, and it houses the 17th-century wooden painted crucifix that inspired Gauguin's *Le Christ Jaune.* After seeing the environs, view the paintings they inspired: the **Musée de L'Ecole de Pont-Aven,** pl. de l'Hôtel de Ville, up the street to the left when facing the tourist office, showcases the works of Gauguin, Serusier, and many of the Pont-Aven school's other artists. (☎02 98 06 14 43. Open daily July-Aug. 10am-7pm; Apr.-Oct. 10am-12:30pm and 2-6:30pm; Feb.-Dec. 10am-12:30pm and 2-6pm. €5, students and ages 13-20 €3, under 12 free.)

The **tourist office,** pl. de l'Hôtel de Ville, is a block from the bus stop on pl. Gauguin. Turn away from the river and walk toward the square and the museum beyond; the office is on the right side of the street. The staff sells a walking-tour guide (€0.50) and organizes **tours,** in French, of the town and museum (town €4). The office can also provide information on the "Fleurs d'ajonc" **folk festival,** on the first Sunday of August. (☎02 98 06 04 70; fax 02 98 06 17 25. Tours June-Sept. daily 11am and 4:30pm. Open July-Aug. M-Sa 9:30am-7:30pm, Su 10am-1pm and 3-6:30pm; Apr.-June and Sept. M-Sa 9:30am-12:30pm and 2-7pm, Su 10am-1pm; Oct.-Mar. M-Sa 10am-12:30pm and 2-6pm.)

QUIBERON

Though it lacks a wealth of museums, monuments, and history, the small peninsula of Quiberon (pop. 4500) does have more than its fair share of summer sunshine. Soak it up on either the Grande plage at the southern tip, or the spectacular, smaller beaches on the eastern side of the peninsula, where surfing, kayaking, and sailing are popular activities among hordes of sun-worshipping tourists. Stunning Belle-Ile is only a 45min. ferry ride away, but the countryside of Quiberon offers many opportunities for excursions. Save time for a hike or bike ride along the peninsula's wave-battered, seaward-facing coast, the Côte Sauvage.

⬛ TRANSPORTATION. Most of the year, the train to Quiberon stops at Auray (☎02 97 24 44 50). A special train connects Auray and Quiberon (1hr., July-Aug. 6-12 per day, €2.60). Trains run through Auray on the way to Brest, Paris, and

Quimper (call ☎ 08 36 35 35 35 for schedules). **TIM buses** (☎ 02 97 47 29 64) run from Auray (1hr., M-Sa 7-9 per day, €6), Carnac (30min., M-Sa 7-9 per day, €3.40), and Vannes (2hr., M-Sa 7-9 per day, €8). Quiberon Voyages, 21 pl. Hoche (☎ 02 97 50 15 30), runs trips all over the province, including an afternoon excursion to Carnac and Vannes (€20) and a €34 full-day trip to Concarneau, Pont-Aven, and Quimper (Open M-Th 9am-noon and 1:30-6pm, F 9am-noon and 1:30-5:30pm. MC/V.) Cruise the beachfront or explore the Côte Sauvage on **bikes**, tandems, or scooters from Cyclomar, 47 pl. Hoche (☎ 02 97 50 26 00), which also has an **annex** at the train station. (Bikes €7 per half-day, €9 per day, €38.50 per week. Scooter €25.50 per half-day, €37.50 per day. Moped €15 per half-day, €24 per day. Insurance for both scooters and mopeds €5.50 per day. 10% off with *Let's Go* guide, ISIC card, or note from the youth hostel. Credit card, personal ID, or passport deposit. Open daily July-Aug. 7:30am-11pm; Oct.-June and Sept. 8:30am-7pm. Annex open July-Aug. daily 8:30am-8pm. MC/V.)

⚡ PRACTICAL INFORMATION. To find the **tourist office**, 14 rue de Verdun, turn left from the train station and walk down rue de la Gare, then right down rue de Verdun. (5min.) The staff distributes a detailed guide to six walking tours. (☎ 02 97 50 07 84 www.quiberon.com. Open July-Sept. M-Sa 9am-1pm and 2-7pm, Su 10am-1pm and 3-7pm, early to mid-Aug. M-Sa until 8pm; Nov. and Feb.-June M-Sa 9am-12:30pm and 2-6pm; Dec.-Jan. M-Sa 9am-12:30pm and 2-5pm. Hours change frequently.) Other services include: a **laundromat** on rue de Port-Maria, near the beach (open daily 9:15am-8pm), **police** (☎ 02 97 30 24 00) at 7 rue Verdun, a **hospital** at the **Centre Hospitalier du Pratel** in Auray (☎ 02 97 29 20 20; open Sept.-June until 8pm), and **emergency services** at the Centre Hospitalier Bretagne Atlantique, bd. Maurice Guillaudot in Vannes (☎ 02 97 01 41 41). The **post office**, pl. de la Duchesse Anne, has **currency exchange.** (☎ 02 97 50 11 92. Open July-Aug. M-F 9am-12:30pm and 2-5:30pm, Sa 9am-noon; Sept.-June M-F 9am-noon and 2-5pm, Sa 9am-noon.) **Postal code:** 56170.

🏠 ACCOMMODATIONS & CAMPING. Quiberon is generally expensive, but the small, comfy **Auberge de Jeunesse (HI)** ❶, 45 rte. du Roch-Priol, will silence any complaints. From the station, turn left and take rue de la Gare toward the beach and the church. Turn left onto rue de Port-Haliguen, then right onto bd. Anatole France, and left onto rte. du Roch-Priol. (12min.) A friendly staff tends four 8-bed rooms and a pleasant outdoor eating area in a quiet neighborhood. (☎ 02 97 50 15 54. Breakfast €3.30. Sheets €2.80. Reception daily 9am-noon and 6-9pm. Open Apr.-Sept. Bunks €7.50. Camping €5.20 per person, tents €1.40.) The **Hôtel Men-Er-Vro** ❹, 22 rue de Port-Haliguen, 10min. from the beach, lets cozy rooms above a *crêperie*. Though small, the rooms are comfortable, individually decorated, and have TV and clean bathrooms with shower and toilet. (☎ 02 97 50 16 08. Breakfast €7. Reception daily 8am-4pm and 6-11pm. Reservations essential June-Sept. Singles €38.20; doubles €52.80-61.50; triples €66; all prices €8-15 lower in the low season. MC/V.) The central **Hôtel de l'Océan** ❸, 7 quai de l'Océan, offers bright, floral rooms, some facing the harbor. An enormous, sunny salon with views of the quai makes a lovely place to people-watch. (☎ 02 97 50 07 58; fax 02 97 50 27 81. Breakfast €6. Singles and doubles €28-38, with shower €38-45, with toilet €44-54. Extra bed €12. MC/V.)

The Quiberon Peninsula has nearly a dozen campsites; the tourist office provides information on all of them. One of the best is just off plage du Goviro. **🏕 Camping Bois d'Amour** ❶ has slick, spacious grounds and a heated pool. (☎ 02 97 50 13 52 or 04 42 20 47 25. Reception daily July-Aug. 9am-8pm; Apr.-May and Sept. 9:30am-12:30pm and 2-6:30pm. €4-8 per person, under 10 €3-5; tent or caravan with car €7-15. Electricity €4. Prices vary based on time of year.)

🖸 FOOD. Quiberon's menus feature seafood and the lollipop-topped, caramel-like *niniche* candy. For a little taste of the sea, try **La Criée ❸**, 11 quai de l'Océan. Displayed on ice, if these fish were any fresher they'd be flopping. The *plateau gargantua*, an awesome array of oysters, crab, and other sea-creatures (€49.50), is perfect for large groups. More modest fish dishes run €16-21. (☎02 97 30 53 09. Open July-Aug. daily noon-2pm and 7-10:30pm; Sept.-Dec. and Feb.-June Tu-Sa noon-2pm and 7-9:30pm, Su noon-2pm. MC/V.) Down the quai toward the Grande plage, **L'Elfenn ❸**, 1 rue de Kervozes, provides a slightly less expensive alternative with great views of the port. (☎02 97 30 40 43. *Menus* €13.30-16.50, fish €7-12, mussels €6-8. Open Su and W-Sa noon-7pm. MC/V.) Set just off the street, **Au Saffran ❹**, 20 rue Verdun, near the tourist office, incorporates various Asian influences to spice up traditional meat dishes. (☎02 97 50 18 64. *Menus* €15, €22, €27.50. Open Tu-Sa noon-2pm and 7:30-10pm, Su noon-2pm. MC/V.)

For groceries, try the extra-large **Marché Plus,** rue de Verdun (open M-Sa 7-9pm, Su 9am-noon), which has a wide variety of inexpensive pre-packaged sandwiches and salads, or the **Casino** supermarket, close to the hostel on rue de Port Haliguen (open M-F 9am-8pm, Sa 9am-noon). Produce **markets** spring up on pl. du Varquez (Sa mornings) and at Port Haliguen (mid-June to mid-Sept. W morning).

🖸 BEACHES. The aptly named Côte Sauvage stretches a wild and windy 10km along the western edge of Quiberon. Though the views from the road are amazing, drivers must take to the foot paths to fully enjoy the boulder-strewn beaches and eroded archways. Heed the signs marked *Baignades Interdites* (Swimming Forbidden); many have drowned in these tempting waters. Green flags mean safe supervised bathing; orange dangerous but supervised bathing; red means bathing prohibited. SOS posts with flotation devices dot the coastline. The weather here can be brutal and mercurial; storms assault the coast, then retreat just as quickly.

Grande plage is the most popular beach, while the small, rocky **plage du Goviro** appeals to those who prefer solitude. To reach it from the port, follow bd. Chanard to the left, along the water as it becomes bd. de la Mer and then bd. du Goviro. The east side of the peninsula is dotted with sandy beaches, perfect for sunbathing.

🖸🖸 ENTERTAINMENT & FESTIVALS. The beaches don't empty until it's too dark to see the volleyball. At 11:30pm, an energized crowd heads to the **Hacienda Café,** 4 rue du Phare, off pl. Hoche. Young teenage *Quiberonnais* drink flaming cocktails and dance until 3am. Black lights illuminate fluorescent murals that cover every surface, including the bar. (☎02 97 30 51 76. *Rhum vanille* or beer €2.50. Open July-Aug. daily 6pm-3am; Oct.-Apr. F-Su 10pm-3am.) To escape the teenybopper crowd, try the nightclub **Le Surtoit,** 29 rue Port Maria, where the clientele tends to be older, probably because they're the only ones who can afford the €5 beer and €8 liquor. (Open daily 11:30pm-5:30am.) In April, the **Journée Océanes** takes the town by storm with dance, music, plays, and even a pirate or two.

NEAR QUIBERON: BELLE-ILE

Boats dock on the northern coast at Le Palais, the island's largest town. SMN, in Port Maria, Quiberon, serves Belle-Ile (45min.) from the gare maritime, quai de Houat. (☎08 20 05 60 00, for foreigners 02 97 35 02 00; fax 02 97 31 56 81. 5-13 per day; round-trip €22.60, under 25 €13.60, seniors €15.50. Bikes €12.60, cars €101-193.) **Buses** run from Le Palais to Belle-Ile's other main towns: Bangor (33min., 7 per day); Locmaria (30min., 5 per day); Sauzon (15-25min., 10 per day). Tickets are available on the bus or at Point Taol Mor, quai Bonelle in Le Palais. (☎02 97 31 32 32. Single ticket €2.50, ages 4-12 €1.60; 2-day pass €10.) Cars Verts, gare maritime at Quiberon, runs one-day **bus tours** of the island. (☎02 97 50 11 60. €11; under 25 €9; over 60 €10.) Rent bikes and mountain bikes at Cyclotour, quai de Bonnelle, near the tourist office. (☎02 97 31 80 68. Bikes €8 per half-day, €10 per day. Passport deposit. Open July-Aug. daily 8:30am-7pm; Sept.-June M-Sa 9am-12:30pm and 2-7pm. No credit cards.) *Bike trails are well marked. The most spectacular area, the island's own Côte Sauvage, is also accessible by boat. See Quiberon Beaches, p. 267, for safety info).*

The coast of Belle-Ile (pop. 4800), an island known as "Le Bien-Nommé" ("The Well-Named"), is even more breathtaking than that of its neighboring *presqu'île*. Through the course of its history, Belle-Ile's high cliffs, crashing seas, and heathered fields have sheltered menhir-carvers, monks, pirates, and German POWs. Belle-Ile, 20km long, is large enough to make bike rental or shuttles necessary.

The massive **Citadelle Vauban,** built in 1549 by Henri II to protect monks from pirates, grew to an impressive network of snaking passageways between 30ft. walls. Today, they protect a grass-roofed museum with displays on famous visitors such as Sarah Bernhardt, Monet, and 400 German WWI POWs. (☎02 97 31 84 17. Open July-Aug. daily 9am-7pm; Apr.-June and Sept.-Oct. 9:30am-6pm; Jan. 11-Mar. 9:30am-noon and 2-5pm. €6.10, ages 7-16 €3.05, under 7 free.)

Belle-Ile's natural treasures lie scattered along the coastline. The **plage de Donnant,** on the western coast, with its expansive dunes and mysterious stone façade, is the widest and most popular beach. Equally gorgeous are the pristine **plage Port-Maria,** on the eastern shore, and the powder-white **plage Grands Sables,** southeast of Le Palais. To see the more rugged side of the island's coastline, head 6km northwest from Le Palais to postcard-like **Sauzon.** The narrow port fills with sailboats rocking gently on the turquoise water. Crisp white houses with multicolored shutters line the port, facing mossy rock cliffs on the other side. Massive rock formations rise over the thunderous **Grotte de l'Apothicairerie,** southwest of **Pointe des Poulains** on the northern tip of the island, and at the **Aiguilles de Port Coton,** where needle-like rocks shoot up through electric-green water. From late July to mid-August, **Lyrique-en-Mer** brings Mozart concerts and several operas to the island. (☎02 97 31 59 59.)

The Palais **tourist office** is on the dock's left end. The energetic staff distributes thorough guides to the island, a French hiking and biking brochure with plans, and a map (€8) that is helpful for exploring the island on foot or bike. They also have info on sailing, sea kayaking, and numerous other island activities. (☎02 97 31 81 93; fax 02 97 31 56 17; www.belle-ile.com. Open July-Aug. M-Sa 9am-12:30pm and 2-6pm, Su 4:30-6:30pm; Apr.-Sept. Su 10am-12:30pm; Oct.-Mar. closed Su.)

CARNAC

TIM bus (☎02 97 21 28 29) goes to Quiberon (30min., 7 per day, €3.70). There are two bus stops corresponding to Carnac's two tourist offices: Carnac-Ville, close to the town center, and Carnac-Plage, near the main tourist office and the beach. Tatoovu, a local shuttle, connects the two. (June-Sept. M-Sa 9:15am-1pm and 2:30-8pm, Su 9:15am-1pm. Tickets €1, carnet of 11 €10.50. Buy tickets on bus. Tourist office has schedules.)

The series of ancient megaliths in Carnac (pop. 4500) is collectively the oldest prehistoric site in Europe. Built from 4500 to 2500 BC, Carnac's 3000 menhirs stretch along the horizon for 4km, steadily increasing in height as they extend westward. A Celtic myth explains that they originated when St-Cornély turned a Roman legion to stone as he fled religious persecution, but recent scholarship suggests they served as ancient astronomic indicators of important sunrises and sunsets.

The closest menhirs to town are the **Alignements du Ménec,** the largest of its kind in the world. More than 1000 menhirs, some over 3m tall, stretch over 2km along the horizon. The somewhat more dynamic **Alignement de Kermario** stands adjacent to the **Géant du Manio** (a big rock) and the **Quadrilatère** (rocks in a square). Call the **Centre d'Accueil,** located in the Archéoscope (see below), to reserve a spot on one of the guided tours. (☎ 02 97 52 89 99; www.culture.gouv.fr/culture/arcnat/mega-lithes. Open daily July-Aug. 9am-8pm; May-June 9am-7pm; Sept.-May 10am-5pm. Hours likely to change; call in advance. Tours in French and occasionally in English. €4, under 25 €3, under 12 free.) Archeology buffs may find the stones more interesting than the uninitiated; the menhirs have been fenced in to prevent erosion, and visitors must keep to the observation boardwalk and surrounding hills.

Behind the church in the town center, the **Musée de Préhistoire**, 10 pl. de la Chapelle, is best summed up as lots of rocks. Though a bit sterile, its displays provide good background for a visit to the megaliths. (☎ 02 97 52 22 04. Open June-Sept. M-F 10am-6pm, Sa-Su 10am-noon and 2-6pm; Oct.-May Su-M and W-Sa 10am-noon and 2-5pm. €5, students €2.50, under 18 free. Combined admission with tour of alignments or Table des Marchands in Locmariaquer available.) The **Archéo-scope**, across the street from the Alignements du Ménec, gives a flashy introduction to the region's megalithic sites using lasers, films, and life-sized moving menhirs. From the church, take a right onto rue St-Cornély, another right on rue de Courdiec, then turn left onto rte. des Alignements. (☎ 02 97 52 07 49. Open July-Aug. daily 9am-6pm; mid-Feb. to mid-Nov. 10am-noon and 1:30-5pm. Showings in French every 30min.; July-Aug. in English 10:30am, 2:30pm, 6pm; also twice daily in German. Call for low season showings. €7, students and ages 13-18 €5, ages 6-12 €4, under 6 free.)

NANTES

The gory history of Nantes (pop. 550,000) would spice up even the dullest text-book. In 1440, the infamous pirate Bluebeard (the Maréchal de Retz) was brought to trial here and burned at the stake for his grisly crimes. Between the 16th and 18th centuries, the city established itself as a nexus of the slave trade, the brutal business making it France's largest port. Putting the efficiency of the guillotine to shame, bloodthirsty and impatient Nantois revolutionaries resorted to mass drownings in the Loire. Modern Nantes successfully blends a high-tech industry and professional population with a large university crowd. Down the street from the modern train station and towering buildings, cafés and 15th- to 16th-century wood-paneled houses line winding cobblestone streets. Street musicians perform on summer nights in the central squares and lively pedestrian streets.

▎ TRANSPORTATION

Flights: the airport is 10km south of Nantes (☎ 02 40 84 80 00). **Air Inter** (☎ 02 51 88 31 08) flies daily to **Lyon, Marseille, Nice,** and **Paris. Air France** (Info ☎ 02 40 47 12 33, reservations ☎ 08 02 80 28 02) sends at least six flights per week to **London.** A **Tan Air shuttle** (☎ 02 40 29 39 39) runs to the airport from pl. du Commerce and the south side of the train station (25min.; 1 per hr. 5:30am-9pm; tickets €6.) Schedule available at the info desk outside train station.

Trains: The train station has two entrances: North, at 27 bd. de Stalingrad, and South, rue de Loumel, across the tracks. Info, tickets at northern entrance. To: **Angers** (40min., every 30min. 5am-11pm, €13.50); **Bordeaux** (4hr., 5 per day, €37); **La Rochelle** (2hr., 7 per day, €20.60); **Paris** (2-4hr., 1 per hr., €49.10); **Rennes** (2hr., 20 per day, €18); **Saumur** (70min., 1 per hr., €17.80). **Luggage check** available at north side of station. (Open 6:15am-11pm. Backpack €3.20, larger luggage €4.80-7. 72hr. limit.)

Buses: Cariane Atlantique goes to **Rennes** (line #10; 2hr.; Sept.-June 2 per day, €23). Info office, 5 allée Duquesne, has schedules. (Open M-F 9:15am-noon and 2:15-6:15pm.) Depart station's south entrance and the parking lot on allée Baco. MC/V.

Public Transportation: TAN, 4 allée Brancas (☎08 01 44 44 44), opposite pl. du Commerce. Runs buses and three tram lines daily until 1am. Ticket €1.20, day pass €3.30. Office open M-F 7:15am-7pm.

Taxis: Allô Radio-Taxis Nantes Atlantique at train station (☎02 40 69 22 22). 24hr.

Car Rental: Europcar is in the parking garage, to the left of the north exit from the train station (☎02 40 29 05 10). Open M-F 7:45am-10:15pm. MC/V. Budget is on the right of the south exit from the train station (☎02 40 35 75 75). Open M-F 7:30am-10pm, Sa 8am-12:30pm and 2:30-6pm. AmEx/MC/V.

Bike Rental: The tourist office provides rental information. Bikes are rented from major parking lots in the city during the summer. Pl. du Commerce pick-up location open year-round. (☎02 51 84 94 51. €3 for half-day, €5 per day. Open daily 9am-7pm.)

Canoe Rental: Contre Courant, on the Ile de Versailles (☎02 40 14 31 24). Take tram line #2 (dir: Orvault Grand Val) to St-Mihiel. Cross the bridge to the island. €5 per hr., €15 per day. Open M-F 10am-noon and 2-7pm, Sa-Su 10am-7:30pm.

■ ORIENTATION

Nantes's tangle of neighborhoods, hills, and pedestrian streets spreads along the north bank of the Loire. Shadowed by a modest skyscraper, the **Tour Bretagne,** the city's axes run east-west along **cours John Kennedy,** which becomes **cours Franklin D. Roosevelt** and later **quai de la Fosse,** and north-south along **cours des 50 Otages.** The pedestrian district between the château and the **place du Commerce** is the liveliest part of town, and pl. du Commerce serves as the hub for local transportation.

⁊ PRACTICAL INFORMATION

Tourist Office: cours Olivier de Clisson (☎02 40 20 60 00; fax 02 40 89 11 99; www.reception.com/Nantes). Excellent maps and free **walking tour guides** in French and English. Ask for all guides and pick and choose where to visit. Tours of the city in French cover a variety of topics, from Nantes's history to its parks. **Accommodations booking** €1. Tours €6, students €3; call for a schedule. Office open M-Sa 10am-7pm. **Branch** at pl. St-Pierre. Open daily 10am-1pm and 2-6pm.

Budget travel: Voyage au Fil (☎02 51 72 94 60), at CRIJ (see below). Ground and air tickets. Matches travelers with drivers. Books nature and adventure trips. Open Tu-W, and F 10am-12:30pm and 2-6:30pm; Th and Sa 2-6:30pm. AmEx/MC/V.

Youth Information: Centre Régional d'Information Jeunesse (CRIJ), 28 rue du Calvaire (☎02 51 72 94 50). Info on youth discounts, housing, and volunteer and employment opportunities. Free **Internet** (30min. limit). Open Tu, W, and F 10am-6:30pm; Th and Sa 2-6:30pm.

Currency Exchange: Good rates at **Change Graslin,** 17 rue Rousseau (☎02 40 69 24 64), in pl. Graslin right next to *La Cigale.* Open M-F 9am-noon and 2-5:45pm, Sa 10am-noon and 2-4:45pm.

English Books: Librairie L. Durance, 4 allée d'Orléans, right turn off cours des 50 Otages. (☎02 40 48 68 79. Open M 2-7pm, Tu-Sa 9:30am-7pm. MC/V.)

Laundromat: 7 rue de l'Hôtel de Ville (open daily 7am-8:30pm); another at 11 rue Chaussée de la Madeleine (open M-Sa 10:30am-8pm).

Police: 6 pl. Waldeck-Rousseau (☎02 40 37 21 21).

Hospital: Centre Hospitalier Régional, 1 pl. Alexis Ricordeau (☎02 40 08 33 33). Women's emergencies ☎02 40 73 57 32.

Youth Hotline: 21 allée Baco (☎02 40 47 71 28). Support hotline for ages 12-25. Free, anonymous emotional counseling. Drop in or call.

Internet: Cybercity, 14 rue de Strasbourg (☎02 40 89 57 92). €3 per hr. Open daily 11am-midnight. **Cyberkebab,** 30 rue de Verdun, also sells falafel and kebabs. €3.10 per hr., €3.10 per kebab. Student discounts. Open daily 9am-2am.

Post Office: 4 rue du Président Edouard Herriot (☎02 40 12 62 74), at pl. de Bretagne near Tour Bretagne. **Currency exchange.** Open M-F 8am-7pm, Sa 8am-noon. **Poste restante:** Nantes RP, 44000. **Postal code:** 44000.

ACCOMMODATIONS & CAMPING

Nantes has plenty of good budget hotels and student dorm space in summer. The hotels across from the station are overpriced and in a seedy neighborhood.

Hôtel St-Daniel, 4 rue du Bouffay (☎02 40 47 41 25; hotel.st.daniel@wanadoo.fr), off pl. du Bouffay, in the heart of the pedestrian district. Clean, well-appointed rooms kept by a sociable owner. Some rooms overlook a graceful church garden. Breakfast €4. Singles €26; doubles with shower and toilet €29; triples and quads €39. AmEx/MC/V. ❷

Hôtel Renova, 11 rue Beauregard (☎02 40 47 57 03; fax 02 51 82 06 39), off cours des 50 Otages. Accommodating proprietor loves to chat with clients. Comfortable rooms with old-style furniture create a homey atmosphere. Central location. Breakfast €3. Singles with sink €21; double with shower €28, with bathtub €34. AmEx/MC/V. ❷

Hôtel du Tourisme, 5 allée Duquesne (☎02 40 47 90 26; fax 02 40 35 57 25). Comfortable rooms with plain walls but nice bathrooms, firm mattresses, TV and phone. For quality star-gazing, request the small single with a skylight. Free bike storage. Breakfast €4.80. Reserve ahead. Singles and doubles with shower €31. Extra bed €8. MC/V. ❷

Auberge de Jeunesse (HI), 2 pl. de la Manu (☎02 40 29 29 20; fax 02 51 12 48 42). From the north exit of the station, go right down bd. de Stalingrad, and left at rue de Manille. The hostel is on the left. (5min.) Located in a former factory, the hostel has an institutional feel. Clean bathrooms and sterile 2- to 5-bed rooms. Good breakfast included. Sheets €2.80. Lockout 11am-3pm. No curfew. €12 per bed. ❶

Foyer des Jeunes Travailleurs Beaulieu (HI), 9 bd. Vincent Gâche (☎02 40 12 24 00; fax 02 51 82 00 05). Only takes guests during August. From the north exit of the station, take tram line 1 (dir: François Mittérand) to pl. du Commerce and switch to line 2 (dir: Trocadie), taking it to Vincent Gâche. Bouleard Vincent Gâche is ahead on the left. By foot, turn left onto cours John F. Kennedy, then left onto av. Carnot and continue straight for about 10-15min., crossing the river. Vincent Gâche is one block up on the left, past the Holiday Inn. (20min.) Modern 1- to 4-person rooms with baths. Nice common rooms give a welcoming feel. Breakfast €2.20. Meals €6.10. Sheets €3. Reception daily 8am-9pm. Beds €12.80, non-members €22.70. ●

Camping du Petit Port, 21 bd. du Petit Port (☎02 40 74 47 94; camping-petitport@nge-nantes.fr). From pl. du Commerce, take tram line 2 (dir: Orvault Grand Val) to Petit Port Facultés. (10min.) Four-star site with plenty of outdoor activities and group events during the summer to keep busy. Laundry, showers, and pool. Reception daily July-Aug. 8am-11pm, Sept.-June 9am-7pm. Reserve in writing or arrive early in summer. €2.80 per person, €4.10 per tent, €5.80 per car. Electricity €3. ●

■ FOOD

Local specialties include *fruits de mer au beurre blanc* (seafood with butter sauce), *canard nantais* (duck prepared with grapes), and Mouscadet and Gros Plant white wines. *Le Petit Beurre* cookies and *muscadines* (chocolates filled with grapes and Muscadet wine) are both local inventions. Explore the streets behind **place du Bouffay,** where the *crêperies* are especially good. The biggest **market** in Nantes is the **Marché de Talensac,** along rue de Bel-Air near pl. St-Similien behind the post office. (Open Tu-Sa 9am-1pm.) On pl. du Bouffay, a smaller market has the same hours, while another stretches down pl. de la Petite Hollande, opposite pl. du Commerce. (Sa 8am-1pm.) The best selection of fresh fruit in town can be found at **Le Fruitier,** 17 rue des Carmes. Pint-sized basket of berries are convenient for snacking. (☎02 40 12 08 09. Open M-Sa 8am-8pm.) **Monoprix,** 2 rue de Calvaire, is off cours des 50 Otages, down from the Galeries Lafayette. (Open M-Sa 9am-9pm. MC/V.) For a quick lunch, head over to **Midi-Pile ●,** 11 chaussée de la Madeleine, a great sandwich shop. (☎02 40 48 46 37. Salads €1.40-3.80, sandwiches €3.20-3.80. Open M-F 11am-3pm.)

▨ **La Cigale,** 4 pl. Graslin (☎02 51 84 94 94), facing Théâtre Graslin, is one of the most beautiful *brasseries* in France. Although some may visit to take pictures of the architecture and intricate décor, the food, especially the *soupe de poisson,* is the real treasure. Diners hand-pick their dinner from a large display of fresh seafood. *Plats* €13; desserts €7; fabulous brunch €15, Sa and Su 10am-4pm. Open daily 7:30am-midnight. ❸

▨ **Le Pain Perdu,** 12 rue Beauregard (☎02 40 47 74 21) serves traditional French seafood dishes with some modern spice and exotic entrées like salmon sushi in a romantic atmosphere. *Menus* €15-20. Open daily noon-2:30pm and 7:30-11pm. ❹

Le Bistrot des Arts, 4 rue Trois Croissants (☎02 40 20 33 86), serves traditional *bistrot* fare fashioned with an eye for form and color, most notably a wide variety of meats in decadent sauces. Lunch *menu* €5.80, dinner *menus* from €9.50. MC/V. ❸

L'Ile Verte, 3 rue Siméon Foucault (☎02 40 48 01 26), makes vegetarian, organic salads and tarts from the freshest market produce. Salads €4.20-8, *plats* €8.80. Open M-Tu and Th-Sa 11:30am-2:30pm. Tea room open 2:30-6:30pm. Closed Aug. ❷

◉ SIGHTS

Ask the tourist office about the **Nantes City Card,** which is a pass covering admission to the château, the Musée des Beaux-Arts, the Musée d'Histoire Naturelle, and the Musée Jules Verne. The pass also includes free access to trams and buses and a tour guided by the tourist office. (€14 for 24hr. access.) Most of Nantes's museums have free entrance one Sunday per month on a rotating basis; check with the tourist office. Walk around the city to experience Nantes's elaborate 19th-century façades fashioned with wrought-iron balconies. Make sure to see **Passage Pommeraye,** an unusual shopping arcade off pl. du Commerce.

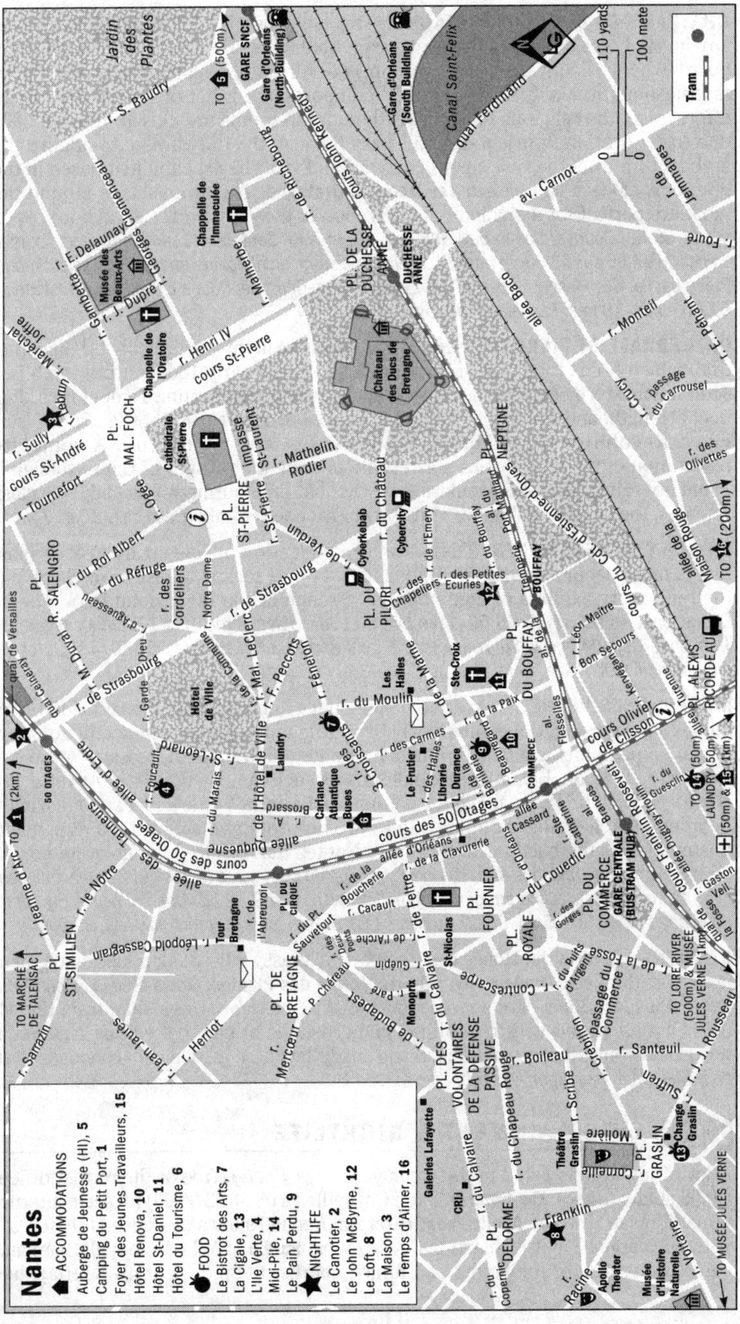
Nantes
ACCOMMODATIONS
Auberge de Jeunesse (HI), 5
Camping du Petit Port, 1
Foyer des Jeunes Travailleurs, 15
Hôtel Renova, 10
Hôtel St-Daniel, 11
Hôtel du Tourisme, 6
FOOD
Le Bistrot des Arts, 7
La Cigale, 13
L'Ile Verte, 4
Midi-Pile, 14
Le Pain Perdu, 9
NIGHTLIFE
Le Canotier, 2
Le John McByrne, 12
Le Loft, 8
La Maison, 3
Le Temps d'Aimer, 16
Tram
110 yards
100 meters
Château des Ducs de Bretagne
Cathédrale St-Pierre
Musée des Beaux-Arts
Chappelle de l'Oratoire
Chappelle de l'Immaculée
Jardin des Plantes
Canal Saint-Félix
GARE SNCF
Gare d'Orléans (North Building)
Gare d'Orléans (South Building)
Hôtel de Ville
Les Halles
Ste-Croix
St-Nicolas
Théâtre Graslin
Musée d'Histoire Naturelle
Apollo Theater
Galeries Lafayette
Monoprix
CRIJ
Cyberkebab
Cybercity
Laundry
Cariane Atlantique Buses
Tour Bretagne
GARE CENTRALE (BUS-TRAM HUB)
PL. DE LA DUCHESSE ANNE
PL. MAL. FOCH
PL. ST-PIERRE
PL. DU BOUFFAY
PL. DU COMMERCE
PL. ROYALE
PL. GRASLIN
PL. DE BRETAGNE
PL. ST-SIMILIEN
PL. R. SALENGRO
PL. DU CIRQUE
PL. FOURNIER
PL. DELORME
PL. ALEXIS RICORDEAU
PL. DES VOLONTAIRES DE LA DÉFENSE PASSIVE
cours des 50 Otages
cours St-Pierre
cours St-André
cours John Kennedy
cours Olivier de Clisson
cours Franklin Roosevelt
r. de Strasbourg
av. Carnot
quai Ferdinand
TO MARCHÉ DE TALENSAC
TO MUSÉE JULES VERNE
TO LOIRE RIVER (500m) & MUSÉE JULES VERNE (1km)

BRITTANY

CHÂTEAU DES DUCS DE BRETAGNE. This château has seen as much history as any in the Loire. Its imposing walls once held Gilles de Retz, the original Bluebeard, who was convicted of sorcery in 1440 for sacrificing hundreds of children in gruesome rituals. In 1598, Henri IV composed the Edict of Nantes here in an effort to soothe religious tensions. Although the rooms are closed off until 2006 due to renovation, tourists can still pass through the drawbridge to admire the architecture from the vast inner courtyard and visit the art exhibits housed in the temporary **Musée du Château des Ducs de Bretagne.** The promenades around the moat are perfect for a picnic or an afternoon in the grass with a good book. (☎02 40 41 56 56. Courtyard open daily July-Aug. 10am-7pm; Sept.-June 10am-6pm. Free. Tours in French July-Aug. daily 3:30pm provide details on history, architecture, and visits to select rooms in the castle. €3. Museum open July-Aug. daily 10am-6pm; Sept.-June closed Tu. €3, students €1.60, under 18 free. Free after 4:30pm.)

CATHÉDRALE ST-PIERRE. Gothic vaults soar 38m in this remarkably bright cathedral, which holds the body of King François II. His early 16th-century tomb is a sculpted masterpiece, with a statue at each corner representing Temperance, Justice, Strength, and Prudence. Built in stages from 1434 to 1891, St-Pierre has survived Revolutionary pillagers, WWII bombs, and a 1972 fire. A complete restoration of the interior has masterfully undone the ravages of time—though it could not salvage the stained glass that was shattered during WWII. Only one glass remains, the largest in France, 25m above François's tomb. (Open daily 10am-7pm.)

MUSÉE DES BEAUX-ARTS. The museum's collection of fine art by French masters is more decorative than definitive, but the real reason to visit is to check out the temporary exhibits of contemporary French art on the ground floor. (10 rue Clemenceau. ☎02 51 17 45 00. Take bus #11, dir: Jules Verne, or #12, dir: Colonière, to Trébuchet. Open M and W-Su 10am-6pm, F until 8pm. €3.10, students €1.60; first Su of the month and F 6-9pm free. Tours M, W, and Su €3.)

MUSÉE JULES VERNE. A creative display pays homage to this local legend. The guided tour through the exhibits may be a little much for the science fiction novice, but a pamphlet available in English provides all the info necessary to wander the museum alone. Beautiful first editions of such famous novels as *Around the World in Eighty Days*, playbills, paraphernalia from Verne's life, and amazingly detailed sketches illustrating his ideas are all proudly displayed. Paintings and posters depict the bustling 19th-century Nantes that inspired the great author. (3 rue de l'Hermitage. Take bus #81, dir: Indre, from pl. du Commerce to Salonges. At the fork, bear right; the museum is at the top of hill on the left. ☎02 40 69 72 52. Open M and W-Sa 10am-noon and 2-5pm, Su 2-5pm. €1.50, students €0.75. Free tours in French July-Aug. 3:30pm.)

GARDENS. Behind the Musée des Beaux-Arts, grassy hills, duck ponds, and greenhouses with exotic flowers await in the **Jardin des Plantes.** (Tours every hr. Open M-Sa 8am-7:45pm, Su 2-5pm.) For a more meticulously landscaped oasis, take tram line #2 (dir: Orvault Grand Val) to St-Mihiel and cross the bridge to the **Ile de Versailles,** a tiny island converted into a peaceful and shady Japanese garden and teahouse. (Open daily Mar.-Sept. 8am-8pm; Oct.-Feb. 8am-5:30pm).

🎵 📷 ENTERTAINMENT & NIGHTLIFE

A lot of nightlife is listed in the weekly *Nantes Poche* (free at the tourist office, €0.50 at any *tabac*). **The Katorza,** 3 rue Corneille (☎08 36 68 06 66) projects international films in *v.o.* The **Apollo Theatre,** on rue Racine, shows movies nightly for €2, with occasional English selections. Nearby **rue Scribe** is full of late-night bars and cafés. A favorite of the young and funky, **quartier St-Croix,** near pl. Bouffay, has about three bars per block and just as many cafés. More clubs and *discothèques* await the adventurous traveler farther from the *vieille ville*.

■ **Le Loft,** 9 rue Franklin, sports a posh lounge with a vast bar. A chic, comfortable place to relax with friends and a cocktail during the week. An eclectic mix of dance music really gets the place banging on weekends. DJ every night from 11pm, except W. No cover. Mixed drinks €7. Open Tu-Sa 9:30am-4am.

La Maison, 4 rue Lebrun (☎02 40 37 04 12), off rue Maréchal Joffre on the other side of town, creates a silly, carefree time in a beach party atmosphere, with primarily young people. Drinks from €4. Open daily 3pm-2am.

Le John McByrne, 21 rue des Petites Ecuries (☎02 40 89 64 46), is a good pub with a lively crowd. The bar is packed on weekends, so gear up for an energetic night out. Live Irish music on Friday nights. Beer €3-5. Open daily noon-2am.

Le Canotier, 21 quai de Versailles (☎02 40 12 06 29), the watering hole for live music aficionados, hosts local musicians 3-4 times per week. Nightly piano bar. Weekend blues, jazz, and French accordion music. Beer €2.80-3.20. Open Tu-Su 2pm-2am.

Le Temps d'Aimer, 14 rue Alexandre Fourny (☎02 40 89 48 60), is Nantes's favorite gay disco with a variety of party music. From pl. de la République on Ile de Nantes, follow rue Victor Hugo to rue Fourny on the left. Or take tram #2 from pl. du Commerce to Wattignies. Walk up the street toward pl. du Commerce and take a left on rue de la Porte Gelée. Continue straight to reach the club. Cover M-Th €5, F-Su €13. Cocktails €5-8. Open daily midnight-7am.

◉ FESTIVALS

Eastern Orthodox chanters, blues rockers from Mali, and masqueraders from Trinidad and Tobago all converge to perform at the international **Festival d'Eté** in early July. Up-and-coming Asian, African, and South American filmmakers walk the red carpet at the **Festival des Trois Continents** (info ☎02 40 69 74 14) in late November and early December. Locals boast that their **Carnaval** (info ☎02 40 35 75 52) is one of the best in France, with parades and an all-night party on Mardi Gras.

BRITTANY

LOIRE VALLEY
(VAL DE LOIRE)

 The Loire Valley, in the heart of France, is known for its châteaux. France owes much to the history of these châteaux, which date back to the 9th century, when France was splintered by Viking invasions. Local communities, under the leadership of feudal lords, erected fortresses to protect landholdings from invaders. Later, the region became a focal point of the incessant Anglo-French wars. In 1429 at Chinon, Joan of Arc persuaded the Dauphin to give her an army to liberate Orléans. During the Renaissance, many castles were converted into comfortable palaces, framed by spectacular gardens and heaped with artistic masterpieces. Today, the rolling hills of the lovely "Garden of France" are perfect for an afternoon bike ride, while its fertile soil grows some of the nation's best wines. Owing to its central location and proximity to Paris, the valley now draws people from all corners of the world.

The cities of the Loire are convenient bases for exploring the region's many castles, but they are also exciting in and of themselves. ◙Tours (p. 292) is a fun, affordable university city that provides quick access to the châteaux of ◙Chenonceau (p. 299) and Azay-le-Rideau (p. 301), as well as to the fortified citadel of Loches (p. 300), and the recreated Renaissance garden of ◙Villandry (p. 300). The city of ◙Blois (p. 284) is located comfortably near the châteaux of ◙Chambord (p. 288), Cheverny (p. 289), Beauregard (p. 289), and Valençay (p. 290). Those who still haven't sated their appetites for châteaux will want to continue on to ◙Amboise (p. 290), famous for its collection of Da Vinci artifacts and bizarre troglodyte dwellings, and to ◙Chinon (p. 297), a quaint village with tunnel-riven château rubble. Orléans (p. 278), Joan of Arc's hometown, grants easy access to Germigny-des-Près (p. 282), the oldest church in France; St-Benoit-sur-Loire (p. 282), an arch-filled Romanesque church; and Sully-sur-Loire (p. 282), a classic fortress complete with requisite towers, turrets, and vast forests. Visitors are also attracted by the lace-making industry of Alençon (p. 316), and the beautiful *vieille ville* and famous annual 24hr. car race of Le Mans (p. 311), the equestrian tradition and mushroom caves of ◙Saumur (p. 302), and the world-famous tapestries of Angers (p. 307).

The rich soil of the Loire Valley nurtures asparagus, strawberries, and sunflowers. In the *caves* once used as quarries for the châteaux, tubs of mushrooms *(champignons)* neighbor barrels filled with wine. Typical French dishes abound here; *rillettes* (potted pork) and pâté often complement regional menus.

▊ TRANSPORTATION

An ambitious itinerary in the Loire Valley can only be realized with a **car**, and three châteaux a day is a good limit. **Trains** often have inconvenient schedules and don't reach many châteaux. Tours is the region's best rail hub, with connections to 12 châteaux, while the smaller city of Blois is also a convenient base from which to explore the area. A group of four renting a car can generally undercut **tour bus** prices, but **biking** is probably the most popular way to see most of the region. Distances between châteaux and hostels tend to be short, and many small, flat roads cut through fields of poppies and grain. Most stations distribute the useful booklet *Châteaux pour Train et Vélo*, which details train schedules, distances, and infor-

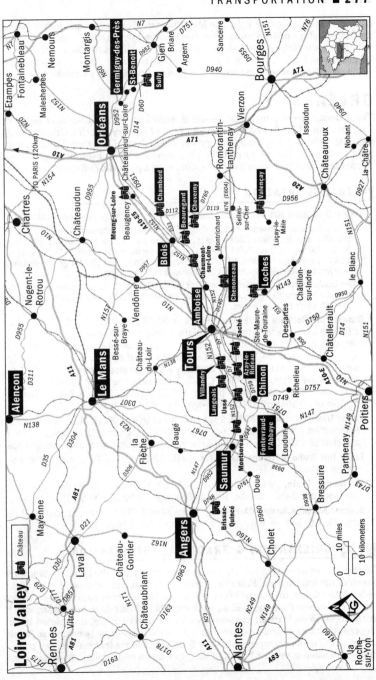

mation on bike and car rentals. The Michelin map of the region and tourist biking guides will steer drivers away from truck-laden highways and onto delightful country roads. Nature buffs should ask at tourist offices for the excellent free bilingual booklet *Loisirs and Randonnées of the Val de Loire*, which has info on **hiking, biking, canoeing, horseback riding, rock climbing,** and **parachuting.**

ORLÉANS

The intimate streets, energetic residents, busy bistros, and historical sights of Orléans (pop. 117,000) make it a unique blend of country and city. Orléans clings tightly to its history, especially the parts involving Joan of Arc: there are at least 45 public statues of the savior of 1429. This, combined with beautifully preserved Renaissance architecture of its *vieille ville*, exert a powerful pull on its neighbors.

▢ TRANSPORTATION

Trains: 2 separate stations. A train shuttles passengers between them every 30min.

Gare d'Orléans, on pl. Albert I (☎ 08 36 35 35 35), is in the center of town and better for tourists. Info office open M-Sa 9am-7:30pm. Ticket booths open daily 5:30am-9pm. To: **Blois** (30min., 6 per day 7:45am-7:50pm, €8.40); **Nantes** (2hr., M-F 3 per day 6:45am-6pm, €31); **Paris** (1¼hr., about 4 per hr. 5am-10:40pm, €15); **Tours** (1hr., every 30min., €14.50). A huge shopping mall, pl. d'Arc, complete with supermarket, is attached to the train station.

Gare Les-Aubrais, rue Pierre Semard (☎ 02 38 79 91 00), is a 30min. walk north from the town center. A train **shuttles** new arrivals from quai 2 to Gare d'Orléans for €1.20, but the transfer is free with a train ticket to Orléans.

Buses: Gare Routiers, 2 rue Marcel Proust (☎ 02 38 53 94 75), connects to the Gare d'Orléans by an overpass to the right of the Carrefour supermarket in the train station shopping mall. Info desk open M-Tu and Th 10am-1pm and 4-6:45pm, W and F 10am-1pm and 3-6:45pm, Sa 10am-1pm. **Les Rapides du Val de Loire** (☎ 02 38 53 94 75; www.rvl-info.com) runs to **Sully** via **Germigny** and **St-Benoit-sur-Loire** (1hr.; M-Sa 5 per day 6:40am-6:25pm, Su 5:30pm; €7.40). **Transbeauce** (☎ 02 37 18 59 00, in Chartres) runs to **Chartres** (1¼hr; 4 per day, M-F 12:50pm-6:50pm, Sa 7am-6:55pm, Su 5:25pm and 8:30pm; €10.60, under age 20 €5.40). Tickets sold on bus.

Public Transportation: SEMTAO, 2 rue de la Hallebarde (☎ 02 38 71 98 38), under pl. Jeanne d'Arc shopping mall. Tickets sold at station machines. €1.20 (good for 1hr.), *carnet* of 10 €10.50, day pass €3. Get a free city bus map here or at the tourist office.

Taxis: Taxi Radio d'Orléans, rue St-Yves (☎ 02 38 53 11 11). €7 to hostel from train station. 24hr.

Car Rental: Ecoto, 19 av. Paris (☎ 02 38 77 92 92). From €40 per day. Open daily 9am-noon and 2-6pm. **Car Go,** 1 rue de Bourgogne (☎ 02 38 53 65 60).

Scooter and Bike Rental: CAD, 95 fbg. Bannier (☎ 02 38 81 23 00). Scooters €24 per day. Bikes €15-18 per day. Open daily 9am-noon and 2-7pm.

✳ ▢ ORIENTATION & PRACTICAL INFORMATION

Most places of interest in Orléans are on the north bank of the Loire, a 5min. walk south of the train station. From the station, go left, and circle around to the right side of the station; the tourist office will be across the street to your right. To get to the city center from the station, walk straight onto **rue de la République,** which leads to **place du Martroi,** the intersection for many streets, dominated by an impressive statue of Jeanne d'Arc. Here, rue de la République becomes **rue Royale** and runs to the river, intersecting **rue de Bourgogne** and **rue Jeanne d'Arc,** two pedestrian-dominated streets with most of the city's sights, restaurants, shops, and bars.

Tourist Office: 6 rue Albert I (☎02 38 24 05 05; fax 02 38 54 49 84). Maps (€0.50) and an excellent walking tour guide of the *vieille ville*. For €2, you can buy a tour book containing info and maps of all of the tourist sites. The office also runs French **tours** (€4.50) with a variety of themes, from Orléans's historic cathedral to the promenades around the Loire (July-Aug. daily 2:30pm; Apr.-Sept. on Su; call office for a schedule). Open May-Sept. W-Sa 9:30am-1pm and 2pm-6pm., Tu open at 10:30am; Oct.-Apr. W-Sa 9:30am-1pm and 2-5:30pm, Tu open at 10:30am.

Budget Travel: Havas Voyages, 34 rue de la République (☎02 38 42 11 80). Open M-F 9:30am-12:30pm and 2-6:30pm, Sa 9am-1pm and 2-6pm. MC/V.

Money: Banks are on rue de la République and pl. du Martroi. For the best **currency exchange,** head to the post office (see listing).

English Bookstore: Librairie Paes, 184 rue de Bourgogne (☎02 38 54 04 50), also carries books in Italian, German, and Spanish.

Youth Information: Centre Régional d'Information Jeunesse (CRIJ), 5 bd. de Verdun (☎02 38 78 91 78; fax 02 38 78 91 71). Provides info on sporting events, jobs, volunteer opportunities, and travel through Europe. Also helps choose courses at the Université d'Orléans. Open M noon-6:30pm, Tu-F 9:30am-6:30pm, and Sa 9:30am-5:30pm.

Laundromat: 26 rue du Poirier (☎02 38 88 23 84). Open daily 7am-11pm. **Laveries du Val de France,** 137 fbg. Bannier (☎02 38 88 23 84). Open daily 7am-7pm.

Police: 63 rue du fbg. St-Jean (☎ 02 38 24 30 00).

Crisis Lines: Battered women (☎08 00 05 95 95); battered men (☎01 40 24 05 05).

24hr. Pharmacy: 7pm-9pm, call ☎15. After 9pm, call police with ID card and prescription.

Hospital: Centre Hospitalier Régional, 1 rue Porte Madeleine (☎02 38 51 44 44).

Internet: Odysseüs Cyber Café, 32 rue du Colombier (☎02 38 77 98 48). €1.50 per 15min., €4.50 per hr. Open M-W 9am-9pm, Th-F 9am-1am, Sa 11am-1am. BizzNet, 256 rue de Bourgogne (☎02 38 24 11 51). Various applications as well as fax, scan, and copying center. €1.60 per 15min., €6 per hr. Open M-F 9am-8pm, Sa 10am-6pm.

Post Office: pl. du Général de Gaulle (☎02 38 77 35 35). Currency exchange. Open M-F 8:15am-7pm, Sa 8:15am-12:15pm. Postal code: 45000.

▟ ACCOMMODATIONS & CAMPING

Cheap hotels are hard to find. Many close in August. Call ahead July-Aug.

Auberge de Jeunesse (HI), 1 bd. de la Motte Sanguin (☎02 38 53 60 06; asse.crju@libertysurf.fr). A 19th-century school for girls has been converted into this 51-bed hostel with large 2- to 4-person rooms. Spotless hallway showers. Kitchen facilities, TV room, parking area, and beautiful views of the Loire. Breakfast €3.40. Sheets €3.20. Reception M-F 8am-7pm, Sa-Su 9-11am and 5-7pm. Dorms €7.80. ❶

Hôtel Charles Sanglier, 8 rue Charles Sanglier (☎02 38 53 38 50). Delightful, immaculate rooms and central location make this a great bargain. Off rue Jeanne d'Arc, with countless restaurants nearby. Breakfast €4.50. Garage available: cars €5.30, bikes €1.50. 1- to 2-person rooms with shower, toilet, and TV €34-38. Extra bed €7.60. ❸

Hôtel de L'Abeille, 64 rue Alsace Lorraine (☎02 38 53 54 87; hoteldelabeille@wanadoo.fr). One block from the station, this 2-star hotel enchants its guests with 31 lovely, whimsically decorated rooms in the *vieille-ville* style. Breakfast in bed for €7. Singles with toilet €35, with shower €39-45; doubles with shower €39-49; triples €51-60. ❹

Hôtel Blois, 1 av. de Paris (☎/fax 02 38 62 61 61), conveniently located across the street from the train station. Clean, simple rooms overlook a busy intersection. The front door locks around 10pm—be sure to get the code from the owner. Breakfast €4.30. Singles and doubles with shower and toilet €31. AmEx/MC/V. ❷

🍴 FOOD

In late summer and autumn, locals feast on *gibier* (game) freshly hunted in the nearby forests. Specialty sausages include the *andouillettes de Jargeau*, while *saumon de Loire* (salmon) is grilled fresh from the river. Orléans's most important culinary contribution are its tangy wine vinegars, which many local *brasseries* serve on salads and in marinades. The local cheeses are *frinault cendré*, a savory relative of camembert, and a mild chèvre. Wash it all down with Gris Meunier or Auvergnat wines, or nearby Olivet's pear and cherry brandies.

Les Halles Châtelet, pl. du Châtelet, is attached to Galeries Lafayette. (Open Tu-Sa 7am-7pm, Su 7am-1pm.) The extensive **Carrefour** that occupies the back of the mall at pl. d'Arc (open M-Sa 8:30am-9pm) is conveniently close to the *centre ville*. Just three blocks from the hostel is a **Marchéplus** supermarket, on the corner of rue de la Manufacture and bd. Alexandre Martin. (Open M-Sa 7am-9pm, Su 9am-1pm.)

At night, the *brasseries* and bars around **Les Halles Châtelet** and **rue de Bourgogne** are the best bet for good, cheap food. Inexpensive Chinese, Indian, and Middle Eastern restaurants lie between rue de la Fauconneries and rue de l'Université, including **Mijana ❷,** 175 rue de Bourgogne, which serves traditional Lebanese cuisine. (☎02 38 62 02 02. Appetizers €5-7, *plats* from €11, *menus* €16-19. Open M 7-11pm, Tu-Sa noon-2pm and 7-11pm. MC/V.) **Les Musardises ❸,** 38 rue de la République, is a classic *salon de thé*, specializing in delectable pastries and truffles. (*Gateaux* €4-6, tea €3.) **L'Arrovoir ❸,** 224 rue de Bourgogne, serves a variety of salads (€7) and classic bistro fare (€14) in an energetic, casual environment. Stick around after dinner for a lively bar scene and a DJ on weekends. **Les Alpages ❷,** 182 rue de Bourgogne, serves traditional French cuisine. The seasonings and prices will keep you coming back. (☎02 38 54 12 34. Open M-Sa 7:30am-10pm. Salads €7.50, *plats* €9-11, *menus* €15-21, fondue for 2 €12-14, dessert €5.20.)

🔎 SIGHTS

Most of Orléans's historical and architectural highlights are near **place Ste-Croix.** These include elegant squares, historic *hôtels*, and stained-glass artwork ranging from the 11th century to the modern renditions found in **Eglise St-Paterne.** *(Orléans Pass gives half-price admission to most sites in town for €11. Passes on sale at tourist office starting May 1.)* In 1429, having liberated Orléans from a seven-month siege, Joan of Arc triumphantly marched down nearby **rue de Bourgogne,** the city's oldest street, a scene vividly captured in "Jeanne d'Arc" at the Musée des Beaux-Arts.

CATHÉDRALE STE-CROIX. With towering Gothic buttresses, an intricate façade, and slender, dramatic interior arches, the cathedral is Orléans's crown jewel. On May 8, 1429, Joan of Arc came here to join the first procession of thanks for the deliverance of the town from the English. Vivid 19th-century stained-glass windows depict her life's story, down to the flames that consumed her. *(Pl. Ste-Croix. Open daily June-Aug. 9:15am-7pm; Sept. 9:15am-5:45pm; Jan.-May and Oct.-Dec. 9:15am-noon and 2:15-5:45pm. Free. Tours of upper sections organized by the tourist office May-Sept. €4.)*

MUSÉE DES BEAUX ARTS. A fine collection contains Italian, Flemish, and French painting, sculpture, and *objets d'art* from the 15th to the 20th centuries. Modern art and archaeological exhibitions come through regularly. *(1 rue Fernand Rabier, to the right as you exit the cathedral. ☎02 38 79 21 55; fax 02 38 79 20 08. Open Su 1:30-6pm, Tu-Sa 10am-noon and 1:30-6pm, W until 8pm. €3, students €1.50, under 16 free.)*

HÔTEL GROSLOT D'ORLÉANS. Built in 1550 by bailiff Jacques Groslot, this beautiful Renaissance mansion was the king's local residence for two centuries. In 1560, François II died here amid scandal. His bedroom is now a popular site for

Orléans

many of Orléans' weddings and receptions. Charles IX, Henri III, and Henri IV also stayed here. The sumptuously decorated rooms evoke the atmosphere of centuries past. Behind the *hôtel*, a peaceful 19th-century garden provides respite from the busy city. Both are now open to the public. *(Pl. de l'Etape. To the left of the Musée des Beaux Arts. ☎02 38 79 22 30. July-Sept. Su-F 9am-7pm, Sat 5pm-8pm; Oct.-June Su-F 10am-noon and 2-6pm, closed Sa. Free tours available through tourist office. Garden open daily Mar.-Sept. 7:30am-8pm; Oct.-Feb. 8am-5:30pm.)*

MAISON DE JEANNE D'ARC. In a reconstruction of the original house where the ill-fated saint stayed during her sojourn in Orléans, models of the city in 1429 and an automated narration in English, Spanish, German, and French depict the events surrounding the 7-month siege of Orléans. The museum also displays reconstructions of clothes and armor from the late Middle Ages. The curators are eager to show visitors around. *(3 pl. de Gaulle. ☎02 38 52 99 89. Open May-Oct. Tu-Su 10am-noon and 2-6pm; Nov.-Apr. 2-6pm. €2, students €1, under 16 free.)*

PARC FLORAL DE LA SOURCE. Originally organized to host the International Flower Show of 1967, this massive park contains intricate gardens of rare flowers, aviaries, a petting zoo, and a butterfly reserve featuring 40 exotic species. The beautiful grounds draw young and old with picnic areas, playgrounds, ducks, and flamingoes. *(By car, take RN-20, dir. Vierzon-Bourges and exit at St-Cyr-En-Val. By tramway, take in direction of Orléans-La Source and exit at the Université-Parc Floral stop. From the train, take a* *right, cross the tracks, and proceed down the path that leads to the park entrance.* ☎ *02 38 49 30 00. Open Apr.-Oct. 9am-6pm; Nov.-Mar. 2-5pm. €3.60, student €3, under 18 €2. Butterfly reserve €2.40. Bike rentals €10.70 per day.)*

OTHER SIGHTS. Popular with school children and nature enthusiasts, the curious **Musée des Sciences Naturelles** makes natural history fun. Collections of bugs are displayed in front of artwork that evokes their natural environment. Tropical and Mediterranean greenhouses heat up the top floor. Don't miss the human skulls in the *Cabinet des Curiosités*. *(6 rue Marcel Proust.* ☎ *02 38 54 61 05. Open daily 2-6pm. €3.10, students and under 16 €1.60.)* Orléans natives are quite proud of the one-room **Musée Historique et Archéologique de l'Orléannais** which displays the treasure of Neuvy-en-Sullias, a remarkable set of Gallo-Roman statues discovered in 1861, along with relics from the Middle Ages to the Neoclassical period. The museum is located within the **Hôtel Cabu**, an old Renaissance mansion designed in the Henry II style. *(Sq. Abbé Desnoyers.* ☎ *02 38 79 21 55. Open July-Aug. daily M 1:30-6pm, Tu-Sa 10am-12:15pm and 1:30-6pm; May-June and Sept. Tu-Su 1:30-6pm; Oct.-Apr. W, Sa, Su 1:30pm-6pm. €3, students €1.50, under 16 free. Admission to the Musée Historique is included with admission to the Musée des Beaux Arts. Tours by reservation only, €3.80 per person or €5 for tours in languages other than French.)*

🎵📷 ENTERTAINMENT & FESTIVALS

Most locals head for the nightlife of Paris, but the bars along **rue de Bourgogne** and near **Les Halles-Châtelet** keep the homefront happy. **Paxton's Head,** 264 rue de Bourgogne, is a laid-back British pub with live jazz on Saturday nights. (☎ 02 38 81 23 29. Beer €7, whiskey €5. Open daily 3pm-3am.) For a lively night with a great crowd, head to **Havana Café,** 28 pl. du Châtelet. (☎ 02 38 52 16 00. Open daily 10pm-3am.) Get into the act at **Entr-acte,** 81 bd. Alexandre, with Thursday night karaoke. (☎ 02 38 62 71 37. Open daily until 11pm). **Bowling,** 2 rue Moreau, proves the universal appeal of smoke, beer, bowling, and billiards. (☎ 02 38 66 31 55. Open M-Th 2pm-1am, F 2pm-2am, Sa 2pm-3am, and Su 2pm-midnight.) **Cabaret Restaurant l'Insolite,** 14 rue du Coq St-Marceau, serves dinner with a cabaret show. (☎ 02 38 51 14 15. *Menus* from €12. Dinner 8:30pm, show begins at 10:30pm. Open F and Sa.)

Select-Studios, 45 rue Jeanne d'Arc, shows a few first-run English-language and French films. (☎ 08 92 69 66 96. €4.50-7.50, matinee €4.) There's also **Cinéma des Carmes,** just up the block at 7 rue des Carmes. The city comes alive with parades, music, and food for the **Fête de Jeanne d'Arc** each May 7-8 in commemoration of the heroine's miraculous victory over the British. During the month of June, Orléans hosts **Jazz d'Orléans,** a festival held in its gardens with musicians from around the world. (www.orleans.fr/orleansjazz. Tickets €13-20, under 26 €10; some concerts free.) In the last week of September, the **Fête de Loire** comes to Orléans with theatrical events, fireworks, and nautical displays on the banks of the Loire (☎ 02 38 79 24 05), while on weekends in November and December, the **Semaines Musicales Internationales d'Orléans (SMIO)** brings the Orchestre National de France to town.

NEAR ORLÉANS

GERMIGNY, ST-BENOÎT, & SULLY

A day's drive eastward along the Loire uncovers these three small towns, each dating from a different era of the Middle Ages. About 30km southeast of Orléans lies the squat Carolingian church of **Germigny-des-Prés.** Though heavily restored, it remains the oldest church in France. The private chapel preserves a restored 9th-century Byzantine-style mosaic. The monks offer a 45min. tour of the church for groups. (☎02 38 58 27 97. Open daily Apr.-Sept. 8:30am-7pm; Oct.-Mar. 8:30am-6pm. Free. Call ahead to arrange a tour; €46 per group.)

The prize of **St-Benoit-sur-Loire**, 35km southeast of Orléans, is an exquisite 11th- and 12th-century Romanesque basilica. Originally part of the Abbaye de Fleury, the church was destroyed during the French Revolution. Its charms now include a Romanesque mosaic floor, intricate carvings, and 75 arched pillars supporting a barrel vault. Twice daily, the church rings with chanted services. The monks offer a tour of the monastery in French (€3) or other languages (€4) by reservation only, at 10am and 1pm. (☎02 38 35 72 43. Masses M-Sa 6am, noon, 9 pm; Su 11am. Church open daily 6am-10pm.)

The 14th-century fortress of **Sully-sur-Loire**, 42km from Orléans, guards the southern bank of the Loire, towering over the village and forest that surround it. The white-turreted castle housed a somnolent Charles VII, a frustrated Joan of Arc, a fleeing Louis XIV, and an exiled Voltaire. Written guides in English explain the details of the artwork and architecture of the château (€1.70). Intricate tapestries and displays recreate life in the age of chivalry. Horse-and-carriage rides are available on the grounds. Throughout the year, special themed tours are given in French. One for children is led by guides in medieval costume, and another focuses on the restoration of the castle. Contact the château for schedules. (☎02 38 89 84 66. Open Su-M and W-Sa Apr.-Sept. 10am-6pm; Feb.-Mar. and Oct.-Dec. 10am-noon and 2-5pm; closed Jan. and every Tu except July-Aug. **Closed until Apr. 1, 2004.** French tours June-Sept. daily, English tours late July to mid-Aug. M 1:30pm. €4.90, students and children €3.40, €1.70 extra for tours.) Sully's grassy grounds and wooded pathways beg for picnics. (Park open daily 9am-nightfall.) In June, the grounds become a stage for a renowned music festival that draws classical musicians from all over the world. (Call tourist office for details.) Two-star **Camping Sully-sur-Loire ❶**, chemin de la Salle Verte, surveys the château from the riverbank. (☎02 38 36 23 93. Reception M-Sa 7am-noon and 2-7pm. Open May-Oct. €2.20 per person, under 7 €1.10; €1.40 per site; €1 per car. Electricity €1.40-2.60.) The **tourist office** is in the center of town on pl. de Gaulle. (☎02 38 36 23 70; fax 02 38 36 32 21. Open May-Aug. M-F 9am-12:30pm and 2-7pm, Sa 9am-7pm, Su 10:30am-1pm; Sept.-June M-Sa 9:30am-noon and 12:30-6:30pm.)

The same **bus** from Orléans also serves Germigny (45min., €5.80); St-Benoît (50min., €6.40); and Sully (1hr., €7.40), five times per day (M-Sa 6:40am-

FROM THE ROAD

UN TOUR DE FRANCE

The French countryside can be a beautiful thing...from a train window as it dashes past you. As a born-and-bred city girl, the thought of moving outside shopping districts and casual sightseeing areas did not even enter my mind—until I tried to visit the château of Beauregard (see p. 289).

Absolutely no transportation was going within a 10km radius of the site. To my dismay, the tourist office handed me a bike rental phone number and a map of bike paths. After one hour spent agonizing over whether I wanted to break a sweat in the name of culture, I decided to do the typical French thing and bike it.

I set out on my country adventure with enthusiasm, which made up for my lack of athletic prowess. Suited up and raring to go, I began cycling through the Loire Valley on a ride that ended up lasting seven hours, all under the hot sun. I am ashamed to admit that many an old man passed me on my way. I almost passed out from dehydration (drink plenty of water), but even so, I would never pass up that cross-country bike trip. Huffing and puffing, I passed acres of grain, the steady flow of the Loire, and at least three country châteaux. My once-in-a-lifetime memories that came from leaving my comfort zone outlasted the sore muscles. And I get lifetime bragging rights about how I toured France by bicycle.

–Gilmara Ayala

6:25pm). Although bus travel between the towns is rather difficult, the pleasant walk from St-Benoît to Germigny takes only 45min. The trek from Sully to St-Benoît takes about 1¼hr. The adventurous may choose to make the challenging 45km **bike ride** to Sully from Orléans, past tiny villages and wheat fields along the scenic south bank of the Loire. **To drive,** take eastbound 152, which becomes the D955, in the direction of Châteauneuf-sur-Loire; signs point you to the D60, which will take you to the three towns.

BLOIS

Blois (pop. 50,000) is one of the Loire's most famous towns. At its heart sits a château that once housed Louis XII and François I. The compressed town manages to encompass the different styles of French architecture from the 12th through the 19th centuries, the most memorable of which are the blue slate roofs, red-brick chimneys, and narrow cobblestone lanes that evoke the simple beauty of a Vermeer village. Blois is a good base for a visit to Chambord and Cheverny, arguably the most famous châteaux in the Loire Valley: each is just an hour's bike trip or a 20min. bus ride away.

▐ TRANSPORTATION

Trains: pl. de la Gare. Ticket office (☎08 92 35 35 35) open M-Sa 5:30am-8:20pm and Su 7:15am-10pm. To: **Angers** via Tours (3hr., 5 per day, €18.40); **Orléans** (30min., 14 per day 6am-11pm, €8.40); **Paris** via Orléans (1¾hr., 8 per day 6am-9pm, €20); **Tours** (1hr., 13 per day 7am-11pm, €8.20); **Amboise** (20min., 15 per day, €5.40).

Buses: Point Bus, 2 pl. Victor Hugo (☎02 54 78 15 66). Open M 1:30-6pm, Tu-F 8:30am-noon and 1:30-5:30pm, Sa 9am-noon. **Transports Loir-et-Cher** (TLC; ☎02 54 58 55 44) sends a bus to nearby **Chambord** and **Cheverny** (mid-May to Aug. 2 per day; 9:10am, returning 1pm, and 1:25pm, returning 6pm; €10, students €8 with ID, under 12 and over 65 free. Reduced entry to châteaux with bus ticket.) Buses leave from the station and from pl. Victor Hugo. Tickets purchased on the bus. Schedules are available at the train station or by calling TLC. Buses also to **Vendôme.**

Taxis: Taxis Radio, pl. de la Gare (☎02 54 78 07 65). €10 to hostel near Blois. 24hr.

Bike Rental: Amster Cycles, 7 rue du Dr. Desfray (☎ 02 54 56 07 73; www.amstercycles.com), one block from train station. Wide selection, including racing bikes. €13 per day, tandem bikes €30. Open M-Sa 9:15am-1pm and 2-6:30pm, Su 10am-1:30pm and 3-6:15pm. MC/V. **Cycles Leblond,** 44 levée des Tuileries and 17 rue de Sanitas (☎02 54 74 30 13). 1km down the river from the city center, near the Verdun bus stop on line #4. The owner rents bikes and gives advice on the best routes to nearby châteaux. €12.20 per day. ID deposit. Open daily 9am-12:30pm and 2-7:15pm.

▟ ▐ ORIENTATION & PRACTICAL INFORMATION

The château and town center are 5min. from the train station, left down av. Jean Laigret. Between the château and **rue Denis Papin** is a bustling pedestrian quarter. When in doubt, descend, as all roads lead down to the city center.

Tourist Office: 3 av. Jean Laigret (☎02 54 90 41 41; www.loiredeschateaux.com), in Anne de Bretagne's Renaissance pavilion, though scheduled to move to pl. de la Voûte du Château. Offers maps of the city (€0.50) and of Loire Valley (€2.60), complete info on châteaux, tickets for bus circuits, **currency exchange** with a €5 fee, and an **accommodations service** €2.30. Open Apr.-Sept. Tu-Sa 9am-7pm, Su-M and holidays 10am-7pm; Oct.-Mar. M 10am-12:30pm and 2-6pm, Tu-Sa 9am-12:30pm and 2-6pm, Su 9:30am-12:30pm. MC/V. Around the corner, **Maison du Loir-et-Cher,** 5 rue de la Voûte

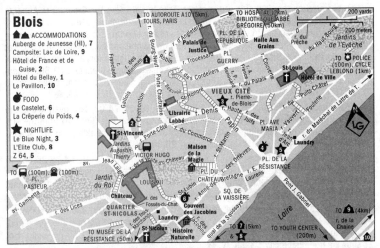

Blois

🏠🏠 ACCOMMODATIONS
Auberge de Jeunesse (HI), 7
Campsite: Lac de Loire, 9
Hôtel de France et de
Guise, 2
Hôtel du Bellay, 1
Le Pavillon, 10

🍴 FOOD
Le Castelet, 6
La Crêperie du Poids, 4

⭐ NIGHTLIFE
Le Blue Night, 3
L'Elite Club, 8
Z 64, 5

du Château (☎02 54 57 00 41; fax 02 54 57 00 47), provides info on events, festivals, lodging, and camping. Open M-F 9am-7pm, Sa-Su 10am-1pm and 1:30-7pm.

Money: Banque de France, 4 av. Jean Laigret (☎02 54 55 44 00), is on the right as you walk down the hill to the tourist office. **Currency exchange** available M-F 9am-12:15pm and 1:45-3:30pm. The post office also exchanges money (see listing).

English Bookstore: Librairie Labbé, 9 rue Porte Chartraine. Open M 2-7:15pm, Tu-F 9:30am-7:15pm, Sa 9am-7:15pm.

Laundromat: Laverie, 11 rue St-Lubin, pl. Louis XII (☎02 54 74 89 82). Open daily 7am-9pm. Wash €4, dry €2. **Laverie du Mail,** 1 rue Jeanne d'Arc (☎ 02 54 75 58 55). Open daily 7am-9pm. Wash €4, dry €1 per 5 min.

Youth Center: Bureau d'Information Jeunesse de Loir-et-Cher, 7 av. Wilson (☎02 54 78 54 87). Brochures, job info, and help planning travel and booking inexpensive tickets. Open M-Sa 9am-12:30pm and 2-5pm.

Police: 42 quai St-Jean (☎02 54 55 17 99).

Hospital: Centre Hospitalier de Blois, mail Pierre Charlot (☎02 54 55 66 33).

Internet: Bibliothèque Abbé Grégoire, pl. Jean Jaurès (☎02 54 56 27 52). €0.20 per 5min., €2.40 per hr. Limit 1hr. Reservations recommended. Open M-Tu and F 1-6:30pm, W 10am-6:30pm, Sa 10am-6pm.

Post Office: 2 rue Gallois (☎02 54 57 17 17). **Currency exchange.** Open M-F 8am-7pm, Sa 8am-12:30pm. **Postal code:** 41000.

🏠 ACCOMMODATIONS & CAMPING

🏠 **Hôtel du Bellay,** 12 rue des Minimes (☎02 54 78 23 62; fax 02 54 78 52 04), at the top of porte Chartraine, near the city center. Small, family-run establishment offers personal attention and spotless, comfortable rooms, the cheapest with a choice of toilet or shower. Breakfast €4.20. Reception 9am-noon and 5-9pm. Closed early to late Jan. Call ahead. Singles and doubles €24-35; triples €45; quads €55. MC/V. ❷

Auberge de Jeunesse (HI), 18 rue de l'Hôtel Pasquier (☎/fax 02 54 78 27 21), 5km west of Blois in Les Grouets. From the tourist office, follow rue Porte Côté, bear right following rue Denis Papin down to the river, and take a right on quai de la Saussaye to the first bus stop on the right side of the street. Take bus #4 (dir: Les Grouets) to Auberge de Jeunesse. (2 per hr. 7am-7pm). The bus also leaves from the SNCF train station at 7:45pm. The hostel's 24 single-sex dorms, of questionable cleanliness, are fairly removed from civilization. Be sure to bring your own dinner, as local restaurants close at 7pm. Attracts a diverse, international crowd. Excellent kitchen facilities and hot press-and-repeat showers in an outdoor bathroom complex. Simple breakfast €3.30. Reception 6:45-10am and 6-10:30pm. Lockout 10am-6pm. Curfew 10:30pm. Open Mar. to mid-Nov. Bunks €15.30, with HI membership €7.40, under 26 €10.70. ❶

Le Pavillon, 2 av. Wilson (☎02 54 74 23 27; fax 02 54 74 03 36), overlooking the Loire. 20min. walk from the train station, or take the local bus (line 3A) from the station. Bright, comfortably furnished rooms right on the Loire. Breakfast €5.30. Singles and doubles €24-38; quads €50. Extra bed €9.30. MC/V. ❷

Hôtel de France et de Guise, 3 rue Gallois (☎02 54 78 00 53; fax 02 54 78 29 45). In an ideal location next to the château, this hotel offers elegantly decorated rooms that recall the days of the 19th century. Breakfast €6. All rooms with toilet, TV, telephone, and shower or sink. Singles €40; doubles €48; triples €57. Extra bed €3. MC/V. ❹

Campsite: Lac de Loire (☎02 54 78 82 05; fax 02 54 78 62 03). From the station or city center, take bus #S7 to Lac de Loire (20min., 3 per day, €1). 2-star site. Open mid-June to mid-Sept. Tent and 1 person €7, €3 per extra person, €1.50 per child. Hot showers free. Electricity €3. MC/V. ❶

▶ FOOD

Locals have been perfecting *le chocolat blésois* ever since Catherine de Medici brought her own pastry-makers from Italy. Sumptuous *pavés du roi* (chocolate-almond cookies) and *malices du loup* (orange peels in chocolate) peer invitingly from *pâtisseries* along **rue Denis Papin.** Traditional, homey restaurants line **rue St-Lubin** and **place Poids du Roi,** and inexpensive Chinese and Greek restaurants are on the streets around the **place de la Résistance.** Bakeries and fruit stands dot the central pedestrian area. An **Intermarché** supermarket is at 16 av. Gambetta (open M-Th 9am-12:30pm and 3-7:15pm, F-Sa 9am-7:15pm) and at **Utile,** 6 rue Drussy (open M-Sa 9am-9pm, Su 9:30am-noon and 5-9pm). **Place Louis XII** bustles with an open-air **market** (Sa morning), while pl. du Château hosts a **gourmet market.** (July-Aug. Th 11am-6:30pm.) *Crêperies* pepper almost every block, but **La Crêperie du Poids ❷,** 3 rue Denis Papin, has the widest selection. (☎02 54 90 01 90. Cheese, egg, or ham crêpe €6-8; ice-cream-and-crêpe sundaes €6. Open Tu-F noon-2pm and 7-10pm, Sa noon-2pm and 7-11pm, Su noon-4pm and 7-10pm; MC/V.) **Le Castelet ❷,** 40 rue St-Lubin, makes regional delicacies with fresh produce for vegetarians (*menu* €12-16), children (€7.50), and everybody else (*formules* from €12). (☎02 54 74 66 09. Appetizers from €5, salads €6. Open July-Aug. M-Tu and Th-Sa noon-2pm and 7-10pm, W and Su 7-10pm; Sept.-June M-Tu and Th-Sa noon-2pm and 7-10pm. MC/V.)

◉ SIGHTS

CHÂTEAU DE BLOIS. Brilliantly decorated with gold trimming, carved pillars, and stained glass that rivals cathedral windows, this château is unique. Home to Louis XII and François I, Blois's château was as influential in the 15th and early 16th centuries as Versailles was in later years, and it combines architectural styles from the reign of each monarch. The motto of François I (1494-1547), *Nutrisco et extingo* (I feed on fire and I extinguish it), explains the abundance of carved and painted fire-breathing salamanders. Though not as grandiose as other châteaux of the

Loire, Blois was meticulously restored by 19th-century architect Félix Duban. It now houses three museums: the recently renovated **Musée des Beaux-Arts**, featuring a 16th-century portrait gallery; the **Musée d'Archéologie**, with a fascinating display of locally-excavated glass and ceramics; and the **Musée Lapidaire,** exhibiting sculpted pieces from nearby 17th-century châteaux. (☎02 54 90 33 33. Open daily July-Aug. 9am-7:30pm; Apr.-June and Sept. 9am-6pm; Jan.-Mar. and Oct.-Dec. 9am-12:30pm and 2-5:30pm. €6, students under 25 and children under 17 €4. Historical tours in French May-Sept. every hr.; depart from the courtyard; free with admission; call ahead to request in English. 25min. tours of the city by carriage depart from the entrance to the château; €5. Son-et-lumière show mid-Apr. to late Sept. daily 10pm; €9.50, students €6.50; English show on W. Combined tickets for the château and son-et-lumière, or for the château and Maison de la Magie €11.50, students €8, and children €5. Ticket for all three attractions €15, students and children €11. MC/V.)

VIEILLE VILLE. The most enjoyable attractions in Blois might be its hilly streets and ancient staircases, outlined in the tourist office's walking guide. Inviting bars and bakeries on **rue St-Lubin** and **rue des Trois Marchands** tempt those en route to the 12th-century Abbaye St-Laumer, now the **Eglise St-Nicolas.** (Open daily 9am-6:30pm.) East of **rue Denis Papin** lie the most beautiful streets of all, lined with timber-framed houses and narrowing into intimate alleys and courtyards. Five hundred years of expansions to **Cathédrale St-Louis** endowed it with a beautiful mix of architectural styles from the 12th to the 17th centuries. (Open daily 7:30am-6pm; crypt open June-Aug.) For splendor and historical appeal, St-Nicolas and St-Louis almost beat out the château. The view of the Loire from the **Jardin de l'Evêché**, behind the cathedral, is utterly spectacular. At sunset, cross the Loire and turn right onto **quai Villebois Mareuil** for a view of the château rising above the roofs of the town.

OTHER SIGHTS. The **Musée de la Résistance, de la Déportation et de la Libération** is a powerful memorial to French Holocaust victims and Resistance fighters from Blois. It is packed with photos, newspaper clippings, and narratives gathered and presented by veterans of the Resistance. (1 pl. de la Grève. ☎02 54 56 07 02. Open M-Sa 9am-noon and 2-6pm. €3, students and children €1). The **Maison de la Magie,** next to the château, entertains with films and displays on magic. A certain amateur trickster was so impressed with the museum's godfather, Blois native Jean-Eugène Robert-Houdin, that he adopted the name Houdini. (1 pl. du Château. ☎02 54 55 26 26. Open July-Aug. daily 10am-6:30pm; Apr.-June and Sept. Tu-Su 10am-12:30pm and 2-6pm. Free tours in French, 1½hr. Live shows 2-3 times per day. €7.50, ages 12-17 €6, ages 6-11 €4.50.)

🎵 ENTERTAINMENT

Blois appears tame—until the sun goes down. Neon signs beckon party-goers to the hip combination *discothèque*, lounge bar, and karaoke joint **L'Z 64,** 6 rue Mal. de Tassigny, near the town center, at around midnight. (☎02 54 74 27 76. Cocktails €5-8. Open Tu-Su 8:30pm-4am.) Near the *place*, **Le Blue Night,** 15 rue Haute, serves 100 international beers (€4-8) in a bar resembling a medieval chapel. Billiard tables are busy and music blasts on the weekends. (☎02 54 74 82 12. Open daily 6pm-4am.) At **L'Elite Club,** 19 rue des Ponts Chartrains, locals gather to rock the night away with house music. (☎02 54 78 17 73. Open Th-Sa 11pm-5am.)

From Sept-May, the city hosts world-class jazz and classical musicians, dancers, and actors in the **Halle Aux Grains,** 1 pl. de la République. Schedules available by phone (☎02 54 90 44 00, Tu-F 1-7pm and Sa 2-7pm. Tickets €18-22, students €16-19.) In July and August, for **Le Soleil a Rendez-Vous avec la Lune,** the city holds free concerts in the street nearly every night, including jazz, classical, and traditional French music. (Schedules available at the tourist office.)

THE BIG SPLURGE

AROUND THE LOIRE IN 80 MINUTES

It takes a lot of patience and time to see all the châteaux in the Loire Valley, but it is certainly possible—and even enjoyable—for those up to the challenge. Some determined châteaux-crawlers will spend hours traveling by bike or car, but more intrepid souls cut the work out of touring by throwing all caution to the wind and visiting the châteaux via hot air balloon. Sightseeing by air is a popular option in France, allowing visitors to see many things at once: river vistas, amazing sunrises, fields of grain, vineyards, and, of course, panoramic views of their favorite châteaux. From the air, all parts of the châteaux estates can be fully appreciated, from the exquisite patterns of the gardens to the buildings' turrets and façades.

Although hot air balloons offer an indisputable source of romance and whimsy, they may be too tame for the most adventurous travelers. Companies also book helicopter tours of the valley or offer opportunities to sky dive onto the lawns of Chambord or Cheverny. Whatever its form, a trip through the air is the "extreme" way to visit châteaux on the Loire.

*To visit châteaux by hot air balloon, contact **France Montgolfieres,** La Riboulière 41400, Monthou-sur-Cher. (☎ 02 54 71 75 40. Tours in English or French. Refundable ticket €250, ages 6-12 €145.)*

CHÂTEAUX NEAR BLOIS

TLC buses, outside the Blois train station, runs a châteaux circuit to Chambord and Cheverny, spending 2hr. at each. For those who prefer to go at their own pace, the châteaux are within easy **biking** range over beautiful terrain. From Blois, it's 10km to **Cheverny** and 6km to **Beauregard.** The châteaux and towns are well-marked along the roads. Cyclists are advised to stay off the major, and narrow, French highways. The **tourist office** branch at the Châteaux de Blois has maps of safe, efficient routes. Pay close attention to route numbers while on the road, as roads are marked by their destination. The **Regional Tourism Committee** (☎ 02 54 78 62 52) offers one-week cycling packages which include bike rental, meals, accommodations, and admission to the châteaux.

CHAMBORD

*Take the TLC **bus** from the SNCF station in Blois (45min., 9:10am and 1:20pm, €10) or enjoy the 1hr. **bike** ride. To bike or **drive,** cross the Loire in central Blois and ride 1km down av. Wilson. At the roundabout, take route D956 south for 2-3km followed by a left onto D33. **Château:** ☎ 02 54 50 40 00. Open daily Apr.-Sept. 9am-6:15pm; Oct.-Mar. 9am-5:15pm. Last entry 30min. before closing. €7, ages 18-25 €4.50, under 18 free.*

Built by François I between 1519 and 1545 for his hunting trips and impressive fêtes, Chambord is the largest and most extravagant of the Loire châteaux, an impressive testament to the monarchy's desire to flaunt their power before visiting dignitaries. With 440 rooms, 365 chimneys, and 83 staircases, the castle is a realization of the ambitious king's interest in a multitude of architectural styles. The Greek cross-floor design used for the keep was formerly reserved for sacred buildings, but François co-opted it for his mansion. In the center of the castle, he built a spectacular double-helix staircase whose design is attributed to Leonardo da Vinci. The ornamentation of the château marks the first influence of the Italian Renaissance in French architecture. François stamped Chambord with 70 of his trademark stone salamanders, commissioned 14 4m tall tapestries of his hunting conquests, and splayed his initials across the large stone chimneys on the rooftop terrace. After all this, François graced Chambord with his presence for 42 days.

The rooms are labeled in English, but more detailed explanations of the architecture are available through rented headsets (€4) in English, German, Spanish, Italian or French. In summer, visitors are given lanterns to visit the castle at their own pace on incomparable **night tours** that feature whispering voices, mysterious eyes peeking through the castle walls, dancing shadows, and colorful frescoes projected onto the outer walls of the castle. (July-Aug. M-Sa 10:30pm-1am, last entry midnight; Sept. F-Sa. €12, ages 12-25 €9, under 12 free). The night tour only passes through the empty front foyers of the castle, so be sure to take the day tour to see the full gamut of castle rooms, their furniture, tapestries, and personal items.

An **ATM** stands next to the snack shops and restaurants outside the tourist office. To explore the surrounding lush forests, **boat** and **bike rentals** are available through **Alizés** from a little shelter at the foot of the château. (☎ 02 54 33 37 54. 2-person boats €10.80 per hr., electric boats €6.10, children €5.30 for 55min. Bikes €5.50 per hr., €9 per half-day, €11 per day. Call ahead to have your bike brought to the SNCF station in Blois at 8am and to return it there 7-8pm. Open daily June-Sept. 10:30am-7:30pm; Oct. and Mar.-Apr. 11am-6pm.) Campers can trek to **Camping Huisseau-sur-Cosson ❶**, 6 rue de Châtillon, about 5km southwest of Chambord on D33. (☎ 02 54 20 35 26. Open May-Sept. 9am-8pm. €2 per tent; €3.50 per person, under 7 €2. Shower included. Electricity €2.50.) Or try **Camping des Châteaux** between Chambord and Cheverny in **Bracieux**. (☎ 02 54 46 41 84; fax 02 54 46 09 15. Open late Mar. to mid-Oct. daily 8:30am-noon and 3-7:30pm. Tent €5, €4.50 per adult, €1.50 per child. Showers included. Electricity €2.)

CHEVERNY

*To **bike** or **drive** to the château, take D956 or D765 south for 45min. Four-star **Camping Les Saules** is 2km away on the road to Contres. (☎ 02 54 79 90 01; fax 02 54 79 28 34. Open Apr.-Sept. 8:30am-8:30pm. €3.80-5.50 per person depending on the season, ages 3-11 €2.60; €4.90-6.10 per tent.) **Château:** ☎ 02 54 79 96 29. Open July-Aug. daily 9:15am-6:45pm; Apr.-June and early Sept. 9:15am-6:15pm; Oct. and Mar. 9:30am-noon and 2:15-5:30pm; Nov.-Feb. 9:30am-noon and 2:15-5pm. €5.90, students €4, ages 7-14 €2.80. MC/V. The same **bus** that leaves from the SNCF station to Chambord also goes to Cheverny after a 2hr. stop at the first château.*

Since its completion in 1634, Cheverny has been privately owned by the Hurault family, whose members have served as financiers and officers to the kings of France. The family's wealth is reflected in the impeccably maintained grounds and luxuriously restored décor of the château, which was inhabited as recently as 1985. Although much smaller than other châteaux, Cheverny retains magnificent furnishings that recreate the feel of a wealthy 17th-century home. Murals, armor, and elegant tapestries cover every inch of the walls. Fans of Hergé's **Tintin** books may recognize Cheverny's Renaissance façade as the inspiration for the design of Captain Haddock's mansion. A gallery of Hergé's art and comics is adjacent to the grounds. Cheverny sheltered the **Mona Lisa** in its Orangerie during WWII. The kennels are home to nearly 70 mixed English-Poitevin hounds still used in hunting expeditions (Oct.-Mar. Tu and Sa.) The **souper des chiens** offers a bizarre opportunity to see these hounds gulp down their dinner of raw meat in less than 60 seconds. (W-F and Su-M 5pm.) Next to the kennels, in the **trophy room**, thousands of antlers poke out of the ceiling and surround a striking stained-glass window depicting a hunt.

BEAUREGARD

*A 30min. **bike ride** from Blois. Off D956, en route to Cheverny. Ask at bike rental for more detailed directions. A **taxi** from Blois costs €14. **Château:** ☎ 02 54 70 36 74 or 02 54 70 40 05. Open July-Aug. daily 9:30am-6:30pm; Apr.-June and Sept. daily 9:30am-noon and 2-6:30pm; Oct.-Jan. M-Tu and Th-Su 9:30am-noon and 2-5pm; early Feb. to Mar. daily 9:30am-noon and 2-5pm. €6.50, students and ages 7-18 €4.50, under 7 free. Gardens alone €4.50.*

Before François I unleashed his fantasies on Chambord, he designed Beauregard as a hunting lodge for his uncle René. Beauregard, 6km south of Blois, is cozier than its flashy cousin, which has subsequently been expanded to a full-blown château. Paul Ardier, treasurer to Louis XIII, commissioned Jean Mosnier to paint what became the world's largest portrait gallery. Today this collection of over 300 wall-to-wall, unframed paintings is a *Who's Who* of European powers, from Philippe de Valois (1378) through Louis XIII (1638) and including all of the Valois monarchs, as well as the faces of Elizabeth I, Thomas More, and Columbus. The 5616 hand-painted Delft tiles that cover the floor portray Louis XIII's army solemnly marching to war, and are currently undergoing a 20-year restoration project. Outside the château, the ruins of a 14th-century chapel invite a walk into the woods. Tours are available in French and English; times vary depending on the season and the availability of guides; call ahead. English guide sheets are always available.

VALENÇAY

Trains run from rue de la Gare to Salbris, which connects to Orléans (2hr.; M-Sa 7 per day, 2 on Su; €15) and Paris (3hr.; M-Sa 7 per day, 2 on Su; €23.80). Buses run to Valençay from the train station in Blois (1½hr., 3 per day 7:40am-5:15pm, €8). To get to the château from the bus stop at pl. de la Halle, continue straight down rue de l'Auditoire and take your second right into pl. Talleyrand. Château: ☎02 54 00 10 66. Open July-Aug. 9:30am-7:30pm; Mar.-June and Sept.-Nov. 9:30am-6pm; call ahead for schedule Nov.-Mar. €8.80, students 18-25 €6. Free shows in French feature actors in traditional dress (daily July-Aug. 11am-5:30pm). The tourist office is on av. de la Résistance. (☎02 54 00 04 42. Open M-Sa 9:30am-7pm, Su 10am-7pm.)

Though farther out than most Loire Valley châteaux, popular Valençay, built in 1540, is a unique mix of interesting history and exquisite furnishings, modeled after the imposing style of Chambord (p. 288). Its owner Jacques d'Etampes intended it to inspire awe for his wealth and strength. After the Revolution, the estate was sold to Napoleon, and the 20,000 hectares of woodlands, vineyards, and fields, became a prized feather in the emperor's cap.

Unlike many châteaux of the Loire, Valençay was built almost entirely in the Imperial style that developed under the reign of Napoleon I. This décor reflects the influence of the château's 19th-century owner, the cunning Charles-Maurice Talleyrand-Périgord. Talleyrand began his career under Louis XVI, but survived the Revolution and was made Minister of Foreign Affairs by Napoleon. The Emperor bought the château for Talleyrand, desiring him to augment the empire's popularity by entertaining important guests here. After Napoleon deposed King Ferdinand VII of Spain in 1808, he sent the Spanish royal family to Talleyrand at Valençay. The Spanish princes and their ladies-in-waiting remained here until 1814, when Ferdinand was reinstated as monarch. The exquisite interior contains a number of remarkable items dating back to the early 19th century, including the table used for the Congress of Vienna and a sumptuous dining room.

Admission to the château includes a free audio guide in English and visits to the wine cellars, underground kitchens, and an animal park complete with peacocks, ponies, goats, hens, and horses. Don't mistake the wallabies for kangaroos. Children will delight in the oversized maze just outside the château.

AMBOISE

One of the oldest cities in the Loire Valley, Amboise (pop. 12,000) was home to the first *Tourangeaux* (people from Tours) in 100 BC. Over 1000 years later, Charles VIII, Louis XI, Louis XII, Catherine de Medici, and François I lived out their days enjoying the peaceful countryside and extraordinary panorama of the river valley from the hillside château. Amboise's most famous former resident may be Leonardo da Vinci, who spent his last years in the town. Not to be missed are the life-size versions of da Vinci's unrealized projects. While Amboise citizens enjoy their grand place in history, their great local vineyards, and a lovely old quarter, they doggedly retain a healthy appreciation for the country life.

■🛈 **ORIENTATION & PRACTICAL INFORMATION. Trains** run from bd. Gambetta to: Blois (20min., 20 per day, €5.40); Orléans (1hr., 6 per day, €12.20); Paris (2¼hr., 7 per day, €23.40); Tours (20min., 11 per day, €4.30). Ticket office (☎02 47 23 18 23) open M-Sa 5:40am-9:30pm, Su 7:15am-9:30pm. **Fil Vert buses** leave the tourist office for **Chenonceau** and **Chambord** (30min., 1 per day, round-trip €29) and **Tours** (35min., 3 per day 6:45am-9am, €2.10). **Taxis,** 12 quai du Général de Gaulle, are easier to find by calling ☎02 47 57 01 54. To rent a **car,** walk to Avis, 12 quai du Général de Gaulle, across the way from the tourist office (☎02 47 23 21 11; MC/V) or Rent-a-Car, 105 av. de Tours (☎02 47 57 17 92; MC/V.) To rent **bikes,** head to Loca Cycles, 3 Jean-Jacques Rousseau, right off quai du Général de Gaulle when walking towards the château. (☎02 47 57 00 28. €14 per day. Passport deposit. Open M-Su 9am-12:30pm and 2-7pm. Cash only.) To reach the **tourist office,** take a left from the station and follow rue Jules-Ferry, crossing both bridges past the residential Ile d'Or. The office is 30m to the right of the bridge, on quai du Général de Gaulle. (15min.) The office posts a list of hotels with vacancies each night, and tourists can call their accommodations hotline for the same information (☎02 47 23 27 42). **Themed tours** available during the summer. Call the tourist office to reserve. (☎02 47 57 09 28; fax 02 47 57 14 35. Open July-Aug. M-Sa 9am-8pm, Su 10am-6pm; Apr.-June and Sept. M-Sa 9:30am-1pm and 2-6:30pm, Su 10am-1pm and 3-6:30pm; Oct.-Mar. M-Sa 9:30am-12:30pm and 2-6:30pm, Su 10am-1pm. Tours W, Sa, and Su €6.) The quai du Général de Gaulle is full of **banks** and **ATMs.** The most central **laundromat** is LavCentre, 5 allée du Sergent Turpin, across the street from the tourist office. (Open daily 7am-8pm. Last wash at 7pm.) The **police** are at 1 bd. A. France (☎02 47 57 26 19), and the **hospital** is on rue des Ursulines (☎02 47 23 33 33). Cyber Café, 119 rue Nationale, provides **Internet** access. (Open Su-M 1-10pm, Tu-Th 10am-10pm, F-Sa 10am-midnight.) The **post office** sits at 20 quai du Général de Gaulle, three blocks down the street to the left as you face the tourist office. **Currency exchange** available. (Open M-Sa 8am-12:30pm and 2-6pm, closed Sa afternoons.) **Postal code:** 37400.

🛏🍴**ACCOMMODATIONS & FOOD.** The **Hôtel Belle-Vue ❹,** 12 quai Charles Guinot, at the end of the two bridges from the train station to the château, offers some of Amboise's nicest rooms, furnished in a charming country style. A flowered terrace overlooking the Loire helps the Hôtel live up to its name. (☎02 47 30 40 40. Breakfast €6. Singles with shower and toilet €45; doubles €55; triples €60.) The best inexpensive accommodations are the **Centre International de Séjour Charles Péguy (HI) ❶,** Ile d'Or. Follow rue Jules-Ferry from the station and head downhill to the right after the first bridge onto Ile d'Or. (10min.) Guests (mostly students or young travelers), are housed in 3- to 4-bed dorm rooms; ask for a room with a view of the Loire and the château. (☎02 47 30 60 90; fax 02 47 30 60 91. Breakfast €2.60. Sheets €3.10. Reception M-F 3-8pm. Dorms €8.60. Free parking.) **Hôtel Le Français,** 6 rue Voltaire, has clean, sleekly furnished rooms in a calm setting just three blocks from the château. (☎02 47 57 11 38. Breakfast €5.80. Singles and doubles with shower €35-45; triples €55.) ▨**Ile d'Or camping ❶** offers such clean, well-maintained facilities it feels like an outdoor hotel. The riverside campsite offers a swimming pool (€2), mini-golf (€2.40), and a peaceful view. (☎02 47 23 47 23. Open early Apr. to Oct. Reception 7am-9pm. €2.30 per person, €3.10 per site, children under 12 €1.60. Electricity €1.90. Shower €1.30. MC/V.)

The rue Victor Hugo and rue Nationale, both at the base of the château, are lined with *brasseries* and bakeries. For a cheap picnic with a great view of the Loire, climb uphill to **ATAC** supermarket, pl. de la Croix Bernard, at rue Grégoire de Tours. (Open M-F 8:30am-12:30pm and 2:30-7:30pm, Sa 8:30am-7:30pm, Su 9:30am-12:30pm.) There's also a **Marché Plus**, 5 quai du Général de Gaulle. (Open M-Sa 7am-9pm, Su 9am-1pm.) Try the local favorite ▨**Le Blason ❸**, 11 place Richelieu, for great regional cuisine, including delicious foie gras and delicate *soufflé glacé* topped with Grand Marnier. (☎02 47 23 22 41. Lunch *menu* €11.50. Dinner *menus* €14.50-25. Entrées €13-20. MC/V.) Even the highest tolerances will be tested by the enormous cocktails at trendy **Le Shaker**, 1 rue de l'Entrepont, on Ile d'Or. (Cocktails €7.50-9. Beers €3-6. Open Su-Th 6pm-2am, F-Sa 6pm-3am.)

❸ **SIGHTS.** Six French kings have held court in the 15th-century château, whose battlements stretch out along the hill, at one time holding as many as 4000 people. In 1560, a failed Protestant conspiracy against the influential arch-Catholic de Guise family led to grisly murder. Some of the rebelling Huguenots were thrown into the Loire in sacks, while others were killed on the château balcony, now described by smiling tour guides as the "Balcony of the Hanging People." Most of the château was destroyed during the French Revolution, but the remaining parts have been restored and opened to the public. The **Logis de Roi**, the main part of the château, remains decorated to fit the 15th- and 16th-century royalty who once inhabited it. Intricately carved Gothic chairs stand over 6 feet high in order to prevent surprise attacks from behind. In contrast, the 2nd floor is furnished with 19th-century pieces that recall the period during which the château was inhabited by nobles of the house of Orléans. The jewel of the grounds is the **Chapelle St-Hubert**, outside the château, the final resting place of Leonardo da Vinci. In summer, people flock to the "Court of King François" **son-et-lumière** staged by 450 Amboise residents and resurrecting everyone from gallant knights to the court jester. (☎02 47 57 00 98. Open daily July-Aug. 9am-7pm; Sept.-Oct. 9am-6pm; Nov.-Jan. 9am-noon and 2-5pm; Mar. 9am-noon and 2-5:30pm; Apr.-June 9am-6:30pm. Nearby park open same hours as château. €7, students €6, ages 7-14 €3.80. *Son-et-lumière* W and Sa June-July 10:30pm, Aug. 10pm. €12.20, children €6.10.)

Built right into the walls of the château, the **Caveau des vignerons**, pl. du Château, offers free tastings of locally made wine, goat cheese, foie gras, and preserved meats. (☎02 47 57 23 69. Apr.-Nov. M-Sa 11am-7pm.) From the château, follow the cliffs along rue Victor Hugo beside the centuries-old **maisons troglodytiques**, houses built in hollowed-out cliffs still inhabited today. Four hundred meters away rests ▨**Clos Lucé**, by far Amboise's most interesting attraction. This Renaissance manor and its gardens were given to Leonardo da Vinci by his biggest fan, François I, who often visited da Vinci using an underground tunnel that connects Clos Lucé to the château. Da Vinci's bedroom, library, drawing room, and chapel are inside, but the main attraction is a collection of 40 machines built from da Vinci's visionary designs with materials contemporaneous to his lifetime. Long before they appeared in the modern world, Leonardo had conceived of everything from the helicopter to the machine gun. (☎02 47 57 62 88; fax 02 47 30 54 28. Open daily July-Aug. 9am-8pm; late Mar. to June and Sept.-Oct. 9am-7pm; Feb. to late Mar. and Nov.-Dec. 9am-6pm; Jan. 10am-5pm. €11, students €9. MC/V.)

TOURS

When the Hundred Years' War (1337-1453) began to threaten the Loire Valley, three small towns united for protection, blending their individual characters to create Tours (pop. 253,000), which became the heart of the French kingdom in the 15th and 16th centuries. This dynamic city is the birthplace of Balzac and the home of 30,000 students. Young people, joggers, musicians, and bar-hoppers fill the strollable paths along the Loire and wide café-lined boulevards. At sunset, the bridges are illuminated prettily above the rushing waters of the river. Tours is conveniently located near about half of the Loire châteaux, making it a good base for budget travelers hoping to visit several châteaux.

TRANSPORTATION

Trains: pl. du Général Leclerc. Info office open M-Th 5:45am-9:45pm, F 5:50am-10:30pm, Sa 5:50am-9:30pm, Su 7:15-11:30am. Many destinations require a change at **St-Pierre-des-Corps,** 5min. outside Tours; check schedule. To: **Bordeaux** (2½hr., 4 per day, €33.80); **Paris** (2¼hr., 7 per day, €25; TGV via St-Pierre 1hr., 7 per day, €35); **Poitiers** (45min., 6 per day, €12.90). No luggage check available.

Local Transportation: Fil Bleu, 5 rue de la Dolve (☎02 47 66 70 70). Office open M-Sa 7am-7pm. Tickets €1.05, *carnet* of 10 €9.20. Day pass €4.20. Buses run 7am-8:30pm; map available from the tourist office or Fil Bleu office near the train station.

Taxis: Artaxi, 13 rue de Nantes (☎02 47 20 30 40), and the train station. 24hr.

Car Rental: The tourist office has a list of companies. **Avis** (☎02 47 20 53 27), in the train station. AmEx/DC/MC/V. **Calypso,** 6 rue George Sand (☎02 47 61 12 28), offers lower rates during the week.

Bike Rental: Amster Cycles, 5 rue du Rempart (☎02 47 61 22 23; fax 02 47 61 28 48). €14 per day, €54 per week. Passport or credit card deposit. Open M-Sa 9am-12:30pm and 1-7pm, Su 9am-12:30pm and 6-7pm. MC/V.

ORIENTATION & PRACTICAL INFORMATION

Place Jean Jaurès is the vertex of four boulevards and the center of the town. The busy **rue Nationale,** once part of the main road between Paris and Spain, runs north to the Loire, while **avenue de Grammont** reaches toward the Cher River to the south. **Boulevard Béranger** and **boulevard Heurteloup** run west and east, respectively, from pl. Jean Jaurès. The mostly pedestrian *vieille ville,* the lively **place Plumereau,** and most historic sites are northwest of pl. Jean Jaurès toward the Loire.

Tourist Office: 78-82 rue Bernard Palissy (☎02 47 70 37 37; www.ligeris.com). From the station, walk through pl. du Général Leclerc, cross the busy bd. Heurteloup and take a right. The office is on the left, past the futuristic Centre des Congrès. Free maps and info booklets as well as **accommodations booking.** Arranges châteaux **tours.** 2hr. historical walking tour departs daily at 10am mid-July to mid-Aug. (€5, ages 6-12 €4.) Call in advance to arrange English tours. The best way to see the city is the 1½hr. walking night tour. (July-Aug. every F 9:30pm from the tourist office. €8, children €6.) The *Carte Multi-Visites,* (€7.70) provides access to six museums and a city tour. Office open mid-Apr. to mid-Oct. M-Sa 8:30am-7pm, Su 10am-12:30pm and 2:30-5pm; mid-Oct. to mid-Apr. M-Sa 9am-12:30pm and 1:30-6pm, Su 10am-1pm.

Money: Banque de France, 2 rue Chanoineau (☎02 47 60 24 00), off bd. Heurteloup, has the best rates. Exchange desk open Tu-Sa 8:45am-noon.

English Bookstore: La Boîte à Livres de l'Etranger, 2 rue du Commerce (☎02 47 05 67 29). Open M 2-7pm, Tu-Sa 9:30am-7pm. Wide selection in many languages. MC/V.

Laundromat: Cyber-Laverie, 16bis pl. de la Victoire. M-F Internet. €1.50 per 15min., €3 per hr. Open M-Sa 10am-7:30pm, Su 11am-7:30pm. Lavo 2000, 17 rue Bretonneau (☎02 47 73 14 69). Open daily 7am-8:30pm.

Police: 70-72 rue de Marceau (☎02 47 60 70 69).

Hospital: Hôpital Bretonneau, 2 bd. Tonnelle (☎02 47 47 47 47).

Internet: Cyber Gate, 11 rue de Prés. Merville (☎02 47 05 95 94). €1 per 15min.; €5 for 1hr., a sandwich, and a drink. Open M 1-10pm, Tu-Sa 11am-midnight, Su 2-10pm. **Top Communication,** 68 rue du Grand Marché (☎02 47 39 09 90). Business center. International calling cards sold. €1 per 20min., €3 per hr. Open M-Sa 10am-10pm.

Post Office: 1 bd. Béranger (☎02 47 60 34 20). **Currency exchange.** Open M-F 8am-7pm, Sa 8am-noon. Branch office on 92 rue Colbert. **Postal code:** 37000.

ACCOMMODATIONS & CAMPING

In peak season, call a week or two in advance. **CROUS** (☎02 47 60 42 42) can provide info about discount meals and long-term housing for students.

- **Hôtel Regina,** 2 rue Pimbert (☎02 47 05 25 36; fax 02 47 66 08 72). Hosts make their guests feel like family. They might even throw in a free knitting lesson. Near river, good restaurants, and city center. Clean hallway showers. Breakfast €4.30. Reception closed noon-2pm and after 1am. Singles and doubles €20-24; triples €23-36. MC/V. ❷

- **Foyer des Jeunes Travailleurs,** 16 rue Bernard Palissy (☎02 47 60 51 51). Centrally located. Feels like a very clean college dorm, and, indeed, many long-term residents are students at the university in Tours. It also draws a crowd of tourists, especially in the summer. Reception open M-F 8am-6:30pm. Breakfast €1.90, other meals €7. One-time €4 restaurant membership. Singles with shower €17; doubles with bath €13. ❷

- **Hôtel des Châteaux de la Loire,** 12 rue Gambetta (☎02 47 05 10 05; fax 02 47 20 20 14). This hotel earns its two stars by providing elegant furnishings and a comfortable ambiance for a reasonable price. Very close to the train station on a quiet street. All rooms come with a shower or bath, toilet, and TV. Breakfast €6.20. Parking €5.30. Singles €38-45; doubles €45-51; triples, quads, and quints available. MC/V. ❹

- **Hôtel Foch,** 20 rue du Maréchal Foch (☎02 47 05 70 59; hotel-foch.tours@wanadoo.fr), just off pl. Plumereau. Large, simple rooms in an unbeatable location, minded by a friendly proprietor. Most rooms have shower; no hallway showers are available. Breakfast €5. Singles €20-34; doubles €23-37; triples €39-45; quads €50-58. MC/V. ❷

- **Camping:** Tourist office lists campsites within 30km. The closest is the three-star **Camping St-Avertin,** 63 rue de Rochepinard in St-Avertin (☎02 47 27 27 60), accessible by bus #5 from Tours. Ask for the stop nearest the campsite and follow the signs. (5min.) Tennis, volleyball, pool. Open Apr. to mid-Oct. Reception 8am-noon and 3-8pm. €5 per person, €2.80 per child under 7, €5 per site, €1.30 per car. Electricity €2.50. ❶

FOOD

Rue Colbert and **place Plumereau** have dozens of pleasant outdoor options with *menus* under €12. Bistros and pubs crowd around **place Jean Jaurès.** Be sure to try the melt-in-your-mouth macaroons *à l'ancienne* and anything *aux pruneaux* (with prunes). Connoisseurs sip the light, fruity whites of Vouvray and Montlouis. The **indoor market,** pl. des Halles, expands outdoors W and Sa mornings. (M-Sa 6am-7:30pm, Su 6am-1pm.) **Marché Gourmand** at pl. de la Résistance (1st and 3rd F of each month 4-10pm) sells only the choicest gourmet products. There is an **ATAC** supermarket, 7 pl. du Général Leclerc, near the station (open M-Sa 8:30am-8pm, Su 9:30am-12:30pm) and a **Monoprix** in Galeries Lafayette on the corner of rue Etienne Pallu and rue Nationale, just north of pl. Jean Jaurès. (Open M-Sa 9am-7:30pm.)

- **La Souris Gourmande,** 100 rue Colbert (☎02 47 47 04 80). Cheese lovers converge at this unique restaurant whose dishes, incorporating an amazing selection of delicious cheeses, are almost overshadowed by the astonishing, bovine-obsessed décor. Fondue €12-14. Open Tu-Sa noon-2pm and 7-10:30pm. ❷

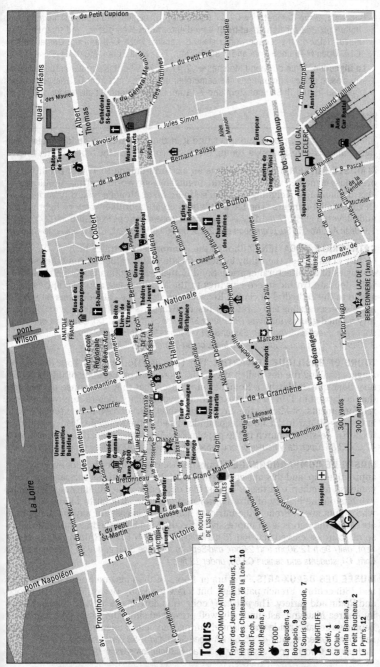

Tours

▲ ACCOMMODATIONS
Foyer des Jeunes Travailleurs, 11
Hôtel des Châteaux de la Loire, 10
Hôtel Foch, 5
Hôtel Regina, 6

● FOOD
La Bigouden, 3
Boccacio, 9
La Souris Gourmande, 7

★ NIGHTLIFE
Le Café, 1
GI Club, 8
Juanita Banana, 4
Le Petit Faucheux, 2
Le Pym's, 12

LOIRE VALLEY

Boccacio, 9 rue Gambetta (☎02 47 05 45 22). Locals know to come to this authentic Italian pizzeria for its market-fresh ingredients, wood-oven pizzas, and tempting tiramasu. Relax on the terrace with a glass of sangría. Pizza €10 and up. Dinner *menus* €14. Open M-Th noon-2pm and 7:30-9:30pm, F-Sa until 10pm. MC/V. ❸

La Bigouden, 3 rue du Grand Marché (☎02 47 64 21 91). This popular *crêperie* spices up classic dishes into pairings like camembert and jam. *Plats* from €7. Desserts €5-8. Open Su-Tu and Th-Sa noon-2pm and 7-11pm. Closed Th and Su afternoons. MC/V. ❷

◉ SIGHTS

Those in search of peace and quiet find it at the beautiful **Lac de la Bergeonnerie** (also called Lac de Tours), a 10min. ride away (bus #1) on the banks of the Cher.

▧ **MUSÉE DU GEMMAIL. Gemmail** is an art form unique to Tours. Brightly colored glass is melded together to form original mosaic works and interpretations of classic paintings, including da Vinci's *Mona Lisa*, Monet's waterlily series, and Dégas's ballet-dancers. The back-lit works create a brilliant play of light on the multi-layered glass. (*7 rue du Murier. Off rue Bretonneau, near pl. Plumereau. ☎02 47 61 01 19. Open Apr.-Nov. Tu-Su 10am-noon and 2-6:30pm. €4.60, students €3.10, under 10 €1.60.*)

CATHÉDRALE ST-GATIEN. Although the interior demonstrates high Gothic architecture at its purest, the wildly intricate façade of this cathedral combines several centuries of architectural caprice. Solid Romanesque columns were embellished with delicate Gothic micro-carvings in the Middle Ages, and two spires were added to the cathedral in classic Renaissance style. The cathedral has one of the Loire's most dazzling and carefully preserved displays of 13th-, 18th-, and 20th-century stained-glass windows. (*Rue Jules Simon. ☎02 47 70 21 00. Cathedral open daily 9am-7pm. Free. Cloister open Easter-Sept. 9:30am-12:30pm and 2-6pm; Oct.-Mar. W-Sa 9:30am-12:30pm and 2-5pm. €2.50. Mass on Su 10am and 6:30pm.*)

TOURS OF BASILIQUE ST-MARTIN. The Tour de l'Horloge and Tour de Charlemagne, flanking rue des Halles, reveal the incredible proportions of the 12th-century Basilique St-Martin, a Romanesque church that they were once part of and that collapsed in 1797, a few years after Revolutionary looters removed its iron reinforcements. St-Martin, the city's first bishop, was carried here after his death in Candes-St-Martin. He now sleeps undisturbed in the Nouvelle Basilique St-Martin, a *fin-de-siècle* church in the popular Neo-Byzantine style. (*Rue Descartes. ☎02 47 05 63 87. Open daily 8am-noon and 2-6:45pm. Closed Jan.-Dec. Mass daily 11am.*)

MUSÉE DE COMPAGNONNAGE. Tours once served as the center for every type of apprenticeship, and this museum exhibits products from these **compagnons** (companions), members of artisans' guilds, that date back to the Middle Ages. While the exhibits on the history of *compagnonnage* may be difficult to follow for those who do not speak French, the intricate handiwork is easy for anyone to appreciate. Amid the curios is an impressively detailed model cathedral and a miniature spiral staircase carved in wood. (*8 rue Nationale. ☎02 47 61 07 93. Open mid-June to mid-Sept. daily 9am-12:30pm and 2-6pm; mid-Sept. to mid-June Su-M and W-Sa 9am-noon and 2-6pm. €4, students and seniors €2.50, under 12 free.*)

MUSÉE DES BEAUX-ARTS. The upper floors of the museum house mostly 17th- and 18th-century French paintings, but a few works by Dégas, Monet, Delacroix, and Rodin add variety. The *primitif* collection downstairs includes two paintings by Andrea Mategna, astoundingly well preserved since the 1430s. The sprawling Lebanese cedar outside was planted during Napoleon's reign. (*18 pl. François Sicard, next to the cathedral. ☎02 47 05 68 73. Open Su-M and W-Sa 9am-12:45pm and 2-6pm. €4, students €2. Gardens open in summer daily 7am-8:30pm; low season 7am-6pm.*)

♫ ◐ ENTERTAINMENT & FESTIVALS

Place Plumereau (or **place Plum**) is the *place* to be, where cheerful students sip drinks and chat at cafés and bars. Three clubs on the square fit snugly together. **Le Pym's**, 170 av. de Grammont, is the most popular club in Tours. Two lively dance floors are hopping almost every night of the week. (Cover €11, closed M.) The **GI Club**, 13 rue Lavoisier, draws a primarily gay crowd and spins house, disco, and techno every night of the week. (☎02 47 66 29 96. Open nightly 11pm-5am.) Those in search of a quieter night can head a few blocks off the pl. Plum to **Le Petit Faucheux**, 23 rue des Cerisiers, for some soul-soothing jazz. (☎02 47 38 29 34. Live combos play weekly; call ahead for a schedule. Cover €7-14, students €10.) **Juanita Banana**, 13 rue du Change, keeps its customers coming back with its spicy food and even spicier salsa music. Cocktails €5. (Open until midnight, 2am on weekends. MC/V.) The hip crowd cools its heels with a cocktail at the trendy **Le Café**, 39 rue Bretonneau, after a night of dancing. (☎02 47 61 37 83. Open daily noon-2am.)

Early July brings the **Fêtes Musicales en Touraine**, a 10-day celebration of music from Saint-Saëns to Gershwin. (☎02 47 21 65 08. €12.20-42.70 per night.) Tours hosts the annual **Jazz en Touraine** festival at the end of September, and the **Acteurs-Acteurs** festival of film and theater the second week of June. The tourist office has more info. **Théâtre Louis Jouvet**, 12 rue Leonardo da Vinci (☎02 47 64 50 50), and at the **Théâtre Municipal**, 34 rue de la Scellerie (☎02 47 60 20 00), have theater all year.

▶ DAYTRIP FROM TOURS: CHINON

Trains and SNCF *buses* run from the station (☎02 47 93 11 04) via St-Pierre-des-Corps to Saumur (1½hr., 2 per day, €10.80) and Tours (45min.; 8 per day M-Sa, 5 on Su; €7.20). A train runs from Saumur to Port Boulet (40min., 5 per day, €3.20), from which a bus continues on to Chinon (15min., 5 per day, €2.80). Ticket office open M-Sa 6am-12:30pm and 1-7:40pm, Su 2:30-8pm.

Perched between the banks of the Vienne River and the majestic, crumbling château where Richard the Lionheart drew his last breath, the quaint village of Chinon (pop. 9000) was one of the most important cities in France under the reign of Henry II and Eleanor of Aquitaine. During the Hundred Years' War, future Charles VII sought refuge in Chinon. Eventually it became part of the estates of the powerful Duke of Richelieu, whose calculated neglect brought the 10th-century château to ruins. Though townspeople remain proud of their rich heritage, Chinon is today more defined by its vineyards, which produce red and white wine and the distinctive *confiture de vin de Chinon*, a delicious wine jam.

The august rubble of Chinon's ▧**château** presides over a hilltop above the Vienne river. Even in their partially crumbled state, the stone walls convey some of their past glory and capture the imagination. The interior of the château displays a number of medieval tapestries with scenes of warriors and court life. The grounds spread between three main fortresses, which are connected by secret underground tunnels. Additional tunnels, just wide enough for a man to crawl through on his stomach, lead to the main well and the town center. Thanks to a belief that anyone who captured the **Tour Marie-Javelle** would die a horrible death, the 14th-century belltower has withstood the Hundred Years' War, the Wars of Religion, and the French Revolution without a blemish; its bell has proudly struck every half-hour since 1399. The **Joan of Arc Museum** that occupies the three-story tower is dedicated to the young warrior who stopped by Chinon to talk with the Dauphin in 1429. Audiovisual presentations about Joan's military travels are given in English and French, and numerous artistic tributes to the young warrior are displayed alongside a copy of her 14th-century signature. (☎02 47 93 13 45. Open daily

THE BIG SPLURGE

BE IT EVER
SO HUMBLE...

Incredibly costly to maintain, hundreds of France's châteaux are being put up for sale. Prices for these classy lodgings range from a few hundred thousand euros to a few million, depending on the size of the building, its condition, and its historical importance. Of course, this does not include the cost of decoration or restoration: a Gothic façade may be romantic, but there's nothing attractive about medieval plumbing.

Château du Soudon, a 12th-century fortress and stronghold during the Hundred Years' War, is one such château. When it was bought by an American company, it had plumbing and electricity, but the grounds looked like a wild jungle of brush, the stained glass could not very well be replaced by the average window worker, and furniture had to be specifically crafted in order to be consistent with its old French décor. After more than a year of repairs, the château is worth much more than its initial €1 million investment.

With these expenses, it's no wonder that many families decide to open their châteaux to the public. Soudon is no exception: it is now a 5-room *chambre d'hôte* surrounded by bike paths, scenic villages, and a pretty river.

(Néons-sur-Creuse. See the website at www.drawbridge-investments.com for more information. Expected to open for guests in spring 2004.)

Apr.-Sept. 9am-7pm; Oct.-Mar. 9:30am-5pm. €6, students €4.60, ages 7-18 €3.20. Free tours are available in either French, English, or German. Night tours July-Aug. €9.50.)

Wine tastings can be enjoyed at **Maison Plouzeau,** 94 rue St-Maurice, where M. Plouzeau's sons conduct free tours in a *cave* beneath the château. (☎02 47 93 16 34. Open Apr.-Oct. Tu-Sa 11am-1pm and 3-7pm.) The **Musée Animé du Vin et de la Tonnellerie,** 12 rue Voltaire, demonstrates the wine-making process and provide free *dégustations* of wine and wine jam. Costumed automatons in bad wigs pepper the 20min. tour with Rabelais quotes. (☎02 47 93 25 63. Tours given in French and English. Open Apr.-Sept. daily 10:30am-12:30pm and 2-6:30pm. €4, children €3.20. MC/V.) The small ■**Maison de la Rivière,** 12 quai Pasteur, devoted to local culture, has everything from a photo exhibit of river life to a workshop demonstrating the traditional boat-building craft. Don't miss the excursions on the Vienne that focus on the river's wildlife. (☎02 47 93 21 34, 02 47 95 93 15 to reserve a boat excursion. Open July-Aug. Tu-F 10am-12:30pm and 2-6:30pm, Sa-Su 3-6:30pm; Apr.-Nov. Tu-F 10am-12:30pm and 2-5:30pm, Sa-Su 2-5:30pm. €3, under 12 €2.50. Free guided tours in French. Boat excursion €2-6.)

Every third Sunday in August, all of Chinon turns out for **Marché à l'Ancienne,** which features regional foods and a parade of citizens costumed in 19th-century Chinonais garb. The **Avoine Zone Blues** brings jazz groups from France and other countries for a weekend of classic and contemporary musical stylings at the beginning of July. (Info ☎02 47 98 11 11. Ticket prices vary.) **Cinéma Le Rabelais,** 7bis rue J. J. Rousseau, plays French films nightly. (☎08 92 68 47 07. Tickets €6.10)

There is a **Shopi** supermarket at 22 pl. de l'Hôtel de Ville (open M-Sa 9am-1pm and 2:30-7pm) and an **open-air market** every Thursday on pl. Jeanne d'Arc and every Sunday on pl. du Général de Gaulle. Stroll along **rue Voltaire** and **place de l'Hôtel de Ville** to find the best cheap meals in town. For tasty regional cuisine, try **La Bonne France ❷,** 4 pl. de la Victoire. This simple restaurant serves up such specials as veal in Touraine wine sauce and rice pudding on gingerbread for dessert. (☎02 47 98 01 34. Appetizers €5, *menus* €9, 14, and 22. MC/V.)

To get to the **tourist office** at pl. d'Hofheim from the station, take a left and walk beside the river, along quai Jeanne d'Arc, towards the *centre ville* (10min.), then turn right at Café de la Paix to pl. de l'Hôtel de Ville. Turn right onto the little road at the back of the square. (☎02 47 93 17 85; fax 02 47 93 93 05. **Walking tours** Apr.-June Su, Th, Sa at 3:30pm; July-Aug. Su

3:30pm, W and F-Sa 10:30am. €4.60, students €2.30. Night tours available July-Aug.; call for schedule. **Accommodations booking** €2.50. **Mini-train tour** July-Aug. daily 6 times per day; Easter-June and Sept. on weekends. €4, students €3. Open May-Sept. daily 10am-7pm; Oct.-Apr. M-Sa 10am-noon and 2-6pm.) For more individualized exploration of the region, **bike rentals** are available at the Hôtel Agnès Sorel, 4 quai Pasteur, located at the end of the quai Jeanne d'Arc. (☎02 47 93 04 37. €8 per half-day, €14 per day.)

CHÂTEAUX NEAR TOURS

Dozens of beautiful châteaux lie within 60km of Tours; *Let's Go* covers the most popular sites, but it is often surprisingly worthwhile to visit the smaller châteaux. **Driving** is the most convenient, though generally the most expensive, way to travel. Highways are well marked with arrow-shaped signs leading to most châteaux. **Biking** between châteaux is extremely popular and beautiful, although **bus tours** are more efficient. Frequent plush minibuses depart from Tours every day; expect to shell out €16-40, which normally includes admission fees to the châteaux. **Valleybus** (www.touring-france.com) offers English-language excursions. The price (from €25) includes one or two châteaux and museums, lunch, and transportation. For other tour companies, contact Saint-Eloi Excursions (☎02 47 37 08 04), Touraine Evasion (☎06 07 39 13 31), Acco-Dispo Excursions (☎02 47 57 67 13), or Quart de Tours (☎06 30 65 52 01). Service Touristique de la Touraine (☎02 47 05 46 09) sits right in Tours's train station but is the most expensive. All tours have English-speaking guides. Most châteaux have free tours (with printed translations or English guides), as well as performances and special events during the summer. *Son-et-lumière* (sound and light shows) are a fun alternative to day visits. Wine cellars often offer free *dégustations*. **Vouvray's** 30 cellars, 9km east of Tours on the N152, specialize in sweet white wine. (☎02 47 52 75 03. Open daily 9am-noon and 2-7pm.) By bus, take #61 from pl. Jean Jaurès to les Patis (20min., M-Sa 14 per day, €3). In **Montlouis,** across the river to the south, 10 *caves* pour forth wonderful dry whites. Trains run from Tours (20min., M-Sa 3 per day, €2.40).

CHENONCEAU

Trains run to Chenonceau from Tours (30min., 8 per day 9am-9pm, €5.10). The station is right in front of the château. Fil Vert **buses** leave for Chenonceau from Amboise (20min., 2 per day, round-trip €1.05) and Tours (1¼hr., 2 per day, €2.10). **Château:** ☎02 47 23 90 07. Open mid-Mar. to mid-Sept. daily 9am-7pm. Call for low season hours. €8, students €6.50. July-Aug. son-et-lumière at 10pm. Entry to Château des Dames wax museum €3.

Perhaps the most elegant château in France, Chenonceau arches gracefully over the Cher River, flanked by woods and gardens. The château owes its beauty to centuries of female designers. Royal tax collector Thomas Bohier originally commissioned the château. While he fought in the Italian Wars (1513-21), his wife Catherine oversaw its practical design, which features straight Italian-style staircases and four rooms branching from a central chamber. In 1547, Henri II gave the château to his mistress, Diane de Poitiers, who added symmetrical gardens and constructed an arched bridge over the Cher so she could hunt in the nearby forest. Later, Henri's widow, Catherine de Médici, forced Diane to give up the castle. She designed her own gardens and the spectacular two-story gallery atop the bridge built by Diane, the site of many Renaissance galas. At Chenonceau, Jean-Jacques Rousseau tutored the boy who inspired his influential work on education, *Emile*.

Chenonceau's kitchens are fully stocked with all the trappings of a 15th-century kitchen. The wine shop at **La Cave Cellar,** on the château grounds, offers tastings for €1.50 (open 10:30am-7pm).

LOCHES

Trains and *buses* cover the 40km from Tours's train station to Loches (50min., 13 per day, €7). The tourist office is in a pavilion near the station on brasserie-lined pl. de la Marne. (☎02 47 91 82 82. Open daily July-Aug. 9am-7pm; Sept.-June 9:30am-12:30pm and 2-6pm.) **Château:** ☎02 47 59 01 32; fax 02 47 59 17 45. Open daily Apr.-Sept. 9am-7pm; Oct.-Mar. 9:30am-5pm. Donjon or Royal Lodge €3.80, students €2.70; both sights €5.10, students €3.50. Son-et-lumière July and Aug. F-Sa at 10pm; call for specific dates. €11, ages 6-12 €6.

Originally built as a solitary tower on a cliff, the walled fortification of Loches was augmented by Louis XI in the 14th century. The wall around this intimate little town has an extravagant royal residence at one extremity of the oval, and an 11th-century Romanesque tower at the other extremity. In the state room of this tower Joan of Arc, on the heels of her 1429 victory over the English at Orléans, told the indifferent Dauphin that she had cleared the way for him to travel to Reims to be crowned king. Louis XI converted the 11th-century keep and watchtowers to the north into a state prison. The "Louis XI" Cage, an intricate, solitary confinement cell, once held da Vinci's protector, Ludovico Sforza, who decorated the walls with frescos are still clear today. Additional curiosities include a torture chamber, underground galleries, and a replica of the suspension cages used to hold revolutionary prisoners. While the floors in the three-story tower have fallen out, the walls and stairs remain and lead up to a remarkable view of the village below. The **Logis Royal**, or Royal Lodge, pays tribute to the famous ladies who once held court here. In Loches, Agnès Sorel, lover of Charles VII, became the first woman to hold the official title of Mistress of the King of France; she was entombed here following her early death at age 28. Anne de Bretagne later added a lacy stone chapel to the logis. The terrace atop the round tower offers a magnificent view of the medieval city. Tours available in French or English by reservation only; €4.

VILLANDRY

Trains leave from the station in Tours to **Savonnières**, 4km from the château (10 min., 5 per day, €2.60). Many **minibus tour** agencies run a circuit to Villandry and Ussé (see p. 299 for phone numbers). From Tours, **cyclists** can travel 15km west along D16, a narrow road that winds along the bank of the Cher past Villandry to Ussé; **drivers** should stick to D7. **Château:** ☎02 47 50 02 09. Open daily July-Aug. 9am-6pm; mid-Feb. to June and Sept. to mid-Nov. 9:30am-5pm. Gardens open daily May-Sept. 9am-7:30pm; Oct.-Apr. 9am-7pm. Château and gardens €7, students €5. Gardens only €5, students €3.50. The **tourist office**, across D7 from the château, has maps and train schedules. (☎02 47 50 12 66. Open daily 9am-12:30pm and 2-6pm.) Although Villandry is one of the closest châteaux, it is still hard to reach from Tours via public transportation.

Villandry lives up to its claim of being *"le plus beau des jardins du jardin de la France"* (the most beautiful of gardens of the garden that is France). With 125,000 flowers and 85,000 vegetables all weeded by hand, it is among the largest. Built on the banks of the Cher by Jean le Breton, minister to François I, the château was purchased in 1906 by Dr. Joachim Carvallo, great-grandfather to the present owner. He renovated the decaying structure and reconstructed the gardens, which had been redone in the English style. Today, the formal French gardens are Villandry's main attraction; their symmetry and intricately planned color design make them incredibly beautiful, especially when viewed from above. The romantic covered arbors and labyrinthine hedgerow mazes are suitable for an afternoon stroll. The kitchen garden, designed in the style of an Italian monastery, produces just enough to sell a little at market. The middle terrace level is the most artistic. The peaceful upper level is lined with lime groves, swan pools, and waterfalls, which provide irrigation for the rest of the garden. Inside the château, the medieval Moorish ceiling is marvelously tiled with 3000 gold-leafed wooden pieces.

LOIRE VALLEY

AZAY-LE-RIDEAU

Trains run from *Tours* to the town of *Azay-le-Rideau (25min., 8 per day 5:30am-8:56pm, €4.30)*, a 2km walk from the château. Turn right from the station and head left on D57. **Buses** run from the *Tours* train station to the tourist office *(45min., daily 3 per day 6:40am-5:50pm, pay on bus). Château:* ☎ *02 47 45 42 04. Open daily July-Aug. 9:30am-7pm; Apr.-June and Sept.-Oct. 9:30am-6pm; Nov.-Mar. 9:30am-12:30pm and 2-5:30pm. Last entrance 45min. before closing. €5.50, ages 18-25 €3.80, under 18 free. Audio commentary available in English €4.* **Son-et-lumière** *daily July 10:30pm; Aug 10pm. €9, joint ticket with daytime visit €12, 18-25 €7, under age 18 €5. The* **tourist office**, pl. de l'Europe, 1km from the train station along av. de la Gare, provides a small map and **accommodations booking**, although few cheap options are available. (☎ 02 47 45 44 40; fax 02 47 45 31 46. Open Apr.-Oct. M-Sa 9am-1pm and 2-6pm, Su 10am-1pm and 2-7pm; Nov.-Feb. M-Sa 2-6pm.) Picturesque **Camping Parc de Sabot** ❶ *is across from the château. (☎ 02 47 45 42 72. Open Easter-Oct. Showers available. Pool July-Aug. €8.60 for 2 people with a tent, €2.50 each additional person, children €1.30. Electricity €2.)*

Surrounded by acres of breeze-ruffled trees and grass atop an island in the Indre, the château at Azay-le-Rideau stands on the ruins of an earlier fortress. The town acquired the nickname "Azay-le-Brulé" (Azay the Burned) in 1418 after Charles VII razed the village in revenge against a Burgundian guard who had refused to let him in. In 1518, the corrupt financier Gilles Berthelot bought the land and his wife Philippa set about designing a new castle. Though smaller than François I's Chambord, the château was intended to rival its contemporary in beauty; the Berthelots succeeded so thoroughly that François seized the château before its third wing was completed. The salamanders without crowns on the exterior walls mark the castle as a non-royal residence built under François. Azay's flamboyant style is apparent in the furniture and the ornate Italian second-floor staircase, the latter carved with the faces of 10 Valois kings and queens lit by open, glassless windows. Azay's *son-et-lumière* is perhaps the most highly rated in the Loire.

LANGEAIS

Trains run directly to Langeais from *Tours (20min., 8 per day, €4.20); the château and centre ville are a mere 100m walk from the train station. The* **tourist office**, place du 14 Juillet, is across the way from the train station and about 600m from the château. (☎ 02 47 96 58 22. Open M-Sa 9:30am-12:30pm and 2-7pm, Su 10am-12:30pm and 3:30-6pm) **Château:** ☎ 02 47 96 72 60. Open daily mid-July to mid-Aug. 9:30am-8pm, Apr. to mid-July and mid-Aug. to mid-Oct. 9:30am-6:30pm; mid-Oct. to Mar. 10am-5:30pm. €6.50, students €4.

One glance at Langeais's towering walls, drawbridge, and arrow-slit windows lays to rest any questions about its historical origins. It has guarded the important royal residences at Tours and Amboise for centuries. East of the other important Loire Valley châteaux, what remains at Langeais is the carefully restored 15th-century fortress built by Louis XI. It incorporates some sections of old ramparts built during the 10th century by Fulk Nerra, Count of Anjou, who needed a base from which to attack and conquer neighboring Blois and Tours. Ownership by members of the house of Anjou continued until the succession of Henri II, after which the French and British clashed over ownership of the property. A 130m stroll along the encircling ramparts invokes thoughts of the numerous intrigues, battles, and sieges Langeais has seen since its construction. Neglected over time, Langeais fell into ruin before undergoing massive restoration efforts in the late 19th century. The château was meticulously rebuilt in its original late Gothic style. Its early Renaissance furnishings, including a vast array of intricate Aubusson tapestries and beautiful, dark-wood 15th-century chairs, chests, and bureaus, prove a seemingly impregnable fortress can also be a comfortable place to live.

SAUMUR

Saumur (pop. 30,000) is best known for its wine, musty mushroom caves, and equestrian tradition. Home to the National Cavalry School, its elite *Cadre Noir* (Black Corps) has trained the country's best riders since the 18th century. An abundance of *tuffeau*, the underground stone quarried to build the châteaux of the Loire, has shaped the city's commerce for the past two centuries. The huge caves left by the mined *tuffeau* have created a prime environment for mushroom farms; Saumur supplies at least 80% of all French *champignons de Paris*, or button mushrooms. Not to be outdone by a humble fungus, the wines of Saumur are also in high demand, endowed by the region's claylike soil with a unique flavor and texture. A refreshing break from the typically castle-heavy Loire, Saumur and its enchanting old quarter have rightfully been awarded a spot on *le pôle touristique*, the official government list of eight places in France that visitors must see.

▚ TRANSPORTATION

Trains: av. David d'Angers, 10min. from pl. Bilange. To get to the station by bus, take bus A from pl. Bilange (dir: St-Lambert or Chemin Vert). Ticket office open until 7:30pm. **SNCF** trains and buses run to: **Angers** (30min., 15 per day, €8.20); **Nantes** (1hr., 9 per day, €16.40); **Paris** (1½hr., 7:50pm, €32); **Poitiers** (2½hr., 6 per day, €15.80); **Tours** (45min., 21 per day, €9).

Buses: Autocars Val de Loire, pl. St-Nicolas (☎02 41 40 25 00), runs buses from here or from the bus parking lot next to the train station. To: **Angers** (1½hr., 6 per day, €5.50); **Fontrevaud** (40 min., 3 per day, €2.30).

Local Transportation: Bus Saumur, 19 rue F. Roosevelt (☎02 41 51 11 87). Office open M 2-6pm, Tu-F 9am-12:15pm and 2-6pm, Sa 9am-noon. Buses run M-Sa 7am-7:30pm. Maps and schedules available, but are unreliable July-Aug. Tickets €1.20.

Car Rental: Ada, 29 av. du Général de Gaulle (☎02 41 50 46 77). Open M-Sa 8am-noon and 2-6:30pm. **Hertz,** 80 av. du Général de Gaulle (☎02 41 67 20 06). Open M-F 8:30am-6:30pm, Sa 8:30am-noon and 2-5:30pm. AmEx/DC/MC/V.

Bike Rental: Camping Municipal (☎02 41 40 30 00; fax 02 41 67 37 81), on Ile d'Offard. €7.50 per half-day, €12.50 per day. Passport deposit.

◼✦ ⁊ ORIENTATION & PRACTICAL INFORMATION

The tourist office and sights are on the left bank of the Loire, a 10-15min. walk from the train station on the right bank; the hostel is on an island between the two. Many of the sights are outside of the center of town, best accessed by bus or bike.

Tourist Office: pl. de la Bilange (☎02 41 40 20 60; fax 02 41 40 20 69). Multilingual staff **books accommodations** for €0.75. Free maps. Open June-Aug. M-Sa 9:15am-7pm, Su 10:30am-5:30pm, May and Sept. closed Su 12:30-2:30pm; Oct.-Apr. M-Sa 9:15am-12:30pm and 2-6pm, Su 10am-noon. French **tours** €7.70.

Currency Exchange: Banque de France, 26 rue Beaurepaire (☎02 41 40 12 00), generally has the best rates. Open M-F 8:45am-noon.

Laundromat: 12 rue du Maréchal Leclerc. Open daily 7am-9:30pm. Also 16 rue Beaurepaire, open daily 7:30am-9:30pm, summer until 10pm.

Police: 415 rue du Chemin Vert (☎02 41 83 24 00).

Hospital: Centre Hospitalier, rue de Fontevraud (☎02 41 53 30 30).

Internet: Welcome Services Copy, 20 rue du Portail-Louis (☎02 41 67 75 15). €5.30 per hr. Open July-Aug. Tu-F 9am-12:30pm and 2-7pm, Sa 9:30am-12:30pm and 2:30-7pm; Sept.-June also open M 2:30-7pm. MC/V.

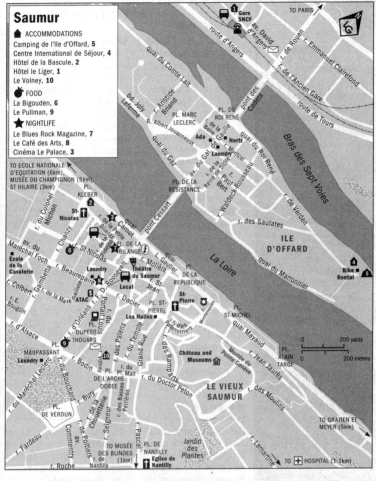

Saumur

🏠 **ACCOMMODATIONS**
Camping de l'Ile d'Offard, **5**
Centre International de Séjour, **4**
Hôtel de la Bascule, **2**
Hôtel le Liger, **1**
Le Volney, **10**

🍎 **FOOD**
La Bigouden, **6**
Le Pullman, **9**

⭐ **NIGHTLIFE**
Le Blues Rock Magazine, **7**
Le Café des Arts, **8**
Cinéma Le Palace, **3**

Post Office: pl. Dupetit Thouars (☎02 41 40 22 08). **Currency exchange.** Open M-F 8am-6:30pm, Sa 8am-noon. **Poste Restante:** Saumur Volney 49400. **Branch** office across from the train station. AmEx traveler's checks sold. **Postal code:** 49400.

🏠 ACCOMMODATIONS & CAMPING

✉ Le Volney, 1 rue Volney (☎02 41 51 25 41; contact@le-volney.com), a few blocks from the *centre ville* and the château. A cheerful owner and comfortable, spacious rooms give this hotel a bed-and-breakfast feel. Breakfast included. Singles and doubles with TV, telephone, and toilet €25-27, with shower €35-49. MC/V. ❷

Hôtel de la Bascule, 1 pl. Kléber (☎02 41 50 13 65), near Eglise St-Nicolas on quai Carnot. These tidy rooms are worth the splurge. Pleasing bedrooms with spotless bathrooms, TV, and showers, and many with excellent views of the river. Breakfast €6.

IN RECENT NEWS

UNE SALADE, SANS OGM

In the Loire Valley, where farmers have prided themselves on producing some of the best fruits and vegetables in France, traditions are meeting modern science with the development of genetically modified products (OGM, or *organismes génétiquement modifiés*). Scientists alter plants' DNA to strengthen resistance to pests and add nutritional value.

These genetically altered products have met with controversy in France due to the lack of information on how the plants could affect consumers. According to the Ministry of Agriculture, consumers may develop allergies to the new foods. The opposition to OGM ranges from the occasional activist who burns down a field of crops to government officials who have refused to allow the sale of OGM. Consumers' interest in the debate is manifested in the new market for food described as *biologique*, grown in conditions that maximize the productivity of the land without adding risk to the consumers' health or the environment. At the end of 2003, a European Union law will require that all products with above 1% of an OGM product be clearly marked.

Despite the concerns, the Ministry of Agriculture maintains that development of OGM, provided that their potential risks are thoroughly researched, are essential in order for France to maintain a dynamic agricultural industry.

Reception closed Su Oct.-June. Singles and doubles €38-42; one large room for 2-4 people €40. Extra bed €7. MC/V. ❹

Centre International de Séjour, rue de Verdun (☎02 41 40 30 00; fax 02 41 67 37 81), on Île d'Offard between train station and tourist office. Adequate rooms with dim bathrooms host a young crowd. Two-bed rooms are especially nice. Helpful English-speaking staff. Foosball, pool, TV, pinball, self-service kitchenette, and laundry. Breakfast and sheets included. Ask at reception for free tickets to Grottien and Meyer *caves*. Reception daily July-Aug. 8am-9pm; Sept. and June 8:30am-12:30pm and 1:30-7pm; Mar.-May and Oct. 9am-noon and 2-7pm. Closed Nov.-Feb. Reservations recommended. 2- to 8-bed dorms €14.50; 2- to 4-bed dorms with shower €22 for first person, €9 each additional person. MC/V. ❶

Hôtel le Liger, 17 av. David d'Angers (☎02 41 67 40 04; fax 02 41 67 40 04), opposite the train station. Friendly proprietors offer neat, if slightly worn, rooms. Restaurant on the ground floor. Breakfast €5. Singles and doubles with sink and toilet €22, with shower €26, with toilet and shower €34. Extra bed €7. ❷

Camping de l'Île d'Offard (☎02 41 40 30 00; fax 02 41 67 37 81), same site as hostel. 4-star site with pool, laundry, tennis, snack shop, mini-golf, and TV. Reception daily July-Aug. 8am-9pm; Sept. and June 8:30am-12:30pm and 1:30-7pm; Mar.-May and Oct. 9am-noon and 2-7pm. Closed Nov.-Feb. June-Aug. €13.50 for 2 people with car, €4 for each additional person, €2 per child. Electricity €3. Tent rental €27-48 per day. MC/V. ❶

🗗 FOOD

Saumur is renowned for its sparkling *crémant de Loire* wine and, of course, mushrooms. Stock up on fungus at the indoor **market** in Les Halles at the far end of pl. St-Pierre (Su-F until 1pm, Sa until noon), or its outdoor equivalents on av. du Général de Gaulle (Th morning) and pl. St-Pierre (Sa morning). The **ATAC** supermarket, 6 rue Franklin D. Roosevelt, sits inside the shopping center across from the Printemps department store with a back entrance on rue St-Nicolas. (☎02 41 83 54 54. Open M-F 9am-1pm and 2:15-7:30pm, Sa 9am-7:30pm, Su 9am-12:30pm.) An assortment of cheap restaurants are sprinkled along **rue St-Nicolas.** Enjoy delicious regional cuisine in the intimate dining room of 🖾**Le Pullman ❸**, 52 rue d'Orléans, charmingly decorated like a 1920s railroad dining car. Fresh food and charming owners keep customers coming back for another ride. (☎02 41 51 31 79. *Plats* €11-15, *menus* €12.50 and €25. Garden dining available in summer. MC/V.) For an extensive menu of salads (€3-8) and crêpes stuffed with everything from fresh seafood to the classic ham and cheese (€6.50-8), try **La Bigouden ❶**, 67 rue St-Nicolas. (☎02 41 67 12 59. Open July-Aug. daily noon-2pm; Sept.-June Su-M and Th-Sa noon-2pm.) **Place St-Pierre** and its off-shoots have several great options for light food and drinks.

🗿 SIGHTS

Three 12th- to 15th-century churches brighten Saumur's main district, and a very pretty **Jardin des Plantes** is tucked between rue Docteur Peton and rue Marceau, on the other side of the château. The picturesque **Pont Cessart** has a fantastic view, and the promenades along the river make for lovely sunset strolls.

ECOLE NATIONALE D'EQUITATION. In 1763, Louis XV chose Saumur as the location for his cavalry training camp, thereby establishing this town as France's top center for horsemanship. The town has continued the spectacular Cadre Noir tradition in this civilian national riding school, whose students compete at an international level and often go on to train equestrians around the country. The palatial, modern premises, located 15min. from the center of town, contain over 50km of training grounds, 400 fine purebreds, and the world's best veterinarians. Since 1825, the school's riders have donned "black dress decorated with gold, and *lampion* hats worn ready for battle." Tours pass through the facilities and explain the rigorous demands of equestrianism; if you visit in the morning, your visit will include a 30min. viewing of daily training. (*☎02 41 53 50 60. Take bus B, dir: St. Hilaire, to Alouette; continue along the road in the same direction until signs direct you the remaining 3km down a sidewalk-free road. Exercise caution. Visitors are only allowed to view the grounds on tours, available in French and English. Apr.-Sept. M 2:30-4:30pm, Tu-F 9:30-11am and 2:30-4:30pm, Sa 9:30-11:30am. €8, children €5. The Ecole also offers shows throughout the year; call ahead for schedule and prices.)*

CHÂTEAU. Saumur's 14th-century château, best known for its cameo appearance in the famous medieval manuscript *Les très riches heures du duc de Berry*, lives up to its reputation as "the very image of a fairy tale château." For two centuries, it housed a prestigious Huguenot academy before being pillaged and abandoned. It was eventually converted into a prison by Napoleon. Today, most of the château is devoted to two exceptional museums. The intriguing **Musée du Cheval** celebrates everything equine, tracing the evolution of the horse and displaying a vast collection of riding gear from China to Argentina. Guided tours, available in French or English, lead the visitor through the **Musée des Arts Décoratifs,** which exhibits medieval and Renaissance painting, sculpture, and tapestries, and brightly decorated *faïence* (potteryware). The south wing of the château, now closed, is undergoing a major restoration that is expected to be completed in 2007; a double spiral staircase, a rare architectural structure for its time, has been discovered during the process. (*☎02 41 40 24 40. Open daily June-Aug. 9:30am-6pm; July and Aug. W and Sa also 8:30-10:30pm; Apr.-May and Sept. 10am-1pm and 2-5:30pm. Closed Oct.-Mar. June-Sept. English and German tours, 40min. €6, students €4, gardens only €2.)*

GRATIEN ET MEYER. Saumur's wines have been in high demand since the 12th century, when Plantagenêt kings took their favorite casks with them to England. Many wine cellars offer tours and tastings. **Caves Gratien & Meyer,** an especially old and well-known vineyard, offers tours (€3) of their cellars and museum and a wine tasting session of their award-winning vintages. (*Rte. de Montsoreau. ☎02 41 83 13 32. Take bus D, dir: Dampierres, from pl. Bilange to Beaulieu. Open Apr.-Nov. daily 9am-noon and 2-6pm, last morning entry 11am, last afternoon entry 5pm; mid-Nov. to Mar. Sa-Su 9am-noon and 3-6pm. Groups of 10 or more may also reserve a visit Nov.-Mar. M-F 9am-noon and 2-6pm.)*

MUSÉE DU CHAMPIGNON. In dark, spooky caves carved out from *tuffeau* stone, this museum gives a sense of the massive mushroom farming industry of the Saumur region. A great variety of mushroom species grow in its dank interior, filling the air with rich aromas. Tours in English trace the history of the mushroom, especially in France, the world's third-largest producer of mushrooms. The mushroom grill outside serves gourmet *hors d'oeuvres* (€4.60-7.10) from noon to 3pm. *(Rte. de Gennes, Ste-Hilaire-St-Florent. ☎02 41 50 31 55. Take bus B, dir: Ste-Hilaire, to Pompiers. From there, follow the signs on the 2km walk to the museum, 20min. Open early Feb. to mid-Nov. daily 10am-7pm. €6.50, students €5.)*

MUSÉE DES BLINDES. Commonly known as "the tank museum," this interesting collection of over 150 tanks from 15 different countries follows the evolution of warfare in the 20th century. Keep an eye out for the camouflaged Tiger I, a monstrous German cruiser, and the Leclerc, France's first tank. Once a year in mid-July French soldiers drive the tanks around to demonstrate that each vehicle on display is still perfectly operational. *(1043 rte. de Fontevraud. ☎02 41 83 69 99. Take bus C, dir: Chemin Vert, to Fricotelle, then walk 1km down rue du Tunnel to the museum. Visit lasts 90min. Open daily May-Sept. 9:30am-6:30pm; Oct.-Apr. 10am-5pm. €5.50, children €3.)*

🎵 📷 ENTERTAINMENT & FESTIVALS

The **Théâtre de Saumur** (☎02 41 83 30 83), next to the tourist office, hosts everything from *galas de danse* to jazz and classical concerts in its 19th-century hall. Dance the night away to live music at the small but friendly ◼**Le Blues Rock Magazine,** 7 rue de la Petite Bilange. (☎02 41 50 41 69. Drinks €3-6. Open May-Sept. daily 11pm-4am; Oct.-Apr. Tu-Sa 11pm-4am. MC/V.) Toss some darts or just toss back an imaginative "beer cocktail" from the extensive menu at **Le Café des Arts,** 4 rue Beaurepaire, a large bar in the *centre ville*. (☎02 41 51 21 72. MC/V.) Late-night lingerers loiter in pl. St-Pierre beside the illuminated cathedral, while livelier crowds and louder music beat around the **Irish pubs** in pl. de la République. Saumur residents line up around the block to catch the latest releases at **Cinéma Le Palace,** 13 quai Carnot. (☎08 92 68 00 73. Tickets €6.50.)

During the first week of July, the three-day **Festivales de Saumur** bring vendors, outdoor dining, music, and free food to rue St-Nicolas. In the third week of September, the Cadre Noir show off their horsemanship with competitions and exhibitions at **La Grande Semaine de Saumur.** The **International Festival of Military Music** occurs in late June every other year; the next one occurs in 2005. Alternating years, also in late June, bring the **Festival des Géants,** a march of oversized puppets that honors Saumur's eternal fascination with carnivals. In late July, the cavalry school and the local tank school join forces in the celebrated **Carrousel.** After 2hr. of graceful equestrian performances, the spectacle degenerates (or evolves) into a 3hr. motorcycle show and dusty tank parade. (Info and reservations ☎02 41 40 20 66. Tickets €20.) Saumur hosts dozens of equestrian events annually, often free.

🏛 DAYTRIP FROM SAUMUR: FONTEVRAUD-L'ABBAYE

*The #16 **bus** makes the 14km trip from the Saumur train station. (25min., 3-5 per day, €2.20.) The **tourist office** dispenses free maps of the town. (☎02 41 51 79 45. Open Easter-Sept. M-Sa 9:30am-12:30pm and 2-6:30pm. Tours of Fontevraud July-Aug. F at 3pm, €4.) One stop before Fontevraud, in **Montsoreau,** are curious **troglodyte cliff dwellings** and a **château.** Call the tourist office in Montsoreau (☎02 41 51 70 22) for info.*

The ◼**Abbaye de Fontevraud,** the largest monastic complex in Europe, has awed visitors for nine centuries. The founder of this now-defunct community, Robert d'Arbrissel, settled in the forest of Fontevraud in 1101. To increase the humility of his monks, he placed a woman at the head of the order. Of its 32 abbesses, 16 were of royal blood; under their rule, the abbey became a place of refuge for women of all classes—from reforming prostitutes to princesses escaping unhappy marriages. Following the Revolution, the abbey became a prison, and so it remained from 1804 until 1963. The 12th-century abbey church also serves as a Plantagenêt necropolis; **Eleanor of Aquitaine,** who lived out her days here after being repudiated by her second husband, **Henry II,** now lies next to him alongside their son **Richard the Lionheart.** The British government has repeatedly sought to transfer the royal remains to Westminster. The abbey's **chapter house** is painted with scenes depicting Christ's last hours. Over time, part of the fresco's chronology has been disrupted by intruding nuns, as seven abbesses have had themselves added to the wall paintings, depicting themselves as witness to the trials of Jesus. Don't miss the 12th-century kitchens and the ceiling model's fascinating architecture. An English booklet and signs help visitors along, but 1hr. tours give the best sense of the abbey's history. Themed visits put a different spin on life in the abbey, but are only available in French. (☎02 41 51 71 41. Abbey open daily June to late Sept. 9am-6:30pm, late Sept to May 9:30am-12:30pm and 2-5pm. Themed tours free with price of admission. Theatrical tours of the abbey nightly in Aug. at 9:30pm.)

ANGERS

Angers (pop. 160,000) is a modern, sophisticated city with illustrious royal roots. From behind the imposing walls of their fortress, the medieval dukes of Anjou ruled over the surrounding territory and a smallish island across the Channel called Britain. Angers's 13th-century château and cathedral and its world-famous apocalyptic tapestry are majestic reminders of the city's past. Today, Jean Lurçat's vibrant 20th-century tapestry, "The Song of the World," reflects the lively atmosphere of modern Angers. Filled with an energetic and youthful population, the town bustles with shops, museums, gardens, and excellent restaurants.

▐ TRANSPORTATION

Trains: rue de la Gare. Information desk open M-Sa 7:30am-9pm, Su 7:30am-10pm. To: **Le Mans** (30min., 6-7 per day, €12.80); **Nantes** (1hr., 9 per day, €13.50); **Orléans** (3-4hr., 6 per day, €24.60) change at St-Pierre des Corps; **Paris** (2-4hr., 3 per day, €43.30); **Poitiers** (2-2½hr., 6 per day, €25.10) change at St-Pierre or Tours; **Tours** (1hr., 12 per day, €14). Locker **luggage check.** (72hr. limit. €3.40-€5. Open M 5am-10pm, Tu-Th 6am-10pm, F 6am-11pm, Sa 6am-10pm, Su 8am-10pm.)

Buses: pl. de la République (☎02 41 88 59 25). To: **Rennes** (3hr., 2 per day, €15.90); **Saumur** (1½hr., 4 per day, €7.60). Open M-Sa 6:30am-7pm.

Public Transportation: COTRA buses (☎02 41 33 64 64). Buses leave from pl. Kennedy or pl. Ralliement 6am-8pm. Limited night service 8pm-midnight. Tickets €1.

Taxis: Angers Taxi-Anjou Taxi (☎02 41 85 65 00). Open daily 5am-11pm.

Car Rental: Hertz, 18 rue Denis Papin (☎01 39 38 38 38). Open M-F 8am-noon and 2-7pm, Sa 8am-noon and 2-6pm. MC/V. Europcar, pl. de la Gare (☎02 41 87 87 10). Open M 7:30am-noon and 2-6pm, Tu-F 8am-6:30pm. AmEx/DC/MC/V.

Bike Rental: Available at the tourist office. €8 per half-day, €11 per day.

▗▐ ORIENTATION & PRACTICAL INFORMATION

Most of the restaurants and nightlife in Angers are concentrated in the pedestrian-only streets radiating outward from pl. du Ralliement. To reach the château and tourist office (when coming from the train station), walk straight onto rue de la

Gare, then turn right at pl. de la Visitation, onto rue Talot. At the traffic light, a left onto bd. du Roi-René will lead to the château. The tourist office is on the right across from the château.

Tourist Office: pl. Kennedy (☎02 41 23 50 00; accueil@angers-tourisme.com). Staff organizes trips to châteaux, **reserves rooms** (€2), rents bikes, **exchanges currency** (€4), and distributes free maps. Open June-Sept. M-Sa 9am-6:30pm, Su 10am-5pm; Oct.-Apr. M 2-6pm, Tu-Sa 9am-6pm, Su 10am-1pm; May M-Sa 9am-6pm, Su 10am-6pm. **Walking tours** in English explore the city's history. (☎02 21 23 50 10. M-Sa 11:30am. €4, students €3.)

Money: Banque de France, 13 pl. Mendès-France (☎02 41 24 25 00), has good rates for **currency exchange.** Exchange desk open M-F 9am-noon.

Youth Services: Centre d'Information Jeunes, 5 allée du Haras (☎02 41 87 74 47). Info on employment, lodging, and discounts. Open M-F 1-3:30pm, Sa 10am-noon.

English Books: FNAC, 23 rue Lenepveu. Open M-Sa 10am-7pm. MC/V.

Laundromat: Laverie du Cygne, pl. de la Visitation (☎02 41 86 11 20). Open M-Th 7:30-11:30am and 2:30-7pm. **Lavarie Des Halles,** 15 rue Plantagenêt. Open daily 8am-9pm.

Police: Gendarmerie, 33 rue Nid de Pie (☎02 41 73 56 10).

Hospital: Centre Hospitalier, 4 rue Larrey (☎02 41 35 36 37).

Internet: Cyber Espace, 25 rue de la Roë (☎02 41 24 92 71). €1 per 15min., €3 per hr. Open M-Th 9am-10pm, F-Sa 9am-midnight, Su 2-8pm.

Post Office: 1 rue Franklin Roosevelt (☎02 41 20 81 81), just off Corneille near rue Voltaire. **Currency exchange.** Open M-F 9am-6:30pm, Sa 9am-12:30pm. **Poste Restante:** "Angers-Ralliement 49052." **Postal code:** 49100.

⌐ ACCOMMODATIONS & CAMPING

▩ **Hôtel Continental,** 12 rue Louis de Romain (☎02 41 86 94 94; le.continental@wanadoo.fr). Near the center of town with large, tastefully decorated, generic rooms. Buffet breakfast €6.50. Singles and doubles with toilet and shower or bath €42-56; triples €64; quads €72. Extra bed €8. ❸

Hôtel de l'Univers, 2 pl. de la Gare (☎02 41 88 43 58; fax 02 41 86 97 28). Kind management welcomes visitors to 45 rooms that are slightly bare but have wide comfortable beds, telephone, and TV. Breakfast €5.60. Hall shower €4. Singles and doubles with toilet €25, with shower €35, with toilet and shower €45-50. MC/V. ❷

Centre d'Accueil du Lac de Maine (HI), 49 av. du Lac de Maine (☎02 41 22 32 10; infos@lacdemaine.fr). Take bus #6 or 16 to Accueil Lac de Maine, turn around, cross the busy road, and follow signs on the right-hand side to the Centre d'Accueil. Proximity to the lake, extensive sporting facilities, mini-golf, and spirited mix of guests justify the 10-15min. bus ride. Breakfast €3.50, meals €7. Call ahead, especially in summer. Individuals may not reserve a room more than 3 weeks in advance. Singles and doubles with shower €25. **Members only.** ❷

Royal Hôtel, 8bis pl. de la Visitation (☎02 41 88 30 25; fax 02 41 81 05 75), straight down rue de la Gare to the corner of rue d'Iena. Spacious, slightly worn, rooms with big windows and TV. Clean hallway shower and free Internet in lobby. Breakfast €5. Singles and doubles with sink €26, with shower and toilet €36; triples €42. AmEx/DC/MC/V. ❸

Hôtel des Lices, 25 rue des Lices (☎02 41 87 44 10), near the château and center. Small, clean rooms above a bistro. Don't fret over the name—it refers to jousting; in this family-run inn, guests do not have to worry about that. Breakfast €4.30. Reception M-F 7am-9pm, Sa-Su 5-9pm. Singles with bath €34; doubles with shower €44. MC/V. ❸

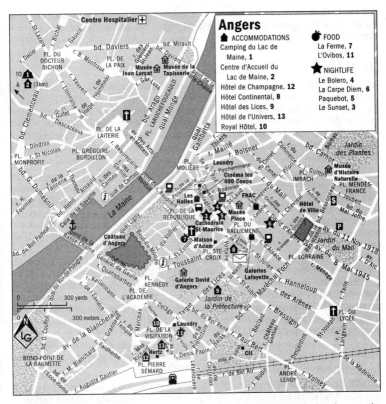

Hôtel de Champagne, 34 rue Denis Papin (☎02 41 25 78 78), A quiet hotel across the street from the station, with private showers and plenty of space. Great value. Book in advance to reserve the cheaper rooms. Breakfast €5.50. Singles with sink and toilet €21-24; doubles with shower €27-39; triples €47-52. MC/V. ❷

Camping du Lac de Maine, av. du Lac de Maine (☎02 41 73 05 03; fax 02 41 73 02 20), near the Centre d'Accueil on CD 111, rte. des Pruniers. Take bus #6 to Camping du Lac de Maine. 4-star campsite on a sandy lakeside offers playgrounds, horseback riding, and bike paths. Open late Mar. to mid-Oct. July-Aug. 2 people with tent and car €15; low season €10.20. Electricity €3. Showers available. MC/V. ❶

🍴 FOOD

Angers caters to its student population with everything from crêpes and pizza to Chinese, particularly along **rue St-Laud, rue St-Aubin,** and **boulevard Maréchal Foch.** A **grocery store** with an excellent bakery resides in the basement of Galeries Lafayette on the corner of rue d'Alsace and pl. du Ralliement. (Open M-Sa 9:30am-7:30pm.) Locals and tourists pack into **La Ferme ❸,** 2 pl. Freppel, at the foot of Cathédrale St-Maurice, to fill up on delicious regional wines, meats, and cheeses. (☎02 41 87 09 90. Appetizers €7, *plats* €9-12, *menus* €15 and €27. Reservations recommended on weekends. AmEx/MC/V.) **L'Ovibos ❸,** 3 rue d'Anjou, grills up a variety of steaks and meats that complement their many salads. Steak platters are named after US states, so pick a region and dig in. (☎02 41 87 48 90. Open daily noon-2pm and 7-11pm. Salads €5-7, meat dishes €8-13, *menus* €9-15. MC/V.)

☉ SIGHTS

A €4.50 ticket provides admission to five museums; the €8 *billet jumelé* also includes the château. Both are sold at the tourist office and at museums. Angers is famous for its cherished tapestries, which are hung in many of the city's main sights. The town is situated near several beautiful parks, including the **Jardin du Mail,** a land-scaped garden with terrific promenades, and the **Jardin des Plantes,** a beautiful, botanical wonder with provocative sculptures and a large, tranquil pond. (Jardin des Plantes open daily until 8:30pm.)

CHÂTEAU D'ANGERS. St-Louis built this 13th-century defensive masterpiece as the symbol of his power. Bristling with 17 towers and protected by a 900m long, 15m high wall, it does its job well. The Renaissance Duke René added an inner courtyard in the 15th century as a shelter for inhabitants of the city and a space for courtly artists and market-vendors. During the Wars of Religion, Henri III ordered the château's demolition; fortunately, his subjects only managed to lower the towers by one story. In the 19th century, the château was converted into a prison. Today, it is a well-preserved monument with enjoyable promenades in the French-syle garden planted where the moat once stood. Among the furnishings in the interior, the most notable is the **Tapisserie de l'Apocalypse,** a 106m tapestry, whose six segments and 74 scenes depict the life of Saint John in his battle against evil, subtly weaving in references to the war between France (represented by John) and Britain, the evil aggressor. The tapestry's gruesome monsters include a seven-headed Satan gobbling down babies. *(2 promenade du Bout du Monde, on pl. Kennedy. ☎02 41 86 81 94. Open daily May-Aug. 9:30am-6:30pm; Sept.-Apr. 10am-5:30pm. Last entrance 45min. prior to closing. French tours leave from the chapel 5 times daily, English tours 1-3 times daily. €6.10, students €4.10, under 17 free.)*

MUSÉE COINTREAU. This factory that has been making the famous liqueur, native to Angers, since 1849. The 2hr. tour discusses the history and production of Cointreau. Free ▨tasting afterwards. Tours in English. *(Bd. des Bretonnières, St-Bar-thélemy-d'Anjou. Take bus #7, which passes by the train station to Cointreau. ☎02 41 31 50 50. Tours Nov.-Apr. M-Sa 3pm, Su 3 and 4:30pm; May-June and Sept.-Oct. M-Sa 10:30am and 3pm, Su 10:30am, 3, and 4:30pm; July-Aug. daily 10:30am, 2:30, 3:30, and 4:30pm. €5.50, under 18 €2.60.)*

GALERIE DAVID D'ANGERS. This beautifully restored Toussaint Abbey, whose vaults have been replaced by a soaring glass roof, now holds a vast collection of David d'Angers's renowned 19th-century sculptures. His subjects are both literary and historical characters, including the artist's personal friends Victor Hugo and Balzac. Among the pieces are a scale replica of David's masterwork for the Pan-théon in Paris and many of the 30 statues he designed for city squares. *(37bis rue Toussaint. ☎02 41 87 21 03. Open mid-June to mid-Sept. daily 9:30am-6:30pm; late Sept. to early June Tu-Su 10am-noon and 2-6pm. €2, under 16 €1. Tours in French M and Th 4pm.)*

MUSÉE JEAN LURÇAT. Angers's second woven masterpiece resides in this former 12th-century hospital. The 80m-long **Chant du Monde** *(Song of the World),* is a symbolic journey through human destiny, representing life's joys and sorrows in ten enormous panels filled with blazing colors and morbid skulls. Lurçat, inspired by the Apocalypse tapestry, abandoned his career as a painter and turned to weaving. Next to the Chant du Monde is the **Musée de la Tapisserie Contempo-raire,** a permanent collection of textiles and tapestry art including pieces by the renowned cloth sculptor Magdalena Abakanowicz. *(4 bd. Arago. ☎02 41 24 18 45. Open mid-June to mid-Sept. daily 9:30am-6:30pm; late Sept. to early June Tu-Su 10am-noon and 2-6pm. €3.50 for each museum, ages 18-25 €1.80, under 18 free.)*

CATHÉDRALE ST-MAURICE. The 12th-century building is a hodgepodge of historical periods with a Norman porch, a 13th-century chancel intersecting a 4th-century Gallo-Roman wall, and some of the oldest stained-glass windows, which in France date back to the 12th and 15th centuries. The single nave of the church is classic Angevin Plantagenêt style with heavily decorated vaults. Like everything in Angers, the church is decorated with a rotating exhibit of beautiful, rare tapestries. Linger long enough and the lovely local nuns might offer a free tour. *(Pl. Chappoulie. ☎02 41 87 58 45. Open daily Apr.-Nov. 8:30am-7pm; Dec.-Mar. 8:30am-5:30pm.)*

OTHER SIGHTS. The **Musée Pince,** housed in a 15th-century building, displays a unique, though small, collection of art from ancient Japan, China, Egypt, and the Roman Empire, from Japanese engravings to miniature statues of horses. Though tiny, these works are all impressively crafted. *(32bis rue Lenepveu. ☎02 41 88 94 27. Open mid-June to mid-Sept. Tu-Su 9:30am-6:30pm; Oct. to early June Tu-Sa 10am-noon and 2-6pm. Adults €2, under 18 €1.)* In the heart of the *vieille ville,* just a few blocks from the château, **place du Ralliement** is home to numerous stores and cafés as well as a magnificent **theater,** which was rebuilt in the 19th century and decorated by local painter Lenepveu. The *vieille ville* derives its name from the ancient, low-roofed, 16th-century stone houses here, among which is the oldest house in Angers, **La Maison d'Adam,** a 16th-century timber-framed house decorated with wooden carvings. (On the corner of pl. Ste-Croix and rue Montault, just behind the cathedral.) In 2004, the **Musée des Beaux-Arts** is set to re-open after a six-year renovation project to create new, modern galleries.

🎵 📷 ENTERTAINMENT & FESTIVALS

The discos have been exiled to the suburbs, but the cafés along **rue St-Laud** are always packed, and bars on student-dominated **rue Bressigny** start getting down before the sun does. **Le Carpe Diem,** 15 rue St-Maurille, a small, chic bar, schedules philosophical discussions and encourages patrons to live by its motto. (☎02 41 87 50 47. Open M-Sa noon-1am.) Shoot a game and taste the local beer in the laidback **Paquebot,** 45 rue St-Laud. (☎02 41 81 06 20. Beer €2-4. Wine €2. Open daily 11am-2pm.) Across the street, **Le Sunset,** 44 rue St-Laud, caters to a feistier crowd and serves glasses of Le Sun, its own tropical punch. (☎02 41 87 85 58. Beer €4-6. Open daily noon-2am. MC/V.) Music of all sorts, echoes through the streets from **Le Bolero,** 38 rue St-Laud. (☎02 41 88 61 19. Cocktails €8.) **Cinéma Les 400 Coups,** 12 rue Calveau, shows international films and Cannes Film Festival selections with French subtitles. (☎02 41 88 70 95. Tickets €6.70, 11am matinee €4.50.)

In late June and early July, Angers attracts renowned French comedy and dramatic troupes to the château for the **Festival d'Anjou,** one of the largest theater festivals in France. Albert Camus once staged a play here before a nationwide TV audience. (Info office at 1 rue des Arènes. ☎02 41 88 14 14; www.festivaldanjou.com. €28 per show, students €12.)

LE MANS

From large, modern apartment buildings and 12th-century churches to ancient Roman walls and a world-famous 24hr. car race, Le Mans (pop. 150,000) is a city of contrasts. Although it may not be the most beautiful city in the Loire Valley, it does have possibly the most beautiful *vieille ville* in France. Interesting sights and an exciting nightlife certainly make it worth a night's stay.

⊫ TRANSPORTATION

Trains: bd. de la Gare (☎08 36 35 35 35), off pl. du 8 Mai 1945. Ticket windows open M-F 5:15am-10:15pm, Sa 6am-10:50pm, Su 6:40am-10:30pm. To: **Nantes** (1hr., 7 per day, €22.50); **Paris** (1-3hr., 12 per day, €31.10); **Rennes** (1hr., 7 per day, €20.60); **Tours** (1hr., 6 per day, €12.40).

Buses: SNCF (☎02 43 25 30 12) sends buses from the station to **Saumur** (1½hr.; 2 per day M-Sa, 1 on Su at 9pm; €13.20).

Public Transportation: SEMTRAM buses, 65 av. Gal. de Gaulle (☎02 43 24 76 76), run 5:30am to 8 or 9pm; the city's **Hi'bus** lines take over until midnight or 1am. Pick up a map at the SEMTRAM office or tourist office. Info office open M-F 7am-7pm, Sa 8:30am-6:30pm. MC/V. Ticket €1, *carnet* of 10 €7.50; sold on bus or in office.

Taxis: Radio Taxi, 2 av. du Gal. Leclerc (☎02 43 24 92 92), at the train station. 24hr.

Bike Rental: Top Team, 9 pl. St-Pierre (☎02 43 24 88 32). From €15 per day. ID deposit. Open Tu-Sa 10:30am-7pm. MC/V.

Car Rental: National Car Rental, in the train station (☎02 43 24 03 34). From €75 per day. Open M-F 8am-noon and 2-6:30pm, Sa 8:30am-noon and 2-5pm. AmEx/MC/V. **Avis,** also in train station. Open M-F 7:30am-7pm, Sa 9am-noon and 2-6pm. AmEx/DC/MC/V. **Sixt Location de Voitures,** av. du Général Leclerc (☎02 43 51 21 21), has more options. Open M-F 8am-noon and 2:30-6pm, Sa by appointment. AmEx/MC/V.

⊁🛈 ORIENTATION & PRACTICAL INFORMATION

Tourist Office: rue de l'Etoile (☎02 43 28 17 22; www.ville-lemans.fr), in the 17th-century Hôtel des Ursulines. Head up rue Gastelier across from the post office and take bus #5 (dir: Villaret) to Etoile. Cross pl. le Couteux and walk down rue de l'Etoile; the office is two blocks down to the left. The staff distributes maps (€4), practical guides, and info booklets. Historical **walking tours** in French depart from the cathedral fountain. Call for a schedule of English tours. (1½-2hr.; July-Aug. M-F 3pm; €5.50, students €3. Night tours W and Sa 9:30pm and 10pm; €10, students €7.) Open June-Aug. M-Sa 9am-6pm, Su 10am-12:30pm and 2:30-5pm; Sept.-May M-F 9am-6pm, Sa 9am-noon and 2-6pm, Su 10am-noon.

Money: Banque de France, 2 pl. Lionel le Couteux (☎02 43 74 74 00), has the best exchange rates. Open M-F 8:45am-noon.

English Bookstore: Thuard Librairie, 24 rue de l'Etoile (☎02 43 82 22 22), also has some Spanish, Italian, and German fiction. Open M-Sa 8:30am-7:30pm. MC/V.

Laundromats: Lav'Ideal, 4 pl. l'Eperon (☎02 43 24 53 99). Open daily 7am-9pm. **Laverie Libre Service,** 4 rue Gastelier (☎02 43 43 99 18). Open daily 7am-9pm.

Youth Information: Ville du Mans Service Jeunesse, 13 rue de l'Etoile (☎02 43 47 38 95). Offers student discounts, organizes sports trips, and has info on jobs and housing. Open M, W, and F 10am-noon and 1:30-6pm; Tu and Th 1:30-6pm; Sa 2-6pm. **SMEBA,** 34 av. François Mitterrand (☎02 43 39 90 20), is a student travel agency that arranges discount tickets and offers health insurance for foreign students in France. Open M-F 9am-6pm. Free **Internet** with sign-up sheets.

Police: Commissariat Central, 6 rue Coeffort (☎02 43 74 40 40).

Hospital: Centre Hospitalier, 194 av. Rubillard (☎02 43 43 43 43).

Internet: Médiathèque, 54 rue du Port (☎02 43 47 48 86). €3.20 per hr. Limit 30min. per day. Reservation required. Open Tu-W and F 10am-6:30pm, Th 1:30-6:30pm, Sa 10am-5pm. **Cyberville,** 8bis rue d'Alger (☎02 43 43 90 90). €0.20 per min. Open M-F 10am-noon and 1:30-6:30pm, Sa 11am-noon and 1:30-6pm. **Cyber@Net,** 27 av. du

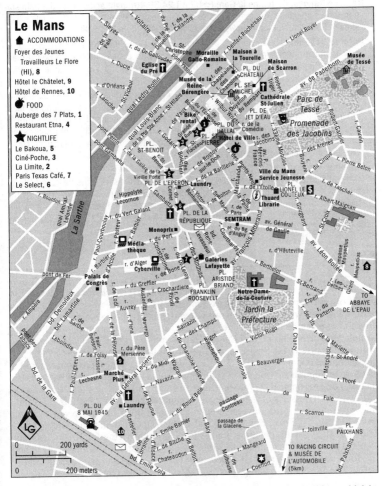

Le Mans

ACCOMMODATIONS
Foyer des Jeunes
  Travailleurs Le Flore
  (HI), **8**
Hôtel le Châtelet, **9**
Hôtel de Rennes, **10**

FOOD
Auberge des 7 Plats, **1**
Restaurant Etna, **4**

NIGHTLIFE
Le Bakoua, **5**
Ciné-Poche, **3**
La Limite, **2**
Paris Texas Café, **7**
Le Select, **6**

Gal. Leclerc (☎02 43 21 45 48). €3 for 30min., €4 per hr. Open M-Sa 10am-midnight, Su 2pm-midnight. Internet is also available for free at Le Mans's major **hostel,** the Foyer des Jeunes Travailleurs Le Flore (see **Accommodations** below).

Post Office: 13 pl. de la République (☎02 43 21 75 00). **Currency exchange.** Open M-F 8am-7pm, Sa 9am-noon. **Branch office,** 1 pl. du 8 Mai 1945, right by the train station. Same hours and services. **Poste Restante** (at main office): République, 72013 Le Mans Cedex 2. **Postal code:** 72000.

▌ ACCOMMODATIONS & CAMPING

It's a good idea to call ahead in Le Mans, as hotels are generally expensive and are often full. Most of the hotels in town are either within a 5min. walk of the train station or on the outskirts of town.

Hôtel de Rennes, 43 bd. de la Gare (☎02 43 24 86 40), right across from the train station, offers spacious, modern rooms in good condition. Breakfast €5.60. Singles with shower €36; doubles with shower and toilet €40-42; triples €45. ❸

Hôtel le Châtelet, 15 rue du Père Mersenne (☎02 43 43 92 36). The worn exterior of this hotel/bar hides nine clean, renovated rooms with a small hallway shower. Breakfast €4. Singles €23; doubles €37; triples €45. Weekend stays require advance notice. No credit cards. ❷

Foyer des Jeunes Travailleurs Le Flore (HI), 23 rue Maupertius (☎02 43 81 27 55; florefjt@noos.fr). This modern complex, close to the city center, serves as a dorm for local students, the town's youth info center, and a hostel. The building has doubles, triples, and quads, plus kitchen, laundry, free Internet, and shared, slightly worn bathrooms. Breakfast included M-Sa. Sheets €2.90. Bunks €11.50, €8.50 when kitchens close. Wheelchair-accessible. **Members only.** ❶

Camping: The tourist office has a list of campsites in the Sarthe region. The closest is the two-star **Camping Le Vieux Moulin,** 9km away in Neuville-sur-Sarthe (☎02 43 25 31 82; fax 02 43 25 38 11). Take the train from Le Mans (8min., 4 per day, €2.50). The riverside site has bikes (€6.10 per day), laundry, a pool, and tennis courts. Open July to early Sept. Call ahead for exact dates. €10.70 for 2 people, €3.10 per extra person. Electricity €3.10. MC/V. ❶

🍴 FOOD

Renowned for its poultry, Le Mans's regional cuisine commonly includes *pintade* (guinea fowl) and *canard* (duck). The succulent *marmite sarthoise,* a warm casserole of rabbit, chicken, ham, carrots, cabbage, and mushrooms bubbling in a bath of Jasnière wine, is an omnivore's dream. Find the best *menus* in the *brasseries* lining **place de la République.** Pleasant, affordable restaurants settle along Grande Rue or behind pl. de l'Eperon in the *vieille ville.* The **indoor market** sells portable goodies in **Les Halles,** pl. du Marché, while an **outdoor market** occupies pl. des Jacobins. (Open W and Su 7am-12:30pm.) There is a **Monoprix** supermarket at 30 pl. de la République (open M-Sa 9am-8pm) and a mid-sized **Marché Plus** at 68 av. du Gal. Leclerc (open M-Sa 7am-9pm and Su 9am-1pm). The nine appetizers, seven *plats,* and ten desserts of the extremely popular **Auberge des 7 Plats** ❸, 79 Grande Rue, are rearranged into diverse combinations on the €14.50 *à la carte menu.* (☎02 43 24 57 77. *Formules* €11.50 and €14.50. Open Tu-Sa noon-1:30pm and 7-10:30pm. MC/V.) With delicious Italian fare, **Restaurant Etna** ❸, 37 rue des Ponts Neufs, a peaceful haven on a busy street, evokes fantasies of northern Italy in both the food and décor. Try their *tagliatelle* with sausage and gorgonzola cheese. (☎02 43 24 18 28. Pizzas and pastas €7-9. *Menus* €14-38. Open Tu-Sa. MC/V.)

👁 SIGHTS

The combined **billet couple** includes visits to two of the following: Musée de Tessé, Musée Vert, or Musée de la Reine-Bérengère. €5.20, students €2.60.

Le Mans holds a remarkable set of **churches,** including the **Maison-Dieu** founded by Henry Plantagenêt. The tourist office brochure *Les Plantagenêts* provides detailed descriptions.

VIEILLE VILLE. Rising up behind thick Roman walls and the river Sarthe, Le Mans's *vieille ville* is considered one of the most picturesque in France, though. The winding streets and alleys, in which *Cyrano de Bergerac* was filmed, are lined with 15th- to 17th-century houses. The tourist office's English brochure "Le Mans: An Art and History Town," helps identify many houses in the area. **Tours**

depart from the cathedral fountain. *(2hr.; daily 3pm; €5.50, students €3. French only.)*
The petite **Musée de la Reine-Bérengère,** 9 rue Reine-Bérengère, inside an impressive 15th-century residence in the *vieille ville,* displays all manner of art and artifacts from Le Mans's past, as well as an impressive collection of ceramics, an industry which has thrived in Le Mans's Sarthe region since medieval times. Note the carvings of the Virgin Mary and Archangel Gabriel on the "Ave Maria" façade; these date from 1530. *(Open Tu-Su May-Sept. 10am-12:30pm and 2-6:30pm; Oct.-Apr. 2-6pm. €2.80, students and children €1.40.)*

CATHÉDRALE ST-JULIEN. One of France's most famous cathedrals, this massive Romanesque and Gothic structure was originally constructed in the 11th and 12th centuries. The sculpted front of the south porch, is considered one of Europe's finest. After a fire destroyed the town in 1134, the cathedral was repaired using Gothic techniques, visible in the pointed arch reinforcements on either side in the nave. The great chancel with twelve chapels was added in the 13th century, doubling the size of the cathedral and necessitating the tangle of flying buttresses around the exterior. The chapel still displays its original 14th-century paint job, with dark violet walls and a blood-red ceiling. *(Pl. des Jacobins. Open daily 8am-7pm. Tours given by tourist office M 3pm, W 10am, Su 3pm. €3.)*

MURAILLE GALLO-ROMAINE. The stocky 4th-century Roman walls hugging the city's southwestern edge helped make the town a strong base for the protection of the *Civitas* territory in ancient Roman times. Punctuated by arched gates and massive towers, the 1.3km long *muraille* is the longest and perhaps best preserved in all of France. Pink mortar gives the entire structure an earthy orange glow, and different-colored stones craft circular, hourglass, and diamond-shaped designs along the wall.

RACING CIRCUIT & MUSÉE AUTOMOBILE. The 13½km stretch of racetrack south of the city is a must-see for car enthusiasts. Since 1923, the circuit has hosted the annual **24 Heures du Mans,** a grueling test of endurance that attracts crowds each June. During the race, drivers receive special massage treatments to help them stay awake. *(Tickets ☎02 43 40 24 75 or 02 43 40 24 77. €2 to enter and walk around track.)* Just outside the track's main entrance, the massive **Musée Automobile de la Sarthe,** which traces the evolution of motor vehicles used in the race with scores of high-tech and vintage models. The slick Ford GT40 is the only one of its kind. *(From bd. Levasseur off pl. de la République, take bus #6 to Raineries, the end of the line; 25min. Continue on foot down rue de Laigne, following signs to the track and museum; 12min. ☎02 43 72 72 24. Open June-Sept. daily 10am-7pm; Oct.-May daily 10am-6pm; Jan.-Feb. Sa-Su 10am-6pm. €6.10, students and ages 12-18 €4.60.)*

MUSÉE & PARC DE TESSÉ. Housed in the former 19th-century bishop's palace, the museum's fabulous collection celebrates over 600 years of art. The modern interior displays 17th- to 19th-century painting and sculpture, temporary exhibits of modern art, and even an Egyptian collection of artifacts and sarcophagi dating from around 1230 BC. Check out the mummy lying next to its full-body X-ray. The highlight is the Egyptian collection's reproduction of the underground tomb of Nofetari, one of the wifes of pharaoh Ramses II, decorated with hieroglyphics and full of dark recesses.

After a visit to the museum, catch some rays in the beautiful **Parc de Tessé** with a fountain, waterfall, shady trees, and acres of grass. *(2 av. de Paderborn, a 15min. walk from pl. de la République. Take bus #3 (dir: Bellevue) from rue Gastelier by the station or from av. du Général de Gaulle, a block down from pl. de la République, to Musée. Bus #9 (dir: Villaret) also goes there from av. du Général de Gaulle. ☎02 43 47 38 51. Open July-Aug. Tu-Su 10am-12:30pm and 2-6:30pm; Sept.-June Tu-Sa 9am-noon and 2-6pm, Su 10am-noon and 2-6pm. €4, students up to 18 €2, half-price Su.)*

LOIRE VALLEY

🎵 📷 ENTERTAINMENT & FESTIVALS

Le Mans packs most of its nocturnal revelry in the narrow side streets off **place de la République.** The young, funky scene is down **rue du Dr. Leroy,** where bars resonate with techno or rock. A few blocks away, the **rue des Ponts Neuf** has its own share of bars that are decorated with everything from model cars to artistic film projections on their walls. **Paris Texas Café,** 21 rue du Dr. Leroy, is a cavernous pub with saloon-like décor and loud music. (☎ 02 43 23 71 00. Beer €4-6. Open daily 11am-2am.) Caribbean-themed ▣**Le Bakoua,** 5 rue de la Vieille Porte, off pl. de l'Eperon, keeps summer alive year-round with its calypso music and rum-based tropical drinks. The bar's fun setting is kept alive by its "mysterious punch." (☎ 02 43 23 30 70. Open daily 6pm-2am. MC/V.) Several *discothèques* sit right in town, including **Le Select,** 44 pl. de la République, with wild strobe lights and good beats. (☎ 02 43 28 87 41. Open Th-Su 11pm-5am. Cover €10, includes 1 drink.) Gay-friendly **La Limite,** 7 rue St-Honoré, has a mixed crowd of partiers depending on the night and type of music. (☎ 02 43 24 85 54. Cover F €6.50, Sa €10. Open Th-Su 11:30pm-4am.)

Cannes film festival winners are featured nightly at the *vieille ville's* ultra-chic **Ciné-Poche,** 97 Grande Rue. (☎ 02 43 24 73 85. €6.30.) For the entire month of April, the city hosts contemporary jazz artists for the **Le Mans Jazz Festival.** (Info and tickets at 9 rue des Frères Greban; ☎ 02 43 23 78 99.) Over 40 theater companies hit the streets the first weekend of July for **Les Scénomanies,** a festival presenting over 100 different shows on the streets of old Le Mans. The excitement brings out all sorts of street entertainment, including international music, dance, and acrobatics. If you've missed Les Scénomanies, don't sweat it—throughout July and August, **Les Soirs d'Eté** features around 50 free theater, comedy, and music performances in the streets on Fridays. Pick up a *L'Eté au Mans* schedule from the tourist office.

▶ DAYTRIP FROM LE MANS: ALENÇON

Trains run from the station on rue Denis Papin to **Le Mans** (30min., 5 per day, €9.20) **Bus** TIS (☎ 02 43 39 97 30) travels to the Le Mans bus station (1½hr., 2 per day, €7.70). For *taxis,* call Radio Taxis (☎ 02 33 28 05 06). The most convenient **car rental** agency is Europcar, 3 rue Demées, one block from the station down av. Wilson and the first street to the left. (☎ 02 33 28 91 11. Open M, F 8:30am-noon and 2-6:30pm; T, W, Th 8am-noon and 2-6pm; Sa 9am-1pm. AmEx/DC/MC/V.)

A small town on the southern border of Normandy, Alençon (pop. 30,000) has humble Gallo-Roman roots but gained international renown in the 1650s for its lacemaking industry, which employed close to 8000 residents during its peak years. The enduring influence of the industry is present today in every window and shop along Alençon's wide avenues, and fine examples of lace craftsmanship are displayed in two museums. A frequent stop-over for those traveling in northwest France, this town's history and love of art make it a wonderful city to explore.

The ▣**Musée de la Dentelle,** 33 rue du Pont Neuf, about the history of Alençon lace, introduces visitors to the development of the unique Alençon point technique of the 1650s, which derived from the intricate needlework of Italian lacemakers. The museum houses samples of lace from both Alençon and other areas and shows a 10min. documentary in French, English, and German. An enthusiastic curator provides magnifying glasses with which to inspect the intricate detail of the lacework, some of which took hundreds of laborers years to complete. Samples of contemporary Alençon lace are available for around €550. (☎ 02 33 26 27 26. Open M-Sa 10am-noon and 2-6pm. €3.10, under 18 €1.80.)

Alençon's gorgeous architecture includes the beautiful 16th-century Eglise Notre-Dame, the towering Château des Ducs, and the elegant 15th-century homes with wrought-iron balconies that pepper the *centre ville*. The town has a great many *places*, tangling intersections, and curving streets, making a stop at the tourist office for a detailed map worthwhile. The massive stone walls of the **Eglise Notre-Dame** dominate the surrounding buildings. Vibrant stained-glass windows, flamboyant carvings on its high vaults, and an intricate, symmetrical Gothic façade ensure that visitors' eyes do not wander from this imposing structure. It contains the chapel where Ste-Thérèse, a native of Alençon, was baptized. *(Pl. de la Magdeleine. Open 9:30am-noon and 2-5:30pm. Free.)*

The **Musée des Beaux-Arts et de la Dentelle**, 12 rue Charles Aveline, housed in an old Jesuit mission, contains a strong collection of 17th- and 18th-century European paintings, an extensive variety of traveling exhibits, and a fascinating display of Cambodian religious, social, and artistic objects that document the country's former standing as a French colony. The museum has also accumulated a large collection of lace from Alençon and around the world. Visitors can drool over the *haute couture* wedding dresses fashioned from contemporary lace. The **National Alençon Point Workshop** puts on lacemaking demonstrations for visitors on Tuesday and Friday afternoons. *(☎02 33 32 40 07. Open July-Aug. daily 10am-noon and 2-6pm; Sept.-June Tu-Sa only. €2.90; students €2.40 or free W.)*

Other great sights include the **birthplace of Saint Theresa**, 50 rue St-Blaise, lovingly preserved in a neoclassical chapel since she was made a saint in 1925. *(Open June-Sept. daily 9am-noon and 2-6pm; Oct.-Dec. and Feb.-May Su-M and W-Sa 9:30am-noon and 2:30-5pm. Free.)* The **Château des Ducs** and the **Palais de Justice**, create an impressive show of grand architecture in pl. Foch. The two 14th-century towers have undergone multiple restorations and were used as a Nazi prison during World War II.

To reach the **tourist office** in pl. de la Magdeleine, cross the parking lot and walk down av. Wilson until the intersection; cross the street and continue down rue St-Blaise, which leads to the tourist office on the left. Housed in the 15th-century Maison d'Onz, the office provides free **accommodations booking** and a **walking guide** of the city, though the staff is much more informative than the pamphlet. A small gallery next door to the main office contains exhibits on the history and architecture of Alençon. *(☎02 33 80 66 33. Open July-Aug. M-Sa 9:30am-7pm, Su 10am-12:30pm and 3-5:30pm; Sept.-June M-Sa 9:30am-noon and 2-6:30pm. City tours of Alençon and the Musée des Beaux-Arts June-Sept.; €4.)*

CHAMPAGNE

Brothers, brothers, come quickly! I am drinking stars!
—Dom Pérignon

According to European law, the word *champagne* may only be applied to wines made from grapes from this region and produced according to a rigorous, time-honored method which involves the blending of three varieties of grapes, two stages of fermentation, and frequent realignment of the bottles by *remueurs* (highly trained bottle-turners) to facilitate removal of sediment. So fiercely guarded is their name that when Yves Saint-Laurent brought out a new perfume called "Champagne," the powerful *maisons* sued to force him to change it—and won. Though Dom Pérignon had to convince his compatriots to try the sweet nectar, few modern-day visitors need further convincing to come quickly to Champagne in order to see (and taste) the *méthode champénoise* at the region's numerous *caves* (wine cellars)—at their best in the glitzy towns of ◼Reims (p. 318) and ◼Epernay (p. 325).

Small as it is, Champagne is strikingly diverse. The golden vineyards and *beaux arts* flavor of the north seem a world away from the quiet citadels and forests of the south. The grape-fed high life may buoy the whole region economically, but smaller towns both near and far from the vines have quite distinct characters. Come to Champagne for the giddy luxury of its namesake *boisson* and the surprisingly boisterous *joie de vivre* of its signature towns, but don't miss out on the region's rich history: the inspiring grandeur of the Reims Cathedral, where French royalty was coronated, the Roman ramparts in sky-high **Langres** (p. 334), and the half-timbered houses and crooked streets of beautifully preserved **Troyes** (p. 329).

Even regional specialties tend to center around a champagne base; try *volaille au champagne* (poultry in a champagne-based sauce) or *civet d'oie* (goose stew).

REIMS

Imagine a sparkling, lively, beautifully laid out city with plenty of diversions for old and young alike. Then add a snazzy, center-of-the-action back story. *Then* add a few million gallons of champagne and you're getting somewhere near Reims (pop. 185,000; pronounced "rrrrahnce") circa 2004. In its pre-modern, pre-photo op medieval days, the city's famous cathedral witnessed some of France's most pivotal moments, from Clovis's baptism in AD 496 to the 1429 crowning of Charles VII, brought to Reims by Joan of Arc. The city also won the dubious honor of witnessing Napoleon's last victory, the so-called "last smile of Fortune." Fortune frowned on another would-be conqueror on May 7, 1945, when the German army surrendered in Reims's little red schoolhouse. Reims has since built over its war scars to return to its 19th-century glory. Bar-packed plazas and tree-lined avenues suit the comfortable lives and *joie de vivre* of the locals, while a thriving artistic scene supports theater, dance, opera, and all those goodies further left of center.

▐ TRANSPORTATION

Trains: bd. Joffre (☎03 26 88 11 65). Info office open M-F 9am-7pm, Sa 9:30am-6pm. To: **Epernay** (20min., 11 per day, €5.20); **Laon** (1hr., 7 per day, €7.70); **Paris** (1½hr., 11 per day, €20.30). SNCF boutique with information and reservations at pl. Myron T. Herrick. (Open M-Sa 10am-7pm.)

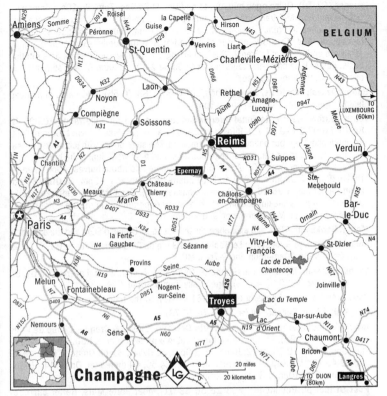

Champagne

Public Transportation: Transport Urbains de Reims (TUR) buses stop in front of the train station. Info office at 6 rue Chanzy (☎03 26 88 25 38). Open M-F 7am-8pm, Sa 7am-7pm. €0.80 per ticket, *carnet* of 10 €6.10, day pass €2.20; buy from driver. All bus lines run 6:35am-9:45pm; 5 lines run until midnight. Regional **buses** leave from the bus station to Troyes and Châlons-en-Champagne. Schedules at the tourist office.

Taxis: ☎03 26 47 05 05 or 03 26 02 15 02. Both 24hr.

Car Rental: Avis, cour de la Gare (☎03 26 47 10 08). Open M-F 8am-noon and 2-7pm, Sa 8am-noon and 2-6pm. **Hertz,** cour de la Gare (☎03 26 77 87 77). Budget, 47 av. Nationale (☎03 26 77 66 66). **Europcar,** 76 bd. Lundy (☎03 26 88 38 38). All accept MC/V, Avis accepts AmEx.

Bike Rental: Centre International de Séjour, chaussée Bocquaine (☎03 26 40 52 60). Half-day €10, full day €15, weekend €25. €77 or passport deposit. MC/V.

■ ⚡ ORIENTATION & PRACTICAL INFORMATION

Tourist Office: 2 rue Guillaume de Machault (☎03 26 77 45 00; www.tourisme.fr/reims), in a pint-sized ruin beside the cathedral. Free map with sights and *caves*, loads of free brochures (in French, English, Spanish, and German), and free same-night **accommodations service** (with deposit). **Currency exchange** on Su. Ask for the student guide *Le Monocle* (only in French). **Tours** of the town with audio guides in 6 languages (€7.70). Office open mid-Apr. to mid-Oct. M-Sa 9am-7pm, Su 10am-6pm; mid-Oct. to mid-Apr. M-F 9am-noon and 2pm-6pm, Sa 9am-6pm, Su 11am-5pm. **Walking tours** of Reims in French July-Aug. Tu and Sa 2:30pm. **Tour of Basilique St-Rémi** in French July-Aug. Th 2:30pm. **Tour of cathedral** July-Aug. daily, except Su morning; 10:30am and 4:30pm in French; 2:30pm in English, Spanish, or German, on a rotating basis. Easter-June cathedral tours in French Sa-Su 2:30pm. Tours €5.40, students and over 60 €3.10, under 12 free.

Budget Travel: Wasteels, 26 rue Libergier (☎08 25 88 70 55). ISIC cards and cheap flights. Open M-Sa 9am-noon and 2-6pm.

Youth Centers: Centre Régional Information Jeunesse, 41 rue Talleyrand (☎03 26 79 84 79; fax 03 26 79 84 72). Info on jobs and local events. Free **Internet;** 30min. limit; no email checking, but policy is loosely enforced. Message board with job offers for seasonal work, including camp counselor positions and field work during the harvest. Contact ANPE Saisonnière (☎03 26 77 62 98) for more info about harvest work. Open M-Th 10:30am-12:30pm and 2-6pm, F 10:30am-12:30pm and 2-5pm. **CROUS,** 34 bd. Henri Vanier (☎03 26 50 59 00; www.crous.reims.fr). Comprehensive info and assistance for students seeking lodging, work, or study opportunities in the area. Hours vary, but generally open M-F 10am-noon and 2-6pm.

Money: Banks with **ATMs** and **exchange** cluster around pl. Drouet d'Erlon and the cathedral.

English Language Bookstore: Le Bookshop, 23 rue du Clou dans le Fer (☎03 26 84 99 80). Open M-Sa 10am-noon and 2-7pm. MC/V.

Laundry: Lavomatique, 49 rue Gambetta. Open daily 7am-9:30pm. **Laverie Chanzy,** 50 rue Chanzy (☎06 20 62 43 64). Open daily 7am-9:30pm.

Police: 40 bd. Louis Roederer (☎03 26 61 44 00), by the train station.

Hospital: 47 rue Cognac Jay (☎03 26 78 78 78).

Internet: Free **Internet** at **CRIJ** (see **Youth Centers**). **Clique & Croque,** 27 rue de Vesle (☎03 26 86 93 92), set back from the street in a plaza. 1st hr. €4.30, €3.80 thereafter. Open M-Sa 10:30am-12:30am, Su 2-9pm. **Ze Cyber,** 31 pl. Drouet d'Erlon (☎03 26 02 45 13), is overpriced but central. 1st hr. €4.50, €4 thereafter. Open M-Th 10am-12:30am, F-Sa 10am-1:30am, Su 2-8pm.

Post Office: pl. Boulingrin (☎03 26 50 58 01), near Porte Mars. Better **currency exchange** rates than the banks. Open M-F 8am-7pm, Sa 8am-noon. Central **branch office,** 2 rue Cérès (☎03 26 77 64 80), on pl. Royale. Open M-F 8:30am-6pm, Sa 8:30am-noon. Also at 8-10 pl. Drouet d'Erlon (☎03 26 09 60 67). Open M noon-7pm, Tu-F 10am-7pm, Sa 10am-5pm. Another branch at 9 pl. Stalingrad (☎03 26 86 69 30), close to the hostel. Open M-F 9am-noon and 2:15-6pm, Su 8:30am-noon. **Poste Restante:** 51084 Reims-Cérès. **Postal code:** 51100.

🏠 ACCOMMODATIONS

Semi-inexpensive hotels cluster west of pl. Drouet d'Erlon, in the region above the cathedral, and near the *mairie*. Reims is a popular destination; call ahead.

🏨 **Centre International de Séjour/Auberge de Jeunesse (HI),** chaussée Bocquaine (☎03 26 40 52 60; fax 03 26 47 35 70), next to La Comédie-Espace André Malraux. Top-notch hostel living, newly revamped and accordingly spiffy. Recall with nostalgia the classic hostel days of ratty housing and squalid communal living, then thank your lucky stars this modern spot is nothing like it. Bright, clean, comfortable new rooms. Friendly staff houses a mix of backpackers and noisy school groups. Breakfast included. Meals €5.50-10.50. Kitchen. Laundry. Reception 24hr. 4- to 5-bed rooms with hall shower €10 per person. Singles €15, with shower €26; doubles €22/€30; triples with shower €36. **Non-members** €2 one-time fee. AmEx/MC/V. ●

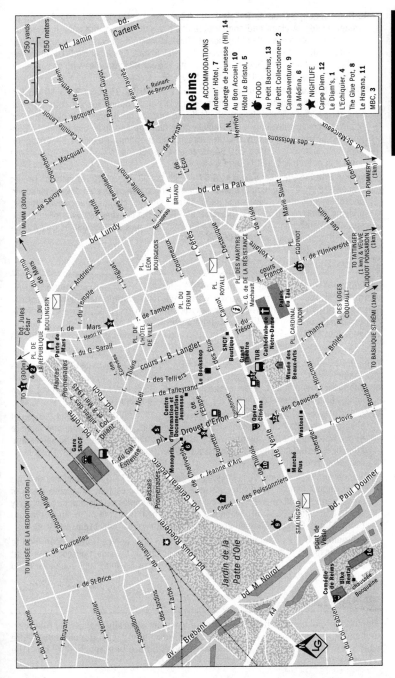

Reims

▲ ACCOMMODATIONS
Ardenn' Hôtel, 7
Auberge de Jeunesse (HI), 14
Au Bon Accueil, 10
Hôtel Le Bristol, 5

● FOOD
Au Petit Bacchus, 13
Au Petit Collectionneur, 2
Canadaventure, 9
La Médina, 6

★ NIGHTLIFE
Carpe Diem, 12
Le Diam's, 1
L'Echiquier, 4
The Glue Pot, 8
Le Havana, 11
MBC, 3

Au Bon Accueil, 31 rue de Thillois (☎03 26 88 55 74; fax 03 26 05 12 38), off pl. Drouet d'Erlon. A clean and comfortable choice, with some of the most inexplicably inexpensive rooms this side of the hostel. Unspectacular, but across the board on a par with hotels at least €10 more expensive. Call well ahead. Breakfast €4.50. Hall shower €1.50. Reception 24hr. Singles €18-21, with shower €27; doubles with shower €30-39. Extra person €7.50, extra bed €15. MC/V. ❷

Hôtel Le Bristol, 76 pl. Drouet d'Erlon (☎03 26 40 52 25; fax 03 26 40 05 08; www.bristol-reims.com). This is most definitely not an option for the currency-challenged traveler. From the elegant, chandeliered lobby to the impressively high-ceilinged rooms decorated with Louis XI- to Louis XV-style furniture and shiny bathrooms, Le Bristol offers comfort and beauty and far outshines other options. Breakfast €7. Reception daily 7am-midnight. Singles €50-54; doubles €55-78; triples €64-74. All rooms with shower or bath, toilet, and TV. AmEx/MC/V. ❺

Ardenn' Hôtel, 6 rue Caqué (☎03 26 47 42 38; fax 03 26 09 48 56), near pl. Drouet d'Erlon and the train station. A step up from super-economical, a step down from super-decadent—for the indecisive splurger. Fourteen romantic, chandeliered, velvety rooms, priced accordingly. All rooms with shower and TV, all but the cheapest with toilet. Breakfast €5.50. Reception M-Sa 24hr., Su after 6pm. Singles €31-41; doubles €47-49; triples and quads €59. Extra bed €6. MC/V. ❸

🞔 FOOD

The heart of Reims's street life, **pl. Drouet d'Erlon** is also its stomach; bakeries and sandwich shops compete for space with cheap cafés and classier restaurants. Kebab stands line rue de Vesle. A **Monoprix** supermarket is at 21 rue Chativesle. (Open M-Sa 9am-8pm. MC/V.) A smaller **Marché Plus** is at 33 rue de Vesle. (Open M-Sa 9am-9pm, Su 9am-1pm. MC/V.) The main **open-air market** is on pl. du Boulingrin near Porte Mars. (Open W and Sa 7am-2pm.)

🞔 **Au Petit Collectionneur,** 123 av. de Laon (☎03 26 83 99 74). A taste of Brittany in this Champagne hotspot. *Galettes* and crêpes (€3-9.50) are seriously stacked with marvelous tasties; salads and meals available as well. Don't leave without downing a few mugs of *cidre bretonne* (from €2.50). Open Tu-Sa noon-2pm and 7-10pm. MC/V. ❶

🞔 **Au Petit Bacchus,** 11 rue de l'Université (☎03 26 47 10 05). Named after the god of champagne and all things scandalous, this beautifully appointed restaurant offers a mouth-watering array of sumptuous meals for the gourmet palette. Exotic spices and attractive presentation make these *plats* hard to resist. *Menus* from €18. Open M-Sa noon-2pm and 7-10pm. MC/V. ❹

Canadaventure, 24bis rue de la Magdaleine (☎03 26 77 97 86). No laughing, eh? This bit of North American woodlands boasts a tasty and impressively exhaustive menu of salmon and, yes, bison specialties. The two-course *formules de saumon* come in every shape and variety (€14.30), while the Canadian beer is a little more straightforward (from €4.30). Open Su-Th noon-2pm and 7:30-10pm, F-Sa until 11pm. MC/V. ❸

La Médina, 13 rue de Chativesle (☎03 26 88 43 34). Serves North African food to Moroccan music, with a pleasant candlelit atmosphere on the side. Couscous with meat €12-17.50, *menus* from €12.50. Open July-Aug. Tu-Sa 7-10pm; Sept.-June also Tu-Su noon-2pm. MC/V after €15.30. ❸

🞔 SIGHTS

The most popular sights near the center of town are all easily reached by foot. Farther out, the champagne *caves*—the biggest draw along with the cathedral—are past a few deserted, run-down neighborhoods and are best reached by bus (the tourist office has details on which bus lines for which *maisons*). Many champagne firms give tours (all available in English); consult the tourist office for more info. It may not be cheaper to buy champagne directly from the firms; ask the advice of wine shops near the cathedral, where there are often sales on local brands, and check the prices at the Monoprix (see **Food**). Good bottles start at €9.50, half the price for champagne outside of France.

■ **CHAMPAGNE CAVES.** Excluding a trip to Epernay (p. 325), this is the best opportunity you'll ever have to fairly swim in bubbly decadence. Four hundred kilometers of *crayères* (Roman chalk quarries) and two hundred kilometers of more modern French-built *caves* shelter the bottled treasures. The cellars are generally kept at 10°C, so a sweater is never a bad idea. The most elegant and impressive tour is at the massive **Champagne Pommery.** Mme. Pommery took over her husband's business and became one of France's foremost vintners; her wealth allowed her to bring art into the workplace, lining the *cave* with exquisite carvings by Gustave Navlet. The firm owns the largest *tonneau* (vat) in the world, carved by Emile Galle and sent to the 1904 World's Fair in St. Louis as a 75,000L gesture of goodwill. *(5 pl. du Général Gouraud. ☎03 26 61 62 56. Tours by reservation only, in French and English. €7, students €3.50, children free.)* **Veuve Clicquot Ponsardin** is slightly less elegant, but with a free tour and tasting, who can complain? Tours pass by a small sample vineyard, wind through cellars made from ancient chalk mines (each named for a past employee of the *maison*), and offer a tasting. *(1 pl. des Droits de L'Homme. ☎03 26 89 53 90. Tours M-Sa 10am-6pm, Nov.-Mar. closed Sa; by reservation only. In English and French. Free.)* The *caves* are the star of **Taittinger's** tour; see the underground remains of the otherwise destroyed Abbaye St-Nicaise while getting some of the most detailed explanations around of the champagne-making process. See the largest champagne bottle in the world and watch the *dégorgement* (on certain days), the term for the sediment removal process. *(9 pl. St-Nicaise. ☎03 26 85 45 35. No reservation necessary. Open Mar.-Nov. M-F 9:30am-1pm and 2-5:30pm, Sa-Su 9am-noon and 2-6pm; last tour 1hr. before closing; Dec.-Feb. closed on weekends. Tours in English and French every 20min. Tours include a winding 100-step staircase and are conducted entirely on foot. €6. AmEx/MC/V.)*

■ **PALAIS DU TAU.** Connected to the cathedral (see below), this former archbishop's residence got its name from its original floor plan, which resembled a "T". Don't miss its dazzling collection, including reliquaries that date back to Charlemagne; the show-stoppers are the sumptuous 50 ft. robes of Charles X and massive statues rescued from crumbling portions of the old cathedral face. *(2 pl. du Cardinal Luçon. ☎03 26 47 81 79. Open May-Aug. Tu-Su 9:30am-6:30pm; Sept.-Apr. Tu-Su 9:30am-12:30pm and 2-5:30pm. €6.10, ages 18-25 €4.10, under 18 free. Tours in English and French €7.50, ages 18-25 €5, under 18 free.)*

CATHÉDRALE DE NOTRE-DAME. The three churches that have stood on this spot held the coronations of Clovis and 25 other French sovereigns. More recently, the current building witnessed the reconciliation between President de Gaulle and German Chancellor Adenauer in 1962. The present cathedral is made of blocks of golden limestone quarried from the *caves*. While WWI bombing destroyed most of the original stained glass, one of the most spectacular elements of the modern building is a sea-blue set of replacement windows by Marc Chagall. Outside, statues of local martyrs decorate the left porch, including the famous smiling angel of Reims. *(☎03 26 77 45 25. Open daily 7:30am-7:30pm. Tours in French and English. Schedule for 2004 not yet set; call ahead or consult tourist office. Tourist office also gives tours. €6, ages 12-25 and seniors €3.50.)*

MUSÉE DE LA REDDITION. Germany signed its surrender to the Allies on May 7, 1945, in a schoolroom across the railroad tracks. That schoolhouse is now the small but fascinating Musée de la Reddition. A short film (in French and English) and several galleries of photos and time lines lead to the preserved, glassed-off room, which contains the thirteen chairs in which the British, French, American, Soviet, and German heads of state sat. Nothing here is sleek or showy, but as a potent historical time capsule, the place itself is powerful. *(12 rue Franklin Roosevelt.* ☎ *03 26 47 84 19. Open Su-M and W-Sa 10am-noon and 2-6pm, Tu 2-6pm. €1.60, children and students free.)*

OTHER SIGHTS. Near the Taittinger *caves,* the **Basilique St-Rémi** rises from a bed of lavender at the other end of town from the cathedral. This Romanesque church with Gothic tinges was built around the tomb of St-Rémi, the bishop who baptized Clovis. *(Pl. St-Rémi. Open daily 9am-7pm. Son-et-lumière July-Aug. Sa 9:30pm.)* Next door, the **Abbaye St-Rémi** shelters an extensive collection of religious art, military uniforms, and artifacts from the Merovingian and Carolingian eras. Look for the Enamels of St-Timothy, a series of engraved tiles depicting life under oppressive Roman rule. *(53 rue Simon.* ☎ *03 26 85 23 36. Open M-F 2-6:30pm, Sa-Su 2-7pm. €1.60, free first Su of every month.)* The largest arch in the Roman empire still rises over the modern pl. de la République. The **Porte Mars** is decorated with reliefs of Romulus and Remus, who gave the city its name.

🎵 🔦 ENTERTAINMENT & FESTIVALS

At night, people concentrate in the cafés and bars of **pl. Drouet d'Erlon.** ◪**The Glue Pot,** 49 pl. d'Erlon, is a popular English-style pub with food at all hours and a big-screen TV featuring all sports, all the time. (☎ 03 26 47 36 46. Beer from €2.70. Open daily 10am-3am. MC/V above €12.) Hidden off rue de Vesle, tropical-style **Le Havana,** 27 rue de Vesle, is the most diverse watering hole in town; live Afro-Cuban music fills the bar every other Friday. (Happy hour daily 6-7pm with 2 beers for €2.50, 2 glasses of champagne for €6, or 2 cups of punch for €2. Open M-Sa noon-midnight. MC/V.) **Carpe Diem,** 6 rue des Capucins, is a mellow gay-friendly bar with three small rooms. (☎ 03 26 02 00 41. Beer €2.50-3.30. Cocktails €3.90-4.60. Open Th 9pm-midnight, F-Sa 9pm-1:30am, Su 4-11pm. MC/V.) The bar-club **MBC,** 12 rue de Mars, is another popular choice with its Indian décor and "kitschy Frenchy" music. (☎ 03 26 09 75 69. Cocktails €4-7. Open Su-Th 4pm-12:30am, F-Sa 4pm-1:30am. MC/V.). The enormous club **L'Echiquier,** 10 av. Jean Jaurès, is just outside the pedestrian district—walk in a group. Three tiers of top-40, techno, and rock make for a flashy, pheromone-filled evening with a generally young crowd. (☎ 03 26 89 12 38. Cover €9 for men, €6 for women, includes one drink. Open Th-Sa 10pm-5am. MC/V.) ◪**Le Diam's,** 15 rue Lesange, is a gay-friendly dance club. Immediately popular upon opening in 2002, it draws an attractive bunch. (☎ 03 26 88 33 83. Cover F-Sa after 1am €12 with 1 drink, free with *Let's Go* guide. Open Th-Su 11pm-4am, F-Sa 11pm-5am. MC/V.)

Like any self-respecting champagne-drenched municipality, Reims offers up a host of cultural activities for the cosmopolitan set. Follow the *trottoir* of playwrights to the **Comédie de Reims,** a regional acting school and theater that stages a host of performances and workshops. (3 chaussée Bocquaine. ☎ 03 26 48 49 00. Open Sept.-June M-F noon-7pm, Sa 1-7pm. Tickets to featured productions €8-15, students €5-8. Prices for other events vary.) **Opéra Cinéma,** 3 rue Théodore Dubois, shows a range of films, some undubbed. (☎ 03 26 47 29 36. Tickets €5.50-7.20. Student discounts with ID. Ticket office open daily 1:30-10pm.) The **Grand Théâtre de Reims,** rue de Vesle, hosts operas and ballets. February will welcome the Peking National Ballet, while *Giselle* floats in at the beginning of May. (☎ 03 26 50 03 92. Box office at 13 rue Chanzy. Open Oct.-June Tu-Sa 2:30-6:30pm. Tickets €7-42, student discounts.) In July and August, less traditional **Le Manège de Reims,** 2 bd. du Général Leclerc, presents dance shows, performance art, and music on its stage, with *les dimanches des curiosités* (Sundays of curiosities) providing special themed performances most Sundays. (☎03 26 47 30 40. Open year-round. Box office open W-Sa 1-7pm. Tickets €5-18.) During the summer, Reims hosts the fantastic ⬛**Flâneries Musicales d'Eté,** with more than 100 free concerts in 60 days. World-famous musicians share the bill with smaller acts, and many of the performances are free. (Late June to early Aug. Call ☎03 26 77 45 00 or stop by the tourist office for more information.) In the fall, **Octob'Rock** brings rock, rap, and reggae sounds to venues all over the city (☎03 26 84 86 37; many performances free.). The **Reims Jazz Festival** (info ☎03 26 47 00 10) lasts through much of November and brings music to the beautifully manicured lawns of the Pommery champagne firm.

EPERNAY

Epernay (pop. 30,000) is every rugged backpacker's secret dream town. Undeniably ritzy and sparklingly seductive, this mascot for Champagne's wealthiest grape-growing regions plays landlord to the world's most distinguished champagne producers. The *maisons* of Moët & Chandon, Perrier-Jouet, and Mercier inhabit the palatial mansions along av. de Champagne and keep their 700 million bottles of the treasured elixir in the 100km of tunnels underneath. Tour a cave, raise a glass, and taste the stars. At the heart of the *Route Touristique du Champagne,* Epernay is also an excellent base for exploring the countryside, including **the Champagne route,** a set of hikes through vineyards, châteaux, and mountains.

▐ TRANSPORTATION

Epernay loses no time introducing you to its main attraction; entering by train from the east, the colorful tiled roofs and blue enameled signs of the de Castellane *maison de champagne* dominate av. de Champagne. The train station is two blocks from the central pl. de la République. **Trains** leave cours de la Gare. (Ticket office open daily 6am-8pm. Info office ☎08 92 35 35 35. Open M 9am-7pm, Tu-F 9:15am-6pm, Sa 8:30am-6pm.) To: Paris (1¼hr., 18 per day, €17.50); Reims (25min., 16 per day, €5.20); Strasbourg (4½hr., 3 per day, €36). **STDM buses** (☎03 26 65 17 07) serve Paris, Reims, and small towns in Champagne. **Local buses** are run by Sparnabus, 30 pl. des Arcades. (☎03 26 55 55 50. Tickets €1, *carnet* of 10 €7.30. Open M 2-6pm, Tu-F 9am-noon and 2-6pm, Sa 9am-noon.) Rent **bikes** at Remi Royer, 10 pl. Hugues Plomb. (☎03 26 55 29 61. €11 per half-day, €17 per day, €77 per week. Open Tu-Sa 9am-noon and 2-7pm. MC/V.)

▐ ORIENTATION & PRACTICAL INFORMATION

To get to the **tourist office,** 7 av. de Champagne, from the station, walk straight ahead through pl. Mendès France, pass a fountain, walk one block up rue Gambetta or rue J. Moët to **pl. de la République,** and turn left onto av. de Champagne. (5min.) The welcoming, English-speaking staff provides free maps, a list of hotels, info on Epernay's *caves,* and suggestions for *routes champenoises,* all available in English. They also publish a free monthly list of local events and festivities, in French. (☎03 26 53 33 00; www.epernay.net. Open Easter to mid-Oct. M-Sa 9:30am-12:30pm and 1:30-7pm, Su 11am-4pm; mid-Oct. to Easter M-Sa 9:30am-12:30pm and 1:30-5:30pm. Train tours 50min.; Tu-Su 7 per day; €4.60, under 16 €2.80. Available in English, French, and German.) **Banks** with **ATM** and **currency exchange** cluster on pl. de la République and pl. Hugues Plomb, including a **Banque de France** on pl. de la République. (Open M-F 8:45am-noon and 1:45-4pm; no bills larger than US$50.) Other services include a **laundromat,** 8 av. Jean Jaurès (☎03 26 54 96 15; open daily 7am-8pm); **police,** 7 rue Jean Chandon-Moët (☎03 26 56 96 60, call here for the **phar-**

ON THE MENU

IT HAD TO BE *BRUT*

While traveling in the birthplace of bubbly, it's easy to be mesmerized by the rivers of delicate amber liquid that course through restaurants and taverns. A visit to any vast wine cellar, where hundreds of thousands of bottles of sparkling white wine are left to age to perfection, is enough to dazzle with the promise of high class refreshment from the likes of Veuve Clicquot, Taittinger, Moët et Chandon, and more. When it comes time to order that first sip of authentic champagne, though, the dizzying array of options and guidelines intimidate all but the most seasoned connoisseur. The following crib sheet will enable any first-time visitor to join the elite drinkers with confidence:

1. What goes with what, now? Before getting a look at the good stuff, choose the appropriate type of champagne for the occasion. *Brut* is an apéritif, vintage *brut* goes with meat and mild cheese. For fish or shellfish, chardonnay is the way to go, while dessert calls for *rosé or demi-sec*. Each variety has a specific culinarily complimentary taste and texture.

2. Only the best. Look at the label. *Tête de Cuvée* comes from the finest juices. Most Champagne houses produce a special bottle in a vintage year, using hand-selected grapes from the highest-quality vineyards. These are normally deemed to be "Pres-

(Continued on next page)

macie de garde); and a **hospital,** 137 rue de l'Hôpital (☎03 26 58 70 70). Access the **Internet** at Cyberm@nia, 11 pl. des Arcades (€2 per hr.; open Tu-Sa 1-10pm, Su-M 2-10pm), l'Icone Café, 25 rue de l'Hôpital Auban Moët (☎03 26 55 73 93. €4.60 per hr.; open M noon-11pm, Tu-Th 11am-11pm, F-Sa 11am-1am, Su 3-11pm; MC/V), or Le Babylone, 25 rue Gambetta. (☎03 26 55 96 44. €4 per hr., pay by the min. Open Tu-Sa noon-8pm). The **post office,** pl. Hugues Plomb, has **currency exchange.** (☎03 26 53 31 60. Open M-F 8am-7pm, Sa 8am-noon.) **Postal code:** 51200.

ACCOMMODATIONS

Epernay caters to the champagne set, so budget hotels are rare. ▨**Hôtel St-Pierre ❷,** 14 av. Paul-Chandon, past the covered market and pl. d'Europe, is the best budget bet. Homey floral wallpaper and three floors of spacious, antique-furnished rooms. (☎03 26 54 40 80; fax 03 26 57 88 68. Breakfast €5. Hall toilets for some rooms. Reception daily 7am-10pm. Singles and doubles €21, with shower €25-32. Extra bed €5. MC/V.) A stone's throw from the station, on the popular pl. Mendès France, **Hôtel de la Cloche ❸** is a pricier, more convenient option. Clean, comfortable rooms all come with shower (or bath), toilet, and TV. (☎03 26 55 15 15; hotel-de-la-cloche.c.prin@wanadoo.fr. Breakfast €6. Reception daily 7am-10pm. Singles and doubles €38-43. MC/V.) For a truly budget option, check in advance to see if the **Foyer des Jeunes Travailleurs ❶,** 2 rue Pupin, is still around. Its future is uncertain after December of 2003 (after this guide went to print), but as long as it remains in Epernay, it provides cheap, clean, decent 4-bed rooms with desks and sinks, laundry facilities, a kitchen, and a cafeteria. From the station, cross the grassy square, turn left onto rue de Reims, and make a quick right onto rue Pupin. Only five rooms are available to travelers; reserve ahead. (☎03 26 51 62 51; fax 03 26 54 15 60. Cafeteria open M-F lunch and dinner, Sa lunch only. Breakfast €2.50. Meals €8-10.50. Reception M-F 9am-8pm, Sa 10am-2pm. Bunks €12. MC/V.) There is a **campground ❶** about 2km from the station (dir: Reims) at allée de Cumières, on the banks of the Marne. (☎03 26 55 32 14. Open mid-Apr. to early Sept. Reception daily June-Sept. 7am-10pm; Apr.-May 8am-1pm and 3-8pm. €3 per person, €1.90 per child, €3.50 per tent and car. Electricity €3.30.)

FOOD

For the most delicious ending to a perfect day of *dégustations* and decadence, head to ▨**Au Bacchus Gourmet ❹,** 21 rue Gambetta (see **The Big Splurge,** p.

328). Otherwise, the pedestrian district around **place des Arcades** and **place Hugues Plomb** is dotted with delis and bakeries. There are Italian, Moroccan, Asian, and Turkish eateries on **rue Gambetta** and a **Marché Plus** at 13 pl. Hugues Plomb. (☎03 26 51 89 89. Open M-Sa 7am-9pm, Su 9am-1pm. MC/V above €7.) Halle St-Thibault hosts a **market.** (Open W-Sa 8am-noon.) The hearty, *brasserie*-style meals are quite tasty at **Le Central ❶**, 11 pl. de la République, a convivial local eatery that also serves crêpes (€3-5.80), *galettes* (€5.10-9), and filling sandwiches for €6-9. (☎03 26 59 19 93. Open daily 11:30am-2pm and 7-11pm. 4-course *menu* €10. MC/V.) For meals with a bubbly twist, **La Cave à Champagne ❸**, 16 rue Gambetta, has composed a menu that incorporates the local product into a wide array of dishes. From *foie gras à la champagne* to oysters in Champagne sauce, every meal is a bubbly delight. (☎03 26 55 50 70. 3-course *menu* €13.50, other *menus* up to €26. Open M-Tu and Th-Su noon-2pm and 7:30-10pm, July-Aug. closed W, Sept.-June closed W night. MC/V.)

When purchasing a souvenir bottle of bubbly, don't assume that prices at the *maisons* themselves will be the best option. Check the local wine shops and discover those very same bottles of *Mercier* that were featured in a *dégustation* for a few euros less than at the manufacturer. The Marché Plus supermarket has a fine selection of champagnes, all priced very low. Of course, the only place to buy a 15L "Nebuchodonosor"-size bottle of *Moët & Chandon* remains the manufacturer's boutique (only €672).

⚡ MAISONS DE CHAMPAGNE

The name says it all: ▓**avenue de Champagne** is a long, broad strip of palatial *maisons de champagne* pouring out bubbly to hordes of visitors. The tours below are all offered in French or English; no reservations are required. All include a *petite dégustation* (ages 16 and up only), and all offer more extensive (and expensive) tastings as well. Take note: without springing for a tour, the only thing visitors get to see at the *maisons* is a liquor-lined boutique. *Caves* are usually around 10°C; bring a sweater. Each firm's tour may give more or less the same explanation of the process, but everything from the dress of the guides to the design of the lobby reflects the status and character of the producer.

For a laid-back and cheap but authentic alternative to the big *maisons*, ask the tourist office about *l'esprit de champagne*, a free presentation and sampling given by several smaller companies in the tourist office. (June to late Oct. F-Sa; July-Aug. Th. 10:30am-noon and 3-6pm. Obtain tickets in advance.)

(Continued from previous page)

tige or Deluxe *Cuvées.*" *Grand Cru* comes from only the highest quality grapes. *Premier Cru* is a step below that, while *Cru* is from the very bottom of the barrel. *Millésime* is a vintage bottle (much less common).

3. Avoid distraction. Eating strongly flavored foods, wearing perfume, and smoking all detract from the experience of champagne tasting. Find another time to sample that plate of local blue cheeses.

4. Before you drink. Raise the glass to the light and examine the contents. When it has been recently poured, the champagne should produce a string of bubbles shooting straight up from the bottom of the glass. The smaller the bubbles, the more delicate the champagne. Make sure to grasp only the stem of the flute to avoid warming the liquid with your hand.

5. Smell that? After it has passed inspection, sniff the champagne once and then swish it around. When you smell it again, the odor will reveal hints of coffee, brioche, lemon, grapefruit, and spice.

6. Drink aready, but no gulping! Sip the liquid delicately, rolling it around the tongue to reveal different tastes. Pay attention to indicators of quality, such as persistence of the flavor (longer-lasting is better) and the mouth feel (relative coarseness and smoothness of their texture). Savor—then rinse and repeat often—you'll pay double for far lowlier champagne back home. Eyes closed, and head back, revel in the decadence of it all.

THE BIG SPLURGE

AU BACCHUS GOURMET

Before you leave the gilded walks of Champagne and reenter the world of the penny-pinching traveler, indulge in some last-minute high culture cravings. The perfect finale to an afternoon of bubbling delights is a meal at classy **Au Bacchus Gourmet** ❹. Its atmospheric seating area, white stone walls, and a low-hanging, wrought-iron chandelier give it a cozy *bistro* feel, while head chef Jean-Paul Fernandès keeps the menu fresh and exciting with near-monthly updates on old favorites.

With a slew of awards to back up his title as *le meilleur saucier de France* (the best sauce-maker in France), Fernandès is famous for his unique and delicious culinary pairings, such as *homard au pamplemousse* (lobster with grapefruit). One particularly fine option is the veal *plat* featuring warm foie gras, asparagus, and various *legumes* (€23.50). The real deal, though, is the full 3-course *menu* (€25), an ever-changing lineup of the chef's most recent all-star dishes. With one last glass of *demi-sec* to go with your dessert of pineapple roasted in butter and exotic *pequillo* pepper jam (€10.50), you can know that, for one day in the heart of Champagne, you sipped some of the high life and ate like a king.

(21 rue Gambetta. ☎03 26 51 11 44. Open W-Su noon-2pm and 7:30-10pm. Reservations suggested. MC/V.)

One of the younger *maisons* that participates, **Esterlin**, 25 av. de Champagne, offers a free tasting and a 10min. video history of the product at its mansion. (☎03 26 59 71 52. Open daily 10am-12:15pm and 1:45-5pm. No reservations necessary.)

■ **MOËT & CHANDON.** The granddaddy of them all, Moët & Chandon, the producer of legendary champagne Dom Pérignon, has been "turning nature into art" since 1743. The mansion is full of as much old-money elegance as one would expect. The 50min. tour, on foot, details the basic steps in champagne production and gives a detailed history of champagne, highlighting at every turn the superior standards of M&C in particular. The *caves* feel authentic, and the 5min. film is a pompous, artistic, and thoroughly amusing bit of highbrow commerce. (20 av. de Champagne. ☎03 26 51 20 20. Open late Mar. to early Nov. daily 9:30-11:30am and 2-4:30pm; early Nov. to Mar. M-F only. Tour with one glass €7.50, two glasses (one vintage) €16, three glasses €20; ages 12-16 €4.50, under 12 free. AmEx/MC/V.)

■ **MERCIER.** Slightly less famous but equally swanky, Mercier, 10min. away from Moët, is in the middle of a vineyard. The self-proclaimed "most popular champagne in France" certainly knows how to market itself. The 30min. tour, in roller-coaster style cars, includes all the same information on production, but it also tells the fascinating history of Mercier himself and his wildly successful advertising schemes of the 19th-century. (He sent a blimp-sized cask of champagne to the 1889 World's Fair in Paris which, according to the tour, "competed only with the Eiffel Tower for the title of most impressive sight.") (70 av. de Champagne. ☎03 26 51 22 22. Open late Mar. to Nov. daily 9:30-11:30am and 2-4:30pm; early to mid-Dec. and early Jan. to Mar. M and Th-Su only. €6, ages 12-16 €3, under 12 free. MC/V.)

OTHER MAISONS. Across the street from Mercier is **De Castellane**, 57 rue de Verdun. A less romantic tour than those of M&C and Mercier, this one gets into the nitty-gritty of champagne production. Visitors during the week can observe factory workers unloading, corking, and labeling. Watching the *dégorgement* is a treat. (☎03 26 51 19 11. Open Mar. to late Dec. daily 10am-noon and 2-6pm, last tours 11:15am and 5:15pm. Full *cave* tour with tasting €8, tower and museum with tasting €4. MC/V.) **Demoiselle Vranken,** 42 rue de Champagne, is a relatively new arrival. The young, hip staff leads small, casual tours. (☎03 26 59 50 50. Open M-Sa 9:30am-noon and 2-5pm; Oct.-Apr. Closed Sa. Tour with tasting €3.50, under 15 free.)

🎵 ENTERTAINMENT

The city's limited selection of watering holes tend to fill up at night. Try **place de la République**, **place Mendès France**, or **place Hugues Plomb** for lively bars and pubs. **Le Progrès**, 5 pl. de la République, draws a mix of 20-somethings and their elders for languorous champagne-sipping on a packed terrace. (☎03 26 55 22 72. Glasses of champagne from €3.90. Food served Tu-Su 6am-midnight, F-Sa until 1am. MC/V.) **Le Chris's Bar**, 38 rue Sézanne, is a bar/club that sometimes features live music and always gives a friendly welcome. (☎03 26 54 38 47. Open M-Sa 3pm-4am. No cover. Cocktails €5. MC/V.)

The **Musiques d'Eté**, a series of free concerts ranging from jazz to classical to modern pop-rock, are held from the end of June to the third week in August (Free. For a guide of locations and times, check with the tourist office.) There is also occasional rock and world music at **place Mendès France.**

TROYES

Troyes (pop. 60,000) has been a prominent city since the Middle Ages. It was here that Chrétien de Troyes wrote *Parsifal*, Jewish scholar Rashi translated the Bible and the Talmud, and a local shoemaker's son became Pope Urbain IV. Today the city is well known for its refreshing combination of well-preserved *vieille ville* beauty and lively urban atmosphere. A pleasure unique to this extraordinary city is the stroll through a beautifully manicured park, past half-timbered fountains and narrow alleyways, into a bustling downtown plaza, all along principal roads that cleverly form the shape of a *bouchon de Champagne* (a champagne cork).

🚃 TRANSPORTATION

Trains: av. Maréchal Joffre (☎08 36 35 35 35; www.voyages-sncf.com for info and reservations). Open M-Sa 4:30am-9pm, Su 6am-9:30pm, help desk open M-Sa 9-11:45am and 2:15-6:30pm. To **Mulhouse** (3hr., 5 per day, €32.90), **Lyon** (6-8hr., €38.50), and **Paris** (1½hr., 14 per day, €8.60). **ATM** and **lockers** available. MC/V.

Buses: Go left after exiting the train station and enter the door just around the corner labeled *gare routière*. **SDTM TransChampagne** (☎03 26 65 17 07) runs to **Reims** (2hr., 2 per day, €20). **Les Rapides de Bourgogne** (☎03 86 94 95 00) runs to **Auxerre** (2½hr., M-Th 1 per day, €15).

Public Transportation: **L'Autoville** (☎03 25 70 49 00; www.tcat.fr), in front of the market. Open M-Sa 8am-12:45pm and 1:30-7pm. Extensive and frequent service (every 12-23min.) service. Tickets €1.10, 3 for €3, pack of 65 for €10. MC/V.

Taxis: **Taxis Troyens** (☎03 25 78 30 30), across the street from the station on the curb in front of the Grand Hôtel. Base charge €2.30; before 7pm €1 per km, after 7pm €1.55 per km. Service Su-Th 4am-midnight, F-Sa 24hr.

Car Rental: Europcar, 6 av. President Coty (☎03 25 78 37 66). Open 7:30am-12:30pm and 1:30-6:30pm. **Budget,** 10 rue Voltaire (☎03 25 73 27 37). Open daily 8am-noon and 2-6:30pm.

◼🧭 ORIENTATION & PRACTICAL INFORMATION

Troyes's train station is just three blocks from the edge of the *vieille ville.* The main tourist office is one block from the train station exit, on the right, at the corner of bd. Carnot; a branch office is near the town center on rue Mignard. (City website: www.ville-troyes.fr.)

Tourist Office: 16 bd. Carnot (☎03 25 82 62 70; www.ot-troyes.fr) and rue Mignard off rue Champeaux (☎03 25 73 36 88). Free detailed **city map**, €1.50 English brochure. Free **accommodations service.** Bd. Carnot office open M-Sa 9am-12:30pm and 2-6:30pm. Rue Mignard branch open mid-Sept. to June M-Sa 9am-12:30pm and 2-6:30pm, Su 10am-noon and 2-5pm; Jul. to mid-Sept. M-Sa 9am-8:30pm (early Sept. 7:30pm) and Su 10am-6:30pm (early Sept. 5pm). The **pharmacie de garde** is always posted in the window of the rue Mignard office. **Currency exchange** available at the rue Mignard office when banks are closed. MC/V.

Money: Banks with **ATMs** and **currency exchange** populate the whole city, although the exchange rate is better at the **post office. Société Générale,** 11 pl. Maréchal Foch (☎03 25 43 57 00; fax 03 25 43 57 57), has **currency exchange** for a hefty commission. Open M-F 8:30am-12:20pm and 1:30-6pm, Sa 8:30am-12:45pm. When banks are closed, the **tourist office** on rue Mignard (see above) will exchange currency.

Cultural Center: Maison du Boulanger, 16 rue Champeaux (☎03 25 43 55 00). Tickets and administration around the corner at 42 Paillot de Montabert. Info on festivals, exhibits, and concerts. Open M-F 9am-noon and 2-6pm, Sa 10am-noon and 2-5pm.

Laundromat: Laverie Automatique, 9 rue Clemenceau (☎03 25 73 93 46). Open daily 7:30am-8pm. **Laverie St-Nizier,** 107 rue Rév. Père Lafra (☎03 25 80 66 37), past the Cathédrale. Open 24hr.

Police: 28 rue Claude Huez (☎03 25 45 17 95).

Hospital: 101 av. Anatole France (☎03 25 49 49 49). For emergency medical service, call ☎03 25 71 99 00.

Internet: Open Games, 24 rue Huez (☎03 25 41 58 71). €1.50 per 30min., €2.80 per hr. Open daily M 2-10pm, Tu-Th 11am-10pm, F-Sa 11am-midnight, Su 2-8pm. MC/V. **L'Espace Viardin,** 10 rue Viardin. €2.50 per hr., a *carte* of 10hr. for €18. Open M-Sa 10am-midnight, Su 2-10pm. MC/V.

Post Office: 2 pl. Général Patton (☎03 25 42 32 32). From the train station, turn right onto bd. Carnot and walk down one block. Open M-F 9am-noon and 1:30-6:30pm, Sa 9am-noon. MC/V. **Currency exchange** available. **Branch office** at 38 rue Louis Ulbach, where rue Claude Huez meets rue de la République. Open Tu-F noon-6pm and Sa 9am-noon. **Poste Restante:** 10013 Troyes-Voltaire. **Postal code:** 10000.

▌ ACCOMMODATIONS & CAMPING

▨ **Les Comtes de Champagne,** 56 rue de la Monnaie (☎03 25 73 11 70; fax 03 25 73 06 02; www.comtesdechampagne.com). On a quiet street minutes from the train station and city center. It's hard to imagine a nicer place to stay in Troyes than this 16th-century mansion with its spacious, modern, tastefully decorated rooms all with TV, toilet, telephone, and shower or bath. Breakfast €5. Reception 7am-10pm. Reserve ahead. Singles start at €28; doubles from €32; triples from €50; quads from €55; some large rooms fit five or six. More expensive, luxurious rooms are available, and are well worth the price (singles up to €55, others up to €75). Extra bed €5. Optional kitchenette €8. MC/DC/V. ❷

Auberge de Jeunesse, 10430 chemin Ste-Scholastique (☎03 25 82 00 65; fax 03 25 72 93 78; www.fuaj.org/aj/troyes). This converted abbey, open all year and clean as a whistle, holds 105 beds. The only catch is that it lies about 5km from the center of town. Take the #8 local bus line from town to the Liberté stop and follow the signs. Reception 8am-11pm. Beds in rooms of five to six, with shower, €8.40. ❶

Hôtel le Trianon, 2 rue Pithou (☎03 25 73 18 52). Clean, moderately sized rooms in a very central location, right next to the Halles outdoor market and above a *tabac*. Breakfast €4.50. Reception 6:30am-8pm. Twin bed €16, with shower €28; big bed €20, with shower €34; two beds €25. Extra person €4.60. MC/V. ❷

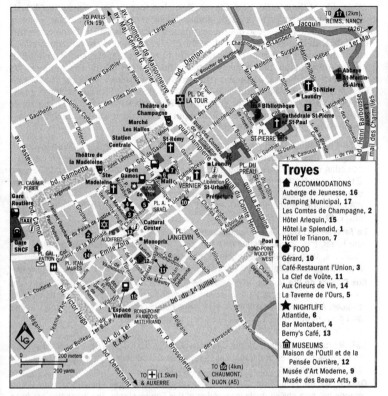

Troyes

🏠 ACCOMMODATIONS
Auberge de Jeunesse, 16
Camping Municipal, 17
Les Comtes de Champagne, 2
Hôtel Arlequin, 15
Hôtel Le Splendid, 1
Hôtel le Trianon, 7

🍴 FOOD
Gérard, 10
Café-Restaurant l'Union, 3
La Clef de Voûte, 11
Aux Crieurs de Vin, 14
La Taverne de l'Ours, 5

⭐ NIGHTLIFE
Atlantide, 6
Bar Montabert, 4
Berny's Café, 13

🏛 MUSEUMS
Maison de l'Outil et de la Pensée Ouvrière, 12
Musée d'Art Moderne, 9
Musée des Beaux Arts, 8

Hôtel Arlequin, 50 rue Turenne (☎03 25 83 12 70; fax 03 25 83 12 99; www.hotelar-lequin.com). This aptly named establishment boasts clean, colorful rooms and suites on the edge of the bustling quartier Vauluisant. Breakfast €6.50. Reception 7am-10pm. All rooms with shower and toilet. Singles €32-50; doubles €35-57; triples €56-59; quads and quints €64-67. MC/V. ❸

Hôtel Le Splendid, 44 bd. Carnot, across from the post office (☎03 25 73 08 52). Le Splendid's clean, attractive rooms, just a block from the station, live up to its ambitious moniker. Most rooms have TV and toilet. Less splendid, however, is the somewhat noisy bd. Carnot just outside. Breakfast €5.50. Singles from €22, with shower €36; doubles with shower €43-47. Extra bed €8. MC/V. ❷

Camping Municipal, 7 rue Salengro (☎03 25 81 02 64), on N60 2km from town. Take bus #1 (dir: Pont Ste-Marie) to this friendly, three-star site. Includes the creature comforts of showers, toilets, TV, and laundry. Open Apr. to mid-Oct. €4 per person, €5.50 per tent or car. ❶

🍴 FOOD

The **quartier St-Jean** is the best place to find a good meal and local chatter. Cafés, restaurants, *brasseries*, and inexpensive *crêperies* line the pedestrian **rue Champeaux** on the way to pl. Alexandre Israël, the center of Troyenne evening life. On another side of the *vieille ville*, the smaller, charming quartier Vauluisant boasts its own pedestrian avenue of gastronomic delights: **rue Général Saussier**. Reasonably priced kebab places also dot the less pleasant **rue de la Cité** near the cathedral.

Les Halles, an English-style market on the corner of rue de la République and rue Général de Gaulle, offers a fresh selection of produce, meats, and baked goods from the Aube region, plus a lively outdoor flea market during the summer. Try *andouillette de Troyes,* a popular tripe sausage, or creamy *fromage de Troyes.* (Open M-Th 8am-12:45pm and 3:30-7pm, F-Sa 7am-7pm, Su 9am-12:30pm. Many stalls take MC/V.) Grab generic grub at the **Monoprix** supermarket, 71 rue Emile Zola (☎03 25 73 10 78; open M-Sa 8:30am-8pm), and make it a spectacular park picnic in pl. de la Libération at the end of rue Emile Zola.

🦪 **La Clef de Voûte,** 33-35 rue Général Saussier (☎03 25 73 72 07). Cheese lovers will delight in this restaurant specializing in *cuisine de fromage,* including an extensive selection of dishes that incorporate both regional and exotic fondues, most around €10-15. The lactose intolerant can order the local specialty *Andouillette AAAAA,* the sausage that comes with a seal of approval from the *Association Amicale des Amateurs d'Andouillettes Authentiques.* Open Tu-F noon-2pm and 7:30-10pm, Sa until 11pm. MC/V. ❸

La Taverne de l'Ours, 2 rue Champaux (☎03 25 73 22 18). Located right off pl. Alexandre Israël, this popular restaurant's terrace is a great place to see and be seen. Their *assiettes,* from *assiette de Troyes* to *assiettes Anglaise* and *Piccadily* run €9.80-12, and their generous salads are €15. Open daily noon-2:30pm and 7-11pm. MC/V. ❸

Aux Crieurs de Vin, 4-6 pl. Jean Jaurès (☎03 25 40 01 01). Part restaurant, part wine cellar, this simple eatery offers about ten times as many wine selections as meal choices. A friendly, knowledgeable staff helps diners choose the perfect vintage. A meal and glass of wine run €13. Open Tu-Sa noon-2pm and 8-10:30pm; bar 11am-midnight; cave M 3-7pm, Tu-Sa 10am-10pm. MC/V. ❷

Café-Restaurant l'Union, 34 rue Champeaux (☎03 25 40 35 76). This recently established hotspot serves traditional Italian favorites to local folk on its private terrace. Pizza €8. Open noon-2pm and 7-11pm, bar 11am-3am. MC/V. ❷

Gérard, 42 rue Emile Zola. Everyone loves a good *boulangerie-patisserie,* and Gérard stands out as a stylish, tasty incarnation of this French staple. The baguettes are fresh, and the *éclairs* are heaven. Open Su-M and W-Sa 6:30am-8pm.

🜊 🜨 SIGHTS & OUTDOORS

CATHÉDRALE ST-PIERRE ET ST-PAUL. The sheer size of this cathedral with fluted pillars is only slightly less stunning than its spectacular, intricate stained-glass designs. Ranging in age from a youthful 100 to an ancient 700 years, the breathtaking *vitraux* dominate a cavernous, but otherwise plain, interior. A long history of fires and other disasters has claimed much of the original architecture, making the surviving windows all the more remarkable. Today, concerts and art exhibitions share the space with daily masses. *(☎03 25 76 98 18. Pl. St-Pierre, down rue Clemenceau past the town hall. Enter the courtyard to the right of the cathedral; the entrance to the museum is on the right. No charge. Open daily 10am-noon and 2-5pm, except M morning.)*

MUSÉE D'ART MODERNE. This attractive, well-designed museum is Troyes's cultural centerpiece, housing over 2000 works of French art from the period 1850-1950, including pieces by Dégas, Rodin, Picasso, and Seurat. The garden contains a diverse collection of statuary, masks, and paintings from Africa and Oceania, works which often inspired, or were inspired by, their European counterparts. *(Pl. St-Pierre; directions as above. €6, under 25 €0.80; free W. Open Tu-Su 11am-6pm.)*

MAISON DE L'OUTIL ET DE LA PENSÉE OUVRIÈRE. This unique collection of over 8000 tools from the 17th-19th centuries is the largest such display in the world. Elaborately arranged in fascinating, bizarre artistic configurations, cleavers and pincers never looked so sleek and pretty. An out-of-place half-sized recreation of the Statue of Liberty's face sits in the courtyard. *(7 rue de la Trinité.* ☎ *03 25 73 28 26; www.maison-de-l-outil.com. Guides available in English and German. €6.50, children 12-17 €5, families €16. Guided tours €1. Open M 1-6pm, Tu-Su 10am-6pm. MC/V.)*

EGLISE ST-MADELEINE. An ornate, colorful 12th-century structure, this church boasts intricate *vitraux* almost as old as those of the Cathédrale. The real sight to see, though, is the impossibly detailed, carved stone *jubé* (gallery) between the nave and the choir. The panels are well-labeled in English, German, and French, dispensing fascinating bits of trivia. *(Just off the ruelle des Chats.* ☎ *03 25 73 82 90. Open Su-M 2-5pm, Tu-Sa 10am-noon and 2-5pm.)*

BASILIQUE ST-URBAIN. At night the basilica's spear-like spires are illuminated against the dark sky, but its flying buttresses are best seen in daylight. The archetypical Gothic structure was commissioned when Jacques Pantaléon became Pope Urbain IV; it rests upon the site of his father's cobbler shop. *(Walk down rue Clemenceau from the Hôtel de Ville.* ☎ *03 25 73 37 13. Open daily 10am-noon and 2-5pm; closed Su and M morning.)*

OTHER SIGHTS. The museum route brings travelers from modern art back through the Renaissance and well into the Stone Age. The city's second largest museum, **Musée des Beaux Arts,** offers a trove of 15th- to 19th-century paintings, regional archaeology exhibits, and some interesting attempts at taxidermy. *(☎ 03 25 76 21 68; museum@ville-troyes.fr. Open Su-M and W-Sa 10am-noon and 2-6pm. €6, not including Musée d'Art Moderne €4.60, students or under 25 €0.80; W free.)* More provincial and less organized, the **Musée Vauluisant** (which also houses the textile-centric **Musée de la Bonneterie**) displays a collection of medieval sculptures from the Troyes school and a hodge-podge of other items. *(4 rue de Vauluisant.* ☎ *03 25 73 05 85. Open Su-M and W-Sa 10am-1pm and 2-6pm.)*

EXCURSIONS. Over 12,500 acres of freshwater lakes dot the region around Troyes. The sunny waters of Lake Orient welcome sunbathers, swimmers, and windsurfers. Wilder Lake Temple is reserved for fishing and bird watching, while Lake Amance roars with speedboats and screaming waterskiers. The **Comité Départemental du Tourisme de l'Aube,** 34 quai Dampierre, provides free brochures of many local and regional outdoor activities. *(☎ 03 25 42 50 00; fax 03 25 42 50 88. Open M-F 8:45am-noon and 1:30-6pm.)* The tourist office has bus schedules for the Troyes-Grands Lacs routes. In July and August, the **Courriers de l'Aube** takes travelers to Lake Orient three times daily. *(☎ 03 25 71 28 40. One-way €5.)*

🎵 ENTERTAINMENT

The size of Troyes's population may be dwarfed by Paris or even Bordeaux, but even the most jaded locals admit that it's a city *"qui bouge bien"* (that moves well). The most concentrated, and the most touristed, swath of local nightlife can be found amid the cafés and taverns of **rue Champeaux** and **rue Mole** off pl. Alexander Israël. **Bar Montabert,** 24 rue Paillot de Montabert, just off rue Champeaux, with a gregarious owner and loyal pub crowd, is one of the many fine bars on this happening street. *(☎ 03 25 73 58 04. Open daily noon-3pm and 6pm-3am. MC/V.)* Friendly, unassuming **Berny's Café,** 43 rule Molé, is the central hang-out spot for Troyes's gay and lesbian population, though much of the clientele at this hotspot is straight. *(☎ 06 22 63 06 62. Open daily 10am-midnight.)* Movie theaters, arcades, and pool halls abut chic boutiques on **rue Emile Zola.** Less consistent and conse-

THE LOCAL LEGEND

A DEVIL OF A PLOY

Langres today doesn't overflow with outrageous parties, but if you look back far enough into local history, you'll encounter one of the most successsful revelers of all time. After all, not too many spirited young lads have been able to sell their souls for a life of good times, then renege on the deal with minutes left on their contract.

Young Chirapa, a self-styled poet, artist, dreamer, and man of the world, generally spent his time carousing around the *Langrois* taverns of the early 14th century, causing trouble. Not shy with the ladies, and well acquainted with all the most disreputable folks in town, Chirapa finally left home to see the world and leave his fiery mark on it. When he returned an old and broken man, the Devil himself felt that this was a spirit who deserved another chance to do some bad in the world. A deal was struck—one soul for 20 years of debauchery—and Chirapa returned to his old life in fine form.

Faced with one candlewick's measure of time left, the clever welcher ran over to the monastery and gave his soul over to the only soul-trading firm with more clout than the Devil. Thus was Chirapa able to live out many more years in pace at the monastery, while the spurned fiend howled and cursed his lost loot. The creakings of houses throughout Langres are to this day attributed to the frustrated demon.

quently less populated entertainment spots can be found all along the small streets **rue de la République** and **rue Raymod Poincaré.**

The hottest nightclub in Troyes changes nightly, but **Atlantide,** 19 rue Claude Huez, is never a bad bet. The crowd is predominantly gay on Sundays and may seem exclusively young on some nights. Locals of all ages, however, agree that it is a consistently good time. (☎03 25 73 85 76; www.club-atlantide.com.) Check out the ubiquitous posters advertising all of Troyes's clubs to get an idea of upcoming events and information, or inquire at the tourist office for a list of *discothèques.*

Lest it become known solely for the art of imbibing bubbly, Troyes hosts a number of festivals and special events. Summer welcomes the extensive **Ville en Musique,** a series of concerts and performances that runs the gamut from modern French rock to classical organ tunes. (Call ☎03 25 43 55 00 or stop by the Cultural Center for more info. Runs mid-June to Aug.) **Le Chemin des Bâtisseurs de Cathédrales,** a free sound-and-light spectacle, is held in the Cathedral of St-Rémy on Friday and Saturday nights at 10pm, from the last weekend in June to the end of the summer.

LANGRES

Perched above the fertile Marne valley, tiny Langres (pop. 10,000) sits comfortably between Champagne, Burgundy, and Franche-Comté. Because of its elevation and central position, the town was founded by the Romans as a stronghold. Years later, it became famous as the birthplace of philosopher Denis Diderot, who ambitiously recorded the known world in his 18th-century encyclopedia. Today the town remains a pleasant blend of vistas and history, a quiet experience to savor and enjoy.

⌐ TRANSPORTATION. Langres sits 3km away—and half a kilometer up—from its train station. (☎03 25 87 75 04. Open M 5:25-11:30am and 1:45-7:20pm, Tu-Sa 8:30-11am and 1:45-6:30pm, Su 2:40-9pm. **Luggage storage** available. AmEx/MC/V.) **Trains** roll from the station to: **Paris** (3hr., 7 per day, €30.10); **Reims** (2½hr., 5 per day, €24.40); **Troyes** (1¼hr., 5 per day, €15.90); and to the hub of **Culmont-Chalindrey** (15min., 10 per day, €2.20). The exciting walk uphill from the station quickly becomes a painful, solemn. Local **buses** run sporadically between the station and the town center (1 ticket €0.85, *carnet of* 10 €5.55). Schedules of departure times and stops are posted at the train station and the tourist office. The impatient can call a **taxi** (☎03 25 87 47 31; €9 from the station to pl. Bel'Air). For the way down, the bravest of travelers will rent **bikes** from **Diderot Cycles et Loisirs,** 67 rue Diderot. (☎ 03 25 87 06 98; cycles.diderot@wanadoo.fr. Open Tu-Sa 9am-noon and 2-6pm; €9 per half-day, €13 per day, €22 for the weekend; €200 deposit. MC/V.)

■ ☷ **ORIENTATION & PRACTICAL INFORMATION.** The **tourist office,** located in sq. Olivier Halle, is just across from the pl. Bel'Air bus stop. The friendly staff provides a free and very useful regional guide (available in English), and **accommodation booking** for €1. **Value tickets** (€5, students €3.50, under 12 free) provide access to all the major local sights. The office also provides **audio guides** for €5 in English, German, Dutch, and Italian. (☎ 03 25 87 67 67; www.paysdelangres.com.fr. Open May-Sept. M-Sa 9am-noon and 1:30-6:30pm, Su 10am-12:30pm and 2-6pm; Apr. and Oct. M-Sa 9am-noon and 1:30-6pm; Nov.-Mar. M-Sa 9am-noon and 1:30-5:30pm.) You can also rumble along the ramparts for an hour on the shameful *train touristique.* (Leaves from the tourist office. Tickets €5, children 4-12 €3.50. July-Aug. 7 per day 10am-6pm; May-June and Sept. W and Sa-Su afternoons 3 per day.) **Banks** with **ATMs** dot the city and line rue Diderot. The **pharmacie de garde** is listed in every pharmacy's window. There is a **laundromat** at pl. de l'Hôtel de Ville. **Internet** is available at Europa, on the corner of bd. de Tassigny and rue Diderot (open M-F noon-midnight, Sa-Su 9am-2am; €1.50 per 30min.), and at the post office (purchase a card, €4.60 per hour). The **police** are at the Hôtel de Ville on rue Charles Beligne (☎ 03 25 87 00 40). Medical care is available at the **Centre Hospitalier,** 10 rue de la Charité (☎ 03 25 87 88 88). On Mondays, the only **currency exchange** option is at the **post office,** rue Général Leclerc. (☎ 03 25 84 33 30. Open M-F 8am-noon and 1:30-6pm, Sa 8am-noon.) **Postal code:** 52200.

☶ **ACCOMMODATIONS & CAMPING.** Set right outside the Porte des Moulins by the tourist office, the **Foyer des Jeunes Travailleurs (HI) ❶,** pl. des États-Unis, offers pleasant, modern dorm rooms, kitchen access, and an adjoining cafeteria. Though slightly institutional, it has outstanding views and is the best bargain in town. From the tourist office, walk out through the 17th-century gateway, then left around the corner. Cross the street to the hostel, marked "Auberge de Jeunesse." (☎ 03 25 87 09 69; courrier@fljt.asso.fr. Breakfast 8:30-9am €2.50. Lunch daily 11:45am-1:30pm, dinner 7-8:30pm. Sheets €3. Reception M-F 9am-12:30pm and 2-7pm, Sa 10:30am-noon. Singles €12; doubles €16. Discount after four nights. Call ahead. Sa-Su by reservation only.) When the Foyer is full, try the **Hôtel de la Poste ❷,** 8-10 pl. Ziegler, a comfortable, inexpensive, and centrally located establishment with medium-sized rooms. (☎ 03 25 87 10 51; fax 03 25 88 46 18. Breakfast €5. Reception open daily 7am-10pm. Singles and doubles start at €22, with shower €35; triples with shower €44. Attached restaurant serves somewhat pricey regional cuisine in a warm, attractive setting. *Menus* start at €15. MC/V.) The smaller and more expensive **Auberge Jeanne d'Arc ❸,** 24-26 rue Gambetta, on pl. Jenson across from Eglise St-Martin, has elegant, comfortable rooms with TV, and a pleasant, pricey restaurant. (☎ 03 25 86 87 88. Breakfast €6.50. Reception daily 7am-11pm. Singles and doubles with shower and toilet €28-55. Extra person €4.60. MC/V.) A more peripheral option is **Les Moulins ❸,** 5 pl. des Etats-Unis, across from the Foyer des Jeunes Travailleurs, which has unexciting, clean singles and doubles €34 and €37, respectively. (☎ 03 25 87 08 12. Breakfast €5.30. Reception open M-Sa 7am-10pm. Reservations suggested during summer. Closed Su and Aug. to mid-Sept. MC/V.)

Camping Navarre ❶ occupies prime hilltop space right next to the 16th-century Tour de Navarre at the edge of the old town, with fabulous views over the ramparts. (☎ 03 25 87 37 92; fax 03 25 90 24 53. Open mid-Mar. to Oct. Reception July-Aug. 6-8am and 4-10:30pm; Sept.-June 6-8am and 4-8pm. Gates closed 10pm-6:30am. €1.70, under 7 €1, €3.50 with tent or car. Electricity €2.75.)

CHAMPAGNE

◘ **FOOD.** From fresh foie gras to the soft orange-cased *fromage de Langres* to the local sweet currant apéritif *rubis de groseilles*, Langrois's *specialités de terroir* are still made the old-fashioned way: on the farm. Many of these farms provide *dégustation* tours; the regional guide available at the tourist office provides contact info. About 10km away in Pouilly-en-Bassigny, **L'Escargotière des Sources** shows visitors the origins of last night's *escargot* platter. A guided tour of this snail farm, complete with tasting, €2.30. (☎03 25 84 29 70. Open June-Sept. Tu-W 2-6pm; M, Th-F with advanced booking.) For those who wish to remain within the city walls, the **market** at pl. Jenson is open Friday mornings, and cafés on the side streets near pl. Diderot offer hearty plates of *fromage de Langres*. Restaurants, like everything else in town, cluster along **rue Diderot.** Lively and friendly ▨**Café de Foy ❷**, pl. Diderot, is a bargain for fresh local specials. Although the salad with walnuts and warm *fromage de Langres* (€6.90) is the most popular dish, the *formule rapide* (€11.90), with appetizer and dessert, comes in a close second. A *petite restauration* of *croque monsiuer* is only €3.35. (☎03 25 87 09 86. Open June-Aug. Su-Th 7am-midnight, F-Sa 7am-1:30am. AmEx/MC/V.) Unique and popular Tex-Mex grill/crêperie **Bananas ❸**, 52 rue Diderot, whips up sample quesadillas with *fromage de Langres* or crêpe tacos from €8-13. (☎03 25 87 42 96. Open M-Sa noon-2:30pm and 7:30-10pm. MC/V.) Pricier, but equally popular, is the restaurant **Hôtel de l'Europe ❸**, 23-25 rue Diderot. *Menus* featuring local wine and (you guessed it) *fromage de Langres* range from €14.50 to 45. (☎03 25 87 10 58; hotel-europe-langres@wanadoo.fr. Open noon-2pm and 7:30-10pm, closed Su night. MC/V.) The **cafeteria** at the Foyer is cheap but surprisingly tasty. (Closed Sa night and Su.) Cheap, generic goods are available at **Aldi** supermarket, rue des Chavannes just before pl. Bel'Air. (Open M-F 9am-12:15pm and 2-7pm, Sa 9am-7pm.)

◙ **SIGHTS.** The ramparts have been the soul of Langres for millennia; a tour of these walls and the stunning views they provide should be visitors' top priority. A good starting point is the squat **Tour de Navarre,** on the southeast corner. Erected in 1521 by François I, this outpost defended the city with 7m thick walls and a spiral ramp for moving artillery. (Open July-Aug. daily 10am-12:30pm and 2-6:30pm; May-June and Sept. Sa-Su 2:30-6pm. €2.50, under 18 €1.50.) Moving clockwise, the first-century AD **Porte Gallo-Romane,** toward the center of the south wall, is the oldest of the seven gates that allow entrance into the fortifications. Farther clockwise stands the 16th-century gunnery **Tour du Petit Sault.** (Open July-Aug. M-Tu and Th-F 2:30-6pm; May-June and Sept. Sa-Su 2:30-6pm.) On the north wall, a single lonely, immobile train car commemorates the **Old Cog Railway,** the original link between the town and the valley below. **Place de la Crémaillère,** just after the railway, overlooks farmland and the glittering **Réservoir de la Liez,** which offers swimming, boating, and camping (swimming and hiking are free, check at the tourist office for info on sailing, waterskiing, and windsurfing). Past the **Table d'Orientation,** a fun 19th-century panel noting visible landmarks as well as far-flung destinations like Moscow and Constantinople, lies the zippy glass-and-steel **Panoramics,** the 20th century's answer to the cog railway, which whisks down the ramparts to the parking lot and road below free of charge.

Moving in from the ramparts, the highest view in town is from the south tower of the 12th-century **Cathédrale St-Mammès,** which dominates the center of town. An impressive combination of Burgundian-Romanesque and Gothic styles, the cathedral's interior is defined by its ornate 13th-century cloister and the various *objets d'art* on display in the treasury. (Cathedral free, treasury €2.50, under 12 €1.50. Tours in French July-Aug. Tu-Su 2:30, 3:30, 4:30, and 5:30pm, Sept.-June Su only. Cathedral open daily 8am-7pm, Nov-Apr. closes at 5pm. Treasury open July-Aug. Su-M and W-Sa 2:30-6pm.) Also in the center of town at pl. du Centenaire, the large and polished **Musée d'Art et d'Histoire** exhibits impressive artifacts from Egypt, Rome, and Langrois prehistory. Eighteenth- and 19th-century paintings by LeBrun and Poussin are also on display. (☎ 03 25 87 08 05. €3.30, students €1.75, under 18 free. Open Apr.-Oct. Su-M and W-Sa 10am-noon and 2-6pm; Nov.-Mar. 10am-noon and 2-5pm. Wheelchair access and tours for the blind available.)

Summer in Langres brings a number of festivals and events, mostly geared toward tourists. For **L'Estival des Hallebardiers,** locals in full Renaissance costume recreate, with active participation from spectators, the night watchman's patrol from more turbulent times. (Aug. F and Sa 9:15pm.) Those whose French is up to par can grab their capes and gallavant about town banishing the bandits and spooks of yore; otherwise, chortle over the entire proceedings along the sidelines. It all ends in music and drink at a Renaissance tavern. (Info ☎ 03 25 90 77 40. €12 to participate, students €9. Begins at the cathedral cloister.) Every Saturday in June, the **Fête du Pétard** celebrates the defense of Langres in 1591 against attackers from Lorraine who unsuccessfully tried to destroy the city gates with a *pétard* (bomb). Dancers, fire eaters, and jugglers mark the three-century-old tradition. (For info, call ☎ 03 25 90 77 40.)

ALSACE, LORRAINE, & FRANCHE-COMTÉ

ALSACE

 German-influenced Alsace and Lorraine are less similar than their hyphenated twinship leads most to believe. In Alsace's Vosges, wooded hills and sunlit valleys are perfect for hiking and are striped vineyards of the Route du Vin, while the well-preserved towns are characterized by crooked streets, canals, and half-timbered houses. Lorraine unfolds to the west among wheat fields and gently undulating plains, her elegant, well-planned cities featuring broad, tree-lined boulevards and stately Baroque architecture. Less touristed but no less entertaining than its neighbors, Franche-Comté rolls out over lush mountains and is home to some of France's finest cross-country skiing in the winter. Alsace's capital, **Strasbourg** (p. 354), is a major intellectual and cultural powerhouse, though vibrant, many-fountained **Nancy** (p. 340) is the intellectual capital of the region. Along with Strasbourg, **Sélestat** (p. 366) and **Colmar** (p. 368) are convenient bases for excursions along the Route du Vin and to other wine tasting centers such as **Arbois** (p. 384). The overwhelming favorite along the Route is lovely, unspoiled **Kaysersberg** (p. 364); other significant stops include **Barr** (p. 365) and heavily touristed **Riquewihr** (p. 365). **Belfort** (p. 374), **Pontarlier** (p. 386), **Lons-le-Saunier** (p. 388), and **Saverne** (p. 362) offer great hiking. For those interested by French history, the WWI memorials at **Verdun** (p. 350), the restored castle of **Haut Koenigsbourg** (p. 367), and the remains of France's only concentration camp at **Natzweiler-Struthof** (see **The Local Story,** p. 382) offer moving history lessons. Party-seekers will want to stop by either the thriving student town of **Besançon** (p. 378) or industrial **Mulhouse** (p. 371), while a calmer time can be found in the gardens and Chagall stained glass of **Metz** (p. 345) or the isolation of Le Corbusier's masterwork cathedral at **Ronchamp** (p. 376).

As top prize in the endless Franco-German border wars, France's northeastern frontier has had a bloody history. Alsace-Lorraine was ravaged during the Franco-Prussian War of 1870-1871, when it was ceded to Germany, then devastated during the French reoccupation in WWI and finally blitzed once again when the Germans retook it in WWII. Just south of Alsace, Franche-Comté was often the pawn of its powerful neighbors. The Franche-Comtois violently opposed France's final 1674 conquest of their land, but they staunchly defended France against the invading Prussians in 1871. Most recently this former frontierland has landed right in the thick of the ever-expanding European unification. Strasbourg is the seat of the European Parliament and an administrative center for the European Union. Miles of borderlands shared with Belgium, Germany, and Switzerland have become mini melting-pots and cultural centers for the newly integrated face of the continent.

Germanic influences are rampant in Alsatian dishes like *tarte à l'oignon* (onion pie), *choucroute garnie* (sauerkraut cooked in white wine sauce and topped with sausages and ham), and *coq au Riesling* (chicken in white wine sauce). Cooks in Lorraine make up in heartiness what they lack in delicacy; bacon, butter, and cream are key ingredients in staple dishes like quiche Lorraine.

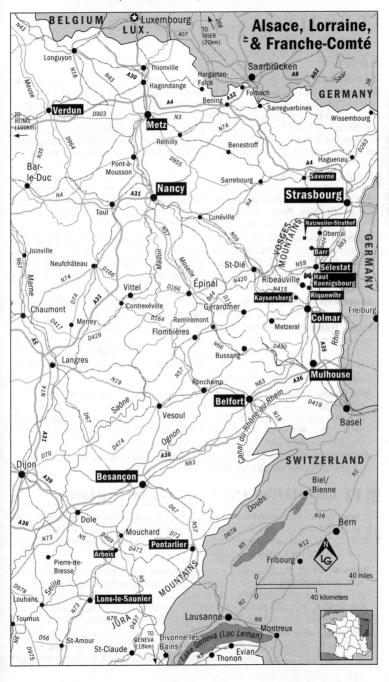

Alsace, Lorraine, & Franche-Comté

LORRAINE

NANCY

Cosmopolitan Nancy (pop. 100,000) owes its gilded beauty to the good Duke Stanislas, whose passion for urban planning transformed the city into a model of 18th-century classicism, with broad plazas, wrought-iron grillwork, and cascading fountains. A hundred years ago, the Nancy School inspired art nouveau sculptors and designers; today Nancy's symphony, opera, jazz, and ballet companies make it an avant-garde cultural center. On top of it all, Nancy's outgoing locals and night-time *joie de vivre* make it one of the most enjoyable cities in northeastern France.

▐ TRANSPORTATION

Flights: Aéroport de Metz-Nancy Lorraine (☎03 87 56 70 00). Flights leave for **Lyon, Marseille, Nice, Paris,** and **Toulouse.** Luggage storage available. Shuttle to the train station (35-40min.; 7 per day; €6.90, students €5.10).

Trains: pl. Thiers (☎03 83 22 12 46). Ticket office open M-F 5:50am-9:35pm, Sa 6:45am-9:35pm, Su 6:45am-9:40pm. To: **Metz** (40min., 24 per day, €8.30); **Paris** (3hr., 14 per day, €35.30); **Strasbourg** (1hr., 17 per day, €18.40). Luggage storage available. **SNCF Boutique** with info and reservations at 18 pl. St-Epvre (Open Tu-F 9:30am-1pm and 2-6pm, Sa 9am-12:30pm and 1:30-3:30pm).

Buses: Rapides de Lorraine buses, 52 bd. d'Austrasie (☎03 83 32 34 20), leave from in front of the train station. Open M-F 9am-noon and 2-6pm.

Public Transportation: STAN. Bus maps at tourist office or **Agence Bus,** 3 rue Dr. Schmitt (☎03 83 30 08 08). Open M-Sa 7am-7:30pm. Most buses stop at Point Central on rue St-Georges. Tickets €1.20, *carnet* of 10 €8.20; available on board, at the station, or from machines. Buses 5:30am-8pm, some to midnight. MC/V at the office.

Taxis: Taxi Nancy, 2 bd. Joffre (☎03 83 37 65 37).

Bike Rental: Cyclotop in the train station near the baggage deposit (☎03 83 22 11 63). €3 per hr., €5 per half-day, €7 per day. Motorbikes €6 per hr., tandems €9 per day. €61 deposit for bike or tandem, €99 for motorbike. ID required. Open Apr.-Dec. Tu-Sa 2-6pm. **Michenon,** 91 rue des 4 Eglises (☎03 83 17 59 59). Bikes €12-21 per day. €160 deposit. Open Tu-Sa 9am-noon and 2-7pm. MC/V.

Car Rental: Avis, 12 rue Crampel (☎03 83 35 40 61), on pl. Thiers. MC/V. **Loca Vu,** 32 rue des Fabriques (☎03 83 15 15 05). MC/V.

▐ ▐ ORIENTATION AND PRACTICAL INFORMATION

The heart of the city is **place Stanislas.** Leaving the station towards pl. Thiers, look left to find rue Raymond Poincaré (*not* rue Henri Poincaré). Follow rue R. Poincaré away from the station, through a stone archway, and continue straight to pl. Stanislas and the tourist office. (5min.)

Tourist Office: pl. Stanislas (☎03 83 35 22 41; www.ot-nancy.fr). Ask for a map, a bus map, and the helpful *Le Fil d'Ariane,* a free French student guide. Other info is available in English. **Currency exchange** only when banks are closed. Same-day hotel **reservation service,** only with partner hotels, €2 plus partial deposit. English spoken. Open Apr.-Oct. M-Sa 9am-7pm, Su 10am-5pm; Nov.-Mar. M-Sa 9am-6pm, Su 10am-1pm.

City Tours: Tourist office leads a few different themed tours, from 1-2hr. July-Aug. Sa 2:30pm, Su 10:30am; Sept.-Oct. and Mar.-June call tourist office for hours. €5, students €3, under 12 free. English tours only available for groups by reservation. Audio

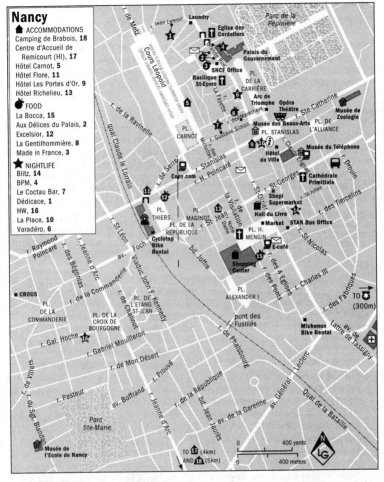

Nancy

ACCOMMODATIONS
Camping de Brabois, **18**
Centre d'Accueil de
Remicourt (HI), **17**
Hôtel Carnot, **5**
Hôtel Flore, **11**
Hôtel Les Portes d'Or, **9**
Hôtel Richelieu, **13**

FOOD
La Bocca, **15**
Aux Délices du Palais, **2**
Excelsior, **12**
La Gentilhommière, **8**
Made in France, **3**

NIGHTLIFE
Blitz, **14**
BPM, **4**
Le Coctau Bar, **7**
Dédicace, **1**
HW, **16**
La Place, **10**
Varadéro, **6**

ALSACE

guide tours (in English, German, and Japanese) €5. Ask about train tours, tours led by actors, and a self-guided walking tour of art nouveau buildings in Nancy.

Laundromat: Self Lav-o-matic, 107 rue Gabriel Mouilleron. Open daily 8am-8pm. **Le Bateau Lavoir,** 125 rue St-Dizier (☎03 83 35 47 47). Open daily 7:45am-9:30pm. **Laverie GTI,** 5 rond-point M. Simon. Open daily 7am-9pm.

Police: 38 bd. Lobau (☎03 83 17 27 37), near the intersection with rue Charles III. Call police for the **pharmacie de garde.**

Hospital: CHU Nancy, 29 av. de Lattre de Tassigny (☎03 83 85 85 85).

Internet: Copy.com, 3-5 rue Guerrier de Dumast (☎03 83 22 90 41). €2 for 30min., €3 per hr. Open M-Sa 8:30am-9pm, Su 2-10pm. **E-café,** 11 rue des 4 Eglises (☎03 83 35 47 34). €5.40 per hr., students €4.80. Open M 11am-9pm, Tu-Sa 9am-9pm, Su 2-8pm. **Musée du Téléphone,** 11 rue Maurice Barres (☎03 83 86 50 00) €2.30 for 30min., €4 per hr. Open Tu-F 10am-7pm, Sa 2-7pm, 1st Su each month 2-6pm.

Money: Banks with **ATMs** and **currency exchange** cluster along rue Stanislas.

English Bookstore: Hall du Livre, 38 rue St-Dizier (☎03 83 35 53 01), has an English book section. Open M-Sa 9am-8pm, Su 11am-7pm. MC/V.

Post Office: 10 rue St-Dizier (☎03 83 39 75 20). Open M-F 8am-6:30pm and Sa 8am-noon. **Branches:** 66 rue St-Dizier (☎03 83 17 39 11). Open M-F 8am-6:30pm, Sa 8am-4pm. 75 Grande Rue. Open M 2-6pm, Tu-F 9am-noon and 2-6pm, Sa 10am-4pm. **Postal code:** 54000.

ACCOMMODATIONS & CAMPING

CROUS, 75 rue de Laxou, helps students find summer accommodations in university dorms, and is a resource for work and study opportunities. Call **Foreign Student Services** at ☎03 83 91 88 26. (Open M-F 9am-5pm. English generally spoken.) There are several nice budget hotels all around the train station, especially on rue Jeanne d'Arc, all about a 10min. walk from pl. Stanislas. The hostel is lovely but far away, and with bus costs and wasted time factored in, maybe not the best value.

Hôtel Flore, 8 rue Raymond Poincaré (☎03 83 37 63 28; fax 03 83 90 20 94). Jovial owners let bright, homey rooms near the station, some tiny, all with shower, toilet, and TV. Bar downstairs attracts young people. Breakfast €4.20. Reception M-Sa 7:30am-2am, Su 11am-11pm. Reserve ahead June-Sept. Singles €26.50-32; doubles €37-40; triples €43. MC/V. ❷

Centre d'Accueil de Remicourt (HI), 149 rue de Vandoeuvre (☎03 83 27 73 67; fax 03 83 41 41 35), in Villers-lès-Nancy, 4km southwest of town. From the station, take bus #122 to St-Fiacre. (Dir: Villiers Clairlieu. 2 per hr., last bus 8pm. St-Fiacre is not always a stop—check with the driver.) Downhill from the bus stop, turn right onto rue de la Grange des Moines, which turns into rue de Vandoeuvre. Look for signs to Château de Remicourt. Hilltop views, a garden, and the location in a château compensate for an institutional interior, but getting to the city can be tricky. Breakfast included. Reception daily 9am-9pm. 3- and 4-bed dorms €12.50; doubles with bath €30. MC/V. ❶

Hôtel Les Portes d'Or, 21 rue Stanislas (☎03 83 35 42 34). A small, sweet surprise just a block from the golden gates of pl. Stanislas, 3min. from the train station. An attractive lobby leads to comfortable, well-decorated rooms, all with shower, bath, toilet, and TV, and worth the price. Breakfast €6. Reception daily 7am-10pm. Reserve ahead. Singles €45-50; doubles €50-60. Extra bed €15. MC/V. ❹

Hôtel Richelieu, 5 rue Gilbert (☎03 83 32 03 03). A good value just off rue St-Jean in the heart of the *centre ville.* Pleasant rooms come with TV, mini-bar, shower or bath, and toilet—take a moment and a few extra euros to live it up in the sauna. Breakfast €6. Reception daily 8am-10pm. Singles €30-42; doubles €45-47; triples €52. MC/V. ❸

Hôtel Carnot, 2-4 cours Léopold (☎03 83 36 59 58). Convenient hotel with a view of the peaceful pl. Carnot or a nice courtyard. The large rooms are comfy, except for their worn-out 70s look. Breakfast €5. Reception 24hr. Singles and doubles with shower €28, with shower and toilet €33-41; triples with shower €50. Extra bed €10. MC/V. ❸

Camping de Brabois, av. Paul Muller (☎03 83 27 18 28), near the Centre d'Accueil. Take bus #125 or 122 to Camping (dir: Villiers Clairlieu). Sweeping hilltop site overlooks the town. Showers, mini tennis court, volleyball, playground, and grocery store make this more a resort than a campground. Access to woodland trails. Reception daily June-Aug. 7:30am-10pm; Apr.-May and Sept.-Oct. 7:30am-12:30pm and 1:30-9pm. Open Apr. to mid-Oct. July-Aug. two people with tent €11.20, Apr.-June and Sept.-Oct. two people with tent €9.80. Extra adult €3.90, children 2-7 €1.80. Electricity €4. ❶

📋 FOOD

Nancy's signature *bergamote* is a bitter hard candy flavored by the orange spice used in Earl Grey tea; all of the *pâtisseries* off pl. Stanislas sell these overpriced suckers. Otherwise, Nancy's regional cuisine, including *quiche Lorraine*, contributes generously to the love-handles of the world. The covered **marché central** is off rue St-Dizier in pl. Henri Mengin (open Tu-Th 7am-6pm, F-Sa 7am-6:30pm), a **Shopi** supermarket at 26 rue St-Georges (☎03 83 35 08 35; open M-F 9am-8pm, Sa 9am-7:30pm; MC/V), and a larger **Monoprix** in the Centre Commercial St-Sebastian off pl. Henri Mengin. (Open M-Sa 8am-8:30pm. MC/V.) Restaurants spill from **rue des Maréchaux** onto pl. Lafayette and up Grande Rue to pl. St-Epvre. For afternoon snacks, there are waffle and crêpe stands behind pl. Stanislas on the **Terrace de la Pépinière,** and cheap kebab joints lining **rue Stanislas** and its surroundings.

Reserve ahead or come early to ■**Aux Délices du Palais ❶,** 69 Grande Rue, a hip sandwich and *tartine* joint, where locals swivel on cowprint stools and munch on meat- or veggie-packed monsters with regional nicknames, such as the over-weight, beefy "Yankee." (☎03 83 30 44 19. Sandwiches €4.50-6. Open M-Sa noon-1:45pm and 7-9:30pm.) One of the classier eateries on restaurant row, **La Gentilhom-mière ❸,** 29 rue des Maréchaux, offers scrumptious regional specialties with a twist, including *magret de canard* with seasonal fruits or *filet de saumon* in wine sauce and truffles, each €13. (☎03 83 32 26 44. Open M-F noon-2pm and 7:30-10pm, Sa 7:30-10pm. Reservations suggested in summer. MC/V.) **La Bocca ❸,** 33 rue des Ponts, is a trendy Italian restaurant with kitschy heart-shaped booths and zebra-print lamp shades. (☎03 83 32 74 47. 3-course *menu* €15.50, pastas and meal salads €7.50-12.50. Open M and W-F 11:30am-2:30pm and 7-11pm, Tu 11:30am-2:30pm, Sa 11:30am-2:30pm and 7pm-midnight. MC/V.) For huge sandwiches, try **Made in France ❶,** 1 rue St-Epvre, a hole-in-the-wall that prides itself on its fresh bread and vegetables. (☎03 83 37 33 36. Sandwiches €2.30-5.10. Open M-Sa 11:30am-9pm. MC/V.) **Excelsior ❹,** 50 rue Henri Poincaré, is a grand old *brasserie* that specializes in *choucroute aux 3 poissons* in Champagne (€17.50) and other *nancienne* cuisine. (☎03 83 35 24 57. Open daily 11:30am-10pm. AmEx/MC/V.)

👁 SIGHTS

■**PLACE STANISLAS.** The city's cultural center and the most impressive sight in Nancy, its three neoclassical pavilions were commissioned in 1737 by Stanislas Lesczynski, the former king of Poland and then-duke of Lorraine, to honor his nephew, Louis XV. The finely molded *Portes d'Or* (the Golden Gates) dazzle during the day, but the nightly *son-et-lumières* (July-Aug. 10pm) are spectacular. From pl. Stanislas, pass through the five-arch **Arc de Triomphe** to the tree-lined **place de la Carrière,** a former jousting ground refurbished by Stanislas with Baroque architecture and wrought-iron ornaments.

■**MUSÉE DE L'ECOLE DE NANCY.** The striking collection in this museum illustrates the development of the Nancy School, part of the turn-of-the-century art nouveau movement. Sculpture, glasswork, and furniture by Emile Gallé (creator of the Paris metro signs) and others leave visitors itching to redecorate. Even the "museumed out" will appreciate the unique artwork on display and the be-fountained, be-statued garden in back. Ask to borrow the detailed English guide at the front desk. (*36-38 rue du Sergent Blandan.* ☎*03 83 40 14 86; www.ecole-de-nancy.com. Take bus #122 or 123, dir. Vandoeuvre Cheminots, to Sédillot or Paul-Painlevé. Open Su and W-Sa 10:30am-6pm. €4.60, students €2.30, under 12 free. An €8 pass buys entry to Nancy's 3 museums. First Su of each month 10am-1:30pm free, W students free. Tours in French F-Su 3pm, €6.10. MC/V over €15.)*

PARC DE LA PÉPINIÈRE. This expansive park is one of the most popular places in the city. Hectares give way to a sprawling zoo and an outdoor café. The aromatic **Roseraie** displays vibrant flowers from around the world. *(Just north of pl. de la Carrière, near pl. Stanislas. Open daily June-Aug. 6:30am-10:30pm; Apr.-May and Sept.-Oct. 6:30am-9pm; Nov.-Mar. 6:30am-8pm. Free.)*

MUSÉE DES BEAUX-ARTS. In a stately Baroque building (whose entrance was designed in 1755 for Stanislas himself), a collection of paintings and sculptures spans the centuries from 1380 to the present. It includes gems by Rubens, Delacroix, Monet, Modigliani, Rodin, and Picasso, and a fantastic exhibit of art nouveau Daum glasswork. *(3 pl. Stanislas. ☎03 83 85 30 72. Open Su-M and W-Sa 10am-6pm. €4.80, students and children €2.30, combined with Musée de l'Ecole de Nancy €6.10. First Su of each month 10:30am-1:30pm free, W students free. Tours in French €1.60.)*

OTHER SIGHTS. Unusual for a French city, the churches here are neither the oldest nor the most noteworthy monuments. The 19th-century **Basilique St-Epvre** is known for its brilliant windows from around the world. It hosts free evening concerts of classical and organ music. *(Off Grande Rue at pl. St-Epvre. Open daily 8am-7pm.)* Notable for its ornate 18th-century painted dome is the **Cathédrale Primitiale.** *(Rue St-Georges, just past rue Montesquieu. Open daily 8am-7pm.)* The innovative little **Musée du Téléphone,** on a quiet street off pl. Stanislas, traces the history of man's quest to reach out, from telegraph stations to today's cordless wonders. Two floors of exhibits are hands-on. Surf the Internet for €4 per hr. *(11 rue Maurice Barres. ☎03 83 86 50 00. Open Tu-F 10am-7pm, Sa 2pm-7pm, 1st Su of the month 2-6pm. €3, students €1.50.)*

🎵 ENTERTAINMENT

Soak up the evening beauty of the illuminated **place Stanislas** from one of its ritzy cafés, or grab a cheaper drink on **rue Stanislas** or **Grande Rue.** Check www.nancy-bynight.com or www.yellownight.com for updates on bars, clubs, concerts, and theater events. ▒**Blitz,** 76 rue St-Julien, is smoky coolness at its best. Red-velvet everything is peppered with Chinese prints and vintage knickknacks. Mellow groove and urban hip-hop play in the background. *(☎03 83 32 77 20. Shots €2, beer €2, absinthe €4, cocktails €2.50. Open Tu-Sa June-Aug. 2pm-2am; Sept.-May 11am-2am. MC/V.)* Trendy 20-somethings also head to **Varadéro,** 27 Grande Rue, a Cuban-style bar with Latin music and a revolutionary flavor. *(☎03 83 36 61 98. Shots €1.50, cocktails €4.50. Open M-Sa 6pm-2am. MC/V.)* **Dédicace,** 9 rue Jean Lamour, is a fun-filled, slightly over-the-top gay bar, with regular drag shows and racy theme nights. Come on Tu to play *poste-éclair,* a mature version of spin-the-bottle. *(☎03 83 36 95 52. Beer €2.50, cocktails €3-7. Open M-Sa 6:30pm-2am, Su 4pm-2am. MC/V.)* A gay bar that caters to its female clientele, friendly-feeling **Le Coctau Bar,** 4 rue Gustave Simon, offers *bonbon*-accompanied cocktails. *(☎03 83 32 02 81. Beer from €2.80, cocktails €3-6. Open Tu-Th 11am-midnight, F-Sa 11am-2am. MC/V.)* Popular with *everyone* in Nancy is the techno/house mix and sleek, chic, *magnifique* setting of gay-friendly ▒**La Place,** 7 pl. Stanislas. Join the city's hippest crowd and party until dawn. *(☎03 83 35 62 63. Open Su-Th 10pm-4am, F-Sa 10pm-5am.)* At **HW,** 1 rue du Général Hoche, young people dance to techno on bars under the lofty ceilings and chandeliers of a converted warehouse. Be cautious, the walk is dark and deserted at night. *(☎03 83 40 25 13. Beer €3. Open M-F 10pm-4am, Sa-Su midnight-6am.)* Laid-back **BPM,** 90 Grande Rue N33, plays reggae, electronica, and drum and bass. *(☎03 83 30 36 01. Beer €2.20, cocktails €5-7. Free concerts. Two-for-one happy hour daily 8-9pm. Open daily 6pm-2am. AmEx/MC/V.)*

For two weeks in October, at the **Jazz-Pulsations** festival in **Parc de la Pépinière,** well-known international musicians set feet a-tapping from dusk until dawn. In summer nightly concerts emanate from the Roseraie. A free sound-and-light show details Nancy's history. (July-Aug. daily 10pm.) In 2004, **Opéra de Nancy et de Lorraine** will present *Don Giovanni, Le Journal Vénitien,* and *Tristan und Isolde* (☎ 03 83 85 33 11; open Oct.-June M-Sa 8am-noon and 1-7pm; tickets available Tu-Sa 1-7pm; tickets €6.10-48.80, discounts for students), and ballets and symphonies. (☎ 03 83 36 72 20. Ticket office open M-F 10am-1pm and 2-6pm.) The **Festival International de Chant Choral** brings 2000 singers from around the world. (Office at 150 rue Jeanne d'Arc. ☎ 03 83 27 56 56. Next concert mid-May 2004. Free.)

METZ

Once capital of the Merovingian kingdom of Austrasia, Metz (pronounced "mess;" pop. 300,000) has changed hands frequently. An independent republican city for centuries, it was seized by Charles V in 1552 and claimed for France, then annexed twice by Germany (after the Franco-Prussian War and during WWII). Modern Metz is a peaceful stroller's heaven, with fountains, cobblestones, canals, and a fabulous cathedral. The *Esplanade*, an impressive walkway packed with tourists and locals, extends to the river Moselle. It is surrounded by immaculately landscaped greenery, while unique yellow stone architecture lends the avenues a sun-drenched glow. Home to a major university, the refreshingly calm city also knows how to kick up its heels at night.

▐ TRANSPORTATION

Trains: pl. du Gal. de Gaulle. Office open Sept. to mid-June M-F 8:30am-7pm, Sa 8:30am-6pm; mid-June to Aug. M-F 8:30am-7:30pm, Sa 8:30am-6pm. Ticket window open longer. Luggage storage €4.50 per bag per day. To: **Luxembourg** (45min., every hr., €10.80); **Lyon** (5hr., 4 per day, €43.60); **Nancy** (40min., 15 per day, €8.30); **Paris** (3hr., 8 per day, €35.30); **Strasbourg** (1½hr., 12 per day, €19.10).

Buses: Les Rapides de Lorraine, 2 rue de Nonnetiers (☎ 03 87 75 26 62, schedules 03 87 36 23 34). Take the underpass to the right of the station, below the tracks, then go left. Ticket window open M-Th 8am-noon and 2-5pm, F until 4pm. To **Verdun** (1hr., 2-3 per day, €12.10) and smaller regional towns. **Eurolines** travels all over Europe.

Public Transportation: TCRM, 1 av. Robert Schumann (☎ 03 87 76 31 11). Office open July-Aug. M-F 9am-6:30pm; Sept.-June M-F 7:30am-7pm, Sa 8:30am-5:30pm. Tickets €0.90, *carnet* of 6 €4, day pass €3. Most lines run M-F 5:30am-8pm, Sa-Su less often. Line #11 runs 10pm-midnight.

THE LOCAL STORY

ALSATIAN IDENTITY

On Old World Alsatian streets cluttered with costumed boutique owners and *kugelhopf* molds, it's easy to imagine you've wandered into Epcot Center's World Showcase rather than a real town surrounded by fields of trailing vines.

For all these cheerful signs of a distinct Alsatian tradition, regional identity has historically been much more complex and far less cheerful. Writer Tomi Ungerer described 20th-century Alsace as a public toilet: always occupied. The lives of the oldest Alsatian grandfathers tell national history on a personal level: they were born German citizens before WWI, grew up French, became German during the Occupation, and will die French. In WWI, Alsatians were forced into the Kaiser's army to fight former compatriots, while in WWII they called themselves the *malgré-nous* (despite ourselves).

Older Alsatians still speak Alsatian, a Low German dialect, and refer to the rest of France as *la France Intérieure.* Many of their middle-aged children can understand the dialect, but the Alsatian language is being lost on the youngest generation, partly due to the lure of French TV, although it is taught as a second language. Even the Alsatian accent—a Germanic twang lamented by generations of uncomprehending outsiders—is losing its edge. The battle over Alsace is still raging, but the struggle has become far more personal.

Taxis: (☎03 87 56 91 92), at the train station.

Car Rental: Avis (☎03 87 50 60 30), at the train station. Open M-F 8am-12:15pm, 1:30-7pm, and 8-9:30pm; Su 4:30-8:30pm; Sa closed. AmEx/MC/V. **Europcar, Budget, National,** and **Hertz** are also at the station.

Bike Rental: Vélocation (☎03 87 62 61 79), at the train station. €3 per half-day, €5 per day, €12 per week. €50 deposit. Open M-F 6am-8pm.

■ 🛈 ORIENTATION & PRACTICAL INFORMATION

The honey-colored *vieille ville* is mostly off-limits to cars. The cathedral dominates the **place d'Armes;** the tourist office is across the street, in the Hôtel de Ville. From the station, take a right, then a left onto rue des Augustins, which becomes rue de la Fontaine, pl. du Quarteau, and pl. St-Louis. At pl. St-Simplice, turn left onto rue de la Tête d'Or, then right onto rue Fabet. Bus #11 (dir: St-Eloy) and #9 (dir: J. Bauchez) go there from pl. Charles de Gaulle. Metz is a big city; though it's safe and clean, always be cautious.

Tourist Office: 2 pl. d'Armes (☎03 87 55 53 76; www.tourisme.mairie-metz.fr). **Currency exchange.** English-speaking staff makes **hotel reservations** (€1.50) and distributes maps. French *Metz en Fête* lists activities. **Internet** with *télécarte* €0.12-0.18 per 3min. Open July-Aug. M-Sa 9am-9pm, Su 11am-5pm; Apr.-June and Sept.-Oct. M-Sa 9am-7pm, Su 11am-5pm; Nov.-Mar. M-Sa 9am-6:30pm, Su 11am-5pm.

City Tours: given by the tourist office M-Sa 3pm in French. €7, under 10 €3.50. English audio guides €7. **Taxi tours** (1hr., 3-4 people, €23.70). Themed tours, night tours, and other special events; check tourist office for information.

Budget Travel: Agence Wasteels, 3 rue d'Austrasie (☎08 03 88 70 47). Student rates and passes. Open M-Th 9am-noon and 2-6pm, F 9am-noon and 2-7pm, Sa 9am-noon.

Youth Center: Centre Régional d'Information Jeunesse, 1 rue de Coëtlosquet (☎03 87 69 04 50). Info on hiking, religious organizations, concerts, travel, lodging, study and work opportunities. Open M and W 10am-6pm; Tu and Th-F 10am-noon and 1:30-6pm.

Laundromat: 23 rue Taison. Open daily 7am-8pm. Also at 22 rue du Pont-des-Morts (☎03 87 63 49 57). Open daily 7am-7pm.

Police: 45 rue Belle Isle (☎03 87 16 17 17), near pl. de Pontiffroy.

Hospital: Centre Hospitalier Regional Metz-Thionville, 1 pl. Phillipe de Vigneulles (☎03 87 55 31 31), near pl. Maud Huy.

Internet: Espace Multimédia, 2 rue du Four du Cloître (☎03 87 36 56 56). Free. Reservations required. Open M 1-6pm, Tu-Sa 9am-6pm. **Boutique des Services,** 9 rue des Clercs (☎03 87 75 97 13). €0.05 per min., €9 for 3½hr. Open M 2-7pm, Tu-Sa 10am-7pm. **Microludique,** 18 rue du Pont des Morts. €4.50 per hr. Open M-Sa 11am–9pm.

Post Office: 9 rue Gambetta (☎ 03 87 56 74 23). **Currency exchange.** Open M-F 8am-7pm and Sa 8:30am-12:30pm. **Branch,** Centre Commercial (☎03 87 37 99 00). Open M-F 9am-7pm, Sa 9am-noon and 1:30-5pm. 3 rue de la Pierre Hardie. Open M-F 9am-7pm, Sa 9am-5pm. 39 pl. St-Louis. Open M 2-6pm, Tu-F 9am-6pm, Sa 9am-noon. **Poste Restante:** 57037. **Postal code:** 57000.

🏠 ACCOMMODATIONS & CAMPING

Relatively inexpensive hotels cluster around the train station. Pricier accomodations are in the pedestrian district .

🛏 **Association Carrefour/Auberge de Jeunesse (HI),** 6 rue Marchant (☎03 87 75 07 26; fax 03 87 36 71 44). Take minibus line B from the station to Ste-Ségolène (every 15min. 7:30am-7:15pm) and go left up the hill. In the *vieille ville*, with clean, bright

ALSACE

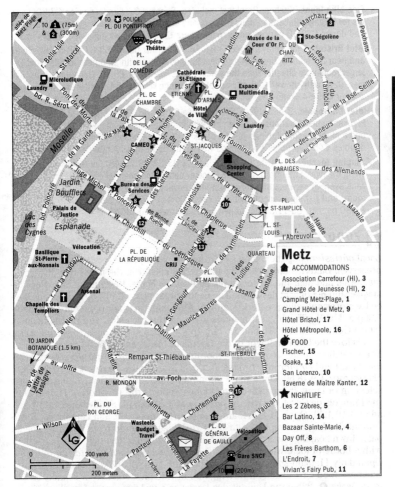

Metz

ACCOMMODATIONS
Association Carrefour (HI), **3**
Auberge de Jeunesse (HI), **2**
Camping Metz-Plage, **1**
Grand Hôtel de Metz, **9**
Hôtel Bristol, **17**
Hôtel Métropole, **16**

FOOD
Fischer, **15**
Osaka, **13**
San Lorenzo, **10**
Taverne de Maître Kanter, **12**

NIGHTLIFE
Les 2 Zèbres, **5**
Bar Latino, **14**
Bazaar Sainte-Marie, **4**
Day Off, **8**
Les Frères Barthom, **6**
L'Endroit, **7**
Vivian's Fairy Pub, **11**

rooms and a friendly atmosphere. Singles and doubles are a great bargain, and many have private shower and toilet. Breakfast included. Meals €6.50. Laundry €3.30. Sheets €3.20. Reception 24hr. 3- and 4-bed dorms €12 per person. Singles and doubles €13.80. **Non-members** €2.90 extra per night for first 6 nights. MC/V. ❶

Grand Hôtel de Metz, 3 rue des Clercs (☎03 87 36 16 33; fax 03 87 74 17 04), a restored 18th-century mansion in the heart of the *vieille ville*. The operative word here is "grand," with comfortable lounges, spacious and gorgeous rooms, and fine views of the old city. Breakfast €3-6.20. Reception daily 7am-11pm. Reservations suggested. Singles €40-70 (most €57); doubles €57-70 (most €70). AmEx/MC/V. ❹

Auberge de Jeunesse (HI), 1 allée de Metz Plage (☎03 87 30 44 02; fax 03 87 33 19 80), on the river. The 30min. walk is tiring; take bus #3 (dir: Metz-Nord; last bus 8:30pm) or #11 (dir: St-Eloy; last bus midnight) from the station to Pontiffroy. Friendly staff tends small, cozy rooms, located on a beautiful river, but there are no door locks.

Free **bike loans.** Kitchen. Breakfast included. Sheets €3. Laundry service €7.50. Lockers for luggage. Reception daily 8-10am and 5-10pm. Reservations suggested. 2- to 6-bed dorms €12.10 per person. **Non-members** €2.90 extra per night. MC/V. ❶

Hôtel Bristol, 7 rue Lafayette (☎03 87 66 74 22; fax 03 87 50 67 89).Small, clean, and near the station, this is Metz's best budget option, with an odd retro 70s look. The larger rooms are cheerier than the smaller ones. Breakfast €5.50. Reception 24hr. Singles €26, with shower €28-41; doubles with shower €29-54; triples and quads with shower €49-54. AmEx/DC/MC/V. ❸

Hôtel Métropole, 5 pl. du Gal. de Gaulle (☎03 87 66 26 22; fax 03 87 66 29 91). Pleasant, classy stationside behemoth with large spotless rooms, with full bath and TV, and a fondness for all things yellow. Breakfast €5.50. Reception 24hr. Singles €38-45; doubles €45-49; triples €53; quads €57. Extra bed €6.80. AmEx/DC/MC/V. ❹

Camping Metz-Plage, allée de Metz-Plage (☎03 87 68 26 48; fax 03 87 32 61 26), lining the river. Enter from rue de la Piscine, behind the hospital on rue Belle Isle. Caravans everywhere. Beautiful views, but little privacy. Showers, grocery store, laundry, TV room, and fishing. Reception daily 7am-10pm. €2.50 per person, €2.50 per tent, €4.30 per car, €5-11.50 per trailer. Electricity included. MC/V. ❶

☐ FOOD

Local *pâtissiers* pop the region's *mirabelles* (plums) into everything from tarts to preserves. Bakeries and other cheap eateries cluster in the **pedestrian district** on **rue Coislin** and near the hostel on **rue du Pont des Morts.** Restaurants line **place St-Jacques** and **rue Dupont des Loges.** The **Centre St-Jacques,** off pl. St-Jacques, has specialty stores and cheap eateries, and an **ATAC** supermarket. (Open M-Sa 8:30am-7:30pm. MC/V.) The biggest **markets** are near the cathedral and pl. St-Jacques. (Open Oct. to mid-Apr. Th and Sa 7am-1pm.) Kebab stands occupy every corner. Locals love the German flavor of the **Taverne de Maître Kanter** ❸, 38 rue des Clercs. The €15.20 *formule taverne* incorporates specialties *tarte flambée* (or *Flammeküche*) and *choucroute brasserie.* (☎03 87 75 01 18. *Tartes à la carte* €7-8, *choucroute* €9-18.50. Open daily noon-midnight. AmEx/MC/V.) A scrumptious selection of large, inexpensive sandwiches, reflects the devotion of **Fischer** ❶, 6 rue François de Curel, to *l'art du pain.* (☎03 87 36 85 97. Sandwiches €3.10, salads €4.10-4.40. Open M-F 6:45am-7pm, Sa 7am-6pm.) At **San Lorenzo** ❷, 8 rue Dupont des Loges, sample the taste of *Italia* as rendered by *la France.* Locals pack down heaping pasta (€7-13) and pizza (€7-12), but maintain their patriotism with a bottle of local wine. (☎03 87 76 15 53. Meal-sized *salade italienne* €9.50. Open daily 11:45am-2pm and 6:45pm-midnight. MC/V.) Unlike Italian food, good Japanese food isn't exactly a thriving nationwide phenomenon in France, so the tasty **Osaka** ❸, 32bis rue Dupont des Loges, is a welcome treat for all sushi and teriyaki fans. (☎03 87 36 68 90. Sushi *menu* €15, skewers €5-10, teriyaki dishes €10-13. Open daily noon-2:30pm and 7-10:45pm. MC/V.)

☑ SIGHTS

■ **CATHÉDRALE ST-ETIENNE.** Thirteenth-century Metz sought to increase its prestige by erecting this spectacular church. The golden cathedral, known to locals as the "lantern of God," is the 3rd-tallest in France and has the world's largest collection of stained glass. Don't miss Chagall's dazzling *vitraux* in the western transept and the brilliantly illuminated glass of Chapelle de St-Sacrement near the welcome desk. Be sure to stop by after dark to see the glowing stained-glass windows. Each summer, a giant *tapis floral* cloaks the pl. d'Armes with elaborate flower arrangements. *(Pl. d'Armes.* ☎*03 87 75 54 61. Open M-Sa 8am-7pm, Su 1-7pm. Desk open M-Sa 10am-1pm and 2-6pm, Su 2-6pm. Tours in French 10:30am and 3pm. €4, with visit to crypt €5. Tours of the Mutte Tower 2, 4:30, 5:30pm; €7.)*

▓**ESPLANADE & GARDENS.** At the other end of rue des Clercs from pl. d'Armes, the Esplanade, an expansive formal garden overlooking the Moselle Valley, is possibly Metz's best feature. The tourist office has a map of its trails. Down the steps from the Esplanade, paths circle the shady. Paddle or pedal your way across the forest-surrounded **Lac aux Cygnes** with rentals from La Flotille. *(1 quai des Régates.* ☎*03 87 36 86 71. Rowboats €9.30 for 30min., motorboats €15 for 30min.)* During the summer, the spectacularly illuminated fountains spurt in tune to music, from Bach to Elvis, for *Les Eaux Musicales du Lac aux Cygnes. (Mid-June to Sept. F-Su at nightfall. Free.)* Swans preen at the **Jardin Botanique,** a taxonomist's heaven, packed with flower beds and tagged trees. In the center, a greenhouse nurtures ferns and palm trees. *(*☎*03 87 55 54 00. Greenhouse open Apr.-Sept. M-F 9am-6:45pm, Sa-Su 9-11:30am and 2-6:45pm; Oct.-Mar. M-F 9:30am-6:45pm, Sa-Su 9-11:30am and 2-6:45pm.)*

OTHER SIGHTS. The **Basilique St-Pierre-aux-Nonnains** is the oldest church in France, erected by the Romans in AD 380 to accommodate large baths and a sports arena. It became a chapel in the 7th century. Settle for being impressed by the history of this sight, as little is left to indicate its age. It is now an exhibition space for modern art. *(*☎*03 87 39 92 00. Open May-Sept. Tu-Su 2-6:30pm; Oct.-Apr. Sa-Su 2-6:30pm.)* Built over a former swamp, the **Place de la Comédie** served a less-than-comedic function during the Revolution: its main attraction was the guillotine. The 1751 Opéra-Théâtre at its center is the oldest functioning theater in France. *(4-5 pl. de la Comédie.* ☎*03 87 55 51 43. For tickets, call the Bureau de Location at* ☎*03 87 75 40 50. Open M-F 1-6pm. Ticket office open M-F 9am-12:30pm and 3-5pm. Tickets €9.20-46.20; students €4.60-12.30. MC/V.)* Along with the usual assortment of local Gallo-Roman remnants, the **Musée de la Cour d'Or** is a notable reconstruction of Roman baths, dimly lit and atmospheric. Upstairs, the **Musée des Beaux-Arts,** highlights local works from the 17th- to 19th-centuries. *(2 rue du Haut-Poirier, in the Cour d'Or.* ☎*03 87 68 25 00. Open M and W-F 10am-5pm, Sa-Su 11am-5pm. €4.60, under 25 €2.30, under 12 free, everyone free Su 11am-1pm and W 10am-1pm. Audio guide in 5 languages €2.30.)*

▟ NIGHTLIFE

Metz has an amazing set of bars and some good clubs. At night, students pack the bars and cafés at **place St-Jacques. Place St-Louis** is another hotspot.

▓ **Bazaar Sainte-Marie,** 2bis-4 rue Ste-Marie (☎03 87 21 05 93). A quirky place full of color and the sort of furniture one might find, well, at a bazaar. Perfect for laid-back types with a yen for some atmosphere. DJ on weekends plays house, groove, funk, and disco. Beer from €2.90. Open July-Aug. M-Th 10am-2am, F-Sa 10am-3am; Sept.-June M 2pm-2am, Tu-Th 10am-2am, F-Sa 10am-3am. AmEx/MC/V.

▓ **Les Frères Barthom** (☎03 87 75 25 52), on the corner of rue du Palais and en Nexirue. Popular and loud chain pub is silly and fun; it has an interior of fake wooden roofs, stone walls, and trees. Beer made by monks €3.80-5. Open Tu-Th 11:30am-1am, F 11:30am-2am, Sa-M 3pm-midnight. AmEx/MC/V.

Vivian's Fairy Pub, 15-17 pl. St-Louis (☎03 87 18 95 01). Decorated *à la* Knights of the Round Table, with round wooden tables and French Celtic music. Beer on tap €4.60-5. Open M 5pm-midnight, Tu-Th 5pm-1am, F-Sa 4pm-3am. MC/V.

Les 2 Zèbres, 4 pl. St-Jacques. A chic young crowd fills this hotspot's see-and-be-seen terrace and cozy cellar bar area. Pop a Zima with the yuppies. Open Su-Th 8am-2am, F-Sa until 3am. MC/V.

Bar Latino, 20 rue Dupont des Loges (☎03 87 36 94 17). The theme is self-explanatory. Come early to drink and listen to hot Latin music; later to drink, listen to hot Latin music and dance. Beer from €2.50. One drink minimum. Open daily 7:30pm-1am.

Day Off, 7 rue Poncelet (☎03 87 78 62 96). A relatively new bar/club, with a young crowd and varied music. Drink prices increase after 1am. Beer €2.90, after 1am €5. Open M-Tu 7:30am-8pm, W-Sa 7:30am-5am, Su 10pm-5am. MC/V.

L'Endroit, 20 rue aux Ours (☎03 87 35 95 64). New gay and lesbian club. L'Endroit promises a glamorous night of dancing, with weekly and special themes to liven things up. Regular themes include "glam" and "kitchissime." Open Th-Su 11pm-5am. MC/V.

🎵 ENTERTAINMENT

During the first half of 2004, the **Opéra-Théâtre** will feature the drama *Hysteria*, directed by John Malkovich, the opera *Médée, The Mikado, Who's Afraid of Virginia Woolf?*, and a number of other notable works (see **Sights: Place de la Comédie**, for ticket info). **Arsenal**, av. Ney, is a beautiful modern concert hall and exposition space hosting a wide range of performances. (☎03 87 39 92 00; reservations ☎03 87 74 16 16; www.mairie-metz.fr/arsenal. Open Tu-Su 1-6:30pm. MC/V.) For bargain-shoppers, Metz's twice-monthly **marché aux puces** (flea market) is France's second largest outside Paris. (Ask tourist office for a brochure or call ☎03 87 55 66 00. Open Sa 6am-noon, Su 7am-6pm.)

Metz En Fête incorporates free outdoor classical concerts and theater, jazz and blues recitals, and organ music in the cathedral. (Info from the tourist office or www.mairie-metz.fr.) These *soirées* culminate in the **Grandes Fêtes de la Mirabelle** at the end of August, a week-long festival held in honor of the noble plum. In the month leading up to Christmas, Metz hosts a particularly elaborate **Marché de Noël**, with over 100 special events held in pl. St-Louis.

VERDUN

France and Germany each lost nearly 400,000 soldiers in the Battle of Verdun (1916), the worst conflict of WWI. Eerie reminders surround the city: 15,000 marble crosses in the National Cemetery; the Trench of Bayonets, where almost all of France's 137th Regiment perished; and the symbol of Verdun, a dove above a pair of clasped hands. Verdun (pop. 20,000) today is caught somewhere between exploiting its tragic past for tourist dollars and trying to distance itself from it. Without its war monuments, though, Verdun is a wholly unspectacular place.

🚌 TRANSPORTATION

Trains: pl. Maurice Genovoix (☎03 29 84 83 02). Ticket booth open M 4:45am-7pm, Tu-F 5:45am-7pm, Sa 9:45am-12:15pm and 2:15-7pm, Su 12:30-7:30pm. To: **Metz** (1½hr., 5 per day, €11.40); **Paris** (1½hr., 4 per day, €29.50).

Buses: Regional buses depart from the parking lot at the end of rue du 8 Mai, just after the Ensemble Sportif on the left. From behind the tourist office, take rue de la Liberté and follow it straight until it becomes rue du 8 Mai. Check tourist office for schedules. To **Metz** (2hr., 4-9 per day, €10.50-16).

Car Rental: Grand Garage de la Meuse, 6 av. Colonel Driant (☎03 29 86 44 05). 21 and over. Open M-F 8am-noon and 1:30-7pm. MC/V. **AS Location,** 22 rue Louis Maury (☎03 29 86 58 58). Open M-F 9am-noon and 2-7pm. MC/V.

Bike Rental: Flavenot Damien, 1 rond-point des Etats-Unis (☎03 29 86 12 43), near the train station. €17.80 per day; passport deposit. Open M 2-7pm, Tu-Sa 9am-noon and 2-7pm. MC/V.

ORIENTATION & PRACTICAL INFORMATION

The train station, cathedral, and hostel are on one side of the **Meuse river;** the tourist office and war memorials on the other. To reach the **tourist office** from the station, take av. Garibaldi (on the left) until it curves to the right and becomes rue Frères Boulhant. Continue to the Port Chaussée, turn left and cross the bridge.

Tourist Office: pl. de la Nation (☎03 29 86 14 18; fax 03 29 84 22 42). English-speaking staff offers a free map of the city center, a larger map (€1), info on the memorials, and **currency exchange** (worse rates than the post office). Hotel and restaurant guides available in English, but only include partners of the tourist office. Daily 4hr. **tour** in French of battlefields and monuments. (May-Sept. 2pm; €25.50, under 16 €16.50; call before noon to reserve a seat.) Somewhat less historical historic tours in French on *dragée* manufacturing. (45min.; daily 9:30, 10:30am, 2:30, 3:30pm; €2.) Open Dec.-Feb. M-Sa 9am-noon and 2-5pm, Su 10am-1pm; Mar.-Apr. and Oct.-Nov. M-Sa 9am-noon and 2-6pm, Su 10am-1pm; May-Sept. M-Sa 8:30am-6:30pm, Su 9:30am-5pm.

Laundromat: 12 av. de la Victoire (☎06 80 12 51 79). Open daily 6:30am-8pm. Also at 56 rue R. Poincaré. Open daily 6:30am-9:30pm.

Police: 2 rue Chaussée (☎03 29 86 00 17). Call for the **pharmacie de garde.**

Hospital: 2 rue d'Anthouard (☎03 29 83 84 85).

Money: Banks with **ATMs** and **currency exchange** dot the pedestrian district. There is a **C/C** at Monument de la Victoire, 63 rue Mazel (☎03 29 83 43 00). Open M-Th 8:45am-noon and 1:30-5:45pm, F 8:45am-noon and 1:30-5:25pm.

Internet: Cyberom@nia, 5 quai de Londres (☎03 29 83 72 11). €3 for 30min., €4 per hr. Open Tu-Su noon-9pm. **Surf'n'Shoot,** 2 rue St-Saveur (☎06 03 51 81 61). €4 per hr. Open M-F 2-9pm, Sa 2pm-midnight.

Post Office: av. de la Victoire (☎03 29 83 45 55). **Currency exchange.** Open M-F 8am-7pm, Sa 8am-noon. **Poste Restante:** 55107 Verdun, B.P. 729. **Postal code:** 55100.

ACCOMMODATIONS AND CAMPING

■ **Auberge de Jeunesse (HI),** pl. Monseigneur Ginisty (☎03 29 86 28 28; fax 03 29 86 28 82), in the Centre Mondial de la Paix, beside the cathedral. From the station, head right to rue Louis Maury, through the square, to rue de la Belle Vierge. (15min.) Simple, renovated rooms in a converted seminary, with great views, a valuable collection of stained glass, and an amazing chapel-like restaurant. 4- to 7-bed dorms (singles available), most with bath. Breakfast €3.20. Sheets €2.70. Kitchen. Reception M-F 8am-12:30pm and 5-11pm, Sa-Su 8-10am and 5-9pm. Lockout 10am-5pm. Bunks €8.90, ages 4-10 €4.20. **Non-members** €2.90 extra per night for first 6 nights. MC/V. ❶

■ **Le Montaulbain,** 4 rue de la Vieille Prison (☎03 29 86 00 47; fax 03 29 84 75 70), near pl. Mal. Foch in the heart of the *vieille ville.* Large, colorful rooms, all with shower, on a quiet side street. Breakfast €5. Reception daily 7:30am-10pm. Reservations recommended July-Aug. Singles and doubles €25-35; triples €38; quads €42. MC/V. ❷

Hôtel Les Colombes, 9 av. Garibaldi (☎03 29 86 05 46), around the corner from the station. Clean, cheery rooms with TV, some family-size. Friendly reception and convenient location. Showerless rooms have no access to showers. Breakfast €5.40. Reception daily 9am-10:30pm. Singles €26, with bath €34-60; doubles with shower €34-40; triples and quads with shower €41-60. €60 for the "honeymoon suite." MC/V. ❸

Hôtel de la Cloche d'Or, 10 pl. St-Paul (☎03 29 86 03 60; fax 03 29 83 73 96). A nicer and pricier option next to the Porte de St-Paul. Simple, spacious rooms with shower or bath, TV, and toilet. Call ahead in the summer. Breakfast €6. Reception daily 7am-10pm. Singles and doubles €40-42. MC/V. ❹

Camping Les Breuils, allée des Breuils (☎03 29 86 15 31; fax 03 29 86 75 76), past the Citadelle Souterraine on av. du Cinquième R.A.P., 1km from town. Take a right onto av. Gal. Boichut and then the first left. Caravans abound at this site, but tall bushes offer some privacy. Pleasant spots by the river. Bar, grocery store, showers, and pool. Reception daily 7am-noon and 2-10pm. Open Apr.-Sept. July-Aug. €4 per person, €4 per site; Apr.-May and Sept. €3.60/€3.60. Electricity €3.50. MC/V. ●

☐ FOOD

Verdun's contribution to confection is the *dragée*, almonds coated with sugar and honey. First engineered by an apothecary in the 13th century to ward off sterility, it is today, appropriately enough, served at weddings and baptisms. The main **covered market** is on rue de Rû. (Open F 7:30am-12:30pm.) Stock up at the **Match** supermarket, in front of the station on rond-point des Etats-Unis. (Open M-Sa 8:30am-7:30pm. MC/V.) Restaurants and cafés are in the pedestrian area along **rue Chaussée** and **rue Rouyers,** and by the canal along **quai de Londres.** ☒**Pile ou Face ●,** 54 rue des Royeurs, serves delicious, elaborate, massive crêpes (€2.50-7.50) and *galettes* (€3.10-9.50) on the terrace or in the bustling dining room. (☎03 29 84 20 70. F nights "all you can eat" €14.40. Open Tu-Su 10am-11pm. MC/V.) Throngs of locals pack **Le Boucher du Quai ❷,** 13 quai de Londres, a self-proclaimed "meat specialist" that also offers sandwiches (€2.90-4.40) and pizza and pasta (€6.20-8.60). Try the *steak frites* and salad for €9 and up. (☎03 29 86 72 01. Open daily 11am-11pm. MC/V.) Ritzy **Restaurant du Coq Hardi ❹,** av. de la Victoire, has mastered *cuisse de lapin* (rabbit thigh; €23) and quiche Lorraine for 2 (€45). On the somewhat cheaper terrace, fancy pizzas go for €9 and full *plats* for €10. (☎03 29 86 36 36. Open daily 12:15-2:30pm and 7:15-9:30pm. Reservations suggested inside. MC/V.)

◉ ♫ SIGHTS & ENTERTAINMENT

The centerpiece of Verdun's pedestrian district is stunning **Le Monument à la Victoire;** the illuminated, fountained av. de la Victoire blazes a path to its feet. The monument stands on an old chapel, the remains of the **Eglise de la Madeleine,** bombed beyond repair in 1916. Inside the chapel, three volumes record the names of soldiers who fought here. (☎03 29 84 37 97. Open daily June 9:30am-12:30pm and 2-6pm; July-Aug. 9:30am-6:30pm; Sept.-Oct. and Apr.-May 9:30am-noon and 2-5:30pm. Free.) The massive **Citadelle Souterraine,** down rue de Rû on av. de la *5ème* RAP, is a reconstructed look at what trench warfare must have felt like. The fortress sheltered groups of 10,000 front-bound soldiers in its 4km of underground galleries. The official *Petit Train* tour (the only means of entering) plays out a bit like Mr. Toad's Antarctic ride for the lightly clothed. Realistic talking holograms depict the underground lives of hungry soldiers and nervous generals. (30min. tours in French or English every 5min. Also available in German, Italian, Dutch, and Spanish. Open daily July-Aug. 9am-6:30pm; Apr.-June and Sept. 9am-6pm; Oct.-Nov. 9am-noon and 2-6pm; Dec. 9:30am-noon and 2-5:30pm. Wheelchair-accessible. €6, ages 5-15 €2.50. MC/V above €15.40.)

Verdun's older, pre-war constructions include the oft-bombed 10th- to 12th-century **Cathédrale Notre-Dame,** rue de la Belle Vierge, which retains a fine set of post-WWI stained-glass windows. *Les Heures Musicales,* a series of choir and organ concerts, fills up the cathedral in summer. (Free to €12. Times vary. Call tourist office for details. Cathedral open daily Apr.-Sept. 8am-7pm; Feb.-Mar. and Oct.-Nov. 8am-6:30pm; Dec.-Jan. 8am-6pm.) Built in 1200, the **Porte Chaussée,** quai de Londres, has served as a prison, a guard tower, and an exit for WWI troops. At the other end of rue Frères Boulhaut, a copy of Rodin's **La Défense** guards the Port St-Paul. The Netherlands created the replica for the town just after the conclusion of the Battle of Verdun. For the battle-weary, **Parc Municipal Japiot,** across from the tourist office, rolls out its green carpet along the shady banks of the Meuse. (Open daily Apr.-Sept. 8:30am-8pm; Mar. and Oct. 9am-6pm; Nov.-Feb. 9am-5pm.)

Le Son et Lumière de la Bataille de Verdun recreates the battle, using over 300 actors and 1000 projectors, for a hushed and appreciative crowd (Info ☎ 03 29 84 50 00. June-July F-Sa night. €18, ages 12-18 €9, under 12 free.) The sounds of **L'Eté Musicale** waft up the river from quai de Londres Sa nights all summer. (Free concerts. All types of music.) Stick around the quai de Londres and neighboring **rue Chaussée** for the best nightlife. The pubs and bars around the river fill up most evenings. **L'Estaminet,** 45 rue des Rouyers, provides a bit of German *bierstub* in the heart of the district, playing jazz and blues some nights. (☎ 03 29 86 07 86. Open M-Sa 2pm-3am. German beer from €1.70, others from €2.30. MC/V.) Verdun's only *discothèque,* **La Bidule,** on the corner of rue Gros Degrès and rue du Rû, fills with mixed beats and a mixed crowd. (☎ 03 29 86 02 86. Open Th-Sa 11pm-4am. €7 cover includes one drink. Cocktails €7-8.)

MEMORIALS NEAR VERDUN

Many sites 5-8km east of Verdun commemorate the battle of 1916. The 4hr. tourist office tour (p. 351) visits all of the memorials mentioned below, describing each in rapid French. Spending more time on the 25km circuit requires a car.

After Alsace and parts of Lorraine were annexed by Germany in 1871, Verdun was thrust within 40km of the German border. France decided to build 38 new forts to protect Verdun and the surrounding area. These fortifications were targeted by German General von Falkenhayn's 1916 offensive. The strongest fort fell first: the immense concrete **Fort de Douaumont,** covering 3km of passageways. Only 57 soldiers remained after most of its force was transferred to weaker areas. The fortress was captured in February 1916, much to the surprise of the French, who shelled it for the next eight months in an attempt to dislodge the German garrison. In October 1916, a fire broke out after heavy shelling, and the Germans fled; a detachment of French-led Moroccan troops retook the fort. The assault of this strategically useless building caused over 100,000 French deaths; a sealed gallery entombs 679 German soldiers killed when a flamethrower set fire to a pile of grenades. (☎ 03 29 84 41 91. Open July-Sept. daily 10am-6:30pm. €3, under 16 €1.80. Informational brochures available in French, English, and German.)

The central and most powerful monument is the austere **Ossuaire de Douaumont,** a vast crypt whose 46m granite tower resembles a cross welded to an artillery shell. The small windows of the vault at the base reveal the remains of 130,000 unknown French and German soldiers. Another 15,000 are buried in the nearby military cemetery. Christian graves are marked by white crosses; Muslim gravestones point toward Mecca. A small monument to Jewish volunteers is 300m from the building. (Open daily May-Aug. 9am-6:30pm; Sept. 9am-noon and 2-6pm; Mar. and Oct. 9am-noon and 2-5:30pm; Apr. 9am-6pm; Nov. 9am-noon and 2-5pm. Ossuary free. Film and tower €3.80, children €2.50. Brochures available in English. Historical film contains a few graphic scenes.) Nearby, the **Tranchée des Baïonettes** holds the bodies of a detachment of France's 137th infantry regiment, buried alive while taking cover from heavy enemy fire. After the battle, the only sign of the men was the points of their bayonets protruding from the ground.

Fort de Vaux, the smallest of the fortifications, surrendered in June 1916 after seven days and nights of murderous hand-to-hand combat. In the dark, the French defenders, who had nothing to drink but their own urine, fended off attacks with gas, grenades, and flamethrowers. Numerous appeals for reinforcements were made to the Verdun garrison, to no avail; inside the fort stands the statue of a carrier pigeon named Valiant, who carried out the last plea. The Germans were so impressed with the resistance they awarded the French commander a saber of honor. (Open daily Apr.-Aug. 9am-6pm; Oct. to mid-Dec. and mid-Feb. to Mar. 9:30am-noon and 1-5pm. €3.30, under 15 €1.30. Info in English available.)

The little town of Fleury at the epicenter of the battle changed hands 16 times during the war. The fighting left the quaint town empty and plantless. The former railway station is now the grim **Musée de Fleury**, built by veterans to honor dead comrades. (Open daily Apr. to mid-Sept. 9am-6pm; Feb.-Mar. and mid-Sept. to Dec. 9am-noon and 2-6pm. €5, under 16 €2.50.)

ALSACE

STRASBOURG

Perhaps the most international city in France, Strasbourg (pop. 450,000) is the administrative center for the European Union. The European Parliament, the Council of Europe, and the European Commission for the Rights of Man are all within its borders. Its defining influence, though, comes from Germany, its former homelands, a few kilometers away. Dodgy accents abound (try saying *Finkwiller* three times fast and see how the tongue muscles evolve), and *winstubs* compete for street space with traditional *pâtisseries* and a host of international restaurants. The end result of this *über-mélange* is an unparalleled experience of cosmopolitan elegance, kept energetic and youthful by the University of Strasbourg.

⌐ TRANSPORTATION

Flights: Strasbourg-Entzheim International Airport (☎03 88 64 67 67; www.strasbourg.aeroport.fr) is 15km from Strasbourg. **Air France,** 7 rue du Marché (☎03 88 15 19 59), and other carriers fly to **London, Lyon,** and **Paris.** Shuttle **buses** (☎03 88 77 70 70) run from the airport to the Strasbourg tram stop Baggarsee (12min., 3-4 per hr., one-way €4.80). Luggage storage available.

Trains: pl. de la Gare (info and reservations ☎08 92 35 35 35). Ticket office open M 5am-9:10pm, Tu-Sa 5:30am-9:10pm, Su 5:55am-9:10pm. To: **Frankfurt,** Germany (3hr., 18 per day, €46.40); **Luxembourg** (2½hr., 14 per day, €26.30); **Paris** (4hr., 16 per day, €37.20); **Zurich,** Switzerland (3hr., 3-4 per day, €34.90). SNCF **buses** run to many surrounding towns from the station; check station or tourist office for schedules. Luggage check 7:45am-8:45pm (€4.50 per bag per 24hr.).

Public Transportation: Compagnie des Transports Strasbourgeois (CTS), 14 rue de la Gare aux Marchandises (☎03 88 77 70 11, bus and tram info 03 88 77 70 70). Open M-F 7:30am-6:30pm, Sa 9am-5pm. Also at the central train station. Open M-F 7:15am-6:30pm. Extensive bus service and 4 brand-new tram lines (4:30am-midnight). Tickets €1.20, *carnet* of 5 €4.70, day pass €3; tickets available at *tabacs.*

Taxis: Taxi 13, pl. de la République (☎03 88 36 13 13). 24hr. Also gives city tours (1-4 people €35) and service to the Route du Vin. **Novo Taxi** ☎03 88 75 19 19. 24hr.

Car Rental: Europ'Car, 16 pl. de la Gare (☎03 88 15 55 66). From €74.80 per day, €84.50 on weekends. 21+. Open M-F 8am-noon and 3-8pm, Sa 8am-noon and 2-5pm. MC/V. **Garage Sengler** (☎03 88 30 00 75), rue Jean Giradow in Hautepierre. €32.30 per day, plus €0.20 per km over 50km; €84.50 on weekends. 21+. Open M-F 8am-12:30pm and 2-6:30pm. MC/V.

Bike Rental: Vélocation, at 4 locations. Main branch at 4 rue du Maire Kuss (☎03 88 23 56 75), near the train station. Bikes €3 per half-day, €4.50 per day. €80-100 deposit with check and photocopy of ID card. Prices will likely change in the near future. Open M-F 6am-7:30pm, Sa-Su 9:30am-noon and 2-7pm. MC/V.

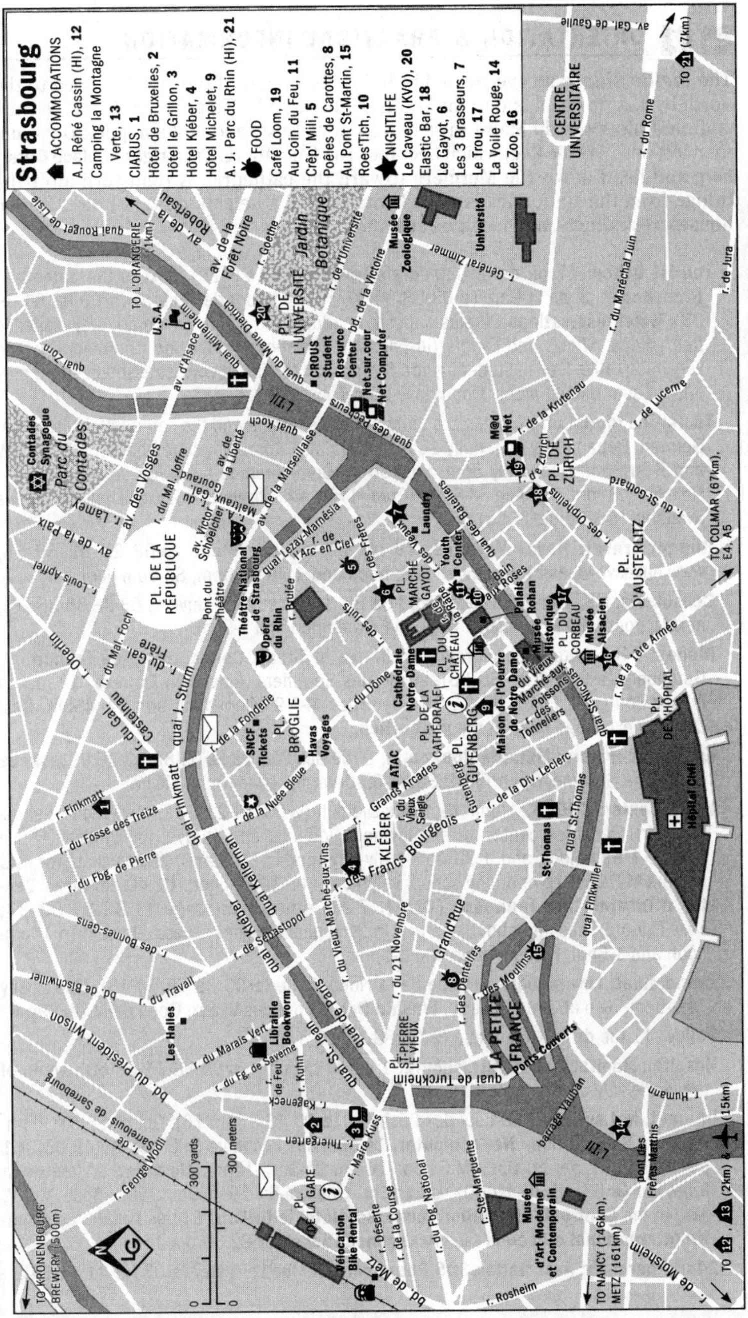

Strasbourg
ACCOMMODATIONS
A.J. Réné Cassin (HI), 12
Camping la Montagne Verte, 13
CIARUS, 1
Hôtel de Bruxelles, 2
Hôtel le Grillon, 3
Hôtel Kléber, 4
Hôtel Michelet, 9
A. J. Parc du Rhin (HI), 21
FOOD
Café Loom, 19
Au Coin du Feu, 11
Crêp' Mili, 5
Poêles de Carottes, 8
Au Pont St-Martin, 15
Roes'Tich, 10
NIGHTLIFE
Le Caveau (KVO), 20
Elastic Bar, 18
Le Gayot, 6
Les 3 Brasseurs, 7
Le Trou, 17
La Voile Rouge, 14
Le Zoo, 16
CENTRE UNIVERSITAIRE
Université
Musée Zoologique
PL. DE L'UNIVERSITÉ
Jardin Botanique
CROUS Student Resource Center
Net.sur.cour
Net Computer
M@d Net
PL. DE ZURICH
PL. D'AUSTERLITZ
Parc du Contades
Contades Synagogue
U.S.A.
TO L'ORANGERIE (1km)
PL. DE LA RÉPUBLIQUE
Théâtre National de Strasbourg
Opéra du Rhin
Pont du Théâtre
PL. BROGLIE
SNCF Tickets
Havas Voyages
Cathédrale Notre Dame
PL. DE LA CATHÉDRALE
PL. DU CHÂTEAU
PL. MARCHÉ GAYOT
Youth Center
Laundry
Palais Rohan
Musée Historique
PL. DU CORBEAU
Musée Alsacien
Maison de l'Oeuvre de Notre Dame
PL. GUTENBERG
PL. KLÉBER
ATAC
PL. DE L'HÔPITAL
Hôpital Civil
St-Thomas
Grand'Rue
LA PETITE FRANCE
Ponts Couverts
PL. ST-PIERRE LE VIEUX
Les Halles
Librairie Bookworm
PL. DE LA GARE
Vélocation Bike Rental
Musée d'Art Moderne et Contemporain
TO KRONENBOURG BREWERY (500m)
TO NANCY (146km), METZ (161km)
TO 12, 13 (2km) & (15km)
TO COLMAR (67km), E4, A5
TO 21 (7km)
0 300 yards
0 300 meters
Ill
quai Koch
quai des Pêcheurs
quai des Bateliers
quai St-Nicolas
quai St-Thomas
quai Finkwiller
quai de Turckheim
quai St-Jean
quai de Paris
quai Kléber
quai Kellermann
quai Finkmatt
quai J. Sturm
quai Lezay-Marnésia
quai Zorn
quai Rouget de Lisle
quai Mullenheim
bd. du Président Wilson
bd. de Metz
bd. de la Victoire
av. des Vosges
av. de la Paix
av. d'Alsace
av. de la Liberté
av. de la Forêt Noire
av. de la Robertsau
av. de la Marseillaise
av. du Gal. de Gaulle
r. des Francs Bourgeois
r. de la Nuée Bleue
r. du Fosse des Treize
r. du Fbg. de Pierre
r. du 21 Novembre
r. du Vieux Marché-aux-Vins
r. de la Div. Leclerc
r. des Juifs
r. du Dôme
r. des Frères
r. de la 1ère Armée
r. de Zurich
r. de la Krutenau
r. de Lucerne
r. du Maréchal Juin
r. de Rome
r. du Général Zimmer
r. de l'Université
r. Goethe
r. de Molsheim
r. Rosheim
r. du Fbg. National
r. Ste-Marguerite
barrage Vauban
pont des Frères Matthis
r. de Jura
r. de St-Gothard
r. des Orphelins
r. des Dentelles
r. des Moulins
r. du Travail
r. de Sébastopol
r. des Bonnes-Gens
bd. de Bischwiller
r. Finkmatt
r. du Gal. Castelnau
r. Oberlin
r. Louis Apffel
r. Lamey
r. du Mal. Joffre
r. du Mal. Foch
r. de la Fonderie
r. Brulée
r. de l'Arc en Ciel
r. des Veaux
r. Marché-aux-Poissons
r. des Tonneliers
r. Gutenberg
r. du Vieux Seigle
r. Grandes Arcades
r. du Marais Vert
r. du Fg. de Saverne
r. Kuhn
r. Kageneck
r. Thiergarten
r. Maire Kuss
r. George Wodli
r. de Sarrelouis
r. de Sarrebourg
r. Déserte
r. de la Course
r. Humann
ALSACE

✈ 🛈 ORIENTATION & PRACTICAL INFORMATION

The *vieille ville* is an eye-shaped island in the center of the city, bounded to the north by a large canal and to the south by the river Ill. To get there from the train station, follow rue du Maire-Kuss across pont Kuss, and make a quick right and then left onto **Grande Rue,** which becomes rue Gutenberg. Turn right at **place Gutenberg** and head down rue Mercière toward the cathedral. A right turn after the bridge from the station leads to **La Petite France,** a neighborhood of old Alsatian houses, restaurants, and narrow canals.

Tourist Office: 17 pl. de la Cathédrale (☎03 88 52 28 28), next to the cathedral. **Branches** at pl. de la Gare (☎03 88 32 51 49) and pont de l'Europe (☎03 88 61 39 23). **Hotel reservations** €2 plus deposit. In addition to a good free map, they dispense free guides: *Shows and Events* (in English), *Strasbourg Magazine* (in French), or the very informative French student guide *Strassbuch* (online at www.strassbuch.com), plus info on surrounding areas. Open daily 9am-7pm. MC/V.

Tours: The **tourist office** organizes tours of the *vieille ville* and the cathedral, in French or German. Departs July-Aug. daily 10:30am, Sa also 3pm; May-June and Sept.-Oct. Tu-W and F-Sa 3pm; Dec. daily 3pm, Su also 4:30pm. Themed tours Apr.-June and Sept.-Nov. Sa 2:30pm; July-Aug. M-Sa 6:30pm. 1½hr. €6, students €3. English audio guides available (€6, students €3). MC/V.

Budget Travel: Havas Voyages, 29 rue de la Nuée Bleue (☎08 25 82 50 55; www.havasvoyages.fr). Open M-F 9am-noon and 1:30-6:30pm, Sa 9am-noon.

Consulates: US, 15 av. d'Alsace (☎03 88 35 31 04, cultural services 03 88 35 38 20), next to pont John F. Kennedy. Open M-F 9am-noon and 2-5pm.

Money: 24hr. automatic currency exchange at **Crédit Commerciale de France,** pl. Gutenberg (☎03 88 37 88 00), at rue des Serruriers. **American Express,** 19 rue du Francs-Bourgeois (☎03 88 21 96 59). Open M-F 9:30am-noon and 2-5:45pm. Best currency exchange rates at the **post office.**

English Bookstore: Librairie Bookworm, 3 rue des Pâques (☎03 88 32 26 99), off rue du fbg. de Saverne. Open Tu-F 9:30am-6:30pm, Sa 10am-6pm. MC/V.

Youth Center: CROUS, 1 quai du Maire-Dietrich (☎03 88 21 28 00; www.crous-strasbourg.fr). Resource center for employment, lodging, and study opportunities. Office open M-F 9am-noon and 1:30-4pm (July-Aug. opens at 10am). Meal tickets for ISIC holders M-F 9am-1pm; during school vacations M-F 10am-noon. €2.40 per meal. **Centre d'Information Jeunesse (CIJA),** 7 rue des Ecrivains (☎03 88 37 33 33; www.cija.org), has info about jobs and lodging plus **Internet** access. Open M-Th 10am-noon and 1-6pm, F 10am-noon and 1-5pm.

Laundromat: Lavomatique, 10 rue de la Nuée Bleue (☎03 88 75 54 18). Open daily 7am-9pm. Also at 2 rue Déserte. **Wash'n Dry,** 13 rue des Veaux. Open daily 7am-9pm.

Police: 11 rue de la Nuée Bleue (☎03 88 15 37 37).

Hospital: Hôpital Civil de Strasbourg, 1 pl. de l'Hôpital (☎03 88 11 67 68), south of the *vieille ville* across the canal.

Internet: Net.sur.cour, 18 quai des Pêcheurs (☎03 88 35 66 76). Open M-F 10:30am-9:30pm, Sa-Su 2-8pm. **Net computer,** 14 quai des Pêcheurs (☎03 88 36 46 05). €1 per 30min, €2 per hr. Open M-F noon-10pm, Sa-Su 2-10pm. **M@d Net,** 21 rue de la Krutenau (☎03 88 36 10 00). €2 per hr. Open M-Sa 10am-9pm, Su 2-8pm. MC/V. Also at the **Centre d'Information Jeunesse, Hôtel le Grillon,** €1 per 15min., and **Centre International d'Accueil** (see **Accommodations**) for €2.30 per 15min.

24hr. Pharmacy: Association SOS Pharmacie, 10 rue Leicester (☎03 88 41 11 34).

Post Office: 5 av. de la Marseillaise (☎03 88 52 31 00). Open M-F 8am-7pm, Sa 8am-noon. **Branches** at cathedral (open M-F 8am-6:30pm, Sa 8am-5pm), at 1 rue de la Fonderie (open M-F 8am-6:30pm and Sa 8:30am-noon), and at 1 pl. de la Gare. (Open M-F 8am-7pm, Sa 8am-noon.) All have **currency exchange. Poste Restante:** 67074. **Postal code:** 67000.

⌐ ACCOMMODATIONS & CAMPING

There are inexpensive hotels all over the city, especially around the train station. Wherever you stay, make reservations early.

⬛ Centre International d'Accueil de Strasbourg (CIARUS), 7 rue Finkmatt (☎03 88 15 27 88; www.ciarus.com). Large, spotless facilities and an international atmosphere. Shower and toilet in all rooms. TV, ping-pong, cafeteria, laundry, and tourism office. Friendly and well-maintained, but with ridiculous Internet prices. "Disco" and "make-your-own-crêpes" nights. Wheelchair access. Breakfast included. Meals €3.50-10. Towels €1.50-2.50. Check-in 3:30pm, call ahead if arriving earlier. Checkout 9am. Reservations advised. 6- to 8-bed dorms €16; 3- to 4-bed dorms €18; 2-bed rooms €21.50. Singles €38. Family rooms €16 per person. MC/V. ❷

Hôtel Kléber, 29 pl. Kléber (☎03 88 32 09 53; www.hotel-kleber.com), steps from the tram line that runs to the station and the airport shuttles. Classy, wide rooms, all with shower, TV, mini-bar, and toilet, some with balconies. Breakfast €6. Reception 7am-midnight. Singles €32-57; doubles €36-66; triples €66-73. AmEx/MC/V. ❹

Hôtel le Grillon, 2 rue Thiergarten (☎03 88 32 71 88; www.grillon.com), 1 block from the station toward the city center. Spacious ski-lodge like rooms above a hip bar where guests get a free drink with a *Let's Go* guide. **Internet** free for 15min. (guests only), €1 per 15min. thereafter. TV in some rooms. Better deals can be found, but this *grillon* has character. Breakfast €7.50. Reception 24hr. Singles €29, with shower €38-53; doubles €36.50/€44-59. Extra bed €10.50. Reservations suggested. DC/MC/V. ❸

Auberge de Jeunesse René Cassin (HI), 9 rue de l'Auberge de Jeunesse (☎03 88 30 26 46), 2km from the station. Turn right from the station onto bd. de Metz, which becomes bd. Nancy and bd. de Lyon, then right onto rue de Molsheim and through the underpass. Be careful here at night. Follow rte. de Schirmeck 1km to rue de l'Auberge de Jeunesse. (30min.) Or, take bus #2 (dir: Illkirch) from the station to Auberge de Jeunesse. The quiet setting by the canal and park is beautiful. Some rooms are spacious with high ceilings and shower and toilet; others are tiny and without facilities. TV room, video games, kitchen, cafeteria, and bar with music and concerts. Friendly young crowd. Breakfast included. Sheets €2. Reception 7am-12:30pm, 1:30-7:30pm, and 8:30-11pm. Curfew 1am. Open Feb.-Dec. 3- to 6-bed dorms €14; singles €32; doubles €44. **Non-members** €2.90 extra. Campground next door. MC/V. ❶

Hôtel Michelet, 48 rue du Vieux Marché aux Poissons (☎03 88 32 47 38). Stellar location near the cathedral with some bargains. Dim hallways lead to carefully decorated, clean rooms; many overlooking a courtyard. Breakfast €4.50. Reception 7:30am-8pm, other hours call ahead. Singles €25, with shower and toilet €36.50; doubles €28/€43; triples €43/€50; quads with shower €55, with toilet €56. Extra bed €6. MC/V. ❷

Auberge de Jeunesse, Centre International de Rencontres du Parc du Rhin (HI), (☎03 88 45 54 20; fax 03 88 45 54 21), on rue des Cavaliers next to the Rhine. 7km from station, but less than 1km from Germany. From the train station, take bus #2 (dir: Pond du Rhin) to Parc du Rhin. (30min.) Go left from the bus stop; rue des Cavaliers is the street with flashing red lights on either side and willow trees on the right side. Follow rue des Cavaliers all the way to the end (18min.). At night the streets are deserted; be careful. Good facilities and great location overlooking the Rhine, with the significant drawback of an unwalkable, 50min. trip to reach the *centre ville*. Volleyball and basketball courts, pool tables, disco, and bar. **Internet** €1 per 15min. Breakfast and sheets included. Reception daily 7am-12:30pm, 2-7:30pm, 8:30pm-7am. Checkout 10am. Fills with school groups in summer; reservations recommended. 3- to 5-bed dorms with shower and toilet €16. **Non-members** €2.90 extra up to first six nights. MC/V. ●

Hôtel de Bruxelles, 13 rue Kuhn (☎03 88 32 45 31; fax 03 88 32 06 22; hotel.bruxelles@wanadoo.fr). Ask to see your room before you take it—some are much smaller than others. Lovely breakfast nook downstairs. Breakfast €5.30. Showers €3. Reception 24hr. 4- to 5-bed rooms €57, with private shower €67; singles and doubles €29/€46; triples €47/€60. Extra bed €8. Jan.-Apr. 10% reduction of some prices. MC/V. ❸

Camping la Montagne Verte, 2 rue Robert Ferrer (☎03 88 30 25 46), down the road from the René Cassin hostel. Spacious and shady riverside campsite. Reception July-Aug. 7am-12:30pm, 1:30-7:30pm, 8:30-10:30pm; Apr.-June, Sept.-Oct., and Dec. 8am-noon and 3:30-7:30pm. Car curfew 10pm. €4.50 per site. €3.40 per person, €1.60 per child under 10. Electricity €3.50. MC/V. ●

◖ FOOD

Local restaurants are known for *choucroute garnie* (sauerkraut with meats), but you also can find delicious €4.50 sausages at stands throughout the city. Other specialties include the ubiquitous *tarte flambée* (much like a thin pizza) and a truckload of local wines from the Route du Vin. The streets around the cathedral are filled with restaurants, particularly **place de la Cathédrale, rue Mercière,** and **rue du Vieil Hôpital.** A little farther away, off pl. Gutenberg, pretty cafés line **rue du Vieux Seigle** and **rue du Vieux Marché aux Grains.** Smaller restaurants in less touristy packages can be found on and around **rue de la Krutenau.** All sorts swarm the cafés and restaurants of tiny **place Marché Gayot,** hidden off rue des Frères. Finer sorts crowd the beautiful, peaceful **quartier des Tonneliers** off rue du Vieux Marché aux Poissons. In **La Petite France,** especially along rue des Dentelles and petite rue des Dentelles, you'll find small **winstubs** (VIN-shtoob)—classic Alsatian taverns with a distinctly German flavor, traditionally affiliated with individual wineries, and characterized by timber exteriors and checkered tablecloths. For anyone tired of sauerkraut and wine, Swiss, German, Indian, Italian, French, and Turkish restaurants reflect Strasbourg's international character. Cheap kebab joints cluster thickly around the train station and on **Grand'Rue. Markets** are held at bd. de la Marne (open Tu and Sa 7am-1pm), pl. de Bordeaux (open Tu and Sa 7am-1pm), pl. de la Gare (open M and Th 10am-6pm), and at many other places in town. Several **supermarkets** are also scattered around the *vieille ville,* including **ATAC,** 47 rue des Grandes Arcades, off pl. Kléber. (☎03 88 32 51 53. Open M-Sa 8:30am-8pm. MC/V.)

▩ **Au Coin du Feu,** 10 rue de la Râpe (☎03 88 35 44 85), between rue des Ecrivains and pl. du Château, presents tasty, voluminous food in a funky but traditional Alsatian interior, where the hip folks start their night. Get a free *kir* if you show your *Let's Go* guide. Two-course dinner *menu* €19.50, *choucroute alsacienne* from €12.50, *tarte flambée* €6.50-10. Open daily noon-2pm and 7-11:30pm. Closed M and Tu lunch. MC/V. ❸

▩ **Crêp' Mili,** 3 rue du Ciel (☎03 88 36 56 88), on a quiet side street off rue des Frères. Fabulous crêpes and *galettes* (€2.50-7.90) served in a stone *cave* dining area. Outdoor seating is available, but this is one atmospheric cellar not to be missed. *Spécialitiés* from €5. Open daily 11:30am-2pm and 6:30-11:30pm. MC/V. ●

▩ **Café Loom,** 33 rue de Zurich (☎03 88 24 26 14). Loom is a laid-back, trendy *tapas* joint with a Latin soundtrack and homemade sangría served at the bar. *Tapas* €1.50-3, sandwiches and quiches from €4, sangría €3.50. Open Tu-F 7am-10pm, Sa 7am-7pm, Su 10am-3pm. MC/V. ●

Au Pont St-Martin, 15 rue des Moulins (☎03 88 32 45 13). At Au Pont St-Martin, you can peer at canals over huge servings of seafood, salad (€7.20), and sauerkraut (€11.50). This popular, consummately German *winstub* in La Petite France is picturesque enough to be featured on postcards of the area. Midweek lunch *menu* €9.20, beer €2.60. Open daily June-Aug. 11:30am-10:30pm; Sept.-May 11:30am-4pm and 6:30-10:30pm. AmEx/MC/V. ❸

Poêles de Carottes, 2 pl. des Meuniers (☎03 88 32 33 23). Poêles de Carottes is a charming, well-priced vegetarian restaurant in the heart of Strasbourg's attractive La Petite France district. Lunch *menu* €9.50, hearty salads €8.50-10.50, vegetable *gratins* €8.50-10.80, pizza €6.30-10.50, pasta €6.50-8.80. Open daily noon-2pm and 7-10:30pm. MC/V. ❷

Roes'Tich, 6 rue du Bain aux Roses (☎03 88 36 25 59). Family-style local favorite serves Swiss specialties, in particular *Roesti*, grated potatoes with a topping (€8.80-10.20). Reservations recommended. Open July-Aug. Tu-Sa noon-2pm and 6:30-10:30pm; Sept.-June daily. MC/V. ❷

🗒 SIGHTS

▩ **CATHÉDRALE DE STRASBOURG.** In Strasbourg, nothing is nearly as impressive, culturally defining, or, well, *tall* as the majestic cathedral. Towering 142m into the sky, Victor Hugo's favorite "prodigy of the gigantic and the delicate" took 260 years to build (it was completed in 1439). **Reliefs** around the three portals depict the life of Christ; the left one shows the Virtues stabbing the Vices. In the southern transept, the massive **Horloge Astronomique** is a testament to the wizardry of 16th-century Swiss clockmakers. At 12:30pm, tiny apostles march out of the face, and a rooster greets a mechanical St. Peter. The tiny automata in an organ chest in the nave once ranted at the minister, much to the amusement of medieval parishioners. The cathedral's central spire, the **Pilier des Anges,** depicts the Last Judgment. Goethe scaled its 332 steps regularly to cure his fear of heights. (☎03 88 24 43 34. *Cathedral open M-Sa 7-11:40am and 12:40-7pm, Su 12:45-6pm. Tours July-Aug. M-F 10:30am, 2pm, 3pm; Sa 10:30am and 2pm; Su 2 and 3pm. €3. Horloge tickets (€0.80) on sale at the postcard stand inside the cathedral 9-11:30am, at the south entrance 11:30am-12:25pm. July-Aug. arrive 30min. early. Choral rehearsals and Gregorian chants Su; check schedule for times. Tower open for climbing Apr.-Oct. M-F 9am-5:30pm, Sa-Su 10am-5:30pm; Nov.-Mar. M-F 9am-4:30pm, Sa-Su 10am-4:30pm. €3, children and students €1.50.)*

▩ **LA PETITE FRANCE.** This lovely old tanners' district, tucked away in the southwest corner of the city center, is characterized by slender steep-roofed houses with carved wood façades in popping pastel colors. Locals flock to this pretty and relaxed neighborhood, chatting in sidewalk cafés to the sound of accordion music and the gurgle of river water. A host of restaurants and *winstubs* also make this the perfect quiet dining spot; many eateries have views of the district's channels.

PALAIS ROHAN. This magnificent 18th-century building houses three small museums. The **Musée des Arts Décoratifs,** once a residence for cardinals, was looted during the Revolution, then refurbished for Napoleon in 1805. The majority of a visit is spent whistling appreciatively at the beautifully restored imperial rooms with gold-encrusted ceilings and immense monochrome expanses of marble, including the bedroom of the Emperor himself. Ask to borrow an informative English guidebook. The unusually appealing and comprehensive **Musée Archéologique** illustrates the history of Alsace from 600,000 BC to AD 800 (written guide in Eng., free audio guide in Fr.). Upstairs, the **Musée des Beaux Arts** displays a solid collection of art from the 14th to the 19th centuries, mostly by Italian and Dutch painters like

Giotto, Botticelli, Raphaël, Rubens, Van Dyck, El Greco, and Goya. *(2 pl. du Château. ☎03 88 52 50 00. Open Su-M and W-Sa 10am-6pm. Each museum €4, students €2.50. A one-day pass for every museum in Strasbourg is €6, students €3. Other combos available.)*

MUSÉE D'ART MODERNE ET CONTEMPORAIN. Opened in 1998, this steel and glass behemoth holds a small but impressive collection of late 19th-century, Impressionist, cubist, and 20th-century painting. Monet, Gauguin, Picasso, Dufy, Kandinsky, and Ernst are featured, though most of the space is devoted to extensive temporary exhibits. Some are more interesting than others, so check the website before going. *(1 pl. Hans Jean Arp. ☎03 88 23 31 31; www.musees-strasbourg.com. Open Tu-Su 10am-6pm. €5, students €2.50, under 18 free. Brochure available in Eng.)*

L'ORANGERIE. Strasbourg's largest, most spectacular park, L'Orangerie was designed by the famed Le Nôtre in 1692 after he cut his teeth on Versailles. It has room for picnics, ponds and waterfalls to be explored by rowboat, a stork-filled mini-farm, a zoo, go-carts, and Le Nôtre's original skateboard park. The vastness of this park makes it seem about as touristed as Uranus. The **Pavillon Joséphine** holds free concerts on summer evenings. *(Take bus #6, 23, 30, or 72 to l'Orangerie. Concerts Su-Tu and Th-Sa 8:30pm.)*

OTHER SIGHTS. The **Palais de l'Europe** houses the Council of Europe and the European Parliament, EU's governing bodies, on av. de l'Europe, at the northwest edge of the Orangerie. Due to the events of September 11, the buildings are closed to the public. The 14th- to 16th-century mansion housing the **Maison de l'Oeuvre Notre-Dame** is dim and stale-smelling, whose main attractions are the glowing rooms of 12th- to 14th-century stained glass. *(3 pl. du Château. ☎03 88 52 50 00. Open Tu-Su 10am-6pm. €4; students, seniors, and large families €2 per person, under 18 free.)* The **Kronenbourg brewery** gives visitors a taste of Germany in France, with tours in French, English, or German; a look at the different stages of brewing; and a tasting session. *(68 rte. d'Oberhausbergen. ☎03 88 27 41 59. Take tram to Ducs d'Alsace. Call for hours and to make reservations. €3, ages 12-18 €2, under 12 free.)* **Heineken** offers free tours of its brewery in French, English, and German, but only for groups and by advance reservation. *(4-10 rue St-Charles, Schiltgheim. ☎03 88 19 59 53. Call to schedule M-F 8am-noon and 1:30-4:30pm.)*

■ NIGHTLIFE

Bars are everywhere. **Place Kléber** attracts a student crowd. **Rue des Frères** and the tiny **place du Marché Gayot** wake up with a mixed crowd after 10pm. The area between **place d'Austerlitz** and **place de Zurich,** across the canal from the *vieille ville,* is slightly seedy but certainly lively. Numerous bars and cafés cluster there, particularly around the tiny **place des Orphelins.** You may want to travel in a group. Grab a free copy of *Le Strassbuch* (in French) from the tourist office, which lists the many nightclubs Strasbourg has to offer.

- **Elastic Bar,** 27 rue des Orphelins (☎03 88 36 11 10). One of the most energetic scenes in the city. Students and regulars fill an interior that took grunge to heart, with graffiti, winding steel staircases, and metal stickers plastered on the walls. Friendly and laid-back, with reggae in the background. Beer from €2.80. Open M-Th 5pm-3am, F 5pm-4am, Sa 6pm-4am, Su 6pm-3am. MC/V.

- **Le Gayot,** 18 rue des Frères (☎03 88 36 31 88). The squished terrace of this friendly bar opens onto lively pl. Marché Gayot and draws a young crowd during the school year, when students frequently play jazz piano. Live music Sept.-June on Th. Open daily June-Aug. 11am-1am; Sept.-May 11am-midnight. MC/V.

Le Zoo, 6 rue des Bouchers (☎03 88 24 55 33). Theme nights, parties, bouncing tunes make this the best gay bar in town. Kitschy décor and a friendly welcome leave little room for improvement. Beer €2.20. Open daily 6pm-2am. AmEx/MC/V.

Le Trou, 5 rue des Coules (☎03 88 36 91 04). Feels like a 40s speakeasy, entertaining raucous students and other young people in a crowded cellar surrounded by dark brick walls and curved ceilings. Not busy until quite late. Beer €2.50-3.50. Open daily July-Aug. 8:30am-4am; Sept.-June 9:30am-4am. AmEx/MC/V.

Les 3 Brasseurs, 22 rue des Veaux (☎03 88 36 12 13). Les 3 Brasseurs is a micro-brewery that serves four different home brews (€4.30 per glass; cheaper beer available at €2), and good food (salad €6.10), all in a dark red and wood interior. A fine place to relax with friends. Happy hour daily 5-7pm with 2 drinks for the price of 1. Open daily 11:30am-1am. MC/V.

Le Caveau (KVO), 1 pl. de l'Université (☎03 88 15 73 70). One of the best-known night clubs in Strasbourg, especially for its student-heavy crowd. Le Caveau is located directly underneath the Strasbourg University restaurant and goes especially wild for any old holiday that comes along. Cover charges vary with the frequent *soirées*. Beer €4. Open nightly 10pm-4am.

La Voile Rouge, quai Mathis (☎03 88 36 22 90), one of the few gay and lesbian night-clubs in Strasbourg, has outfitted a large barge (with a red sail) with a lounge and dance floor. Beer €5, liquor €8. Open Th-Su 11pm-5am.

ENTERTAINMENT

The **Orchestre Philharmonique de Strasbourg** performs at the Palais de la Musique et des Congrès, located just behind pl. de Bordeaux. (Tickets ☎03 88 15 09 09, info 03 88 15 09 00. Student tickets half-price or less. Oct.-June. MC/V.) The **Théâtre National de Strasbourg,** 1 av. de la Marseillaise, performs Sept.-May. (☎03 88 24 88 24; www.tns.fr. €16-23, students €11.70-16. Th shows €8. MC/V.) The **Opéra du Rhin,** 19 pl. Broglie, features opera and ballet in its 19th-century hall. (☎03 88 75 48 23. Tickets €11.60-55, students under 26 half-price; rush tickets from €16, students from €12. MC/V.)

Summer in Strasbourg is all about the **place de la Cathédrale,** which becomes a stage every afternoon and evening for all manner of performers, mostly a troupe of musicians, flame-eaters, acrobats, and mimes. The **cathedral** itself hosts organ concerts inside throughout the summer. (Free concerts June-Sept. Su 5:30pm. Organ recitals W 8:30pm. €11, students €5.50.) Also on summer nights, pl. du Château hosts the **Nuits de Strass,** a funny and free projection show; **water-jousters** match weapons on the River Ill outside the Palais Rohan.

FESTIVALS

One of Strasbourg's most popular festivals is the annual June **Festival de Musique de Strasbourg,** a two-week extravaganza attracting some of Europe's best classical musicians. The **Festival de Jazz,** spanning the first two weeks of July, draws giants of the jazz world. (Tickets €15, students €11.50, under 5 €5.50.) For information on either of these two festivals, contact the helpful Wolf Musique, 24 rue de la Mésange (☎03 88 32 43 10). L'Orangerie park hosts countless free concerts in the lavish Pavillion Joséphine June-Aug. Su-Tu and Th-Sa 8:30pm.

Musica, a contemporary music festival held annually from mid-September to early October in Strasbourg, includes an array of popular concerts, operas, and films. (☎03 88 23 47 23.) For info on exhibitions, concerts, and films, visit www.musees-strasbourg.org.

ALSACE

NEAR STRASBOURG

SAVERNE

The 3rd-century Roman travel guide *Itinerarium Antonin* recommended Saverne (pop. 12,700) as a "good place to rest." This 21st-century guidebook agrees. According to legend, an appreciative *licorne* (unicorn) rendered Saverne's Roman baths magical with his touch; the pretty, fountain-happy passages of the *vieille ville* are still brimming with his watery vitality. Party animals may be disappointed here, but others who stay within the cobbled town center will be dazzled by the beautiful gardens and canals.

🏛🚂 ORIENTATION & PRACTICAL INFORMATION. Trains leave from pl. de la Gare. (☎08 92 35 35 35. Ticket office open M-F 6:30am-7:30pm, Sa 8:30am-6pm, Su 10:15am-8:30pm.) To: Metz (1hr., 5 3per day, €14.80); Nancy (1hr., 8-9 per day, €13.80); Paris (4-6 hrs.; 6 per day; €39); and Strasbourg (30min., 29 per day, €6.90). Ask at ticket window for luggage storage. SNCF **buses** run from the station to nearby Molsheim, Hugueneau, and Marlenheim (€2-5.50). **Rent bikes** at Ohl, 10 rue St-Nicolas (☎03 88 91 17 13. Open Tu-F 9:30am-noon and 2-7pm, Sa 9:30am-noon and 2-5:30pm. Half-day €11.50, full day €14.50. ID deposit. AmEx/MC/V.)To get to the **tourist office,** 37 Grande Rue, from the train station, cross the square and bear right (diagonally) onto rue de la Gare. Cross the Zorn River and take a left onto Grande Rue. A helpful, English-speaking staff dispenses town and trail maps, and info on local sights, accommodations, and hiking (most available in English). (☎03 88 91 80 47; info@ot-saverne.fr. Open M-Sa 9:30am-noon and 2-6pm; May-Sept. also Su 10am-noon and 2-5pm.) Other services include: **banks** with **ATMs** and **currency exchange** along Grande Rue, a **Société Générale** on pl. de Gaulle (☎03 88 71 57 00; open Tu, Th, F 8:30am-noon and 1:30-5:45pm, W 8:30am-noon and 1:30-6:20pm, Sa 8:30am-noon), a **Wash'n'Dry** at 7 rue des Clés (open daily 7am-9pm), **police** at 29a rue St-Nicolas, off the end of Grande Rue (☎03 88 91 19 12; call here for the **pharmacie de garde**), **Hôpital Ste-Catherine** at 19 côte de Saverne, east of the town center, near the forest (☎03 88 71 67 67), **Internet** at Fight Club, 3 rue des Murs, just off rue Poincaré (☎03 88 03 14 47; €3 per hr.; open M-F 8am-10pm, Sa 10am-1am), or at Cappadoce, 5 rue des Clés (☎03 88 71 06 91; €3 per hr.; open daily 10am-1am. €2 for 30min.), and a **post office** at 2 pl. de la Gare. (☎03 88 71 56 40. Open M-F 8am-noon and 1:30-6pm, Sa 8am-noon.) **Postal code:** 67700.

🏠🍴 ACCOMMODATIONS & FOOD. The Auberge de Jeunesse ❶ occupies the 4th floor of the Château des Rohan, right in the center of town. Recently renovated but crowded rooms have amazing views. (☎03 88 91 14 84; fax 03 88 71 15 97; aj.saverne@wanadoo.fr. Internet. Breakfast €3.30. Sheets € 2.80. Reception 8-10am and 5-10pm; ask for a key and code if you plan to be out late. Lockout 10am-5pm. Curfew 10pm. Reserve during summer. 8-bed dorms €8.40 per person; €2.90 extra for **non-members** the first 6 nights. Closed part of Dec. and Jan. MC/V.) **Hôtel National ❸,** 2 Grande Rue, is located just a 2min. walk from the station and a 2min. walk from the center of town. Rooms are clean and spacious, if not exactly elegant, and they come fully loaded with TV, toilet, and shower/bath. (☎03 88 91 14 54; fax 03 88 71 19 50. Breakfast €6. Reception daily 6:30am-midnight. Singles €38-43; doubles €43-47; triples €54-57. MC/V.) **Camping de Saverne ❶,** 40 rue du Père Libermann, is a three-star campground near tennis courts, trails to the Vosges, and good views. (☎03 88 91 35 65. Reception Apr.-Sept. 7am-10pm. Tax and insurance €0.30 extra. €3.20 per person, children €1.70; €2 per tent, €2.90 with car. Electricity €2.50. MC/V.)

Most food options, like everything else here, can be found along **Grande Rue,** including kebab stands and a **Coop** supermarket, 118 Grande Rue. (Open M-F 8am-12:15pm and 3-7pm, Sa 8am-12:15pm and 2:30-5pm. MC/V.) Look for the **market** at pl. de Gaulle. (Th mornings, with a smaller version Tu and Sa.) 🗟**Muller Oberling ❶,** 66-68 Grande Rue, is a charming *salon de thé* that provides a bit of atmospheric Saverne, outdoors in good weather. Come for the quiche (€2.30), *tarte à l'oignon,* pizza (€3), an exceptional range of baked goods, and great views of the *place.* (☎03 88 91 13 30. Open M-F 7am-7pm, Sa 7am-6pm, Su 7am-12:30pm and 1:30-6pm; July-Aug. Su no break for lunch. More extensive *plats* available €7-10. MC/V.) **S'zawermer Stuebel ❷,** 4 rue des Frères, serves filling pasta (€6.90-7.40), pizzas (€6-9.20), and *Rapzepfles* (potatoes with flour, €7.80-13.20) on a shady terrace and in a tiny converted wine cellar with vaulted ceilings. (☎03 88 71 29 95. Open daily 11:30am-2:30pm and 6:30-10:30pm. MC/V.)

🖸🎭 **SIGHTS & ENTERTAINMENT.** Site of the famous Affair of the Necklace, the **Château des Rohan** spreads its elegant Neoclassical arms along pl. de Gaulle in the center of town. Less scandalously, the château now contains a dry archeological museum and the engaging **Musée de Louise Weiss,** a tribute to the local feminist, journalist, and Resistance fighter. (Both open mid-June to mid-Sept. Su-M and W-Sa 10am-noon and 2-6pm; Mar. to mid-June and mid-Sept. to Nov. Su-M and W-Sa 2-5pm; Dec.-Feb. Su 2-5pm. €2.50, students €1.70.) The "City of Roses," Saverne's pride and joy is its **Roseraie,** a botanical garden along the banks of the Zorn off route de Paris. In 1993, the garden christened a new rose variety—appropriately tall and prickly—the "Louise Weiss." The first Saturday in August and March sees the **Cours de Greffe,** a contest for the most exquisite hybrid rose, while an exposition of new rose varieties takes up the last Sunday of August. (Open June to mid-July daily 9am-7pm, mid-July to mid-Sept. 10am-6pm. €2.50.)

On Friday and Saturday nights from July to August, the Château opens up for themed performances and walks around the grounds. (€13, more with a meal included, reserve at the tourist office.) A mellow pub scene lines Grande Rue. **Le Commerce,** 3 pl. de Gaulle, provides the mid-20s set with a slick décor and a hip, attractive staff. (☎03 88 02 05 37. Open M-Sa 10am-1:30am, Su 11am-10pm. Beer from €2.50, food from €2. MC/V.) Try some *Bière de la Licorne,* produced in Saverne and available at most pubs along Grande Rue.

🥾 **HIKES.** One of Saverne's greatest assets is an endless network of forested **hiking** and **biking** trails. Club Vosgien maintains phenomenal trails and runs hikes in the area; ask the tourist office for info. Bikers can pick up the free brochure *Cyclo Tourisme,* (available in English), which includes a map and suggested routes, from the tourist office. Some trails are best left to experts, but many are quite welcoming to the non-Shirpa set. All levels can take on the 45min. jaunt through shaded woods to the lovely 12th-century castle **Le Haut Barr;** pick up a map at the tourist office and follow rue du Haut Barr (D17) southwest. Nearby is the **Tour du Télégraphe Chappe,** the first telegraph tower along the Paris-Strasbourg line. (☎03 88 52 98 99. Open June to mid-Sept. Tu-Su noon-6pm. €2.30, children €1.80.)

ROUTE DU VIN (WINE ROUTE)

The vineyards of Alsace flourish along a 150km corridor along the foothills of the Vosges from Strasbourg to Mulhouse known as the Route du Vin. The Romans were the first to ferment Alsatian grapes. Today Alsatians sell over 150 million bottles yearly. Hordes of tourists are drawn to the medieval villages along the route, by picture-book half-timbered houses and wineries giving free *dégustations.*

ON THE MENU

THE GOÛT DU VIN

You've been in France for two weeks and thus far you've managed to avoid looking like an amateur by waving vaguely at your menu and demanding, "of course...ahem...the most obvious choice for this meal...right... *there*." But the wine lists along the Route du Vin are more daunting than your average *carte*. It's time to learn if the wine you've been drinking was a *première cuvée* or just has a *bouquet* of walnuts and dirty old socks:

Gewurztraminer: This dry, aromatic white wine has been called "The Emperor of Alsatian wines." Drink it as an apéritif, with foie gras, pungent cheeses, or Indian, Mexican, or Asian cuisine.

Riesling: Considered one of the world's best white wines, Riesling is fruity, dry, and drunk with white meats, *choucroute*, and fish.

Sylvaner: From an Austrian grape, Sylvaner is a light, fruity, slightly sparkling white that goes well with seafood, *charcuterie*, and salads.

Muscat: A sweet and highly fruity white wine, often an apéritif.

Pinot family: *Pinot Blanc* is an all-purpose white wine for chicken, fish, and all sorts of appetizers; *Pinot Gris* is a smoky, strong white wine that can often take the place of a red wine in accompanying rich meats, roasts, and game; and *Pinot Noir*, the sole red wine of the Alsatian bunch, tastes of cherries and complements red meats.

Spread out over nearly 100 towns, though, these tourists still leave room quiet exploration and an authentic Alsatian experience.

Consider staying in **Colmar** (p. 368) or **Sélestat** (p. 366), larger towns that anchor the southern Route. Buses run frequently from Colmar to surrounding towns, but smaller northern towns are a little more difficult to get to. **Car rental** from Strasbourg or Colmar smooths out transportation problems, but would drain any wallet. **Biking**, especially from Colmar, is only for those with the stamina to gut out lengthy journeys, but trails and turn-offs are well marked. **Trains** connect Sélestat, Molsheim, Barr, Colmar, and Mulhouse. Country roads have minimal sidewalks for walking. The best source of info on regional *caves* is the **Centre d'Information du Vin d'Alsace,** 12 av. de la Foire aux Vins, at the Maison du Vin d'Alsace in Colmar. (☎03 89 20 16 20; fax 03 89 20 16 30. Open M-F 9am-noon and 2-5pm.) Tourist offices in Strasbourg (p. 354) or any of the towns along the Route dispense helpful regional advice, including the excellent *Alsace Wine Route* brochure.

If you only have the time or interest to cover one destination, *Let's Go* advises that you take the bus from the Colmar train station to **Kaysersberg** (see below), one of the Route's prettiest and most characteristic towns.

KAYSERSBERG

If you only have time for one town on the Route, make it Kaysersberg (pop. 2720). The exceptionally charming and relatively untouristed town bursts with flowers during the summer. Its name, from the Latin *Cœsaris Mons* (Caesar's Mountain), dates to Roman times, when it commanded one of the most important passes between Gaul and the Rhine Valley. Many local vineyards can trace their roots to the 13th century. The ruined castle on the hill above town is now privately owned and not open to visitors, but make the hour-long trek to the top for a peek. The pastel-green **Musée Albert Schweitzer,** 126 rue du Général de Gaulle, contains memorabilia retracing the life and works of the Nobel Peace prize winning doctor. The glassblowing studio **Verrerie d'art de Kaysersberg,** 30 rue du Général de Gaulle, offers tours of its workshops. (☎03 89 47 14 97. Workshop open Tu-Sa 10am-noon and 2-6pm, Su 2-6pm. Brochures in Eng. €3, students €2.)

The **tourist office,** 39 rue du Gal. de Gaulle, is in the Hôtel de Ville; cross the bridge behind the bus stop and walk straight to a little square with a fountain. (☎03 89 78 22 78; www.kaysersberg.com. Open mid-June to mid-Sept. M-Sa 9am-12:30pm and 2-6:30pm,

Su 10am-2pm; mid-Sept. to mid-June M-Sa 9am-noon and 1:30-5:30pm. Guided tours in French given July-Aug. M, Th, Su at 10:30am and 3pm. €4.50. Brochures in English, French, German.) Kaysersberg has no train station, but **buses** run to **Colmar** (20min., 1 per hr. M-Sa 6:30am-7pm, €2.30).

RIQUEWIHR

One of the most visited villages along the Route and headquarters of a number of Alsace's biggest wine-shipping firms, the 16th-century walled hamlet of Riquewihr (pop. 1288) maintains a beautiful, accessible *vieille ville*. On the flip side, it's accessible to a distracting number of tourists in summer. The beautiful **Tour des Voleurs** (Tower of Thieves) has an eerily enthralling torture chamber. (Open Apr.-Oct. daily 9:15am-noon and 1:30-6:15pm. €2, under 10 free. Free audio guides available in English, French, German.) Less ghastly, and less enjoyable, is the 13th-century **Tour du Dolder**, rue du Gal. de Gaulle, once a sentinel post, now a museum of local heritage. (Open July-Aug. daily 9:15am-noon and 1:30-6:15pm; Apr.-June and Sept.-Oct. Sa-Su only. €1.50, under 10 free. Sound and light show June-Sept. F at 10pm.; €2, under 10 free.) Riquewihr celebrates a number of alcohol-related holidays. In nearby **Ribeauvillé** the **Foire Aux Vins** takes place on the second-to-last weekend in July, and on the first Sunday of September, music accompanies the clink of glasses during the **Minstrel's Festival,** free *cave* tours and tastings.

The **tourist office,** 2 rue de la Première Armée, offers the usual array of free maps and guides (most available in English and German) and leads free walking **tours** in French. (☎03 89 49 08 40; www.ribeauville-riquewihr.com. Tours July-Aug. Su-M and W-Sa 5pm. Open May-Oct. M-Sa 9am-noon and 2-6pm, Su 10am-noon and 2-5pm; Nov.-Apr. M-Sa 9am-noon and 2-6pm.) Pitch a tent at the small but four-star **Camping Intercommunal ❶,** 1½km from the town center. (☎03 89 47 90 15. Reception July-Aug. 8:30-11am and 2:30-8pm; Apr.-June and Sept.-Dec. 8:30-11am and 3-7pm. Open Apr.-Dec. €3.70, children €1.70, €4 per site. Electricity €4.10.)

BARR

Of the Route du Vin towns, Barr (pop. 6000), on the slopes of Mont Ste-Odile, seems most tied to its grapes: two minutes from the town center, you can sip a glass of white wine while strolling between the rows of vines that created it. To reach the lovely *vieille ville* from the train station, turn right onto rue de la Gare and left onto av. des Vosges. Follow this past the roundabout, bearing left, avoiding what becomes rue de l'Hôpital de la Gare, and continuing for several blocks to rue St-Marc. Take a right here, walk two blocks, and turn right onto rue des Bouchers. From the pl. de l'Hôtel de Ville, a right on rue du Dr. Sultzer leads to several *caves*. To the left is the massive, unornamented **Eglise Protestante,** starting point for the **sentier viticole** (vineyard trail). The highlight of any trip to Barr, the path winds 2km through bright fields of glistening grapes during the summer, walkable alone or in a tourist office tour. (Tours in French July-Aug. Th at 4pm; otherwise by reservation. Free, with complementary tastings.) The local *vigniers* pull out their best bottles for the **Foire aux Vins** in the second week of July, and the first weekend in October brings music, markets, and, of course, more wine for the **Fête des Vendanges.** Call the tourist office for festival info.

Trains to Barr run from Sélestat (25min., 9 per day, €2.90) and Strasbourg (50min., 10 per day, €5.50). The **tourist office,** with an English guide to Barr, is at pl. de l'Hôtel de Ville. (☎03 88 08 66 65; www.pays-de-barr.com. Open Sept.-June M-Sa 9am-noon and 2-6pm; July-Aug. M-F 9am-12:30pm and 1:30-7pm, Sa 9am-noon and 2-6pm, Su 10am-noon and 2-6pm.) Sleep by a tiny vineyard just outside the *centre ville* at two-star **Camping St-Martin ❶,** rue d'Ile. (☎03 88 08 00 45. Reception 9-11am, 3-6pm, and 8-9pm. Adult €3, child €1.50, car €1.70. Electricity €2.70.)

SÉLESTAT

Halfway between Colmar and Strasbourg, Sélestat (pop. 17,200) lacks the crowds of its fellow anchors on the Route du Vin. Once part of the Holy Roman Empire and a center of Renaissance humanism, Sélestat today is a laid-back Alsatian hamlet with a proudly preserved cultural heritage. Light on the "authenticity" of some other Route du Vin towns, but heavy on the beautiful views, Sélestat is a friendly haven of good vines and good vibes.

■ ■ **ORIENTATION & PRACTICAL INFORMATION.** From pl. de la Gare, **trains** (☎08 92 35 35 35) run to Colmar (15min., 20 per day, €3.70) and Strasbourg (30min., 20 per day, €6.50). **Buses** run from the station to a number of surrounding towns (the tourist office provides a guide of bus companies and schedules). The **tourist office,** 10 bd. Gal. Leclerc, in the Commanderie St-Jean, is north of the town center, 10min. from the train station. Go straight on av. de la Gare, through pl. Gal. de Gaulle, to av. de la Liberté. Turn left onto bd. du Maréchal Foch, which becomes bd. Gal. Leclerc after pl. Schaal. The efficient staff doles out expert advice and trilingual guides, and rents **bikes.** (☎03 88 58 87 20; www.selestat-tourisme.com. Open July-Aug. M-F 9:30am-noon and 1:30-6:45pm, Sa 9am-12:30pm and 2-5pm, Su 11am-3pm; Sept.-June M-F 9am-noon and 2-5:45pm, Sa 9am-noon and 2-5pm. Bikes €5.50 for 2hr., €8 per half-day, €12.50 per day, €55 per week. €150 deposit. MC/V.) **Banks** with **ATMs** and **currency exchange** line av. de la Gare and cluster thickly in the *vieille ville* along **rue des Chevaliers.** Access the **Internet** and find work opportunities and listings of lodgings and events at Info Jeunesse, rue du Sel behind the Maison du Pain. (☎03 88 58 85 92; service.jeunesse@ville-selestat.fr. Open M noon-6pm, Tu 1-8pm, W 1-7pm, Th noon-8pm, F 9-7pm. Opens at 9am during school vacations. €2 per hr.) Internet is also available at Médiathèque, 2 espace Gilbert Estève. (☎03 88 58 03 22. Open Tu 5-11pm, W 10am-noon and 2-6pm, Th-F 2-6pm, Sa 10am-noon and 2-5pm. €2 per hr.) Other services include: **police** at bd. du Général Leclerc (☎03 88 58 84 22; call here for the **pharmacie de garde**), a **hospital** is at 23 av. Pasteur (☎03 88 57 55 60), behind the train station, and a **post office,** complete with ATM, at 5 rue de la Poste, near the Hôtel de Ville. (☎03 88 58 80 10. Open M-F 8am-noon and 1:30-6pm, Sa 8am-noon.) **Postal code:** 67600.

■ ■ **ACCOMMODATIONS & FOOD.** The ▓**Hôtel de l'Ill ❷,** 13 rue des Bateliers, on a peaceful residential street in the *vieille ville,* is the best deal in town. From the train station, take av. de la Gare, turn right onto av. de Gaulle, which becomes av. de la Liberté, rue du 4e Zouaves, and rue du Président Poincaré. Make a left onto rue de l'Hôpital and follow it to pl. du Marché aux Choux. Rue des Bateliers is on the right. The hotel packs 15 cozy, colorful, and modern rooms onto three floors presided over by a purring tabby cat. All rooms have shower, toilet, and TV. (☎03 88 92 91 09. Breakfast €5. Reception daily 7am-3pm and 5-11pm. Singles €23; doubles €37.30; triples with bath €55. MC/V.) The bright, simple rooms at **Auberge des Alliés ❸,** 39 rue des Chevaliers, have the best location, above a bustling restaurant in the *vieille ville.* (☎03 88 92 09 34. Breakfast €7. Reception 7am-9am. Reservations suggested. All rooms with toilet, TV, and bath. Singles €46; doubles €50; triples €58; quads €61. *Menu du jour* at the restaurant €14. AmEx/MC/V.) Small, shaded **Camping Les Cigognes ❶,** rue de la Première D.F.L., is outside the ramparts on the southern edge of the *vieille ville,* near tennis courts, parks, and a lake. (Mid-June to Aug. ☎03 88 92 03 98, Sept. to mid-June 03 88 58 87 20. Reception daily July-Aug. 8am-noon and 3-10pm; May-June and Sept.-Oct. 8am-noon and 3-7pm. Open May-Oct. €7.70-9.20 per person, €10.70-12.20 for 2-3 people.)

  Cobbled streets and culinary treats, from *boulangeries* and grocery stores to fine sit-down meals, define the lovely **rue des Chevaliers.** A **market** fills the town center with breads, meats, and produce (Tu 8am-noon); another for **regional specialties** fills sq. A. Ehm. (Sa mornings.) A casual local favorite, with outdoor dining and a dazzling selection of pastries and ice cream flavors, is ▧**J P Kamm ❶**, 15 rue des Clefs. (☎03 88 92 85 25. Pizza €3.40, quiche €4.50, ice cream from €1.20. Open Tu 8am-7pm, W-F 8:30am-7pm, Sa 8am-6pm, Su 8am-1:30pm. MC/V after €8.) **Au Bon Pichet ❸**, 10 pl. du Marché aux Choux, serves up hearty Alsatian fare in a cheerful interior. (☎03 88 82 96 65. Salad from €7.50, *magret de canard* €15.50. Open Su-M 10am-2pm, Tu-Sa 10am-3pm and 6-10pm. AmEx/MC/V.)

▣▨ **SIGHTS & FESTIVALS.** According to legend, Sélestat was founded by a giant. His thigh bone (a mere mammoth tusk, some claim) graces Sélestat's impressive ▧**Bibliothèque Humaniste,** 1 rue de la Bibliothèque, a storehouse for ancient texts from Sélestat's 15th-century humanistic boom. Its collection spans 13th-century students' diligently annotated translations of Ovid to the 16th-century *Cosmographie Introductio*, the first book to mention America by name. (☎03 88 58 07 20. Open M and W-F 9am-noon and 2-6pm, Sa 9am-noon; July-Aug. also Sa-Su 2-5pm. €3.50, students and seniors €2. Audio guide €1.50, available in English) The **FRAC** modern art gallery, 1 espace Gibert Estève, has a rotating schedule of free exhibitions within its massive, sleek glass and intriguing artist-created gardens. (☎03 88 58 87 55; www.culture-alsace.org. Open W-Su 2-6pm.)

The 60m tower of the striking 13th- to 14th-century **Eglise St-Georges,** rue de l'Eglise, at the north end of the *vieille ville,* marks the site where Charlemagne spent Christmas in AD 775. It's worth a peek inside to glimpse the vibrant 14th-century stained glass with Max Ingrand's 1960s additions. Surrounded by ivy-covered homes, the 12th-century **Eglise Ste-Foy** at pl. Marché aux Poissons was constructed by Benedictine monks but later taken over by Jesuits. Hints of the imperial Hohenstaufen family (look for their insignia, a grimacing lion) contrast with striking floor mosaics of the Ganges and Euphrates, rivers key to man's earliest civilizations, and the signs of the zodiac. The **Maison de Pain,** rue du Sel, appropriately located in the former seat of the breadmakers' guild, provides a rollicking and drool-inducing history of breadmaking from 12,500 BC to the present. (☎03 88 58 45 90. Open Jan.-June and Sept.-Nov. Tu-F 10am-noon and 2-6pm, Sa-Su 2-6pm; July-Aug. Tu-F 10am-6pm, Sa-Su 10am-5pm. Dec. daily 10am-7pm. €4.60, students €2.30, under 12 free. MC/V.)

Bars and pubs, like everything else in the *vieille ville,* cluster along **rue des Chevaliers.** For a livelier time, visit the *winstubs* of **rue Poincaré,** just along the old town's southern wall. Sélestat's major festival is the **Corso Fleuri,** or flower festival, on the second Sunday in August. Street artists perform, wine is tasted, and gnomes invade the streets on floats of over 500,000 dahlias. It ends in a giant fireworks display. (Info at corso@ville-selestat.fr, or call the Service Culturel. €6.60, under 12 free.) Home to the first recorded Christmas tree in Europe, Sélestat decks itself out in evergreen for the weeks leading to Dec. 25.

▣ **DAYTRIP FROM SÉLESTAT: HAUT KOENIGSBOURG.** On a rocky outcropping far above the spreading *plaine d'Alsace,* this highly touristed **château** is an early 20th-century masterpiece of medieval forgery. When the people of Sélestat presented Germany's Kaiser Wilhelm II with the ruins of a 12th-century Hohenstaufen fortress demolished in the Thirty Years' War, he rebuilt the once-grand château on its original site. This towering recreation strikes a note of falseness with its undamaged gorgeousness—the unending stream of neck-craning tourists doesn't help—but there is no denying the appeal of the views from the towers, its marvelous architecture, its **Donjon,** and the 15th- to 17th-century collection of medieval weaponry. In the gloriously appointed **Salle des Fêtes,** the *Salle du Kaiser* dazzles with polished decadence. (*☎03 88 82 50 60. By car from Sélestat, take*

*A35 to sortie 17 via Kintzheim or 18 via Saint-Hippolyte, then take N59 via Lièpvre. A taxi is about €20 each way from Sélestat. Ask the Sélestat tourist office advises on other methods of travel. Open daily June-Aug. 9:30am-6:30pm; Apr., May, Sept. 9:30am-5:30pm; Mar., Oct. 9:45am-5pm; Nov.-Feb. 9:45am-noon and 1-5pm. €7, ages 18-25 €4.50, under 18 free, first Su of month Oct.-Apr. free. **Dungeon** tours July-Aug. 10:45am, noon, 1:45pm, 3pm, 4:15pm. €1.50. Free brochures in English, German, French. Audio guide in English, German, French. €4. Free tours in French 11am and 2:30pm.)*

COLMAR

The largest town on the Route du Vin, and the birthplace of Statue of Liberty sculptor Auguste Bartholdi, Colmar (pop. 68,000) contains a smattering of worthwhile sights. The endlessly winding cobbled streets of its bustling *vieille ville* house a typical Alsatian assortment of stubby pastel houses, German street names, and *choucroute*-happy *winstubs*. The city's main attractions include the German Renaissance masterpieces of Grünewald and Haguenauer's *Issenheim Altarpiece* and Schongauer's *Virgin in the Rose Bower*. Colmar makes for a gorgeous summer sojourn—just beware the scads of tourists with this thought.

☐ TRANSPORTATION

Trains: pl. de la Gare (☎08 91 67 68 69). Info office open M-F 9am-7pm, Sa 8:30am-6pm. To: **Lyon** (4½-5½hr., 7 per day, €36); **Mulhouse** (19min., 36 per day, €6.50); **Paris** (5hr., 21 per day, €40.80; only one is direct); **Strasbourg** (40min., 36 per day, €10). AmEx/MC/V.

Buses: on pl. de la Gare, to the right of the station exit. Buses generally go 6am-7pm. Buses run to small towns on the Route du Vin, including **Kayersberg** (9 per day, €5-10) and **Riquewihr** (10 per day, €6-11). The tourist office has a bus schedule in *Actualités Colmar*. Most accept MC/V.

Public Transportation: Trace on rue Unterlinden (☎03 89 20 80 80), in a covered *galerie* to the right of the tourist office. Open M-F 8:30am-12:15pm and 1:30-6:15pm, Sa 8:30am-12:15pm. Tickets €0.90, *carnet* of 10 €6.40. Buses run 6am-8pm; infrequent night *Somnabus* M-Sa 9pm-midnight.

Taxis: pl. de la Gare (☎03 89 41 40 19 or 03 89 80 71 71). 24hr.

Bike rental: Colmar à Bicyclette (☎03 89 41 37 90), an orange building in the pl. Rapp near av. de la République. €3 per half-day, €4.50 per day. €45.50 cash deposit and ID required. Helmets not rented. Open June-Sept. M-Tu and Th-F 8:30am-noon and 2-8pm, W and Sa-Su 8:30am-8pm; Apr.-May and Oct. daily 9am-noon and 2-7pm. Also at **La Cyclothèque**, 31 rte. d'Ingersheim (☎03 89 79 14 18). €5 per half-day; €9.40 per day. €30.50 deposit. Open M-Sa 8:30am-noon and 2-6:30pm. MC/V.

☒ ☐ ORIENTATION & PRACTICAL INFORMATION

To get from the station to the tourist office, go left onto av. de la République. Follow it as it becomes rue Kléber and curves right through pl. du 18 Novembre into the main pl. Unterlinden; the tourist office is straight ahead. (15min.)

Tourist Office: 4 rue des Unterlinden (☎03 89 20 68 92; www.ot-colmar.fr). German- and English-speaking staff has free, hard-to-follow maps, cash-only **currency exchange**, and **reservations service** with a night's deposit. The free *Actualités Colmar* (in French) lists local events. **City tours** in French and German Apr.-Oct. €4, ages 12-16 €2.60. Office open July-Aug. M-Sa 9am-7pm, Su 9:30am-2pm; Apr.-June and Sept.-Oct. M-Sa 9am-6pm, Su 10am-2pm; Nov.-Mar. M-Sa 9am-noon and 2-6pm, Su 10am-2pm.

Police: 6 rue du Chasseur (☎03 89 24 75 00).

Hospital: Hôpital Pasteur, 39 av. de la Liberté (☎03 89 12 40 00).

Internet: Planetcafé, 1-3 rue Mercière (☎03 89 24 45 07). €2.50 per hr., €6 per day, 10% reduction with student ID. Open M 1:30pm-1am, Tu-W and F-Sa 11:30am-1am, Su noon-midnight. **Infr@ Réseau,** 12 rue du Rempart (☎03 89 23 98 45). €3 per hr. Open school year M 2-8:30pm, Tu 10am-1:30pm and 2:30-8:30pm, W 10am-6:30pm, Th 10am-1:30pm and 2:30-8:30pm, F 10am-1:30pm and 2:30-9pm, Sa 10am-9pm, Su 2-7pm; school vacation Su-M 1:30-8pm, Tu-Sa 10am-noon and 1:30-9pm.

Laundromat: 1 rue Ruest. Open daily 7am-9pm.

24hr. Pharmacy: The number for the **pharmacie de garde** is posted at the tourist office.

Post Office: 36-38 av. de la République (☎03 89 24 62 00), across from the Champs de Mars. **Currency exchange, Cyberposte,** and **ATM.** Open M-F 8am-6:30pm, Sa 8:30am-noon. Branch office on the corner of rue Etroite and rue du Nord open M-F 9am-6pm, Sa 9am-noon. **Postal code:** 68000.

ACCOMMODATIONS & CAMPING

Auberge de Jeunesse (HI), 2 rue Pasteur (☎03 89 80 57 39). Take the underground passage in the train station and exit to the right onto rue du Tir; with the railroad tracks on your right, follow it as it becomes av. du Gal. de Gaulle, rue Florimont, and then rue du Val St-Grégoire. Cross the tracks with a right onto rue du Pont Rouge; continue through the intersection on the rte. d'Ingersheim to rue Pasteur. (20min.) Or, take bus #4 (dir: Europe) to Pont Rouge. Plain, crowded dorm rooms and hallway showers, but singles are a bargain. Kitchen. Breakfast included. Sheets €3.50. Reception Apr.-Sept. 7-10am and 5pm-midnight; Oct.-Mar. closes at 11pm. Lockout 10am-5pm. Curfew midnight. June-Aug. reserve in advance. Closed mid-Dec. to mid-Jan. 6- to 8-bed dorms €11.50; singles €16.50; doubles €28. MC/V. **Members only.** ❶

Hôtel Kempf, 1 av. de la République (☎03 89 41 21 72; hotel.kempf.free.fr). Large, simple rooms with a homey atmosphere, in the middle of the *vieille ville.* Breakfast €6. Reception 8am-midnight. Closed mid-Jan. to early Feb. and for two weeks June-July. Singles and doubles €28 plus €2.50 for hall shower, €35 for private shower; triples with bath and toilet €55. MC/V. ❸

Hôtel Primo, 5 rue des Ancêtres (☎03 89 24 22 24; www.hotel-primo.com), near pl. Unterlinden. A stone's throw from the town center, bright, clean rooms have TV and Internet. Breakfast €6. Reception 24hr. Singles and doubles €29-52; triples €44-62. Wheelchair-accessible. MC/V. ❸

La Chaumière, 74 av. de la République (☎03 89 41 08 99), near the station, 10min. from the center of town. Kind hostess lets pleasant, clean, and simple rooms with TV, some around a cement balcony overlooking a courtyard. Breakfast €5. Reception 7am-11pm. 4-6 people with bath €80-86. Singles and doubles €28-30, with shower €37-40; triples €43. Jan.-Feb. prices €2 lower. MC/V. ❸

Camping de l'Ill, rte. de Neuf-Brisach (☎03 89 41 15 94; www.camping-alsace.com), is two laurel-scented kilometers from town on a wooded river in view of the Vosges. Take bus #1 (dir: Horbourg-Wihr) to Plage d'Ill. Reception July-Aug. 8am-9pm; Mar.-June and Sept.-Dec. 8am-8pm. Fills quickly in summer. Open Mar.-Dec. €3 per person, under 10 €1.80; €3.30 per site. Electricity €2.40. ❶

FOOD

Colmar has a wealth of gastronomic goodies for the thrifty diner. There is a **Monoprix** supermarket at pl. Unterlinden (open M-F 8am-8pm, Sa 8am-8pm. AmEx/MC/V), and **markets** in pl. St-Joseph (Sa morning) and pl. de l'Ancienne Douane (Th

ALSACE

morning), a popular café spot. **La Cassolette ❷**, 70 Grand'Rue, prepares an exhaustive selection of delicious sandwiches and large salads (€7-11.50) on a meters-tall menu in its cozy, flower-filled interior. (☎03 89 23 66 30. Open M-Th 8am-7pm and F-Sa 8am-9:30pm. MC/V.) **Brasserie Schwendi ❷**, 23-25 Grand'Rue, is open late and serves generous portions of *tartes flambées* (€5.90-8.10) and other Alsatian staples, as well as a great selection of local beer and wine. (☎03 89 23 66 26. *Plats* €6.40-13. Open daily 10am-12:30am, hot food served noon-11pm. MC/V.) For upper-end Alsatian cuisine in a whimsical setting, head to the **Maison des Têtes ❹**, 19 rue des Têtes, housed inside the famously be-noggined monument. (☎03 89 24 43 43. Reservations suggested in summer. *Choucroutes à la carte* start at €15, *menus* from €25. Open Tu 7-9:30pm, W-Sa noon-2pm and 7-9:30pm, Su noon-2pm. AmEx/MC/V.) For those exploring the local viticulture, a friendly welcome, a great selection of local wines (€3.90 and up), and a 400-year legacy await at **Robert Karcher et Fils**, 11 rue de l'Ours, in the *vieille ville*. (☎03 89 41 14 42. Open daily 8am-noon and 2-6pm. MC/V.)

🅖 SIGHTS

A fair number of Colmar's sights can be seen from outside. Get acquainted with the inimitable (and rather bizarre) traditional style of Alsatian houses, glistening in Easter egg colors, that cluster thickly in the **quartier des Tanneurs** and **la petite Venise** (little Venice). On rue des Têtes, 105 grotesque stone heads stare out from the 1609 **Maison des Têtes**, a must-see for its sheer creepiness. The **Collégiale St-Martin**, pl. de la Cathédrale, boasts an attractive, speckled exterior.

MUSÉE D'UNTERLINDEN. Converted from a 13th-century Dominican convent, this museum holds Mathias Grünewald and Nikolaus Haguenauer's *Issenheim Altarpiece* (1500-1516), which depicts scenes from Christ's life in stunning iconographic detail. The rest of this busy museum's collection is interesting for its wild variety. (*1 rue d'Unterlinden. ☎03 89 20 15 58; www.musee-unterlinden.com. Open May-Oct. daily 9am-6pm; Nov.-Apr. Su-M and W-Sa 9am-noon and 2-5pm. €7, students €5, under 12 free. Free audio guides in Fr., Eng., Ger. MC/V.*)

EGLISE DES DOMINICAINS. This church is little more than a showroom for Martin Schongauer's exquisite *Virgin in the Rose Bower* (1473), a lushly colored panel overwhelmed by an outrageous neo-Gothic frame. German-captioned paintings on the walls date to the German occupation of Alsace during the Franco-Prussian War; their return was a provision of the Treaty of Versailles. (*pl. des Dominicains. Open Apr.-Dec. daily 10am-1pm and 3-6pm. €1.30, students €1, ages 14-16 €0.50.*)

MUSÉE BARTHOLDI. Noted French sculptor Frédéric Auguste Bartholdi (1834-1904), best known for a 47m statue of his mother entitled *Liberty Enlightening the World* (known to some as the Statue of Liberty), has been memorialized in this peculiar museum, whose drawings and models reveal the amusing and distressing fact that nearly all his figures sport a familiar pose, with one arm raised. A giant plaster ear here was a full-scale study for Ms. Liberty's *oreille*. (*30 rue des Marchands. ☎03 89 41 90 60. Open Mar.-Dec. Su-M and W-Sa 10am-noon and 2-6pm. €4, students €2.50. Brochures in English.*)

MUSÉE DU JOUET ET DES PETITS TRAINS. The tiny Museum of Games and Little Trains is full of everything you ever wanted to play with but didn't have when you were a kid. A small town-sized population of dolls, a Cinderella's coach exhibit, and a 1000m network of model trains stand out among the diminutive collection. (*40 rue Vauban. ☎03 89 41 93 10; www.musee-jouet.com. Open July-Sept. daily 9am-6pm; Oct.-June Su-M and W-Sa 10am-noon and 2-6pm. €4, students €3.*)

🎵 🔲 ENTERTAINMENT & FESTIVALS

A wide selection of pubs and bars dot the *vieille ville*, particularly around the Cathédrale and along **Grand' Rue**. *Petits plats* are available into the wee hours at **Brussel's Café**, 18 pl. de la Cathédrale, in a jovial, relaxed atmosphere. (☎03 89 41 43 12. Beer from €2.80. Open daily 11am-1am. MC/V.)

The 10-day **Foire aux Vins d'Alsace** in mid-August is the region's largest wine fair. Popular European musicians hold concerts at 9pm; free tastings and exhibitions take place daily. (☎03 90 50 50 50; www.foire-colmar.com. Festival entrance until 5pm €2.50, after 5pm €5.50. Concerts €12-25.) In the first two weeks of July, the more highbrow **Festival International de Colmar** features two dozen classical concerts and a slew of international talent (Tickets €10-50, under 25 €5-18. For more info call ☎03 89 20 68 97 or visit www.festival-colmar.com.) The Collégiale St-Martin's organists play for the **Heures Musicales** (July-Aug. Tu 8:45pm; €8, students €6.50), and the **Soirées Folkloriques** offer up free folk music concerts Tu nights at 8:30pm in pl. de l'Ancienne Douane (call the tourist office for details).

MULHOUSE

There is just enough going on in this bustling town to avoid dullness, and everyone is welcomed into the local mix. Once an industrial powerhouse, Mulhouse (pop. 110,000) may not have Nancy's architecture or Metz's gardens, but it atones for its bland and occasionally kitschy façades with a slew of fabulous museums.

🔲 🔢 TRANSPORTATION & PRACTICAL INFORMATION

Trains run from bd. Gal. Leclerc to Basel, Switzerland (20min., 7 per day, €6.50); Belfort (30min., 28 per day, €7.40); Paris (4½hr., 8 per day, €44.60); and Strasbourg (1hr., 14 per day, €13.80). Local **buses** run from Porte Jeune, north of the pedestrian district. (☎03 89 66 77 77. Most routes 7am-7pm; evening routes 8:30-11:30pm. Tickets €1.15, *carnet* of 10 €8.20, day pass €3. Tickets available at station or on the bus. MC/V in station.) For a **taxi**, call ☎03 89 45 80 00. (24hr. service. €10-16 from train station to hostel.) **Car rental** is available at **Hertz**, 94 rue de Bâle (☎03 89 65 15 04; MC/V) or at **Budget**, 217 rue de Bâle (☎03 89 65 52 20; MC/V).

The **tourist office**, 9 av. Foch, is two blocks ahead of the right edge of the station, across from a park. Friendly staff provides **reservations service** and walking tour maps. (☎03 89 35 48 48; www.tourism-mulhouse.com. Tours in French and English on request July-Aug. M, W, Sa 10am. €4, under 12 free. Main office open M-F 9am-7pm.) The **annex** is in the Hôtel de Ville. (☎03 89 66 93 13. Open July-Aug. M-Sa 10am-7pm, Su 10am-noon and 2-7pm; Sept.-June daily until 6pm.) Other services include: **banks** with **ATMs** and **currency exchange** around the city, especially pl. de la Réunion; **laundromats** at 1bis rue des Halles (☎06 62 86 55 43; open daily 7am-8pm) and 65 av. de Colmar (☎03 89 42 23 26; open daily 7am-8pm); **police** at 12 rue Coehorn (☎03 89 60 82 00; call here for the **pharmacie de garde**), off bd. de La Marseillaise; a **hospital** at 20 rue du Dr. Laënnec (☎03 89 64 64 64), behind the station; **Internet** at **Semaphore l'Info Jeunesse**, 9 rue du Moulin (☎03 89 66 33 13; www.semafore.org; free for 1hr. per person per day; no email or chat; open M, W-F 8am-5pm and Tu, Sa 10am-5pm), **Noumatrouff**, 57 rue de la Mertzau (☎03 89 32 94 17; free with reservation), and **Brasserie Le Convivial**, 5 rue de la Sinne. (☎03 89 46 11 06. €3.50 per hr. Open daily 7am-1:30am, closes W at 5pm, opens Su at 9am.) The central **post office**, 3 pl. de Gaulle, offers **currency exchange** and has an **ATM**. (☎03 89 66 94 00. Open M-F 8am-7pm, Sa 8am-noon.) A convenient **branch** is located at pl. de la Réunion. (Open M 1-6pm, Tu-Sa 10am-6pm, Su 10am-12:30pm.) **Poste Restante:** 68074. **Postal code:** 68100.

ACCOMMODATIONS

Dirt-cheap rooms in Mulhouse are elusive, but there are many comfortable two-stars. Rates often drop on weekends. The newly refurbished **Auberge de Jeunesse (HI) ❶**, 37 rue d'Ilberg, offers clean, sparse, 3-, 4- and 6-bed rooms with coed bathrooms. Take bus #2 (dir: Coteaux; bus #S1 after 8:30pm) to Salle des Sports. (☎03 89 42 63 28; mulhouse@fuaj.org. Breakfast included. Luggage storage. Linen €2.80. Reception daily July-Aug. 8am-noon and 5pm-midnight; Sept.-June until 11pm. Wheelchair-accessible. Dorms €11.90. MC/V. **Members only.**) Homey, family-run **Hôtel St-Bernard ❸**, 3 rue des Fleurs, conveniently located near the town center, maintains spacious if unspectacular rooms. Guests have access to showers, 32-channel TVs, free Internet, bikes, a small library, and, most importantly, an irresistible St. Bernard. (☎03 89 45 82 32; fax 03 89 45 26 32; stbr@evhr.net. Breakfast €6.50. Reception daily 7am-9:30pm. Singles with shower €31; doubles with shower €33-47. Extra bed €9. AmEx/DC/MC/V.) **Hôtel de Bâle ❸**, 19-21 Passage Central, is a decent alternative with a friendly staff and pleasant rooms but not the extra niceties. (☎03 89 46 19 87; www.ot.ville-mulhouse.fr. Breakfast €6.50. Reception 24hr. TVs in rooms. Singles €28, with shower €33, with shower and toilet €40; doubles €30, with shower or bath and toilet €42-49. MC/V.) The **Camping de l'Ill ❶**, rue Pierre de Coubertin, has an on-site grocery store. (☎03 89 06 20 66. Reception daily 8am-1pm and 3-9pm. Open Apr.-Oct. €3.40 per person, €3.40 per lot. Electricity €3.20. Tax €0.15 per person per day. MC/V.)

FOOD

Mulhouse tries to price like the Swiss (steeply), but the student community necessitates cheap kebab joints and pizzerias (on **rue de l' Arsenal**). A **Monoprix** supermarket at the corner of rue du Sauvage and rue des Maréchaux sells the usual staples. (Open M-F 8:15am-8pm and Sa 8:15am-7pm. MC/V.) A few doors down, **Le Globe** grocery also sells Alsatian *choucroute* (sauerkraut), local sausages, and delicacies from pâté to handmade marzipan. (☎03 89 36 50 50. Open M-Th 9:30am-6:30pm, F-Sa 9am-6:45pm. MC/V.) On a quiet street off the main drag, the unassuming façade of ▣**Le Maharadjin ❸**, 8 rue des Tanneurs, conceals a beautiful dining area, particularly scrumptious Indian cuisine, and friendly service. (☎03 89 56 48 21. Vegetarian specialties €10-18, *saag paneer* €13.50, *menu du jour* €9. Open daily 11:45am-2:30pm and 6:45-11:30pm. MC/V.) **Auberge du Vieux Mulhouse,** pl. de la Réunion, cooks up *La Mulhousienne*, a pork and saurkraut confection with apples (€11.70) in a large, timbered restaurant. (☎03 89 45 84 18. *Menu du jour* €10.80. Open daily 10am-10pm, F-Sa until 11pm. MC/V.) Cheap gyros (€2.50-4), salads (€2.50-4), cold sandwiches (tuna, cheese, or shrimp; €2.50), and desserts (€2.50) await at **Le Bosphore ❶**, 13 av. de Colmar, the prettiest quick-service joint in town. (☎03 89 45 16 00. Open daily 9am-1am. MC/V.)

SIGHTS

Mulhouse's historical district centers around the festive **place de la Réunion,** named for the joyful occasions in 1798 and 1918 when French troops reunited the city with France, though most interesting sights are outside the *vieille ville.*

MUSÉE NATIONAL DE L'AUTOMOBILE. Worshippers of the internal-combustion wonders of the automobile will be in heaven; others will at least find their interest piqued. The brothers Schlumpf once owned the 500-plus mint-condition automobiles on display. The staggering collection ranges from an 1878 steam-driven *Jacquot à Vapeur* to the bubbly electric cars of the future, all shined to a blindingly impressive polish. The room of *chefs d'œuvres* contains cars once owned by the likes of Charlie Chaplin and Emperor Bao Dai. *(192 av. de Colmar. Take bus #1, 4, 11, 13, or 17 north to Musée Auto. ☎03 89 33 23 23; www.collection-schlumpf.com. Free audio guides in English, French, German, and Spanish. Open daily Apr.-Oct. 9am-6pm, Nov.-Mar. 10am-6pm. €10, students €7.50, ages 7-18 €5, under 7 free. Wheelchair-accessible. MC/V.)*

MUSÉE FRANÇAIS DU CHEMIN DE FER. The slick engines and railway cars appeal to the slackjawed gawker in everyone. Peer into the perfectly restored compartments of such railroad legends as the Orient Express. Every hour a massive 1949 steam engine (the last of its kind) chugs away in place to viewers' delight. The one-room **Musée du Sapeur-Pompier** celebrates France's heroic firemen-*cum*-medics. *(2 rue Alfred de Glehn. ☎03 89 42 83 33. Take bus #17 (dir: Musées) from Porte Jeune Place, or #18 (dir: Technopole) from the train station; 1 per hr. On Su, use line M. Open daily May-Sept. 10am-6pm; Oct.-Apr. 10am-5pm. €7.60, students and children 6-18 €4, under 6 free. Wheelchair-accessible. MC/V.)*

ELECTROPOLIS. This zippy new museum introduces kids of all ages to the wonderful world of energy with hands-on exhibits, films, and historical collections. *(55 rue du Pâturage, next to the railway museum. ☎03 89 32 48 60; www.electropolis.tm.fr. Open Tu-Su 10am-6pm. €7.30, students and children 6-18 €5.80, under 6 free; combined ticket with railroad museum €12.20. Wheelchair-accessible. MC/V.)*

TEMPLE DE ST-ETIENNE. The bustling pl. de la Réunion center's on one of France's few Protestant Gothic cathedrals. If the church seems distinctly modern, it's because the Protestants acquired it from the Catholics in 1890, then tore it down and built it back up again. The temple's original 14th-century stained-glass windows, were preserved and now line the galleries. *(☎03 89 66 30 19. Open May-Sept. M and W-Su 10am-noon and 2-6pm, Sa 10am-noon and 2-5pm, Su 2-6pm. Free.)*

OTHER SIGHTS. To escape the ubiquitous machinery in town, visit the blossoming gardens of the **Parc Zoologique et Botanique,** a well-maintained collection of endangered animals and plants. *(Take bus #12, dir: Moenschsberg, to Zoo. ☎03 89 31 85 10; www.zoo-mulhouse.com. Open daily May-Aug. 9am-7pm; Apr. and Sept. 9am-6pm; Mar. and Oct.-Nov. 9am-5pm; Dec.-Feb. 10am-4pm. Mar.-Oct. €7.40, Nov.-Feb. €4, students and ages 6-16 €4.)* The miles of textile swatches from the last 250 years at **Musée de l'Impression sur Etoffes** are startlingly beautiful. Those interested can learn more about the history of this industry here. *(14 rue J. J. Henner. ☎03 89 46 83 00. Open May-Sept. Tu-Su 10am-noon and 2-6pm; Oct.-Mar. closed Tu. €6, students €3, children 12-18 €2, under 12 free. Guide available in French, English, and German.)*

NIGHTLIFE & FESTIVALS

Fun-loving Mulhouse is especially busy in the center of town. **Rue Henriette** buzzes with pub chatter late into the night, and the area between **rue du Sauvage** and **place de la Réunion** boasts a high concentration of nightlife. Students flock to the crowded **O'Bryan Pub,** 5 pl. des Victoires, off rue du Sauvage. *(☎03 89 56 25 58. Beer from €2.40. Open daily 10am-1:30am. MC/V.)* There are a few gay-friendly bars in town, but the **Jet 7 Bar,** 2bis passage de l'Hôtel de Ville, is probably the friendliest, a sleek, happening spot with happy hour 6:30-8pm. *(☎03 89 56 04 21. Open Tu-Sa 11am-1:30am; post-Saturday-night breakfast Su 5-9am. MC/V.)* At the nightclub **Salle des Coffres,** 74 rue du Sauvage, right outside the *vieille ville*, a young crowd keeps jumping late into the night each weekend. *(☎03 89 56 34 98. Cover €8 with one drink, students €5. F-Sa 10pm-4am.)* **J.H.,** 1 rue Ste-Thérèse just off quai du Forst, is the best gay club in town. Theme nights rotate through the week; some themes try to welcome more women. *(☎03 89 32 00 08; www.jh-clubgay.com. M, Th free, F-Sa €8 with one drink. Open M and Th-Su 10:30pm-4am.)*

Throughout the year, especially in summer, Mulhouse comes alive with a number of **concerts** and **festivals. Bêtes de Scène,** in mid-July, brings a series of rock concerts to various venues. (For ticket info call ☎08 92 68 36 22 at €0.34 per min. or the tourist office for details. Ticket prices vary, some events free.) Every year, the city comes out for a **Carnaval** party from late February to early Mar., and for **street theater** in August. The tourist office has a full calendar.

FRANCHE-COMTÉ

ALSACE

BELFORT

Occupying a valley between the mountains of the Vosges and the Jura, Belfort (pop. 50,000) has been a favorite target of invading armies for centuries. In recent years the old town has become an industrial powerhouse, home to the factories that produce TGV trains and Peugeot automobiles. Happy with its growth, the town nevertheless manages to retain a small, charming *vieille ville* of bustling shops and strolling locals. Don't miss the Chapelle de Notre-Dame-du-Haut in nearby Ronchamp, one of Le Corbusier's masterpieces.

🖪🖬 TRANSPORTATION & PRACTICAL INFORMATION. Trains (☎08 36 35 35 35) run to Besançon (1hr., 17 per day, €12.50); Mulhouse (30min., 17 per day, €7.40); Paris (4hr., 9 per day, €40.40); Strasbourg (1½hr., 8 per day, €18.20). Office open M-F 5:30am-8pm, Sa 8:40am-6:30pm, Su 8:50am-8pm. AmEx/MC/V. CTRB, pl. Corbis, sends **buses** around Belfort. (☎03 84 21 08 08. Office open M-F 9am-12:15pm and 1:45-8:15pm. Lines run 6am-8pm. Tickets €1.10, *carnet* of 10 €8.) For **taxis,** call Radio Belfortains at 44 rue André Parant. (☎03 84 22 13 44. Base €1.25, €1.25-1.60 per km. 24hr.) **Car rental** is available at Hertz, 17 rue Aristide Briand (☎03 84 28 26 23; open M-Sa 9am-noon and 2-7pm; MC/V) and Budget, 63 fbg. de Montbéliard. (☎03 84 22 70 23. Open M-Sa 9am-noon and 2-7pm. MC/V.)

To get from the station to the **tourist office,** 2bis rue Clemenceau, head left down av. Wilson, then bear right on fbg. de France. When you see the river, turn left on fbg. des Ancêtres and follow it to rue Clemenceau; the office, set back from the road, is right of the mammoth Caisse d'Epargne. Friendly staff has free maps, hotel and restaurant listings, info on excursions, *Le Petit Géni,* a guide to Belfort with discounts to local stores and restaurants, and *Spectacles,* a free guide to restaurants and clubs. A helpful 24hr. electronic information center is outside the door, beside many free maps. (☎03 84 55 90 90. Open late June to Aug. M-Sa 9am-12:30pm and 1:30-6:30pm; Sept. to late June M-Sa 9am-12:30pm and 1:45-6pm.) There is an automatic **currency exchange** machine and **ATM** at Caisse d'Epargne, pl. de la Résistance (☎03 84 57 77 77), and other **banks** with currency exchange and ATMs on bd. Carnot and in the *vieille ville.* Other services include: a **laundromat** at 60 fbg. de Montbeliard (☎03 84 21 84 10; open daily 7am-9pm), **police** at 1 rue du Monnier (☎03 84 58 50 00; call here for the **pharmacie de garde**), a **hospital** at 14 rue de Mulhouse (☎03 84 57 40 00), **Internet** at Belfort Information Jeunesse, 3 rue Jules Vallès, (☎03 84 90 11 11; open M-Sa 10am-noon and 1:30-6pm; closed Tu and Sa mornings), and a **post office,** complete with ATM, at 19 fbg. des Ancêtres. (☎03 84 57 67 56. Open M-F 8am-7pm, Sa 8am-noon. MC/V.) **Postal code:** 90000.

🖪 ACCOMMODATIONS & CAMPING. Belfort has a smattering of one- and two-star hotels, but few truly budget places, except for ▧**Hôtel au Relais d'Alsace ❸,** 5 av. de la Laurencie (see **The Hidden Deal,** p. 375). **Résidence Madrid ❶,** 6 rue Madrid, a cheap option 10min. from the station, away from the *centre ville,* provides dorm-style rooms and singles of adequate quality, a friendly international crowd of residents, sinks in every room, and co-ed toilets and showers on each floor. From the train station, turn left onto av. Wilson, left again on rue Michelet, crossing over the railroad tracks, then right onto rue Parisot, which becomes av. Général Leclerc. Rue Madrid will be on the left after about seven minutes. Exercise caution in this neighborhood at night. (☎03 84 21 39 16; www.ufjt.org/adresse/belfort-madrid. Breakfast €2.50, full meal €6.80, main course €4.50. Reception daily 8:30am-12:30pm, 2-7:30pm, and 10:30pm until the morning. Dorms €14, with HI card €11.50. MC/V.) **Hôtel du Centre ❷**, 11 rue du Magasin, near the tourist office, has dark, cramped hallways, but the eight rooms are spacious and comfortable. Downstairs is a friendly little bar. (☎03 84 28 67 80. Reception 8am-10pm. Singles €21, with shower €27; doubles €23/€27-32. Extra bed €10. Reserve ahead. MC/V.) **Hôtel St-Christophe ❹**, pl. d'Armes, is in a prime location across from the cathedral in the heart of the *vieille ville*. The main hotel rents large, comfortable rooms with TV and bath, but the annex across the square is a better deal. (☎03 84 55 88 88; fax 03 84 54 08 77. Breakfast €7. Reception 6am-10pm. Singles with shower €51; doubles with bath €58. Annex: singles €41; doubles €52. MC/V.)

The three-star **Camping International de l'Etang des Forges**, 4 rue du Général Bethouart, is ideally located on the Etang des Forges, a sparkling lake 10min. by car from the *centre ville*. The open grounds afford little privacy, but plenty of space, good views, and squeaky-clean bathrooms. (☎03 84 22 54 92; fax 03 84 22 76 55. Reception daily 8am-12:30pm and 2:30-10pm. Open mid-April to late Sept. Two people with tent €13.50, ages 5-10 €2. Electricity €2.80.)

❏ **FOOD.** The local pastry is the *belflore*, a raspberry-almond tart. Finding food is delightfully easy along **Faubourg de France**, which cuts from the river to the train station, or nearly anywhere in the *vieille ville*. Cafés, *boulangeries*, and restaurants cluster around **place des Armes**. Supermarket **Petit Casino** is by the hostel at rue Léon Blum (open daily 7am-noon and 3-7pm. MC/V), **Monoprix** at the corner of bd. Carnot and av. Foch. (Open M-Sa 8:30am-8pm; MC/V.) Find good vegetarian dining at █**Gazelle d'Or ❸**, 4 rue des 4 Vents, a quiet eatery off pl. des Armes which specializes in couscous. (☎03 84 58 02 87. *Menu* €8.50. Open M-Sa noon-1:30pm and 7-11pm. MC/V.) **Aux Crêpes d'Antan ❶**, 13 rue du Quai, presents a formidable selection of creamy, artistically folded crêpes and *galettes* (€2.40-9) in a Provençal-themed shop around the corner from the cathedral. (☎03 84

THE HIDDEN DEAL

HÔTEL AU RELAIS D'ALSACE

One could not find a warmer welcome than at the **Hôtel au Relais d'Alsace ❸**. Kim and Georges, the English-speaking Franco-Algerian couple who run and own the hotel, must be the sweetest people on the planet. Kim's motherly enthusiasm is limitless, while Georges gives better advice than the tourist office about trails to take around town (ask for a map). Attracting families, backpackers, and traveling musicians from all over the world, the lobby is often filled with lively conversation, and adoring souvenir pictures drawn for the owners by past guests cover the walls. Kim and Georges offer spacious rooms with phone and TV, which they decorated by hand. The top floor gives a prized view of the nearby Château de Belfort. At breakfast, sip fresh-squeezed juice as you add your name to their lengthy guest book.

(5 av. de la Laurencie. ☎03 84 22 15 55; www.arahotel.com. From the station, take av. Wilson left until you hit Faubourg de France on the right. Take it to the vieille ville. At the cathedral, make a left onto rue Gal. Roussel, then a right onto Grande Rue, then left onto rue Grande Fontaine. Pass through the Porte de Brishac (an old gate) and continue straight. Av. de la Laurencie will be on the left. Breakfast €5. Washer and dryer available. All rooms with shower. Singles €27; doubles €36; triples €45; quads €50. Extra bed €6. MC/V.)

22 82 54. Open noon-2pm and 7-10pm. MC/V.) For a change of pace from the French pancake, **La Patate Gourmande ❷**, 12bis fg. des Ancêtres, fills the stomach with garnished, baked, and *au gratin* potatoes (€7.50-14) and elaborate salads (€4.50-9.50). The restaurant resembles a cabin in the woods transplanted to a tiny alley. (☎03 84 21 88 44. *Franc-Comtoise* potato with melted *comté* cheese and sausage €12. Open daily noon-2pm and 7-9:30pm. MC/V.)

◪ SIGHTS. At the top of any list of Belfort's sights—and at the top of the hill overlooking the town, on the winding road from pl. des Bourgeois—sits its medieval **château**, a military fortress during the Thirty Years' War but now a scenic hodgepodge of historical attractions. A circuit of the grounds provides a lesson in military history. The best place for a view of the land below is the **terrace** above the museum. (☎03 84 54 25 51. Open daily Apr.-Sept. 10am-6:30pm; Oct.-Mar. 10am-5pm. Free tours in French July-Aug. daily 10am-5pm.) A passageway on one of the lower levels leads to the viewing platform of the **Belfort Lion,** a monument to those who fell during the 1870 siege, carved entirely of red Vosges sandstone by the man who crafted the Statue of Liberty. (Platform open daily June-Sept. 9am-7pm; Apr.-May 9am-noon and 2-7pm; Oct.-Mar. 10am-noon and 2-5pm. €1, under 18 free. €5.60, students €4; includes the Musée d'Art et d'Histoire, Tour 46, and the Donation Jardot. MC/V.) Less impressive, but odd enough to intrigue, the **Musée d'Art et d'Histoire** displays a stuffy but extensive collection of outdated weaponry. Next to the guns and bayonets is an assortment of regional 19th-century clothing, dolls, and trinkets. (Open Apr.-Sept. Su-M and W-Sa 10am-noon and 2-5pm; Oct.-Mar. daily. €2.90, students €1.90, including Tour 46; 2nd Su of every month free. MC/V.) Along the route back into town, remnants of the octagonal fortifications that once surrounded the *vieille ville*, including several guard towers, remain intact.

The city has a pair of unique museums. **Tour 46,** on the corner of rue Bartholdi and rue Ancien Théâtre, presents special exhibits by great modern artists. (Open May-Sept. Su-M and W-Sa 10am-noon and 2-6pm. Prices vary. Call the château for info on the exhibit.) The **Donation Maurice Jardot**, 8 rue de Mulhouse, surrounded by the floral abundance of **square Emile Lechten,** has an impressive rotating collection of sketches and paintings by modern greats like Picasso, Braque, Léger, Chagall, and architect Le Corbusier. (☎03 84 90 40 70. Open daily July-Sept. 10am-6pm; Apr.-June 10am-noon and 2-6pm; Oct-Mar. 10am-noon and 2-5pm. €4, students €2.40. Wheelchair-accessible. AmEx/MC/V.) Walk along av. Jean Jaurès away from the museum to find the dazzling flowers of the **Rosière garden.**

Back in the *vieille ville*, on the other side of the ramparts from rue des Bons Enfants, Vauban's perfectly preserved 1687 **Porte de Brisach,** rue des Mobiles, bears the motto of the ever-humble Louis XIV: *Nec Pluribus Impar* ("superior to all others"). The **Cathédrale St-Christophe** presides over pl. des Armes in the heart of Belfort. Made of the same Vosges sandstone as the château, its graceful classical façade shelters a chilling transept with paintings by Belfort native G. Dauphin.

A 20min. train ride west, in the tiny village of Ronchamp (pop. 3000), Le Corbusier's famous 1954 **Chapelle de Notre-Dame-du-Haut** stands on the site of a disastrous 1944 German attack. The mushroom-shaped chapel, which draws architecture students from the world over, was meant to be a testament to hope in the wake of World War II. Le Corbusier used thick slabs of concrete, receding walls, and a sparsely decorated candlelit worship space "to create a space of silence, prayer, peace, and interior joy."

To reach Ronchamp, hop on an SNCF **bus** or **train** at the SNCF station in Belfort (20min.; M-F 9 per day, Sa 6, Su 2; €4.10). To reach the chapel from the train station, follow rue de la Gare left, turn left onto rue Le Corbusier, and left again onto rue de la Chapelle, then climb the steep, winding road for 1½km. For those with neither car, bike, nor legs of steel, Hôtel Pomme d'Or near the base of the hill will call a **taxi,** which will cost about €5 round-trip. (☎03 84 20 65 13. Open daily Apr.-Sept. 9:30am-6:30pm; Oct.-Mar. 10am-4pm. €2, students €1.50, children 5-12 free. Wheelchair-accessible. MC/V after €15.)

🎭🎉 **ENTERTAINMENT & FESTIVALS.** Belfort's dance clubs are relegated to the suburbs; think long and hard about getting home once the buses have stopped. The center of town has several fun bars. ▧**Farlo,** 14 rue des Capucins, attracts wild students with alternative rock, salsa, and Latin music, cages for dancing, waitresses grinding on bars, cocktails invented on-the-spot by the barmaids, and balconies from which to watch it all. (☎03 84 26 07 67. Beer €2.60, cocktails €6.50. Open Tu-F 5pm-12:30am, Sa-Su 5pm-1am. MC/V.) **Café Brussels,** 3 pl. des Armes, is a good place for people-watching in the heart of the *vieille ville.* (☎03 84 38 06 01. Beer on tap €2.10-3.20, coffee €1.50. Open daily 7:30am-1am. MC/V.) Beer of all kinds can be had at **Bistro des Moines,** 22 rue Dreyfus Schmidt, a lively bar-restaurant with an extensive brewery selection. (☎03 84 21 86 40. Beer €2.20-6.40; meals €7.50-12.50. Open M-F 10:30am-1am, Sa 10:30am-2am. MC/V.)

The château hosts free **jazz** July-Aug. (W 8:30pm). The cathedral holds cheap classical **concerts** on Thursday nights. The tourist office has details. In the first weekend in July, 85,000 music fans from all over Europe descend upon Belfort for **Les Eurockéennes,** France's largest open-air rock festival. A recent lineup featured Radiohead, Massive Attack, the Roots, Dépêche Mode frontman Dave Gahan, and nearly 60 other acts from rock to rap. Get tickets early. (For info call ☎08 92 68 85 88 at €0.34 per min.; www.eurockeennes.fr. Tickets sold at FNAC stores.) At the beginning of June, over 2000 musicians from around the world hit town for the **Festival International de Musique Universitaire,** a three-day extravaganza offering over 200 concerts, many of them free, running the gamut from classical and jazz to rock and world. Reserve accommodations well in advance; rooms are next to impossible to find during the event. (☎03 84 22 94 42; www.fimu.com.) The tourist office has a free guide of other concerts and festivals throughout the summer. The last week of November brings the film festival **Entrevues,** which showcases fresh, young directors and retrospectives. (For info on all festivals, call Cinéma d'Aujourd'hui ☎03 84 54 24 43.)

🏞 **EXCURSIONS.** Belfort has nearly 550km of marked hiking trails. The tourist office has many pamphlets that list nearby walks, hikes, and biking trails, including *Country Walks* (available in English). A popular nearby route circles Bessoncourt, 4km to the east. The town is the departure point for the daunting E5 trail that stretches from the Adriatic to the Atlantic, but following one of the many *petites randonnées* around the area provides a fairly flat 10-14km circuit. (3-5hr.) To the north, the towering summit of the Ballon d'Alsace (1247m) is a meeting point for three major long-distance trails: the GR5, GR7, and GR59. The taxing 7km hike to the peak should only be attempted by the fit, but the panoramic view of the glacial Doller valley and the Rhine and Saône valleys is spectacular.

The warm **Lac de Malsaucy,** west of Belfort, offers hiking, swimming, sunning, fishing, and outdoor performances. Small **boats, nautical bicycles,** and **mountain bikes** can be rented from the Base de Loisirs du Malsaucy, rue d'Evette (☎03 84 29 21 13). The nearby **Maison Départmentale de l'Environnement** (☎03 84 29 18 12) offers expositions on everything from frogs to weather. Throughout the summer, puppeteers, acrobats, comedians, and musicians perform here. In July, **Les Eurockéennes** (see **Entertainment**) stops by. Outdoor movies are shown on Thursday nights in late July and August. Free outdoor movies are shown on Tuesday nights at 10pm. To get to the lake, take bus #17 from town. (See bus schedule for details.) For more info on **fishing** in and around Belfort, contact the Fédération du Territoire de Belfort pour la Pêche. (☎03 84 23 39 49; www.unpf.fr/90.)

ALSACE

BESANÇON

Bounded by the river Doubs on three sides and a steep bluff on the fourth, Besançon (pop. 120,000) has baffled military strategists from Julius Caesar to the great military engineer Vauban 1800 years later. The city is known for its delightful setting, fine parks, and healthy supply of *joie de vivre*. A major university and an international language center give it a large student population, including a diverse international contingent, and an impressive number of museums and discos.

TRANSPORTATION

Trains: av. de la Paix. Office open M-F 9am-6:30pm, Sa 10am-5:20pm. To: **Belfort** (1hr., 18 per day, €12.50); **Dijon** (1hr., 22 per day, €11.90); **Lyon** (2½hr., 11 per day, €30.60); **Paris** (2hr., 8 per day, €43.50) via **Dole** (29 per day); **Strasbourg** (3hr., 8 per day, €26.40). Minor station at av. de Chardonnet. AmEx/MC/V.

Buses: Monts Jura, behind 9 rue Proudhon; office at 17 rue Proudhon (☎08 25 00 22 44). To **Pontarlier** (1hr., 6 per day, €8). Office open M-Sa 8-10am and 4-6:30pm.

Public Transportation: Ginko, 4 pl. du 8 Septembre (☎08 25 00 22 44; www.ginko-bus.com). Open M-Sa 10am-12:45pm and 1:15-7pm. Night buses run sporadically until midnight. Tickets €0.90, *carnet* of 10 €7.80, 24hr. pass €3. Buy tickets on bus.

Taxis: (☎03 81 88 80 80). Minimum charge €4.60. 24hr. service.

Bike Rental: Cycles Pro Shop, 18 av. Carnot (☎03 81 47 03 04). €9 per half-day, €13 per full day, helmet €3. Deposit €150-300. ID required. Open M-Sa 9am-noon and 2-7pm. MC/V.

Car Rental: Europcar, straight across from the train station on av. Foch. (☎08 21 80 58 08). Open M 8am-noon and 2-6pm, Tu-F 9am-noon and 2-6pm. AmEx/MC/V.

ORIENTATION & PRACTICAL INFORMATION

Most areas of interest in Besançon lie within a thumb-shaped turn of the Doubs River. To reach the tourist office, cross the train station's parking lot and head down the stairs. Follow av. de la Paix, which turns into av. Foch, but stay to the right. Continue to veer left at the river, and turn onto av. de l'Helvétie. Follow this to pl. de la Première Armée Française. The office is in the park to the right, and the *vieille ville* is across the bridge. (10min.)

Tourist Office: 2 pl. de la 1ère Armée Française (☎08 20 32 07 82; www.besancon-tourisme.com). Lists hotels and restaurants and provides free **accommodations service,** a free copy of the comprehensive student guide *La Besace,* and info on excursions and festivals. **Tours** May-Sept. for individuals (in French; €6, students €4) and groups (in French, English, or German, by reservation). **Currency exchange** at the same rate as the banks. Open July-Aug. M 10am-7pm, Tu-Sa 9am-7pm, Su 10am-noon and 3-5pm; Oct.-Mar. M-Sa until 6pm; Sept.-Apr. closed Su 3-5pm. MC/V.

Youth Center: Centre Information Jeunesse (CIJ), 27 rue de la République (☎03 81 21 16 16; www.crijfc.com). Info on internships, jobs, events, and apartments. HI cards. Free **Internet** with a Carte Avantage Jeunes (€6 for a year membership. The card also gets discounts on everything from lodging to sights. Limit 2hr. per week.) Open M 1:30-6pm, Tu-F 10am-noon and 1:30-6pm, Sa 1:30-6pm.

English Bookstore: Campo Novo, 50 Grande Rue (☎03 81 65 07 70), has a small selection of books in English. Open M 10am-7pm, Tu-Sa 9am-7pm. MC/V.

Laundromat: Blanc-Matic, 54 rue Bersot, near the bus station. Also 57 rue des Cras, near the Foyer Mixte. Both open daily 7am-8pm.

Police: 2 av. de la Gare d'Eau (☎03 81 21 11 22). Near pl. St-Jacques.

Hospital: Centre Hospitalier Universitaire, 2 pl. St-Jacques (☎03 81 66 81 66).

Internet: At the **CIJ** (see **Youth Center**). **T@cybernet,** 18 rue de Pontarlier (☎03 81 81 15 74). €3.60 per hr., €2.40 with a Carte Jeunes. MC/V. Open M-Sa 11am-10pm, Su 2-8pm. **Foyer des Jeunes Travailleurs** has free access for guests.

Post Office: 4 rue Demangel (☎03 81 53 81 12). **Postal code:** 25000. Open M-F 8am-7pm, Sa 8am-noon. **Branches** at 23 rue Proudhon (☎03 81 65 55 82), off rue de la République, and pl. Jouffroy d'Abbans (☎03 81 65 55 82). **Currency exchange** and **Cyberposte.** Branches open M-F 9:30am-noon and 1:30-6:30pm, Sa 9am-noon. **Poste Restante:** 25031 Besançon-Cedex. **Postal code:** 25019.

■ ACCOMMODATIONS & CAMPING

Hostels are a trek from the *vieille ville* (30min.), but offer excellent facilities at a bargain and are easily accessible by convenient daytime and nighttime bus lines (until midnight). Besançon's central hotels are closer to the action, but require advance reservations and aren't the most value-packed bargains around.

Foyer Mixte des Jeunes Travailleurs (HI), 48 rue des Cras (☎03 81 40 32 00; fax 03 81 40 32 01). Take bus #7 (or night line A) from pl. Flore (dir: Orchamps; 3-5 per hr., €0.90). To get to pl. Flore, cross the train station parking lot, head down the stairs, take av. de la Paix, and keep to the left as the road bends and turns into rue de Belfort. Turn right onto av. Carnot, walk for a block until the green lights of the pharmacy in pl. Flore come into view, then take a sharp left onto rue des Chaprais. The stop is on the same side of the street as a Casino grocery. To go by foot, follow the above directions onto rue Belfort. After 10min., turn left on rue Marie-Louise, which becomes rue des Cras after crossing over the railroad tracks. Follow rue des Cras up a large hill and over a smaller one; the hostel entrance is just after rue Resal on the right. (30min.) Locals refer to it as "Foyer Les Oiseaux." Large, bright white rooms with private bathrooms in a large, friendly facility. Frequent concerts, movies, and other special events. Free Internet in the lobby. Breakfast included. 5-course cafeteria meal €6.60. Reception daily 8:30am-1am. No lockout times. No reservations. Dec.-Feb. only two rooms available. Singles €17, 2nd night €15; doubles €25/€23. AmEx/MC/V. ❷

Hôtel du Nord, 8-10 rue Moncey (☎03 81 81 35 56; fax 03 81 81 85 96), on a charming sidestreet in the heart of the old town. Attentive reception and large attractive rooms with cable TV—the height of budget-travel luxury. Breakfast €4.60. Reception 24hr. Parking. Check-in and checkout noon. Reserve well in advance. Singles and doubles with shower or bath €30-52; triples and quads with shower €54. AmEx/DC/MC/V. ❸

Centre International de Séjour, 19 rue Martin-du-Gard (☎03 81 50 07 54; fax 03 81 53 11 79; cis.besancon@wanadoo.fr). Take bus #8 (dir: Campus, or the Campus night bus) from the Foch stop near the station to Intermarché. To get to Foch from the station, cross the parking lot, go down the stairs, and head down the road that leads downward at a slight diagonal to the left (av. de la Paix, which turns into av. Foch). The stop is half a block down on the left. Getting off the bus, walk back up the hill and turn left at the hostel's sign. Another large, friendly place with clean rooms and many non-backpackers. Restaurant, TV room, and foosball. Breakfast €4.40. Meals €6.30-10.30. Reception 7am-1am. Check-in 3pm; checkout 9am. Singles €18, with shower, toilet, and TV €27.30; doubles €22.60/€30.80; triples (no shower) €25.50. AmEx/MC/V. ❷

Hôtel du Levant, 9 rue des Boucheries (☎03 81 81 07 88), on pl. de la Révolution. Just off popular rue des Granges and Grande Rue, this old hotel is inexpensive and well-located, although the rooms are old and somewhat run-down. Breakfast €3.80. Reception daily 10am-3pm and 6-9pm. Reservations recommended for the summer. Singles €18, with shower €23-28; doubles €23/€33-35; triples €30/€43-45; quads with shower €49-52; quint with shower €56. MC/V. ❷

ALSACE

Hôtel de Paris, 33 rue des Granges (☎03 81 81 36 56; www.hotel-deparis.com). Step into the lap of luxury in these large, fully-equipped, shiny rooms overlooking a garden. Free Internet for guests. Breakfast €6.50. Reception 24hr. Reserve in advance. Singles M-Th €45-50, F-Su €36; doubles €53-58/€36. AmEx/MC/V. ❹

Camping de la Plage, rte. de Belfort in Chalezeule (☎03 81 88 04 26; fax 03 81 50 54 62), northeast of the city. Take bus #35 (dir: Palente) to the terminus. (5min.) Shuttle bus *(navette)* leaves site five times per day (mid-June to Aug.) Otherwise it's a 35min., 5km walk down rte. de Belfort. Four-star campground with free access to a pool June-Aug. Near a highway, although the site itself retains a certain rural charm. Breakfast €4.10. Reception daily 9am-noon and 2-10pm. Open Apr.-Sept. €7.70 for one person with car. Electricity €3.10. AmEx/MC/V. ❷

🍴 FOOD

Besançon's dining options are plentiful and reasonably priced. **Rue Claude Pouillet** and **rue des Granges** dish out many tempting options at tourist-level prices, while out-of-the-way eateries appeal to the student budget. For the do-it-yourself shopper, pl. de la Révolution, hosts outdoor covered **markets.** (Open Tu and F 6am-12:30pm, Sa 6am-7pm.) Groceries are always available at one of the **Petit Casino** supermarkets that dot the city. (One at 12 Grande Rue. Open M-Sa 8:30am-8pm. MC/V.) Sharp *comté* cheese is Besançon's speciality. Wash it down with *vin jaune*, one of the more famous Arbois wines. *Charcuteries* along rue des Granges sell *saucisse de Marteau*, a regional sausage specialty, while *chocolatiers* in the center of town will offer up *releuleu*, also known as *boulets de la Citadel*, a layered chocolate, nut, and sugar confection. Two lesser-known great deals are just south of the main drag. **🔲Au Gourmand ❶**, 5 rue Megevand, serves an astonishing array of hearty dishes at incredibly low prices. Canary-yellow walls, vintage chocolate advertisements, and collections of teapots and cat figurines conjure images of the eccentric grandmother you never had. (☎03 81 81 40 56. Rice and pasta dishes €5.40-7.70; omelettes €3.10-5.40; warm salads with potatoes €4.60-6.10. Open Tu-F 11:30am-1:45pm and 6:45-9pm. MC/V.) **🔲La Boîte à Sandwiches ❶**, 21 rue du Lycée, is a well-hidden hole-in-the-wall off rue Pasteur. Exotic ingredients like heart of palm fill over 50 wittily-named sandwiches like *La Geisha, La Bohémienne, Le Communiste*, and *Le Franc Comtoise* (which features local *saucisse* and creamy melted Comté cheese). (☎03 81 81 63 23. Sandwiches and salads €2.30-5.40. Open M-Sa 11:30am-2pm and M-F 7pm-midnight. MC/V.) Pricier, prettier options include the vertically splendid **Brasserie du Commerce ❷**, 31 rue des Granges, whose towering ceiling and ornate décor complement the regional delicacies on the menu. (☎03 81 81 33 11. *Andouilletes du Côté de Jura* with *crème vin jaune* €11. Open M-Sa 8am-1am, Su 9am-1am. AmEx/MC/V.) **Rosa Bianca ❸**, pl. Granvelle, is an Italian *brasserie* with a park view and a fine terrace. Pastas, meats, and a slew of salads pack the menu. (☎03 81 81 05 60. Pastas €8-15, salads €7-11. Open daily 8am-1am. MC/V.)

👁 SIGHTS

Besançon's *vieille ville* is a bustling but manageable circuit graced by a trio of worthwhile museums and remarkably well-preserved Renaissance buildings.

CITADEL. Vauban's Renaissance citadel, built during the reign of Louis XIV, was once a brooding military fortification, but today the citadel houses excellent museums, zoos galore, and stunning views. A visit requires a grueling trek uphill from the town, but is worth every step. Although this 17th-century stronghold is a conspicuous tourist spot, this at least means that detailed English explications are

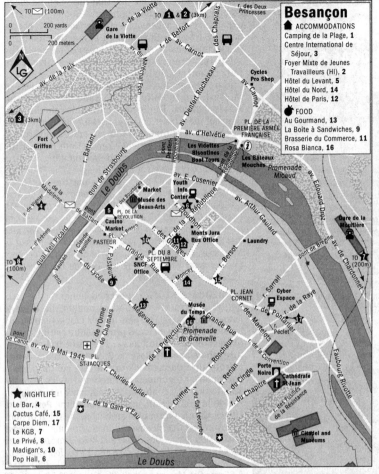

Besançon

↑ ACCOMMODATIONS

Camping de la Plage, **1**
Centre International de Séjour, **3**
Foyer Mixte de Jeunes Travailleurs (HI), **2**
Hôtel du Levant, **5**
Hôtel du Nord, **14**
Hôtel de Paris, **12**

🍴 FOOD

Au Gourmand, **13**
La Boîte à Sandwiches, **9**
Brasserie du Commerce, **11**
Rosa Bianca, **16**

★ NIGHTLIFE

Le Bar, **4**
Cactus Café, **15**
Carpe Diem, **17**
Le KGB, **7**
Le Privé, **8**
Madigan's, **10**
Pop Hall, **6**

provided for many of the extensive collections. After passing through the free park area overlooking the city below, a first priority should be the ▨**Musée de la Résistance et de la Déportation.** One hundred members of the French Resistance were shot at the citadel during the German occupation of Besançon. This comprehensive collection of letters, artifacts, and often graphic photographs chronicles the Nazi rise to power, the Holocaust, and the invasion of France in a deeply affecting manner. Ask a guard to open the exhibition room on the third floor, which contains a collection of sculptures and drawings by two local men who were deported to concentration camps. Audio guides, available in English (€2), play survivors' recorded accounts. (☎03 81 65 07 55. No children under 10.)

More lighthearted and appealing to children is the fine **zoological** area that spans the back wall of the fortification. The main park houses the always-entertaining primate wing, as well as a small hands-on farm for children. The **insectarium** next door is fascinating, but not for the weak-stomached: a mock kitchen exhibit

THE LOCAL STORY

NATZWEILER-STRUTOF

In the course of five years, over 10 million men, women, and children were brutally murdered by a Nazi regime bent on power and racial dominance. Most of these murders were committed in concentration camps in Poland and Germany, but Nazis spread as far west as Natzweiler-Strutof (30km from Obernai), the only concentration camp on French soil.

Ten to twelve thousand Jews and French resistance fighters were massacred at Natzweiler. In one of the most horrific acts of the Holocaust, hundreds of prisoners met their dooms in twisted scientific experiments on chemical warfare and diseases like hepatitis and typhus. Some prisoners were killed solely to provide skeletons for anatomical research.

The remains of the Natzweiler camp are open to the public, continuing to stand as a frightening reminder of the brutal capacity of human cruelty. Visitors can see the guard towers, four crematoria, and the gas chamber. A museum converted from a barracks displays pictures, diagrams, and items that tell the intensely human side of the story of inhuman deportation and execution. It is simple but powerful, and well-worth a visit.

(Natzweiler-Strutof can only be reached by car. From Obernai, take D426, D214, and D130, then follow signs for Camp du Strutof. €2.50.)

reveals all the little nasties that hide behind clean countertops and inside cupboards. Rounding out the experience, an **aquarium,** a **climatorium,** and a **noctarium** strive to dazzle with their respective scientific preoccupations, to varying degrees of success. The nighttime creepy-crawlies of the noctarium are rather poorly exhibited.

More conventional in nature, but nevertheless of interest, are the informative **Salle de Vauban** and **Musée Comtois.** The former chronicles the life and times of the citadel's famous creator, while the latter displays an assortment of folk art, crafts, and archeological finds from Franche-Comté. Both lie near the **Tour de la Reine,** from which the surrounding countryside can be observed at a royal height. The **Petit Train** rides to the top and gives a tour along the way. (☎ 03 81 63 44 44. Pick-up at pl. du 8 Septembre every hr. from 10:15am to 6:15pm except 1:15pm. €5.50, students €3. Citadel ☎ 03 81 65 07 54; fax 03 81 83 04 66; sem.citadelle@wanadoo.fr. Open daily July-Aug. 9am-7pm; Apr.-June and Sept.-Oct. 9am-6pm; Nov.-Mar. 10am-5pm. Closed Tu Nov.-Easter. €7, students €6, under 14 €4, includes entrance to every museum and facility. Audio guide €2. Wheelchair access to most sites. MC/V.)

CATHÉDRALE ST-JEAN. Perched beneath the citadel, this attractive cathedral boasts the **Horloge Astronomique,** a 30,000-part indoor clock visible only by tour. Fifty-seven faces provide information on the planets, eclipses, and more. The cathedral also features the elaborate **Rose de St-Jean,** a circular white marble altar dating back to the 11th century, and a dark interior that mixes architectural styles from the 12th to the 18th centuries. A walk back into town on rue de la Convention, passes through the **Porte Noire** (Black Gate), a triumphal arch from the reign of Marcus Aurelius that is covered in scaffolding. *(Cathedral ☎ 03 81 83 34 62. Open Su-M and W-Sa 9am-6pm., except during mass. Free. Horloge ☎ 03 81 81 12 76. Tours Apr.-Sept. Su-M and W-Sa 9:50, 10:50, 11:50am, 2:50, 3:50, 4:50, 5:50pm.; Oct.-Mar. no tours W. Closed Jan. €2.50, under 18 and students free.)*

MUSÉE DES BEAUX-ARTS ET D'ARCHÉOLOGIE. The oldest public museum in France houses an exceptional collection of more than 6000 works by Ingres, Van Dyck, Rubens, Matisse, Picasso, Renoir, and other masters in a capacious, well-presented space. Interesting, but not nearly as fine as the wonderful painting exhibits, are the Egyptian rooms of mummies and sarcophagi. *(1 pl. de la Révolution. ☎ 03 81 87 80 49. Open Su-M and W-Sa June-Oct. 9:30am-12:30pm and 2-6pm; Nov.-May 9:30am-noon and 2-6pm. €3, students with ID and all on Su and holidays free. Tours in French €1.50. Wheelchair-accessible. MC/V.)*

MUSÉE DU TEMPS. This brand-new museum—appropriately situated in the watch-making capital of France—takes a concrete approach to the grand question of time. The extensive collection of clocks and related gadgets is interactive, attractively displayed, and high-tech. The museum itself has a relaxed notion of time: it opened two years behind schedule and is closed on Mondays and Tuesdays. (*Palais Granvelle, 96 Grande Rue. ☎03 81 87 81 50; musee-du-temps@besancon.com. Open Su and W-Sa May-Sept. 1-7pm; Oct.-Apr. 1-6pm. €3, Sa €1.50, students with ID and all on Su free, ticket valid 2 days. English and German guides available at desk. Wheelchair-accessible.*)

BOAT TRIPS. **Les Vedettes Bisontines** runs boat cruises on the Doubs and the citadel canals from pont de la République, near the tourist office. (*☎03 81 68 13 25; www.sautdudoubs.fr. Operates Apr.-Oct. 100min.; hours vary, usually 3-4 per day. €8.50, children €7.*) Or cross rue de la République to **Les Bâteaux Mouches** (*Le Pont Battant. ☎03 81 68 05 34. Operates Apr.-Oct.; Nov.-Mar. by reservation only. 100min.; 4-5 per day. €8.50, children €7. Days and tours vary; call ahead.*)

NIGHTLIFE

Most nights of the week, Besançon's students pack bars and discos until early morning, especially in the area from **rue Claude Pouillet** over **Pont Battant** to **place Jouffroy d'Arbans**. Small, friendly bars proliferate in the pedestrian section of town.

▓ **Carpe Diem,** 2 pl. Jean Gigoux (☎03 81 83 11 18), is a bar with an eponymous philosophy. Run by a delightful owner according to his ideas on *le rôle sociale* of the pub, this much-appreciated hotspot brings together students and non-students for drinks and discussion. Events, films, and concerts happen regularly. Beer €2. Open M-Th 7am-1am, F-Sa 7am-2am, Su 8am-11pm. MC/V.

▓ **Pop Hall,** 26 rue Proudhon (☎03 81 83 01 90), across from the post office, is the hippest pool hall in town. A nondescript façade hides everything from antique chandeliers and gondolas to cars appropriated from amusement parks. The high point is the bathrooms, which feature chipped Victorian mirrors, Roman vases, bronze cowhead sinks, and a toilet bowl lamp. Kitschy/casual/retro/cool, this bar attracts all ages, but especially the young. Beer €2, cocktails €2.50-4.50. Happy hour 6-8pm, drinks half-price. Open Su-Th 2pm-1am, F-Sa 2pm-2am. MC/V.

Madigan's, 17 pl. 8 Septembre (☎03 81 81 17 44), brings the Irish pub experience across the Channel. Students and tourists share in the Guinness drinking. Margaritas €2.50, beer €2-2.80. Open Su-Th 7:30am-1am, F-Sa 7:30am-2:30am. MC/V.

Le Bar, 15 rue de Vignier (☎03 81 82 01 00), seems to overcompensate for being one of the only gay bars in town. The basic theme is sex, from the porn playing on a big-screen TV to the condoms and gloves available downstairs. Ring bell to enter, but make sure not to ring the bell of the family next door by accident. Beer on tap €2.50, cocktails €5. Open M-Th 8pm-1am, F-Sa 9pm-2:30am, Su 9pm-2am. MC/V.

The Cactus Café, 79 rue des Granges (☎03 81 82 01 18), provides its semi-rowdy student crowd with 7000 karaoke-ready tracks Th-Sa 10pm-2am. Beer €2-2.60 on tap. Open M-Th 9am-1am, F-Su 9am-2am. MC/V.

Le Privé, 1 rue Antide Janvier (☎03 81 81 48 57). Follow rue d'Arênes straight past the Lycée Condé to a stoplight. Go left onto rue A. Janvier. The club is on the right. This gay and lesbian nightclub is geared more toward men than women (witness the 19th-century dandy grinning from the sign outside). The 22-year-old establishment feels like it never left the 80s, blasting a variety of French and American music from that fabled decade and sporting fluorescent green neon lights, red- and black-striped couches, and prominent mirrors. Nicely packed on the weekends. Cover Tu-Th €8, F €9, Sa €10; includes one drink. Open Tu-Su 11pm-5am.

ALSACE

Le KGB, 8 av. de Chardonnet (☎03 81 61 17 49), about 1km from the tourist office, is the best of Besançon's dance clubs. A large dance floor with London Underground décor is surrounded by plush couches, two bars, and many drunken students. Different music in each room, plus **Le Lounge** for the 30-40 set. Be cautious on the poorly lit av. de Chardonnet. Cover €8, F-Sa €9.50; W-Th students €4.10. Open W-Th 10:30pm-4am, F-Sa 10:30pm-5am. MC/V.

🎵 FESTIVALS

The tourist office publishes several comprehensive lists of events; make sure to get *Les Temps Chauds de l'Été* for up-to-date summer information. In July and August, the city sponsors **Festiv'été,** with theater, music, dance, expositions, and a film festival. (Many events are free. Call the tourist office for info.) **Jazz en Franche-Comté** brings a flurry of concerts in June and July, uniting jazz musicians from across France and abroad. (Call ☎03 81 83 39 09 or visit www.multimania.com/festivaljazz for info. Most tickets €5-16, all with student discounts, many free.)

Les Concerts de Granvelle bring a wide range of free musical acts to the open-air Palais Granvelle Friday nights throughout July and August. (Call the tourist office for more info.) The **Festival International de Musique** fills the air with nightly classical concerts during mid-September. Orchestras from across Europe perform well-worn favorites as well as more recent compositions in 85 concerts, most of which are free. (☎03 81 25 05 80; fax 03 81 81 52 15; contact@festival-besancon.com. Tickets €11-36 depending on locale, student discounts up to 25%.)

For more info on everything that's planned for this year, check out Besançon's website at www.besancon.com. The Foyer les Oiseaux hostel (see **Accommodations**) sponsors an array of events; pick up a schedule at the tourist office.

JURA MOUNTAINS

The Jura mountain range is often overlooked by travelers who flock to the Alps farther south. Much older than its neighbor, the Jura range has become rounder and smoother with age and is covered with dense pine forests, sunny meadows, and countless hiking, biking, and skiing trails.

ARBOIS

Though buzzing with tourist-centered industry, this peaceful wine-tasting center (pop. 3960) has not lost its down-to-earth, regional feel. Residents are still firmly tied to the local vineyards: for every air-conditioned tour bus zipping by, a tractor rattles through town. Combined with a healthy splash of the locally produced *vin jaune*, the sandy-colored stones, medieval ramparts, and cascading river of Arbois make it a picturesque and worthwhile visit.

◪🛈 ORIENTATION & PRACTICAL INFORMATION. Trains and SNCF buses will take you to **Besançon** (45min., 5 per day, €7.50) and **Dole** (5 per day, €6.40). The train station is a good 15min. hike from the town center. Go straight from the station onto av. de la Gare, take the second left onto av. Pasteur, and follow it straight into town as it becomes rue de Courcelles and, a block later, Grande Rue, until it reaches the central **place de la Liberté.** The train station itself, with one automatic ticket machine, only functions as a departure point for trains; the building is not open. The SNCF office inside the tourist office functions as the ticket/information center. Also note: while trains depart from the station, SNCF buses often depart from the center of town on rue des Fossés. Check with the office before heading to the station. (☎03 84 66 25 00. Open M-Sa 9:30am-noon and 2-6pm.)

To get to the **tourist office** and SNCF office from the train station, follow the directions above to pl. de la Liberté. From there, turn right onto rue de l'Hôtel de Ville; both offices are on your right, just after the Hôtel de Ville. Pick up a free **map**, a list of hotels and restaurants, a flood of brochures, and, in July-August, a **free tour** of the town in French. Audio tours available in English and German for €1.60. (☎03 84 66 55 50; www.arbois.com. Open July-Aug. M-Sa 9:30am-noon and 2-6pm, Su 10am-noon; low season hours vary.) The **police station,** 17 av. Général-Delort, can be reached at ☎03 84 66 14 25. The **hospital** is at 23 rue de l'Hôpital (☎03 84 66 44 00). The **pharmacie de garde's** number is posted on the window of any pharmacy. **Banks** with **ATMs** can be found along Grande Rue in the center of town. **Internet** is available at the public library (bibliothèque), 9 Grande Rue (☎03 84 37 41 90; open Tu 10:30am-noon and 4-6:30pm, W and Sa 10:30am-noon and 2-6:30pm, Th 4:30-6pm, F 9am-noon and 4:30-6pm; €1 per hr.), and at Château Pécauld, rue des Fossés. (☎03 84 66 26 14. Open Tu-Th afternoons. Call ahead. €1.60 per hr.) The **post office** is on av. Général Delort just past the police station. (☎03 84 66 01 21. Open M-F 8:30am-noon and 2-6pm, Sa 8:30-noon.) **Postal code:** 39600.

⚑ ACCOMMODATIONS & FOOD. While some ritzy Arbois hotels reach ungodly prices (up to €275 for a suite at the four-star Château de Germigney just outside of town), there are a few decent, centrally located options for the budget traveler. **Hôtel de la Poste ❷,** 71 Grande Rue, is the only truly inexpensive accommodation, with simple but clean rooms above a bar. (☎03 84 66 13 22. Shower on first floor, toilets on every floor. Breakfast €5. Reception July-Aug. daily 7am-11pm; closed Tu Sept.-June. Singles €17; doubles €22; triples €27; quads €33. MC/V.) The next best option is well worth the price. **Hôtel les Messageries ❸,** 2 rue de Courcelles, a Victorian-style establishment, has stone archways, bright rooms, floral trimmings, and great views. (☎03 84 66 15 45. Reception 7am-10pm. Breakfast €6. Singles with hall shower €27, with private shower €33, and toilet €45; doubles €30/€36/€51. Extra bed €8, under 10 free. Closed Dec.-Jan. and W night Sept.-Nov. and Feb.-June. MC/V.) The three-star **Municipal des Vignes ❶** campsite, nearby on av. du Général Leclerc, offers modern amenities including hot showers, snack bar, nearby pool, laundry, and TV. (☎/fax 03 84 66 14 12. Reception open Apr.-Sept. 7am-noon and 4pm-10pm. Open Apr.-Sept. July-Aug. 1-2 people €10.60; electricity €11.70. Apr.-June and Sept. 1-2 people €9.60; electricity €10.80. €1.50 per child. Bank cards and traveler's checks accepted.)

The mysteriously compelling *vin jaune*, fermented from Sauvignon grapes for six years in an oak cask, is the pride of Arbois, as is the even more elaborate *vin de paille*, made from grapes that have been dried on beds of straw. Many *caves* in Arbois offer free *dégustations*, and upscale restaurants have local wines by the glass. For a free tour and tasting, visit the *caves* of **Henri Maire,** pl. de la Liberté, one of the larger establishments in town. (☎03 84 66 15 27. Tours given daily. Make reservations a day in advance. MC/V.) Not nearly as glamorous, but much cheaper, are the exquisite wines at **Spar** supermarket, 55 Grande Rue, including a large selection of *vins jaunes*. (☎03 84 37 44 47. Open M-Sa 7:30am-12:30pm and 3-7:30pm, Su 7:30am-12:30pm. MC/V.) Outdoor **markets** are held every Friday just off pl. de la Liberté.

A bit off the main drag, lively, friendly **Bar Le 33 ❶,** 43 pl. Faramand, prepares quick sandwiches for €2.45 or heartier grub for €6. (☎03 84 66 08 74. Open Su-Tu and Th-Sa 11:30am-midnight. MC/V.) Popular **La Balance ❸,** 47 rue de Courcelles, has a vegetarian *menu*, and outdoor dining with a lovely fountain view. (☎03 84 37 45 00. Reservations recommended for summer. Open July-Aug. Tu-Su noon-2:30pm and 7:30-10pm; closed Su night Sept.-June. Closed for three weeks in Dec. MC/V.) **La Cuisance ❷,** 62 rue de Faramand, fills with locals who delight in the generous *plats* (€6) and *menus* (€7.20). Kids eat for €5.70. (☎03 84 37 40 74. Open

Su-M and Th-Sa 9am-3pm and 5pm-midnight, Tu-W 9am-3pm. MC/V.) For a quick bite, head to **Restaurant Agor Kebab ❶**, 73 Grande Rue, a cheerful, crowded Middle Eastern stronghold in a land of expensive *coq-au-vin-jaune* eateries. (☎03 84 66 33 64. Falafel and kebab sandwiches €3.50-5, platters €7.50. Open M-F noon-2pm and 6-10pm, Sa-Su 6pm-midnight.) Bring a date with a sense of humor to the atmospheric **La Finette: Taverne d'Arbois ❸**, 22 av. Louis Pasteur, a rustic place with candles, wooden tables, animal heads, shotguns, and €15.50 3-course meals. (☎03 84 66 06 78. Open daily 11am-midnight. AmEx/MC/V.) The homemade ice cream and chocolate at ▨**Hirsinger's Chocolatier and Salon de Thé ❶**, 38 Grande Rue, is acclaimed by glossy gourmet magazines and locals alike. (☎03 84 66 06 97. One scoop €2, two scoops €3. MC/V for over €15.)

◩◪ SIGHTS & FESTIVALS. Arbois is proud to be known as Louis Pasteur's "favorite town." The enjoyable **Maison de Pasteur**, 83 rue de Courcelles, showcases the original vineyards and laboratory where he made several crucial observations on the nature of alcoholic fermentation. It continues to bottle wine under Pasteur's name. (☎03 84 66 11 72. Open June-Sept. daily 9:45-11:45am and 2:15-6:15pm; Apr.-May and Oct. daily 2:15-5:15pm. €5.35, children €2.75.) Surrounded by working vineyards, the **Musée de la Vigne et du Vin,** in **Château Pécauld** on rue des Fossés, gives a fascinating in-depth look at the ins and outs of wine production. (☎03 84 66 40 45. Open July-Aug. 10am-12:30pm and 2-6pm, Mar.-June and Sept.-Oct. 10am-noon and 2-6pm; Nov-Feb. 2-6pm. July-Aug. guided tours available, with wine-tasting afterward. €3.30, students €2.50.) The tower of **Eglise St-Just** and the nearby 16th-century ramparts provide exquisite views.

Nightlife in Arbois consists of some quiet wine-sipping at a pub (most likely on pl. de la Liberté), but a series of events liven up the town in summer. The newly jazzed-up **Fête des Vins** pairs a little mood music with a lot of wine-tasting during the last two weekends in July. During the **Fête du Biou**, the first Sunday in September, a procession of *vignerons* (wine makers) offers the first grapes of the season to God. The **Festival Orge et Musique** brings classical music into the churches of Arbois and around the town during July and August. If the outdoors are calling, the Arbois area supports 110km of marked **hiking trails** and nearly 60km of **mountain biking trails.** (Contact the tourist office for detailed maps and descriptions.)

PONTARLIER

Pontarlier (pop 18,400), 840m above most of Alsace, is the gateway to some of life's highest pleasures: the oft-overlooked Haut-Jura mountains. Although known as a slow, friendly, not-so-happening town, it was once the absinthe capital of Europe (until the hallucinogenic liqueur was banned in 1915). In addition to great mountain views and wide boulevards, Pontarlier serves as a good base for hiking, riding, skiing, and biking in the Jura or for a trip to Switzerland, just 12km away.

▣◪ TRANSPORTATION & PRACTICAL INFORMATION. The **train station** is on pl. de Villingen-Schweningen. (☎03 81 46 56 99. Open M-F 5am-12:30pm and 1:40-10:55pm, Sa 5am-12:30pm and 1:30-10:40pm, Su 7am-12:40pm and 1:30-10:40pm.) **Trains** go to: Dijon (1½hr., 5 per day, €18.70); Geneva (3hr., 5 per day, €33.50); Paris (3½hr., 5 per day, €55.20). Monts Jura **buses** leave from in front of the train station for **Besançon** (55min., 6 per day, €8). The **tourist office** is at 14bis rue de la Gare. From the train station, cross through the rotary and head left one block on rue de la Gare. The office is left of the bus station, down rue Michaud. The staff has info on Pontarlier, hiking, skiing, and other outdoor sports, and free regional guides *Le Doubs: Massif de Jura* and *Guide Pratique*, which list cheap mountain lodgings. (☎03 81 46 48 33; info@pontarlier.org. Office open M-Sa 9am-6pm,

July-Aug. also Su 10am-noon. Guides available in English and German.) Cycles Pernet, 23 rue de la République, rents **bikes**. (☎ 03 81 46 48 00. €15 per day, €34 for 3 days. Passport deposit. Open Tu-Sa 9am-noon and 2-7pm; May-Aug. also M 3-6pm. MC/V.) Other services include: **banks** with **ATMs** along **rue de la République**; a **laundromat** at 13 rue du Moulin Parnet (open daily 7am-9pm); **police** at 19 Rocade Pompidou (☎ 03 81 38 51 10; call here for the **pharmacie de garde**); a **hospital** at 2 fbg. St-Etienne (☎ 03 81 38 53 60); and **Internet** at Cyber @rena, 8 rue de la République (☎ 03 81 46 98 33. Open M 1-11pm, Tu F 10am-noon and 1pm-midnight, W-Th 10am-noon and 1-11pm; Sa 9am-midnight. €2.50 per 20min., €5 per hr.) The **post office**, 17 rue de la Gare, has a **Cyberposte**. (☎ 03 81 38 49 44. Open M-F 8am-6:30pm and Sa 8am-noon.) **Postal code:** 25300.

ⓕⒸ ACCOMMODATIONS & FOOD. The best buy in town is the quiet, centrally located **Auberge de Pontarlier (FUAJ) ❶**, 2 rue Jouffroy. From the tourist office, go left on rue Marpaud; the hostel is the white stucco building on the left. The spotless, attractive dorm-style rooms have four beds each, and the friendly folk at reception have many suggestions for activities, and organize hiking and skiing trips. (☎ 03 81 39 06 57; fax 03 81 39 06 57. Common room with big-screen TV. Breakfast €3.25. Kitchen. Sheets €2.75. Reception 8am-noon and 5:30-10pm. Reservations advised for summer. Dorms €8.40 per bed. **Members only.**) TVs, wood paneling, spacious rooms, and a central location make the rooms of the **Hôtel de France ❷**, 8 rue de la Gare, another good bargain, although some are quite dim. (☎ 03 81 39 05 20; fax 03 81 46 24 43. Reception daily 7am-11pm. Breakfast €5. Singles with hall shower €16, with private shower €27; doubles €26/€27; triples with no private shower €33; quads with shower €50. MC/V.) At the upscale **Hôtel St-Pierre ❸**, 3 pl. St-Pierre, guests enjoy bright, spacious, tastefully decorated rooms in a classy establishment, with a restaurant downstairs that serves everything from *petite restauration croque monsieurs* (€3) to regional *comtoise menus* (€11). Reserve well in advance during summer. (☎ 03 81 46 50 80. Reception daily 7am-10pm. Singles €27.50-35; doubles €33-43.50; triples €45-58. MC/V.)

The most scenic accommodations are at the three-star **campground** on rue du Tolombief. From the station, turn right onto Rocade Georges Pompidou, cross the river, and bear left onto rue de l'Industrie. Take the first right onto av. de Neuchâtel and follow the signs. (15min.) Amenities include a TV, ping-pong, a game room, and a bar. (☎ 03 81 46 23 33; fax 03 81 46 23 34. July-Aug. 1 person and tent/car €9.60, 2 people and tent/car €12.50; Sept.-June €8.70/€11.10; children €1.20. Electricity €3.10. Châlets July-Aug. €54 per day for 2 people, Sept.-June €46; €366/€275 per week, €1250/€963 per month. Extra person €3.10. 6-person max.)

Although it may not pack the hallucinogenic punch it was once known for, a modern version of **absinthe Pontarlier** is available at every bar and café around town for €3-4. Try a bit of the anise-flavored concoction and be transported to the high-flying times of raucous yesteryear. Do as the Pontarliens do and buy your own food at the **Casino** supermarket, 75 rue de la République. (☎ 03 81 46 51 22. Open M-F 8:30am-12:30pm and 2:30-7pm, Sa 8:30am-7pm. MC/V.) Outdoor **markets** appear Th and Sa mornings at pl. Jules Pagnier year round. Good dining opportunities are concentrated around the well-traveled **rue de la République**. Right in the thick of things, sprawling **Le Grand Café Francais ❷**, 36 rue de la République, a gives a good bang for your buck. The *plat du jour* costs €6.90 and specialty *FlammeKüche* (a quiche-like dish) with Alsatian trimmings, cheese, and a salad goes for €7.10. (☎ 03 81 39 00 72. Open May-Aug. noon-midnight; Sept.-April closes Su at 1pm. MC/V.) The wood oven of **Pizzeria Gambetta ❷**, 15 rue Gambetta, off rue de la Gare, cooks over 20 varieties of pizza, ranging from pepperoni to eggs, tuna, and potatoes. Pizza, regional meat dishes, and pasta can be made to go, but stay for the incredible chocolate mousse. (☎ 03 81 46 67 17. Pizza from €6, design-your-own

€8.90; meal salads €7-9; mousse €3.80. Open Tu, Th-Su noon-1:30pm and 7-9:30pm. Closed much of Sept. MC/V.) Sample the *menu régional* (€11.50), featuring *fondue au Comté* and local *saucisse de Marteau* at **La Pinte Comtoise ❸**, 4 rue Jeanne d'Arc, an inviting place just off rue de la République. (☎03 81 39 07 35. Open Su-Tu and Th-Sa afternoon noon-2pm and 7-9:30pm. MC/V.)

📱 **SKIING, HIKING, BIKING, & RIDING.** The smooth, pine-covered Jura mountains, have 74km of long-distance **cross-country skiing** trails. Nine trails on two slopes (**Le Larmont** and **Le Malmaison**) span every level of difficulty. (Daily pass for cross-country skiing €6, under 17 €3.50; for downhill skiing €10/€7. MC/V.) Le Larmont (☎03 81 46 55 20), the alpine ski area nearest to Pontarlier, offers toboggan and snowshoe trails. For ski conditions, call **Info-Neige** (☎03 81 39 91 66), Massif de Jura. The Jura are much colder than the Alps, so wear layers. **Sport et Neige,** zac des Grands Planchants, sud rue Mervil, is the nearest store that rents ski equipment. (☎03 81 39 04 69. €9 per day, €40 per week; children €7/€40. Open M-Sa 9am-noon and 2-7pm. MC/V.) Prices are far cheaper than in the Alps, but the snow quality is less reliable. **Metabief Mont d'Or,** accessible by shuttle bus from Pontarlier, has day and night skiing. (☎03 81 49 13 81. Shuttle 30min., 3-4 per day from Mont Jura bus station, €8. Lift tickets €19.50 per day, under 12 €12. MC/V.)

In the summer, skiing gives way to fishing, hiking, and mountain biking. There are two mountain bike departure points in Pontarlier, one to the north just off rue Pompée and one to the south, about 2km west of Forges. Hikers can choose between the **GR5,** an international 262km trail accessible from Larmont, and the **GR6,** which leads to a narrow valley dominated by the dramatic **Château de Joux.** The massive 1000-year-old castle houses an extensive series of dungeons and a collection of rare arms. July-Aug. it hosts concerts, theater, and general merriment during the **Festival des Nuits de Joux.** (☎03 81 69 47 95; www.chateaudejoux.com. Open July-August daily 9am-6pm; Apr.-June and Sept.-Oct. 9:45-11:45am and 2-4:30pm; Nov.-Mar. 10-11:30am and 2-4pm; mid-Nov. to mid-Dec. by request only. €5.10, students €4.10.) The tourist office gives out a map (€2.50) that marks departure points for biking and hiking around town, including one near the train station at pl. St-Claude. More detailed maps can be found at **Librairie Rousseau,** 20 rue de la République. (☎03 81 39 10 28. Open M-Sa 9am-noon and 2-7pm. Closed M afternoon. **English books** also available here. MC/V.) **Le Poney Club,** rue du Toulombief, adjacent to the campground, rents well-trained horses for riders of all skill levels. (☎03 81 46 71 67. Take bus #2, dir: Poney Club. €7 for 30min., €10.50 per hr. For rides with a free guide, call a day in advance.)

In town, be sure to visit the local **Musée,** 2 pl. d'Arçon, if only for the immeasurable pride it takes in showcasing the absinthe-soaked history of liqueur production in Pontarlier. (☎03 81 38 82 14. Open M, W-F 10am-noon and 2-6pm, Sa 2-6pm, Su 3-7pm. €3.20, students €1.60.) The **Porte St-Pierre** at the head of rue de la République is an exact copy of the 18th-century Porte St-Martin in Paris.

LONS-LE-SAUNIER

Lons-le-Saunier (pop. 20,000) is a freshly scrubbed, green gem of a mountain town, not quite so convenient a base as Pontarlier for exploring the Jura. Best known as the birthplace of Rouget de Lisle, composer of *La Marseillaise,* Lons is also an ancient Roman spa site, with saltwater baths and preserved ruins. Most visitors come for the nearby mountains and the locals' highly developed *joie de vivre.*

📟 **TRANSPORTATION. Trains** run to: Besançon (10 per day, €11.70); and Lyon (5 per day, €15.80). **Local buses** run to outlying villages (☎03 84 86 07 74, usually 6am-6pm. Inquire at the tourist office for a schedule.) **Taxis** are available outside the station. (☎ 03 84 24 11 16. €1.70 base fee; €1.30 per km before 7pm, €1.77 after 7pm. 24hr.) Rent **bikes** at Dominique Maillard, 17 rue Perrin. (☎ 03 84 24 24 07. Open M-F 9am-1pm and 2-6:30pm. MC/V.)

█ PRACTICAL INFORMATION. To get to the **tourist office**, pl. du 11 Novembre, cross the street in front of the station and head up rue Aristide Briand until it forks. Take the right fork (av. Thurel) to rue Rouget de Lisle on the left. Continue straight across rue Jean Jaurès. The office is in the old theater to your left. They offer free maps, hotel and restaurant listings, guides to excursions in the Jura (available in English), and a mountain of friendly suggestions for what to do in town. The office leads French **tours** (€3) of the town and into the Jura on a highly variable schedule. (☎ 03 84 24 65 01; fax 03 84 43 22 59; www.ville-lons-le-sau-nier.fr. Open M-F 8am-noon and 2-6pm, Sa 8am-noon and 2-5pm.) For info on countryside **tours** (available in English and German) with groups of ten or more, contact Juragence, 19 rue Jean Moulin. (☎ 03 84 47 27 27. Open M-F 9am-12:30pm and 2-7pm, Sa 9am-noon and 2-5:30pm.) Other services include: **banks** with **ATMs** on rue Aristide Briand and pl. de la Liberté; a **laundromat** at 26 rue des Cordeliers (☎ 06 80 92 08 37; open daily 7am-9pm); **police** at 6 av. du 44ème R.I. (☎ 03 84 35 17 10; call here for the **pharmacie de garde**); a **hospital** at 55 rue Docteur Jean Michel (☎ 03 84 35 60 00); **Internet** at Car'Com, at the tourist office (€3.80 per hr.; open M-F 8am-noon and 2-6pm, Sa 10am-noon and 2-6pm), e' pl@net, 13 rue Aristide Bri-and (€3 per hr; open M-F 10am-7pm, Sa 1-7pm), and Info Jeunesse, 2 pl. de la Lib-erté. (☎ 03 84 87 02 55. €3.80 per hr. Open M-F 10am-noon and 2-6pm, Sa 10am-noon.) Info Jeunesse also sells **discount cards** good for discounts or free access to museums, lodgings, cinemas, and concerts (€5 for those under 26). The **post office** is on av. Aristide Briand. (☎ 03 84 85 83 60. Open M-F 8am-7pm, Sa 8am-noon.) **Poste Restante:** 39021. **Postal code:** 39000.

▐ ACCOMMODATIONS. Lons has a few decent, less expensive hotels located near pl. de la Liberté, but no hostels to speak of. Reserve a week in advance during the summer. The central **Hôtel des Sports ❷**, at 21 rue St-Desiré, is the best. Go four blocks from the train station on av. Aristide Briand and follow it around an abrupt left, then right onto rue St-Desiré. The hallways are dark and cramped, but the rooms are surprisingly spacious and bright. Roll out of bed and get breakfast at the daily market next door. (☎ 03 84 24 04 42. Breakfast €5. Reception M-Sa 6am-10:30pm, Su 8:30am-1:30pm and 5-10pm. Singles and doubles with shower €22; tri-ples €33. AmEx/MC/V.) At **Hôtel les Glaciers ❷**, 1 pl. Philibert de Chalon, nine bright though somewhat institutional rooms go for snap-'em-up rates. From rue St-Desiré, walk one block to pl. Liberté; diagonally across the *place* is the arcaded rue du Commerce. Take this for two blocks to a fork at pl. de l'Hôtel de Ville, then veer to the left and continue to the end of the block. The hotel is on the right. (☎ 03 84 47 26 89. Breakfast €5. Reception 7am-11pm. Singles €20, with shower €25; doubles €23/€28. MC/V.)

▐ FOOD. *Charcuteries, pâtisseries,* and *boulangeries* line **rue du Commerce**. A produce **market** appears at **pl. Verdun** each Thursday morning; find goodies the rest of the week at the local markets, cafés, and restaurants around the **place de la Lib-erté**, or at the **Casino** supermarket, 41 rue du Commerce. (☎ 03 84 24 48 64. Open Tu-Sa 7:30am-12:30pm and 3-7:30pm, Su 8am-noon.) The small, cheerful market **La Ferme Comtoise,** 23 rue St-Desiré, will help indecisive customers find the perfect variety of *miel de Jura* (honey) or *fromage de Comté.* (☎ 03 84 24 06 16. Open M-Sa 7am-7pm, Su 8am-1pm. MC/V.) Locals leisurely sip their *kirs* at the **Grand Café du Théâtre,** 4 rue Jean-Jaurès on pl. de la Liberté, an ornate and classy *fin de siècle* eatery with a Jurassienne salad featuring *fromage de Comté* for €8.40. (☎ 03 84 24

ALSACE

18 45. Open daily 7:30am-1am. MC/V.) **Le Strasbourg ❸**, around the corner, next to the tourist office, offers up regional *plats* in a sleek dining area. *(L'assiette Franc-Comtoise*, with Marteau sausage and potatoes, €10.90. (Open daily noon-2pm and 7-10pm. MC/V.)

SIGHTS. Lons-le-Saunier has two important bases for exploration. **Place de la Liberté**, with its open promenade and glittering fountain, is the center of Lons's tiny universe. It is also the site of the old theater, whose Rococo façade, reconstructed in 1901 after a devastating fire, has been equipped with a clock that chimes a refrain from *la Marseillaise* on the hour. The houses of the bustling **rue du Commerce**, just off the *place*, were also rebuilt—in stone—after a great fire in 1637. A few blocks down av. Jean Moulin is the second base, the beautiful gardens of **Parc des Bains**. Within the tree-lined gates lie the popular **Thermes Ledonia**, a luxurious salt-water spa whose ancient spring water allegedly cures ailments like rheumatism and cellulite. Full-scale treatment costs thousands of euros, but €9 will buy a dip in the pool and a sauna session. (☎03 84 24 20 34; lons@villegiatherm.com. Open Apr.-Oct. M-Sa 6:30am-12:30pm and 1:45-8pm; closes at 7pm F-Sa. MC/V.)

The museums of Lons, while not the central reason for any visit, possess their own character and charm. The birthplace of Rouget de Lisle, at 24 rue du Commerce, is now the tiny **Musée Rouget de Lisle.** Its cracked walls and four rooms hold enough *Marseillaise*-related memorabilia to make anyone salute—or go mad: the French anthem plays on a constant loop in the background. (☎03 84 47 29 16. Open mid-June to mid-Sept. M-F 10am-noon and 2-6pm, Sa-Su 2-5pm. Free.) Following the rue du Commerce to its end and bearing right onto rue Richebourg leads to the small but stylish **Musée d'Archéologie,** 25 rue Richebourg, which exhibits artifacts from excavations around Lons, including France's oldest dinosaur skeleton, the Plateosaurus. (☎03 84 47 12 13. Open M-F 10am-noon and 2-6pm, Sa-Su 2-5pm. €2, students €1, under 18 free; W and first Su of every month free.) To the left off rue du Commerce, **Musée des Beaux Arts,** pl. Philibert de Chalon boasts a splendid collection of Perraud statuary. (☎03 84 47 64 30. €2, students €1, under 18 free. Open M and W-F 10am-noon and 2-6pm, Sa-Su 2-5pm.) Following rue Richebourg back toward the center of town from the Parc leads to **Promenade de la Chevalerie** and an astonished-looking statue of Rouget de Lisle sculpted by Bartholdi.

EXCURSIONS. Nestled between some of the Jura's most breathtakingly beautiful peaks, 10km from Lons, slumbers the little town of **Baume-les-Messieurs** and its well-known **abbey.** (☎03 84 44 99 28. Open mid-June to mid-Sept. daily 10am-noon and 2-6pm.) Monts Jura **buses** run from Lons June-Aug. (☎03 84 86 08 80. Ask the tourist office for bus schedules.) There is an extensive network of caves near the town, with underground lakes and vaults up to 80m high. (☎03 84 48 23 02. €3.50, under 14 €2.50. Caves open Apr.-Sept. M-Su 10am-6pm.) The cliffs surrounding Baume are an incredible sight by starlight; one can spend the night outdoors at **Campground La Toupe,** a well-placed sight with showers but no laundry service. (☎03 84 44 63 16. Reception open 7am-noon and 2-8pm. €2.50 per person, €2 per car or tent. Electricity €2.50.)

BURGUNDY (BOURGOGNE)

A battleground for Gallic border wars in the first century BC, Burgundy was a major player in the Roman conquest. **Autun** (p. 405) was founded as a Roman capital. In the 5th century, the Burgundians, one of many Germanic tribes to pour across the Empire's borders during its final years, settled on the plains of the Saône and modestly named the region after themselves. During the Middle Ages, the duchy of Burgundy built magnificent cathedrals, and the powerful abbey of **Cluny** (p. 405) governed over 10,000 monks. During the Hundred Years' War, the Burgundians allied with the English to betray young Joan of Arc.

Encompassing miles of gorgeous vineyards, pretty old villages, and the wild, forested Morvan, largely rural Burgundy is known for its wine (**Beaune,** p. 398, and the **Côte d'Or,** p. 401), mustard (**Dijon,** p. 391), porcelain (**Nevers,** p. 408), and rich cuisine (just about everywhere). Burgundy is also home to a wealth of stately churches, dream-like châteaux (**Rochepot,** p. 403; **Gevrey-Chambertin,** p. 402; and **Val Lamartinien,** p. 405) and adorable medieval streets, the most beautiful of which may be at **Vézelay** (p. 412) and **Sémur-en-Auxois** (p. 414). The area contains a number of old towns, such as **Mâcon** (p. 403) and **Auxerre** (p. 409), that are now fairly quiet but retain some of their older charm.

Burgundy's diverse wines may stretch the limits of your vocabulary, but don't miss other regional delicacies: *gougères* (puffed pastry with cabbage or cheese), *hélix pomatia* (snails) in butter and garlic, and the esteemed *bœuf bourguignon*. The *jambon persillé* (a gelatin of ham and parsley) may be an acquired taste, but the traditional *coq au vin* (chicken in wine) is fantastic from the start.

DIJON

The regional capital of Burgundy and the tangy hub of French mustard production, Dijon (pop. 160,000; annual mustard produced 84,000 tons) combines gritty urbanity with provincial charm. In the late Middle Ages, the powerful Dukes of Burgundy exercised a prestige and influence from Dijon that the weak Parisian monarchy could not hope to match. The *maisons en bois* and *hôtels particuliers* of the *vieille ville* seem comfortably frozen in the past, but Dijon is clearly speeding into the 21st century as both an industrial and administrative center. Reflecting the town's large population of students and backpackers, Dijon's night scene stays lively until the wee hours.

◧ TRANSPORTATION

Trains: cours de la Gare, at the end of av. Maréchal Foch. Info office open M-F 9am-7pm, Sa 9am-6pm. To: **Beaune** (30min., 27 per day, €5.70); **Clermont-Ferrand** (4hr., 5 per day, €29.70); **Lyon** (2hr.; 5 trains, 2 TGV per day; €21.20); **Nice** (6-8hr.; 4 trains, 2 TGV per day; €57); **Paris** (1¾-3hr.; 7 trains, 13 TGV per day; €25.80). **SOS Voyageurs** (☎03 80 43 16 34), in the train station, has travel information. Open M-F 8:30am-7pm, Sa 8:30am-5pm. **Luggage storage** open Sept.-June M-F 8am-7:15pm, Sa-Su 9am-12:30pm and 2-6pm; July-Aug. M-F 8am-7:15pm; €3 per bag, €5 for 2 bags.

BURGUNDY

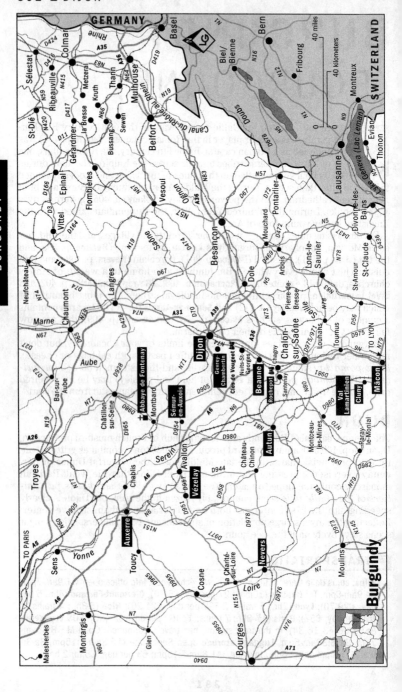

Buses: TRANSCO, av. Mal. Foch (☎03 80 42 11 00), connected to the train station, left from the exit. Ticket and info office open M-F 5:30am-8:30pm, Sa 6:30am-12:30pm and 4-8:30pm, Su 9:30am-12:30pm and 4:40-8:30pm. Schedule posted outside the terminal. Or, buy tickets on the bus or at the *chef de gare*'s office near the bus terminal. To: **Beaune** (1hr.; 9 per day M-Sa 6:35am-7:25pm, Su only 11:10am; €5.80), **Autun** (2¼hr., M-Sa 12:15pm, Su 11:10am, €12), and various stops in the **Côte d'Or.**

Public Transportation: STRD (☎03 80 30 60 90), pl. Grangier. Office open M-F 7:15am-7:15pm, Sa 8:30am-noon and 2-7:15pm. Map at the tourist office. Tickets €0.80; 12-trip pass €7; 1-day pass €2.70; 1-week pass €7.30; all available on board. Buses run 6am-8pm; limited night bus service until 12:30am, Su morning until 1am.

Taxis: Taxi Dijon (☎03 80 41 41 12). 24hr. Under €10 from center to periphery.

Car Rental: Avis, 7bis cours de la Gare (☎03 80 42 05 99). €90 per day. 25+. Open M-F 8am-12:30pm, 2-8pm, and 8:30-9:30pm; Sa 8am-12:30pm and 2-6pm; Su 5:15-9:15pm. AmEx/MC/V.

Bike Rental: EuroBike, 4 rue du fbg. Raines (☎03 80 45 32 32), rents bikes, scooters, motorcycles, and in-line skates; recommends other locations. €10-12 per half-day, €18-20 per day. Open Apr.-Oct. M-Sa 8am-noon and 2-6:30pm, Su 9:30-10:30am and 6:30-7pm; Nov.-Mar. M-Sa 9am-noon and 2-6pm. Low-season prices lower.

■✦❷ ORIENTATION & PRACTICAL INFORMATION

The main axis of the *vieille ville*, the pedestrian **rue de la Liberté,** runs roughly from **place Darcy** (recognizable by its big arch) and the tourist office to **place St-Michel.** From the train station, follow av. Mal. Foch. The **place de la République,** northeast of pl. Darcy, is the central roundabout for roads leading out of the city.

Tourist Office: pl. Guillame Darcy (☎03 80 44 11 44). Gives free map and sells a more detailed version (€4.80). Organizes themed **city tours,** some in English (June-Aug. daily; €6, students €3; reserve ahead), and vineyard tours (€45-95). **Accommodations service** €2.30 plus 10% deposit. **Currency exchange.** Open May to mid-Oct. daily 9am-8pm; mid-Oct. to Apr. M-Sa 10am-6pm, Su 10am-noon and 2-6pm. **Branch** at 34 rue des Forges (☎03 80 44 11 44). Open May to mid-Oct. M-Sa 9am-1pm and 2-6pm; mid-Oct. to Apr. M-F 9am-noon and 2-6pm. **Branch** in the Palais des Ducs. Open M-F 8am-7pm, Sa 8am-12:30pm and 1:30-6pm, Su 9am-12:30pm and 1:30-6pm.

Youth Information: Centre Régional d'Information Jeunesse de Bourgogne (CRIJ), 18 rue Audra (☎03 80 44 18 44).Info, most in French, on lodging, classes, grape-picking, summer jobs, and travel. Open M-Tu and Th-F 10am-1pm and 2-6pm, W 10am-6pm.

Laundromats: 36 rue Guillaume Tell. Open daily 6am-9pm. Wash €3.50, dry €1.50. At 28 rue Berbisey, open daily 7am-9pm. At 8 pl. de la Banque, open daily 7am-8:30pm.

Police: 2 pl. Suquet (☎03 80 44 55 00). Call here for the **pharmacie de garde.**

Medical Assistance: Centre Hospitalier Regional de Dijon, 3 rue fbg. Raines (☎03 80 29 30 31). **SOS Médecins** (☎03 80 59 80 80) has doctors on call.

Internet: Multi Rezo, in station, cours de la Gare (☎03 80 42 13 89). Open M-Sa 9am-midnight, Su 2-10pm. €1 for 12min., €5 per hr., €15.20 for 5hr. **Reveil Informatique,** 38 rue Planchettes (☎03 80 63 89 71). Open M-F 9am-noon and 2-6pm. €9 per hr.

Post Office: pl. Grangier (☎03 80 50 62 19), near pl. Darcy. **Currency exchange.** Open M-F 8am-7pm, Sa 8am-noon. **Poste Restante:** 21031. **Postal code:** 21000.

▌ ACCOMMODATIONS & CAMPING

Dijon's budget accommodations can be uninvitingly dark and impersonal, so travelers may want to opt for the cheaper hotels listed below. Reserve ahead.

B U R G U N D Y

■ **Hôtel Victor Hugo,** 23 rue des Fleurs (☎03 80 43 63 45; fax 03 80 42 13 01). Quiet and convenient Immaculate, spacious rooms have shower or bath and toilet make it worth every penny. Breakfast €4.80. Reception 24hr. Singles €29-36.50; doubles €36.50-45. MC/V. ❸

■ **Hôtel Montchapet,** 26-28 rue Jacques Cellerier (☎03 80 53 95 00; www.hotel-montch-apet.com). In a quiet neighborhood. Kind proprietors let bright, comfortable rooms with TV. Breakfast €5. Reception 7am-10:30pm. Check-out 11am. Singles €26, with toilet €31, with shower €39; doubles with toilet €36, with shower €36-46; triples and quads with shower €54-59. Extra bed €5. AmEx/MC/V. ❷

Hôtel du Sauvage, 64 rue Monge (☎03 80 41 31 21; fax 03 80 42 06 07). Tucked away from the street on a cobblestone driveway, the fairy-tale, half-timbered façade of this 15th-century post office overlooks a flowery courtyard. Breakfast €5.50. Reception 7am-11pm. June-Aug. reserve 2 weeks in advance. Clean singles with shower €34-43, with bath €39-57; doubles €35-64. Huge 5-person loft €80. Extra bed €10. MC/V. ❸

Auberge de Jeunesse (HI), Centre de Rencontres Internationales, 1 av. Champollion (☎03 80 72 95 20; fax 03 80 70 00 61), 4km from the station. Take bus #5 (or night bus A) from pl. Grangier to Epirey; the bus stops right in front of this concrete megahostel with dark hallways. **Internet** €2 per 15min. Laundry. Breakfast included. Lunch or dinner from €4. Lockers €2. No keys before midday. Reception 24hr. Reservations recommended. Dorms €15; singles with shower €28-30; doubles and triples with shower €16-19; prices slightly lower for 2- to 3-night stays. MC/V. ❶

Foyer International d'Etudiants, 6 rue Maréchal Leclerc (☎03 80 71 70 00; fax 03 80 71 60 48). A very long walk (30-40min.) or bus #4 from pl. Darcy (dir: St-Apollinaire) to Parc des Sports will take you to this hostel. From av. Paul Doumer, turn right onto rue du Stade, then take the first left onto rue Maréchal Leclerc. An international crowd inhabits this colorless, dormitory-like hostel. TV rooms, ping-pong and tennis courts, laundry, kitchen, and a lawn. Push-button, sometimes cold showers. Cafeteria open daily. Reception 24hr. Huge singles with shared, coed bathrooms €14. AmEx/MC/V. ❶

Camping Municipal du Lac, 3 bd. Kir (☎03 80 43 54 72). Exit the back of the station and turn right on av. Albert I. After 1km, turn left on bd. Kir and follow the signs; if you cross a bridge, you've gone too far. Or take bus #12 from pl. Darcy (dir: Fontaine d'Ouche) to Hôpital des Chartreux. Park and canal with bike path nearby. This grassy site gets crowded in the summer. Reception July-Aug. 8:30am-8pm; June and Sept. 8:30am-noon and 1:30-5pm; Apr.-May and Oct. daily 8:30am-noon and 2:30-7pm. Open Apr. to mid-Oct. €2.60 per person, under age 7 €1.45; €1.50 per car; €2.10 per site. Electricity €2.60. ❶

🍴 FOOD

Dijon's reputation for high cuisine is well deserved—and restaurant prices reflect it. *Charcuteries* are an economical way to sample specialties like *tarte bourguignonne*, mushroom quiche, and *jambon persillé* (ham with parsley).

Rue Berbisey, rue Monge, rue Musette, and **place Emile Zola** host a variety of reasonably priced restaurants. The narrow, pedestrian **rue Amiral Boussin** behind the pl. de la Liberté provides dining in the most classically Continental setting. Several *brasseries* and a sea-themed *crêperie* spill onto the street. Shoppers can find local produce at a colorful **market** in the pedestrian area around Les Halles. (Open Tu and Th-F mornings, all day Sa.) There's a **supermarket** in the basement of Galeries Lafayette, 41 rue de la Liberté (open M-Sa 8:15am-7:45pm), and within **Monoprix,** 11 rue Piron, off pl. Jean Macé. (Open M-Sa 9am-8:45pm.)

■ **Les Clos du Cappucines** ❸, 3 rue Jeanin, serves Burgundian masterpieces of asparagus, *chèvre*, and banana-and-mango desserts in a 17th-century cobblestone courtyard, pleasantly removed from the busy *centre ville*. (☎03 80 65 83 03. 2-

BURGUNDY

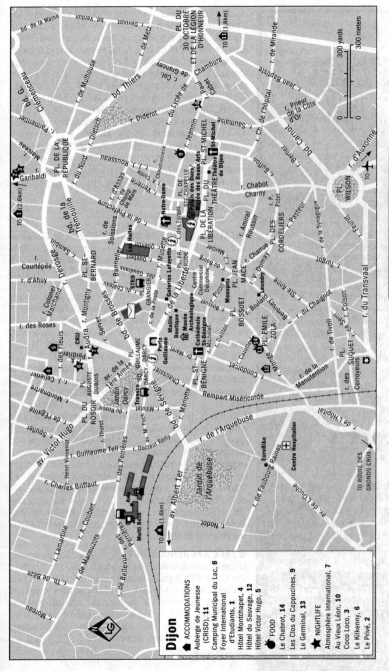

Dijon

▲ ACCOMMODATIONS
Auberge de Jeunesse (CRISD), **11**
Camping Municipal du Lac, **8**
Foyer International d'Etudiants, **1**
Hôtel Montchapet, **4**
Hôtel du Sauvage, **12**
Hôtel Victor Hugo, **5**

🍴 FOOD
Le Chabrot, **14**
Les Clos du Cappucines, **9**
Le Germinal, **13**

★ NIGHTLIFE
Atmosphère International, **7**
Au Vieux Léon, **10**
Coco Loco, **3**
Le Kilkenny, **6**
Le Privé, **2**

THE LOCAL LEGEND

CUTTING THE MUSTARD

Mustard has been spicing up Burgundian palettes since the Middle Ages, when it was also used as animal feed, oil, and fertilizer. To people in the mustard business, the Biblical "seed of Senève" refers to mustard.

Locals love to tell the story of how mustard got its name. When Philip the Bold brought the Burgundian specialties of wine and mustard to his home in Flanders, his flag carried the words "Moult me tard" (I am in a hurry to return). Blowing in the wind, the flag read as "Moutard"—the first mustard advertising campaign.

The yellowish condiment is made by sifting, washing, and pressing the brown or black seeds, adding vinegar, and grinding it after a 58hr. storage period. Rich in vitamin C, mustard wards off scurvy and helps digest rich Burgundian cuisine. Mustard plaster placed on the chest is an old home remedy.

For those who want to learn more and eat copious amounts of ·mustard seeds, the **Amora/ Maille factory** on quai Nicolas Rolin offers daily tours of its **Musée de Moutarde** in English and French at 3pm. Tickets (€3) are available at the tourist office.

No trip to Dijon would be complete without a stop at the source of **Grey Poupon**, the **Maille Boutique**, 32 rue de la Liberté, which sells twenty different mustards. (☎ 03 80 30 41 02. Open M-Sa 9am-7pm. MC/V.)

course *menu* €12; 3 courses €16; 4 courses €28. Open Tu-F for lunch and dinner, Su-M and Sa for dinner only.) Light green decor, an aquarium underfoot, display cases full of frog paraphernalia, and a menu listing *jambes de grenouille* (frog legs) are all symptomatic of a full-fledged croaker obsession at **Le Germinal ❷**, 44 rue Monge. (☎ 03 80 44 97 16. *Menus* €7.50-10, generous dinner *plats* from €9.50. Reserve ahead. Open Tu-Th noon-2pm and 7-10:30pm, F-Sa noon-2pm and 7-11pm. MC/V.) Restaurant and *cave du vin* **Le Chabrot ❸**, 36 rue Monge, serves mouthwatering smoked fish appetizers, a special Burgundy cheese plate, and chocolate-vanilla-banana mousse. (☎ 03 80 30 69 61. Lunch *menu* €11, dinner *menu* €27. Open M-Sa 10am-10:30pm. MC/V.)

🜄 SIGHTS

PALAIS DES DUCS DE BOURGOGNE. The Dukes of Burgundy (1364-1477) were the best sort of rulers: fearless (Jean sans Peur), good (Philippe le Bon), and bold (Philippe le Hardi and Charles le Téméraire). At the center of the *vieille ville*, the 52m Tour Philippe le Bon is the most conspicuous vestige of ducal power. A climb up the tower for a view of the *vieille ville* is a good way to begin a Dijon visit. (☎ 03 80 74 52 71. Tours Easter to mid-Nov. daily every 45min. 9am-5:30pm; mid-Nov. to Easter W 2-6pm, Sa-Su 9-11am and 1:30-3:30pm. €2.30, students €1.20.)

Most of the buildings in the palace currently function as administrative offices, but the east wing of the complex houses the quite elegant **Musée des Beaux-Arts,** pl. de la Ste-Chapelle. The chapel housing the Duke's funerary monuments is breathtakingly ornate. One of the lifelike figures on the base of Philippe le Bon's tomb, sculpted by Dijon's prodigal son sculptor Claus Sluter, is depicted holding his nose because of the rotting corpse's smell. The section dedicated to "modern" art includes a Cézanne and 20th-century technicolor paintings by Lapicque. (Pl. de la Libération. ☎ 03 80 74 52 70. Open M and W-Su May-Oct. 9:30am-6pm; Nov.-Apr. 10am-5pm. Modern art wing closed 11:30am-1:45pm. €3.40, groups and seniors €1.60, students with ID free, Su free.)

MUSÉE ARCHÉOLOGIQUE. Next door to the palace is the Musée Archéologique, which displays layers of the Côte d'Or's past, from prehistoric jewelry and Gallo-Roman sculpture to 17th-century mustard crocks. Claus Sluter's emotionally arresting sculpture "Head of Christ" graces the first stairway landing. (5 rue Dr. Maret. ☎ 03 80 30 88 54. Open Tu-Su June-Sept. 9am-6pm; Oct.-May 9am-noon and 2-6pm. €2.20, students free, Su free.)

EGLISE NOTRE-DAME. The 11th-century cult statue of the Black Virgin in the cathedral is credited with the liberation of the city on two desperate occasions: in 1513 from a Swiss siege and in 1914 from the German occupation. Two sumptuous tapestries depicting the miracles were commissioned for the Virgin in gratitude—unfortunately, they have been moved due to vandalism. The **Horloge à Jacquemart** clock, above the church's tower was hauled off as plunder by Philippe le Hardi after his 1382 victory over the Flemish. As you leave the church via rue de la Chouette, remember to rub the well-worn **chouette** (owl) for good luck. *(Pl. Notre Dame.* ☎ *03 80 74 35 76. English pamphlet well worth the €0.50.)*

EGLISE ST-MICHEL. While the inside of this church has the dark, vaulted interior of a Gothic cathedral, it switched style mid-construction, resulting in a unique, colonnaded Renaissance façade. Like the Eglise Notre-Dame, it suffered severe damage during the Revolution, but was lovingly restored by Abbé Deschamps, who is buried in one of the chapels. *(Pl. St-Michel.* ☎ *03 80 63 17 84.)*

CATHÉDRALE ST-BÉNIGNE. This Gothic cathedral, recently renovated and recognizable by its distinctive brightly tiled Burgundian roof, commemorates a 2nd-century missionary whose remains were unearthed nearby in the 6th century. Don't miss the 18th-century organ designed by Charles Joseph Riepp and the unusual circular crypt, pitch-black in places; flowers indicate Bénigne's grave. *(Pl. St-Bénigne.* ☎ *03 80 30 39 33. Open daily 9am-7pm. Crypt €1.)*

OTHER SIGHTS. The **Jardin de l'Arquebuse** boasts reflecting fountains, pools, an arboretum, and 3500 species of flora meticulously laid out. A giant sequoia makes for a grand entrance. Cross under the tracks that are to your left as you approach the station. *(1 av. Albert I.* ☎ *03 80 76 82 84. Open July-Sept. daily 7:30am-10pm; Oct.-Feb. 7:30am-5:30pm; Mar.-June 7:30am-7pm.)* The **Côte d'Or** (p. 401) makes a great daytrip.

🎵 🍷 ENTERTAINMENT & FESTIVALS

Rue Berbisey is lined with bars and cafés. ◪**Le Privé,** 20 av. Garibaldi, just north of pl. de la République, pulses with energy from students and 20-somethings draped over leopard-skin couches or dancing to techno and hip hop under golden palm trees and in steel cages. *(*☎ *03 80 73 39 57. F-Sa cover €8; includes one drink. Su-Th cover €5, with one drink €8. Open Tu-Sa 10pm-5am, Su-M 11pm-5am.)* The club starts rocking at 2am, after closing time at other bars like the Latin-themed **Coco Loco,** 18 av. Garibaldi—where jumping throngs of youngsters really go *loco.* *(*☎*03 80 73 29 44. Open Tu-Sa 5pm-2am.)* ◪**Au Vieux Leon,** 52 Rue Jeanin, attracts a merry bohemian crowd. Discussion is the stimulant of choice, whether over beer at large outdoor picnic tables or the café with angsty intellectuals downstairs, complemented by jazz music. *(*☎ *03 80 30 98 29. Beer €3-4.)* At **Atmosphère Internationale,** 7 rue Audra, local students let loose on the dance floor while aloof foreigners watch from the nearby pool tables. The party starts late. *(*☎ *03 80 30 52 03. No cover for international students with ID; Su-W free for everyone; Th-Sa cover €5, includes a drink. Soirées internationales W and Th night. Open daily 5pm-5am. MC/V.)* Across the street, **Le Kilkenny,** 1 rue Auguste Perdrier, serves a great selection of beers on tap under arched stone ceilings. *(*☎ *03 80 30 02 48. Open Tu-Sa 7pm-3am, Su-M 6pm-3am. Draft beers €4-6, Irish specialty beers €4.30-7.50.)*

The beautiful 18th-century **Théâtre de Dijon,** pl. du Théâtre, right next to St-Michel, puts on operas from mid-October to late April. *(*☎ *03 80 68 46 40. Tickets €21.40-42.70, students €9.20 1hr. before curtain. Office open M-F 1-7pm and Sa 4-7pm during production months.)* Check out the plays (both classic and contemporary) at the **Nouveau Théâtre de Bourgogne,** Théâtre du Parvis St-Jean, rue Danton. *(*☎ *03 80 30 12 12. Open Oct.-June M-F 1-7pm, Sa 4-7pm; performances M, F, Sa*

8:20pm and W 7:30pm. Dijon's **Estivade** brings dance, music, and theater to the streets and indoor venues from late June to mid-July. Pick up a program at the tourist office. (☎03 80 30 31 00. Tickets free and up to €8.) The city devotes a week in late summer to the **Fêtes de la Vigne** and the **Folkloriades Internationales,** a celebration of grapes accompanied by over 20 foreign dance and music troupes. (☎/fax 03 80 30 37 95. Tickets €10-46, most €10-15; ask about youth discounts.)

BEAUNE

The puns are easy enough to make—*le vin de Beaune, c'est du bon vin*—but the throngs of dapper 40-somethings and red-faced septuagenarians who come to this viticulture hot spot (pop. 24,000) often don't speak enough French to understand them. The crowds of visitors share with locals their deep love of the liquid that Louis Pasteur called "the healthiest and most hygienic drink," grown here since Roman times. The atmosphere at Beaune is decidedly *bourgeois:* the cobblestone streets, stunning roof of the hospital, and the taste of fine vintages are universally accessible, but the prices at boutiques and restaurants are not. More fiscally challenged travelers might find it an ideal daytrip.

▐ TRANSPORTATION

Trains (☎03 80 22 13 13) depart av. du 8 Septembre for Dijon (25min.; 33 per day, 4 TGV; €5.70); Lyon (1½hr., 11 per day, €18.10); Paris (2hr., 11 per day, €38.40). The info office is open M-F 10am-noon and 2-7pm. **TRANSCO buses** go to Dijon (1hr., 10 per day, €5.80) from rues Buttes, Clémenceau, Jules Ferry, Pasteur, and St-Nicolas. (☎03 80 42 11 00. Stops along the Côte d'Or; schedule at tourist office.) **Allo Beaune Taxi** (☎06 09 42 36 80) has 24hr. service. **Cars** can be rented at ADA, 26 av. du 8 Septembre, across from the train station. (☎03 80 22 72 90. Open M-Sa 8am-noon and 2-6pm. MC/V.) The knowledgeable English-speaking staff at **Bourgogne Randonnées,** 7 av. du 8 Septembre, near the station, **rents bikes,** gives free maps with routes, suggest itineraries, and store luggage, space permitting. (☎03 80 22 06 03. €3 per hr., €15 per day, €28 for 2 days, €69 per week. Credit card deposit. Open M-Sa 9am-noon and 1:30-7pm, Su 10am-noon and 2-6pm. MC/V.)

▐ ▐ ORIENTATION & PRACTICAL INFORMATION

The streets of the town center run in concentric rings around the **Basilique Notre-Dame.** Almost everything there is to see lies within the circular ramparts enclosing Beaune's *vieille ville.* From the station, head straight on av. du 8 Septembre, which becomes rue du Château. Once inside the city walls, turn left onto rue Thiers and follow it for about 10min. until you cross **rue de l'Hôtel-Dieu,** which leads to the Hôtel-Dieu and the **tourist office,** 1 rue de l'Hôtel-Dieu. (15min.) The staff provides free maps, lists of *caves,* a **reservations service** with 10% deposit, **tours** of the *vieille ville* (July to mid-Sept. daily at noon; €6.50 per person, €10.50 per couple), a €14.50 *Pass Beaune* to three sights of choice, and **currency exchange** (€5) Sa-Su. (☎03 80 26 21 30; fax 03 80 26 21 39. Open mid-Nov. to Mar. M-Sa 10am-6pm, Su 10am-12:30pm and 2-5pm; end of Mar. to end of June M-Sa 9:30am-7pm, Su 10am-12:30pm and 2-5pm; end of June to mid-Nov. an hour later.) The staff also runs an **information booth** at Porte Marie de Bourgogne, 6 bd. Perpeuil. (Open June-Nov. M-F 9:30am-noon and 2-6pm.) The **Point Information Jeunesse,** 8 av. de Salins, has info on work, study, and sports. (☎03 80 22 44 95. Open M-Th 1:30-6pm, F 1:30-5pm.) Other services include a **laundromat** at 19 rue fbg. St-Jean (☎03 80 24 09 78; open daily 6:30am-9pm), **police** at 5 av. du Général de Gaulle (☎03 80 25 09 25), a **hospital** at 120 av. Guigone de Salins, northeast of the town center (☎03 80 24 44

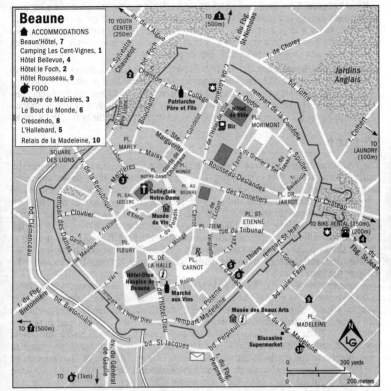

Beaune

⌂ ACCOMMODATIONS
Beaun'Hôtel, 7
Camping Les Cent-Vignes, 1
Hôtel Bellevue, 4
Hôtel le Foch, 2
Hôtel Rousseau, 9
🍎 FOOD
Abbaye de Maizières, 3
Le Bout du Monde, 6
Crescendo, 8
L'Hallebard, 5
Relais de la Madeleine, 10

44), **24hr. ambulance** service (☎ 03 80 20 20 09), and **Internet** at Diz, 28 rue de Lor-raine (☎ 03 80 26 36 01. €1 for 10min., €5.50 per hr. Open M-Sa 11am-9pm.) The **post office,** bd. St-Jacques, has **currency exchange, Internet,** and **Poste Restante.** (☎ 03 80 26 29 50. Open M-F 8am-7pm, Sa 8am-noon.) **Postal code:** 21200.

🛏 ACCOMMODATIONS & CAMPING

Visitors swarm to Beaune Apr.-Nov.; reserve at least a week in advance.

🛏 **Hôtel Rousseau,** 11 pl. Madeleine (☎ 03 80 22 13 59). Comfortable rooms open onto a courtyard. Plenty of company from pigeons and the owner's tropical birds. Breakfast included. Shower €3. Curfew 11:30pm. Singles €23-39; doubles €29-46, with shower €50-54; triples and quads €46-73. ❷

Beaun'Hôtel, 55 fbg. Bretonnière (☎ 03 80 22 11 01; fax 03 80 22 46 66). Southwest of the center, off bd. Clemenceau. Pretty, bright rooms in yellow, blue, and purple; many are quite large. Buffet breakfast €6.50. Reception 8am-6pm. Doubles €44-58; triples €60; family suite for 4-5 people €78. Closed Dec.-Feb. MC/V. ❸

Hôtel le Foch, 24 bd. Foch (☎ 03 80 24 05 65; fax 03 80 24 75 59). Le Foch features several pleasant, colorful rooms, near the ramparts and a quiet park. Breakfast €5.40. Reception 7am-9pm. Singles and doubles €25, with shower €33-54; triples €38. Extra bed €6. MC/V. ❷

Hôtel Bellevue, 5 rte. de Seurre (☎03 80 24 05 10). From the station, make a left onto av. des Lyonnais and then another left onto rue Bellevue, and follow it to the corner (7 min.). Above a large restaurant, a somewhat grouchy owner maintains clean, plain rooms for 2 people at a great price. 10min. walk from the town center. Doubles with sink €25, with shower or toilet €27, with both €30. ❷

Camping: Les Cent-Vignes, 10 rue Dubois (☎03 80 22 03 91), 500m from the town center off rue du fbg. St-Nicolas. Head north on rue Lorraine from pl. Monge. Arrive early in summer. Graveled or grassy sites made pleasantly private by hedges. Ping-pong, tennis, laundry, restaurant, and grocery store. Open mid-Mar. to end of Oct. Reception 8am-9:30pm. €3.10 per person. Site €4.20, car included. Electricity €4.10. MC/V. ❶

◖ FOOD

The restaurants around **place Madeleine** and **place Carnot** serve the least exorbitantly priced *menus*, but even here prices for local wine are high. **Casino supermarkets** are at 28 rue du fbg. Madeleine (open M-Sa 8:30am-8pm); rue Carnot (open M 3-7pm, Tu-Sa 7:30am-12:30pm and 3-7:30pm, Su 8:30am-noon); and 15 rue Maufoux (open M-Sa 7:30am-12:30pm and 3-7:30pm.) A large and popular open-air **market** opens on pl. de la Halle W and Sa mornings, and M afternoons from June to mid-Sept. Those willing to dispense with formality can eat a full meal for under €9 at the locally popular cafeteria **Crescendo ❷,** Centre Commercial Champion, 9 av. Charles de Gaulle, 12min. from the center. (Open daily 11:30am-2:30pm and 6:30-9:30pm; tea 9am-10pm.)

Monsieur Neaux, chef of **Relais de la Madeleine ❷,** 44 pl. Madeleine, wants diners to try everything he cooks—he'll come by at the end of a meal to make sure his patrons are satisfied. A cut above the rest, Madeleine features house specialties like duck *pâté* with pistachio, a wondrous *mousse au chocolat*, and peppered trout. (☎03 80 22 07 47. *Menus* €11.50, €14.50, and €23. Open Su-Tu and Th-Sa noon-2pm and 7-10pm. AmEx/MC/V.) For a tasty dinner that takes you back in time, head into the dimly-lit 12th-century wine cellar at **Abbaye de Maizières ❸,** 19 rue Maizières, near the Musée du Vin and the cathedral. (☎03 80 24 74 64. 3-course *menu* of regional specialties €16, 4 courses €23. Open daily noon-2pm and 7-9pm.) The traveler who hasn't yet had enough to drink can have an *apéritif* or a *vin au verre* at the wine bar **Le Bout Du Monde ❶,** 2 rue du fbg. Madeleine. (☎03 80 24 04 52. Wine €3-7 per glass. Open daily 6pm-2am. MC/V.) The nearby German-themed **L'Hallebard ❶,** 25 rue d'Alsace, serves a cherry-flavored beer in a garden setting (☎03 80 22 17 68. Beer €3-6. Open daily 1-11pm.)

◉ ⚡ SIGHTS & SIPS

▨ **HÔTEL-DIEU.** In 1443, Nicolas Rolin, chancellor to the Duke of Burgundy, built this hospital to help the city's poor recover from the ravages of war and famine. Patients were treated here until 1971. Today, the building is the town's best non-potable tourist attraction. In the courtyard, visitors ogle the colorful tiled roofs that make this one of France's architectural icons. In the *Salle des Poivres*, the communal patients' room, mannequins of the nuns who nursed them bend over red curtained beds. The room's elegant decor explains why the hospital was called "the palace of the poor." The *Hôtel*'s great treasure is **The Last Judgment,** carved panels by Roger van der Weyden. The exquisite details of the blessed and the damned are fully appreciated only with a giant magnifying glass. The hospital maintains 143 acres of vineyards; each year, on the third Sunday of November, the most recent vintages go up for sale at a charity auction. *(Open daily 9am-6:30pm. €5.10, students €4.10; tour €1.60.)*

PATRIARCHE PÈRE ET FILS. At the foot of a winding staircase behind a chapel, a labyrinth of wine bottles matures to perfection in Beaune's largest *cave*. A friendly, English-speaking staff point the way along 5km of musty corridors lined with over four million bottles. In the final *caves*, a *dégustation* of 13 different wines is led by expert *sommeliers*. (*5-7 rue du Collège.* ☎ *03 80 24 53 78. Open daily 9:30-11:30am and 2-5pm; arrive at least 1hr. before closing. €9; all proceeds to charity.*)

OTHER SIGHTS. Inside the 15th-century Hôtel des Ducs de Bourgogne, the **Musée du Vin** shows visitors its wine cellar, vats, and immense presses for free and traces the history of wine from Roman times. (*Rue d'Enfer, off pl. Général Leclerc.* ☎ *03 80 22 08 19. Open Apr.-Nov. daily 9:30am-6pm; Dec.-Mar. W-Su 9:30am-5pm. €5.10, students €3.10. Includes Musée des Beaux Arts and Musée Etienne-Jules Marey.*) In addition to a small collection of Gallo-Roman sculpture, the **Musée des Beaux Arts** houses paintings by 15th- and 16th-century Dutch and Flemish artists and 18th- and 19th-century French artists, including a collection by painter Felix Ziern, famous for his Mediterranean landscapes. (*Porte Marie de Bourgogne, 6 bd. Perreuil.* ☎ *03 80 24 56 92, weekends* ☎ *03 80 24 98 70. Open daily Apr. to late Sept. 2-6pm, Mar. 2-5pm, late Sept. to Dec. 10am-5:30pm. For admission, see Musée du Vin.*) In a pink-and-white stone interior, the Burgundian-Romanesque **Collégiale Notre-Dame** draws visitors to a set of 15th-century tapestries behind the altar that illustrate the life of the Virgin. (*Open daily 8:30am-7:30pm. Tapestries open M-Sa 9:30am-12:30pm and 2-7pm, Su 1-7pm. Tours of the tapestries on request €2.30, students €1.50.*)

CÔTE D'OR

The 60km of Golden Slopes that run from Dijon to the tiny village of Santenay, 20km south of Beaune, have nurtured grapes since 500 BC. Limestone-laced soil, the right amount of rainfall, and perfect exposure and soil drainage, make it a godsend for viticulturists, as well as some of the most valuable real estate in the world.

The Côte d'Or is divided into two regions. The **Côte de Nuits,** stretching south from Dijon through **Nuits-St-Georges** to the village of **Corgoloin,** produces red wines from the Pinot Noir grape. Running from Corgoloin south to **Santenay,** the **Côte de Beaune** produces great white wines from Chardonnay grapes.

Transportation around the vineyards can be difficult. The most intimate way to see the vineyards near either Beaune or Dijon is to **bike** down the **Route des Grands Crus.** Bike rental shops in both cities arrange

NO WORK, ALL PLAY

IF IT AIN'T BAROQUE...

Beaune's most publicized festival, like Beaune itself, is for those with a taste for the elegant and old-fashioned. Since 1983, Beaune has held the **International Festival of Baroque Music,** featuring concerts of sacred and secular music and opera from the 17th and 18th centuries. This signature musical celebration takes place over four weekends from early July to early August. Beaune's wine cellars provide a forum for young composers of the Baroque style to premier their works.

Concert-goers usually get to sit in Beaune's most famous spot—the courtyard of its hospice, whose tiled roof, lit up at night, creates a concert forum unique in the world. Other concerts are held in the white-tiled interior of the Basilique Notre Dame. While the distinctly classical tone of this *fête* may be more appealing to Beaune's distinguished wine-tasting visitors than to young mosh pit fans, the chance to hear live Mozart in the hospice courtyard is a truly special one. Besides, the Baroque festival is as lively as it gets. It is *the* Saturday night option in downtown Beaune. Students and members of large groups can sit in on a concert for as little as €8.

(☎ *03 80 22 97 20 or 03 80 26 21 33; www.festivallbeaune.com. Festival office at Beaune tourist office. Open late Mar. to June M-Sa 9am-noon and 2-6pm; July daily 9am-6pm.*)

tours of differing lengths that can get you where you want to go. Renting a **car** in Dijon or Beaune (around €90 per day including tax, insurance, and gas) is the easiest way to the grapes, but if you are planning on taking part in the wine tasting, this might not be the best choice. **TRANSCO buses** (☎ 03 80 42 11 00) run from Dijon to Beaune (1hr.; 9 per day, Su only 11:10am; €5.80); **Gevrey-Chambertin** (30min., 19 per day, €2.40); Nuits-St-Georges (45min.; 11 per day, Su only 12:34 and 6:24pm; €4). TRANSCO will take you from Beaune to Château de Rochepot (5 per day, fewer on Su; €3.20).

Lodging on the Côte is expensive; your best bet—for both bargain and experience—is to reserve a room days in advance at one of the many *chambres d'hôte* that dot the villages. The tourist office in Beaune or Gevrey-Chambertin will supply you with a copy of *Chambres et Tables d'hôte*, a comprehensive list of bed and breakfasts. The Dijon and Beaune tourist offices also offer the *Bourgogne Hôtes* guide, which lists almost every hotel and campsite in the region.

ROUTE DES GRANDS CRUS

From Eurobike (p. 393) turn right on av. de l'Hôpital, bear left at the intersection to av. Jean Jaurès, then right at the Port du Canal. Follow the signs to Chenove or Route des Grands Crus. This heavenly, mostly flat road, which loses its congestion after a mile or two, winds through **Chenove, Marsennay-La Cote, Couchey, Fixin, Brochon,** and finally **Gevrey-Chambertin,** each village more enchanting than the next. Among the green hills speckled with church spires, omnipresent vineyards make the air intoxicating. Family-owned *caves* along the route offer free *dégustations*, but most will expect you to buy something. Drink and bike at your own risk. (Dijon to Gevrey-Chambertin by bike, about an hour. By foot, about 2½ hours.)

GEVREY-CHAMBERTIN

Perhaps the finest vineyards in all of France are around Gevrey-Chambertin, 10km south of Dijon. Nine of the Côte's 29 *grands crus* are grown here, all with "Chambertin" in their name. Perched atop the vineyards, the **Château de Gevrey-Chambertin** is a perfect place to unwind, especially after a long bike ride. The gracious proprietress will take you through her 10th-century château, built to protect the wine and the villagers (in that order). The tour ends with a taste of the prized vintages, which cost €14 and up. (☎ 03 80 34 36 13. Get off at the bus stop near the entrance to the village, go left up the hill, left again, and the château will be on your left. Open daily mid-Apr. to mid-Nov. 10am-noon and 2-6pm; Jan. to mid-Apr. and mid-Nov. to late Dec. 10am-noon and 2-5pm. Tour €4.50, includes tasting.)

The Gevrey-Chambertin **tourist office** is small, but very helpful. (☎ 03 80 34 38 40. Open M and Sa 9:30am-12:30pm and 1:30-5:30pm, Tu-F 9am-12:30pm and 1:30-6pm, Su 10am-12:30pm and 1:30-5pm; July-Aug. M and Sa open until 6pm.) Bunk down in rural easy living at the **Marchands ❸**, 1 pl. du Monument aux Morts. (☎ 03 80 34 38 13; fax 03 80 34 39 65. Singles €28; doubles €39-43; triples €54-59; quads €69-74. MC/V.) Reserve early in summer.

ABBAYE DE FONTENAY

To get to Fontenay from Dijon, take the TGV or TER from Dijon to Montbard (3-4 per day, €10). Taxis are usually waiting at the train station to take tourists on to the Abbey, but if you can't find one, ask at the station or the hotel across the street for individual drivers' numbers (about €22 round-trip).

This beautiful restored remnant of monastic life lies in the hills above the village of Montbard. The overwhelming sense of peace and order here romanticizes the life of a monk. The Abbey was founded in the 12th century by Cistercian monks, known for their strict devotion and self-denial, and flourished until the 1600s, when it was converted into a paper mill. The visit includes the now restored **Abbey Church,** known for its architecture and for its **Virgin of Fontenay** statue, set off by spine-chilling streams of sunlight. Also on view are the monks' dormitories, the bubbling fountains in the garden, and the forge that was the sight of the first water-powered hammer. There is no picnicking on the grounds, but a small cafeteria and an ample front lawn with a flowing stream are ideal spots for refreshment. For a site so off-the-beaten-path, *c'est bon.* (☎03 80 92 15 00; www.abbayedefontenay.com. Admission €8, students and senior citizens €4. Hour-long tours available, some in English, but most visitors choose to go it alone with multilingual pamphlets from the information office.)

CHÂTEAU DE ROCHEPOT

The **Château de Rochepot,** 15km southwest of Beaune, springs straight out of a (distinctly Burgundian) fairy tale, with its wooden drawbridge, slate roof, and pointed, colorfully tiled turrets. "To enter, knock three times," declares the ancient sign. The 45min. tour of this 13th century medieval fortress includes a peek at the Guard Room, the ingenious kitchens, the dining room, the old chapel, and the "Chinese" room, a gift of the last empress of China. (☎03 80 21 71 37. Open Su-M and W-F Apr.-June 10:30-11:30am and 2-5:30pm; July-Aug. 10am-6pm; Sept. 10-11:30am and 2-5:30pm; Oct. 10-11:30am and 2-4:30pm. Admission €5.50.)

While lodging is scarce in this tiny town, ▨**Le Relais du Château ❸,** rte. de Nolay, has a friendly, English-speaking proprietor, and the bright, clean rooms are a fantastic deal. (☎03 80 21 71 32. Breakfast €5.80. Restaurant *menus* €10.50-26. Doubles with shower €28, with shower and toilet €41. MC/V.)

MÂCON

Laid against the right bank of the Saône, "Matisco" was an important Roman colony and later became a frontier city between French lands and the Holy Roman Empire. Romantic poet, politician, and ladies' man Alphonse de Lamartine (1790-1869) was *mâconnais,* but his fame and fervor far outstripped his quiet birthplace. This working class hub (pop. 40,000) has none of the fairy tale charm of its cobblestoned Burgundian neighbors and few sights, but is a decent base for exploring the Beaujolais vineyards and Cluny.

◈🛈 ORIENTATION & PRACTICAL INFORMATION

Trains and buses run from rue Bigonnet to Dijon (1¼hr., 19 per day, €16) and Lyon (1hr., 20 per day, €11.70). The info desk is open M-F 9am-noon and 1:20-6:30pm, Sa 9am-noon and 1:20-5:30pm. **TGVs** stop at Mâcon-Loche, 6km away. SNCF bus #7 (dir: Chalon-sur-Saône) shuttles to the TGV station (12min., 4 per day, €1.80). Call ☎06 07 36 57 06 for a **taxi.** (24hr. About €15 from Mâcon-Loche to Mâcon.) Pro' Cycles, 45 rue Gambetta, **rents bikes.** (☎03 85 22 81 83. €14 per day, €70 per week. Open M 3-7pm, Tu-Sa 9am-noon and 2-7pm.)

The compact town center is framed by rue Gambetta, rue Victor Hugo, cours Moreau, and the Saône. To reach the **tourist office,** 1 pl. St-Pierre, from the station, go straight down rue Gambetta and left onto rue Carnot. The staff provides an **accommodations service** €2.30 with 10% down payment and 6 themed **tours** in French. (☎03 85 21 07 07; fax 03 85 40 96 00. Open June-Sept. M-Sa 10am-7pm, Su and holidays 3-7pm; Mar.-May and Oct. M-Sa 10am-12:30pm and 1:30-6pm; Nov.-Feb. M-Sa 10am-12:30pm and 2-6pm. Tours July-Sept. Sa 2:30pm; €6, under 12 free; in English July-Aug.) Other services include a **laundromat,** 20bis rue Gambetta

BURGUNDY

(☎06 15 31 68 68; open daily 7am-10pm), **police** at 36 rue Lyon (☎03 85 32 63 63; call here for the **pharmacie de garde**), a **hospital** at bd. de l'Hôpital (☎03 85 20 30 40), **Pharmacie de la Pyramide** at 362 rue Carnot (☎03 85 38 04 99; open M 1:45-7:30pm, Tu-Sa 8:30am-12:30pm and 1:45-7:30pm), **Internet** at Le Victor Hugo Café, 37 rue Victor Hugo (☎03 85 39 26 16; €4 per hr.; open M-Sa 8am-1am, Su 3pm-midnight, and a **post office** at 3 rue Victor Hugo with **currency exchange** and **Poste Restante.** (☎03 85 21 05 50. Open M-F 8:30am-7pm, Sa 8:30am-noon.) **Postal code:** 71000.

▊ ◖ ACCOMMODATIONS & FOOD

Reserve in advance July-Aug. **Hôtel Escatel ❶**, 4 rue de la Liberté, is a hike from the station but extremely well priced. From the station, turn left onto rue V. Hugo and follow it past pl. de la Barre as it runs into rue de l'Héritan. The hotel is to the right across from the intersection of rue de l'Héritan and rue de Flace. (15min.) The hum of traffic from the intersection fills its long college-dorm hallways and modern, cheerful rooms. (☎03 85 29 02 50; fax 03 85 34 19 97. Breakfast €5.80. Reception 24hr. Checkout noon. Singles €15.10, with shower €26, with bath €33.60; doubles €26/€30.50/€40. Extra bed €7.70. AmEx/MC/V.) If you want something in the *centre ville*, stay at **Le Promenade ❷**, 266 quai Lamartine. From the station, walk straight down rue Gambetta and make a left onto quai Lamartine. A neat, accommodating, sometimes crowded hotel provides rooms of varying quality, all with toilet and shower; treat yourself to a room with heavenly blue skylight if you can. (☎03 85 38 10 98; fax 03 85 38 94 01. Reception 10am-3:30pm and 6:30pm-midnight. Singles and doubles €20-31; triples €32.50-34. AmEx/V.)

Situated between Burgundy and the Beaujolais, Mâcon enjoys the best of both wine worlds. It also produces its own Chardonnays, *Pouilly Fuissé* and *Mâcon Clessé*, which go well with *quenelles* (smooth, creamy fish dumplings) and *coq au vin*. A small **market** is held daily on pl. aux Herbes; a larger one is held on espl. Lamartine. (Sa 7am-1pm.) There's also a **Marché Plus** on 18 rue Lacretelle off rue V. Hugo. (Open M-Sa 7am-9pm, Su 9am-1pm.) Much of Macon's budget eating consists of busy *brasseries*, located on the *quais* next to the noisy highway.

◉ ♫ SIGHTS & ENTERTAINMENT

Among the slim pickings of Mâcon's sights, the **Musée des Ursulines,** rue des Ursulines, is by far the best, with a diverse collection ranging from ancient chess pieces to a history of the Saône. Archaeological exhibits include the gruesome stone coffin of a Frankish warrior, opened to reveal the bones and possessions of the original tenant. (☎03 85 39 90 38. Open Tu-Sa 10am-noon and 2-6pm, Su 2-6pm. €2.30, students and under 26 free.) **The Résidence Soufflot,** 249 rue Carnot, designed in 1752 by Soufflot, architect of the Panthéon in Paris (p. 126), continues to serve as a hospital. Its multi-level Italianate chapel enabled the sick to join in mass without descending to the ground floor. A *tonneau tournant* (revolving cupboard) allowed mothers to orphan children anonymously. (Ask for the chapel key at the tourist office. Open only to groups until completion of renovations in spring 2004. Open M-F 10am-7pm.) At rue Dombey and pl. aux Herbes, the **Maison de Bois,** now a friendly bar, is one of several medieval houses on rue Carnot and rue Dombey. Built in 1510, the house is one of only four in France with such grotesque carvings. The **Pont St-Laurent** provides a good view of the city and its old buildings.

Just behind quai Jean Jaurès are lively concert-bars like **Bar l'Insolite,** 65 rue Franche, with nightly karaoke. (☎03 85 38 07 63. Open Tu-Sa 10am-2am.) The big summer event is the four-week festival **L'Eté Frappé,** from early July to mid-August, which features films, jazz, classical music, comedians, and dancing. The tourist office has the free *Les Rendez-vous* or *L'Eté Bleu,* which lists events.

► DAYTRIPS FROM MÂCON

CLUNY

Cluny has no train station; buses are tortuously routed and irritatingly infrequent. SNCF (☎03 85 59 07 72; open Tu-F 9am-noon and 1:30-5:30pm, Sa 9am-noon) runs buses to Cluny from Mâcon (40min., 7 per day, €3.90). To get from the bus stop to the tourist office, 6 rue Mercière (☎03 85 59 05 34; fax 03 85 59 06 95), walk against the traffic on rue Porte de Paris, turn right at pl. du Commerce, and continue for 5min. Helpful map and a free guide pratique. (Open June-Sept. M-Sa 10am-7pm, Su and holidays 3-7pm; Mar.-May and Oct. M-Sa 10am-12:30pm and 1:30-6pm; Nov.-Feb. M-Sa 10am-12:30pm and 2-5pm.) Tours mid-July to Aug.; inquire at the Cluny Abbey info desk (open daily May-Aug. 9:30am-6pm; Sept.-Apr. 9:30am-noon and 1:30-5pm).

At its height, Cluny and its nearly omnipotent abbot led a vast network of daughter abbeys. By virtue of the order's unique charter, it escaped the control of every ruler except the pope. The Romanesque abbey church, **Cluny III**, dedicated to St-Pierre and St-Paul, produced almost a dozen popes and was the largest church in the world until the construction of St. Peter's in Rome. During the Wars of Religion, the Revolution, and its aftermath, the abbey was looted, sold, and used as a quarry. A mental reconstruction of the abbey's scale requires some effort, but its former wealth is apparent in the ornamentation of the Gothic **Pope Gelasius** façade. The remains are now home to the **Ecole Nationale Supérieure d'Arts et Métiers,** whose central cloister is surrounded by student rooms. To get to the abbey from the tourist office, follow rue Mercière one block and turn right onto rue de la République. This area, particularly rue d'Avril and rue Lamartine, is home to the best of the well-preserved **maisons romanes** (medieval houses) which dot the city. (☎03 85 59 23 97; fax 03 85 59 16 34. Open daily May-Aug. 9:30am-6:30pm; Sept.-Apr. 9:30am-noon and 1:30-5pm. Closed May 1, Nov. 1, Nov. 11, Dec. 25, and Jan. 1. Abbey tours in English July-Aug. W and F 10:15am, 2:15, 4:15pm; tours also available in French. €5.50, under 26 €3.50. Ask about night tours July-Aug.)

VAL LAMARTINIEN

The sights and roadsides of the area around Cluny are dotted with signs bearing verses by Romantic poet Alphonse de Lamartine (1790-1869). Châteaux also abound in this valley, most notably the ■**Château de Cormatin,** complete with moat, formal gardens, aviary, and maze. The monumental open-well staircase in the north wing was the height of sophisticated engineering at the time of its construction (1605-1616). The Italian-style rooms, though unrestored, are well preserved. The tour features a plethora of interest-piquing historical details—once the Marquis died, the Marquise, then 22, lived the rest of her life in black—and even a brief meditation session. You can **bike** by taking car-free **la Voie Verte,** a 44km stretch of road devoted to bikers and bladers, which covers a good deal of fairly flat countryside near Cluny. The **SNCF bus** from **Cluny** (25min., 8 per day 5:20am-8:13pm, €2.40) or **Mâcon** (1hr., 7 per day 7:58am-7:40pm, €5.60) will take you to the château. (☎03 85 50 16 55; fax 03 85 50 72 06. Open Apr. to mid-Nov. daily 10am-noon and 2-5:30pm. Tours in French with written English translation every 30min. €6.50, students ages 18-26 with ID €5, ages 10-17 €4. Park only €4.)

AUTUN

"Rome? Non…Autun" is the slogan splashed across billboards pictures of Roman gateways. True to self-advertisement, Autun (pop. 18,000), originally Augustodunum, was founded around 15 BC by Emperor Augustus as a "sister and rival of Rome." In addition to its impressive collection of ancient rubble, Autun has (some-

BURGUNDY

what) more recent architectural prizes, such as the Cathédrale St-Lazare (1120-1146), erected to compete with nearby Vézelay in the lucrative medieval pilgrimage business. Still standing after the ravages of eight none-too-kind centuries, the cathedral houses some of the most arresting Romanesque sculpture in the world. Despite these ancient treasures, the town's contemporary life feels rather listless.

⚅⚆ ORIENTATION & PRACTICAL INFORMATION. The main street, **avenue Charles de Gaulle,** connects the station to the central **place du Champ du Mars,** up a slow, steady hill. (10min.) To get to the *vieille ville* from there, follow the signs from rue aux Cordeliers or rue St-Saulge.

Trains run from pl. de la Gare on av. de la République, but Autun is far from any major railway line and thus difficult to get to. Most journeys to and from Autun require a change at regional stops Châlon-sur-Saône or Etang, and many involve tortuous connections. It is possible to get to Dijon almost directly by train (2hr., 8 per day, €15.10) via Etang. **TGVs** leave Gare Le Creusot for Paris (1½hr., 5 per day, €41.90-55.30). The quickest way to get to Lyon is to catch a bus to regional transport hub Gare Le Creusot (45min., 5 per day, €5.40) and take the TGV from there (50min., 3 per day, €22.40). **SNCF buses** leave from outside the Autun station for Chalon-sur-Saône (2hr., 3 per day, €8.80). The helpful station office is open M-F 7:05am-7:10pm, Sa 9:05am-12:30pm and 2:30-6:30pm, Su 12:05-7:30pm. **TRANSCO buses** (☎03 80 42 11 00) leave for Dijon from pl. de la Gare (2¼hr., daily 5:10pm, €12). For a **taxi,** call ☎03 85 52 04 83. (24hr.)

The **tourist office,** 2 av. Charles de Gaulle, off pl. du Champ de Mars, offers various themed city **tours,** as well as nocturnal tours of the *vieille ville* in summer that mix music and historical sketches. Self-guided city brochure €3 in French. (☎03 85 86 80 38; fax 03 85 86 80 49. City tours €5.50, children €2.40. Night tours daily July-Aug. 9:30pm; €7.60, under 12 free. Bike tours €9.90. Office open daily May-Oct. 9am-7pm; Nov.-Apr. 9am-noon and 2-6pm.) There's an **annex** at 5 pl. du Terreau, next to the cathedral. (☎03 85 52 56 03. Open May-Sept. 9am-7pm.) The **hospital** is at 9 bd. Fr. Latouche (☎03 85 52 09 06). The **police** are at 29 av. Charles de Gaulle (☎03 85 52 14 22); call them for **pharmacie de garde** info. The **Cybercafé Explorateur,** 17 rue Guerin, caters to **Internet** addicts. (☎03 85 86 68 84. €6.10 per hr. Open Tu-Sa 10am-7:30pm.) Do your **laundry** at **Salon Lavoir,** 1 rue Guerin. (☎03 85 86 14 12. Wash and dry €4-5. Open daily 6am-8pm.) You can **exchange currency** and pick up mail through **Poste Restante** at the **post office,** 8 rue Pernette. (☎03 85 86 58 10. Open M-F 8:30am-6:30pm, Sa 8:30am-noon.) **Postal code:** 71400.

⚇⚈ ACCOMMODATIONS & FOOD. The city's cheap hotels are across from the train station. Reserve a couple of weeks in advance in summer. The **Hôtel de France ❷,** 18 av. de la République, is a plain hotel across from the train station, over a quiet bar/restaurant. Most rooms are large, but the little rooms under the slope of the roof are charming, if warm in summer. (☎03 85 52 14 00; fax 03 85 86 14 52. Breakfast €4.70. Reception daily 8am-11pm. Singles and doubles €20-22, with toilet €24, with shower €26; triples €33-39; quads €39-46; quints €54. MC/V.) Next door are the inviting rooms of the **Hotel of Commerce and Touring ❷,** 20 av. de la République, in raspberry and pink accents. (☎03 85 52 17 90; fax 03 85 52 37 63. Breakfast €5. Reception 6:30am-11pm. Closed Jan. Singles and doubles €25, with shower €30-38, with shower and toilet €33-39. MC/V.) The **Camping Municipal de la Porte d'Arroux ❶,** located just an easy 20min. walk from town, rides the soft banks of a river in the fields. From the train station, turn left on av. de la République, left on rue de Paris, and go under the Porte d'Arroux. Cross the bridge and veer right on rte. de Saulien; the campground is on your left. The standard, graveled sites have hedges for privacy. There is a restaurant and a grocery store; a few feet away is a small pond for fishing and swimming. (☎03 85 52 10 82; fax 03 15 52 88 56.

Open Apr.-Oct. Office open daily July-Aug. 7am-8pm; Apr.-June and Sept.-Oct. 9-11am and 6-9pm. Check-out noon. €2.50 per person; €3.50 per tent, €1.30 per car. Electricity €2.50.)

Autun's ruins are prime picnicking territory. Prepare your feast at **Intermarché,** pl. du Champ du Mars (open M-Th 8:30am-12:45pm and 2:30-7:30pm, F-Sa 8:30am-7:30pm), where some markets come Wednesday and Friday mornings. Bright little restaurants line the cobblestone streets of the upper city. **Le Petit Rolin ❷,** 12 pl. St-Louis, serves crêpes and salads for under €10 and drinks all day in the shadow of the cathedral, with romantic terrace seating at night. (☎03 85 86 15 55. *Menu* €15-25. Open daily 11am-3pm and 6-11pm. MC/V.)

⬛ SIGHTS. At the top of the upper city, the **Cathédrale St-Lazare** rises above the Morvan countryside; the uphill walk feels like a pilgrimage. During a clerical quarrel, one group objected to the marvelous **tympanum** above the church doors and covered it in plaster, unwittingly protecting the masterpiece from the ravages of the Revolution. The relief sculpture depicts the Last Judgment in figures that are incredibly expressive and full of movement for the era. **Gislebertus,** the artist's name, is visible below Jesus's feet. In the dimly lit nave, intricately carved capitals illustrate biblical scenes; to see them at eye level, climb up to the *salle capitulaire* above the sacristy. Beware the basilisk, an imaginary serpent whose gaze reputedly turns people to stone. (Open daily 8am-7pm.)

The **Théâtre Romain,** near the lake northeast of the *vieille ville,* is delightfully unrestored. Its stones, vivid and fresh, emerge from a grassy hillside, and picnickers relax where 12,000 enthralled spectators once sat. Today the theater faces the local soccer field and a pretty lake. During the first three weekends in August, 600 locals bring chariot races and Roman games to life in the much-hyped **Augustodunum** show. (Info ☎03 85 86 80 13. €12, children under 12 €8. Tickets sold at tourist office.) From the theater's rear you see the **Pierre de Couhard,** a 30m pile of bricks. Its purpose remained unknown until excavations unearthed a 1900-year-old plaque that cursed anyone who disturbed the man inside's eternal slumber. *Let's Go* does not recommend incurring dormant wrath. To reach the site, leave the *vieille ville* through the Porte de Breuil and climb into the hills.

The **Musée Rolin,** 3 rue des Bancs, next to the cathedral, has a diverse historical collection in the 15th-century mansion of Burgundian chancellor Nicolas Rolin. Its highlight is Gislebertus's relief sculpture of Eve at the Fall, which scandalized audiences of its day for depicting female nudity and for imbuing the sinful foremother with real sadness. (☎03 85 52 09 76; fax 03 85 52 47 41. Open Apr.-Sept. Su-M and W-Sa 9:30am-noon and 1:30-6pm; Oct.-Mar. M and W-Sa 10am-noon and 2-5pm, Su 10am-noon and 2:30-5pm. €3.10, students €1.60.)

There are a few signs that Autun was once the largest city in Roman Gaul. The cushy way to see them is on the **Petit Train,** which leaves from pl. du Champ de Mars and from the tourist office annex near the cathedral (45min.; June-Aug. 7 French tours per day 10am-6pm; €5, children €3). If you go solo, arm yourself with a free map from the tourist office. Standing in the fields behind the train station, across the river Arroux, is the huge brick first-century **Temple de Janus.** The two remaining walls tower over cow pastures, white clouds drifting through their eroded, gaping windows. To reach them from the train station, walk northeast along av. de la République and take a left onto rue du fbg. d'Arroux, passing under one of the city's two remaining Roman gates: the still impressive, double-decker **Porte d'Arroux,** conveniently located near an idyllic river park. These two large arches for vehicles and two smaller ones for pedestrians led to the **Via Agrippa,** the main trade road between Lyon and Boulogne. Better preserved, the other gate, **Porte St-André,** at the intersection of rue de la Croix Blanche and rue de Gaillon, is more impressive still.

Autun's ramparts and towers are best seen from the hills above; to get there, take the path from near the cathedral to the Pierre de Couhard, or rent a **bike** from the Service du Sports on the far side of the lake. (☎03 85 86 95 80. €8.60 per half-day, €14.50 per day. Open July-Sept. 8:30am-6pm.)

NEVERS

A budding tourist destination in western Burgundy, Nevers (pop. 55,000) is a relatively undiscovered city of medieval and Renaissance architecture, and green parks. Ravaged by WWII bombing, Nevers has rebounded with significant restorations. It is now an ideal base for picturesque châteaux and countless outdoor activities along the Loire.

🖥🔖 TRANSPORTATION & PRACTICAL INFORMATION. Trains pass through Nevers to: Bourges (38-55min., 16 per day, €9.60); and Clermont-Ferrand (1½hr., 11 per day, €19). (Ticket windows open M 5:35am-9pm, Tu-Sa 6:05am-9pm, Su 6:45am-9pm.) **Local buses** depart from rue de Charleville, left of the train station as you exit. (☎03 86 57 16 39 or 03 86 71 94 20. €1 to the city center. Transit maps available at the main office, 31 av. Pierre Bérégovoy.) For a **taxi**, call ☎03 86 57 19 19 (7am-11pm) or 03 86 59 58 00. To explore the numerous bike trails of the region, Nièvre Aventure, 6 quai des Mariniers, **rents bikes**, complete with repair kit and helmet. (☎03 86 57 69 76. €18 per day, €75 for 5 days. Open M-Sa 8am-12:30pm and 1:30-7pm.) The town center is an easy 8min. walk away. From the station, head four blocks up av. Général de Gaulle to Nevers's main square, **place Carnot.** Diagonally across the square from av. de Gaulle is rue Sabatier, where the sleek multilingual **tourist office,** 4 rue Sabatier, has free maps of the city, biking trails, self-guided walking tours, and information on boat excursions, all in several languages. (☎03 86 68 46 00; www.ville-nevers.fr. Open Apr.-Sept. M-Sa 9am-7pm, Su 10am-7pm; Oct.-Mar. M-Sa 9am-noon and 2-6pm; Oct. and Mar. also Su 9:30am-12:30pm. July-Aug. city tours in French daily 10am and 3pm; €5.) Other services include: **police** at 6bis av. Marceau (☎03 86 60 53 00); a **hospital** at 1 av. Colbert (☎03 86 68 30 30); **Internet** at Pain et Friandises, 5 rue de la Pelleterie (☎03 86 59 26 69; €0.06 per min.; open M-Sa 9am-7pm), or Forum Espace Culture, a large bookstore at the corner of rue du Nièvre and rue de la Boucherie (☎03 86 59 93 40; €2.30 for 30min., €3.10 per hr.; open M 2-7pm, Tu-Sa 10am-7pm); and **currency exchange** at Crédit Municipal, pl. Carnot (open M-F 8:15-11:45am and 1:15-5:15pm, Sa 8:15-11:45am), and at the **post office,** 25bis av. Pierre Bérégovoy, which also has **ATMs** nearby. (☎03 86 59 87 00. Open M-F 8am-6:30pm, Sa 8am-noon.) **Poste Restante:** 58000. **Postal code:** 58019.

🏠 ACCOMMODATIONS. Left of the train station, opposite the convent, **Hôtel Beauséjour ❷,** 5bis rue St-Gildard, has tidy rooms with firm beds and stenciled wooden furniture. (☎03 86 61 20 84; hbeausejour@wanadoo.fr. Breakfast €5.50. Reception daily 7am-10pm. Singles and doubles with sink €23.50, with shower €29.50, with shower and toilet €31-38. Extra bed €8. MC/V.) **Hôtel de Verdun ❸,** 4 rue de Lourdes, overlooking the Parc Salengro, has spacious, renovated rooms, an elevator, and English-speaking owners. (☎03 86 61 30 07; fax 03 86 57 75 61; hotel.de.verdun@wanadoo.fr. Breakfast €5.50. Reception M-Sa 7am-9pm, Su 7am-noon. Singles €32-43; doubles €42-52. MC/V.)

🍴 FOOD. Skip the *brasseries* in the *vieille ville* for the cheaper, more interesting restaurants off pl. Carnot. The tourist office distributes a restaurant guide featuring the city's *toques Nivernais,* which offer reasonably priced gourmet menus. **Marché Carnot** hosts a covered **market** on av. du Gal. de Gaulle and rue St-Didier.

(M-F 7am-12:40pm and 3-6:55pm, Sa 6:30am-7pm.) A **Champion** supermarket, 12 av. du Gal. de Gaulle, is half a block from pl. Carnot. (Open M-F 9am-7:30pm, Sa 8:30am-7:30pm, Su 9am-noon.) The sassy decor of **Tandem Café ❷**, 7 pl. Guy Coquille, complements its playfully color-coded *menus* of salads, *tartines*, and pastas. (☎03 86 59 24 15. *Menus* €9-10, including wine. Open M-W 8am-8pm, Th-Sa 8am-midnight. Food served at lunch only.) **Autour du Monde ❸**, pl. Carnot, dishes up Greek and Turkish specialities like moussaka (€13) in a spirited setting. (☎03 86 57 68 72. Entrées €7.50-19. Open daily noon-11pm. MC/V.) For a special night out, try **La Cour Ste-Etienne ❹**, 33 rue Ste-Etienne, which has rotating *menus* (€15-27) fashionably presented in the courtyard of the Eglise Ste-Etienne. (☎03 86 36 74 57. Open Tu-Sa noon-1:15pm and 7:30-11pm. MC/V.) **Le Goemon Crêperie ❶**, 9 rue du 14 Juillet, serves omelettes and creative crêpes (€2.30-5.50) in a wood-trimmed interior. (☎03 86 59 54 99. Open daily noon-2pm and 7-10pm.)

🔲 **SIGHTS.** The most visible building in Nevers, the Renaissance **Cathédrale St-Cyr et Ste-Juliette**, off pl. Carnot and up rue du Doyenné, was bombed nearly to rubble in WWII. Astonishing reconstruction has restored it almost to its original splendor. The windows, striking reminders of the war's destruction, are intriguing examples of modern stained glass. (☎03 86 59 06 54. Open June-Sept. Tu-Sa 10am-noon and 2-7pm. Free tours 11am, 3, and 6pm.)

Opposite the cathedral, fairy tale turrets ornament the 15th-century **Palais Ducal**, once the seat of regional government. A modest museum of local porcelain resides within, but the exquisite exterior is the real draw. (☎03 86 68 46 00. Enter from tourist office. Free.) From the tourist office, go down the hill to pl. Carnot, turn right onto rue des Ourses, and follow it to the pedestrian rue François Mitterrand, which is lined with classy stores. Venture toward rue St-Etienne to visit a neighborhood that flourished during the monastic boom of the 11th century. Almost one millennium old, the **Eglise Ste-Etienne** is remarkably well preserved.

🔲 **EXCURSIONS.** A walk through the gardens lining the **Promenade des Remparts**, from the Loire to av. Général de Gaulle, passes the crumbled remains of 12th-century Nevers. In the center of the city, just off pl. Carnot, the **Parc Roger Salengro** has sprawling paths through manicured flower gardens, tall trees providing shade, and picnic-ready lawns. On the way out of Nevers, visitors who cross the **Pont de Loire** will delight in a final view of the gentle green slopes and blue water of the Loire and its banks.

The tourist office provides maps and information on a wide range of outdoor activities in the Loire region, from mountain biking to horseback rides. Hikers tired of toting their loaded backpacks can rent a donkey at **Les Aubues**. (☎/fax 03 86 22 89 83; www.un-ane-en-morvan.com. €30-35 per half-day, €235-265 per week.) For a slow meander down the Loire, **Les Settons**, plage du Midi, offers 35min. boat cruises with commentary in French and English. (☎03 86 84 51 97. Open Easter-Oct. daily 9:30am-7pm. €4.60, children €2.30.)

AUXERRE

A prime piece of riverfront real estate, the city of Auxerre (pop. 40,000) has always been defined by its location on the banks of the Yonne River. Originally a Roman hub along the via Agrippa, Auxerre became an early center for French Christendom under the learned bishop Germain (AD 378-448) and his various successors. Many of the city's most impressive sights have ecclesiastical ties, but modern Auxerre also has a bustling *vieille ville* with timbered *ancien regime* houses, superb vineyards, famously pristine fishing areas, and its very own, thoroughly cherished national champion soccer team.

BURGUNDY

✦ 🛈 ORIENTATION & PRACTICAL INFORMATION

Trains: Gare Auxerre-St-Gervais, rue Paul Doumer, east of the Yonne (☎08 92 35 35 35). Info office open M-F 5:15am-8:30pm, Sa 6:15am-8:30pm, Su 6:45am-9:30pm. To: **Avallon** (1hr., 10 per day, €8); **Dijon** (2½hr., 10 per day, €20.20); **Lyon** via Dijon (3-5hr., 19 per day, €35.70); **Marseille** via Laroche-Migenne (4 hr. TGV, 1 per day, €60.70); **Paris** (2hr., 12 per day, €20). Also a hub for regional bus routes and regional trains. No luggage storage. MC/V.

Public Transportation: Le Bus (☎03 86 94 95 00) runs through town M-Sa 7:30am-7:30pm. Tickets €1.10, *carnet* of 10 €8.30. Schedules at tourist office.

Taxis: ☎03 86 52 30 51 or 03 86 46 78 78. 24hr.

Tourist Office: 12 quai de la République (☎03 86 52 06 19; www.ot-auxerre.fr). Follow the signs from the train station to the *centre ville*, cross pont Bert, and take a right onto quai de la République. The office is 2 blocks down on the left (12min.). **Accommodations service** (€2.30 plus 10% of the first night's cost up front), **currency exchange** Su, **walking tours** (June-Sept. daily, Oct.-May Sa or Su by reservation. €4.50), and **bike or boat rental** on the Yonne (bikes €8 per half-day, €13 per day, €150 and ID deposit; boats €17 per hr., €45 per half-day). Open mid-June to mid-Sept. M-Sa 9am-1pm and 2-7pm, Su 9:30am-1pm and 3-6:30pm; mid-Sept. to mid-June M-F 9:30am-12:30pm and 2-6pm, Sa 9:30am-12:30pm and 2-6:30pm, Su 10am-1pm. Services available 24hr. at confusing outdoor "Cyber Office."

Police: 32 bd. Vaulabelle (☎03 86 51 85 00). Call for the **pharmacie de garde.**

Hospital: 2 bd. de Verdun (☎03 86 48 48 48). 24hr.

Laundromat: Lav-o-Clair, 138 rue de Paris.

Internet: Bureau d'Information Jeunesse de l'Yonne, 70 rue du Pont (☎03 86 51 68 75). €1.60 per 15min., 25 and under €0.80 per 30min. Open M-Th 10:30am-12:30pm and 2-6pm, F until 5pm. **Média 2,** 17 bd. Vauban (☎03 86 51 04 35). €4.60 per 30min., €9 per hr. Open M-Th 9am-noon and 2-7pm, F until 6pm. **Monoprix** supermarket, pl. Charles Surugue (☎03 86 52 19 90), has télécartes on the 1st (not the ground) floor. Open M-Sa 8:30am-8pm.

Post Office: pl. Charles-Surugue (☎03 86 72 68 60). **Currency exchange, Poste Restante** and **Cyberposte.** Open M-F 8:30am-7pm, Sa 8:30am-noon. Branch location: 110 rue du Pont. **Postal code:** 89000.

🏠 ACCOMMODATIONS & CAMPING

🏨 **Hôtel le Seignelay,** 6 rue du Pont (☎03 86 52 03 48; www.leseignelay.com). Set around a luscious garden/dining area, the rooms are clean, bright, and comfy. Large buffet breakfast €6. Reception daily 7am-11pm. Closed Feb. Reserve ahead June-Aug. Singles €25-31.50, with bath €38-41.50; doubles €29-45/€50.50; triples and quads with bath €58-64.50. AmEx/MC/V. ❸

Foyer des Jeunes Travailleurs (HI), 16 bd. Vaulabelle (☎03 86 52 45 38), in an apartment building back from the street. Follow the signs from the train station to the *centre ville*, cross pont Bert, and turn left on quai de la République; rue Vaulabelle is the first right. (15min.) Clean, smartly arranged rooms provide a sink, a wardrobe, and a desk. Hall showers and toilets. The striking lobby—a hall of mirrors—is a communal hangout. Breakfast included. Other meals €3.40. Reception daily 2-8pm. Singles €13. ❶

Hôtel La Poste, pl. de Cordeliers (☎03 86 52 12 02; fax 03 86 51 08 61). Centrally located near the Cathédrale St-Etienne, this tidy, welcoming hotel offers friendly service and cozy rooms. Breakfast €6, room service €10. Reception M-Sa 7am-10pm. Closed Su and Feb. Singles from €29, doubles from €33, triples from €54, quads from €60. €0.50 tax per person per night. MC/V. ❸

Hôtel Saint Martin, 9 rue Germain Benard (☎03 86 52 04 16), off bd. Davout. Clean, simple rooms with hall bathrooms, above a *bar-tabac*. Breakfast €4. Reception M-Sa 6:30am-9pm. Closed Su, holidays, and Aug. Singles €17-20; doubles €20-26; 4-person suite €40. MC/V. ❷

Camping, 8 rte. de Vaux (☎03 86 52 11 15), south of town on D163. Reception 7am-10pm. Open Apr.-Sept. €2.30 per site, €2.60 per person. Electricity €2.10. ❶

🍴 FOOD

Markets are held on pl. de l'Arquebuse (Tu and F) and on pl. Dégas, on the outskirts of town (Su morning). The **Monoprix** supermarket, 10 pl. Charles Surugue, in the heart of the old town, also operates a cheap cafeteria with a 3-course *formule* for €6. (Supermarket open M-Sa 8:30am-8pm. Cafeteria open M-Sa 11:30am-6pm.) Rue du Pont has the best and widest variety of flavors and prices. Night owls will appreciate 🏠**La Tour d'Orbandelle** ❷, parking des Cordeliers (☎03 86 52 31 46), a refreshing Italian option. (Open daily 11:30am-midnight. Tasty pizza from €5.50, pasta from €8. AmEx/MC/V.) Locals, young and old alike, go to **Primavera** ❸, 39 rue du Pont, for its Greek specialties *(souvlaki, moussaka)* served in a classy outdoor setting. (Open M-Sa 12:30-2pm and 7:30-10pm. Fixed *menus* €12-24. MC/V.) The amusing **Au Grand Gousier** ❷, 45 rue de Paris (☎03 86 51 04 80), advertises, among other things, a children's menu *"pour les petits ogres."* (Open M-Tu and F-Sa 12:15-2:30pm, W-Th 12:15-2:30pm. Escargot starts at €5.20. MC/V.)

👁 SIGHTS

Utterly charming and picturesque, the petite **Passerelle footbridge** (up the quai de la République from Pont Bert) makes a perfect starting point for an exploration of Auxerre. The tourist office right across the road provides free guides in English, French, German, Italian, and Dutch to **The Thread of History,** a colored line on the ground that weaves past every monument in the city, although the weary traveler might curse its comprehensiveness.

The towering **Cathédrale St-Etienne,** begun in 1215, is a must-see. Its wounded façade still displays statuettes decapitated by Huguenots when they occupied the city in 1567. Inside, the hulking organ is an impressive sight, while down below lies an 11th-century Romanesque **crypt,** which preserves an ochre fresco of Christ on horseback. The **treasury** on the south wall guards relics, illuminated manuscripts, and St-Germain's 5th-century tunic. (Cathedral open mid-Mar. to mid-Oct. M-Sa 9am-6pm, Su 2-6pm; mid-Oct. to mid-Mar. M-Sa 10am-5pm, closed Su. Crypt €2.50, treasury €1.50, student entry to treasury free with payment for crypt, under 14 free. Son-et-lumière with audioguides in English and German, nightly June-Aug. 10pm, Sept. 9:30pm; €5. Call ☎03 86 52 23 29 for details. AmEx/MC/V.)

The Gothic **Abbaye St-Germain,** 2 pl. St-Germain, commissioned around 500AD by Clothilde, attracts pilgrims and tourists to the tomb of the former bishop of Auxerre. The dark and chilly crypt holds some of France's oldest frescoes. (Open Su-M and W-Sa June-Sept. 10am-6:30pm; Oct.-May 10am-noon and 2-6pm. Crypt tours €5.80 including Musée Leblanc, €4.20 in the winter, students under 26 free. Parts are handicapped accessible. Abbaye **Museum** next door.) Visitors wandering near pl. de l'Hôtel will certainly be charmed by the **Tour de l'Horloge,** a turreted 15th-century clock tower in white and gold, but they may be slightly unnerved by the boldly painted wooden statues of Auxerrois celebrities that dot the area. Those with an interest in pottery and tapestries might enjoy the **Musée Leblanc-Duvernoy,** 9bis rue d'Egleny, with special exhibits each summer. (☎03 86 51 09 74. Open Su-M and W-Sa 2-6pm. €2, students under 26 free, first Su of every month free.)

🎵 🎭 ENTERTAINMENT & NIGHTLIFE

Concerts descend on Auxerre in summer, beginning with the *"Garçon, la note!"* series July 1st through August (free concerts M-Sa 11pm in the city's cafés; call tourist office for details). The Cathédrale St-Etienne presents free organ concerts in the summer (July-Aug. Su 5pm). Auxerre also plays host to a piano festival in September and an international music and film festival in November (ask tourist office for this year's details). The **Théâtre of Auxerre**, 54 rue Joubert (☎03 86 72 24 24), is closed during the summer, but from September to May it sings and dances with a variety of musical and dramatic events (prices vary widely depending on event). Enthusiastic pub-crawlers can find satisfaction in any of the bars that line the rue du Pont, but none stay open much later than midnight.

Those more interested in outdoor sports can take advantage of the great fishing in Auxerre and the Yonne region. Contact the **Fédération de Pêche de l'Yonne** (☎03 86 51 03 44). The **Société Mycologique Auxerroise,** 5 bd. Vauban (☎03 86 46 65 96), organizes mushroom-hunting expeditions in spring and autumn.

VÉZELAY

High above the breathtaking Vallée de Cousin, Vézelay (pop. 492) watches over dense forests, golden wheat, and white flecks of cattle in distant pastures. Vézelay's small, sloping, shop-lined streets; its untarnished medieval hilltop; and its splendid views distinguish it as one of the most beautiful villages in France. Tiny and peaceful, but certainly well-touristed, Vézelay is famous for its Basilique Ste-Madeleine, which has housed the relics of Mary Magdalene since the 11th century.

🔁 🔢 ORIENTATION & PRACTICAL INFORMATION. There's no train station in Vézelay; **trains** run from Paris via Auxerre to Sermizelles (2½hr., 5 per day, €12.60). From here you can take **Taxi Vézelay** for the 10km ride to Vézelay (☎03 86 32 31 88 or 06 85 77 89 36; 24hr.). An easier option is to take the **SNCF bus,** which leaves the train station at Avallon for Vézelay (July-Aug. daily 9:37am and 10:46am, return 5:24pm.) **Taxis** from Avallon are about €20. Call Alain Taxi (☎03 86 34 31 08), which is open 24hr., or Taxi Avallon (☎03 86 34 09 79). Vézelay is also easily reached by **bike.** The tiny **tourist office,** rue St-Pierre, just down the street from the church, has free maps and a very helpful *guide pratique* that lists all local accommodations and businesses. The office also has **Internet** access (€2 per 10min.), group tours by reservation, and individual tours July-Aug. (☎03 86 33 23 69; fax 03 86 33 34 00. Office open May-Oct. daily 10am-1pm and 2-6pm; Nov.-Apr. closed Th.) For the **pharmacie de garde,** check the window of the Pharmacie Meslin at 25 rue St-Etienne. Renting **bikes** at **A.B. Loisirs,** Route du Camping in nearby Saint-Père, requires a short downhill walk of 2km along D957, heading toward Avallon. (☎03 86 33 38 38. Bikes €16 per half-day, €23 per day. Open daily 9:30am-7pm.) The **post office,** rue St-Etienne, has both an **ATM** and **currency exchange.** (☎03 86 33 26 35. Open July-Aug. M-F 8:30am-12:30pm and 1:30-5pm, Sa 8:30am-noon; Sept.-May M-F 9am-noon and 2-5pm, Sa 8:30-11:30am.) **Postal code:** 89450.

🏠 🍴 ACCOMMODATIONS & FOOD. The **Auberge de Jeunesse (HI) ❶.** Follow the signs downhill from the bus stop on Route de l'Etang. Pleasant dorm-style rooms have 4-6 beds and kitchen access. (☎03 86 33 24 18. Closed Jan. Beds €7-9). Only a block away from the hilltop and the church, ⬛**Maison Les Glycines ❸,** rue St-Pierre, is a three-star hotel with 11 attractive, spacious rooms, each with a bath/sink/toilet. An attached *salon de thé* offers wisteria-shaded outdoor dining area and food from €7. (☎03 86 32 35 30; perso.wanadoo.fr/relais-des-gourmets/glycines. Breakfast €6. Reservations required. Singles €30-52; doubles €52-64; extra bed €14. MC/V.) An option used primarily by pilgrims, but open to all, is the *maison* run by the Fraternité Monastique de Jerusalem and the sisters of Ste-Madeleine, who organize days of prayer, silence, and study. Contact the tourist office for information, or call the Fraternité at ☎03 86 33 39 53. Right by the bus stop, **Le Cheval Blanc ❷** offers travelers nine bright, tidy rooms. Attached to the hotel, a restaurant serves salads (€8-8.30) and three *menus* (€14-22.50). (☎03 86 33 22 12. Breakfast €6. Reservations required. Closed mid-Dec. to mid-Jan. Singles and doubles with shower and toilet €19-38. MC/V.)

With its ruddy tile floor and smoky fireplace, the rustic **🏠Auberge de la Coquille ❷**, 81 rue St-Pierre, perfectly suits the local specialties it serves, such as spicy escargot and crumbling rounds of *fromage époisses*. The *menu bourguignon* (€11)—a *galette bourguignon*, *crêpe miel* (honey), and a glass of red wine—makes a perfect light lunch. (☎03 86 33 35 57. 3- and 4-course *menus* €8-24.50. Reservations suggested June-Aug. Open daily noon-10pm. MC/V.) Vegetarians can dive into the 4-course *menu végétarien* (€19) while their carnivorous friends enjoy a *menu* featuring *noix de porc à la moutarde* (€15) at **Le Bouganville ❸**, 28 rue St-Etienne. (☎03 86 33 27 57. *Carte* options from €10. Reservations suggested. Open Su-M and Th-Sa 12:30-2:30pm and 6:30-9:30pm. Closed Dec.-Jan. MC/V.) Casual types and those who just don't want to climb the hill should try **La Fortune du Pot ❸**, pl. du Champ-de-Foire across from the bus stop, with *menus* of hearty favorites from *jambon* to *anduoillette* €10.50. (☎03 86 33 32 56. Open 12:30-9:30pm. MC/V.) Groceries can be found at the **Vival** supermarket, near the bottom of rue St-Etienne. (Open July-Aug. daily 8am-8pm, Sept.-June M-Sa 8:15am-8pm, Su 9am-8pm. MC/V.)

◎ SIGHTS. All roads in Vézelay converge at the famous hilltop **Basilique St-Madeleine**. The Gothic and Romanesque church stands as an impressive, if typical, member of medieval France's old-church club, with an intricately sculpted tympanum and a cavernous interior. A strange *mélange* of camera-clad tourists and praying pilgrims fills the welcome center. The underground crypt housing the relics of Mary Magdalene would be otherworldly were it not for the tour guides and stage lighting. The basilica is also the site where St. Bernard of Clairvaux launched the Second Crusade and Richard the Lionheart set off for the Third Crusade. (☎03 86 33 39 50. Open daily 7am-8:30pm, though hours vary. Closed during mass. Tours in English with reservation; pamphlets in English.) **Concerts and performances** take place in the basilica and all over town most nights throughout the summer months; call tourist office for details. A peaceful and attractive spot for a bit of fresh air or a snack can be found along the southern ramparts behind Ste-Madeleine, which look out over vineyards that have been producing Chardonnay, Mélon, and Pinot Noir since the 9th century. The *caves* (cellars) of local winery **Caves de la Ville**, 32 rue St-Etienne, for a guided tour and tasting. (☎03 86 33 29 62. Multi-level tours July-Sept. daily 2-5pm, Oct.-June on weekends. €5, under 18 free. MC/V.) The **Maison Jules Roy**, rue des Ecoles (facing downhill from the church, make a right through the parking lot and follow the signs), makes for a thoughtful visit to the home of the late Algerian-born French author known for denouncing France's treatment of Algeria and Indochina. Guest writers and literary readings take place here. (☎03 86 33 35 01. Open June-Sept. Su-M and W-Sa 2-6pm.)

If you find yourself in nearby **Avallon** on your way to Vézelay, visit the uniquely enjoyable **🏠Musée du Costume**, 6 rue Belgrand, off Grande Rue A. Briand, historical narrative meets fashion show with rooms full of 18th- to 20th-century *haute couture* on amusingly up-close display. The mannequins strike witty poses, and the tour guides provide charming patter that will entertain both fashionistas and history lovers. (☎03 86 34 19 95. Open Easter-Nov. daily 10:30am-12:30pm and 1:30-5:30pm. Tours in French. €4, students €2.50.).

OF MICE & STRONG MEN

Sémur-en-Auxois may *look* like a petite, unassuming town. No burly train stations to muscle visitors through the city limits. A real pipsqueak of a place, the classic 98-pound weakling.

If some classic (and we do mean *classic*) lore has anything to say about it, though, not even Paris itself can measure up to the long shadow cast by this *très vieille ville*. According to legend, Hercules himself founded tiny Sémur-en-Auxois during a trek from Spain to Italy after demolishing some hapless, weaker foes. After spending a night in Auxois (then the ancient country of the *Mandubiens*), the story goes, he halted his army at present-day Sémur and established a rigorous training camp for his men. Games were organized, prizes awarded, and a city of strong character was born.

To this day, locals have retained a taste for festive games and competitions. Each spring at the end of May they host a medieval *course des chaussés* (footrace to win a pair of knitted stockings) in a show of sportive *esprit*. This is no town of braggarts and brutes. These people of Herculean heritage prove that a small and peaceful village might just be the fitting remainder of an ancient quest for strength and renown.

(To learn more about the town and its annual course des chaussés, *visit www.ville-semuren-auxois.fr.)*

SÉMUR-EN-AUXOIS

The crumbling towers that protect the *vieille ville* of Sémur-en-Auxois (pop. 5100) and its 7th-century castle have long defined its identity over the years. The town's name is derived from its Roman appellation, "Sene Muros," meaning "old walls." The unspoiled provincial town of cobblestones and archways overlooking a bend in the Armençon provides serenity, but don't come here if you're looking for much more than a mild, relaxing night.

TRANSPORTATION. TRANSCO (☎03 80 42 11 00) runs **buses** from Semur to Avallon (45min., 3 per day, €6.50); and Dijon (1½hr., 3 per day, €9.70). Schedules at the tourist office. For a **taxi**, call ☎03 80 96 60 18 or 03 80 97 34 67.

PRACTICAL INFORMATION. The tourist office, pl. Gaveau, where rue de la Liberté meets the gates of the *vieille ville*, has bus schedules, free maps, a list of hotels, and an **SNCF info and reservation office.** The info office staff runs **group tours** in English and French. (☎03 80 97 05 96. Tourist office open midJune to Sept. M-Sa 9am-7pm, Su 10am-noon and 2-6pm; Oct. to mid-June M 2-6pm, Tu-Sa 9am-noon and 2-6pm. SNCF info office open mid-June to Sept. Tu-F 9am-noon and 2-6pm, Sa 9am-noon and 2-5pm. Tours by reservation €3.10.) Other services include: **bike rental** at R.D.X., *2ter* rue du Bourg Voisin (☎03 80 97 01 91; €7 per half-day, €11 per day; open Tu-Sa JuneAug. 9am-noon and 2-7pm, Sept.-May 9:30am-6:30pm; MC/V); **Laundromat La Buanderie** at the Centre Commercial Champlon (open daily 9am-7pm); **police** (☎03 80 97 11 17) and a **hospital** (☎03 80 89 64 64; 24hr.) on av. Pasteur, east of the center; a **pharmacie de garde,** which is listed on every pharmacy's window; **Internet** at the Cyber KFÉ inside the bar at the Hôtel du Commerce, 19 rue de la Liberté (☎03 80 96 64 40; KFÉ hours vary, usually open until 11:30pm. €2 per 30min.); and **ATMs** and **banks** around pl. de l'Ancienne Comédie, which also has a **post office** with **Poste Restante** and **currency exchange.** (☎03 80 89 93 06. Open M-F 8:30am-noon and 1:30-5:30pm, Sa 8:30am-noon.) **Postal code:** 21140.

ACCOMMODATIONS & CAMPING. Hôtel du Commerce ❸, 19 rue de la Liberté, close to both the bus stop and the *vieille ville*, lets spacious rooms, with TV, shower, sink, toilet, and access to a sleek terrace bar. (☎03 80 96 64 40; fax 03 80 97 00 18. Breakfast €5. Reception daily 7am-9pm. Most singles and doubles €31.30, some €45-55. Reservations suggested during summer. AmEx/MC/V.) The **Hôtel des**

Gourmets ❷, 4 rue Varenne, offers large, beautifully furnished rooms in an old house near the heart of the *vieille ville*. The attached restaurant serves local favorites from €14. (☎ 03 80 97 09 41; www.hotellesgourmets.fr.st. Breakfast €6. Free parking. Closed Dec. and year-round M-Tu. Reservations suggested in summer for both hotel and restaurant. Singles €25.50; doubles €25.50-40, with bath €40; triples and quads €40; 6-person room €58. Extra bed €5. AmEx/MC/V.) **Hôtel des Cymaises ❹**, 7 rue du Renaudot, around the corner from rue Buffon, has quiet, spacious rooms and pretty grounds. (☎ 03 80 97 21 44; www.proveis.com/lescymaises. Reservations suggested. Singles and doubles equipped with shower/toilet/sink €47-56. MC/V.)

Camping Municipal du Lac de Pont ❶, 3km south of Sémur, offers a spot in the sun next to a scenic lake with a beach, tennis courts, bike rental, laundry, and a minimart. From Place de l'Ancienne Comédie, follow signs to "camping." (☎ 03 80 97 01 26. Reception 9am-noon and 4-8pm. Open May to mid-Sept. €3.10 per person, €1.80 per site or child, €1.60 per car. Electricity €2.50.)

⌂ FOOD. A stroll along rue Buffon reveals a number of attractive dining options, although the tasty *crêpes bourguignonnes* (€7) make ▧**La Goulue ❷**, 15 rue Buffon, a standout, with colorful decor, outdoor dining, and huge portions. (☎ 03 80 97 28 97. Crêpes start at €5.50 and up, *tartiflettes* and *bourguignonne* specialties €7-18, *menu du marché* €9.50, dessert €4. Open 11am-3pm and 7-11pm. MC/V.) **Le Calibressane ❸**, 16 rue Févret, located just around the corner from rue Buffon, provides a taste of California. Enjoy their special *chile con carne de Jill* (€12) served in a wood trimmed dining room. (☎ 03 80 97 32 40. Fish starts at €11; *menus* from €13. Open Tu-Th noon-2pm and 7-9:30pm, F until 10pm, Sa until 10:30pm. Closed Sa afternoon, Su night, and M. Reservations suggested in summer. MC/V.) **Le Sagittaire ❷**, 15 rue de la Liberté, has tasty, inexpensive Italian dishes. (☎ 03 80 97 23 91. 3-course weekday lunch *menu* €9. Open daily noon-2:30pm and 7-11pm. AmEx/MC/V.)

For groceries, stop in at the **Petit Casino** supermarket, located directly across from the church. (☎ 03 80 96 61 21. Open Tu-Sa 8am-12:30pm and 3-7:30pm, Su 9am-12:30pm. MC/V.) Small **markets** open at pl. Charles de Gaulle (Th morning), and at pl. Notre Dame (Su morning).

◙ ⌂ SIGHTS & ENTERTAINMENT. The tourist office schedules walking tours of the city, offers free brochures with self-guided itineraries, and also runs a 45min. **petit train** in the summer. (July-Aug. Tu-Su 3 per day; Sept.-June schedules vary. Groups must reserve in advance. €4, children €2.50.) Walk around the ramparts and the orchard-lined Armençon river. Romantics can take a moonlit walk down to the charming and little-touristed **Pont Pinard** for a breathtaking view of the illuminated *vieille ville* (From the rue du Rempart, walk away from the city and make a left onto rue du Fourneau, then follow the signs. Watch for cars. *Vieille ville* illuminated mid-June to Sept. 10pm-midnight.)

In the medieval town, down rue Buffon, mossy gargoyles menace the *place* from the 15th-century Gothic facade of the **Collégiale Notre-Dame.** The 13th-century tympanum on the **porte des Bleds** faces rue Notre Dame, and two sculpted snails slime their way to St. Thomas's feet on the skinnier left pillar—no doubt seeking divine intervention to save them from their likely fate in Alsace—a quick dip in a bowl of tasty butter-and-garlic sauce. Be sure to check out the church interior, if only for a glimpse of a surprising memorial to fallen American WWI soldiers. A **son-et-lumière** run by the church recounts the city's history. (Open daily 9am-noon and 2-6pm. English, Dutch, Spanish, and German pamphlets available. *Son-et-lumière* July-Aug. Tu, F, Sa 10:30pm, Sept.-May by reservation.) Behind the church lies a quiet **park** perfect for a picnic.

BURGUNDY

The comprehensive **Musée**, rue Jean-Jacques Cottenot, dabbles in a bit of everything—the eerie zoology room is worth a look. (Open Su-M and W-Sa 2-6pm. €3.10, €1.10 for students.)

⚅ ⚄ ENTERTAINMENT & NIGHTLIFE. At around 300 seats, the **Théâtre Municipale**, 11 rue du Rempart, is the smallest opera house in France. Stop by and enjoy the impressive acoustics and unique *architecture à l'italienne* (check the tourist office for the season's schedule). To seek out **bars** and **brasseries** at night, walk the rue Buffon or rue de la Liberté.

MASSIF CENTRAL

Many tourists find escape from Paris in the coastal regions of Provence and the Riviera, but the lucky few who penetrate the Auvergne, in France's interior, will find rugged unadulterated beauty. Giant lava needles, extinct volcanic craters, and aromatic pine forests rise out of the Massif Central. University town **Clermont-Ferrand** (p. 417) serves as a good hiking base and the towering, dormant volcano **Puy-de-Dôme** (p. 423) has prime views of the Volcanic Park, though the real hiking (and skiing) mecca is **Le Mont-Dore** (p. 423), near a string of dormant volcanoes. **Le Puy-en-Velay** (p. 427) builds on the volcanic theme with pumice-paved streets and statue-topped volcanic needles. The mineral waters of Le Mont Dore, Bourbelle, and **Vichy** (p. 431), a city stymied in the *Belle Epoque*, attract both the *curistes* (those who believe in the healing powers of the springs) and the curious. During World War II, the region was the seat of the Nazi-controlled French government, but was also rife with small bands of Resistance fighters. Although fairly quiet, Auvergne has picturesque scenery and a wealth of outdoor adventures.

Auvergne kitchens simmer with rich food. Pork, cabbage, and potatoes are combined in the regional stew *potée auvergnate*. Local cheeses include St-Nectaire, Bleu d'Auvergne, Cantal, and Fourme d'Ambert. Tarts and jams are filled with apricots from local orchards, while apple pudding dishes *(pompes aux pommes)* are a festival favorite.

CLERMONT-FERRAND

During the Middle Ages, Clermont-Ferrand (pop. 137,000) was two distinct cities, Clermont and Montferrand. Economic and political rivalry festered between them until Louis XIII ordered their merger in 1630. Clermont got the better deal: the "combined" city's walls excluded Montferrand. Forty minutes away by foot, the outcast city is now nearly forgotten. During the 20th century, Clermont became synonymous with Michelin tires (rubber was first used in bicycle tires here) and the gastronomically revered *Red Guides*, thanks in part to brothers André and Edouard Michelin. Despite its college-town appeal and cobblestone streets, Clermont-Ferrand is perhaps best as a base for trips to the surrounding mountains.

▐ TRANSPORTATION

Trains: av. de l'Union Soviétique. Info office open M-F 4:45am-11:15pm, Sa 5:30am-11:15pm, Su 6:60am-11:15pm. To: **Le Puy** (2½hr., 2 per day, €17.10); **Lyon** (3hr., 10 per day, €21.80); **Paris** (3½hr., 7 per day, €37.50).

Buses: 69 bd. F. Mitterrand (☎04 73 93 13 61), near the Jardin Lecoq. Buses to destinations throughout the Auvergne, including **Vichy** (1¾hr., 2 per day, €9). Office open M-Sa 8:30am-6:30pm.

Public Transportation: 15-17 bd. Robert Schumann (☎04 73 28 56 56; www.smtc-clermontferrand.com). Buses cover the city 5am-10pm. Ticket €1.20, day pass €4.60; available from vending machines at pl. de Jaude and throughout the city.

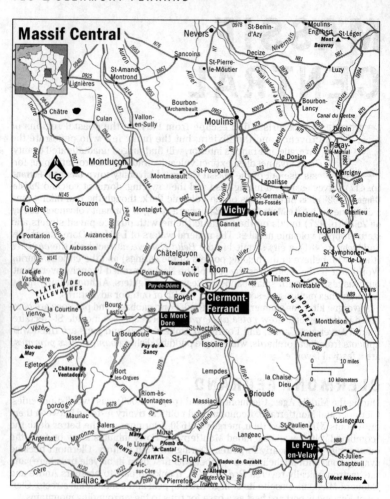

Taxis: Taxi 63 (☎ 04 73 31 53 15), **Taxis Radio** (☎ 04 73 19 53 53).

Bike Rental: Léovélo, 20 pl. Renoux or 43 av. de l'Union Soviétique, across from the train station (both ☎ 04 73 14 12 36). Open M-Sa 7:30am-7pm.

◀▓ 🔢 ORIENTATION & PRACTICAL INFORMATION

The *centre ville* of Clermont-Ferrand is in Clermont, between pl. Delille and pl.de Jaude. The train station is a 25min. walk from the city center, but buses #2, 4, and 14 travel from the station to **place de Jaude.** Several restaurants, a theater, and the large shopping complex, **Centre Jaude,** surround the *place.* From the station, go left onto av. de l'Union Soviétique, left again onto bd. Fleury, and take a quick right onto av. Carnot. Continue on this road through several name-changes and bends to pl. de Jaude. Pick up a map at the tourist office in the train station.

Tourist Office: pl. de la Victoire (☎04 73 98 65 00; www.clermont-fd.fr). From the train station, make a left onto av. de l'Union Soviétique. Take a left at pl. de l'Esplanade and a quick right onto av. Carnot (changes names several times), walk about 10min., and make a right onto rue St-Gènes. The office will be on the right, before the cathedral. (20min.) Excellent map, bus schedules, and helpful staff. Located in the same building, **L'Espace Massif Central** has further info on natural attractions in the Auvergne, including an impressive selection of maps and outdoor activity guides. French and English walking tours July to mid-Sept. €5.50, students €3. Office open May-Sept. M-F 9am-7pm, Sa-Su 10am-7pm; Oct.-Apr. 9:15am-12:15pm and 1:15-5:15pm.

Budget Travel: Voyages Wasteels, 11 av. des Etats-Unis (☎08 25 88 70 34). Open M-F 9:30am-noon and 2-6pm, Sa 9:30am-noon.

Youth Centers: Espace Info Jeunes, 5 av. St-Genès (☎04 73 92 30 50; www.crij.org/auvergne). Open M-F 10am-6pm, Sa 10am-1pm. Info on jobs, travel, and schools aimed at French youth.

Laundromat: 55 rue du Port. Open daily 7am-11pm. Also at 6 pl. Hippolyte Renoux. Open daily 7am-8pm.

Police: 2 rue Pélissier (☎04 73 98 42 42).

Hospital: Centre Hospitalier Universitaire de Clermont-Ferrand, rue Montalembert (☎04 73 75 07 50). 24hr. **SOS Médecins,** 28 av. Léon Blum (☎04 73 42 22 22).

Poison Control: ☎04 72 11 69 11.

24hr. Pharmacy: Pharmacie Ducher, 1 pl. Delille (☎04 73 91 31 77). Night fee €3.90 (10pm-7am).

Internet: Cyber Strike, 31 av. de Grande Bretagne. Incredible €2.50 per hr. Open daily 11am-midnight.

Post Office: 1 rue Busset (☎04 73 30 65 00). **Currency exchange** and **Cyberposte.** Open M-F 8am-7pm, Sa 8am-noon. **Branch** at 2 pl. Gaillard (☎04 73 31 70 00). Open M-F 9am-7pm, Sa 8:30am-12:30pm. **Postal code:** 63000.

⌐ ACCOMMODATIONS & CAMPING

Most inexpensive hotels are located just outside of the center of town, about half-way between the train station and the *vieille ville*. Several older, less attractive hotels cluster near the train station.

▨ Foyer des Jeunes Travailleurs (Corum Saint Jean), 17 rue Gauthier de Biauzat (☎04 73 31 57 00; fax 04 73 31 59 99). Great location near the *vieille ville*. Modern complex has simple rooms (some with private showers), a bar, and laundry facilities (€3). Breakfast included. Meals €5-8. Reception daily 9am-7pm. Often full during school year; call 2-3 days ahead. Singles or doubles €17-23 per person. ❷

Hôtel Ravel, 8 rue de Maringues (☎04 73 91 51 33; fax 04 73 92 28 48; hotelravel63@wanadoo.fr). This charming hotel, with an English-speaking owner and an intricate mosaic façade, sits just outside Clermont-Ferrand's city center. All rooms here come equipped with shower and bathroom. Breakfast €5. Singles €33; doubles €39; triples €45; quads €56. MC/V. ❸

Hôtel Zurich, 65 av. de l'Union Soviétique (☎04 73 91 97 98), to the right of the train station, past the hostel. Homey rooms with plush, red curtains, gold bedspreads, and a grandmotherly *patronne*. Call ahead for reception. 1 single at €18; other singles and doubles €23-27, with shower €23-35. Reduced rates for stays over 1 week. ❸

Dav'Hôtel Jaude, 10 rue des Minimes (☎04 73 93 31 49; fax 04 73 34 38 16; www.davhotel.fr). Fresh, colorful rooms minutes from the cathedral. Reception 24hr. Breakfast €7. Singles €44.50-47.50; doubles €47.50-52; triples €64. AmEx/MC/V. ❹

Auberge de Jeunesse "Cheval Blanc" (HI), 55 av. de l'Union Soviétique (☎04 73 92 26 39; fax 04 73 92 99 96). Across from the station and to the right. Characterless 1- to 8-bunk rooms look out on concrete. Squat-style toilets. Kitchen. Breakfast included. Sheets €2.70. Reception daily 7-9:30am and 5-11pm. Lockout 9:30am-5pm. Curfew 11pm. Open Apr.-Oct. €11.20 per person. **Members only.** ❶

Camping: Le Chancet, av. Jean-Baptiste Marrou (☎04 73 61 30 73). 6km outside Clermont, on the Nationale 89 (dir: Bordeaux). From the station, take bus #4C (dir: Ceyrat) to Préguille. 3-star site has sports, activities, and biking and hiking excursions during the summer. Laundry. Reception July-Aug. daily 8am-10pm. €2.50, ages 4-10 €1.70; €5 per tent; €1.40 per car. Caravan site with electricity €9. ❶

🍴 FOOD

Michelin may have created the most influential French restaurant guide, but Clermont-Ferrand is not generally known for its cuisine. A few quaint restaurants are tucked along side streets in the city center, fast food joints pepper **avenue des Etats-Unis**, and some *brasseries* surround the tourist office and cathedral.

There is a **Champion** supermarket on rue Giscard de la Tour Fondue. To get there from the train station, make a left at pl. de la Résistance and take a right onto rue Giscard. (Open M-Sa 8:30am-8:30pm, Su 9am-12:30pm.) Local produce and cheese are sold at the **Marché Couvert/Espace St-Pierre**, off pl. Gaillard, a huge covered market selling hundreds of regional specialties. (Open M-Sa 7am-7:30pm.)

Aux Délices de la Treille ❸, 33 rue de la Treille, prepares delicious regional *menus* (€11-22) in a quirky restaurant that toes the delicate line between tacky and cool. Yannick, the charismatic owner, happily chats up his customers. (☎04 73 91 26 90. Open daily 11:30am-2:30pm and 6-11pm.) **Ah! St-Tropez ❹**, 10 rue Massillon, near pl. de Victoire, serves tasty, gourmet *menus* (€15-18) within vibrantly colored walls and playful, Provençal murals. (☎04 73 90 44 64. Open Tu-Sa noon-11pm. MC/V.) **Le Pescajoux ❶**, 13 rue du Port, overcomes bad décor with over 160 types of delicious crêpes from basic nutella (€3) to the "Popeye" (€6.40), with fresh spinach. (☎04 73 92 12 26. Open M-F noon-2pm and from 7:30pm, Sa from 7:30pm. MC/V.)

👁 SIGHTS

The *vieille ville* of Clermont, called the **Ville Noire** (Black City) for its black-stone buildings, blend typical French country architecture with volcanic stone. Although the town's museums are interesting, some of the best sights lie in the mountains beyond the city. The **Passe Découverte** (€9) is accepted at the city's five major museums. All museums give free admission the first Sunday of each month.

CATHÉDRALE NOTRE-DAME DE L'ASSOMPTION. First built in AD 450 and completely reconstructed in the Gothic style between 1248 and 1295, this massive church now commands attention from miles away. The strength of the lava-based material allowed the architects to elongate the church's graceful, jet-black spires to a height of 100m; climb the 252-step tower for a panoramic view. Within the dark, airy interior, three massive rose windows gleam brilliantly. *(Pl. de la Victoire. http://cathedrale-catholique-clermont.cef.fr. Open June to mid-Sept. M-Sa 8am-noon and 2-6pm, Su 9:30am-noon and 3-7pm; mid-Sept. to late May 8am-noon and 2-6pm. Tower open 10am-5:15pm. €1.50. Info available in 11 languages.)*

BASILIQUE DE NOTRE-DAME-DU-PORT. This 12th-century church was built in the local Auvergnat Romanesque style; its intricately carved capitals depict Bible stories. Pope Urban II is believed to have urged the First Crusade here. The first Sunday after May 14, pilgrims come to see the icon of the Black Virgin. *(Pl. Notre-Dame-du-Port. ☎04 73 91 32 94. French tours July-Aug. W and F at 3pm. Open daily 8am-7pm.)*

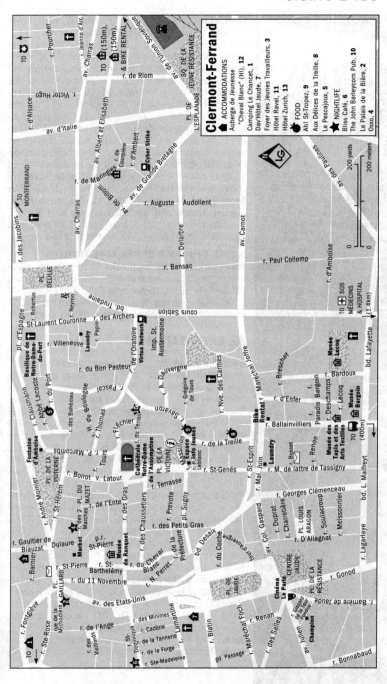

Clermont-Ferrand

▲ ACCOMMODATIONS
Auberge de Jeunesse
"Cheval Blanc" (HI), 12
Camping Le Chancet, 1
Dav'Hôtel Jaude, 7
Foyer des Jeunes Travailleurs, 3
Hôtel Ravel, 11
Hôtel Zurich, 13

● FOOD
Ah! St-Tropez, 9
Aux Délices de la Treille, 8
Le Pescajoux, 5

★ NIGHTLIFE
Bliss Café, 6
The John Barleycorn Pub, 10
Le Palais de la Bière, 2
Oxxo, 4

MASSIF CENTRAL

FROM THE ROAD

FRIENDS IN THE END

It started out as a game to see how my French was progressing. When curious locals asked where I was from, I would invariably challenge them to guess. They usually progressed from Dutch, to German, to English, to no idea. "No," I would smile, "I'm American."

When I left the states, several people expressed pity that, as an American, I *had* to go to France. What my little game quickly revealed was that attitudes on this side of the Atlantic were far from frosty—in fact I was welcomed more warmly here than I have been perhaps anywhere else in Europe. Locals offered me special menu items and often invited me in for a drink with the family.

I did engage in my fair share of political discussions, but most often with people eager to understand why they kept hearing reports of Americans hating the French. They insisted, many sounding hurt, that while they did not always agree with the actions of the US government, they thought nothing less of the American people. The French people I met were eager for me to relay their friendly feelings back home. As one man said as I ate dinner with his family, "the French and the Americans have always been friends, though we may not always agree politically. We hope that we can move past the ill feelings and return to that friendship...soon."

—Marit Dewhurst

MONTFERRAND. Most of Montferrand's best sights are inconspicuous **hôtels particuliers,** private mansions which date from the Middle Ages and the Renaissance. The best way to visit the town, which rises above an unattractive commercial district and is a 40min. walk up av. de la République, is on the tourist office's 2hr. **walking tour.** (Tu, Th, and Sa 3pm from pl. Louis Deteix; €5.50, students €3.) Take bus #17 (dir: Blanzat or Cébazat) or bus #10M (dir: Aulnat) from the train station. Like Clermont, Montferrand also has a volcanic stone church, though its version is somewhat less impressive. **Notre-Dame-de-Prospérité** stands on the site of the long-demolished château of the Auvergnat counts. The 18th-century convent on rue du Seminaire is now the **Musée d'Art Roger-Quillot,** pl. Louis Deteix, which exhibits paintings, sculpture, and artifacts from the 12th through the 20th centuries. *(Musée ☎04 73 16 11 30. Open Tu-Su 10am-6pm. €4, students €2.50, free first Su of each month.)*

MUSÉE DES TAPIS ET DES ARTS TEXTILES. This museum has exhibits on the various uses, techniques, and international differences of textile art. *(45 rue Ballainvilliers. Bargoin ☎04 73 91 37 31, Tapis ☎04 73 90 57 48. Both open Tu-Su 10am-6pm. Each museum €4, students €2.50. Info available in French, English, and braille.)*

🎵 ENTERTAINMENT

Clermont's students complain that the city's nightlife is sluggish, but there are a few popular nightspots; check *Le Guide de l'Etudiant Clermont-Ferrand* (available at the tourist office) for complete listings. Pool tables and cheap beer are the main attractions at the many bars across from the train station. **Le Palais de la Bière,** 3 rue de la Michodière, on the corner of pl. Galliard and av. des Etats-Unis, lacks a little in ambiance, but compensates with international beers and late-night *brasserie* fare. (☎04 73 37 15 51. Open Tu-Sa 7:30pm-1:30am. Closed Aug.) Imbibe with students and townies at **The John Barleycorn Pub,** 9 rue du Terrail. The bearded and tattooed bartender entertains with stories of the sea-life. (☎04 73 92 31 67. Open daily 5pm-2am.) **Bliss Café,** 36 rue St-Dominique, a gay-friendly nightclub, has zebra print tables, green chairs, and a lively dance floor with house and techno music. (☎04 73 30 88 53. Open Tu-Sa 5pm-1:30am, Su 6:30pm-1:30am.) For a late night of clubbing, **Oxxo,** 16 rue de Deux Marchés, has two dance floors that keep hopping until the early morning. (☎04 73 14 11 11. Cover Th €2; F-Sa €7 with drink, €5 without. W free. Open W 10pm-4am, Th-Sa 10pm-5am.) **Cinéma Le Paris,** 8 pl. de la Résistance, runs recent films and some classics. (€7.50, students €6.)

During the first week of February, European filmmakers gather for Clermont-Ferrand's annual **Festival International du Court Métrage**, considered the Cannes of the short film. For more info, contact La Jetée, 6 pl. Michel de l'Hospital. (☎04 73 91 65 73. Pass for 5-6 films €2.50.)

NEAR CLERMONT-FERRAND

PUY-DE-DÔME

Clermont-Ferrand's greatest attraction is its proximity to a terrain of extinct volcanoes, crater lakes, and picturesque mountains. Puy-de-Dôme, the mountain in the middle, is part of the **Parc Naturel Régional des Volcans d'Auvergne**, west of Clermont-Ferrand. (☎04 73 65 64 00; fax 04 73 65 66 78.) Hikers, bikers, and skiers alike enjoy the unspoiled terrain of France's largest national park. A booklet available at the Clermont-Ferrand tourist office indicates hiking paths through the area. There are three main sections in the protected area: the **Mont-Dore**, the **Monts du Cantal**, and the **Monts Dômes**—the best base for exploring the well-marked mountains.

From the top of the massive, flat-topped **Puy-de-Dôme** (1465m), there is a clear view of the teacup-shaped **Chaîne des Puys**, a green ridge of extinct volcanoes which runs north-south. In late autumn, the *mer de nuages* (sea of clouds), a blanket of clouds that obscures the plains below such that only isolated peaks protrude into the sky, seems straight from a postcard. (Puy-de-Dôme open Mar.-Oct. daily 7am-10pm, weather permitting. Call ☎04 73 62 12 18 to see if the road to the top is open.) Brave Icarus-types can take to the skies with help from **Volcan Action** (☎04 73 62 15 15), which offers a 15min. paragliding flight with an instructor for €65 (all gear provided). At the peak, the **Centre d'Accueil de Puy-de-Dôme** has regional info, maps, informative displays on volcanoes, and free, geologically rich tours of the summit nearly every hour. (☎04 73 62 21 46. Open July-Aug. daily 9am-7pm; May-June and Sept. M-F 10am-6pm, Sa-Su 10am-7pm; Oct. daily 10am-6pm.)

Although Puy-de-Dôme is only 12km from Clermont-Ferrand, getting there can be an exercise in strategic planning. The Clermont tourist office's **Espace Massif Central** desk has info on how best to make the trip. **Voyage Maisonneuve**, 24 rue Clemenceau, organizes infrequent **bus excursions** to the summit and other parts of the Auvergne. (Office ☎04 73 93 16 72. Open M-F 8:30am-noon and 2-6:30pm, Sa 9am-noon. Bus service available July-Aug. see tourist office for details. 5hr., €13 to Puy-de-Dôme.) The best bet, though, is to hike or drive. Hikers take bus line #14 to Royat from the stop at Place Allard. Follow the signs for the Hôtel Paradis to reach the first yellow markers that guide the rest of the wide, graveled 3hr. hike along the PR Chamina to the summit. Buy a good **map** (such as the IGN *Chaîne des Puys*, available in Clermont-Ferrand *tabacs*) and listen to the weather forecast for the day, as conditions change rapidly—hailstorms at the summit are not uncommon, even in June. Bring warm clothes and rain gear. From 10am to 6pm in July and August, and weekends and holidays in May, June, September, and October, drivers must leave their cars at the base and take a bus (last bus descends at 7pm; round-trip €3.50; free parking at base and summit); otherwise, the toll is €4.50.

LE MONT-DORE

Located in an isolated valley amid primordial scenery, Le Mont-Dore (pop. 1700) sits at the foot of the largest volcano in a dormant range. Elephants, rhinos, and tigers once roamed through bamboo forests here, and their fossils remain encrusted in the area's volcanic rock. A premiere ski resort in the winter and a hiking mecca year-round, Mont-Dore attracts summer *curistes* seeking health in the warm, mineral-rich waters that seep up through cracks in the lava.

⑦ PRACTICAL INFORMATION. Trains run from pl. de la Gare (☎04 73 65 00 02) to **Clermont-Ferrand** (1½hr., 6 per day, €10.40). Info desk open M-Th 5:50am-9pm, F until 9:40pm, Sa until 7:45pm, Su 9:30am-noon and 2-7pm. **Taxis** are operated by **Claude Taxi** (☎04 73 99 80 61) and **Taxi Sepchat** (☎04 73 65 09 38). Rent **bikes** and **skis** at **Bessac Sports,** rue de Maréchal Juin. (☎04 73 65 02 25. Bikes €12 per half-day, €15 per day. Passport deposit. Skis €7-24 per day.) Snowboards and hiking equipment also available. Open July-Aug. daily 9am-noon and 2-7pm; Sept.-June during school vacations Sa-Su 8:30am-7pm. MC/V.)

From the train station, head up av. Michel Bertrand and follow the signs to the **tourist office,** av. de la Libération, behind the ice-skating rink across the Dordogne. Staffers distribute a practical city guide, help with **accommodations booking** (for stays over 3 days), and organize summer hikes and bike tours. **Internet** with *télé-cartes* is also available. (☎04 73 65 20 21; fax 04 73 65 05 71. Open daily July-Aug. 9am-1pm and 2-7pm; Sept.-June 9am-12:30pm and 2-6:30pm. Hikes €5.50.) Other services include: **police** (☎04 73 65 01 70 or 17) on av. M. Bertrand; a **hospital** at 2 rue du Capitaine-Chazotte (☎04 73 65 33 33), off pl. Charles de Gaulle; the **Pharmacie du Parc** at 17 rue Meynadier. (☎04 73 65 02 86 or 06 03 78 20 93. Open M-Sa 9am-12:30pm and 2:30-7:30pm.) The **pharmacie de garde** alternates between **Parc** or **Pharmacie de l'Etablissement,** 1 pl. du Panthéon (☎04 73 65 05 21). The **post office,** pl. Charles de Gaulle, **exchanges currency** and has an **ATM** just outside. (☎04 73 65 37 10. Open M-F 8:30am-noon and 1:30-5:30pm, Sa 8:30am-noon.) **Postal code:** 63240.

⚐ ACCOMMODATIONS & CAMPING. Le Mont-Dore has over a dozen hotels with rooms starting in the low €20s, making it relatively easy to find an affordable bed, though reservations are usually recommended during summer and peak winter skiing periods. Pull into **Hôtel Le Parking ❷,** 19 av. de la Libération, behind the tourist office. This quaint, partially pink hotel has sizable, comfortable rooms and spectacular views. (☎04 73 65 03 43. Breakfast €3.90. Reception daily 7am-9pm. Closed Nov. Singles and doubles €21.40-24.50, with shower €26-29, with bath €30.50-37.50; triples with bath €38.10-45. MC/V.) Modern wood paneling creates a clean, bright feel at **Castel Medicis ❷,** 5 rue Duchatel, right at the top of the main part of town. (☎04 73 65 30 50; hotelcastelmedicis@wanadoo.fr. Breakfast included. Reception daily 8:30am-8pm. Singles and doubles €20, with shower €28, with bath €31. Extra bed €8. MC/V.) The **Grand Hôtel ❸,** 2 rue Meyandier, in the center of town, looks like a castle, with four turrets and simple rooms for a happily-ever-after evening. (☎04 73 65 02 64; fax 04 73 65 27 72. Breakfast €4. Singles and doubles with toilets €24, with shower €29; triples and quads with bath €34. MC/V.) Overlooking the city park, **Hôtel le Londres ❸,** 45 rue Meyandier, has fresh rooms, some with balconies, and an elevator. (☎04 73 65 01 12. Closed in Apr. Singles and doubles with bathroom €30.50-37; triples and quads €43-47. MC/V.) The **Auberge de Jeunesse "Le Grand Volcan" (HI) ❶,** rte. du Sancy, is 3km from town. From the station, climb av. Guyot-Dessaigne, which becomes av. des Belges. Continue on D983 (through several name changes) into the countryside. The hostel is on the right, after the ski lifts. The train station supplies info on local buses that run near the hostel. This chalet's spartan 1- to 6-bed rooms aren't very appealing, but it compensates with an idyllic setting at the foot of Puy de Sancy. Avoid the cramped loft singles. (☎04 73 65 03 53; fax 04 73 65 26 39. Kitchen, bar, and laundry facilities. Breakfast and bunk €11.30. Lunch and dinner €8. Reception daily June-Aug. 8am-noon and 6-11pm; Sept.-May 8am-noon and 6-9pm. **Members only.**)

There are four **campsites** in Le Mont-Dore. The most convenient is the site at **Des Crouzets ❶,** av. des Crouzets, across from the station, in a pleasant, crowded hollow on the Dordogne. Set up first and pay later. (☎/fax 04 73 65 21 60. Office open M-Sa 9am-noon and 3-6:30pm, Su 9:30am-noon and 4-6:30pm. Open mid-Dec. to mid-Oct. Reservations not accepted. €2.50 per person; €2.30 per site; car included. Electricity €2.50-5.) Located one kilometer behind the train station, the gravel sites of **L'Esquiladou ❶**, rte. des Cascades, are better suited to caravans, but it's less crowded than at Des Crouzets. (☎/fax 04 73 65 23 74; camping.esquiladou@wanadoo.fr. Reception daily July-Aug. 9am-noon and 3-7pm; May-June and Sept.-Oct. 9am-noon and 3-6pm. €2.60 per person; €2.40 per tent. Electricity €2.50-5.)

⬛ FOOD. Restaurants take a backseat to outdoor pursuits in Le Mont-Dore. However, the small spots serving regional dishes like potato and cheese *truffade*, or its creamed cousin aligot, are ideal after a day of exploring. Many restaurants in Mont-Dore are affiliated with a hotel; these pensions serve everyone, but usually give discounts to guests. Most *menus* begin at €11; the good ones run €13-15. **Le Bougnat ❸**, 23 rue Georges Clemenceau, serves regional fare in a beautiful, flower-trimmed stone building. The delicious *aligot* goes for €12.50. (☎04 73 65 28 19. Entrees €11-13. Open Tu-Sa noon-2pm and 7:30pm-11pm. MC/V.) In a 1920s salon, **Café de Paris ❷**, pl. du Panthéon, cooks up local café food (including *truffade*, €9), on a quiet pedestrian street, and has an occasional evening piano bar. (☎04 73 65 01 79. Open daily 8am-11pm.) Mountaintop picnics make the most scenic meals: pick up a wedge of St-Nectaire cheese and a length of uniquely flavored dry sausage from one of the street side shops specializing in tasty local food, or try the **Utile** supermarket on rue du Cap-Chazzotte. (Open July-Aug. M-Sa 7am-7:30pm, Su 7am-12:30pm and 3-7:30pm; Sept.-June M-Sa 7am-12:30pm and 3-7:30pm.)

⬛ SIGHTS. Every morning in the May-October thermal season, *curistes* seeking the healing power of Le Mont-Dore's springs descend upon the ornate **Etablissement Thermal**, 1 pl. du Panthéon (see **The Big Splurge**, at right). Five springs used today were channeled by the Romans, who discovered that the pure water did wonders for their horses' sinuses. Today, a French-led tour of the *thermes* ends with a dose of the *thermes'* celebrated *douche nasale gazeuse*, a tiny blast of carbon and helium that evacuates sinuses more effectively than any sneeze. (☎04 73 65 05 10. Tours M-Sa every hr. 2-5pm. €3.) Down the hill on av. Michel Bertrand, the **Musée Joseph Forêt** honors the celebrated art editor, a Mont-Dore native who bequeathed his collection to the town in 1985. Before his death, Forêt recruited seven painters and seven writers to collaborate in the publication of the world's largest book. *Le Livre de l'Apocalypse*,

THE BIG SPLURGE

SOAKING IT UP

People seeking to cure a laundry list of ailments flock to the mineral water springs of Auvergne's volcanic region. Discovered by the Romans, the *thermes* were forgotten until the 1700s and 1800s, when Byzantine-style bath houses were built in a small string of cities throughout the Auvergne. Now they draw a rich clientele into the mountains for weeks of treatment.

Today, dedicated *curistes*, doctors' notes in hand, line up as early as 6am every morning for their daily *cures*, which involve everything from inhaling the humid vapors to being sprayed with a large hose from head to foot. The majority of bathers are on three-week prescriptions.

Newcomers eager to test the waters should try the **Etablissement Thermal** in Le Mont-Dore. Even without a prescription, one can sign up for a morning *découverte* package (€43), which includes fabled treatments like a high-powered whirlpool, a precisely placed vapor shower, a nasal humidifer, a powerful hosing down, and a communal sauna. "Patients" in thick pink robes are whisked from one small tiled room to the next for their various water *cures*. For those recovering from yesterday's hike, a brief thermal infusion may be just what the doctor ordered.

(1 pl. du Panthéon. ☎04 73 65 05 19; fax 04 73 65 09 37. Reservations recommended.)

weighing a quarter-ton, incorporates works by Dalí and Cocteau. The original was sold in bits to pay for printing, but a copy is displayed in the back of the museum. (☎ 04 73 65 20 21. Call 12:30-3pm to set up a visit. €2.)

🖪 **HIKING & BIKING.** Trails through the volcanic mountains span dense forests, rushing waterfalls, and jagged rocks, then plunge into farming valleys. Scaling the peaks is relatively easy—the summit of Puy de Sancy (1775m) awaits at the end of a languorous 6hr. hike. Those planning an extended hike should review their route with the tourist office, which has maps and multilingual guidance. Leave an itinerary of multi-day routes with the **peloton de montagne** (mountain police; ☎ 04 73 65 04 06), on rue des Chaussers at the base of Puy de Sancy. All hikers should acquire maps and weather reports—mist in the valley often signifies hail or snow in the peaks. The tourist office's pocket-sized *Massif du Sancy* (€6.90) maps out hiking circuits. Their *Massif du Sancy et Artense* (€14.40) covers 47 hikes originating in all areas of Le Sancy. An **IGN map** (either Massif du Sancy or the larger Chaîne des Puys) is essential for any serious trek (€5.40).

For all the views without all the exertion, the **téléphérique** transports people from the base station by the hostel to the Puy de Sancy. (☎ 04 73 65 02 73. Departs daily July-Aug. every 10min. 9am-6pm; Oct.-Apr. 8:45am-4:45pm, Oct.-Nov. only Sa-Su; May-June and Sept. 9am-12:30pm and 1:30-5pm. One-way €4.90, round-trip €6.) The oldest electric **funicular** in France scales 1245m up to Salon des Capucin from near the tourist office. (Departs daily every 20min. July-Aug. 9am-6:40pm; May and Sept. 10am-12:10pm and 2:10-6:40pm. One-way €3.30, round-trip €4.20.)

Bikers and drivers should check out the calm volcanic lakes, such as **Lac Servière** (15km northeast), which pool in the craters of the Mont-Dore region. Most of the lakes have small pebble beaches and are suitable for windsurfing, sailing, fishing, and swimming. **Lac d'Aydat,** to the northeast, offers paddle-boats and other amusements, as does **Lac Chambon,** 20km east of Le Mont-Dore via D996E, near Murol.

Hikes are indicated by yellow trail signs, often accompanied by detailed maps of the surrounding area. For an **easy hike** (1½hr., 3½km round-trip), try the **Grande Cascade** waterfall. From the *thermes,* follow rue des Desportes a few meters to the right and climb the stairs on the left to join the chemin de Melki Rose, which leads into the rte. de Besse and the chemin de la Grande Cascade. After crossing a road, the trail runs through birch woods and winds up a narrow, pine-covered gorge. A quick climb up the metal stairway leads to the top of the waterfall. Another easy option is the **Salon du Capucin** (1½hr., 4½km round-trip). From the tourist office, take av. Jules Ferry and follow the signs.

A low-grade **intermediate hike** (1½hr., 6km round-trip) starts at the Salon du Capucin trail convergence point, near the funicular drop-off point. From the lodge, head toward Le Bourgeat along the wide trail. Keep straight; 5min. of moss-covered slopes open into a shrub-filled meadow with a great view of the surrounding mountains. Traverse the off-trail meadow until reaching a yellow sign, and head toward Crève-Cœur; after five more minutes, a wonderful chasm view will suddenly appear. Head toward Rigolet-Haut and Choucailles, then come back along a paved road to Creve-Cœur to pass lovely rural houses, cows, and great mountain views. From Creve-Cœur, it's an easy 0.9km walk back to Salon du Capucins.

A great **intermediate hike** (3-4hr., 8km round-trip) begins at the base of the Puy de Sancy, near the hostel. Ascend the mountain via the Val de Courre, clearly labeled with yellow markers. At **Puy Redon,** the trail joins the GR30, which winds to the summit of Puy de Sancy. Summer snow patches are not uncommon, but on clear days the Alps are visible to the east. On the south side of the peak, wildflowers and other rare vegetation carpet the immense **Vallée de la Fontaine Salée.** Smart hikers who don't want to follow the GR4 all the way back (see below) retrace their steps along the Val de Courre instead of suffering through the marked ski trails of the

GR4e. Another **half-day hike** (5-6hr. round-trip) starts just off the D996, a few hundred meters west of **le Marais.** Follow the yellow-marked PR as it curves right and ascends through a thick wood. At the juncture of the GR30, turn left and follow a 2km detour to climb the **Puy Gros.** Otherwise, continue right for several kilometers, passing by another yellow-marked PR, and on to the Lac de Guery.

The ambitious, **full-day advanced hike** (6hr.) follows a series of trails that loop around town, passing all the major natural attractions on the way. Beginning from the tourist office, follow the signs to the Salon du Capucin, a towering mass of rocks overlooking town. Another vertical 200m reaches the **Pic du Capucin,** where the trail meets with the GR30, marked with parallel red and white lines. The GR30 follows a narrow ridge, then skirts the summit of Puy Redon, which hovers over beautiful Val de Courre, then ascends 100m to the summit of **Puy de Sancy,** the highest peak in the Massif Central. From here, follow the GR4 as it loops back north and descends a series of ski trails before climbing back into the trees. The weary can take the GR4e, which descends straight to the base of the ski mountain.

NEAR LE MONT-DORE

The region surrounding Le Mont-Dore is peppered with small, picturesque towns within easy driving or hiking range. **La Bourboule,** which can also be reached by a shuttle service from Le Mont-Dore, was established in the 1875 upon the discovery of its thermal springs and became a widely popular destination in the 1920s. The city, just 15min. from Le Mont-Dore, maintains its "Roaring Twenties" atmosphere with exquisite art nouveau architecture, glamorous plazas, and charming hotels and restaurants. Information on thermal visits, shuttles from Mont Dore, and lodging is available at the **tourist office,** pl. de la République. (☎04 73 65 57 71; www.bourboule.com. Open June-Aug. daily 9am-7pm; Sept.-May 9am-12:30pm and 2-7pm.) On the opposite side of the mountain, **Besse,** an ancient lava stone cobbled village once frequented by the Medici family, is lined with small bakeries, *fromageries*, and stores displaying regional specialties. The freshest St-Nectaire cheeses, *saucissons*, and wines from the Côtes d'Auvergne are sold in the charming, timber-lined streets. The helpful staff at the **tourist office,** pl. Pipet, provide advice on daytrips, *dégustations*, and hiking trails. (☎04 73 79 52 84; www.super-besse.com. Open daily 9am-12:30pm and 2-7pm.)

LE PUY-EN-VELAY

Jutting crags of volcanic rock pierce the sky near Le Puy (pop. 20,500), punctuating an horizon dominated by rolling expanses of gentle green hills. A pilgrimage site since the first churches were built atop these natural skyscrapers, Le Puy has always been a popular travel destination in France. Its lava-stone cobbled streets are lined with countless traditional *dentelle*, lace-making shops, and window displays of the local lentil crop. Although a predominantly tranquil town, Le-Puy-en-Velay comes alive during the busy July-September festival season, with an event held nearly every week.

◗ TRANSPORTATION

Trains: pl. Maréchal Leclerc. Info and ticket offices open M 4:25am-7pm, Tu-Sa 5:40am-7pm, Su 10:05am-8:10pm. To: **Clermont-Ferrand** (2½hr., M-F 1-3 per day, €17.10); **Lyon** (2½hr., M-F 4 per day, €17.10); **St-Etienne-Châteaucreux** (1¼hr., M-F 13 per day, €11.40). Most trains arriving from the south or from Clermont-Ferrand require a change at Brioude; trains from Lyon or Paris change at St-Etienne-Châteaucreux. Trains marked "car" are buses.

Buses: pl. Maréchal Leclerc, next to the train station (☎04 71 09 25 60). Open M-F 8am-noon. Transportation by bus can be spotty. **Chavanelle** runs to **St-Etienne** (2¼hr., M-Sa 3 per day, €8.80). Those traveling south should bus to **Langogne** (2hr., M-F 7:50am and 4:15pm, €7.30) to catch a train. Buy tickets on bus.

Public Transportation: S.A.E.M. TUDIP, pl. du Breuil. Info and map at the tourist office. Tickets on bus €1, *carnet* of 10 at the tourist office €6.90. Runs daily 7am-7:25pm.

Taxis: Radio-Taxis, pl. du Breuil (☎04 71 05 42 43). 24hr.

■ ⚐ ORIENTATION & PRACTICAL INFORMATION

From the station, walk left along av. Charles Dupuy, cross sq. H. Coiffier, and turn left onto bd. Maréchal Fayolle. A 5min. walk leads to adjacent squares **place Michelet** and **place du Breuil.** The tourist office and most hotels are here and on nearby bd. St-Louis; the cathedral, hostels, and *vieille ville* are uphill to the right.

Tourist Office: pl. du Breuil (☎04 71 09 38 41; www.ot-lepuyenvelay.fr). Free **accommodations service.** Free, well-marked map with 3 walking tours. Open July-Aug. M-Sa 8:30am-7:30pm, Su 9am-noon and 2-6pm; Sept.-June M-Sa 8:30am-noon and 1:30-6:15pm, Su 9am-noon and 2-6pm; Oct.-Mar. Su 10am-noon only. Daily guided tours of the cathedral or the nearby geological sites are given early July to early Sept.

Laundromat: 12 rue Chèvrerie. Open M-Sa 7:45am-noon and 1-7pm. **Lav'Flash,** 24 rue Portail d'Avignon. Open M-Sa 8am-8pm, Su 9:15am-6:30pm.

Police: rue de la Passerelle (☎04 71 04 04 22).

Medical Assistance: Centre Hospitalier Emile Roux, bd. Dr. Chantemesse (☎04 71 04 32 10). 24hr. **Clinique Bon Secours,** 67bis av. M. Foch (☎04 71 09 87 00). **Ambulance** ☎04 71 90 30 34. For the **pharmacie de garde,** call ☎04 71 04 04 22.

Internet: Forum Café, 5 rue Gal. LaFayette (☎04 71 04 04 98), is dirt cheap at €1.50 per hr. Open Tu-Sa 1-6pm. **Planet Phone,** 33 pl. du Breuil (☎06 25 10 17 13), has an international phone booth. Open daily 9am-11pm. Both have only two computers.

Post Office: 8 av. de la Dentelle (☎04 71 07 02 05). **Currency exchange** with small commission, Western Union. **Cyberposte.** Open M-F 8am-7pm, Sa 8am-noon. **Branch office:** 49 bd. St-Louis (☎04 71 09 77 61). Open M-F 9am-noon and 2-5:30pm, Sa 9am-noon. **Postal code:** 43000.

⌂ ACCOMMODATIONS & CAMPING

▨ **Gite des Capucins,** 29 rue des Capucins (☎04 71 04 28 74), off bd. St-Louis. White boards on every door encourage guests to make their own nameplates at this small, extremely friendly stop. Immaculate 4- to 6-bed dorms, each with private bath. Kitchen facilities and quaint garden in back. Breakfast €4.60. Sheets €1.60. Reception until late; there is usually someone around to answer calls. Beds €12.20. Well-furnished, colorful 2-person apartments €51.80; 4-person apartments €64. ❶

Centre Pierre Cardinal (HI), 9 rue Jules Vallès (☎04 71 05 52 40; fax 04 71 05 61 24). Numerous quads and one 18-bed dorm in a clean and beautiful former barracks. Excellent kitchen. Breakfast €3.20. Sheets €3.50. Reception daily 7:30am-8:30pm. Lockout Su 10am-8pm. Curfew 11:30pm. Closed holidays, Christmas vacation, and during the July Festival des Musicales. Bunks €7. **Members only.** ❶

Maison St-François, rue St-Mayol (☎04 71 05 98 86; fax 04 71 05 98 87). Soothing peach- and white-trimmed rooms, practically *in* the cathedral. Kitchen, convent garden, and joyful common room. Caters primarily to pilgrims in summer, but other travelers are welcome. Breakfast included. Meals €9.50. No sheets available. Reception 2-8pm. Check-out by 8:30am. Call a few days ahead. Beds €15. ❶

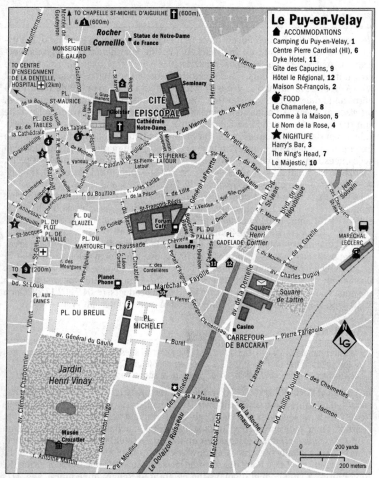

Le Puy-en-Velay

▲ ACCOMMODATIONS
Camping du Puy-en-Velay, **1**
Centre Pierre Cardinal (HI), **6**
Dyke Hotel, **11**
Gîte des Capucins, **9**
Hôtel le Régional, **12**
Maison St-François, **2**

🍴 FOOD
Le Chamarlene, **8**
Comme à la Maison, **5**
Le Nom de la Rose, **4**

★ NIGHTLIFE
Harry's Bar, **3**
The King's Head, **7**
Le Majestic, **10**

MASSIF CENTRAL

Hôtel le Régional, 36 bd. Maréchal Fayolle (☎04 71 09 37 74), near pl. Michelet. Large, clean, colorful rooms in a noisy area with sound-proofed windows. Attached to a small café. Breakfast €4.50. Reception daily 7am-10pm. Singles and doubles €21.50, with shower from €26; triples from €34; quads €47.50. AmEx/MC/V. ❷

Dyke Hotel, 37 bd. Maréchal-Fayolle (☎04 71 09 05 30; fax 04 71 02 58 66). The name, pronounced *deek*, refers to tall points of rock in le Puy. Modern, well-equipped rooms painted in cheerful yellow tones overlook a busy street. Breakfast €5.40. Singles and doubles with shower €31-43. MC/V. ❸

Camping du Puy-en-Velay, chemin de Bouthezard (☎04 71 09 55 09), near the Chapelle St-Michel and the river. Walk up bd. St-Louis, continue on bd. Carnot, turn right at the dead end onto av. d'Aiguille, and look to the left. (15min.) Or take bus #6 (dir: Mondon) from pl. Michelet (10min., 1 per hr., €1). Grassy, but not very private. Reception daily 8am-noon and 2:30-9pm. Open Easter to Sept. €2.20 per person; €2.40 per tent; €1.60 per car; €7.80 for 2 people, site, and car. ❶

FOOD

Recognized by the French government as a city of high-quality local food, le-Puy-en-Velay's many restaurants and markets provide mouth-watering regional specialties. Nearly every restaurant serves *lentilles vertes et saussicon*, as lentils are grown in mass, quality-controlled quantities around the region. Complete a meal with Verveine, an alcoholic *digestif* with a sweet mint flavor, made from local herbs and honey (€10-22 per bottle). Inexpensive restaurants line the side streets off **place du Breuil**. A **Casino** supermarket occupies the corner of av. de la Dentelle and rue Farigoule (open M-Sa 8:30am-8pm), with a **cafeteria** above (meals €4.60-7.30; open daily 11:30am-9:30pm). On Saturdays (6am-12:30pm), farmers set up fresh produce **markets** in practically every square. The market in pl. du Plot also sells cheese, mushrooms, and a few live chickens and rabbits; the adjacent pl. du Clauzel hosts an antique market. (Open Sa 7:30am-1pm.) At pl. du Breuil, the biggest spread of all includes clothing, hardware, toiletries, and shoes.

Le Nom de la Rose ❷, 48 rue Raphaël, presents an odd but eminently satisfying combination of French-cooked Mexican food, though not as spicy as on the other side of the Atlantic. (☎04 71 05 90 04. *Menu* €14.80, *chili con carne* €7.20, *quesadillas* €5.40. Open daily noon-3pm and 7pm-midnight. MC/V.) In a tastefully renovated 17th-century house, small, hip **Comme à la Maison ❸**, 7 rue Séguret, serves simple, delicious *menus du jour* (€12-16) named after local celebrities. (☎04 71 02 94 73. Open daily noon-3pm and 7-11pm. MC/V.) In homey, wood-decorated **Le Chamarlene ❸**, 19 rue Raphaël, diners sample fresh cheeses and yogurts made on the spot. Daily *menus* (€9-14) feature local farm products. (☎04 71 02 17 72. Open M-W noon-4:30pm, Th-Sa noon-11pm; closed M in the winter. MC/V.)

 SIGHTS

The **billet jumelé** *(sold Feb.-Oct. at tourist office and all sites; €7) provides admission to all the sights in the Cité Episcopale, as well as the Musée Crozatier, Chapelle St-Michel, and Rocher Corneille. An English-language* **guide pratique** *has descriptions of each site.*

CATHÉDRALE NOTRE-DAME. Towering over the lower city, the **Cité Episcopale** has attracted pilgrims and tourists for over 1000 years. It was built on a rock known as "le puy," where, legend holds, the Virgin appeared and healed a woman in the 5th century. Though designed as a Christian cathedral, much of it was built by Muslim workers, whose influence is apparent on the doors to either side of the entrance, where "There is only one true God" is written in Arabic. At the altar, a copy of Le Puy's mysterious **Vierge Noir** (Black Virgin) has replaced the one burned during the Revolution. A side chapel displays the celebrated Renaissance mural *Les Arts Libéraux*. It is thought to be unfinished: of the seven arts, only Grammar, Logic, Rhetoric, and Music are represented. *(☎04 71 05 98 74. Open daily 7am-8pm. Free tours are offered early July to late Aug.)*

CLOISTER. The most remarkable of the sights near the cathedral, the cloister's black, white, and peach stone arcades reflect an Islamic influence from Spain. Beneath flame-red tiling and black volcanic rock is an intricate frieze of grinning faces and mythical beasts. Amid the Byzantine arches of the **salle capitulaire**, a vivid and well-preserved 13th-century fresco depicts the Crucifixion. The same ticket allows a peek at the **Trésor d'Art Religieux**, which contains walnut statues and jeweled capes. *(☎04 71 05 45 52. Both open daily July-Sept. 9am-6:30pm; May-June 9am-noon and 2-6pm; Oct.-Mar. 9am-noon and 2-5pm. €4.60, ages 18-25 with ID €3.10.)*

STATUE DE NOTRE-DAME DE FRANCE. At the edge of the *vieille ville* is the **Rocher Corneille,** the eroded core of a volcano. The summit overlooks a dreamscape of jagged crags and manicured gardens. For a windy view through windows below the Virgin's arm, climb to the top of the cramped 16m **Notre-Dame de France,** a statue cast from cannons captured during the Crimean war. Notre-Dame earned national fame in 1942, when 20,000 young people came here to pray for the liberation of France. *(Open daily July-Aug. 9am-7:30pm; mid-Mar. to Apr. 9am-6pm; May-June and Sept. 9am-7pm; Oct. to mid-Mar. 10am-7pm. €3, students €1.50.)*

MUSÉE CROZATIER. This grand cultural history museum overlooks the shaded benches, children's areas, and manicured plants in the **Jardin Henri Vinay.** Exhibits highlight centuries-old traditional craftsmanship such as *dentelle* (lace-making) and the intricate wood carving of the Puy region. In addition to a small painting collection, the museum also displays some of the early patented designs of native son Emile Reynaud, who invented the precursor to the film projector. *(☎04 71 06 62 40. Open May-Sept. Su-M and W-Sa 10am-noon and 2-6pm; Oct.-Apr. Su-M and W-Sa 10am-noon and 2-4pm, Su 2-4pm. €3, students and under 25 €1.20, under 18 free.)*

CHAPELLE ST-MICHEL D'AIGUILHE. Just outside the old city, this primitive chapel crowns an 80m spike of volcanic rock. Its stained glass dimly illuminates a faded 12th-century fresco and the almost voodoo-like 10th-century woodcut crucifix uncovered during excavations. The chapel was built in 950 by the first pilgrim to complete the Chemin de St-Jacques, a trail from Le Puy to Spain still trod by the pious. *(☎04 71 09 50 03. Open daily May-Sept. 9am-6:30pm; Feb. to late Mar. 2-4pm; late Mar. to late Apr. and Oct. to mid-Nov. 9:30am-noon and 2-5pm. €2.50, under age 14 €1.)*

🔲🔲 NIGHTLIFE & FESTIVALS

The best of Le Puy's many bars is 🔳**The King's Head,** 17 rue Grenouillit, a relaxed English pub that serves beer (€2.50) and fish and chips, in addition to curries and whatever else the friendly Dave concocts. (☎04 71 02 50 35. Open M-Th noon-1am, F-Sa noon-2am, Su 5pm-1am.) **Harry's Bar,** 37 rue Raphaël, cultivates a chic, low-key, dimly-lit environment, where locals chat amiably amid Latin, Eastern European, and jazz music. (☎04 71 02 23 02. Beer €2-2.50, cocktails €4. Open M-Th 5pm-1am, F-Sa 5pm-2am.) **Le Majestic,** 8 bd. Maréchal Fayolle, is a *brasserie* by day but spills out onto a terrace at night. Art exhibits and low, colorful chairs give this nightspot a creative flair. (☎04 71 09 06 30. Techno F-Sa. Open M-Sa 7am-1am, Su 10am-1am.) Although the **Municipal Theater** is closed until 2005, information on theater and dance performances can be found at the **Centre Culturel de Vals,** av. Charles Massot (☎04 71 05 61 24). A **cinéma** is located at 29 pl. du Breuil. (☎04 71 09 00 35. €6.40, students €5.30.)

From early July, Le Puy hosts a different festival each week, ranging from music to theater and culminating at the mid-September **Fête Renaissance du Roi de L'Oiseau.** Jugglers, minstrels, and costumed locals wander the streets; food and drink are bought with specially minted festival currency. A centuries-old tunnel system carved into the rock below the *vieille ville* is opened and turned into one great party hall, where beer and wine flow freely. (☎04 71 02 84 84. €2-5, depending on activity. Free to those in costume. For costume rentals call ☎04 71 09 16 53.)

VICHY

With lacy ironwork and resplendant *Belle Epoque* architecture, Vichy (pop. 78,000) seems entrenched in its past as a city that once drew royals, celebrities, and wealthy *voyageurs* to the mineral-rich waters that flow here. Despite its splendor, Vichy's past is darkened by its use as the capital of France from 1940 to 1944. Forced to evacuate Paris, the French administration selected Vichy, with its large hotels and strong cultural life, as the seat of the Nazi puppet government.

THE LOCAL STORY

VICHY'S WILLFUL AMNESIA

Until the 1970s, the details of Vichy's *années noires* (black years) were largely swept aside by historians and politicians in favor of heroic tales of the Resistance championed by Charles de Gaulle. Today, residents remain silent about the town's past.

"They prefer to forget that era," says Priscille Bonnefoy, a discount clothing store employee. "It's not very pleasant." Ann Auguste, owner of the Juice Café, agrees. "It's a bit of a taboo. There's no museum, no monument. People start to wonder, why not?"

When asked about the apparent absence of WWII-era monuments, a representative at the city hall deflects the questions. Instead, she carefully notes the distinction between the *Vichysstes* (Pétain supporters) and the *Vichyssois* (normal Vichy citizens).

Residents interviewed at a *boulodrome* defended the Vichy people, some blaming Pétain's top aide Pierre Laval instead. Paul Deschamps, 86, says residents "aren't responsible for the *bêtises* of the Vichy government."

Other aging *Vichyssois* talk vividly about Pétain propaganda films and of how the Gestapo tortured resisters in the town's casino. "I find it more frustrating that they don't just let it go—there's a monument, there's everything you need to know," Auguste says. "And that way people won't bother about it anymore."

Maréchal Philippe Pétain, a WWI hero, was elected leader of this new state (p. 72). Amidst decorative art nouveau promenades and fancy *confiseries*, an absence of major WWII monuments and museums, or plaques to designate buildings used by Pétain's government, creates an eerie historical gap.

⁊ PRACTICAL INFORMATION. The **train** station on pl. de la Gare sends cars to: Clermont-Ferrand (35min., 11 per day, €7.80); Nevers (1hr., 15 per day, €13.60); Paris (3hr., 6 per day, €33.80). (Ticket counters open M-Th 5:40am-8:50pm, F 5:40am-9:50pm, Sa 6:30am-8:50pm, Su 6:45am-9:50pm; info desk open M-Sa 9:40am-5:50pm and on Su June-Aug.) The **bus station** is in a brick building next to the train station. (Office open M-F 8am-noon and 2-6pm. Reduced hours during the July-Aug. school vacation.) **Public buses** run through town from 6:30am to 8pm (€1). Schedules are available at the tourist office and at Bus Inter (☎04 70 97 81 29), on pl. Charles de Gaulle near the post office. Purchase tickets on the bus or in various kiosks throughout town. For a taxi, call **Vichy Taxis** (☎04 70 98 69 69).

Both Vichy's well-managed **tourist office,** 19 rue du Parc, and the popular *sources* sit in the **Parc des Sources.** From the station, walk straight on rue de Paris; turn left at the fork onto rue Clemenceau, then right onto rue Sornin. The tourist office is straight across the park, in the Hôtel du Parc that once hosted Pétain's government. (10min.) The staff provides a good map, a list of hotels and restaurants, free **accommodations service,** and French-led **walking tours** (€5). They also have a booklet of suggested regional tours and events. (☎04 70 98 71 94; fax 04 70 31 06 00; www.ville-vichy.fr. Office open July-Aug. M-Sa 9am-7:30pm, Su 9:30am-12:30pm and 3-7pm; Apr.-June and Sept. M-Sa 9am-12:30pm and 1:30-7pm, Su 9:30am-12:30pm and 3-7pm; Oct.-Mar. M-F 9am-noon and 2-6:30pm, Sa 9am-noon and 2-6pm, Su 2:30-5:30pm.) Other services include: **police,** 35 av. Victoria (☎04 70 96 11 11); the **Centre Hospitalier,** 15 bd. Denière (☎04 70 97 33 33); **La Grande Pharmacie,** 46 rue de Paris (☎04 70 98 23 01; open M 2:30-7:15pm, Tu-Sa 9:30am-12:15pm and 2:30-7:15pm); a **pharmacie de garde** (dial ☎15); a **Wash'n Dry** at 3 bd. Gambetta (☎06 78 78 08 9; open daily 7am-9pm). The **post office** at pl. Charles de Gaulle **exchanges currency** at 1.5% commission. (☎04 70 30 10 75. Open M-F 8am-7pm, Sa 8am-noon.) **Postal code:** 03200.

⌐◧ ACCOMMODATIONS & FOOD. In keeping with Vichy's long-standing tradition of pampering, even its budget hostels are deluxe. Hotels jostle for business on tiny streets throughout the city; rooms

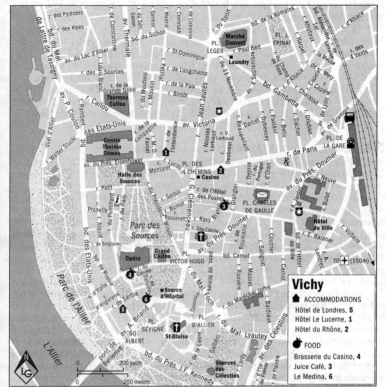

Vichy

⌂ ACCOMMODATIONS

Hôtel de Londres, 5
Hôtel Le Lucerne, 1
Hôtel du Rhône, 2

◆ FOOD

Brasserie du Casino, 4
Juice Café, 3
Le Medina, 6

typically start around €22. The friendly, multilingual owner of **Hôtel du Rhône ❸,** 8 rue de Paris, between the train station and the *thermes,* offers delightful, well-decorated doubles and triples and an air-conditioned salon. The restaurant downstairs offers regional specialties. *Let's Go* readers staying more than two nights receive a free breakfast. (☎04 70 97 73 00; fax 04 70 97 48 25. Breakfast €3, buffet €6. *Menus* €12-39. Reception 24hr. Singles and doubles with shower €25-46; triples €36-68; deluxe rooms with bath €54-79. Extra bed €5. AmEx/MC/V.) **Hôtel Le Lucerne ❷,** 8 rue de l'Intendance, centrally located on a hotel-lined side street, has well-maintained rooms, delicately tiled floors, and an old-fashioned elevator. (☎04 70 98 24 46; fax 04 70 31 71 61. Breakfast €5. Reception daily 7am-9pm. Open Apr.-Oct. Singles €22-24, with shower €26-29; doubles and triples €32-35. MC/V.) The historic, restored **Hôtel de Londres ❷,** 7 bd. de Russie, has large, clean rooms around a quiet, flower-filled inner courtyard. (☎04 70 98 29 27; fax 04 70 98 29 37; hotel.londres@wanadoo.fr. Open Jan. to late Oct. Singles with shower €18-22; doubles €24-29; triples €41; quads €45. MC/V.) The four-star, riverside **Camping Les Acacias ❷** has a market, pool, and laundry. Take bus #7 from the train station (dir: La Tour) to Charles de Gaulle, then bus #3 to Les Acacias; it's 3.5km on foot. (☎04 70 32 36 22; www.camping-acacias.com. Open Apr. to mid-Oct. Reception daily 8am-10pm. €4.50 per person, €4.50 per tent; electricity €2.50.)

There is a **Casino** supermarket on pl. Charles de Gaulle and l'Hôtel des Postes. (Open M-Sa 8:30am-12:30pm and 2:30-7:30pm, Su 9am-noon.) A covered **morning**

market is on pl. Léger where rue Jean Jaurès and bd. Gambetta intersect. (Open Tu-Sa.) Most restaurants in Vichy are affiliated with hotels and are rather expensive. **La Medina ❸**, 7 rue de Banville, serves delicious Moroccan food in a beautiful North African-style *salon*, complete with petal-strewn tables. (☎04 70 98 54 03. Couscous and *tijanes* €9-13. Open Tu-Su Sept.-June noon-2pm and 7-11pm, July-Aug. noon-2pm. MC/V.) Across the street from the opéra, **Brasserie du Casino ❹**, 4 rue du Casino, creates a 1920s look with plush carpet and walls lined with photos of old Vichy. (☎04 70 98 23 06. *Menus* €14-24. Open Su-M and Th-Sa noon-1:15pm and 7:30-10:30pm. MC/V.) For a satisfying smoothie in a sunny interior, the **Juice Café ❶**, 16 rue Ravy Breton, whips up fruit- or veggie-filled concoctions. (☎04 70 97 93 86. Smoothies €4-4.50. Open Tu-Sa noon-7pm and Su-M 3-7pm.)

◙ ▣ SIGHTS & ENTERTAINMENT. The only way to see Pétain's Vichy is to take a French **tour** from the tourist office—significant buildings of the World War II era are not marked and information on the dark years is difficult to find. (Tours 3:30pm July-Aug. W and Sa; June and Sept. W only. €3.80.)

A sip of Vichy's nectar makes one wonder how the town ever made it big—the water tastes disgusting. The *sources* bubble free of charge at the cold springs of **Sources des Célestins** on bd. Kennedy. (Open Apr.-Sept. M-Sa 7:45am-8:30pm, Su 8am-8:30pm; Oct.-Mar. daily 8am-6pm.) The heart of the action, though, is the **Halle des Sources** at the edge of the **Parc des Sources**. Anyone can drink for €1.50. Regulars bring their own glass encased in a special woven carrying basket, available for purchase at Vichy pharmacies for €7.50, though visitors may purchase a less-classy plastic cup for €0.15. (☎04 70 97 39 59. Open M-Sa 6:15am-8:30pm, Su 7:45am-8:30pm.) If you go, take small swigs—it looks like plain water, but it's powerful stuff. **Célestins** is easiest to digest and was proven to relieve arthritis in a 1992 study by the Hôpital Cochimin in Paris. **Parc** is tougher on the stomach, and **Lucas** is chock-full of sulphur, hence the rotten-egg smell. Still thirsty? The **hot springs** are even more vile. (Open M-Sa 6:30am-8:30pm, Su 7:45am-8:30pm.) **Hôpital**, which also flows freely behind the Grand Casino, is used for stomach problems—**Chomel** is the most popular; **Grand Grille** is the most potent. Visitors can recover with older *curistes* in the beautiful Parc des Sources. Surrounded by a wrought-iron art nouveau promenade and flanked by the Opéra, it is Vichy elegance at its height.

Manicured floral displays and thick shade trees fill the English-style gardens in the elegant riverside **Parc de l'Allier**, commissioned by Napoleon III. Across the river and a brisk 20-25min. walk along the promenade to the right of Pont de Bellerive lies Vichy's ultimate recreational facility.

The tourist office posts a daily list of upcoming events in Vichy. There are cheap gaming thrills at the **Grand Casino** in the Parc des Sources. (Open daily noon-4am.) **Operas** and **concerts** take place during the summer in the beautiful **Opéra**, 1 rue du Casino. (☎04 70 30 50 30. Open Tu-Sa 1:30-6:30pm, until curtain time on performance nights; by phone only Tu-F 10am-12:30pm. Operas €27-59, under 25 €24-53; concerts €17-40/€8-21, a few concerts are free.)

RHÔNE-ALPS

The Alps-bound train ride is an experience not soon forgotten. Camera-clutching visitors cannot believe the vibrant wildflowers, distant snowpatches, and tinkling cowbells. The curves of the Chartreuse Valley, the rugged crags in the Vercors range, and the glaciers in the shadow of Mont Blanc, Europe's highest peak, create a wonderland for skiers, hikers, and gazers. Summer and winter visitors will find the most dependable weather, but also the biggest crowds.

The Alps are split between two historical provinces, Savoie and the Dauphiné. Savoie, which includes the peaks of Haute Savoie, the Olympic resorts located in the expansive Tarentaise valley, and the awe-inspiring Vanoise park, bears the name of the oldest royal house in all of Europe. The Dauphiné includes the Chartreuse Valley, Vercors regional park, Ecrins national park, and the Belledonne and Oisans mountains.

This entire region first became independent in the 11th century, under Guiges I. His great-grandson Guiges IV took the surname "Dauphin" (dolphin). In the 14th century, when the last independent Dauphin finally sold all of his lands to France, the French monarchs adopted the practice of ceding the province to the heir to the throne, the Dauphin. In the 15th century, Louis XI established a permanent *parlement* (court) in **Grenoble** (p. 452), which has become the area's cultural and intellectual capital.

Towns of the region are well touristed and often pricey, but the beauty of their natural landscape makes them irresistible. ⬛**Annecy** (p. 463), a flower-filled, fairytale city, is an alpine hiker's dream. Skiers flock to ⬛**Chamonix** (p. 468), a famous mountain-sports town dominated by Mt. Blanc, as well as to **Megève** (p. 460) and **Val d'Isère** (p. 477), two posh and pricey towns known for their excellent skiing and hiking trails. Skiing arrangements should be made a couple of months in advance. The surreal, arabesque fortress of ⬛**Hauterives** (p. 459) makes the town a necessary stop in the area. **Lyon** (p. 435), a vibrant cultural center and culinary capital, rounds out the region's collection of breathtaking towns.

As would be expected, the food in the French Alps has a Swiss twist. Regional specialties include *fondue savoyarde* (bread dipped in a blend of cheeses, white wine, and kirsch), *raclette* (pungent cheese melted and served with boiled potatoes and onions), and *gratin dauphinois* (sliced potatoes baked in a creamy cheese sauce).

LYON

Culinary capital, former center of the silk trade and the French Resistance, and ultramodern city, Lyon (pop. 1.2 million) is friendlier and more relaxed than Paris, with a few centuries' more history. Roman roads connected this provincial capital of Gaul to Italy and the Atlantic, permanently establishing Lyon's status. During the Renaissance, foreign merchants and bankers set up shop here, encouraged by the city's tax-free permanent markets, while in the 15th century Lyon became Europe's printing house. Silkworms imported from China in the 16th century contributed to the city's rise to economic power. Spared from the urban renewal of the early 1960s, the ornate façades and elegant courtyards of the 16th-century townhouses in *Vieux Lyon* attest to this period of wealth. These buildings played

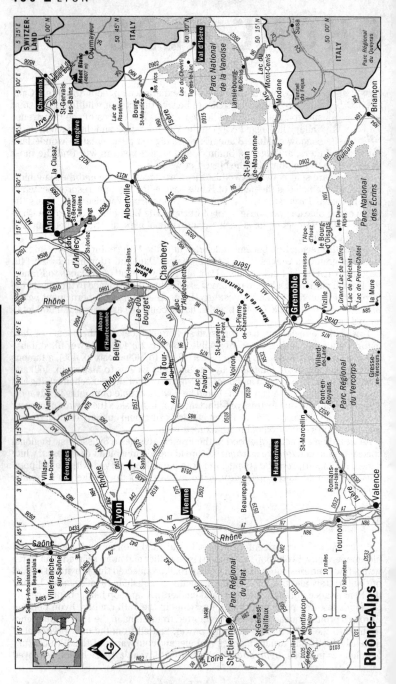

RHÔNE-ALPS

Rhône-Alps

a major role in the city being named a UNESCO World Heritage sight in 1998. Today, Lyon is the stomping ground of world-renowned chefs Paul Bocuse, Georges Blanc, and Jean-Paul Lacombe, and an incubator of new culinary geniuses. There's no doubt one can eat well at one of the masters' spin-off restaurants, and just about anywhere else in the city.

■ INTERCITY TRANSPORTATION

Flights: Aéroport Lyon-Saint-Exupéry (☎04 72 22 72 21). The TGV, which stops at the airport, is cheaper and more convenient than the 50 daily flights to Paris. **Satobuses/ Navette Aéroport** (☎04 72 68 72 17) **shuttles** to Gare de la Part-Dieu, Gare de Perrache, and subway stops Grange-Blanche, Jean Mace, and Mermoz Pinel (every 20min., €8.20). **Air France**, 17 rue Victor Hugo, 2ème (☎08 20 82 08 20), has 6 daily flights to both Paris's Orly and Roissy airports (€101-207).

Trains: SNCF trains go to: **Dijon** (2hr., 6 per day, €21.20); **Geneva,** Switzerland (2hr., 13 per day, €18.80); **Grenoble** (1¼hr., 21 per day 6:10am-12:20am, €17.10); **Marseille** (3hr., 17 per day, €39); **Nice** (6hr., 12 per day, €47.70); **Paris** (2hr., 26 TGV per day, €54-68); and **Strasbourg** (5½hr., 5 per day, €38.40). Trains passing through Lyon stop at **Gare de la Part-Dieu,** bd. Marius Vivier-Merle (M: Part-Dieu), in the business district on the Rhône's east bank. Info desk open M-F 9am-7pm and Sa 9am-6:30pm; ticket windows open M-Th and Sa 5:15am-11pm, F and Su 5:15am-midnight. The **SNCF Boutique,** 2 pl. Bellecour across from the tourist office, solves traveling quandaries in a slighter calmer atmosphere, but lines are long everywhere. Open M-Sa 9am-7pm. Lockers and **baggage storage** open daily 6am-midnight. €4.50 for 2 bags. Trains terminating in Lyon continue to **Gare de Perrache,** pl. Carnot (M: Perrache).

Buses: On the lowest level of the Gare de Perrache, at the train station, and at Gorge de Loup in the 9ème (☎04 72 61 72 61 for all three). Perrache station open daily 5am-12:30am. Domestic companies include **Philibert** (☎04 78 98 56 00) and **Transport Verney** (☎04 78 70 21 01), but it's almost always cheaper, faster, and simpler to take the train. **Eurolines** (☎04 72 56 95 30; fax 04 72 41 72 43) travels out of France.

Bike Rentals: Holiday Bikes, 199 rue Vendôme, 3ème (☎04 78 60 11 10). €12 per day; €250 deposit. Open M-Sa 9am-12:30pm and 3-7pm, Su 9am-noon and 6:30-7pm. AmEx/MC/V. Pleasant bike paths run up and down the Saône.

▐ LOCAL TRANSPORTATION

TCL (☎04 78 71 70 00) has info offices at both stations and all major metro stops. *Plan de Poche* (pocket map) available from the tourist office or any TCL branch. Tickets are valid for all methods of mass transport, including the **metro, buses, funiculars,** and **trams.** Tickets €1.40; *carnet* of 10 €10.60, student discount includes 10 passes valid for one month €9.10. One pass is valid 1hr. in 1 direction, connections included. *Ticket Liberté* day pass (€3.80) is a great deal for short-term visitors. The efficient **metro** runs 5am-midnight, as do **buses** and **trams,** which have two different lines; T1 connects Part-Dieu to Perrache directly. **Funiculars (cable cars)** swing between the Vieux Lyon metro stop, pl. St-Jean, and the top of Fourvière and St-Just until midnight.

Taxis: Taxi Radio de Lyon ☎04 72 10 86 86. Perrache to airport €36 during the day, €49 at night; Part-Dieu to airport €31/€49. 24hr. **Allô Taxi** ☎04 78 28 23 23.

▐ ORIENTATION

Orient yourself using Fourvière, the basilica, and the **Tour Métallique,** a mini-Eiffel Tower, in the west, and the **Tour du Crédit Lyonnais,** a reddish-brown "crayon" towering over Part-Dieu, in the east. Lyon has two major squares; pl. Bellecour, containing the tourist office and numerous bookstores, is south, while pl. des Terraux, with the Hôtel de Ville and its giant statue of four horses, is to the north.

Lyon is divided into nine **arrondissements;** the 1*er*, 2*ème*, and 4*ème* lie on the **presqu'île** (peninsula), a narrow strip of land jutting south toward the confluence of the Saône and Rhône rivers. Starting in the south, the 2*ème* (the city center) includes the Perrache train station and **place Bellecour,** as well as most of the city's boutiques, hotels, and fast-food joints. The 1*er* is home to the nocturnal Terreaux neighborhood, with its sidewalk cafés and student-packed bars. Farther north, the *presqu'île* widens into the 4*ème* and the Croix-Rousse, a residential neighborhood that once housed Lyon's silk industry. The main pedestrian arteries of the *presqu'île* are **rue de la République,** affectionately known as "la Ré," to the northeast of pl. Bellecour, and **rue Victor Hugo,** to the south of Bellecour.

To the west lies the oldest part of the city: Vieux Lyon, with narrow streets and traditional restaurants, and the **Fourvière** hill, with a Roman theater, a basilica, and fabulous views. Most people live east of the Rhône (3*ème* and 6*ème*-8*ème*), also home to the **Part-Dieu** train station and modern commercial complex.

Most trains terminating in Lyon stop at both the **Gare de Perrache** and the **Gare de la Part-Dieu.** Perrache is more central and considered safer at night, but both are connected to Lyon's highly efficient **metro,** which is the fastest way to the tourist office in the **tourist pavilion** on pl. Bellecour. To walk from Perrache, head straight onto rue Victor Hugo and follow it until it ends at pl. Bellecour; the tourist office will be on the right. (15min.) From Part-Dieu, leave the station by the fountains and turn right, walk for three blocks and turn left onto cours Lafayette, cross the Rhône on pont Lafayette and continue as the street changes to pl. des Cordeliers, then turn left on rue de la République and follow it to pl. Bellecour. (30min.) Lyon is a reasonably safe city, though travelers should watch out for pickpockets inside Perrache, at pl. des Terreaux, and in pl. Bellecour's crowds.

◨ PRACTICAL INFORMATION

TOURIST & FINANCIAL SERVICES

Tourist Office: In the Pavilion, at pl. Bellecour, 2*ème* (☎04 72 77 69 69; fax 04 78 42 04 32). M: Bellecour. Incredibly efficient, and eager for tourism. Brochures and info on rooms and restaurants. **Hotel reservation** office. Free, indispensable "Map & Guide" in seven languages has museum listings, a subway map, and a blow-up of the city center. Ask about the wide range of excellent **city tours** in French (and English during the summer). Tours €9, students €6.50. 3hr. audio tours of the city are available in 4 languages; €6.10. Also available is an insightful, anecdotal book that describes walking tours through the five quarters included in the UNESCO World Heritage list (€5.35), which humbles even the best of guidebook writers (i.e., *Let's Go* researchers). Equally invaluable is the **Lyon City Card,** which authorizes unlimited public transportation along with admission to the 14 biggest museums, tours, audio tours, and boat tours. Valid for 1, 2, or 3 days; €15, €25, and €30, respectively. **Internet** available but expensive. Office open May-Oct. M-Sa 9am-7pm; Nov.-Apr. daily 10am-6pm. For info on entertainment and cinema, try the weekly "Lyon Poche" (€1) or the seasonal "Lyon Libertin" (€3) and "Guides de l'été de Lyon: Restaurant Nuits" (€2), all available in *tabacs*. For longer stays, pick up the free gold mine of all goings-on, "Le Petit Paumé." Tours of the old city depart from in front of the Cathédrale St-Jean in Vieux Lyon (M: Vieux Lyon).

Bus Tours: Philibert (☎04 78 98 56 00; fax 04 78 23 11 07; webescapes@philibert.fr). 1½hr. tour of Lyon, with audio guides in 6 languages. Tour starts at Perrache. Get on or off at any point and reconnect later on. Late Mar. to Oct. daily. €17. Also goes to nearby Perouges and the Beaujolias (p. 450).

Consulates: Canada, 21 rue Bourgelat, 2*ème* (☎04 72 77 64 07), 1 block west of the Ampère-Victor Hugo metro. Open M-F 9am-noon. **Ireland,** 58 rue Victor Lagrange, 7*ème* (☎06 85 23 12 03). Open M-F 9am-noon. **UK,** 24 rue Childebert, 2*ème* (☎04 72 77 81 70). M: Bellecour. Open M-F 9am-noon and 2-5pm. **US,** in the World Trade Center, 16 rue de la République, 2*ème* (☎04 78 38 33 03). Open by appointment only daily 10am-noon and 2-5pm.

Money: Currency exchange in the tourist office, or for no commission at **Goldfinger S.A.R.L.,** 81 rue de la République (☎04 72 40 06 00). Open M-Sa 9:30am-6:30pm.

LOCAL SERVICES

English Bookstore: Decitre, 6 pl. Bellecour, 2*ème* (☎04 26 68 00 12). Fantastic selection and English-speaking salespeople to advise. Open M-Sa 9:30am-7pm. MC/V.

Bureau d'Informations de Jeunesse (BIJ), 9 quai des Célestins (☎04 72 77 00 66), lists jobs and more. Open M noon-6pm, Tu and Th-F 10am-6pm, W 10am-7pm, Sa 10am-1pm and 2-5pm. Closed Sa July-Aug.

Women's Center: Centre d'Information Féminine, 18 pl. Tolozan, 1*er* (☎04 78 39 32 25). Open M-F noon-1pm and 1:30-5pm.

Gay Support: Maison des Homosexualities, 16 rue St-Polycarpe (☎04 78 27 10 10). Social and cultural center, with library. Call for schedule of events.

24hr. Pharmacy: Pharmacie Blanchet, 5 pl. des Cordeliers, 2*ème* (☎04 78 42 12 42).

Laundromat: Lavadou, 19 rue Ste-Hélène, north of pl. Ampère, 2*ème*. Open daily 7:30am-8:30pm. **Laverie,** 51 rue de la Charité, 2*ème*. Open daily 6am-10pm.

EMERGENCY & COMMUNICATIONS

Police: 47 rue de la Charité (☎04 78 42 26 56).

Crisis Lines: SOS Amitié (☎04 78 29 88 88). **SOS Racisme** (☎04 78 39 24 44). Open Tu 6-8pm. **AIDS info service,** 2 rue Montebello, 3*ème* (toll-free ☎0800 840 800).

Hospitals: All hospitals should have English-speaking doctors on call. **Hôpital Edouard Herriot,** 5 pl. Arsonval. M: Grange Blanche. Best for serious emergencies, but far from the center of town. More central is **Hôpital Hôtel-Dieu,** 1 pl. de l'Hôpital, 2*ème*, near quai du Rhône. The central city hospital line, ☎08 20 08 20 09, will tell you where to go. There's also **Hôpital Antiquaille,** rue de l'Antiquaille, in Roman Lyon.

SOS Médecins, 10 pl. Dumas de Loire (☎04 78 83 51 51), arranges home visits.

Internet: Taxiphone Communications, 15-17 rue Montebello (☎04 78 14 54 25). €0.80 for 15min., €1.50 for 30min., €3 per hr. Open daily 8:30am-10:30pm. **Connectix Café,** 19 quai St-Antoine, 2*ème* (☎04 72 77 98 85). €7 divisible card allows 1hr. of use. Open M-Sa 11am-7pm.

Post Office: pl. Antonin Poncet, 2*ème* (☎04 72 40 65 22), next to pl. Bellecour. **Currency exchange.** Open M-F 8am-7pm, Sa 8am-12:30pm. **Poste Restante:** 69002. **Postal codes:** 69001-69009; last digit indicates *arrondissement*.

⚑ ACCOMMODATIONS & CAMPING

France's second-largest financial center (after Paris, *bien sûr*) is filled on most weekday nights with businessmen who leave town on the weekends. Fall is the busiest season for accommodations in Lyon; it's easier and cheaper to find a place in the summer, but it is still prudent to make reservations ahead of time. Budget hotels cluster east of pl. Carnot. Prices rise as one approaches pl. Bellecour, but there are some inexpensive options just north of pl. des Terreaux. The accommodatins in Vieux Lyon tend to break budgets.

RHÔNE-ALPS

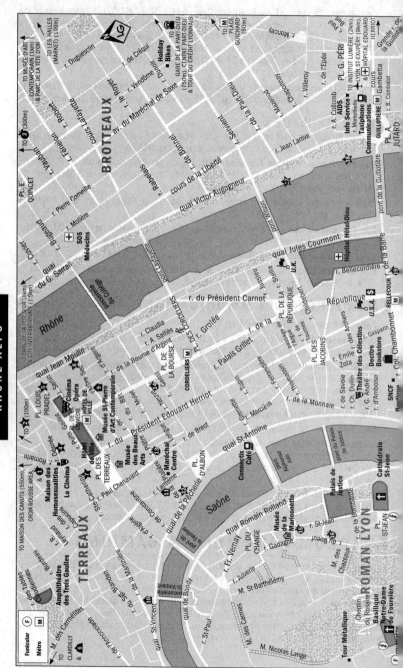

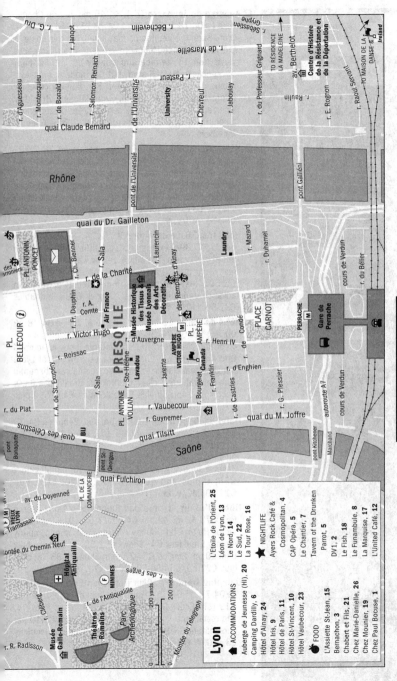

RHÔNE-ALPS

Lyon

▲ ACCOMMODATIONS
Auberge de Jeunesse (HI), **20**
Camping Dardilly, **6**
Hôtel d'Ainay, **24**
Hôtel Iris, **9**
Hôtel de Paris, **11**
Hôtel St-Vincent, **10**
Hôtel Vaubecour, **23**

◆ FOOD
L'Assiette St-Jean, **15**
Bernachon, **3**
Chabert et Fils, **21**
Chez Marie-Danielle, **26**
Chez Mounier, **19**
Chez Paul Bocuse, **1**

L'Etoile de l'Orient, **25**
Léon de Lyon, **13**
Le Nord, **14**
Le Sud, **22**
La Tour Rose, **16**

★ NIGHTLIFE
Ayers Rock Café &
Cosmopolitan, **4**
CAP Opéra, **4**
Le Chantier, **7**
Tavern of the Drunken
Parrot, **5**
DV1, **2**
Le Fish, **18**
Le Funambule, **8**
La Marquise, **17**
L'United Café, **12**

THE LOCAL STORY

CHEF OF THE CENTURY

Let's Go *was about to interview world-renowned chef* **Paul Bocuse** *from a telephone booth in Lyon when Bocuse suggested that* Let's Go *come out to his place at Collonges-au-Mont-d'Or for lunch.* Let's Go *obliged, rushing to the hostel to put on something approaching its Sunday best.*

Paul Bocuse is the original celebrity chef. His exhausting list of awards includes Commander of the National Order of Merit, one of France's highest honors. The prestigious international culinary competition named in his honor, the **Bocuse d'Or** *(Bocuse gold medal), reflects the luster of his international reputation.*

Let's Go *found Bocuse to be warm and assured. An imposing man in his mid-70s who recovered from a WWII wound under American care, he has often said he has American blood in his veins.*

Q: The title "Chef of the Century," the sculpture of you in the Musée Grevin, international fame and success—did you ever think all this was possible?

A: [chuckles softly] "Chef of the Century" is not a big deal...I think that we have a craft, a manual craft, and I believe it is important to work hard. Above all, it is necessary to pass on our craft to future generations. That is what's most important.

Q: Explain your cooking philosophy.

A: The most important thing in cooking is first to use good prod-

(Continued on next page)

Auberge de Jeunesse (HI), 41-45 montée du Chemin Neuf (☎04 78 15 05 50; fax 04 78 15 05 51). M: Vieux Lyon. Sure, the bathrooms may smell, but this hostel is the place to meet fellow travelers in Lyon. Gorgeous views from the terrace and a lively bar attract many backpackers. Helpful staff, but the modern, split-level rooms can get hot in summer. Bar, laundry (€4.50), Internet (€2.25 per 15min.), and kitchen. Breakfast included. Sheets €2.70. Reception 24hr. Reservations recommended. 4- to 8-bunk rooms. €12.20 per bed. V. **Members only. ❶**

Hôtel St-Vincent, 9 rue Pareille, 1er (☎04 78 27 22 56; fax 04 78 30 92 87), just off quai St-Vincent. The St-Vincent's friendly owners rent simple, elegant rooms, within stumbling distance of much nightlife. Breakfast €5.50. Reception 24hr. Reserve ahead. Singles with shower €31, with toilet €38; doubles €38-48; triples €50-53. MC/V. ❸

Hôtel Iris, 36 rue de l'Arbre Sec (☎04 78 39 93 80; fax 04 72 00 89 91). Iris is a cozy little spot filled with return customers. The sunny yellow walls of the breakfast room match the smiles of the owner. Breakfast €5.50. Reservations recommended two weeks in advance during the summer. Singles €29-40; doubles €32-50. MC/V. ❸

Hôtel de Paris, 16 rue de la Platière, 1er (☎04 78 28 00 95; fax 04 78 39 57 64), this hotel bursts with color and character. The comfortable lobby is adorned with black-and-white Impressionist drawings of Lyon. Ranging from classic to futuristic, rooms have beautiful curtains and large, clean bathrooms. Breakfast €6.50. Reception 24hr. Singles €42; doubles €49-75; triples €78; quads €81. AmEx/MC/V. ❹

Hôtel Vaubecour, 28 rue Vaubecour, 2ème (☎04 78 37 44 91; fax 04 78 42 90 17). Good budget spot somewhat hidden away on the 3rd floor of an antique building. Breakfast €3.85. Reception daily 7am-10pm. Reserve June-Aug. Singles from €22.90; doubles from €26; triples and quads from €54.20. Extra bed €12.20. MC/V. ❷

Hôtel d'Ainay, 14 rue des Remparts d'Ainay, 2ème (☎04 78 42 43 42; fax 04 72 77 51 90). M: Ampère-Victor Hugo. The d'Ainay offers basic, cheap, sunny rooms. Breakfast €4. Shower €2.50. Reception daily 6am-10pm. Singles €24-27, with shower €33-38; doubles €27.50/€34-38.50. MC/V. ❷

Camping Dardilly, 10km from Lyon in a dull suburb (☎04 78 35 64 55). From the Hôtel de Ville, take bus #19 (dir: Ecully-Dardilly) to Parc d'Affaires. Pool, TV, and restaurant. Reception daily 8am-10pm. €3.10 per person; tent €6.10, caravan €7.60, car free. Electricity €3. MC/V. ❶

🖸 FOOD

The galaxy of Michelin stars adorning the city's restaurants confirms that this is the gastronomic capital of the Western world. Lyonnais food is bizarre, elegant, creative, and always delicious. A typical delicacy consists of cow their feet prepared in a subtle, creamy sauce. Even inexpensive restaurants maintain. the city's culinary tradition.

THE PRIDE OF LYON

The pinnacle of the Lyonnais food scene is 🖸**Chez Paul Bocuse ❺**, 9km out of town, where meals cost approximately the equivalent of Andorra's GNP. For Lyonnais master Jean-Paul Lacombe's cuisine, head to **Léon de Lyon ❺**, 1 rue Pléney, 1er (☎04 72 10 11 12. *Menus* €55, €86, and €135. Open Tu-Sa noon-2pm and 7:30-10pm). For Philippe Chavent's, try **La Tour Rose ❺**, at 22 rue du Boeuf, 5ème. (☎04 78 92 69 11. *Menus* €53, €91, and €106. Open M-Sa noon-1pm and 7-9:30pm.) Some of these restaurants have occasional weekend buffet brunches hovering around €30-40; check outside or call. Wannabe gourmands need not sell their internal organs to enjoy Bocusian cuisine, however: the master has several spin-off restaurants in Lyon. At **Le Nord ❹**, 18 rue Neuve, 2ème, Bocuse's traditional food graces the €18 *menu* in a famed century-old *brasserie*. (☎04 72 10 69 69; fax 04 72 10 69 68. Extravagant desserts €5-6. Open daily noon-2:30pm and 7pm-midnight. AmEx/MC/V.) Bocuse's kitchens serve up Mediterranean fare at the appropriately named **Le Sud ❸**, 11 pl. Antonin Poncet, 2ème, which has an €18 *menu*, plus pizza and pasta from around €11, in a beautiful formal setting. (☎04 72 77 80 00. Open daily noon-2:30pm and 7pm-midnight. AmEx/MC/V.) Whether you're heading north or south, reserve a few days ahead.

Locals snap up the tasty *cocons* (chocolates wrapped in marzipan), made in the grand *pâtisserie* 🖸**Bernachon**, 42 cours F. Roosevelt, 6ème (see **On the Menu**, p. 444).

OTHER FLEURS-DE-LYON

For a happy medium between *haute cuisine* and university canteens, try one of Lyon's many **bouchons,** descendants of the inns where travelers stopped to dine and have their horses *bouchonné* (rubbed down). These cozy restaurants serving local fare can be found along **rue Mercière** and **rue des Marronniers** in the 2ème. Although frowned on by locals as touristy, most places in Vieux Lyon are sure to satisfy with style. The *bouchons* along **rue St-Jean** have €13-16 *menus*. The trendy locals eat at lantern-strewn **rue**

(Continued from previous page)

ucts. It's also important to have a team that understands my craft. This is a craft that requires companions.

Q: Do you feel a high creativity level is essential to contemporary cuisine?
A: Here, we do *la cuisine classique.* Yes, there is much creativity—I believe that's an important part of the craft. But our cuisine is, how shall I say, that of the old style. We do not seek out new influences. *Bien sûr,* there are many restaurants that are very interesting, but we do not seek out Japanese influences, Asian influences, Californian influences. We remain within the cuisine of the region, as we have done for fifty years. We do not do *cuisine fusion.* That is a cuisine of confusion.

Q: What is your advice for travelers who don't have a lot of money?
A: *Alors,* the *brasseries*—one can eat much more cheaply there.

Q: What do you think of patrons who drink Coca-Cola with their meals?
A: I believe that in life people must remain free. If you drink Coca-Cola, well, why not? It's perhaps not the...ideal...drink for a *repas* in France, but *pourquoi pas?*

Q: For the grand dinners at big international conferences—for example, the G7 Summit conference of 1997—do you ever get a bit nervous? Stage fright, so to speak?
A: No, no, no [chuckling]. It's exactly like here. *Et maintenant,* [pointing to the first course, which is already sitting on the table], leave this and eat. Eat that there.

THE HIDDEN DEAL

CHOCOLATE HEAVEN

On the wide, ritzy cours F. Roosevelt, a monogrammed "B" adorns a set of red awnings, at first indistinguishable among the flashy clothing displays that flank it—until you notice the steady stream of well-dressed locals heading inside. The famous chef Bocuse is not the only great "B" in town: this B stands for ■ **Bernachon,** Lyon's grandest *pâtisserie.*

Bernachon's designer-label chocolate is made entirely from scratch. Inside the gilded walls, the immaculately dressed staff can help awestruck visitors choose from hundreds of tiny, delicious specialties—both pure chocolates and pastries that far outshine the other local *viennoiseries.* The showcases sparkle with the ambrosial *palets d'or,* which are recognized as the best chocolates in France—and not only because they're made with gold dust. Lyon residents also take particular pride in their *cocons* (chocolates wrapped in marzipan).

The mini chocolate *gâteaux,* which go for €6 at local restaurants, are only €1 here. Bernachon also sells savory snacks and small sandwiches at reasonable prices (€3-6), so it's a great spot to buy picnic goodies of all kinds.

(42 cours F. Roosevelt, 6ème. ☎04 78 24 37 98. Individual delicacies €1-3. Open M-F 9am-7pm, Sa 8:30am-7pm, Su 8:30am-5pm. Closed Aug.)

Mercerie; dinner *menus* tend to be €16-20. Cheaper Chinese fast-food restaurants and *brasseries* line the wide streets off **rue de la République** (*2ème*), and dozens of kebab joints surround the Hôtel de Ville.

■ **Chez Mounier,** 3 rue des Marronniers, 2ème (☎04 78 37 79 26). Mounier specializes in tasty, hearty traditional dishes in a sparsely decorated but still cozy setting, with cheerful waitstaff. 4-course *menus* €9.60, €13.60, and €15.10. Open Tu-Sa noon-2pm and 7-10:30pm, Su noon-2pm. ❸

■ **Chabert et Fils,** 11 rue des Marronniers, 2ème (☎04 78 37 01 94). One of the best- known *bouchons. Museau de bœuf* (snout of cattle) is only one of many strange Lyonnais concoctions on the €16 *menu.* For dessert, try the exquisite, creamy *guignol* (€5.40), but plan to take an after-dinner nap. Lunch *menus* €8-12.50, dinner *menus* €16-27.50. Open daily noon-2pm and 7-11pm, F-Sa until 11:30pm. MC/V. ❸

Chez Marie-Danielle, 29 rue des Remparts d'Ainay (☎04 72 43 09 25), is a refreshing change from the male-dominated chef scene in Lyon—Marie-Danielle has received dozens of awards for her Lyonnais fare served in a *brasserie*-style dining hall. Lunch *menu* €14, dinner *menu* €21.50. Open Tu-Sa noon-2pm and 7:30-10pm. MC/V. ❹

L'Assiette St-Jean, 10 rue St-Jean, 5ème (☎04 72 41 96 20). An excellent *bouchon,* with unusual, archaic décor. *Gateau de foies de volaille* (chicken liver) €6.60, *menus* €13-27.50. Open June-Aug. Tu-Su noon-2pm and 7-10:30pm; Sept.-May W-Su 7-10:30pm. AmEx/MC/V. ❸

L'Etoile de l'Orient, 31 rue des Remparts d'Ainay, 2ème (☎04 72 41 07 87). M: Ampère-Victor Hugo. Be sure to have some tea at this intimate Tunisian restaurant, run by an exceedingly warm couple. Tajine lamb €11.50, couscous dishes €11-13. *Menus* €10-25. Open M noon-2pm, Tu-Su noon-2pm and 7-11pm. ❸

SUPERMARKETS

Markets open on the quais of the Rhône and Saône every morning 8am-1pm, except for Mondays, and small **supermarkets** and **épiceries** are close to nearly every major square, including Bellecour, pl. St-Jean, and pl. des Terreux. Ultra-gourmet products are sold at **Maréchal Centre,** rue de la Platière at rue Lanterne, 1er. (☎04 72 98 24 00. Open M-Sa 8:30am-8:30pm.) Lyon's many university restaurants may not boast any culinary masterpieces, but they're sure to please the wallet. One is **Résidence la Madeleine,** 4 rue Sauveur, 7ème. (☎04 78 72 80 62. Meals about €2.50. Open M-F 11:30am-1pm and 6:30-8pm, Sa 11:30am-1pm. Closed Aug.)

◎ SIGHTS

VIEUX LYON

Stacked against the Saône at the foot of the Fourvière hill, Vieux Lyon's narrow streets wind between lively cafés, tree-lined squares, and magnificent medieval and Renaissance homes. The colorful *hôtels particuliers*, with their delicate carvings and ornate turrets, sprang up between the 15th and 18th centuries, when Lyon controlled Europe's silk and publishing industries. The regal homes around rue St-Jean, rue du Bœuf, and rue Juiverie have housed Lyon's elite for 400 years.

TRABOULES. The distinguishing features of Vieux Lyon townhouses are the **traboules**, tunnels leading from the street through a maze of courtyards, often with vaulted ceilings and statuary niches. Although their original purpose is still debated, later *traboules* were constructed to transport silk safely from looms to storage rooms. During WWII, the passageways proved invaluable as info-gathering and escape routes for the Resistance (though some *résistants* found their way blocked by Germans at the exits). Many are open to the public at specific hours, especially in the morning. An inexpensive, 1hr.+ tour beginning near the Cathédrale is the ideal way to see them, or pick up a list of addresses from the tourist office. (*Tours in English and French in summer daily at 2:30pm, irregular hours during rest of year; consult tourist office. €9, students €5.*)

CATHÉDRALE ST-JEAN. The southern end of Vieux Lyon is dominated by soaring columns of the Cathédrale St-Jean. Some of its multicolored stained-glass windows are replacements of the ones destroyed by Lyon's exploding bridges during the Nazis' hasty retreat in 1944. In the gallery, the shift from Romanesque to Gothic is evident where the rows of arches begin to have pointed tops. Henri IV met and married Maria de Médici here in 1600. Inside, every hour between noon and 4pm, automatons pop out of the 14th-century **astronomical clock** in a charming reenactment of the Annunciation. The clock can calculate Church feast days until 2019. (*Cathedral open M-F 8am-noon and 2-7:30pm, Sa-Su 8am-noon and 2-7pm.*)

MUSEUMS. Down rue St-Jean, turn left at pl. du Change for the **Hôtel de Gadagne**, a typical 16th-century Vieux Lyon building, and its relatively minor museums. The better of the two is the **Musée de la Marionnette**, which displays puppets from around the world, including models of **Guignol**, the famed local

cynic, and his quite inebriated friend, Gnaffron. *(Pl. du Petit Collège, 5ème. M: Vieux Lyon. ☎ 04 78 42 03 61. 1hr. tours on request. Open Su-M and W-Sa 10:45am-6pm. €3.80, students €2, under 19 free.)*

FOURVIÈRE & ROMAN LYON

From the corner of rue du Bœuf and rue de la Bombarde in Vieux Lyon, climb the stairs heading straight up to reach **Fourvière Hill,** the nucleus of **Roman Lyon.** From the top of the stairs, continue up via the rose-lined **Chemin de la Rosaire,** a series of switchbacks that leads through a garden to the **esplanade Fourvière,** where a model of the city indicates local landmarks. Most prefer to take the less strenuous **funicular** (known as *la ficelle*) to the top of the hill. It leaves from the head of av. A. Max in Vieux Lyon, off pl. St-Jean. The **Tour de l'Observatoire,** on the eastern edge of the hilltop basilique, offers a more acute angle on the city. On a clear day, scan for Mont Blanc, about 200km to the east. *(Jardin de la Rosaire open daily 6:30am-9:30pm. Tour open W-Su 10am-noon and 2-6:30pm. €2, under 15 €1.)*

▧ **BASILIQUE NOTRE-DAME DE FOURVIÈRE.** Lyon's archbishop vowed to build a church if the city was spared attack during the Franco-Prussian War. It was, and the bishop followed through. The basilica's white, meringue-like exterior is imposing from a distance—gorgeous or bizarre, depending on taste. The highlight of the ornate interior is the group of shimmering, gigantic mosaics that depict religious scenes, Joan of Arc at Orléans, and the naval battle of Lepante. The low, heavy crypt used for mass, was conceived by the architect Pierre Bossan to contrast with the impossibly high and golden Byzantine basilica above. *(Behind the Esplanade at very top of the hill. Chapel open daily 7am-7pm; basilica open 8am-7pm.)*

MUSÉE GALLO-ROMAIN. The rooms and corridors of this brilliant museum circle deep into the historic hillside of Fourvière, housing a collection of arms, pottery, statues, and jewelry. Romaholics will appreciate six large, luminous mosaics, a bronze tablet inscribed with a speech by Lyon's favorite son, Emperor Claudius, and a huge, half-cracked eggshell pot. Artifacts are labeled in English and French. *(Open Tu-Su Mar.-Oct. 10am-6pm; Nov.-Feb. 10am-5pm. €3.80, students €2.30. Th free.)*

PARC ARCHÉOLOGIQUE. Just next to the Minimes/Théâtre Romain funicular stop, the Parc holds the almost too well-restored 2000-year-old **Théâtre Romain** and the smaller **Odéon,** discovered when modern developers dug into the hill. Both still function as venues for shows during the **Nuits de Fourvière** (see **Festivals**). *(Open Apr. 15-Sept. 15 9am-9pm; Sept. 16-Apr. 14 7am-7pm. Free.)*

LA PRESQU'ILE & LES TERREAUX

Monumental squares, statues, and fountains are the trademarks of the *presqu'île,* the lively area between the Rhône and the Saône. At its heart is **place Bellecour,** from which pedestrian **rue Victor Hugo** unfurls quietly south, lined with boutiques and bladers. To the north, crowded **rue de la République,** or "la Ré," is the urban aorta of Lyon. It runs through **place de la République** and ends at **place Louis Pradel** in the 1er, at the tip of the Terreaux district, once a marshy wasteland. The area was filled with soil, creating a chic neighborhood of dry terraces *(terreaux).* Now bars, clubs, and sidewalk cafés fill up after 8pm and keep this area hopping quite late into the night.

Across the square at **place Louis Pradel** is the spectacular 17th-century façade of the **Hôtel de Ville,** framed by an illuminated cement field of miniature geysers. The **Opéra** building, looking out over pl. Louis Pradel nearby, is a 19th-century Neoclassical edifice supporting what looks like an outsized airplane hangar, alluringly lit in dark red at night.

■**MUSÉE DES BEAUX-ARTS.** This unassuming but excellent museum includes a comprehensive archeological wing, a distinguished collection of French, Dutch, and Spanish paintings, works by Picasso, a section devoted to the Italian Renaissance, and a lovely sculpture garden. Surrounded by all-star pre-, post-, and just-plain-Impressionist collections, even the museum's esoteric local works are delightful. A few nice surprises await explorers of the museum, including a Rodin bust of national hero Victor Hugo at the end of his life (1883), and an unbelievably large French coin collection. (20 pl. des Terreaux. ☎04 72 10 17 40. Open W-Th and Sa-M 10am-6pm, F 10:30am-8pm. Sculptures closed noon-1pm; paintings closed 1-2pm. €3.80, under 26 €2, students under 26 with ID free.)

LA CROIX-ROUSSE & THE SILK INDUSTRY

Though mass silk manufacturing is based elsewhere today, Lyon is proud of its historical dominance of the industry in Europe. Lyon's few remaining silk workers perform delicate handiwork, reconstructing and replicating rare patterns for museum and château displays.

■**MUSÉE HISTORIQUE DES TISSUS.** In dark rooms, rows of costumes recall skirt-flouting, ruffle-collared and bosom-baring characters of the past. The collection also includes examples of 18th-century elite garb (such as Marie-Antoinette's Versailles winter wardrobe), scraps of Byzantine textiles, and silk wall-hangings that resemble stained-glass windows. Included in the price is admission to the neighboring **Musée des Arts Décoratifs,** housed in an 18th-century **hôtel.** (34 rue de la Charité, 2ème. ☎04 78 38 42 00. Tissus open Tu-Su 10am-5:30pm. Arts Décoratifs open Tu-Su 10am-noon and 2-5:30pm. Maps in English. Tour in French Su 3pm. €4.60, students €2.30.)

LA MAISON DES CANUTS. Some old silk looms in a tiny back room are all that remain of the weaving techniques of the *canuts* (silk weavers.) The Maison's shop sells silk made by its own *canuts.* A scarf costs €30 and up, but silk enthusiasts can take home a silkworm cocoon for €7 or less, or maybe just a handkerchief for €7. (10-12 rue d'Ivry, 4ème. ☎04 78 28 62 04; fax 04 78 28 16 93. Tours by arrangement. Open M-F 9am-noon and 2-6:30pm, Sa until 6pm. €4, students €2.30.)

EAST OF THE RHÔNE & MODERN LYON

Lyon's newest train station and monstrous space-age mall form the core of the ultra-modern Part-Dieu district. Locals call the commercial **Tour du Crédit Lyonnais** *Le Crayon* for its unintentional resemblance to a giant pencil standing on end. Next to it, the shell-shaped **Auditorium Maurice Ravel** hosts major cultural events.

CENTRE D'HISTOIRE DE LA RÉSISTANCE ET DE LA DÉPORTATION. In a building where Nazis tortured detainees during the Occupation, the center houses an impressive but sobering collection of documents, photos, and films of the Resistance, which was based in Lyon. There's also a space set up for children. (14 av. Bertholet, 7ème. M: Jean Macé. ☎04 78 72 23 11. Open W-Su 9am-5:30pm. €3.80, students €2. Admission includes an audio guide in French, English, or German.)

MUSÉE D'ART CONTEMPORAIN. This extensive, entertaining mecca of modern art resides in the futuristic **Cité International de Lyon,** a super-modern complex with offices, shops, theaters, and Interpol's world headquarters. All the museum's exhibits are temporary; the walls themselves are built anew for each installation. (Quai Charles de Gaulle, next to Parc de la Tête d'Or, 6ème. Take bus #4 from M: Foch. ☎04 72 69 17 17. Open W-Su noon-7pm. €3.80, students €2, under 18 free.)

INSTITUT LUMIÈRE. A must for film buffs, the museum's exhibits chronicle the exploits of the brothers Lumière, who invented the motion picture in 1895. The relatively small museum is full of intriguing factoids: Louis created a forerunner to holograms in 1920. The Institut's complex also includes a movie theater, "Le Hangar du Premier-Film," and a park. *(25 rue du Premier-Film, 8ème. M: Monplaisir Lumière.* ☎ *04 78 78 1895. Open Tu-Su 11am-7pm. €5.50, students €4.50.)*

PARC DE LA TÊTE D'OR. This massive park, one of the largest in Europe, sprawls over 259 acres. Its name derives from the legend that a golden head of Jesus lies buried somewhere on its grounds. In summer, paddle boats are available for a visit to its artificial green lake and island. Reindeer, elephants, and other animals fill the zoo, and giant greenhouses encase a botanical garden. The 60,000-bush rose gardens are magnificent. *(M: Charpennes or Tram T1 from Perrache, dir: IUT-Feyssine.* ☎ *04 78 89 02 03. Open mid-Apr. to mid-Oct. 6am-11pm; mid-Oct. to mid-Apr. 6am-9pm.)*

🈲 NIGHTLIFE

Nightlife in Lyon is fast and furious. There is a row of semi-exclusive joints off the Saône, on quais Romain Rolland, de Bondy, and Pierre Scize in Vieux Lyon (5ème), but the city's best and most accessible late-night spots are a strip of riverboat dance clubs by the east bank of the Rhône. Students buzz in and out of a series of tiny, intimate bars on **rue Ste-Catherine** (1er) until 1am, before heading to the clubs. For those in search of a more mellow (and expensive) evening, the streets off **rue Mercerie** host several **jazz and piano bars.** When school is out of session for the summer, the scene is only lively on weekends. More suggestions can be found in "Lyon Libertin" (€3) and "Guides de l'Eté de Lyon: Restaurant/Nuits" (€2), available at *tabacs.* The tourist office's city guide lists spots that cater to Lyon's active gay community, and "Le Petit Paumé" offers superb tips. The most popular gay spots are in the 1er.

🈲 **Le Fish,** across from 21 quai Augagneur (☎ 04 72 87 98 98), plays salsa, jungle, hip-hop, disco, and house on a swank boat. This club is the choice spot for Lyonnais youngster. F-Sa cover €11-13 includes first drink, free before 11pm. Open W-Th 10pm-5am, F-Sa 10pm-6am. **Students only.**

Ayers Rock Café, 2 rue Désirée (☎ 04 78 29 13 45), an Aussie bar, and the **Cosmopolitan** (☎ 04 72 07 09 80), with New-York-themed drinks, right next door. Be sure to stumble over, as both places are usually packed with students. Both have shooters for €3 and cocktails starting at €6. Cosmo is a little darker, a little less international, and a little more restrained. Ayers open daily 6pm-3am; Cosmo open M-Sa 8pm-3am.

Tavern of the Drunken Parrot, next door to Le Chantier (☎ 04 78 28 01 39), serves homemade, extremely potent rum drinks (€2); try the citron or coco. Combined with the dark-and-dirty ship motif, the drinks have eager customers walking the plank into oblivion. Open daily 6pm-3am.

Le Funambule, 29 rue de l'Arbre Sec (☎ 04 72 07 86 70), is a darkly lit, hip bar for the late-20s crowd. Open Tu-Th 7pm-1am, F-Sa 7pm-3am.

Le Chantier, 20 rue Ste-Catherine (☎ 04 78 39 05 56), offers 12 tequila shots for €15.25. Slip down a spiral slide to reach the dance floor downstairs, which is filled with students and locals. Open Tu-Sa 9pm-3am, sometimes later.

La Marquise (☎ 04 78 71 78 71), next door to Le Fish, spends less on the boat but more on big-name jungle and house DJs. Cover €6 for occasional *soirées à thème.* Open W-Sa 11pm-dawn.

L'United Café, impasse de la Pêcherie (☎ 04 78 29 93 18), in an alley off quai de la Pêcherie. The weekend club circuit starts here around midnight, with American and Latino dance hits. Theme nights range from post office to beach party—and there are lip-shaped urinals to boot. No cover. Drinks €3-6. Open daily 10:30pm-5am.

DV1, 6 rue Violi (☎04 72 07 72 62), off rue Royale, north of pl. Louis Pradel. Drag queens nightly, with a huge dance floor. A mostly male, mid-20s to mid-30s crowd. Drinks €3.50-4. Open W-Th and Su 10pm-3am, F-Sa 10pm-5am.

CAP Opéra, 2 pl. Louis Pradel (☎04 72 07 61 55), is a popular gay pub, with red lights to match the Opéra next door. Occasional *soirées à thème*. Open daily 2pm-3am.

▪ SHOPPING

Serious shoppers and awestruck admirers of French fashion will enjoy Lyon. The Centre Part-Dieu, across bd. Marius Vivier-Merle from Gare de la Part-Dieu, is the closest thing homesick Americans will find to the local **mall**, containing chain clothing stores, food shops, a movie theater, bowling alley, and a huge Galleries Lafayette. The 1*er* and 2*ème arrondissements*, particularly **rue de la République** and the charming **passage de l'Argue**, are where it's at for upscale brand names. Funky ethnic **boutiques** and poster stores cluster around rue St-Jean in Vieux Lyon, and **bookstores** surround pl. Bellecour. Bargain-hunters will enjoy the massive **flea market** that sets up on Mondays on the quais to the east of the Saône.

▪ ENTERTAINMENT

LIVE PERFORMANCES

Lyon's major stage theater is the **Théâtre des Célestins**, pl. des Célestins, 2*ème* (☎04 72 77 40 00; box office open Tu-Sa noon-7pm. Tickets €8-29, discounts for under 26 and over 65). The **Opéra**, pl. de la Comédie, 1*er* (☎04 72 00 45 45), has pricey tickets (€10-72), but €8 tickets for those under 26 and over 65 go on sale 15min. before the show. (Reservations office open M-Sa noon-7pm.) The acclaimed **Orchestre National de Lyon** plays a full season. (☎04 78 95 95 95. Oct.-June. Tickets €15-50.) The **Maison de la Danse**, 8 av. Jean Mermoz, 8*ème* (☎04 72 78 18 00; tickets €12-38), keeps pace with the dance scene.

CINEMA

As the birthplace of cinema, Lyon is indeed a superb place to see quality film. Both the **Cinéma Opéra**, 6 rue J. Serlin (☎04 78 28 80 08), and **Le Cinéma**, 18 impasse St-Polycarpe (☎04 78 39 09 72), specialize in black-and-white undubbed classics offered every night of the week (€5.20-6.10).

▪ FESTIVALS

During the summer, Lyon has a festival or special event nearly every week. The **Fête de la Musique** (June 21) and **Bastille Day** (July 14) entail major partying, as with elsewhere in France. The end of June sets off the two-week **Festival du Jazz à Vienne** (p. 450). **Les Nuits de Fourvière** is a three-month summer festival held in the ancient Théâtre Romain and Odéon at Lyon, from mid-June through mid-Sept. Popular performers are interspersed with classical concerts, movies, dance, and plays. (☎04 72 32 00 00. €10-35 tickets and info at the Théâtre Romain or the FNAC shop on rue de la République.)

The biennial **Festival de Musique du Vieux Lyon**, 5 pl. du Petit Collège, 5*ème*, brings artists from around the world to perform in Lyon's old town in early and mid-December. (☎04 78 38 09 09. Tickets €15-36.) Every December 8, locals place candles in their windows and ascend with tapers to the basilica for the **Fête des Lumières**. The celebration (which turns into a city-wide block party) honors the Virgin Mary for her protection of Lyon from the Black Plague.

RHÔNE-ALPS

⚡ DAYTRIPS FROM LYON

▓ PÉROUGES

*Trains run from Lyon (30min.; M-Sa 16 per day, Su 7 per day; €5.60) to Mexiemeux-Pérouges. From the station, go straight, turn left onto rue Lyon, take a right at the round-about and head straight to a steep dirt road on the right, which runs right to the city gates. Arriving in the morning is the best chance to appreciate the silence and peace before English-speaking tour groups flood the main square. Or take a **Philibert Tour** from Lyon with commentaries in English. (Tours leave Apr.-Oct. Sa from Part-Dieu at 1:15pm, Bellecour at 1:30pm, and Perrache at 1:45pm, returning by 6pm. €32.)*

This tiny, historic hilltop hamlet is such a source of pride for Europe that it was the site of the G-7 summit in 1996. Pérouges's streets, affectionately called **galets,** are made with rounded stones collected from nearby rivers; their shape and color blend into the structure of the homes. Exquisitely preserved, the houses, streets, and gardens, complemented by draping flora, invoke romantic visions of royalty. While legend has it that Pérouges was built by a tribe of Gauls from Italy, the town has changed nationalities many times due to various feuds between dukes and kings. Most of the buildings in the town date to the 15th century, a period of prosperity during which weaving was preeminent. The town's culinary specialty is *galette de Pérouges* (a doughy pastry made with sugar and butter), which is served with *cerdon*, a magnificent wine.

A superb way to see the evolution of the area's history is to stop in at the **Musée de Vieux Pérouges,** in the Maison des Princes, to which citizens have donated ancient wares. Its turret has a fabulous view of the rooftops and gardens below. (Open M-F 10am-noon and 2-6pm, Sa-Su 10am-7pm. Closed Nov.-May. €4, children €2.) The **tourist office** can assist in getting around. (☎04 74 61 01 14. Open May-Sept. M-F 9am-noon and 2-5pm. During the low season, call ahead.)

BEAUJOLAIS

The very mention of Beaujolais provokes a thirst for the cool, fruity wine that is one of this region's main exports. The Beaujolais, between the Loire and the Saône, with Lyon at its foot and Mâcon at its head, is home to an important textile and lumber industry, especially in the mountainous areas to the west. The tourist offices dotting the countryside can provide suggested bike or car routes that wind through endless vineyards, sleepy villages, and medieval châteaux, with a couple of *dégustations* (tastings) thrown in for good measure. The most touristy spot is in the town Romaneche-Thorins—called "Le Hameau." It offers exhibits, tastings, and a *vinothèque*. (☎03 85 35 22 22; www.hameuenbeaujolais.com). Devoted wine enthusiasts, though, are better off getting a list of serious wine growers.

Unfortunately, the most beautiful and authentic areas in the Beaujolais are difficult to access by public transportation; trains run between Mâcon and Lyon, but stop mostly in uninteresting industrial towns like Villefranche. The best option is to rent a **car** in Lyon or Mâcon or venture in by **bike.** In Lyon, try Holiday Bikes (☎04 78 60 11 10), or in Mâcon, try Pro' Cycles (☎03 85 22 81 82). **Bus tours** from Lyon in English are available through the tourist office with Philibert, which leads a tour of the Beaujolais culminating in a *dégustation* in Le Hameau. (☎04 78 98 56 98. Apr.-Oct. Th-F and Su around 1:15pm; return to Lyon at 7pm. €34.)

VIENNE

In the days of the Roman Empire, Vienne was made a Roman colony, which entitled her inhabitants to the privileges of Roman citizens. The impressive remnants of these glory days dot the town center and spread along a giant stretch of land across the Rhône river. Now, Vienne is practically syonymous with the world-renowned **Festival du Jazz à Vienne**, at the end of June and beginning of July each year. During the festival, musicians from all over the world come to play at both pricey and free venues, and spotlights illuminate the town's most revered Roman ruins. Jazz enthusiasts consume gallons of locally made Côtes du Rhône wine. Vienne's current status as a cultural capital is nothing new, though.

🖃🖬 TRANSPORTATION & PRACTICAL INFORMATION. Trains leave from pl. de Pierre-Semard at the end of Cours Brillier to both of Lyon's stations (20-30min., 40 per day, €5.60). Ticket booth open daily 5:15am-8pm, Su until 10:15am. **Buses** are to the left after exiting the train station. **Taxi Mounier** (☎ 06 80 59 37 17) congregates in front of the gare. From the station, walk straight on cours Brillier almost until the river to get to the **tourist office,** cours Brillier. The helpful staff at the has free maps, brochures, and sporadic themed city tours. They can help with railroad schedules, accomodations and of course, tickets to the jazz festival. (☎04 74 53 80 30; www.vienne-tourisme.com. Open M-Sa 9am-noon and 1:30-6pm, Su 10am-noon and 2-5pm.) Above and behind the train station is Mt. Pipet, with the Roman amphitheater, while St-Romain-en-Gal and its treasure trove of ruins sit directly across the Rhône.

🖪🖸 ACCOMMODATIONS & FOOD. To reach the **Auberge de Jeunesse ❶,** 11 quai Rondet, from the tourist office, take a left along the river. (5min.) Huge, coed dorms and bathrooms create a chatty, late-night atmosphere on three floors overlooking the Rhône. (☎04 74 53 21 97; mjcvienne@wanadoo.fr. Reception July to mid-Sept. daily 9am-8pm, mid-Sept. to June closed Sa and Su. Small bar and kitchen. Sheets included. Dorms €8, with breakfast €11.20.)

Cafés line **cours Brillier** towards the *gare,* while **cours Romestang** has dozens of *pâtisseries/salon de thés* serving sandwiches and drinks. For picnics among the Roman ruins or in the Jardin de Ville, **Intermarché** is at pl. Camille Joffray, just off Cours Brillier to the left behind the parking lot (☎04 74 85 38 23. Open M-Sa 8:30am-7:45pm). Those craving nearby Lyon's delicacies should head to **La potin'noise ❷,** 14 Rue Henry Jacquier, an appealing restaurant tucked away on a street above the Hôtel de Ville. (☎04 74 78 19 19. 4-course Lyonnais *menu* €16, other *menus* €23 and €28. Open Tu-Sa noon-2pm and 7-9pm. MC/V.) **La Medina ❷,** 71 rue de Bourogne (☎04 74 53 51 35), a popular Moroccan restaurant, has *menus* for €10.50. (Open daily noon-2pm and 7-10pm. Closed M, Tu lunch. MC/V).

🖸 SIGHTS. The most spectacular of Vienne's Roman ruins is the well-preserved **Temple of Augustus and Livia,** which rises in the middle of a square. On the hillside, at the foot of **Mt. Pipet,** the dark, steeply-plunging **Théâtre Romain** is the venue for dozens of outdoor concerts, but is worth applause in itself, as are the views from Mt. Pipet. Below the amphitheater, the **Jardin Archéologique de Cybèle** contains remnants of archways from the old Roman forum. It is a nice spot for a picnic and a pleasant venue for early-evening jazz. The small **Pyramide du Cirque Romain** rises sharply above the traffic on bd. Fernand-Point, not far from the hostel, the only vestige of a vast Roman circus.

The granddaddy of them all is the Gallo-Roman city, across the river at **St-Roman-en-Gal,** accessible by a pedestrian walkway from the quai. It contains a forum, main streets, public bathrooms, baths, and underground storerooms. Analysis of amphoras found here revealed the date of the Italian vintage inside to be AD 124. Some of the fountains have been restored and gurgle amid the ancient streets. The **museum** contains an impressive collection of restored mosaics, recovered cutlery, amphorae, old coins, and a hall for rotating exhibits. The museum recently drew raves with a show that compared Andy Warhol's pop art to the mass production of images for political propaganda in ancient Rome. (☎04 74 53 74 01. Open Tu-Su Mar.-Oct. 10am-6pm; Nov- Feb 10am-5pm. Admission to museum and sites €3.80, students €2.30, Th free.)

Impressive churches cluster around the *centre ville.* The cavernous **Cathédrale St-Maurice** has an intricate and somewhat decaying façade, and an array of Romanesque capitals. (Open daily 8am-8pm.) **Eglise St-Pierre,** at pl. St-Pierre, from the 5th century AD, now has a small archeological museum with a lovely collection of Gallo-Roman sculpture. North of the temple, **St-André-le-Bas,** has a cloister and several revolving exhibits. (St-Pierre ☎04 74 85 20 35; St-André ☎04 74 85 18 49. Both open Jan.-Mar. and mid-Nov. to Dec. Tu-F 9:30am-12:30pm and 2-5pm, Sa-Su 2-6pm; Apr. to mid-Oct. Tu-Su 9:30am-1pm and 2-6pm. Admission for each €2.)

🔎🔲 **ENTERTAINMENT & FESTIVALS.** During the two-week summer **jazz festival,** mainline concerts featuring world-renowned jazz, Latin, and cabaret artists are held at 8:30pm in the **amphitheater.** Tickets are €15-25, but *musique gratuit* that bookend the main shows make the festival accessible to all. Schedules are available at the box office or tourist office. Free music, often featuring young bands or singers, comes every evening at about 7:30pm to a makeshift stage at the **Jardins de Cybèle.** Another bandstand gives musicians a chance to serenade onlookers even earlier (6pm) at **L'Académie,** part of a square right in front of the **Hôtel de Ville.** At midnight, the free 🔲**Club de Minuit** sets up in the Théâtre de Vienne, behind the Cybèle gardens, packing awestruck crowds into an intimate, cabaret-style venue. Schedules and tickets are available at the tourist office, the amphitheater box office at 4 rue de Pipet (☎08 99 27 02 07), the Théâtre de Vienne (☎04 74 85 00 05), various music stores across France, and www.jazzavienne.com. The amphitheater hosts pop, jazz, and classical artists all summer as well; the tourist office and the theater box office both have concert schedules.

Popular bars and cafés cluster on rue du Musée, cours Romenstang, and rue Orfèvres. **Almodobar,** 17 rue du Musée, is a Spanish-themed bar and café that serves *tapas* for €4-8. (☎04 74 85 78 85. Open 1pm-midnight.)

GRENOBLE

A dynamic university town full of nightlife, earnest politics, shaggy radicals, and charming sidewalk cafés, Grenoble (pop. 156,000) is cherished by hikers, skiers, bikers, aesthetes, and set designers for its snow-capped peaks and sapphire-blue lakes. An influx of immigrants to France in the 1960s gave Grenoble a sizable North and West African population, which helped to establish the cosmopolitan feel of the unoffical capital of the Alps.

▐ TRANSPORTATION

Flights: Aéroport de Grenoble St-Geoirs, (☎04 76 65 48 48) St-Etienne de St-Geoirs, 41km from city center. Buses leave 1¼hr. before each flight from bus station (€13). Domestic flights only.

Trains: Gare Europole, pl. de la Gare. Open daily 6am-9pm. To: **Annecy** (2hr., 18 per day, €15.90); **Lyon** (1½hr., 27 per day, €17.10); **Marseille** (2½-4½hr., 15 per day, €32.30); **Nice** (5-6½hr., 5 per day, €47.20); **Paris** (3hr., 6 per day, €58.80-78.60).

Buses: left after exiting the train station. Open M-Sa 6:15am-7pm, Su 7:15am-7pm. **VFD** (☎08 20 83 38 33; www.vfd.fr) runs to **Geneva,** Switzerland (3hr., 1 per day, €25.50) and **Nice** (10hr., 1 per day, €52.40). Frequent service to ski resorts and outdoor areas.

Public Transportation: Transports Agglomération Grenobloise (TAG) (☎04 76 20 66 66). Only really useful for transport to and from the *gare,* as the city center is very walkable. Info desk in the tourist office open July-Aug. M-Sa 9am-6pm; Sept.-June M-F 8:30am-6:30pm, Sa 9am-6pm. Ticket €1.10, carnet of 10 €8.90. Day pass €3, week pass €10.60. Two tram lines run July-Aug. and Sept.-June Su-W about every 5-10min. 5am-midnight; Th-Sa 4 lines run 6am-8:30pm and 9pm-midnight.

Taxis: (☎04 76 54 42 54). 24hr. €55 to the airport.

Car Rental: Self Car, 24 rue Emile Gueymard (☎04 76 50 96 96), located right by the train station. Insurance included in rental fee. 21 and over. Open July-Aug. M-F 8am-noon and 2-6pm, Sa 8am-noon; Sept.-June M-F 7:30am-noon and 1:30-6:30pm; Sa 8am-noon. AmEx/MC/V.

◤◢ ☒ ORIENTATION & PRACTICAL INFORMATION

To get to the tourist office and the center of town, turn right from the station onto pl. de la Gare and take the third left onto av. Alsace-Lorraine, following the tram tracks. Continue along the tracks on rue Félix Poulat and rue Blanchard; the tourist complex will be on the left, just before the tracks fork. (15min.) The primarily pedestrian *vieille ville* stretches from the tourist office to the river, bounded by the Jardin de Ville and Musée de Grenoble. The winding streets intersect with innumerable *places* and squares, making it difficult to navigate the city. The Bastille looms ominously above the town from across the river.

Tourist Office: 14 rue de la République (☎04 76 42 41 41; www.grenoble-isere.info). From the train station, tram lines A and B (dir: Echirolles or Universités) run to Hubert Dubedout-Maison du Tourisme. Hosts an **SNCF** counter, local **bus** office, and **post office.** Good maps, hotel info, and train and bus schedules. Provides free copies of every local tourist publication. **Tours** of the old city July-Aug. daily; Sept.-June 2 per month. €6.50. Office open M-Sa 9am-6:30pm, Su 10am-1pm and 2-5pm.

Hiking Information: Bureau Information Montagne, 3 rue Raoul Blanchard (☎04 76 42 45 90; infos.montagne@grande-traversee-alpes.com), across from the tourist office. Info on hiking, mountaineering, biking, and cross-country skiing trails. Free brochures, maps, expert advice. Sells detailed guides, maps. Open M-F 9am-noon and 2-6pm, Sa 10am-1pm and 2-5pm. **Weather:** ☎08 36 68 02 38. **Snow info:** ☎08 92 68 10 20.

Ski and Climbing Equipment Rental: Borel Sport, 42 rue Alsace-Lorraine (☎04 76 46 47 46; fax 04 76 46 00 75). Skis, boots, and poles €10-19 per day. Snowboard package €16 per day. Cross-country package €8-11 per day. Via Ferrata climbing ensemble (harness, cord, helmet) €11 per day. Snowshoes €5-7 per day. Open June-Aug. Tu-Sa 10am-noon and 2-6pm; Sept.-May daily 9am-noon and 2-7pm. MC/V.

Budget Travel: Voyages Wasteels, 7 rue Thiers (☎08 25 88 70 39; www.wasteels.fr). Student travel packages. Open M-F 9am-noon and 2-6pm, Sa 9am-1pm and 2-5pm. MC/V.

Laundromat: Lavomatique, 14 rue Thiers (☎04 76 96 28 03). Open daily 7am-10pm.

Police: 36 bd. Maréchal Leclerc (☎04 76 60 40 40). Take bus #31 (dir: Malpertuis) to Hôtel de Police.

Hospital: Centre Hospitalier Régional de Grenoble, La Tronche (☎04 76 76 75 75).

Internet: E-toile, 15 rue Jean-Jacques Rousseau (☎04 76 00 13 60), is the cheapest bet. €1.50 for 15min., €2 for 30min., €3.50 per hr. Open M-F 10am-11pm, Sa-Su 10am-midnight. **L'Autre Monde,** 4 rue Jean-Jacques Rousseau (☎04 76 01 00 20). €2.30 for 30min., €4.50 per hr. Open M-F 10am-1am, Sa 1pm-1am, Su 1-10pm.

Post Office: 7 bd. Maréchal Lyautey (☎04 76 43 51 39). Open M-F 8am-7pm, Sa 8am-noon. **Branch office,** 12 rue de la République (☎04 76 63 32 70), inside the tourist complex. Open mid-July to Aug. M-F 9am-noon and 2-5:30pm, Sa 9am-noon; Sept. to mid-July M 8am-5:45pm, Tu-F 8am-6pm, Sa 8am-noon. **Postal code:** 38000.

ACCOMMODATIONS & CAMPING

Budget hotels dot downtown Grenoble. It's wise to call ahead. The student guide *Le Guide de l'Etudiant*, free at the tourist office, has info on long-term stays. The HI Auberge de Jeunesse in Echirolles/Grenoble is closed for 2003 with indefinite plans to reopen in the spring of 2004; visitors should consult www.fuaj.com for updated information on the expected reopening date.

Le Foyer de l'Etudiante, 4 rue Ste-Ursule (☎04 76 42 00 84; www.multimania.com/foyeretudiante). A budget traveler's best bet for July-Aug., when it ceases to be a dorm and welcomes tourists. Stately old building encloses a courtyard where backpackers and students mix. Spacious rooms with desks and high ceilings. Kitchen, piano, free **Internet**. Sheets €8. Laundry €2.20. Reception 24hr. July-Sept. 3-night min. for room; 5-night max. for dorm. Oct.-June 6-month min. stay. Dorms €8. July-Sept. singles €14; doubles €22. Oct.-June singles €243; doubles €364. **Oct.-June women only.** ❶

Hôtel de la Poste, 25 rue de la Poste (☎/fax 04 76 46 67 25), in the heart of the pedestrian zone. Cheap rooms have antiquated charm at this homey refuge. Those in showerless rooms should get comfortable with the 26-year owner and friendly staff: the only public shower is 4ft. from the reception desk. Reception daily 8am-midnight. Singles €22, with shower and TV €26; doubles €28/€35; triples €32; quads €37. ❷

Hôtel Victoria, 17 rue Thiers (☎04 76 46 06 36; fax 04 76 43 00 14). Friendly owner takes good care of visitors at this super-clean hotel. Though a bit dark, rooms are spacious and have firm beds. Breakfast €5.50. Reception daily 7am-11:30pm. Curfew 11:30pm. Closed Aug. Singles with shower €29, with toilet €34; doubles €34/€40-45; triples €48; quads €51. AmEx/MC/V. ❸

Hôtel du Moucherotte, 1 rue Auguste Gache (☎04 76 54 61 40; fax 04 76 44 62 52), offers small, slightly stuffy rooms and a dark entrance hall, but has a pleasant owner and location right in the *vieille ville*. Breakfast €5.50. Reception daily 8am-11pm. Singles €24-32; doubles €32-40; triples €35.60-41.10. Cash only. ❸

Camping: Les 3 Pucelles, 58 rue des Allobroges (☎04 76 96 45 73; fax 04 76 21 43 73), in Seyssins, just on the southwest corner of Grenoble. Take tram A (dir: Fontaine-La Poya) to Louis Maisonnat, then take bus #51 (dir: Les Nalettes) to Mas des Iles; turn left and the site is a couple of blocks down. Small and suburban, this is the closest campsite to town and the only one open all year. 70 sites and a swimming pool. Reception daily 7:30am-11pm. Laundry €2.20. Call ahead June-Aug. 1 person, tent, and car €7.50. Extra person €2.80. Electricity €2.20. MC/V. ❶

FOOD

The most lively of Grenoble's 16 **markets** can be found on on pl. St-André, pl. St-Bruno, pl. Ste-Claire, and pl. aux Herbes. (All Tu-Su 6am-1pm; pl. Ste-Claire also F 3-8pm.) A particularly well-stocked **Monoprix** is across from the tourist office (open M-Sa 8:30am-8pm); a **Casino** is at 46 cours Jean Jaurès, about 10min. from the youth hostel. (Open M-Sa 8:30am-8pm.) Grenoble has many affordable restaurants, some with discounts and student *menus*. **University Restaurants (URs)** (☎04 76 57 44 00) sell meal tickets (€2.40) during the school year. Two URs are in Grenoble *ville*: 5 rue d'Arsonval (open M-F 11:30am-1:30pm and 6:30-7:45pm), and rue Maurice Gignoux. (Open daily noon-1:15pm and 6:30-7:50pm.) There's also a **Casino Cafeteria** on rue Guetal with cheap, fast service. (Salads €2.20-4.50, appetizers €1-3.80, hot dishes €3.50-6.40. Open daily 11am-9:30pm.)

Regional restaurants cater to locals around **place de Gordes**, between pl. St-André and the Jardin de Ville. Asian eateries abound between **place Notre-Dame** and the river and **rue Condorcet**; *pâtisseries* and North African establishents congre-

Grenoble

▲ ACCOMMODATIONS
Camping Les 3 Pucelles, 3
Le Foyer de l'Etudiante, 11
Hôtel du Moucherotte, 13
Hôtel de la Poste, 14
Hôtel Victoria, 4

● FOOD
La Belle Etoile, 5
Tête à l'Envers, 9
Le Tonneau de Diogène, 10

★ NIGHTLIFE
L'Absolu and George V, 2
Le Couche-Tard, 7
Cybernet Café, 12
L'Entrepôt, 1
London Pub, 8
Les Trois Canards, 6

Tram Stops
Tramway B
Tramway A

LG

Parc Paul Mistral

200 yards
200 meters

RHÔNE-ALPS

r. de Jeanne d'Arc
av. de Verdun
r. Malakoff
Hôtel de Ville
Musée d'Histoire Naturelle
Jardin des Plantes
bd. Jean Pain
av. de Verdun
r. Hebert
bd. des Adieux
r. Chanrion
r. Joseph
r. des Dauphins
r. Eug. Faure
r. D. Villars
r. Génissieu
r. Haxo
r. Fourier
PL. DE VERDUN
Préfecture
r. Fantin Latour
r. de la Liberté
PL. DE METZ
r. Casimir Perier
bd. Maréchal Lyautey
Beyle Stendhal
bd. Maréchal Lyautey
r. Hoche
Youth Center
r. Lesdiguières
r. Raoult
r. Condillac
r. de Sault
r. St-Jacques
r. de la Poste
Casino Cafeteria
cours Lafontaine
bd. Gambetta
r. Thiers
Voyages Wasteels
r. Lakanal
r. Lesdiguières
r. Génissieu
Laundry
r. Bergers
cours Berriat
TO CASINO (4km)
r. Condorcet
r. Colbert
av. de Vialle
r. Joseph Rey
PL. ST-BRUNO
r. Chorier
r. Sémard
TO ① & ③ (3.5km)
TO ② (600m)
r. la Genin
PL. DE LA GARE
Self Car
r. Emile Gueymard
r. Jean Macé
quai de la Graille
quai Claude Bernard
autoroute A48
TO LYON (105km)
bd. de l'Esplanade
rte. de Lyon
Parc Guy Pape
Jardin des Dauphins
PL. HUBERT DUBEDOUT
quai de France
pont de la Porte de France
l'Isère
PL. BRIAND
ESPLANADE
Maurice Gignoux
Parc A. Michalon
quai Xavier Jouvin
pont Marius Gontard
Téléphérique to La Bastille
Fort de la Bastille
TÉLÉPHÉRIQUE TERMINAL (150m)
Musée Dauphinois
Musée de Grenoble
r. St-Laurent
pont St-Laurent
quai Perrière
Montée Chalemont
Jardin de Ville
r. Hector Berlioz
r. M. Gontard
r. Deprez
bd. Edouard Rey
r. Docteur Mazet
r. Créqui
bd. Gambetta
PL. VICTOR HUGO
cours Jean Jaurès
r. Lorraine
r. Jay
r. Lafontaine
Laundry
r. Agutte Sembat
PL. GRENETTE
Grande Rue
r. de la République
r. Montorge
PL. ST-ANDRÉ
Collégiale St-André
Palais de Justice
r. des Clercs
L'Autre Monde
Etoile
Monoprix
r. J. Rousseau
r. Raoul Blanchard
r. Vicat
Bureau Information Montagne
Laundry
r. Abbé de la Salle
Cathédrale Notre-Dame
PL. NOTRE-DAME
Très-Cloîtres
r. Ste-Ursule
r. Très-Cloîtres
r. du Vieux Temple
r. Chenoise
r. Brocherie
r. Bayard
r. de la Paix
r. Voltaire
PL. CLAIRE
La New Age
Barnabé
r. Duclot
r. Bonne
r. Félix Poulat
r. de Belgrade
r. de Palanka
r. Millet
r. St-Laurent
quai de la Perrière
Cimetière St-Roch
bd. Maréchal Leclerc
Parc A. Michalon
r. du Souvenir
r. Verte
r. Ammon de Crissée
r. Bizanet
r. Masséna
r. de l'Alma
r. Bergès
av. Félix-Viallet
r. Casimir Brenier
Borel Sport
av. Alsace
r. Denfert-Rochereau
r. Crépu
r. Sté-Claire
r. Montorge
r. Bayard
PL. ST-CLAIRE
pont St-Laurent

gate around **rue Chenoise** and **rue Lionne**, between the pedestrian area and the river. Cafés and restaurants cluster around pl. Notre-Dame and **place St-André**, in the heart of the *vieille ville*. Lively, cheap pizzerias line **quai Perrière** across the river.

■ **Tête à l'Envers**, 12 rue Chenoise (☎04 76 51 13 42). This seven-table gem specializes in a *mélange* of international cuisine. The menu changes daily, depending on what's fresh at the market and in the creative mind of the expert chef. Guess the identity of 5 of the 6 desserts and win a prize. Mention *Let's Go* for a free coffee or digéstif. Entrées €7, *plats du jour* €8.30, dessert €7, lunch *menu* €11-12.20. Reservations recommended. Open Tu-F noon-3pm and 7:30pm-1am, Sa 7:30pm-1am. MC/V. ❷

La Belle Etoile, 2 rue Lionne (☎04 76 51 00 40). This family establishment specializes in Tunisian cuisine, with some of the best couscous in Grenoble (€7.40-13). Large salads €2.30-8.40, omelettes €2.60-5.60, *tagines* €9.50, fresh pastries €2.30. Closed mid-July to mid-Aug. Open Tu-Su noon-2pm and 7-11pm. AmEx/MC/V. ❷

Le Tonneau de Diogène, 6 pl. Notre-Dame (☎04 76 42 38 40). Nothing beats the philosophical discussions held by local intellectuals one night per week Sept. to mid-July; check the front of the store for times and topics. Salads €6.10, omelettes €3.50-5, and meat dishes €2.90-9.40, 3-course *menu* €6.50. Open daily 8:30am-1am. A set of back stairs leads to **Le Sphinx** (☎04 76 44 55 08), Grenoble's finest philosophy library/bookstore. Open M-F noon-8:30pm, Sa 10am-7pm. AmEx/MC/V. ❶

👁 SIGHTS

■**TÉLÉPHERIQUE GRENOBLE-BASTILLE.** The icons of Grenoble, these gondolas depart from the city every 10min. and head for the **Bastille**, a 16th-century fort perched ominously 475m above the city. From the top, on a clear day, visitors can look north toward the Lyon valley and its two converging rivers, or south over the ridge of snow-capped mountains. Sporty types can continue 1hr. up to **Mont-Jalla**, but views don't improve much. At the cable station, practice alpine climbing skills on the **Via Ferrata**, the first urban climbing site in the world, or walk down via the **Parc Guy Pape** through the other end of the fortress to the Jardin des Dauphins. (1hr.) Be cautious: the trail is isolated and passes through several dark tunnels. (*Téléphérique: quai Stéphane-Jay. ☎04 76 44 33 65; www.telepherique-grenoble.com. Open July-Aug. M 11am-12:15am, Tu-Su 9:15am-12:15am; Nov.-Feb. M 11am-6:30pm, Tu-Su 10:45am-6:30pm; Mar.-May and Oct. M 11am-7:25pm, Tu-Sa 9:15am-11:45pm, Su 9:15am-7:25pm; June and Sept. M 11am-11:45pm, Tu-Sa 9:15am-11:45pm, Su 9:15am-7:25pm. Closed mid-Jan. One-way €3.80, students €3; round-trip €5.50/€4.40.*)

■**MUSÉE DE GRENOBLE.** Art lovers will swoon over one of France's most prestigious collections of fine art. Its masterpieces include larger-than-life canvases by Rubens, de la Tour, and Zubararàn, and a top-notch 20th-century collection with an entire room devoted to Matisse. A fair amount of space is devoted to local artists' depictions of the mountains, perfect for drumming up enthusiasm for outdoor pursuits. (*5 pl. de Lavalette. ☎04 76 63 44 44; www.ville-grenoble.fr/musee-de-grenoble. Open July-Sept. M and Th-Su 10am-6pm, W 10am-9pm; Oct.-June M and Th-Su 11am-7pm, W 11am-10pm. €4, students €2; with temporary and permanent collections €6, students €3. Guided 1½hr. visits in French Sa-Su 3pm; €4.*)

■**MUSÉE D'HISTOIRE NATURELLE DE GRENOBLE.** Children in particular love this museum, but anyone not sqeamish about taxidermy should check it out. Dioramas of alpine animals, including lynx, bears, and birds, line a stately wooden hall. The second floor presents gruesome insects from around the world and a glittering display of gems. Many of the exhibits have English descriptions, but the beautiful displays need little introduction. (*1 rue Dolomieu. ☎04 76 44 05 35; www.museum-grenoble.fr. Open M-Th 9:30am-noon and 1:30-5:30pm, Sa-Su 2-6pm.*)

MUSÉE DAUPHINOIS. This is one regional ethnographic museum definitely worth a visit. Situated on the north bank of the Isère in a beautiful 17th-century convent, this museum boasts multimedia extravagance, futuristic exhibits, and sound effects. The two permanent exhibits have English explanations. The "Gens de l'Alpe" (People of the Alps) explores the history of the hearty souls who first carved out a livelihood in the mountains. Check out "La Grande Histoire du Ski" (The Great History of Skiing), featuring a vast collection of early and modern skis. *(30 rue Maurice Gignoux. Cross the Pont St-Laurent and go up Montée Chalemont. ☎04 76 85 19 01; www.musee-dauphinois.fr. Open M and W-Su June-Sept. 10am-7pm; Oct.-May 10am-6pm. €3.20, under 25 free. W afternoon free.)*

VIEILLE VILLE. Built over 17 centuries, Grenoble's *vieille ville* is a motley but charming collection of old-time squares, fountains, and parks. Vestiges of the Roman ramparts are most visible near the town's historic center, **place St-André,** now transformed into Grenoble's most popular student hangout. The 13th-century **Collégiale Saint-André** was the traditional burial place for Dauphins before the French crown acquired both land and title in 1349. *(Open 8am-5pm.)* Directly across, you can't miss the flamboyant Gothic **Palais de Justice,** built by Dauphin prince and future king Louis XI in 1453 to house the Dauphiné region's parliament. *(Tours depart from the tourist office Su-F 10:15am. €6.50, students €5.20.)* The **Café de la Table Ronde,** built in 1739, is the second-oldest coffee shop in France. *(☎04 76 44 51 41. Open M-Sa 9am-1am. Coffee €1.)*

🎵 ENTERTAINMENT

Grenoble has the funky cafés and raucous bars of a true college town, most located in the area between **place St-André** and **place Notre-Dame.** Covers for clubs range €8-10, and drinks are nearly as much. Hours listed here are for the school year; most places have more limited hours in summer. The **Maison de la Culture** in the tourist office is so hip it calls itself **Le CARGO.** (☎04 76 01 21 21. Open Sept.-June Tu-Sa 9am-6:30pm.)

Le Couche-Tard, 1 rue du Palais (☎04 76 44 18 79), a small bar with graffiti-covered walls, neon lights, and a dance area, is where drunken scholars mix it up. Happy hour M-Sa 7-10:30pm; cocktails €2. Open M-Sa 8pm-2am.

Les Trois Canards, 2 av. Felix Viallet (☎04 76 46 74 74), by the Jardin de Ville, has €1.60 shooters and a mind-boggling selection of flavored vodka (€2) for students and 20-somethings. Relax in the spacious interior with a live DJ, seahorses, disco ball, and various Budweiser paraphernalia. Open daily 8am-1am; July-Aug. closed Su.

Cybernet Café, 3 rue Bayard (☎04 76 51 73 18), has **Internet,** but it's not for cybernerds. A funky crowd loves this mellow, artfully decorated spot. Happy hour 6-8:30pm; drinks €2-4. Internet €3 for 30min., €5 per hr. Open Tu-Sa 3pm-1am.

London Pub, 11 rue Brocherie (☎04 76 44 41 90), is a slightly kitschy but friendly home-away-from-home for expats, with a more local crowd in the student-deprived summer. The two-floor establishment has an outgoing staff and flag-adorned interior. After a few drinks, the bar area morphs into a de facto dance floor. Happy hour daily 6-9pm; drafts from €1.60. Open M-Sa 6pm-1am.

L'Entrepôt, 5 rue Auguste Genin (☎04 76 48 21 48; www.entre-pot.com), near the *gare,* hosts local musicians of varying genres. Grenoble citizens rave about its laid-back but festive atmosphere. Cover €5-9. Open Th-Su 9pm-3am. MC/V.

L'Absolu and George V, 124 cours Berriat (☎04 76 84 16 20), are two of the only gay clubs in Grenoble. Intimate red lounge area, dance floor, and theme nights twice a month. Cover €10, includes one drink. Open Th-Su midnight-5:30am.

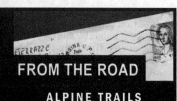

FROM THE ROAD

ALPINE TRAILS

The ice-capped mountains, half-frozen lakes, vibrant wildflowers, and well-worn footpaths looked like those I've seen trekking in the western United States. Almost immediately, however, I noticed how vastly different these mountains were from home.

Dozens of locals were sunbathing at the lake or sipping Perrier on a café terrace. Yes, a café, even here, in the midst of a wilderness preserve. As I passed elderly women with hiking poles, teenagers with rolled cigarettes tucked behind their ears, and men tugging their six-year-old sons by the hand, something occurred to me: in France, the mountains are everyone's territory. These unfathomably beautiful vistas in Washington state require a week of serious backcountry camping, but in France they are easily reached by *navette* or *téléphérique*. This accessibility is refreshing—there's no cult surrounding synthetic socks, top-grade boots, or ultralight sleeping bags. High-tech folks come here, too, but their numbers are equaled by shirtless 60-year-old men meandering along the mountain trails.

It's sometimes irksome never to be able to enjoy the surroundings in complete solitude, but by the end of my trek, I was happily saying *"bonjour"* every five minutes, and my smiles were reflected back at me on the faces of hikers I passed.

–Sarah Seltzer

FESTIVALS

On July 14, Grenoble blazes with fireworks over its very own Bastille. The **Festival du Court Métrage** celebrates short films in early July. Contact the **Cinémathèque**, 4 rue Hector Berlioz (☎ 04 76 54 43 51). The **Festival de Théâtre Européen** hams it up in July. (Info ☎ 04 76 44 60 92. Shows free to €16.) In late November, the two-week **Festival 38ème Rugissants** (info ☎ 04 76 51 12 92) features contemporary music. **Cabaret Frappe** celebrates singers and songwriters from around the world, from late June to early July with both free outdoor and €11 indoor concerts. Info and tickets for most events are available at the **Billetterie**, next the tourist office. (☎ 04 76 42 96 02. Open M-Sa 9am-noon and 1:30-6pm.) The weekly *Le Petit Bulletin*, free in cinemas and some restaurants, has full movie schedules.

SKIING

Rent equipment in town to avoid high prices at the resorts. The biggest ski areas are to the east in **Oisans**. The **Alpe d'Huez**, rising above one of the most challenging legs of the Tour de France, boasts an enormous 3330m vertical drop and sunny, south-facing slopes; 220km of trails span all difficulty levels. (Tourist office ☎ 04 76 11 44 44; fax 04 76 80 69 54; ski area ☎ 04 76 80 30 30. €33 per day, €171.50 per week.) Popular with advanced skiers, **Les Deux Alpes** has the largest skiable glacier in Europe, limited summer skiing, and a slope-side youth hostel. Its lift system, including two gondolas, runs up the 2000m vertical. (Tourist office ☎ 04 76 79 22 00; fax 04 76 79 01 38. Ski area ☎ 04 76 79 75 00. Youth hostel ☎ 04 76 79 22 80; fax 04 76 79 26 15. Lift tickets €32 per day, €137.70-153 per week.)

The **Belledonne** region, northeast of Grenoble, lacks the towering heights and ideal conditions of the Oisans but compensates with lower prices. **Chamrousse** is its biggest and most popular ski area, offering a lively atmosphere and a youth hostel. If conditions are right, there's plenty of good alpine and cross-country skiing for a great value, especially for beginners. (Tourist office ☎ 04 76 89 92 65; fax 04 76 89 98 06. Youth hostel ☎ 04 76 89 91 31; fax 04 76 89 96 66. Lift tickets €23 per day, €79-113 per week.) Only 30min. from Grenoble, the resort makes for an ideal daytrip in the summer (bus ride €8.70). Chamrousse maintains four **mountain bike** routes of varying difficulty in addition to a 230km network of **hiking** trails. In January, the town plays host to a renowned comedy film festival.

The neighborly slopes of the **Vercors** region, south of Grenoble, are popular with locals. In traditional villages with small ski resorts, such as **Gresse-en-Vercors**, vertical drops range around 1000m. Rock-bottom prices make the area a stress-free option for beginners or those looking to escape the hassles of the major resorts. The drive from Grenoble takes about 40min. (Tourist office ☎ 04 76 34 33 40; fax 04 76 34 31 26. Tickets €8.80-12.20 per day, €52.90-72.10 per week.) Saturated with quaintness and with ibex, Vercors and its regional park offer plenty of great **hikes**, as well as **mountain bike** circuits in and around the villages of **Meaudre** and **Autrans**, which has a sleepy hostel and lots of farmland for the peace-seeker. Contact **Bureau Info Montagne** (p. 453) for maps and details. **Mountain climbers** should ask specifically for the free *Carte des Sites d'Escalade de l'Isère* or purchase a comprehensive topo-guide for about €16.

The four slopes around Grenoble aren't the only source of daytrips in the area. The Dauphiné region is proud of its *"Huit Merveilles"* (Eight Wonders), which include elaborate natural caves. The tourist office has information on excursions to towns such as **Pont-en-Royans** and other natural beauties.

HIKING

A number of popular hikes lie just a short bus ride away. In Vercors, views from the top of **Le Moucherotte** (1901m) are unparalleled. Take VFD bus #510 (dir: Plateau du Vercors) to St-Nizier du Moucherotte (40min., 2 per day, €4.40) and head to the center of town. In front of the church, an easy trail starts to the right of the orientation table and quickly joins the **GR91**, which passes the remains of an old *téléphérique* before reaching the mountain's summit via a former ski trail. Descend along the same route. (Round-trip 4hr.) A steeper trail reaches the summit of the **Chamechaude** (2082m) in the heart of the Chartreuse natural park. Take VFD bus #714 to Col de Porte. Then follow the dirt trail leading from behind Hôtel Garin to the right until reaching the middle of a field; to the left, a second trail leads into the forest and joins the main path, a zig-zag ascent up to the **source des Bachassons**. From here hikers can stop to admire the view or continue to the top of the mountain. Before ascending, pick up the free trail map, *La Carte des Sentiers des Franges Vertes*, at the Bureau Info Montagne (p. 453).

DAYTRIP FROM GRENOBLE: HAUTERIVES

*To reach the site, take the **train** from Grenoble to Romans (1hr., 11 per day, €10.50), then pick up a La Régie Drôme **bus** to Hauterives (☎ 04 75 02 30 42. 30min.; July-Aug. W 8am and 4, F 7:15, 8, 11:30am, 4pm; Sept.-June M-Tu and Th 6:15pm, F 9:30, 11:30am, 4pm, 6:15pm; €4.40). Call to be sure there is a bus back the same day. A better option, if possible, is to **drive** from Grenoble. Take A48 north; at Voreppe, switch to A49 toward Romans. At Romans, take D538 north to Hauterives. (1hr.) From Lyon, head south on A7 and change to D538 at Vienne.*

This village has put itself on the map with a whimsical palace and the intriguing story behind it. In 1879, the local postman, Ferdinand Cheval, tripped over an oddly shaped rock while on his daily rounds. He began to collect piles of odd little rocks and over the next 33 years, he shaped them into a fantasy palace outside the village. Rock by rock, it grew into an unbelievably detailed world of grimacing giants, frozen palms, and swirling staircases. When he finally laid down his trowel, the ⧫**Palais Idéal** (Ideal Palace) was almost 80m long and over two stories high. The palace, an indescribable mix of Middle Eastern architecture and hallucinatory images, has become a national monument. Visitors can climb all over it to explore its caves and crevices, mottoes and mysteries sculpted by the postman's two hands and unshakable faith. (☎ 04 75 68 81 19; www.facteurcheval.com. Open daily

July-Aug. 9am-12:30pm and 1:30-7:30pm; Sept. and Apr.-June 9am-12:30pm and 1:30-6:30pm; Oct.-Nov. and Feb.-Mar. 9:30am-12:30pm and 1:30-5:30pm; Dec.-Jan. 9:30am-12:30pm and 1:30-4:30pm. €4.80, students €3.80, under 16 €3.30.)

Hauterives's **tourist office,** rue du Palais Idéal, provides info on the palais and the surrounding region. (☎04 75 68 86 82; fax 04 75 68 92 96. Open daily Apr.-Sept. 10am-12:30pm and 1:30-6pm; Oct.-Nov. and Feb.-Mar. 10am-12:30pm and 1:30-5:30pm; Dec.-Jan. 10am-12:30pm and 1:30-4:30pm.)

MEGÈVE

Nestled in a lush valley, shopping and gambling mecca Megève is one of the posh-est alpine resorts, ideal for beginning skiers and those who prefer an off-slopes experience in a chic French town. Despite heavy tourism, the tiny alleyways over rushing mountain streams retain old-fashioned appeal; and visitors don't have to part with (all) their fortunes to enjoy its charms. Though the town inspires the most admiration when lit up for the winter holidays, it remains adorable all year.

▐ TRANSPORTATION

Geneva International Airport is 1hr. away. €32 bus rides from the airport to Sal-lanches are available twice daily through S.A.T. **Trains** run from 116 rte. 212 to St-Gervais (7min., 10-12 per day, €4); Annecy (1½hr., 5 per day, €10.50); Lyon (4hr., 5 per day, €17); and Paris (4½hr., 3 per day, €25). **Buses** (office open daily 9am-noon and 2-6:15pm) also run from 116 rte. 212, and go to Sallanches (1hr., 5 per day, €8.50); Chamonix (1¼hr., 1 per day, €8.40). **Luggage storage** €4.50. **Taxis** wait at at the train station. (☎04 50 21 28 20. 24hr.)

▌ ▐ ORIENTATION & PRACTICAL INFORMATION

The **place de l'Eglise,** with its oft-photographed spire, is the closest equivalent to a central square. On one side, pedestrian **avenue Charles Feige** and **rue St-François** run past lively cafés, shops, and bars on the way to **rue du Mont D'Arbois** and **rue Edmund Rothschild.** The latter leads to **Mt. d'Arbois,** the golf course, hotel, *téléphérique,* and ski area, a trek by foot. In the summer a marked footpath cuts up the hill; in the winter the best way to reach the summit is to take the Chamois and Rocharbois **gondolas.** On the other side of the *place,* **rue Monseigneur Conseil** goes to the tourist office, 70 rue Monseignuer Conseil. The staff provides maps and info on hiking, skiing, camping, and *chambres d'hôtes,* **Internet** (€2.50 for 15min. with an ATM card), **accommodations booking** (☎04 50 21 29 52; reservation@megeve.com), and **currency exchange** with €5 commission. (☎04 50 21 27 28; megeve@megeve.com. Open mid-June to early Aug. and mid-Dec to late Apr. daily 9am-7pm; late Apr. to mid-June and early Aug. to mid-Dec. M-Sa 9am-12:30pm and 2-6:30pm. **Internet** is also available at Bar des Alpes, 273 rue de la Poste (☎04 50 93 08 15), across from post office. (Open only during high season). Other services include: **police** off pl. de l'Eglise (☎04 50 93 29 22), and at the train station, 1436 rte. 212 (☎04 50 91 28 10), **mountain rescue** (☎04 50 91 28 18), and a **post office,** 276 rue de la Poste (☎04 50 21 04 64), down the street from the bus station, that **exchanges currency** at good rates. Open M-F 8:30am-noon and 2-5:30pm, Sa 8am-noon. **Postal code:** 74120.

▐ ACCOMMODATIONS & CAMPING

Many hotels charge the same for singles as for doubles. The best deals are doubles and ski apartments for multiple people. Most cheaper hotels are about a 20min. walk outside the *centre ville,* toward either Sallanches or Rocheburne. Camping is an inexpensive summer option, while in the winter, reserving a *demi-pension* may save money. The best deal by far for groups of two is to take a room at one of several local ⬛**chambres d'hôtes**, which tend to charge less than €30 per person per night with breakfast included. Arrangements must be made well in advance through the Megève reservation office (see **Practical Infomation**). Because this is a ski town, rates rise and fall with snow. Always call ahead for winter reservations. Those traveling Apr.-June or Sept.-Dec. are advised to call the tourist office to verify the opening dates of hotels.

The English-speaking management at **Hôtel le Rond-Point d'Arbois ❸**, 111 rte. Edmund Rothschild, rents large doubles, some with balconies, on the road up to Mt. d'Arbois near the skibus stops. (☎44 12 23 47 76; www.stanfordskiing.co.uk. Breakfast €5. Doubles from €47. Open June-Sept. and Dec.-Apr. MC/V.) **La Croix du Savoie ❹**, offers spacious apartments with small kitchens and bathrooms in the Demi Quartier neighborhood, a 25min. walk out of town along rte. 212 toward Sallanches. (Breakfast included. Open mid-June to late Aug. and Dec.-Apr. Singles from €38; doubles €49-73; 3- to 4-person suites €70-120 in summer, €90-150 in winter. MC/V. A 30min. walk from town, **Camping Bornand ❶** has small sites, some graveled, and a playground. From rte. 212, toward Sallanches, turn right at the sign for "Tleecabin Princesse." Follow signs for "camping." (☎04 50 93 00 86; camping.bornand@tiscali.fr. Open May-Sept. €3.30 per person, €3.50 per site. MC/V.)

🎵 FOOD

For a day of hiking the mountains or a night spent in a ski chalet, store-bought goodies hit the spot. Along the streets of the *centre ville*, dozens of *épiceries* specializing in Savoyard food open their doors, and there are multiple supermarkets, the most centrally located of which is **Sherpa**, 150 rue Ambroise Martin (☎04 50 21 46 92. Open M-Sa 9am-12:15pm and 4-7pm, Su 9am-12:15pm). There are also a **Casino** across from the tourist office and several large supermarkets on rte. 212 toward Sallanches. *Brasseries* with less expensive *menus* abound on the main pedestrian streets; those in the mood for serious upscale dining among the elite can kiss their budget goodbye at one of the town's famously top-notch hotels. The ⬛**Chalet du Mont d'Arbois ❺**, 447 chemin de la Rocaille, has been a Megève institution for nearly a century. (☎04 50 21 25 03. Reservations required. *Plats* from €28, *menus* €45-55. Open late June to Sept. and mid-Dec. to Mar. only noon-2pm and 7:30-10pm. AmEx/MC/V.) If you want to eat without breaking your budget, **Petite Crêperie Bretonne ❷**, 91 rue St-François, is located in a charming little alleyway (☎04 50 21 63 49. Takeout crêpes €3, sit-down *menu* with salad, *galette*, and sweet crêpe €10. Open M-Sa noon-10pm. No credit cards.)

🎿 HIKING, SKIING, & THE OUTDOORS

The **ski areas** surrounding Megève offer solid intermediate terrain. The largest complex, **Mt. d'Arbois/Mt. Joly**, offers the most varied and challenging terrain, much of it above tree line, through a large network of lifts. It is serviced from either the Princesse or Mt. d'Arbois *téléphériques*. Skiing is also available in the nearby hamlets of **Rocheburne, Jaillet,** and **Combloux,** connected by lifts from St-Gervais. From the town center, the **Chamois lift** enables skiers to head to the Rocheburne or Mt. d'Arbois areas. The base areas are connected by a **skibus,** which is included in Megève lift passes. At the Maison de la Montagne, a bulletin board and ski map list lift and trail openings and closings.

Because the town is a giant base for several **ski schools,** it attracts beginners and families in droves. Two main ski schools compete for Megève children: the **Ecole de Ski Français,** 76 rue Ambrose Montin (☎04 50 21 00 97), is in the Maison de La

Montagne. The **Ecole de Ski Internationale** (☎ 04 50 58 78 88) meets under the Mt. d'Arbois cable car. Both offer private and group lessons, including multi-day morning packages for skiing, snowboarding, and ski racing. Several smaller ski schools meet as well; ask at the tourist office.

Ski rental is possible in dozens of places throughout town and is best done by the week. Budget travelers might want to rent skis in Megève's neighboring towns for the best deals. The cost of **ski passes** depends on ability. A simple Megève pass includes all the areas listed above for €29.50 per day, children €23.50. For beginners, there's a pass that serves only the Jaillet and Combloux resorts for €19.50 per day, children €15.50. Multi-day passes save about €4 per day. For those who want access to the real *hors-piste* stuff, a 6- or 7-day Mt. Blanc pass provides access to the slopes in nearby Chamonix and Courmayer, Italy. (6 day pass €205, children €164.)

During the **summer,** three principal *téléphériques* offer hikers and visitors expansive mountain views and hiking opportunities. (**Mt. d'Arbois gondola:** ☎ 04 50 21 22 07. Mid-June to Aug. one-way €5.50, round-trip €8.50. **Jaillet gondola:** ☎ 04 50 21 01 50. Late June to mid-Sept. €4.60/€8.50. **Rocheburne cable car:** ☎ 04 50 21 01 51. Late June to early Aug. €5.50/€9.60) The █walk up to Mt. d'Arbois's base from town departs from rue Edmund de Rothschild, about 5min. outside of town. Marked "Mt. Arbois/Calvaire," the steep 20-30min. trail passes several gorgeous churches and hundreds of photo opportunities.

From the top of Mt. d'Arbois's chairlift, it's a 1½hr. walk to the summit of Mt. Joly. A network of **"fitness" trails** cover this mountain, which has the best views of Mt. Blanc. The tourist office sells a trail map for €6 and gives a free French brochure, *Promenades à Pied*, that describes popular hikes in the area. The Compagnie des Guides, in the Maison de la Montagne, offers **guided multi-day hikes, alpinism courses, climbing, mountain biking,** and **canyoning.** Several facilities are available for **horseback riding, tennis,** and **golf;** there are also four or five **spas** and a **swimming pool.** The magazine *Megève Eté,* free at the tourist offices in Megève or in Chamonix, has an extensive list of things to do.

🎵 🎭 ENTERTAINMENT & FESTIVALS

Upscale *après-ski* and late-night options await skiers on **route Edmund de Rothschild.** The **Pallas** disco, 96 rte. Edmund de Rothschild (☎ 04 50 91 82 70), is one of the more popular clubs in town. (Cover €9. Open during ski season nightly 11pm-3am.) The starkly trendy bar **Wake Up,** 131 rte. Edmund de Rothschild, is another well-populated option. (☎ 05 50 58 25 79. Beer €3-6. Open July-Aug. and Dec.-Apr. daily 4pm-midnight; Sept.-Nov. and May-June Th-Sa only.) Most night spots in the center of town are found on rue Ambrose Martin and rue Charles Feige. Famous and intimate, the **5 Rues Jazz Club,** quartier des 5 Rues (☎ 04 50 91 90 69), off pl. de l'Eglise in the basement of an old stone building, draws crowds and luminaries during ski season. The **Cargo Club,** 30 rue Ambrose Martin, often brings in DJs from around the region for Friday and Saturday night parties. (☎ 04 50 58 25 79. Cover €7-12. Open in winter Th-Sa 11pm-3am; in summer call for hours.) A simple bar, **La Calèche,** 4 rue Monseigneur Conseil, caters to locals with its dark interior and extensive beer menu. (☎ 04 50 21 21 32. Open M-Sa noon-10pm.)

A **casino,** 199 rue Charles Freige, beckons with the usual slot machines, poker, roulette, and blackjack. (☎ 04 50 93 01 83. Open daily 1pm-2am, Sa-Su until 3am. MC/V.) **Cinémas Rocheburne** (☎ 04 50 21 03 52) plays movies July-Aug. and Dec.-Apr. **Le Canadien Bowling Alley** is at 370 rte. de Sallanches (☎ 04 50 21 18 40).

Summer brings great jazz music to Megève. In the middle of July is the annual **Megève Jazz contest,** with over fifty free open-air concerts, while August heralds the week-long **Megève Jazz festival.** More information available at the tourist office.

ANNECY

In the *vieille ville* of Annecy (pop. 50.300), far from the noisy thoroughfares and high-rises of downtown, narrow cobblestone streets, winding canals, turreted castles, and overstuffed flower boxes look more like a the makings of a fairy-tale than a modern city. Bordering the man-made charms of this "Venice of the Alps," massive mountains and the purest lake in Europe provide a stunning sight for windsurfers below and paragliders above.

▐ TRANSPORTATION

Trains: pl. de la Gare. Open daily 5am-10:30pm. Ticket window open M 4:45am-9:15pm, Tu-Sa 6:10am-9:15pm, Su 6:40am-10:40pm. **Luggage storage** July-Aug. daily 8am-7:15pm; Sept.-June M-Sa 8am-noon and 2-5pm (€4.50). To: **Chamonix** (2½hr., 7 per day, €16.70); **Grenoble** (2hr., 12 per day, €14.10); **Lyon** (2hr., 9 per day, €18); **Nice** (7-9hr., 2 per day, €54.20); **Paris** (4hr., 8 per day, €57.60-72.40).

Buses: adjacent to the train station. Office open M-F 7:45-11am and 2-7:15pm, Sa 7:45-11am. **Autocars Frossard** (☎04 50 45 73 90) runs to **Geneva, Switzerland** (1¼hr., 6 per day, €9); **Lyon** (3½hr., 2 per day, €16.40).

Public Transportation: SIBRA (☎04 50 10 04 04). Info booth across from the train station open M-F 8:30am-7pm, Sa 8:30am-6pm. Extensive service; July-Aug. and weekends in June summer line stops at the hostel. Tickets €1, *carnet* of 8 €6.50.

Bike, Ski, and In-line Skate Rental: Little Big Shop, 38 av. de la Maveria-Annecy-le-Vieux (☎04 50 67 42 13). Bikes €10.50 per half-day, €15 per day. Ski, boot, and pole packages €14.50-25.50 per day. Open Tu-Sa 9am-noon and 2-7pm. MC/V. **Golf Miniature de l'Imperial,** 2 av. du Petit Port (☎04 50 66 04 99), beside plage de Paquier. In-line skates €5 per hr., €8 per half-day, €9 per day. Bicycles €8 per half-day, €15 per day, €20 for two days. Open daily 9am-7pm.

Taxis: at the station (☎04 50 45 05 67). 24hr. About €7 to the Auberge de Jeunesse.

▐▐ ORIENTATION & PRACTICAL INFORMATION

Most activity centers around the lake southeast of the train station. The canal runs east-west through the old town; the elevated château is on one side and the main shopping area, closer to the center of Annecy, is on the other. To reach the tourist office from the train station, take the underground passage to rue Sommeiller. Turn left onto rue Vaugelas and follow it for four blocks. The tourist office is straight ahead in the large Bonlieu shopping mall.

Tourist Office: 1 rue J. Jaurès (☎04 50 45 00 33 or 04 50 45 56 66; ancy-tour@noos.fr), at pl. de la Libération. Detailed maps, info on hiking, lodging, excursions, and climbing. The bilingual *Annecy Guide* describes nearby sights. *Sentiers Forestiers* (€3.10) details hiking paths in the Semnoz forest. Comprehensive French topo-guide of the region (€9.60). **Tours** of the *vieille ville* (2hr.; July-Aug. French tours M-Sa 3:30pm, English tours M and F 4pm; €5.20). Office open July-Aug. M-Sa 9am-6:30pm, Su 9am-12:30pm and 1:45-6:30pm; Sept.-June daily 9am-12:30pm and 1:45-6pm.

Youth Center: Bureau Information Jeunesse, 1 rue Jean Jaurès (☎04 50 33 87 40; infojeunes@ville-annecy.fr), in the Bonlieu center. Info on study options, housing, jobs, and leisure activities. Free **Internet.** Open M 3-7pm, Tu-F 12:30-7pm, Sa 10am-noon.

Laundromat: Lav'Confort Express, 6 rue de la Gare, across the canal. Wash €2, dry €2. Open daily 7am-9pm.

Police: 17 rue des Marquisats (☎04 50 52 32 00).

Hospital: 1 av. de Trésum (☎04 50 88 33 33).

RHÔNE-ALPS

Internet: Free at the **Youth Center** (see listing). **Syndrome Cyber-café,** 3bis av. de Chevenes (☎04 50 45 39 75), near the train station. €2 per 15min., €6 per hr. Open July-Aug. daily noon-10pm; Sept.-June M-W noon-7:30pm, Th-Sa noon-10pm. **L'Emailerie,** fbg. des Annonciades (☎04 50 10 18 91), in the *vieille ville,* has American keyboards. €1.50 per 15min., €6 per hr. Open June-Aug. daily 10am-8pm; Sept.-May M-Sa 10:30am-12:30pm and 2:30-7:30pm.

Post Office: 4bis rue des Glières (☎04 50 33 68 20), off rue de la Poste, down the street from the train station. **Currency exchange** at good rates, no commission. Open M-F 8:30am-6:30pm, Sa 8am-noon. **Poste Restante:** 74011. **Postal code:** 74000.

▐ ACCOMMODATIONS & CAMPING

Annecy's priciest accommodations are in the charming *vieille ville* and by the lake. Reservations are recommended, especially during ski season and in summer.

▨ **Auberge de Jeunesse "La Grande Jeanne" (HI),** rte. de Semnoz (☎04 50 45 33 19; annecy@fuaj.org). The summer line goes to the hostel from the station (dir: Semnoz; 7am-6:30pm; July-Aug. daily 6 per day, June and Sept. Sa-Su 6 per day; €1). Or take bus #1 (dir: Marquisats) from the station to Hôpital, in front of the police station. Walk straight on av. de Tresum, away from the lake, and follow the signs pointing to Semnoz. Take a left onto bd. de la Corniche and a right onto chemin du Belvédère for a steep ascent to the hostel. (15min.) Clean modern building perched excitingly between the forest and the lake. Tiny 4- to 5-bed dorms, with shower. Single-sex rooms available. Game room, kitchen, TV room, small bar, and laundry. Breakfast included. Dinner €8. Sheets €2.70. Reception Apr.-Nov. 8am-noon and 3-10pm; mid-Jan. to Mar. 8am-noon and 5-10pm. Reservations via the Internet (www.iyhf.net) suggested June-Aug., but you must pay half in advance. Closed Dec. to mid-Jan. Bunks €12.70. MC/V. ●

Hôtel Savoyard, 41 av. de Cran (☎04 50 57 08 08), in a pretty Savoyard mansion with courtyard. Attentive managers let spacious rooms with floral wallpaper and wooden floors. Breakfast €4. Reception daily 7am-10pm. Open May-Oct. Singles and doubles €20, with shower and bath €27-35; triples €25/€31-41; quads with bath €41. ❷

Hôtel Plaisance, 17 rue de Narvik (☎/fax 04 50 57 30 42), a right off av. de Cran (see above directions to Hôtel Savoyard). Charming manager caters to international clientele with intimate rooms, a woodsy breakfast area, and a TV salon. Ultra-clean and quiet. Breakfast €3.90. Showers €2. Reception daily 7am-midnight. Singles and doubles €23, with shower and toilet €32; triples €38.20; quads €45.80. MC/V. ❷

Hôtel du Château, 16 rampe du Château (☎04 50 45 27 66; hotelduchatea@noos.fr). Gorgeous views and pristine white rooms at the best option in the *vieille ville.* All rooms have shower and bath. Breakfast €6.50. Open mid-Dec. to mid-Nov. Reception daily 7am-9pm. Singles €46; doubles €50-55; triples €69. MC/V. ❸

Camping le Bélvèdere, 8 rte. de Semnoz (☎04 50 45 48 30; camping@ville-annecy.fr), just above the youth hostel. Pretty site. Small grocery store, TV, ping-pong, *pétanque,* and forested hiking trails nearby. Electricity €2.30. Laundry €5.40. Reception July-Aug. 8am-9pm; mid-Apr. to June and Sept. to mid-Oct. 8am-8pm. July-Aug. reserve via email or fax. Open mid-Apr. to mid-Oct. Sept.-June 1-2 people with tent and car €9.90-10.70; July-Aug. €13. Extra person €3.80-4.60, extra tent €1.60-2.30. MC/V. ●

▐ FOOD

Annecy's *vieille ville* is lined with affordable restaurants, each more charming than the next. Fill a picnic basket with the soft local *reblochon* cheese at the **markets** on pl. Ste-Claire (Tu, F, and Su 8am-noon) and on bd. Taine. (Sa 8am-noon.) Grocery stores line av. de Parmelan. A **Monoprix** supermarket fills most of pl. de

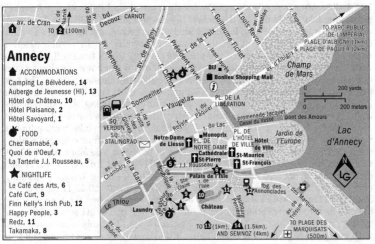

Notre-Dame. (☎04 50 45 23 60. Open M-Sa 8:30am-7:30pm.) A **Casino** supermarket is at 10 rue des Glières, across from the post office. (☎04 50 51 38 31. Open M-F 8am-12:15pm and 3-7:30pm, Sa 8am-12:15pm and 3-7pm.) Tiny restaurants with affordable menus line fbg. Ste-Claire, presenting the best options for budget-conscious *gourmands*. The popular ◼**Quoi de n'Oeuf ❸**, 19 fbg. Ste-Claire, serves plentiful portions on orange tablecloths that spill onto a *vieille ville* street. Eggheads jump at the €10.50 *tartiflette*, salad, and dessert. (☎04 50 45 75 42. Open M-Sa noon-2pm and 7-9:45pm. MC/V.)

For an escape from fondue, try **La Tarterie J.J. Rousseau ❷**, 14 rue J. J. Rousseau. The €9.10 *menu* includes *tarte salée* (in salmon, chicken, vegetarian, and cheese variations), *tarte sucrée*, and drink. (☎04 50 45 36 25. Open M-Tu noon-2pm, W-Sa noon-2pm and 7-9pm. MC/V.) With so many lovely gardens around, picnics are a great option. Paper-bag it at **Chez Barnabé ❶**, 29 rue Sommeiller. (☎04 50 45 90 62. Salad bar €2.70-5.30, homemade hot dishes €2.10-5.30, sandwiches €2.50-3.10, pizza €1.60-2. Open M-Sa 10am-7:15pm.)

👁 SIGHTS

VIEILLE VILLE. A stroll through the *vieille ville* will cost several rolls of film. **The Palais de l'Isle,** a 13th-century château first occupied by the counts of Geneva after their hometown came under Episcopal control, is a beautiful, turreted building, located strategically on a narrow island in the canal. It served as a prison, most recently for WWII Resistance fighters, whose impassioned carvings mark the walls. (☎04 50 33 87 30. Open June-Sept. daily 10:30am-6pm; Oct.-May Su-M and W-Sa 10am-noon and 2-5pm. €3.10, students €0.80.) Beneath the towers of the castle on the opposite side of the canal, **quai Perrière, rue de l'Isle,** and **rue Ste-Claire** are some of Annecy's most charming streets, despite their abundant arcades.

Straddling the town's narrowest canal, the large and bare church **Eglise St-Maurice,** consecrated in 1442, is well-known for the rare 15th-century painting that marks the tomb of Philibert de Monthoux, a one-time Annecy noble; look for it on the choir's left wall as you enter. This macabre mural of a decomposing corpse—finished a whole two years before its patron's death—is thought to reflect anxiety over the Hundred Years' War.

THE LAKE. After a stroll through the bustling streets, a brisk swim in Annecy's crystalline lake could be just the ticket. In summer, **plage d'Albigny**, 2-3km up av. d'Albigny, draws tourists and locals for **windsurfing, sailing**, and **kayaking**, as well as dining in trendy, coastal restaurants. Swimmers beware: despite regular extermination efforts, an infestation of the *puce de canard* (duck flea) still haunts the lake. The *puce* penetrates human skin in search of a warm home, producing mosquito-like bite symptoms that last 4-5 days, occasionally causing a fever. The best preventative measures are to avoid swimming when it's very hot, remain within 2m of the shore, use sunscreen, and shower after swimming. The smaller and more crowded **plage des Marquisats**, south of the city down rue des Marquisats, also permits swimming. The Club de Voile Française on the lake rents a limited selection of watercraft. Rent **pedal boats** at one of the numerous companies along the port or, for better deals, on the south side of the Champ de Mars. *(€8 for 30min., €12 per hr.; lake tours €6-14.)* For €3.50, the young at heart can frolic in the **Parc Public de l'Impérial,** an aquatic wonderland with waterslides, sailing, tennis, swimming, and a casino. *(20min. up av. d'Albigny beside plage d'Albigny. ☎ 04 50 23 11 82. Open May-Sept. daily 11am-7:30pm.)* Views of the lake from above are as breathtaking as plunging into its turquoise depths. Annecy is one of the best places in the world for **paragliding** *(parapenting)*, and plenty of companies help fuel this reputation, most with comparable prices. **Takamaka** helps little Daedali fly above the crystal-blue waters. *(Tandem €80; 5-day course €427.)*

GARDENS. Graced by manicured hedges, fountains, and the occasional long-necked swan, the shaded **Jardin de l'Europe** is Annecy's pride and joy. At its north side, the **Pont des Amours** (Lover's Bridge) connects the European gardens to the **Champ de Mars**, a grassy esplanade frequented by picnickers, sunbathers, and frisbee-throwers. Residents aren't quick to gloat, but such gardens have won it victory in the national *Ville Fleurie* (Flower City) contest three times in the last decade.

CHÂTEAU. The 12th-century château, a short, steep climb from the *vieille ville*, towers over Annecy. Once a stronghold of the Genevan counts, the castle and its imposing parapets now contain slightly dull archeological and artistic exhibits. Inside the main building, the museum's welcome desk occupies an enormous hearth that once fed a lively court. The 15th-century wooden statuary in the next room is interesting, as is the original ceiling of the banquet hall upstairs, the lone survivor of a 1952 fire. The **Observatoire Régional des Lacs Alpins,** in the rear of the castle, has exhibits about lake ecosystems, an aquarium, and a view that trumps the other attractions. *(☎ 04 50 33 87 30. Open June-Sept. daily 10:30am-6pm; Oct.-May Su-M and W-Sa 10am-noon and 2-5pm. Château €4.60, students €1.50, entrance to grounds free.)*

⚡ HIKING

Annecy's nearby Alpine forests shelter excellent hiking and biking trails. Dozens of hikes begin on the **Semnoz**, a limestone mountain south of the city. The **Office National des Forêts** (☎ 04 50 23 84 10) distributes a color map, *Sentiers Forestiers*, with several routes (€3.10 at the tourist office or hostel). The *Guide Pratique* also has lots of info on outdoor recreation. One of the best hikes begins at the **Basilique de la Visitation,** close to the hostel. From town, take bus A to its terminus, Visitation. From the basilica, continue along the road until you reach a small parking lot. Follow signs for *"la Forêt du Crêt du Maure."* The easy Ste-Catherine trail, marked "perimeter," follows a meandering circle around the Semnoz forest, leading past breathtaking views. (2hr.) After about an hour, the trail intersects with the red-and-yellow-marked **GR96**, on which long-haulers sometimes opt for a 38km circuit of the lake. An exquisite, scenic 16km *piste cyclable* (bike route) hugs the eastern shore of the lake. At the end of the piste, the entire loop can be completed on the main road (D909a), but be wary of traffic. The tourist office has a free lake map that includes the bike route and some departure points for hikes. The **Bureau des Guides** and **Takamaka,** 17 fbg. Ste-Claire, run excursions for mountaineering activities, including hiking, biking, rock-climbing, ice-climbing, paragliding, and canyoning. (☎04 50 45 60 61; www.takamaka.fr. Open July-Aug. daily 9am-7pm; Sept.-June M-F 9am-noon and 2-6pm. Hikes €20 per half-day, €30 per day. Canyoning €45-80. Sign up the night before. MC/V.)

ENTERTAINMENT & FESTIVALS

Relaxing bars line the canal in the *vieille ville* and the lake. The scene in Annecy revolves more around mellow outdoor drinking than wild dancing, but something exists for everyone. Artsy bar **Le Café des Arts,** 4 pass. de l'Isle, has a choice spot next to the cathedral. (☎04 50 51 56 40 Beer €1.10-3.90. Open daily 8:30am-2am.) Easy-going **Café Curt,** 35 rue Ste-Claire, is crowded with students and backpackers. (Wine €1.30-3, Kronenbourg €2, cognac €5-55. Open daily June-Sept. 10am-2am; Oct.-May 10am-1am.) The most beloved bar in town is **Finn Kelly's Irish Pub,** 10 fbg. des Annonciades, where locals chat by the bar and anglos converge at outdoor tables. (☎04 50 51 29 40. Draft beer €3. Happy hour 6:30-8pm; buy one drink, get one free. Open daily 3pm-3am.) The flashiest, however, is **Redz,** 14 rue Perrière, which puffs smoke out of its perpetually open doors. It draws an older clientele with theme nights and DJs nightly June-Aug. (☎04 50 45 17 13. Beer €2.40-6, cocktails €9-16. Open daily Apr.-Oct. 11am-3am; Nov.-Mar. 5pm-3am.) **Happy People,** 48 rue Carnot , lives up to its name. Wild nights are the norm at this gay and lesbian disco, perhaps because of the pitch-black make-out room in back. (☎04 50 51 08 66. Drinks €9-12. Cover F-Sa €12, includes one drink. Open daily 11pm-5am.)

Performing arts and films are the realm of the **Théâtre d'Annecy** in the Bonlieu Mall across from the tourist office. (☎04 50 33 44 11. Tickets €15-23, students €11.50-20.) Pick up festival schedules at the tourist office. There's a film festival the first weekend of June, but the biggest party is the **Fête du Lac,** with fireworks and water shows every first Saturday in August (€6-41.50).

AROUND LAC D'ANNECY

The smaller, more peaceful villages on the Lac d'Annecy, within 20km of Annecy, are accessible by bus and boat and make excellent daytrips. Voyages Crolard **buses** departing from the train station, stop in front of the tourist office, and near plage d'Albigny circle the lake. (☎04 50 45 08 12; www.voyages-crolard.com. 10 per day, Su less frequently. Tickets €2.70-3.10.) D909 also circles the lake, intersecting N508 at Doussard, the lake's southernmost point. Many of the attractions around the lake are poorly marked and not easily accessible with limited weekend bus schedules. The tourist office in Annecy can help avoid confusion.

The spectacular **Gorges du Fier** is a canyon etched by water erosion, 10km west of Annecy. The 256m long suspended walkway across the gorges yields spectacular views. (Info ☎04 50 46 23 07. Open mid-June to mid-Sept. daily 9am-7pm; mid-Mar. to mid-June and early Sept. to mid-Oct. 9am-noon and 2-6pm. €4.20.)The **Château de Montrottier,** 5min. from the canyon entrance, was formerly owned by the region's foremost art collectors and displays centuries-old Asian costumes, armor, and pottery. (☎04 50 46 23 02. Open June-Aug. daily 10am-1pm and 2-7pm; mid-Mar. to May and Sept. Su-M and W-Sa 10am-1pm and 2-6pm; early Oct.-June Su-M and W-Sa 2-6pm. €5.40, students €4.60.) To get there, take SIBRA **minibus** A from the train station to Poisy-Moiry (30min., 5 per day, €1) and walk away from the town center, following signs for **Lovagny** to the gorges. (40min., 3km.) The route is poorly marked at first: walkers should remember to head away from the town center and get directions from the bus driver or tourist office. For those who would rather avoid the walk, Voyages Crolard runs a **bus** tour that includes admission to the gorges and the château. (☎04 50 45 00 56. July-Aug. W 2pm, returns 7pm. €18.)

Talloires, 13km from Annecy, is a good starting point for the 1hr. hike to the impressive waterfalls at **La Cascade d'Angon** and to the beautiful gardens of the **Ermitage de St-Germain.** Take the Closettaz path out of the village, which is a right up the hill, around the corner from the bus stop and away from the beach, following the signs. The hike begins behind the Talloires Ecoles bus stop. At the trail's first division, about 40min. into the climb, make a sharp right through an old iron gate to skirt the side of the gorge and view the cascade with (perhaps) canyoners rappelling down its sides. Talloires has a lovely beach and several posh restaurants. (Talloires tourist office ☎04 50 60 70 64; fax 04 50 60 76 59.) Visitors can hop on the **omnibus** back to Annecy. It circumnavigates the lake, stopping at several towns 3 times per day. (Compagnie de Navigation: ☎04 50 51 08 40; www.annecy-crosieres.com. Taillores to Annecy €7.20). South of Annecy, **Doussard** is noteworthy for being Lac d'Annecy's source and for its surrounding nature preserves. (Tourist office ☎04 50 44 30 45; fax 04 50 44 81 75.) Nearby **St-Jorioz** is known for its great mountain views. (Tourist office ☎04 50 68 61 82; fax 04 50 68 96 11.)

A sumptuous 12th-century **château** across the lake from Annecy marks the birthplace of St-Bernard de Menthon, who made his name in the business of dog breeding. His ridiculously wealthy descendants still live in the castle, but the lower floors—including a walnut-paneled library, music salon, and 14th-century bedroom—are open to the public. (☎04 50 60 12 05. Open July-Aug. daily noon-6pm; May-June and Sept. F-Su 2-6pm. €5.50, weekend tours in period dress €6.)

The nearest **ski resort** is **La Clusaz,** 32km away, with 130km of trails and 56 lifts. Contact the **tourist office** in La Clusaz for info. (☎04 50 32 65 00; www.laclusaz.com.) The international youth hostel **La Grande Jeanne ❶,** outside La Clusaz on rte. du Col de la Croix Fry, has mostly quads with showers. (☎04 50 02 41 73; fax 04 50 02 65 85. Reception daily 8am-noon and 5-8pm. Open mid-Dec. to mid-Sept. Breakfast included. Mid-May to mid-Sept. dorms €15. Mid-Dec. to mid-May weekly stays only; *demi-pension* €289, full *pension* €329. MC/V.)

▶ DAYTRIP FROM ANNECY: ABBAYE D'HAUTECOMBE

Give or take a few counts, the entire House of Savoy is entombed in the Abbaye d'Hautecombe. The only part of this former Benedictine abbey open to visitors is its flamboyant Gothic **church,** the lavish result of eight centuries of necropolistic excess. Poor, exiled Umberto II, the last Savoy king, is the most recent occupant; he was stuffed inside in 1983 among 200 statues and 40 other tombs. One masterpiece is a marble statue of Marie Christine de Bourbon, who oversaw the church's restoration; the intricate sculpture, taken from a single block of stone, took eight years to make. A marble *pietà*, the church's prized possession, is given a proud place in the chapel to the left of the choir. (☎04 79 54 26 12; www.chemin-neuf.org/hautecombe. Open M and W-Sa 10-11:30am and 2-5pm, Su 10:30am-noon and 2-5pm. Entrance only with audio guide; English guide by request. Free.) The only way to get to the church is to take the train to Aix-les-Bains, and then the **boat** from Grand Port. (☎04 79 88 92 09; www.gwel.com. Round-trip 2½hr. Su-M and W-Sa July-Aug. 4 per day; Sept.-June 1-2 per day. €10.10.)

CHAMONIX

The train station is called "Chamonix-Mt. Blanc," for more than just a convenience: the city and the mountain are intimately connected. Chamonix (pop. 10,000) hosted the first Winter Olympics in 1924 and never extinguished the torch.

Whether they've come for the skiing, hiking, cycling, or rock-climbing, people in Chamonix eat, sleep, and dream mountains. Those who glance away from the snow-capped Mont Blanc, Europe's tallest peak, will notice a friendly town with authentic chalets, bustling pedestrian streets, and a bilingual population.

TRANSPORTATION

Trains: av. de la Gare (☎04 50 53 12 98). A special local train runs from **St-Gervais** to **Martigny**, stopping at Chamonix. Ticket sales daily 6:10am-8:10pm. Info kiosk July-Aug. daily 9:20am-noon and 1:15-6:18pm. **Luggage storage** €3 for 1st bag, €1.50 per additional bag. Open daily 6:30am-8:10pm. From St-Gervais to: **Annecy** (2½hr., 7 per day, €16.80); **Geneva** (2½hr., 7 per day, €20.80); **Grenoble** (4hr., 4 per day, €26.20); **Lyon** (4hr., 6 per day, €29.60); **Paris** (6-7hr., 9 per day, €50-70).

Buses: Société Alpes Transports, at the train station (☎04 50 53 01 15). Ticket office open July-Aug. M-Sa 7:45-8:15am, 9:30am-12:15pm, and 1:20-6:30pm; Su 8-8:30am, 9:30am-12:15pm, and 2-6:15pm. Call for office hours during other seasons. To: **Courmayeur**, Italy (50min.; July-Aug. 6 per day, Sept.-June M-Sa 2 per day; €9.50), and **Geneva**, Switzerland (1hr.; July-Aug. M-Sa 3 per day, Su 1 per day; Sept.-Nov. and May-June M-Sa 1 per day; Dec.-Apr. M-F 4 per day, Sa-Su 5 per day; €29 to town, €32 to airport). **Voyages Crolard** (☎04 50 45 08 12) runs to **Annecy** (2¼hr., M-F 1 per day, €15).

Public Transportation: Chamonix Bus (☎04 50 53 05 55) runs to ski slopes and hiking trails. Follow signs from pl. de l'Eglise to the main bus stop. Chamonix hotels and *gîtes* dispense the **Carte d'Hôte,** which gives free travel on all buses. Tickets €1.50.

Taxis: at the station (☎04 50 53 13 94). **Alp Taxi Rochaix** (☎04 50 54 00 48). 24hr. About €12 to the Auberge de Jeunesse.

ORIENTATION & PRACTICAL INFORMATION

The center of town is the intersection of av. Michel Croz, rue du Docteur Paccard, and rue Joseph Vallot, each named for a past conqueror of Mont Blanc's summit. South of the **Arve** river is the train station. Most everything else, including the tourist office, is on the other bank (closer to the slopes); from the station, follow av. Michel Croz through town, turn left onto rue du Dr. Paccard, and take the first right to the pl. de l'Eglise. (5min.)

Tourist Office: 85 pl. du Triangle de l'Amitié (☎04 50 53 00 24; www.chamonix.com). English-speaking staff has lists of hotels and dorms, campgrounds map, hiking map *Carte des Sentiers d'Eté* (€4), *Chamonix Magazine* (free), info on cable cars, and weather conditions. **Internet** with a *télécarte.* Open daily July-Sept. and mid-Dec to Apr. 8:30am-12:30pm and 2-7pm; May-June, Oct. and Nov. to mid-Dec. 9am-12:30pm and 2-6pm. **Centrale de Reservation** (☎04 59 53 23 33; reservation@chamonix.com) books apartments or hotels for stays of 2 nights or more.

Currency Exchange: Comptoir de Change, 21 pl. Balmat (☎04 50 55 88 40), has the most competitive rates. 24hr. **exchange** machine. Also changes American Express traveler's checks for €4.90 commission and sells cheap **film.** Open daily 8am-8pm.

Laundromat: Cham'Laverie, 98 via d'Aoste, located just off of av. de l'Aiguille du Midi, does your laundry for you at €9 per load (detergent not included). Open M-Sa 9am-noon and 3-6pm. Also available to do laundry in Chamonix is **Laverie Automatique,** 65 av. du Mont Blanc, in the Galerie Commerciale Alpina. Wash, dry, and detergent €8. Open M-Sa 8:30am-7pm, Su 10am-5pm.

Hospital: Centre Hospitalier, 509 rte. des Pèlerins (☎04 50 53 84 00). **Ambulance:** (☎04 50 53 84 00); night doctor (☎04 50 53 48 48).

RHÔNE-ALPS

Police: 48 rue de l'Hôtel de Ville (☎04 50 55 99 58).

Internet: Plenty of downtown bars have web access. The best deal is **Cybar,** 80 rue des Moulins (☎04 50 53 69 70). €1 per 10min. Open daily June-Nov. 11am-1:30am; Dec.-May 10am-1:30am. **I-Guest** (☎04 50 55 98 58), in the Galerie Blanc Neige, off rue du Dr. Paccard, charges €7.50 per hr., €20.50 for 3½hr., using a divisible card. Open daily 10am-1pm and 4-8pm. MC/V.

Post Office: pl. Jacques-Balmat (☎04 50 53 15 90), below the tourist office. Open M-F 8:30am-noon and 2-6pm, Sa 8:30am-noon. **Postal code:** 74400.

SKIING, BIKING, & HIKING RESOURCES
Hiking Information:

Office de Haute-Montagne (☎04 50 53 22 08; www.ohm-chamonix.com), on the 3rd floor of the Maison de la Montagne, across from the tourist office. An expert staff helps plan your adventures, gives info on weather conditions, and sells detailed maps (€4-9). Open July-Aug. daily 9am-noon and 3-6pm; closed Su Sept.-June and Sa Oct.-Nov.

Club Alpin Français, 136 av. Michel Croz (☎04 50 53 16 03; infos@clubalpin-chamonix.com). Best source of info on mountain *refuges* and road conditions. Guides available: register 6-7:30pm the day before hikes. Bulletin board matches drivers, riders, and hiking partners. Hikers from far and wide convene in the office to plan the weekend's trips and excursions (F 7pm). **Members only;** email to inquire about membership. Open July-Aug. M-Sa 9:30am-noon and 3:30-7:30pm, closed W morning; Sept.-June M-Tu and Th-F 3:30-7pm, Sa 9am-noon.

Skiing and Hiking Lessons and Info: Ecole du Ski (☎04 50 53 22 57), on the 2nd floor of the Maison de la Montagne. Half-day group lessons €42; 2hr. private lesson €95; guided group descent of Vallée Blanche €58. Open Dec.-Apr. daily 8:15am-7pm. On the main floor, the **Compagnie des Guides** (☎04 50 53 00 88; www.cieguides-chamonix.com) gives skiing and climbing lessons and leads guided summer hikes and winter ski trips. Group ski excursions €56 per person. Register 5:30pm the evening before. Open Jan.-Mar. and July-Aug. daily 8:30am-noon and 3:30-7:30pm; Sept.-Dec. and Apr.-June Tu-Sa 10am-noon and 5-7pm.

Cycling Information: Pick up the free, invaluable map and guide, *Itinéraires Autorisés aux Vélos Tout Terrain,* at the tourist office or at mountain bike rental shops.

Weather Conditions: at Maison de la Montagne, Club Alpin Français, and the tourist office. Call ☎08 92 68 02 74 for a French recording of road and weather conditions.

Mountain Rescue: PGHM Secours en Montagne, 69 rte. de la Mollard (☎04 50 53 16 89). 24hr. emergency service.

Hiking Equipment: Sanglard Sports, 31 rue Michel Croz (☎04 50 53 24 70). Boots €7-8 per day, €43-50 per week. Open daily July-Aug. 9am-7:30pm; Sept.-June 9am-12:30pm and 2:30-7:30pm. Closed early to mid-Oct. AmEx/MC/V.

Bike and Ski Rental: Dozens of places rent skis, snowboards, bikes, and climbing equipment. Skis should not be more than €8-16 per day or €40-65 per week, depending on quality. Snowboards should not exceed €16 per day and €80 per week.

▮ ACCOMMODATIONS & CAMPING

Chamonix's hotels are expensive, but the *gîtes* and dormitories are quite cheap. All are packed in the winter and summer; reserve up to six weeks in advance. For a truly unforgettable experience, stay at the ▮**Red Mountain Lodge** (see **The Hidden Deal**). The hardest time to get a room is early February, when the city hosts a car race. Call the tourist office for available places; the accommodations listed by *Let's Go* fill up fast.

The area's far-flung mountain *refuges* tend to be remote, with few facilities, and are frequently unattended. For info on these mountain *refuges*, see the **Outdoors** section of Chamonix (p. 474).

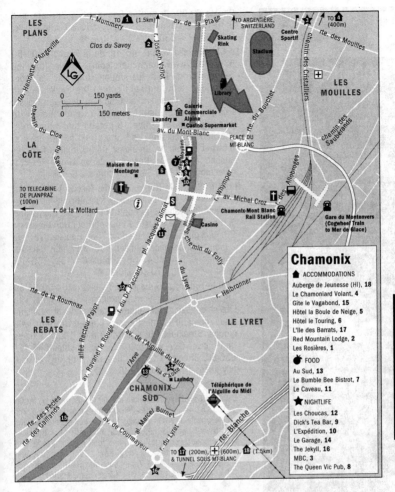

RHÔNE-ALPS

Chamonix

▲ ACCOMMODATIONS

Auberge de Jeunesse (HI), **18**
Le Chamoniard Volant, **4**
Gite le Vagabond, **15**
Hôtel la Boule de Neige, **5**
Hôtel le Touring, **6**
L'Ile des Barrats, **17**
Red Mountain Lodge, **2**
Les Rosières, **1**

🍴 FOOD

Au Sud, **13**
Le Bumble Bee Bistrot, **7**
Le Caveau, **11**

★ NIGHTLIFE

Les Choucas, **12**
Dick's Tea Bar, **9**
L'Expédition, **10**
Le Garage, **14**
The Jekyll, **16**
MBC, **3**
The Queen Vic Pub, **8**

Gite le Vagabond, 365 av. Ravanel le Rouge (☎04 50 53 15 43; gitevagabond@hot-mail.com). Friendly *gite* near the center of town. Cozy bunkrooms encourage bonding between backpackers. Popular bar, **Internet** (€0.15 per min.), and climbing wall. Breakfast €5. Dinner €10.50. Kitchen. Luggage storage. Laundry €7.70. Reception 8-10:30am. 4- to 8-bunk dorms €12.50. Credit card deposit. MC/V. ❶

Auberge de Jeunesse (HI), 127 montée Jacques Balmat (☎04 50 53 14 52; www.aj-chamonix.fr.st), in Les Pélerins, at the foot of the Glacier de Bossons. Take the bus from the train station or pl. Mont Blanc (dir: Pélerins) to Pélerins Ecole (€1.50), and follow the signs uphill to the hostel. On the special train, get off at Les Pélerins and follow the signs. By foot, walk down rte. des Pélerins. (30min.) A beautiful modern chalet practically on top of a glacier, but a bit removed and impersonal. Many groups fill 2- to 6-person bunks in a separate building. Reductions on practically everything in town. All-inclusive winter ski packages €389-481 per week. Breakfast included. Dinner €8.

THE HIDDEN DEAL

RED MOUNTAIN LODGE

The **Red Mountain Lodge ❷** is achieving legendary status among backpackers in the French Alps. The lodge was born when its snow-boarding Aussie owner figured he'd turn his spacious chalet into a backpacker's haven. Guests, cozy in the plush couches on the ground floor, joke that it's the "Hotel California" because "you can check out any time you like, but you can never leave." It's a normal occurrence for two-night stays to become two weeks, or for travelers to meet at the lodge and then continue on together.

Gites and dorms abound in the Chamonix mountains, but the Red Mountain Lodge actually feels a lot like home. Students, climbers, and couples introduce themselves over a breakfast of müesli and yogurt, regale each other with tales of mountains conquered, or sit on the lawn at twice-weekly barbecues (€10 including beer and wine), listening to guitars.

The camaraderie is facilitated by staff who point out hikes from the balcony, and by groups who head off together to pubs at night. Next summer, they're planning to add a pool. For all this luxury, the price remains one of the most competitive in town: €16 for dorm rooms including breakfast, and €20-30 per person for private rooms.

(435 rue Joseph Vallot. From the station, walk down av. Michel Croz and take a right onto rue Joseph Vallot. ☎04 50 53 94 97; www.redmountainlodge.co.uk.)

Sheets €2.90. Reception 8am-noon, 5-7:30pm, and 8:30-10pm. Dorms €13; singles €15.30, with shower €16; doubles €30.60/€32. MC/V. ❶

Le Chamoniard Volant, 45 rte. de la Frasse (☎04 50 53 14 09; www.chamoniard.com), 15min. from the center of town. From the station, turn right, go under the bridge, and turn right across the tracks, left on chemin des Cristalliers, and right on rte. de la Frasse. This *gite* has a rustic, camplike atmosphere with wooden walls, massive 18-person bunkroom, red-checked tablecloths, and lots of ski paraphernalia. **Internet** €9 per hr. Breakfast €4.30, dinner €10.20. Kitchen. Sheets €4. Reception 10am-10pm. Reservations required. 4- to 8-person dorms €12. ❶

Hôtel la Boule de Neige, 362 rue Joseph Vallot (☎04 50 53 04 48; laboule@claranet.fr). Cute, ski-instructor-run alpine chalet with small but spotless rooms and firm beds, above a bar in a busy part of town. Breakfast €6. Reception 7am-noon and 5-7pm. Dec.-Feb. reserve 2 months in advance. Singles €35, with bath €40-50; doubles €35-40/€45-55; triples €45-51/€55-65; quads with bath €70-80. MC/V. ❸

Hôtel le Touring, 95 rue Joseph Vallot (☎04 50 53 59 18; www.hoteltouring-chamonix.com). Large hotel with English-speaking staff, charming alpine décor, and spacious rooms. It's almost always packed Dec.-Apr. with groups. Breakfast €6. Reception 8am-10pm. Singles with shower €37, with bath €56-60; doubles €44-47/€56-60; 3rd bed €10, 4th bed €6. Late Aug. to mid-July prices €10-15 lower. MC/V. ❹

Campsites:

L'Ile des Barrats, 185 chemin de l'Ile des Barrats (☎/fax 04 50 53 51 44), off rte. des Pèlerins, has great views and amiable crowds. Friendly manager keeps a well-maintained site. With your back to the cable car, turn left, pass the busy roundabout, continue 5min., and look right. Luggage storage. Reception daily July-Aug. 8am-10pm; May-June and Sept. 9am-noon and 4-7pm. Open May-Sept. Laundry €5. €5 per person, €4.60 per tent, €2 per car. Electricity €2.80. ❶

Les Rosières, 121 clos des Rosières (☎04 50 53 10 42; www.campinglesrosieres.com), off rte. de Praz, is close to Chamonix Sud and often has room. Small sites among chalets with stunning views. Follow rue Vallot for 1½km or take a bus to Les Nants. Reception daily July-Aug. 8am-9pm; Sept.-June 9am-noon and 2-7pm. Open early Feb. to mid-Oct. €4.70-5.50 per person, €2.20-2.50 per tent, €2.10-3 per car. Electricity €2.70-3. ❶

🍴 FOOD

Tourist-driven Chamonix produces better restaurants than you might expect. Bars and ski lodges serve good meals as well. Regional fare like fondue and *raclette* shares menu space with international ski staples. There is a **Super U,** 117 rue Joseph Vallot (☎04 50 53 12 50; open M-Sa 8:15am-7:30pm, Su 8:30am-noon), and a **Casino** supermarket at 17 av. du Mont Blanc, inside the Galerie Commerciale Alpina. (☎04 50 53 11 85. Open M-Sa 8:30am-7:30pm; July-Aug. also Su 8:30am-12:30pm.) A morning **market** is held on pl. du Mont Blanc. (Sa 7:30am-1pm.)

RESTAURANTS

▨ **Le Bumble Bee Bistrot,** 65 rue des Moulins (☎04 50 53 50 03), has a creative *tapas*-style menu featuring such diverse dishes as falafel, tandoori chicken, steak, ale pie, and marsala duck (€2–8.50). There's a good selection of vegetarian options and delicious desserts. Light-yellow walls and soft tunes keep patrons mellow. Open Dec. to mid-May daily 6:30pm-2am; June-Oct. M-Sa noon-3pm and 6:30pm-2am. MC/V. ❸

▨ **Au Sud,** 67 prom. Marie Paradis (☎04 50 53 42 97), offers a mix of regional specialties and traditional cuisine under a ceiling of hanging baskets. Try the excellent *entrecôte au poivre* (€12) or the *menu* (€14.50), which includes salad and *jambon cru, fondue savoyard,* and sorbet or *dessert du jour.* Thursday nights, have *couscous royal* (€13.50). Open June-Sept. and mid-Dec. to Mar. daily noon-2pm and 6pm-midnight; Apr.-May and Oct. to mid-Nov. Su-M and W-Sa noon-2pm and 6pm-midnight. ❸

Le Caveau, 13 rue du Dr. Paccard (☎04 50 55 86 18). This 300-year-old former wine and cheese cellar serves brick-oven pizzas (€6.70-12.50), vegetarian options (€8.50-9.50), and Swedish specialties (€11-12) like meatballs, courtesy of the Swedish owner. It claims to have the world's best garlic bread. Open Dec. to mid-June and mid-July to Sept. daily 6:30pm-2am; Oct.-Nov. Su-M and W-Sa 6:30pm-2am. MC/V. ❷

RESTAURANT/BARS

▨ **The Jekyll,** 71 rte. des Pèlerins (☎04 50 55 99 70). In an old stone barn, this popular Irish pub serves huge portions of hearty, traditional Irish and international food, like couscous, with live music on many weekend nights. Entrées €5.20-8. Open daily Dec.-Apr. 4pm-2am; July-Oct. M-Sa 6pm-2am; July-Aug. closed Su. MC/V. ❷

MBC Micro Brasserie de Chamonix, 350 rte. du Bouchet (☎04 50 53 61 59). A 10min. walk from the center of town, just across from the Centre Sportif. Anglo and French locals rave about this mellow, untouristy micro-brewery with three ales and lots of food. Lounge on couches beneath Christmas lighting, large windows, and sleds on the walls. *Plats* €6.50-10, pints €4.50, pitchers €12. Open daily 4pm-2am. ❷

◢ NIGHTLIFE

Chamonix's nightclubs and pubs are popular in the winter when people shake what's left of their ski-weary bodies after the bars shut down. Pubs are open year-round, although they can be painfully empty during the summer. Locals offer great tips on where to drink, but even the uninitiated won't have to crawl far between drinks on bar-filled **rue des Moulins.**

▨ **L'Expédition,** 26 rue des Moulins (☎04 50 53 57 68). A chic crowd of ski instructors, *hôteliers,* and guides schmooze in this mainstay's small, intimate interior. Dec.-Apr. Tu and Th theme nights, including comedy, graffiti, and gangsta. Draft beer €5.50. Cocktails €4.20-7.80. Open daily June-Oct. 5:30pm-4am; Nov.-May 4pm-4am. Closed some Su nights in the low season.

▨ **The Queen Vic Pub,** 74 rue des Moulins (☎04 50 53 91 98). Energetic English pub draws a young, mixed, easygoing crowd. Pool tables and loud music in an elegant 2-floor chalet. Happy hour 6-9pm. Beer €2.50. Open daily 6pm-2am.

Les Choucas, 206 rue du Dr. Paccard (☎04 50 53 03 23). Alpine swank in a revamped chalet. Cow-skin lounges and giant TV screen showing extreme skiing. Beer €3.40

THE BIG SPLURGE

L'AIGUILLE DU MIDI

With a touch of pride, Chamonix residents boast that more people ascend the *Aiguille du Midi* (Needle of the South) cable car than do the Eiffel Tower. Those with acrophobia (fear of heights) or argentophobia (fear of expenditure) might be tempted to avoid the 20min., €33.80 ride over towering forests and snowy peaks, but few who make the journey are disappointed. As the summit of Mt. Blanc gets closer and closer, the *oohs* and *aahs* from large groups of tourists begin to mount.

Peak-worshippers should head out early, as clouds and crowds gather by mid-morning. The first stop, **Plan de l'Aiguille** (€12, round-trip €14), is a starting point for hikes (see **Hiking,** p. 476), but is otherwise not worthwhile. For the best views, as well as a look at ice-climbers, summer skiers, and other hardcore adventurers, continue to **l'Aiguille du Midi,** which is nearly twice as high as the first stop. At the Aiguille, the panorama is breathtaking, as is the head-lightening 3842m high air. Warm clothes are essential for the trip. A touch of wooziness might set in; take it slow up the stairs to the *terrasse.* For an additional €3, an elevator will take you right to the summit, where there's a glorious 360° view. Take some once-in-a-lifetime pictures and forget about your newly emptied wallet; after all, things are supposed to be lighter at this altitude!

before 10pm. Cocktails €7-10.50, including "Multiple Orgasm up Against the Wall." Open Dec.-Sept. daily 4pm-4am; Oct.-Nov. Th-Sa only. **Closed in 2003.**

Dick's Tea Bar, 80 rue des Moulins (☎04 50 53 19 10), is the flagship of this bar-saturated street. London DJs keep the dance floor thumping at this hotspot, one of three Dick's in the Alps. Shots €3-6. Dec.-Apr. cover €11, includes one drink. Open Dec.-Apr. daily 10pm-4am; July-Aug. open biweekly: call for details.

Le Garage, 200 av. de l'Aiguille (☎04 50 53 64 49), is generally considered the best Chamonix disco. Caters to anglos and Scandinavians. Stainless steel, neon-blue lights and lots of booze. Party doesn't start until 1am. No cover, but one drink required (€3.50-10). Open Dec.-Apr. daily 10pm-4am; July-Aug. daily 11pm-4am; May-June and Sept.-Nov. Th-Sa 10pm-4am.

⬛ OUTDOORS

Whether you've come to climb mountains or ski down them, expect a challenge in this area. Steep grades, potential avalanches, and unique terrain make this entire region ill-suited for beginners to the world of ice.

TÉLÉPHERIQUES. Hikers and skiers will probably need to take a *téléphérique* (cable car) during their stay in Chamonix, and others will probably want to take the ride just for the views. A board on pl. de l'Eglise lists the lifts that are currently open. Those who desire a spectacular trip should consider taking the **Aiguille du Midi** (see **The Big Splurge**).

High-altitude escapades don't end with a view of Europe's tallest peak; from the Aiguille du Midi summit, hikers continue to **Helbronner,** where they can straddle the French-Italian border (May-Sept. only; round-trip €18) and eat a picnic lunch on the Glacier Géant. The slightly rickety four-person gondolas run into the glacial heart of the Alps and provide views of the **Matterhorn** and **Mont Blanc.** From Helbronner, a final *téléphérique* descends into Italy to **La Palud,** near the resort town of **Courmayeur.** Bring a passport and cash—the Italian side doesn't accept credit cards for the cable car. Check at the tourist office that the entire *téléphérique* route is in operation before setting out for this trip. (*Téléphérique* open daily Sept.-June 8am-3:45 or 4:45pm; July-Aug. 6am-5:40pm.)

Several *téléphériques* run year-round to the opposite side of the valley (away from Mt. Blanc), which is known for popular hiking trails and panoramic restaurants. Cars on **Le Brévent** (2525m) leave from the corner of rte. Henriette and La Mollard, up the street from the tourist office. (☎04 50 53 13 18. Open daily

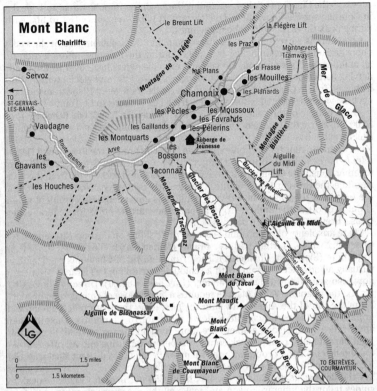

Mont Blanc

------- Chairlifts

le Breunt Lift

la Flégère Lift

Montagne de la Flégère

les Praz

les Plans

la Frasse

les Mouilles

Servoz

TO ST-GERVAIS-LES-BAINS

Montnevers Tramway

Mer de Glace

Chamonix

les Planards

les Pècles

les Moussoux

les Favrards

Vaudagne

les Gaillands

les Pélerins

Montagne de Blaitière

Route Blanche

les Montquarts

Arve

les Bossons

Auberge de Jeunesse

Aiguille du Midi Lift

les Chavants

Taconnaz

Glacier des Pélerins

les Houches

Glacier des Bossons

L'Aiguille du Midi

Montagne de Taconnaz

Tunnel sous Mont Blanc

Mont Blanc du Tacul

Dôme du Goûter

Mont Maudit

Aiguille de Bionnassay

Mont Blanc

Glacier de la Brenva

Mont Blanc de Courmayeur

TO ENTRÈVES, COURMAYEUR

N

0   1.5 miles

0   1.5 kilometers

July-Aug. 8am-6pm; Sept.-June 9am-5pm. One-way €12, round-trip €15.) Another great option is **La Flégère,** 2km east of the city in Les Praz, on rue Joseph Vallot. The car stops at an eponymous plateau on the way to **l'Index** (2595m), a starting point for most ice climbs in the area. (☎ 04 50 53 18 58. One-way €12, round-trip €15. Open July-Aug. daily 7:40am-5:50pm; June and Sept. daily 8:40am-4:50pm.)

A special train (not a *téléphérique*) runs up to the **Mer de Glace,** France's largest glacier (97km long). The train departs from a small station next to the main one. (☎ 04 50 53 12 54. Daily July-Aug. every 20min. 8am-6pm; May-June and early to mid-Sept. every 30min. 8:30am-5pm; mid-Sept. to Apr. every hr. 10am-4pm. €10, round-trip €13.) From the Mer, a cable car runs to an **ice cave** that is carved afresh every year—the glacier slides 30m per year, so last year's cave is farther down the wall of ice (car descent €2.10, cave admittance €3). Consider riding the train to the Mer and taking the downhill hike back. Just as you get out of breath on the way down, the **Luge d'Eté,** a concrete chute, will whisk you to the bottom. (☎ 04 50 53 08 97. Open July-Aug. daily 10am-7:30pm, also M and Th 8:30-10:30pm; Sept. and June daily 1:30-5:30pm; Oct.-Nov. Sa-Su 1:30-6pm. €5.)

SKIING. Those aiming to ski for only a few days should buy daily lift tickets at the different ski areas—one area is more than enough for each day. If your trip plans extend to a week, buy a **Cham'Ski** pass, available at the tourist office or major *téléphériques* (Brévent, Flégère, Aiguille du Midi). The ticket gives unlimited access to the Chamonix Valley, excluding the small Les Houches area, and one day in Courmayeur-Val-Veny, Italy (€171; passport photo required). Get to lifts early during peak times to avoid unbearable lines.

Chamonix is surrounded by skiable mountains. The **southern side** of the valley opposite Mont Blanc, drenched in sunlight during the morning, offers terrain for all abilities. In the afternoon, the sun and extreme skiers head over to the death-defying **north face**, which has mostly advanced, off-*piste*, and glacial terrain. Public buses (free to Cham'Ski holders) and the trains of the Mont Blanc tramway connect the valley's string of resort villages, from Les Bossons to Le Tour.

At the bottom of the valley, near the Swiss border, **Le Tour-Col de Balme** (☎04 50 54 00 58), above the village of **Le Tour,** is the first of Chamonix's ski areas. Its sunny trails are the most suitable for beginning to intermediate skiers (day pass €24.60). More dramatic runs for the non-expert can be found around the **Brévent** and **Flégère** *téléphériques* closer to town. Connected by a cable car, Brévent and Flégère together constitute Chamonix's largest ski area; located a few steps from the tourist office, the Brévent *téléphérique* is particularly convenient. Note, however, that the terrain at the top of the Brévent gondola is advanced; less confident skiers should get off at the middle stop **Planpraz,** the starting point for several easier trails. (Brévent and Flégère day pass €26.)

There are plenty of opportunities for off-*piste* skiing on the opposite side of the Chamonix valley, starting with **Les Grands Montets** (☎04 50 54 00 71; 3275m), in Argentière (8km from Chamonix). The *grande dame* of Chamonix's ski spots is virtually all advanced terrain. With a remodeled half-pipe, Les Grands Montets is now also geared toward **snowboarding.** (Day pass €31.80). Directly above Chamonix, the infamous **Vallée Blanche** requires a hearty dose of courage and insanity. From the top of the Aiguille du Midi *téléphérique*, the ungroomed, unmarked, unpatrolled 20km trail cascades down a glacier to Chamonix. Despite their appearance from below, glaciers are more icefield than snowfield. Stay within sight of trail markers and check conditions before venturing out. All off-*piste* skiers should check their route with the **ski patrol** or the **Office de Haut Montagne.** Skiing with a guide who knows the terrain is highly recommended. Never ski alone. Try the **Compagnie des Guides.** (p. 470; from €55 per person.) English-speaking guides tailor the itinerary to you and make all the necessary arrangements, from equipment rental to lift reservations. Otherwise, you'll need to reserve a spot on the *téléphérique* in high season (☎08 92 68 00 67). Those who don't want to ski on a glacier can ski beside one at the **Glacier du Mont Blanc** in Les Bossons, even at night. (☎04 50 53 12 39. Day pass €14. Night skiing W-F; €10.)

HIKING. Chamonix has 350km of hiking trails, marked by signs, in terrain ranging from forests to glaciers. A map, available at the tourist office, lists all the mountain *refuges* and gives departure points and estimated lengths for all the trails (€4). Climbers should buy the **IGN topographic map** (p. 470), available at the **Office de Haute Montagne** and local bookstores (€9).

The following are several recommendations for intermediate, half-day hikes that have the best views for the effort and are easily accessible from Chamonix. Grades are steep, but using cable cars for either the trip up or back saves time and energy. Those with bad knees should avoid prolonged downhill walks. Most hikes can be extended by avoiding the cable cars. Walkers who would rather just look at the mountains can meander the trail that follows the Arve River through the valley. It begins by the river next to the sports center.

Chalet Floria is the perfect introduction to the mountains surrounding Chamonix. Turning left on rue Mummery, follow the signs to an uphill track that eventually becomes a narrow uphill trail. The walk is 45-50min. to an adorable restaurant with red umbrellas, hundreds of colorful flowers planted by the owners, and views of Mt. Blanc. The botanical owners allow picnics with the purchase of a drink (€3), but the price is really for the gorgeous setting. (1½-2hr. round-trip.) Another, far steeper, hour and a half leads to the top of Flégère and the cable car down.

Two intermediate hikes lead to **Mer de Glace.** The **Grand Balcon Nord,** on the opposite side of the valley at a higher altitude, passes by jagged ice cascades and peaks. Take the Aiguille du Midi cable car to the first stop, Plan de l'Aiguille, and descend to the Refuge du Plan de l'Aiguille. (☎06 65 64 27 53. Open mid-June to mid-Sept. Breakfast and dinner €19. Rooms €10.) Keep to the trail that heads horizontally to the right, and after 2½ unforgettable hours, hit the **Hôtel Montenvers** at the foot of the Mer de Glace glacier. Mountaineers use the *refuge* as a base for ice climbing. (☎04 50 53 87 70. Breakfast and dinner included. Open mid-June to mid-Sept. €35.) The less pricey trip begins from the valley, 900m up from the Montenvers train station, marked by signs. It ascends to the Mer at a moderate-to-steep grade for 2½hr. The train can whisk tired hikers back to Chamonix.

On the south side of the valley, the **Grand Balcon Sud** is a picturesque, wildflower-studded trail linking the Brévent and Flégère *téléphériques.* From the Flégère cable car station, descend slightly to the path that heads right toward a chimney. After 2hr., the trail meets the Planpraz cable car station (2000m; the middle station of Brévent), where you can hike or ride back to town or embark on a difficult, scenic ascent to the **Col de Brévent** (2368m), the top of the Brévent lift. (1¾hr.) From the top of the Flégère cable car station and the Flégère *refuge,* follow the signs on a breathless 1¾hr. ascent to **Lac Blanc,** a turquoise alpine lake that stays frozen through June. Hikers can picnic, sun themselves on rocks, and watch ice climbers descend a steep bowl. Those with spending money can sit at tables in the restaurant at **Refuge du Lac Blanc,** which offers rooms with breakfast and dinner for €44.50. (☎04 50 53 49 14. Reservations required.)

Experienced mountain climbers, of course, come to Chamonix to ascend **Mont Blanc** (4810m), a two- or three-day climb. Don't try it solo. Climbers can be caught by vicious blizzards, even in August. The Maison de la Montagne, the Compagnie des Guides, and the Club Alpin Français all have info on this most classic of alpine climbs (see **Skiing, Biking, and Hiking Resources**).

VAL D'ISÈRE

Although less accessible than other ski towns in the Alps, Val d'Isère (pop. 1750) attracts people from all over the world for hiking, skiing that lasts until August on the Glaciers du Pissailles, and other outdoor pursuits. This world-class ski resort's main occupation is worshipping the mountains, snow, and native son Jean-Claude Killy, who won gold in every single men's downhill event in the 1968 Grenoble Winter Olympics. Killy brought Olympic events to Val d'Isère in 1992 and helped turn its main street into a tourist-laden strip of expensive hotels, restaurants, and ski boutiques.

During the summer, snow and prices melt, and bikers and climbers fill the few open hotels. The town officially "opens" in late June and then again in early December, and can be eerily quiet during the low season. Mid-December is a particularly crazy time, when the Criterium de la Première Neige, one of the first international competitions of the season, comes to Val.

☞ TRANSPORTATION

Trains: pl. de la Gare in Bourg St-Maurice. Open daily 5am-10:30pm. To: **Annecy** (3hr., 6 per day, €21.30); **Grenoble** (3hr., 6 per day, €19.80); **Lyon** (3-4hr., 10 per day, €25.70). **Luggage storage** €4.50 per item. Available July-Aug. and mid-Dec. to Apr. daily 10am-6pm; after-hours inquire at ticket window.

Buses: Autocars Martin (☎04 79 06 00 42), at the bus station by the roundabout 150m down the main drag from the tourist office. Open July-Aug. M-Tu and Th-F 10-11am and 1:45-8:15pm, Sa 7-10am and 1:15-7:30pm; Dec.-Apr. M-F 9-11:30am and 1:30-7:45pm, Sa 6:30am-8:30pm, Su 7:30-11:30am and 1:30-7:45pm. **Main office** at pl. de la Gare in Bourg St-Maurice (☎04 79 07 04 49). Open daily 8am-noon and 2-6pm. Dec.-Apr. buses to **Geneva,** Switzerland (4-4½hr.; M-Th 3 per day, F-Su 4 per day; €48) via **Annecy** (3½hr., €40.40); and **Lyon airport** (4hr.; M-F 2 per day, Sa-Su 3 per day; €50.30). Also, upon request, to the hostel in **Les Boisses** (15min.; early Dec. to early May M-F 4 per day, Sa 1 per day, Su 2 per day; early May to early Dec. M-F and Su 3 per day, Sa 4 per day; €2.80). **SNCF** info and reservation desks (☎04 79 06 03 55) are in the same building. Open July-Aug. Tu-Sa 9am-noon and 2-6pm; Dec.-Apr. M-Sa 9am-noon and 3-6:30pm.

Public Transportation: Val d'Isère runs **free shuttles** *(navettes)* around town. **Train Rouge** runs between La Daille and Le Fornet (Dec.-Apr. every 5-30min. 8:30am–2am), while **Train Vert** runs from the tourist office and the bus station up to the Manchet Sports complex and the entrance to the Vanoise national park (July-Aug. only). Both shave time off trips to the *refuges.*

Taxis: ABC ☎04 79 06 19 92; **Altitude Espace Taxi** ☎04 79 41 14 15. €46-68 to the train station in Bourg St-Maurice. €15 from Val to the hostel.

Bike and Ski Rental: About 30 locations in town offer rental; ask at the tourist office.

◼ 🛈 ORIENTATION & PRACTICAL INFORMATION

Val d'Isère has no train station. The nearest one is in **Bourg-St-Maurice,** 30km to the north; a bus leaves there for Val d'Isère (Su-F 3 per day, Sa 8 per day; Apr.-Nov. last bus 6:35pm; Dec.-Mar. extended hours; €10.50). To get to the hostel, get off at **Tignes-Les-Boisses,** 7km from Val d'Isère (€9.40). The Val d'Isère mega-resort comprises three villages in a line: **Le Fornet** at the top, **La Daille** below at the valley's entrance, and **Val Village** in the middle, home to most accommodations and the **tourist office.** Unless otherwise stated, listings below are in Val Village, the most substantial of the three towns. Although street names are neither used nor clearly indicated, the town is navigable with the tourist office's *Practical Guide* map.

Tourist Office: (☎04 79 06 06 60; www.valdisere.com), in Val Village. From the bus station, it's a 5min. walk along the main road toward Le Fornet. The office is on the left at the roundabout. Distributes practical guides in six languages that detail prices and schedules and suggests where to hike and ski. Open May-June and Sept.-Nov. daily 9am-noon and 2-6pm; July-Aug. daily 8:30am-7:30pm; Dec.-Apr. Su-F 8:30am-7:30pm, Sa 8:30am-8pm. **Annex** (☎04 79 06 19 67) at the town entrance; it's a small wooden hut to the right on the way up from La Daille. Open July-Aug. daily 9am-noon and 3-6pm; Dec.-Apr. Sa-Su 9am-noon and 2-7pm.

Laundromat: Laverie Automatique, just above the Casino supermarket, on the way up the roundabout. Open daily 8am-9:30pm. **Laverie Linge** (☎06 11 84 29 33), on the right about 300m down from the bus station. Wash and dry €8 at both.

Weather, Ski, and Road Info: Call the tourist office or listen to French-language **Radio Val** (96.1FM; ☎04 79 06 18 66). **Weather forecast:** ☎08 36 68 02 73. **Ski Lifts:** ☎04 79 06 00 35. **Ski Patrol:** ☎04 79 06 02 10.

Police: (☎04 79 06 03 41), above the tourist office, across from Casino supermarket.

Hospital: (☎04 79 41 79 79), in Bourg St-Maurice.

Internet: Lodge Bar (☎04 79 06 19 31). Turn right at roundabout above the bus station. €3 for 15min., €5.50 for 30min., €9 per hr. Open mid-Nov. to Apr. daily 4:30pm-1:30am; July-Aug. 6pm-1:30am. Also **Dick's Tea Bar** (see **Entertainment**).

Post Office: (☎04 79 06 06 99), across from the tourist office in Vieux Val. **Currency exchange** with good rates. Open July-Aug. M-F 9am-noon and 1:30-4:30pm, Sa 8:30-11:30am; Dec.-Apr. M-F 8:30am-noon and 2-6pm, Sa 8:30am-noon; Sept.-Nov. and May-June M-F 10am-noon and 1:30-3:30pm, Sa 9:30-11am. **Postal code:** 73150.

ACCOMMODATIONS & CAMPING

World-class slopes feet away make it tough to find a room in winter. An inexpensive option for groups during non-peak times is to rent an apartment or "tourist residence" in one of the many chalets in town. **Val Location** at the tourist office does the booking (www.vallocation.com). The hotels that remain open in the low season maintain very reasonable prices. The cheapest beds are at the *refuges*, **Le Prariond** and **Le Fond Des Fours**, each at least a 2hr. hike from downtown (see **Hiking**). Cheaper **gîtes** in Le Fornet offer an alternative to downtown hotels; the tourist office has a complete list. During the ski season, **Moris Pub**, 75m up from the tourist office, rents bright rooms upstairs for super-cheap prices. (☎04 79 06 22 11. Breakfast included. €22.90 per person. MC/V.)

Auberge de Jeunesse "Les Clarines" (HI) (☎04 79 06 35 07; reservations 04 79 41 01 93; tignes@fuaj.org), in the village of **Les Boisses.** To walk from Val d'Isère, a pleasant, well-marked trail begins at La Daille. Follow the river down to the lake and bear left along the shore: ford the cascading creek. Turn right, cross the bridge, and take the small, unmarked path ascending to the right until it meets the road. To the right is Les Boisses and the hostel. (1½hr.) Call ahead to see if the trail is open. Or take the Tignes/Val Claret bus to Les Boisses from Bourg-St-Maurice (€9.40) or Val d'Isère (€2.80). A free shuttle runs between Tignes and Les Boisses (Apr.-Nov. 4 per day; Dec.-Mar. more). Wooden rooms for 4-6 people off of bright orange hallways, all but 3 with toilets. Friendly staff. Safe atmosphere overlooking the Lac du Chevril. Discounts on rentals. **Skiing, hiking, biking,** and **water sports** packages (from €9-30 per day). **Paragliding** excursions (€90) and **horseback riding, biking,** and **rock climbing** trips. Reception daily 7:30-9am and 5-10pm. Entry code after 10pm. Reserve far in advance. Closed May to late June and Sept.-Nov. June-Aug. bed and breakfast €13, with dinner €20.30; week with *demi-pension* €120. Dec.-Mar. bunks with breakfast €13, with dinner €21, with alpine day pass €38. MC/V. ❶

Gîtes Bonnevie (☎04 79 06 06 26; fax 04 79 06 16 65), in Le Fornet (accessible by the *train rouge*. Cross the bridge and it's the first building on the right. Gorgeous wood-trimmed chalet-style studios for 2 or 10 people, all with bathroom, kitchen, TV, and splendid views. About as cheap as it gets. Apr.-Nov. €20 per person. Dec.-Mar. weekly rentals only: doubles €310, 10-man €1448. Winter prices fluctuate; call to verify. ❷

Hôtel Sakura (☎04 79 06 04 08; www.sakura7.com). Turn right at the roundabout above the bus station. Spacious rooms with handmade wood furniture, shower or bath, toilet, TV, telephone, and kitchen. Breakfast €6. Reception daily 8am-8pm. Open July-Aug. and Dec.-May. July-Aug. singles €50; doubles €56; triples and quads €100; quints €110. Dec.-May singles and doubles €99; triples and quads €169; quints €184. MC/V. ❹

Le Relais du Ski (☎04 79 06 02 06; lerelaisduski@valdisere.com), 500m up from the tourist office, on the left. Small, wood-paneled rooms with hall showers. Breakfast €9, automatically included. Dinner €17. Reception 24hr. June-Sept. singles €25-49; doubles €32-56; triples €39-60; quads €44-64. Dec.-Apr. singles €40-53; doubles €50-74; triples €66-84; quads €76-100. AmEx/MC/V. ❸

Camping les Richards (☎/fax 04 79 06 26 60), 1km up from the tourist office. Take the free *train rouge* shuttle to Les Richards. Plain campground in a beautiful valley close to town. Crowded mid-Aug. during the 4x4 competitions. Open mid-June to mid-

Sept. Reception daily June and Sept. 9am-noon and 5-8pm; July-Aug. 7:30am-12:30pm and 2-8pm. €2.40 per person; €1.50 per tent; €1.40 per car. Electricity €1.90-3.80. Shower €1. MC/V above €15. ❶

FOOD

A **Casino** is in the *centre ville*, just up the roundabout by the bus station (☎04 79 06 02 66. Open daily July-Aug. 7:30am-1pm and 3:30-8pm; Dec.-Apr. 7:30am-1pm and 2:30-8:30pm.) Another one is in the **Les Hameaux** store, 500m up from the tourist office. (☎04 79 06 12 24. Open July-Aug. and Dec.-Apr. daily 7:30am-1pm and 3:30-8pm; May-June and Sept.-Nov. M-W, F, and Su 9am-12:30pm and 4-7:30pm.) In the low season, only a few *brasseries* and standard restaurants are open.

Le Bananas (☎04 79 06 04 23) is up the roundabout and near the base of the *téléphériques*. Ski instructors and wannabes pack this rockin' chalet for delicious Tex-Mex bites and beers inches from the slopes. Quesadillas €15, salads €4-12, *menus* €17 and €20. Happy hour Dec.-Apr. 7-8pm. Open daily 1pm-1am. MC/V. ❸

La Casserole (☎04 79 41 15 71) is just up the roundabout. Enjoy Savoyard specialties like fondues and *tartiflettes* (€13-20) in a dark wood chalet hung with animal skins. Meat dishes €14-22, salads €3.50-11.50. Open July-Aug. Tu-Sa noon-1:45pm and 6:30-10pm, Su noon-1:45pm; Nov.-Apr. daily 6:30-10:30pm. AmEx/MC/V. ❸

Maison Chevallot (☎04 79 06 02 42) is 20m up from the bus station. Delicious home-made options like *tourte au beaufort*, *quiche lorraine*, *tartiflette*, *fougasse*, and sandwiches are served with a salad (€4-5). For dessert, don't miss the excellent pastries, including nut cake (€2.29) and *fondant chocolat* (€2.30). Open daily 6:30am-7:30pm; May and Oct.-Nov. closed 1-3pm. MC/V. ❶

Le Canyon (☎04 79 06 18 19). Across the street from the bus station and to the left. Keeps itself in business as the only restaurant in town open almost all year. Serves locally endorsed Savoyard specialties like *gratin dauphinois* (€13.50), in addition to salads, pastas, and pizzas. For sandwiches and crêpes (€5-10), ask for their lighter menu. Entrées €7-15. Open daily 8am-10pm. MC/V. ❸

ENTERTAINMENT

In addition to being a haven for pizzerias, the roundabout above the bus station serves as Val d'Isère's unofficial nightlife strip. Start a night of drinking at **Lodge Bar**. (See **Internet**. Cocktail *du jour* €5. Happy hour 4:30-7pm; beer €1.50-3. Live music Dec.-Apr. Tu and F.) Then stumble up the block to **Café Face** and groove to the sounds of DJs and sax players. (☎04 79 06 29 80. Open daily Dec.-May 4pm-2am; July-Aug. 10pm-2am.) Across the street, **Dick's Tea Bar** is the best late-night option. A touristy crowd packs the dance floor of this Val mainstay. (☎04 79 06 14 87. Happy hour Dec.-Apr. 6-8pm; beer €3. Paninis €3-4. Shooters €6-8, cocktails €13-19. **Internet** for €5 per 30min. Open Dec.-Apr. daily 3pm-4am; July-Aug. Tu-Su 10:30pm-4am). Across from the bus station, **Le "XV"** serves drinks in beach chairs on the terrace, creating a suitable summer option. Drinks €4-10. (☎04 79 41 90 55. Open late June to Sept. and Dec.-Apr. 1pm-midnight. **Café Fats** or **Le Bananas** also stay busy long into the night (see **Food**).

OUTDOOR ACTIVITIES

SKIING. Over 100 lifts, several of them originating right in Val d'Isère and Tignes, provide access to 300km of trails. One can ski for a week without repeating a run. Lift tickets are valid on the entire Espace Killy, which includes every lift and run from Val d'Isère to Tignes, a ski station 7km away. The mountains are generally skiable from late November to early May, with optimum conditions in mid-winter. (Lift tickets €26 per half-day, €36.50 per day, €196 per week.)

Most good beginner runs are at higher altitudes, around the Marmottes and Borsat lifts on the south side of Bellevarde (that's the back side; take the Bellevarde lift up) and in the super-scenic **Pissaillas** area (take the Solaise cable car, then the Glacier and Leissier lifts). Intermediate and advanced skiers frequent the slopes surrounding Tignes, while the north side of Bellevarde is known for expert runs. There's a giant **snow park** between Val and Tignes; a classic border run starts at the top of the Mont Blanc lift and whirls its way through the park to La Daille, where a Funival car whisks boarders back to the Bellevarde summit for an encore.

Val d'Isère is most proud of its off-*piste* opportunities. Skiers of the **col Pers** region, accessible from the Pissaillas glacier, speed past wildlife in the Gorges de Malpassaet. Check weather conditions, leave an itinerary with the ski patrol, and never go alone. Hire a **guide** (☎ 04 79 06 02 34) if unfamiliar with the area.

Late June to mid-July, Pissaillas and **La Grande Motte** in Tignes offer **summer skiing.** For Pissailles, lift tickets are available at the Le Fornet cable car (see **Hiking**); a free bus heads to the top. The hostel arranges packages for Tignes. Conditions deteriorate and prices drop after 11am; there's no skiing after 1:30pm. (€17 per half-day, €21 per day. Lifts open at 7:30am.)

HIKING. Before hiking around Val, check the weather report and bring warm clothing—snowstorms and winter weather strike even in summer. Hikers should check ahead to make sure *gîtes* and trails are open. Some intermediate trails are suitable only for those with the proper equipment and experience. Trails around Val are well-marked with blazes and signs, but hikers should buy the detailed *Val d'Isère—Balades et Sentiers* (€3.80) and a hiking map in English at the tourist office (€6.90), which describe over 40 routes spanning 100km.

Until the construction of modern ski areas in the 60s, **Le Fornet** (1950m) was the highest continuously inhabited village in the French Alps. It can be reached by an easy 4km hike. (1½hr.) Starting from the church in Val Village, follow the sign for Le Fornet. The trail leads through the *Vieux Val* to a small pedestrian road and then briefly joins up with the **GR5** before forking again toward Le Fornet. Just before the village, the trail allows hikers to double back via the beautiful 45min. **sentier écologique,**

NO WORK, ALL PLAY

SUMMER SKIING

At 1pm, a bus rolls into the parking lot in Tignes, and a stream of ski- or snowboard-toting youngsters swing their poles and discuss their jumps. The scene is normal for winter, but this is no December afternoon. It's early July, the sun is shining, and everyone else sports hiking boots or biker shorts. In Val d'Isère, the skiing never stops. The glaciers behind the villages of Le Fornet and Tignes hold on to their snow as long as possible, becoming the national centers of *ski d'été.*

Summer skiers rouse themselves at 6am, and hit the snow hard by 7 or 7:30am. By 1pm, it's all over: the snow is, as the French say, *"comme la soupe."*

On a typical morning, small teenager-heavy French ski teams practice their slalom and downhill courses, boarders cruise over jumps in the snow park, and elite groups of skiers train with year-round instructors. A few skiers just cruise down the hill, enjoying the sunshine and the sport. For those who ski or snowboard, *ski d'été* might be worth a shot just for the thrill of it. Those less inclined to participate will still enjoy watching skiers huff and puff while working on a tan at the base of the slopes.

(Rental at the base of the slopes €20-30 per day; lift passes €17 per half-day, €22.50 per day. Hostellers can arrange €29 rental and lift packages through the hostel in Tignes. See p. 479.)

which meets up with the GR5 once again and returns to town. Another nice promenade for the less hardy leads under the Solaise cable car toward Le Manchet. The hum of the town fades almost immediately and is replaced by cowbells. It's about 1hr. to the waterfall at the park entrance, which is a departure point for *refuge* hikes and an ideal picnic spot.

Val d'Isère's classic **intermediate** hikes lead to the two closest *refuges*, through the **Vanoise National Park**, France's premiere wildlife reserve. The trail to the **Refuge de Prariond** (one-way 3km; 1¾hr.; 300m vertical) begins in Le Fornet. It is a must for animal lovers; acrobatic *bouquetin* (ibex), *chamois* (the antelope's smaller cousin), and furry marmots roam the areas around the trail. From the center of Le Fornet, cross the bridge and follow the signs to **pont St-Charles.** After the bridge, the marked trail switchbacks several times out of the far end of the parking lot before beginning a steep ascent to the **Gorges du Malpasset.** The trail plateaus, continuing to the *refuge.* (*Refuge* ☎ 04 79 06 06 02. Staffed late Mar. to mid-May and mid-June to mid-Sept. Mid-May to mid-June and mid-Sept. to late Mar. wood, gas, utensils, covers, and a tin box are provided with payment. Breakfast €5.60, *à la carte* lunch €14, dinner €14. Shower €2. Animal-skin sleeping sacks €2.30. Reserve and get directions at the tourist office. €11.50 per person, students €8.50.) From Prariond, it is another 2hr. and a 600m vertical ascent to the **Col de la Galise** pass (2987m), one of the most stunning panoramas in the region. Coming out of the *refuge*, take the trail to the right. At the **Roche des Coses** (2750m), branch right for a 45min. excursion into Italy with more stupendous vistas. Take care: this trail is usually snow-covered year-round.

The second *refuge* hike leads through alpine meadows to the **Refuge des Fours,** in the Vanoise National Park. Take the free shuttle to **Le Manchet** (see **Public Transportation**) and continue up the road to the beginning of the trail near a cluster of old stone farmhouses. Take the trail on the right marked "refuge des fours." From there, it's a steady climb to the hut in a high valley across from the **Méan Martin** glacier and alpine lakes. (One-way 1¾hr.; 560m vertical. *Refuge* ☎ 04 79 06 16 90; staffed same months as Fornet. Breakfast €5.50, lunch €14, dinner €9.60. Sleeping sack €2.60. Showers €2.50. €11.50 per person, students €8.50.) To return to Val, one option is to cross the **Col des Fours** pass and head back to town via the **GR5.** Continue along the trail that runs to the *refuge*, then turn left onto the path that ascends the neckline between the 3135m **Pelou Blanc** and the 3072m **Pointe des Fours.** (1¼hr.; 450m vertical). Where the trail ends, hang a left on the red-and-white marked **GR5** for a scenic descent to town on the **Col d'Iseran,** a popular leg of the Tour de France (6km; 1½-2hr.; 900m vertical).

A full-day **advanced** trek heads from le Fornet to the **Lac de la Sassière.** From the *téléphérique*, descend slightly and turn right at the trail marker for the Balcon des Barmettes. At the Balcon, head right on Trail #36, the **Bailletta,** which climbs steeply for 800m to the small **Lac de la Bailletta** (2½hr.), where the trail reaches a pass and then descends gradually to the larger **Lac de la Sassière.** This man-made lake is packed with trout and surrounded by *chamois*, ibex, and marmots. Return by the same path for several hundred meters until the sign for **Picheru,** a steeper trail than the *Bailletta* route. Picheru passes over several exposed knife-edge ridges before crossing just to the right of **Le Dome** and descending gradually into town. (Round-trip to Lac de la Sassière 12.2km; 940m vertical; 7hr.) Another advanced trek heads from the *Camping les Richardes;* pick up the treacherous **GR5** (marked with red and white) and brave the harrowing ascent to the **Col de l'Iseran** (2770m). About halfway up, the path crosses the **RD902.** From the top a different glacier is visible in every direction. (One-way 6km; 474m vertical; 3hr.) Not all hiking is based in Val: several *refuge* hikes in the Vanoise also depart from Tignes, from both the upper town and the hostel. A map is available in the Tignes tourist office, and staff at the hostel have loads of advice for guests.

OTHER OUTDOOR ACTIVITIES. Mountain Guides (☎04 79 06 06 60) teaches ice climbing (morning session €76) and rock climbing (afternoon session €28), and leads full-day canyoning trips (€64). Nature expeditions are offered for all levels.

For a relaxing trip to the summit of Val d'Isère, take a *téléphérique* (cable car) over peaks, glaciers, and valleys up to the top of the mountain. In the summer, a chairlift runs to **Solaise,** a small summit surrounded by a lake and easy hiking trails, and to the higher **Bellevarde,** site of the 1992 Olympic downhill. (Cable cars to Solaise Dec.-Apr. every 10min. 8:45am-5pm; July-Aug. every hr. 9am-noon and 2-4:50pm. To Bellevarde Dec.-Apr. every 10min. 9am-4:45pm. Chairlift July-Aug. 9:30-11:30am and 2:30-4:30pm. Cable cars €7, round-trip €8.) Trail #17, **Chemin de l'Ouillete,** which starts near Chapelle St-Jean at the base, also runs to Solaise. (Round-trip 2½hr.) This trail is for all experience levels and provides wonderful views. From Bellevarde, a steep trail descends along the front of the mountain to Val d'Isère, and another runs down the back to La Daille; be cautious walking it, as most of the terrain has been sliced and ground by **mountain bikers** and 4x4s.

Before attempting uncharted mountains, advanced **climbers** should call the **Bureau des Guides** (☎04 79 06 06 60). Beginners will appreciate **Via Ferrata** in La Daille. This 2-3hr. climb (360m vertical) via metal footholds and ropes hugs the side of the mountain facing the valley; there is also a more demanding 4-6hr. climb that requires a guide. Signs at the La Daille chapel point to the climbing site.

PROVENCE

From the tiny vineyards that stretch into radiant rows of sunflowers to the vibrant North African fabrics and spices sold in the Marseille marketplace, travelers to Provence are greeted with picture-perfect views and a colorful welcome warmer than the hottest days of July. ◼**Marseille** (p. 484), with 2600 years of history, is the second-largest city in France. ◼**Avignon** (p. 504) retains the formidable Palais des Papes, a relic of the town's brief stint as home to the medieval papacy. The elegant university city of ◼**Aix-en-Provence** (p. 498) is the third major locale in the region. The smaller towns throughout the Lubéron and the Vaucluse are most popular for their festivals, though their beauty and history are also appealing. Roman ruins still stand at the ◼**Pont du Gard** (p. 540), in **Nîmes** (p. 534), **Orange** (p. 540), in Provençal favorite ◼**Arles** (p. 519), and the ancient ghost town of **Oppède-le-Vieux** (p. 516). The ruins in arresting ◼**St-Rémy** (p. 529) cast shadows over the footprints of Van Gogh, one of many artists drawn by the region's beautiful landscape. The ◼**Fontaine de Vaucluse** (p. 514) is most notable for its sublime flowing fountain, **l'Isle-sur-la-Sorgue** (p. 513) for its canal-entangled streets, and ◼**Les Baux-de-Provence** (p. 526) for its gigantic castle and vineyards.

The secret to Provence's appeal lies partly in the diversity of its offerings. Roman relics are interspersed with Arabic food stalls, while artists continually find inspiration in Provence's varied landscape, including the astonishing red, yellow, and orange cliffs of the "ochre hills" (◼**Roussillon**, p. 518), the jewel-green resort town of **Cassis** (p. 497), and the perfumed fields of lavender in **Gordes** (p. 518). Fierce *mistral* winds cut through the olive groves and tranquil fountains in the north, and the steep white cliffs of the ◼**Calanques** (p. 497) and marshy ◼**Camargue** (p. 530) to the south.

Provence has simple, fresh food. Regional specialties include *bouillabaisse* (a hearty seafood stew), *soupe au pistou* (with pine nuts, fresh basil, and garlic), *aïoli* (creamy garlic dip), and fresh seafood. For dessert, *calissons* (almond-flavored pastries) are a traditional delight.

MARSEILLE

Marseille (pop. 800,000), France's second-largest city, is like the *bouillabaisse* soup for which it is famous: steamy and pungently spiced, with a little bit of everything mixed in. A jumble of color and commotion, the city that Alexandre Dumas once called "the meeting place of the entire world" remains an alluring center of international influence. Although Marseille does inherit a history similar to that of many French cities, complete with Roman ruins, Byzantine churches, and 18th-century art workshops, a walk through the sidestreets is punctuated by the vibrant colors of West African fabrics for sale in markets, the sounds of Arabic music from car stereos, and the smells of North African cuisine wafting out of hole-in-the-wall restaurants. A true immigrant city, Marseille offers a taste of both the ancient and modern cultures of the entire Mediterranean.

Its origins date back to 600 BC, when Phoenician Greeks sought shelter in Marseille's port. The well-located city quickly grew into a trading center and an independent ally of Rome. The city has long held its own through bouts with warfare, plague, and more recently, economic hardship, developing a reputation for resilience and toughness. As a gateway to Europe, Marseille has welcomed Spanish, Armenian, and West African immigrants through the decades, and, since the

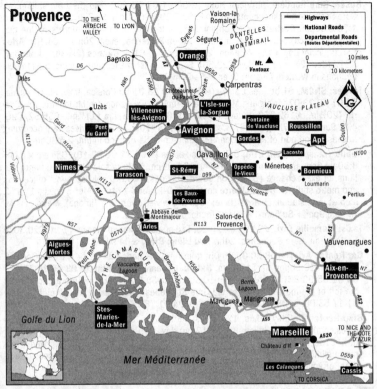

Provence

Mer Méditerranée

1960s, increasing numbers of Jews and Muslims from France's former colonies. After years of living in the shadow of gay Paris and the rest of Provence, Marseille is finally receiving the cultural recognition it truly deserves, largely thanks to the interesting *Euroméditerranée* development projects, designed to encourage tourism to the city.

TRANSPORTATION

Flights: Aéroport Marseille-Provence (☎04 42 14 14 14; www.marseille.aeroport.fr). Flights to: **Corsica** (**Air Littoral,** ☎08 25 83 48 34; **Air Lib Express,** 08 25 80 58 05); **Lyon** (**Air France,** ☎08 20 82 08 20); **Paris** (Air France and Air Lib Express). Shuttle buses connect airport to Gare St-Charles 5:30am-9:30pm (every 20min., €8.50). Taxis from the *centre ville* to the airport €36 during the day, €45 at night.

Trains: Gare St-Charles, pl. Victor Hugo. M: Gare St-Charles. Info and ticket counters open daily 4:30am-1am. To: **Lyon** (1½hr., 21+ per day, €47.50); **Nice** (2¾hr., 21 per day, €24.50); **Paris** (3hr., 17 per day, €68). **Baggage service** open daily 7:15am-11pm (€3.20-7 per bag, held for up to 72hr.) **SOS Voyageurs** (☎04 91 62 12 80), in the station, helps tourists find lodgings. Open M-Sa 9am-7pm. **Note:** While listed on train schedules, many trains to nearby cities, like **Aix-en-Provence,** may actually be buses, and thus will be marked as "car" on the schedule.

Buses: Gare Routière, pl. Victor Hugo (☎04 91 08 16 40), near the train station. M: Gare St-Charles. Ticket counters open M-Sa 6:30am-6:30pm, Su 7:30am-12:30pm and 1:30-6:30pm. **Cartreize** is an organization of local operators. Buy tickets on the bus (except to Nice) with exact change. To: **Aix-en-Provence** (every 20min., €4.10); **Arles** (2-3hr., 7 per day, €13); **Avignon** (2hr., 5 per day, €15); **Cannes** (2¼-3hr., 4 per day, €21); **Nice** (2¾hr., 1 per day, €22.50). **Eurolines** also makes international trips to destinations in Western Europe. Open M-Sa 9am-6pm.

Ferries: SNCM, 61 bd. des Dames (☎08 91 70 18 01 for Corsica, Italy, and Sardinia; 08 91 70 28 02 for Algiers, Morocco, and Tunisia; www.sncm.fr). M: Joliette. To: **Algeria** (20½hr., €162-250, reduced price €110-165); **Corsica** (11½hr., €35-52/€26-40); **Sardinia** (17hr., €58-67/€41-50); **Tunisia** (20hr., €144). Prices vary according to season and port of arrival. Open M-F 8am-6pm, Sa 8am-noon and 2-5:30pm.

Public Transportation: RTM, 6-8 rue des Fabres (☎04 91 91 92 10). Office open M-F 8:30am-6pm and Sa 9am-12:30pm and 2-5:30pm. **Tickets** sold at bus and metro stations, or exact change (€1.40) on board. Day pass (€3.80) sold at tourist office, bus and metro stations. **Carte Liberté** costs €6.50-13 for 6-12 trips. **Metro** lines #1 and 2 stop at train station. Line #1 (blue) goes to the *vieux port* (dir: Timone). Metro runs M-Th 5am-9pm, F-Su 5am-12:30am. Tourist office has map.

Taxis: Marseille Taxi, ☎04 91 02 20 20. Taxi stands surround the *vieux port*. €20-30 to hostels from Gare St-Charles. 24hr. **Taxi Blanc Bleu,** ☎04 91 51 50 00.

Car Rental: Avis, (☎08 20 05 05 05, from Gare St-Charles 04 91 64 71 00). Open M-F 6:30am-10:30pm, Sa 7am-8pm. **National/Alamo Car Rental,** (☎08 25 16 12 12/ 04 91 05 90 86). Open M-F 8am-10:30pm, Sa-Su 8:30am-8pm. Both are located to the left of the main entrance to the Gare St-Charles. **Europcar,** in the Hôtel Ibis (☎04 91 17 53 00, or 08 25 35 23 52). Call ☎04 91 78 78 78 for road conditions.

Bike Rental: Holiday Bikes, 129 cours Lieutaud (☎ 04 91 92 76 04; www.holiday-bikes.com). M: Cours Julien. Bikes €12 per day, €65 per week. Mopeds €25-120 per day, €150-720 per week. Motorcycles €53-215 per day, €300-1200 per week. Helmet, unlimited mileage, and insurance included in price. Open Tu-Sa 9am-noon and 3-7pm, or any other time if you call ahead.

■ ORIENTATION

The city is divided along major streets into 16 *arrondissements*, referred to in town as *quartiers*. **La Canebière** is the main artery of the city center, funneling into the **vieux port** (old port) to the west and becoming bland urban sprawl as it heads to the east. North of the *vieux port* and west of rue de la République lies **Le Panier**, Marseille's oldest remaining neighborhood. Surrounding La Canebière are several African and Arabic communities, including the African-market-filled Belsunce *quartier*. Although travelers should be wary here at night, these areas are great for daytime exploration.

Upscale restaurants and nightlife cluster around the *vieux port* on quai de Rive Neuve, cour Estienne d'Orves, and pl. Thiers. East of the *vieux port*, La Canebière, rue St-Ferreol, and rue Paradis contain the city's largest stores and major fashion boutiques. The areas in front of the **Opéra** (near the port) and around **rue Curiol** (near rue Sénac) are known to be meeting grounds for prostitutes and their clients; be particularly cautious after dark. A few blocks southeast, **cours Julien,** with funky shops and tiny concert spaces, has an artsy countercultural feel.

The city of Marseille has just two metro lines, and they are clean and easy to use. The bus system is thorough but a little more complex than the subway—a route map from the tourist office helps enormously. Use the buses to access the beach, which stretches along the coast southwest of the *vieux port*.

PRACTICAL INFORMATION

Tourist Office: 4 bd. de la Canebière (☎04 91 13 89 00; www.marseille-tourisme.com). Extremely helpful multilingual staff provides brochures of walking tours, free maps, accommodation service, excursions, and **RTM day pass**. **City tours** daily 10am and 2pm, €6.50. Open July-Aug. M-Sa 9am-8pm, Su 10am-6pm; Oct.-June M-Sa 9am-7pm, Su and holidays 10am-5pm. **Annex** (☎04 91 50 59 18) at train station. Open daily 10am-6pm, Sa-Su closed 3-4pm.

Consulates: UK, 24 av. du Prado (☎04 91 15 72 10). **US,** 12 bd. Paul Peytral (☎04 91 54 92 00). Both open by appt. M-F 9am-noon and 2-4pm.

Money: La Bourse, 3 pl. Général de Gaulle (☎04 91 13 09 00). Open M-F 8:30am-6:30pm, Sa 9am-5:30pm. **Comptoir Marseillais de Bourse,** 22 bd. de la Canebière (☎04 91 54 93 94). Both with good rates and no commission. Only accepts European traveler's checks and cash. Open M-Sa 9am-7pm. **American Express,** 39 bd. de la Canebière (☎04 91 13 71 21), located in Afat Voyages. Open M-F 9am-6pm, Sa 9am-noon and 2-5pm. **ATMs** line rue Canebière.

English Bookstore: Ad Hoc Books, 8 rue Pisançon (☎04 91 33 51 92). Open M-Sa 10am-7pm. Well-stocked English-language bookstore owned by a charming Brit.

Youth Information: Centre Régional Information Jeunesse, 96 La Canebière (☎04 91 24 33 50; crijpa@wanadoo.fr). Info on sports, short-term employment, leisure activities, and services for the disabled. Open July-Aug. M-F 9am-1pm; Sept.-June M and W-F 10am-5pm, Tu 1-5pm. **CROUS,** 42 rue du 141*ème* R.I.A. (☎04 91 62 83 60), has info on housing, work, and travel. Open M-F 9am-12:30pm and 1:30-4:30pm.

Laundromat: Point Laverie, 56 bd. de la Libération and 6 rue Méry. Wash €3.50-7, dry €0.40 per 5min. Open daily 7am-8pm. Also at 8 rue Bruetil. Open daily 6:30am-8pm.

Gay Support: Lesbian & Gay Pride, 8 bd. de la Liberté (☎04 95 08 21 72).

Rape Hotline: SOS Femmes, 14 bd. Théodore Thurner (☎04 91 24 61 50). 24hr.

Traveler Emergency: SOS Traveler, St-Charles station (☎04 91 62 12 80). **Lost and Found** (☎04 91 90 99 37). Open M-F 8:30-11:30am and 2:30-5:30pm.

Police: 2 rue du Commissaire Becker (☎04 91 39 80 00). Also in the train station on esplanade St-Charles (☎04 91 14 29 97). Dial ☎17 in emergencies.

Hospital: Hôpital Timone, bd. J. Moulin (☎04 91 38 60 00). M: Timone. **SOS Médecins** (☎04 91 52 91 52) and **SOS Dentist** (☎04 91 85 39 39) have on-call doctors.

24-Hour Pharmacy: Pharmacie le Cours Saint-Louis, 5 cours Saint-Louis (☎04 91 54 04 58). Open daily 8:30am-7:30pm. Serves as one of five rotating *pharmacies de garde;* check pharmacy windows, *La Provence,* or with the police for up-to-date info.

Internet: Cyber Café de la Canebière, 87 rue de la Canebière (☎04 91 05 94 24). €2 per hr. Open daily 9am-11pm. **Info Café,** 1 quai Rive Neuve (☎04 91 33 53 05). €3.80 per hr. Open M-Sa 8:30am-10pm. **Le Rezo,** 68 cours Julien (☎04 91 42 70 02). €4.60 per hr. Open M-W 9:30am-8pm, Th-F 9:30am-10pm, Sa 10am-10pm.

Post Office: 1 pl. Hôtel des Postes (☎04 91 15 47 00). Follow rue de la Canebière toward the sea and turn right onto rue Reine Elisabeth as it becomes pl. Hôtel des Postes. **Poste Restante** and **currency exchange** at this branch only. Open M-F 8am-7pm, Sa 8am-noon. **Branch office** at 11 rue Honnorat (☎04 91 62 80 80), near the station. Open M-F 8am-6:45pm, Sa 8am-noon. **Postal code: 13001.**

ACCOMMODATIONS

Marseille has a range of hotel options, from pricey three- and four-star hotels near the *vieux port* to the less reputable but temptingly cheap hotels in the quartier Belsunce. Hotels listed here prioritize safety and location. Both hostels are located far from the city center, offering an escape from the fast pace of the city, but bus access is infrequent in the summer. Most places fill up quickly on weekends and in the summer, so call at least a week in advance. Large blue signs throughout the city provide directions to the major hotels.

▨ **Hôtel du Palais,** 26 rue Breteuil (☎04 91 37 78 86; fax 04 91 37 91 19). Competent, kind owner runs a tight ship. Large, well-maintained, soundproofed rooms have A/C, TVs, and showers or baths. Breakfast €5. Singles €38; doubles €45; triples €53; students can get a triple for €38. Extra bed €8. MC/V. ❹

Hôtel Alexandre I, 111 rue de Rome (☎04 91 48 67 13; fax 04 91 42 11 14). Hôtel Alexandre I is a high-quality choice for those staying in Marseille. The quite spacious rooms all come with showers. Breakfast €5. Reception 24hr. Singles €29; doubles €37-40; triples €48; quads €64. MC/V. ❸

Auberge de Jeunesse Bonneveine (HI), impasse Bonfils (☎04 91 17 63 30; fuaj.net/homepage/marseille), off av. J. Vidal. From the station, take metro line #2 to Rond-Point du Prado, and transfer (keeping your ticket) onto bus #44 to pl. Bonnefon. At the bus stop, walk back toward the traffic circle and turn left at J. Vidal, then turn left onto impasse Bonfils; the hostel is on the left. Swimming and sunbathing areas are just 200m away. A well-organized hostel filled with a young, international crowd. The brightly colored, modern building houses a bar, restaurant, Internet (€0.15 per min.), pool table, video games, vending machines, and 160 beds. Rooms are basic but adequate. Breakfast included. Lockers €1.50. Laundry: wash €3.50, dry €2. Bike rental €10 for 4hr. July-Aug. 3-day maximum stay. Reception 9am-noon and 2-6pm. Curfew 1am. Reserve ahead in summer. Closed late Dec. to Feb. Dorms Apr.-Aug. €14 1st night, €12.10 thereafter; doubles €16.70/€14.80. Feb.-Mar. and Sept.-Dec. dorms €13.40/€11.50; doubles €15.60/€13.70. MC/V. **HI Members only.** ❶

Auberge de Jeunesse Château de Bois-Luzy (HI), allée des Primevères (☎/fax 04 91 49 06 18). Take bus #6 from cours J. Thierry at the top of La Canebière to Marius Richard. 10m up the hill from the bus stop, take a right onto bd. de l'Amandière and walk to the soccer fields. Follow the road down to the right and around the fields to reach the hostel. Or take bus #8 (dir: Saint-Julien) from La Canebière to Felibres Laurient, walk uphill, and make the first left; the hostel will be on your left. Night bus "T" also leaves La Canebière for Marius Richard. A beautiful 19th-century château that once housed a count and countess now provides 90 beds for youth and families. Mostly three- to six-bed dorms and a few doubles. Breakfast €3. Dinner €7.50. Luggage storage €2 per bag per day. Sheets €1.80. Reception 7:30am-noon and 5-10:30pm. Lockout noon-5pm. Dorms €10.40 for first night, €8.40 thereafter; singles €14.40/€12.40; doubles €11.40/€9.40. Cash only. **HI Members only.** ❶

Hôtel Béarn, 63 rue Sylvabelle (☎04 91 37 75 83; fax 04 91 81 54 98). On a quiet side street between rue Paradis and rue Breteuil. Adequate rooms with high ceilings and large windows. Internet €4 per hr. Breakfast (with homemade jam from a local monastery) €4. Reception 7am-11pm. Singles and doubles with shower and/or bath €35-40; triples with bath €41-42. AmEx/MC/V. ❸

Hôtel Saint-Louis, 2 rue des Recollettes (☎04 91 54 02 74; fax 04 91 33 78 59). Saint-Louis features countless pretty, high-ceilinged rooms in cheerful colors, located just off noisy rue de la Canebière. Some with balcony, nearly all with satellite TV. Breakfast €5, in bed €6. Reception 24hr. Singles €30; doubles with bath €38-45; triples €53. Extra bed €7. AmEx/V. ❸

Grand Hôtel de la Préfecture, 9 bd. Louis Salvator (☎04 91 54 31 60). A welcoming staff operates this safe, clean hotel. Sizeable rooms, most with private bathrooms, all with TV and A/C. Breakfast €5. Reception 24hr. Singles €29-37; doubles €40; triples €40-50. AmEx/MC/V. ❸

🍎 FOOD

Marseille's restaurants reflect the cultural diversity of this dynamic international port city. From the small African eateries and *kebab* stands along rue de la Canebière, to the Provençal places lining rue St-Saens and rue Fortia, diners can choose among the finest flavors from around the world. The streets surrounding the *vieux port* are packed with countless restaurants, many of which serve steaming dishes of the city's trademark *bouillabaisse* (a full meal comprising various Mediterranean fish, fish broth, and a spicy sauce called "rouille" or "rust"). A more artsy dining experience can be found at the cours Julien, where an eclectic collection of small restaurants are tucked along the side streets and in the main pedestrian mall. Locals stock up at the fish market, picking up ingredients for their homemade *bouillabaisse* just inches from the fishing boats on quai des Belges (daily 8am-noon). There is a vegetable market on cours Julien (M-Sa 8am-1pm) and an open-air market on cours Pierre Puget, beginning at rue Breteuil (M-Sa, starts at 8am). Before heading for the hostels, stock up at the **Monoprix** supermarket, on bd. de la Canebière, across from the American Express office. (Open M-Sa 8:30am-8:30pm.)

Ivoire Restaurant, 57 rue d'Aubagne (☎ 04 91 33 75 33). This simple restaurant offers a taste of West African cuisine, complete with fresh peanuts and Senegalese beer. A friendly local crowd comes for the typical West African dishes such as Yassa and Maffé (€6-10). Open daily noon-midnight. ❷

La Kahena, 2 rue de la République (☎ 04 91 90 61 93). M: Vieux Port. Incredibly spiced couscous dishes (€8-14) are the specialty at this Tunisian restaurant on the corner of the *vieux port.* Blue tile mosaics and smells of warm spices complement its North African aura. Open daily noon-2:30pm and 7:30-11:30pm. MC/V. ❸

Baba of Marseille, 14 rue St-Pons (☎ 04 91 90 66 36). A collision of past and present, the décor underneath the arched stone ceiling of this 14th-century building features hip furniture, eclectic lighting, and photos of past diners. Friendly owner Baba serves southern French dishes such as the *Rocamadour salade* with chèvre, *poire* (pear), and *alcool de poire* (€10), and the *mille feuille d'agneau* (€17). Look for the owner's baby picture on the menu. Occasional live jazz music. Open W-Sa noon-midnight. ❸

Le Sud du Haut, 80 cours Julien (☎ 04 91 92 66 64). M: Cours Julien. Inviting décor and outdoor seating make this the ideal place for a leisurely meal of tasty, traditional Provençal cuisine with a modern flair. The *petit légumes provençal* (€9) and the *Saint Marcellin Rôti* (€13) are highly recommended. Funky bathrooms supply markers and paper so patrons can contribute their skills to the wall art. Open W-Sa noon-2am. ❸

Le Restaurant Végétarien, 53 rue St-Pierre (☎ 04 91 42 75 06). M: Cours Julien. Steps from cours Julien, this quiet outdoor garden provides a respite from the city. Enjoy one of the appetizing *plats du jour* or salads (€9-12) on the full vegetarian menu to the accompaniment of soothing music. Open M-Sa noon-2:30pm and 7:30-11:30pm. ❸

Country Life, 14 rue Venture (☎ 04 96 11 28 00), off rue Paradis. Tasty all-you-can-eat vegan food under a huge skylight, amid a near-forest of foliage. Big buffet plate €6; small plate €2.90. Open M-F 11:30am-2:30pm; health food store open M-Th 9am-6:30pm, F 9:30am-3pm. MC/V. ❶

🔍 SIGHTS

A walk through the city's streets tops any other sights-oriented itinerary, providing glimpses of the lively African and Arabic communities' influence amidst ancient Roman ruins. Walking trips and longer daytrips are easily planned with maps and

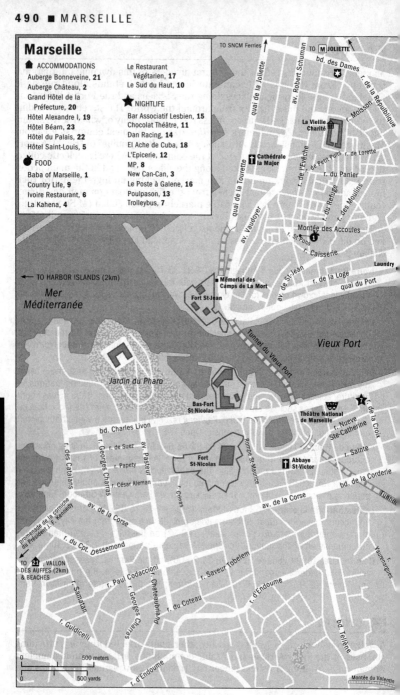

Marseille

🏠 ACCOMMODATIONS

Auberge Bonneveine, **21**
Auberge Château, **2**
Grand Hôtel de la
Préfecture, **20**
Hôtel Alexandre I, **19**
Hôtel Béarn, **23**
Hôtel du Palais, **22**
Hôtel Saint-Louis, **5**

🍴 FOOD

Baba of Marseille, **1**
Country Life, **9**
Ivoire Restaurant, **6**
La Kahena, **4**

Le Restaurant
Végétarien, **17**
Le Sud du Haut, **10**

⭐ NIGHTLIFE

Bar Associatif Lesbien, **15**
Chocolat Théâtre, **11**
Dan Racing, **14**
El Ache de Cuba, **18**
L'Epicerie, **12**
MP, **8**
New Can-Can, **3**
Le Poste à Galene, **16**
Poulpason, **13**
Trolleybus, **7**

PROVENCE

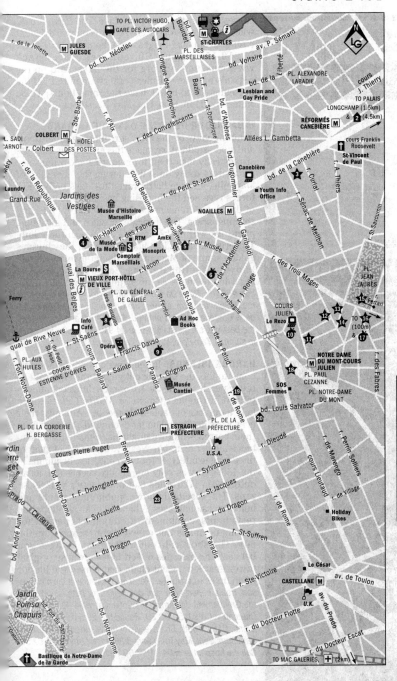

THE INSIDER'S CITY

COURS JULIEN

An eclectic collection of wall murals, vintage music and clothing shops, bookstores, comic book shops, theaters, and countless cafés and restaurants, cours Julien is one of Marseille's most interesting districts and the perfect place for a bargain. On Sundays and Mondays, many shops are closed.

1 Cartoonish humor and bright colors fill the impressive **murals** on **rue Crudère** and **rue Pastoret**.

2 **Black Music**, 2 rue de la Bibliothèque (☎04 91 92 07 14), has a large assortment of classical and contemporary black music.

3 **Kaleidoscope**, 3 rue des Trois Mages (☎04 91 47 48 56), offers a sweet selection of used records.

4 Tiny **Baluchon Boutique**, 11 rue des Trois Rois (☎04 91 48 14 26), features the best vintage digs.

5 Immerse yourself in paperbacks at **Librairie du Cours Julien**, cours Julien. (☎04 91 47 57 85)

6 **La Passerelle**, 26 rue des Trois Mages (☎04 91 48 77 24), features a large selection of comic books and a snappy café and bar.

suggestions from the tourist office. The *Petit Train*, which gives tours of the city, departs on two different circuits from quai Belges every hour. (☎04 91 40 17 75. 10:15am-5pm. €5, children €3.) Check www.museum-paca.org for the latest info on the region's museums. Unless otherwise noted, all the museums listed below have the same hours: Tu-Sa June-Sept. 11am-6pm; Oct.-May 10am-5pm.

■ **BASILIQUE DE NOTRE DAME DE LA GARDE.** A stunning view of the city, surrounding mountains, and stone-studded bay made this church's hilltop site strategically important for centuries and a must-see for visitors today. In WWII, during the liberation of Marseille, a fierce battle raged for days before FFI forces regained the imposing basilica. The east face of the church remains pocked with bullet holes and shrapnel scars. The intricate mosaics and intriguing paintings within the basilica are worth the climb. Towering nearly 230m above the city, the church's golden statue of Madonna cradling the infant Christ, known affectionately as *"la bonne mère,"* is regarded by many as the symbol of Marseille. *(Take bus #60 (dir: Notre Dame); or, from the tourist office, walk up rue Breteuil and turn left onto rue Grignon, which becomes bd. de la Corderie. Turn left onto bd. André Aune and you will see the basilique's huge staircase. ☎04 91 13 40 80. Open daily in summer 7am-8pm; in winter 7am-7pm.)*

HARBOR ISLANDS. Resembling a child's sandcastle come to life, the **Château d'If** guards the city from its rocky perch outside the harbor. Its dungeon, immortalized in Dumas's *Count of Monte Cristo*, once held a number of hapless Huguenots. Although their cells were drafty and under-decorated, the view from their barred windows might have made a life sentence almost bearable. Nearby, the **Ile Frioul** quarantined plague infectees for two centuries, beginning in the 1600s. It was only marginally successful, as an outbreak in 1720 killed half of the city's 80,000 citizens. The **hospital** is now a public monument and holds occasional raves. A handful of small shops and restaurants, combined with tiny inlets perfect for swimming, make this an excellent escape from the city. The short ride out to the islands takes you between the batteries of **Fort St-Jean**, whose original tower guarded a giant chain that closed the harbor off in times of trouble. *(Reserve in advance in the high season. Boats depart from quai des Belges for both islands. Call the Groupement des Armateurs Côtiers at ☎04 91 55 50 09. Château ☎04 91 59 02 30. Round-trip 20min.; €9 for each island, €15 for both. Boats leave for the islands June-Aug. daily 9am-5pm; Sept.-May Tu-Su 9am-3:30pm. €4, under 25 €2.50. Call the hospital at ☎04 91 57 00 73 for event info.)*

LA VIEILLE CHARITÉ. A formidable example of the famous 17th-century work of local architect Pierre Puget, La Charité sheltered orphans, the elderly, and others in need. It broke new ground in the field of child abandonment: parents could leave their unwanted children in front, where a wooden turnstile near the gate kept the nuns inside from seeing their faces. Now home to many of Marseille's cultural organizations, it contains several of the city's museums, including the Egyptian, prehistoric, and anthropological collections held in the **Musée des Arts Africains, Océaniens et Amérindiens.** Temporary art exhibits are displayed in the central building, and **Le Miroir,** a small cinema, screens old films. The complex is defined by both grace and balance with high, blank exterior walls facing the **Panier** district and a contrasting sunny interior with colonnades and a stunning Baroque chapel. *(2 rue de la Charité. ☎ 04 91 14 58 80. Temporary exhibits €3, permanent collections €2, students with ID half-price.)*

MUSÉE CANTINI. This memorable museum chronicles the region's artistic successes of the last century, with major fauvist and surrealist collections, including limited works by Henri Matisse and Paul Signac. The works of Auguste Chabaud, a painter from Provence, will be on display until February 2004. *(19 rue Grignan. ☎ 04 91 54 77 75. €3, students €1.50, over 65 and under 10 free.)*

MÉMORIAL DES CAMPS DE LA MORT. This small but moving museum recalls the death camps of World War II and Marseille's role in them. In 1943, nearly 2,000 buildings housing Jews were destroyed in the *vieux port.* Sobering quotes by Primo Levi, Louis Serre, and Elie Wiesel, and a disturbing collection of ashes are displayed. *(Quai de la Tourette. ☎ 04 91 90 73 15. Free.)*

ABBAYE ST-VICTOR. St-Victor, an abbey fortified against pirates and Saracen invaders, is one of the oldest Christian sites in Europe. The eerie 5th-century catacombs and basilica contain both pagan and Christian relics, including the remains of two 3rd-century martyrs. Sarcophagi pile up along the walls; some, partially excavated, remain half-embedded in the building's foundations. The abbey hosts a concert festival each year from March to December. *(Perched on rue Sainte at the end of quai de Rive Neuve. Follow the signs from the quai. ☎ 04 96 11 22 60. Open daily 9am-7pm. €2 for crypt entrance. Call ☎ 04 91 05 84 48 for festival info. Tickets €26, students €23.)*

PALAIS LONGCHAMP. Inaugurated in 1869, the palace was built to honor the completion of a canal which brought fresh water to alleviate Marseille's cholera outbreak. Endowed with towering columns and flowing water, the monument itself is only the center of the complex, which includes two museums, a park, and an observatory. The **Musée des Beaux-Arts** features dramatic Biblical works and paintings of 19th-century Provence. The **Musée de l'Histoire Naturelle** includes a wide assortment of stuffed animals and temporary exhibits on subjects as diverse as the histories of dinosaurs and milk. *(Take metro #1 to Cinq Avenues Longchamps.* **Musée des Beaux-Arts** ☎ 04 91 14 59 30. €2, students €1. **Musée de l'Histoire Naturelle** ☎ 04 91 14 59 50. Open Tu-Su 10am-5pm. €3.20.)*

OTHER SIGHTS. The **Musée de la Mode** carries fluctuating exhibits of contemporary fashion. *(Espace Mode Méditerranée, 11 La Canebière. ☎ 04 91 56 59 57. Free tours in French W and Sa-Su 4pm. €2, students €1, over 65 free.)* Millennia-old artifacts are displayed in the adjoining **Musée d'Histoire de Marseille,** which include pottery pieces and the skeleton of an ancient boat, though there is little explanatory text. *(Enter through the lowest level of the Centre Bourse mall. Museum ☎ 04 91 90 42 22. €2, students €1, over 65 and under 10 free.)* The **MAC, Galeries Contemporaines des Musées de Marseille,** features art from the 1960s to today, including works by César and Wegman. *(69 av. d'Haifa. ☎ 04 91 25 01 07. Bus #23 or 45. Open Tu-Su 11am-7pm. €3, students €1.50.)*

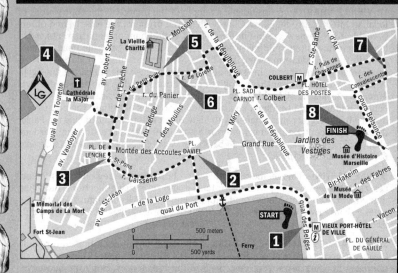

QUAI DES BELGES. Every morning the smell of fish fills the air as fishmongers sell the freshest of the day's catch along the entrance to the *vieux port*. Around noon, the city cleans up with large firehoses.

> **START:** quai des Belges
> **FINISH:** bd. de la Canebière
> **DISTANCE:** 2.7km/1.7 mi.
> **DURATION:** 3-4hr.

CLOCHER DES ACCOULES. Follow the quai du Port to the passage Petécontore, and head up the stairs to the remains of one of Marseille's oldest churches. The towering 11th-century clock has become the symbol of the Panier district.

PLACE DE LENCHE. Though it is now filled with small cafés and *brasseries*, this square is presumed to be the site of the ancient Greek city center. It offers an excellent view, through modern buildings, of Notre-Dame-de-la-Garde and the *vieux port*.

CATHÉDRALE DE LA MAJOR. From pl. de Lenche, bear right onto rue de l'Evêché and follow it for three blocks, passing some tiny bakeries and left onto rue de Chapitre. The huge Roman-Byzantine cathedral appears suddenly on the coast. Built under the direction of young Napoleon III, it contains beautiful mosaics.

VIEILLE CHARITÉ. Built between 1671 and 1749, the Vieille Charité formerly served as an orphanage and a shelter for the poor. It now houses the **Musée d'Archéologie,** the **Musée d'Arts Africain, Océanien, et Amérindien,** and a small cinema.

ARTERRA. One of many shops on rue Petit Puits continuing the 200-year-old Marseille tradition of *santon* making. This traditional workshop demonstrates how *santons* are made, from the initial mold to the final detailed painting. (3 rue Petit Puits. ☎04 91 91 03 31. Open M-F 9am-1pm and 2-6pm, Sa hours vary.)

RUE DU BAIGNOIR. Head past rue d'Aix and the miniature Arc de Triomphe on rue Puvis de Chavannes, which changes to rue des Dominicaines, until arriving at rue du Baignoir. The small shops in this neighborhood sell goods from North Africa ranging from vibrant fabrics to fragrant incense.

MARCHÉ DE BELSUNCE. Cut down rue Nationale to this daily market known for its Mediterranean imports as well as pungent stalls overflowing with fresh garlic.

▶ ALONG THE SHORE

From the Palais du Pharo to the av. du Prado, the **promenade de la corniche du Président J.F. Kennedy** runs along Marseille's most beautiful stretch of beaches and inlets. The typically heavy traffic is made more bearable by the picturesque views of the Mediterranean. Make a stop at **Vallon des Auffes.** This hidden fishing port looks much the same today as it did 50 years ago, with rows of brightly painted, traditional fishing boats dipping and pulling at their moorings. Pedestrians take bus #83 from the *vieux port* (dir: Rond-Point du Prado) to Vallon des Auffes.

Bus #83 continues on to Marseille's **public beaches.** Get off just after it rounds the statue of David and turns away from the coast. (20-30min.) Or take #19 (dir: Madrague) from M: Castellane or M: Rond-Point du Prado. Both **plage du Prado** and **plage de la Corniche** offer wide beaches, clear water, grass for impromptu soccer matches, and good views of the cliffs surrounding Marseille. **Supermarché Casino et Cafeteria,** across from the statue, provides for the traveler's every need. (Open M-Sa 8:30am-8:30pm. Cafeteria open daily 8:30am-10pm.)

🎵 🎭 ENTERTAINMENT & NIGHTLIFE

There are a few late-night restaurants and a few nightclubs centered around **place Thiers,** near the *vieux port.* A more creative crowd unwinds along the **cours Julien.** Tourists should exercise caution at night, particularly on the dimly-lit streets of the quartier Belsunce, bd. d'Athènes, and in the more far-flung areas of the city, since night buses are scarce, taxis expensive, and the metro closes early (Su-Th 9pm, F-Sa midnight).

Though often overshadowed by that of Paris, Marseille's vibrant entertainment scene includes the best of international theater, music, art, and more. The ticket office at **L'Espace Culture,** 42 rue de la Canebière (☎ 04 96 11 04 60; www.espaceculture.net), provides detailed information and publications on current cultural events throughout the year. Several small theaters and music venues throughout the city assure Marseille's reputation as a theater and music town. Theater buffs should check out the program at the **Théâtre National de Marseille La Criée,** 30 quai de Rive Neuve. (☎ 04 91 54 70 54. Tickets €9-25. Box office open by telephone Tu-Sa 10am-7pm, in person 1-7pm.) Music lovers will not be disappointed by **L'Opéra de Marseille,** 2 rue Molière (☎ 04 91 55 11 10; www.mairie-marseille.fr. Tickets €8-60, under 25 €7-39. Open Su and Tu-F 10am-5:30pm.) Smaller theaters include **Marseille Théâtre Municipal, L'Odéon,** 162 bd. de la Canebière (☎ 04 96 12 52 70), and **Théâtre Gymnase,** 4 rue du Théâtre Français. (☎ 08 20 00 04 27. Box office open Sept.-July M-Sa noon-6pm. Call from 11am-6pm. Tickets €20-28, students €12.) **Cité de la Musique** (☎ 04 91 39 28 28; www.citemusique-marseille.com) offers monthly programs. Unwind with the latest French and American films at **Le César,** 4 pl. Castellane (☎ 04 91 37 12 80; €6.50), or **Variétés,** 37 rue Vincent Scotto, just off rue Canebière. (☎ 04 96 11 61 61. €6.50.)

BARS & CLUBS

El Ache de Cuba, 9 pl. Paul Cézanne (☎ 04 91 42 99 79 or 06 88 21 19 52). Music blares from the speakers and onto the sidewalk from this little slice of Havana. Oct.-June weekly Latin dance and Spanish lessons. You must buy a card (€2) to order something, but those with cards are welcomed into the community. Afterwards, drinks run about €2.50, including the "House Punch." Open W-Sa 5pm-2am.

Trolleybus, 24 quai de Rive Neuve (☎ 04 91 54 30 45; info 06 14 68 88 14). Has to be seen to be believed. This mega-club, occupying an 18th-century warehouse, has separate rooms for house-garage, rock, pop-rock, and soul-funk-salsa. A chic local crowd

IN RECENT NEWS

DEATH IN THE AFTERNOON

Bullfighting is not just for hot-blooded Spaniards. French writer Prosper Merimée put the romance in bullfighting with his short story "Carmen," and a French composer, Georges Bizet, gave it lyrical beauty in his opera. Bullfights are still held in several cities in the south of France, and most fights are modeled after the Spanish version, in which six bulls are killed.

According to the Society for the Prevention of Cruelty to Animals, 90% of bulls used in French bullfights are imported from Spain, and many are sick animals that would not be allowed to fight in Spain. France has also gained the reputation for "doctoring" bullfights—sawing off and rebuilding horns with resin to make them painful for the bull to use.

Today, polls indicate that roughly 80% of the French do not support bullfighting. The cultural capital of the south, Marseille, has been a no-bullfight zone since 1962, and protestors hope to make it the rule rather than the exception. In the meantime, a French tradition is slowly replacing the violent Spanish one. In the Provençal *cocarde camarguaise*, players distract the bull with mitted hands while swiping at pompoms between the bull's horns. During these bullfights, the only blood shed is that of the occasional inexperienced matador.

gets down to the winning lineup of French and international DJs who have been spinning here for 14 years. Beer from €5, drinks €6.50. F nights no cover; Sa cover €10, includes 1 drink. Open July-Aug. W-Sa 11pm-7am; Sept.-June closed W.

Dan Racing, 17 rue André Poggioli (☎06 09 17 04 07). M: Cours Julien. Patrons speak "the universal language" of music in nightly ad hoc performances. Drums, guitars, and other music-makers are provided so anyone can join in on stage. Fun auto- and bike-racing décor adds to the mystique of this casual bar. Drinks €2.30-3.50. Open W-Sa 10pm-2am.

Poulpason, 2 rue André Poggioli (☎04 91 48 85 67). M: Cours Julien. The Poulpason's underwater theme, complete with a giant octopus reaching out from the wall, creates a cool atmosphere for DJs and live rock. Drinks €2.50-5. Open W-Sa 10pm-2am.

MP, 10 rue Beauvau (☎04 91 33 64 79) This friendly, quiet gay bar is frequented mostly by men, though women are also welcome. Light snacks and tall wire stools add charm to this laid-back bar near the *vieux port.* Drinks €2.50-9. Open daily from 6pm.

Bar Associatif Lesbien, 3 rue St-Pierre (☎04 91 48 76 36; www.aux3g.com). M: Cours Julien. Rainbow décor brightens up this social, two-room lesbian bar off cours Julien. A relaxed atmosphere turns into late-night dancing to techno and house music. Drinks €2.60-4. Open Th and Su 6:30pm-midnight; F-Sa 6:30pm-2am.

New Can-Can, 3 rue Sénac (☎04 91 48 59 76). A perpetual weekend party for the city's gay community. Cool *discothèque* setup, with red leather couches. Su-Th no cover; F free before midnight, then €13; Sa €8 before midnight, €14 after. Open 10pm-6am.

LIVE PERFORMANCE

For more info on performance or cultural activities, call **Espace Culture,** 42 La Canebière. (☎04 96 11 04 60. Open M-Sa 10am-6:45pm.)

L'Epicerie, 17 rue Pastoret (☎04 91 42 16 33; www.epicerie-marseille.fr). M: Cours Julien. A creative showcase for budding artists, this funky new theater, gallery, café, and bar all rolled into one features everything from jazz and poetry performances to tango lessons and art conferences. Already getting rave reviews from the press, this little gem is a *salon de thé* by day and a hip, casual performance venue by night. Open W-Sa 4-11pm in the summer; noon-10pm in the winter.

Chocolat Théâtre, 59 cours Julien (☎04 91 42 19 29). A perfect dinner and theater combo. Shows mostly comic pieces. Open Tu-Sa 11:30am-1am. Tickets Tu-Th €13.30, F €15, Sa €18. Dinner and show €23-39, students Tu-Th €11.

La Poste à Galene, 103 rue Ferrari (☎04 91 47 57 99), features both local groups and world-famous acts on the cutting edge. Techno and everything else. Tickets €5-17. Open M-F from 8:30pm, shows at 9:30pm.

⚆ FESTIVALS

Experience the **International Documentary Film Festival** in June and the **Lesbian and Gay Pride March** in late June and early July. Multiple small neighborhood and cultural festivals bring to life the local atmosphere. Information on these can be found in both the tourist office and Espace Culture. The **Festival de Marseille Méditerranée** keeps Marseille full of music, dance, and theater in July. December brings the **Festival de Musique,** a week-long jubilee of jazz, classical, and pop music at l'Abbaye de St-Victor. Call the tourist office or **Espace Culture** (see above) for info.

◪ DAYTRIPS FROM MARSEILLE

LES CALANQUES

The stunning result of underground rivers and sea level fluctuations over centuries, the magnificent rock formations of the Calanques jut into the sea. Stretching from Marseille to Toulon, these towering cliffs of steep near-white rock provide spectacular natural scenery and shelter a fragile balance of terrestrial and marine plants and wildlife, including foxes, bats, and peregrine falcons. Bleached white houses skirt the hills, overlooking swarms of scuba divers, mountain climbers, cliff divers, and nudists.

A marvelous way to view the *calanques* from the water is with G.A.C.M., 1 quai des Belges (☎ 04 91 55 50 09), which operates 4hr. **boat trips** along the Calanques to Cassis and back (mid-June to Sept. daily, mid-July to Sept. 9:30am and 2pm W and Sa-Su 2pm; €25). Hiking is possible, though it can be rather challenging, given the steepness of the Calanques; those interested should check with the tourist office for local conditions.

A cheaper option is to take bus #21 to Luminy (€1.40), which stops near the calanques **Morgiou** and **Sormiou.** The first of the inlets, **Callelongue,** also lies at the farthest reaches of Marseille bus line. Take #19 from M: Castellane to its terminus, La Madrague de Montredon, then catch #20 and follow the coastal roads until its terminus. Service on #20 is sporadic (about one bus per hr. from La Madrague, 6:57am-7:20pm). Explore the trails in the nearby hills to kill time while waiting. Line #20 often ends prematurely at **Goudes** (the town before Callelongue), which is a good base for trails to secluded inlets; ask the driver to take you all the way to Callelongue when you get on.

CASSIS

*Since the train station is 3km outside town, it's easiest to take a **bus** from Marseille (40-50min.; 10 per day 9:15am-7:30pm; leaves from the bus station at M: Castellane).* ***Trains,*** *however, conveniently run at later hours. (21-22min.; 25 each day from Marseille 6am-11:06pm; 25 each day from Cassis 5:16am-10:04pm; €4.40.) For a **taxi** from the train station to town (about €7-8), call ☎04 42 01 78 96 or 06 81 60 48 51. From the bus stop, go right and walk for 5min., following the signs for the centre ville. Turn left on rue Victor Hugo to reach the port. At the water, you will find the **tourist office,** quai des Moulins. (☎04 42 01 71 17; fax 04 42 01 28 31. Open June-Sept. M-F 9am-12:30pm and 2-7pm, Sa-Su 9:30am-12:30pm and 3-6pm; Mar.-May and Oct. M-F 9:30am-12:30pm and 2-6pm, Sa 10am-noon and 2-5pm, Su 10am-noon; Nov.-Feb. M-F 9:30am-12:30pm and 2-5pm, Sa 10am-noon and 2-5pm, Su 10am-noon.)*

The charming resort town of Cassis, 23km from Marseille, clings to a hillside overlooking the Mediterranean. Between immaculate white villas around the slopes above and a jewel-green port below, the town is a network of winding staircases, slender alleyways, and thick gardens. Summer crowds the town with tourists. Parking becomes a competitive sport. Fortunately, the relative peace and unquestionable beauty of the *calanques* are nearby; follow the signs to the **Calanque de Port-Pin,** about an hour east of town. From there, it's a 30min. hike to the popular, otherworldly **Calanque En Vau** and beach.

Explore the crystalline water with a **kayak** at Club Sports Loisirs Nautiques, plage de la Grande Mer. (☎04 42 01 80 01; single kayak €40 per day, double €65), or see the cliffs on a **boat tour.** (☎04 42 01 90 83. 45-90min. Boats leave regularly from port Feb. to mid-Nov.; make reservations Jan.-Feb. €10-15.) The *calanques* are also known for great **diving:** for information, contact Diving Cassis Services Plongée, 3 rue Michel Arnaud. (☎04 42 01 89 16; www.cassis-services-plongee.fr. €28.50 per trip, €43 with equipment rental.)

AIX-EN-PROVENCE

Aix (pronounced "Ex"; pop. 137,000) is one of those rare cities that caters to tourists yet remains unspoiled by their influence. This is the city of Paul Cézanne, Victor Vasarely, and Emile Zola, where nearly every golden façade or dusty café has had a brush with artistic greatness. The town is sprinkled with markers that trail in the footsteps of Cézanne through his favorite haunts on the Chemin de Cézanne. The tourist office provides excellent narrative maps in several languages. Fountains spring up at nearly every small square along the twisting sidestreets of the city center. Aix's student population ensures a lively nightlife scene all year long and keeps it in the cultural forefront of Provence. From the end of June through early August, dance, opera, jazz, and classical music take over the city.

▐ TRANSPORTATION

Trains: at the end of av. Victor Hugo, off impasse Gustave Desplace. Ticket window open M-F 5am-9:25pm, Sa-Su 6am-9:25pm. Reservations and info offices open M-F 8am-7:30pm, Sa 8am-7pm; be prepared for a long wait. Almost every train goes through Marseille; information on schedules can be found in the waiting area. To: **Cannes** (3½hr., 8 per day 5:10am-9pm, €25.10); **Marseille** (35min., 21 per day 5:10am-9:25pm, €5.70); **Nice** (3-4hr., 8 per day 5:10am-9pm, €27.60). Note: Some trains to and from Marseille are actually buses; check the departure info before leaving. If it says "car," your "train" is actually a bus.

Buses: av. de l'Europe (☎04 42 91 26 80), off av. des Belges. Info desk open daily 7:30am-7pm; tickets 6:30am-7pm. Companies compete for the heavy commuter traffic to **Marseille,** with buses almost every 10min. **Phocéens Cars** (☎04 93 85 66 61) goes to **Cannes** (1¾hr., 2 per day, €21) and **Nice** (2¼hr., 5 per day, €20.60). **C.A.P.** (☎04 42 97 52 12) runs to **Arles** (1¾hr.; M-Sa 5 per day, 1 on Su; €11.40). Ask for under-26 student discounts for Nice or Cannes (ISIC required).

Public Transportation: Aix-en-Bus (☎04 42 26 37 28) runs buses around the city. Maps and *carnets* available at the tourist office. (€1.10, €7.30 for a *carnet* of ten).

Taxis: Radio Aixois, ☎04 42 27 71 11. €10 from train station to hostel 3km west of *centre ville.* 24hr.

Bike Rental: La Rotonde, 2 av. des Belges (☎04 42 26 78 92). Bikes €15 per day, €60 per week; students and under 12 years €13/€55. Includes helmet and repair kit. ID and deposit required. Open M-Sa 9:30am-12:30pm and 2:30-6:30pm.

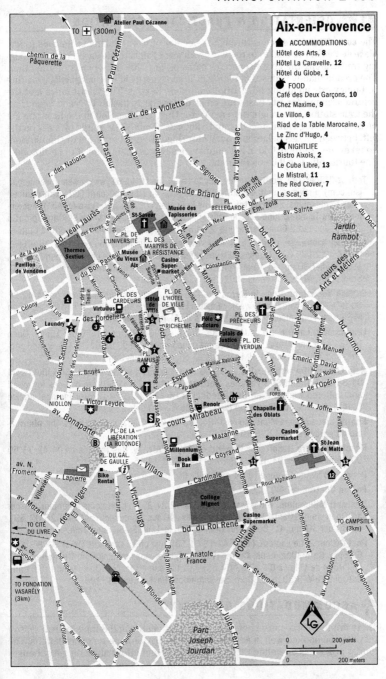

Aix-en-Provence

ACCOMMODATIONS
Hôtel des Arts, **8**
Hôtel La Caravelle, **12**
Hôtel du Globe, **1**

FOOD
Café des Deux Garçons, **10**
Chez Maxime, **9**
Le Villon, **6**
Riad de la Table Marocaine, **3**
Le Zinc d'Hugo, **4**

★ **NIGHTLIFE**
Bistro Aixois, **2**
Le Cuba Libre, **13**
Le Mistral, **11**
The Red Clover, **7**
Le Scat, **5**

PROVENCE

⚜ 🛈 ORIENTATION & PRACTICAL INFORMATION

The **cours Mirabeau** sweeps through the center of town, linking **La Rotonde** (a.k.a. **place du Général de Gaulle**) to the west with **place Forbin** to the east. Fountain-dodging traffic along the cours separates cafés on one side from banks on the other. The predominantly pedestrian *vieille ville* snuggles inside the **périphérique**—a ring of boulevards including bd. Carnot and cours Sextius. The **tourist office** and the central terminus for city buses are on **pl. du Général de Gaulle.** To reach them from the train station, go straight onto av. Victor Hugo and bear left at the fork, staying on av. Victor Hugo until it feeds into **La Rotonde.** (5min.) The tourist office is on the left, between av. des Belges and av. Victor Hugo. To get there from the bus station, go up av. de l'Europe, take a left onto av. des Belges, and follow it to La Rotonde. The tourist office will be on the right.

Tourist Office: 2 pl. du Général de Gaulle (☎ 04 42 16 11 61; www.aixenprovencetourism.com). Provides multi-lingual guides to Aix, "Visa for Aix" card (€2) with reduced rates to museums, and **city tours,** some in English (€8, €4 with "Visa for Aix"). **Accommodation booking** June-Aug. M-Sa 9am-7pm. Open July-Aug. M-Sa 8:30am-8pm, Su 10am-1pm and 2-6pm; Sept.-June M-Sa 8:30am-7pm, Su 8:30am-1pm and 2-6pm.

Currency exchange: L'Agence, in Afat Voyages, 5 cours Mirabeau (☎ 04 42 26 93 93; fax 04 42 26 79 03). American Express affiliate; takes traveler's checks. Open July-Aug. M-Sa 9am-7:30pm, Su 10am-2pm; Sept.-June M-F 9am-6:30pm, Sa 9am-1pm and 2-5pm. 24hr. **ATMs** line cours Mirabeau.

English Bookstore: Book in Bar, 1 rue Cabassol, just off cours Mirabeau (☎ 04 42 26 60 07). Also a café. Hosts weekly English language events, readings, and music. Open M-Sa 9am-7pm. Also, check out the **Cité du Livre** (see **Sights**).

Laundromat: Laverie, 35 cours Sextius. Wash €2.90-6.80, dry €0.30 per 15min. Open Tu-Su 7am-8pm. Also at 15 rue Jacques de la Iroquois (☎ 06 08 01 02 13), 3 rue Fonderie, and 3 rue Fernand Dol. Branches all open daily 7am-8pm.

Help Lines: SIDA Info Service (☎ 08 00 84 08 00) is an AIDS hotline. **SOS Viol** (☎ 04 91 33 16 60) and **SOS Femmes Battues** (☎ 04 91 24 61 50) are hotlines for raped and battered women. Call **SOS Médecins** (☎ 04 42 26 24 00) for medical advice (24hr.). **Service des Etrangers** (☎ 04 42 96 89 48) aids foreigners.

Pharmacie: 17 cours Mirabeau (☎ 04 42 93 63 60). Operates a rotating 24hr. **pharmacie de garde** (☎ 04 42 26 40 40).

Hospital: Centre Hospitalier Général du Pays d'Aix, av. des Tamaris (☎ 04 42 33 50 00). **Ambulance** ☎ 04 42 21 37 37 or 04 42 21 14 15.

Police: 10 av. de l'Europe (☎ 04 42 93 97 00), near the Cité du Livre.

Poison Control: ☎ 04 91 75 25 25.

Internet: Millennium, 6 rue Mazarine (☎ 04 42 27 39 11), off cours Mirabeau. €3 per hr. Open daily 10am-11pm. Also **Virtu@us,** 40 rue Cordeliers (☎ 04 42 26 02 30). €2.30 per 30min., €3.80 per hr. Open M-F 9am-1am, Sa-Su noon-1am.

Post Office: 2 rue Lapierre (☎ 04 42 16 01 50), just off La Rotonde. Open M-F 8:30am-6:45pm, Sa 8:30am-noon. **Currency exchange** for small commission. The **annex,** 1 pl. de l'Hôtel de Ville (☎ 04 42 63 04 66), has the same services. Open M and Th-F 8am-6:30pm, Tu-W 8:30am-6:30pm, Sa 8am-noon. **Postal code:** 13100.

🏠 ACCOMMODATIONS & CAMPING

There are few inexpensive hotels near the city center, and during festival season they may be booked well in advance. Reserve early or hope for cancellations. The tourist office has an online reservation service and information on guest houses and nearby châteaux that take in guests. Campgrounds and chain hotels surround the periphery of Aix.

Hôtel du Globe, 74 cours Sextius (☎04 42 26 03 58; fax 04 42 26 13 68). Spacious rooms with pristine bathroom, oversized armchair, and TV; some have balconies. Rooftop terrace. Breakfast €8. Reception 24hr. Singles €35, with shower €40; doubles with shower €54, with bath €59; two small beds with shower €54, with bath €57; triples with bath €63-69; quads with bath €85. Extra bed €9. AmEx/MC/V. ❹

Hôtel des Arts, 69 bd. Carnot at rue Portalis (☎04 42 38 11 77; fax 04 42 26 77 31). Identical, compact, modern rooms, all with shower, toilet, phone, and TV. Breakfast included. Reception 24hr. Singles and doubles €31-44, depending on whether the room faces noisy bd. Carnot. MC/V. ❸

Hôtel La Caravelle, 29 bd. du Roy-René (☎04 42 21 53 05; fax 04 42 96 55 46). Appealing, moderately sized rooms with cool lighting, several blocks south of the *centre ville*. Breakfast €5.50. Reception 24hr. Singles €39; doubles €43-58; doubles on garden and quad €66. AmEx/MC/V. ❹

Campsites:

Arc-en-Ciel, rte. de Nice (☎04 42 26 14 28), is 2km from the city center. Take bus #3 from La Rotonde at the Trois Sautets stop. Small, comfortable campsite is divided by the Arc. Several sites have a view of Cézanne's Pont des Trois Sautets. Pool, hot showers, and multilingual management who allege that this is the oldest continuously operated campsite in Europe. €5.20 per person, €5.80 per site, parking included. ❶

Chantecler, av. St-André (☎04 42 26 12 98; fax 04 42 27 33 53), by rte. de Nice, is 2km from the city center. Take bus #3 from La Rotonde at the Val St-André stop. Sites have views of Mont Ste-Victoire on a quiet, wooded hill. Pool, impeccable hot showers and restrooms, restaurant, and bar. Open year-round. Reception 8am-11pm. June-Aug. €12 per person, €15.50 with electricity; low season €11.10/€14.30. ❶

⚑ FOOD

Aix's culinary reputation rests on its sweets. The city's *bonbon* is the **calisson d'Aix,** a small iced marzipan-and-melon treat. Other specialties include soft nougat and hard praline candies. Check out the *pâtisseries* on rue Espariat or rue d'Italie; rue d'Italie also has bakeries, *charcuteries*, and fruit stands. The roads north of cours Mirabeau are packed with restaurants, as is **rue de la Verrerie,** off rue des Cordeliers. For the freshest fruits and vegetables, in addition to spices, soaps, and country products, markets open on pl. de la Madeleine (Tu, Th, Sa 7am-1pm) and pl. Richelme (daily, same times). Three **Petit Casinos** serve supermarket shoppers: 3 cours d'Orbitelle (☎04 42 27 61 43; open M-Sa 8am-1pm and 4-7:30pm); 16 rue d'Italie (open Tu-Sa 8am-8pm, Su 8am-1pm); 5 rue Sapora (open Tu-Sa 8:30am-7:30pm, Su 8:30am-12:30pm).

The *Aixois* like nothing better than a cool leisurely drink or a long meal at the cafés along **cours Mirabeau.** Though eating on Mirabeau is generally expensive, an espresso at the ancient gilt-and-mirrored **Café des Deux Garçons ❶** won't empty the wallet. The former watering hole of Cézanne and Zola, affectionately known as the "Deux G's," charges only €1.50 for a coffee. (☎04 42 26 00 51. Open daily 7am-2am.) At lunch and dinner time, colorful tables spill from small restaurants into the squares and side streets of Aix. **Le Villon ❸,** 14 rue Félibre Gaut, off rue des Cordeliers, has calm outdoor seating, a friendly waitstaff, and an excellent *tarte citron* (€4.60). Inside there's candlelit jazz, classical, or French music, even at lunchtime. (☎04 42 27 35 27. Lunch *menu* €9.60, dinner *menu* €11.50-18. Open M-Sa noon-2pm and 7-11pm. MC/V.) For tasty, if pricey, Moroccan fare at tables canopied by a huge tree, head to **Riad de la Table Marocaine ❹,** 21 rue Lieutaud. (☎04 42 26 15 79. Most couscous dishes €18 or less; *menus* €28-34. Open Su-M and W-Sa noon-3pm and 7-11pm.

PROVENCE

ON THE MENU

CALISSONS D'AIX

Some believe that the trademark almond-shaped candy of Aix-en-Provence, the **calisson,** dates back to antiquity. A more probable story places its origin in 1474, at the time of the marriage of René d'Anjou and Jeanne de Laval. According to legend, the new queen never smiled. In an attempt to break her perpetually solemn expression, the royal cook whipped up a confection of sugar, almonds, and crystallized fruit. Upon tasting the delicacy, Jeanne burst into a grin. Her confused courtesans asked what was making her smile; one of them responded that *"Ce sont des câlins"* (it is hugs), which in Provençal was *"di calin soun."*

Calissons consist of melons and almond paste topped with communion wafers and icing. An authentic *calisson* must weigh 10-14 grams and contain exclusively Mediterranean almonds—from Italy, Spain, Maghreb, or, of course, Provence. The world's leading producer of almonds, Aix began making *calissons* in factories in the 19th century using a secret recipe. Many of the *confiseries* in Aix will allow visitors to watch them being made in certified *calisson*-manufacturing shops. All the producers of *calissons* today come from families who have made the confection for at least two generations.

Calissons d'Aix make an ideal gift for those at home, if they make it out of the store uneaten.

AmEx/MC/V.) The highly praised **Chez Maxime ❹,** 12 pl. Ramus, serves excellent Provençal cuisine, from fresh meats to an impressive wine menu. (☎04 42 26 28 51. €13-20; *menus* €21-28. Open M 6pm-midnight; Tu-Sa noon-midnight. MC/V.) For traditional *Aixois* food with a modern twist, **Le Zinc d'Hugo ❸,** 22 rue Lieutaud, serves creative dishes on a quiet street. (☎04 42 27 69 69. *Plats* €8.50-14, *menus* €12-24. Open Tu-Sa noon-midnight. MC/V.)

🄖 SIGHTS

Every corner of Aix is marked by a remarkable edifice, and nearly every fountain has a history. Individual exploration is the best way to experience Aix's charm. Narrative maps from the tourist office provide interesting facts on the various squares, markets, and fountains of the city. The "Visa for Aix" (€2), sold at the tourist office or participating museums, gives reduced admission at museums, a free tour of Thermes Sextius, and half-price on the tourist office's town tour.

FONDATION VASARELY. This trippy black-and-white museum is a must-see for both modern art fans and those who know nothing about the "plastic alphabet." Designed in the 1970s by Hungarian-born artist Victor Vasarely, the father of optical illusion art, or "op art," the building resembles a beehive from above and displays some of Vasarely's most monumental work in eight huge hexagonal spaces. The almost entrancing audio guide probes Vasarely's attempts to create a "polychromatic city of happiness." *(Av. Marcel-Pagnol, Jas-de-Bouffan, next to the youth hostel; take bus #4 or 10 from near the bus station. ☎04 42 20 01 09. Open June-Sept. M-F 10am-1pm and 2-7pm, Sa-Su 10am-7pm; Oct.-May closes at 6pm. €7, students and ages 7-18 €4, under 7 free.)*

CHEMIN DE CÉZANNE. A self-guided 2hr. walking tour winds through the haunts of Aix's most famous son. In his studio, the **Atelier Paul Cézanne,** the artist's beret still hangs in the corner of a room filled with paint-smeared palettes and the props he used for still-lifes, as though he might step inside from the overgrown garden at any moment and pick them up. Multi-lingual guides can match objects in Cézanne's most famous works to those on the shelves. *(9 av. Paul Cézanne. Take bus #21 north of Aix, or just walk 10min. uphill on av. Paul Cézanne. ☎04 42 21 06 53. Open daily mid-June to Sept. 10am-6:30pm; Oct.-Mar. 10am-noon and 2-5pm; Apr. to mid-June 10am-noon and 2:30-6pm. €5.50, students €2, children under 16 and seniors free.)*

CATHÉDRALE ST-SAVEUR. An intriguing mix of Romanesque, Gothic, and Baroque naves built on (and with) stones from a preexisting Roman site, this church is pure architectural whimsy. Carved panels from the 15th-century main portal remain in mint condition. During the Revolution, the bas-relief representing a "transfiguration" was completely destroyed, leaving a blank space above the doors, and all the statues in the great front were decapitated. They were recapitated in the 19th century with disappointing new heads. *(Rue Gaston de Saporta, on pl. de l'Université. ☎04 42 23 45 65. Open daily 9am-noon and 2-6pm, except during services.)*

CITÉ DU LIVRE. This former match factory is now a cultural center with three major sections. The **Bibliothèque Méjanes** contains the largest library in the region and a gallery of contemporary art. Bookended by giant, rusty steel replicas of French classics, this bright library stocks current *Newsweeks* and a good collection of British and American literature. The **Discothèque** loans a wide selection of music from around the world. The air-conditioned **Videothèque d'Art Lyrique** screens operas, ballets, and concerts of past **Festivals d'Aix** for free. *(8-10 rue des Allumettes, southeast of La Rotonde. ☎04 42 91 98 88. Open Tu and Th-F noon-6pm, W and Sa 10am-6pm. Borrowing from the Bibliothèque requires a €20 membership.)*

OTHER SIGHTS. A fine collection of 17th- and 18th-century tapestries hangs in the **Musée des Tapisseries.** The highlight is the series depicting the story of Don Quixote. *(Palais Archiépiscopal, 2nd fl., 28 pl. des Martyrs de la Résistance. ☎04 42 23 09 91. Open Su-M and W-Sa 10am-5pm. €2, under 25 free. July-Aug. free tours in French and English. Call ☎04 42 21 05 78 for info on tours.)* For fans of city history, the **Musée du Vieux Aix,** 17 rue Gaston de Saporta, highlights a random assortment of *Aixois* history, from *santon* molds to popular puppets from early festivals. *(☎04 42 21 43 55. Open Tu-Su Apr.-Oct. 10am-noon and 2:30-6pm; Nov.-Mar. 10am-noon and 2-5pm. €4.)* Antique lovers might enjoy the 17th-century **Pavillon de Vendôme,** which houses paintings and furniture from the turn of the 18th century, as well as temporary exhibits in the summer. *(32 rue Célony. ☎04 42 21 05 78. Museum open Su-M and W-Sa Apr.-Sept. 10am-noon and 2-6pm; Feb.-Mar. and Oct. 10am-noon and 1:30-5:30pm; Nov.-Jan. 10am-noon and 1-5pm. €2, under 26 free. Gardens open daily 9am-5:30pm. Free.)*

■ NIGHTLIFE

Partying is a year-round pastime in Aix. Most clubs open at 11:30pm but don't get going until 2am. Pubs and bars hold earlier hours, often with happy hours. **Rue de la Verrerie** has the highest concentration of bars and clubs; candlelit cafés line the **Forum des Cardeurs,** behind the Hôtel de Ville. Get down to techno, dance, R&B, and house at **Le Mistral,** a big chic dance club at 3 rue F. Mistral; don't show up in shorts, jeans, or sandals. *(☎04 42 38 16 49. €16 cover includes one drink. Tu women free with one drink. Open Tu-Sa 11:30pm-5am.)* **Bistro Aixois,** 37 cours Sextius, lures loads of international students and alcohol into a compact space with a Caribbean beach party motif. *(☎04 42 27 50 10. Open daily 6:30pm-4am. MC/V.)* **The Red Clover,** 30 rue de la Verrerie, is a lively bar with an overflowing international crowd. Happy hour 6-8pm, glass of wine €1.20. *(☎04 42 23 44 61. Open daily 8am-2am.)* **Le Scat,** 11 rue Verrerie, is a happening jazz, rock, and dance club. *(☎04 42 23 00 23; scatclub.free.fr. Nightly free concerts M-Sa 1am. €13 cover includes one drink. Open M-Sa 11pm-6am.)* For salsa, jazz, hip hop, and rock in a more laid-back atmosphere, **Le Cuba Libre,** 4 bd. Carnot, sits just outside the *périphérique* *(☎04 42 21 47 44. Happy hour 6-10pm. Open M-Sa 5pm-2am. Drinks €2.50-5.)* **Ciné Mazarin,** 6 rue Laroque, off cours Mirabeau, and **Renoir,** 24 cours Mirabeau, screen French, foreign, and some English-language films. *(Both ☎04 42 26 99 85. €7.50, students €6, under 6 €4.50.)*

● FESTIVALS

Aix's overwhelming festival season kicks off in the beginning of June with the week-long **Cinestival**. With the free **"billet scoop"** from the tourist office, films cost €3. The **Festival d'Aix-en-Provence**, a famous series of operas and orchestral concerts, lasts from June to July. (Ticket office at 11 rue Gaston de Sapora. ☎04 42 17 34 34; www.festival-aix.com. Tickets start at €6.) For two weeks at the end of July and the beginning of August, the city hosts **Danse à Aix**, which features ballet, modern, and jazz performances. (☎04 42 23 41 24. Call M-F 2-5pm. €11-38, students €11-30.) Tickets are available at the tourist office or at 1 pl. John Rewald. (M-Sa 9am-noon and 2-6pm.) In early July, the city puts on a two-week **Jazz Festival** (Tickets €20). **Aix-en-Musique**, 3 pl. John Rewald (☎04 42 21 69 69), sponsors concerts year-round.

AVIGNON

Its bridge memorialized by the children's song "Sur le pont d'Avignon," the city of Avignon is a medieval maze of fashionable boutiques, intriguing museums, and the unparalleled Palais des Papes, a sprawling Gothic fortress known in its time as "the biggest and strongest house in the world."

Some 700 years ago, political dissent in Italy led the homesick French pontiff Clement V to shift the papacy to Avignon. During this "Second Babylonian Captivity of the Church," as it was dubbed by the stunned Romans, seven popes erected and expanded Avignon's Palais, making the city a "Rome away from Rome." Gregory XI returned the papacy to Rome in 1377, but his reform-minded Italian successor so infuriated the cardinals that they elected an alternate pope who again set up court in Avignon, beginning the Great Schism. In 1403 the last "anti-pope" abandoned the luxurious ecclesiastical buildings, but the town remained Papal territory until the Revolution. Though the popes have gone, the city seems to persist as a capital of Catholicism, the fervor of the papal courts spilling out of history into the tourist-popular modern Avignon.

Avignon (pop. 100,000) is today chiefly known for its two theater festivals—first and foremost, the famous **Festival d'Avignon,** the largest theatrical celebration in Europe, held since 1947, and also the younger, more experimental **Festival OFF.** For three weeks in July, performers, singers, and artists fill the streets with a creative electricity. Although prices soar and accommodations fill up quickly, the thrilling festival weeks are worth the extra tourist frenzy. The city quiets down rather significantly after the festivals have passed, but its monuments, museums, and performer-filled streets maintain their liveliness throughout the year. The city is also a good base for trips to some of Provence's most idyllic villages: the hamlets of the Alpilles (p. 526) and the perched towns of the Lubéron and Vaucluse (p. 513).

▐ TRANSPORTATION

Trains: bd. St-Roch, porte de la République (☎04 90 27 81 89). Info desk and ticket counters open daily 4:30am-12:30am. To: **Arles** (30min., 19 per day, €5.70); **Lyon** (2hr., 7 per day, €25.40); **Marseille** (70min., 15 per day, €15.50); **Montpellier** (1hr., 11 per day, €13); **Nice** (3hr., 7 per day, €35); **Nîmes** (30min., 12 per day, €7.10). **TGV** ticket counters open daily 5:40am-10pm. To: **Dijon** (2¾hr., 16 per day, €41); **Lyon** (1hr., 12 per day, €35.70); **Paris** (3½hr., 13 per day, €79.20). **Note:** The TGV departs from a second train station outside of town, in quartier de Courtine. A Navette **shuttle** bus (€1) runs every 20min. between the two train stations; it also stops just in front of the post office on rue de la République.

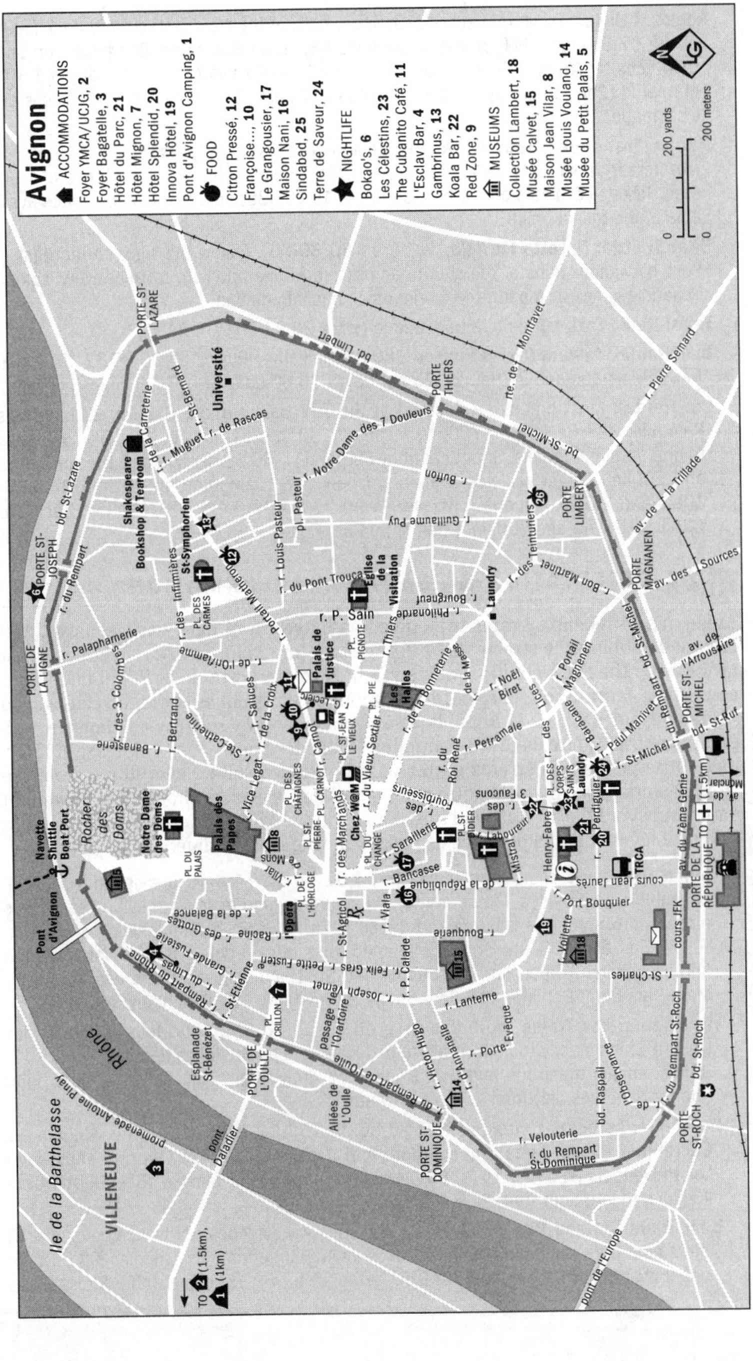

Avignon
ACCOMMODATIONS
Foyer YMCA/UCJG, 2
Foyer Bagatelle, 3
Hôtel du Parc, 21
Hôtel Mignon, 7
Hôtel Splendid, 20
Innova Hôtel, 19
Pont d'Avignon Camping, 1
FOOD
Citron Pressé, 12
Françoise..., 10
Le Grangousier, 17
Maison Nani, 16
Sindabad, 25
Terre de Saveur, 24
NIGHTLIFE
Bokao's, 6
Les Célestins, 23
The Cubanito Café, 11
L'Esclav Bar, 4
Gambrinus, 13
Koala Bar, 22
Red Zone, 9
MUSEUMS
Collection Lambert, 18
Musée Calvet, 15
Maison Jean Vilar, 8
Musée Louis Vouland, 14
Musée du Petit Palais, 5
200 yards
200 meters
Rhône
Ile de la Barthelasse
VILLENEUVE
Pont d'Avignon
Palais des Papes
Notre Dame des Doms
Rocher des Doms
Palais de Justice
Les Halles
Université
TRCA
PORTE DE LA RÉPUBLIQUE
PORTE ST-LAZARE
PORTE THIERS
PORTE LIMBERT
PORTE MAGNANEN
PORTE ST-MICHEL
PORTE ST-ROCH
PORTE ST-DOMINIQUE
PORTE DE L'OULLE
PORTE DE LA LIGNE
PORTE ST-JOSEPH

Regional Buses: Gare Routière, bd. St-Roch, right of the train station. Info desk (☎04 90 82 07 35) open M-F 8am-noon and 1:30-6pm, Sa 8am-noon. Buy tickets on bus. **CTM** goes to: **Arles** (45min., 5 per day, €7.80); **Les Baux** (1hr., 2 per day, €7.80); **Marseille** (2hr., 5 per day, €15.20); **St-Rémy** (45min., 10 per day, €5.20). Buses are less frequent Sept.-June.

Public Transportation: TCRA, av. de Lattre de Tassigny (☎04 32 74 18 32; www.tcra.fr), near porte de la République. Office open M-F 8:30am-12:30pm and 1:30-6pm. Tickets (€1) sold on the bus, *carnet* of 10 (€7.80) sold at the office. Maps available at the tourist office.

Boat Shuttle: Navette Fluviale, (☎04 90 80 80 00). Follow the signs to the right of Pont d'Avignon. Runs a free shuttle across the Rhône mid-Feb. to Dec. every 15min. Schedule varies by month; the tourist office has information.

Taxis: Radio Taxi, porte de la République (☎04 90 82 20 20). 24hr.

Bike Rental: Aymard Cycles Peugeot, 80 rue Guillaume Puy (☎04 90 86 32 49). Open Tu-Sa 8am-noon and 2-7pm. €9.20 per day, €36.60 per week. €120 deposit. MC/V.

Car Rental: Most offices are located at the TGV train station. **Car Go,** 141 rue des Rémouleurs (☎04 90 800 700; www.cargo.fr), at the TGV station, will drive customers to and from their hotels. Smart car from €9 per day, €0.32 per km, or €186 for 5 days and 500km. Larger vehicles available. Open M 7:30am-noon and 2-6pm, Tu-Sa 8-10am and 2-6pm. National/Citer, (☎04 90 27 30 07), at the TGV station. Basic car €261 for 5 days and 700km. Open M-Sa 9am-6pm.

➤ 🛈 ORIENTATION & PRACTICAL INFORMATION

Avignon's 14th-century ramparts enclose a labyrinth of alleyways, squares, and cramped cobblestone streets that are excellent for exploring. To reach the tourist office from the train station, walk straight through porte de la République onto cours Jean Jaurès. The tourist office is about 200m uphill on the right. Cours Jean Jaurès becomes rue de la République and leads directly to **place de l'Horloge**, Avignon's central square, below the looming Palais des Papes. Just southeast of l'Horloge, little pedestrian streets glitter with boutiques selling everything from the latest fashions to Provençal pottery. At night, lone travelers should stay on well-lit paths and avoid the area around rue Thiers and rue Philonarde. Avignon is a haven for car thieves and pickpockets, especially during festival time.

Tourist Office: 41 cours Jean Jaurès (☎04 32 74 32 74; www.ot-avignon.fr). Knowledgeable staff provides info on housing, restaurants, and regional activities, as well as maps and **tours** of the Lubéron and the city. (2hr. tours in several languages Apr.-Oct. Tu, Th, Sa 10am. €8, students €5. Themed tours offered during the festival d'Avignon and for children.) Open July M-Sa 9am-7pm, Su 10am-5pm; Apr.-June and Aug.-Sept. M-Sa 9am-6pm; Oct.-Mar. M-F 9am-6pm, Sa 9am-5pm, Su 10am-noon.

Train Tours: Les Trains Touristiques (☎06 11 35 06 66). Short tour of Rocher des Doms €2; longer city tour €6. Train tours leave from pl. du Palais des Papes every 15-35min. Longer trains run mid-Mar. to mid-Oct. daily 10am-7pm; July-Aug. until 8pm. Shorter train runs only from 1:30pm onwards.

Bus Tours: Autocars Lieutaud (☎04 90 86 36 75) runs excursions to the **Alpilles, La Camargue, Nîmes, Arles,** the **Lubéron,** and **Orange** for €15-28. (Apr. to early Nov.) **Les Provençals** (☎04 90 14 70 00) also tours many nearby locales. (See **Sights.** €25-45. June to late Sept. Tu-F €5-9 discount with pass.)

Boat Tours: Bateau Bus (☎04 90 85 62 25; www.avignon-et-provence.com/mireio) offers boat trips along the Rhône (1-2hr.; July-Aug. 6 per day; €7, children €3.50). For longer river cruises, **Compagnie G.B.P.** (☎04 90 85 62 25; same web address) rides up and down the Rhône, stopping in Arles, Tarascon, Châteauneuf-du-Pape, and the Camargue, among others. (Tour options alternate throughout the year; €24.70-57, depending on meals and length).

English Bookstore: Shakespeare Bookshop and Tearoom, 155 rue de la Carreterie (☎04 90 27 38 50), down rue Carnot toward the ramparts. English-cream teas, and excellent homemade brownies (€1.30). Open Tu-Sa 9:30am-12:30pm and 2-6:30pm.

Youth Information: Espace Info-Jeunes, 102 rue de la Carreterie (☎04 90 14 04 05). Info on jobs, study, health care, housing, work. Open M-F 8:30am-noon and 1:30-5pm.

Laundromat: 66 pl. des Corps Saints. Also 48 rue Carreterie. Both open daily 7am-8pm. For a more exciting way to pass the time doing laundry, **Le Café Lavoir,** 101 rue de la Bonneterie (☎04 90 27 91 06; le-cafe-lavoir@wanadoo.fr), is a funky café and laundromat, complete with a tiny art gallery and lavender-soap sale. Wash €4-8, dry €1 per 15min. Open daily 10am-8pm.

Police: bd. St-Roch (☎04 90 16 81 00), left of the train station.

Lost and Found: at Municipal Police Office, 13 quai St-Lazare (☎04 32 76 01 73).

Hospital: 305 rue Raoul Follereau (☎04 32 75 33 33), south of the town center. 24hr.

24hr. Pharmacy: 11-13 rue St-Agricol (☎04 90 82 14 20). Open daily 8am-7:15pm. For the nightly **pharmacie de garde,** call the police.

Internet: Webzone, 3 rue St-Jean le Vieux (☎04 32 76 29 47), at pl. Pie. A fair number of computers and chatty English-speaking staff. €2.50 for 30min., €4 per hr. Open daily 9am-midnight, Su noon-8pm. **Chez W@M,** 41 rue du Vieux Sextier (☎04 90 86 19 03). New computers and Ben & Jerry's mini-ice cream; €3.50 per hr. Open M-F 8am-1am, Sa-Su noon-1am.

Post Office: cours JFK (☎04 90 27 54 00), near porte de la République. **Currency exchange. Western Union.** Open M-F 8am-7pm, Sa 8am-noon. **Branch office** on pl. Pie (☎04 90 14 70 70). Open M-F 8:30am-12:30pm and 1:30-6:30pm, Sa 8:30am-noon. For **Poste Restante,** specify "Poste Restante: Avignon." **Postal code:** 84000.

ACCOMMODATIONS & CAMPING

In general, Avignon's budget offerings are pleasant and plentiful. Unfortunately, unreserved beds vanish once the theater troupes hit town. All prices increase (often by €10 for hotels) during July festival season. (Many hotels fill up by March for the July-Aug. holiday). The tourist office lists organizations that set up cheap housing during the festival; if hotels are full, festival-goers might also consider staying in Arles, Nîmes, Orange, or Tarascon and commuting by train (€5.50-7.10).

Hôtel Splendid, 17 rue Agricol Perdiguier (☎04 90 86 14 46; fax 04 90 85 38 55), near the tourist office. Charming, recently redone rooms with new wooden furniture on a quiet street in a busy area; the smallest rooms have names like Lavender and Olive. Breakfast €5. Reception 7am-11pm. Singles with shower €30-34; doubles with shower €40-46. Extra bed €5. AmEx/MC/V. ❸

Foyer YMCA/UCJG, 7bis chemin de la Justice, Villeneuve (☎04 90 25 46 20; fax 04 90 25 30 64; info@ymca-avignon.com). From the train station, turn left and follow the city wall; cross the second bridge (pont Daladier) and the Ile Barthelasse. Continue straight for 200m, then take a left onto chemin de la Justice; the foyer will be up the hill on your left. (30min.) From the post office, take bus #10 (dir: Les Angles-Grand Angles) to Général Leclerc or #11 (dir: Villeneuve-Grand Terme) to Pont d'Avignon. Clean, sparsely decorated, cheerful rooms with terraces; great views of the Palais, the surrounding countryside, or the inviting pool. Internet €2.80 per hr. Breakfast €5. *Demi-pension* obligatory in July. Reception 8:30am-noon and 1:30-6pm. July-Aug. F-Su reception is at on-site restaurant. Reserve ahead. Apr.-Oct. singles €15 per person, with shower and toilet €30; doubles €26-40; triples €31-52. Rates drop 20% in other months. MC/V. ❶

Foyer Bagatelle, Ile de la Barthelasse (☎04 90 86 30 39 or 04 90 85 78 45; fax 04 90 27 16 23). Take bus #10 or 11 to La Barthelasse. Incomparable view of the city from the banks of the Rhône. Simple 2-, 4-, 6-, or 8-bed rooms with soft colors. Internet €4.60 per 30min. Supermarket, two cafeterias, and bike rental (€16 per day with ID deposit). Breakfast priced à la carte. Reception 11am-8pm. Lockout 2-5pm. Dorms €10.20; doubles €23-31. Excellent **camping** facilities available in the dense shade of plane trees. Reception 8:30am-8:30pm. 1 person and tent €7.40, 2 people and tent €10.20. Electricity €2.40. MC/V. ❶

Hôtel Mignon, 12 rue Joseph Vernet (☎04 90 82 17 30; www.hotel-mignon.com). Charming hotel on a chic street near great shopping. Provençal fabrics adorn each comfortable, plush, carpeted, well-equipped room. Breakfast included. Singles €33; doubles with shower €50-55; triples with shower €60; quads €78. Rates increase by €4-5 July-Aug. MC/V. ❸

Hôtel du Parc, 18 rue Perdiguier (☎04 90 82 71 55; fax 04 90 85 64 86). Modern, understated rooms with handmade bedspreads and curtains that give it a personal feel. Right across from the Hôtel Splendid. Breakfast €5. Shower in hall €2. Reception noon-10pm. Reserve well ahead. Singles €29, with shower €36; doubles with bath €42; triples with bath €55. MC/V. ❸

Innova Hôtel, 100 rue Joseph Vernet (☎04 90 82 54 10; fax 04 90 82 52 39; hotel.innova@wanadoo.fr). Within footsteps of everything, with clean and simple rooms. Smiling owner goes out of his way to assist guests. Breakfast €5. Bike storage available. Singles €28; doubles with shower €35-55; quads €65. MC/V. ❸

Camping: Pont d'Avignon, 300 Ile de la Barthelasse (☎04 90 80 63 50; www.camping-avignon.com), 10min. past Foyer Bagatelle. Hot showers, laundry, restaurant, supermarket, pool, and tennis and volleyball courts in a four-star site that feels like a hotel, except that it's outdoors. 300 spots. Reception July-Aug. 8am-10pm; June and Sept. 8:30am-8pm; Mar.-May and Oct. 8:30am-6:30pm. Open Mar.-Oct. July 1 person and tent €14.60; 2 people and tent €20.10; extra person €4. Electricity €2.50-2.90. Prices significantly lower in low season. MC/V. ❷

☐ FOOD

There's a delicious selection of lively and creative restaurants on the crooked **rue des Teinturiers.** The cafés of **place de l'Horloge** are good for a drink after dinner, when mimes and street musicians milk the crowds for smiles and centimes. The Vietnamese restaurants throughout the city on small impasses or in alleys off major thoroughfares are often great budget options. For those with midnight snacking tendencies, **snack bars** line the boulevards and *places* of Avignon, serving up all manner of hot, greasy sandwiches, crêpes, and ice cream. **Parc de Rocher des Doms,** overlooking the Rhône, provides good picnic spots and has an outdoor café near the pond. **Les Halles,** the large indoor **market** on pl. Pie, promises endless amounts of regional produce, chèvre, meats, and wines. (Tu-Su 7am-1pm.) The same food may be less expensive at the **open-air markets** outside the city walls near porte St-Michel (Sa-Su 7am-1pm) and on pl. Crillon (F 7am-1pm). **Shopi** supermarket, rue de la République, about 100m from the tourist office, offers quick grocery fixes (open M-Sa 8:30am-8pm), as does the reliable **Petit Casino** on rue St-Agricol (open M-Sa 8am-8pm, Su 9am-8pm) and at 3 rue Corps Saints. (Open M-Sa July-Aug. 8am-12:45pm and 4-7:45pm; Sept.-June 8am-12:30pm and 3-7:30pm.) Most restaurants stay open an hour or two later and seven days a week during the festivals. For bread and pastry lovers, **Le Fournil des Papes,** 45 cours Jean Jaurès (☎04 90 85

80 62), just inside of the Porte de la République, has a wide selection of freshly baked goods, including breads with black olives or chèvre baked inside. (Open M-Sa 7:15am-8pm; open Su in July.)

Françoise..., 6 rue Général Leclerc (☎04 32 76 24 77), near pl. Pie. Gourmet, home-style meals can be eaten at common tables with large plates of bread in the center, or as take-out. Lots of vegetarian options, sandwiches, salads, and soups (all €3-5), as well as full meals (€8-10). Welcomes diners to a home-like feel with special touches, including the warm out-of-the-oven *pomme-framboise* crumble (€2.90) served in little baskets with wooden "silverware." Open daily noon-3pm and 7-10pm; non-stop during the July festival season. ❷

Sindabad, rue des Teinturiers (☎04 90 85 99 50). A recent addition to the delicious finds on this narrow street, Sindabad serves zesty vegetarian Indian/Provençal cuisine with unique blends of spices and flavors, such as in their avocado-laced *lasagne aux légumes* (€10). Entrées €5-10; 5% less for take-out. Open daily 11am-2:30pm and 7pm-12:30am. MC/V. ❷

Terre de Saveur, 1 rue St-Michel (☎04 90 86 68 72), just off pl. des Corps Saints. Homey Provençal restaurant serves hearty dishes with organic veggies in a cozy dining room filled with locals. Vegetarian *menu* €13; omnivore version €15. *Plats* €9-11.50. Open M-Sa 11:30am-2:30pm, F-Sa and nightly during Avignon Festival 7-9:30pm. MC/V. ❸

Le Grangousier, 17 rue Galante (☎04 90 82 96 60). This small, funky, art-filled restaurant specializes in slow-cooked food: each menu item has been cooked for 4-28hr. The food's rich flavor attests to the care put into it. *A la carte* options €7-10, full *menus* €20-25. ❷

Maison Nani, rue de la République (☎04 90 82 60 90), near H&M. A jovial crowd of regulars satisfy their appetites with heaping salads (€9-14.50) at this lively restaurant amidst the action of rue de la République. The *"Don Nani" salade de penne* (€8.90) gives off the smell of fresh basil. Open M-Sa 11:30am-2:30pm, F-Sa 7-11pm. ❸

Citron Pressé, 38 rue Carreterie (☎04 90 86 09 29). This small restaurant offers tasty and filling Lebanese, Indian, and Provençal meals for astonishing prices (€3.50-6). Open June-Sept. daily noon-2am; Oct.-May M-W noon-2pm, Th-F noon-2pm and 7:30pm-2am, Sa 7:30pm-2am. ❶

SIGHTS

*Avignon's sights, at least all those listed here, operate on a **Pass** system. At the first monument or museum you visit, you'll pay full admission (regardless of age or status); at sights visited for 15 days thereafter, you pay the reduced price (which also applies to students and seniors).*

PALAIS DES PAPES. This golden Gothic palace, the largest in Europe, thrusts gargoyles out over the city and the Rhône. Its sheer, battlemented walls are interrupted by the tall, ecclesiastical windows of the Grande Chapelle and the dark cross of arrow-loops. Begun in 1335 by the third pope of Avignon, Benoît XII, and finished less than twenty years later by his successor Clément VI, the papal palace is neatly divided into two sections with the contrasting styles of their builders: the strict, spare grandeur of the Cistercian Benoît and the astonishing scale and ostentation of the aristocratic Clément. Although Revolutionary looting stripped the interior of its lavish furnishings, the giant rooms and their frescoed walls are still remarkable, with brightly colored tiles and slowly flaking paint in some of the inner chambers. What dazzles the viewer most is the way the Palais unrolls almost endlessly, chamber after chamber. A comprehensive audio guide, available in eight languages and offered free with admission, provides history and architectural explanations. From May to September, the most beautiful rooms in the Palais are given over to diverse exhibitions, which have recently included Picasso and a creatively contrasting retrospective of contemporary artists. *(☎04 90 27 50 74; www.palais-des-papes.com. Open daily July-Sept. 9am-8pm; Oct.-June 9am-7pm. Last ticket 1hr. before closing. Palace and exhibition €9.50, with pass €7.50.)*

PONT ST-BÉNÉZET. This 12th-century bridge is known to all French (and many non-French) children as the "Pont d'Avignon," immortalized in the famous song. In 1177, Bénézet, a shepherd boy, was commanded by angels to build a bridge across the Rhône. He announced his intentions to the population of Avignon, but the people, thinking he was "a man inhabited by fairies," laughed at him. The Archbishop, pointing to a gigantic boulder, told Bénézet that he would have to place the first stone himself. Miraculously, the shepherd heaved the rock onto his shoulder and tossed it into the river. The holy shot put convinced the townspeople, who responded quickly with shovels and mortar, finishing the bridge in 1185. Despite the divinely chosen location, the bridge has suffered a number of destructive incidents at the hands of warfare and the once turbulent Rhône. It costs €3.50 (with pass €3) to walk on the bridge; there is no extra charge for dancing round and round. *(☎04 90 85 60 16. Includes a detailed audio guide in 7 languages. Open daily Apr.-Nov. 9am-7pm; July-Sept. 9am-8pm; Nov.-Mar. 9:30am-5:45pm.)* Farther down the river, **Pont Daladier** makes it all the way across the river to the campgrounds, offering free views of the broken bridge and the Palais along the way.

COLLECTION LAMBERT. Highlighting the oft-misunderstood art of the period from the late 1960s through the present, this excellent museum presents three exhibits per year. Past artists have included Sol LeWitt and Jean-Michel Basquiat. The high-quality museum displays two permanent pieces: a digitized message from Jenny Holzer, and a throbbing red neon room on the top floor. *(5 rue Violette. ☎04 90 16 56 20; www.collectionlambert.com. Open Tu-Su July-Aug. 11am-7pm; Nov.-Feb. until 6pm. €5.50, with pass €4.)*

OTHER SIGHTS. On the hill over the Palais, the beautifully sculpted **Rocher des Doms Park** has vistas of Mont Ventoux, St-Bénézet, and the fortifications of Villeneuve. (Open during daylight hours.) Next to the Palais, the 12th-century **Cathédrale Notre-Dame-des-Doms** contains the dramatically lit Gothic tomb of Pope John XXII. *(Open daily 10am-7pm.)* The **Musée du Petit Palais,** pl. du Palais des Papes, is crowded with religious art and Roman sculptures. *(☎04 90 86 44 58. Written guides available in English, German, and Italian for €2. Open M and W-Su June-Sept. 10am-1pm and 2-6pm; Oct.-May 9:30am-1pm and 2-5:30pm. €6, with pass €3.)* The **Musée Calvet,** an elegant 18th-century hôtel particulier, exhibits art from the 17th to 20th centuries, highlighting pieces by French artists like Camille Claudel. *(65 rue Joseph Vernet. ☎04 90 86 33 84. Open Su-M and W-Sa 10am-1pm and 2-6pm. €6, with pass €3.)* For those with a penchant for finer things, a 19th-century hôtel houses the small but intriguing decorative arts collection of the **Musée Louis Vouland.** *(17 rue Victor Hugo. ☎04 90 86 03 79; www.vouland.com. Visits available in English with reservation. Open May-Oct. Tu-Sa 10am-noon and 2-6pm, Su 2-6pm; Nov.-Apr. Tu-F 10am-noon and 2-6pm, Sa-Su 2-6pm. €4, pass €2.50.)*

🎵 📷 ENTERTAINMENT & FESTIVALS

Regular performances of opera, drama, and classical music take place in the **Opéra d'Avignon,** pl. de l'Horloge (☎04 90 82 81 40). **Rue des Teinturiers** is lined with theaters holding performances from the early afternoon through the wee hours of the morning. These include the **Théâtre du Chien qui Fume,** 75 rue des Teinturiers (☎04 90 85 25 87), the **Théâtre du Balcon,** 38 rue Guillaume Puy (☎04 90 85 00 80), and the **Théâtre du Chêne Noir,** 8bis rue Ste-Catherine (☎04 90 82 40 57). The **Utopia Cinéma,** behind the Palais des Papes on 4 rue Escalier Ste-Anne, screens a wide variety of movies in *version original*. (☎ 04 90 82 65 36; www.cinemas-utopia.com. €5, 10 showings €40.) The **Maison Jean Vilar** (see **Other Sights**) shows free videos.

Although the best nightlife in Avignon is found throughout the weeks of the festival when bars, cafés, shops, and restaurants stay open until early in the morning, the rest of the year still promises nighttime amusement that is only slightly tamer. *Brasseries* on **cours Jean Jaurès** and **rue de la République** stay open late to entertain quiet crowds on their terraces. A few lively bars color **place des Corps Saints. The Cubanito Café,** 52 rue Carnot, features nightly dancing to Cuban music, including salsa, in a boisterous, kick-back atmosphere. Free salsa lessons Tu-Sa 9-10pm. (☎ 04 90 27 90 59. Open daily 8am-1am. Beers from €2.20.) **Les Célestins,** 38 pl. des Corps Saints, is a mosaic-tiled, red and orange glittering café whose fun-loving crowd fills the outdoor seating that takes over the *place*. (Beer from €2, drinks €3-5. Open daily 9am-1am.) The newest club on the scene for those seeking ultraviolet-lit dance floors and chic drinking, **Bokao's,** 9bis bd. St-Lazare, just outside the porte St-Lazare, is filled with glowing white lanterns and palm trees. (☎ 04 90 82 47 95. Drinks from €5. Cover Sa only, €10. Open W-Sa 10pm-5am.) For an equally snazzy gay- and lesbian-only club, **L'Esclav Bar,** 12 rue du Limas, near the Pont d'Avignon, has heavy techno and house with a bouncer who enforces the private club policy. (☎ 04 90 85 14 91. Cover €5, includes a drink. Open daily from 11pm.) **Red Zone,** 25 rue Carnot, fulfills its role as a student club with later hours and music ranging from salsa to house to R&B. (☎ 04 90 27 02 44. Open daily 9am-3am; closed Su Nov.-Feb.) Cheap suds and a crackling sound system draw talkative Australians and backpackers to the **Koala Bar,** 2 pl. des Corps Saints. (☎ 04 90 86 80 87. Beer from €2.50, drinks from €2. Happy hour daily 9-10pm. Open 8:30pm-1:30am, until 1am Nov.-Feb.) Speedy bar-restaurant **Gambrinus ❷,** 62 rue de la Carreterie, near porte St-Lazare, has six beers on tap and 60 in bottles, as well as mussels, from traditional *moules marinières* with fries (€7.30) to *moules à la bière* (€8.70), in huge portions. (☎ 04 90 86 12 32. Drafts €2.20-3.10. Billiards €1.50. Open M-Sa 8am-1:30am. Closed early Aug. and early Jan. MC/V.)

July brings the definite highlight of Avignon's calendar, a month filled with poster wars and more theater than is imaginable. During the riotous **Festival d'Avignon,** Gregorian chanters rub shoulders with all-night *Odyssey* readers and African dancers. The official festival, also known as the **IN,** is the most presti-

IN RECENT NEWS

FESTIVAL OFF

Following a summer of nationwide workers' strikes, fears of similar protests in Avignon were raised before the opening of its world-renowned theater festival. Avignon's theater workers were angered by a negotiation process regarding nationally controlled pay structures for theater employees. The proposal, which saw little union support, would put theater professionals at risk of losing unemployment benefits that sustain them in the low season.

The combined IN and OFF Festivals in Avignon run throughout the month of July, bringing over 700 productions to the stage. In the days prior to the scheduled July 8th opening of the festival, posters throughout the city warned of the possible "death of culture" if the theater workers were not supported. On July 8th, instead of the roar of applause, Avignon was greeted with a truly theatrical strike of over 10,000 protestors. Waving SOS flags, shouting for public support, and even "crucifying" a stagehand in front of the Palais des Papes, protestors descended upon the city, bringing the opening festivities to a standstill. While city officials worried about the economic loss caused by canceling the festival, the strikes went on. On July 10th, the director of the Festival d'Avignon reluctantly called off the festival for the first time ever; similar cancellations occurred in Montpellier, Marseille, and Aix.

gious theatrical gathering in Europe, appearing in at least 30 different venues from factories to cloisters to palaces. (Info and tickets ☎04 90 14 14 14. Festival office ☎04 90 14 14 60; www.festival-avignon.com. Tickets free to €33. Reservations accepted after mid-June. Rush tickets at venue 45min. before the show; students and those under 25 get a 50% discount.) The cheaper and more experimental (although equally established) **Festival OFF** presents over 700 pieces, some in English, over the course of three weeks in July. (OFFice on pl. du Palais. ☎01 48 05 01 19; www.avignon-off.org. Tickets free to €16; purchased at the venue or the OFFice, not available over the phone.) One doesn't need a ticket to get in on the act—fun, free theater overflows into the streets during the day and particularly at night. The Centre Franco-Américain de Provence sponsors the **Euro-American Film Workshop** in late June at the Cinéma Vox. The festival showcases feature-length and short films directed by young French and American aspirants. Meals, parties, and lectures give an opportunity for rubbing shoulders with the next big thing. Films are in *v.o.* with French or English subtitles. (☎04 90 25 93 23. Night showings €6, morning films €1.50, day pass €55.)

▓ DAYTRIP FROM AVIGNON: VILLENEUVE-LÈS-AVIGNON

*From Avignon, **bus** #11 (every 20min.) to Villeneuve will take you to the tourist office. Otherwise, a 25-30min. walk over the Le Pont Daladier, just below Pont d'Avignon, provides scenic views along the Rhône. Follow the signs to Villeneuve. The Bâteau Bus **boat,** allées de l'Oulle, near the Pont Daladier, cruises past Pont St-Bénézet and docks at Villeneuve. From there, a Petit Train (€1) will take you to the town center. (☎04 90 85 62 25. July-Aug. 6 per day 10:30am-7:20pm. Roundtrip €7, children €4.50; 20% off with pass. Tickets on board or at tourist office in Avignon.)*

Founded in the 13th century to intimidate France's Provençal neighbors, Villeneuve-lès-Avignon ("new town by Avignon") sits on a hill overlooking Avignon. The so-called "City of Cardinals" was the home of many of the dignitaries and attendants to the papal court.

La Chartreuse du Val de Bénédiction, rue de la République, is one of the largest Carthusian monasteries in France and home to la Chartreuse-Centre National des Ecritures du Spectacle, which hosts artists and creative performances throughout the year. The collapsed back wall of the church affords a dramatic view of Fort St-André. (☎04 90 15 24 24. Open daily Apr.-Sept. 9am-6:30pm; Oct.-Mar. 9:30am-5:30pm. €6.10, students and those with pass €4.10.) Info regarding regular special events is available at the front desk. Crowning Mont Andaon is the Gothic **Fort Saint-André,** built by King Philip the Fair in the 14th century. The towers served as prisons after losing their strategic value; the stone floors and walls still bear the marks of the prisoners' desperate carvings. (☎04 90 25 45 35. Open Apr.-Sept. daily 10am-1pm and 2-6pm, Oct.-Mar. 10am-noon and 2-5pm. €4.60, students and those with pass €3.10.)

Situated within the fortress is the 11th-century Benedictine **Abbaye St-André.** Its original buildings were mostly destroyed during the Revolution but have been replaced with a manicured, fairy-tale French garden, complete with purple lilies, olive trees, and the occasional live goat. Between the hidden fountains and arcades of cypresses are views of the Rhône valley and Avignon. (☎04 90 25 55 95. Open Tu-Su Apr.-Sept. 10am-12:30pm and 2-6pm; Oct.-Mar. 10am-noon and 2-5pm. €4, with pass €3.)

The Gothic **Tour Philippe Le Bel,** located right at the intersection of av. Gabriel Péri and Montée de la Tour, provides a dizzying view from its wind-swept platform. (☎04 32 70 08 57. Tower open daily Apr.-Sept. 10am-12:30pm and 3-7pm; Oct.-Mar. 10am-noon and 2-5:30pm. €1.60, students and pass €0.90.)

THE LUBÉRON & THE VAUCLUSE

This region fulfills every romanticized vision of sunny French countryside. Nestled between two picturesque mountain ranges, the Parc Naturel Régional du Lubéron and the Vaucluse, stretch neat rows of vineyards and perfumed, radiant fields of lavender dotted with haunting medieval châteaux and tiny villages perched precariously on rocky escarpments. For centuries, this mini-Eden has been a home and inspiration to writers, from Petrarch to the Marquis de Sade to Samuel Beckett. Small wonder: from the fiery reds of the ochre hills to the deep greens of the olive-tree farms, this is Provence's living poetry. Although *Let's Go* lists a few famous beauties here, this region is ideal for discovering hidden surprises on one's own. A guidebook should only be a starting point.

TRANSPORTATION. The majority of the Lubéron can easily be covered in two to three days by **car**, by far the easiest option. Avignon is filled with rental companies happy to provide maps and suggestions. N100 blows right through the middle of the Lubéron park and branches off to the smaller towns, but the twisting, narrow roads from one town to the next are usually far more picturesque. Expect to pay €2-3 for parking in most villages. However, combining occasional bus trips with walks or bike rides between towns (usually 7-15km) will let you experience Provence at its pristine finest, albeit in more time. Biking, though common, is not for the faint of heart, as the mountains climb steeply here. A few of the bike rental companies offer to drop renters off at cities that allow for strategic downhill coasting. Locals sometimes choose to hitch, but rides for tourists are difficult to come by and *Let's Go* does not recommend hitchhiking at any time. Avignon **buses** leave from the central bus terminal. Voyages Arnaud (☎04 90 38 15 58) runs buses from Avignon to Isle-sur-la-Sorgue (40min., 8 per day, €3.10); Fontaine de Vaucluse (55min., 4 per day, €3.90); and Bonnieux (70min., 1 per day, €3). Les Express de la Durance (☎04 90 71 03 00) buses head to Cavaillon (40min., 12 per day, €3.10), which also serves as a hub for bus excursions. TransVaucluse (☎04 90 82 07 35) covers most of the Vaucluse and Lubéron including Apt (1hr., 7 per day, €6.90). Its schedules change regularly; information is posted at the *gare routière* in Avignon. Autocars Barlatier (☎04 90 73 23 59) goes to the train station at **Bonnieux** (1hr., 5 per day, €5.30), sometimes via Oppède-le-Vieux (1 per day, €5). However you travel, good walking shoes are a must for the hilly, often unpaved roads.

L'ISLE-SUR-LA-SORGUE

L'Isle-sur-la-Sorgue (pop. 17,500) is the first step from Avignon and into the Vaucluse countryside. Entangled in the green ribbon of its river, this tranquil town echoes with the rushing currents of water that twist around the *centre ville*. The sparklingly clear, shallow waters of the Sorgue are split into numerous channels to the east of the city, surrounding and running beneath the town center, aptly nicknamed "the Venice of Vaucluse." Founded in the 12th century, l'Isle-sur-la-Sorgue has long depended on its narrow waterways for fish, industry, and now tourism. The mossy spokes of waterwheels once used to power grain and textile mills still turn, splashing cool water and occasionally disrupting the path of the traditional three-plank low fishing boats (called *Nego-Chin* or "Drowning Dog"). For travelers, the gardens along the river, particularly the **Jardin Public**, provide idyllic views for a picnic lunch. Antique and art collectors will find small treasures in tiny galleries throughout the center of the town, most of which are closed on Mondays.

The town's main attraction is its **open-air market**. (Th and Su 8am-1pm.) On the first Sunday of August, the **water market** crowds the Sorgue with small boats and *Nego-Chins* full of hawkers' wares. In July, the city and its neighbors host the **Fes-**

tival de la Sorgue, celebrating the river with water jousting and concerts. The **tourist office,** in the church on pl. de la Liberté, supplies comprehensive info on festivals, markets, lodging, shopping, and outdoor activities for the entire region around the town and in the Vaucluse. (☎04 90 38 04 78; www.ot-islesurlasorgue.fr. Open July-Aug. M-Sa 9am-1pm and 2:30-6:30pm, Su 9am-1pm; Sept.-June M-Sa 9am-12:30pm and 2-6pm, Su 9am-12:30pm.)

The easiest way to l'Isle-sur-la-Sorgue is by the TransVaucluse **train** from Avignon (☎04 90 82 07 35; about 20min., 14-15 per day, €4). Cheaper accommodations are mostly located on the outskirts of l'Isle-sur-la-Sorgue. The tourist office provides an excellent guide to the hotels, bed and breakfasts, and campgrounds in the region. **La Gueulardière ❹,** 1 cours René Char, near the rotary, offers five quiet, well-kept rooms in a dignified old hotel where tree leaves flutter in the breeze and old paintings decorate the walls. (☎04 90 38 10 52; fax 04 90 20 83 70. Breakfast €4. Reception 8am-9pm. Doubles €53. MC/V.) Camping at **La Sorguette ❶,** on rte. d'Apt (RN100), along the river 2km north of the town center, is a great base for exploring the Vaucluse. (☎04 90 38 05 71; www.camping-sorguette.com. Showers, laundry, snack bar, and ping pong. July-Aug. kayaks €8 per hr., €16 per half-day. Reception 8:15am-7:30pm. Open mid-Mar. to mid-Oct. July to late Aug. 2 people with car €18.80; Mar. to early July and late Aug. to Oct. €15.30. Extra person and children under 7 €4.50-6.20. Electricity €3.50-6.) **Isle 2 Roues (Cycles Peugeot),** on av. de la Gare right outside the train station, rents **bikes.** (☎04 90 38 19 12. Open Tu-Sa 8am-noon and 2-7pm. €13 per day. Passport deposit.) **Provence Vélos Location,** a family-run, friendly, English-speaking rental place, will drop off customers with their rental bikes in the village of their choice to avoid painful uphill climbs. Optional picnic lunches can be arranged. (☎/fax 04 90 60 28 07. Check www.guideweb.com/provence-velos for their four locations in Provence, including Isle-sur-la-Sorgue. €14.50 per day. 10% reduction for groups of three or more. All offices open daily 7am-7pm.) The **post office,** av. de Quatre Otages, across from the Jardin Public, provides **currency exchange.** (☎04 90 21 28 22. Open M-F 8:30am-noon and 1:30-5:30pm, Sa 8:30am-noon.) **Postal code:** 84803. Crédit Agricole, 7 quai Jean Jaurès, has a 24hr. **ATM** across the river from the post office. The **laundromat** on l'Impasse de la République is open daily 8am-8pm. (Wash €3-15, dry €2 per 35min.) **Taxi** services can be reached at ☎06 08 09 19 49. For the **police station,** quai Jean Jaurès, call ☎04 90 20 81 20. The **tourist office,** in the church on pl. de l'Eglise, supplies info on festivals, markets, and hiking. (☎04 90 38 04 78; fax 04 90 38 35 43. Open July-Aug. M-Sa 9am-1pm and 2:30-6:30pm, Su 9am-1pm; Sept.-June M-Sa 9am-12:30pm and 2-6pm, Su 9am-12:30pm.) For medical needs, use the small **Hôpital de l'Isle-sur-la-Sorgue** (☎04 90 21 34 00) and **ambulance** service (☎04 90 38 00 00). The **Pharmacie de la Sorgue** on rue de la République is open M-F 8am-noon and 2-6pm; the **pharmacie de garde** can be found by calling ☎04 90 78 58 00.

FONTAINE DE VAUCLUSE

Tucked into the base of 230m cliffs, with an emerald spring so clear that it gives off an other-worldly glow, Fontaine de Vaucluse (pop. 500) is a refreshing oasis. The Sorgue rushes full-speed here from **Le Gouffre,** one of the largest river sources in the world. At its spring peak, Le Gouffre pours 90 cubic meters of water per second into the Sorgue. The underground cavern of water gushes below the cliffs to unknown depths; neither Jacques Cousteau and his team of explorers nor modern-day robotics have discovered the bottom of this mysterious water source. Equally fruitless were the quests of Petrarch, who pined on the banks of the river after "Laura," the lovely wife of the Marquis de Sade. After spotting Laura in an Avignon church on April 6, 1327, Petrarch spent two decades composing sonnets in Fontaine, a melancholy time recounted in *De Vita Solitaria*. In July and August, tourists swarm into Fontaine only a little less ferociously than its river does, bringing out the worst of Provençal kitsch. Luckily, the overwhelming beauty of the fountain and the hum of cicadas wipe out the plastic impression left by this tourist trap.

The 10m **Colonne** in the center of town commemorates Petrarch's life and labor, as does the small **Musée Petrarque** across the bridge. (☎04 90 20 37 20. Open June-Sept. Su-M and W-Sa 10am-12:30pm and 1:30-6pm; early Apr. to May and early Oct. Su-M and W-Sa 10am-noon and 2-6pm; Mar. to early Apr. and late Oct. Sa-Su 10am-noon and 2-6pm; Nov.-Mar. closed except to groups. €3.50, students €1.50.) The opposite side of the river is scattered with several small museums, including the **Musée d'Histoire 1939-1945,** which reconstructs daily life in the Vaucluse region under the *années noires* ("dark years") under Vichy rule. Through sleek exhibits with intriguing artifacts, original documents, and narrative films, the museum details the impact of the Nazi occupation as well as the importance of the resistance movements that sprang up in the Vaucluse. (☎04 90 20 24 00. Open June-Sept. Su-M and W-Sa 10am-6pm; early Apr. to May Su-M and W-Sa 10am-noon and 2-6pm; early Oct. Su-M and W-Sa 10am-noon and 2-5pm; mid-Oct. to Dec. Sa-Su 10am-noon and 2-5pm; Mar. to mid-Apr. Sa-Su 10am-noon and 2-6pm. €3.50, students €1.50, under 12 free.)

There's also the surprisingly informative **Le Monde Souterrain,** which offers underground tours through slightly artificial-looking caverns that have been reconstructed for tourists. (☎04 90 20 34 13. Open June-Sept. daily 9:30am-7:30pm; Feb.-May and Oct.-Nov. 9:30am-noon and 2-6pm. Last tour 1hr. before closing. Tours in French with written English translation €5, under 18 €3.30.) The **tourist office,** along the chemin de la Fontaine towards the Gouffre, has helpful hotel and camping listings as well as English information about activities in the area. (☎04 90 20 32 22; fax 04 90 20 21 37; officetourisme.vaucluse@wanadoo.fr. Open M-Sa 9am-1pm and 2-7pm.)

Surprisingly inexpensive lodgings can be found at the ▓**Hôtel Font de Lauro ❸,** 1½km from Fontaine de Vaucluse, right off the road to l'Isle-sur-la-Sorgue. Rooms have a quiet Provençal feel and views of vineyards. A pool completes this bargain package. The sign is small, so be on the lookout. (☎/fax 04 90 20 31 49. Breakfast €5.70. Gate closes at midnight. July-Aug. reservations required. Doubles with shower €27, with bath €37.50; one triple with bath €50. MC/V.) The rural **Auberge de Jeunesse (HI) ❶,** chemin de la Vignasse, is 1km from town. Follow signs from the Colonne or ask the bus driver to let you off near the *auberge.* Wake to a chorus of roosters in this rustic, spacious stone country house. (☎04 90 20 31 65; fax 04 90 20 26 20. Breakfast €3.20. Dinner €8.40. Kitchen access. Sheets €2.70. Laundry €3.20. Reception 8-10am and 5:30-11pm. Curfew 11pm. Open Feb. to mid-Nov. Bunks €8, **camping** €5. **Members only.)** The hostel also offers suggestions for **hiking** in the Lubéron, especially on the nearby national hiking trails GR6 and GR91, although hiking is prohibited in July and August for fear of fires in the extremely dry Lubéron.

The outfitting company **Kayak Vert,** located about 500m from Fontaine on the road to l'Isle-sur-la-Sorgue, **rents kayaks** for the 8km trip down to L'Isle-sur-la-Sorgue. A friendly (and mandatory) guide escorts you down, and a minibus takes you back up to Fontaine. The Sorgue is a Class 1 river, meaning it's safe and suitable for all skill levels. (☎04 90 20 35 44; www.canoefrance.com. Two-person canoes €36; one-person kayak €17; university students with ID €14. Open mid-Apr. to Oct., weather permitting. Reserve ahead.) There is a **post office** with a rare **ATM** up the street from the Colonne, away from the river. (Open M-F 9am-noon and 2-5pm, Sa 8:30-11:30am.) A **mini-market** is across the street. (Open July-Aug. Tu-Su and holidays 8:15am-8pm; low season daily 7:15am-12:30pm and 3:30-7pm, closed W afternoon.)

OPPÈDE-LE-VIEUX

The ghost town of Oppède-le-Vieux (pop. 0) clings to the mountainside below an exquisitely ruined château and above gardened terraces of lavender and olive groves. Slowly abandoned in the 16th century for more agriculturally advantageous regions, Oppède-le-Vieux was completely deserted by the early 20th century. The only hints of this once-bustling market town are sun-baked stone buildings, a couple of artists' studios, and a tiny square. Oppède-le-Vieux has recently begun to restore the ancient ruins, some of which predate the 13th century. In the process, the town has become a popular tourist destination, complete with tiny cafés. Parking is allowed below the village (€2), from where small, hand-painted signs direct pedestrians up a winding, stony path to the 11th-century **Eglise Notre-Dame d'Alidon**, next to the **château** (20min). The walk through vine-covered ruins provides stunning views of the tidy vineyards in the valley below. Warning signs around the castle should be heeded: overhanging arches and clifftop towers have been known to drop loose stones on unaware trespassers.

LACOSTE & BONNIEUX

Curling, cobblestoned alleyways in Lacoste lead to exceptional views of tidy *vignobles,* perilous cliffs, and seemingly enchanted forests. The lovely ruins of the château that towers over tiny Lacoste (pop. 440) was home from 1774 to 1778 to the **Marquis de Sade,** who abducted local peasants to satisfy his sexual needs before being arrested and imprisoned. Nowadays, the raciest thing left in the village is a group of American art students who rush around trying to find inspiration in the picturesque countryside and deserted châteaux. Bonnieux (pop. 1420), though only slightly larger than its neighbors, is the capital of the Lubéron. Flowers burst from the balconies and windows of the well-restored houses that cluster along the hillside of this *village perché.*

Lacoste is home to one of the few affordable accommodations in the valley. The **Café de Sade ❶** rents hotel rooms named after the colors in which they are monochromatically decorated, as well as a large 32-bed dormitory overlooking the valley. (☎04 90 75 82 29; fax 04 90 75 95 68. Breakfast €5.50. Sheets €4. Closed Feb. or Mar.; call to find out. Bunks €13; *demi-pension* €28; doubles €36-37, with bath €42-46; triples €56.) **Rent bikes** at Mountain Bike Lubéron, rue Marceau, which organizes free delivery within 15km of Bonnieux, including Lacoste. (☎04 90 75 89 96; mobile 06 83 25 48 07. €8 per half-day, €14 per day, €74 per week. Open Mar.-Nov. 8:30am-noon and 1:30-6:30pm.)

APT

Best known for its candied fruits and seemingly endless fields of sweet-smelling lavender, Apt (pop. 11,200) is lined with small shops and cafés that make it an excellent base for short excursions into the Lubéron. Established as a Roman military base in 1 BC, Apt's claim to religious fame are the relics of Sainte-Anne, which are thought to aid in fertility and are celebrated every year at the procession of Sainte-Anne on the last Sunday of July. The twisting streets of Apt are filled with pottery boutiques specializing in *faïence,* a ceramic technique that produces swirling colorful patterns. In July, the bright purple lavender fields surrounding the nearby villages of Saignon and Auribeau perfume the air with fresh blossoms.

In the center of town, the **Cathédrale de Sainte-Anne,** lined with crystal chandeliers, holds the remains of Ste-Anne that were supposedly miraculously brought to Apt by Charlemagne in 776. (Open Tu-Sa 10am-noon and 4-6pm.) Off of pl. Jean Jaurès, the **Maison du Parc** has a permanent educational exhibit on the natural and cultural history of the Lubéron National Park. The information desk also answers questions about various **hiking, canoeing,** and **biking** routes throughout the Park. Maps and natural guide books for sale at the info desk. (☎04 90 04 42 00. Open Apr.-Sept. M-Sa 8:30am-noon and 1:30-7pm; Oct.-Mar. M-F 8:30am-noon and 1:30-6pm.)

With a Saturday produce market recognized as one of France's top 100, a centuries-old tradition of candied fruit production, and vineyards stretching out beyond the city limits, Apt's abundance of delicious cuisine is no surprise. For those interested in learning about the various cheeses of France, **Picodon & Pélardon ❸,** 23 rue de la Sous-préfecture, serves delicious *dégustations* of ten cheeses, various breads, a flower-filled salad, wine, and decadent chocolate dessert at red-checkered tables for a mere €11. The smiling owner will patiently explain the various cheeses and breads. (☎/fax 04 90 04 01 78. Open daily 9:15am-7pm. *Dégustations* Apr.-Oct. daily 12:15-2:30pm; Nov.-Mar. Th-Sa or by reservation.) Hidden behind hanging vines, **Le Plantane ❸,** 13 pl. Jules Ferry, serves delectable Provençal and Mediterranean dishes (€8-16), including several vegetarian options, in a restaurant filled with flowers and eclectic art. The changing menu often features an excellent €14 *filet de sole avec vanille.* (☎04 90 04 74 36. Reservations recommended. Open M noon-1:30pm, Tu 7:30-9:30pm, W-Sa noon-1:30pm and 7:30-9:30pm. MC/V.) For Moroccan cuisine, **Le Fibule ❸,** 128 rue de la République, offers mouth-watering *tagines* (€6-18), stews cooked in clay pots, in a mesmerizingly tiled and glittering *salon de thé.* (☎04 90 74 05 29. Open Apr.-Aug. M-Sa noon-3pm and 4-10pm; Sept.-Mar closed Su-M.)

The **Hôtel le Palais ❸,** 24 pl. Gabriel Péri, has clean, simple rooms in the center of town. (☎04 90 04 89 32; fax 04 90 04 71 61. Breakfast €6.50. Reception 8am-noon and 4-8pm; if closed call ☎06 86 68 44 50. Singles and doubles €32, with shower €35-46; triples €46-54, with balcony €48-56; quads €84. MC/V.) For camping, the *pays d'Apt* has several options. The **Camping Municipal les Cèdres ❶,** route de Rustrel, is the closest option to the city and offers 75 shady spots for campers. (☎04 90 74 14 61; camping.lescedres@free.fr. Open mid-Feb. to mid-Nov. Electricity, hot showers, laundry, and snack bar. €9.60 for two adults and a car.). For a slightly more expensive but far more convivial experience, the region surrounding Apt is filled with small *chambres d'hôtes,* bed and breakfast options amid lavender fields, in working farms, or in smaller villages with expansive views. **Le Moulin des Fondons ❹,** outside of Auribeau (☎/fax 04 90 75 10 63), offers luxuriously large rooms (doubles €38-58) with touches of lavender from the field just outside. The kind-hearted owners lay out a full family-style *table d'hôte* (€17) for dinner and fresh jams and breads for breakfast. A pool and several paths for exploring the area allow visitors to feel right at home.

Autocars Barlatier (☎04 90 73 23 59) runs **buses** from Avignon to the *gare routière* in Apt (50min., 3 times a day, tickets available from driver). The *gare routière* is at av. de la Libération. (☎04 90 74 20 21. Info office open M-Sa 9am-noon.) From Avignon, Sumian buses (☎04 91 49 44 25) serve Aix-en-Provence (1hr. 50min., 2 per day) and Marseille (2¼hr., 2 per day). For **taxis,** call ☎04 90 04 70 70 or 04 90 04 73 20.

The **tourist office** in pl. de la Bouquerie (☎04 90 74 03 18; fax 04 90 04 64 30; www.ot-apt.fr) has a friendly staff that provides a hotel **reservation service,** advice on regional activities and festivals, and walking tour maps of Apt and its environs. (Open July-Aug. M-Sa 9am-7pm and Su 9:30am-12:30pm; Sept.-June M-Sa 9am-noon and 2-6pm; Sept.-May Su 9:30am-12:30pm.) Several pharmacies share the **pharmacie de garde,** for more information check the window at the **Grande Pharmacie de la Cathédrale,** 17 rue des Marchands. (☎04 90 74 02 53. Open M-F 8:30am-12:30pm and 2:30-7:45pm, Sa until 7:15pm.) The **police** are located just off of pl. Gabriel Péri (☎04 90 74 00 13). Apt's main health center is the **Centre Hospitalier,** route de Marseille (☎04 90 04 33 00). The laundromat, **La Lavandière II,** 4 av. Victor

PROVENCE

Hugo (☎04 90 04 86 11), is open daily 7am-8pm. The **post office**, av. Victor Hugo, just across from the tourist office, offers **currency exchange.** (☎04 90 04 42 42. Open M-F 8am-12:30pm and 2-6pm, Sa 8:30am-1pm.) **Poste Restante. Postal code: 84400.**

ROUSSILLON

Its radiant oranges, surprisingly bright yellows, and earthy reds have made Roussillon (pop. 1200) the most famous of the ochre villages. Its stunning natural ochre park can be seen from as far away as Gordes, a wild, red-orange incision in the otherwise gray-green countryside. In this village built on the world's largest vein of natural ochre, every doorway, windowsill, and wall is tinted with the warm and vibrant shades of the earth. An exploration of the ⬛**Sentier des Ochres** is indispensable: visitors can walk through a vast, dusty ochre deposit between steep, wind-sculpted cliffs. White shoes and clothing will quickly change colors after a few minutes here. (Open July-Aug. daily 9am-7:30pm; Mar.-June and Sept. to mid-Nov. M-Sa 9:30am-5:30pm, Su 9:30am-6pm. €2. Closed on rainy days for safety's sake.) Just 1km outside the town, the **Conservatoire des Ocres et Pigments Appliqués,** route d'Apt, has restored an old pigment-making factory and offers tours (€5) and classes (prices vary) throughout the year. Short-term classes for children and adults range from painting and photography to fabricating dyes from natural resources. A large bookstore and a pigment store abut the conservatory. (☎/fax 04 90 05 66 69; info@okhra.com. Open Tu-Su July-Aug. 9am-7pm; Sept.-June 9am-6pm. 30min. tour; times vary but are frequent in summer.

The **tourist office,** pl. de la Poste, has hotel listings and information on the annual Samuel Beckett event, a tribute to the author who completed *Waiting for Godot* in Roussillon. Past summer events have included art exhibits, readings, and performances. (☎04 90 05 60 25; www.roussillon-provence.com. Open daily June-Aug. 9am-noon and 1:30-6:30pm; Sept.-May M-Sa 10am-noon and 2-5:30pm.) There's **currency exchange** and a 24hr. **ATM** at the **post office** next door. (Open Apr. to mid-Nov. M-F 9am-noon and 2-5pm, Sa 9am-noon; mid-Dec. to Feb. closes at 4:30pm.) A pharmacy is located in pl. du Pasquier. (☎04 90 05 66 15. Open M-Sa 9am-noon and 2:30-7pm.) A few expensive hotels can be found in the city, though the tourist office can help with cheaper options farther afield. **L'Arc en Ciel,** route de Goult (☎04 90 05 73 96), has 70 camping spots complete with a *boules* court, hot showers, bike rental, and a pool. (Open mid-Mar. to mid-Oct. €11.20 for a tent and two adults.)

GORDES

Considered by many to be the most picturesque of the hillside towns, Gordes (pop. 2050) is perched precariously over remarkable views that seem to stretch to the ocean. The small city center is a tourist haven sprinkled with a few small shops and cafés. This region of Provence is particularly recognized for its **bories,** drystone huts and dwellings built through the skillful placement of stone upon stone without the use of mortar. Often seen in the middle of fields or lost in the tangled undergrowth of the hills, they predate the Romans but continued to be built and used by the locals until the 18th century. The **Village des Bories** outside town is a unique hamlet of *bories* inhabited until a little over 150 years ago. (☎04 90 72 03 48. Open daily 9am to around sunset. €5.50, ages 10-17 €3.) A 4km twisting, narrow drive beyond Gordes leads to the **Sénanque Abbey,** an active Cistercian community surrounded by perfumed fields of lavender. The exceedingly touristed site was occupied by monks from AD 1148 until the Revolution, then repopulated and restored in the mid-19th century. Today it sells honey, lavender products, and *sénacole,* a liqueur produced by the local monks. Despite recent efforts to curb tourist intrusions, visitors continue to flock to this postcard-perfect abbey. It is, however, a place of prayer requiring visitors to dress conservatively and respect the peace of the abbey. (☎04 90 72 05 72. Visits by tour only; times vary by season. The information office and www.seanque.fr can provide detailed schedules. €5, under 18 €2.) The **château** in the middle of town, originally a fortress, houses the Hôtel de Ville, the tourist office, and a collection of 200 sensual paintings and photo montages in the **Musée Pol Mara**. (Open daily 10am-noon and 2-6pm. €4, ages 10-17 €3.)

A large **market** surrounds the château on Tuesday mornings, selling everything from pottery and paintings to sausage and socks. L'Eglise St-Firmin, just below the château, has unusual, brightly painted walls in turquoise and brick-red, punctuated with framed paintings and frescoes. Above the château, the Charité St-Europe hosts the annual **Bazart** sale from July to September featuring the work of 32 young artists. (€60-170; www.bazart.com has information on the touring sale as well as works for purchase.)

Many of the restaurants in Gordes are filled with photo-taking tourists, but **Le Bouquet de Basilic,** route de Murs, just above the château, serves changing pesto dishes deliciously laden with basil (€9-12) in a peaceful garden terrace. (☎04 90 72 06 98. Open daily noon-2:30pm and 7:15-11pm, closed Th lunch. MC/V.)

The **tourist office** is in the château. (☎04 90 72 02 75. Open daily 9am-noon and 2-6pm.) There's a 24hr. **ATM** in the *place* in front of it. The **post office** is located in the center of town and **exchanges currency.** (Open May-Sept. M-F 9am-noon and 4-7pm, Sa 9-11:30am; Oct.-Apr. M-F 9-11:30am and 2-5pm, Sa 9-11:30am). A **pharmacy,** 2 rue de l'Eglise, faces the church. (☎04 90 72 02 10. Open M-Sa 9am-12:30pm and 2-7pm, Su 10am-12:30pm.) **Taxis,** though expensive, are available at ☎04 90 72 61 43 or 04 90 72 11 24.

ARLES

Each street in Arles (pop. 35,000) seems to run into or out of the great Roman arena. The one-time political capital of Roman Gaul, Arles (pop. 35,000) was nearly destroyed by invasions in the Middle Ages. Since the 12th century, however, the city has remained an important city for trade and culture. With locals who speak in hearty Provençal tones and enthusiastically don traditional garb for festivals, Arles has been a favorite among visitors to Provence and a magnet for artists as much for its relative intimacy as for its ancient ruins. Van Gogh lost two years and an ear here, Picasso loved Arles's bullfights enough to produce over 150 drawings in 35 days (he donated 70 to the city), and every year the annual International Photography Festival fills every nook and cranny in Arles with exhibits. For the adventurous, the hills of the Alpilles and the Camargue marshlands are an easy daytrip away.

P R O V E N C E

▟ TRANSPORTATION

Trains: av. P. Talabot. Ticket counters open M-Sa 5:50am-9:50pm, Su 5:50am-9:40pm. To: **Avignon** (20min., 17 per day, €5.60); **Marseille** (50min., 20 per day, €11.20); **Montpellier** (1hr., 5 per day, €11.80); **Nîmes** (20min., 7 per day, €6.30).

Buses: av. P. Talabot (☎04 90 49 38 01), outside the train station. Info desk open M-F 9am-4pm. **Les Cars de Camargue,** 24 rue Clemenceau (☎04 90 96 36 25). Info desk open M-Th 8:15am-noon and 2-5:30pm, F 8:15am-noon and 2-4:30pm. To **Nîmes** (1hr., M-Sa 6 per day, €5.20). **Cars Ceyte et Fils** and **CTM,** 21 chemin du Temple (☎04 90 93 74 90), go to **Avignon** (45min.; M-Sa 7 per day, Su 2 per day; €8.10). Buses may drop passengers at bd. Georges Clemenceau rather than the *gare routière.*

Public Transportation: (☎08 10 00 08 16; www.star-arles.fr). Serves both central Arles and the local suburbs.

Taxis: A.A.A. Arles Taxis (☎04 90 93 31 16); **Arles Taxis Radio** (☎04 90 96 90 03).

Car Rental: National/Citer, 4 av. Paulin Talabot (☎04 90 93 02 17; fax 04 90 93 18 83). Located a block from the train station toward the city center.

Bike Rental: Peugeot Cycles, 15 rue du Pont (☎04 90 96 03 77). €14 per day. Open Tu-Su 8am-noon and 2-7pm.

■✦ 🛈 ORIENTATION & PRACTICAL INFORMATION

Arles follows the curve of the Rhône River in the north near the train station. The tourist office, bd. des Lices, south of the old city center, divides the commercial areas from the residential areas farther south.

Tourist Office: Espl. Charles de Gaulle, bd. des Lices (☎04 90 18 41 20; www.ville-arles.fr). Turn left outside the station and walk to pl. Lamartine; after the Monoprix turn left down bd. Emile Courbes. Continue to the big intersection by the southeast old city tower, then turn right onto bd. des Lices. Excellent free maps and brochures. **Accommodations service** €1 plus down payment. Open Apr.-Sept. daily 9am-6:45pm; Oct.-Mar. M-Sa 9am-5:45pm, Su 10:30am-2:30pm. **Branch** in the train station (☎04 90 18 41 20. Open M-Sa 9am-1pm.)

Money: Arène Change, 22bis rond-point des Arènes (☎04 90 93 34 66). No commission on US dollars. Accepts traveler's checks. Open Apr.-Oct. M-Sa 9am-6:45pm, hours decrease in winter. **ATMs:** Several 24hr. ATMs surround pl. de la République.

Laundromat: Lincoln Laverie, 6 rue de la Cavalerie. Wash €3.50-7.50. Open M-Th 9am-6pm.

Lockers: 1 pl. Lamartine (☎ 04 90 96 01 24). From the train station, half a block towards the city center at Hôtel de France (see **Accommodations**). €10 per day.

Police: on the corner of bd. des Lices and av. des Alyscamps (☎04 90 18 45 00).

Hospital: Centre Hospitalier J. Imbert, quartier Fourchon (☎04 90 49 29 29).

Ambulance: 7bis bd. Emilie Combes (☎04 90 49 79 79 or 04 90 96 04 27).

Poison Control: ☎04 91 74 66 66.

AIDS Info Service: ☎08 00 23 13 13.

SOS Femme: Marseille-based women's health and rape hotline (☎04 90 24 61 50).

24hr. Pharmacy: Pharmacie de l'Hôtel de Ville, 31 rue de l'Hôtel de Ville (☎04 90 96 01 46). Open M-Sa 8:30am-7:30pm, Su 10am-12:30pm. Arles's **garde de ville** (24hr. pharmacy) changes each weekend; call the police for info.

Internet: Point Web, 10 rue du 4 Septembre (☎04 90 18 91 54; www.hexaworld.net/pointweb). €1 for 10min. English keyboards available. Open M-Sa 9am-7pm.

Post Office: 5 bd. des Lices (☎04 90 18 41 10), between the tourist office and the police station. **Currency exchange.** Open M-F 8:30am-6:30pm, Sa 8:30am-12:30pm. **Postal code:** 13200.

▐ ACCOMMODATIONS & CAMPING

Arles has plenty of inexpensive hotels, especially in the area around **rue de l'Hôtel de Ville** and **place Voltaire.** The tourist office provides comprehensive guides to the area's hotels, as well as several *chambres d'hôtes* and camping options. Reservations are crucial during the photography festival in July and should be made a month or two in advance.

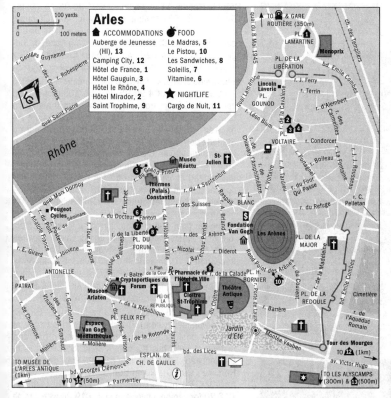

Arles

🏠 ACCOMMODATIONS   🍴 FOOD

Auberge de Jeunesse (HI), **13**
Camping City, **12**
Hôtel de France, **1**
Hôtel Gauguin, **3**
Hôtel le Rhône, **4**
Hôtel Mirador, **2**
Saint Trophime, **9**

Le Madras, **5**
Le Pistou, **10**
Les Sandwiches, **8**
Soleilis, **7**
Vitamine, **6**

⭐ NIGHTLIFE

Cargo de Nuit, **11**

PROVENCE

Saint Trophime, 16 rue de la Calade (☎04 90 96 88 38; fax 04 90 96 92 19). Fairy tale rooms are painted in different lively colors with high ceilings and large stone-walled bathrooms. Located within steps of the Arènes and the city center. Breakfast €5.95. Reception 24hr. Singles €34-40; doubles €47, with bath €50-55; triples €65-70; quads €70. AmEx/MC/V. ❹

Hôtel Gauguin, 5 pl. Voltaire (☎04 90 96 14 35; fax 04 90 18 98 87). Framed prints of Gauguin's paintings decorate the cheerful yellow walls of this warm hotel. Although not for the bug-phobic, the Gauguin offers several rooms with balconies looking onto pl. de Voltaire. Breakfast €5. Reception 7am-10pm. Doubles with shower €29-33.50; 2-bed doubles with bath €36; triples €42. Extra bed €8. MC/V. ❸

Hôtel de France, 1 pl. Lamartine (☎04 90 96 01 24; fax 04 90 96 90 87). Clean, simple rooms a block from the train station and across the street from the Monoprix. English-speaking owner runs adjoining restaurant. Breakfast €4. Singles and doubles with shower €30-38; triples €46; quads €54. MC/V. ❸

Hôtel Mirador, 3 rue Voltaire (☎04 90 96 28 05; fax 04 90 96 59 89). Friendly English-speaking owner welcomes guests into clean and simple rooms. Internet €7 per hr. Breakfast €4.30. Reception 7am-11pm. In summer singles and doubles with shower €30-38, with bath €41; low-season singles and doubles €30-33/€36. Extra bed €9.20. AmEx/MC/V. ❹

THE LOCAL STORY

THE QUEEN OF ARLES

The Queen of Arles, chosen from a group of 18- to 24-year-old single applicants, is elected every three years along with her six demoiselles through a comprehensive process during the annual **Fête des Gardians.** *Selected based on their ability to represent the arlesienne culture, applicants are required to be native to the pays d'Arles, able to speak Provençal, and familiar with the traditions, history, dances, and cultural practices of the Provençal people. As queen, the winner must wear the traditional costume and hairstyle to a variety of occasions.*

Let's Go was lucky enough to have a few moments to talk with 20-year-old Florence Disset, the endearing 18th Queen of Arles, as she celebrated both the beginning of the Fête d'Arles and her own completion of the baccalauréat.

Q: Why did you apply for this prestigious position?
A: Ever since I was a girl, I wore the customary Arles costumes, spoke Provençal, and danced the traditional dances. [Becoming Queen of Arles] was a dream, as it is for most girls in Arles.

Q: How do you balance your duties as queen with schoolwork?
A: It is not easy. I have to plan things out very well. And now with my exams, it has been very difficult.

Q: The dresses you wear are beautiful and truly authentic, but do you have to wear them every day?

(Continued on next page)

Hôtel le Rhône, 11 pl. Voltaire (☎04 90 96 43 70; fax 04 90 93 87 03). Inviting breakfast loft and charming Provençal pastel-painted rooms, some with TV or balcony. Breakfast €5. Reservations recommended. Singles and doubles €26, with shower €30-33; triples with shower €36, with toilet €43. MC/V. ❸

Auberge de Jeunesse (HI), 20 av. Maréchal Foch (☎04 90 96 18 25; fax 04 90 96 31 26), 10min. from the center and 20min. from the station. From the station, take the Starlette bus to Clemenceau, then take the #4 bus (dir: l'Aurélienne) to Foch (€0.80). There are no Starlettes on Su, and the last bus to Clemenceau from the station leaves Clemenceau at 6:34pm. To walk from the station, follow directions to the tourist office, but instead of turning on bd. des Lices, cross it and continue down av. des Alyscamps; follow the signs. Modern, with a quiet garden and ramshackle toilets. 8-bed dorms and a few 3-, 4-, and 5-bed rooms. Near the municipal pool and cinema. Personal lockers. Breakfast and sheets included. Dinner €8 on nights when there are groups eating. Bar open until midnight. Reception 7-10am and 5-11pm. Lockout 10am-5pm. Curfew 11pm in winter, midnight in summer. Reservation (by letter or fax) recommended Apr.-June. Bunks €13.70; €11.80 after first night. MC/V. ❶

Camping: City, 67 rte. de Crau (☎04 90 93 08 86; www.camping-city.com). The closest site to town. 2-star site with pool, snack bar, showers, laundry, bar, and restaurant. Take bus #2 from station (Starlette bus to Clemenceau). Then take bus #2 (dir: Pont de Crau) to Hermite (€0.80). Reception daily 8am-8pm. Open Apr.-Oct. €4 per person; €2.80 per child under 7; €16.20 for person, child, and site, €19.20 with car. ❶

◘ FOOD

Situated on the edge of the Camargue, Arles's cuisine benefits from both fresh seafood and hearty Carmargue *taureau* meat. Anchovies, *saucisson d'Arles*, *saucisson de taureau*, and sea salt are staples of any traditional *arlesienne* meal. Restaurants serving up these local delicacies are tucked into the small squares and line the narrow streets, particularly in pl. du Forum and around the Arènes. Regional produce fills the **open air markets** on bd. Emile Combes (W 7am-1pm) and bd. des Lices (Sa 7am-1pm). There are two **supermarkets** in town: **Monoprix** on pl. Lamartine, close to the train station and the city gates (open M-Th 8:30am-7:30pm, F-Sa 8:30am-8pm), and **Petit Casino,** 26 rue Président Wilson, off bd. des Lices toward the center of town. (Open M-Sa 7:30am-12:30pm and 3:30-7:30pm, Su 8:30am-12:30pm; July-Aug. also open M 8:30am-12:30pm.)

▓ **Les Sandwiches,** 46 rue des Arènes. Behind forest-green shutters, this tiny yellow sandwich counter serves an ideal alternative to the *paninis* found at most cafés. The sandwiches here are sure to satisfy both vegetarians and meat-lovers. Fresh ingredients include basil picked off the plant before your eyes. *Le Nelly* (€3.50) consists of avocado, tomatoes, chèvre, and lettuce. Sandwiches €2-4. Open daily noon-3pm and 4-11pm, closed for dinner in winter. ❶

▓ **Soleilis,** 9 rue Docteur Fanton (☎04 90 93 30 76). After dinner, try a *boule* or two of perhaps the most delicious ice cream in all of Provence. A must, especially for their unusual flavors made with freshly picked fruit. €1.80 for one scoop and homemade waffle cone, €1 for regular cone. Mountainous sundaes €5.20. Open daily July-Aug. 2-7pm and 8:30-10:30pm or later; Mar.-June and Sept.-Oct. 2-7pm. ❶

Le Pistou, 30bis rond-point des Arènes (☎04 90 18 20 92; www.lepistou.com). Overlooking the street, Pistou's gourmet cuisine matches its magical setting. Serves local specialties including an excellent *gardienne de torreau,* bull meat cooked in a wine sauce. Entrées €9-20. Open noon-3pm and 6-11pm. MC/V. ❸

Le Madras, 1 pl. Constantin (☎04 90 96 39 09). In honor of the owner's Indian and Antiguan sons-in-law, the cuisine here represents a spicy Provençal-Indian-Creole blend. The local shrimp marinated in Creole and Indian spices (€11) is a unique treat. Open Su-Tu and Th-Sa noon-10:30pm. MC/V. ❸

Vitamine, 16 rue du Docteur Fanton (☎04 90 93 77 36). Heaven-sent for vegetarians, Vitamine offers delectable salads in a Crayola-color setting. The *prix fixe menus* are appropriately titled for those interested in a taste-specific meal such as *le sportif* (€10.50) or *le plein air* (€12.80). Pasta and 38 salads (€4.60-7.70). Reserve for terrace seats. Open M-Sa noon-3pm and 7-10:30pm or midnight. Closed Jan. MC/V. ❷

👁 SIGHTS

Ancient Roman ruins hide below the surface of the 17th- and 18th-century architecture of the *centre ville.* Markers tracing important monuments crisscross the city and are explained in a guide available at the tourist office. The city's **Pass Monuments** (€12, students and under 18 €10) will give you access to all the major sights in Arles, including Les Arènes, Cryptoportiques, Musée Réattu, Muséon Arlaten, Musée d'Arles Antique, Théâtre Antique, Les Alyscamps, and Cloître St-Trôphime. The times here listed indicate the last chance to purchase tickets; most sights close 30min. later. For info, call the **Régie des Monuments** at ☎04 90 49 36 74.

(Continued from previous page)

A: [Laughs] Oh no! I wear modern clothes and am usually in jeans!

Q: May I ask how many bobby pins it takes to hold your hairstyle in place?

A: [laughing] It definitely changes by the day. On a good day, it takes five; on a bad day, it may take a whole army of bobby pins to keep it up.

Q: Have you thought of what you will do when your reign as Queen is over?

A: I am finishing my studies in the hopes of being a teacher for children under 6 years of age.

Q: Now that exams are over, are you free to tend to your royal duties?

A: Ah no. I will start right away with an organization working as a personal aid with both physically and mentally handicapped people. I will take a couple days off in August to relax.

Q: What has been the best part of being the Queen thus far?

A: I have met such interesting people, from government officials to Japanese delegates—I was there on a cultural exchange. I have also learned much about myself—how to relate to people and handle such a large responsibility. To represent one's own culture and city at only 20 years of age is certainly a learning experience.

Q: You must have some advice for visitors: what's so special about Arles?

A: (smiling) This is my city. To me, Arles is very special because it cares so deeply about maintaining and celebrating its traditions. Elsewhere in France, cities have lost touch with their cultural heritage; it has been replaced by modernization. In Arles we not only guard our history, but we share the culture with others.

LES ARÈNES. It's always a surprise to emerge from the medieval network of streets here and meet the towering layered arches of a Roman amphitheater. Built in the first century AD, this structure—the largest of its kind surviving in France—was so cleverly designed that it could evacuate all 20,000 spectators in five minutes. In the 8th century, homes were built on and in the original structure, converting it into a fortified village, and two towers built during that era still remain. The highest tower, which is inaccessible, bears witness to a thousand years of vandalism, including names scratched in by WWII American GIs. The smaller tower, however, offers a nice view of all of Arles—and a heavenly breeze on hot summer days. *Corridas* staged here from Easter through September are as exciting as anything the Romans watched. *(Arenas ☎ 04 90 49 36 86. Open daily May-Sept. 9am-6:30pm; Mar.-Apr. and Oct. 9am-5:30pm; Nov.-Feb. 10am-4:30pm. Without Monument Pass €4, children and students €3. Corridas and cocardes ☎ 04 90 96 03 70. Bullfights from €14, children €7.)*

FONDATION VAN GOGH. You'll find no Van Goghs here—only tributes to him by other artists. From innovative sculpture and paintings to creative musical compositions and poetry, the pieces here reflect the tremendous impact Van Gogh continues to have on the art world. Each work is accompanied by French and English text explaining how the artist was touched by Van Gogh's work. *(26 rond-point des Arènes. ☎ 04 90 49 94 04. Open daily 10am-7pm. €5, students and children 8-18 €3.50.)*

CRYPTOPORTIQUES DU FORUM. A visit to the underground galleries of this former Roman forum is an eerie walk through history. Dating from the first century BC, the damp and gloomy underground galleries run below the pl. du Forum to the city hall, revealing the extent of the ancient foundations of the Roman forum. *(Rue Balze. Open daily May-Sept. 9am-6:30pm; Mar.-Apr. 9-11:30am and 2-5:30pm; Oct. 9-11:30am; Nov.-Feb. 10-11:30am and 2-4:30pm. €3.50, students and under 18 €2.60.)*

MUSÉE RÉATTU. Once a stronghold of the knights of St-John, this spacious museum now houses a collection of captivating contemporary art that contrasts with the gargoyles and arched ceilings of the medieval building. At the heart of the museum, near exhibits of work by Henri Rousseau and Réattu, are the 57 drawings with which Picasso honored Arles in 1971; most attempt to capture the many "faces" (literally) of the town. *(Rue du Grand Prieuré. ☎ 04 90 49 37 58. Open May-Sept. daily 10am-noon and 2-6:30pm; Mar.-Apr. and Oct. 10am-noon and 2-5pm; Nov.-Feb. 1-5pm. €4, students €3.)*

MUSÉON ARLATEN. An extensive collection of Provençal artifacts, recreating a vision of 19th-century daily life, are brought together in this quite comprehensive and interesting folk museum founded by turn-of-the-century poet Frédéric Mistral, who dedicated his life to safeguarding local traditions in the region. Items here range from parasols, hairpieces, and drawings to temporary exhibits on the modern lives of Arlesiens. *(29 rue de la République. ☎ 04 90 93 58 11. Open June-Aug. daily 9:30am-1pm and 2-6:30pm; Apr.-May and Sept. Tu-Su 9:30am-12:30pm and 2-6pm; Oct.-Mar. Tu-Su 9:30am-12:30pm and 2-5pm. €4, students €3. Audio guides in French, Provençal, English, German, and Italian. €2.)*

MUSÉE D'ARLES ANTIQUE. This ultramodern blue building contains a well-assembled set of Roman tools, mosaics, sarcophagi, and other local artifacts. Free multilingual brochures help interpret the dioramas of the major Roman structures in Arles. The museum also includes spectacular, almost complete mosaics dating from the 2nd century, and large to-scale models of Roman architecture, including the ingenious pontoon bridge that was once the symbol of Arles. *(Av. de la 1ère D.F.L. ☎ 04 90 18 88 80. 10min. from the center of town. With your back to the tourist office, turn left, walk along bd. G. Clemenceau to its end, and follow the signs. Open daily Mar.-Oct. 9am-7pm; Nov.-Feb. 10am-5pm. €5.40, students €3.80. Tours in French by reservation.)*

THÉÂTRE ANTIQUE. Squeezed between the amphitheater and the gardens, this partially ruined theater is a reminder of the art-loving side of Roman culture. Capitols lie haphazardly around the flower-filled backstage, and only two columns of the stage wall stand, but enough remains for modern productions to take advantage of the theater's magnificent acoustics and monumental atmosphere. *(Rue de la Calade. For reservations call the Théâtre de la Calade at ☎ 04 90 93 05 23 or the tourist office. Open May-Sept. daily 9am-6:30pm; Oct. 9-11:30am; Nov.-Feb. 10-11:30am and 2-4:30pm; Mar.-Apr. 9-11:30am and 2-5:30pm. €3, students and children €2.20.)* Just behind the theater, the shady **Jardin d'Eté** is a great place to picnic, eavesdrop on concerts, or cuddle with your *chéri*. *(Open daily May-Sept. 7am-8:30pm; Oct.-Apr. 7am-5:30pm.)*

ALYSCAMPS. Meriting mention in Dante's *Inferno*, one of the most famous burial grounds from Roman times until the late Middle Ages is at Alyscamps, whose name is a twist on Champs-Elysées, or "Elysian Fields." Consecrated by St-Trôphime, first bishop of Arles, it now holds 80 generations of locals. The most elaborate sarcophagi have been destroyed or removed, though some can be found in Musée d'Arles Antique. A sense of unbreakable peace hangs heavily in the poplared avenues and the 12th-century abbey at their end. In the deathly cool lower level of the abbey, one cough brings an otherworldly echo. *(10min. from the center of town. From the tourist office, head east on bd. des Lices to its intersection with bd. Emile Courbes. Turn left onto av. des Alyscamps and cross the tracks. ☎ 04 90 49 36 87. Open daily May-Sept. 9am-6:30pm; Mar.-Apr. 9-11:30am and 2-5:30pm; Oct. 9-11:30am; Nov.-Feb. 10-11:30am and 2-4:30pm. €3.50, students and under 18 €2.60.)*

CLOÎTRE ST-TRÔPHIME. This medieval cloister is an oasis of calm and shade. Each carved column in its arcades is topped by lions in brushwood, saints in stone leaves, and the occasional fluttering bird. Attached is the Eglise St-Trôphime, built between the 11th and 15th centuries and adorned with an intricately carved façade. *(Pl. de la République. ☎ 04 90 49 33 53. Open daily May-Sept. 9am-6:30pm; Mar.-Apr. and Oct. 9am-5:30pm; Nov.-Feb. 10am-4:30pm. €3.50, students €2.60. Church free.)*

🎭 NIGHTLIFE & FESTIVALS

Deep respect for traditional culture is evident in the many local Provençal festivals and celebrations held throughout the year. The biggest of these, the weeks-long **Fête d'Arles,** begins with the lighting of a midsummer's fire on June 23. Evening parties and events culminate in the prestigious equestrian *courses carmarguaises*, when riders race bareback through the bd. des Lices. Every three years, the city elects *la reine d'Arles* and her six *demoiselles* who represent the city's language, customs, and history at local events and international exchanges. Other local festivals include the **Fête des Gardians** on May 1, which celebrates the "brotherhood of herders" of the Camargue's wild horses, and the several *férias*, or **bullfights,** held on Easter and during early September in the Arènes. (Tickets €12-83. For more info, contact the Bureau des Arènes at ☎ 04 90 96 03 70; www.label-camargue.com.)

The major draw for tourists is the annual **Rencontres Internationales de la Photographie,** held in the first week of July. Undiscovered photographers from around the world court agents by roaming around town with portfolios under their arms. Visitors also benefit from more famous, established photographers who present their work in 15 locations, conduct nightly slide shows (€6.50-8), participate in debates, and offer colloquia with artists, some free. When the festival crowd departs, the remarkable exhibits are left behind. (€3.30-5 per exhibit, all exhibits €18.50; under 25 free.) For more info, visit the tourist office or contact **Rencontres,** 10 rond-point des Arènes (☎ 04 90 96 76 06; www.rencontres-arles.com). During the festival, tickets can be bought in the Espace Van Gogh.

Although Arles is hardly a town for night-owls, the cafés along bd. Georges Clemenceau attract an animated crowd for drinks and music at night. **Cargo de Nuit**, 7 av. Sadi Carnot, is the only nightclub within the central city. The cargo-ship-themed hotspot attracts locals and visitors with a wide range of music and a small art gallery. (☎04 90 49 55 99; www.cargodenuit.com. Drinks €3.80-4.50. Open daily noon-4pm for lunch, Th-Sa 8pm-3am for dancing.) For theater-goers, the **Théâtre d'Arles**, bd. Georges Clemenceau (☎04 90 52 51 55; accueil@theatre-arles.com), showcases drama, dance, and musical performance from October to June.

ALPILLES

Home to the remaining traces of Roman history, several famous artists and poets, and the tidy fields of olive groves and vineyards, the hills of the Alpilles are a tranquil tourist retreat. Its small towns provide clear vistas similar to those of the Vaucluse to the north and the relaxed atmosphere of Arles and Nîmes to the south.

LES BAUX-DE-PROVENCE

Les Baux-de-Provence is known for its medieval ruins, demolished castle, and breathtaking panoramas of the vineyards and villages below. The village sits 245m up on a defensively strategic rocky spur of the Alpilles. The Baux lords plundered medieval Provence from this eagle's nest of a town, managing at one point to hold 72 towns in the region. Even Dante came to their court—it's thought that he found inspiration for his *Inferno* in the twisted gorges of the Val de l'Enfer ("Valley of Hell"), so named for its tortuous cliffs below the castle. The Baux line died out in the 14th century, and Louis XIII humiliated the town by destroying its castle and ramparts in 1632. A narrated, self-paced tour of the ruins of Les Baux takes tourists through the remaining ruins, an impressive testament to the powerful lords who once inhabited the immense stone structures.

The ruined halls and towers of the mountaintop **Château des Baux** cover an area five times that of the village below. Treacherously slim limestone stairs offer brave visitors a magnificent view of the cliffs and farmland in the valley below. A giant *trébuchet*, the largest medieval siege warfare engine, stands out on the plateau. A great number of tourists flock here, audio guides clamped to their ears: those who arrive early will enjoy the eerie treat of having the mountaintop, valley, and distant Mediterranean all to themselves. Hold on to children and lighter possessions, as gusting *Mistral* winds are strong on the unprotected cliff. Housed in a cool Romanesque chapel inside the château's gates, the tiny **Chapelle St-Blaise** has a delightful slide-show of van Gogh and Cézanne's paintings of olive trees. (☎04 90 54 55 56. Open daily July-Aug. 9am-8:30pm; Dec.-Feb. 9am-5pm; Sept.-Nov. and Mar.-May 9am-6:30pm. Thorough audio guide in 7 languages. €6.50, students €5, under 18 €3.50.) Les Baux is also known for its limestone quarries, one of which has been converted into the **Cathédrale d'Images.** From the bus stop, continue down the hill, turn right at the crossroads, and follow the sign. (7min.) Dozens of projectors splash 3000 images from above into gigantic walls cut deep into the limestone. 2004 will bring a series of photographs from the ancient Greek city of Alexandria. (☎04 90 54 38 65. Open daily 10am-7pm, last show at 6:15pm. €7, ages 8-18 €4.10.) Walk down the hill to the **Fondation Louis Jou**, rue Frédéric Mistral, which commemorates Les Baux's favorite son with major works by the printmaker himself as well as engravings by Dürer and Goya. If it seems shut down, continue 50m and inquire at the small shop; it may not really be closed. (☎04 90 54 34 17. Open Apr.-Oct. Su-M and F-Sa 2-5pm, Tu-Th by reservation; Nov.-Mar. by reservation. €3, students €1.50.)

■Mas de la Fontaine ❹, at the foot of the village in the Val d'Enfer, offers seven elegant and fashionably decorated rooms in a traditional *mas* (Provençal farm) with a garden and pool. This place is worth the splurge, and travelers know it, so make reservations. Follow signs to the Gendarmerie; the hotel is then two minutes downhill on your right. (☎04 90 54 34 13. Breakfast €6. Open mid-Mar. to Oct. Doubles with shower €40-47, with bath €51-55; triples €6. Extra bed €10.) Most backpackers bring picnics to the Cité Morte for picturesque meals atop the hill; for picnic supplies, the small **bakery** in the parking lot has fresh breads, fruit, and sandwiches. (Open daily Mar.-Dec. 8:30am-8pm; Jan.-Feb. 10:30am-5pm.) Otherwise, there are plenty of sandwich stands and *crêperies* in the touristy center of town.

The **tourist office** in the Hôtel de Ville, about halfway up the hill between the parking lot and the Cité Morte, gives out a free map and short history of the city, as well as lodging and transportation info. (☎04 90 54 34 39. Open daily Apr.-Sept. 9am-7pm; Oct.-Mar. 9am-12:30pm and 1:30-6pm.) CTM **buses** from Les Baux run to Arles. (☎04 90 93 74 90. 30min., M-Sa 4 per day 11:45am-6:45pm, €4.80.) Conseil Général des Bouches-du-Rhône has **bus** service between Avignon, St-Rémy, and Les Baux (☎ 04 32 76 00 40. 1hr. July-Aug. daily 7:40am-4:20pm; June and Sept. Sa-Su only; May and Oct. Su only. €5.40.) **Taxis** can be obtained at ☎06 80 27 60 92.

TARASCON

Tarascon (pop. 13,000) is intimately linked to Provençal folklore through its namesake, *la tarasque*, a legendary monster that once terrorized the village. For four days over the last weekend of June, during the **Fête de la Tarasque,** the replica of the monster is paraded through the town, accompanied by concerts, bullfights, horse shows, and dancing. When Tarascon is not *en fête*, it is a quiet southern town with calm cobbled streets, refreshing breezes off the Rhône, and serious *boules* games in the municipal *boules* courts. Tarascon's proximity to Arles (17km), Avignon (23km), and Nîmes (24km) and less expensive lodgings make it a good base from which to explore the surrounding cities.

The prize of Tarascon is the imposing 15th-century **Château de Tarascon,** perched above a wedge of the Rhône. This luxurious fortress, built by Louis II of Anjou, saw few years of warfare, serving mainly as a prison; it is, therefore, well-maintained, with the star-painted ceiling in the Queen's chambers still easily visible. Surrounded by a now-dry grassy moat, it boasts a lovely Provençal garden, medieval graffiti, an apothecary, and detailed tapestries. A climb to the roof reveals a picture-perfect view of Tarascon's rival château, the ruined Château de Beaucaire, across the river, and of the surrounding countryside clear to the Camargue. (☎04 90 91 01 93. Open daily 10am-7pm. €5.50, ages 18-25 €3.50, under 18 free.)

PROVENCE

QUIT HOGGING THE TRUFFLES! If you see a group of diners in a French restaurant with their napkins over their heads, don't be alarmed. They're merely savoring the delicate aroma of the most sought-after mushroom in the world—the *truffe noir*, or black truffle. Not to be confused with the Belgian chocolate blobs that bear a minimal visual resemblance to them, the real, honest-to-goodness truffle grows in the roots of oak and hazelnut trees. Picked fresh, a truffle is worth its weight in gold to the gastronomically obsessed. Why so dear? The truffle hides underground and defies systematic cultivation. Fortunately, nature has blessed the French with the truffle-hunter *par excellence*. Pigs, which are attracted to the truffle's sexy odor, can snuffle out these delicacies in no time. The biggest obstacle is making off with the treasured *truffe* with a greedy pig in hot pursuit.

THE LOCAL LEGEND

LA TARASQUE

Often depicted with the small kicking legs of a child hanging ferociously from its mouth, *la tarasque* has haunted both children and adults in southern Provence for centuries. According to legend, the green, spiked, toothy cross between a crocodile and a small dinosaur terrorized the region surrounding the Rhône. Creeping onto farms in the middle of the night, it made off with whole cows or unsuspecting children.

Luckily for the villagers of this region, Ste-Martha arrived. The saint, on her quest from Saintes-Maries-de-la-Mer to introduce the Provençal people to Christianity, agreed to confront the terrible animal and relieve the people from its horrible appetite. Entering the forest unarmed, she miraculously tamed the beast with her wooden cross, bringing it into the town attached to her rope belt. The monster was captured by the people in the village and a marvelous celebration ensued, resulting in the naming of the town, Tarascon. Since the joyous death of the *tarasque*, villagers have feasted each year at the annual **Fête de la Tarasque** in honor of the conquered creature. A parade featuring a model of the animal is led through Tarascon by local *chevaliers*, and dancing, fireworks, and much eating and drinking follow. Today, candies and cakes are sold in bakeries throughout Tarascon, allowing children to take their revenge on the green beast.

To reach the **Auberge de Jeunesse (HI) ❶**, 31 bd. Gambetta, from the train station, turn right and follow the tracks until you reach bd. Victor Hugo. Cross the street and follow the path between the tracks and the wall for 20m, turning left on the next major road, bd. Gambetta. Following the signs, the hostel is another 5min. farther, on your left near a phone booth. It has comfortable beds in 8- to 12-bed dorms, kitchen facilities, a secure bike area, and free parking. Reservations are accepted by email (tarascon@fuaj.org), but this gem of a hostel, with its charming British-accented, Marseille-born owner, is rarely full. (☎ 04 90 91 04 08. Breakfast €3.20, obligatory first morning. Sheets €2.70. Reception 7:30-10am and 5:30-10:30pm. Lockout 10am-5:30pm. Beds €8.40. **Members only.**) **Hôtel du Viaduc ❷**, 9 rue du Viaduc, has clean, cozy rooms, some of them newly renovated. From the train station, cross under the tracks and head left. (5min.) Popular with cyclists, it maintains a locked bike area and free parking. Jovial proprietors, who speak some English, generate a convivial atmosphere. (☎ 04 90 91 16 67. Breakfast €5, *petit déjeuner* €2.50. Doubles €20, with shower €25, with toilet €28-34. Internet €3 per 30min.) **Camp** at **Tartarin ❶**, bd. du Roy René, behind the château on the Rhône, a simple site with a bar, snack stand, free showers, and lots of shade. The ground, unfortunately, is hard, with spotty grass. (☎ 04 90 91 01 46; fax 04 90 91 10 70. Reception 9am-noon and 3-7pm; after-hours until 11pm try the bar. Open Apr.-Oct. €3.40 per person, €3 per tent, €1.70 per car. Electricity €2.70.)

Bistrot des Anges ❸, located in the pl. du Marché, serves up daily Provençal *menus* (€16) and extraordinary chocolate cake (€3.90) in a hip, relaxed setting. (☎ 04 90 91 05 11. Open M-Th 9am-6pm, F-Sa 9am-6pm and 8-10pm. MC/V.) The bakery across from the tourist office, 56 rue des Halles (☎ 04 90 91 01 17), serves up melt-in-your-mouth treats, including hazelnut truffles shaped like the *tarasque*. (Open Tu-Su 6:30am-1pm and 3-7:30pm.)

Trains from Tarascon go to Arles (10min., 7 per day, €2.60) or Avignon (10min., 16 per day, €3.50). Ticket window open M 6:10am-7pm, Tu-F 6:20am-7pm, Sa 6:40am-7pm, Su 9:35am-noon and 1:25-6pm. Cevennes Cars (☎ 04 66 29 27 29) sends **buses** from the train station to Avignon (35min., M-Sa 4 per day 6:50am-7pm, €7.60) and St-Rémy (25min.; M-F 3 per day 7:55am-6:05pm, 2 on Sa; €3.10). In a pinch, call **Espace Taxi** (☎ 06 08 40 75 31 or 04 90 91 34 50). For the **pharmacie de garde**, call the **police**, 3 rue du Viaduc (☎ 04 90 91 52 90). The multilingual staff of the **tourist office**, 59 rue des Halles, provide free guides and maps. From the train station, walk across the common and turn left on cours A. Briand; walk for two minutes, and rue des Halles will be on your right. (☎04 90 91 03 52. Open M-Sa 9am-noon and 2-6pm.) There are no currency exchange bureaus in town, but a **24hr. ATM** lies just to the left of the tourist office. The **post office** is to the left of the train station. (☎04 90 91 52 00. Open M-F 8:30am-5:30pm, Sa 8:30am-noon.) **Postal code:** 13150.

ST-RÉMY

A little town approached through luminous arcades of plane trees, St-Rémy's artistic flair shines through in its numerous boutiques, artists' galleries, and the oft-told stories of Van Gogh's years here. Just outside the maze of charming streets that make up the *centre ville* lie a small group of Roman remnants and the ancient city of Glanum, now a major archeological site.

Nestled in the heart of the town are a few interesting museums. The **Centre d'Art Présence Van Gogh** housed in the 253-year-old Hôtel Estrine, 8 rue Estrine, features contemporary artists. Although it lacks original Van Gogh paintings, the mid-sized museum has rotating exhibits on the master's work. (☎04 90 92 34 72; fax 04 90 92 36 73. Open Tu-Su 10:30am-12:30pm and 2:30-6:30pm. €3.20, students and seniors €2.30.) The 15th-century **Hôtel de Sade,** rue de Parage, holds all the best finds from nearby Glanum, including well-preserved glasswork and pottery. (☎04 90 92 64 04; fax 04 90 92 64 02. Open daily July-Aug. 11am-6pm; Apr.-June and Sept. 10am-noon and 2-6pm; Jan.-Mar. 10am-noon and 2-5pm. €2.50.)

Glanum, a settlement from the 7th century BC, lies nearly 1km south of the town center, past the tourist office on av. Vincent Van Gogh. (15min.) Discovered eighty years ago, the sprawling collection of houses, temples, springs, and sacred wells unearthed here are still being studied by an on-site archeological team. The town once prospered as a stop on the main road from Spain to Italy (the *Via Domitia*) and now provides fascinating insight into the hybrid Gallo-Roman culture that emerged in Provence. (☎04 90 92 23 79. Open daily Apr.-Sept. 9am-7pm; Oct.-Mar. 9am-noon and 2-5pm. €5.50, ages 12-25 €3.50.) Standing in solitary splendor across the street are the well-preserved **Antiques,** a commemorative arch and mausoleum built during the reign of Augustus. Across the street, the still-functioning **Saint-Paul de Mausole,** chemin des Carrières, offers tranquil gardens and breezy corridors to visitors and residents of the therapeutic center where Van Gogh spent just over a year producing over 100 drawings and 150 of some of his most famous paintings. Above the flowered cloister, visitors can tour the three rooms in which the artist spent the last year of his life, including one just for his materials. A small gallery now shows very creative exhibits by current patients, produced through the center's art therapy program. (☎04 90 92 77 00. Open daily Apr.-Oct. 9:30am-7pm; Nov.-Mar. 10:30am-1pm and 1:30-5pm. €3, students €2.20, under 12 free.) The Monday after Pentecost brings a veritable stampede of farm animals—mostly sheep—through the town center during the **Fête de la Transhumance,** a celebration of the traditional migration of Provençal flocks from the plains to the Alpine pastures. The **Carreto Ramado,** a pagan festival dedicated to field work, in which 50 horses draw an enormous cart of fruits and vegetables, and the big **Féria Provençale,** in which bulls are teased but not killed, take place in mid-August. The tourist office distributes the free *Patrimoine* handbook, with tons of cultural info as well as guided tours of Van Gogh's hangouts in St-Rémy.

Restaurants are on the pricier side here; however, **Lou Planet,** 7 pl. Favier, serves fresh produce-filled crêpes and salads (€4.80-7) in an umbrella-topped courtyard. The *légumes de saison et chèvre crêpe* (€6.50) gives an excellent taste of the season's finest veggies. (☎04 90 92 19 81. Open Apr.-Oct. noon-2:30pm and 7-10pm.) For slightly more expensive and substantial dining, **Bistrot Découverte,** 19 bd. Victor Hugo, serves full Provençal meals, such as *pavé de taureau* (€13.50), to a jovial crowd in a fiery orange-colored restaurant. (☎ 04 90 92 34 49. Open Tu-Su noon-2pm and 7-10pm. MC/V.) Near the statue of Nostradamus are a handful of good *brasseries* and a **Petit Casino** supermarket on rue de la Résistance. (Open M-W and F-Sa 7:30am-12:30pm and 3:30-7:30pm, Su 7:30am-12:30pm.) To take in the vistas that Vincent loved, get the pamphlet that includes the *Promenade sur les lieux peints par Van Gogh* from the **tourist office**, pl. Jean Jaurès. From the bus stop, walk up av. Durand Maillane; the office will be on the left, in a parking lot, next to the **police station** (☎ 04 90 92 00 47). The tourist office provides info on housing, restaurants, and local activities, and conducts group **tours** in English, German and Spanish from late Apr. to mid-Sept. (☎ 04 90 92 05 22; fax 04 90 92 38 52. Free map. Tours of old St-Rémy, the Alpilles, and Vincent's sights €6.10-6.40, not including St-Paul entrance fee. Open daily early Apr. to Oct. 9am-12:30pm and 2-7pm; Nov. to early Apr. 9am-noon and 2-6pm.) **Buses** (☎ 04 90 14 59 00) come from **Avignon** (45min., 8 per day 7:15am-5:15pm, €5.20). The **Pharmacie Cendres**, 4 bd. Mirabeau (☎ 04 32 60 16 43) has up-to-date info on the **pharmacie de garde**, as do the **police** at ☎ 04 90 24 22 00 or 04 90 92 58 11. For health emergencies, an **ambulance** can be reached at ☎ 04 90 92 11 88. **Taxis** are available at ☎ 06 09 52 71 54.

CAMARGUE

In stark contrast to the Provençal hills to the north, the Camargue is a vast delta lined with tall grasses and prowled by all manner of wildlife. Pink flamingos, black bulls, and the famous local white horses roam freely across the flat expanse of wild marshland, protected by the confines of the national park. The human inhabitants include **gardians,** rugged herders from a 2000-year-old line of cowboys, and the Gypsies who have made the area a stopping point for 500 years. The Camargue is anchored in the north by Arles and in the south by Stes-Maries-de-la-Mer; Stes-Maries serves as the best base for excursions into the region.

STES-MARIES-DE-LA-MER

According to legend, in AD 40 Mary Magdalene, Mary Salomé (mother of the Apostles John and James), Mary Jacobé (Jesus's aunt), and their servant Sara were put to sea to die. Their ship washed ashore here. Stes-Maries's dark, fortified church was built to house their relics. The tourist traffic it occasions has made Stes-Maries into a sort of monster, surrounded by a honky-tonk collection of over-priced snack trailers and stores willing to cast anything Provençal in plastic. The town is still worth a visit, though; besides possessing the aforementioned church, Stes-Maries is the unofficial capital of the Camargue, and most expeditions into that strange wilderness depart from here. The town is also dear to Gypsies who come here from all over Europe on pilgrimages every May.

■ ⃞ **ORIENTATION & PRACTICAL INFORMATION.** The town is wedged between untouched conservation land to the north, sea to the south, and marshes to the east. **Buses** leave from Arles (50-55min.; 7:50am-6:10pm daily, M-Sa 5 per day, Su 4 per day; €4.80); contact Les Cars de Camargue (☎ 04 90 96 36 25) for info. The bus stop in Stes-Maries-de-la-Mer lies in pl. Mireille. Once here, **rent bikes** at Le Vélo Saintois, 19 rue de la République. (☎ 04 90 97 74 56. €6.50 for 2hr., €8 per half-day, €14 per day; passport or ID deposit. Open daily July-Aug. 8am-7pm; Sept.-Nov. and Feb.-June 9am-6:30pm.) A few minutes up the road at the entrance to the town, Le Vélociste, route d'Arles, offers the same prices for rentals, as well as packages that include **horse rides.** (☎ 04 90 97 83 26. Passport or ID deposit. Open Su-M and W-Sa 9am-12:30pm and 2-7pm.) If you get stuck in the Camargue's mud, call **Allô Taxi** at ☎ 04 90 97 94 49 or 06 18 63 08 59. From center of town to Musée Camarguais €32, to Auberge de Jeunesse €13-17.

To get to the **tourist office**, 5 av. Van Gogh, walk toward the ocean down rue de la République from the bus station or down rue Victor Hugo from the church. The office gives out a free guide to the region, which lists biking, hiking, boating, and horseback tours in the area, and provides a helpful list of the area lodgings. (☎04 90 97 82 55; www.saintesmaries.com. Open daily July-Aug. 9am-8pm; Apr.-June and Sept. 9am-7pm; Oct.-Feb. 9am-5pm.) Crédit Agricole, on pl. Mireille, also has a 24hr. **ATM** outside the tourist office. (☎04 90 97 81 17. Open Tu-W and F 9am-4:30pm, Th 10am-12:30pm and 1:45-4:30pm, Sa 9am-12:15pm.) **Pharmacie Cambon-Neuville-Corus** is at 18 rue Victor Hugo. (☎04 90 97 83 02. Call for urgent service during off-hours. Open M-Sa 9am-12:30pm and 3-7:30pm, Su 10am-12:30pm.) The **police** are on av. Van Gogh (☎04 90 97 89 50), right next to *les arènes*. The **post office** is at 6 av. Gambetta. (☎04 90 97 96 00. Open M-F 9am-noon and 1:30-4:30pm, Sa 8:30am-11:30pm.) **Postal code:** 13460.

⋔ ACCOMMODATIONS & CAMPING. Rooms fill quickly in summer, and most are over €35: the town may be cheaper as a daytrip from Arles. The **Hôtel Méditerranée ❹**, 4 bd. Frédéric Mistral, is a pretty, quiet hotel blooming with flowers. Some rooms have little terraces. (☎04 90 97 82 09; fax 04 90 97 76 31. Breakfast €5. Reception 24hr. Reserve ahead in summer. Closed for part of Jan. Doubles €38.50-43; triples €58. About €4 cheaper in the low season. MC/V.) Green-shuttered **Hôtel Le Castelet ❹**, 10 rue des Launes, offers clean, basic rooms and a front breakfast terrace on a quiet street. (☎04 90 97 83 47; www.hotellecastelet.com. Doubles €40-49; triples €59; quads €65. Prices reduced €10 in the low season.) North of Stes-Maries, in the heart of the Camargue, is the **Auberge de Jeunesse Hameau de Pioch Badet (HI) ❷**. To get there, take the bus that runs between Stes-Maries and Arles to Pioch Badet (from Stes-Maries 5min., 6 per day, €1.90; from Arles 40min., €4.50). The quiet, camp-style hostel fills early in summer, so take the first bus you can. (☎04 90 97 51 72. Kitchen. Bike rental €10 per day plus passport deposit. Horse tours €11.50 per hr., €53.50 per day. Sheets €2.75. Reception daily 7:30-10:30am and 5-11pm; call ahead if you plan to arrive later. Lockout 10:30am-5pm. July-Aug. curfew 11pm; extended during festivals. Reserved primarily for groups Nov.-Jan. Obligatory *demi-pension* €20.60. **Members only.**)

If you're in the mood for a big splurge, a night at the three-star **Mangio Fango ❺**, on the rte d'Arles 10min. from the center of town, will allow you to live in splendor. Enjoy the excessively large, exquisite rooms, the heated pool, outdoor terrace, and garden—at a price. (☎04 90 97 80 56. Breakfast €9.50. Reception 9am-9pm. Doubles €84-107, €58-88 low season. AmEx/MC/V.)

The starry sky of the Camargue may be more fun to sleep under than a roof: in that case, **camp** at **La Brise ❶**, an expansive site crossed by watery ditches and stands of reeds and dotted with purple-pink trees. Take the bus from Arles to La Brise, 5min. east of the city center. The site has a pool and laundry. Be warned: the Camargue breeds mosquitoes. (☎04 90 97 84 67; labrise@laposste.net. Reception 8:30am-8:30pm. July-Aug. , €6.50 per person, 1 person with tent €9.70, 2 people with car €17.60; Apr.-June €6.10/€9.20/€16.80; significantly lower in low season. Electricity €4.)

⌂ FOOD. The Camargue's main crop is a sweet, fat-grained rice; you will find it in gelatinous cakes sold at *pâtisseries*, at local restaurants, and on the shelves of **supermarkets** like the Petit Casino on av. Victor Hugo. (☎04 90 97 90 60. Open in summer daily 8am-8pm; in winter 8am-noon and 4-8pm.) A **market** fills pl. des Gitanes on Mondays and Fridays (7am-noon). Restaurants cluster near the waterfront and around **rue Victor Hugo**, especially on **place Esprit Pioch,** where they serve seafood, heaping portions of steaming paëlla, *pavé de taureau*, and refreshing sangría. Most *menus* start around €12, but €9 is reasonable for lunch. Near the beach, **Le Piccolo ❷**, 7 rue Leon Gambetta (☎04 90 97 82 82), serves fresh *coquillage* (mussels and oysters; €6.50-13) amid cool ocean breezes and chandeliers made of colored bottles. (Open daily noon-11:30pm. MC/V.)

⑥ SIGHTS. The only major sight in town, and the focus of Stes-Maries, is the gray 12th-century **fortified church** looming above the town's menagerie of snack bars. A picturesque view of the surrounding sea and marshland greets those who climb the vertigo-inducing staircase. The dark Romanesque interior offers a cool respite from the heat. In the crypt, the relics of the saints are displayed, and a statue of Ste-Sara glimmers in the corner, almost obscured by her layers of gilt and brocaded cloaks. The saint's power supposedly has cured the blind, healed the lame, and halted the harsh *mistral* winds of 1833. (☎04 90 97 87 60. Church open daily 8am-12:30pm and 2-7pm. Roof and tower open daily in summer 10am-8pm; in winter 10am-noon and 2-5pm. €2.)

■ FESTIVALS. According to legend, the family chief of the region's native Gypsies, Sara, greeted the Stes-Maries when they arrived and asked that she and her people be baptized as Christians. The **Pèlerinage des Gitans** is a yearly event uniting Gypsy pilgrims from all over Europe (May 24-25). A costumed procession from the church to the sea bears statues of the saints and reenacts their landing. A **festival** on the weekend around October 22 honors the Maries, with similar ceremonies for non-Roman pilgrims. In the second week of July, the **Féria du Cheval** brings horses from around the world for shows, competitions, and rodeos at the Stes-Maries and Méjanes arenas. (Call the Arènes de Méjanes at ☎04 90 97 10 60 for details. €24-70.) During July, August, and September, **bullfights** and **horse shows** occur regularly at the modern arenas. (Call the Arènes at ☎04 90 97 85 86. Tickets from €14.)

◪ EXCURSIONS. Stes-Maries is undoubtedly the capital of the Camargue, and most organized visits to the region leave from here. While some tours are listed here, the tourist office is teeming with more information. The best way to see the Camargue is on **horseback.** The region is dotted with stables offering tours throughout the park on horses. The beautiful beasts can go far into the marshes, wading through deep water into the range of birds and bulls inaccessible by any other means. Most rides are oriented toward novices. For the sake of mosquito protection and comfort, most riding places recommend wearing long pants and sneakers or boots. The stables are all united under a single association, the Association Camarguaise de Tourisme Equestre, and their prices remain within a few euros of one another. (☎04 90 97 10 10; fax 04 90 97 70 82. €12 per hr., €23 for 2hr., €33 for a half-day; picnic usually included on daytrips.)

Although most of the trails are open only to horseback riders and walkers, **bicycle touring** is a great way to see much of the area. Keep in mind that bike trails may be sandy and difficult to ride. Trail maps indicating length, level of difficulty, and danger spots are available from the Stes-Maries tourist office. Bring an ample supply of fresh water—it gets hotter than Hades, and there are few bathroom stops along the way. A 2hr. pedal will reveal some of the area, but you'll need a whole day if you plan to stop along the wide, deserted white-sand beaches that line the trail. Aspiring botanists and zoologists should stop at the **Centre d'Information de Ginès,** on the bus line between Stes-Maries and Arles, which distributes info on the region's unusual flora and fauna. (Pont de Gau, 10min. from Stes-Maries. ☎04 90 97 86 32. Open Apr.-Sept. daily 10am-6pm; Oct.-Mar. Su-Th and Sa 9:30am-5pm.) Next door, the **Parc Ornithologique de Pont de Gau** provides several kilometers of paths through the marshes and offers views of birds and grazing bulls. (☎04 90 97 82 62. Park open daily Apr.-Sept. 9am-sunset; Oct.-Mar. 10am-sunset. Reception office opens at 10am. €6, under age 17 €3.)

The final two options for visiting the area are by boat or jeep. Camargue, 5 rue des Launes, sends **boats** from Port Gardian deep into the Petit Rhône for up-close bird- and bull-watching. (☎04 90 97 84 72; fax 04 90 97 73 50. Open Mar.-Nov. 1½hr.; Mar.-Sept. 3-4 per day, Oct. 2 per day. July-Aug. first departure 10:30am, last departure 5:55pm; Sept.-May last departure 4:10pm. €10, children €5.) For **jeep safaris,** contact Le Gitan, 13 av. de la Plage, in Stes-Maries. Safaris explore the banks of the Grand and Petit Rhône. The jeeps hold 7-8 people. (☎04 90 97 89 33. 2hr. trips €31 per person; 4hr. trips €37. July-Sept. trips depart between 10am-6pm; low season the last trip leaves at 4pm. Open daily 9am-8pm.)

AIGUES-MORTES

Built in the 13th century by Louis IX as a port city from which the Seventh and Eighth Crusades were launched, Aigues-Mortes was an important trading port for several centuries. During the conflicts between Catholics and Protestants, many Huguenots were imprisoned within the city towers. This curiously inland port city, whose name means "Dead Waters," controls the largest sea salt production in France, along the edge of the Carmargue. In summer, the water here takes on a purplish hue as it evaporates, creating its famous salt formation, the *fleur du sel de Camargue*. Herons, egrets, and flamingos dot the marshes around the city's thick defensive wall. Aigues-Mortes's primary attractions are history and scenery. Inside its slow-paced walls, boutiques and restaurants sell the specialty foods of the Camargue while tourists peek out of windows along the ancient ramparts.

☰☷ TRANSPORTATION & PRACTICAL INFORMATION. SNCF **buses** run to Nîmes (50min.; 4 per day 6:40am-7pm; €6), as do STDGard buses (1hr., 5 per day, €5.70). Les Courriers du Midi run buses to Montpellier (1½hr., M-Sa 2 per day, €6). It is not easy to get to Aigues-Mortes from the east; from Arles a train or bus to Nîmes will get you within shouting distance, and there is **public transportation** from Stes-Maries-de-la-Mer only between July and August. The tourist office has the most up-to-date information. If you are really desperate, call **Aigues-Mortes Taxi** (☎06 11 56 20 12 or 06 20 96 44 16). To get to the local **tourist office,** located on pl. St-Louis, from the bus stop, enter the city through the porte de la Gardette and continue walking straight through to the main square; the tourist office is in the far left corner. (☎04 66 53 73 00; www.ot-aiguesmortes.fr. Open July-Aug. M-F 9am-8pm, Sa-Su 10am-8pm; June and Sept. M-F 9am-6pm, Sa-Su 10am-6pm; Oct.-May 9am-noon and 1-6pm.) The **post office** is several blocks east on rue Baudin. (☎04 66 53 60 02. Open M-F 8:30am-noon and 2:30-6pm, Sa 8:30-11:30am.) The **police** (☎04 66 53 69 73) are at 1 bd. Gambetta. The most convenient **pharmacy** is Pharmacy Cathala, 5 rue J. Jaurès. (☎04 66 53 68 00. Open M-Sa 8:45am-12:15pm and 2:30-7:15pm.) In case of an **emergency** at night, call Cathala or the other two pharmacies (☎04 66 53 61 30 or 04 66 53 83 09). Crédit Agricole, 6 rue A. Courbet, **exchanges currency** for a commission charge (open M-F 8:45am-12:30pm and 1:30-5pm), and there are several **ATMs** around the central pl. St-Louis.

☱☐ ACCOMMODATIONS & FOOD. The cheapest option in town is the **Hôtel L'Escale ❸**, 3 av. Tour de Constance, directly across the street from the tower, whose white walls and wooden furniture retain the appealing scent of the sea. (☎04 66 53 71 14; fax 04 66 53 76 74. Reception 6:30am-11pm. Reservations usually required mid-July to mid-Aug. Singles and doubles with sink and shower €26, with toilet €30; triples €29; quads €40; one quint €57. AmEx/MC/V.) The **Hôtel Tour de Constance ❹**, 1 bd. Diderot, is slightly more expensive with a welcoming lobby and views of the ramparts. (☎04 66 53 83 50. Breakfast €5. Reception until 10pm. Doubles €42; triples €50; quads €58; all with shower. MC/V.)

Crêperies and small boutiques can be found on **rue Jean Jaurès,** while lively, well-priced eateries fill **pl. St-Louis.** A **market** often spans the length of the wall just outside the city's fortifications (W and Su 8am-12:30pm). In an animated and funky atmosphere, **Le Café de Bouzigues ❸,** 7 rue Pasteur, serves *tien d'agneau* (€18) and other delicious local specialties with a fun twist. (☎04 66 53 93 95. Entrées €10-20. Open daily noon-11:30pm. MC/V.) Along a quiet side street, **La Guinguette de la République ❸,** 25 rue de la République, has regional cuisine in a charming setting, complete with red-checkered tablecloths. (☎04 66 51 66 09. *Menu* €10, entrées €9-14.50. Open daily noon-11pm. MC/V.) Less expensive but just as satisfying, **Chez Léo ❷,** 11 rue Victor Hugo (☎04 66 51 45 88), serves excellent crêpes, including the *Nîmoise* with a *branade* of codfish (€5.40), and salads and *tapas.* (Open daily noon-2:30pm and 6-10pm. Closed W in winter. MC/V.) The **Barthélémy Boulangerie-Pâtisserie ❶,** 32 rue Emile-Jamais, has large pieces of the town's special dessert, *fougasse d'Aigues-Mortes,* a sugary treat with orange-flower flavoring. (☎04 66 53 73 42. Open Su-Tu and Th-Sa 6am-1pm and 4-7pm.)

◧ ⛴ **SIGHTS & ENTERTAINMENT.** Louis IX (St-Louis) built this *bastide* as a springboard from which to reconquer the Holy Land; he launched the Seventh and Eighth Crusades from Aigues-Mortes in 1248 and 1270. Though the crusades were fatal for St-Louis—he was captured on the first and died on the second—the town has weathered several sieges, its planned grid still enclosed by 13th-century walls. The **Tour de Constance,** keystone of the city's defensive fortifications, has been well preserved, probably as a result of its impenetrable 6m-thick walls. Multilingual brochures provide some history for the walk around the top of the ramparts and into the towers surrounding the entire city. An optional tour in French takes you to the top of the tower, which offers a picturesque view of the densely packed town and of the reddish water around it, and through the vaulted prison on the way down. (☎04 66 53 61 55. Tower and ramparts open daily July-Sept. 10:30am-7:30pm; mid-May to June 10am-7pm; Mar. to mid-May 10:30am-6pm; Jan.-Feb. and Oct.-Dec. 9:30am-5pm. All times include a 1-2pm lunchtime closing. 40min. tours in French; 9 per day. €5.50, under age 26 €3.50.) On the corner of the *place* is the 13th-century **Notre Dame des Sablons,** St-Louis's final stop in France before his first crusade. St-Louis turned the church's walls from wood into fortified stone; it now features modern, colorful, childlike painted-glass windows. (Open daily 8:30am-noon and 2-6pm.)

Les Salins de Midi provides 1¼hr. train or bus tours in several languages of the rose-colored **salt extraction lakes.** (☎04 66 73 40 24; www.salins.fr. Open daily Mar. to mid-May and Sept. to early Nov. 10am-5:15pm; mid-May to late Aug. 9:30am-6:45pm. Trips every 15-30min. €6.80, under age 13 €5.) L'Aventure runs daily **boat tours** into the Camargue. (☎06 03 91 44 63. €7 for 1½hr., €8.50 for 2hr.)

The first week in August brings Mediterranean singers to the town for the **Festival des Nuits d'Encens.** (Info ☎04 66 73 90 95. Concert tickets €14-23, students €11-18.) The second weekend of October sees the **Fête Votive's** *Course Camarguaise.* In this Camarguaise tradition, a bull is released into an arena with a tassel attached to his horns. A prize is awarded to the *raseteur* who can detach the tassel. On the last weekend of the month, the **Fête de St-Louis** recreates the past with historical pageants, jousting, and a medieval market.

NÎMES

It is the Spanish feel of Nîmes (pop. 132,000) that draws the vacationing French. They flock here in particular for the *férias,* with their bull runs, bullfights, flamenco dancing, and lots of other hot-blooded Latin activity. Nîmes also serves as an excellent base for short excursions to some of the Roman ruins in the area, including the architecturally impressive Pont du Gard aqueduct. Despite the lively *féria* season, however, Nîmes doesn't merit a long-term stay, lacking both the intimacy of other Provençal cities and the glitz of the Côte d'Azur.

☐ TRANSPORTATION

Trains: bd. Talabot. Info office open M-F 5:45am-9:30pm, Sa 6:45am-9:45pm, Su 6:45am-10pm. To: **Arles** (20min., 13 per day, €6.30); **Bordeaux** (5hr., 10 per day, €46.40); **Marseille** (1¼hr., 20 per day, €15.30); **Montpellier** (30min., 50 per day, €7.20); **Paris** (3hr., 10 per day, €75.90); **Toulouse** (3hr., 8 per day, €29.30).

Buses: rue Ste-Félicité (☎04 66 29 52 00), behind the train station. Info office just inside the train station open M-F 8am-noon and 2-6pm. Société des Transports Départementaux du Gard (STDG; ☎04 66 29 27 29) runs to **Avignon** (1½hr.; M-F 8 per day, Sa 6 per day, Su 2 per day; €6.70). Cars de Camargue (☎04 90 96 36 25) serves **Arles** (M-F 5 per day, 3 on Sa; €5.40) and **Montpellier** (M-Sa 2 per day; €8.40).

Public Transportation: T.C.N. (☎04 66 38 15 40). Maps and schedules available at the tourist office. Buses stop running at 9:30pm. Tickets good for 1hr. Ticket €0.95, *carnet* of 5 €3.80. Single tickets available on the bus, *carnets* at the station kiosks near the Station Esplanade or the *gare routière*.

Taxis: TRAN office (☎04 66 29 40 11) in train station. Base €1.80; €0.58 per km until 7pm, €0.83 per km after 7pm. 24hr.

⚡❷ ORIENTATION & PRACTICAL INFORMATION

Nîmes's shops, museums, and cafés cluster in the *vieille ville* between bd. Victor Hugo and bd. Admiral Courbet. To get there from the train station, follow av. Feuchères, veer left around the park, then clockwise around the arena. To reach the tourist office, follow the signs and go straight on bd. Victor Hugo for five blocks until you reach the Maison Carré, a Roman temple in the middle of pl. Comédie, whose façade looks out upon rue Auguste and the tourist office.

Tourist Office: 6 rue Auguste (☎04 66 58 38 00; www.ot-nimes.fr). Free **accommodations service,** detailed map, and festival info. The free *Nîmescope* lists events. Info on bus and train excursions to Pont du Gard, the Camargue, and nearby towns. Open July-Aug. M-F 8am-8pm, Sa 9am-7pm, Su 10am-6pm; May and Sept. M-F 8am-7pm, Sa 9am-7pm, Su 10am-6pm.

Tours: Le Petit Train (☎04 66 70 26 92). Leaves almost every hr. from espl. Charles de Gaulle in front of the Palais de Justice. Open daily July-Aug. 9:30am-7:30pm; Apr.-June and Sept.-Oct. 9:30-11:30am and 2:30-5:30pm. €5, ages 2-11 €2.

Budget Travel: Nouvelles Frontières, 1 bd. de Prague (☎04 66 67 38 94; fax 04 66 78 38 62). Open M-F 9am-7pm, Sa 9pm-6pm.

Bureau Information Jeunesse, 8 rue de l'Horloge (☎04 66 36 56 86). Provides information on employment, education, and travel opportunities geared toward students. Also has free **Internet** by reservation only. Open Tu-F 9am-6pm, Sa 2-6pm.

Money: Banque de France, 2 sq. du 11 Novembre (☎04 66 76 82 00), offers **currency exchange** with no commission. Exchange desk open M-F 8:30am-12:15pm.

Laundromat: Lavomatique, 5 rue des Halles. Open daily 7am-8pm. **Laverie Libre Service,** 22 rue de Vérone. Open daily 7am-9pm.

Police: 10 rue de la Trésorerie (☎04 66 67 84 29).

Hospital: Hôpital Caremeau (☎04 66 68 68 68), rue Professeur Robert Debré.

SOS Médecins: Emergency doctor ☎04 66 23 69 23. On-call doctor ☎04 66 76 11 11.

PROVENCE

Internet: Net's Games, 22 rue de l'Horloge, pl. de la Maison Carré (☎04 66 36 36 16), is packed with videogame-playing teens. €3.80 per hr. Open daily 10am-midnight. Also available at dark and smoky **PC Gamer,** 2 rue de Nationale (☎04 66 76 27 85). €4 per hr., 10am-noon €3 per hr. Open M-Sa 10:30am-1am, Su 2pm-1am.

Post Office: 1 bd. de Bruxelles (☎04 66 76 69 50), across from the park at the end of av. Feuchères. **Currency exchange** with no commission. Open M-F 8am-7pm, Sa 8am-noon. **Branch offices:** 19 bd. Gambetta and 11 pl. Belle Croix. **Poste Restante:** 30006. **Postal code:** 30000 and 30900.

▌ ACCOMMODATIONS & CAMPING

The *vieille ville* is dotted with pricey hotels. If you are up for a long walk or bus ride every morning, the hostel is unquestionably the best option. Reserve a couple of weeks in advance during festivals and summer concerts.

▨ **Auberge de Jeunesse (HI),** 257 chemin de l'Auberge de la Jeunesse (☎04 66 68 03 20; fax 04 66 68 03 21), off chemin de la Cigale, 4½km from quai de la Fontaine. On foot, pass the Maison Carré on bd. Victor Hugo and continue straight on bd. A. Daudet. Go left at sq. Antonin onto quai de la Fontaine. The Jardins de la Fontaine will be on your right; continue alongside the garden straight on av. Roosevelt. Follow the signs for the Auberge; they will lead you right onto rte. d'Alès and left onto chemin de la Cigale. Follow the small Auberge signs uphill. (45min.) Or take bus #2 (dir: Alès or Villeverte) to Stade, Route d'Alès, and follow the signs. After buses stop running at 8pm, the hostel minibus (call ahead to arrange) will pick you up at the station for free. It will also bring you back to the station in the morning for €1.30. This delightfully modern and friendly hostel is well worth the difficult trek. The comfortable dorms are kept by a warm staff and surrounded by well-kept botanical gardens. 4- to 6-bed dorms with bath and magnetic key-card access. Some family rooms available. Ping-pong, *pétanque*, foosball, laundry, kitchen, snacks, and bar until 1am. **Internet** €3.80 per hr. Bikes €8.20 per day. Scooter €22 per day. May-Oct. bike/kayak tour combo to Pont du Gard €20. Breakfast €3.20. Dinner €9.10. Sheets €2.70 per week. Individual, locking cupboards for luggage. Reception Mar.-Sept. 24hr. (night guard). No curfew. Reservations advised. Bunks €9.50. **Camping** €5.50, with tent rental €7.50. MC/V. **Members only. ❶**

▨ **Hôtel Cat,** 22 rue Amiral Courbet (☎04 66 67 22 85; fax 04 66 21 57 51). Each clean and sizeable room features photographs of a different regional site, from Aigues-Mortes to the Pont du Gard. Breakfast €4. Reservations recommended, especially during *férias*, when prices increase slightly. Singles €21; singles or doubles with shower €25-35. MC/V. ❷

Hôtel Concorde, 3 rue des Chapeliers (☎/fax 04 66 67 91 03), off rue Régale. A friendly staff cares for clean but cramped rooms in this small hotel. Just around the corner from the *arènes*, but away from the noise. Breakfast €4. Singles €21-24, with shower €26-29; doubles €28-34; triples with shower €38. MC/V. ❷

Hôtel de l'Amphithéâtre, 4 rue des Arènes (☎04 66 67 28 51; perso.wanadoo.fr/hotel-amphitheatre). Though pricier, these elegant rooms, each named after a Provençal poet or writer, are meticulously well-kept and centrally located. Breakfast €5.70. Singles €30; doubles €39-55 depending on size and if it has a balcony. Rates increase significantly in the high season. Extra bed €15. AmEx/MC/V. ❸

Campsite: Domaine de La Bastide, rte. de Générac (☎/fax 04 66 38 09 31), 5km south of the train station. Take bus D (dir: La Bastide, last bus 7:30pm) to its terminus. By car, drive towards Montpellier and get off at rte. de Générac. Three-star site with grocery store, laundry, and recreational facilities. €7.30 per person, €11.60 for two. Caravan with electricity €10.40 per person, €14.70 for two. ❶

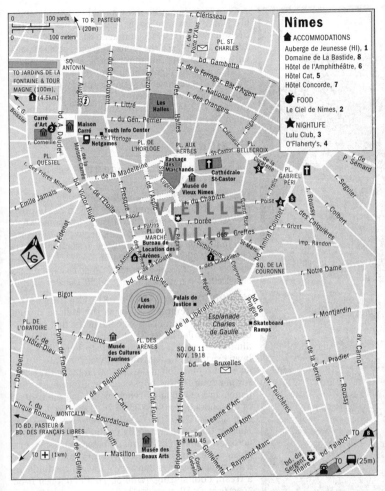

Nîmes

🏠 ACCOMMODATIONS
Auberge de Jeunesse (HI), **1**
Domaine de La Bastide, **8**
Hôtel de l'Amphithéâtre, **6**
Hôtel Cat, **5**
Hôtel Concorde, **7**

🍴 FOOD
Le Ciel de Nîmes, **2**

★ NIGHTLIFE
Lulu Club, **3**
O'Flaherty's, **4**

PROVENCE

🍴 FOOD

Local chefs employ generous amounts of *herbes de Provence* (a mixture of local herbs) and *aïoli* (a thick sauce of garlic and olive oil). Nîmes specializes in *la brandade de morue*, dried cod crushed with olive oil and packed in a turnover, pastry, or soufflé. Unfortunately, even the more expensive restaurants in Nîmes are unspectacular. If you have access to a kitchen, you can prepare better meals yourself, with fresh produce from the various markets. Stock up at the **open-air market** on bd. Jean-Jaurès (F 7am-1pm), the **market** in Les Halles (daily 6am-1pm), or the large **Marché U,** 19 rue d'Alès, just down the hill from the hostel. (Open M-Sa 8am-12:45pm and 3:30-8pm.) The terraced herb gardens and ponds on the back slopes of the **Jardins de la Fontaine** are great places to bring a picnic basket.

ON THE MENU

BATHE YOUR BREAD

Provence has boundless pride in its cuisine: the flavors of the local *terroir* are simple, fresh, and rich. The quality of the vegetables here is particularly prized. Especially in warmer months, as towns and villages on the Riviera begin to sell delicious summer greens, any traveler to the region should sample the freshness of Provençal produce by indulging in the traditional *pan bagnat.*

Approximately translated as "bathed bread," the *pan bagnat* is a sandwich made out of a round, crusty roll and filled with vegetables, tuna, and olive oil. It began as a version of the *salade Niçoise*—a salad with tuna into which Provençal locals crumbled hard bread. Today the sandwich's popularity is easy to understand as it is delicious, filling, and easy to make. Purchase fresh vegetables at the nearest *marché* and attempt the recipe at home:

Step 1: Purchase a roll at the local *boulangerie* and cut it in half, rubbing each side with garlic, quality olive oil, and a touch of vinegar or vinaigrette. Season with salt and pepper to taste.

Step 2: Fill the sandwich with thinly sliced tomatoes, small onions, cucumbers, hard boiled eggs, tuna, red or green peppers, olives, French beans, artichokes, and fresh basil leaves.

Step 3: Chill the sandwich before eating to allow the garlic to penetrate the bread.

Caladons, honey cookies sprinkled with almonds, are Nîmes's favorite sweet. Cafés and bakeries line the squares; *brasseries* dominate **bd. Victor Hugo, bd. Admiral Courbet,** and the arena. Terraced **pl. du Marché** with its crocodile fountain reverberates with laughter late into the night. On the 3rd floor of the Carré d'Art, **Le Ciel de Nîmes ❸** serves artful delights before a beautiful view of the entire city. (☎04 66 36 71 70. Entrées €12-14, excellent salads, and fresh juices. Open Tu-Su 10am-8pm. MC/V.)

🇬 SIGHTS

A three-day pass to all sights is sold at every sight (€9.80, students €4.90).

LES ARÈNES. The city's pride and joy is the best-preserved Roman amphitheater in France. Impressive when empty, the amphitheater is awesome when packed with screaming crowds during its concerts and bullfights. The elliptical stone arena, built in AD 50, seats 23,000 people. (☎*04 66 76 72 77. Open M-F summer 9am-7pm; winter 9am-6pm. Closed on days of* férias *or concerts; call in advance to verify. €4.50, students €3.20.)*

MAISON CARRÉ & CARRÉ D'ART. The imposing rectangular temple known as the **Maison Carrée** served as the center of public life in the first century of Roman rule. Louis XIV liked it so much that he almost ordered it to be brought to Versailles as a lawn ornament. In 1992 the roof was renovated to be an exact replication of the original large flat tiles. The former temple now houses a few informative text panels in English and French explaining the history of the building. (☎*04 66 36 26 76. Open daily June-Sept. 9am-7pm and 2:30-7pm; Oct.-May 10am-6pm. Free.)* The Maison Carrée is gracefully counter-balanced from across the square by Norman Foster's ultra-modern glass cube, housing the city library and the **Carré d'Art,** which displays impressive traveling exhibits in a fresh, cool setting. (☎*04 66 76 35 70. Open Tu-Su 10am-6pm. €4.50, students €3.20.)*

MUSÉE DES CULTURES TAURINES. This new museum offers a playful and compelling glimpse into the culture of bullfights and the importance of the *férias* to the city and the surrounding region, especially if you're able to read the French text. Videos, images, clothing, and even mounted bulls' heads from ancient and modern *férias* describe in vivid detail the various components of the bullfighting culture, from the types of bulls in the region to the role of female *toreras.* (6 *rue Alexandre Ducros.* ☎*04 66 36 83 77; www.musee.taureaux@ville-nimes.fr. Open May-Oct. Tu-Su 10am-6pm, until 8pm on* féria *days. €4.60, students €3.30.)*

JARDINS DE LA FONTAINE. Created in the 18th century, this typically French garden is filled with the sounds of games of *boules*, mothers pushing strollers, children racing after each other, and the splash of tall fountains. An ideal picnic spot, the gardens offer plenty of shade and a slight breeze on hot summer days. *(Off pl. Foch to the left along the canals from the Maison. Garden open daily Apr. to mid-Sept. 7:30am-10pm; mid-Sept. to Nov. 7:30am-6:30pm; Nov.-Mar. 8am-7pm. Free.)* Rising majestically above the park is the **Tour Magne.** Built in the Iron Age and modified by Augustus in 15 BC, this massive tower, essentially a blunt stone spike, once represented a corner of the Roman empire. Now the eroded ruins offer an exhilarating view of Nîmes and the surrounding countryside. *(☎04 66 67 65 56. Open daily July-Aug. 9am-7pm; Sept.-June 9am-5pm. €2.40, students €1.90.)*

MUSÉE DES BEAUX ARTS & MUSÉE DU VIEUX NÎMES. The **Musée de Beaux Arts,** a Neoclassical building accented with marble pillars and Roman mosaic floors, features paintings of the French, Italian, Flemish, and Dutch schools from the 15th to 18th centuries. The **Musée du Vieux Nîmes,** in a 17th-century Episcopal palace, displays 17th-century artifacts as well as a cool modern exhibit on the history of blue jeans which honors Nîmes as the birthplace of denim. *(Beaux-Arts: rue de la cité Foule. ☎04 66 67 38 21. Vieux Nîmes: pl. aux Herbes, next to the cathedral. ☎04 66 36 00 64. Both open Tu-Su July-Aug. 10am-6pm; Sept.-June 11am-6pm. €4.30, students €3.)*

🎵 🍺 ENTERTAINMENT & FESTIVALS

Outside of the festival season, Nîmes is a pretty lousy place to party. Bars are lively during the *férias* (see below), but otherwise they shut down relatively early. Check out the cafés along the pl. du Marché. Bustling **O'Flaherty's,** 21 bd. Amiral Courbet, has €3.50-5 pints of beer and live music on Thursday nights in winter. The dart-filled, Guinness-sloppy bar is a favorite of both anglophone visitors and friendly *Nîmois.* *(☎04 66 67 22 63. Open M-F 11am-2am, Sa-Su 5pm-2am.)* Locals fill the outside tables at the **Café Carré,** 1 pl. de la Maison Carrée, which is a café overlooking the Maison Carrée by day and a lively bar at night. *(☎04 66 67 50 05. Drinks €1.50-3. Open daily 7am-2am.)* **Lulu Club,** 10 impasse de la Curaterie, off rue de la Curaterie, is a gay dance bar. *(☎04 66 36 28 20. €8 cover includes 1 drink. Mixed drinks €4; straight alcohol €8. Open Tu-Sa 11pm onward.)* **Cinéma Le Sémaphore,** 25 rue Porte de France, plays non-French films in their original languages. *(☎04 66 67 83 11. €5.20, under 25 €4.30, noon shows €4.)*

In the summer, students in Nîmes head for the beach, where temporarily constructed restaurant-bars open in June and entertain until early September. Although it is difficult to get there and even harder to find a cheap way back to Nîmes, bus #6 runs along the plage de la Corniches. Party-goers can get off at Les Passantes or Les Amours d'Antan.

Concerts, movies, plays, and operas take place at *les arènes* throughout the year (€9-46). Summer acts have included Ray Charles and Ben Harper. For info and reservations, contact the **Bureau de Location des Arènes,** 4 rue de la Violette. *(☎04 66 02 80 80. Open M-F 10am-6pm.)* The **Théâtre de Nîmes,** 1 pl. de la Calade, offers over 70 shows per year, ranging from theater to dance to musical performances. *(☎04 66 36 65 00. Tickets €9-30, with some reduced rates for students.)*

It is worth changing travel plans to see one of the famous *férias.* Nîmes holds three important *férias*: the **Féria de Primavera** in mid-February, the **Féria des Vendages** in mid-September, and the most boisterous, the **Féria de Pentecôte** (during Pentecost). For five days, the streets resound with the clattering of hooves as bulls are herded to the *arènes* for combat, and the nights are full of revelry.

The **Courses Camarguaises,** held at varying dates in June, July, and August, provide more humane entertainment. Fighters strip decorations from the bulls' horns,

PROVENCE

narrowly avoiding the lethal points, and then vault over barriers to safety. (Tickets €10.50-53.50. Purchase at the arena ticket office, 4 rue de la Violette. Cheap seats usually available on the day of the event.) During **les Marchés du Soir** (AKA **Jeudis de Nîmes**), the city center fills with local painters, artists, and musicians late into the night (July-Aug. Th 7-11pm).

⚑ DAYTRIP FROM NÎMES: PONT DU GARD

The Pont du Gard is the centerpiece of a 50km Roman aqueduct that once supplied Nîmes with water. Its three diminishing levels of arches bridge the 275m-wide valley of the Gardon River at a height of 48m. Built in 19 BC under the direction of Roman engineers to transport water from the springs near Uzès to Nîmes, the entire aqueduct, an architectural *coup de grace*, slopes at a mere rate of 25cm per km, at an average gradient of 0.34 degrees. Close to 90% of the aquaduct is underground, a Roman feat of near-perfect construction.

Although a walk across the bridge itself is free, the helpful welcome center houses several interpretive activities, including a sleek, educational museum (€6), a 25min. film in English and French about the construction of the bridge (€3, screening times available at the information desk), and a children's learning center (€4.50). Guided tours of the bridge are available in several languages (€5). Packages of all four activities are available for €10, students €9. Swimming in the refreshing river below the Pont du Gard offers a cool view of the bridge; stairs down to the rocky beach are on either side of the bridge itself.

If you have a whole day to spare, the best way to experience the Pont du Gard is to start from **Collias**, 6km toward Uzès. Here **Kayak Vert** rents two-person canoes, kayaks, and bikes. The pleasant two- to three-hour paddle takes you down river past the Château de St-Privat (sight of a famous treaty signing) to the Pont du Gard, where a bus shuttles you back to Collias. (☎04 66 22 80 76. Kayak/canoe rental €14 per day, with shuttle €16; bikes €17 per day, €15 per half-day. 15% discount for students or guests of the hostel in Nîmes.)

The Société des Transports Départementaux du Gard (STDG; ☎04 66 29 27 29) runs **daily buses** from the bus station to the Pont du Gard (30min.; M-Sa 5 per day, 2 on Su; €4.80). Buses also leave for the Pont du Gard from Avignon (45min., 7 per day, €5). The bus stops Sept.-June at the roundabout by the Hôtel L'Auberge Blanche—AKA, the middle of nowhere; July-Aug. the bus stops at the Pont du Gard Welcome Center. The Nîmes **tourist office** leads **tours** to the Pont du Gard every Tuesday July-Aug. 2:30-7:30pm, meeting at the main entrance of the Jardins de la Fontaine at 2:30pm. €13, students €9.

Camping le Barralet, rue des Aires in Collias, offers a pool and hot showers in addition to river bathing. A grocery store is 200m away. (☎04 66 22 84 52; fax 04 66 22 89 17. Open Mar.-Sept. 1 person €6-7.40, 2 people €11-13.50, 3 people €13.50-16.50. Lower prices Apr.-June and Sept. MC/V.)

ORANGE

Despite its name, this northern Provençal town has never tended a single citrus grove in all of its colorful two-millennium history. *Orange* is a perversion of the original Roman name of the city: *Arausio*. Orange's juice, the Côtes du Rhône vintage, originates in its renowned vineyards, not in groves. *Caves* throughout the region offer *dégustations* of the fine liquid. An immense Roman theater and intricately decorated triumphal arch, in addition to summer festivals, are the chief reasons for making a visit to Orange.

⊞ 🔋 ORIENTATION & PRACTICAL INFORMATION

Trains run from av. Frédéric Mistral to Avignon (20min.; M-Sa 19 per day, Su 13 per day; €4.70); Marseille (1¼hr., 11 per day, €17.10); Lyon (2½hr.; M-Sa 7 per day, Su 4 per day; €21.60); and Paris (3½hr., 2 TGV per day, €62.50). The info office is open daily 5:30am-7:45pm. **Buses** (☎04 90 34 15 59) run from cours Pourtoules to Avignon (55min.; M-Sa about every hr., Su 4 per day; €4.80). The ticket office is open M-Tu and Th-F 8am-12:30pm and 3-5pm, W 8am-noon and 3-5pm. For a **taxi**, call Taxi Monge at ☎04 90 51 00 00.

To reach the **tourist office**, 5 cours A. Briand, from the station, follow the signs along av. F. Mistral to the *centre ville;* keep left as the road becomes rue de la République. (15min.) Multilingual staff provides maps, daytrip ideas, and 1hr. tours (July-Aug. 1 per day, price varies) of Théâtre Antique in English. (☎04 90 34 70 88; fax 04 90 34 99 62. Open Apr.-Sept. M-Sa 9:30am-7pm, Su 10am-6pm; Oct.-Mar. M-Sa 10am-1pm and 2-5pm. **Branch office**, pl. des Frères Mounet, opposite Théâtre Antique. Open Apr.-Sept. M-Sa 10am-1pm and 2:15-7pm.) Other services include: a **laundromat** at 5 rue St-Florent, off bd. E. Daladier (open daily 7am-8pm); **police** at 427 bd. E. Daladier (☎04 90 51 55 55); the Louis Giorgi **hospital** at chemin de l'Abrian, on av. H. Fabré (☎04 90 11 22 22); **ambulances** at ☎04 90 34 02 66; a **24hr. pharmacy**, Pharmacie St-Martin, 18 rue St-Martin (☎04 90 34 02 82; open M-F 8:45am-12:15pm and 2-7:45pm); **Internet** at Atlas Télécom, 22 rue V. Hugo (☎04 90 11 04 60; €3.50 per hr; open daily 10am-11pm), which has international phone booths; and a **post office** with **currency exchange** at 679 bd. E. Daladier, cours Pourtoules. (☎04 90 11 11 00. Open M-F 8am-6:30pm, Sa 8am-noon.) **Postal code:** 84100.

📫 📋 ACCOMMODATIONS & FOOD

Orange's hotels fill up fast in July and August for the Festival d'Avignon. Every wall of the brightly colored, family-owned **Hôtel St-Florent ❸**, 4 rue du Mazeau, near pl. aux Herbes, is painted with frescoes. Some rooms have TV. (☎04 90 34 18 53; fax 04 90 51 17 25. Breakfast €6. Closed Dec.-Feb. Singles €24, with shower €27-34; doubles with shower €34, with bath €40-65; triples with bath €50; family suites with bath €60-70. Extra bed €8. July-Aug. prices slightly higher. MC/V.) **Arcôtel ❷**, 8 pl. aux Herbes, rents simple, cheery, comfortable rooms, close to both the central *place* and the Roman theater. Some triples and quads are particularly huge. (☎04 90 34 09 23; fax 04 90 51 61 12. Breakfast €5.50. Reception 7am-11pm. Singles €18; doubles €27-38; triples with bath €42; quads with bath €50. MC/V.) **Camping: Le Jonquier ❶**, on rue A. Carrel, is a hike. From the tourist office, walk toward the *autoroute*, turn right after the school onto av. du 18 Juin 1940, and left onto rue H. Noguères. After 5min., go right on rue A. Carrel. Take the middle road through the rotary; the site will be on the left. (15min.) The three-star site has a pool, tennis, mini-golf, showers, and mini-mart. (☎04 90 34 49 48; www.avignon-et-provence.com/le-jonquier. Reception daily 8am-8pm. Open Apr.-Sept. 1-2 people, car, and tent €20.50; €4 per additional person. Electricity €1. MC/V.)

The eateries on pl. aux Herbes and pl. de la République serve standard café fare, from goat cheese salads to steaming pizzas. For groceries, head to the **Petit Casino**, 16 rue de la République. (Open M-Sa 7:30am-12:30pm and 3:30-7:30pm.) Place République, pl. Clemenceau, and cours A. Briand host an **open-air market** selling everything from produce to handmade jewelry (Th 7am-1pm), and a food-less Provençal market (Sa 10am-3pm). **The Festival Café**, 5 pl. de la République, serves delicious *menus* (€11-20), including an incredible *mousse au chocolat*, on a purple-trimmed terrace. (☎04 90 34 65 58. Open daily 7:30am-midnight. MC/V.)

🔲 🎵 SIGHTS & ENTERTAINMENT

Built in the first century, Orange's striking **Théâtre Antique** is the best-preserved Roman theater in Europe. Its 3811 sq. ft. stage wall is one of three remaining in the world; Louis XIV is said to have called it the most beautiful wall in his kingdom. The theater originally held 10,000 spectators and was connected to a gymnasium complete with running tracks, combat platform, sauna, and a temple. After the fall of Rome, this locus of pagan entertainment fell into disrepair; local homes sprung up in and around its walls. In the mid-19th century, engineers rediscovered its great acoustics and used the three remaining rows as a template for reconstructing the seating area. Above the theater, amid the ragged remnants of the Prince of Orange's castle, the overgrown park **Colline St-Eutrope** offers a panoramic view and free, though acoustically poor, standing room for concerts.

Across the street, a ticket to the theater provides access to the **Musée Municipal,** which exhibits many antique objects uncovered by excavations around Orange, as well as rooms dedicated to more recent history and to the fabrication of Provençal cloth. (☎ 04 90 51 17 60 for both theater and museum. Open daily June-Aug. 9am-8pm; Apr.-May and Sept. 9am-7pm; Mar. and Oct. 9am-6pm; Jan.-Feb. and Nov.-Dec. 9am-5pm. Combined ticket €7, students €5.50.)

Orange's other major monument, the **Arc de Triomphe,** stands on the Via Agrippa, which once connected Arles to Lyon. Built during Augustus's time, the arch's façades depict Roman victories over the Gauls. A *Petit Train* visits it June-Sept. from -the Théâtre Antique. (☎ 04 90 37 28 68. 30min. €5, under age 10 €2.50.)

From early July to August, the **Théâtre Antique** regains its original function with the **Chorégies,** a series of grand opera and choral productions. Info available from the Maison des Chorégies, 18 pl. Sylvain, next to the theater. (☎ 04 90 34 24 24. Open June-Aug. M-Sa 10am-7pm; Feb.-May M-F 11am-1pm and 2-5pm. Tickets €4-160; students under 28 can buy tickets for as little as €2.) In August, rock concerts, films, and variety shows take the stage. For info, call the **Service Culturel,** next door to Maison des Chorégies, where visitors can also inquire about other performances, including several small art festivals in mid- to late June. (☎ 04 90 51 57 57. Open M-Th 8:30am-noon and 1:30-6pm, F 8am-noon and 1:30-4:30pm, on the nights of performances.)

CÔTE D'AZUR

Between Marseille and the Italian border, the sun-drenched beaches and warm waters of the Mediterranean form the backdrop for this fabled playground of the rich and famous. Sunbathers bronze *au naturel* on pebbly beaches, high rollers drop millions in casinos, cultural types wander abandoned coastal fortifications, and trendy youth swing until dawn in Europe's most exclusive nightclubs.

Now one of the most touristed parts of France, the Côte d'Azur began as a Greco-Roman commercial base. Forts, ports, and prosperous villages sprang up here around 600 BC, only to be razed by barbarian invaders toward the middle of the first millennium. With the 16th-century arrival of the French monarchy, the region started to take its modern form. The Riviera's resort status began to develop when in the late 18th-century, English and Russian aristocrats took up the habit of wintering on the Côte in order to escape their native countries' abominable weather. Nice was soon drawing a steady crowd of the idle rich. In the 1920s, Coco Chanel popularized the Provençal farmer's healthy tan; parasols went down, hemlines went up, and the upper class's ritual sun-worship began.

The Riviera has been the passion and the death of many a famous artist, including F. Scott Fitzgerald, Picasso, and Renoir. Most towns along the eastern stretch of the Côte boast a chapel, room, or wall decorated by Matisse or Chagall. The ultimate celebrity accessory is a vacation home in St-Tropez, and each May high society makes its yearly pilgrimage to the Cannes Film Festival and the Monte-Carlo Grand Prix. Less exclusive are Nice's raucous *Carnaval* in early February and various summer jazz festivals. Penny-pinching travelers can soak up the spectacle, as well as plenty of sun, sea, and crowded sand.

The towns of the Côte range from quiet seaside villages to glitzy resorts. Nearly all visits to the Riviera include a stop in **Nice** (p. 545), the area's budget mecca and anglophone party town. From there, daytrips to quintessential Côte d'Azur coastal villages abound (🖾**St-Paul**, p. 555; 🖾**Villefranche-sur-mer**, p. 556; 🖾**St-Jean-Cap-Ferrat**, p. 558; **Beaulieu-Sur-Mer**, p. 557; and **Eze**, p. 558). No trip to the area is complete without extensive lounge time on the amazing beaches along the coast. Some of the best are found in the exclusive town of 🖾**Antibes** (p. 569), but less pricey options are plentiful around small villages such as **St-Raphaël** (p. 586) and **Fréjus** (p. 587). Nude beaches await the brave on the **Iles d'Hyères** (p. 595). Those seeking solitude and adventure will enjoy the deep, hikeable 🖾**Canyon Du Verdon** (p. 585) and its bases at either **Castellane** (p. 585) or perfume capital **Grasse** (p. 583). The gamblers' havens of **Monaco and Monte-Carlo** (p. 559) offer plenty of opportunities to lighten a heavy wallet, as do the glam-town of **Cannes** (p. 577) with its famous film festival, and the celebrity-favored 🖾**St-Tropez** (p. 590). The party continues for the young and hedonistic at 🖾**Juan-les-Pins** (p. 575), the prime spot for late-night action. For more genuine coastal charm, **Menton** (p. 566) makes a pleasant, quiet stopover, as do **Biot** (p. 574), renowned for its glass-blowing industry, and the medieval, cobblestoned town and castle at **Grimaud** (p. 594).

🝗 BEACHES

In summer, the best time to swim is from 7pm to 9pm, just before sunset. Bring a beach mat (€3.50 at supermarkets) as even the sand beaches are a bit rocky. Almost all the towns on the Côte lie along one local rail line, making exploration easy. The largest cities have the worst or least-convenient beaches: Marseille's are

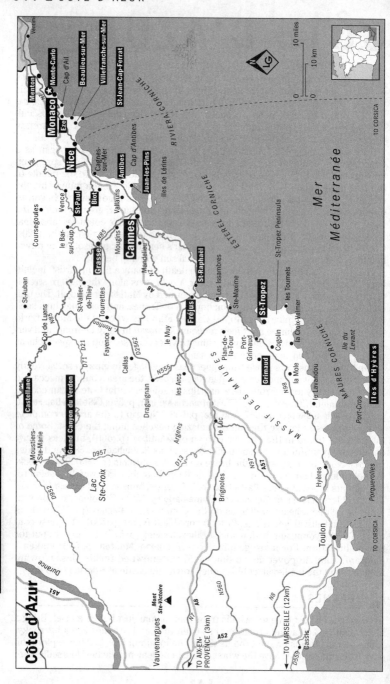

artificial, Nice's rocky, Cannes's private, and St-Tropez's, though beautiful, are remote. Smaller beaches between towns, like **Cap Martin** (between Monaco and Menton), **St-Jean-Cap-Ferrat** (between Monaco and Nice), and **St-Raphaël-Fréjus** (between Cannes and St-Tropez), are better options. Nearly all beaches are topless or top-optional, and it's seldom hard to find a secluded spot to go bottomless, too. Nudity is the norm at the astounding **Héliopolis** on the **Ile du Levant** (p. 595), and in the *calanques* near **Eze-sur-Mer** (p. 558). Don't neglect less-frequented islands: Porquerolles, the Ile du Levant, and the Iles des Lérins off Cannes all have fine rock ledges and secluded coves. Nice's beach is notoriously unsafe at night. In classier towns like Cannes, beaches are a nighttime hangout for local drug dealers, while many kids earn their summer salaries in tourists' jewelry, mopeds, and cash.

NICE

Sun-drenched and sizzling, Nice (pop. 380,000) is the unofficial capital of the Riviera. The former vacation haunt of dukes and czarinas continues to seduce tourists with non-stop nightlife, extreme shopping, and first-rate museums. No matter the season, the old town's maze of pedestrian streets buzzes with shoppers by day and lively bar-goers by night. Excellent transportation and budget lodgings make the fifth-largest city in France an inexpensive base for sampling the Côte d'Azur's pricier delights. Be prepared to make new friends, hear more English than French, and have more fun than you'll be able to remember.

✈ INTERCITY TRANSPORTATION

Flights: Aéroport Nice-Côte d'Azur (☎08 20 42 33 33). **Air France**, 10 av. Félix-Faure (☎08 20 82 08 20). Open M-F 9am-6pm. Outbound flights to **Bastia** in Corsica (€115; under 25, over 60, and couples €57) and **Paris** (€93; under 25, over 60, and couples €46). **EasyJet** flies to **London** (see **Travelling from the UK:** p. 37). Sunbus #23 goes to the airport from the train station (☎04 93 13 53 13. Every 15min. 6am-8:30pm, €1.30). The pricier ANT airport bus runs from the bus station (☎04 93 21 30 83. M-Sa every 20min., Su every 30min.; €3.50).

Trains: There are two primary train stations in town: **Gare SNCF Nice-Ville,** av. Thiers (☎04 93 82 62 11, call M-F 9am-noon or 3-6pm for lost luggage, missed trains, and special assistance). Open daily 5am-12:15am. To: **Cannes** (45min., every 15-45min., €5); **Marseille** (2½hr., every 30-90min., €24); **Monaco** (15min., every 10-30min., €3.70); **Paris** (5½hr., 6 per day, €76). Ticket office open daily 5:30am-8:30pm. Luggage storage (☎04 92 14 82 68) open M-Sa 8:15am-noon and 2-5pm. Small locker €3.20, large €7, max. storage 72hr. **Gare du Sud,** 4bis rue Alfred Binet (☎04 93 82 10 17), 800m from Nice-Ville. Private trains to **Plan-du-Var** and **Digne-les-Bains.**

Buses: 5 bd. Jean Jaurès (☎04 93 85 61 81), left at the end of av. Jean Médecin. Info booth open M-Sa 8am-6:30pm. If booth is closed, buy tickets on the bus. To: **Cannes** (1½hr.; M-Sa 3 per hr. 6:10am-9:45pm, Su every 30min. 8:30am-8:30pm; €6) and **Monaco** (40min., M-Sa 4 per hr. 6am-8pm, Su every 30min. 6am-7:50pm; €3.50).

Ferries: Corsica Ferries (☎04 92 00 42 93, reservations ☎08 25 09 50 95; www.corsicaferries.com) and **SNCM** (☎04 93 13 66 66, reservations 04 93 13 66 99; fax 04 93 13 66 91) take high-speed ferries out of the port. Take bus #1 or 2 (dir: Port). To: **Corsica** (€40, bikes €3-13, small cars €45). See **Corsica** (p. 759) for more info.

⬛ LOCAL TRANSPORTATION

Public Transportation: Sunbus, 10 av. F. Faure (☎04 93 13 53 13), near pl. Leclerc and pl. Masséna. Info booth open M-F 7:15am-7pm, Sa 7:15am-6pm. Buses operate daily 7am-8pm, but schedules vary; the tourist office provides the **"Sunplan"** bus map and the **"Guide Infobus."** Individual tickets €1.30, day pass €4, 5-day pass €13, weeklong pass €16.80, 8-ticket *carnet* €8.30. Buy passes at office or on board. **Noctambus,** aptly named, operates 4 routes when the sun goes down, daily 9pm-2:40am. Inquire at the tourist office for info. Use caution when traveling around Nice after dark.

Taxis: Central Taxi Riviera (☎04 93 13 78 78; fax 04 93 13 78 79). Get a price range before boarding and make sure the meter is turned on. From the airport to the center of Nice €18-28. Night fares are more expensive.

Bike and Car Rental: JML Location, 34 av. Auber (☎04 93 16 07 00), opposite station. Bikes €7 per half-day, €11 per day, €42 per week; €228 credit card deposit. Scooters €23/€37/€196/€900. Cars €45 per day, €0.12 each km over 200km. 23+. Open June-Sept. daily 9am-6:30pm, Oct.-May M-Sa 8am-1pm and 2-6:30pm. MC/V. **Nicea Location Rent,** 12 rue de Belgique (☎04 93 82 42 71; nicealocation@aol.com), around the corner from the station. Scooter €49.50 per day, €167 per week; deposit €600 and up. Rents bikes, in-line skates, motorcycles. 5-10% student discount, 10% if you reserve by email. Open daily Dec.-Sept. 9am-6pm. AmEx/MC/V. **Budget Rent-a-Car,** 23 rue de Belgique, opposite the station (☎04 92 16 24 16; nice-gare@comeback.fr). Open M-F 8am-6:30pm, Sa 8am-noon and 2-6pm, Su 9am-noon. MC/V.

✦ ❷ ORIENTATION AND PRACTICAL INFORMATION

The train station, **Gare Nice-Ville,** is surrounded by cheap restaurants, budget hotels, and triple-X video stores. Exiting the station, to the left is **avenue Jean Médecin,** a main artery that meets the water at **place Masséna.** (10min.) To the right is **boulevard Gambetta,** the other main water-bound thoroughfare. The **promenade des Anglais,** which becomes **quai des États-Unis** east of av. Jean Médecin, hugs the coast and is a people-watcher's paradise, as are the cafés, boutiques, and pricey restaurants west of bd. Jean Medecin in the **rue Masséna** pedestrian zone. Below and to the left of Jean Médecin lies the pulsating **Vieux Nice.** Continuing along past the old city, you'll find **Port Lympia,** a warren of alleyways, *brasseries,* and *tabacs.*

Unfortunately, Nice's big-city appeal also means big-city crime. Women should avoid walking alone at night, and everyone should **exercise caution** around the train station, in Vieux Nice, and on the Promenade des Anglais.

Tourist Office: av. Thiers (☎08 92 70 74 07; www.nicetourism.com). Genial, English-speaking staff makes same-day reservations for hotels and provides the English-language *Nice: A Practical Guide* and a map (essential in Vieux Nice). The *Semaine des Spectacles* (€1 at *tabacs*) lists entertainment for the entire Côte. Open M-Sa June-Sept. 8am-8pm, Su 9am-7pm; Oct.-May 8am-7pm. **Branches:** 5 prom. des Anglais (☎/fax 04 92 14 48 03). Same hours, but closed on Su Oct.-May. Also at airport terminal 1 (☎/fax 04 93 21 44 50). Open June-Sept. daily 8am-10pm; closed Su Oct.-May.

Budget Travel Offices: USIT, 15 rue de la France (☎04 93 87 34 96; fax 04 93 87 10 91), near pl. Masséna. Books cheap international flights as well as bus and train trips within France, and arranges excursions and camping trips. Open M-Sa 9:30am-6:30pm.

Consulates: Canada, 10 rue Lamartine (☎04 93 92 93 22). Open M-F 9am-noon. **UK,** 26 av. Notre Dame (☎04 93 62 13 56). Open M, W, F 9:30-11:30am. **US,** 7 av. Gustave V (☎04 93 88 89 55; fax 04 93 87 07 38). Open M-F 9-11:30am and 1:30-4:30pm.

Currency Exchange: Cambio, 17 av. Thiers (☎04 93 88 56 80), opposite the train station. 5% commission on European traveler's checks. Open daily 7:30am-8pm. **Change,** 10 av. Félix Faure (☎04 93 80 36 67). Open M-Sa 9:30am-12:30pm and 2-5:30pm. **American Express,** 11 prom. des Anglais (☎04 93 16 53 53; fax 04 93 16 51 67), at the corner of rue des Congrès. Open daily 9am-8:30pm. **Travelex,** 12 av. Thiers (☎04

93 82 13 00), outside the train station. Open daily 9am-5:30pm. Also located at pl. Masséna. Open daily 9:20am-11:30pm; Oct.-June 9:20am-10pm.

English Bookstore: The Cat's Whiskers, 30 rue Lamartine (☎04 93 80 02 66). Great selection, from bestsellers to cookbooks. Open July-Aug. M-Sa 10:30am-12:30pm and 3-7pm; Sept.-June M-F 9:30am-noon and 2-6:45pm, Sa 9:30am-noon and 3-7pm. Sometimes closed M morning. AmEx/MC/V.

Youth Center: Centre d'Information Jeunesse, 19 rue Gioffredo (☎04 93 80 93 93; www.crij.org/nice), near the Museum of Contemporary Art. Posts student summer jobs. Most useful if you speak French. Open M-F 10am-7pm, Sa 10am-5pm.

Laundromat: Laverie Niçoise, 7 rue d'Italie (☎04 93 87 56 50), near Basilique Notre Dame. Wash €4, dry €2 per 20min. Open M-Sa 8:30am-12:30pm and 2:30-7:30pm.

Police: 1 av. Mal. Foch (☎04 92 17 22 22), at the opposite end from bd. J. Médecin.

Hospital: St-Roch, 5 rue Pierre Devoluy (☎04 92 03 33 75).

24hr. Pharmacy: 7 rue Masséna (☎04 93 87 78 94).

Internet: Teknosoft, 16 rue Paganini (☎04 93 16 89 81). €2 per 30min., €4 per hr. Open daily 9am-10pm. **Alexso Info,** 1 rue de Belgique (☎04 93 88 65 02). Open 10am-8pm daily. €0.90 per 10 min., €3.90 for 50min. Both have American keyboards. Also at 2 pl. Magenta, near pl. Masséna (☎04 93 82 29 69). **The NetGate,** 40 rue de la Buffa (☎04 97 03 27 97). Friendly service. €5 per hr., students €4 per hr. 16 computers, all with English keyboards. Open daily.

Post Office: 21 av. Thiers (☎04 93 82 65 22; fax 04 93 88 78 46), near the station. Open M-F 8am-7pm, Sa 8am-noon. **Postal code:** 06033 Nice Cédex 1.

ACCOMMODATIONS

Nice's hostels are remote and often full. Reserve 2-3 weeks ahead in summer. The city has two clusters of budget hotels. Those by the train station badly located but newer than those closer to Vieux Nice and the beach. Particularly those traveling alone or planning to sample Nice's nightlife would be wise to stay near Vieux Nice.

HOSTELS (OUTSKIRTS OF NICE)

Relais International de la Jeunesse "Clairvallon," 26 av. Scudéri (☎04 93 81 27 63; clajpaca@cote-dazur.com), in Cimiez, 4km out of town. Take bus #15 to Scudéri (dir: Rimiez; 20min., every 10min.) from the train station or pl. Masséna; after 9pm, take the N2 bus from pl. Masséna. Disembark and turn right, heading uphill, and take the first left. To walk from the station, turn left and left again on av. J. Médecin, then right before the overpass on bd. Raimbaldi. Go 6 blocks and turn right on av. Comboul, then left on bd. Carabacel, which becomes bd. de Cimiez. Turn right onto av. de Flirey, and keep trudging uphill until you reach av. Scudéri. Turn left and follow the signs. (30min.) A mini-football field, lovely dining room, garden with fountain, swimming pool (open 5-7 or 8pm), and TV access in this luxurious villa of a deceased marquis help to keep the 160 guests entertained. 4- to 10-bed rooms. Breakfast included. 5-course dinner €9. Laundry €4, dryer €2. Check-in after 5pm, but luggage can be dropped off anytime. Lockout 9:30am-5pm. Curfew 11pm. No reservations, but with 160 beds space is not usually an issue. Dorms €14. Half board available for €22.50. ●

Auberge de Jeunesse (HI), rte. Forestière du Mont-Alban (☎04 93 89 23 64; fax 04 92 04 03 10), 4km from the city center. To get there from the bus station, take #14 (dir: Mont Boron) to l'Auberge (every 30-45min.; last bus 7:50pm). To get there from the train station, take #17 and switch to #14 at the Sunbus station. If going on foot, from the train station, turn left and then right on av. Jean Médecin. Follow it through pl. Masséna and turn left on bd. Jaurès. Turn right on rue Barla, following the signs up the hill. (50min.) Ultra-clean hostel draws a cool, friendly crowd. 6- to 10-bed dorms.

Kitchen with supplies provided. Lockers in dorms. Internet with phone card, €5 per 30min., €7 per hr. Breakfast included. Sheets €2.70. Laundry €6. Lockout 10am-5pm. Curfew 12:30am. Dorms €13.90. ❶

NEAR THE TRAIN STATION

▓ **Hôtel Belle Meunière,** 21 av. Durante (☎04 93 88 66 15; fax 04 93 82 51 76), opposite the train station. Birds chirp in the spacious garden courtyard of this former mansion where backpackers relax over free breakfast and nighttime drinks. 4- to 5-bed co-ed dorms. Showers €2. Luggage storage €2. Laundry €5.50-9.50 including drying and folding. Reception 7:30am-midnight, access code after hours. Dorms €14; with shower €19; doubles with shower €47.50; triples €57; quads €76. MC/V. ❷

▓ **Hôtel Pastoral,** 27 rue Assalit (☎04 93 85 17 22), on the far side of av. Jean Médecin near the train station. Simple but spacious rooms with elegant hardwood décor and a caring owner create a comfortable atmosphere. No sleeping late here: you must be out of your room for the day by 10am. Breakfast €4. Reception 8am-6pm; access code after-hours. Free luggage storage. Singles with shower €20; doubles €25, with shower and toilet €30; triples €37.50; quads €50. ❷

Hôtel des Flandres, 6 rue de Belgique (☎04 93 88 78 94; fax 04 93 88 74 90), 100m from the train station and 800m from the beach. With an imposing entrance, large bedrooms and bathrooms, and high ceilings, this hotel appears more expensive than it is. Friendly owner and charming breakfast room. Breakfast €5. Reception 24hr. Singles €35-45; doubles €45-51; triples €60; quads €67. Extra bed €12. MC/V. ❹

Hôtel Notre Dame, 22 rue de Russie (☎04 93 88 70 44;jyung@caramail.com), at the corner of rue d'Italie, 1 block west of av. Jean Médecin. Friendly owners rent huge, fresh-scented rooms in Grecian white and blue. An intimidating dog protects guests. All rooms with sparkling toilet and shower. Breakfast €4. Free luggage storage. Reception 24hr. Singles €39; doubles €45; triples €57; quads €60. Extra bed €10. MC/V. ❹

Hôtel Les Orangers, 10bis av. Durante (☎04 93 87 51 41; fax 04 93 82 57 82), across from the train station. Behind a beautiful exterior lie bright co-ed dorms with closely packed beds, showers, and fridges (hot plates on request). Friendly English-speaking owner loans beach mats and stores luggage for free (non-guests €2). 2-night min. Reception 8am-9pm. Lock-out June-Aug. 11am-1pm. Reserve ahead for singles. Closed Nov. Dorms €16; singles €20-26; doubles €38-40; triples €54; quads €60. MC/V. ❶

NEAR VIEUX NICE & THE BEACH

Hôtel Petit Trianon, 11 rue Paradis (☎04 93 87 50 46), left off rue Masséna. A budget oasis in lively pl. Masséna. Rooms are small, simple, but with elegant chandeliers, pastel décor, and firm beds. Friendly English-speaking staff. Free beach towel loan. Reservations essential. Singles €15; doubles €31, with shower and toilet €39; triples €60; quad €50. Prices higher Apr.-Sept. Extra bed €8. MC/V. ❶

Star Hôtel, 14 rue Biscarra (☎04 93 85 19 03; info@hotel-star.com), in a quiet part of town midway between the station and Vieux Nice. Spacious, charming pastel rooms, some with luxurious bath, all with TV, A/C, phone, and hairdryers. Singles €35; doubles with shower €45, with bath €50; triple with bath €60. Prices €10 higher May-Sept. ❹

Hôtel Little Masséna, 22 rue Masséna (☎/fax 04 93 87 72 34). Worn, clean rooms with TV and kitchenette in a touristy part of town. Friendly owners. Breakfast €4.50. Reception daily 8am-noon and 2-9pm. Singles and doubles €28, with shower €38, with shower and toilet €48. Extra person €6.10. Oct.-May prices €2-5 lower. MC/V. ❸

Hôtel Au Picardy, 10 bd. Jean Jaurès (☎/fax 04 93 85 75 51), across from the bus station. Ideally located near Vieux Nice. Brown paint and a lack of natural light keep the rooms dark. Street-side rooms can be noisy, but the windows are soundproof. Breakfast €3. Showers €1.50. Reception 8am-5pm. Singles €19, with shower €28; doubles €24-27, with shower and toilet €33; triples €34-38; quads €38-48. Extra bed €5. ❷

⎁ FOOD

Nice is a city of restaurants, from four-star establishments to holes-in-the-wall. *Pâtisseries* and bakeries sell inexpensive local specialties flavored with North African spices or olives. Try the crusty *pan bagnat*, a loaf of bread with tuna, sardines, vegetables, and olive oil; *pissaladière* pizza topped with onions, anchovies, and olives; *socca*, thin, olive-oil-flavored chickpea bread, served hot with pepper; or *bouillabaisse*, a hearty stew of mussels, potatoes, and fish. The famous *salade niçoise* combines tuna, potatoes, tomatoes, and a spicy mustard dressing.

Cafés and food-stands along the beach are expensive. The **market** at cours Saleya is a good place to pick up fresh olives, cheeses, and melons (Tu-Su 6am-1:30pm). A produce **market** also springs up on av. Maché de la Libération (Tu-Su 6am-12:30pm). Expensive gourmet establishments line rue Masséna, which offer nothing cheaper than a €9 pizza. Avenue Jean Médecin features reasonable *brasseries* and *panini* vendors, and gems hide amid the tourist traps on Vieux Nice. Retain some semblance of literacy at **Restaurant Université ❶**, 3 av. Robert Schumann, which serves students filling meals for €5, with student ID €3. (☎04 93 97 10 20. Open Sept.-June daily 11:30am-1:30pm.)

▨ **La Merenda,** 4 rue de la Terrasse. Those lucky enough to get a table can savor the work of a culinary master who turned his back on one of the most renowned restaurants in Nice to open this affordable 12-table gem which only stocks enough fresh food to last the day. Nothing about the menu is constant except its exotic flair, evidenced by fried zucchini flowers, stockfish, and veal head. The chef recommend *pâtes au pistou*. Reserve in the morning, in person, for dinner. 2 seatings at 7 and 9pm. Cash only. *Plats* €10-15. Open M-F noon-1:30pm and 7-9:30pm. ❸

▨ **Lou Pilha Leva,** 13 rue du Collet (☎04 93 13 99 08) in Vieux Nice. Tourists and locals pack outdoor wooden benches and chow down on inexpensive tasty local food. Pizza slice €3; *socca* €2; *pissaladière* €2; *moules* €5. Open daily 8am-11pm. ❶

Le Restaurant d'Angleterre, 25 rue d'Angleterre (☎04 93 88 64 49), near the train station. This local favorite serves delicious French specialties in a pleasant, intimate setting. Friendly, English-speaking owner, fast service, and large portions ensure a great value. The *menu sâge* includes bread, large salad, main course, side dish, dessert, and an after-dinner cordial (€11.50). Open Tu-Sa 11:30am-1:45pm and 6:45-10pm. ❸

People, 12 rue Pastorelli (☎04 93 85 08 43). With friendly owners, hearty regional dishes like foie gras, and an excellent wine selection, this local favorite is well worth the walk from Vieux Nice. The clientele is young and the menu affordable. *Plats* €12-17. Open M noon-2:30pm, Tu-Th noon-2:30pm and 7-10:30pm, F-Sa 5pm-midnight. ❸

Acchiardo, 38 rue Droite (☎04 93 85 51 16), in Vieux Nice. Simple but appetizing Italian and French dishes served in a charming country setting with gingham, hanging corn husks, grape vines, and bronze pans. Pastas (€6) and classic French meats (house escallop specialty €11.50) are popular with a local clientele loyal to the family-run business. Open M-F noon-1:30pm and 7-10pm. ❶

Speakeasy, 7 rue Lamartine (☎04 93 85 59 50). Alas, there's no illicit liquor here. But there are delectable vegan lunch options, prepared by an American chef/animal-rights activist in a very intimate setting. All customers share three tables at this tiny hole-in-the-wall. Organic bean patties, couscous, and daily specialties satisfy even the staunchest carnivores and convert some along the way. Testimonials of famous vegetarians from Gandhi to Martina Navratilova are painted around the entrance. €11-12 for 2 courses. Open M-Sa noon-2:15pm. ❸

J. Multari, 58bis av. Jean Médecin (☎04 93 92 01 99). This graceful *salon de thé*, bakery, and sandwich shop serves excellent, inexpensive fare. Try a goat cheese, chicken, or ham sandwich on fresh baguette (€3.10), salad (€3), pizza (€1.50), crêpe (€5), or

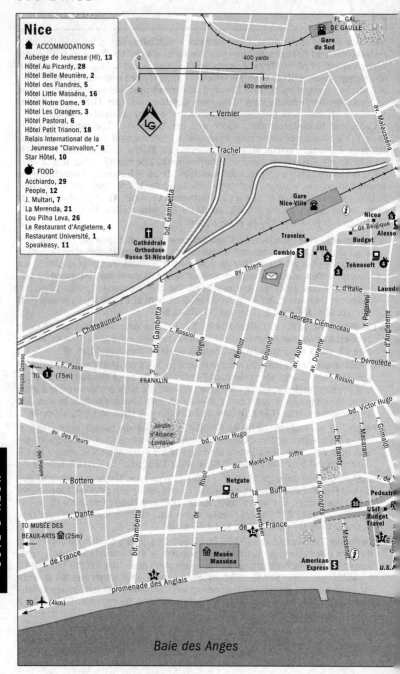

Nice

🏠 ACCOMMODATIONS

Auberge de Jeunesse (HI), **13**
Hôtel Au Picardy, **28**
Hôtel Belle Meunière, **2**
Hôtel des Flandres, **5**
Hôtel Little Masséna, **16**
Hôtel Notre Dame, **9**
Hôtel Les Orangers, **3**
Hôtel Pastoral, **6**
Hôtel Petit Trianon, **18**
Relais International de la
  Jeunesse "Clairvallon," **8**
Star Hôtel, **10**

🍅 FOOD

Acchiardo, **29**
People, **12**
J. Multari, **7**
La Merenda, **21**
Lou Pilha Leva, **26**
Le Restaurant d'Angleterre, **4**
Restaurant Université, **1**
Speakeasy, **11**

PL. GAL DE GAULLE

Gare du Sud

r. Vernier

r. Trachel

av. Malaussèna

Gare Nice-Ville

Nicea

r. de Belgique

Alexso

Budget

Travelex

Camblo

JML

Teknosoft

Cathédrale Orthodoxe Russe St-Nicolas

bd. Gambetta

av. Thiers

r. d'Italie

Laund

r. d'Angleterre

r. Paganini

r. Châteauneuf

bd. Gambetta

r. Rossini

r. Guiglia

r. Berlioz

r. Gounod

av. Georges Clémenceau

av. Auber

av. Durante

r. Rossini

r. Déroulède

bd. François Grosso

r. F. Passy

TO ❶ (75m)

PL. FRANKLIN

r. Verdi

av. des Fleurs

Jardin d'Alsace Lorraine

bd. Victor Hugo

bd. Victor Hugo

r. Grimaldi

r. Macarani

r. du Maréchal Joffre

r. Dr. Barety

r. Bottero

r. de Rivoli

Netgate

r. de la Buffa

r. du Congrès

r. de

Pedestr

USIT
Budget
Travel

r. Dante

r. Meyerbeer

TO MUSÉE DES BEAUX-ARTS 🏛 (25m)

r. de France

bd. Gambetta

r. de France

r. Masséna

Musée Masséna 🏛

American Express

U.S.A

promenade des Anglais

TO ✈ (4km)

Baie des Anges

CÔTE D'AZUR

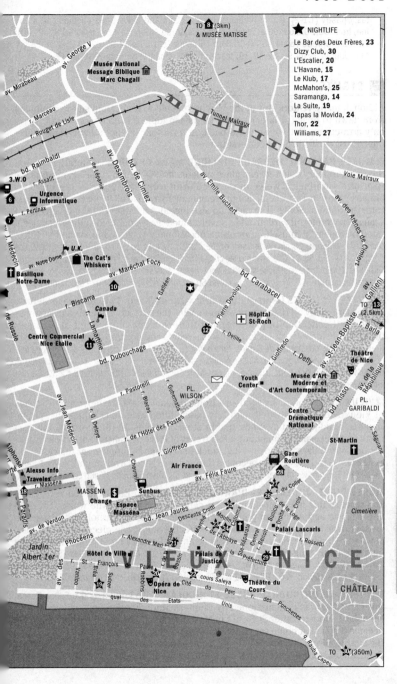

★ NIGHTLIFE

Le Bar des Deux Frères, 23
Dizzy Club, 30
L'Escalier, 20
L'Havane, 15
Le Klub, 17
McMahon's, 25
Saramanga, 14
La Suite, 19
Tapas la Movida, 24
Thor, 22
Williams, 27

TO 8 (3km)
& MUSÉE MATISSE

Musée National
Message Biblique
Marc Chagall

av. George V

av. Mirabeau

r. Marceau

r. Rouget de Lisle

Tunnel Malraux

Voie Malraux

bd. Raimbaldi

r. Assalit

3.W.0

6

Urgence
Informatique

r. Pertinax

7

r. J. Médecin

av. Notre Dame

av. de Lépante

bd. de Cimiez

av. Desambrois

av. Émile Buchert

Tunnel Malraux

av. des Arènes de Cimiez

av. Gallieni

U.K.

The Cat's
Whiskers

Basilique
Notre-Dame

av. Maréchal Foch

10

r. Gubernatis

r. Biscarra

Canada

Lamartine

Centre Commercial
Nice Etoile

11

bd. Dubouchage

bd. Carabacel

r. Pierre Dévoluy

Hôpital
St-Roch

12

r. Delille

r. Gioffredo

r. Defly

av. St-Jean-Baptiste

r. Barla

Théâtre
de Nice

av. de la République

de Russie

r. Pastorelli

r. Blacas

PL.
WILSON

Youth Center

Musée d'Art
Moderne et
d'Art Contemporain

bd. Risso

PL.
GARIBALDI

r. Ségurane

av. Jean Médecin

r. de l'Hôtel des Postes

r. Gioffredo

Centre
Dramatique
National

St-Martin

Alphonse

Alexso Info
Travelex

18

r. Masséna

PL.
MASSÉNA

Change

Espace
Masséna

Sunbus

bd. Jean Jaurès

Air France

av. Félix Faure

Gare
Routière

28

r. du Collet

26

r. de la Loge

Droite

r. Rossetti

Cimetière

av. de Verdun

Phocéens

r. Alexandre Mari

r. de la Terrasse

r. Grasin

Descente Crotti

Marché
r. de l'Abbaye

Moulin

r. Benoît

Centrale

Ste-Réparate

Buicci

Palais Lascaris

Jardin
Albert 1er

Hôtel de Ville

St-
François

Bréa

Suffer

r. Robbins

19

20

Opéra de
Nice

Palais de
Justice

Cité

cours Saleya

du

Parc

Théâtre du
Cours

VIEUX NICE

CHÂTEAU

quai

des

Etats

Unis

r. des Ponchettes

q. Rauba Capeu

TO 30 (350m)

tasty pastry (€1-2). Go for breakfast before 11am and enjoy three pastries and a coffee, from €2.20. Four other locations in Nice: 2 rue Alphonse Karr (☎04 93 87 45 90); 22 rue Gioffredo (☎04 93 80 00 31); 13 cours Saleya (☎04 93 62 31 33); and 8 bd. Jean Jaurès (☎04 93 62 10 39, take-out only). Open M-Sa 6am-8:30pm. ❶

👁 SIGHTS

Although many visitors stay at the beaches people-watching and sun-worshipping from dawn to dusk (or later), azure waters and topless sunbathers are not Nice's only attractions. Put your clothes back on for a tour of Nice's impressive museums. Trust us, it's in all of our best interests.

▓ MUSÉE NATIONAL MESSAGE BIBLIQUE MARC CHAGALL. Chagall founded this extraordinary concrete and glass museum in 1966 to showcase his 17 *Message Biblique* paintings. Twelve of these colorful canvases illustrate the first two books of the Old Testament, and the remaining five, done all in shades of red, illustrate the Song of Songs. The museum also includes a cursory photo-biography of Chagall, a wonderful garden, and a small stained-glass-encircled auditorium, decorated by the artist himself. Auditorium occasionally stages concerts and lectures. *(Av. du Dr. Ménard. 15min. walk north of the station, or take bus #15 (dir: Rimiez) to Musée Chagall. ☎04 93 53 87 20; www.musee-chagall.fr. Open Su-M and W-Sa July-Sept. 10am-6pm; Oct.-June 10am-5pm. Last tickets sold 30min. before closing. Guided tours in French, English, and Italian by appt. €5.50, under age 26 and Su €4, under 18 and first Su of the month free.)*

▓ MUSÉE MATISSE. Henri Matisse first visited Nice in 1916 and never left its shores. Originally a 17th-century Genoese villa, the museum contains a disappointingly small collection of paintings, but there is a dazzling exhibit of Matisse's three-dimensional work, including bronze reliefs and dozens of cut-and-paste tableaux. *(164 av. des Arènes de Cimiez. Take bus #15, 17, 20, 22, or 25 to Arènes. Free bus tickets between Musée Chagall and Musée Matisse; ask at either ticket counter. ☎04 93 81 08 08. Open M and W-Su Apr.-Sept. 10am-6pm, Oct.-Mar. 10am-5pm. €3.80, students €2.30. Call for info on lectures.)*

▓ VIEUX NICE. Sprawling southeast from bd. Jean Jaurès, the labyrinthine streets of Vieux Nice are crowded with tiny pansy-filled balconies, fountains, public squares, hand-painted awnings, and pristine churches. In the morning, the area hosts bustling **markets**, including a fish frenzy at **Place St-François** and a flower market on **Cours Salaya.** In the evening, knick-knack stands supplement the cafés and restaurants, and the quarter becomes the center of Nice's lively nightlife. *(Fish frenzy Tu-Su 6am-1pm; flower market Su 6am-noon, Tu and Th-F 6am-5:30pm, W and Sa 6am-6:30pm.)*

MUSÉE D'ART MODERNE ET D'ART CONTEMPORAIN. Enter the concrete, glass, and steel of this museum's minimalist galleries and admire the work of French new realists and American pop artists like Lichtenstein, Warhol, and Klein. The museum showcases European and American avant-garde pieces with a gallery devoted to the fantastic statues of Niki de St. Phalle and a reputation for attracting interesting traveling exhibits. *(Prom. Des Arts, at the intersection of av. St-Jean Baptiste and Traverse Garibaldi. Take bus #5 (dir: St-Charles) to Musée Promenade des Arts. The museum is behind the bus station. ☎04 93 62 61 62. Open Tu-Su 10am-6pm. €4, students €2.50.)*

CATHÉDRALE ORTHODOXE RUSSE ST-NICOLAS. Also known as the **Eglise Russe,** this cathedral was commissioned by Empress Marie Feodorovna, widow of Tsar Nicholas I. Modeled after St-Basil's in Moscow, the onion-domed structure quickly became a spiritual home for exiled Russian nobles. The gilded screen concealing the altar also sets it apart from French cathedrals. There's one hint, however, that the cathedral is influenced by the Riviera: its dominant colors are Mediterranean light blue and yellow rather than dark and somber blues and grays. *(17 bd. du Tsarevitch, off bd. Gambetta.* ☎ *04 93 96 88 02. Open daily June-Aug. 9am-noon and 2:30-6pm; Sept.-May 9:30am-noon and 2:30-5pm. €1.80.)*

LE CHÂTEAU. At the eastern end of the promenade, Le Château—the formal name for the remains of an 11th-century cathedral—sits in a pleasant green hillside park ornamented by an artificial waterfall. Don't be fooled: there hasn't been a château here since an 8th-century battle. The top does, however, provide a spectacular view of the rooftops of Nice and the sparkling Baie des Anges. The vista can be reached by climbing 400 steps or catching the elevator at the Tour Bellanda. *(Park open daily 7am-8pm. Elevator runs 9am-7:30pm. €1.)*

MUSÉE DES BEAUX-ARTS. The former villa of Ukraine's Princess Kotschoubey has been converted into a celebration of French academic painting, including Van Dongen and Raoul Dufy. Dufy, Nice's second greatest painter, celebrated the spontaneity of his city with sensational pictures of the town at rest and play. *(33 av. Baumettes. Take bus #38 to Chéret or #12 to Grosso.* ☎ *04 92 15 28 28. Open Tu-Su 10am-noon and 2-6pm. €3.80, students €2.30.)*

JARDIN ALBERT I & ESPACE MASSÉNA. Jardin Albert I is the central city park. In addition to the usual repertoire of benches and fountains, its outdoor Théâtre de Verdun presents jazz and plays in summer. Contact the tourist office for a schedule. *(Between av. Verdun and bd. Jaurès, off prom. des Anglais and quai des Etats-Unis. Box office open daily 10:30am-noon and 3:30-6:30pm.)*

OTHER SIGHTS. Named by the rich English community that commissioned it, the **Promenade des Anglais,** a posh, palm-lined seaside boulevard, is Nice's answer to the great pedestrian thoroughfares of Paris, London, and New York. Today the promenade is lined by luxury hotels like the stately **Négresco** (toward the west end), where the staff still don top hats and 19th-century uniforms. Just east of the Négresco, the **Espace Masséna** gives romantic picnickers a lovely shady area in which to woo each other beside lavish fountains. **Private beaches** crowd the seashore between bd. Gambetta and the Opéra, but public strands west of bd. Gambetta compensate for the exclusivity. Many travelers are surprised when they actually see Nice's beaches, which are no more than stretches of rocks smoothed by the sea. Bring a beach mat.

🎵 📷 ENTERTAINMENT & FESTIVALS

The Nice party crowd is still swinging, toasting the sunrise on the beach after all the discos have closed and revelers in St-Tropez and Antibes have called it a night. The hotspots around rue Masséna and Vieux Nice pulsate with dance, jazz, and rock. As night falls, the promenade des Anglais fills with street performers, musicians, and pedestrians along the beach and boardwalk. The free brochure *l'Excés* (www.exces.com), available at the tourist office and in bars, provides information. Local men have a reputation for harassing people on the promenade and around the train station: lone women beware. Exercise caution after dark; avoid traversing untrafficked streets and walking in the city alone. The dress code at all bars and clubs is simple: look good. Some pubs serve to patrons not sporting designer threads, but almost all will turn away shorts, sandals, sneakers, or baseball caps. Dressing *classé* ("in good taste") is paramount. So leave the fishnets on the beach.

BARS

McMahon's, 50 bd. Jean Jaurès (☎ 04 93 13 84 07). Join the locals and expats who lap up Guinness and shoot pool at this friendly Irish pub. Happy hour daily 3-9pm; €3 pints and €2 wine. Cocktail hour 9-10pm with €4.50 drinks. Karaoke on Th, request DJ and free shots on Sa, and dancing barmaids nightly. Make sure to head over on "cheap Tuesday" for €2 vodka, gin, or whiskey cocktails. Open daily 3pm-2am.

Thor, 32 cours Saleya (☎04 93 62 49 90; www.thor-pub.com). In this raucous Scandinavian pub, a favorite among Nice residents in the know, svelte blonde bartenders pour pints, and backpackers and locals alike let loose to daily live music. Happy hour 6-9pm with €4 pints. Music starts 10pm. Open daily 6pm-2am.

Le Bar des Deux Frères, 1 rue du Moulin (☎04 93 80 77 61). This hip local favorite is hidden behind the façade of an old restaurant. A young, lively crowd downs tequila (€3.10) and beer (€5) amid red curtains and smoky tables. Happy hour Tu-Sa 6:30-10pm with all drinks €1.60-4. June-Sept. live DJ daily, W Afro/Latin night. Open Tu-Sa 6pm-2:30am, Su-M 10pm-2:30am.

L'Havane, 32 rue de France (☎04 93 16 36 16). This hip Latin bar caters to a mid-20s crowd with nightly live salsa bands. Fun-loving locals sip cocktails and dance amidst the tables. Open daily 5pm-2:30am.

L'Escalier, 10 rue de la Terrasse (☎04 93 92 64 39). A lively mix of locals and tourists fills this bar long after the other bars have locked their doors for the night. With plenty of seating and a separate billiards area, L'Escalier can be a pleasant place to relax for a drink, but the real party starts late when the DJ picks up the pace and the line outside extends down the street. Open daily 10pm-5am.

Tapas la Movida, 2bis rue de l'Abbaye (☎04 93 62 27 46), an intimate little bar, resembles a secret revolutionary meeting spot, but the only plotting you'll do is figuring out how to crawl home after braving the *bar-o-mètre* (€15), a meter-long wooden box of shots. Live reggae and rock concerts M-Th (€1.50). Open M-Sa 8pm-12:30am.

Williams, 4 rue Centrale (☎04 93 62 99 63). After the other bars have called it a night, Williams keeps the kegs flowing for a tourist-heavy crowd. Get up your nerve for karaoke nights M-Th with €8 pints and cocktails. Live music F-Sa. Open daily 9pm-7am.

NIGHTCLUBS

Nice's nightclubs can quickly drain your funds, though reductions on exorbitant covers are generally offered on Thursdays, Sundays, all days before midnight, and to all smartly-dressed females. Cover at most places usually includes the first drink. The scene in Nice is in constant flux: new clubs replace old ones almost daily and the hot spot shifts rapidly.

Dizzy Club, 26 quai Lunel (☎06 12 16 78 81). Pulsating house music moves locals and tourists alike amidst boxes and pillars decorated in the fantastical style of Paul Klee. Art deco tables, plush black chairs, and modern art fight against an orange background.

Saramanga, 45-47 prom. des Anglais (☎04 93 96 67 00). A club so hot that showgirls play with fire for the patrons' entertainment. Hawaiian-shirted bartenders pour exotic drinks. Cover €15. Open F-Sa 11pm-6am.

La Suite, 2 rue Bréa (☎04 93 92 92 91). This small club attracts a funky, well-dressed, and well-moneyed crowd. Velvet theater curtains drape the walls, but not much clothing drapes the go-go dancers on the weekends. Cover €13. Open Tu-Su 11pm-2:30am.

Le Klub, 6 rue Halévy (☎06 60 55 26 61). Nice's most popular gay club caters to a gorgeous, well-tanned crowd with a cocktail lounge and video projections on the dance floor. Cover €11 on Sa. Open July-Aug. Tu-Su 11:30pm-6am; Sept.-June open W-Su.

CULTURE

The **Théâtre du Cours,** 5 rue Poissonnerie in Vieux Nice, stages traditional drama. (☎04 93 80 12 67. €12.20, students €9.20.) The grand **Théâtre de Nice,** on the promenade des Arts, hosts all sorts of theatrical performances, concerts, and marionettes (☎04 93 13 90 90. €10-30, students €7-25.) Visiting symphony orchestras and soloists perform in the **Opéra de Nice,** 4-6 rue St-François de Paule (☎04 93 13 98 53 or 04 92 17 40 00. €8-40.) The **FNAC,** 24 av. Jean Médecin in the Nice Etoile shopping center, sells tickets for virtually every musical or theatrical event in town. (☎04 92 17 77 77. www.fnac.com.)

❑ FESTIVALS

In mid-July, the **Nice Jazz Festival** attracts 45,000 visitors, who enjoy over 500 musicians in 75 concerts over an 8-day period. Ticket holders can attend nightly concerts by the likes of B.B. King, George Clinton, and Ani DiFranco. Concerts 7pm-midnight. (Arènes et Jardins de Cimiez. ☎08 20 80 04 00; www.nicejazzfest.com. Tickets €30 per night; 3-day pass €76; 8-day pass €152.) During the 📷**Carnaval** in Lent (Feb. 21-Mar. 5), Nice gives Rio a run for its money with two weeks of parades, fireworks, outlandish costumes, and, of course, partying. Call the tourist office for more info.

NEAR NICE

Inland from Nice, the small towns of St-Paul and Vence hide their art treasures removed from the mania of the coast.

◧ TRANSPORTATION. SAP Buses (☎04 93 58 37 60) sends buses #400-410 to Vence and St-Paul from **Nice** (60min.; 28 per day; €4.10 to **St-Paul,** €4.50 to **Vence**). To get to St-Paul from **Cannes,** take the train to Cagnes-sur-Mer and change to bus #400-410 (€1.50). The last of the #400-410 buses leave St-Paul for Nice and Cagnes-sur-Mer at 7:20pm from the stop just outside the town entrance. The trip from Vence to St-Paul costs €1.20.

ST-PAUL

If you visit one medieval village on the Côte D'Azur, make it St-Paul. A quaint walled hamlet built on a clifftop, some of St-Paul's churches and ruins date from the early Middle Ages. With incredible views of the surrounding countryside, it has been an artists' paradise for years: Chagall, Picasso, Léger, and Soutine all came here for inspiration, and many modern artists have followed in their footsteps. Eighty galleries sell local paintings, pottery, handicrafts, and works by the likes of Léger and Ernst. As you stroll through the well-trampled village, stop at Chagall's gravestone (cemetery open daily 8am-6pm) and the exquisite *église collégiale,* home to the mounted skull of St-Etienne. (Open daily 8am-8pm.)

Much of St-Paul's art is in nearby **Fondation Maeght,** 1km from the town center. From the St-Paul bus stop, take a right onto chemin de Ste-Claire, passing Chapelle St-Claire on your right, and you will see blue signs for the foundation. Designed by Joseph Sert to showcase modern and contemporary art, the foundation is part museum and part park, with works by Miró, Chagall, Calder, Arp, and Léger integrated into the surrounding shrubs and fountains. Maeght, an art dealer, commissioned a small, somber chapel in memory of his son, who died of leukemia. Filled with stained glass by Braque and Ubac, the chapel is now part of the museum. The museum also features a labyrinth designed by Miró. (☎04 93 32 81 63; www.fondation-maeght.com. Open daily July-Sept. 10am-7pm; Oct.-June 10am-12:30pm and 2:30-6pm. €10, students €8, under 10 free. Photography permit €2.50.)

The **tourist office,** 2 rue Grande, just inside the walls of St-Paul, dispenses free maps and info on galleries and exhibitions. (☎04 93 32 86 95; fax 04 93 32 60 27; art-devivre@wanadoo.fr. Open June-Sept. daily 10am-7pm; Oct.-May 10am-6pm.) It also gives personal one-hour tours of the medieval city in English by request. (10am-

5:30pm. €8 per person.) You can also rent a set of balls for a game of *pétanque* for €3 per person or schedule a game with an inhabitant of the village (€61 for 1hr. plus €3 per person).

CORNICHES

Rocky shores, pebble beaches, and luxurious villas line the coast between hectic Nice and high-rolling Monaco. More relaxing and less touristed than their glam-fab neighbors, these tiny towns sparkle quietly with interesting museums, architectural finds, and breathtaking countryside. The train offers an exceptional glimpse of the coast up close, while buses maneuvering along the high roads of the *corniches* provide a bird's-eye view of the steep cliffs and crashing sea below.

▐ TRANSPORTATION. Trains and buses between Nice and Monaco serve most of the Corniche towns. With a departure about every hour, **trains** from Nice to Monaco stop at Villefranche-sur-Mer (7min., €1.30), Beaulieu-sur-Mer (10min., €1.70), and Eze-sur-Mer (16min., €2).

Several numbered RCA **buses** (☎04 93 85 64 44; www.rca.tm.fr) run between Nice and Monaco, making stops along the way. #111 leaves Nice, stopping in Villefranche-sur-Mer (9 per day). Two buses continue on to St-Jean-Cap-Ferrat (M-Sa 9:10am and 12:15pm). #100 runs between Nice and Villefranche-sur-Mer 11 times daily. #112 runs 7 times per day (3 on Su) between Nice and Monte-Carlo, stopping in Eze-le-Village. RCA and Broch (☎04 93 85 61 81 or 04 93 07 63 28; daily every hr.) run between Nice and Villefranche-sur-Mer (15min., €1.60), Beaulieu-sur-Mer (20min., €2), Eze-le-Village (25min., €2.40), Monaco-Ville (40min., €3.70), and Monte-Carlo (45min., €3.70). Most tickets sold include a free same-day return, though you should make sure before you purchase. Last buses from the Corniches to Nice and Monaco leave 7:20-7:40pm.

VILLEFRANCHE-SUR-MER

The stairwayed streets and pastel houses of 700-year-old Villefranche-sur-Mer have earned the town a reputation as one of the Riviera's most photogenic gems. The backdrop for dozens of films, including a James Bond installation, *Dirty Rotten Scoundrels*, and movies by Hitchcock and Cocteau, the town has enchanted artists and writers from Aldous Huxley to Katherine Mansfield. Tina Turner makes an annual pilgrimage to her hillside villa here. Despite the celebrity presence, Villefranche remains an authentic Provençal town with an excellent beach.

As you walk from the station along quai Courbet, a sign for the *vieille ville* directs you along the 13th-century **rue Obscure,** the oldest street in Villefranche. A right at the end of rue Obscure takes you to the **Eglise Saint-Michel,** which contains an impressive wooden statue of a martyred Christ sculpted by an anonymous slave. At the end of the quai stands the pink and yellow 14th-century **Chapelle St-Pierre,** painted in simple lines from floor to ceiling by Jean Cocteau, former resident, film-maker, and jack-of-all-arts. Chapel motifs are divided between religious images of the life of Saint Peter and depictions of fishermen during their daily Provençal life. (☎04 93 76 90 70. Open Tu-Su summer 10am-noon and 4-8:30pm; autumn 9:30am-noon and 2-6pm; winter 9:30am-noon and 2-5pm; spring 9:30am-noon and 3-7pm. €2.) The rather dull 16th-century **Citadelle** houses three small museums, the most interesting of which is the rustic **Musée Volti,** dedicated to Antoniucci Volti, who created curvaceous female forms out of bronze, clay, canvas, and copper. (☎04 93 76 33 27; musees@villefranche-sur-mer.fr. Open July-Aug. M and W-Sa 10am-noon and 2:30-7pm, Su 2:30-7pm; June and Sept. M and W-Sa 9am-noon and 2:30-6pm, Su 2:30-6pm; Oct.-May W-Sa 9am-noon and 2-5:30pm, Su 1:30-6pm. Free.)

If you're dead-set on spending a night in the Corniches rather than the nearby budget-friendly Nice, Villefranche has few options. **La Régence ❹**, 2 av. Maréchal Foch, rents carpeted rooms on top of an all-night bar along the main drag. (☎04 93 01 70 91; laregence@caramail.com. Internet €5 per 30min., €8 per hr. Breakfast €5. Reception 6am-2am. All rooms have shower and toilet. Singles €40; doubles €49; triples €54. AmEx/MC/V.)

The popular Australian bar, Internet café, and DVD rental store, **Chez Net**, pl. du Marché, behind Hôtel Welcome, is the one-stop nightlife location in Villefranche. Laid-back Australian/French couple serve everything from beer (Foster's €4 per pint; Guinness €5 per pint) to smoothies. They broadcast major international sports events for a mainly anglo crowd in a friendly atmosphere with outdoor seating. (☎04 93 01 83 06. Open Su-Tu 5pm-2:30am and F-Sa 11am-2:30am. **Internet café** has 6 computers with English keyboards (€5 per hr.). Next door, the local favorite **Loco Loco ❷** serves delicious food at low prices, including big plates of mussels (€11), salads (€5-9), sandwiches (€3.50-5), pastas (€8), and steaks (€10-11). (Open daily 11am-3pm and 7-11pm.)

To reach the **tourist office** from the train station, exit on quai 1 and head inland on av. G. Clemenceau. Continue straight as it becomes av. Sadi Carnot. The office is at the end of the street in the Jardin François. It distributes a walking tour of the town and suggests excursions to nearby villages. (☎04 93 01 73 68; www.ville-franche-sur-mer.com. Open July-Aug. daily 9am-7pm; June and Sept. M-Sa 9am-noon and 2-6:30pm; Oct.-May 9am-noon and 2-6pm.)

BEAULIEU-SUR-MER

Reportedly named by Napoleon, who called it a *"beau lieu"* (beautiful place), this seaside resort's *Belle Époque* villas, classy casino, and waterfront four-star hotels attest to its previous status as *the* place to go in winter for elite folk from all over Europe. Today, the big money has since moved to quieter mansions in nearby St-Jean-Cap-Ferrat, but Beaulieu still attracts a few stars. For those of lesser means, the main justification for a visit to this relatively uninteresting town is its spectacular villa. Beaulieu also serves as a nice starting point for the lovely seaside walk to Saint-Jean-Cap-Ferrat.

On a plateau overlooking the sea, Renaissance man Theodore Reinach built his dream villa ▓**Kérylos**, which today stands as proof that money can buy happiness. This home perfectly imitates an ancient Greek dwelling: columns, mosaics, and marble sculptures are all copied from original specimens, and the frescoes in the foyer have been artificially aged. On one of the coast's prettiest terraces, the villa is encircled by gardens with statues of the Olympian gods. (Tours only. 90min. audio guide in English, German, Italian, or French. Open July-Aug. daily 10am-7pm; early Feb.-June and Sept.-early Nov. daily 10am-6pm; early Nov.-early Feb. M-F 2-6pm and Sa-Su 10am-6pm. €7, students €5.50.)

If you're planning on spending the night in Beaulieu, the best option is probably **Le Riviera ❹**, 6 rue Paul Doumer. (☎04 93 01 04 92. Breakfast €6. Reception 7am-12:30pm and 4-8pm. Singles with sink €36, with shower €49; doubles with shower €55; triples €58, with shower €67. Prices €5 lower Nov.-Jan. AmEx/MC/V.) Pricier **Hôtel Select ❺**, 1 rue André Cane, pl. du Général de Gaulle (☎04 93 01 05 42), provides spacious rooms in shades of teal, all with bathroom, TV, fridge, and phone. (Singles €51-59; doubles €59-65.)

A promenade along the waterfront passes by the major hotels. If you'd rather walk than gawk, the **tourist office**, pl. Georges Clemenceau, suggests scenic routes to nearby towns. (☎04 93 01 02 21; www.ot-beaulieu-sur-mer.fr. Open July-Aug. M-Sa 9am-12:30pm and 2-7pm, Su 9am-12:30pm; Sept.-June M-F 9am-12:15pm and 2-6pm, Sa 9am-12:15pm and 2-5pm.)

CÔTE D'AZUR

ST-JEAN-CAP-FERRAT

As if the Riviera needed a trump card! Quietly wealthy St-Jean-Cap-Ferrat is a haven for the upper-class—the King of Belgium still makes a yearly appearance. The town is serviced by **bus** #111, but nothing compares to the 40min. ◪**seaside walk** from Beaulieu (access the path in front of the Beaulieu casino). Passing lavish villas, rocky beaches, and once-beautiful docks, it could take up to an hour with all the photo opportunities.

The **Fondation Ephrussi de Rothschild** is just off av. D. Semeria, between the tourist office and the Nice-Monaco road. The foundation holds the furniture and art collections of the eccentric Baroness de Rothschild and her famous father, encompassing Monet canvases, Gobelins tapestries, Chinese vases, and a stunning tea room. Outside, each of seven lush gardens reflects the Baroness's love of travel. One is Japanese, one is Spanish, and another is an "exotic" garden. The villa can be accessed directly from Beaulieu. Follow the shore path toward St-Jean, turning right after the three-pronged tree and before the pink villa that separates the path from the Mediterranean. From the top of this walled shore access, turn left and follow the road uphill, turning right at the sign to the Fondation. (☎04 93 01 45 90; www.villa-ephrussi.com. A guided tour in French is the only way to see the first floor: 11:30am, 2:30, 3:30, and 4:30pm; €2. Tea salon open 11am-5:30pm; gardens until 7:30pm. Open July-Aug. daily 10am-7pm; Sept.-Oct. and mid Feb. to June daily 10am-6pm; Nov. to mid-Feb. M-F 2-6pm, Sa-Su 10am-6pm, gardens until 6:30pm. €8.50, students €6.)

St-Jean's **beaches** have earned the area the nickname *presqu'île des rêves*, "Peninsula of Dreams" Mainly attracting locals who descend from their villas to bask in the sun, the beaches feel secluded and peaceful. With so many options, you'll want to pass by the aptly named **plage Passable**, just down the hill from the tourist office, and hit Cap's best beach, the wide **plage Paloma**, past the port on av. Jean Mermoz. For a more solitary sunbath, make a right off av. Mermoz at the junction of pl. Paloma and try **Les Fossettes** and, farther on, **Les Fosses**. These beautiful rocky stretches look out on a quiet and unpopulated bay. You should also consider walking around Pointe de St-Hospice. The 30min. walk affords secluded sunbathing spots and stunning vistas.

The tiny **tourist office**, 59 av. Denis Séméria, is halfway along the winding street that runs from Nice and Monaco to the port. It distributes free maps and free walking tours of the peninsula's 14km of trails. (☎04 93 76 08 90; fax 04 93 76 16 67. Open July-Aug. M-Sa 8:30am-6:30pm; mid-June and early Sept. M-Sa 8:30am-6pm; early Sept. to mid-June M-Sa 8:30am-noon and 1-5pm.)

EZE

Centuries ago Théodore de Banville explained that "to reach Eze one has to climb up from the sea or drop down from the sky." Today, roads make the Roman-village-turned-medieval-citadel at **Eze-le-Vilage** far more accessible. In spaces carved into 429m cliffs over the sea, the houses in Eze have been inhabited for over 25 centuries by everyone from the Moors to Piedmontese. Now only 50 of Eze's 2700 residents live there. Most live in **Col d'Eze** or the seaside town **Eze Bord-de-Mer** (also called **Eze-sur-Mer**), whose pebble beach is popular with windsurfers, kayakers, and sailors.

A favorite of photo-snapping tourists, Eze-le-Village is a living testament to the Riviera's past. The **Porte des Maures,** erected in remembrance of a devastatingly successful surprise attack by the Moors, dates to the tumultuous 10th century, when much of the Côte was in Moorish hands. The **Eglise Paroissial,** an 18th-century structure with a somber façade, has a 17th-century-style baroque interior with sleek Phoenician crosses. (☎04 93 41 00 38. Open daily 9am-7pm.) The **Jardin Exotique,** which offers fabulous views of the sea and the Cap d'Antibes, is planted around a Savoy fortress that was razed in 1706 by the invading armies of Louis XIV. (☎04 93 41 10 30. Open daily Sept.-June 9am-noon and 2-6pm; July-Aug. 9am-8pm. €2.50, students €1.60.)

Eze-le-Village offers more than narrow streets and nice vistas—the second-largest factory of the **Fragonard Parfumerie** is located here. Perfumes are sold at warehouse prices and free 15min. tours in English, Spanish, German, Italian, Russian, or Dutch explain the perfume-making process. (☎04 93 41 05 05; www.fragonard.com. Open daily 8am-6:30pm.) The more intimate **Parfumerie Galimard** has a free **museum** and guided visits. (☎04 93 41 10 70. Open daily 9am-6:30pm.)

It was on the long climb from the seaside to Eze-le-Village that Nietzsche composed the third part of *Thus Spake Zarathustra.* To see the stunning views of the coast that inspired Nietzsche, robust hikers can follow the 1hr. climb to the top along the winding **Sentier Friedrich Nietzsche.** The trail begins in Eze Bord-de-Mer, 100m east of the train station, and ends at the base of the medieval city, near the *parfumerie.* If you give it a go, wear hiking shoes and bring a camera. For those less inclined to hike to the village, **bus #112** connects Nice, Eze-le-Village, and Beausoleil seven times per day.

Eze annually hosts two major festivals, each attracting about 4000 people. In early July, the **Festival Latino** fetches salsa, theater, and art notables from Latin America. In late July, inhabitants of the village don costumes for **Eze d'Antan,** a festival that illuminates the history of Eze in the Middle Ages. Each year the village focuses on a different theme: recent years' themes include "charms and magic spells of the Middle Ages" and "Sarrazin invasions." For details on both festivals, call the tourist office.

The friendly English-speaking staff at the **tourist office,** pl. de Gaulle, provides free maps and info. (☎04 93 41 26 00; www.eze-riviera.com. Open daily Apr.-Oct. 9am-7pm; Nov.-Mar. 9am-6:30pm.) Guided tours of the medieval village and exotic garden are offered daily by request (€5 per person; try to call 1 day in advance to make a reservation). To get there, take the Navette mini-bus from the train station. There's an **annex** right next to the train station. (☎04 93 01 52 00. Open May-Oct. 10am-1pm and 3-6:30pm.)

To get to Eze, take the **train** from Nice (14min., €2). The train station is in Eze-Bord-de-Mer, but from May-Sept. a Navette **mini-bus** connects Eze's three tiers, stopping in Eze Bord-de-Mer in front of the tourist office annex and in Eze-le-Village where the main road meets the path to the medieval city (8 per day 9:35am-6:45pm; one-way €3.80, round-trip €6.90). If you miss the bus, a **taxi** ride (☎06 18 44 77 93) to the top costs about €20.

MONACO & MONTE-CARLO

In 1297, François Grimaldi of Genoa established his family as the rulers of Monaco (native pop. 7106) after overthrowing the town with the help of a few henchmen disguised as monks. Ever since, the tiny principality has jealously guarded its independence and exclusivity.

Although the rest of the Côte d'Azur may be defined by conspicuous consumption, Monaco doesn't flaunt its glamor as prominently as its neighbors do: and anyway, its wealth is proven aptly enough by its ubiquitous surveillance cameras, security officials, high-speed luxury cars, multi-million dollar yachts, and the famous casino in Monaco's capital city of Monte-Carlo. The sheer spectacle of it all—not to mention the juicy tabloid allure of Monaco's royal family—is definitely worth the daytrip from Nice.

⌐ TRANSPORTATION

Trains: The new Gare SNCF has 4 points of access: galerie Prince Pierre (behind the old train station), pl. Ste-Dévote, galerie Ste-Dévote (at the beginning of rue Grimaldi) and bd. Princesse Charlotte. Info desk and ticket window open daily 5:45am-8:30pm. To: **Antibes** (1hr., every 30min., €6.40); **Cannes** (65min., every 30min., €7.10); **Menton** (11min., every 30min., €1.70); **Nice** (23min., every 30min., €2.90).

Buses: Buses leave from bd. des Moulins and av. Princesse Alice, both near the tourist office. Two lines: **TAM** and **RCA** (☎04 93 85 64 44). To: **Nice** (45min., every 15min., €3.70) and **Menton** (20min., every 15min., €2.10). **Cap d'Ail, Eze-sur-Mer, Beaulieu-sur-Mer, Villefranche-sur-Mer,** and **St-Jean-Cap-Ferrat** accessible via Nice route. Same day return tickets to Monaco free.

Public Transportation: 6 bus routes (☎97 70 22 22) serve the entire principality (M-Sa every 11min. 7am-9pm, Su and holidays every 20min. 7:30am-9pm). Bus #4 links the av. Prince Pierre train station entrance to the casino; bus #2 connects the *vieille ville* and *jardin exotique* via pl. d'Armes; lines #5 and 6 connect Fontvielle with the rest of the city. Tickets €1.40, *carnet* of 4 €3.30, *carnet* of 8 €5.40. The €3.30 *carte touristique* offers unlimited travel on the day of purchase. Tickets on board.

Taxis: ☎93 15 01 01 (24hr). 11 taxi stands. Phone ☎93 50 56 28 for a complete list. €10 minimum charge; €12.20-15.30 to the Relais de Jeunesse in Cap d'Ail.

Car rental: Avis, 9 av. d'Ostende (☎93 30 17 53). Open M-Sa 8am-noon and 2-7pm, Su 9am-noon. AmEx/MC/V. **Hertz,** 27 bd. Albert I (☎93 50 79 60; fax 93 25 47 58). Open M-Sa 8:30am-noon and 2-7pm, Su 8:30am-1pm. AmEx/MC/V. **Europcar,** 47 av. de Grande-Bretagne (☎93 50 74 95; fax 93 25 78 38). Open M-Sa 8am-noon and 2-6pm. Closed Su. AmEx/MC/V.

Scooter Rental: Auto-Moto Garage, 7 rue de Millo (☎93 50 10 80). Open M-F 8am-noon and 2-7pm, Sa 8am-noon. €23 for 9am-7pm, €26 for 24hr., €145 per week. Credit card deposit. AmEx/MC/V.

✴🛈 ORIENTATION & PRACTICAL INFORMATION

This compact but jam-packed principality can best be understood as five distinct neighborhoods (from east to west): **Fontvieille, Monaco-Ville, La Condamine, Monte-Carlo/Larvotto,** and **Le Jardin Exotique.** Fontvieille is home to a large shopping center and **Carrefour**, perhaps the most economical shopping option in Monaco. Monaco-Ville, rising fortress-like over the harbor, is the historical heart of the principality: home to the Palais Princier, the Cathédrale de Monaco, and café-lined pedestrian avenues. La Condamine, near the main port, bustles with a colorful morning market, train station, and lively bars. The glitz associated with Monaco, however, is concentrated in Monte-Carlo/Larvotto. There one finds the fabled tables of the Monte-Carlo casino and the *Carré d'Or*, a cluster of thoroughfares lined with luxury boutiques. Monte-Carlo/Larvotto also boasts Monaco's only beach, the **plage du Larvotto**. A 5min. walk uphill from the casino takes you across the border to **Beausoleil,** France, a more down to earth, economical option for those wanting to stay a stone's throw from the *richesse* of the pl. du Casino.

Tourist Office: 2a bd. des Moulins (☎92 16 61 16; fax 92 16 60 00; www.monaco-congres.com; dtc@monaco-congres.com), near the casino. A friendly, English-speaking staff provides city maps, events brochures, and hotel reservations free of charge. Open M-Sa 9am-7pm, Su and holidays 10am-noon. There are **annexes** in the train station at the av. Prince Pierre exit and in the port mid-June to Aug.

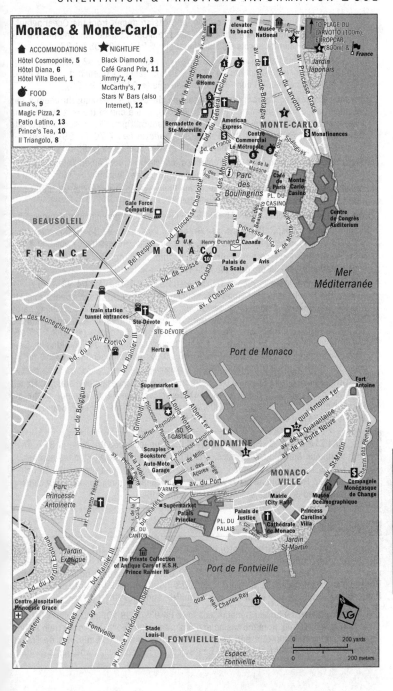

Monaco & Monte-Carlo

🏠 ACCOMMODATIONS
Hôtel Cosmopolite, 5
Hôtel Diana, 6
Hôtel Villa Boeri, 1

🍴 FOOD
Lina's, 9
Magic Pizza, 2
Patio Latino, 13
Prince's Tea, 10
Il Triangolo, 8

⭐ NIGHTLIFE
Black Diamond, 3
Café Grand Prix, 11
Jimmy'z, 4
McCarthy's, 7
Stars N' Bars (also
    Internet), 12

CÔTE D'AZUR

Tours: Mini-train tours to the port, palace, and casino depart from the Oceanography Museum (June-Sept. 10:30am-6pm; Oct.-May 11am-5pm; closed Jan. and mid-Nov. to late Dec.). Thirty minute tickets €6, children under 5 free. (☎92 05 64 38)

Embassies and Consulates: Canada, 1 av. Henry Dunant (☎97 70 62 42); United Kingdom, 22 bd. Princesse Charlotte (☎93 50 99 66); France, 1 Chemin du Ténao (☎92 16 54 60). The nearest US consulate is in Marseille (☎04 91 54 92 00).

Currency Exchange: Compagnie Monégasque de Change, parking du chemin des Pêcheurs, av. de la Quarantaine (☎93 25 02 50), at the end of the port, has reasonable rates and a €1 commission. Open Su-F 9:30am-5:30pm. Closed early Nov. to late Dec. **American Express,** 35 bd. Princesse Charlotte (☎97 70 77 59). Open M-F 9:30am-noon, 2-6:30pm. **Monafinances,** 17 av. des Spélugues (☎93 50 06 80).

ATMs: ATMs can be found throughout Monaco, principally on bd. Albert I along the main port. **CFM Monaco** has an "automatic currency exchange" machine.

English-Language Bookstore: Scruples, 9 rue Princesse Caroline (☎/fax 93 50 43 52). Open 9:30am-noon and 2:30-7pm. AmEx/MC/V.

Police: 3 rue Louis Notari (☎93 15 30 15). 5 other stations throughout the principality.

Hospital: Centre Hospitalier Princesse Grace, av. Pasteur (☎97 98 99 00; emergency ☎97 98 97 69), off bd. Rainier III, along the train tracks. Accessible by bus line #5.

24hr. Pharmacy: Monaco has a rotating schedule of *pharmacies de garde*. Call the police station or look in the daily *Monaco-Matin*.

Internet: Phone@Home, 3 rue du Marché (☎04 93 41 99 99, fax 04 93 41 93 44), next to the Hôtel Diana and Hotel Cosmopolite in Beausoleil. Owner speaks English, French, and Chinese. Internet, fax, telephone, and photocopying services; calling cards sold. Internet €4 for 30min., €6.50 per hr. Faxes within France €2, within Europe €2.50, international €3.50. **Stars 'N' Bars,** 6 quai Antoine I (☎97 97 95 95; www.starsnbars.com). 2 computers, €5 for 30min. Open daily 10am-midnight. Gale Force Computing, 13 av. St-Michel (☎93 50 20 92; gfc@monaco.mc). €4.50 for 30 min. Open M-F 9am-12:30pm and 2-6pm, F closes at 5pm.

Post Office: Palais de la Scala (☎97 97 25 25). Monaco issues its own stamps; French stamps cannot be used there. **Branch office** across from Hôtel Terminus at the av. Prince Pierre train station exit. 5 additional branches. All offices open M-F 8am-7pm, Sa 8am-noon. **Postal code:** MC 98000 Monaco.

CALLING TO & FROM MONACO. Monaco's country code is 377. To telephone Monaco from France, dial 00377, then the 8-digit Monaco number. To call France from Monaco, dial 0033, and drop the first zero of the French number. French phone cards will not work in Monaco's public phones, but cards purchased in Monaco will work throughout Europe.

ACCOMMODATIONS

If you choose to stay within a stone's throw of the casino, forget those college plans for your children. Your best bet is to stay in **Beausoleil,** where prices are nearly halved. The hotels in Beausoleil are closer to the casino and the best nightlife than some of those in Monaco itself. The only other viable options are in **La Condamine,** along rue de la Turbie, rue Grimaldi, and av. Prince Pierre.

Hôtel Villa Boeri, 29 bd. du Général Leclerc (☎04 93 78 38 10; fax 04 93 41 90 95), in Beausoleil, 10min. from the casino and 5min. from the beach. Leave the train station at bd. Princesse Charlotte and keep to the left. Walk about 15min. Bd. de France changes to bd. du Général Leclerc in Beausoleil. English-speaking owner rents a variety of rooms, from *luxe* doubles with bathtubs to single rooms with double bed and shower. All have A/C, TV, and phone. Breakfast €5. Singles and doubles €40-48, deluxe doubles €46-60, triples €69; quads €81. Prices rise 10% June-Sept. AmEx/MC/V. ❹

Hôtel Cosmopolite, 19 bd. du Général Leclerc (☎04 93 78 36 00; fax 04 93 41 84 22), in Beausoleil, next door to Hôtel Diana. Amiable English-speaking Italian owners run this simple but genial hotel. The cheapest rooms are small but well-equipped with comfortable beds, A/C, TV, phone, and hairdryer. Breakfast €7. Reception 24hr. Singles with shower €38, Sept.-June €34, with shower and toilet €56-73/€51-66; doubles with shower and toilet €66-88/€60-76; triples €84-94/€76-85. AmEx/MC/V. ❹

Hôtel Diana, 17 bd. du Général Leclerc (☎04 93 78 47 58; fax 04 93 41 88 94; www.monte-carlo.mc/hotel-diana-beausoleil), next to Hôtel Cosmopolite. Thirty-five clean, if slightly run-down, rooms at reasonable prices. Breakfast €6. Reception 24hr. Reservations required. Singles €32, with shower €35, with shower and toilet €45; doubles (with one bed) €32-55; triples with bath and toilet €63. AmEx/MC/V. ❸

🄕 FOOD

Not surprisingly, Monaco has little budget fare. Go *à la carte* at the fruit and flower market on pl. d'Armes at the end of av. Prince Pierre (open daily 6am-1pm), the huge **Carrefour** in Fontvieille's shopping plaza (☎92 05 57 00; open M-Sa 8:30am-10pm), the **Casino** supermarket on bd. Albert I (☎93 30 56 78; open M-Sa 8:30am-8pm), or **Marché U** at 30 bd. Princesse Charlotte (☎97 97 14 01; open M-Sa 8:30am-7:15pm). For sweeter snacks, try **Prince's Tea ❷**, 26 av. de la Costa (☎93 50 63 91), a charming *pâtisserie* and *salon de thé* near the tourist office that offers a mouthwatering array of desserts for around €1 each.

Monaco enjoys an inordinate number of Italian restaurants and pizzerias. Local favorite **Il Triangolo ❸**, 1 av. de La Madone (☎93 30 67 30), serves enormous, heavenly pizzas (€9-14) in a cozy, relaxed atmosphere. Friendly Italian owners speak French, English, and a smattering of Spanish. Plats du jour €12-16. Save those extra euros for the slot machines and enjoy free delivery on delicious made-to-order sandwiches or one of 23 varieties of pizza (€5 to €9) at **Magic Pizza ❷**, 27 bd. du Général Leclerc (☎04 93 41 86 86). **Lina's ❶**, in *Le Métropole* shopping center, makes affordable sandwiches of all kinds. (☎93 25 86 10; www.linascafe.com. €3-7. Open M-Sa 9:15am-7:30pm.) Tired of pizza? The newly opened **Patio Latino ❶**, quai Charles Jean Rey in Fontvieille (☎92 05 67 37), sheds its inhibitions and becomes a lively Spanish-themed bar. Head over for *tapas* (€3-9) and sangría (€5), then let loose to the salsa and merengue rhythms.

🄖 SIGHTS

■**MONTE-CARLO CASINO.** At this famously alluring gambling house, Richard Burton wooed Liz Taylor and Mata Hari shot a Russian spy. Its position along the rocky coast is convenient for suicide, an end once sought by as many as four bankrupts per week. Even those too prudent to gamble away their life savings will find the extravagant, red-curtained, gilt-ceilinged interior worth a peek. While optimists test their luck with **slot machines** (M-F from 2pm, Sa-Su from noon) or **blackjack** and **roulette** (daily from noon), the less intrepid can entertain themselves at the ornate **Atrium du Casino** theater. While all casinos have **dress codes** that frown upon shorts, sneakers, sandals, and jeans, the exclusive *salons privés* require coat and tie and charge a €10 cover to join in elite games like *chemin de fer* and *trente et quarante*. The more relaxed **Café de Paris** next door opens for gambling at 10am and charges no cover fee. The 21+ rule is strictly enforced, so bring a passport. (☎92 16 20 00; www.casino-monte-carlo.com. €10.)

CÔTE D'AZUR

PALAIS PRINCIER. Perched on a cliff, the palace is the occasional home of Prince Rainier and his tabloid-darling family. The palace guard nominally protects the palace entrance and changes with great fanfare daily (11:55am). Only when the prince is away does the flag lower, and the doors then open to tourists. At these times, tours in French, English, and Italian wind through the small but lavishly decorated palace. Stops include the hall of mirrors, Princess Grace's official state portrait, Prince Rainier's throne, and the chamber where King George III of England died. (☎ 93 25 18 31. Open daily June-Sept. 9:30am-6pm, Oct. 10am-5pm. €6, students and children 8-14 €3.)

PLAGE DU LARVOTTO. Though Monaco's beaches can't compare to the rest of the Riviera, residents and tourists fill this lovely, umbrella-speckled beachfront. (Off av. Princesse Grace. The public elevator from the bd. des Moulins drops passengers off just to the right of the beach.)

MUSÉE OCÉANOGRAPHIQUE. An educational break from Monaco's excesses, the oceanographic museum was founded by Jacques Cousteau and prince-cum-marine biologist Albert I. The main attraction is a 90-tank aquarium, featuring both Mediterranean and tropical sealife, and filled with seawater pumped directly from the harbor. Kids will enjoy the shark lagoon and 1.9m green moray eel, the largest on display in the world. (Av. St-Martin. ☎ 93 15 36 00. Open daily Apr.-Sept. 9am-7pm, Oct.-Mar. 10am-6pm. €11, students and children 6-18 €6. Audio guide €3.10.)

CATHÉDRALE DE MONACO. Thirty-five generations of Grimaldis rest inside this white neo-Romanesque-Byzantine church, which hosted the 1956 wedding of Prince Rainier and Grace Kelly. The victim of a tragic car accident, Princess Grace lies in a tomb behind the altar emblazoned with her Latin name, "Patritia Gracia." To the right of Grace's tomb, encased in glass, is a newly restored painting of Saint Nicolas, by *niçois* painter Louis Brea. (Pl. St-Martin, near the Palais. ☎ 93 30 87 70; fax 93 25 32 59; monacathedrale@aol.com. Mass Su 10pm and Sa 6pm. Open daily Mar.-Oct. 7am-7pm; Nov.-Feb. 7am-6pm. Free.)

JARDIN EXOTIQUE. A photographer's dream, this meticulous garden offers sweeping views that extend over the entire principality, all the way to Italy, as well as an extensive cactus collection. Free tours (on the hour) explore stalagmites and stalactites in the park's dungeon-like grottos. (62 bd. du Jardin Exotique, up the public elevators on bd. de Belgique. The last stop on the #2 bus line. ☎ 93 15 29 80; www.monte-carlo.mc/jardinexotique. Open daily mid-May to mid-Sept. 9am-7pm, mid-Sept. to mid-May 9am-6pm or until sundown. €6.60, students and children 6-18 €3.20, under 6 free.)

CAR COLLECTION. As if marrying a prince weren't good enough, when Grace Kelly wedded Prince Rainier III, she also became the owner of 105 of the sexiest cars in the world, now displayed in the **Private Collection of Antique Cars of H.S.H. Prince Rainier III.** Gawk at Prince Albert's toy race cars, the 1956 Rolls Royce Silver Cloud that carried Prince Rainier and Grace Kelly on their wedding day, and the auto that captured the first *Grand Prix de Monaco* in 1929. (Terrasses de Fontvieille. ☎ 92 05 28 56. Open daily 10am-6pm. €6, students and children 8-14 €3.)

OTHER SIGHTS. Napoleonophiles and war enthusiasts will appreciate the **Musée des Souvenirs Napoléoniens et Collection des Archives Historiques du Palais,** just to the left of the palace entrance. The small museum was assembled by Prince Louis II, an aficionado of Napoleonic history and great-grandson of Napoleon's adopted daughter, to house Napoleonic paraphernalia. It also explains Monaco's history through coins, documents, and paintings. (Next to the Palais Princier entrance. ☎ 93 25 18 31. Open June-Sept. daily 9:30am-6:30pm; Oct. daily 10am-5pm; Dec.-May Tu-Su 10:30am-12:30pm and 2-5pm. €4, students €2.) When visiting the palace or the cathedral, take a stroll along the seaside **Jardin St-Martin,** next to the Oceanographic Museum.

Though not as large or unique as the Jardin Exotique, the gardens boast a dramatic statue of Albert I and good views of the coast. *(Open daily 9am-sunset.)* Keep your eyes peeled for **Princess Caroline's villa,** a pink oasis just outside the gardens between the cathedral and the oceanography museum. Guards are forbidden to disclose the location, but the armed monk insignia on its gates should tip you off. If you've come to Monaco for enlightenment, question your sanity and stroll through the tranquil cherry trees and tiny brooks in the **Jardin Japonais.** *(Open daily 9am-sunset. No charge.)* For high fashion at *nearly* affordable prices, the **Second Hand Bernadette de Sainte Moreville** in Beausoleil can help you spend those last few traveler's checks. *(Bd. de France. ☎04 93 78 31 53. Open M-F 10:30am-1:30pm and 4-7:30pm, Sa 10:30am-1:30pm.)*

NIGHTLIFE

Monaco is the place to see and be seen. Its chic nightlife is accordingly *très cher*, but certainly not to be missed.

Stars N' Bars, 6 quai Antoine I (☎97 97 95 95; fax 93 50 85 75), a portside restaurant by day, is one of the liveliest clubs in Monaco by night. Teenagers and tourists in tight clothes and slick hair work up a sweat on the dance floor, then cool off with cocktails at the tables outside. Restaurant open daily 10am-midnight. DJ spins Sept.-June Tu-Th 10pm-2am. 21+. Cover €8. Disco open July-Aug. daily midnight-5am; Sept.-June F-Sa midnight-5am.

Café Grand Prix, quai Antoine I (☎93 25 56 90), a short stroll down from Stars N' Bars, replaces throbbing techno with live music in a cozy, streamlined interior. Open daily 10am-5am. Live music 11:30pm. Happy hour daily 6-9pm with drinks half-price.

McCarthy's, 7 rue du Portier (☎93 25 87 67), lets the Guinness flow in true Irish pub fashion, but does so from within an appropriately ritzy Monaco address amid mahogany paneling. Comfortable outdoor seating allows patrons to ogle passing glitterati. 18+. Open daily 6pm-dawn. Occasional live music beginning at 11:30pm; check "By Night" for details (available at the Tourist Office and most bars.)

Black Diamond, 11 av. Princesse Grace (☎97 77 00 24). Although the swank interior and steep prices may be intimidating, the bartenders are friendly, the outdoor seating relaxed, and the DJ takes requests. Happy hour daily 6-9pm. Drinks €12. Bar open daily July-Aug. 5pm-5am; Sept.-June 5pm-3am.

Jimmy'z, 26 av. Princesse Grace (☎92 16 22 77), on the beach and away from the *bourgeoisie*. Jimmy'z has been *the* hotspot in Monaco for 30 years and is still unmatched for its size, sophistication, celebrity, and prices. The dance floor fills around 1am. Open daily from 11pm until the party stops.

FESTIVALS

Each January, Monaco kicks off the new year with the **Festival International du Cirque** (☎92 05 26 00), an exhibition of the world's best circus acts, then follows with the **Flower-Arranging Competition** in mid-May (call the tourist office for details). But the real party doesn't start until the end of May, when the city hosts the prestigious **Formula One-Grand Prix,** one of the jewels in the crown of the World Drivers' Championship (May 29-June 1). Tourists and celebrities alike look in awe at the world's best race car drivers. Travelers not as impressed by snazzy paint jobs and thick exhaust fumes should think twice before visiting during the race, as prices skyrocket, most tourist attractions close, and access to the waterfront is limited to paying spectators. (Tickets are on sale at the booking office of the ACM, 23 bd. Albert I. ☎93 15 26 24; location@acm.mc. Tickets €35-420.)

MENTON

Often called the "Secret Riviera," Menton (pop. 30,000) remains blissfully removed from the glitter and glare of nearby tourist traps but offers the picturesque white-sand beaches, lush gardens, and medieval alleys that made the Riviera famous. On France's eastern border, it is also a gateway to Italy.

◰ TRANSPORTATION

Trains: pl. de la Gare (☎08 36 35 35 35). Trains operate 5am-11:45pm. Reservations 5am-noon and 12:45-7:35pm; self-service machines at other times. Trains leave every 30min. to: **Cannes** (1¼hr., €7.70); **Monaco** (11min., €1.70); **Nice** (35min., €3.80). Also to: **Ventimiglia** (10min., €1.20) and **Genoa** (2½hr., 8-12 per day, €16.60) in Italy.

Buses: prom. Maréchal Leclerc (☎04 93 35 93 60); walk straight and to the left of the train station. Open M-F 8am-noon and 1-5pm, Sa 9-11am. Buses operate 7am-8pm. **Rapides Côte d'Azur** (☎04 97 00 07 00) runs buses every 15min. to **Monaco** (€2.10, same day return included) and **Nice** (€4.30).

Taxis: (☎04 92 10 47 02). 5 central taxi stands serve the city from 5am-11pm; reserve in advance by phone during off hours. Taxi from the train station to the hostel costs €7.

Bike Rental: L'Escale du 2 Roues, 105 av. de Sospel (☎04 93 28 86 05). €13 per day. **Holiday Bikes,** 4 espl. G. Pompidou (☎04 92 10 99 98; www.holiday-bikes.com). Scooters, motorcycles, and cars also available. Bikes €12.20+ per day, €60+ per week, with a €230 deposit. Scooters €30+ per day with a €500 deposit. AmEx/MC/V.

◰◰ ORIENTATION & PRACTICAL INFORMATION

Menton is divided into the *vieille ville*, the new town, and the beach. **Avenue du Verdun** or **avenue Boyer** (depending on the side of the street) is the main thoroughfare of the new town, and ends at a casino. A left turn at the casino leads to the crowded pedestrian **rue St-Michel** and the heart of the *vieille ville*, a surprisingly untouristed tangle of serpentine streets and stairwells. The liveliest beach is **plage des Sablettes,** located below the Basilique St-Michel.

Tourist Office: 8 av. Boyer (☎04 92 41 76 76; fax 04 92 41 76 78; www.villedementon.com). From the train station, walk straight out onto av. de la Gare. After a block, cross av. de Verdun and turn right onto av. Boyer. An extremely helpful, English-speaking staff provides free maps and practical guidebooks. Open July-Aug. M-Sa 9am-7pm, Su 9:30am-12:30pm; Sept.-June M-F 8:30am-12:30pm and 1:30-6pm, Sa 9am-noon and 2-6pm.

Garden Tours: Service du Patrimoine, 5 rue Ciapetti (☎04 92 10 33 66). Two 2½hr. tours daily at 10am and 2:30pm. Call ahead for English tours.

Currency Exchange: Crédit Lyonnais, 4 av. Boyer (☎04 92 41 81 11). Open M-Th 8:20am-12:05pm and 1:30-5:30pm, F 8:20-11:55am and 1:30-5:30pm, Sa 8:20-11:55am.

Police: 9 rue Partouneaux, (☎04 93 28 66 00). The **local police** is located on rue de la République (☎04 92 10 50 50).

Hospital: La Palmosa, rue Antoine Péglion (☎04 93 28 77 77). For emergencies, call ☎04 93 28 72 40.

Internet: Passion Informatique, 2 av. Thiers (☎04 92 10 32 80). 5 computers with fast connections. €1.50 for 15min., €5 per hr. **Le Café des Arts,** 16 rue de la République (☎04 93 35 78 67). 2 computers. €1.50 for 15min., €6 per hr. M-Sa 7:30am-10pm. **L'Espace Arts et Communications,** av. Edouard VII (☎04 93 28 10 24). 1 computer. €0.15 per min. Open M-F 9am-noon and 3-6pm.

Post Office: cours George V (☎04 93 28 64 84), facing the tourist office. **Currency exchange.** Open M-F 8am-6pm, Sa 8am-noon. **Postal code:** 06500.

▶ ACCOMMODATIONS & CAMPING

Auberge de Jeunesse (HI), plateau St-Michel (☎04 93 35 93 14; fax 04 93 35 93 07; menton@fuaj.org). Head straight from the train station along av. de la Gare. Cross the first boulevard you hit and take a left. Take the first right, following the sign for "Camping St-Michel." Continue straight ahead on rue des Terres Chaudes, with the train tracks on your right. Turn left at Escalier des Rigaudis. At the level point, turn right up the steep stair section. At the top of the stairs, turn left and follow the path to a clearing. The hostel is on your left, 60m past the campsite. Alternatively, take bus #6 (8:40am, 11:10am, 2pm, and 5pm; €1.10). This hostel compensates for its remoteness with a friendly atmosphere, fabulous vistas, and free breakfast served on a terrace overlooking the bay. 80 beds (8 per room). Maximum stay 6 days. Dinner €4.80 (pay in advance). Sleepsack €2.80. Laundry €6. Reception 7am-noon and 5pm-midnight. Strictly enforced **curfew** at midnight. Open Mar.-Oct. Beds €12. ❶

▨ **Hôtel Beauregard,** 10 rue Albert I (☎04 93 28 63 63; fax 04 93 28 63 79; beauregard.menton@wanadoo.fr). Take an immediate right out of the train station and go down the steps behind Le Chou Chou *brasserie*. Turn right, and the hotel is 80m down on the right. A friendly staff lets 18 airy, spacious rooms with rich peach walls, blue carpet, and TV. Breakfast €4.90. Reception 6:15am-10pm. Reserve 1-2 months in advance July-Aug. Singles and doubles €28-31, with toilet and shower €34; triples with toilet and bath €45-52. Extra bed €8. ❸

Hôtel de Belgique, 1 av. de la Gare (☎04 93 35 72 66; fax 04 93 41 44 77; perso.wanadoo.fr/hotel.de.belgique). 20 spacious, attractively furnished rooms with floral wallpaper, all equipped with TV and telephone. Breakfast €5. Singles €27.50; doubles €35, with toilet and shower €48; triples €58. Extra bed €10. MC/V. ❸

Hôtel Richelieu, 26 rue Partouneux (☎04 93 35 74 71; fax 04 93 57 69 61; hotelrichelieu.menton@wanadoo.fr). Take a left turn off av. Boyer just before the tourist office; the hotel is 3 blocks down to the right. A marble staircase immediately lends elegance to this charming 43 room hotel. Recently renovated by friendly, English-speaking owner. Breakfast included. Singles with shower and toilet €50; doubles €62-73. Extra bed or person €15. AmEx/MC/V. ❹

Camping Municipal du Plateau St-Michel, rte. des Ciappes de Castellar (☎04 93 35 81 23; fax 04 93 57 12 35), 50 steps shy of the hostel. A quiet, adult crowd enjoys free hot showers, an affordable restaurant-bar, and a panoramic sea view in this isolated spot. Reception M-Sa 8:30am-noon and 3-6:30pm, Su 8:30am-noon and 3:30-6:30pm. €2.90 per person; €3.50 per small tent; €4.70 per large tent; €3.20 per car. Electricity €2.40. Laundry July-Sept. Reception 8:30am-noon and 3-6:30pm. Prices €0.30-0.60 higher mid-June to mid-Sept. MC/V.❶

◖ FOOD

Menton prides itself on the quality of its fruits and vegetables—not too surprising for a city with the slogan "my town is a garden." Test the freshness of *Mentonnaise* produce at one of the town's three markets: the small **Marché Carëi** (av. Sospel at the end of av. Boyer, open daily 7am-12:30pm), **Marché Couvert,** or **Les Halles** (Quai de Monléon, off rue St-Michel; open every morning), and **Marché du Bastion** (near the Musée Jean Cocteau, quai Napoléon III, open Saturday mornings). Restaurants, including some good Italian places in bustling **place du Cap,** dot the waterfront and **rue St-Michel** in the *vieille ville*. Street vendors bring an Italian flair, selling *panini* (Italian-style sandwiches) and *glace italienne*.

CÔTE D'AZUR

Le Café des Arts, 16 rue de la République (☎04 93 35 78 67). The stone walls and eclectic art collection in this cheerful café contribute to an enjoyable dining experience. Check your email while you wait for the friendly, English-speaking waitstaff to serve you delicious salads, pastas, or *plats du jour* (€8-10). Open M-Sa 7:30am-10pm. ❷

Le Retro, rue St. Michel (☎04 93 28 18 02), serves sandwiches (€3-4) and salads (€7). A *croque-monsieur* and salad will total a mere €4.60. Outdoor seating makes this a pleasant place to stop as you explore the *vieille ville*. Open until 7:30pm. ❶

Leur Enceau, rue St. Michel, outside pl. Georges, is another pleasant stop. Here, a sandwich, drink, and 2 scoops of ice cream or dessert costs €5.90. ❶

👁 📷 SIGHTS & FESTIVALS

The *vieille ville* and the beaches are reason enough to venture into Menton. Plentiful but rocky beaches stretch along the coast from quai Napoléon III east to Monaco. **Plage du Borrigo, plage du Casino,** and **plage du Marché** combine to form the longest stretch of beach in Menton, but if you prefer sand, head west of quai Napoléon to local favorite **plage des Sablettes.** Also on quai Napoléon is Menton's main attraction, the **Musée Jean Cocteau,** also known as **the Bastion.** Follow the prom. du Soleil towards the plage des Sablettes. Best known for his work in film and drama, Jean Cocteau experimented in the studio arts, and this 17th-century building showcases the interesting results. (☎04 93 57 72 30. Open Su-F, 10am-noon and 2-6pm. €3, students under 25 €2.30, 18 and under free. First Su of the month free.) Truly devoted Cocteau fans can declare their love by visiting the **Salle des Mariages** in the Hôtel de Ville, the only marriage site sanctioned by the state. Cocteau decorated this wonderfully odd, windowless room as a Greek temple and then added leopard rugs and red velvet chairs for Vegas-like effect. (☎04 92 10 50 00. Open M-F 8:30am-noon and 2-5pm. €1.50, students €1.20, under 18 no charge.)

The bell tower of the **Basilique St-Michel** rises majestically above rue St-Michel in the *vieille ville*. From rue St-Michel, take a left onto rue des Logettes, and then ascend the steps of rue des Ecoles Pie. Despite many renovations since the first stones were laid in 1619, including a complete restoration after a devastating earthquake in 1887, the church's Italianate façade remains distinctly Baroque. Twelve side-chapels exhibit crimson tapestries donated by the princes of nearby Monaco. (Open Su-F 10am-noon and 3-5:15pm. Su mass 10:30am.) Next door is the charming **Chapelle des Pénitents Blancs,** unconventionally decorated with shellfish. The sea-stone mosaic of **pl. St-Michel,** between the two churches, provides an ideal location to gaze onto the plage des Sablettes and the coast of the Italian Riviera.

From the dominating height of 225m, the **Monastère Annonciade** overlooks Menton. To see the view for yourself, take the 30min. hike up the **Chemin de Rosaire** (just west of the bus station, before the police station), which passes 15 chapels built by Princess Isabelle of Monaco in gratitude to the Virgin of the Annonciade for curing her leprosy. The small monastery at the top is eerily beautiful, ornamented with a set of femurs, some bones of unknown origin, and a gift shop. (☎04 93 35 76 92. Open daily 8am-6:30pm; mass M-Sa 11:15am, Su 10am.)

Plant lovers will appreciate Menton's gardens—the small town's pride and joy. Beginning in the late 18th century, winter residents began designing elaborate and exotic gardens, perfectly suited to Menton's temperate climate. Among the most exceptional is **Serre de la Madone,** 74 rte. de Gorbio (☎04 93 57 73 90), at the Mer and Monts stop on the #7 bus. The Parisian-born American resident Lawrence Johnston designed this garden in 1924 after travelling the world for 30 years to find exactly the right combination of exotic plants. Today, the garden is a designated *monument historique*. (Open Feb.-Sept. Tu-Su by guided visit only. English, Italian, and French tours available through reservation at the Service du Patrimoine;

€8.) June is Menton's official "month of gardens," when private gardens open to the public. The tourist office provides a schedule of openings; contact the Service du Patrimoine to make reservations.

Each February brings some 250,000 visitors sweet on honoring sour fruit at the **Fête du Citron (Lemon Festival)**. What began as a small flower and citrus exhibition in 1929 has become a joyous 15-day festival culminating in a parade of floats decorated with 120 tons of citrus fruit.

ANTIBES

While most Riviera towns flaunt sun and sand like cheap costume jewelry, demure Antibes (pop. 78,000) is the real gem of the coast. Though blessed with beautiful beaches, a charming *vieille ville*, and a renowned Picasso museum, the city is less touristed than Nice and more relaxed than St-Tropez. Wild locals, wealthy ex-patriots, and a recent inundation of young anglophones make for scandalous summer nights in the neighboring town of Juan-les-Pins.

▉ TRANSPORTATION

Trains: Pl. Pierre Semard, off of av. Robert Soleau. Ticket counter open daily 5:30am-10:45pm; information desk open 7:15am-7:50pm. Station open daily 5:25am-12:05am. To: **Cannes** (15min., 20 per day, €2.30); **Nice** (15min., 20 per day, €3.50); **Marseille** (2¼hr., 10 per day, €23.70); **Avignon** (1¾hr., 3 per day, €38.40); **Monaco** (1hr., 7 per day, €6.20).

Regional Buses: RCA (☎04 93 39 11 39) sends buses from pl. de Gaulle to: **Cannes** (20min., every 20min. 7am-11pm, €2.50); **Nice** (45min., every 20min. 6:15am-9pm, €4.10); and the **Nice airport** (30min., every 20min. 6:15am-9pm, €7). Bus schedules available at the tourist office.

Public Transportation: Local buses leave from the *gare routière*, on pl. Guynemer (☎04 93 34 77 60). On-site office provides transit maps. Tickets €1.10, *carnet* of 10 €10.50, unlimited one-day pass €4.50, unlimited three-day pass €10.50. Office open M-F 8am-noon and 2-5:30pm, Sa 9am-noon and 2-4:30pm.

Taxi: Allô Taxi Antibes (☎04 93 67 67 67) wait at the train station. Around €12-15 from the train station to Juan-les-Pins. 24hr.

Bike and Scooter Rental: ScootAzur, 43 bd. Wilson (☎04 93 67 45 25; fax 04 93 67 45 26). Bikes from €12 per day, €56 per week; €150 deposit. Scooters €33-50/€175-250/€900. Open M-Sa 9am-noon and 2-7pm. AmEx/MC/V.

Car Rental: Europcar, 26 bd. Foch (☎04 93 34 79 79; www.europcar.com). From €319 per week with a €450 deposit. 21+. Cars can be returned elsewhere. Open May-Sept. M-Sa 8am-noon and 2-7pm, Su 8am-noon; Oct.-Apr. M-Sa 8am-noon and 2-6pm. AmEx/DC/MC/V.

▉ ▉ ORIENTATION & PRACTICAL INFORMATION

Av. Robert Soleau connects the train station with **place de Gaulle** and the tourist office. From here, a short walk along rue de la République passes the bus station and heads into the heart of **Vieux Antibes**. Follow tree-lined bd. Albert I from pl. de Gaulle and turn right at the water to reach a long stretch of beach and the beginning of **Cap d'Antibes**. (15min.) The hostel and the tip of the peninsula are 30min. from the base of the Cap.

Tourist Office: 11 pl. de Gaulle (☎04 92 90 53 00; www.antibes-juanlespins.com). Free maps, info on restaurants, camping, and festivals, and help with **hotel reservations.**

Open July-Aug. daily 9am-7pm; Sept.-June M-F 9am-12:30pm and 1:30-6pm, Sa 9am-noon and 2-6pm. **Branch** at the train station (☎04 97 21 04 48). Open July-Aug. daily 9am-7pm; Sept.-June M-F 9am-12:30pm and 1:30-5pm.

Tours: Tours of the *vieille ville* depart from the Archaeology Museum every Tu at 9:30am. Longer excursions around Cap d'Antibes also leave from the Garoupe beach every W at 9:30am. (Both are conducted in French and take 2½-3hr. English tours available by reservation. €7.50). Mid-July to Aug., additional 2hr. tours are offered Su-M and W-Sa at 10am and 2:30pm (€2, under 18 free). Consult the tourist office for more information.

Currency Exchange: Bureau de Change, 17 bd. Albert I (☎04 93 34 12 76). **No commission** on foreign currencies. Open M-Sa 9am-noon and 2-6:30pm. **Eurochange,** 4 rue G. Clemenceau (☎04 93 34 48 30). Open M-Sa Apr.-Oct. 9am-7pm; Nov.-Mar. 9am-5pm. Those with a *Let's Go* guide do not have to pay the 4% commission.

English Bookstore: Heidi's English Bookshop, 24 rue Aubernon (☎/fax 04 93 34 74 11). Largest English bookshop, with budget-friendly used-book section. Open daily 10am-7pm. MC/V.

Laundromat: Lave Plus, 44 bd. Wilson (☎06 61 86 06 19). Wash €3.40-7.70, dry €0.50 per 5min., detergent €0.40. Wash, dry, and fold service €10 for 5kg, with ironing €16. Open daily 7am-8:30pm. Right next door, **Blanpress** (☎04 93 67 65 93) offers dry-cleaning. Pants €5.20, shirts €5. Open M-Sa 7:30am-7pm.

Police: 5 rue des Frères Oliviers (☎04 92 90 78 00).

Hospital: Chemin des Quatres Chemins (☎04 92 91 77 77).

24hr. Pharmacy: Call the police or consult the local *Nice Matin* newspaper.

Internet: Xtreme Cyber, 8 bd. d'Aguillon (☎04 93 34 09 96), at the Galérie du Port. €0.12 per min., €5 for 50min. Open M-F 9am-7pm, Sa 10am-2pm.

Post Office: Av. Paul Doumer (☎04 92 90 61 00), behind the playground on rue de la République. Open M-F 8am-7pm, Sa 8am-noon. **Postal code:** 06600.

▛ ACCOMMODATIONS & CAMPING

Antibes has a few budget hostels, though fewer than Nice and Cannes. Sight-seers should stay in the *vieille ville;* those interested in beach and nightlife should stay in Juan-les-Pins.

▨ **Relais International de la Jeunesse (Caravelle 60),** 25 av. de l'Antiquité (☎04 93 61 34 40; www.riviera-on-line.com/caravelle), at the intersection of bd. de la Garoupe and av. de l'Antiquité. To reach the hostel, walk 40min. along the shore in the direction of Cap d'Antibes. Or take bus #2A from the bus station at pl. Guynemer in Antibes to La Bouée (every 40min. 6:50am-7:30pm, €1.10). From there, walk back along the coast in the direction of Antibes for 5min. From mid-June to mid-Sept., line 2Abis stops directly in front of the hostel (5 per day 9am-5:30pm, €1.10). Originally owned by a colonel in the British army, this pink stucco mansion is located right next to the ocean. The main building has marble floors, high ceilings, and enormous sunny windows. Breakfast included. Dinner €8. Luggage drop-off all day. Sheets €3. Reception daily 8-10am and 5:30-10:30pm. Lockout 10am-5:30pm. Reserve one month in advance July-Aug. 4- to 10-bed single-sex dorms €14.40. **Camping** €8 per person, no breakfast. ❶

The Crew House, 1 av. St-Roch (☎04 92 90 49 39; fax 04 92 90 49 38; workstation_fr@yahoo.com). From the train station, walk down av. de la Libération until it turns into av. de Verdun after the rotary, then make a right onto av. St-Roch. Attracting a fun anglo crowd, this centrally located hostel provides bare rooms with 4-8 metal bunks. Internet €0.12 per min., €5.40 per hr. Lockers available; bring your own lock. Reception M-F 8am-8pm, Sa-Su 9am-6pm. Dorms Apr.-Oct. €20, €100 per week; Nov.-Mar. €15/€75. AmEx/MC/V. ❷

Stella's, 5 av. Paul Arène (☎04 93 34 12 14). From the train station, cross the street and take av. de la Libération toward the port, continuing until the third right after the roundabout, at av. Paul Arène. 10 beds in two co-ed rooms fill the top floor of Stella's beautiful, well-located Mediterranean home. There are usually vacancies; call 10am-5pm to be sure. Dorms €20, €120 per week. ❷

Hôtel Mediterranée, 6 av. Marechal Reille (☎04 93 34 14 84; http://hotel.mediterranee.free.fr), 2 blocks away from the bus station. This 2-star hotel has tastefully decorated rooms modernized with A/C, TV, telephone, soundproof windows, shower, and toilet. Breakfast (€6) is served under vines in the middle of an outdoor terrace. Reception daily 8am-10pm. Closed most of Dec. Reserve one month ahead July-Aug. May-Sept. singles €42; doubles €55-61; triples €69; quads €77. Oct.-Apr. prices €7-13 lower. Reduced prices for stays of more than 7 days. Extra bed €5. MC/V. ❹

Nouvel Hôtel, 1 av. du 24 Août (☎04 93 34 44 07; fax 04 93 34 44 08). Between the old and new town, this hotel's plain rooms all come with TV and large windows. Breakfast €4.60. Reception daily 6am-8pm. Singles €30.70; doubles €45.40-49.40, with shower €52.40, with shower and toilet €55.40. Extra bed €14.70. MC/V. ❸

◖ FOOD

Popular restaurants fill Vieux Antibes. Cours Masséna hosts the fantastic **marché Provençal,** considered one of the best markets on the Côte d'Azur (open Tu-Su 6am-1pm), the cheapest pizzerias in town, and, at night, local artists selling paintings and ceramics. A few blocks away, lively **place Nationale** is known for its excellent people-watching and reasonably priced restaurants. The largest local supermarket is **Intermarché,** 1 bd. Albert I. (☎04 93 34 19 10. Open M-Sa 8:15am-8pm.)

▨ **Le Brulot,** 3 rue Frédéric Isnard (☎04 93 34 17 76; www.brulot.com), right off av. G. Clemenceau, is the hot local place for sit-down meals. Specializing in Provençal cuisine *au feu de bois* (wood-fired), this two-level restaurant serves delicious meats (€12.50-21) and fish (€18-28.50) in an intimate basement hollowed out of a cave. Le Brulot cooks an excellent steak (€17-21). The fresh *bouillabaisse* must be ordered 24hr. in advance. Duck with pepper sauce €17, appetizers €5-11, *menus* €13-35. Reservations necessary. Open July and Sept. daily 7pm-midnight; Oct.-June M-W 7pm-midnight, Th-Su 1:30am-3pm and 7pm-midnight. Closed Aug. AmEx/MC/V. ❸

THE HIDDEN DEAL

WATER INTO WINE

France pumps out vast quantities of wine for unbeatable prices. That €4 *bouteille de vin* from the local supermarket may seem to be a good deal right now, but a visit to the **Cave Raymond,** 6 av. Guillabert, will forever transform your frugal palate. Disguised behind a classy store front and expensive bottles of local *pastis,* the owners keep three enormous vats of red, white and *rosé* wine. From these metal barrels, customers use a garden hose to transfer the store's wine into their own empty bottles for a mere €2 per liter. If you're worried about the quality of the wine you're getting, you can taste it before buying.

The only tricky part of the exchange is that the *cave* requires patrons to use a specific type of bottle decorated with elevated glass stars. Finding the appropriate bottle may take some extra time at the supermarket, but the effort is worthwhile. Those that give up on locating the necessary starred items can buy pre-bottled wine for €1.80, although the quality is slightly lower and the fun garden hose is not put into effect. Either way, you'll pay as much for a small bottle of Evian water. Thrifty travelers of the world, remember: in France, it's cheaper to keep yourself intoxicated than to keep yourself hydrated.

(☎04 93 34 08 68. Open M-F 9am-noon and 3:30-7pm, Sa 9am-noon. AmEx/MC/V.)

Le Broc en Bouche, on the corner of rue des Palmiers and rue Aubernon (☎04 93 34 75 60), sells everything from the exotic dishes (€10) on its menu to the art hanging on its walls. Although the restaurant only serves 8 starters and *plats*, the selections change every day to ensure fresh produce. Wine tasting is also offered in the *cave* below. Open July-Aug. M-Sa 7:30-11pm; Sept.-June Tu-Sa noon-2pm and 8-10:30pm. MC/V. ❸

Les Saveurs d'Asie, 2bis rue de la République (☎04 93 34 98 28), near pl. de Gaulle. The counter displays over 80 Chinese dishes, including ten types of spring rolls (€1.30-1.80), and about a dozen chicken platters (€4.20-4.50). Open daily 9am-10pm. V. ❶

🆔 SIGHTS

Popular with artists, Antibes was once home to Pablo Picasso, Graham Greene, and Max Ernst. A **combined ticket** allows entrance to the Musée Picasso, the Musée Archéologique, the Fort Carré, Musée Napoléonien, and Musée de la Tour. *(Cours Masséna. ☎04 93 34 13 58. €10, valid for 7 days, available at each of the six museums.)* The **🄼Musée Picasso,** pl. Mariejol, in the Château Grimaldi, displays an excellent collection of Picasso's paintings and sculptures, among them several of his representations of the town of Antibes and his famous painting, *Joie de Vivre.* *(☎04 92 90 54 20; fax 04 92 90 54 21. Open Tu-Su mid-June to mid-Sept. 10am-6pm; July-Aug. until 8pm on W and F; mid-Sept. to mid-June 10am-noon and 2-6pm. €6, students €3, under 18 free. Audio guide in English €3.)* The **Musée Archéologique,** on the waterfront in the Bastion St-André-sur-les-Remparts, displays archeological finds and small exhibits on the history of ancient Antibes. *(☎04 93 34 00 39. Same hours as the Musée Picasso. 45min. guided tours in French F at 3pm. €3, students €1.50, under 18 free.)* The largest private marina on the Mediterranean, **Port Vauban** harbors an enormous fleet of spectacular white yachts, guarded by the 16th-century **Fort Carré.** This military base housed important prisoners of war. Napoleon was imprisoned there when Robespierre and the Reign of Terror collapsed. Outside, a statue of a French soldier commemorates the citizens of Antibes who died in WWI. The soldier is mistakenly holding his gun in his left hand instead of his right one: the sculptor is said to have killed himself upon learning of this error. *(☎06 14 89 17 45. Tours every 30min. in French or English. Open Tu-Su mid-June to mid-Sept. 10:15am-5:30pm; mid-Sept. to mid-June 10:15am-4pm. €3, students and seniors €1.50, under 18 free.)* The attractive **Musée Napoléonien,** bd. Kennedy in Cap d'Antibes, is housed in an old watch-tower built by Bonaparte in 1794, before his coup d'état. Take bus #2A from pl. Guynemer to Eden Roc (every 40min. M-Sa 6:50am-7:30pm, €1.10). The museum contains Bonapartist paraphernalia such as an empirical bust by Canova and a pair of Josephine's red velour shoes. *(☎04 93 61 45 32. Open Tu-Su mid-June to mid-Sept. 10am-6pm; mid-Sept. to mid-June 10am-4:30pm. €3, students €1.50, under 18 free.)* Next door, the renowned **Hôtel du Cap-Eden-Roc** has hosted celebrities from Winston Churchill to Madonna. Buy drinks at the outdoor bar in order to view the luxurious lobby and grounds. *(☎04 93 61 39 01. Beer €6-7, alcohol €15-35, bellinis €24. Reserve for July-Aug. in Jan. Closed mid-Oct. to mid-Apr. Singles €240-infinity. Cash only.)*

Beginning across from the Port de la Salis, the Chemin du Calvaire is decorated with the "Twelve Stations of the Cross," dedicated to Christ's last struggle. The stations lead up to the small chapel of **Notre-Dame du Bon-Port,** overlooking the Garoupe beaches. According to an ancient legend, an old man went to the church on a stormy night and saw the Virgin Mary drenched in seawater. She declared that she had just prevented the sinking of a fishing boat and saved all of the sailors on board. In honor of this sighting, the people of Antibes dress up in nautical costumes every year on the first Thursday in July and carry the Virgin statue down to the shore. The chapel is now cluttered with model boats; many people leave them as thanks for a returned sailor or as a prayer for a missing one.

COTE D'AZUR

A small city of **theme parks** has emerged 3km up the northern shore on rte. de Biot. **Aquasplash** has a salt water wave pool and 13 enormous water slides. (☎04 93 33 49 49. Ticket office open mid-June to mid-Sept. daily 10am-6pm. €17, ages 3-12 €14.). Dolphins, killer whales, and sea lions perform impressive tricks at **Marineland.** (☎04 93 33 49 49; www.marineland.fr. Ticket office open Feb.-Dec. daily 10am-10:30pm. €28, ages 3-12 €21. Oct.-Mar. prices €6 lower.) At night, **Antibesland** lights up with roller coasters, bumper cars, and cotton candy stands. (Open July-Aug. M-Sa 4pm-2am, Su 2pm-2am; Sept. Sa-Su 4pm-2am; Apr.-May Sa-Su 2-7pm; June M-F 8:30pm-2am, Sa 4pm-2am, Su 2pm-2am. Entrance free, rides from €1.50.) Take bus #200 (dir: Nice) from pl. de Gaulle to Biot Gare (every 20min. 6:15am-8:50pm, €1.50). From there, keep walking in the same direction along rte. de Nice and turn left at the rotary.

🏢🎭 NIGHTLIFE & FESTIVALS

Juan-les-Pins is the place to be at night, though you can have a good time pre-partying in the Antibes bars. The bars and pubs along **boulevard d'Aguillon** hold happy hours (usually around 6pm) for a cosmopolitan crowd of anglophones. **Cinéma Casino,** across from the bus station at 6 bd. du 24 Août, shows several modern films in English. (☎04 93 34 04 37; www.cinefil.com. €7.50, M-Tu and F afternoons €6.) During the first week of July, the **Festival d'Art Lyrique** brings world-class soloists and orchestras to the old port. (☎04 92 90 53 00. €13-65.) Antibes celebrates **Bastille Day** on July 13th, while Juan-les-Pins lights fireworks on the 14th.

> **La Gaffe,** 6 bd. d'Aguillon (☎04 93 34 04 06), is frequented almost exclusively by hip young anglophones. Fruity "alco-pops" €6. Live rock bands W and F-Sa. Half-price drinks round M-Tu and Th-F 6-7pm. Buy one, get one free June-Sept. M-Tu and Th-Sa 11pm-midnight, W 9-10pm, Sa 10pm-midnight. Open daily June-Aug. 11:30am-2am; Sept.-May 11:30am-12:30am.

> **Le Blue Lady,** rue Lacan (☎04 93 34 41 00), across the street, is a low-key, anglo bar with pool tables and a popular terrace. Open M-W and F 7:30am-midnight, Th 6:30am-midnight, Sa 8:30am-midnight.

> **Xtreme Café,** 6 rue Aubernon (☎04 93 34 03 90), draws a good-looking crowd to its classy wine bar and stone interior. Beer €3, other alcohol €7. Theme nights. Open daily June-Sept. noon-2:30am; Oct.-May noon-12:30am.

> **The Hop Store,** 38 bd. d'Aguillon (☎04 93 34 15 33), has all the trimmings of an Irish pub but is more sedate. Beer from €3.40, pints €5.40. Happy hour 7-8pm with €3.40 pints. Live music on weekends. Open daily May to mid-Sept. 8:30am-2:30am; mid-Sept. to Apr. 3pm-12:30am.

🏖 BEACHES

The two main public beaches in Antibes, **plage du Ponteil** and neighboring **plage de la Salis,** are crowded all summer. Less crowded and cleaner, the breathtaking rocky beach on **Cap d'Antibes** has clear blue water perfect for snorkeling and an almost idyllic landscape of white cliffs. Bring sandals and chairs. Take bus #2A from the bus station to Tour Gandolphe (every 40min. M-Sa 6:50am-7:30pm, €1.10). With the map from the tourist office, find av. Mrs. L. D. Beaumont and follow it to the end. Turn left onto the pedestrian road, which leads to the water. Turn right when a small door appears in the surrounding walls and follow the dirt path until you find an isolated beach cove occupied by a handful of bathers. Also on Cap d'Antibes, the sandy paradise of the **plage Garoupe** put itself on the map in the 1920s when celebrities such as Cole Porter, F. Scott Fitzgerald, Ernest Hemingway, and Pablo Picasso began to frequent it. Fitzgerald even used Garoupe as the setting for his novel *Tender is the Night*, while Picasso paid tribute to the sandy strip through a series of paintings.

Côte Plongée, on the rocky beach below the Musée Napoléonien, at the corner of bd. Kennedy and bd. du Maréchal Juin, provides **scuba diving.** Take bus #2A (every 40min. 6:50am-7:30pm, €1.10) from pl. Guynemer to Eden Roc, and then walk along bd. Kennedy until it meets the coast. Descend the stone steps and turn left. (☎06 72 74 34 94; www.coteplongee.com. Ages 8 and up. Open May-Oct. daily 9am-6pm. Intro dive €25, from boat €33, at night €40, with guide €39.)

In **Juan-les-Pins**, 35 beach clubs of comparable quality stretch the length of the coast. On the bridge across from rue Esterel, a little stand offers **parasailing.** (☎06 03 47 96 00. Open mid-July to Sept. daily 9am-7pm; Oct. to mid-July by reservation. It is best to call in advance. 1 person €50, 2 people €70, 3 people €90. Cash or check only.) On the same bridge, a competing stand advertises **jet-skiing.** (☎06 08 56 95 14. €25, with an instructor €40. Cash or check only.) Jet-skiing was invented in Juan-les-Pins in 1932 when Norwegian downhill skiing champion Emil Peterson decided to tie himself to a boat and ski on the water.

■ DAYTRIP FROM ANTIBES: BIOT

*Biot's train station (☎08 92 35 35 35) is 2mi. from the town center; the most convenient way to travel from Antibes is by **bus** (Sillages, ☎04 93 64 88 84). Bus #10A connects Biot Village and the bus station in Antibes (20min.; M-Sa 12 per day, Su 8 per day; €1.10). The last bus from Biot to Antibes departs at 6pm. Bus #1 connects the **train** station to the village (10min.; every hr. M-F 7:30am-7:45pm, every 2hr. Sa 9am-7pm).*

Biot has for centuries been known for its production of yellow clay *jarres*, once used to transport oil. Originally settled by the Greeks and Romans, Biot was left desolate after the Black Plague. In 1470 some 50 families returned, planting the 10,000 orange trees that still flourish in the surrounding countryside, reconstructing Biot's narrow streets, fortified gates, and *bougainvillea*-covered homes, and producing the pottery for which it was renowned. Biot has since become a center of artistic creation; an enchanted Fernand Léger spent the end of his life painting here, and Eloi Monod invented the town's distinctive "bubble glass." Today, visitors can watch master glassblowers in action, visit the plentiful galleries and boutiques that line the village streets, and explore the Léger museum.

Biot's 15th-century cobblestone streets, open *places*, fountains, and flower-covered homes make for pleasant strolls. Boutiques and art galleries showcase glasswork and pottery, and art exhibitions are often organized in the **place des Arcades.** The tourist office distributes a 1hr. self-guided **tour** of the village, but wandering without a map is just as easy. Be sure to see the **Eglise de Biot,** constructed atop the ruins of an ancient 12th-century Roman church. At the bottom of some 20 steps awaits the stunning 15th-century red and gold *rétable, La Vierge au Rosaire*, by Louis Bréa, and the newly restored *Ecce Homo* by Guillaume Canavesio. (☎04 93 65 00 85. Open daily 9am-6pm. Free.) The lovely pl. des Arcades at the center of the village contains the ancient forum; some of it dates to the 13th century. It contains the delightful **Galerie Jean-Claude Novaro** (or Galerie de la Patrimoine), 2 pl. des Arcades, run by Novaro's daughter. The gallery is devoted to the colorful work of Novaro, known as the Picasso of glasswork, and other up-and-coming artists. (☎04 93 65 60 23. Open daily 11am-12:30pm and 2:30-6:30pm. If the Galerie is closed, call Lea Novaro's mobile phone at ☎06 12 78 27 27; she is never far from the gallery.)

The stunning **Verrerie de Biot,** chemin des Combes, is the source of much of Biot's modern-day renown. The Verrerie was created in 1956 by Eloi Monod, a ceramist from the prestigious Ecole de Sèvres who decided to reproduce the famous Biot pottery in a new medium. In the process, he invented "bubble glass," formed by imprisoning air between two layers of glass at temperatures around 1100° F. This enthralling art form is displayed here by master glassblowers, whose title means they have studied the art for at least 16 years. While here, be sure to stop by the **Galerie International du Verre**, a gallery displaying and selling unique glass creations by 35 international artists. (☎04 93 65 03 00; www.verrerie-biot.com. Open June-Sept. M-Sa 9am-8pm, Su 10:30am-1pm and 3-7:30pm; Oct.-May M-Sa 9:30am-6pm, Su 10:30am-1pm and 2:30-6:30pm. Free.) Also at the edge of town is the **Musée National Fernand-Léger**, chemin du Val-de-Pome. (☎04 92 91 50 20; fax 04 92 91 50 31. Open M and W-Su July-Sept. 11am-6pm; Oct.-Mar. 10am-12:30pm and 2-5:30pm; Apr.-June 10am-12:30pm and 2-6pm. €6.) Before glass, Biot was known for its pottery, some of which is on display and for sale at the **Poterie Provençal**, 1689 rte. de la Mer, 5min. from the train station, the oldest *poterie* in Biot. It continues to produce the traditional Biotoise *jarres* once used to transport olive oil; most others were put out of business with the advent of metal containers. (☎04 93 65 63 30; fax 04 93 65 02 82. Open M-Sa 8am-noon and 2-6pm, Su 2-6pm.) A free shuttle runs July-Aug. every 10min. from the parking lot at the entrance of the village to the Verrerie, the Musée Fernand-Léger, and the Poterie Provençal. In the low season, take bus #10a (the same bus that goes to Antibes; €1.10), which stops several times between the village and the train station.

Crêperie du Vieux Village ❶, 2 rue St-Sébastien, whips up delicious sweet crêpes (€3-6, with ice cream €6-7), salty crêpes (€7-10), and their speciality €7-10 crêpe pizzas. (☎04 93 65 72 73. Omelettes €5-8, salads €3-9. Open M-W and F-Su noon-3pm.) Family-run **Chez Odile ❸** (☎04 93 65 15 63), chemin des Bâchettes, specializes in Provençal food, large portions, and cheerful service. (Lunch *menu* €15. Open July-Aug. noon-2pm and 6-9pm, closed W and Th for lunch; Sept.-June also closed Th dinner.)

The **tourist office**, 46 rue St-Sébastien, is located in the village. A friendly English-speaking staff distributes walking tours of the village and information about Biot's *verreries*, each with its own trademark form of glasswork. (☎04 93 65 78 00; fax 04 95 65 78 04; tourism@biot-coteazur.com. Open July-Aug. M-F 10am-7pm, Sa-Su 2:30-7pm; Sept.-June M-F 9am-noon and 2-6pm, Sa-Su 2-6pm.)

NEAR ANTIBES: JUAN-LES-PINS

Under the Romans, Antibes was a major port and fishing base. To protect Antibes from the stench of the incoming seafood, nearby Juan-les-Pins was constructed to store and ship out the fish. It consisted mainly of houses for the sailors and sea-food factories, until the 1920s, when Juan-les-Pins was completely revamped by the infamous robber baron Jay Gould. Lined with bars and beach clubs, the modern town is now packed with seekers of sun, sea, and sex (not necessarily in that order). In the summer, boutiques stay open until midnight, and nightclubs blast music until the first rays of sunlight summon the dancers to the beach.

🖪🅿 TRANSPORTATION & PRACTICAL INFORMATION. The **train station** is on av. l'Estérel, where it joins av. du Maréchal Joffre. (Open daily 6:40am-9:10pm.) Trains run to: Antibes (5min., 25 per day, €1.30); Cannes (10min., 25 per day, €1.80); Nice (30min., 25 per day, €3.80); Monaco (1hr., 9 per day, €6.30). By **bus** from pl. Guynemer in Antibes, take Sillages #1A (10min., every 20min. 7am-7:40pm, €1.10). Line 1Abis Noctantibes shuttles between the pl. de Gaulle in Antibes and Juan-les-Pins (July-Aug. 8pm-12:20am). **Le Petit Train** (☎06 03 35 61 35) goes from rue de la République in Antibes, through the *vieille ville*, to Juan-les-Pins. Although touristy, the little train serves both as a guided tour of Antibes and as a means of transportation. (30min.; every hr. July-Aug. 10am-11pm, May-Oct. 10am-7pm; round-trip €6.50, ages 3-10 €3.50.) **Taxis** usually wait at the Jardin de la

Pinède and outside the train station. (☎04 92 93 07 07. From the station to Antibes around €12-15.) To **walk** from pl. du Gal. de Gaulle in Antibes, head along bd. Wilson for 1½km and follow the bikini-clad masses to the beach.

To get to the **tourist office,** 51 bd. Guillaumont, walk straight on av. du Maréchal Joffre from the train station and turn right onto av. Guy de Maupassant; the office is 2min. away on the right, at the intersection of av. Amiral Courbet and av. Guillaumont. The office makes same-day **hotel reservations** and provides free maps. (☎04 92 90 53 05; www.antibes-juanlespins.com. Open July-Aug. daily 9am-7pm; Sept.-June M-F 9am-noon and 2-6pm, Sa 9am-noon.) Other services include: a **laundromat** at 2 av. l'Esterel, near the train station (☎04 93 61 52 04; wash €3.90-9, dry €0.50 for 5min., detergent €0.40; open daily 7am-9pm) and a **post office** on av. Joffre, across from the train station. (☎04 92 93 75 50. Open M and W-F 8am-noon and 1:45-6pm, Tu 8am-noon and 2:15-6pm, Sa 8am-noon.) **Postal code:** 06160.

⌐⌐ ACCOMMODATIONS & FOOD. Although packed with luxury hotels, Juan-les-Pins has very limited budget lodging. **Hôtel Parisiana ❹,** 16 av. de L'Estérel, has rich carpets, bright silk flowers, and sunny rooms with fridge, shower, toilet, and TV. (☎04 93 61 27 03; fax 04 93 67 97 21. Breakfast €5. Reception daily 7am-10pm. Singles €35; doubles €49; triples €59; quads €67. Extra bed €11. Sept.-May prices €7-11 lower, even lower for stays of more than five nights. AmEx/MC/V.) The friendly manager of **Hôtel Trianon ❸,** 14 av. de l'Estérel, offers modest rooms with TV and free Internet. (☎/fax 04 93 61 18 11; www.trianon-hotel.com. Breakfast €4. Reception daily 7am-midnight. Reserve one week in advance July-Aug. Singles €32; doubles with toilet €36, with toilet and shower €46-48; triples €46-54. Sept.-June prices €5-13 lower. AmEx/MC/V.) In a pink stucco villa about 100m from the beach, the **Hôtel Alexandra ❹,** rue Pauline, has tastefully decorated rooms equipped with A/C, telephone, TV, and shower. Friendly owners serve breakfast in the enclosed terrace outside amid palm trees and bright flowers. (☎04 97 21 76 50; www.hotelalexandra.net. Reception daily 8am-11pm. Open Mar.-Oct. Reserve one month in advance for July-Aug. Breakfast €6, dinner €16. July-Aug. singles €49; doubles €61-76; triples €84-88. May-June and Sept. prices €6-8 lower; Mar.-Apr. and Oct. €11-14 lower. AmEx/DC/MC/V.)

The **Casino** supermarket is on av. Admiral Courbet, across from the tourist office. (☎04 93 61 00 56. Open daily 8am-1pm and 3-8pm. MC/V.) At the incomparable **Ruban Bleu ❸,** on Promenade du Soleil, by the ocean, diners can people-watch while eating fresh fish and filling pizzas. Outdoor tables have a great view of the Bastille Day fireworks. (☎04 93 61 31 02; fax 04 93 67 13 45. Fish and meat dishes €13.50-15, pizza €7-12, pasta €9-22. Lunch *formule* M-Sa €14. Open daily 7:30am-1am. MC/V.) Farther from the water, **La Bamba ❷,** 18 av. Dautheville, bakes hot pizzas (€7.50-10.50), pastas (€6.50-10.50), and meat and fish dishes (€9.50-22.50) from its wood-burning oven. (☎04 93 61 32 64. *Menu* €17. Open Apr.-Oct. daily 5:30pm-1am. AmEx/MC/V.)

♫♬ ENTERTAINMENT & NIGHTLIFE. The heart of Juan-les-Pins nightlife is the Casino area, where cruising the strip is entertainment in itself. Wild *discothèques* open from midnight to 5am with cover charges around €16. The flavor of the moment is **◼Milk,** av. Gallice, where a hip crowd beautifies the dance floor and plush red sofas. (☎04 93 67 22 74. Cover €16, includes one drink. Open July-Sept. daily midnight-5am; Oct.-June F-Sa midnight-5am.) In psychedelic **Whisky à Gogo,** 5 rue Jacques Leonetti, a young crowd dances to house, hip-hop, and Latin beats amid water-filled columns. (☎04 93 61 26 40; wagogo.juan@wanadoo.fr. Cover €16, beer €8, margaritas €5. 18+. Open Apr. to mid-Oct. daily 12:30am-6am.) An older, more sedate crowd frequents **Le Village,** on the corner of av. Georges Gallice and bd. Baudoin, whose Mexican theme includes pueblo façades and life-size *bur-*

ros. (☎04 92 93 90 00. Cover €16. M white party, Tu and Su ladies night, Th Latin, F-Sa international music. Open July-Aug. daily midnight-5am.)

Most *discothèques* are only open weekends in the low season. Fortunately, bars pick up the slack. At the tropical-themed **Pam Pam Rhumerie,** 137 bd. Wilson, bikinied showgirls vibrate to drumbeats and down flaming drinks like the Waikiki. (☎04 93 61 11 05. Open mid-Mar. to early Nov. daily 3pm-5am.) The jointly owned **Ché Café,** on carrefour de la Nouvelle Orléans (open Apr.-Oct. daily 5pm-4am), and **La Réserve,** across the street, host pre-clubbing crowds on their large patios. (☎04 93 61 20 06. Open daily July-Aug. 8am-5am; Sept.-June 8am-3am.) Across from Ché, **Zapata's** lassos, sombreros, and jalapeño pepper lights attract a fun, light-hearted crowd. (Open Apr.-Oct. daily 5:30pm-4am.) New-comer **Kelly's Irish Bar,** 5 bd. de la Pinède, targets the ubiquitous anglo population. (Pints €5-6.10. July-Aug. live music F-Sa from 11:30pm. Open daily June-Aug. 6pm-5am; Sept.-May 6pm-1am.) Lose any remaining money at the gaudy **Eden Casino,** bd. Baudoin. (☎04 92 93 71 71. No cover. 18+. Slot machines open 10am-5am. Roulette and blackjack tables open 9:30pm-5am; €11 cover; strict formal dress code.)

■ **FESTIVALS.** In mid-July, Juan-Les-Pins puts on the massive **Festival International de Jazz (Jazz à Juan).** Lasting 1½ weeks, the concerts usually draw a few big names. (Info at jazzajuan@antibes-juanlespins.com. Tickets €20-59, students and under 18 €10-18; available at the tourist offices in Juan-les-Pins and Antibes.)

CANNES

The name Cannes (pop. 70,000) no doubt conjures images of Catherine Deneuve sipping champagne by the pool, Marilyn Monroe posing red-lipped on the beach, and countless other starlets competing for camera time. With its renowned annual film festival, these associations are not at all inaccurate. But the festival happens only once a year—at other times, Cannes is the most accessible of the Riviera's glam-towns, lacking the wealth of Monte-Carlo and the exclusivity of St-Tropez. The palm-lined boardwalk, gorgeous sandy beach, and innumerable boutiques are open to all; if your legs are bronze, your sunglasses stylish, and your shopping bags full, you belong here.

▄ TRANSPORTATION

Trains: 1 rue Jean-Jaurès (☎08 92 35 35 35). Train station open daily 5am-12:30am. Info desk and ticket sales open daily 5:30am-10:30pm. Luggage storage €3.20-7 for 72hr. Open daily 9am-12:15pm and 3:30-5:30pm. To: **Antibes** (15min., €2.30); **Monaco** (1hr., €7.80); **Nice** (40min., €5.20); **Marseille** (2hr., 6:30am-11:03pm, €22.30); **St-Raphaël** (25min., €4.10); and other coastal towns. TGV to **Paris** (5hr.) via Marseille €79-97.

Buses: Rapide Côte D'Azur, pl. de l'Hôtel de Ville (☎04 93 39 11 39). To: **Nice** (1½hr., every 20min., €5.80) and **Nice airport** (60min.; every 40min. M-Sa 7am-7pm, Su 8:30am-7pm; €12.40, under 25 €9.25). Buses to **Grasse** (50min., every 30min., €3.80) leave from the train station.

Public Transportation: Bus Azur, pl. de l'Hôtel de Ville (☎04 93 45 20 08). Info desk and ticket sales M-F 7am-7pm, Sa 8:30am-6:30pm. Bus tickets €1.30; *carnet* of 10 €8.50, weekly pass €9.45. Purchase on board.

Taxis: Allô Taxis Cannes (☎04 92 99 27 27).

Bike and Scooter Rental: Holiday Bikes, 32 av. du Maréchal Juin (☎04 93 94 30 34). Bikes from €12.20 per day, €60 per week; €230 deposit; scooters from €30/€145/€500. Open M-Sa 9am-7pm, Su 10am-noon and 7-8pm. AmEx/MC/V.

THE LOCAL LEGEND

A CANNES DEBUT

A few short days in celebrity-filled Cannes makes most visitors wish they were just a *bit* more glamorous. In 1800, however, Cannes was little more than a tiny fishing village, inhabited by the monks of St-Honorat abbey.

The city was transformed in 1834 by **Lord Henry Brougham,** a radical 48-year-old English member of Parliament, anti-slavery activist, champion of educational reform and women's rights, and opponent of political corruption. On December 28, 1834, Lord Brougham was headed to Nice, hoping that a warm orange tree climate would mend his daughter's failing health. He found Nice under quarantine due to a sudden cholera epidemic, and was forced to spend the night in Cannes.

Thirty-four years later, Brougham was still there. He had built a lovely château, planted grass seeds imported from English lawns—and entertained. Well-connected Brougham drew to his frequent dinner parties both English and French aristocracy. Cannes rapidly gained a reputation for being *the* place for the European aristocracy to winter. Villas and luxury hotels transformed the Croisette from a simple dirt path along the seashore into a posh boulevard. Guy de Maupassant joked wryly: "I met three princes one after the other on the Croisette!" Cannes's transformation took merely 30 years, and it has never looked back.

■ ORIENTATION

The *centre ville,* between the station and the sea, is the city's shopping hub; **rue d'Antibes** runs through its center. Heading right from the station on rue Jean-Jaurès, one finds the old city, **le Suquet,** where flea-markets dominate **rue Meynadier** by day and upscale dining enlivens **rue St-Antoine** by night. Stargazers or tourist office-seekers should follow **rue des Serbes** (opposite the station) to **bd. de la Croisette,** Cannes's long and lavish coastal promenade. The tourist office is on the left in the huge **Palais des Festivals,** which is encircled by celebrity handprints. Cannes's beautiful **beach** begins here and stretches along the peninsular land of clubs known as **Palm Beach.**

🛈 PRACTICAL INFORMATION

Tourist Office: 1 bd. de la Croisette (☎04 93 39 24 53; fax 04 92 99 84 23; www.cannes.fr). 2½hr. guided **tours** with French-English bilingual guide every 2nd and 4th Sa, 2pm (☎04 92 99 84 22; €7). Open daily July-Aug. 9am-8pm, Sept.-June 9am-7pm. **Branch** office at train station (☎04 93 99 19 77). Open M-Sa 9am-7pm. For hotel reservations, call **centrale de reservation** (☎04 93 99 99 00) daily 9am-7pm.

Currency Exchange: Office Provençal, 17 rue Maréchal-Foch (☎04 93 39 34 37), across from train station. Open daily 8am-8pm. **American Express,** 1bis rue Notre Dame (☎04 93 99 05 45). Open May-Sept. M-F 9am-5:30pm, Sa 9am-noon; Oct.-Apr. closed Sa.

English Bookstore: Cannes English Bookshop, 11 rue Bivouac Napoléon (☎04 93 99 40 08). Open M-Sa 10am-1pm and 2-7pm. AmEx/MC/V.

Laundromat: Salon Lavoir GTI, 26 rue Merle (☎06 62 84 00 20). Open daily 7am-9pm.

Youth Center: Cannes Information Jeunesse, 5 quai St-Pierre (☎04 93 06 31 31). Info on jobs and housing. Open M-F 8:30am-12:30pm and 2-5pm.

Police: 1 av. de Grasse (☎04 93 06 22 22) and 2 quai St-Pierre (☎08 00 11 71 18).

Hospital: Hôpital des Broussailles, 13 av. des Broussailles (☎04 93 69 70 00).

Internet: CyberCafé Institut Riviera Langues, 26 rue de Mimont (☎04 93 99 14 77). €4 per hr. Open M-F 10am-9pm, Sa noon-9pm and Su 2-9pm.

Post Office: 22 rue Bivouac Napoléon (☎04 93 06 26 50), off allée de Liberté. Open M-F 8am-7pm, Sa 8:30am-noon. Also 37 rue de Mimont (☎04 93 06 27 00). Open M-F 8:30am-noon and 1:30-5pm, Sa 8:30am-noon. **Postal code:** 06400.

▐ ACCOMMODATIONS

For most of the year, it's not hard to get a good night's sleep at a reasonable price. During the film festival, however, hotel rates triple and rooms need to be reserved at least a year in advance. Plan early for high season, particularly August.

Hostel Les Iris, 77 bd. Carnot (☎/fax 04 93 68 30 20 or 06 09 45 17 35; lesiris@hotmail.com). Take a right onto rue Jean-Jaurès and another right onto bd. Carnot. The hostel is on the left, about 50m before Hôtel Amarante. (7min.) Young, friendly, English-speaking owners converted a hotel into this clean, bright hostel. Light blue doors and yellow hallways lead to rooms containing 2-6 firm beds. Terrace restaurant is open until 11pm and serves pizzas (€5), pastas (€6), and cheap beer (€1.50). Reception 10am-9pm; make reservations in advance and reception will wait up. Key code access after-hours. Check-in 10am, checkout 9am. All rooms have keys. Dorms €18, linens included. MC/V. ❷

Auberge de Jeunesse: Le Chalit, 27 av. du Maréchal Gallieni (☎/fax 04 93 99 22 11 or 06 03 40 70 86). Take stairs to a passage under the train station; signs will point to the hostel. (5min.) At night, travelers should avoid the dark tunnel; instead, turn right on bd. Carnot after exiting the station and follow it straight until av. 11 Novembre. Take a right on 11 Nov. and a left onto av. Gallieni. Bunk beds and movie posters fill the small, bright 4- to 8-bed dorms. Restaurant in basement. Sheets €3. Reception daily May-Sept. 8:30am-9:30pm; Oct.-Apr. 8:30am-3pm and 5-7pm. Lockout 10:30am-5pm. 24hr. access with door code. Reservations required May-Sept. Luggage storage €3. Dorms €20. ❷

Hôtel Mimont, 39 rue de Mimont (☎04 93 39 51 64; fax 04 93 99 65 35; canneshotelmimont@wanadoo.fr). Rue de Mimont is two streets behind the train station. Either take the infamous underground passage (see hostel directions) for two blocks, or exit the train station to the left, turn left on bd. de la République, then make another left on rue de Mimont. The best budget hotel in Cannes. Clean, spacious rooms made up in cheerful shades of yellow, blue, and teal and lovingly maintained by friendly English-speaking owners. All rooms have new beds with thick duvets, TVs, and direct-line telephones. Breakfast €5.50. Free luggage storage. Reception 8am-11pm. Singles €29, with toilet €36; doubles €36.50/€42; triples with toilet €51. Extra person €10. Prices 10% higher July-Aug. AmEx/MC/V. ❸

Hôtel de Bourgogne, 11 rue du 24 Août (☎04 93 38 36 73; fax 04 92 99 28 41), off rue Jean-Jaurès. 21 well-maintained rooms in muted shades of pink. Not bursting with charm, but in the heart of the town. Breakfast €5. Reception 24hr. Singles €25-33 with shower €35, with shower and toilet €45; doubles €35-37/€37-45/€42-50; triple with shower €50. July-Aug. €5-15 more. AmEx/MC/V. ❸

▐ CAMPING

Le Grand Saule, 24 bd. Jean Moulin (☎04 93 90 55 10; fax 04 93 47 24 55; www.legrandsaule.com), in nearby Ranguin. Take bus #9 from pl. de l'Hôtel de Ville toward Ranguin, stop at Le Grand Saule (20min., €1.15). A three-star site with swimming pool, snack bar, 8 tennis courts, ping pong, billiards, and pinball machine feels more like a resort than the great outdoors. Sauna €6; tennis €10 per hr. July-Aug. 1 person €16, 2 people €22; May-June and Sept. €12/€16. Car €3. Electricity €3. Showers free. Laundry €3. Bungalows and chalets for 4-6 people also available for rental by the week (€400-730). MC/V. ❶

Parc Bellevue, 67 av. M. Chevalier (☎04 93 47 28 97; fax 04 93 48 66 25), in La Bocca. Take bus #2 to Chevalier and walk straight for 500m, following signs for the campground. 211 sites with beautiful views, trails, and a pool (open 10am-7pm). As

THE BIG SPLURGE

LA GROSSE TARTINE

Surrounded by the rich, the famous, and the devastatingly well-dressed, you will doubtlessly get the urge to experience the high life in Cannes during your visit. For a wonderful meal, pass on the tourist-saturated rue du Suquet and head over to 🗹 **La Grosse Tartine ❹**. The friendly manager will greet and usher you to a table on the sunny terrace or in the cozy yellow interior with tropical hints and vintage French posters.

Though the restaurant offers a budget-oriented selection of *tartines* (open-faced sandwiches), including lamb *confit*, chicken, goat cheese, and *foie gras poêlé* (€11-18.50), you should consider splurging on three courses from the main menu. To begin, try the house speciality: homemade warm foie gras (€17), accompanied by grapes and figs. For a main course, the chef suggests fish dishes (€16-30) from *saumon tartare* to royal king prawns, and a varied listing of meats (€18-30), including beef, lamb, steak tartare, and duck. For dessert (€8-9), do not miss the to-die-for *gâteaux fondant au chocolat*, a rich dark chocolate cake with a molten chocolate center.

Three courses and wine may force you to budget for a few days, but the generous plates of rich cuisine will ensure good memories for your future empty stomach.

(☎04 93 68 59 28. 9 rue du Bateguier. Open daily noon-2pm and 7-10pm. AmEx/MC/V.)

many mobile homes as tents. Reception daily 8am-7pm. Showers free. Laundry €3. July-Aug. 1 person with tent €14, 2 people with tent €17, electricity €3; Apr.-June and Sept. €10/€13/€2. Car €2. ❶

🗓 FOOD

Though the city is dominated by higher-end restaurants, good food for a reasonable price does exist in Cannes. There are **markets** on pl. Gambetta and on pl. du Commandant Maria, but even better is the **Forville** market on rue Meynadier and rue Louis Blanc, which offers a large selection of fruit, vegetables, fish, and flowers. (All open Tu-Su 7am-1pm.) Or try **Champion** supermarket, 6 rue Meynadier. (☎04 93 39 62 13. Open M-Sa June-Aug. 8:30am-7:30pm; Sept.-May 8:30am-7:45pm.)

Tasty and reasonably priced restaurants pepper the pedestrian zone, particularly along **rue Meynadier.** Farther along, the narrow streets of **le Suquet** beckon, but the ambiance will add to the bill.

🗹 **La Grosse Tartine,** 9 rue du Bateguier (☎04 93 68 59 28), is a glamorous dining experience. (See **The Big Splurge,** at left.) ❹

🗹 **Aux Bons Enfants,** 80 rue Meynadier, offers 3 savory courses for €17. This 3rd-generation restaurant will not disappoint. The menu changes according to what catches the chef's eye at the nearby marché Forville. Open May-July and Sept. M-Sa noon-2pm and 7-9:30pm; Oct.-Apr. M-F noon-2pm and 7-9:30pm, Sa noon-2pm. No credit cards. ❹

La Fregate, 26 bd. Jean Hibert (☎04 93 39 45 39). This large brasserie, popular with local youth, serves large portions of Italian-inspired cuisine on a bright green and yellow seaside terrace. Enormous selection of pizzas (€8-12), pastas (€7-11), and meats (€13-22). Non-stop summer service makes this a reliable pleasure. Open June-Sept. 24hr.; Oct.-May daily 6am-1am. AmEx/MC/V. ❷

Belliard, 1 rue Chabaud (☎04 93 39 42 72; fax 04 93 38 96 62; gbelliard@aol.com). Belliard has been treating locals since 1930. This nationally recognized bakery, pastry shop, *salon de thé,* and restaurant offers a gourmet €8 plate. Choose from 3-4 meat and fish options and 7-8 *légumes.* Open M-Sa 7am-8pm. No foreign credit cards. ❷

Le Bourgogne, 13 rue de 24 Août (☎04 93 38 33 27), located right next to the Hôtel de Bourgogne. In this simple restaurant, a friendly chef concocts delicious pastas (€8-10), pizzas (€7.50-9), and French *plats du jour* in a rustic interior. €16 *menu.* Open daily 11am-2:30pm and 7-11pm. ❸

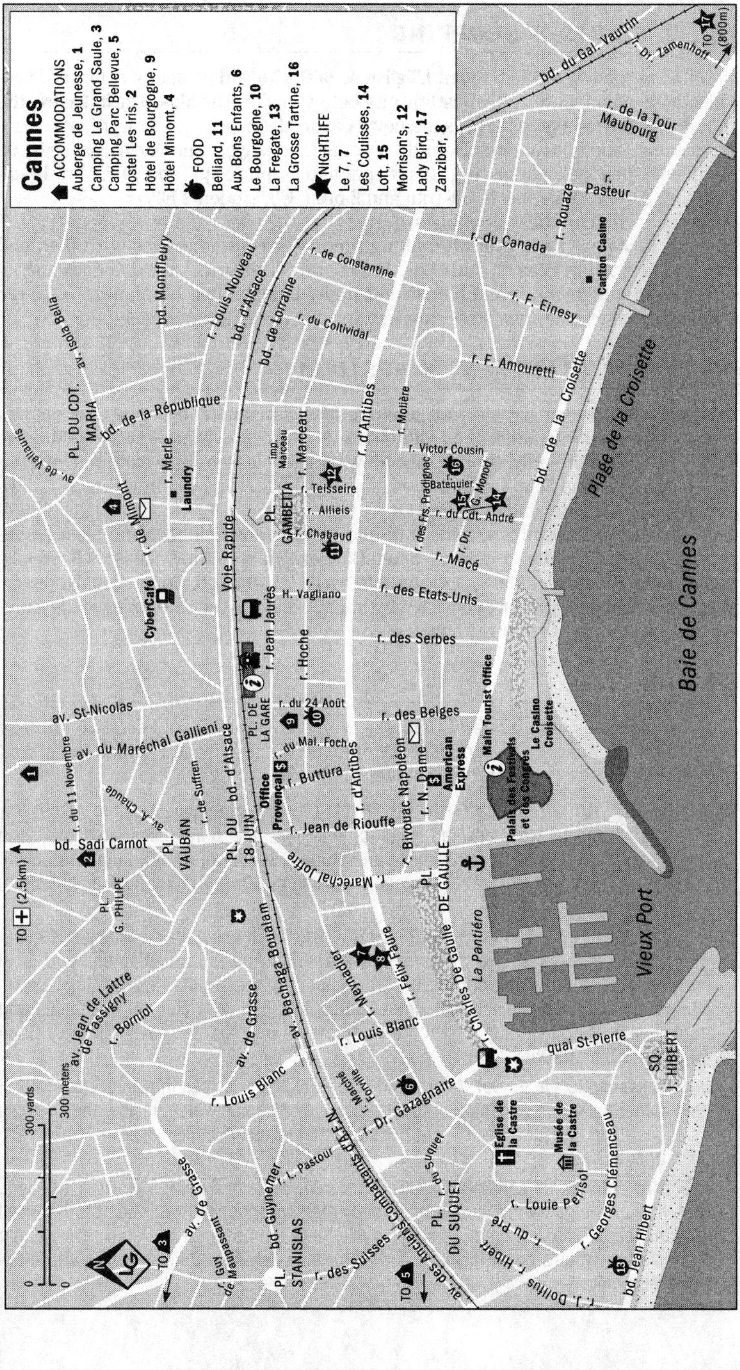

Cannes
ACCOMMODATIONS
Auberge de Jeunesse, 1
Camping Le Grand Saule, 3
Camping Parc Bellevue, 5
Hostel Les Iris, 2
Hôtel de Bourgogne, 9
Hôtel Mimont, 4
FOOD
Belliard, 11
Aux Bons Enfants, 6
Le Bourgogne, 10
La Fregate, 13
La Grosse Tartine, 16
NIGHTLIFE
Le 7, 7
Les Coulisses, 14
Loft, 15
Morrison's, 12
Lady Bird, 17
Zanzibar, 8
Baie de Cannes
Vieux Port
Plage de la Croisette
bd. de la Croisette
Main Tourist Office
Palais des Festivals et des Congrès
Le Casino Croisette
Carlton Casino
American Express
Office Provençal
Laundry
CyberCafé
Eglise de la Castre
Musée de la Castre
La Pantiéro
quai St-Pierre
r. d'Antibes
bd. Sadi Carnot
Voie Rapide
300 yards
300 meters

👁 🔅 SIGHTS & SHOPPING

Perched at the top of the Suquet, **L'Eglise de la Castre** and its shady courtyard provide an excellent view of the bustling city below. Inside, the **Musée de la Castre,** the remains of the monks of Lérins's medieval castle, displays collections of art, weapons, masks, and instruments from the Pacific, Himalayas, and Americas. (☎04 93 38 55 26. Open Tu-Sa June-Aug. 10am-1pm and 3-7pm; Sept. and Apr.-May 10am-1pm and 2-6pm; Oct.-Mar. 10am-1pm and 2-5pm. €3, students €2.)

Blessed with countless boutiques, Cannes has the best window-shopping on the Riviera. **Boulevard de la Croisette,** along the waterfront, is graced with high-end names like Cartier, Chanel, and Dior. The (barely) less pricey **rue d'Antibes** and its environs mix high-end brand names and funky independent boutiques. Go to **rue Meynadier,** a carnivalesque street market, for dirt-cheap alternatives.

🎵🎭 ENTERTAINMENT & FESTIVALS

The world of cinema arrives with pomp and circumstance in Cannes for the legendary ▓**Festival International du Film,** to be held in 2004 from May 15 to May 26. The festival is invite-only, though the sidewalk show is free. July 4 and 14 bring the **Fête Américaine** and **Fête Nationale,** respectively, boisterous celebrations of American and French independence days.

Cannes's three casinos provide multiple ways to lose money. The least exclusive, **Le Casino Croisette,** 1 espace Lucien Barrière, next to the Palais des Festivals, has slot machines, blackjack, and roulette. (☎04 92 98 78 00. Cover €10. No jeans, shorts, or T-shirts; jacket necessary for men. 18 and over. Gambling daily 8pm-4am, slots open at 10am. Free entry.)

🔊 NIGHTLIFE

Those looking to get into one of Cannes's elite nightspots should dress to kill. The cafés and bars near the waterfront stay open all night for just as much fun at half the price. Nightlife thrives around **rue Dr. G. Monod.**

▓ **Morrison's,** 10 rue Teisseire (☎04 92 98 16 17; www.morrisonspub.com). Guinness posters, mahogany walls covered in quotations from Irish playwrights, and a massive Irish flag please pub-lovers from France and abroad. Beer from €4.90, Guinness €6.10. All pints €3.90, half-pints €2. Live music W-Th from 10pm. Happy hour daily 5-8pm. Open daily 5pm-2:30am.

▓ **Loft,** 13 rue du Dr. G. Monod (☎04 93 39 40 39). The hot spot for the young and beautiful—dress to impress. Live DJ spins house and hip hop for the jet-setting and local crowds alike. Always crowded on the weekends, it's a guaranteed good time. Downstairs, the chic Asian-French restaurant **Tantra** morphs into a club on weekends, and tables serve as dance floors until the party moves upstairs. No cover. Live DJ. Open daily 10:30pm-2:30am.

Les Coulisses, 29 rue du Cor. André (☎04 92 99 17 17). Across the street from Tantra, this corner bar is the perfect spot to sit outside and people-watch. Inside, the DJ spins house and hip hop for a crowd—and bar staff—that loves to dance. No cover. Open daily 10:30pm-2:30am.

Lady Bird, 115 av. de Lérins (☎04 93 43 20 63), by Palm Beach. After the party ends at Loft, torches guide the way to this trendy nightspot, packed with men on the prowl and the ladies who love them. DJ spins house till dawn. Cover €15.30, includes 1 drink; F ladies free, men's cover includes 4 drinks. Open July-Aug. daily 11pm-dawn, Sept.-June F-Sa only.

Le 7, 7 rue Rougières (☎04 93 39 10 36). Guaranteed to supply a fun night, Le 7 is known for its nightly drag shows in a catwalk-style, intimate interior. Cover €15, includes one drink. Drag shows start at 1:30am. Open daily 11:30pm-dawn.

Zanzibar, 85 rue Félix Faure (☎04 93 39 30 75). Europe's oldest gay bar, serving drinks since 1885. Intimate patio and candle-lit cavern have a marine theme: silver Poseidons, boat parts—the works. Cocktails €9. Theme parties 2nd Sunday of every month; inquire for details. Open daily 6pm-dawn, closed Tu Oct.-Apr.

GRASSE

You'll know you're in Grasse (pop. 45,000) when the smell of sea foam turns to citronella and tanning oil to tea rose. Capital of the world's perfume industry for over 200 years, Grasse is home to France's three largest, oldest, and most distinguished *parfumeries.* The sunny beach town is also located near the GR4 trail and serves as an excellent base for exploration of the Grand Canyon du Verdon (p. 585).

▉⃟ TRANSPORTATION & PRACTICAL INFORMATION. Grasse's proximity to Cannes (15km) makes it a pleasant afternoon excursion. Most tourist destinations are concentrated in the *vieille ville* and on the south-facing hillside. As you face the sea, the bus station is to the immediate left of the old city; **boulevard de Jeu de Ballon,** just above the station, is home to the **tourist office annex** and the **casino.** A few steps away is **place du Cours,** a large plateau overlooking the valley, within easy reach of the Fragonard perfumery and several museums.

The **bus station,** pl. Notre Dame des Fleurs, has service daily to Cannes (40min.; M-Sa every 30min. 5:40am-9:10pm, Su every hr. 5:40am-7:30pm; €3.70) and Nice (1hr.; July-Aug. 10 per day, Sept.-June 23 per day; €6.20), through the RCA bus lines #600 and 500, respectively. (RCA ☎04 93 36 08 43. Office open M-Tu and Th-F 7:30am-noon and 1:30-5pm, W 7:30-11:30am and 2-5pm.) Although no trains stop at Grasse, there's an **SNCF info office** across the *place.* (Open M-F 9am-5pm, Sa 9am-noon and 1:30-5pm.) Below the Palais des Congrés on cours Honoré Cresp, the **tourist office** hands out maps with a 1½hr. annotated walking tour of the city. For further information on the town's history, free 1hr. tours in English are available by reservation. (☎04 93 36 66 66; fax 04 93 36 86 36. Open July-Sept. M-Sa 9am-7pm, Su 9am-1pm and 2-6pm; Oct.-June M-Sa 9am-1pm and 2-6pm.) Get **currency exchange** at Change du Casino, 6 cours Honoré Cresp, several doors down from the tourist office. (☎04 93 36 48 48. Open M-Sa 9am-12:30pm and 2-6:30pm.) The **post office** is in the parking garage under the bus station. (☎04 92 42 31 40. Open M-F 9am-noon and 2-5pm, Sa 9am-noon.) **Postal code:** 06130.

▉⃟ ACCOMMODATIONS & FOOD. Grasse has several budget hotels. To get to **Hôtel Ste-Thérèse ❸,** 39 bd. Y. E. Baudoin, climb the street behind the tourist office annex, keeping left and continuing uphill on bd. Y. E. Baudoin. (15min.) This clean, modest hotel is surrounded by a terrace with sunbathing chairs. Though it was once a church, all that remains of its past are a few remaining stained-glass windows. All rooms come with TV and a panoramic view stretching all the way to Cannes. (☎04 93 36 10 29; fax 04 93 36 11 73; hotelstetherese@wanadoo.fr. Breakfast €5, dinner €16. Reception daily 7am-11pm. Same-day reservations are often possible. Singles €27, with shower and toilet €36; doubles €37/€55-58; triples with shower and toilet €68; quads with shower and toilet €95. Extra bed €16. MC/V.) **Hôtel Les Palmiers ❸,** 17 bd. Y. E. Baudoin, on the way to Hôtel Ste-Thérèse, has bare rooms with a high ceiling, large windows, slightly weak bedsprings, shower, and TV. (☎/fax 04 93 36 07 24. Breakfast €5. Reception 24hr. Reserve 2 weeks in advance for July-Aug. Singles €22-38; doubles €24-45; triples €38-61; quads €42-

A NOSE BY ANY OTHER NAME The celebrities of the scent industry are known as "noses," the trade name for the master olfactors who produce *haute couture's* most famous fragrances. The best noses train for 15 years before ever extracting an essence; by the time they're ready to mix a scent, the sniffling students have memorized around 2000 smells. It can take up to two years for a nose to mix a new scent. Numbering 10 in all of France, noses are hot commodities and are required by contract to renounce alcohol, cigarettes, and spicy foods.

69. AmEx/MC/V.) Near the bus station, the **Hôtel Napoléon** ❷, 6 av. Thiers, equips most of its rooms with soundproof windows and TV, though it is in need of renovation. (☎04 93 36 05 87; fax 04 93 36 41 09; napo.grasse@aol.com. Breakfast €5. Hallway shower available. Reception daily 6:30am-10pm. Frequent vacancies. Singles with or without toilet €21.40, with shower and toilet €29; doubles €27.50-30.50, with toilet €32.10, with shower and toilet €38.20; triples with shower and toilet €45.80; quads with shower and toilet €56.50. MC/V.)

A morning **market** fills pl. aux Aires. (Open Tu-Su 7am-1pm.) Dozens of specialty food stores, *crêperies*, and little cafés occupy the *vieille ville*. Centering around the cobblestone **place aux Aires,** Grasse's most affordable restaurants also have the best ambiance. Stock up on groceries at the **Monoprix** supermarket, rue Paul Goby, near the bus station. (☎04 93 36 44 36. Open M-Sa 8:45am-7:30pm.)

◪ **SIGHTS & SMELLS.** Follow the aroma of musky cologne and *eau de toilette* to Grasse's three largest *parfumeries*. The best, ◪**Fragonard,** 20 bd. Fragonard, gives free tours of its 220-year-old factory, still in use today. On display upstairs is a large collection of perfume bottles ranging from ancient Egyptian to the minimalist chic of Calvin Klein. (☎04 93 36 44 65; www.fragonard.com. Free 20min. tours in English. Open daily June-Sept. 9am-6:30pm; Oct.-May 9am-12:30pm and 2-6pm.) **Molinard,** 60 bd. Victor Hugo, 5min. from the center of town, has a newer factory designed by Gustave Eiffel, the architect of Paris's famous tower. The *parfumerie's* free tours end with a visit to their tastefully decorated boutique. Concoct your own *eau de parfum* at the 1½hr. "Sniffer Workshop" for €40. (☎04 93 36 01 62; www.molinard.com. Free tours in English. Open July-Aug. daily 9am-7pm; May-June and Sept. daily 9am-6:30pm; Oct. and Apr. daily 9am-12:30pm and 2-6pm; Nov.-Mar. M-Sa 9am-12:30pm and 2-6pm.) **Galimard,** 73 rte. de Cannes, was founded in 1747 by Louis XIV's perfume and pomade maker. The factory now offers 2hr. sessions with one of their professional "noses," who'll help you create a personal fragrance for €34. From the *gare routière* or tourist office, take bus 1PA to Blauquière. (☎04 93 09 20 00; www.galimard.com. Free 30min. tours in English. Open daily June-Sept. 9am-6:30pm; Oct.-May 9am-12:30pm and 2-6pm.) To make sense of all these scents, head to the superb **Musée International de la Parfumerie,** 8 pl. du Cours Honoré Cresp. The 2nd floor houses a 3000-year-old mummy's scented hand and foot, while the rooftop greenhouse displays the natural components of perfume. (☎04 93 36 80 20; www.museedegrasse.com. Open June-Sept. daily 10am-7pm; Oct. and Dec.-May Su-M and W-Sa 10am-12:30pm and 2-5:30pm. €4, students and ages 10-16 €2, under 10 free. 1hr. guided visits in English €5.50, students and children €3.50.)

Housed in its namesake's 17th-century villa, the **Musée Jean-Honoré Fragonard,** 23 bd. Fragonard, features originals and reproductions of the libertine painter's florid work. (☎04 93 36 01 61. Hours and prices are the same as those for the Musée International de la Parfumerie.) In the town of Grasse's *vieille ville*, the Romanesque **Cathédrale Notre-Dame-du-Puy** displays three works by Peter Paul Rubens, as well as Jean-Honoré Fragonard's only religious painting, *Lavement* *des Pieds*, commissioned especially for the lavish Baroque chapel housed inside. (☎ 04 93 36 11 03. Open July-Sept. daily 9:30-11:30am and 3-6:30pm; Oct.-June M-Sa 9:30-11:30am and 3-5:30pm.)

■ **FESTIVALS.** In the middle of May, **Expo-Rose** attracts rose growers from around the world for the largest exhibition of its kind (€7.70). The *Grassois* put down their eyedroppers again in early August for the **Fête du Jasmin.** This fragrant festival centers around flower competitions and the election of Ms. Jasmin.

■ **DAYTRIP FROM GRASSE: GRAND CANYON DU VERDON.** Sixty kilometers off the coast in Provence's rocky interior is the Grand Canyon du Verdon, Europe's widest and deepest gorge. The canyon is a memorable (if slow) way to move between the Riviera and the Alps; Napoleon did it in 1816. Its plunging cliffs and topaz streams are especially worth a visit if you like water sports; the nearby town of Castellane is home to a micro-industry of adventure outfits. The tree-speckled, chalky canyon is itself appealing, but most people come for the Verdon River and the immense Lac de Ste-Croix into which it flows. The canyon's most beaten track is **Sentier Martel,** a.k.a. the **GR4** trail. The six- to eight-hour hike traces the river from La Maline east to Point Sublime as the gorge widens and narrows, passing through tunnels and caves rumored to have once hidden fugitives. Flashlights are useful for the tunnels.

The Verdon River's water ends up in **Lac de Ste-Croix,** a mellow emerald lake at the mouth of the gorge that's perfect for canoeing and kayaking. The GR4 trail past La Palud-sur-Verdon will eventually take you there by foot. By car, take D952 past La Palud to Moustiers and then follow signs to Ste-Croix-de-Verdon, or take D957 before Moustiers to Les Salles-sur-Verdon.

Castellane, 17km east of the canyon and the largest village in the area, is, unfortunately, a bit of a pain to reach from the coast. The canyon itself can be nearly inaccessible from Castellane outside of July and August. VFD **buses** (☎ 08 20 83 38 33) run from Grasse (70min., 1 per day, €11.60).

Before venturing into the canyon, stock up on hiking gear at **L'Echoppe,** rue Nationale, Castellane's only outdoor outfitter. (☎/fax 04 92 83 60 06. Open Apr.-May M-Sa 9:30am-noon and 3-7pm; June and Sept. M-Sa 9am-12:30pm and 2:30-7:30pm; July-Aug. daily 8:30am-8pm. Closed Oct.-Mar. MC/V.)

A number of **water sport** outfits run trips through the canyon. **Aboard Rafting,** 8 pl. de l'Eglise (☎/fax 04 92 83 76 11; www.aboard-rafting.com), offers all types of trips with an anglophone staff; **Acti-Raft,** rte.des Gorges du Verdon (☎ 04 92 83 76 64; fax 04 92 83 76 74; www.actiraft.com); **Aqua Viva Est,** 12 bd. de la République (☎/fax 04 92 83 75 74; www.aquavivaest.com); and **Aqua Verdon,** 9 rue Nationale (☎/fax 04 92 83 72 75; www.aquaverdon.com), all run comparable outfits. Though **rafting** is the most conventional way to go down the river, summer water levels are only high enough about twice a week. (Usually Tu and F; for information on water levels call ☎ 04 92 83 69 07. 1½hr. trip €28-30, half-day trip €37-55, day trip €59-75. Reserve ahead.) The adventurous can try a number of other water sports, including **aqua-rando, canyoning, hydrospeeding,** and **water rambling** (call companies for descriptions and rates). Equestrian types can trot their way through the canyon on **horseback** with **Les Pionniers** in La Palud-sur-Verdon. (☎/fax 04 92 77 38 30. €25 for 2hr., €34 per half-day, €61 per day. Make reservations in advance.)

ST-RAPHAËL & FRÉJUS

Situated along the Estérel Hills, the twinned cities of St-Raphaël and Fréjus provide an excellent base for a visit to St-Tropez. Package tourists flock to the beach town of St-Raphaël for its inexpensive accommodations, rollicking nightlife, and proximity to the sea. More independent tourists also find it invaluable for its train and bus stations, which provide convenient springboards for exploring the area. For those more keen on charm and history than golden sand, the nearby city of Fréjus harkens back to its Roman and Episcopal past, and is home to what is perhaps the Riviera's best hostel. Though both towns may play second fiddle to St-Tropez, they are far more friendly to budget travelers.

ST-RAPHAËL

St-Raphaël (pop. 32,000) is charming only around the beach. The boardwalk turns into a carnival midway through summer evenings, packed with ice cream vendors, gaming booths, and flirting teenagers. While St-Raph lacks the sophistication of Cannes and St. Tropez, its long, sandy beach, lively port, and relative affordability make it an attractive base from which to visit St-Tropez or Fréjus. It's best to stick to the beach and avoid the town itself, which is devoid of charm.

▣ ⁊ TRANSPORTATION & PRACTICAL INFORMATION. St-Raphaël is a major stop on the coastal train line, separated from Cannes by the **Massif de l'Estérel,** 40km of volcanic rock and dry vegetation. There are hotels and restaurants near the train station, a few blocks from the rue Waldeck Rousseau exit.

Trains run from pl. de la Gare to: Cannes (25min., every 30min., €4.10); Marseille (1¾hr., every hr., €19.30); Nice (1hr., every 30min., €9.20). Ticket booths open daily 6:45am-9:45pm. Info office open daily 6:30am-9:30pm. **Luggage storage** open M-F 8:30am-noon and 2-5:30pm. €18 per bag. MC/V. **Buses** leave from behind the train station. **Esterel Cars** (☎04 94 95 16 71) serves Fréjus (25min., every hr. 7:30am-6:40pm, €1.40). More frequent service July-Aug.; pick up a schedule from the bus station or tourist office. **Sodetrav** (☎04 94 95 24 82) goes to St-Tropez (1½hr., 11 per day 6:25am-9pm, €8.40). **Beltrame** (☎04 94 95 95 16) goes to Cannes (1¼hr., 8 per day, €5.50) and to the airport in Nice (2¼hr., 4 per day, €17.70). **Taxis** (☎04 94 83 24 24) wait outside the train station. Les Bateaux de St-Raphaël **ferries** at the old port go to St-Tropez. (☎04 94 95 17 46; fax 04 94 83 88 55. 50min.; July-Aug. 5 per day, Sept.-June 2 per day; €10 one-way, €19 round-trip. Those staying at the hostel in Fréjus should ask about 10% fare reductions.)

The **tourist office,** opposite the train station on rue Waldeck Rousseau, books accommodations. (☎04 94 19 52 52; fax 04 94 83 85 40; www.saint-raphael.com. Open July-Aug. daily 9am-7pm; Sept.-June M-Sa 9am-12:30pm and 2-6:30pm.) Pick up info about jobs, housing, French courses, and cheap travel at **Information Jeunesse,** 21 pl. Gallieni, on the main thoroughfare between the train station and the beach. (☎04 94 19 47 38. Open M-Th 8am-noon and 1:30-5pm; F 8am-noon and 1:30-4:30pm.) The **police** (☎04 94 95 24 24) are on rue de Châteaudun. For **laundry,** check out Top Pressing, 34 av. Général Leclerc. (Open M-Tu and Th-F 8am-12:15pm and 2:30-7pm, W and Sa 8am-12:15pm.) Cyber Bureau, 123 rue Waldeck Rousseau, beside the train station, provides **Internet.** Six computers. (☎04 94 95 29 36. Open Sept.-June M-F 9am-6:30pm, Sa 10am-3pm. Longer hours July-Aug. €2 for 15min., €4 for 30min, €7 per hr.) The **post office** is on av. Victor Hugo, behind the station. (☎04 94 19 52 00. Open M-F 8am-6:30pm, Sa 8am-noon.) **Postal code:** 83700.

⬘ ACCOMMODATIONS. St-Raphaël's intense package tourism can make one feel like the only person in the world traveling independently, but accommodations are more plentiful here than in Fréjus, and far cheaper than in St-Tropez. Be sure to book ahead in July and August. Fréjus's hostel is a short ride away (p. 588). The best deal in town is **Hôtel les Pyramides ❸,** 77 av. Paul Doumer, on a calm street just minutes from the waterfront. Relax in the spacious lounge and outdoor patio or in large green and white rooms with TV, toilet, and shower, some with balcony.

Rooms in the back overlook the train station and can be a bit noisy with an open window. To get there, leave the station to the left, make a right onto av. Henri Vadon, and take the first left onto av. Paul Doumer. (☎04 98 11 10 10; fax 04 98 11 10 20; www.saint-raphael.com/pyramides. Breakfast €7. Open mid-Mar. to mid-Nov. Reception daily 7am-9pm. Check-in July-Aug. 2pm; mid-Mar.-June and Sept.-mid-Nov. 1pm. Reservations required. Singles €26; doubles €36-55; triples €56; quads €66. Extra bed €13. Prices €5 higher July-Aug. MC/V.) Right on the lively waterfront, **Le Touring** ❹, 1 quai Albert I, has cushioned furniture, firm beds, welcoming rooms in every shade of brown, and its own bar and *brasserie*. Exit the station on the right; Albert I is the third left at the water. (☎04 94 95 01 72; fax 04 94 95 86 09; letouring@wanadoo.fr. Breakfast €4. Reception 24hr. Closed mid-Nov. to mid-Dec. Reservations necessary. Singles and doubles with one bed and shower €32-41, with toilet €40, in summer €54, sea views €4 extra; triples with shower and toilet €54. MC/V.) Near the train tracks, **La Bonne Auberge** ❷, 54 rue de la Garonne, has colorful rooms of varying quality, as well as a restaurant. (☎04 94 95 69 72. Breakfast €5. Dinner *menus* from €11.50. Free luggage storage. Open Feb.-Nov. Reception 7am-9pm. Reservations necessary. Singles €21-35; doubles €31-40; triples and quads €38-50. MC/V.)

◼◼ FOOD & NIGHTLIFE. It's hard to come by interesting dining spots in a town where most people's meals are packaged with their rooms. The most lively and affordable restaurants are near the **old port,** quai Albert I. The **Monoprix** supermarket is at 14 bd. de Félix Martin, off av. Alphonse Karr near the train station. (☎04 94 19 82 82. Open M-Sa 8:30am-7:30pm.) **Morning markets** color pl. Victor Hugo, down the hill from the bus station, and pl. de la République. Fresh fish can be bought at the old port. (All markets daily 7am-12:30pm.) Right on the waterfront towards Fréjus plage, a pleasant 10 minute walk along the water from the old port, **La Romana** ❷, a local favorite, serves delicious pizzas (€6.50-9), and meat and seafood dishes (€8-16). Another option for a good, dependable meal is **Le Grillardin** ❸, 42 rue Thiers. Friendly staff serves salads (€5.50-10), tasty pizzas (€6.40-10), meats *au feu de bois* (€10.70-21.10), and fresh fish (€10-18.30). The house speciality is the *soupe du poissons* (€16). (☎04 94 40 46 14. *Menus* €16 and €25. Open July-Sept. daily 7pm-1am, Tu and Th-Sa noon-2pm; Oct.-May Su-Tu and Th-Sa noon-2pm and 7-11pm. MC/V.) **Le Mille Pâtes** ❷, 138 rue J. Barbier off quai Albert I, a small, simple restaurant with cheerful yellow walls, serves pizzas and pastas (from €7) on green floral tablecloths. (☎04 94 83 94 10. *Menu* €12 and €14. Open daily 9:30am-3pm and 5:30pm-midnight. AmEx/MC/V.) At night, sunbaked clubbers head to **La Réserve,** promenade René Coty. It lacks the edge of clubs in Cannes or St-Tropez, but it's the only place to go in St-Raphaël. (☎04 94 95 02 20. Cover €13, includes one drink. Open Th-Sa 11pm-5am.)

◪◼ BEACHES & FESTIVALS. Thirty kilometers of golden sand run along the coast from St-Raphaël west through Fréjus and east through Boulouris, which is more isolated and consequently less crowded. Most of the beach is public and dotted with snack stands. The first weekend in July brings the free **Compétition Internationale de Jazz New Orleans,** a 23-year-old tradition in St-Raphaël. Hundreds of musicians face off in the streets and around the port. The festival culminates in a final competition on the Palais des Congrès concourse. Call the cultural center (☎04 98 11 89 00) or the tourist office for details.

FRÉJUS

Founded by Julius Caesar in the first century BC, Fréjus is a charming town filled with Roman ruins that have earned it the nickname "Pompeii of Provence."

Although Fréjus is far from the beach and surrounded by a sprawl of high-rises, its varied sights, appealing center, and superb hostel make it well worth a visit.

▟ TRANSPORTATION

Regular **buses** connect Fréjus to St-Raphaël until 7:10pm (6:05pm on Su) and later July-Aug.; ask for a schedule at the tourist office. Fréjus's **train station** on rue Martin Bidoure (☎ 08 92 35 35 35) is little-used—St-Raphaël processes most of the town's traffic. Limited service runs to: St-Raphaël (5min., 12 per day, €1.20); Cannes (25min., 12 per day, €5.80); Nice (1½hr., 12 per day, €8.80); and Marseille (1¾hr., 5 per day, €19). **Local buses** (€1.10) connect the *vieille ville* with the beach, daytrips, and St-Raphaël. The **bus station,** pl. Paul Vernet (☎ 04 94 53 78 46), is next to the tourist office. (Open M-F 9:15am-12:15pm and 2:30-5:30pm, Sa 9:15am-12:15pm.) For **taxis,** call ☎ 04 94 51 51 12; there's a stand in pl. Vernet.

◢ ▟ ORIENTATION & PRACTICAL INFORMATION

Fréjus's 7km beach, a 20min. walk from the town center, is closer physically and spiritually to St-Raphaël than to Fréjus; visitors should stick to the *vieille ville* here and its surrounding sights. To get to the **tourist office,** 325 rue Jean Jaurès, from St-Raphaël, take bus #6 to pl. Paul Vernet. The office offers guided **tours** in English once a week July-Aug.; contact the office for details. (☎ 04 94 51 83 83; fax 04 94 51 00 26; www.ville-frejus.fr. Tours €5, students €3. Office open July-Aug. M-Sa 10am-noon and 2:30-6:30pm, Su 10am-noon and 3-6pm; Sept.-June M-Sa 9am-noon and 2-6pm, Su 10am-noon and 3-6pm.) The **Hôpital Inter-communal** (☎ 04 94 40 21 21) is on the corner of av. André Léotard and av. de St-Lambert. The **police** (☎ 04 94 51 90 00) are on rue de Triberg. The **post office,** av. Aristide Briand, is just down the hill from the tourist office. (☎ 04 94 17 60 80. Open M-F 8am-6:30pm, Sa 8am-12:30pm.) **Postal code:** 83600.

▟ ▟ ACCOMMODATIONS & FOOD

One of the best hostels on the Côte (although a hike from St-Tropez) is the ▓**Auberge de Jeunesse de St-Raphaël-Fréjus (HI) ❶,** chemin du Counillier. From the Fréjus tourist office, take av. du 15*ème* Corps d'Armée, then turn left on chemin de Counillier after the second roundabout. (20min.) From Fréjus, bus #10 (€1.10) leaves from behind the bus station for the hostel at 6:30pm. From St-Raphaël, local buses run every hour from 7:20am to 7pm; get off at "Les Chênes" (or "Paul Vernet," a farther but more frequent stop), and walk up av. Jean Calliès to chemin du Counillier. There is a shuttle from the *auberge* to the beach and to the St-Raphaël train station daily at 8:50am. Owners Charles and Chantal make visitors feel right at home at this peaceful, secluded hostel (1km off the freeway), complete with wooden dining rooms and a lovely 170-acre spread of tree-cloaked parkland. Four- to eight-person single-sex dorms are incredibly clean and have beautiful views of the inland valley. Ask about discounts on bike rentals, canoes, and St-Tropez ferry tickets. (☎ 04 94 52 93 93; fax 04 94 53 25 86; youth.hostel.frejus.st.raphael@wanadoo.fr. Breakfast included, 7-9am. Kitchen 6-9pm. Sheets €2.70. Laundry €6. Reception daily 8-10am and 6-8pm; phone for reservations during these hours. Lockout 10am-6pm. Curfew July-Aug. midnight, Sept.-June 10pm. Closed Nov.-Feb. Dorms €13; quads with shower and toilet €60. Camping €10 per person with tent. Cash only.)

In the center of town, **La Riviera ❸,** 90 rue Grisolle, has simple, functional light-green rooms and a friendly, English-speaking staff. To get there from pl. Paul Vernet, walk straight down rue Jean Jaurès past pl. de la Liberté, and turn left on rue

Grisolle. (☎ 04 94 51 31 46; fax 04 94 17 18 34. Breakfast €5. Reservations necessary in the summer. Singles and doubles €27-29, with shower €36-39; triples €39.50-47.10; quads €47.60-55.20. MC/V.)

The **marché Provençal** fills **rue de Fleury** and **place Formigé** on Wednesday and Saturday mornings with fresh fruits and vegetables along with Provençal knick-knacks. The bus from the hostel will drop shoppers off directly. There's an **Intermarché** supermarket, av. de l'Europe, at the second roundabout on the way to the hostel. (☎ 04 94 53 30 70. Open M-Th 8:30am-12:30pm and 3-7:30pm, F-Sa 8:30am-7:30pm, Su 9am-12:30pm.) Budget restaurants cluster around **place de la Liberté.** Nearby, **Les Micocouliers ❸,** pl. Paul-Albert Février, serves reliably delicious Provençal cuisine in a pleasant outdoor terrace. (☎ 04 94 52 16 52. *Plats du jour* €8-10, pasta €7.50, *salade niçoise* €8. 3-course *menu provençal* €15.50. Open T-Su 11am-2pm. MC/V.) The unassuming **Faubourg de Saigon ❷,** 126 rue St-François de Paule, off rue Jean Jaurès, serves excellent Vietnamese dishes (around €8) in a fan- and lantern-filled interior. (☎ 04 94 53 65 80. *Menu* €15. Open daily noon-2pm and 7-10pm, no lunch service on M. AmEx/V.) Try the restaurant at **La Riviera ❷,** 90 rue Grisolle, for simple but tasty French dishes. (☎ 04 94 51 31 46. Salads €2.80-7.60, omelettes €3.50-7.50, pasta €5.80-7.40, meat €8.50-14.50, fish €5.80-13. *Menus* €12 and €15. Open Tu-Su noon-2pm and 7-10pm). **Les Saveurs d'Eugenie ❷,** 48 rue Grisolle, is a small, friendly take-out place with delicious sandwiches, paninis (€3.50-4), and salads (€6.50). Try the *poulet à la provençal*, sliced thin and served in a panini (€4). (☎ 04 94 17 04 76. Open daily 10am-7pm. Cash only.)

🄶 SIGHTS

FRÉJUS EPISCOPAL BUILDINGS. The first mention of a bishop in Fréjus dates all the way back to AD 374. In the middle of the *vieille ville*, Fréjus's remarkable baptistry and cathedral are the products of 2000 years of building and rebuilding. Visible from a side entrance on pl. Formigé, the octagonal **baptistry,** dating back to the 5th century, is one of France's oldest buildings. It is supported by eight pillars, each constructed from a single block of granite. The spectacular 12th- to 14th-century **cloisters** feature marble columns culled from Roman ruins. Wood-beamed ceilings are decorated with over 1200 miniature paintings, 500 of which are still clearly visible, painted alternately on red and blue backgrounds, and depicting fantastical beasts, human-animal hybrids, and bawdy medieval scenes. Far less riotous—or interesting—is the austere Gothic **cathedral,** whose walnut doors were carved in 1530. (*Pl. Formigé. ☎ 04 94 51 26 30. Cloister open Apr. to mid-Sept. daily 9am-7:30pm; mid-Sept. to Mar. Tu-Su 9am-noon and 2-5:30pm. €4.60, students €3.10. Doors and baptistry accessible only by 40min. guided tour in French. Accompanying English, German, or Italian written explanations available. Cathedral open daily 8am-noon and 2:30-7pm.*)

ROMAN RUINS. Built in the 1st and 2nd centuries to entertain rowdy, homesick soldiers, the **Roman Amphitheater** lacks the embellishments of those in Nîmes or Arles, which were designed for more discerning patrician eyes. Today, gladiators have been replaced by musicians and matadors, as the amphitheater hosts rock concerts and two bullfights per year. (*Rue Henri Vadon. ☎ 04 94 51 34 31. From the tourist office, take rue Jean Jaurès to pl. de la Liberté, then turn right on rue de Gaulle. Open Apr.-Oct. M and W-Sa 10am-1pm and 2:30-6:30pm; Nov.-Mar. M and W-F 10am-noon and 1-5:30pm, Sa 9:30am-12:30pm and 1:30-5:30pm, Su 8am-5pm. Free. Bullfights July 14 and Aug. 15; €22-61. Contact tourist office for concert schedule.*) The original wall of Fréjus's other ancient forum, the **Roman Theater,** remains intact; the rest of the structure now hosts concerts and plays. (*☎ 04 94 53 58 75. From the roundabout at the tourist office, go about 250m on rue G. Bret. Open Apr.-Oct. M-Sa 10am-1pm and 2:30-6:30pm, Su 8am-7pm;*

CÔTE D'AZUR

Nov.-Mar. M-F 10am-noon and 1:30-5:30pm, Su 8am-5pm. Free.) Pillars and arches are all that remain of an ancient Roman **aqueduct,** which once stood past the theater along av. du 15ème Corps d'Armée.

OTHER SIGHTS. Fréjus's other sights, neither medieval nor ancient, can be ignored by those pressed for time. **Villa Aurélienne,** on the hill next to the hostel and surrounded by an immense park, is an elegant 19th-century private home which features photographic exhibits. *(Av. du Général d'Aimée Calliès. Call the tourist office for info.)* **The Pagode Hong-Hiên** was built in 1917, partly by Vietnamese soldiers who decided to settle in Fréjus after fighting alongside the French in WWI. Surrounded by noisy freeways, the Pagode is the closest Buddhism gets to kitsch. A weird assemblage of large plaster figures recounts the life of Buddha. It is occasionally used as a place of worship. *(13 rue H. Giraud, 10min. up av. Jean Calliès from the hostel. ☎04 94 53 25 29. Open daily 9am-noon and 2-7pm. €1.50.)* Two minutes farther up av. Jean Calliès is the **Mémorial des Guerres en Indochine,** a stone monument to the French soldiers killed in the Indo-Chinese war, as well as a one-room photographic history display. *(☎04 94 44 42 90. Open daily 10am-5:30pm. Museum closed Tu. Free.)* Diehard fans of Jean Cocteau, film director, artist, and poet, can visit the circular **Cocteau Chapel,** which he designed and built, although it was left unfinished after his death in 1963. *(Av. Nicola on the RN7 to Cannes. Bus #3/13 from "pl. Paul Vernet," 11 per day. ☎04 94 53 27 06. Open Apr.-Oct. M and W-F 2:30-6:30pm, Sa 10am-1pm and 2-6:30pm; Nov.-Mar. M and W-F 1:30-5:30pm, Sa 9:30am-12:30pm and 1:30-5:30pm.)*

ST-TROPEZ

Nowhere is the glitz and glamour of the Riviera more apparent than in St-Tropez (pop. 5400). The town is named after Torpes, the highest steward of the Roman emperor Nero. In AD 68, Torpes's profession of Christianity so angered Nero that he decapitated the steward. In modern times, there is little dispute over matters of devotion: St-Tropez is devoted to sun, sand, and big boats. Originally a small fishing hamlet, St-Tropez first came into public view in 1892 with the arrival of Paul Signac and other Post-Impressionist artists. Sixty-four years later, Brigitte Bardot's nude bathing scene in *Et Dieu Créa la Femme (And God Created Woman)* sealed the town's celebrity status. Ever since, the former village has bewitched everyone from Hollywood stars and corporate giants to daytripping backpackers, all of whom flock to the sleek yachts, exclusive clubs, and nude beaches that make St-Tropez famous.

⌸ TRANSPORTATION

Reaching the so-called "Jewel of the Riviera" requires some effort, as it lies well off the rail line, and it's another hassle altogether to leave town for the outlying beaches and villages.

The fastest and cheapest way to get here is by **boat.** Les Bateaux de St-Raphaël (☎04 94 95 17 46; fax 04 94 83 88 55), at the old port, sail in from St-Raphaël (1hr.; July-Aug. 5 per day, Sept.-June 2 per day; €10 one-way, €19 round-trip). Otherwise, Sodetrav **buses** (☎04 94 97 88 51) leave from av. Général Leclerc, across from the ferry dock, for St-Raphaël (1½-2¼hr.; July-Aug. 14 per day, Sept.-June 8 per day; €8.40) and Toulon (2¼hr.; July-Aug. 15 per day, Sept.-June 8 per day; €15.90). **Bus station** open July-Aug. M-Sa 8:15am-8pm, Su 10:15am-1:30pm; Sept.-June M-F 9:30am-noon and 2-6pm, Sa 10am-noon. Rent a **bike** or **moped** at Louis Mas, 3-5 rue Quarenta. (☎04 94 97 00 60. Bikes €8 per day; deposit €153. Mopeds €32/€915. Open Easter to mid-Oct. M-Sa 9am-7pm, Su 10am-1pm and 4-7pm. AmEx/MC/V.) For **taxis,** call ☎04 94 97 05 27, or hail one from the Musée de l'Annonciade.

🛈 PRACTICAL INFORMATION

The town itself is condensed and pedestrian-friendly, with constant activity between the **port** and **place des Lices**. The **tourist office** is on quai Jean Jaurès. After arriving by bus or ferry, walk into town along the waterfront for about 10min. until reaching a series of cafés. The tourist office is the one without outdoor seating. The tan and well-dressed staff distributes schedules for the municipal system of *navette* (shuttle; €1) transport, and also the *Manifestations* event guide. They also assist with same-night **accommodations booking.** (☎04 94 97 45 21; fax 04 94 97 82 66; www.saint-tropez.st; tourism@saint-tropez.st. Open daily late June to early Sept. 9:30am-8:30pm; early Sept. to early Oct. and mid-May to late June 9:30am-12:30pm and 2-7pm; late Mar. to mid-May 9:30am-12:30pm and 2-6:30pm; early Nov. to late Mar. 9am-noon and 2-6pm.) **Master Change,** 18 rue Allard, offers **currency exchange** at the old port. (☎04 94 97 80 17. Open Mar.-June and Sept.-Oct. M-Sa 9am-8pm, Su 10am-noon and 5-8pm; July-Aug. 9am-10pm.) There's **Internet** as well as cocktails at La Girafe, 16 rue du Portail Neuf, 2min. from the tourist office. Six computers. (☎04 94 97 13 09. €2.50 for 15min., €0.12 per additional min., approx. €4 for 30min. Beer €2.50-6, cocktails €6-11. Open daily 10am-3am.) **Laverie du Port "Anne-Marie,"** 13 quai de l'Epi, charges €5.50 to wash clothes. Open M-Sa July-Aug. 7am-9pm, Sept.-June 9am-1pm and 3-7pm. The **police** (☎04 94 56 60 30) are on rue François Sibilli, near the church, and on av. Général Leclerc by the new port. The **hospital** (☎04 94 79 47 30) is on av. Foch, off pl. des Lices. There is a **post office** on pl. A. Celli between the new and old ports. (☎04 94 55 96 50. Open M-F 8:30am-noon and 2-5pm, open at 9:30am on the 2nd and 4th Th of every month; Sa 8:30am-noon.) **Postal code:** 83990.

🛏 ACOMMODATIONS

Hotels are scarce and expensive in St-Tropez; without a reservation made far in advance, it's difficult to get here and find available same-day accommodations. A stay in St-Raphaël or Hyères is easier on the wallet but forces visitors to limit their time here—though staying up all night in St-Tropez and heading out the next day may be an option. The closest **hostel** is in Fréjus. **Camping** is the best and cheapest option. Though no sites are within walking distance of the town, a frequent ferry connects the large campsite at Port Grimaud with the peninsula (see **Daytrips**). The campgrounds flanking St-Tropez's famous beaches are smaller and often full; book them months in advance for the summer months. Camping on the beach is actively prohibited.

One of the most budget-friendly, central hotels is **Lou Cagnard ❹,** 18 av. Paul Roussel, about a 3min. walk from pl. des Lices. 19 spacious, well-maintained rooms overlook the avenue or a peaceful garden in the back. White bedspreads and bright curtains leave rooms feeling airy and clean. All rooms have a shower and telephone. Charming breakfast room is decorated in bright reds and yellows. Reservations are essential. (☎04 94 97 04 24; fax 04 94 97 09 44. Breakfast €8. Closed early Nov. to late Dec. Reception 8am-9pm. Singles and doubles €43-54, with toilet €55-92. MC/V.) Another good option is **La Belle Isnarde ❹,** rte. de Tahiti, about a 20min. walk from the tourist office. From the pl. des Lices, take a right on av. du Maréchal Foch, a quick right onto rue de la Résistance, and a left onto av. de la Résistance, which becomes chemin des Belles Isnarde. From there, the hotel is 2min. up on the left. Though farther from town, this peaceful hotel boasts spacious pastel rooms and a pleasant garden. (☎04 94 97 13 64 and 04 94 97 57 74. Closed mid-Oct. to mid-Apr. Breakfast €6. Singles and doubles with shower €50-55, with shower and toilet €60-63. Cash only).

ON THE MENU

TARTE TROPÉZIENNE

One of the special delights of France is the *pâtisserie*, tempting passersby with endless little pastries. In St-Tropez, the most reputable local *pâtisserie*, **La Tarte Tropézienne**, offers an unparalleled pastry with a colorful history.

In 1955, while searching through his grandmother's recipe box, Alexandre Micka, local *pâtissier*, found a strange recipe for a soft pastry covered in sugar and filled with a cream. Micka began producing and perfecting this treat for a local audience.

Eventually, Micka was hired as a caterer for the cast of the French film *Et Dieu Crea La Femma*, starring Brigitte Bardot. Bardot loved the pastry and suggested that Micka call it *La Tarte de St-Tropez*. Thanks to her star power, Micka's *tarte* grew in popularity. In 1985 he sold his business to Albert Dufrène, sales manager of La Tarte Tropézienne, who marketed the *tarte* throughout France.

Today the nationwide production of the *tarte* requires 4000 eggs, 500kg of flour, and 500kg of milk each day, and two tons of butter and three tons of sugar each week. Despite this scale of production, the ingredients are still weighed in a ladle, the sugar still boiled in copper cauldrons, and the pastry still made by hand.

(36 rue Georges Clémenceau, just off pl. des Lices. ☎ 04 94 97 71 42. Open daily July-Aug. 6:30am-11pm; Sept.-June 8:30am-8pm.)

🏕 CAMPING

Campazur runs three campsites close to St-Tropez. Campers have it lucky at **Les Prairies de la Mer ❶**, Port Grimaud. The huge, extremely social site is near a beach and the canals of Port Grimaud, "France's Venice." Amenities include hot showers, tennis, and water sports. (☎ 04 94 79 09 09; fax 04 94 79 09 10; www.campazur.com. Open early Apr. to early Oct. Early Apr. to early July 2 people, tent, and car €20-27, extra person €5, electricity €5; early July to late Aug. €35, extra person €10, electricity included; late Aug. to early Oct. €17-25, extra person €5, electricity €5. Laundry available.) The MMJ ferry leaves the *capitainerie* three minutes away for St-Tropez once per hr. (☎ 04 94 96 51 00; €9 round-trip.) The smaller **Kon Tiki ❶** has a choice location near the northern stretch of Pampelonne beach. Campers can soak up sun by day and the beach's wild nightlife (including Kon Tiki's own bar) by night. (☎ 04 94 55 96 96; fax 04 94 55 96 95; kontiki@campazur.com. Same dates and prices as above.) Next door is **Toison d'Or ❶**, the smallest of the three sites. (☎ 04 94 79 83 54; fax 04 94 79 85 70; toison@campazur.com. Same dates and prices as above.) The complex boasts a supermarket, laundromat, tennis, ping-pong, and a scuba diving instruction center. In July and August, Sodetrav sends a bus from the St-Tropez station to both sites daily. (11:35am, 2:10, 4, 5:40pm; €1.60.) Otherwise, take the free municipal shuttle (M-Sa 4 per day) from pl. des Lices to Capon-Pinet and walk along the beach until reaching the site. (30-40min.)

🍴 FOOD

St-Tropez's vibrant restaurant and café scene lies along the old port and the narrow streets behind the waterfront. Of course, like everything else, eating is a glamorous and costly affair. Budget travelers will do best to forgo the swanky restaurants and grab paninis from the snack shops. For fruits and vegetables, try the fabulous **grand marché** on **place des Lices** (Tu and Sa 7:30am-1pm), or the **morning market** on **place aux Herbes,** behind the tourist office. There's a **Monoprix** supermarket, 9 av. Général Leclerc (☎ 04 94 97 07 94; open daily July-Aug. 8am-10pm; Sept.-June 8am-7:50pm) and a **SPAR** market, 16 bd. Vasserot, on pl. des Lices. (☎ 04 94 97 02 20. Open Apr.-Sept. M-Sa 7:30am-7:30pm, Su 8am-1pm and 4-7:30pm; Oct.-Mar. M-Sa 7:30am-1pm and 3:30-7:30pm, Su 8am-1pm and 4-7:30pm.) **La Tarte Tropézienne ❷**, pl. des Lices, is a *boulangerie* and *pâtisserie* with simple but excellent cuisine, including their famed, eponymous pastry. (See **On the Menu,** p. 592). Candlelit tables on the winding cobblestone roads behind the waterfront will seduce any visitor to St-Tropez. One won't regret splurging at **l'Aventure ❸,** 21 rue du Portail Neuf, a small local favorite that specializes in traditional regional cuisine and serves creative and exquisitely presented *plats du jour* for €10. (☎04 94 97 44 01. Open July-Aug. daily noon-2pm and 7-11pm. Closed W Sept.-June.) For a slice of Americana, head to **Basilic Burger ❷,** pl. des Remparts, where fresh salads and juicy hamburgers (€6.90-7.60) are served amid American pop music and Coca-Cola memorabilia. Paninis and sandwiches (€4.70-6.70, take-out €3.50-5.30) also available. (☎04 94 97 29 09. Open daily July-Aug. 9:30am-11pm; Sept.-June 9:30am-7pm. V.) The popular **Délice des Lices ❶,** pl. des Lices, is *the* place to go for a late-night snack. Hot and cold sandwiches (€3.10-4.60) and a wide selection of condiments not often found at sandwich stands. (☎04 94 54 89 84. Open 24hr.)

🗿 SIGHTS

Most travelers don't come to St-Tropez for the museum scene. Nevertheless, **Le Musée de l'Annonciade,** pl. Grammont, right on the port, is a good break from all that sun-worshipping. This lovely converted chapel houses Fauvist and neo-Impressionist paintings by Signac, Bonnard, and Matisse, among others, and plentiful images of the Riviera and St-Tropez. (☎04 94 97 04 01. Open Su-M and W-Sa June-Sept. 10am-1pm and 4-9pm; Oct.-May 10am-1pm and 4-7pm. €5.50, students €3.50.) **The Citadel** above the port contains the **Musée Naval,** which follows St-Tropez's interesting military history through WWII. (☎04 94 97 59 43. Open daily Apr.-Sept. 10am-12:30pm and 1:30-6:30pm; Oct. and Dec.-Mar. 10am-12:30pm and 1:30-5:30pm. €4, students €2.50.)

🏖 BEACHES

St-Tropez's pride and joy is its white, sandy, endless coastline. Unfortunately, the beaches are rather inaccessible without a car. There is a *navette* municipal shuttle that leaves from pl. des Lices (schedule varies seasonally, ask the tourist office for current timetable). It heads to **Les Salins** (M-Sa 6 per day, last return shuttle leaves around 6:10pm; €1), a rather secluded sunspot, and to **Capon Pinet** (M-Sa 4 per day, last return shuttle leaves around 5:20pm; €1), the first stretch of the famous Pampelonne beachline. Walking south along the beach, exclusive beach clubs alternate with public sand. Some of the most popular beaches among the young jet-set crowd are **plage Tahiti** and **Key West Beach.** Be warned that lounge chairs in these clubs will cost €14 per day; one is better off simply walking along the coast to find a desirable spot to stretch out.

A quieter option is to take the *navette* to Les Salins and explore the beaches to the left, or follow the beautiful, rocky **sentier littoral** along the coast to the right until it melds with the Pampelonne beachline, passing a handful of unpopulated swimming spots and celebrity villas on the way. (1hr.) Sunbathers who miss the shuttle back to town can take a taxi from Pampelonne Beach to the port, but it will cost €20-30. Fifteen kilometers along the peninsula, great swimming and good rock climbing await at the intimate **plage de L'Escalet,** but it's unfortunately only accessible by foot or private car.

For those without the time or inclination to head to Pampelonne or Cap des Salins, there's a decent spot 10min. from the old port. Facing the port, head to the citadel and find chemin des Graniers, which curves around the citadel and the water to the small, uncrowded **plage des Graniers.** Most spots allow or expect nude sunbathing—in St-Tropez, only the tourists have tan lines.

CÔTE D'AZUR

🎵 🎭 ENTERTAINMENT & NIGHTLIFE

At the height of St-Tropez's excess and exclusivity is its wild nightlife. One night-time locus is the beachfront, which is not so convenient for travelers without cars or coastal villas of their own. Those without transportation have many options within town itself: when the sun sets, the port and the streets behind the water-front become a playground for the tanned and the glam. **Les Caves du Roy,** in Hotel Byblos on av. Paul Signac, nabs the title of the most elite club. Slip on Gucci sun-glasses and try a €23 vodka and tonic or the €20,000 Methusalem Cristal Roederer White while hobnobbing with celebrities. (☎04 94 56 68 00; www.lescavesdu-roy.com. Open July-Aug. daily 11:30pm-4am; June and Sept. F-Sa 11:30am-4am.) Asian-influenced restaurant/bar **Bodega de Papagayo** (☎04 94 97 76 70), on the old port, and its accompanying nightclub **Le Papagayo** (☎04 94 97 20 01), attract mon-eyed youth and soccer stars. (Open June-Sept. daily 8:30pm-4am, club gets crowded after 1am; Oct.-May M-Tu and Th-Su, hours according to how good the party is. Cocktails €13. Club cover €25, includes first drink. No cover if you "look good.") **VIP Room,** Résidence du Port, is in the vein of Caves and Papagayo. The dance floor is crowded as the young and rich let loose to hip hop and house. (☎04 94 97 14 70. Open daily 8pm-5am. No cover.) A pleasant place to have a quiet drink away from the tourist crowds is local favorite **Le Loft,** 9 rue des Remparts. The small, candlelit space is decorated with exposed wood, wrought iron, warmly col-ored cushions, and plush chairs. Try the Loft (€10), a vodka-based cocktail filled with freshly cut kiwi. (☎04 94 97 60 50. Open daily 10pm-3am.) A down-to-earth anglo crowd frequents **Kelly's Irish Pub,** a pretension-free joint toward the end of the old port. Even the fashion-challenged are allowed to order a beer (€3) and lis-ten to the live music here. (☎04 94 54 89 11. Open daily 10:30am-3am.) The epitome of sedentary style (i.e. no dancing) is the **Café de Paris,** a gold, velvet, and crystal-chandeliered café with an enormous patio in the center of the port. At night, house music and funky green-and-blue lighting transform the slightly stuffy restaurant into a mellow bar. (☎04 94 97 00 56; www.cafedeparis.fr. Beer and wine €4.50-8.50. Cocktails €11-13. Open daily 7am-3am.) **Le Pigeonnier,** 13 rue de la Ponche, is a less elite nightclub that caters to both gays and straights. (☎04 94 97 84 26. Open daily 11:30pm-5am. No cover. Cocktails €13.)

🎉 FESTIVALS

St-Tropez celebrates its historic ties to the idle rich with a yearly string of golf tournaments and yacht regattas. Every May 16-18, during **Les Bravades,** locals pay homage to their military past and patron saint with costumed parades. June 29 brings **St-Peter's Day** and a torch-lit procession honoring the saint of fishermen.

🗺 DAYTRIPS FROM ST-TROPEZ

GRIMAUD

> **Sodetrav** (☎04 94 97 88 51) sends **buses** from St-Tropez (30min., M-Sa 7 per day, €3.30). Or take the **ferry** to Port Grimaud (20min., every hr.), and catch the **Petit Train** at the top of the Prairies de la Mer campsite (every hr.).

Less ritzy than the city but more endearing, the inland villages of the St-Tropez peninsula make excellent daytrips. With their picture-perfect hilltop settings and memorable views, these secret gems are quickly becoming highly prized real estate. Tour groups have started to discover them, so come quickly, before the bottled water prices double.

The best of the peninsula is delightful **Grimaud**. Until the 17th century the castle of Grimaud, set high on a hill, controlled the Gulf of St-Tropez, which was in fact known as the "Gulf of Grimaud" until the end of the 19th century. From the castle, one can look down upon the medieval village itself, nestled into the deep green countryside. This dream-like setting doesn't dissipate within the village itself. Few can resist the charm of Grimaud's narrow cobblestone lanes, fountain-filled *places*, and stone houses covered in bright pink *bougainvillea*. The narrow streets by **pl. Neuve** are home to boutiques and some expensive restaurants. Above pl. Neuve, signs point to the simple, Romanesque **Eglise St-Michel,** one of three chapels in Grimaud. (Open daily 9am-6pm.)

For non-campers Grimaud has to be a daytrip; it has no budget hotels. The **tourist office** is at 1 bd. des Aliziers, a few doors down from the museum. (☎04 94 43 26 98; fax 04 94 43 32 40; www.grimaud-provence.com. Open July-Aug. M-Sa 9am-12:30pm and 3-7pm, Su 10am-1pm; Apr.-May, June, and Sept. M-Sa 9am-12:30pm and 2:30-6:15pm; Oct.-Mar. M-Sa 9am-12:30pm and 2:15-5:30pm.)

ILES D'HYÈRES

*Ferries to the island depart from the town of Hyères, to the east of Toulon. **Trains** run from Toulon (2 per day, €5.10) and Marseille (2 per day, €13.10). Sodetrav **buses** (☎04 94 12 55 00) run to Toulon (1hr., every 15min., €5.70) and St-Tropez (1½-2hr., 8 per day, €13), while Phocéens-Cars (☎04 93 85 66 61) go to Cannes (1½hr., 2 per day, €22) and Nice (2hr., 2 per day, €22). To get to the ferry ports, catch Sodetrav local bus #67 to Port La Gavine (€2.10) or La Tour Fondue (€2.80).*

These exotic, underpopulated islands lie off the coast between St-Tropez and the grimy metropolis of Toulon. Nicknamed the "Iles d'Or" or "Golden Islands" by Henry II, the islands draw tourists for three main reasons: nature, *natation* (swimming), and, of course, nudity.

TLV Ferries (☎04 94 58 95 14; www.tlv-tvm.com) run to Porquerolles from Tour Fondue (20min.; July-Aug. every 30min. 9am-12:30pm and every hr. 2:30-6:30pm; Sept.-June 6-16 per day; round-trip €14.30, bikes €12.) Ferries (☎04 94 57 44 07) also run to Port-Cros (1hr.) and Ile du Levant (1½ hr.) from Port D'Hyères (July-Aug. 4 per day, Sept.-June 2 per day; round-trip €21). In July and August, a **boat** from Hyères connects Port-Cros with Ile du Levant (round-trip €24). For those wishing to see both islands in the low season, Le Lavandou **shuttles** between the two, but be prepared for a hostile reception when you admit another company got you to the mainland. (☎04 94 71 01 02. Boats depart Port-Cros for Le Levant at 10:15am, 12:15, 5:15pm, though schedule varies. One-way €6.70.)

The largest of the three islands and the one most easily accessed from the coast, **Porquerolles** (pop. 342) has the most colorful history. It was home to a religious order until François I, in a stroke of genius, granted it as an asylum to convicts who won pardon in exchange for their promise to defend the mainland against pirates. The criminals promptly transformed the island into a base for their own piratical activities. A century later, Louis XIV put a violent stop to their raiding. Today, mainlanders and tourists seek respite from the hectic Riviera in the island's rugged cliffs and small, hidden coves. On Porquerolles, the Hyères **tourist office,** 3 av. Ambroise Thomas, below the Casino, supplies free maps and ferry schedules. (☎04 94 01 84 50; www.ot-hyeres.fr. Open July-Aug. M-Sa 8:30am-7:30pm, Su 3:30-7:30pm; Sept.-June M-F 9am-6pm, Sa 10am-4pm.)

Like its neighbor, the **Ile du Levant** was originally settled by monks. Its former inhabitants would be shocked if they could see it today, a haven for asceticism in one regard only: clothing. Home to **Héliopolis,** Europe's oldest nudist colony, islanders go *au naturel* on the beaches and wear the legal minimum (not much) in the port and village. The clothing-inclined can head for the narrow, winding hiking trails within the **Domaine des Arbousiers,** a substantial natural reserve, instead. The Héliopolis map includes seven trails. Walk straight uphill from the port to reach what passes for a town square, with restaurants, hotels, and a nightclub. (15min.) To spend the night on the island, try **Hôtel La Source ❺,** about 5min. from the port. The garden setting is calm and peaceful, with the exception of the chirping *cigales.* Simple rooms get the job done. (☎ 04 94 05 91 36; fax 04 94 05 93 47. Breakfast €6. Open Mar.-Oct. Reception daily 8am-midnight. Singles €58; doubles €65. Extra bed €16. MC/V). For camping, try **Colombero ❶,** just 2min. from the port. (☎ 04 94 05 90 29. €7 per person. No electricity.)

The smallest and most rugged of the three islands, **Port-Cros** is a stunning national park that offers hours of fun for hikers. Its mountainous terrain is home to 114 species of migratory birds, 602 indigenous plants, and 48 non-indigenous human beings. The well-trodden **sentier des plantes** (plant trail) passes by several forts and the beautiful but crowded **plage de la Palud.** To find a more solitary swimming hole, continue on the **sentier de Port Man,** reached by a 4hr. hike that circles the north end of the island and penetrates its wild, unpopulated interior. A national park info booth on the port provides maps of the island (€1.50) and suggests activities. (☎ 04 94 01 40 70. Open July-Aug. daily 9:15am-12:45pm and 3:15-5:40pm; Sept.-June whenever boats arrive and depart.) **Scuba dive** in the clear water off Port-Cros to view the area's many wrecks and search for the 40lb. brown *mérou,* a massive grouper once thought to be extinct. Sun Plongée, beside the Sun Bistro, runs **open-water dives.** (☎ 04 94 05 90 16; www.sun-plongee.com. With equipment €37, without equipment €28. Beginners €10 extra.)

The **Hôtel du Portalet ❷,** 4 rue de Limans, has tasteful rooms and can be used as an island-hopping base. The friendly owners who are experts on the town supply TVs, high ceilings, and firm beds in a nice area of town. (☎ 04 94 65 39 40; fax 04 94 35 86 33; chbenit@oreka.com. Breakfast €5.50. Free luggage storage. Reception 8am-10:30pm. Reserve ahead in high season. Singles €26-28, with shower and toilet €30-39, with bath €37-41; doubles €32-44, with bath €42-56. AmEx/MC/V.)

A **Casino** supermarket is on av. Gambetta, across from the McDonald's. (Open Tu-Sa 7:30am-12:30pm and 4-7:30pm, Su 8am-noon.) For a sit-down meal, try **La Brasserie ❸,** 2 rue Léon Gautier, within La Coupole. The large outdoor terrace, good variety, and excellent service are matched by reasonable prices. (☎ 04 94 12 88 00. Salads €4.50-8, pastas €8, fish €11.50-16.50, meat €11-14.50, and *coquillages,* or seashells—a local speciality. Lunch *menu* €10.50, dinner *menu* €13. Open Su-Th noon-10pm, F-Sa noon-11pm. MC/V.)

CÔTE D'AZUR

LANGUEDOC-ROUSSILLON

Occitania, independent of both France and Spain, once stretched from the Rhône valley to the foothills of the Pyrénées. Its people spoke the *langue d'oc*, a Romance language whose name comes from their word for "yes." In the mid-12th century, Occitanians adopted the heretical Cathar brand of Christianity, which triggered the Church's Albigensian Crusade (named for the Cathar stronghold of Albi) against the so-called heretics; the slaughter that followed resulted in Occitania's political and linguistic integration into France.

Roussillon, in the far southwest corner of France, was historically part of Catalunya, not France, and **Perpignan** (p. 620) was the capital of the Kings of Majorca. Today, Roussillon's locals identify with Barcelona more than with Paris. Many speak Catalan, a relative of the *langue d'oc*, which sounds like a hybrid of French and Spanish. Perfectly situated between the sandy coasts of the Mediterranean and the gorgeous peaks of the Pyrénées, the region attracts an interesting mix of sunbathers and backpackers. Tiny fortified **Villefranche-de-Conflent** (p. 616) and **Foix** (p. 614) serve as a perfect hiking bases into the mountains. The latter also attracts visitors with its impregnable castle, navigable underground river, and prehistoric caves. Perpignan provides an economical base for visits to the beautiful towns of **Collioure** (p. 618) and **Canet-Plage** (p. 624) on the coast of the Mediterranean. Farther north, the medieval ramparts of **Carcassonne** (p. 609) and the lovely one-street town of **Cordes-sur-Ciel** (p. 608) look like they come straight from the pages of a fairy tale. Adding to this mix are the remarkable pink buildings of **Toulouse** (p. 597), the lively theater and gay scene of college town **Montpellier** (p. 630), and heavily Italian **Sète** (p. 638), France's largest Mediterranean fishing port. Visitors also seek out the excellent museums of **Castres** (p. 604), **Béziers** (p. 636), and **Albi** (p. 605), which also has a colossal red-brick cathedral.

A popular regional dish in the Languedoc is *cassoulet*, a hearty stew of white beans and meat. The area is also known for its peaches and cherries.

TOULOUSE

Sassy, headstrong Toulouse (pop. 350,000) is known as *la ville en rose* (the city in pink)—the place to come when all French towns begin to look alike. The city's magnificent buildings, from the stately homes of 16th-century pastel merchants to the striped Capitole, are built of local rose-colored bricks. Many of them are trimmed with white marble, giving Toulouse a grandeur befitting France's 4th-largest city. Politically, Toulouse has always been a free-thinking place. Its powerful counts made life miserable for French kings in the Middle Ages, and it wasn't until the Revolution that France finally got a firm grip on the *capitouls* (town councillors) of its unique 12th-century government. Still pushing the frontiers of knowledge, this university town, where Thomas Aquinas made Aristotle palatable to medieval theologians, now serves as the capital of France's aerospace industry. During the school year, 100,000 students flood the pizzerias of rue du Taur, the city's countless museums, and the quais of the Garonne.

Languedoc-Roussillon

■ TRANSPORTATION

Flights: Aéroport Blagnac (☎05 61 42 44 00). **Air France** (☎08 02 80 28 02) flies to **London** (2 per day, round-trip from €210) and **Paris** (25 per day, round-trip from €115). **Navettes Aérocar** (☎05 34 60 64 00; www.navettevia-toulouse.com) serves the airport from the bus station and allée Jean Jaurès (30min.; every 20min.; €3.70, under 25 €2.90).

Trains: Gare Matabiau, 64 bd. Pierre Sémard. To: **Bordeaux** (2-3hr., 14 per day, €27.70); **Lyon** (6½hr., 3-4 per day, €48); **Marseille** (4½hr., 8 per day, €38.50); **Paris** (8-9hr., 4 per day, €74.50); **Perpignan** (2½hr., 6 per day, €25); **Carcassonne** (24 per day, €13.20). Ticket office open M-Sa 9am-7:30pm.

Buses: Gare Routière, 68-70 bd. Pierre Sémard (☎05 61 61 67 67), next to the train station. Open M-Sa 7am-7pm, Su 8am-7pm. To: **Albi** (1½hr., 4 per day, €11.20); **Carcassonne** (2¼hr., 3 per day, €10.60); **Foix** (2hr., 1 per day, €8.90); **Montauban** (70min., 4 per day, €6.50). Buy tickets on the bus. **Eurolines** (☎05 61 26 40 04; www.eurolines.fr) with an office in the station, runs buses to most major cities in Europe. Open M-F 9:30am-6:30pm, Sa 9:30am-5pm. To: **Berlin** (3¼hr., F and Su 1 per day, €184); **Brussels** (21hr.; Tu-W, F, and Su 2 per day; €115); **London** (20hr.; Tu-W, F, and Su 1 per day; €135); **Barcelona** (6hr., M-Sa 1-2 per day, €45-58); **Casablanca** (32hr., W and Sa 1 per day, €210); **Amsterdam** (20½hr., Tu-W and F-Su 1 per day, €133); **Prague** (24hr.; W, F, and Su 1 per day; €146).

Metro: SEMVAT, 49 rue de Gironis (☎05 61 41 70 70 or 05 62 11 26 11). Buy tickets just inside the station (€1.20 per ticket). Maps at ticket booths and tourist office. Open daily 8am-midnight.

Taxis: Taxi Bleu (☎05 61 80 36 36). Between the train and bus station. €16-20 to the airport. 24hr.

✈ 🛈 ORIENTATION & PRACTICAL INFORMATION

While residential Toulouse sprawls ever outward along both sides of the Garonne, tourist Toulouse, along with the thriving student quarter, are within a small section east of the river, bounded by rue de Metz in the south and by bd. Strasbourg and bd. Carnot to the north and east. The metro is useful for reaching your hotel from the train station, but after you've dropped off your pack, there should be no need to venture underground again. Even the walk from the train station to the main part of town takes only about 15min. The center is the huge stone plaza known as the **Capitole.**

Tourist Office: Donjon du Capitole, on rue Lafayette at pl. Charles de Gaulle (☎05 61 11 02 22; www.ot.toulouse.fr), in the park behind the Capitole. From the station, take the metro to Capitole or turn left along the canal and then right onto allée Jean Jaurès. Walk two-thirds of the way around pl. Wilson (bearing right), then take a right onto rue Lafayette. The office is in a small park on the left of the intersection with rue d'Alsace-Lorraine. Free **accommodations** service. City **tours** in English (July-Sept. Sa at 3pm, €7.70; in French M-F 3 per day). Lists of hotels, restaurants, and cultural events. Office open June-Sept. M-Sa 9am-7pm, Su 10am-1pm and 2-6pm; Oct.-May M-F 9am-6pm, Sa 9am-12:30pm and 2-6:15pm, Su and holidays 10am-12:30pm and 2-5pm.

Budget Travel: OTU Voyage, 60 rue de Taur (☎05 61 12 54 54). Cheap fares for students. Open M-F 9am-6:30pm, Sa 10am-1pm and 2-5pm. **Nouvelles Frontières,** 2 pl. St-Sernin (☎05 61 21 74 14, national 08 25 00 08 25). Open M-Sa 9am-7pm. MC/V.

Consulates: UK, 20 chemin de Laporte (☎05 61 15 02 02). Open M-Tu and Th-F 10am-noon and 2-5pm. **US,** 25 allées Jean Jaurès (☎05 34 41 36 50). Open by appointment only.

Currency Exchange: Banque de France, 4 rue Deville (☎05 61 61 35 35). No commission, good rates. Open M-F 9am-12:20pm and 1:20-3:30pm.

English Bookstore: The Bookshop, 17 rue Lakanal (☎05 61 22 99 92). Collection of novels, French history books, and travel guides. Open M-Sa 10am-7pm. MC/V.

Youth Center: CRIJ (Centre Regional d'Info Jeunesse), 17 rue de Metz (☎05 61 21 20 20). Info on travel, work, and study. Open mid-July to mid-Sept. M-Sa 10am-6pm; mid-Sept. to mid-July M-Sa 10am-1pm and 2-7pm.

Laundromat: Laverie St-Sernin, 14 rue Emile Cartailhac. Wash and dry €7. Open daily 7am-10pm.

Hospital: CHR de Rangueil, av. du Prof. Jean Poulhes (☎05 61 32 25 33).

Police: Commissariat Central, bd. Embouchure (☎05 61 12 77 77).

S.A.M.U. (Emergency Medical Aid): ☎05 61 49 33 33.

Night Pharmacy: 70-76 allées Jean Jaurès (☎05 61 62 38 05). Open daily 8pm-8am.

Internet: New House, 7 rue des 3 Renards, near St-Sernin (☎05 61 21 98 42). English keyboards. €3 per hr. Open M-Sa 10am-11pm, Su noon-6pm. **Adéclik,** 5 pl. St-Pierre (☎05 61 22 56 48). €2 per hr.

Post Office: 9 rue Lafayette (☎05 34 45 70 51). **Currency exchange** with good rates. Open M-F 8am-7pm and Sa 8am-noon. **Poste Restante:** 31049 Toulouse Cedex. **Postal code:** 31000.

ACCOMMODATIONS & CAMPING

Hotels line the blocks near the train station, but cheaper, more comfortable hotels can be found in the city center or on the outskirts of town. Toulouse's lack of a youth hostel is made up for by a host of welcoming, hostel-priced hotels.

Hôtel des Arts, 1bis rue Cantegril (☎05 61 23 36 21; fax 05 61 12 22 37). M: pl. Esquirol. Low prices and spacious rooms in a perfect location. Breakfast €4. Reception daily 7am-11pm. Singles €15-21, with shower €23-25; doubles €25/€26-28. Extra bed €5. MC/V. ❷

Hôtel du Grand Balcon, 8 rue Romiguières (☎05 61 21 48 08; fax 05 61 21 59 98), off pl. du Capitole. Worn 1920s luxury overlooking the bustle of the pl. du Capitole. The official hotel of the French airborne postal service, this hotel is classified as a historical monument by UNESCO; author of the beloved *Le Petit Prince* Antoine de St-Exupéry stayed in room #32 (€31). Breakfast €5. Reserve ahead. Singles and doubles €26, with shower €33, with bath €35.10; triples with bath €45; quads €35.10. ❸

Hôtel Beauséjour, 4 rue Caffarelli (☎/fax 05 61 62 77 59), just off allée Jean Jaurès, close to the station. Bright rooms with new beds at the lowest prices in Toulouse. Ask about tiny singles that usually go to long-term guests (€14). Breakfast €4. Shower €1. Reception daily until 11pm. Huge singles and doubles €20, with shower €23, with bath €25. Extra bed €8. AmEx/MC/V. ❷

Hôtel Anatole France, 46 pl. Anatole France (☎05 61 23 19 96; fax 05 61 21 47 66). In a calm *place* next to the student quarter. Bright, airy rooms. Breakfast €4.50. Singles and doubles €21, with shower €24, with TV and toilet €32. Extra bed €5. MC/V. ❷

Camping:

Pont de Rupé, 21 chemin du Pont de Rupé (☎05 61 70 07 35; fax 05 61 70 00 71), at av. des Etats-Unis (N20 north). Take bus #59 (dir: Camping) from pl. Jeanne d'Arc to Rupé. Restaurant, bar, and laundry. €9 per person, €8 with car, €3 per additional person. ❶

La Bouriette, 201 chemin de Tournefeuille (☎05 61 49 64 46), 5km outside Toulouse along N124 in St-Martin-du-Touch. Take bus #64 (dir: Colomiers) from metro stop Arène and ask for "St-Martin-du-Touch." Open year-round. €4 per person, €2.80-4 per site, car included. ❶

FOOD

Any budget traveler should head directly to the **rue du Taur** in the student quarter, where cheap eateries serve meals for €5.50-10. Lebanese, Chinese, and Mexican restaurants coexist on **rue des Filatiers** and **rue Paradoux.** On Wednesdays (6am-6pm), **place du Capitole** becomes an open-air department store and on Saturday mornings (6am-1pm) it hosts an **organic market.** Other markets are held at **place Victor Hugo, place des Carmes,** and **boulevard de Strasbourg.** (Open Tu-Su 6am-1pm.) There's a **Monoprix** supermarket at 39 rue Alsace-Lorraine (open M-Sa 8:30am-8:50pm) and a **Casino** near pl. Occitane at the Centre Commerciale St-Georges. (Open M-Sa 9am-7:30pm.) Students who want a good, hot meal at low rates (€2.40) should head to the **restaurants universitaires.** The nearest student cafeteria to town is the **Arsenal Restaurant Universitaire,** 2 bd. Armand Duportal, near rue du Taur (☎05 61 23 98 48). For info on the 13 other student cafeterias scattered around Toulouse, head to the **CROUS,** 58 rue du Taur. (☎05 61 12 54 00. Open M-F 8:30am-5:30pm; cafeterias open 11:30am-1:30pm and 6:30-8pm. ISIC required.) The *brasseries* that crowd busy pl. Wilson offer €8.50-15 *menus.*

Le Grand Rideau, 75 rue du Taur (☎05 61 23 90 19), is a cross between a small restaurant, art gallery, and theater, serving regional food in a three-course lunch (€8.90) and a generous evening *menu* (€14). In keeping with the theme, dishes have names like "Shakespeare" and "Molière." Some concerts are planned, but impromptu performances spring up all the time. Animation Th-F nights. Open M noon-2pm, Tu-F noon-2pm and 7pm-midnight. ❸

Jour de Fête, 43 rue du Taur (☎05 61 23 36 48), is right down the street from Le Grand Rideau. This relaxed *brasserie* with brick walls and old posters serves a large *plat du jour* for €6.50 and a salad for €4.50. Open daily noon-midnight. ❷

La Faim des Haricots, rue du Puits Vert (☎05 61 22 49 25), between pl. Capitole and the student quarter, is a vegetarian's haven. Simple veggie-heavy menu with salad bar, omelettes, and pastas. *Menus* €8-15. Open Th-Sa noon-3pm and 7:30-10pm. ❸

🖸 SIGHTS

Toulouse is famous for the red-brick **stone mansions** of the town's wealthy 15th- and 16th-century dye merchants, which can be seen on the tourist office's 2hr. **tour.** (In French. July-Sept. M-Sa 10am. €7.70.) From local artists to canonized painters, the diversity of Toulouse's art makes for a nice afternoon of museum-hopping. Most museums are free to students. Multi-sight passes are sold at all museums: €3 gives entry to any three museums, €4.50 to six.

LE CAPITOLE. The city's most prominent monument is this mammoth brick palace and the huge stone plaza in front, which is ideal for people-watching. The building was once home to the bourgeois *capitouls*, who unofficially ruled the city (technically controlled by counts) for many years. All people in Toulouse who marry must pass through the **Salle des Illustres,** beside the Mairie. **La Salle Henri Martin,** next door, includes 10 post-Impressionist *tableaux* by Henri Martin, representing Toulouse in all four seasons. *(Salles open M-F 8:30am-noon and 1:30-7pm, Sa and Su 10am-noon and 2-6pm. Free.)*

BASILIQUE ST-SERNIN. St-Sernin is the longest Romanesque structure in the world, but its most visible feature is an enormous brick steeple that rises skyward in five ever-narrowing double-arched terraces like a massive wedding cake. **St-Dominic,** head of the Dominican order of friars, made the church his base in the early 13th century, though he departed a bit from the ascetic monastic traditions. Behind the left side of the ornate **altar** in the back of the church, the **crypt** conceals a treasure trove of holy relics, from engraved silver chests to golden goblets, some from the time of Charlemagne. *(☎05 61 21 70 18. Church open July-Sept. M-Sa 8:30am-6:15pm, Su 8:30am-7:30pm; Oct.-June M-Sa 8:30-11:45am and 2-5:45pm, Su 8:30am-12:30pm and 2-7:30pm. Tours in French July-Aug. 2 per day. €5.50. Crypt open July-Sept. M-Sa 10am-6pm, Su 11:30am-6pm; Oct.-June M-Sa 10-11:30am and 2:30-5pm, Su 2:30-5pm. €2.)*

RÉFECTOIRE DES JACOBINS & CHURCH. This 13th-century southern Gothic church is the final resting place of St. Thomas Aquinas. His ashes take center stage in an elevated, under-lit tomb. *(Rue Lakanal. Open daily 9am-7pm. Weekly summer piano concert €16-28, students €9. Tickets at tourist office. Cloister €2.20.)* The Réfectoire des Jacobins presents regular exhibitions of archeological artifacts and modern art. *(69 rue Pargaminières. ☎05 61 22 21 92. Open daily 10am-7pm during expositions; otherwise, same hours as church. €5.)*

MUSEUMS. The huge **Musée des Augustins** displays an unsurpassed assemblage of Romanesque and Gothic sculptures, including fifteen snickering gargoyles, in a gorgeous redone Augustine monastery. *(21 rue de Metz, off rue des Arts. ☎05 61 22 21 82. Free organ concert W 8:30pm. Open Su-M and W-Sa 10am-6pm, W until 9pm. €2.20, students free.)* The striking **Hôtel d'Assezat** hosts the Fondation Bemberg, which displays 28 Bonnards, a modest collection of Dufys, Pissarros, and Gauguins, as well as the odd Picasso, Renoir, and Matisse. *(Pl. d'Assézat. ☎05 61 12 06 89. Fondation*

☎ *05 61 12 06 89. Open Tu and F-Su 10am-12:30pm and 1:30-6pm, Th 10am-12:30pm and 1:30-9pm. Groups €2.75.)* The **Musée St-Raymond** holds a decent collection of archeological finds. Especially fascinating is a hall lined by the ominous sculptures of hundreds of Roman emperors. *(Pl. St-Sernin.* ☎ *05 61 22 31 44. Open daily June-Aug. 10am-7pm; Sept.-May 10am-6pm. English text guide available. €2.20, students free.)* **Les Abbatoirs** is a vast space dedicated to cutting-edge, constantly revolving exhibits of contemporary art, reached by walking across either the St-Pierre or Pont Neuf bridges. *(76 allées Charles-de-Fitte.* ☎ *05 62 48 58 00. Open Tu-Su noon-8pm. €6.10, students €3.10.)*

CITÉ DE L'ESPACE. Opened in 1997, the fantastic **Cité de l'Espace** park is devoted to Toulouse's space program, complete with interactive games, a planetarium, and the Mir space station. Avoid crowds in summer by arriving before noon. *(Take A612 exit 17 to Parc de la Plaine, av. Jean Gonord, or bus #19 (dir: pl. de l'Indépandance), and follow the signs. M-F the bus does not stop at the park; get off the bus at Ivoire, walk down the main street, and turn right at the roundabout.* ☎ *05 62 71 64 80. Open July-Aug., Feb., and Apr. daily 9am-7pm; Sept.-Jan. Tu-F 9am-6pm, Sa-Su 9am-7pm; Mar. and May-June M-F 9am-6pm, Sa-Su 9am-7pm. Closed 2nd week of Jan. English audio guide available. €12, students €10, ages 6-12 €9. Tickets to planetarium included.)*

🎵 🎭 ENTERTAINMENT & FESTIVALS

Toulouse has something to please almost any nocturnal whim, although the city is liveliest from October to May, when the students come out in full force. The numerous cafés, *glaciers*, and pizzerias flanking **place St-Georges** and **place du Capitole** are open late, as are the bars off **rue St-Rome** and **rue des Filatiers.** Locals like to café-hop, drinking *kir* and beer all afternoon, take a break for dinner, and then hit the bars and clubs hard at night. During the school year, students head to **place St-Pierre** to watch rugby in one of the small bars while drinking *pastis.* From September to June, the weekly *Flash* keeps up on the latest in restaurants, bars, and clubs (€1 at *tabacs*). The July-August issue *Flash Eté* is a big festival listing. CD and book megalith **FNAC,** at the intersection of bd. Strasbourg and bd. Carnot, has cultural pamphlets, club advertisements, and tickets to large concerts. (☎ 05 61 11 01 01. Open M-Sa 9:30am-7:30pm.)

■**Au Père Louis,** 45 rue des Tourneurs, is always packed by well-dressed crowds who drink the regional wines by the glass (€2.30)—and bottle (€10). The *maison* (with a lunchtime restaurant) has been around since 1889. (☎ 05 61 21 33 45. Open M-Sa 8:30am-3pm and 5-10pm.) **Café Populaire,** 9 rue de la Colombette, is a hot and smoky destination for the financially strapped. Groups come here for the cheapest beer in Toulouse. A box of 13 bottles of beer costs €19, or a mere €13 on Mondays. (☎ 05 61 63 07 00. Happy hour 7:30-8:30pm: buy one *pastis*, get one free. Open M-F 9pm-2am, Sa 2pm-4am.) **La Ciguë,** 6 rue de la Colombette, just off bd. Lazare Carnot, is a friendly gay bar and a great place to ask about the discos *du jour.* Every night, a different DJ plays the same hard rock. (☎ 05 61 99 61 87. Beer €3. Open daily 6pm-2am. MC/V.) **Bodega-Bodega,** 1 rue Gabriel Péri, just off bd. Lazare Carnot, a wildly popular destination for young crowds, is a bar that turns into a club after the clock strikes twelve. It's hard to guard your money when the poker chips given as change make it easy to buy another drink. (☎ 05 61 63 03 63. Beer €2.50, margaritas €6, *tapas* €7 until midnight. €6 cover Th-Sa 10pm-2am. Open Su-F 7pm-2am, Sa 7pm-6am. MC/V.)

Cave Poésie, 71 rue du Taur (☎ 05 61 23 62 00), hosts plays and performances. The full moon is the catalyst for an "open door" night (starting 9pm) of comedians, poets, and musicians. Pick up their schedule outside the door or at the tourist office. **Cour de l'Ecole des Beaux Arts,** quai de la Daurade, stages classic plays with a modern twist. (☎ 05 61 23 25 49 or 05 61 23 25 45.)

Toulouse

■▲ ACCOMMODATIONS

Camping La Bouriette, **5**
Camping Pont de Rupé, **1**
Hôtel Anatole France, **6**
Hôtel des Arts, **13**
Hôtel Beauséjour, **4**
Hôtel du Grand Balcon, **7**

🍎 FOOD

La Faim des Haricots, **11**
Le Grand Rideau, **2**
Jour de Fête, **3**

★ NIGHTLIFE

Bodega-Bodega, **8**
Café Populaire, **10**
La Cigüé, **9**
Au Père Louis, **12**

Most of Toulouse's **movie theaters** are located in and around pl. Wilson. **UGC,** 9 allée du Président Roosevelt (☎05 62 30 28 30), plays mostly American new releases, some of them dubbed in French. Everything is shown in its original language at **Utopia Cinemas,** 23 rue Montardy (☎05 61 23 66 20), including artsy films from around the world.

From July to September, **Musique d'Eté** brings classical concerts, jazz, gospel, and ballet to a variety of outdoor settings, including the Jacobins courtyard and the Halle aux Grains. Tickets are sold at concert halls and the tourist office (€13). Traditional music and dance groups parade through the streets on the last Sunday in June for the festival known as the **Grand Fénétra.** (Info ☎05 61 49 18 36.) The **Festival International de Piano aux Jacobins** tickles Toulousian ivories every couple of days at 8:30pm during September at the Jacobins cloister. (Bureau du Festival ☎05 61 22 40 05; www.pianojacobins.com. Tickets available at the Bureau or the tourist office. €16-28, students €9.)

🔡 DAYTRIPS FROM TOULOUSE

CASTRES

The **train station,** av. Albert I (open M-F 6:30am-6pm, Sa-Su 6:30am-7pm), has service to Toulouse (1hr., 9 per day, €12.10). Though trains from Albi do eventually arrive in Castres, **buses** are cheaper and more direct. They run from the **bus station,** pl. Soult (☎05 63 35 37 31), to Albi (45-55min., 8 per day, €6) and Toulouse (1½hr., 7 per day, €10).

When Castres (pop. 48,000) acquired the 11th-century bones of St-Vincent, the city became an essential pilgrimage stop for those en route to Santiago de Compostela. This prominence ended when his basilica was destroyed during the Wars of Religion. The city compensated by constructing two museums, each worth their own brief pilgrimages—the **Musée Goya** and the **Musée Jaurès.**

In front of the shrubs of the perfectly-groomed **Jardin de l'Evêché,** the **Musée Goya** houses the world's second-largest collection of Spanish painting, along with works by Catalan and Aragonese masters. The paintings inside the ancient Episcopal palace are centered around four series of Goya's sardonic engravings on subjects as diverse as the horrors of war and the humor of daily life. (☎05 63 71 59 27. Open July-Aug. M-Sa 10am-6pm, Su 10am-noon and 2-6pm; Sept.-June Tu-Sa 9am-noon and 2-5pm, Su 10am-noon and 2-5pm. €3, students €1.50, under 18 free.)

While art lovers enjoy the Goya museum, the **Centre National et Musée Jean Jaurès,** 2 pl. Pélisson, caters to those interested in France's social history—or those just curious about why every single town in the country seems to have an avenue Jean Jaurès. A brilliant scholar and professor of philosophy, prominent socialist Jaurès led the striking glass-workers of Carmaux in 1896 and vehemently supported Alfred Dreyfus, a Jewish officer framed as a traitor by the army, before Jaurès's assassination in 1914. The modern, sleek building is packed with political cartoons, photographs, and newspaper articles that recount the spirited life and rhetoric of the man himself. (☎05 63 72 01 01. Open July-Aug. daily 9am-noon and 2-6pm; Apr.-June and Sept. Tu-Su 9am-noon and 2-6pm; Oct.-Mar. Tu-Su 9am-noon and 2-5pm. €1.50, students €0.80.) The **Centre d'Art Contemporain,** 35 rue Chambre de l'Edit, is a space for temporary exhibits of current artists. (Open July-Aug. daily 10am-noon and 2-6pm; Sept.-June W-F 10am-noon and 2-5:30pm, Sa-M 3-6pm. €1.80, students €1.) The Musée Goya and Musée Jaurès both sell a €3.80 ticket for adults that allows admission to all three of Castres's museums.

For two weeks in mid-July, the **Festival de Dance** celebrates international Hispanic culture with concerts, exhibitions, flamenco, and ballet performances. Many events are free; tickets to others are available at the tourist office or by calling the **Théâtre Municipale.** (☎05 63 71 56 57. Open M-F 10:30am-12:30pm and 3-6:30pm.)

When hunger strikes, try the **markets** on **place Jean Jaurès** (Tu and Th-Sa 7:30am-1pm) and **place de l'Albinque.** (Tu-Su 8:30am-1pm.) **Monoprix** is on rue Sabatier at pl. Jean Jaurès. (Open M-Sa 8:30am-7:30pm.) There are a few bakeries on **rue Gambetta** and **rue Victor Hugo** in the town center, while restaurants surround the **Pont Vieux, place Jean Jaurès,** and **rue Villegoudou.** For a sit-down meal, try **La Mandragore ❸,** behind pl. Jean Jaurès on rue Malpas. The restaurant serves regional French cuisine with an extra touch of herbs—try the *crème brulée* perfumed with lavender. (☎05 63 59 51 27. Three-course *menu* with wine €12. Open Tu-Sa noon-2pm and 7:30-10pm.) Traditional *Nougatines Castraises* (€9 for 200g) is the specialty of **Cormary ❶,** 13 rue Victor Hugo, which also sculpts fine chocolates, marzipan, and pastries into animal shapes. (☎05 63 59 27 09. Open M-F 6am-1pm and 1:30-7:30pm, Sa 6am-5:30pm, Su 6am-1pm. MC/V.)

To get to the **tourist office,** 3 rue Milhau Ducommun, from the train station, turn left onto av. Albert I and then bear right onto bd. Henri Sizaire. At pl. Alsace-Lorraine, continue straight over the bridge, ignoring signs for the *centre ville* (follow-

LANGUEDOC

ing signs and bearing left will take you right to the Musée Goya). Turn left onto bd. Raymond Vittoz, then turn left onto rue Villegoudou and veer right onto rue Leris. It's on the right at the very end of the street by the river. (20min.) Across the river is pl. Jean Jaurès. From the bus station, walk across pl. Soult and continue straight on rue Villegoudou, then see the directions from the train station above. (☎05 63 71 37 00 or 05 63 62 63 62; www.ville-castres.fr. Open July-Aug. M-Sa 9am-12:30pm and 1:30-6:30pm, Su 10:30am-noon and 2:30-5pm; Sept.-June M-Sa 9:30am-12:30pm and 2-6pm, Su 2:30-4:30pm.)

MONTAUBAN

Montauban is accessible from Toulouse by train (25min., every hr., €7.60; info office open M-F 7am-7:30pm, Sa 9am-7:30pm) and by bus (☎05 63 22 55 00; 1hr., 4 per day, €6.30). Local buses are run by Transports Montalbanais, bd. Midi-Pyrénées (☎05 63 63 52 52; €0.90, carnet of 10 €7; runs 6:30am-8pm). Catch taxis at the train station or call ☎05 62 88 70 70.

The ochre-tinted medieval architecture of Montauban (pop. 55,000) dates back to 1144, when the Count of Toulouse incited enraged local artisans to sack the wealthy abbey at Montauriol ("golden mountain") and use its stones to start construction of present Montauban. Never on good terms with mainstream Catholicism, Montauban was one of the last bastions of Protestantism in France following the revocation of the Edict of Nantes in 1685. The birthplace of celebrated 19th-century painter Jean-Auguste Dominique Ingres (1780-1867), the town merits a stop for its impressive **Musée Ingres**, 19 rue de l'Hôtel de Ville, which occupies the 17th-century Bishop's palace. While the museum is not exclusively devoted to the Neoclassical painter and his predilection for nude female forms, its upper floors spotlight hundreds of his sketches and some minor paintings. The highlight of the museum is the large, vaulted medieval hall, the only remnant of the château built by the Prince Noir in 1362. (☎05 63 22 12 91. Open July-Aug. daily 10am-6pm; Sept.-June Tu-Su 10am-noon and 2-6pm, mid-Oct. to mid-Apr. closed Su mornings. Tours in French July-Aug. daily 2:30pm; €6, students €3. Museum €4, students free, 1st Su of month free.)

Just after revoking the Edict of Nantes, Louis XIV spitefully constructed Montauban's classical cathedral, **◧Notre Dame de l'Assomption.** Four enormous sculptures of the Evangelists keep solemn watch over *Le Vœu de Louis XIII*, one of the most impressive religious works by Ingres. Detailed murals decorate the smaller side chapels, and the entrance façade is the highest in Europe. (Open daily 9am-noon and 2-6pm.)

Alors Chante is a festival where revelers play various traditional French tunes for one week at the end of May and beginning of June (☎05 63 63 02 36; tickets €10-32), while a **Jazz Festival** swings through on the third week of July. Big-name concerts are all ticketed events, but between the 17th and 21st of July the streets of the *vieille ville* resound with free concerts, usually held at noon and 7pm. (Info ☎05 63 63 60 60; www.jazzmontauban.com. Tickets €16-39, students €11-14; available at tourist office.)

ALBI

Dominated by the magnificent Cathédrale Ste-Cécile, the narrow, cobblestone streets of Albi (pop. 50,000) twist down to the tree-lined river Tarn. Native son Henri de Toulouse-Lautrec was lured away by the lights of Paris and the Moulin Rouge, though visitors to Albi will wonder why he left. Those who come for the cathedral and the Toulouse-Lautrec museum often end up staying longer than planned, entranced by the peaceful, relatively untouristed city.

THE LOCAL LEGEND

DEATH ON THE MONT

The region around Carcassonne, known as the *pays Cathar*, is the one-time haunt of the Cathars, once the most powerful sect in France. At the height of their influence, the Cathars networked with various centers throughout Europe, including Switzerland, Serbia, Croatia, and Bulgaria—perhaps also with the Muslim Sufi communities in Spain and the Middle East, and with nearby Jewish Kabbalist scholars.

In some way prefiguring Protestantism, the Cathars reacted against the excesses and shallow spirituality of the Church. They believed in two creators: God, who created the soul, and an evil creator, who made the body. They considered baptism unfair to those too young to choose a faith for themselves, viewed the Christian symbol of the cross to be the glorification of a torture device, and rejected materialism: the so-called "Cathar castles" were not built by the Cathars, but merely used by them for protection against the Crusaders. Cathari priests, called *parfaits* or *perfecti* (perfects), diligently kept vows of chastity, poverty, and obedience. They allowed women to be *perfecti*: many noblewomen, including wives and sisters of the counts of Foix, were therefore attracted to the faith. The sect's sworn enemies labeled them *Cathar*, derived from the Greek word for purity, as a mockery; the members of the

(Continued on next page)

🚆 TRANSPORTATION. Trains run from pl. Stalingrad to: Castres (1½hr., 3 per day, €12.80) via St-Sulpice; and Toulouse (1hr., 15 per day, €12.30). Info office open M-F 5:30am-9:45pm, Sa 6am-9:45pm, Su 6:50am-10:10pm. **Buses** depart pl. Jean Jaurès (☎05 63 54 58 61) for Castres (1hr., M-Sa 8 per day, €5.50) and Toulouse (M-Sa 5 per day, 1 on Su; €10). **Local transportation** is run by Espace Albibus, 14 rue de l'Hôtel de Ville. (☎05 63 38 43 43. M-Sa 7:30am-7:30pm; €0.80.) **Albi Taxi Radio,** 64 impasse Jean de la Fontaine (☎05 63 54 85 03), waits at the station.

🛈 PRACTICAL INFORMATION. To reach the **tourist office,** Palais de la Berbie, at pl. Ste-Cécile, turn left from the station onto av. Maréchal Joffre, then left on av. du Général de Gaulle. Bear left over pl. Lapérouse to the pedestrian *vieille ville*. Rue de Verdusse leads to pl. Ste-Cécile; signs point the way from there. (10min.) The office **books rooms** (€1.50) and offers guides to the city, tours in French (mid-June to mid-Sept. M-Sa 12:15pm, €4), and **currency exchange** on bank holidays. (☎05 63 49 48 80; www.tourisme.fr/albi. Open July-Aug. M-Sa 9am-7pm, Su 10:30am-12:30pm and 2:30-5pm; May-June and Sept. M-Sa 9am-12:30pm and 2-6:30pm, Su 10:30am-1pm and 2:30-6:30pm; Oct.-May M-Sa 9am-12:30pm and 2-6pm.) Other services include: **ATMs** and **currency exchange** at Crédit Agricole, pl. du Vigan (☎05 63 92 66 11; open Tu-Th 9am-noon and 1:45-5:30pm, F 9am-noon and 1:45-6:30pm, Sa 9am-1pm and 1:45-4pm); a **laundromat** at 8 rue Emile Grand, off Lices Georges Pompidou (☎05 63 54 51 14; open daily 7am-9pm); **police** at 23 rue Lices Georges Pompidou (☎05 63 49 22 81); a **hospital** on rue de la Berchère (☎05 63 47 47 47); and **Internet** at Ludi.com, 62 rue Séré-de-Rivière. (☎05 63 43 34 24; €4.60 per hr.; open M-Sa 2pm-midnight). The **post office,** pl. du Vigan, offers **currency exchange.** (☎05 63 48 15 63. Open M-F 8am-7pm, Sa 8am-noon.) **Postal code:** 81000.

🛏🍴 ACCOMMODATIONS & FOOD. Be sure to reserve ahead, especially for summer weekends. For info on *gîtes d'étape* and rural camping, call **ATTER** (☎05 63 48 83 01; fax 05 63 48 83 12). The antiquated **🏨Hôtel La Régence ❷,** 27 av. Maréchal Joffre, near the train station, is a good deal with its brightly wallpapered rooms and homey feel. (☎05 63 54 01 42; fax 05 63 54 80 48. Breakfast €5. Singles €23; singles and doubles with shower €27-41. Extra bed €8. MC/V.) Elegant **Hôtel Saint-Clair ❹,** 8 rue St-Clair, has large, immaculate rooms overlooking a small courtyard. (☎05 63 54 25 66; andrieu.michele.free.fr/HSC.htm. Breakfast €7. Reception daily 8am-9pm. Singles with shower €36-38; doubles €45-54; triples €55-65. MC/

V.) **Camp** near a pool at **Parc de Caussels ❶,** 2km east of the town center, toward Millau on D999. Take bus #5 from pl. Jean Jaurès to Camping (M-Sa every hr. until 7pm). Or walk (30min.), leaving town on rue de la République and following the signs. (Reception daily 7am-10pm. Open Apr. to mid-Oct. €7.50 for 1 person, €10 for 2 people with car, extra person €3.)

Near Albi, the vast region of **Gaillac** shelters *vignoble* estates that prepare some of the best wines of the southwest. **Markets** are held indoors at pl. du Marché near the cathedral (Tu-Su 8am-1pm) and outdoors at pl. Ste-Cécile (Sa 8am-1pm). An organic market is at pl. du Jardin National (Tu and Th 5-7pm). Stock up on groceries at **Casino,** 39 rue Lices Georges Pompidou. (Open M-Sa 9am-7:30pm.) ▓**La Table du Sommelier ❸,** 20 rue Porta, a wine cellar and restaurant, serves carefully-prepared, modern cuisine. (☎05 63 46 20 10. *Plats* €10, 2-course meal €12.50, 3-course €15. Open Tu-Sa noon-2pm and 7-10pm. MC/V.) Regional specialties like foie gras, duck salads, and creative grilled meats are presented at **La Tête de l'Art ❸,** 7 rue de la Piale. Try the local tripe flavored with saffron. (☎05 63 38 44 75. *Menus* €14-30, *plats* €15-22. Open July-Aug. daily noon-2pm and 7:30-10pm; Sept.-June closed Tu-W. MC/V.) **Le Tournesol ❷,** rue de l'Ort en Salvy, a popular vegetarian restaurant behind pl. du Vigan, has vegan pâté, as well as hummus, cheese, and heavenly homemade desserts. (☎05 63 38 38 14. *Plat du jour* €7.80. Open Tu-Th and Sa noon-2pm, F noon-2pm and 7:30-9:30pm. MC/V.)

◙ **SIGHTS.** The pride of Albi, eclipsing even the Lautrec museum, is the ▓**Cathédrale Ste-Cécile.** Stained-glass windows, lavish gold-and-blue walls, and graphic frescoed representations of hell combine to create an impressive physical manifestation of the power of the Church. It was built between the 13th and 15th centuries as a fortress cathedral to enforce "the one true religion" after the Church's Albigensian Crusade stamped out the Cathar sect. Magnificent stone carvings line the choir walls in patterns so intricate they look like lace. The bright, unrestored fresco covering the entire ceiling, painted in 1512, is the largest Italian painting in France. (☎05 63 43 23 43. Open daily June-Sept. 9am-6:30pm; Oct.-May 9am-noon and 2-6:30pm. 11am services. Free. Choir €1; treasury €3, ages 12-25 €2. Free organ concert W 5pm and Su 4pm. Tours July to early Sept. daily 10am and 2:30pm. €5, English audio guide €3.)

The **Palais de la Berbie,** the 13th-century bishop's palace, was constructed in a similar defensive style owing to the tense relations between the church and the ruling family. The fortress showcased the clergy's wealth and power and served as both the tribunal

(Continued from previous page)

sect called themselves "Christians" or "good men."

The Cathars were tolerated until the turn of the 12th century, when they responded to the Inquisition with a bloody Cathar raid in Avignonet. The Pope excommunicated the Cathars and sent Crusaders into Languedoc. Catholics and Cathars alike were killed in the conquest, following the Pope's dictate: "Kill them all, for God knows his own." The Cathar bishop of Toulouse, Guilhabert de Castres, retreated to the Château de Montségur (Secure Mount), perched on the highest point of a commanding outcropping of rocks known as "the pog." The Pope's forces laid siege to the castle from May 1243 until March 1244, slowly advancing up the pog. When the castle keep finally succumbed, the surviving Cathars were told to renounce their beliefs or burn at the stake. On March 16, 1244, 200 Cathars gave their answer, throwing themselves into a pyre at the base of the pog.

The bloody conquest of Montségur wiped out the sect and all of its writings. Today, massive crumbling walls and a broken vault are the only evidence of the last bastion of Catharism. Some allege, however, that on the night before the mass suicide the Cathar bishop entrusted the sect's treasure to four *perfecti*, who escaped into the mountains and were never found. Whether or not these material remnants were rescued, Catharism's spirit of tolerance and personal liberty is still championed by many today.

courts and prison for those charged of crimes by the church. Beautiful gardens and walkways, crafted after the building was converted into a residence, offer splendid views of the Tarn River. (Gardens open daily Sept.-June 8am-noon and 2-6pm; July-Aug. 9am-6pm. Free.) The palace now contains the ■**Musée Toulouse-Lautrec.** The son of the Count of Toulouse by his cousin and wife, **Henri de Toulouse-Lautrec** (1864-1901) suffered from a congenital bone defect that left him significantly shorter than average. He led a life of debauchery in the cafés, cabarets, and brothels of Paris, but his keen sense of caricature, satiric wit, and accomplished brush transformed his racy experiences into a lasting homage to Parisian nightlife. The museum's impressive collection of his oil paintings and ink prints includes all 31 of the famous posters of Montmartre nightclubs. Sculptures and paintings by Dégas, Dufy, Matisse, and Rodin are displayed upstairs. (☎05 63 49 48 70. Open July-Aug. daily 9am-6pm; June and Sept. daily 9am-noon and 2-6pm; Nov.-Feb. M and W-Su 10am-noon and 2-5pm; Mar. and Oct. M and W-Su 10am-noon and 2-5:30pm; Apr.-May daily 10am-noon and 2-6pm. €4.50, students €2.50. Tourist office gives **tours** June-Sept. 8 at 11am and 4pm. €8.50, students €6.50, audio guide in English €3.)

■■ **ENTERTAINMENT & FESTIVALS.** When the sun goes down, the crowds come out along **place de l'Archevêché** in front of the Palais de la Berbie and on **Lices Georges Pompidou** near pl. du Vigan. Salsa and merengue flows from **Le Patio Latino,** 10 rue de l'Ort en Salvy, with its brightly colored café and dance floor. (☎05 63 38 68 16. Drinks €3-6. Lessons Tu and Th 8pm. Rock and pop W. Open July-Aug. Tu-Su 7pm-2am; Sept.-June closed Su. MC/V.) Popular **Café Le Grand Pontie,** pl. du Vigan, doles out beer, sundaes, loud music, and billiards amid stream-lined booths and neon signs. (☎05 63 49 70 75. Beers €3, *plats* €7.90. Open daily 7am-1am. MC/V.) Innovative plays organized by the **Théâtre de la Croix Blanche,** 14 rue de Croix Blanche, take place in various town centers during the first two weeks of July. (☎05 63 54 18 63 for schedules, tickets around €11.) **L'Athanor Scène Nationale,** pl. de l'Amitié Entre les Peuples, off bd. Carnot and opposite Parc Rochegude, often screens foreign art films. (☎05 63 38 55 56. Open Tu-F 2-7pm, Sa 10am-noon and 2-7pm. €6, students and seniors €4.)

Albi revels in an abundance of celebrations, all listed in *Sortir à Albi,* available at the tourist office. In early July, the **Albi Music Festival** brings concerts (up to €13) and a variety of free shows. The **Festival Théâtral** takes place the first week of July. (Tickets €18, students €16.)

NEAR ALBI

CORDES-SUR-CIEL

True to its name, medieval Cordes-sur-Ciel is a celestial city. Perched among the clouds and bounded by a crumbling double wall sprouting flowers between its stones, the tiny city 24km from Albi rises to a summit accessible only by a steep, cobblestone street that twists through multiple gates.

Much of the town's medieval architecture was preserved by the efforts of archeologist Charles Portal. **Musée Charles Portal,** located in Portail Peint when first approaching from pl. de la Bouteillerie, chronicles the town's history with a varied collection of his finds. (Call tourist office for info ☎05 63 56 00 52. Open July-Aug. daily 11am-noon and 3-6pm; Apr.-June and Sept.-Oct. Su and holidays 3-6pm. €3.50, students €2.) The **Musée de l'Art du Sucre,** a few steps farther down Grande Rue Raymond VII, sells all kinds of candied treats and intricate sugar models. (☎05 63 56 02 40. Open Feb.-Dec. daily 10:30am-12:30pm and 2:30-6:30pm. €2.30.)

Across the street, **place de la Bride** once served as the town's defensive platform in place of a more formal central fort. Today it provides a panoramic view of the countryside. Next to **Eglise St-Michel,** the highest point in town (open daily 3-5:30pm), rests the **Puits de la Halle,** a 114m deep well constructed in 1222 by tunnelling through an entire mountain. The bottomless oasis supplied Albi with water during sieges of the area.

For four days around July 14th, fire-eaters play to a costumed crowd during the **Fête du Grand Fauconnier,** which offers plays, concerts, magic shows, banquets, and a medieval market. (Reservations and info ☎ 05 63 56 00 52. Entrance €7, children €3, free if costumed.) The **Festival Musique** sponsors classical music concerts during late July. (For information, call ☎ 05 63 56 00 75. Tickets €15-25, students €10.)

Sudcar Rolland (☎ 05 63 54 11 93) runs two buses from Albi to Cordes (M-Sa; last return bus 6pm; €5, students €2.50). **Trains** from Albi go via Tessonnières to Vindrac (1 hr., 2 per day, €6), where travelers can avoid the nightmarish walk by calling the **Barrois minibus** (☎ 05 63 56 14 80), which runs the last 5km to Cordes (€5).

The **tourist office,** pl. de Halle in Maison Fontpeyrouse, offers guided **tours** and **books rooms.** (☎ 05 63 56 00 52; www.cordes-sur-ciel.org. Tours Tu-F 11am; €3.80. Open July-Aug. Tu-F 9am-6pm, Sa-M 2-5:30pm; Sept.-June daily 10am-noon and 2-5:30pm.) There is also an **annex** in the lower city, in the Maison du Pays Cordais. (Open daily 10:30am-12:30pm and 2-6pm.) A **navette** shuttles between the annex in the *haute ville* and the lower part of Cordes. (Departs daily every 12min. €2, children €1.30.) A **market** takes place at the bottom of the hill. (Sa 8am-noon.)

CARCASSONNE

Carcassonne is where Cinderella lost her glass slipper, Beauty nursed the Beast, and Jack's giant lived a happy life until that whole beanstalk affair. Round towers capped by red tile roofs and an undulating double wall guard the approach to the city. As you walk through the stone portals, the ramparts still seem to resound with the clinking of armor and sharpening of steel. The dream, though, fades fast once you clear the city walls. The "battle sounds" are actually the shouts of thousands of photo-taking visitors jostling for space on the narrow streets. Carcassonne has become one of France's largest tourist traps, for a reason. Try to experience it late in the evening, when the streets are clear of crowds and the flood-lit fortress echoes with free concerts.

▀ TRANSPORTATION

Trains: behind Jardin St-Chenier (☎ 04 68 71 79 14). Info office open M-Sa 9am-noon and 1:30-6:15pm. To: **Lyon** (5½hr., 2 per day, €49.30); **Marseille** (3hr., every 2hr., €35.10); **Montpellier** (2hr., 14 per day, €19.50); **Nice** (6hr., 5 per day, €52); **Nîmes** (2½hr., 12 per day, €24.60); **Perpignan** (2hr., 10 per day, €17); **Toulouse** (50min., 24 per day, €13.20).

Buses: regional buses leave from the *gare routière* on bd. de Varsovie. From the train station, cross the canal, turn right onto bd. Omer Sarrut, and then left at the fork. Check schedules at the station and the tourist office. To: **Toulouse** (2½hr., 3 per day, €8). **Cars Teissier** (☎ 04 68 25 85 45) runs to **Lourdes** (€23).

Public Transportation: a free **shuttle** *(navette)* takes you from sq. Gambetta (in the lower city) to the citadel gates. (☎ 04 68 47 82 22. Mid-June to mid-Sept. M-Sa every 15min. 8:30am-12:30pm and 2-6pm.) **CART,** sq. Gambetta (☎ 04 68 47 82 22), runs **buses** throughout the city, including from the train station to the citadel gates and the campground. To get from the station to the *cité,* take bus #4 (dir: Gambetta) and then bus #2 (dir: La Cité. M-Sa every 20-40min. 7am-7pm. €0.90.)

Taxis: Radio Taxi Services (☎04 68 71 50 50). At the train station or across the canal by Jardin Chenier. 24hr. €6-7 from the station to the *cité*.

◆ 🛈 ORIENTATION & PRACTICAL INFORMATION

The **bastide St-Louis,** once known as the *basse ville* (lower town), recently changed its name to recruit daytrippers who might otherwise pass it over. Its main attractions are shops, hotels, the **train station,** and most importantly the **shuttle** and **TOUC,** which both run to the citadel. Otherwise, it's a pleasant but steep 30min. hike. To get from the station to the *cité*, walk straight down av. de Maréchal Joffre, which turns into rue Clemenceau. Just past the clearing of pl. Carnot, turn left onto rue Verdun, which leads to sq. Gambetta and the **tourist office.** Bear right through the square and turn left up the narrow road that leads to Pont Vieux. Continue straight up the hill to the *cité*. The **tourist office annex** will be on the right as you enter the castle.

Tourist Office: 15 bd. Camille Pelletan (☎04 68 10 24 30; fax 04 68 10 24 38; www.carcassonne-tourisme.com), at sq. Gambetta. Free map, list of accommodations, and oodles of brochures. Open daily July-Aug. 9am-7pm; Sept.-June 9am-12:30pm and 1:30-6pm. Annex in the *cité's* porte Narbonnaise (☎04 68 10 24 36). Open daily July-Aug. 9am-7pm; Sept.-June 9am-1pm and 2-6pm. Also annex near the station on av. de Maréchal Joffre (☎04 68 25 94 81). Hours same as *cité* annex.

Money: Banque Nationale, 50 rue Jean-Bringer (☎08 02 35 01 03), **exchanges currency** at decent rates. Open M-F 8am-noon and 1:30-5pm, Sa 8am-noon.

Internet: Alerte Rouge, 73 rue de Verdun (☎04 68 25 20 39). €4 per hr. Open M-Sa 10am-11pm.

Police: La Comissariat, 4 rue Barbès (☎04 68 11 26 00).

Medical Assistance: Centre Hospitalier, rte. de St-Hilaire (☎04 68 24 24 24).

Post Office: 40 rue Jean Bringer (☎04 68 11 71 00). **Currency exchange.** Open M-F 8am-7pm, Sa 8am-noon. **Branch office** (☎04 68 47 95 45) also offers currency exchange on both rue de Comte Roger and rue Viollet-le-Duc in the *cité*. **Poste Restante:** 11012. **Postal code:** 11000.

🛏 ACCOMMODATIONS & CAMPING

Carcassonne's comfortable hostel is a gift from above to budgeteers, with 120 beds right in the middle of the *cité*. Hotels in the Bastide St-Louis, a hefty walk from the sights of the *cité*, are surprisingly cheap; those in the *cité* itself are ferociously expensive. If you find crowds unbearable, the Sidsmums hostel is in the beautiful countryside 10km outside the city.

🏠 **Auberge de Jeunesse (HI),** rue de Vicomte Trencavel (☎04 68 25 23 16; fax 04 68 71 14 84; carcassonne@fuaj.org), in the *cité*. The only place worth staying if you want to see the castle late at night. Bunkbeds with shower and sink in crowded, clean co-ed rooms. Breakfast included. Kitchen. Sheets €2.70. Bike rental €8 per day. Laundry. Snack bar. Internet €3 per hr. Lockout 10am-4pm. Reception 24hr. Reserve a few days ahead, earlier in July and August. Bunks €12.50. MC/V. **Members only. ❶**

🏠 **Sidsmums Travelers Retreat,** 11 chemin de la Croix d'Achille (☎04 68 26 94 49 or 06 16 86 85 00; www.sidsmums.com). This 10-bed hostel, set in the countryside against the peaceful town of Preixan, will seem like paradise after the crowds in town. Sid and his Mum will offer you advice on the best hikes in the area, drive you to nearby pubs, or serve you cool lemonade in the garden. Call for pick-up from the station (€5) or take the bus headed for Limoux from the canal side of the *gare routière* (ask for Preixan; 4-6

Carcassonne

🏠 ACCOMMODATIONS
Auberge de Jeunesse (HI), **7**
Camping de la Cité, **4**
Hôtel Le Cathare, **2**
Hôtel Montmercy, **9**
Sidsmums Travelers Retreat, **1**

🍴 FOOD
Le Bar à Vins, **10**
Blanche de Castille, **6**
Les Fontaines du Soleil, **8**

⭐ NIGHTLIFE
O'Sheridans, **3**
La Bulle, **5**

per day, last bus at 6:15pm). Kitchen. Mini-store. Bikes €8 per day. Reception 24hr. Reserve ahead. Bunks €18; 1 double €35. ❶

Hôtel Le Cathare, 53 rue Jean Bringer (☎04 68 25 65 92; fax 04 68 47 15 02), near the post office in the lower town. Older rooms are cheap, but bright, well-renovated rooms are worth the extra money. Restaurant. Breakfast €5. Reception daily 8am-7pm. Four tiny, aging singles for €14; renovated singles and doubles €18, with shower €26; triples €46-53. MC/V. ❷

Hôtel Montmercy, 2 rue Camille St-Saens (☎04 68 11 96 70; fax 04 68 11 96 79; le.montmercy@wanadoo.fr), right below the parking lot at the gates to the *cité*. Swimming pool, charming café, and spacious rooms steps away from the *cité*. Breakfast €6.50. Reception daily 8am-8pm. Reserve ahead July-August. Singles and doubles €40-55; triples and quads €65-105. MC/V. ❹

Camping de la Cité, rte. de Ste-Hilaire (☎04 68 25 11 77), has lots of wide open grassy space across the Aude; from the lower town, turn right immediately after you cross Pont Vieux down rue du Jardin and follow the footpath. (30min. from train station.) Or take the shuttle from the train station. (15min.) English-speaking staff. Pool, tennis courts, and a grocery store. Reception daily 8am-9pm. Open mid-Mar. to early Oct. Mid-Mar. to mid-June and mid-Sept. to early Oct. €12.20 per site and 1-2 people, €3.70 per extra person; mid-June to early July and late Aug. to mid-Sept. €15 per site, €4.50 per extra person; early July to late Aug. €16.80 per site, €4.60 per extra person. ❶

LANGUEDOC

ON THE MENU

CASSOULET DE CASTELNAUDARY

For rich, phenomenally flavorful eats, no one can beat the best of French cuisine, and few French meals are more savory than Languedoc **cassoulet,** a thick hearty stew of white beans and meat. *Pays Cathar* residents are proud of their native *cassoulet,* and top-notch chefs feature it front and center on their menus. The dish originated in Castelnaudary, a small town located between Toulouse and Carcassonne, which is denoted on the highway by a small icon symbolizing *cassoulet:* delicious fumes wafting toward the sky.

Requiring days of preparation and a rich variety of ingredients, *cassoulet de Castelnaudary* can be rather difficult and quite expensive to make. The hopeful gourmet chef must soak 800g of white beans *(haricots blancs)* in water for 12 hours, cook them with lard and onions, and then add garlic and an assortment of meat. A leading French culinary society has proclaimed that authentic *cassoulet* must contain at least 30 percent *saucisson de Toulouse* (a pork sausage), goose or duck liver, or mutton. The remaining ingredients include pork rinds, stock, and aromatic vegetables and herbs. The whole concoction is simmered in layers for up to three days. Finally, it is placed in a pan and cooked for 2½hr. until there's a fine *croustillant,* or crust, on top. It is eaten warm with salad and a strong red wine.

🍴 FOOD

Carcassonne's specialty is the inexpensive *cassoulet* (see **On the Menu**). There is a food **market** on pl. Carnot (open Tu, Th, and Sa 7am-1pm) and a **Monoprix** on rue G. Clemenceau at rue de la République. (Open M-Sa 8:30am-8pm.) Restaurants on **rue du Plo** offer €8.50-10 *menus;* save room for dessert at one of the outdoor *crêperies* on **place Marcou.** Restaurants in the *cité* tend to close in winter. Simple and affordable options line **boulevard Omer Sarraut** in the lower city. ◨**Les Fontaines du Soleil ❷,** 32 rue du Plo, is one of Carcassonne's most lauded restaurants, with a sunny garden courtyard and a fountain. The €9.50 weekly lunch *menu* includes a salad, *cassoulet,* and a pitcher of wine. (☎04 68 47 87 06. Open daily 11:30am-3pm and 7-10:30pm. MC/V.) **Le Bar à Vins ❶,** 6 rue de Plo, has snacks and *tapas* (€3-10) as well as tons of festive drinks in a courtyard with an outdoor bar and laid-back atmosphere. Be sure to stop by late at night for the only real nightlife in the *cité.* (☎04 68 47 38 38. Open June-Sept. daily noon-2am. No credit cards.) **Blanche de Castille ❶** is a *salon de thé* next to the tourist office annex at the Porte Narbonnaise, serving what seems like the only frozen coffee in France (€3.80), ice cream, crêpes (€2-7), and foie gras with toast (€11.50) on a secluded *terrasse.* (☎04 68 25 17 80. Open daily 8am-6pm. MC/V.)

👁 SIGHTS

The entire *cité,* with its turrets, ramparts, windy streets, and touristy souvenir shops, is a sight in itself. The walls and **fortifications** date back to the first century, unsurprising since this hill above the sea road to Toulouse is a strategically valuable spot. An early Visigoth fortress here repelled Clovis in AD 506. The town was finally taken after many centuries of unsuccessful sieges, falling with Languedoc during the Albigensian Crusade. The *cité* eventually came under the control of the French crown. King Louis IX built the 2nd outer wall, copying the double-walled fortresses he had observed in Palestine during the Crusades. Untended, the city deteriorated until the architect Viollet-le-Duc restored it in 1844.

Intended at the time of its construction in the 12th century to be a palace, the **Château Comtal,** 1 rue Viollet-le-Duc, was transformed into a citadel when Carcassonne submitted to royal control in 1226. Entrance to the outer walls is free, but you can enter the château only on a paid tour. The **Cour du Midi,** a stop on the tour, holds the remains of a Gallo-Roman villa, once home to the troubadours for which Carcassonne's court was famous. The **Tour de la Justice's** treacherous staircase, which ends in a dead end, was a stairway to heaven (or hell) for ill-fated invaders who rushed upstairs to find themselves trapped. Thirty-minute tours in French run continuously. English tours mid-June to mid-Sept. daily at 11:45am and 2:45pm. (☎04 68 25 01 66; fax 04 68 25 65 32. Open daily June-Sept. 9am-7:30pm; Apr.-May and Oct. 9:30am-6pm; Nov.-Mar. 9:30am-5pm. €6.10, ages 18-25 €4.10.) The Romanesque nave and Gothic choir of the **Basilique St-Nazaire and St-Celsois,** at the end of rue St-Louis, is an interesting juxtaposition of architecture. On a sunny day the simple rose windows on either side of the transept are especially eye-catching. (Open daily 8am-8pm.)

The *cité* of Carcassonne is filled with small museums, most of which are kitsch shops in fancy dress. An exception is the **Musée de l'Ecole,** 3 rue du Plo, in the city's old schoolhouse. In reconstructed classrooms, the museum displays a fascinating collection of textbooks, certificates, and letters from the late 1800s, when Jules Ferry was in the process of transforming the French education system. (☎04 68 25 95 14. Open daily July-Aug. 10am-7pm; Sept.-June 10am-6pm.)

The lower town—the **Bastide St-Louis**—was born when Louis IX, afraid enemy troops might find shelter close to his fortress, burned the houses that clung to the city's outside walls and relocated their residents, whom he gave their very own walled fortifications and church. Converted into a fortress after the Black Prince razed Carcassonne during the Hundred Years' War in 1355, the *basse ville's* **Cathédrale St-Michel,** rue Voltaire, still sports fortifications on its southern side facing bd. Barbès. Don't miss the gargoyles snarling down from their high perches. (Open M-Sa 7am-noon and 2-7pm, Su 9:30am-noon.)

🎵 🎭 ENTERTAINMENT & NIGHTLIFE

The evening is the best time for wandering the streets of Carcassonne's *cité* and relaxing in the cafés in **place Marcou.** Bars and cafés along **boulevard Omer Sarraut** and **place Verdun** are open until midnight. Grab a Guinness (€5.50 per pint) at **O'Sheridans,** 13 rue Victor Hugo off pl. Carnot, a friendly Irish pub filled with French and anglo crowds. (☎04 68 72 06 58. Open daily 4pm-2am. Live music W and Th. AmEx/MC/V.) At the base of the *cité,* nocturnal locals dance the night away at **La Bulle,** 115 rue Barbacane. (☎04 68 72 47 70. €9 cover includes first drink. Open F-Sa until dawn.)

🎇 FESTIVALS

In July, the month-long **Festival de Carcassonne** brings dance, opera, theater, and concerts to the Château Comtal and the ancient amphitheater, both of which are known for having great acoustics. (Info and reservations ☎04 68 11 59 15; www.festivaldecarcassonne.com. €21-42, most shows €10 for students.) The **Festival Off** showcases smaller bands as well as mildly alternative free comedy and dance performances in the *places* of the *cité* and in the Bastide St-Louis. On **Bastille Day,** deep red floodlights and smoke set the entire *cité* ablaze in remembrance of the villages burned by the inquisitorial jury headquartered here in the Tour de l'Inquisition. The fireworks display is the second best in France. For two weeks in early August, the entire *cité* returns to the Middle Ages for the **Spectacles Médiévaux.** Locals dressed in medieval garb talk to visitors, display their crafts, and pretend nothing has changed in eight centuries. Every afternoon at 5:30pm, there is an equestrian show with mock jousting and pitched battles. Even non-French speakers will enjoy the nightly 9:30pm *spectacle*—a huge multimedia drama that brings the 13th century to life. For ticket info, contact Compagnie Mystère Baiffe (☎06 86 86 31 33).

FOIX

Il était une fois (once upon a time, as French fairy-tales begin), the powerful counts of Foix decided to show off their might by building a massive château over-looking the town of Foix. Today, the towers of the magnificent château look down on the busy marketplace below, cobblestone streets lead through a maze of red-roofed houses, and nearby caves and grottos still bear the marks of the prehistoric peoples who first settled the Ariège region. In the summer, the whole town turns out for an enormous medieval spectacle to relive the days of yore. The city is a good base for hiking and kayaking nearby. Strongly consider renting a car—the Château de Montségur, prehistoric caves, and serene Ariège passes are poorly served by public transportation.

▐▋ TRANSPORTATION & PRACTICAL INFORMATION. The **train station** (☎ 05 61 02 03 64), av. Pierre Sémard, is north of town off the N20. (Info open M-Sa 8:10am-12:20pm and 1:25-8:30pm, Su 8:15am-1:55pm and 2:15-10:20pm.) Trains go to Toulouse (1hr., 10 per day, €11). By bus, **Salt Autocars**, 8 allées de Villote (☎ 05 61 65 08 40), also runs to Toulouse (1¼hr., 2 per day, €8).

To reach the **tourist office**, 29 rue Théophile Delcassé, leave the train station and turn right. Follow the street until you reach the main road (N20). Follow this high-way to the second bridge, cross it, and follow cours Gabriel Fauré for about three blocks. Rue Théophile Delcassé is on your right. The office provides a free small map and tons of information on exploring the region. (☎ 05 61 65 12 12; www.mai-rie-foix.fr. Open July-Aug. M-Sa 9am-7pm, Su 9am-noon and 2-6pm; June and Sept. M-Sa 9am-noon and 2-6pm, Su 10am-12:30pm; Oct.-May M-Sa 9am-noon and 2-6pm.) For **police**, call ☎ 05 61 05 43 00. The **hospital** (☎ 05 61 03 30 30) is 5km out of town in St-Jean de Verges. For **Internet**, drop by the **Bureau d'Information Jeunesse (BIJ)**, pl. Parmentier. (☎ 05 61 02 86 10. €2.50 per hr. Reserve ahead. Open M 1-5pm, Tu and Th-F 10am-5pm, W 10am-6pm.) There is a **laundromat** at 32 rue de la Faurie. (☎ 05 61 02 72 15. Open daily 8am-8:30pm.) The **post office**, 4 rue Laffont, has **currency exchange**. (☎ 05 61 02 01 02. Open M-F 8am-7pm, Sa 8am-noon.) **Poste Restante**: 09008. **Postal code**: 09000.

▐▘ ACCOMMODATIONS & FOOD. The best option for budget travelers is unquestionably the █**Foyer Léo Lagrange ❶**, 16 rue Peyrevidal. To get there, turn right onto cours Gabriel Fauré out of the tourist office and right again onto rue Peyrevidal just after the Halle Aux Grains; the *foyer* will be on your right. A cross between a nice hotel and a friendly hostel, it offers privacy and sociability in 22 clean 1- to 4-bed rooms, each equipped with a sink, closet, desk, and private shower. Rooms facing the street in back have impressive views of the château. (☎ 05 61 65 09 04; fax 05 61 02 63 87. Free Internet. Kitchen available. Reception daily 8am-11pm; call ahead if arriving late. €14 per person.) Opposite the *foyer* is centrally-located **Hôtel Eychenne ❸**, 11 rue Peyrevidal, which rents large rooms above a smoky but lively bar. (☎ 05 61 65 00 04; fax 05 61 65 56 63. Breakfast €4.60. Reception 8am-8pm; call ahead if arriving late. Singles and doubles with shower €29, with toilet €37; triples or quads with shower €55. MC/V.) Classy **La Barbacane du Château ❸**, 1 av. de Lérida, is just past the flowered roundabout to the right on cours Gabriel Fauré, about 5min. from the tourist office. The price is reasonable for the elegance of mahogany, large beds, sparkling bathrooms, and glossed tables. Several rooms have excellent views of the château. (☎ 05 61 65 50 44; fax 05 61 02 74 33. Elevator. Breakfast €7. Open Apr.-Oct. daily 7am-11:30pm. Singles and doubles €32, with bath €45. MC/V.) **Camping du Lac/Labarre ❶** is a three-star site on a lake 3km up N20 toward Toulouse. Buses from Toulouse stop at the camp. From the train station, head left along N20 until you see the signs for the campground on your left. **Rent canoes and kayaks** from lakefront Base Nautique (half-day €8) down the street. (☎05 61 65 11 58; www.campingdulac.com. July-Aug. €6.50 per person, €15 for 2 people, car, tent, and electricity; Sept.-May €3.50 per person, €10 for 2 people, car, tent, and electricity; June €5 per person; €12 for 2 people, car, tent, and electricity.)

Foix's restaurants serve specialties of the Ariège region. Try *truite à l'ariègeoise* (trout), *cassoulet* (white-bean and duck stew), or the wonderfully messy *écrevisses* (crayfish). Restaurants with moderately priced local specialties line **rue de la Faurie.** For regular supplies, head to the **Casino** supermarket, rue Laffont. (Open M-Sa 9am-7pm.) On Fridays, **open-air markets** sprout up all over Foix, with meat and cheese at the Halle aux Grains, fruit and vegetables at pl. St-Volusien, and clothing along the allées de Villote. (Food 8am-12:30pm; clothes 8am-4pm.) The star restaurant in town is undoubtedly **La Sainte Marthe ❹,** pl. Lazema, which exudes an air of mastery over every dish made with water-fowl. Menus featuring dishes like foie gras, *magret de canard*, and, of course, *cassoulet*, aren't cheap, but the array of culinary awards in the window make them seem like bargains. (☎05 61 02 87 87. *Menus* €24-44, *cassoulet* €16. Open Su-M and W-Sa noon-2:30pm and 7-10pm. MC/V.) For good prices on regional food, try the casual **Le Jeu de l'Oie ❷,** 17 rue de la Faurie. €6.90 will get you a generous *plat du jour;* the three-course lunch *menu* allows you to sample the taste of local cuisine. (☎05 61 02 69 39. Open July-Aug. M-Sa noon-2:30pm and 7-11pm; Sept.-June M noon-2:30pm, Tu-F noon-2:30pm and 7-11pm, Sa 7-11pm. AmEx/MC/V.) For those who want to escape the *cassoulet* glut, **l'Atlas ❸,** 14 pl. Pyrène, serves many varieties of couscous and *tagines* (a casserole of lamb or chicken and vegetables) under Moroccan tapestries and a vine canopy. (☎05 61 65 04 04. Three-course *menu* with wine €10. Open Tu-F and Su 11:30am-3pm and 7-10:30pm, Sa 11:30am-3pm.)

◙◙ SIGHTS & EXCURSIONS. The **Château de Foix,** the prototypical medieval castle, is unique for its collection of three stunning towers, all perched protectively on a high point above the city. The towers were built centuries apart. The round tower, from the 15th century, is a particularly impressive piece of architecture. Inside the well-preserved castle, the small **Musée de l'Ariège** displays a collection of armor, stone carvings and artifacts from the Roman Empire to the Middle Ages. After its glory days, the castle was used as a garrison and later a prison: inside the round tower, graffiti written by desperate prisoners is still legible. Be sure to take the free tour in English, which is chock full of historical details. After the tour, visitors haul themselves up the towers of the castle for an impressive panoramic view of the Pyrenean foothills. (☎05 34 09 83 83. Both open July-Aug. daily 9:45am-6:30pm; June and Sept. daily 9:45am-noon and 2-6pm; Oct.-May W-Su 10:30am-noon and 2-5:30pm. Included with admission are tours in French every hr., in English 1pm. €4, students €2.) Down the hill at pl. St-Volusien, the 9th-century **Abbaye Saint-Volusien** pre-dates the château by a couple of hundred years. The streets radiating out from in front of it indicate its once-central location; in medieval times it dominated the religious life of the region. Now its large, simple interior is worth several minutes of contemplation. (Church open daily 8am-8pm.)

The Ariège region boasts some of the most spectacular **caves** in France. The **Grotte de Niaux** would be a stunning cave in its own right, but it becomes spectacular when lanterns illuminate the prehistoric wall drawings of bison, horses, and ibex that date from around 12,000 BC. Reservations are required to enter the cave. 20km south of Foix, the grotto is only accessible by car. (☎05 61 05 88 37. Open Apr.-Oct. daily; Nov.-Mar. Tu-Su. €9, students €7.50, children €5.50.) An hour-long boat ride navigates the **Rivière Souterraine de Labouiche,** the longest navigable underground river in Europe. The small metal boat cruises through galleries of stalactites and stalagmites, pulled along by wisecracking guides who can give the tour in both French and English. There is no public transportation to this site. Arrive before 3:30pm to avoid extreme crowds. (☎05 61 65 04 11. Open July-Aug. daily 9:30am-6pm; Apr. to late May M-Sa 2-6pm, Su 10am-noon and 2-6pm; late May to June and Sept. daily 10am-noon and 2-6pm; Oct. to mid-Nov. Su 10am-noon and 2-6pm. €7.50, children €5.50.)

■ **FESTIVALS.** From the end of July though the middle of August, on weekends at 10pm, an extravagant medieval spectacle, **Il était une Foix...l'Ariège,** enlivens the area around Foix's château. Villagers wrestle bears, fight battles, and shoot off more fireworks than some major cities use on Bastille Day. (For info and tickets call the Théâtre de Verdure de l'Espinet at ☎05 61 02 88 26. €10-22, students €5-11.) In the second week of July, the **Résistances** festival brings 100 art films—many of which premiere in Cannes—to Foix. (☎05 61 05 13 30; www.cine-resistances.com. €5 per film, €60 per week; students half-price.) There's also a **jazz festival** at the end of July, with concerts nightly at 9pm and jazz playing from speakers around the *centre ville* all day. (☎06 86 58 00 71; www.jazzafoix.com. €15 per night, students €10, weekly pass €50-70.)

VILLEFRANCHE-DE-CONFLENT

Deep in the mountains of the Conflent range, the miniscule Villefranche-de-Conflent (pop. 220) occupies a once-prized position. For almost 300 years, the walled city kept an active garrison to protect the borders arbitrated by Louis XIV in the 1659 Treaty of the Pyrénées. Since its decline in military importance, the idyllic town has gained recognition instead for its magnificent Fort Liberia and nearby stalagmite caves. The gorgeous surrounding Pyrénées and their scenic mountain trails also make Villefranche a perfect home base for hikers.

7 PRACTICAL INFORMATION. Trains (☎04 68 96 63 62) run from Perpignan to the outskirts of Villefranche (50min., 8 per day, €6.90). From the station, take the only road to the highway and turn right toward the town center. (5min.) Surrounding the entire city, the enormous rampart walls have two open gates that lead to the town's parallel main streets. The left one will bring you to the rue St-Jacques; the right one opens onto the rue St-Jean. The **tourist office,** 32bis rue St-Jacques, has lodging info and sells IGN hiking maps for €9-11. (☎04 68 96 22 96; fax 04 68 96 07 24. Open daily July-Aug. 10am-8pm; June and Sept. 10am-7pm; Oct.-Dec. and Feb.-May 10:30am-12:30pm and 2-5pm. Closed Jan.)

Running 63km through the Pyrénées, the tiny **Train Jaune** links Villefranche to Latour-de-Carol (2½-3hr., 5 per day, €15.50). The train runs over deep mountain valleys on spectacular viaducts, stopping at many small towns along the way. From Latour you can either turn around and head back to Villefranche or switch to a regular train and continue on to Toulouse (2¾hr. from Latour-de-Carol, 4 per day, €19). If you don't have too much time to spare, shorter scenic trips can be made from €3.10. During the winter months, the train also hauls **skiers** off to the fashionable **Font-Romeu** (30min., 5 per day, €9.40). Equipped with snow machines and chair lifts, this resort offers first-rate skiing. (**Tourist office** in Font Romeu ☎04 68 30 68 30). The Train Jaune does not take reservations, so be sure to arrive at the station an hour in advance to ensure a spot. Children 4-12 are half-price.

⌂ ACCOMMODATIONS. Villefranche has few cheap hotels, and even the expensive ones fill quickly during the summer. **L'Auberge du Cèdre,** a few buildings down to the right of the tourist office, has ten rooms equipped with TVs and toilets, all with free access to a hallway shower. (☎04 68 96 05 05; fax 04 68 96 35 39. Breakfast €5. Reservations recommended. Singles and doubles €41; triples €56; quads

€66. AmEx/MC/V.) The *mairie* (town hall) on pl. de l'Eglise rents out small studio apartments with kitchens and antique wooden furniture. However, to take advantage of these **gîtes communaux ❸**, you must stay for a full week (Sa-Sa)—or at least pay the weekly rate. (☎04 68 96 10 78. Town hall open M-Tu and Th-F 9am-noon and 2-6pm. July-Aug. €150 for 2 people, €200-215 for 4-6 people; Sept.-June €125/€165-180.) If you succumb completely to the lure of the Pyrénées and the tiny Train Jaune, continue on from Villefranche to the stop Thuès Carança (30min., 5 per day, €5 from Villefranche). The *gîte-camping* **Mas de Bordes ❶** is perched beside a crumbling church in a canyon nook, right by a natural hot spring. (☎04 68 97 05 00. Small bungalows with kitchen access €10-65; camping €4 per person, €1 per tent.) The *gîte* is a 3hr. walk from an entrance to the **GR10,** the hiking trail which stretches from the Atlantic to the Mediterranean.

◙◪ SIGHTS & OUTDOORS. Built into the mountainside high above the town, the impressive **Fort Liberia** takes the form of two overlapping hexagons. The stronghold was constructed in 1681 by Vauban in order to protect Villefranche and the rest of the Catalan region from Spanish attacks. Buy tickets at the info desk inside the town, next to the tourist office on rue St-Jacques. (☎04 68 96 34 01; fax 04 68 05 21 78. €5.50, students €4.60, ages 5-11 €2.60. Open daily June-Sept. 9am-7pm; Apr.-May 10am-7pm; Oct.-May 10am-6pm.) To reach its fortified heights, hike (20min.) or catch the *navette* from the Porte de France (July-Aug. every 30min.; Sept.-June request at the St-Jacques info desk. Round-trip €2.50, ages 5-11 €1.50). Vauban left towers to climb and passageways to navigate, but it is the view of the impossibly picturesque Villefranche from above that makes the trip worthwhile. There are actually only 832 steps in the subterranean "Staircase of 1000 Steps" which leads back down to the city, but you probably won't mind.

Accessible from the tourist office, the fortified **ramparts** of Villefranche offer more bare rock passageways to wander around in. Be careful not to get lost in the maze of stone tunnels, as the endless walls and empty rooms all begin to look alike after a while. (☎04 68 96 16 40. Open daily July and Aug. 10am-8pm; June and Sept. 10am-7pm; Oct.-Dec. and Feb.-May 10:30am-12:30pm and 2-5pm. Closed Jan. Guided visits in French July-Aug. M-Th 11am and 3pm. €3.50, students €2.50, under 10 free. 1hr. cassette tour in English or French €3.) Just 200m from the town, visitors can walk through endless white chambers of stalagmites and stalactites at the **Grand Carolettes.** Created thousands of years ago by an underground river, the cave contains natural stone columns that jut out from pools of water. (☎04 68 96 23 11. Open mid-June to mid-Sept. daily 10am-6:30pm; Apr. to mid-June and mid-Sept. to Oct. daily 10am-6pm; Nov.-Mar Su 2-5pm. €7, children €3.)

◙ FESTIVALS. Celebrated throughout the Catalonian region on June 23, the **Fête des Feux de St-Jean** burns brightly in Villefranche. Torches lit on the Canigou mountain return sacred fire to the village, where locals dance the traditional *sardane*, drink wine, and leap over bonfires. People dressed as giants appear in the village every Sunday in April in recognition of **Pâques.** Instead of Bastille Day, Villefranche-de-Conflent celebrates the **Fête de St-Jacques** during the third weekend in July with fireworks and dancing.

The biggest festival in the area is in the nearby city of **Prades,** which for 23 years was home to the great Catalan cellist Pablo Casals during his political exile from Franco's Spain. The annual **Festival Pablo Casals,** from the late July through the middle of August, attracts international musicians for three weeks of chamber music and workshops. The **Bureau du Festival Pablo Casals** in Prades sells tickets. (☎04 68 96 33 07; fax 04 68 96 50 95; www.prades-festival-casals.com. Tickets €15-30, students €12-25, under 13 €7-13. Open M-F 9am-noon and 2-6pm. MC/V.)

LANGUEDOC

COLLIOURE

Collioure (pop. 2930) is nestled at the idyllic spot where the Pyrénées tumble through emerald vineyards and orchards to meet the shores of the Mediterranean. The rocky harbor of this small port captured the fancy of Greeks and Phoenicians long before it modeled for a then-unknown Matisse, who baptized the town an artist's mecca in 1905. Matisse was soon followed by Dérain, Dufy, Dalí, and Picasso. With one glimpse of the expansive sea and the stone lighthouse bathed in the late afternoon sun, you too will feel inspired. On market days, fishermen and farmers offer organic products direct from the boat or the homestead. Freshly picked apricots and peaches are sold alongside anchovies and regional Banyul wines.

■∎ TRANSPORTATION & PRACTICAL INFORMATION. The **train station** (☎04 68 82 05 89), at the top of av. Aristide Maillol, sends trains north to Perpignan (20min., 15 per day, €4.70). You can also go south to Barcelona (3¾hr., 5 per day, €12.10) and Port Bou (30min., 5 per day, €2.90). Ticket office and information desk open M 7:35am-1pm and 2:30-4:30pm, Tu-Sa 7:50am-1pm and 2:30-4:30pm, Su 12:10-6:05pm. **Cars Inter 66** (☎04 68 35 29 02) travels to nearby coastal towns and Perpignan (45min., 8 per day, €5.40). X-Trem Bike, 5 rue de la Tour d'Auvergne, has good prices on **bike rentals.** (July-Aug. ☎04 68 82 59 77, Sept.-June 06 23 01 93 01. Open daily 8:30am-12:30pm, 1:30-2:30pm, and 6-7pm. Half-day €8-10, full day €14-18, week €60-85; €100 deposit.)

To get to the **tourist office** from the train station, walk downhill on av. Aristide Maillol until you reach pl. du Mal. Leclerc. Continue down along the canal and take a left onto pl. du 18 Juin. The office provides maps of the town and suggestions for 1-7hr. hiking trails. (☎04 68 82 15 47; www.collioure.com. Open July-Aug. daily 9am-8pm; Sept.-June M-Sa 9am-noon and 2-6:30pm.) **Crédit Agricole**, 28 rue Pasteur, **exchanges currency** for a €2 commission and traveler's checks for a €3.50 commission. **ATMs** are outside. (☎04 68 82 03 82. Open M-W and F 8:30am-noon and 1:30-5pm, Th 9:30am-noon and 1:30-5pm). There is also a currency exchange at the post office (see below). The **police station** (☎04 68 82 09 53) and the **post office** are on rue de la République. The post office **exchanges money** without a commission and has **ATMs** outside. (☎04 68 98 36 00. Open M-Tu and Th-F 8:30am-noon and 1:30-4pm, W 8:30am-12:30pm; Sa 8:30-11:30am.) **Postal code:** 66190.

∎∎ ACCOMMODATIONS & FOOD. Collioure fills its hotels and beaches to the brim during July and August. **Hôtel Triton ❸**, 1 rue Jean Bart, is in a bright pink villa on the waterfront. The charming rooms have A/C, TVs, soundproof windows, and showers for comparably low prices. From the train station, follow av. Aristide Maillol to pl. du Maréchal Leclerc and then take a right over the bridge onto rue de la République. At the small rotary, take a left onto av. du Général de Gaulle and follow this street down to the beach. (☎04 68 98 39 39; www.aswfrance.com/hotel-triton. Breakfast €6. Reception daily 8am-7pm. Reserve ahead July-Aug. Doubles €33, with toilet €46, with view of the sea €55; triples with toilets and a view of the sea €65. AmEx/DC/MC/V.) The **Hostellerie des Templiers ❹** is on av. Camille Pelletan (mailing address: 12 quai de l'Amirauté), a block away from the tourist office. Tiled stairways lead to hallways covered top to bottom with over 2000 original paintings—gifts of lodgers such as Matisse, Picasso, and Dalí. The individualized rooms come equipped with original works of art, Catalan furniture, TV, A/C, toilet, and shower. Two annexes in the back offer cheaper rooms with fewer amenities. (☎04 68 98 31 10; www.hotel-templiers.com. Breakfast €6. Reception daily 8am-midnight. Closed early Jan. to early Feb. July-Sept. doubles €62-75; quads €93-112; annex doubles €36-50. Apr.-June and Oct. €55-65/€83-88/€34-47. Nov.-Mar. €46-55/€73-78/€39-41. AmEx/MC/V.) **Camping la Girelle ❷**, on plage de l'Ouille, is a scenic 15min. hike from the town center. Nestled between two protective hills, the campsite is located on an idyllic shaded beach. Restaurant, bar, and hot showers available. (☎04 68 81 25 56; campinglagirelle.66@wanadoo.fr. Reception daily 9am-noon and 5-8pm. Open Apr.-Sept. July-Aug. €21 for 2 people and tent; Apr.-June and Sept. €17. Electricity €3.80.)

Local produce is sold at a fantastic **market** centered on pl. du Maréchal Leclerc and spilling out along the canal toward the Château Royal. (Open W and Su 8am-1pm.) Reasonably priced *crêperies*, pizzerias, and cafés crowd **rue St-Vincent** near the port. For pre-packaged goods, head to the **Shopi** supermarket, 18 av. de la République. (Open mid-June to mid-Sept. M-Sa 8:30am-7:30pm, Su 8:30am-1pm and 4-8pm; mid-Sept. to mid-June M-Sa 8:30am-12:30pm and 3:30-7:15pm.) On bd. Boramar, the **San Vincens ❹** café provides cushioned chairs that spill out onto the rocky beach. Local seafood specialties include Catalan *bouillabaisse* (€20), paëlla for two (€37), and mussels with creamy garlic sauce (€9.50). The breath-taking view of the nearby mountains, harbor, and châteaux compensates for inflated prices. (☎04 68 82 05 12; fax 04 68 82 15 69. Open daily 9am-2am. Closed mid-Oct. to mid-Jan. AmEx/MC/V.)

◙ SIGHTS. Extending from pl. du 8 Mai 1945 to the port, the hulking white stone **Château Royal** sheltered the kings of Majorca in the 13th century and was later for-tified by both French and Spanish kings during the unending border wars. The château is worth visiting for its spooky underground tunnels and its spectacular view of the harbor below. (☎04 68 82 06 43; www.cg66.fr. Open daily July-Aug. 10am-7pm; June and Sept. 10am-6pm; Oct.-May 9am-5pm. English brochures. 1¼hr. tours in French and English available by reservation. €4, students and ages 12-18 €2, under 12 free.)

A 30min. hike through the **Parc Pams,** behind the Musée d'Art Moderne, will give a good view of the 16th-century **Fort Saint Elme.** Back across the bay, a walkway built into the bottom of the cliffs continues for several kilometers along an iso-lated coastline and leads to the town of **Argelès.** Hikers can get info from the tour-ist office on these and other magnificent trails nearby.

To retrace the steps of Matisse and Dérain, follow the **Chemin du Fauvisme.** The *chemin* begins and ends in front of the tourist office, where you can pick up a map and itinerary. In the small ivy-covered Villa Pams on rte. de Port-Vendres, the **Musée d'Art Moderne-Fonds Peské** houses a modest collection of paintings and ceramics by minor artists. At any one time, the museum will display either its per-manent or temporary exhibits, as the building is not large enough to accommodate both. (☎04 68 82 10 19. Open Su-M and W-Sa July-Aug. 10am-noon and 2-7pm; Sept. and June 10am-noon and 2-6pm; Oct.-May 10am-noon and 2-5pm. €2, students €1.50, under 12 free.)

Those with a taste for the harbor should stop by **Les Anchois Desclaux** on the cor-ner of av. du Général de Gaulle and rte. d'Argelès. Besides selling anchovies, the store allows visitors to watch them being prepared and to taste a series of ancho-vies preserved in vinegar with flavors like lemon, curry, and pimento. (☎04 68 82 05 25. Open daily July-Aug. 8am-8pm; Sept.-June 9am-noon and 2-7pm.)

▶◙ EXCURSIONS & FESTIVALS. The **Centre International de Plongée,** 15 rue de la Tour d'Auvergne, offers scuba diving lessons and rents the necessary under-water equipment. (☎04 68 82 07 16; www.cip-collioure.com. Initation lesson for beginners (ages 8 and up) €39, second lesson in the ocean €45, combined price for 2 lessons €75. 8-session course during July €240; ages 14 and up only. €20 per dive with scuba card, €25 per dive with scuba card and guide. Open Apr.-Christ-mas M-Sa 10am-noon and 3-7pm, Sa 10:30am-noon and 5:30-7pm. MC/V.)

From August 14 to 18, the streets of Collioure fill with dance and music for the **Festival de St-Vincent.** Midway through the festival, on August 16, a **corrida** (bullfight) at the arena (5pm) is followed by a **fireworks** display over the sea (10pm).

PERPIGNAN

The hot and crowded city of Perpignan (pop. 108,000) is only a few kilometers from the transparent waters of the Mediterranean, but the distance feels much larger when you're stuck in the midst of this congested city. Although the Catalan influence permeates the town, with brilliant "blood and gold" flags hanging everywhere, there is little to see or do in central Perpignan. What makes Perpignan worthwhile, however, are cheap hotels, a good transportation system, and friendly locals. The town also provides a reasonably priced base for visits to the more expensive and beautiful towns of Collioure or Canet-Plage.

▐ TRANSPORTATION

Flights: Aéroport de Perpignan-Rivesaltes, 4km northwest of the town center, just outside of town along D117 (info and reception desk ☎04 68 52 60 70; aeroport@perpignan.cci.fr). **Ryanair** (☎04 68 71 96 65; www.ryanair.com) offers the cheapest flights to **London** (€60-350, depending on date and availability). **Hertz** rents **cars** at the airport. (☎04 68 61 18 77. Cheapest car is €300 per week with a €730 deposit. Cars can be returned elsewhere. 21+. Open Su-F 8am-noon, 1-6:30pm, and 8:30-11pm; Sa closed during the late-night shift. MC/V.) **Navette Aéroport** runs shuttles from the SNCF train station, pl. Catalogne, and the *gare routière* to the airport. (☎04 68 55 68 00. €4.50, ages 4-10 and groups €3. Around 6 per day, depending on the flight schedule.)

Trains: rue Courteline. Info office open M-Sa 8am-6:30pm. To: **Carcassonne** (1½hr., 3 per day, €15); **Lyon** (5½hr., 4-5 per day, €43.70); **Montpellier** (1½-2hr., 8-10 per day, €18.70); **Paris** (5-6hr., 4 per day, €74.80); **Toulouse** (3hr., change at Narbonne; 10 per day; €23.20); **Marseille** (5hr., change at Narbonne; 7-8 per day; €33.10).

Buses: Regional buses depart the *gare routière*, 17 av. Général Leclerc (☎04 68 35 29 02) to: **Collioure** (45min., 8 per day, €5.40); **Villefranche-de-Conflent** (1hr., 4 per day, €8.30). Office open M-Sa 7am-6:45pm. They also offer a **tourist pass** good for 8 days within the *département* (€23). From June to September, the **Cars Verts Voyages,** 10 rue Jeanne d'Arc (☎04 68 51 19 47), organizes **daytrips** to: **Carcassonne** (€23), **Andorra** (€26), **Barcelona** (€28-32), and the peak of nearby **Mt. Canigou** (€38).

Local Transportation: CTP, pl. Gabriel-Péri (☎04 68 61 01 13), runs **buses** throughout Perpignan and **shuttles** over to Canet-Plage. Tickets within Perpignan €1.05; *carnet* of 10 €7.50. First bus in any direction 6am, last bus 8:30pm. Office open M-F 7:30am-12:30pm and 1:30-6:30pm, Sa 8:30am-noon.

Taxis: Accueil Perpignan Taxi (☎06 68 35 15 15), by the train station. €2.30 starting fee, €1.24 per km. Around €12-15 to the airport, €20-25 to Canet-Plage. 24hr.

Car Rental: Europcar (☎04 68 34 89 80) is located inside the train station. Car rentals from €296 per week with a €600 deposit. Cars can be returned elsewhere. 21+. Open M-F 8am-7pm, Sa 8am-noon and 2-6pm.

Bike Rental: Bouti Cycle, 20 av. Gilbert Brutus (☎04 68 85 02 71). €38 for 5 days. €150 deposit. Open Tu-Sa 9am-12:30pm and 2:30-7:15pm.

◢▚ ▐ ORIENTATION & PRACTICAL INFORMATION

Perpignan's train station, once referred to as "the center of the world" by a rather off-center Salvador Dalí, is almost constantly packed with weary travelers, making connections to Catalonia, Spain, 50km to the south, and to the Pyrénées, whose foothills begin rolling 30km to the west. The city itself stretches out for a long way from the station, but most of the action takes place in the labyrinth of small streets in the heart of the *vieille ville*. The area makes a triangle, bounded on the far side by the regional tourist office, the **place de Catalogne** up the canal toward the train station, and the **Palais des Rois de Majorque** to the south. Most of Perpignan's gypsy population lives on the hilltop past the *vieille ville* in the **Quartier St-Jacques,** near the intersection of bd. Jean Bourrat and bd. Anatole France. In the day, this neighborhood's residents sit outside, chatting noisily, but it's best to avoid it at night.

Tourist Office: Palais des Congrès, pl. Armand Lanoux (☎04 68 66 30 30; www.perpignantourisme.com), at the opposite end of the town center from the train station. From the train station, follow av. de Gaulle to pl. de Catalogne, then take bd. Georges Clemenceau until you reach pl. de la Résistance. Take a slight left onto cours Palmarole and continue down this street until you see a large glass-paneled building in the middle of the garden on your right. (20min.) Multilingual staff offers comprehensive **tours** in French (2½hr.; June-Sept. W and Sa at 2:30pm; €4, under 14 free). Year-round tours in English or French available by reservation. For tours in English, call ☎04 68 22 25 96. Office open mid-June to mid-Sept. M-Sa 9am-7pm, Su 10am-4pm; mid-Sept. to mid-June M-Sa 9am-6pm, Su 10am-4pm.

Money: BNP Paribas, 19 quai Vauban (☎08 20 82 00 01), offers currency exchange for a €5.40 commission, as well as having ATMs located just outside. Open for exchange M-F 9-11:30am and 1:30-4pm. The post office also exchanges money with no commission (see listing).

Laundromat: Laverie Foch, 23 rue Maréchal Foch. Open daily 7am-8:30pm. Wash €3.50-6.10, dry €0.50 for 7min.

Police: av. de Grande Bretagne (☎04 68 35 70 00).

Hospital: av. du Languedoc (☎04 68 61 66 33).

24hr. Pharmacy: The local newspaper *L'Indépendant* (€1.30), sold at every *tabac,* lists the rotating **pharmacie de garde.**

Internet: Cyber Espace, 45bis. av. du Gal. Leclerc, facing the *gare routière* (☎04 68 35 36 29). Two floors hold 46 PCs equipped with games. €2 per 30min., €3 per hr., €9 for a 7:30am-12:30pm, 1-6pm, or 8pm-1am slot. Open July-Aug. M-F noon-1am, Sa 1pm-1am, Su 2-8pm; Sept.-June M-F 7:30am-1am, Sa noon-1am, Su 2-8pm. **Hôtel Méditerranée,** 62bis av. de Gaulle (☎04 68 34 87 48). €4 per hr., after 9pm €2. Open daily 7am-2am. The best deal is at the **youth center.**

Post Office: quai de Barcelone (☎04 68 51 99 12). **Currency exchange** with good rates. Cyberposte. Open M-Tu and F 8am-7pm, W-Th 9am-7pm, Sa 8am-noon. **Poste Restante:** 66020. **Postal code:** 66000.

▌ ACCOMMODATIONS & CAMPING

The cheapest hotels are near the train station on av. du Général de Gaulle. From these hotels and the nearby Auberge de Jeunesse, it's only about a 10min. walk to the city center.

▓ **Hôtel de l'Avenir,** 11 rue de l'Avenir (☎04 68 34 20 30; fax 04 68 34 15 63; www.avenirhotel.com), off av. du Général de Gaulle. Colorful rooms, terraces, and a rooftop garden give the feel of a beautiful summer home, with furnishings and wall decoration handpainted by the owner. Reserve ahead. Breakfast €4. Shower €2.80. Reception M-Sa 7am-11pm, Su 7-11am and 6-11pm. Singles €15.30; doubles and larger singles €18.30-€22.20, with toilet €23.70, with shower and toilet €32; triples with shower €35.10; quads with shower €38.20. Prices for everything except singles drop €1.50-2.30 mid-Sept. to mid-June. Extra bed €5.40. AmEx/MC/V. ❷

Auberge de Jeunesse La Pépinière (HI), allée Marc-Pierre (☎04 68 34 63 32; fax 04 68 51 16 02), on the edge of town between the highway and the police station. From the train station, take a few steps down av. de Gaulle and turn left onto rue Valette. At the end of this street, turn right onto av. de Grande Bretagne, left onto rue Claude Marty (rue de la Rivière on some maps) just before the police station, and right onto allée Marc-Pierre. (10min.) Six to eight small metal bunks are crowded into each room of this old stucco building. Outdoor terrace with flowers provides a refreshing break from the somber bedrooms. Kitchen available daily 7:30-11am and 5-11pm. Breakfast €3.20. Sheets €3. Checkout 10am, strictly enforced. Lockout 10am-5pm. Closed late Dec. to late Jan. Bunks €8.60, €11.50 for non-HI members. Cash or check only. ❶

Hôtel Express, 3 av. du Général de Gaulle (☎04 68 34 89 96). A block from the train station. Clean, functional rooms come with wooden floors and old furniture. Breakfast €4. Shower €2.50. Reception 24hr. Often full during the summer; call ahead. Singles €17-29; doubles €19-35; triples €31-43; quads €37-42. MC/V. ❷

Camping Le Catalan, rte. de Bompas (☎04 68 63 16 92). Take the bus (dir: Bompas) from the *gare routière* and ask to be let out at Camping Catalan (15min., 2 per day, €1.80). Ninety-four spots have access to a snack bar, pool, and hot showers. Closed late Oct. to Mar. July-Aug. 2 people with car €14.40, extra person €4, electricity €2.60; Apr.-June and Sept.-Oct. €11.10/€3/€2.50. MC/V. ❶

◖ FOOD

Perpignan's best culinary feature is its spread of reasonably priced restaurants serving Catalan specialties. If you've been waiting to try *escargots*, don't slither an inch farther; *cargolade* smothers your shell-wearing garden friends with garlic *aïoli*. The specialty *touron* nougat is available in flavors such as caramel, almond, and dried fruit. **Place Jean Jaurès de la Loge, place Arago,** and **place de Verdun** in the *vieille ville* are filled with restaurants that stay lively at night. Pricier options and candle-lit tables line **quai Vauban** along the canal, while **avenue de Gaulle,** in front of the train station, has cheaper alternatives. A wide variety of fresh produce can be found at the **open-air markets** on pl. Cassanyes (open daily 7am-12:30pm) and pl. de la République (open Tu-Sa 7am-12:30pm and 4:30-7:30pm, Su 7am-1pm; M 7am-1pm fruits and vegetables only). Place de la République also holds an assortment of fruit stores, *charcuteries,* and bakeries, as well as the **Marché République.** (Open Tu-Su 7am-1pm and 4-7:30pm.) **Casino** supermarket stockpiles food on bd. Félix Mercader. (☎04 68 34 74 42. Open M-Sa 8:30am-8pm.)

The best location in the city is held by the ◼**Bistrot St-Jean ❸,** 1 rue Cité Bartissol, which sets its tables in the courtyard of the cathedral. Specialties include their *pause terroir* (€9.50), a hearty concoction of grilled bread smothered with cheese and toppings such as onions, potatoes, and anchovies. (☎04 68 51 22 25. *Menus* €17-19; meat and fish dishes €12-20. Open July-Aug. daily noon-2pm and 7-10:30pm; Sept.-June closed Su. MC/V.)

◗ SIGHTS

A **museum passport,** valid for one week (€6), allows entrance to the Musée Hyacinthe Rigaud; the Casa Pairal; the Musée Numismatique Joseph Puig, 42 av. de Grande-Bretagne (☎04 68 66 24 86); and the Musée d'Histoire Naturelle, 12 rue Fontaine Neuve (☎04 68 66 33 68). Purchase at any of the listed museums.

An uphill walk across the *vieille ville* brings you to the sloping red-rock walls of Perpignan's 15th-century Spanish **citadel.** Concealed inside is the simple, square 13th-century **Palais des Rois de Majorque,** where the Majorcan kings bred lions. Although the castle's main chambers are bare and generally unimpressive, its tow-

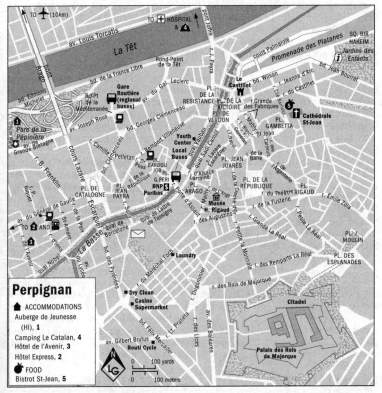

Perpignan

⬆ ACCOMMODATIONS
Auberge de Jeunesse
(HI), 1
Camping Le Catalan, 4
Hôtel de l'Avenir, 3
Hôtel Express, 2

🍎 FOOD
Bistrot St-Jean, 5

ers give an amazing view of the surrounding city. The courtyard below also serves as a concert hall throughout July, hosting a variety of plays and musical performances; tickets cost €22-49 and can be purchased next to the tourist office, at the Palais des Congrès. (Enter from rue des Archers. Palais ☎ 04 68 34 48 29. Open June-Sept. daily 10am-6pm; Oct.-May 9am-5pm. 1hr. French tours available if reserved in advance. €4, students €2, under 12 free. Ticket sales end 45min. before closing.)

Back in the *vieille ville*, the **Musée Hyacinthe Rigaud**, 16 rue de l'Ange, contains a small but impressive collection of paintings by 13th-century Spanish and Catalan masters, as well as canvases by Rigaud, Ingres, Picasso, and Miró. (☎ 04 68 35 43 40. Wheelchair-accessible. Open Su-M and W-Sa noon-7pm. €4, students and ages 15-18 €2, under 15 free.) Guarding the entrance to the city's center, **Le Castillet** was originally built in 1368 by the Spanish as part of the fortifications intended to repel French invaders. After the Treaty of the Pyrénées in 1659, the small castle was transformed into a prison and torture chamber for those who refused to acknowledge the victorious French crown. Now that relations between France and Spain are slightly less hostile, the Castillet is used to hold the small **Casa Pairal**, a museum of Catalan domestic ware and religious relics. (☎ 04 68 35 42 05. French guided tours mid-June to mid-Sept. M and Th at 3pm. Open Su-M and W-Sa May-Sept. 10am-7pm; Oct.-Apr. 11am-5:30pm. €4, students €2, under 15 free.)

A paragon of Gothic architecture, the striking **Cathédrale St-Jean** at pl. Gambetta is partly supported by a macabre pillar depicting the severed head of John the Baptist. The side chapels also have stunning oil paintings, colorful stained glass, and crystal chandeliers. (☎04 68 51 33 72. Open daily 7:30am-noon and 3-7pm. Su mass 8, 10:30am, 6:30pm.)

♫ ◉ ENTERTAINMENT & FESTIVALS

Perpignan is a big city that keeps small-town hours. Everything seems to shut down by 8pm, and even the restaurants usher out their last customers around 10:30pm. If you're looking for a night on the town, prepare yourself for a calm and café-centric experience. The open-till-dawn clubs lining the beaches at nearby **Canet-Plage** (p. 624) constitute the wildest nightlife, but unless you can make the night last until 6:50am (9:10am on Sunday morning), getting back to Perpignan will mean paying €20-25 for a taxi.

In July and August, the town hosts free musical performances and traditional Catalonian dancing every Thursday from 7:30 to 11:30pm at various locations. **Procession de la Sanch** takes over the streets of the *vieille ville* on Good Friday. Although the hooded, solemn ceremony feels a little like the rites of some secret cult, everyone in town is welcomed to watch. As in most of southwestern France, sacred fire is brought down from Mt. Canigou on June 23 for the **Fête de St-Jean.** (☎04 68 35 07 60. Office open daily 5-8pm.) The two weeks surrounding the celebrated day are filled with continuous dancing, music concerts, and food tasting. For two nights at the end of June, **La Fête des Vins** makes the entire town a little more jolly. Between bd. Wilson and the cours Palmarole, over 50 stands hand out wine samples for free and full glasses for €3. Cheese, foie gras, and catalan lamb are also available. (☎04 68 51 59 99; fax 04 68 51 62 06.) In July, the **Estivales de Perpignan** (www.estivals.com) brings world-renowned theater and dance to Perpignan. (Tickets €22-49, under 21 €11-23, young children €9. Tickets can be purchased next to the tourist office, at the Palais de Congrès.) During the first two weeks in September, Perpignan hosts **Visa Pour l'Image,** an international festival of photojournalism (☎04 68 66 32 17; www.visapourlimage.com).

▶ DAYTRIP FROM PERPIGNAN: CANET-PLAGE

*CTP Shuttles (☎04 68 61 01 13) runs **buses** to Canet-Plage; catch the #1 in Perpignan at pl. Arago or at prom. des Platanes on bd. Wilson. (30min.; every 30min.; departing from Perpignan July-Aug. M-Sa 6:15am-8:10pm, Su 8:20am-8:10pm; Sept.-June M-Sa 6:15am-7:40pm, Su 1:25-7:50pm; departing from Canet July-Aug. M-Sa 6:50am-9pm, Su 9:10am-9pm; Sept.-June M-Sa 6:50am-8:20pm, Su 2:10-8pm. €2.10, round-trip €3.60.) Get off at the Canet-Plage CTP bus stop, right in front of the post office. **Taxis** are on av. de la Méditerranée near the beach. Call **A.G. Taxis** if you need vehicles with 5-9 seats. (☎04 68 73 08 62. During the day €1.24 per km, at night €1.86, starting fee €2.30. €20 to Perpignan, €26-€30 to the airport.) Rent **bikes** at Sunbike, 122 Promenade Côte Vermeille. (☎04 68 73 88 65. €8 for 2hr., €14 for 8hr., €45 per week. ID card and €150-200 deposit required. Open July-Aug. daily 9am-7:30pm; Sept.-June Tu-Sa 9:30am-12:30pm and 2:30-7pm. Closed for two weeks in Feb. and Dec. AmEx/MC/V.)*

For sunbathing and swimming, Perpignan residents commute to **Canet-Plage,** a 30min. bus ride from the main city. The town's main attraction is its long stretch of sandy beach clubs, each separated from the other by trampolines, playgrounds, and mini-golf courses. At night the beachfront shimmers with neon lights. Vendors line the boardwalk, children crowd onto the musical carousels in the Espace Méditerranée, and parents sit in one of the surrounding cafés, most of which bring in live music after 8pm. The **casino,** at the edge of the Espace Méditerranée, is a good place to lose your money. (☎04 68 80 14 12. Open July-Aug. daily 10am-4am; Sept.-June Su-Th 10am-2am, F-Sa 10am-4am. Slot machines open all day; roulette and black-jack tables open at 9pm. 18+. Dress code not strictly enforced.) A 20min. walk away from the beach toward Canet, the *discothèque* complex **La Luna**, in the Colline des Loisirs, is packed with people once the bars close around 2am. From the bus stop, walk to the rotary on your right and take another right onto av. de la Méditerranée. After two more rotaries, continue straight onto the highway; the discos will be on your right past the big Casino supermarket. (☎04 68 73 31 01; www.luna.fr. Open July-Aug. daily midnight-6am; Sept.-June F-Sa midnight-5am. €12 cover, including one drink, at each of the three discos.) The most youthful disco scene is found at **Voice&BDF**—groups can call ahead for a bus from Perpignan. **Paradisko** draws a slightly older crowd, while **Full Moon** hosts a good mix of guests. Next door, **Le Fly Bar** serves drinks until the clubs open. (☎04 68 80 80 49. Open F-Sa 8pm-2am. Beer €5.)

On the beachfront, it's not hard to find a good, cheap meal. **Gallerie Cassanyes,** leading away from the Espace Méditerranée, is packed with sandwich shops and restaurants that improve in quality the farther you get from the plaza. Pizza and pasta usually go for around €7. The **market** near the beach on pl. Foment de la Sardane sells produce and cheap clothes. (Open Tu-Su 7:30am-12:30pm.) There is a smaller **market** in the village, 45min. from the beach, at pl. St-Jacques. (Open W and Sa 7:30am-noon.) Pick up supplies at the **Petit Casino** supermarket, 12 av. de la Méditerranée. (☎04 69 80 36 34. Open July-Aug. daily 8am-12:30pm and 3:30-7:30pm, Su 8am-12:30pm. Closed M Sept.-June.) Bakeries and *charcuteries* cluster along the same avenue toward the port.

The Canet-Plage **tourist office**, av. de la Méditerranée, doles out free brochures and maps. From the bus stop next to the post office, turn right and head to the rotary. From there, take a left onto av. de la Méditerranée; the tourist office will be down the street on your right. (☎04 68 86 72 00. Open July-Aug. daily 9am-7pm; Sept. and June M-Sa 9am-noon and 2-6pm, Su 10am-noon and 2:30-5:30pm; Oct.-May M-Sa 9am-noon and 2-5pm, Su 10am-noon and 3-5pm.)

MILLAU

Located in a small valley between the Tarn and Dourbie rivers, Millau (pop. 25,000) originally put itself on the map as a Roman industrial center acclaimed for its sturdy red pottery. Several centuries later, the town shifted its focus to the production of fine leather and continues to export its handmade gloves to elegant shops in Paris and New York City. Visitors now come mainly for the town's gorgeous hiking trails and abundant mountain sports. Positioned in the center of the idyllic **Parc Naturel Régional des Grands Causses,** the modern town of Millau provides a reasonably-priced home base for nature lovers and adventure-seekers alike. Nearby, Roquefort's cheese factories and the canyons in Gorges du Tarn make perfect daytrips.

▣ TRANSPORTATION & PRACTICAL INFORMATION. Infrequent **trains** travel to: Paris (10hr., 2 per day, €58.60); Montpellier (2½hr., 2 per day, €14.40); Béziers (2hr., 3 per day, €15.20). Information desk (☎05 65 61 56 63) open M-Sa 7am-9pm, Su 7am-1pm. More convenient **buses** run from outside the Millau train station to Montpellier (2hr., 6 per day, €15.30) and Toulouse (4hr., 1 per day, €23). The information desk inside the train station (☎05 65 59 89 33) is open M-Tu and Th 8:30am-noon and 2:30-6:30pm, W and F 8:30am-12:30pm and 2:30-6:30pm, Sa 9am-noon. **Taxis** (☎06 73 00 53 58 or 06 85 74 05 07) are sometimes outside the train station. **Europcar**, 3 pl. Frédéric Bompaire, **rents cars.** (☎05 65 59 19 19; fax 05 65 59 22 50; www.europcar.fr. Cars from €282 per week, €810 per month. 21+. Open M-F 8:30am-noon and 2:30-7pm, Sa 9am-noon. AmEx/MC/V.)

THE BIG SPLURGE

CHÂTEAU DE CREISSELS

Just 3km from Millau, the **Château de Creissels** guards the expansive valley at its doorstep. Originally a 12th-century fort, the building was first owned by Raimond de Roquefeuil, a direct ancestor of the American Rockefellers. The French monarchy gained possession of the castle in 1589, and the château became a hotel in 1960.

Although the small, modern rooms are impressive, the large bedrooms in the *partie ancienne* are simply breathtaking. The latter are decorated with oriental rugs, white floor-to-ceiling curtains, marble fireplaces, and sometimes a crystal chandelier. The library and billiard rooms that grace the first floor are similarly exquisite. The château also offers delicious 5-course *menus* (€30-38), either in its medieval vaulted cellar or its attractive outdoor *terrasse* overlooking Millau.

(Rte. de Ste-Affrique, in the town of Creissels. ☎05 65 60 19 59; www.chateau-de-creissels.com. To get there from the train station in Millau, walk 3km uphill to the town of Creissels or take a short €6 cab ride. Breakfast €7.70. Closed mid-Jan. to mid-Mar. Reception daily 7am-11:30pm. Reserve one week in advance. Modern doubles and triples with TV, toilet, and bath or shower €46.50-60; triples and doubles in the old section €78. Extra person €18. AmEx/MC/V.)

To get to the center of town, take a right out of the train station and walk a block down rue Georges Pompidou until you see rue du Barry on your left. As this street turns into rue Droite, you will find the **tourist office** on your left, at 1 pl. du Beffroi. The helpful staff makes **hotel reservations** and provides free maps of the town. (☎05 65 60 02 42; fax 05 65 60 95 08; www.ot-millau.fr. Open July-Aug. M-Sa 9am-7pm; Sept.-June M-Sa 9am-12:30pm and 2-6:30pm, Su 10am-12:30pm and 3-6:30pm.) The tourist office also offers **tours** from the last week in June until the first week in September. (M 10am and Th 4:30pm. €5.) The **police** can be found at 14 rue de la Condamine (☎05 65 61 23 00), while the **hospital** is located at 265 bd. Achille Souquest. (Info ☎05 65 39 30 00, emergencies ☎05 65 59 31 55.) The **pharmacie de garde** is posted outside the tourist office or in the local *Midi Libre* newspaper. There is a **laundromat** at 14 av. Gambetta. (Open daily 7am-9:45pm. Wash €3-6, dry €0.50 per 5min., detergent €0.50.) The cheapest **dry-cleaning** service can be found at 66 rue Jean Jaurès. (☎05 65 61 16 28. Pants €5, shirt €4.60, dress €6.10. Open M 2-4:40pm, Tu-F 8:45am-noon and 1:45-7pm, Sa 9am-noon.) Check your email at **Posanis**, 5 rue Droite. (☎05 65 60 68 53. €3 per hr.; photocopies €0.15 per page. Open M-Sa July-Aug. 10am-10pm; Sept.-June 2-10pm.) The **post office,** 12 Alfred Merle, has a **Western Union** desk and **ATMs** outside. It also offers a **currency exchange** with good rates. (☎05 65 59 20 50. Open M-F 8am-7pm, Sa 8am-noon.)

⌂ ACCOMMODATIONS & CAMPING. Most of the hotels in Millau are expensive and thoroughly unimpressive. One exception to the rule is the **Hôtel de Paris et de la Poste ❷**, 10 av. de Alfred Merle, across from the train station. This hotel's colorful rooms have antique furniture and large sunny windows. (☎05 65 60 00 52; fax 05 65 60 71 34. Breakfast €5. Reception 7am-11pm. July-Aug. reserve 1 week in advance. Singles and doubles €22, with shower €25, with shower and toilet €35, with bath and toilet €40. Extra bed €6. MC/V.) Another good deal can be found at the two-star **Hôtel du Commerce ❷**, 8 pl. de Mandarous. From the train station, walk straight on av. de Alfred Merle and turn right onto av. de la République. The hotel is at the end of this street, on the fourth floor of a small office building. Although plain and nondescript, the rooms are clean and come with TVs. (☎05 65 60 00 56; fax 05 65 60 96 50; www.hotel_du_commerce.com. Breakfast €4.50. Reception M-F 7am-1pm and 3:30-11pm, Sa-Su 7:45am-1pm and 3:30-11pm. July-Aug. reserve 1 week in advance. Singles €19, with toilet €23, with toilet and shower €29; doubles with bath and toilet €32-

35.10; triples with bath and toilet €38.20-40; quads with bath and toilet €43. Extra bed €8. Wheelchair-accessible. AmEx/DC/MC/V.) Those that reserve months in advance may just be lucky enough to ensure a spot at the **Gîte de la Maladrerie ❶**, av. Louis Balsan. Owned by a sweet older man, this small cottage offers homey 2- to 6-bed rooms. Stop at the tourist office for a map, as the *gîte* is far from the center of town. (☎ 05 65 61 41 84 or 05 65 60 41 84; fax 05 65 60 26 02. Reception daily 6-8pm. Beds €10; camping €2 per person. Cash only.) Although it does not come highly recommended, there is an **Auberge de Jeunesse ❶**, 26 rue Lucien Costes, on the outskirts of town. The hostel is located in a modern cement building monitored by an unfriendly staff. (☎ 05 65 61 27 74; fax 05 65 61 90 58. Reception M 8am-7:30pm, Tu-Th 8am-1:30pm and 4:30-7:30pm, F 8am-6:30pm, Sa 3-7pm. Those who have previously reserved a room may also arrive at the hostel Sa 7am-11pm and Su 11am-midnight. Sheets €2.80. 2- to 4-bed rooms €10 per person. **HI members only.** Cash only.) For a night of luxury, check into the **Château de Creissels,** rte. de Ste-Affrique, a converted medieval fort (see **The Big Splurge,** p. 626).

There are also six campsites on the other side of the Tarn River, about 5min. from the town center. About 500m from the pont de Cureplat, the four-star **Camping Les Rivages ❶**, av. de l'Aigoual, is the best site in Millau. Catering to athletes and children, the shaded grounds offer two badminton courts, three ping-pong tables, two pools, three tennis courts, three squash courts, a volleyball net, a basketball court, a river beach, a playground, and a jacuzzi. (☎ 05 65 61 01 07; fax 05 65 59 03 56; www.campinglesrivages.com. Open May-Sept. Reception daily July-Aug. 8am-9pm.; May-June and Sept. 8am-noon and 2-7pm. July-Aug. 2 people and tent €20.50, with electricity €23.50, with water €26; 4-person mobile home €380-530 per week; late June and early Sept. €16/€19/€20, 4-person mobile home €39-51 per night; May to mid-June and late Sept. €13/€15/€17/€39-51. MC/V.)

❏ **FOOD.** There is an enormous **Super U** on av. du Pont Lerouge, on the other side of the Tarn river. (Open M-Sa 8:30am-8pm, Su 8:30am-2pm.) In the center of town, there is a much smaller **Petit Casino**, 11 av. Jean Jaurès. (Open July-Aug. Tu-Sa 7:30am-7:30pm, Su 7:30am-12:30pm; Sept.-June Tu-Sa 7:30am-12:30pm and 3:30-7:30pm, Su 7:30am-12:30pm.) At pl. Foche and pl. des Halles, **markets** provide fresh meat and vegetables (W and F 7am-noon). Selling over 100 varieties of cheese, **Le Buron**, 18 rue Droite, has a variety of pungent Roquefort cheeses stashed among its crowded shelves. (☎ 05 65 60 39 88. Open M 9am-noon and 3-7pm, Tu-Sa 8am-12:30pm and 3-7:30pm. MC/V.)

Although more expensive than along the coast, restaurants in Millau offer gourmet food produced with fresh local ingredients and an abundance of Roquefort cheese. In the heart of the *vieille ville*, bd. and rue de la Capelle have a pleasing mixture of elegant restaurants and cheap pizzerias. **Le Chien à la Fenêtre ❶**, 10 rue Peyrollerie, serves elaborate *galettes* (€2-7.50) topped with salmon, cheese, or duck. For dessert, the sugary crêpes (€2-5.30) come with bananas, chocolate, coconut, and ice cream. The open kitchen lets diners watch their food being prepared. (☎ 05 65 60 49 22. Salads €3.20-7.50. Open July-Aug. M-Sa 10am-2pm and 7-10pm; Sept.-June closed M. MC/V.) **Mand-Arielle ❷** serves filling portions of pizza (€5.80-7.80) and homemade pasta (€6.30-7.50) for the cheapest prices around. The €12 *menu* includes a drink, pizza, and movie ticket to the nearby cinema. (☎ 05 65 60 66 25. *Menus* €11-14, meat or fish dishes €6-11.20. Open July-Aug. daily noon-2:30pm and 7-11pm; Sept.-June closed Su lunch. MC/V.) The upscale restaurant **Capion ❸**, 3 rue Jean-François Almeras, serves regional specialties made entirely with locally grown produce. The delicious foie gras and duck breast come especially recommended. (☎ 05 65 60 00 91; fax 05 65 60 42 13. *Menus* €11-19, fish or meat dishes €10-16. Open Su-M and Th-Sa 9am-4pm and 6pm-midnight, Tu 9am-4pm. Closed the last 3 weeks in July. MC/V.)

LANGUEDOC

THE BIG SPLURGE

THESE GLOVES AREN'T FOR KIDS

Although small boutiques specializing in leather products line the streets of Millau, none is as authentic as the famous **Maison Fabre**. Run by the same family since 1924, the store offers handmade gloves produced with the softest and most durable leather available. Each pair is meticulously cut and sewn together by two older women who sit in the basement at antique iron machines amid piles of fabric and thread. The colored leather is lined with cashmere or rabbit fur and then carefully decorated with beads and Swarski crystals.

Although the Maison Fabre has been selling its products to the most fashionable stores in Paris for over sixty years, their label has just recently been introduced in the United States. Saks Fifth Avenue has picked up one of their models, selling the $176 gloves at triple their original price. Their quality goes virtually unrivaled. Friendly and energetic staff wait on customers, repeatedly running to the basement to dig out correct sizes, colors, and models.

(20 bd. Gambetta. ☎ 05 65 60 58 24; www.maisonfabre.fr. Gloves with slight defects €22, other defect-free gloves €35-100. Imported leather jackets and purses also available. Store open M-F 9am-noon and 2-7pm, Sa 10am-noon and 2-6pm. MC/V.)

◙ **SIGHTS.** Occupying one corner of pl. Maréchal Foch, the interesting **Musée de Millau** displays local artifacts dating back to the prehistoric period. Fossilized dinosaur footprints and primitive skulls line the basement walls, while the top floor is covered with an extensive exhibit on glove-making. (☎ 05 65 59 01 08; fax 05 65 61 26 91. Open July-Aug. daily 10am-6pm; May-June and Sept. daily 10am-noon and 2-6pm; Oct.-Apr. closed Su. €5, ages 19-25 €3.50, under 18 free.)

Three blocks farther down rue Droite, the ancient tower of the **Beffroi** looms high above the city. Originally built in the 12th century as a medieval *donjon*, the belfry remained an active prison until just after the French Revolution. Today visitors can wander through the ancient jail cells and observe the tower's enormous iron bell. A steep climb up the narrow, crumbling staircases leads to a breathtaking view of the orange roof tiles of Millau and the gorgeous surrounding mountains. (July-Aug. guided visits at 10 and 11am, self-guided visits 2:30-6pm; late June and most of Sept. guided visits at 3, 4, and 5pm; Oct.-May open by reservation only. Guided tours €3.50, self-guided €2.50, under 19 free.)

The ruined Roman pottery factories lie 2km from the city at **Gaufresenque**. During the 1st century BC, the red ceramic bowls and vases produced here were exported from England to India. Today, all that remains of this mighty industrial center are the low stone walls that outline the ancient town's foundations. (☎ 05 65 60 11 37. Open daily May to mid-Sept. 9am-noon and 2-6:30pm; mid-Sept. to Oct. and mid-Nov. to late Dec. 10am-noon and 2-6pm. €4, ages 19-25 €2.50, under 18 free. Combined ticket to the Gaufresenque and the Musée de Millau €6.)

🎭🎪 **ENTERTAINMENT & FESTIVALS.** The town of Millau does not offer much in terms of nightlife. Catering to an older crowd, several café-bars sprinkled at the ends of **boulevard de Bonald** serve drinks in a calm, subdued atmosphere. Farther from the heart of the city, the popular **Locomative,** 33 av. Gambetta, offers refuge for young locals and foreigners. Fondly referred to as "Le Loco," the bar hosts music concerts every Friday year-round, and also every Wednesday in July and August. (☎ 05 65 61 19 83. Beer €2, other alcohol from €1.50. Happy hour Th 6:30-7:30pm. Open M-Sa 9am-1am.)

For six days in the middle of August, thousands of *pétanque* players from around the country fly to Millau to compete in the town's annual **Mondial Pétanque** tournament. In an effort to raise female participation, two days are now devoted entirely to women competitors, while the last day consists of a mixed gender tournament. The tournament is free to viewers. In the middle of July, the **Millau en Jazz** festival brings eight days of musical concerts. (☎05 65 60 82 47; www.millauenjazz.net. Tickets free to €19; sold at the tourist office.)

▨ OUTDOORS. Perhaps the town's greatest asset is the beautiful **Parc Naturel Régional des Grands Causses** that stretches throughout the region and centers around Millau. Primitive humans first discovered this idyllic region over 200,000 years ago and left behind various carved statues and cave paintings as proof of their inhabitancy. Today the 315,000-hectare park offers excellent mountain trails as well as an unlimited number of sporting activities. The tourist office sells hiking maps (€3-12) and mountain biking maps (€4.60-6.10), while the park's office, 71 bd. de l'Ayrolle, can answer any ecological questions you may have. (☎05 65 61 35 50. Open M-F May-Sept. 9am-12:30pm and 2-6pm; Oct.-Apr. 9am-noon and 2-5pm.)

Taking advantage of the park's natural beauty, companies fill Millau to the brim, advertising every sporting activity imaginable. Providing the largest selection in town, **Antipodes,** 6 pl. des Halles, organizes underground cave climbing, mountain biking, ropes courses, rafting, kayaking, bungee jumping, and hang gliding. (☎05 65 60 72 03; fax 05 65 60 72 10; www.antipodes-millau.com. Hang gliding €65 per person; bungee jumping €40; ropes course €10-20. Office open M 2:30-7:30pm, Tu-Sa 9:30am-12:30pm and 2:30-7:30pm. V.)

Horizon Loisirs, 6 pl. Maréchal Foch, offers most of the same activities, but specializes in hang-gliding. (☎05 56 59 78 60; fax 05 65 59 78 59; www.horizon-millau.com. Hang-gliding €45-65, 5-session initiation course €350. Office open July-Aug. daily 9:30am-noon and 2-7pm; Mar.-June and Sept. to mid-Nov. 10am-noon and 2-5pm. MC/V.) **Organisation Roc et Canyon,** 55 av. Jean Jaurès, differentiates itself from the masses by providing paintball for those with their own means of transportation. (☎05 65 61 17 77; fax 05 65 60 84 57; www.roc-et-canyon.com. Paintball €23 per person; rafting €24; 5-8km kayak trip €17-20; 5-17km canoe trip €25-42; mountain biking €16 for a half-day; 50m bungee jumping €39; cave climb €29; 120m rock climb €34. Open daily mid-June to Sept. 8am-8pm; Oct. to mid-June 9am-6pm. Cash only.)

▨ DAYTRIPS FROM MILLAU

ROQUEFORT

Surrounded by herds of white goats, the small town of Roquefort (pop. 800) has become famous for its beautiful countryside and pungent blue cheese. Granted the sole right to produce cheese under the prestigious Roquefort label, the tiny village somehow churns out enough moldy goat milk to support the entire nation. This impressive feat is accomplished by seven main producers, the largest of which is the well-respected **Société.** Guided tours of the caves lead visitors to where the cheese is wrapped and stored on wooden shelves. After walking through a museum on Roquefort's history, the tour ends with a sampling of three cheeses. (☎05 65 59 93 30; fax 05 65 58 57 17; www.roquefort-societe.com. Open daily mid-July to Aug. 9:30am-6:30pm; Sept. to mid-July hours fluctuate every few weeks, call ahead for specific times. 1hr. tour €2.30, students €1.60, under 16 free.)

In a similar presentation, the **Papillon** company, rue de la Fontaine, takes visitors through each phase of the cheese process and provides free samples. An interesting documentary summarizes the effects past political leaders have had on the town of Roquefort and its famous product. (☎05 65 58 50 08; fax 05 65 58 50 31. Guided tours free. Caves open daily July-Aug. 9am-6:30pm; Apr.-June and Sept. 9:30-11:30am and 1:30-5:30pm; Oct.-Mar. 9:30-11:30am and 1:30-4:30pm.)

For further knowledge on moldy blue cheese, visit the **tourist office** on av. de Lauras. (☎05 65 58 56 00; fax 05 65 58 56 01; www.roquefort.com. Open July-Aug. daily 9am-7pm; Apr.-June and Sept.-Oct. M-Sa 9am-6pm; Nov.-Mar. M-F 10am-5pm.) Although it is easy to find your way around the tiny town of Roquefort, getting there is a more difficult matter. During July and August, one **bus** travels between Roquefort and the Millau train station. (30min.; M, W, F 1 per day leaves Millau at 10am, return trip 1:30pm; round-trip €9, under 10 €5.) During the rest of the year, buses going in the direction of Toulouse can drop you off at Lauras, a town 3km away from Roquefort (25min., M-Sa 7am and 12:35pm, €4.80). From there, walk uphill through pastures while paying close attention to road signs.

GORGES DU TARN

With its base only 10km away from Millau, the Gorges du Tarn slice dramatically through the rocky mountainside above. Considered to be a small, vegetated version of the Grand Canyon, the Gorges attract visitors with their natural beauty and plentiful water activities. The canyon is lined by several old villages, each a blur of red-tiled roofs and crumbling cobblestone streets. The farthest from Millau, **Ste-Enimie,** also happens to be the largest and most infused with tourists. At the intersection of Gorges du Tarn and Gorges de la Jonte, the tiny town of **Rozier** benefits from both the Tarn and Jonte rivers. Closer to Millau, **Aguessac** and **Rivière-sur-Tarn** make beautiful 10-15km hikes.

Perhaps the best way to see the canyon is to float down its middle. On rte. des Gorges du Tarn in Aguessac, **Escapade** rents **canoes** and **kayaks,** among many other modes of transportation. (July-Aug. ☎05 65 59 72 03, Sept.-June ☎06 87 01 02 94; fax 05 65 59 08 70; c-escapade@wanadoo.fr. 7-14km canoe trip €22-27, 7-14km kayak trip €14-18. Open July-Aug. daily 9am-7pm; Sept.-June by appointment.) Another option is to rent **horses, ponies,** or **donkeys** from Ferme Equestre du Puech Capel, in Rivière-sur-Tarn. The stables take riders for short walks or long excursions lasting up to 15 days. (☎05 65 59 86 32; fax 05 65 60 41 74; ferme-de-puech-canal@wanadoo.fr. €11 per hr., under 6 €5 for 30min. Excursions €40 per day.)

For a change, the **Grotte de Dargilan** allows visitors to view its rock formations from the inside. The natural underground cave offers a mile-long trail of breathtaking stalagmites and rock columns. (☎/fax 04 66 45 60 20; www.dargilan.com. Open daily July-Aug. 10am-6:30pm; Apr.-June and Sept. 10am-noon and 2-5:30pm; Oct. 10am-noon and 2-4:30pm. Closed Nov.-Easter. €8, ages 12-18 €6, ages 6-12 €4.)

For a list of hotels and campsites, visit the **tourist office** on rte. des Gorges du Tarn in Rivière-sur-Tarn. The friendly staff hands out maps and lists of water activities. (☎/fax 05 65 59 74 28; www.ot-gorgesdutarn.com. Open July-Aug. daily 10am-12:30pm and 3-7pm; June and Sept. M-F 9am-noon and 3-7pm; Oct.-May M-F 9am-noon and 2-5pm.) From Millau, **buses** run to the tourist office (25min., 3 per day, €3), as well as to the towns of Aguessac, Rozier, Meyrueis, and Ste-Enimie. Prices and travel time vary greatly depending on the distance.

MONTPELLIER

College town Montpellier (pop. 230,000), the capital of Languedoc, has earned the reputation of being the most light-hearted place in the south. Amateur theatrical performances sprout up on every street corner, academics and posers browse fabulous bookstores, and the city puts together a vibrant annual avant-garde dance festival. Cafés on pl. de la Comédie, fondly known as *l'Oeuf* (the egg), sell expensive coffee with complimentary five-star people-watching. Stores on every street sell to the trendy and the retro alike. Come sundown, students hit the bars around pl. Jean Jaurès. The city floods with tourists during the summer, but the wide avenues and sunny streets maintain a relaxed and airy feeling.

LANGUEDOC

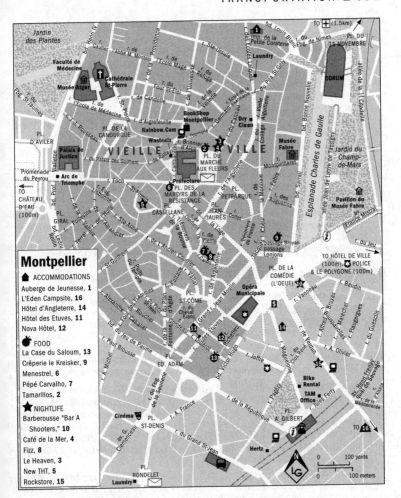

Montpellier

⌂ ACCOMMODATIONS
Auberge de Jeunesse, **1**
L'Eden Campsite, **16**
Hôtel d'Angleterre, **14**
Hôtel des Etuves, **11**
Nova Hôtel, **12**

🍴 FOOD
La Case du Saloum, **13**
Crêperie le Kreisker, **9**
Menestrel, **6**
Pépé Carvalho, **7**
Tamarillos, **2**

★ NIGHTLIFE
Barberousse "Bar A
    Shooters," **10**
Café de la Mer, **4**
Fizz, **8**
Le Heaven, **3**
New THT, **5**
Rockstore, **15**

▶ TRANSPORTATION

Flights: Planes take off from the **Aéroport Montpellier Méditerranée** (☎04 67 20 85 00; fax 04 67 22 02 12), in nearby Mauguio. **Air France** flies to London daily. Info office in the Polygone (☎08 20 82 08 20; www.airfrance.fr). **La Navette Aéroport** shuttles between the airport and the *gare routière* on rue du Grand St-Jean (20min., 11 per day, €1.10). Contact the TAM office (see **Public Transportation**) for a bus schedule.

Trains: Pl. Auguste Gibert (☎08 92 35 35 35). Office open M-F 5am-10pm, Sa 6:15-10am, Su 6:45-10am. To: **Avignon** (1¼hr., 10 per day, €13); **Perpignan** (1½hr., 13 per day, €21); **Marseille** (1¾hr., 9 per day, €20.80); **Toulouse** (2½hr., 10 per day, €28.60); **Nice** (4hr., 2 per day, €39); **Paris** (3½hr., 12 per day, €83.30).

Regional Buses: Rue du Grand St-Jean (☎04 67 92 01 43), on the 2nd floor of a parking garage next to the train station. Info office open M-F 8am-7pm, Sa 8am-6:30pm.

Les Courriers du Midi (☎04 67 06 03 67) travel to **Béziers** (1¾hr.; M-Sa 8 per day, Su 4 per day; €11.10).

Public Transportation: TAM, 6 rue Jules Ferry (☎04 67 22 87 87; www.tam-way.com), operates the local buses and a tramway that connects the city center to its outskirts. Trams every 10-30min. 5am-12:30am; buses less regularly and only until 6-9pm. 1hr. tickets for trams and buses €1.10, 24hr. pass €3.20, weekly pass €11.10. Buy bus tickets from the driver and tram tickets from automated dispensers at the train stops. **Rabelais** connects the city center and the train station 9pm-1am. **L'Amigo** connects Corum (near the city center) to popular night clubs on the outskirts of town. Buses leave Corum Th-Sa at midnight, 12:45, and 1:30am, and return at 2:30, 3:30, and 5am.

Taxis: TRAM (☎04 67 58 10 10) wait at the train station. €1.24 per km during the day, €1.86 at night, €1.70 starting fee. €8-10 from station to hostel. 24hr.

Bike Rental: TAM Vélo (TAM), 27 rue Maguelone (☎04 67 92 92 67). €1.50 per hr., €6 per day. ID and €150 deposit. Electric bicycles and tandem bicycles also available. Open M-Sa 9am-7pm, Su 9am-1pm and 2-7pm. MC/V.

Car Rental: Hertz, 18 rue Jules Ferry (☎04 67 58 65 18; fax 04 67 58 63 15), to your left as you walk out from the train station. Cars from €251 per week, with a €620 deposit. Those under 25 must pay an additional €25 per day. 21+. Open M-F 7am-1pm and 2-7pm, Sa 8am-noon and 2-6pm, Su noon-8pm. AmEx/DC/MC/V.

✴ ⁊ ORIENTATION & PRACTICAL INFORMATION

Across from the train station, **rue Maguelone** leads to fountain-filled **place de la Comédie,** Montpellier's modern center. To reach the tourist office from the *place,* turn right and walk past the cafés and street vendors. It's behind the right-hand corner of the Pavillon de l'Hôtel de Ville. (10min.) The *vieille ville* is bounded by bd. Pasteur and bd. Louis Blanc to the north, esplanade Charles de Gaulle and bd. Victor Hugo to the east, and bd. Jeu de Paume to the west. From pl. de la Comédie, **rue de la Loge** ascends to the center of the *vieille ville,* **place Jean Jaurès.**

Tourist Office: 30 allée Jean de Lattre de Tassigny (☎04 67 60 60 60; www.ot-montpellier.fr). Free maps and same-night **hotel reservation service.** Distributes the weekly *Sortir à Montpellier* and *L'INDIC,* a student guide published in October. **Currency exchange** with no commission. Wheelchair-accessible. Open M-F 9am-6:30pm, Sa 10am-6pm, Su 10am-1pm and 2-5pm; July-Aug. M-F 9am-7:30pm, Sa 10am-6pm, Su 9:30am-1pm and 2:30-6pm. **Branch office** at the train station (☎04 67 92 90 03). Office open M-F 9:30am-1pm and 2-6pm.

Tours: City tours in English (2hr.) given in June every Sa at 3:30pm, July-Aug. Tu and Sa at 10:30am, Sept. Sa at 10:30am. French tours depart Oct.-May W at 5pm. Reservations must be made at least 2 days in advance. €6.50, students €5.50.

Budget Travel: Wasteels, 1 rue Cambacérès (☎08 25 88 70 48), offers good plane, train, and bus prices. Open mid-Sept. to June M-F 9:30am-12:30pm and 2-6:30pm, Sa 9:30am-1pm; July to mid-Sept. closed Sa.

Money: Banque Courtois, pl. de la Comédie (☎04 67 06 26 16; fax 04 67 92 65 49), exchanges money with no commission. 1.1% commission on traveler's checks. Open M-Tu and Th-F 9am-noon and 2-6pm.

English Bookstore: BookShop Montpellier, 6 rue de l'Université (☎04 67 66 09 08). Browse bestsellers and language guides while sipping complimentary coffee. Open Sept.-July M-Sa 9:30am-1pm and 2:30-7pm; closed M in Aug.

RainbowCom, 2 rue Fournarié (☎04 67 91 20 75), supplies information about gay life in Montpellier and other towns in the south. They also write the free IB News magazine, which lists all upcoming gay events. Office open M-Sa 2-7pm.

Laundromat: Lavo Sud, 70 rue des Ecoles Laïques. Open daily 7am-9pm. **Laverie Repasserie,** 12 rue St-Denis. Open daily 7:30am-9pm. For both: wash €3-6.80, dry €0.50 per 5min. There is also a dry-cleaning service at **Pressing Notre Dame,** 51 rue de l'Aiguillerie (☎04 67 60 67 38). Pants and shirts €5.20, dresses €8.80. Open M 2-7pm, Tu-Sa 8am-noon and 2-7pm.

Police: In the Hôtel de Ville (☎04 67 34 71 00).

Hospital: 191 av. du Doyen Guiraud (☎04 67 33 81 67).

Internet: Cybercafé www, 12bis rue Jules Ferry (☎04 67 06 59 52), across from the train station. €0.80 for 30min., €1.50 per hr. Fax, photocopier, and scanner available. Open daily 9am-1am. **Planète 2000,** 21 rue de Verdun (☎04 99 13 35 15 or 04 99 13 35 16). €1.80 per hr. Open daily 9:30am-midnight.

Post Office: Pl. Rondelet (☎04 67 34 52 40). **Currency exchange** with no commission. **Western Union** office. Open M-F 8am-7pm, Sa 8am-noon. **Branch office** at pl. des Martyrs de la Résistance (☎04 67 60 03 60). Open M-F 8am-6:30pm, Sa 8:30am-noon. **Postal code:** 34000.

▛ ACCOMMODATIONS & CAMPING

Except for the campsite, all listings are in the large *vieille ville.* The cheapest is the youth hostel, although several hotels offer great bargains as well. Search **rue Aristide Olivier, rue du Gal. Campredon** (off cours Gambetta and rue A. Michell), and **rue A. Broussonnet** (off pl. Albert I) for other reasonably priced hotels.

Auberge de Jeunesse (HI), 2 impasse de la Petite Corraterie (☎04 67 60 32 22; fax 04 67 60 32 30; montpellier@fuaj.org). From the train station, walk straight on rue Maguelone and across pl. de la Comédie onto rue de la Loge. Turn right onto rue Jacques Cœur, continue until the end of the *vieille ville,* and turn right on impasse de la Petite Corraterie, just before bd. Louis Blanc. (20min.) The hostel's large windows make up for its unappealing bathrooms and pesky 2am curfew. 90 beds in 2- to 10-person single-sex rooms. Pool table €2 per game. Breakfast €3.30. Sheets €2.80 per week. Reception daily 8am-noon and 1pm-midnight. Lockout 10am-1pm. Reserve in advance. Dorms €8.40. MC/V. ❶

Hôtel d'Angleterre, 7 rue Maguelone (☎04 67 58 59 50; www.hotel-d-angleterre.com), right off pl. de la Comédie. Perfectly located between the train station and the Oeuf, this hotel has sunny rooms. The hotel's somewhat haughty owner doesn't mind making you wait. Breakfast €5.50. Reception 24hr. Reserve several weeks in advance. Singles with shower and TV €28; doubles with TV €28, with shower and TV €38-50. Extra person €5. AmEx/MC/V. ❸

Nova Hôtel, 8 rue Richelieu (☎04 67 60 79 85; fax 04 67 60 89 06; hotelnova@wanadoo.fr). From the train station bear left on rue de la République. Turn right onto bd. Victor Hugo, left onto rue Diderot, and right onto rue Richelieu. (5min.) Warm, comfortable, sunlit rooms. 5% discount for students with a *Let's Go* guide. Breakfast €4.60. Reception M-Sa 7am-11:30pm, Su 8am-11:30pm. Reserve several weeks in advance in the summer, earlier in festival season. Singles €20.90; doubles €23.90, with shower €27.70-34.10, with shower, toilet, and TV €32.70-38.60; triples with shower €40, with shower, toilet, and TV €44.70; quads with shower, toilet, and TV €51. AmEx/MC/V. ❸

Hôtel des Etuves, 24 rue des Etuves (☎04 67 60 78 19; www.hoteldesetuves.fr). From the train station, follow directions to Hôtel Majestic, but continue straight on rue des Etuves instead of turning onto rue du Cheval Blanc. Personable atmosphere and 13 fresh, spacious rooms, all with wooden furniture, showers, and toilets. Breakfast €4.20. Reception daily 7am-11pm, closed Su noon-6pm. Reserve one week in advance. Singles €20.50-28, with TV €31; doubles €32-34. Cash only. ❷

L'Eden Campsite, Rte. de Palavas (☎04 67 15 11 05; fax 04 67 15 11 31), 3km away in coastal Lattes. To reach L'Eden, take the Tram (dir: Odyssaeum) to the Port Marianne stop. From here, switch to bus #17 and get off at Oasis Palavasienne in Lattes. (20min.) Four-star camping with tennis courts, pool, and restaurant. Free showers, electricity, and shuttles to the beach. (15min.) July-Aug. 1-2 people and car €25.30, 3 people €30.80, 4 people €34.10; Sept.-June €17.60/€22/€24.20. V. ❷

🔲 FOOD

Montpellier has many reasonably priced restaurants. Standard French cuisine dominates the *places* of the *vieille ville*. **Rue des Ecoles Laïques** in the old city has Greek, Egyptian, Italian, and Lebanese food. Students frequent the eateries on **rue de Fbg. Boutonnet,** halfway between the *vieille ville* and the university. Morning **markets** set up daily at Les Halles Castellane, on rue de la Loge, and Plan Cabanes, on cours Gambetta. The excellent supermarket **INNO,** in the basement of the Polygone commercial center, just past the tourist office, offers great bargains. (Open M-Sa 9am-8:30pm.)

Crêperie le Kreisker, 3 passage Bruyas (☎04 67 60 82 50), near pl. de la Comédie. This small restaurant serves over 50 tasty meal crêpes (€1.90-6.40) topped with buttered snails, mushrooms, artichokes, seafood, and bacon. Speedy and attentive staff also dishes out large salads (€2.30-6.40) and 30 types of dessert crêpes. Open M-Sa 11:45am-2pm and 7-11pm. MC/V. ❷

Pépé Carvalho, 2 rue Cauzit (☎/fax 04 67 66 10 10; pepcarvalho@free.fr), near pl. St-Ravy. Named after the Catalan hero of Manuel Vásquez Montalbán's detective stories, this Spanish restaurant has a lively atmosphere and offers cheap *tapas* (€2.70-4.80) in 30 varieties. €9 *menu* includes 5 *tapas.* Three-person special gives you 15 *tapas* and a bottle of wine for €35. Sangría €1.90, paëlla €9.90. Open July-Aug. M-Sa noon-3pm and 7pm-1am, Su 7pm-1am; closed Su early Sept. to June. AmEx/MC/V. ❷

La Case du Saloum, 18 rue Diderot (☎04 67 02 88 94). Hip, unassuming establishment serves Senegalese dishes and homemade fruit juice. Knock yourself out with their popular specialty, ginger punch, made from natural ginger, orange juice, and rum (€3 per glass). *Plats* €7-12, *menus* €12-18. Open M 3pm-1am, Tu-Sa 11:30am-1am. AmEx/MC/V. ❷

Tamarillos, 2 pl. du Marché au Fleurs (☎04 67 60 06 00; www.philippechapon.biz). Located in a blossoming town square, this upscale restaurant creates elaborate dishes garnished with fruit and flowers. Healthy vegetarian options are also available upon request. Appetizers €12-20, meat and fish dishes €12-23. Open daily noon-3pm and 8am-midnight. MC/V. ❹

Menestrel, impasse Perrier (☎04 67 60 62 51; www.le-menestrel.com), tucked back from pl. des Martyrs de la Résistance. This family-oriented restaurant offers medieval food inside an ancient cellar vault. Friendly waitstaff dons costumes while serving basil-flavored wine (€3 per glass) and boar meat covered with apples (€9). To aid in further recreating the past, diners can request to borrow monk outfits while eating. *Menu* €19.50, *plats* €12-14. Open M-Sa 7-11pm. MC/V. ❸

🔘 SIGHTS

The gigantic **Musée Fabre,** at 39 bd. Bonne Nouvelle (☎04 67 14 83 00), holds one of the largest collections of fine art outside of Paris. Although the museum is closed for renovations until late 2006, the small pavilion annex on the other side of Esplanade Charles de Gaulle displays samples of the collection. (☎04 67 66 13 46; fax 04 67 66 09 20. Open Tu-Su 1-7pm. As the museum's hours may vary depending on the exhibition, it is best to call in advance. €3, students and ages 6-25 €1, 1st Su of each month free.) Right beside the pavilion, small **ponies** can be rented for a 10min. stroll around the Esplanade gardens for €3. (Open June-Sept. daily 2-8pm.)

The old city's pedestrian streets and bookstores as well as its sprawling pl. de la Comédie have some of the best entertainment in Montpellier. The secret courtyards and intricate staircases of 17th- and 18th-century *hôtels particuliers* hide behind grandiose oak doors. Especially notable are the **Hôtel de Varennes**, 2 pl. Petrarque, and the **Hôtel des Trésoriers de France**, rue Jacques Cœur. The tourist office distributes a walking guide to help visitors find the most impressive *hôtels*. Rue Foch, off pl. des Martyrs in the northwest corner of the old city, leads to the grassy **promenade du Peyrou**, which links the **Arc de Triomphe**, erected in 1691 to honor Louis XIV, to the **Château d'Eau**, the arched terminal of an aqueduct. Locals may tell you it dates back to antiquity, but it only just turned 100. Boulevard Henri IV leads to the **Jardin des Plantes**, France's first botanical garden. (Open June-Sept. M-Sa noon-8pm; Oct.-Mar. M-Sa noon-6pm. Free.)

If you're tired of sights and shopping, the sandy **plage de Palavas** provides a relaxing refuge. Take the tram (dir: Odysseum) to Port Marianne and switch to bus #17. The beaches are a short walk from the *gare routière* in Palavas. (20min.)

⬛ NIGHTLIFE

The most animated bars are scattered along **place Jean-Jaurès**. At sundown, **rue de la Loge** fills with vendors, musicians, and stilt-walkers. The extremely popular ◪**Barberousse "Bar A Shooters,"** 6 rue Boussairolles, just off pl. de la Comédie, sells 73 different flavors of rum for €2 each. (☎ 04 67 58 03 66. Beer €3. Happy hour 6-8pm. Open M-Sa 6pm-2am.) **Fizz**, 4 rue Cauzit, is a hot live-music dance club. Foreign students meet each other on the first floor and dance close on the second. (☎ 04 67 66 22 89. Cover F-Sa €8, includes one drink; Tu-Th free. Beer €5.50, hard stuff €6.50. Open July-Aug. Tu-Su midnight-4am; Sept.-June midnight-5am.) At the dance spot **Rockstore**, 20 rue de Verdun, a young crowd grinds to hip hop on the first floor and gyrates to techno music above. The disco also hosts live concerts 3-5 times per week from Sept. to June. (☎ 04 67 06 80 00. No cover. Beer €2. Bar open M-Sa July-Sept. 6pm-6am; Oct.-June 6pm-4am. Discos open at 11:30pm.)

There is vibrant **gay nightlife** in Montpellier. The best discos, such as **La Villa Rouge**, rte. de Palavas (☎ 04 67 06 52 15 or 04 67 06 52 58), in Lattes, lie on

THE INSIDER'S CITY

r. de Candolle · r. d'Aigrefeuille · r. de l'Université · r. Germain · r. du Cannau · r. Vieille Intendance · r. Fournarié · r. Castel Moton · r. de Ratte · r. Bonnier d'Alco · r. Chebrolé · PL. DU MARCHÉ AUX FLEURS · **Préfecture** · r. Cambacérès · r. de la Barbalerie · r. Massin · PL. DES MARTYRS DE LA RÉSISTANCE · r. Foch · PL. PÉTRARQUE · r. Rebuty · St-Firmin · ① ② ③ ④ ⑤ ⑥

GAY MONTPELLIER

With its great location near the Mediterranean, Montpellier has become one of France's unofficial gay capitals.

1 **IB News** is a journal on the gay scene in southern France, and can answer any questions about the hottest beaches, bars, and bums (for more information, see p. 632).

2 Shop for club wear at **Le Village**, a hip boutique with upscale men's clothing. (3, rue Fornarié, ☎ 04 67 60 29 05.)

3 Run by a gay owner, **Bistro d'Alco** serves upscale traditional French fare in a queer-friendly atmosphere. (4, rue Bonnier-d'Alco.)

4 The terrace of **Café de la Mer** is ideal for people-watching over a post-dinner coffee. It is the unofficial *rendez-vous* point for gay partiers about to hit the town (p. 636).

5 At **New THT**, young chic clubbers rock to disco. Once known for public debauchery, it's now more low-key (p. 636).

6 **Le Heaven** serves the same crowd as THT, but with less talking and more of said debauchery (p. 636).

the outskirts of town; the Amigo buses (p. 632) are a good way to get there. Gay bars are sprinkled throughout the *vieille ville* (see **The Insider's City,** p. 635). Pre-party at **Café de la Mer,** 5 pl. du Marché aux Fleurs, known as the gay hub of Montpellier. (☎04 67 60 79 65. Open M-Sa 8am-2am, Su 3pm-2am.) **New THT,** 10 rue St-Firmin, off rue Foch, becomes very popular during the later hours. (☎04 67 66 12 52. No cover. Beer €3.10, straight liquor €5.40. 2-for-1 Happy hour 8-10pm. Open daily mid-June to mid-Sept. 9am-1am; mid-Sept. to mid-June 8pm-1am.) Wilder **Le Heaven,** 1 rue Delpech, provides a perfect atmosphere for meeting men. (☎04 67 60 44 18. Beer €3, liquor €5.50. No cover.)

🎵🖼 ENTERTAINMENT & FESTIVALS

The **Corum,** at the far end of Esplanade Charles de Gaulle, hosts weekly theatrical performances and concerts. (☎04 67 61 67 61. Operas and philharmonic orchestras €14-23, students and children €11-18; plays €8-46.50/€7-40.50. Office open M-F 8am-7pm.) **Cinéma Le Diagonal,** 18 pl. St-Denis, shows foreign films in their original languages with French subtitles. (☎04 67 92 91 81. €5.80, under 13 €4. MC/V.)

During the last two weeks of June and the first week of July, the open-air **Printemps des Comédiens pac Euromédecine** arrives in Montpellier. For details, contact the Opéra Comédie, pl. de la Comédie. (Info ☎04 67 63 66 67, reservations 04 67 63 66 66; www.printempsdescomediens.com. Tickets €6-21, under 25 and seniors €6-18.) In the first two weeks of July, the **Festival International Montpellier Danse** organizes performances, workshops, and films on local stages and screens. (☎04 67 60 83 60, reservations 04 67 60 07 40. Tickets €3.80-27.50.) The rest of July is taken up by the opera, jazz, and classical music performances of **Festival de Radio France et de Montpellier.** (Info and tickets ☎04 67 02 02 01; www.festivalradiofrancemontpellier.com. Most concerts are free; others cost €11-34, students and seniors €6-25.)

NEAR MONTPELLIER

BÉZIERS

Trains leave the station, bd. Verdun, for Montpellier (50min., 20 per day, €9.70) and Toulouse (1½hr., 6 per day, €20). The station is open M 5:25am-9:05pm, Tu-Th 5:40am-10:35pm, F-Su 5:40am-9:05pm. From the station, take the underpass, climb rue de la Rotonde, and turn left on allées Paul Riquet. Behind the statue of Riquet is the **tourist office**, 29 av. St-Saëns. (15min.) Helpful brochures and city guides direct you to the local wineries or nearby beaches. ☎04 67 76 47 00; www.ville-beziers.fr. Open July-Aug. M-Sa 9am-7pm, Su 10am-1pm and 3-6pm; Sept.-June M-Sa 9am-noon and 2-6pm. Guided visits depart from the office July-Aug. M-W at 10:30am; Sept.-June by reservation. €4, students and children under 12 €2.50.

Although modern Béziers (pop. 70,000) is an archetypal Languedoc city, Celts, Iberians, Phoenicians, Greeks, Romans, Arabs, and Franks have all passed through and left their mark. The monuments here aren't spectacular, but its diverse past has left pleasant historical surprises. Béziers is also the starting point of the manmade **Canal du Midi,** which serves as a 240km link between the Atlantic Ocean and the Mediterranean Sea. Before the construction of the Suez canal, the channel was the only alternative to the Strait of Gibraltar.

🍴🎭 FOOD & ENTERTAINMENT. *Biterroise,* the sweet local specialty cake, is flavored with almonds and filled with a pâté of grapes and wine. You can find this sweet dessert along with other fresh produce at the indoor **market** at Les Halles, pl. Pierre Sémard. (Open Tu-Su 5:30am-1:30pm.) Across the street, on the corner of

allées Paul Riquet and rue Flourens, the **Marché Plus** has a reasonable selection of food along with a dry-cleaning service, fax machine, and photocopier. (Open M-Sa 7am-9pm, Su 7am-noon.) There is a larger **Monoprix** at 5 allées Paul Riquet. (Open M-Sa 8:30am-8pm.) At lunchtime, rue Paul Riquet, toward to the Théâtre Munici-pal, is a giant blur of reasonably priced restaurants and cafés. For dinner, elegant but surprisingly inexpensive restaurants line the small av. Viennet between pl. G. Péri and the Cathédrale St-Nazaire at pl. de la Révolution.

The biweekly magazines *Pau's Café* and *Olé* list clubs, bars, and upcoming events. *Exit* magazine has information on the town's disco scene. All three of these publications can be obtained at the tourist office free of charge. After 10pm, many of the cafés on allées Paul Riquet attract crowds with pounding music and small bar sections. A fashionable set at **Ness Café**, 36 allées Paul Riquet, sits on leopard-print stools or outdoor café tables. (☎04 67 49 07 19. Beer €2.30, fish and meat dishes €10-12, pizza €6.50-9. Live DJ F and Sa night. Open M-Sa June-Sept. 5pm-2am; Oct.-May closes at 1am. AmEx/MC/V.) The slightly older clientele at **Le Dollar**, 20 allées Paul Riquet, is treated to live music several times a month. (☎04 67 28 20 84. Beer €2.20, paëlla €8, *moules-frites* €7.50. Open June-Sept. M-Sa 7:30am-2am, Su 5pm-2am; Oct.-May closes around 12:30am. AmEx/MC/V.)

In mid-August, a **féria** that has earned Béziers the nickname "the French Seville" fills the town with five days of *corridas*. Beginning early July, tickets to individual events are sold at the arena on av. Emile Claparède (€24-83); from early to late June, reservations for the entire five days can be made by telephone or on the web. (☎04 67 76 13 45; www.arenes-de-beziers.com. €132-375.) Book hotels months in advance during the *féria*, as the town becomes absolutely mobbed with visitors.

◧ SIGHTS. The four museums of Béziers can be accessed with one pass sold at all museums (€3.10, students and under 12 €2.40). **Le Musée du Biterrois,** pl. St-Jacques (☎04 67 36 71 01), pulls together fascinating regional objects from the pre-historic era until WWII, including Roman funerary monuments and a 1913 Renault driven by "the youngest driver in the world" (4-year-old Jean Lovign). Guided visits in French available if reserved in advance. The second floor houses the **Musée d'Histoire Naturelle,** showcasing stuffed birds, pinned insects, and a small aquar-ium. It may be closed in 2004 due to a lack of staff, but if it is the curators of the Musée Biterrois will open the doors during the week upon request. **Musée Fabré-gat,** 6 pl. de la Révolution (☎04 67 28 38 78), next to the cathedral, displays paint-ings and sculptures by regional artists from the 15th to 20th centuries. An annex to the Fabrégat, the **Musée Fayet,** 9 rue du Capus (☎04 67 49 94 66), houses local art produced from 1830 to 1930, most notably a collection of sculptures by Béziers native Jean-Auguste Injalbert. (All four museums have same hours and prices. Open Tu-Su July-Aug. 10am-6pm; Apr.-June and Sept.-Oct. 9am-noon and 2-6pm; Nov.-Mar. 9am-noon and 2-5pm. €2.40, students and under 12 €1.60.)

The **Cathédrale St-Nazaire,** built on the ruins of a pagan temple in pl. de la Révolu-tion, was destroyed by fire in 1209 and later rebuilt in the French Gothic style. Musicians from all over France and Canada host weekly organ concerts July-August. (Open daily July-Aug. 9:30am-6pm; Sept.-June 9:30am-noon and 2:30-5pm. Concerts Su at 7pm, free.) Nearby, the **Eglise de la Madeleine** witnessed the massa-cre of Béziers townspeople by the violent hands of the Albigeois Crusaders in 1209. To complete its bloody past, the church was also later transformed into a *baïonnette* factory, during the French Revolution. (Open M 3-6pm, Tu-Sa 9am-noon and 3-6pm.)

Linking the Atlantic to the Mediterranean via the river Garonne, Paul Riquet's **Canal du Midi** lies at the base of the city, down quai Port Neuf. Built between 1667 and 1681 by over 15,000 workers, the canal currently helps to irrigate the town and transport small boats around the city.

▨ EXCURSIONS. Fifteen kilometers from Béziers, the one-time fishing village of **Valras** has become a family beach resort graced with 4km of pure white sand. Take bus #212 from the *autogare* at pl. du Gal. de Gaulle and get off in Valras. Most of the campsites lie beyond the town center, at the Porte de Valras bus stop; ask the bus driver to be sure. (☎04 67 28 36 41. 35min.; July-Aug. 17 per day, last return 10:30pm; Sept.-June M-Sa 12 per day, Su 6 per day, last return at 7pm; round-trip €6.) From the *autogare* in Valras, turn left onto rue Charles Thomas and then take your next right onto bd. Capitaine Espinadel, where the **tourist office** provides info on jet skis, tennis courts, and sailboat rentals. (Pl. René Cassin. ☎04 67 32 36 04; www.valras-plage.net. Open daily 9am-12:30pm and 2-7pm.)

For those blessed with their own transportation, most of the nearby private vineyard and *cave* cooperatives give tours ending with wine sampling. The tourist office in Béziers can help direct you to the region's acclaimed *appellations:* Minervois, St-Chinian, Faucères, and a spicy red Cabrières.

SÈTE

The **train station**, quai M. Joffre, sends trains to: Béziers (30min., 25 per day, €6.80); and Montpellier (20min., 30 per day, €4.70). Info office is open M-F 5:50am-7:45pm, Sa-Su 6:40am-7:45pm. **Taxis** wait at the train station. (☎04 67 20 49 00. €1.24 per km during the day, €1.82 at night; €1.07 starting fee. Approximately €7 to the hostel.) **Sétoise buses** shuttle passengers throughout town until 6:30-8:45pm. (☎04 67 74 18 77; 1hr. ticket €1.) As some lines do not run over the weekend, it is best to pick up a schedule at the tourist office. Bus #2 goes from the train station to the tourist office; ask to get off at La Marine. To continue on to both beaches, get off at Les Quilles.

Strategically situated between the Mediterranean and the Bassin Thau, Sète (pop. 42,000), was founded in 1666 as a port town. It is now the largest Mediterranean fishing town in France. Its hybrid Italian-French culture, the result of an early 20th-century exodus from the Italian village of Gaet during the depression in Italy, produces unusual maritime festivals and the lovely *Sètois* accent made famous by folk singer Georges Brassens. Heavy machinery blots the otherwise picture-perfect shoreline, though there is a certain industrial poetry to the rusty ships and screeching gulls—appropriately enough, since the town gave birth to Paul Valéry, one of France's greatest modern poets. Nearby, the two local beaches offer a sunny respite from the bustle of everyday life.

Sète's **tourist office,** 60 rue Mario Roustan, behind quai Général Durand, provides €1 maps, free city guides, and daily themed **tours** in French July-Aug., including a nighttime boat ride along the canal. (☎04 67 74 71 71. Office open July-Aug. daily 9:30am-7:30pm; Sept. and June daily 9:30am-12:30pm and 2-6pm; Oct.-May M-Sa 9am-noon and 2-5:30pm. Currency exchange open M-F 9:30am-noon and 2:30-6pm, Sa 9:30am-noon. Tours vary in price €4.50-10, children €2-5.)

◖ FOOD. During festivals and holidays, *frescati* can be found on every dessert menu. The sweet raisin biscuit is soaked in rum and topped with a layer of coffee cream and soft meringue. Invented in Sète, *tielle* was originally given to fishermen about to embark on long sea voyages. The round pie contains octopus, tomatoes and spices in a flaky crust. Vendors on the canal offer them for €2; inland bakeries sell less authentic versions for €1.50. The restaurants lining **Promenade J. B. Marty,** at the end of rue Mario Roustan near the *vieux port*, serve the catch of the day in unusual ways for €9 and up. Cheaper pizza, pasta, and seafood are the specialties of the less touristy eateries on **rue Gambetta** and its offshoots. The **Monoprix** supermarket is located at 7 quai de la Résistance (☎04 67 74 39 38. Open M-Sa 8:30am-9pm, Su 9am-noon.) The **daily market** at **Les Halles,** just off rue Alsace-Lorraine, provides an abundance of fresh vegetables, fruit, and flowers. (7am-12:30pm.)

🟥 **SIGHTS.** The **Société Nautique de Sète**, on Môle St-Louis, at the southern end of town, is one of France's oldest yacht clubs. All summer, yacht races, including the famed **Tour de France à la Voile**, sail by the Môle. The best place to watch is in front of the café **Les Jardins de L'America's Cup**. The **plage de la Corniche** in the southwest corner of town starts off a 12km stretch of sandy beaches, accessible by bus #6 (departs from the tourist office July-Aug. daily 10am-7pm) and #7 (departs from the Hôtel de Ville year-round W and Sa 8:35am-11:25am). Bus #2 stops a few blocks away from the beach at Les Quilles. (Departs from quai de la Résistance, the train station, and Pont de Pierre year-round M-Sa 7am-7:30pm, Su 2:30-7pm.) All buses are €1. The tourist office has a full list of beach activities, such as **scuba diving** and **sailboat rentals**. Sète Croisières offers **boat rides** and **fishing excursions** July-Aug. (Quai Gal. Durand. ☎04 67 46 00 46; www.setecroisiers.com. 1hr. canal ride €10, ages 3-12 €5; one-day excursion along the Canal du Midi €29/€19; 4hr. sea-fishing trip with bait and equipment included €19, ages 8-12 €15. Reserve 2 days in advance.)

A walk to the *vieux port* and up the hill along rue Haute gets you to the **maritime cemetery** that inspired Valéry's poem *Le Cimetière Marin*. The poet himself is interred here. (Open July-Sept. 8am-7pm, Oct.-June 8am-6pm.) The modern building above the cemetery, the **Musée Paul Valéry**, rue François Desnoyer, displays a large collection of model ships, archeological finds, and local art. (☎04 67 46 20 98. Open July-Aug. daily 10am-noon and 2-6pm; Sept.-June Su-M and W-Sa. July-Aug. €4.60; Sept.-June €3; students and children 12-18 €1.50; first Su of each month free.) On the other side of the city is **L'Espace Georges Brassens**, 67 bd. Camille Blanc, a multimedia museum that pays homage to the irreverent folk singer from Sète. (☎04 67 53 32 77; www.ville-sete.fr/brassens. Take bus #2 or 3. Open daily July-Aug. 10am-noon and 2-7pm; Sept.-June 10am-noon and 2-6pm; Oct.-May. closed M. €5, students €2.)

If you're physically fit, climb chemin de Biscan-Pas from the hostel to the top of **Mont St-Clair** (183m) for a great view of Sète, its canals, and the sea. (15min.) The church **Notre Dame de la Salette**, with wall murals from the 1950s, is the destination of fishermen's wives on a pilgrimage in late September for the **Feu de la St-Jean.**

🟥 **ENTERTAINMENT & FESTIVALS.** Every evening the popular **La Bodega**, 21 quai Noel Guignon, plays live music, from Brazilian jazz to hip hop, and serves over 25 types of whiskeys and 100 cocktails. (☎04 67 74 47 50. Open June-Sept. daily 10pm-4am; Oct.-May closed Su.) **La Dolce Vita**, 21 quai Rhin et Danube, offers dancing, karaoke, and live music. (☎04 67 74 80 73. Open Tu-Su 10pm-3am.) At pl. Edouard Herriot, **Casino de Sète** opens its slot machines early for the morning gamblers. (☎04 67 46 65 65. 18+. Roulette and blackjack open Tu-Sa at 9pm. Piano bar July-Aug. daily 10:30pm; Sept.-June F-Sa 10:30pm. Casino open daily 10am-4am.)

For six days in late August, locals celebrate **La Fête de St-Louis** with fireworks and street performances. The festival centers around the animated **Tournois de Joutes Nautiques**, in which participants joust from oversized rowboats. Arrive early to secure a spot on quai de la Résistance for the competition. On most other summer weekends at 2:30pm, gladiators stage exposition battles in preparation for the tournament. **La Fête de St-Pierre,** the first weekend in July, brings solemn religious rites in the morning and loud festivities at night. On Sunday morning, during the **Bénédiction de la Mer,** fishermen invite the crowds onto their decorated boats and throw flowers into the water to commemorate those lost at sea. For five days in July, Sète draws a few big names to its annual jazz festival, **Jazz à Sète.** (☎04 67 51 18 11; www.jazzasete.com. Tickets €22-25, students €18-20.)

LANGUEDOC

AQUITAINE
& PAYS BASQUE

The southwest corner of France has some of the country's most varied cultures and landscapes. On the geographical extremity of two nations, the region has suffered centuries of international and civil wars. Aquitaine was in English hands from the 12th to 15th centuries; the Pays Basque was part of Basse-Navarre until its ruler inherited the French throne in 1598 as Henri IV. A small Basque separatist minority maintain that their *Euzkadi* homeland is independent, part of neither France nor Spain.

Below the sprawling vineyards of the Médoc that surround ▓**Bordeaux** (p. 640), the pine forest of Les Landes opens onto the windswept sands of the **Côte d'Argent** and **Arcachon** (p. 650). South of Aquitaine, France's border with Spain is a jumble of sensory impressions, from the blinding glitter of the casino of **Biarritz** (p. 652) and the surfer heaven of **Anglet** (p. 662), to the clinking of cow bells on the fields of ▓**St-Jean-Pied-de-Port** (p. 667) and the sharp smell of seafood throughout ▓**St-Jean-de-Luz** (p. 663). The bilingual signs of ▓**Bayonne** (p. 657) proclaim, amid red and green houses, the city's status as the capital of the Pays Basque. Among these typically Basque towns are both quaint medieval villages (▓**St-Emilion,** p. 648; and **Col de St-Ignace,** p. 667) and impressive châteaux (**Pau,** p. 670).

Aquitaine's glory is its wine, which complements food flavored with the elusive *truffe noir* (black truffle). In Gascony, Moulard duck and Roquefort cheese are menu essentials, accompanied by Armagnac, a local brandy. The Pays Basque has a distinctly Spanish influence. The *jambon cru* (cured ham) of Bayonne, the *thon* (tuna) of St-Jean-de-Luz, and the ubiquitous *piperade* (omelette filled with green peppers, onions, tomatoes, and thyme) are notable regional dishes.

AQUITAINE

BORDEAUX

Bordeaux's aromatic wines, grown on the *bords d'eaux* (riverbanks) of the Garonne and Dordogne, are some of the best in the world. Without them, Bordeaux (pop. 280,000) might never have thrived. Until someone, probably an ancient Roman, discovered that the soil was perfect for growing grapes, the sandy, rocky land around the city was useless. Today, the city hosts summer wine festivals and provides a base for tours of legendary vineyards like St-Emilion, Médoc, Sauternes, and Graves. A university town, Bordeaux's diverse, youthful atmosphere makes for great nightlife. Bordeaux is currently undergoing extensive reconstruction as it builds a new tramway system through the city's center, which will probably not be finished until well into 2004.

▐ TRANSPORTATION

Flights: Airport in **Mérignac** (☎05 56 97 11 27), 11km west of Bordeaux. A shuttle bus (☎05 56 34 50 50) connects the airport to the train station and the pl. Gambetta (45min. daily every 45min. 6am-9:45pm. €6; students, under age 26, over 60, and

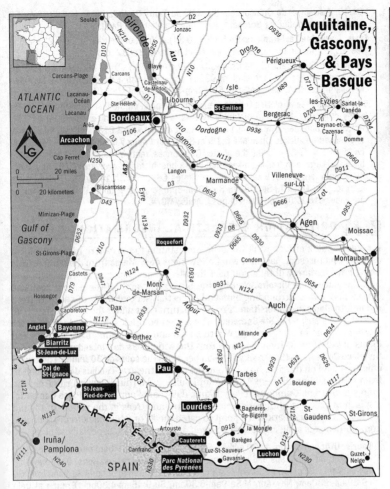

Aquitaine, Gascony, & Pays Basque

families of 3 €4.50). **Air France** (☎08 20 82 08 20) flies one plane to **London** daily for around €575. Their main office in Bordeaux makes reservations and provides various flight schedules (37 av. de Tourny; open M-F 9:30am-6:30pm, Sa 9:30am-1:15pm. AmEx/MC/V).

Trains: Gare St-Jean, rue Charles Domercq (☎05 56 33 11 06). Information office open M-Sa 9am-7pm. To: **Lyon** (8-10hr., 3 per day, €53.50); **Marseille** (6-7hr., 12 per day, €56.50); **Nantes** (4hr., 4 per day, €36); **Nice** (9-10hr., 5 per day, €70); **Paris** (TGV: 3-5hr., 15-25 per day, €57.50); **Rennes** (6hr., 1 per day, €46.50); **Poitiers** (2hr., 10-20 per day, €28); **Toulouse** (2-3hr., 11 per day, €27).

Public Transportation: The **CGFTE bus system** (☎05 57 57 88 88) serves the city and suburbs. Maps at the train station and info offices at 4 rue Georges Bonnac (M-Sa 8am-7:30pm) and at pl. de Quinconces (M-Sa 7am-7:30pm). The *Carte Bordeaux Découverte* allows unlimited city bus use (1-day €3.75, 3-day €8.40); otherwise, fare is

€1.15. Also in pl. de Quinconces, the **Réseau Trans Gironde** buses travel to over 50 small towns surrounding Bordeaux, including Martillac and Pauil.

Taxis: Aquitaine Taxi Radio (☎05 56 96 00 34), in front of the train station. €2 starting fee, €1.15 per km during the day, €1.75 at night. €23/€32 to the airport.

Car Rental: Europcar, 35 rue Charles Domercq (☎08 25 00 42 46; fax 05 56 31 26 94), connected to the train station. €316+ per week, with a €450 deposit. 21+. Open M-F 7am-11:30pm, Sa 8am-8pm, Su 10am-7:30pm. AmEx/MC/V.

Bike Rental: Free at pl. des Quinconces with ID deposit on the first Su of the month. On every other day, the more distant **Vélo Bus,** 10 pl. Stalingrad (☎05 57 80 04 79), across the pont de Pierre, lends their bikes out for free with a €183 deposit, an ID card, and a used bus ticket. Open M-F 6:15am-8pm. **Bord'eaux Vélos Loisir,** quai Louis XVIII (☎05 56 44 77 31), facing the pl. des Quinconces, rents bikes, in-line skates, electric bikes, go-karts, and "talking bikes" that give a brief historical overview of 16 major landmarks in 4 languages. Bikes and in-line skates €8 for 4hr., €14 for 8hr. Talking bikes €15 for 2hr. Open Tu-Sa 1-8pm, Su 10am-8pm, and other times if you call 24hr. in advance. €150-200 and ID as deposit. AmEx/MC/V.

✈️ 🛈 ORIENTATION & PRACTICAL INFORMATION

It takes about 30min. to walk from the train station to the *centre ville*, the oldest and most picturesque part of town. Follow **cours de la Marne** from the station. This busy thoroughfare will take you past the **Marché des Capucins** on your right and into the **place de la Victoire.** Nearby, the huge stone arch of the **porte d'Aquitaine** towers above the surrounding bars and clubs that serve crowds of students from the nearby **Domaine Universitaire.** From here, turn right under the arch of the *porte* onto the pedestrian **rue Ste-Catherine.** The patterned brick sidewalks lead to *vieux Bordeaux*, the hub of the city, where shops and restaurants draw tourists and locals alike. After 10-15min., you'll cross the wide **cours de l'Intendance** and enter the **place Comédie** as the street you're on becomes the **cours du 30 Juillet.** The **tourist office** is ahead on the right, just beyond the Grand Théâtre. The **bus depot** is right in front of the station. Buses #7 (dir: Saint-Louis) and 8 (dir: Bacalan) run from the train station to pl. Gambetta (every 10min. daily 5am-9pm, €1.15). **Place Gambetta,** a splash of greenery with park benches, lawns, and trees in the middle of the old town, is a good landmark and a point to catch the #7 or 8 bus back to the train station. Bordeaux is a big city; guard yourself and your wallet, especially at night.

Tourist Office: 12 cours du 30 juillet (☎05 56 00 66 00; www.bordeaux-tourisme.com). Well stocked with maps and brochures; also makes **hotel reservations.** Open July-Aug. M-Sa 9am-7:30pm, Su 9:30am-6:30pm; Sept.-Oct. and May-June M-Sa 9am-7pm, Su 9:30am-6:30pm, Nov.-Apr. M-Sa 9am-6:30pm, Su 9:45am-4:30pm. **Branch** at train station (☎05 56 91 64 70) makes hotel reservations. Open M-Sa 9am-7pm.

City Tours: Several in French and English are given by the **tourist office.** Walking tours Apr. to mid-Nov. Su-Tu and Th-F 10am, mid-Nov. to Mar. daily 10am. 2hr. bus tours Apr. to mid-Nov. W and Sa 10am. Each tour €6.50, students €6.

Local Vineyard Tours: Half-day bus tour Apr. to mid-Nov. daily 1:30pm; mid-Nov. to Mar. W and Sa 1L30pm. €26, students and seniors €23.

Budget Travel: Wasteels, 13 pl. de Casablanca (☎08 25 88 70 32; fax 05 56 31 91 48), across the street from the station, books charter flights. Open M-F 9am-12:45pm and 2-6:15pm, Sa 9:30am-12:30pm. MC/V.

Consulates: UK, 353 bd. du Président Wilson (☎05 57 22 21 10; fax 05 56 08 33 12). Open M-F 9am-noon and 2-5pm. **US,** 10 pl. de la Bourse (☎05 56 48 63 85; fax 05 56 51 61 97). For security reasons, the office is only open by reservation. To reach other foreign consulates, contact the tourist office.

AQUITAINE

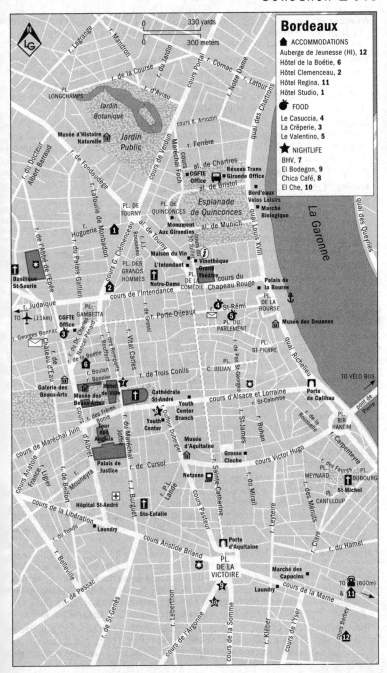

Bordeaux

ACCOMMODATIONS
Auberge de Jeunesse (HI), **12**
Hôtel de la Boétie, **6**
Hôtel Clemenceau, **2**
Hôtel Regina, **11**
Hôtel Studio, **1**

FOOD
Le Casuccia, **4**
La Crêperie, **3**
Le Valentino, **5**

NIGHTLIFE
BHV, **7**
El Bodegon, **9**
Chica Café, **8**
El Che, **10**

American Express: 11 cours de l'Intendance (☎05 56 00 63 36). Open M-F 9:30am-12:30pm and 1:30-5pm. For 24hr. refund assistance, call ☎08 00 90 86 00 for lost traveler's checks, 01 47 77 72 00 for credit cards).

Youth Center: Centre d'Information Jeunesse d'Aquitaine, 5 rue Duffour Dubergier (☎05 56 56 00 56). Information about activities, jobs, and GBLT services. Open M-Th 9:30am-6pm, F 9:30am-5pm. Free Internet for up to 10min. **Branch,** 2 blocks away at 125 cours d'Alsace Lorraine (☎05 56 56 00 41), sells train tickets and provides free Internet use for 45min. Open M-Th 9:30am-6pm, F 9:30am-5pm.

Laundromat: 57 cours de la Marne. Open daily 7am-10pm. Wash €3-7, dry €0.50-1, detergent €0.50. Also at 39 rue Docteur Charles Nancel-Penard. Open daily 7:30am-9:30pm. Wash €3.50-7, dry €0.50, detergent €0.50. Also at 43 cours de la Libération. Open daily 7am-9pm. Wash €3.50-6, dry €1, detergent €0.50.

Police: 87 rue de l'Abbé de l'Epée (☎05 56 99 77 77). **Branch** at train station.

Hospital: 1 rue Jean Burguet (☎05 56 79 56 79).

Internet: Netzone, 209 rue Ste-Catherine (☎05 57 59 01 25), 3 blocks away from pl. de la Victoire. €3 per hr., students €2.50. Open M-Sa 9:30am-midnight, Su noon-midnight. Free Internet at the two youth centers; available for a small fee at the Hôtel Studio and the post office (see listings).

Post Office: 52 rue Georges Bonnac (☎05 57 78 85 25), off pl. Gambetta. **Currency exchange** with no commission. Open M-F 8:30am-6:30pm, Sa 8:30am-noon. **Cyberposte. Branch** (☎05 57 14 32 00) at the corner of rue St-Rémi and rue des Piliers-de-Tutelle is open M 2-6pm, Tu-F 10am-6pm, Sa 10am-12:30pm. **Postal code:** 33065.

▌ ACCOMMODATIONS & CAMPING

Despite being in the run-down outskirts of town, Bordeaux's main hostel is close to the train. A few great deals can be found on the side streets around the pl. Gambetta and the cours d'Albret. Reserve at least a few days in advance in summer.

▨ **Hôtel Studio,** 26 rue Huguerie (☎05 56 48 00 14; www.hotel-bordeaux.com), is a backpacker favorite. Walk 1 block down rue Clemenceau from pl. Gambetta, turn left on rue Lafaurie de Montbadon, and left on rue Huguerie. The tiny clean rooms have telephone, toilet, shower, and cable TV at the lowest prices around. The walls are paper-thin, and the rooms are a little dark on the lower floors, but with all the perks and the comfortable beds you might not even notice. Internet: hotel guests €2.25 per hr., others €4.50. Breakfast €4. Reception 7am-midnight. Reserve ahead. Small singles €16, larger singles €24; doubles €20/€27; triples €30.50; quads and quints €38. MC/V. ❷

Hôtel de la Boétie, 4 rue de la Boétie (☎05 56 81 76 68; fax 05 56 81 24 72). Check-in is at Hôtel Bristol around the corner, 4 rue Bouffard. Run by the same family as Hôtel Studio, La Boétie offers similar amenities. Each plain white room comes with shower, cable TV, telephone, and nondescript prints of minor paintings. Breakfast €4. Reception 7am-midnight. Singles €20-24.50, doubles €27.50; triples €30.50; quads and quints €38. Larger rooms available. AmEx/MC/V. ❷

Hôtel Clemenceau, 4 cours Georges Clemenceau (☎05 56 52 98 98; clemenceau@hotel-bordeaux.com). In the heart of old Bordeaux, 20m from where buses #7 and 8 stop in pl. Gambetta. This 2-star hotel was built during the 18th century, but has since been modernized to include cable TV, A/C, telephones, mini-bars, and showers in every room. Breakfast €4.50. Reception 6am-1am; after-hours ask for code. Su-Th singles €26-35; doubles €31-38. F-Sa singles €26; doubles €29. AmEx/MC/V. ❸

Hôtel Regina, 34 rue Charles Domercq (☎05 56 91 66 07; fax 05 56 94 32 88). Beautiful old white building across from the train station offers modest pastel rooms in an out-of-the-way location that is nevertheless perfect for late arrivals and passers-through.

Noise from the street and the bus stop may be bothersome. Breakfast €4.70. Singles with toilet and bath €20, with shower €23; doubles with shower €29, with shower and toilet €32. Extra person €4.70. AmEx/MC/V. ❷

Auberge de Jeunesse (HI), 22 cours Barbey (☎05 56 33 00 70; fax 05 56 33 00 71). Large modern rooms are decorated with shiny metal furniture and patches of bright colors. Near the station, the hostel is in a neighborhood filled with seedy characters who can make the 30min. walk from the city center a harrowing experience at night. Breakfast included. Wheelchair-accessible. Curfew 2am. 2- to 6-person dorm rooms with showers €16.20. Non-members pay an extra €1.60 per night. MC/V. ❶

🖪 FOOD

Center of the self-proclaimed *"région de bien manger et de bien vivre"* (region of fine eating and living), Bordeaux takes its food as seriously as its wine. Local specialties include oysters, foie gras, and beef braised in wine sauce. Most restaurants are scattered around the **rue St-Rémi** and **place St-Pierre.** Here, candlelit tables fill the alleyways that converge on **place du Parlement.** For Middle Eastern specialties, try the area around **St-Michel.** Most *Bordelais* don't eat before 9pm in the summer, and restaurants usually serve until 11pm or midnight.

There's fruit at the **market** in pl. des Grands Hommes (M-Sa 7am-7pm), fish at the **marché des capucins** (Tu-F 6am-1:30pm, Sa-Su 6:30am-2:30pm), and organic food in the **marché biologique** on quai Louis XVIII. (Th 5am-5pm.) For prepackaged goods, try the enormous **Auchan** supermarket, near the post office at the huge Centre Meriadeck mall on rue Claude Bonnier. (Open M-Sa 8:30am-10pm.)

La Casuccia, 49 rue St-Rémi (☎05 56 51 17 70). Intimate, romantic restaurant, perfect for a candlelit *tête-à-tête* or an outing with friends. Especially good are their pizzas (€5.50-10) and *gratin d'avocat au crabe* (€8.50). Filling 3-course *menus* start at €10, 4-course *menu* €15.50. Open Tu-Sa noon-3pm and 7-11:30pm, Su 7-11:30pm. Taking the food to go is 10% cheaper. MC/V. ❷

Le Valentino, 6 rue des Lauriers (☎05 56 48 11 56), is an inexpensive oasis in the pricey quarter of Bordeaux. Beautifully presented cuisine tastes just as good as it looks. Appetizers €6.50-12, main course €8-15. 2-course *menu* €10, 3-course €12-22. Open daily 7-11pm. AmEx/MC/V. ❸

La Crêperie, 20 rue Georges Bonnac (☎05 56 51 02 33; www.lacreperie.com). The delicious dessert crêpes (€2.20-7.20) at this small restaurant take the French staple to a whole new level. The saltier *galettes* (€2.20-9.20) come complete with a mound of potatoes, bacon, goat cheese, smoked salmon, raisins, mushrooms, and duck. Salads €2-6.80. Open daily noon-midnight. MC/V. ❶

🖸 SIGHTS

Admission to all museums in Bordeaux is free on the first Sunday of every month. Opening hours of all sights may change once street construction is finished.

CATHÉDRALE ST-ANDRÉ. Nearly nine centuries after its consecration by Pope Urban II and one century since its renovation, this building is still the centerpiece of Gothic Bordeaux. On the façade of the church are statues of angels and apostles—many apparently deranged or deformed—surrounding reliefs from the life of Christ. The cathedral hosted the wedding of Eleanor of Aquitaine and the future Louis VII in 1137, as well as the marriage of Louis XIII and Princess Anne of Austria in 1615. *(Pl. Pey-Berland. ☎05 56 87 17 18. Open Apr.-Oct. daily 8-11am and 2-5:30pm; Nov.-Mar. W and Sa 2:30-5:30pm. Guided tours for groups offered year-round if you call in advance.)* Its bell tower, the **Tour Pey-Berland,** juts 50m into the sky, with a large statue of Notre-Dame d'Aquitaine on top for good measure. The tower was placed 15m away from the cathedral, Italian-style, because its masons feared that the vibrations of the massive bells might make the cathedral collapse. Climb the 229 spiraling steps for the view of your life. (☎ *05 56 81 26 25. Temporarily closed for renovations. Will be open June-Sept. daily 10am-6:30pm; Oct.-May Tu-Su 10am-noon and 2-5pm. €4, under 25 and seniors €2.50.)*

MUSÉE DES BEAUX ARTS. Originally used to display Napoleon's captured war booty, Bordeaux's impressive fine arts museum now houses a multitude of great works by painters such as Titian, Caravaggio, Rubens, Matisse, Picasso, Seurat and Renoir. The permanent collection is held in the two buildings that frame the Hôtel de Ville; the temporary exhibits are across the street in the *Galeries des Beaux Arts. (20 cours d'Albret, near the cathedral. ☎ 05 56 10 20 56. Open M and W-Su 11am-6pm. €4, students free. Guided tours in French W 12:30pm. Joint ticket for the temporary and permanent collection €5.50, over 65 €3; ticket solely for the permanent collection €4/ €2.50. Students and under 18 free.)*

EGLISE ST-MICHEL. The best cityscape of Bordeaux can be seen from the 114m tower of the Eglise St-Michel. On ground level, you can catch even more of the world sitting in one of the many cafés that surround the church or browsing the different markets that fill the courtyard each morning. As one local describes the area, "Here we have a bit of Portugal, a bit of Morocco, a bit of Algeria, and a bit of Aquitaine." This is the most Bohemian district of Bordeaux, the place where students hang out and sip mint tea with their friends. *(Church open M-Sa 9am-6pm, Su 9am-12:30pm; free. Tower open June-Sept. 2-7pm; €2.50, under 12 free.)*

MONUMENT AUX GIRONDINS. Several avenues in Bordeaux converge on pl. de Quinconces, at whose center is a much-adorned marble pole topped by a stone Lady Liberty. The monument commemorates the moderate group of Girondin leaders—so named because they came from towns bordering the Gironde—who were guillotined in 1797 by their deranged political rivals, the Montagnards. Before losing their heads, they produced the Revolution's most important document, the **Declaration of the Rights of Man.** The event is commemorated in the bicentennial date inscribed on the monument's side (1989). The hundred-year-old monument is filled with symbols: the three women on the side facing town represent Bordeaux, the Dordogne, and the Garonne, and empty pedestals facing the river remind us of the murdered Girondins—most famously poor Pierre Vergniaud, who argued so eloquently for the King's life.

GRAND THÉÂTRE. The rather austere colonnaded Neoclassical façade of this 18th-century opera house conceals a breathtakingly intricate interior. Probably the most strictly classical opera house in the world, it is certainly one of the most impressive. Attend an opera, concert, or play, or take a daytime tour conducted in English. *(On pl. de la Comédie. Tickets ☎ 05 56 00 85 95; www.opera-bordeaux.com. Open Tu-Sa 11am-6pm. Tickets €8-70, 50% discount for those under 25. 1hr. tours through tourist office ☎ 05 56 00 66 00, frequency depends on theater's production schedule. €5; students, children, and over 65 €4.)*

PALAIS DE LA BOURSE. The construction of the Palais de la Bourse, with its ornately adorned pillars, fountain, and wrought-iron façades, was the most important step in the 18th-century modernization of Bordeaux. To the left of the building, the interesting **Musée National des Douanes,** or National Customs Museum houses quirky exhibits devoted to tariffs and excise taxation that require an understanding of French to be appreciated. *(☎ 05 56 48 82 82. Open Tu-Su 11am-6pm. €3; students, ages 10-18 and over 60 €1.50.)*

MUSÉE D'AQUITAINE. A historic and ethnographic collection of Aquitaine's classical and folk art from prehistory to the present, this museum displays Neanderthal skulls, ancient stone tools, Roman sculptures, and Gothic religious art. *(20 cours Pasteur. ☎ 05 56 01 51 02. Open Tu-Su 11am-6pm. Audioguides in 3 different languages €2.50. Museum €4; students, disabled visitors and children under 18 free.)*

⬛ NIGHTLIFE

Youthful Bordeaux's lively bars and nightclubs seem endless. *Clubs and Concerts*, a free brochure at the tourist office, gives an overview of them. **Place de la Victoire** and **place Gambetta** are mobbed by 70,000 students during the school year and continue to serve as the hotspots for entertainment during the summer. **St-Michel** has a more mellow atmosphere, with locals gathering at the café tables around 6pm and often staying until midnight. After the clubs close, you can eat and drink at **place Marché des Capucins** and hang out with early-morning market workers. In addition, Bordeaux's gay scene is second only to Paris.

El Bodegon, on the pl. de la Victoire (☎ 05 56 94 74 02). Dominating the nightlife in this popular square, the enormous El Bodegon draws wild students from all across the city. On Wednesday nights, crowds gather to watch soccer games at 8pm and then to sing karaoke at 10:30pm. Theme nights with free giveaways every weekend. Mondays bring special deals such as half-price *Desperados*. Beer €2.50. Happy hour 6-8pm. Open M-Sa 7am-2am, Su 2pm-2am.

BHV (Bar de l'Hôtel de Ville), 4 rue de l'Hôtel de Ville (☎ 05 56 44 05 08), across from the Hôtel de Ville. Flashing lights spin off the mirrors in this small but fashionable gay bar, which is filled most nights of the week. Beer €3. Daily theme nights with free giveaways in July-Aug. Theme nights W. Drag shows Sept.-June Su at 10pm. Open daily 6pm-2am. MC/V.

Chica Café, 3 rue Duffour Dubergier (☎ 05 56 51 70 66), in the shadow of the cathedral. This friendly, boisterous Latino bar is a pool hangout spot for older men during the day, and a students' dance venue at night. The bare concrete dance floor in the basement stages occasional concerts and dance lessons. Beer €2; daiquiris €5.20; shots €1.50. Happy hour 6-8pm. Open M-Sa 11am-2am.

El Che, 34 cours de l'Argonne (☎ 05 56 92 33 98). A funky Afro-Cuban *bar-rhumerie* near pl. de la Victoire. Sip on homemade rum cocktails (€3.50) in this bit of tropical Ile des Antilles transported to the gray streets of Bordeaux. Free salsa lessons Sept.-May W and F 8:30pm. Beer €2.50. Currently open M-Sa 7pm-2am, open daily once the street construction outside is finished. MC/V.

⬛ WINERIES & VINEYARDS

A HISTORY OF CLARET

Bordeaux's reputation for wine is the product of 20 centuries of shameless (but justifiable) self-promotion. The wines were of variable color and quality until Louis IX snatched the port of La Rochelle from the English in 1226. Not to be deprived of his claret (as the English call red Bordeaux wine), King Henry II bestowed generous shipping rights on Bordeaux, making it England's wine cellar. At first citizens simply shipped out wines produced farther up the Garonne River, but the money flowing in sparked a local planting mania. Soon Bordeaux's port made the decision to ensure its monopoly over the market by refusing to accommodate other wines. In the 18th century, the vineyards spread from the Médoc region to areas south of the Dordogne. Today, they produce almost 500 million bottles per year.

TASTING IN BORDEAUX

If you're just in town for a day or two and are desperate for the full wine experience, head to the **Maison du Vin/CIVB,** 1 cours du 30 juillet, where there's a wine bar, professionals on hand to tell you what you're drinking, and even a tasting course. The 2hr. "Initiation to Wine Tasting" program, available in English, teaches the subtle art of oenophilia through comparative tasting and will leave you confident enough to waltz into any four-star restaurant. (☎05 56 00 99 30; www.vins-bordeaux.fr. Open M-Th 8am-12:30pm and 1:30-5:15pm, F 8:30am-12:30pm. Wine tasting course twice weekly €20.) Locals buy their wine and crystal pitchers at the classy **Vinothèque,** 8 cours du 30 Juillet. (☎05 56 52 32 05. Open M 2-7:30pm, Tu-Sa 10am-7:30pm. AmEx/MC/V.) Across the street at 2 allée de Tourny, the smaller and more intimate **L'Intendant** is run by a knowledgeable and helpful owner. (☎05 56 48 01 29. Open M-Sa 10am-7:30pm. AmEx/MC/V.)

VISITING THE CHÂTEAUX

It's easiest to explore the area with a car, but some vineyards are accessible by train—St-Emilion and Pauillac in particular make good daytrips. The tourist office gives afternoon tours of the more popular vineyards in English. (Apr. to mid-Nov. daily 1:30pm, mid-Nov. to Mar. W and Sa 1:30pm. St-Emilion tours W and Su, Médoc tours Th and Sa, Graves and Sauternes F. €26, students and seniors €23.) Bring a good map if you're biking or walking because local roads are hard to navigate. The owners of the châteaux are usually happy to give private tours, but call ahead or ask the tourist office to call for you. All of the châteaux sell wine directly.

ST-EMILION

The viticulturists of St-Emilion (pop. 2850), just 35km northeast of Bordeaux, have been refining their technique since Roman times; theirs is, not surprisingly, among the best appellations in France. Today they gently crush 12,850 acres of grapes to produce 23 million liters of wine annually. Quite apart from its main industry, the medieval village's yellow stone buildings, twisting narrow streets, and religious monuments are a pleasure to visit. The **Eglise Monolithe,** carved by Benedictine monks over three centuries, is the largest subterranean church in all of Europe. The damp underground **catacombs** nearby served as the burial place for a series of Augustine monks when the cemetery became too small. As a tribute to its religious origins, the town also proudly holds the hermitage of **St-Emilion** himself. The three monuments can only be accessed through the guided visits that depart from the tourist office daily at 10am (Tours 45min.; €5.50, students and children ages 12-17 €2.90. Normally held in French, but English guides can be reserved in advance).

The **Maison du Vin de St-Emilion,** pl. Pierre Meyrat, offers a 1hr. course on local wines in both French and English. Their wine shop has wholesale prices and a free exhibit. (☎05 57 55 50 55; www.vins-saint-emilion.com. Open daily Sept.-July 9:30am-12:30pm and 2-6:30pm; Aug. 9:30am-6:30pm. Wine course offered mid-July to mid-Sept. daily 11am. €17. MC/V.)

The **tourist office,** near the church tower at pl. des Créneaux, distributes the *Grandes Heures de St-Emilion,* a list of **classical concerts** and **wine tastings** hosted by nearby châteaux. To get to the tourist office, take a right on the main road from the station; when you reach town, walk straight up rue de la Porte Bouqueyre toward the tower (2km). Take the bus from the train station. (☎05 57 55 28 28; www.saint-emilion-tourisme.com. Open July-Aug. daily 9:30am-8pm; mid- to late June and early to mid-Sept. 9:30am-7pm; Apr. to mid-June and mid-Sept. to Oct. 9:30am-12:30pm and 1:45-6:30pm; Nov.-Mar. 9:30am-12:30pm and 1:45-6pm.) In addition to renting **bikes,** they offer tours in English to local châteaux. (Bikes €10 per half-day, €14 per day; credit card deposit required. Tours July-Aug. M-Sa

2 and 4:15pm; May-June and Sept. 3:30pm. €9, children €6.) **Trains** come here from Bordeaux (35min., 4 per day, €7). It's the second stop from Bordeaux and the tiny station is poorly marked, so don't miss it.

MÉDOC, GRAVES, & SAUTERNES REGIONS

Though St-Emilion is probably the best vineyard for a first visit, there are other worthwhile regions near Bordeaux. The **Médoc** area north of Bordeaux, between the Gironde estuary and the ocean, gets its name from the Latin *medio-acquae*, meaning "between the waters." This region is home to some of the world's most famous red wines: Lafite-Rothschild, Latour, Margaux, Haut-Brion, and Mouton-Rothschild. To access the vineyards, book one of the organized tours that depart from Bordeaux, or take the *Réseau Trans Gironde* from the depot in the pl. de Quinconces to Pauillac, the most renowned village of the region (1hr., M-Sa 6-10 per day). The **tourist office**, at La Verrerie, can provide free maps, suggest hiking trails, and help make reservations to visit local châteaux. (☎ 05 56 59 03 08; www.pauillac-medoc.com. Open July 1 to mid-Sept. M-Sa 9:30am-7:30pm, Su 10am-6pm; mid-Sept. to Oct. and June M-Sa 9:30am-12:30pm and 2-6:30pm, Su 10:30am-12:30pm and 2-6pm; Nov.-May M-Sa 9:30am-12:30pm and 2-6pm, Su 10:30am-12:30pm and 2:30-6pm.)

South of the Garonne is the **Graves** region, named for its gravelly topsoil. Graves's dry and semisweet wines were the drink of choice in the time of Eleanor of Aquitaine, before the reds of Médoc overtook them 300 years ago. In the southeastern end of Graves is the **Sauternes** region, celebrated for its sweet white wines.

The charming château **Smith Haut Lafitte**, in the town of Martillac, is located less than a 20min. drive from Bordeaux. Proprietors Daniel and Florence Cathiard bought the crumbling vineyard in 1990 and saved it from corporate ownership. Now a small but luxurious château with peacocks strolling in its garden, Smith Haut Lafitte gives detailed tours and tastings by reservation (☎ 05 57 83 11 22; www.smith-haut-lafitte.com).

Across the street from the vineyards, the four-star luxury hotel **Les Sources des Caudalie,** run by the friendly Cathiard daughters, overindulges the likes of Madonna and Princess Caroline of Monaco (among others) with a revolutionary *vinothérapie* spa. (☎ 05 57 83 82 82; www.caudalie.com. 30min. barrel bath in grape extract €45.70. Bath, massage, jet shower, and honey and wine wrap €130. Reservations must be made 10 days in advance.)

THE LOCAL LEGEND

SAINTLY SOIL

Originally from the small town of Vannes, **St-Emilion** deserted his friends and family at an early age in order to join a strict Catholic order. Around AD 740, he became a Benedictine monk in a convent in Saintonge and started a new life of unblemished devotion. Within a short time, the young man began to attract attention for his generosity and selflessness. Although his gifts to others originally were of a secular nature, they started to take on a magical quality, which many people attributed to the hand of God. He is believed to have restored sight to a blind woman and to have performed other small, but impressive, miracles.

As a result of his infallible virtue and rumored spiritual powers, Emilion attracted a large, rather unwanted, devotional following. After several months of living as a local celebrity, the monk fled to the forest of Combes. He traveled alone for several days until reaching the future site of the town of St-Emilion. Here he set down his bags, built a small house, and began an isolated life in contact only with God. At his death on January 6, 767, pilgrims began traveling to the newly holy site and eventually constructed the **Chappelle de la Trinité** in the monk's honor. Still centered around this rather small church, the town of St-Emilion has now become a vineyard paradise.

ARCACHON

Arcachon (pop. 11,450) is one of the best in a chain of beach towns on the **Côte d'Argent** (Silver Coast), the thin strip of sand which runs along 200km of France's southern Atlantic seaboard. It's known in particular for two silicon landmarks: the **Dune du Pyla**, Europe's highest sand dune, and the **Banc d'Arguin**, a 1000-acre sand bar. Arcachon is a resort town at heart, full of vacationing families in summer and despondent hotel owners in the winter. During its high season, the town is a perfect daytrip—easygoing, unpretentious, and naturally stunning.

■ ⟨⟩ ORIENTATION & PRACTICAL INFORMATION. Trains, pl. Roosevelt, go only to Bordeaux (55min.; 10-20 per day, last train M-Sa 8:15pm, Su and holidays 9:50pm; €8.40.) **City bus** #611 runs from a stop in front of the train station to "Pyla-sur-Mer," site of the dune (25 min.; July-Aug. 15 per day, Sept.-June 8 per day; €2.70. Office at 47 bd. du Général Leclerc, ☎05 57 72 45 00.) If the bus does not stop at Pyla, the Haitza stop is only a 10min. walk from the dune. Walk uphill between the two hotels; at the three-star hotel near the bend in the road, turn right and take the wooden stairway down to the sea. **Locabeach 33,** 326 bd. de la Plage, rents two-wheeled transportation. (☎05 56 83 39 64; www.locabeach.com. Open daily July-Aug. 9am-8pm; Sept.-June 9am-12:30pm and 2-7pm. Bikes €7-10 per half-day, €10-13 per day; deposit €130-155. Scooters and mopeds €39-59 per day; driver's license required; deposit €760-1200 with an ID card. AmEx/MC/V.)

Arcachon's **tourist office,** pl. Roosevelt, is one block left of the station. (☎05 57 52 97 97; tourisme@arcachon.com. Open July-Aug. daily 9am-9pm; Apr.-May M-Sa 9am-6pm, Su 10am-1pm and 2-5pm; June and Sept. M-Sa 9am-6:30pm, Su 10am-1pm and 2-5pm; Oct.-Mar. M-Sa 9am-7pm.) Wash beach towels at the **laundromat** on the corner of bd. du Général Leclerc and rue Molière. (Open July-Aug. daily 7am-10pm, Sept.-June daily 7am-8pm. Wash €5-8, dry €5 per 30min., detergent €0.50.) The **police** (☎05 57 72 29 30) are on pl. de Verdun. The **hospital** (☎05 57 52 90 00) is on bd. Louis Lignon. The **post office,** 1 pl. Franklin Roosevelt, opposite the tourist office, has a **currency exchange** with no commission for US dollars. (☎05 57 52 53 80. Open M-F 8:30am-6pm, Sa 8:30am-noon. **Cyberposte.**) **Postal code:** 33120.

ⓕ ACCOMMODATIONS. In the summer, rooms here start at €36 for a double; even in the low season, the prices begin at €27. Unfortunately, the best value in town seems to be at **Le Bordeaux ❹,** 39 bd. du Général Leclerc, a two-star hotel 20m from the train station and 300m from the beach. Directly over a bar and restaurant, Le Bordeaux offers 14 modest white rooms that come complete with shower and toilet. (☎05 56 83 80 30; le.bordeaux@discali.fr. Breakfast €6. Reserve a week in advance. Singles €35, with TV €40; doubles €55; triples €70; quads and quints €70; July-Aug. prices €10-60 more expensive. AmEx/MC/V.) **The Auberge de Jeunesse (HI) ❶,** 87 av. de Bordeaux, is in Cap-Ferrat. To get there, take a ferry from Arcachon's Jetée Thiers on av. Gambetta. (☎05 56 54 92 78. July-Aug. daily at least 1 per hr. 9am-7pm. one-way €6, children €4, bikes €3; round-trip €10/€5/€4.) From the Cap-Ferrat ferry pier, take av. de l'Océan and continue as it becomes rue des Bouvreuils after the roundabout. (15min.) Turn left onto av. de Bordeaux, and the hostel will be on your right after a few minutes. (☎05 56 60 64 62. Reception 8am-1pm and 6-9pm. 60 beds available. Open July-Aug. only. €7. **HI members only.**)

In Arcachon, the very social **Camping Club d'Arcachon ❷,** 5 allée de la Galaxie, lies in the middle of a beautiful pine forest 2km from the beach. The three-star site has a two-tiered pool, jacuzzi, billiards table, and a bar-restaurant. (☎05 56 83 24 15; www.camping-arcachon.com. Laundry €5. Checkout noon. Closed mid-Nov. to mid-Dec. €6 per person, €2 per child ages 4-10, €13 per tent, €4 per car. Electricity €4. Bungalows €390-400 per week; mobile homes €520-540; chalets €550. All prices are significantly cheaper Sept.-June. AmEx/MC/V.) There are five campsites within a few kilometers of each other in **Pyla-sur-Mer** along the rte. de Biscarrosse, although it's quite a trek to any of these. The closest is the three-star **Camping de la Dune ❷**, 300m from the beach on rte. de Biscarrosse. Take bus #611 from the SNCF station of Arcachon to Camping de la Dune (dir: Le Pyla; 4 per day go directly to the campsite, 6 others stop at Haitza or the Dune du Pyla; €2.70). A pool, tennis court, bar, grocery store, and laundromat are located on the campsite. (☎05 56 22 72 17; www.campingdeladune.fr. Open late-Apr. to late-Sept. Two people with a tent and car July €17, Aug. €20, Apr.-June and Sept. €12; renting a mobile home €20/€26/€15; extra person €6/€8/€4. Electricity and showers included. MC/V.)

❏ FOOD. It would be a crime to leave Arcachon without savoring a few ounces of the 15,000 tons of oysters gathered here annually. Beach cafés line **avenue Gambetta** and **boulevard de la Plage,** offering copious seafood platters and €10 *moules frites* (mussels-'n'-fries). **Le Commerce ❷**, 9 av. Gambetta, spills into the street, providing a perfect vantage point from which to watch sunbathers strut by while munching on shellfish. (☎05 56 83 05 17. Fish €7-17.50, meat €6.10-12, salad €3-7.50. Open daily 7am-1am. AmEx/MC/V.)

A bit of a splurge, **Le Pavillon d'Arguin ❹**, 63 bd. du Général Leclerc across the street from the tourist office, serves fresh and plentiful seafood platters, duck, and veal with asparagus for €16-28. (☎05 56 83 46 96. Sa-Su reservations recommended. Open July-Aug. noon-2:30pm and 7-10:30pm; Sept.-June Su 7-10:30pm, Tu-Sa noon-2:30pm and 7-10:30pm. AmEx/MC/V.) A cheaper option chosen by many French tourists is to buy bread from one of the many *boulangers artisanals* and produce from the **Marché Municipal,** rue Jehenne. (Open daily 8am-1pm.)

◧❐❏ SIGHTS, ENTERTAINMENT, & FESTIVALS. Rising suddenly from the edge of a pine forest, the 117m ▨**Dune du Pyla** looks more like a transplanted section of the Sahara than a French beach. Wind races furiously across the face of the dune, creating an ocean of white sand unblemished by vegetation. For courageous souls who are willing to cross the entire dune, there is a protected area at the edge where wading is possible, although a fierce undertow makes deeper swims too dangerous. Farther along the water, there are separate beaches for the clothed and the nude. From the bus stop in Pyla-sur-Mer, continue in the same direction down bd. de l'Océan and take a left at the rotary onto av. de Biscarrosse; follow this road for 10min. and the dune area will be on your right. The **Ecole Professionnelle de Vol Libre du Pyla (EPVLP)** has **hang gliding** from the dune; ask at the tourist office. (☎05 56 22 15 02. €61 per flight, €400 per week.)

Arcachon's bird sanctuaries and nature parks attract flocks of tourists. **UBA boats** take 2hr. excursions to the Dune du Pyla, the Cap Ferret lighthouse, and the oyster beds around **L'Ile aux Oiseaux** (Apr.-Oct. 3 per day; €12.50, children €9.50). The same company also offers trips to **Arguin Sandbar** from the Jetée Thiers pier. (☎05 56 54 92 78. July-Aug. daily at 11am, June and Sept. approximately one excursion per week. €15, children €10.) About 15km out of town, the **Parc Ornithologique du Teich** shelters 260 species of migrating birds in one of France's most important sanctuaries. (☎05 56 22 80 93; www.parc-ornithologique-du-teich.com. Open June-Aug. daily 10am-8pm; Sept.-May 10am-6pm. Binoculars and seeds available. €6.20, ages 5-14 €4.50. Guided visits with a reservation.)

In the hilly town of Arcachon itself, **Ville d'Hiver,** an arboreal district of turn-of-the-century villas, lies across from the **Parc Mauresque** north of the beach. Doctors designed the neighborhood's curving streets to protect invalids from the ocean winds; this "winter village" is 2°C warmer on average than its beachfront counterpart. Now the fairy-tale villas, which range in style from faux Swiss chalet to pseudo-Gothic castle, make up a quiet suburban neighborhood, removed from the tourist rat race below. The village is accessible by foot or via French **tours** in a shameful mini-train. (Office at 47 bd. du Général Leclerc. ☎ 05 57 72 45 00. Tours 35min.; July-Aug. 6 per day, June and Sept. reserve in advance. €4, children €3.) The **Ste-Cécile** observatory, across the park on the way back from the Ville d'Hiver, offers a stunning view of Arcachon. The spiral staircase is not easy to climb and worse to descend. (Open 9am-6pm. Free.)

Arcachon's younger set run to several beachfront *discothèques* as soon as night falls. There's also the **Casino d'Arcachon,** 163 bd. de la Plage, a fairy-tale creation containing, besides the obvious, several bars and a nightclub. Strict dress code prohibits flip-flops, sleeveless T-shirts, frayed jeans, and beach attire. (☎ 05 56 83 28 67; casino-arcachon@g-partouche.fr. 18+. Nightclub open 10:30pm-5am; slot machines open daily 10am-4am; roulette, blackjack, and stud poker open Su-M and F-Sa 9:30pm-4am. AmEx/MC/V.)

For one night in late June, the town of Arcachon hosts the annual **Fête de la Musique,** where bands playing music of all different genres, including jazz, gospel, heavy metal, and pop, give free performances from 7pm-1am. (Call ☎ 05 56 22 01 10 for more information.)

PAYS BASQUE

BIARRITZ

Once a minor whaling village, the town of Biarritz, at the base of the Pyrénées, became the playground of aristocrats in the mid-19th century. Napoleon III, Alphonse XIII of Spain, Nicholas II of Russia, and the Shah of Persia were all drawn to the town's shores by its natural beauty and fashionable reputation (which persists to this day). Still glistening with money, sleek Biarritz remains a theme park for a select few; thankfully, its gorgeous stretches of beach attract a much more democratic mix.

⌐ TRANSPORTATION

Flights: Aéroport de Parme (☎ 05 59 43 83 83), 7 esplanade de l'Europe. M-Sa take bus #6 (dir: Bayonne Gare) from Hôtel de Ville to Parme Aéroport (every 30min. 7am-7:20pm), Su take bus C (dir: Aéroport. 9:05am, then every 30min. noon-7:15pm.) **Ryanair** (☎ 05 59 43 83 93) flies to **London** daily for €32-55 one-way.

Trains: Biarritz-la-Négresse (☎ 05 59 50 83 07), 3km from town. Information desk open daily 7:45am-8pm. To: **Bayonne** (10min., 17 per day, €2, TGV €3.50); **Bordeaux** (2hr., 7per day, TGV €25.50); **Paris** (5hr., 5 per day, TGV €67); **Pau** (2hr., 4 per day, €14.40); **Toulouse** (4-5hr., 5 per day, €32.70). **SNCF office,** 13 av. Foch. Open M-F 9-11:45am and 2-5:45pm.

Buses: ATCRB (☎ 05 59 26 06 99) shuttles over to **St-Jean-de-Luz, Anglet, Bayonne,** and **Saint Sebastien;** main office in St-Jean-de-Luz. Bus stops on rue Joseph Petit, next to the tourist office. Buy tickets (€2.80) on the bus.

Local Transportation: STAB (☎ 05 59 52 59 52). Office with maps and schedules on rue Louis-Barthou, near the tourist office (☎ 05 59 24 26 53. Open M-Sa 8:15am-noon and 1:30-6pm). 10 min. to Anglet and 20min. to Bayonne (M-Sa 6am-8:30pm bus #1, 2, or 6; Su 7:30am-8:30pm bus A, B, or C). 1hr. tickets €1.20; *carnet* of 10 €9.50, students during school year €8.

Taxis: Atlantic Taxi Radio (☎ 05 59 03 18 18). 24hr. €2 to begin trip, €0.72 per km. Approximately €10 from the taxi stand to either the train station or the airport.

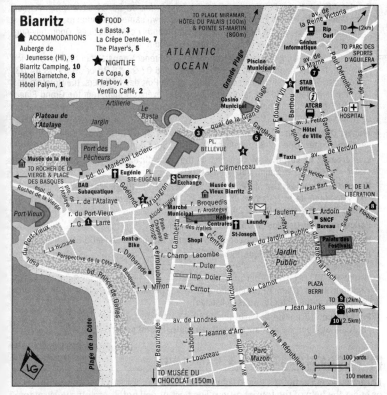

Biarritz

▲ ACCOMMODATIONS
Auberge de
Jeunesse (HI), **9**
Biarritz Camping, **10**
Hôtel Barnetche, **8**
Hôtel Palym, **1**

🍴 FOOD
Le Basta, **3**
La Crêpe Dentelle, **7**
The Player's, **5**

★ NIGHTLIFE
Le Copa, **6**
Playboy, **4**
Ventilo Caffé, **2**

Bike and Scooter Rental: Rent-a-Bike, 24 rue Peyroloubilh (☎05 59 24 94 47 or 06 80 71 72 88; sobilo.location@wanadoo.fr). Bikes €12 per day, €5 for *Let's Go* users. Scooters €31 per day, rollerblades €12, Harley Davidsons €230. Deposit €75-150. Open daily 9am-7pm. MC/V.

Surfboard Rental: Rip Curl Surf Shop, 2 av. Reine Victoria (☎05 59 24 38 40), one block from Grande Plage. €10 per half-day, €15 per day, €85 per week; ID and €300 deposit. Open July-Aug. daily 10am-8pm; Sept.-June M-Sa 10am-1pm and 3-7pm. For **lessons,** contact **Rip Curl** at ☎05 59 24 62 86. 1 person for 2hr. €35, 3 people €90, 6 people €160.

⊞ 🔀 ORIENTATION & PRACTICAL INFORMATION

The train station, **Biarritz-la-Négresse,** is 3km from the *centre ville,* so buses are more convenient when coming from areas around Biarritz. For those traveling from greater distances, buses #2 (dir: Sainsontan) and 9 (dir: La Barre or Ste-Madeleine) run from the train station to the city center and the tourist office (every 20min. M-Sa 6:30am-9pm, €1.20). On Sundays, bus B (dir: Sainsontan) travels the same route (every 30min. 8am-8pm). Arriving from Biarritz-la-Négresse, turn left onto **allée du Moura,** which becomes av. du Président Kennedy. Turn left a few kilometers later onto **avenue du Maréchal Foch,** which continues to **place Clemenceau,** Biarritz's main square. (40min.)

AQUITAINE

Tourist Office: 1 sq. d'Ixelles (☎05 59 22 37 10; fax 05 59 24 97 80; biarritz.tourisme@biarritz.fr), off av. Edouard VII. Staff tracks down same-night hotel rooms or campsites for free. Pick up the free *Biarritzscope* for monthly events listings. Open July-Aug. daily 8am-8pm; Sept.-June M-Sa 9am-6pm, Su 10am-5pm.

Tours: Guided walking tours of the town center (in French) depart from the tourist office July-Aug. M 10am and F 6pm. **Le Petit Train** (☎06 07 97 16 35 or 05 59 03 44 03) also offers 30min. French guided train rides of the Port des Pêcheurs, the Hôtel de Palais, the Port Vieux, and the Jardin Public Departs every 30 min. from the Grand Plage. July-Aug. daily 10am-6pm., Apr.-June and Sept.-Oct. daily 2-6pm. Open year-round for groups with reservation. €5.

Money: Change Plus, 9 rue Mazagran (☎05 59 24 82 47). No commission and good exchange rates. Open M-Sa July-Aug. 9am-7pm, Sept.-June 9am-noon and 2-6pm.

Laundromat: Le Lavoir, 4 av. Jaulerry, by the post office. Open daily 7am-9pm. Wash €4-7, dry €0.30 per 5min., detergent €0.60.

Beach Emergencies: Grande Plage ☎05 59 22 22 22. **Plage Marabella** ☎05 59 23 01 20. **Plage de la Milady** ☎05 59 23 63 93. **Plage Miramar** ☎05 59 24 34 98. **Plage du Port Vieux** ☎05 59 24 05 84.

Police: rue Louis-Barthou (☎05 59 01 22 22).

Hospital: Hôpital de la Côte Basque, av. Interne Jacques Loëb (☎05 59 44 35 35).

Internet: Génius Informatique, 60 av. Edouard VII, in the back of a toy store (☎05 59 24 39 07). €0.15 per min., €9 per hr. Color photocopies €1.50 per page, black and white €0.30. Fax €1.50 per page. Open July-Aug. daily 9am-8pm; Sept.-June M 2-7:30pm, Tu-Sa 10am-12:30pm and 2-7:30pm. Internet is also available at the post office and at the Hotel Palym (see listings).

Post Office: 17 rue de la Poste (☎05 59 22 41 10). **Currency exchange** open M-F 8:30am-6:30pm, Sa 8:30am-noon. **Cyberposte. Postal code:** 64200.

▐▌ ACCOMMODATIONS & CAMPING

Bargains do exist, but it's best to plan a month ahead for stays in July and August, or enlist the help of the tourist office. The best-priced hotels are off rue Mazagran, around rue du Port-Vieux. The youth hostel is newly renovated but far from the city center; all other hotels listed are centrally located.

▨ **Auberge de Jeunesse (HI),** 8 rue de Chiquito de Cambo (☎05 59 41 76 00; fax 05 59 41 76 07; aubergejeune.biarritz@wanadoo.fr), a 40min. walk or a 10min. bus ride from the beaches in Biarritz. To get to the hostel from the town center, take bus #2 (dir: Gare SNCF) to Francis Jammes or #9 (dir: Labourd; mid-June to mid-Sept.) to Bois de Boulogne. Walking, take av. Maréchal Foch as it becomes av. du Président J. F. Kennedy. Turn right on rue Philippe Veyrin; the hostel is at the bottom of the hill on the right. Situated near a beautiful lake, this young, social hostel plays nightly movies in its common room and provides a well-stocked bar from mid-June to Sept. Large, sunny rooms are decorated with bright blue sheets, wooden furniture, and lockable cabinets. Breakfast included. Dinner €8.40. Bike rentals €12 per day, €9 after noon. Laundry: wash €3.50, dry €2.50. Internet €2.50 per 30min. Reception 8:30am-12:20pm and 6pm-10pm. 2- to 4-bed dorms €17.10 the first night, subsequent nights €14.30. Locked bike-and-car garage available. Non-HI members €2.90 extra per night. AmEx/MC/V. ❶

Hôtel Palym, 7 rue du Port Vieux (☎05 59 24 16 56; www.le-palmarium.com). Antique wood furnishings and cable TV in clean rooms about 50m from the ocean. Breakfast €4.50. Reception 8am-1am. Internet €10 per hour. Singles €28; doubles €35-38, with shower €47.50; triples €47/€62-67; quads with shower, kitchen, and mini-bar €70-80. Sept.-June doubles €35, with shower €40; triples and quads €45/€50. MC/V. ❸

Hôtel Barnetche, 5bis rue Charles-Floquet (☎05 59 24 22 25; www.hotel-barnetche.fr), in the center of town. From pl. Clemenceau, take rue du Helder through pl. Libération to rue Charles Floquet. This hotel offers a rustic, 12-bed dorm room perfect for travelers on a budget, in addition to more expensive individual rooms decorated with old wooden furniture. No-nonsense, energetic owner keeps everything ship-shape. Breakfast (with homemade croissants) €6. In Aug., obligatory (and tasty) *demi-pension* €17 extra. Reception 7:30am-11pm, May-June and Sept. until 10:30pm. Reservations by phone or web recommended. Open May-Sept. Dorms €20 per person. Singles €35; doubles €58; triples €75; quads €100. Passport deposit required. Cash only. ❸

Camping: Biarritz, 28 rue d'Harcet (☎05 59 23 00 12; www.biarritz-camping.fr). A 10min. walk from Milady and 45min. from town. Take the Navette-des-Plages bus (#9; mid-June to mid-Sept.) or walk down av. Kennedy from the station following signs. Quiet, unshaded plots separated by perfect hedges. Restaurant, bar, washing machines, individual safes, jacuzzi, and heated pool on site. Wheelchair-accessible. Free showers Open early May-late Sept. Reservations are mandatory early July-late Aug. Early July-late Aug. 2 people with tent €19, mobile homes €460-580 per week, electricity €3.50; start of July and end of Aug. €17/€380-445/€3; May-June and Sept. €13.50/€200-245/€2.30. MC/V and traveler's checks. ❶

▸ FOOD

In dining, as with everything in Biarritz, style trumps substance. Expect impressive elegance and high prices around **Grande Plage** and **place Ste-Eugénie.** More mid-priced eateries can be found on **avenue de la Marne** as it splits from av. Edouard VII. Cheap crêpes and sandwiches can be found along **rue Mazagran** and **placeClemenceau.** The **Marché municipal** on rue des Halles offers local produce and an abundance of specialties. (Open daily 8am-2pm.) Next door is a **Shopi** supermarket, 2 rue du Centre. (☎05 59 24 18 01. Open 9am-12:45pm and 3:30-5pm. MC/V.)

Le Basta, 31 bd. du Général de Gaulle (☎05 59 22 22 58). Enjoy a stunning view of the Port des Pêcheurs and the Eglise Ste-Eugénie from the terrace of this seaside café. Seafood and Basque *plats* €7.50-12. 3-course *menu* €12-13. Open Apr.-Sept. M-W and F-Su 8:30am-midnight. Cash only. ❸

La Crêpe Dentelle, 6 av. de la Marne (☎05 59 22 28 29). Delicious and substantial crêpes derived from the owner's imagination, modeled on traditional Breton recipes. From July-Jan., the restaurant prepares crêpes

ON THE MENU

A SPANISH MÉLANGE

As a result of their proximity to Spain, Biarritz and Bayonne have adopted various cultural traditions and tasty dishes from their southern neighbor. One such incorporation is the mixed seafood and vegetable platter, paëlla, that can be found at most restaurants in the towns. The dish originated in the 18th century, when Spanish peasants became frustrated with having to throw away the remains of their lunchtime feasts and finally decided to toss all the leftovers into one large bowl. Vegetables, poultry, and seafood were mixed together and later reheated for dinner in order to conserve money and time. The Spanish later dignified this mélange by giving it a name and presenting it as a local specialty.

Today, the regions surrounding the Pyrénées are filled with the enormous copper bowls in which chefs prepare the now famous mixture of crayfish, mussels, shrimp, chicken, rice, green peppers, onions, tomatoes, and saffron. For travelers in Biarritz wishing to sample the local paëlla, the restaurant at the **Hôtel Palym** serves all-you-can-eat platters for €12, and one take-out portion for €8. *(6 rue de Port-Vieux. ☎05 59 24 25 83. Open daily 10am-10pm. MC/V).* In Bayonne, **Chez Txotx** sells a very authentic version for €14. *(40 rue Port Neuf. ☎05 59 59 33 66. Open July-Aug. daily 8am-8pm; Sept.-June closed Su. Cash only.)*

topped with fresh mussels and shrimp imported directly from nearby Bretagne. 3-course lunch *menu* €10. Crêpes €2-8.30, salads €3.80-8.50. Open M-Sa noon-2:30pm and 7pm-1am. V. ❷

The Player's, 2 rue Gardères (☎05 59 24 19 60). Perfectly situated next to the Grand Plage and the casino, this pizzeria and bar serves tasty food for reasonable prices. The delicious homemade *tarte aux pommes* with buttery crust and whipped cream comes especially recommended (€5). Meat and fish €6-14.50; filling pizzas €6-9.20; pitchers of local sangria €6. Open Dec.-Oct. noon-midnight. MC/V. ❷

SIGHTS & BEACHES

All of Biarritz is designed in consideration of its beaches. The **Grande Plage** is nearly covered in summer by thousands of perfect bodies and talented surfers. On the walkway behind the beach is the immaculate white **Casino Municipal.** Walk left along av. de l'Impératrice to reach the **Pointe St-Martin** and the tall lighthouse, **Le Phare de Biarritz.** From here, it is possible to see the sands of the Landes region separating from the rocky coast of the Basque country. Inland, the **Hôtel du Palais** overlooks the **Plage Miramar.** Constructed in 1845 by Emperor Napoleon III for Princess Eugénie, the E-shaped palace has since been converted into a hotel. Rooms begin at €325 in high season, but those without such royal wallets can soak up the atmosphere of Biarritz's best four-star hotel in the terrace café with a cup of coffee (€4-5.50). Across av. de l'Impératrice is the old **Hôtel Continental,** where Russian nobles fled after the Bolshevik Revolution in 1917.

On the other side of the Grande Plage, jagged rock formations provide shelter in the **Port des Pêcheurs** for small fishing boats. **BAB Subaquatique,** near the Port des Pêcheurs, organizes scuba excursions. (☎05 59 24 80 40. Open July-Aug. €18, with guide €21, for beginners €28. Diving excursions to the *Vieux Port* and nighttime trips available. Cash and traveler's checks only.) Walk from the point over the steel bridge and through the **Rocher de la Vierge,** a tooth-like rock with a statue of the Virgin Mary, to gaze at breathtaking sunsets. The **Plage des Basques** stretches on the other side of the jetty. Endless paths cut into the flowered coast two minutes from the town center, but check the tides before traipsing onto the rocks. At low tide, this deserted beach has the cleanest water and sand in town.

Finally, trek out of town to the **Musée du Chocolat,** 14-16 av. Beaurivage, to learn about the historical background of chocolate and consume delicious hand-made samples from **Henriet,** the small candy shop on pl. Clemenceau. (☎05 59 41 54 64. Open July-Aug. daily 10am-6pm, Sept.-June M-Sa 10am-noon and 2:30-6pm. Guided tours in French or English usually depart every hour. If there are not enough visitors, the museum will give out hand-held audio guides instead. Wheelchair-accessible. €6, students and ages 13-18 €5, ages 4-12 €3.)

ENTERTAINMENT & FESTIVALS

Casino Barrière de Biarritz gloats over the Grande Plage in all its art-deco glory, but in order to enter the ocean of slot machines, gamblers must leave their flip flops, ripped jeans, and beach gear at the door. (1 av. Edouard VII. ☎05 59 22 77 77. 18+. Open Su-Th 10am-3am, F-Sa until 4am.) Hang out around the **Port des Pêcheurs** until 11pm or midnight, when the rich and reckless strap on their party boots. Things pick up early at the **Ventilo Caffé,** 30 rue Mazagran, a popular bar where a young crowd drinks and chats while sitting in exotic, red velvet chairs. (☎05 59 24 31 42. Beer €2.50, alcohol €5. Open daily 8am-2am. MC/V.) Once all the local bars close at 2am, the more persistent party-goers flock to the town's two main nightclubs. Lively **Le Copa,** 24 av. Edouard VII, has a large tropical bar on its main floor and a dance club downstairs that plays Latin music, techno, and hip hop (☎05 59 24 65 39. No cover. Beer and alcoholic drinks €8, glass of champagne €10. Bar open daily 11pm-6am, dance club opens at 2am.) A few streets away, the competing nightclub **Playboy**, 15 pl. Clemenceau, attracts a younger crowd by blasting rap and dance music until the early morning hours (☎06 63 60 39 20. €10 cover with drink. Beer €5, alcohol €8. Open midnight-6am, although no one comes until 2am). On weekend nights, many head for cheaper, wilder **San Sebastián** just over the border in Spain.

The **International Festival of Biarritz** celebrates the cinema and culture of Latin America during the first week of October. Throughout September, **Le Temps d'Aimer** will please the culturally inclined with music, ballet, and art exhibits. (Tickets at the tourist office. €16-30; student discounts.) In July and August, *pelote* and Basque dancing hit **Parc Mazon** Mondays at 9pm. Two *cesta punta* tournaments animate the **Fronton Euskal-Jai** in the **Parc des Sports d'Aguiléra**. For two weeks in mid-July, Biarritz hosts the international **Biarritz Masters Jaï-Alaï** tournament, while at the end of August, the town is taken over by the **Gant d'Or**, a tournament among big-name players. The winning teams from each tournament compete for the **Trophée du Super Champion** in mid-September. (For all three, call tourist office at ☎05 59 22 37 00. Tickets €10-20.) As a tribute to its other primary sport, Biarritz hosts a **Surf Festival** for two weeks in July, the **Junior Pro Competition** at the end of August, and the **Biarritz Surf Trophy** at the beginning of November. The city also celebrates its Spanish roots year-round with free **Basque music concerts** (pl. des Halles, third Sa of month 11:30am) and **dance shows** (first Su of month 11:30am; July-Oct. at the esplanade Casino Municipal, Nov.-June at the pl. de la Mairie).

BAYONNE

Although only a few kilometers from the center of Biarritz, Bayonne (pop. 42,000) seems hundreds of years removed from its more fashionable neighbor. The pace of life has not changed here since the 17th century, which is reflected even in the language of the region: the verb for "walk" is *flâner* (meaning "stroll"). Bayonne rises early, when lively markets crowd the banks of the Nive, but then slows down again in the afternoon as people retreat indoors behind exposed wooden beams and colorful shutters. Towering above it all, the grand Gothic cathedral marks the lazy passing of time with the tolling of its bells. It is only in the middle of July and August that things pick up, when hurried tourists flock to Bayonne to watch traditional Basque festivals, bullfights, and sports matches.

▐▀ TRANSPORTATION

Trains: pl. de la République (☎08 36 84 58 45). Info office open M-Sa 9am-noon and 3-6:15pm. To: **Biarritz** (10min., 11 per day, €2); **Bordeaux** (2hr., 9 per day, €22); **Paris** (5hr., 7 TGV per day, €71.60); **Toulouse** (4hr., 5 per day, €32). Also to **San Sebastián, Spain** via Andailles (1½-2hr., M-F 6 per day and Sa-Su 5 per day, €8).

Public Transportation: STAB, Hôtel de Ville (☎05 59 59 04 61). Office open M-Sa 8:15am-noon and 1:30-6pm. Buses run every 20-30min. Lines #1, 2, and 6 serve **Biarritz**. Lines #1, 2, and 7 stop in the center of **Anglet**. Line #4 follows the river Adour through Anglet. Buses run from around 6:30am-8pm (7pm on Su). 1hr. ticket €1.20; *carnet* of 10 €9.50, during the school year students €8.

Taxis: Both **Radio Taxi** and **Taxi Gare** are stationed outside the train station and at pl. Charles de Gaulle (☎05 59 59 48 48). 24hr. €2 starting cost, €1.24 per km during the day, €1.85 per km at night. Around €12-20 to get to Biarritz.

AQUITAINE

⚔️ 🛈 ORIENTATION & PRACTICAL INFORMATION

Bayonne is on two rivers that join to split the city into three sections. The train station is in **St-Esprit,** on the northern side of the wide river **Adour.** From here, the pont St-Esprit, usually lined with fishermen, connects to budget-friendly **Petit-Bayonne,** home of Bayonne's museums and smaller restaurants. Five small bridges from Petit-Bayonne cross the much narrower Nive to Grand-Bayonne on the west bank. This oldest part of town has a buzzing pedestrian zone where red-shuttered houses *(arceaux)* perch over ground-floor shops and *pâtisseries.* The center of town is manageable on foot, and an excellent bus system makes Anglet and Biarritz a snap to reach. To get to the **tourist office** from the train station, follow the signs to the *centre ville,* crossing the main bridge (pont St-Esprit) to Petit-Bayonne. Continue through pl. du Réduit and cross the next bridge on the right (pont Mayou) over to Grand-Bayonne. Take a slight right onto rue Bernède, and continue walking 300m as the street becomes av. Bonnat. The tourist office is on the left. (10min.)

Tourist Office: pl. des Basques (☎05 59 46 01 46; www.bayonne-tourisme.com). Free **city map,** hotel reservations, and *Fêtes en Pays Basque* brochures. Open July-Aug. M-Sa 9am-7pm, Su 10am-1pm; Sept.-June M-F 9am-6:30pm, Sa 10am-6pm.

Tours: The tourist office organizes 2hr. walking tours of neighborhoods and old ramparts. (July-Sept. M-F 10am; Oct.-June Sa at 3pm in French. €5, children under 12 free.) Tours given in English July-Aug. Th 10am. **Bâteau le Bayonne,** allée Boufflers (☎06 80 74 21 51), runs 2hr. guided boat trips along the Adour river. Excursions leave year-round upon demand; call for departure times. €14, group members €12, ages 5-12 €8.

Budget Travel: Pascal Voyages, 8 allées Boufflers (☎05 59 25 48 48). Open M-F 8:30am-6:30pm, Sa 9am-noon.

Money: Banque Inchauspe et Cie, 12 bd. Alsace-Lorraine (☎05 59 55 65 55), in St-Esprit. No commission, good rates. Open M-F 8:30am-noon and 1:45-5pm. Those on the other side of the river can try the **BNP Paribas,** 1 pl. de la Liberté (☎08 02 35 58 71). €5.40 commission for cash, no commission on traveler's checks. Open for exchange M-Tu and Th 8:30am-noon and 1:30-5:15pm. **ATMs** outside.

Laundromat: Lavopratic, 57 rue Bourg-Neuf (☎06 82 02 41 55). Open daily 8am-8pm. Wash €3.40-6.80, dry €0.40 per 5min. Ironing available daily 8am-noon and 2-5:30pm (T-shirt €0.60, long-sleeved shirt €0.75, jeans €0.90). Directly across the street, **Pressing Laverie,** 54 rue Bourg-Neuf (☎06 86 49 89 61), offers dry-cleaning service (€4-6 per piece of clothing). Open M-F 9am-noon and 2:45-6pm, Sa 9am-noon.

Police: av. de Marhum (☎05 59 46 22 22).

Hospital: 13 av. Interne Jacques Loëb (☎05 59 44 35 35), St-Léon.

Internet: In St-Esprit, **Cyber-net Café,** 9 pl. de la République (☎05 59 50 85 10). €0.15 per min., €4.50 per hr. Color photocopies €2.30 per page. Open M-Sa 7am-8pm, Su 10am-8pm. Internet is also available at the **post office** (see below).

Post Office: 11 rue Jules Labat (☎05 59 46 33 60), Grand-Bayonne. **Currency exchange** with no commission. Open M-F 8am-6pm, Sa 8am-noon. **Cyberposte. Branch office,** on the corner of bd. Alsace-Lorraine and rue de l'Este (☎05 59 50 32 90). Open M-F 8:30am-5:30pm, Sa 8:30am-noon. **Poste Restante** (at main branch): 64181. **Postal code:** 64100.

▌ ACCOMMODATIONS & CAMPING

Reasonably-priced lodgings dot **St-Esprit's** train station area. Hotels in **Grand-Bayonne** are pricier; hunt around **place Paul Bert** in **Petit-Bayonne,** but expect a noisy night near nightlife. Hotels fill quickly in festival season—reserve ahead. The closest hostels are in Anglet (p. 662) and Biarritz (p. 652), each a 20min. bus ride away.

AQUITAINE

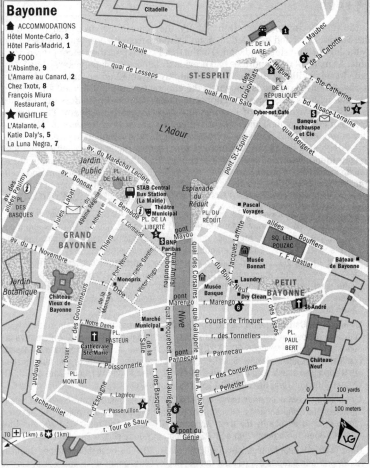

Bayonne

🏠 ACCOMMODATIONS
Hôtel Monte-Carlo, 3
Hôtel Paris-Madrid, 1

🍴 FOOD
L'Absinthe, 9
L'Amarre au Canard, 2
Chez Txotx, 8
François Miura
  Restaurant, 6

⭐ NIGHTLIFE
L'Atalante, 4
Katie Daly's, 5
La Luna Negra, 7

🏨 **Hôtel Paris-Madrid,** pl. de la Gare (☎05 59 55 13 98; fax 05 59 55 07 22; sorbois@wanadoo.fr), located to the left of the train station. A 3min. walk from Petit-Bayonne. Large individualized rooms are decorated with old wooden furniture and hand-painted purple grapes on the walls. The 4th floor has personal balconies overlooking pl. de la Gare. Gracious, English-speaking husband and wife are more knowledgeable and forthcoming than 20 tourist offices. TV/reading room. Breakfast €4. Hall shower €1. Reception July-Aug. 24hrs., Sept.-June 6:30am-12:30am. Singles and doubles €16-22, with shower €23-25, with shower and toilet €28; triples and quads with bath, toilet ,and TV €44. MC/V. ❶

  Hôtel Monte-Carlo, 1 rue Hugues (☎05 59 55 02 68), located just to the right of the train station. Check in at the lively bar/restaurant next door. Colorful rooms are decorated with old, local posters and occasionally a TV. Breakfast €4.50. Reception 6:30am-9pm. Singles and doubles €25, with shower €30; triples €33; quads with shower €39. MC/V. ❷

FOOD

At the very beginning of the 18th century, the Spanish monarchy heightened its anti-Semitic laws and expelled all non-Christians from its borders. Jews escaped by the hundred on ships and landed in the first French port they encountered, Bayonne. As many of the deportees had previously been chocolate-makers, they introduced their skills to the region and quickly established an enormous candy market. Today Bayonne is known as the chocolate capital of France and honors this title with its large array of chocolate shops. Along with its desserts, the city has also borrowed most of its meat and fish recipes from Spain. The narrow streets of Petit-Bayonne and St-Esprit offer €8-10 *menus* of *jambon de Bayonne* (dry cured ham) and *poulet à la basquaise* (chicken wrapped in large peppers). Grand-Bayonne, the city's cloth-napkin zone, serves regional specialties in a less budget-oriented atmosphere. Vendors sell meats, fish, cheese, and produce at the **marché municipal**, on quai Roquebert. (Open M-Th 7am-1pm, F 7am-1pm and 3:30-7pm, Sa 6am-2pm.) There is also a **Monoprix** supermarket on the corner of rue Orbe and rue Port Neuf. (☎05 59 59 00 33. Open M-Sa 8:30am-7:30pm. AmEx/MC/V.)

▓ **François Miura Restaurant,** 24 rue Marengo (☎05 59 59 49 89). In terms of luxury and decadence, this restaurant is far and away #1 in Bayonne. Amid fresh roses and modern art, patrons dine on sophisticated Basque food, such as squid marinated in pork juice and its own ink (€16). The unobtrusive restaurant is tucked away down a street; look for a foggy glass door decorated with the recommendation stickers of a dozen different travel guides. Appetizers €13.50-19, 3-course *menu* €18.50-29; main dishes of lamb, veal, pigeon, or filet mignon €16-21. Open M-Tu and Th-Sa noon-2pm and 8-10pm, Su noon-2pm. Although not mandatory, reservations are strongly recommended. AmEx/MC/V. ❹

L'Amarre au Canard, (☎05 59 50 16 77), directly across from the train station. Specializing almost exclusively in duck, this new restaurant serves over 20 different variations of the tender fowl (€6.90-14.20). €10 lunch *menu* includes duck platter, dessert, coffee, and a glass of wine. Salad €6.90, 3-course *menu* €15, beef and lamb dishes that somehow snuck onto the menu €11.50-12. Open M and W-F noon-2pm and 7:30-11pm, Tu noon-2pm, Sa-Su 7:30-11pm. MC/V. ❸

L'Absinthe, 15 quai Jauréguiberry (☎05 59 25 60 13), has delicate cuisine in small, intensely flavorful servings. Dinner served within the purple and yellow, art deco-ed room or on a terrace by the river. Appetizers €7-8, fish and meat €13-20, absinthe €4.50. Open Tu-Su noon-2pm and 7:30-10pm. Oct.-June closed Su. MC/V. ❹

Chez Txotx, 49 quai Jauréguiberry (☎05 59 59 16 80). This bullfighting-themed Spanish *brasserie* with a *tapas* bar (€1 per *tartine*) fills its seats on the dock with a lively crowd. Fresh fish come directly from the covered market next door (€10.50-13.50). Paella €14. Live music Su and Th at 9pm. Open daily 10am-2am. Cash only. ❸

SIGHTS

The works of Bayonnais painter Léon Bonnat (1833-1922) are displayed along with his extensive art collection at the ▓**Musée Bonnat,** 5 rue Jacques Laffitte. The walls of this four-story museum are hardly large enough to fit all of the stunning paintings by Dégas, Ingrès, Van Dyck, Reubens, Rembrandt, and Goya. (☎05 59 59 08 52. Open Su-M and W-Sa May-Oct. 10am-6:30pm; Nov.-Apr. 10am-12:30pm, 2pm-6pm. €5.50, students €3, under age 18 free. Entrance is free the first Su of each month.) Holding the title of world's largest ethnographic museum on the Pays Basque, the **Musée Basque,** 37 quai des Corsaires, has everything from traditional religious objects to fishing equipment to portraits of important local celebrities. Explanations are written in French, Spanish, and Basque, so non-locals may find the museum less interesting. (☎ 05 59 46 61 90; www.musee-basque.com. Open May-Oct. Tu-Su 10am-6:30pm; Nov.-Apr. Tu-Su 10am-12:30pm and 2-6pm. €5.50, students €3, under 18 free. Entrance is free on the first Su of each month. The tourist office leads French guided visits through the museum July-Sept. Th at 10am. Combined ticket for the Basque Museum and the Bonnat Museum €9, students €4.50.) On Sundays at 10:30am, the **Eglise St-André** (☎ 05 59 59 18 72) holds a traditional Basque mass with Basque chants.

The 13th-century **Cathédrale Ste-Marie**, pl. Pasteur, whose spiny steeples pierce the sky above Bayonne, seems disproportionately tall in relation to the town it serves. Although the church has endured sporadic fires, weathered a brief stint as a cemetery, and suffered massive destruction during the secularizing zeal of the Revolution, renovations have completely erased all traces of decay. (☎ 05 59 59 17 82. Church open M-Sa 7:30am-noon and 3-7pm, Su 3:30-8pm. Cloister open daily 9am-12:30pm and 2-6pm; Oct.-May closes at 5pm. Entry to both is free.) The prison block of the **Château-Vieux de Bayonne** on nearby rue des Gouverneurs has held such notorious villains as Don Pedro of Castille in 1367. The inside of the fort can only be viewed through the tourist office's guided tours in French. (July-Sept. every M and Sa at 10am; Oct.-June first Sa of every month at 3pm.) Around the corner on av. du 11 Novembre, Bayonne's refreshing **botanical gardens** flourish atop the battlements with 1000 species of Japanese flora, including a miniature bamboo forest. (Open mid-Apr. to mid-Oct. daily 9am-noon and 2-6pm.)

Those looking for a beach that is more secluded than the crowded plots of sand in Anglet or Biarritz should try the **Metro plage** in Tarnos; take bus #10 from the train station (every 20 min. M-Sa 7:20am-7:25pm). Lifeguards are only on duty during July and August, but the 2km walk is beautiful all year.

🎵 🎭 ENTERTAINMENT & FESTIVALS

Nightlife is nearly nonexistent in this quiet town of long afternoons and short evenings. The main bars grouped on the streets between **place Paul Bert** and **quai Galuperie** in Petit-Bayonne cater mostly to aging local men. Travelers seeking a more lively atmosphere often take the 10min. bus ride to Biarritz or head for the border to San Sebastian. In Bayonne, the Irish pub **Katie Daly's**, 3 pl. de la Liberté, serves expensive pints to animated crowds on the weekends. A large screen is set up by the door so that locals can watch soccer games while drinking. Live

IN RECENT NEWS

BASQUE CASE

In Bayonne, the capital of France's Basque region, restaurants post signs reading *Euskara badikigu*. Years of Latin lessons won't help you discover that this means "Basque spoken here," for Basque is the only non-Indo-European language spoken in Western Europe. Basque might not be the language of Babel, as believed in the 18th century, but Basques are tied to an ancient past. Geneticists recently found a link between Basques and Celts, suggesting both are close ancestors to European pre-farming communities.

Recent talk of Basque identity, however, has focused on the ETA (Basque Homeland and Liberty), a radical movement based in Spain that organizes attacks in the name of independence. As violence continues in Spain, France has cracked down on ETA training cells and imprisoned members for acts of terrorism.

Yet only 10% of French Basques vote for Basque parties, and even fewer support the ETA's radical ideology. How has France escaped Spain's problems? French Basques did not experience the cultural oppression as their Spanish counterparts did under Franco, and scholars suggest that tolerance toward French Basques has actually aided in their assimilation with the larger nation. The Pays Basque remains the middle ground, balancing its cultural identity between extremes of separatism and assimilation.

pop and rock music F-Sa. (☎ 05 59 59 09 14. Pints of Guinness €6, €5 7-9pm. Open Su-F 5pm-2am, Sa 2pm-2am.) **La Luna Negra,** in an alleyway off rue de la Salie, presents a cornucopia of music styles at its cabaret-style bar and stage. W is blues night; Th-Sa entertainment ranges from mimes to storytellers to classical concerts. (Bar open W-Sa 5pm-2am, shows start 9-9:30pm. Blues night €4, other shows €6-8; beer €2.50.) **L'Atalante,** 7 rue Denis Etcheverry, in St-Esprit, shows artsy international films in their original language. (☎ 05 59 55 76 63; www.cinema-atalante.org. Wheelchair-accessible. €5.70, students and children €3.80, €25 for 5 tickets. Movies begin every 2hr. from 2:30-8:30pm. Closed 2 weeks late July-early Aug.)

Bayonne's festivals take over the city from the end of June to the very beginning of October. June 21 brings the **Fête de la Musique,** where rock bands, jazz ensembles, breakdancers, and Basque crooners perform at various free concerts. The orchestra **Harmonie Bayonnaise** stages jazz and traditional Basque concerts in the pl. de Gaulle gazebo. (July-Aug. Th 9:30pm. Free.) After the first Wednesday in August, unrestrained hedonism breaks out during the **Fêtes Traditionelles,** as the locals immerse themselves in five days of concerts, bullfights, fireworks, and a chaotic cow race. July through September, Bayonne holds several bullfights or *corridas* in the **Plaza de Toros** (☎ 05 59 46 61 00). Tickets (€18-92) sell out fast, but the cheap, nose-bleed section usually has seats available on fight days. The Hôtel de Ville, on rue Bernède, provides information about local bullfights at the **Bureau des Arènes** (☎ 05 59 46 61 00) and about the city's festivals at the **Bureau d'Information Municipale** (☎ 05 59 46 60 41). Both are open M-F 9:30am-noon and 3-6pm. Year-round, the **Théâtre Municipale** hosts various musical performances. (☎ 05 59 59 07 27. Ticket office open Tu-F 1-6pm, Sa 10am-1pm and 3-6pm. Tickets approximately €10-20, although they vary for every show.)

▶ DAYTRIP FROM BAYONNE OR BIARRITZ: ANGLET

Known as the surfing capital of France, Anglet's *raison d'être* are its 4km of fine-grained white sand, parcelled out into nine sparkling beaches. The waves are strongest at the **plage des Cavaliers,** where most of Anglet's surfing competitions are held, but swimmers all along the coast should be wary of the strong undertow. When in doubt, swim near a lifeguard (they're on all the beaches except the plage du Club and the plage des Dunes). Pine needles cover the walking trails at the **Fôret du Chilberta,** which has a newly constructed adventure and ropes course. Contact Evolution 2 Pays Basque, 130 av. de l'Adour, which runs the course and offers **river-rafting trips** (€24.50 per half-day), **scuba diving** (€28 per 2hr.) and **surfing lessons** (€35 per 2hr.) at separate locations within an hour's drive of Anglet. (☎ 05 59 42 03 06; www.evolution2.com/paysbasque. Open mid-May to Oct. Beginner's ropes course for children ages 5-10 €8, 1½hr. intermediate course for adults €17, 2hr. advanced course €25. Office open July-mid-Sept. daily 10am-8pm, April-June and mid-Sept.-Oct. Sa-Su 2-6pm.) To get there, take STAB line #4 M-Sa from Bayonne, #9 M-Sa from Anglet's beaches or Biarritz, and bus C on Su from Bayonne, Biarritz, and Anglet's beaches, and get off at La Barre. Along the coast, professional surf competitions are held throughout the summer and are free for spectators. Starting off the season in the beginning of August, the **O'Neill Pro Competition** is held for six days on the plage des Cavaliers. About a week later, pro and amateur surfers demonstrate their skills at the **Quicksilver Air Show.** The qualifying rounds take place during the day at the Sables d'Or, followed by the final match-up at 9pm. For five days at the end of August, women take over the scene to compete in the longboard and bodyboard divisions of the **Kana Miss Cup.** Prepare for these title challenges by renting a board and taking lessons at one of the many surf shops along the beaches. On av. des Dauphins, **Freestyle** provides surfboards, wetsuits, bikes, beach cruisers, snowboards, and skis, depending on the season (☎ 05

59 03 27 24; freestyle.surfacademy@wanadoo.com. 1½hr. Lessons €30, €150 for 6 people. Surfboards €9 per half-day, €15 per day, €75 per week; wetsuits €5-6/€8-10/€40-50; bikes and beach cruisers €7/€10/€50; skis and snowboards with boots €140 per week. Photocopy of credit card required as a deposit. Open June to mid-Sept. daily 10am-8pm, mid-Sept. to May W-Su 10am-12:30pm and 2:30-7pm). Anglet Olympique Canoe Kayak on pl. du Docteurs Gentilhe (☎06 15 54 60 41), also rents out **jet skis** and **sea kayaks,** both €12 per hr. and €34 per day. Open July-Aug. daily 10am-5pm, Sept.-June W and Sa 2-6pm.

Those too sunburned to stand another day at the beach can head over to the town's **skating rink,** 299 av. de l'Adour, near the ropes course (☎05 59 57 17 30. Visitors €2, skaters €3.50, skate rentals €2.50. Open July-Aug. M-Sa 3-5:30pm and 9-11:30pm, Su 10am-noon and 3-5:30pm; Sept.-Apr. M and W-Th 2-5pm, Tu 2-5pm and 9-11pm, F 2-5pm and 9pm-midnight, Sa 2-6pm, Su 9:30-11am and 2-6pm. Closed May-June.)

In the Fôret du Chilberta, the Club Hippique provides **riding lessons** and **horseback tours** of the forest. The stables are on rue du Petit Palais, off Promenade de la Barre (☎05 59 63 83 45; fax 05 59 63 95 59; clubhippique@wanadoo.fr. 1hr. lesson or forest-walk €19, on ponies €17. Horseback excursions €36 per half-day, €46 per day. Open July-Aug. M-Sa, Sept.-June M-W and F-Su. If there is no one at the office, speak to a stable hand. Reservations are mandatory.)

The well-equipped **tourist office,** 1 av. de la Chambre d'Amour in pl. Général Leclerc, is a good 10-15min. walk from the sea. (☎05 59 03 77 01; fax 05 59 03 55 91. Open July to mid-Sept. M-Sa 9am-7pm; mid-Sept. to June M 9:30am-12:30pm and 2:30-6pm, Tu-F 9am-12:30pm and 2-6pm, Sa 9am-12:30pm.) There is an **annex** closer to the shore on av. des Dauphins. (Open July to mid-Sept. daily 10am-7pm, Apr. daily 10:30am-1pm and 3-6:30pm; mid-Sept. to Mar. and May-June Sa-Su 10:30am-1pm and 3-6:30pm.) **STAB** buses (€1.20) run throughout Anglet about every 15min., but less frequently on Sundays and holidays. Get a map or schedule from the tourist office in Anglet, or the train stations in Biarritz and Bayonne. From these two neighboring towns, the #1, 2, 6, and 7 buses M-Sa and the A and B buses on Su travel to the center of Anglet, while the #9, 7, and C buses run along its coast. The #9 and C buses stop near the youth hostel.

ST-JEAN-DE-LUZ

St-Jean-de-Luz (pop. 13,000; Basque name Donibane Lohitzun) has always lived off the sea. Its early wealth came from whaling and the Basque *corsaires* (pirates) who raided British merchants throughout the 1600s. These high-seas riches are responsible for the finest examples of Basque architecture, from the octagonal belltower above Ravel's birthplace to the elaborate interior of the Eglise St-Jean-Baptiste. This Basque town is certainly worth a visit for its charm and architecture, but budget travelers may want to daytrip from the more affordable Bayonne.

▐▌ TRANSPORTATION

Trains: bd. du Cdt. Passicot. Info office open M-F 10am-12:30pm and 2:10-6:30pm. To: **Bayonne** (30min.; 7 per day; €3.90, TGV €5.60); **Biarritz** (15min.; 10 per day; €2.50, TGV €4.20); **Paris** (5½hr., 10 per day, TGV €73.20); **Pau** (2½ hr.; 5 per day; €15.70).

Buses: across from the station. **ATCRB** (☎05 59 26 06 99) runs to **Bayonne** (35min., 7-13 per day, €3.60) and **Biarritz** (25min., 7-13 per day, €2.80). Also to **San Sebastian,** Spain (45min.; Apr.-June and Sept. Tu and F 9:50am and 2:50pm, July-Aug. M-F 9:55am and 3:10pm; €3.60 one way, €6.80 round-trip). Buy tickets on bus. Office open M-F 9am-noon and 2-6pm.

AQUITAINE

Taxis: at the train station (☎05 59 26 10 11). €6.50 flat rate to anywhere in town. Approximately €25 to get to Biarritz during the day, €30 at night. Open 24hrs.

Bike Rental: Fun-Bike Location (☎05 59 26 75 76 or 06 23 42 01 82), at the station. Bikes €15 for 24hr., €59 per week, €250 deposit; scooters €37/€229/€800. Open daily 9am-7:30pm. It is recommended that customers call in advance Sept.-June because the owner will often leave the office for hours at a time if there is a lack of customers. MC/V accepted July-Sept., Oct.-June cash only.

Car Rental: AVIS (☎05 59 36 76 66; fax 05 59 36 19 42), at the station. €291 per week and up. Photocopy of credit card required as a deposit. Cars can be returned at other locations. 25+. Office open M-F 8am-noon and 2-6pm, Sa 9am-noon and 2-6pm. AmEx/MC/V.

✴ 🔁 ORIENTATION & PRACTICAL INFORMATION

From the train station, bear left diagonally across the rotary onto bd. du Commandant Passicot. The **tourist office**, pl. Foch, is on the right, just past the 2nd rotary. From pl. Foch, rue de la République runs two short blocks to **place Louis XIV**, the center of town. The beach is 50m straight ahead, and the pedestrian **rue Gambetta** runs perpendicular to the right. **Ciboure**, the section of St-Jean-de-Luz on the other side of the river **Nivelle**, can be reached by crossing the pont Charles de Gaulle.

Tourist Office: pl. Foch (☎05 59 26 03 16; fax 05 59 26 21 47). Maps and info on accommodations, events, and excursions. 2hr. tours of the town offered in French Apr.-June and Sept.-Oct. Sa at 3pm, July-Aug. Tu and Sa at 10am. English tours available if reserved in advance. €4.60, children €2.30. Open July-Aug. M-Sa 9am-7pm, Su 10am-1pm and 3-7pm; Sept.-June M-Sa 9am-12:30pm and 2-7pm, Su 10am-1pm.

Money Exchange: Banque Inchauspé et Cie, 16 bd. Victor Hugo (☎05 59 26 24 71). Good exchange rates and no commission. Open Tu-Th 8:30am-12:15pm and 1:45-5:15pm, F 8:30am-12:20pm and 1:45-5:45pm, Sa 8:30am-12:30pm. **ATMs** directly across the street.

Laundromat: Laverie Automatique, at the intersection of bd. Victor Hugo and rue Chauvin Dragon. Wash €4-7, dry €0.40 per 4min., detergent €0.50. Open daily 8am-10pm.

Surf Shop: Le Spot, 16 rue Gambetta (☎05 59 26 07 93; www.surf-oceanic.com). 2hr. lesson €35. Wet-suit €8 per half-day, €14 per day; bodyboard €6/€10; surfboard €10/€15. Deposit €200. Open July-Aug. M-Sa 10am-1pm and 2:30-7:30pm, Su 11am-1pm and 2:30-7:30pm; Mar.-June and Sept.-Oct. M 3-7pm, Tu-Sa 10am-1pm and 2:30-7:30pm; Nov.-Feb. M 3-7pm, Tu-Sa 10am-12:30pm and 3-7pm. Cash only.

Police: av. André Ithurralde (☎05 59 51 22 22).

Hospital: 19 av. André Ithurralde (☎05 59 51 45 45). 24hr. emergency service at the private hospital **Polyclinique,** 10 av. de Layats (☎05 59 51 63 63).

Post Office: 44 bd. Victor Hugo (☎05 59 51 66 50). Open July-Aug. M-F 8:45am-6:30pm, Sa 8:45am-noon; Sept.-June M-F 8:45am-noon and 1:45-5:30pm, Sa 8:45am-noon. **ATM** outside. **Postal code:** 64500.

🏠 ACCOMMODATIONS & CAMPING

Hotels are expensive and fill up rapidly in summer. Reserve early, especially in August. It may be best to commute from Bayonne or Biarritz. However, those who do stay in St-Jean-de-Luz can expect nice rooms and good service for the prices.

Hôtel Bolivar, 18 rue Sopite (☎05 59 26 02 00; fax 05 59 26 38 28), on a central but quiet street near the beach. Sparkling rooms with shining floors are rented by a no-nonsense owner. Breakfast €6. Reception 7:30am-9:30pm. Open May-Sept. Singles with toilet €34, with toilet and shower €48; doubles €38-40/€60; triples with bath, toilet, and TV €65. May-June and Sept. prices slightly lower. AmEx/MC/V. ❸

Hôtel Verdun, 13 av. de Verdun (☎05 59 26 02 55), across from the train station. Well-kept, pastel-colored rooms with huge bathrooms for the lowest prices in St-Jean. The hotel's restaurant serves an €11 *menu* which includes soup, a main course, and an all-you-can-eat dessert tray. Breakfast €4. July-Sept. singles and doubles €38, with shower €42; triples and quads with shower €44, with shower and toilet €49. Obligatory demi-pension adds €13. Jan.-Apr. and Nov.-Dec. 1-4 people €23-28; May-June and Oct. 1-4 people €26-32. Reception 9am-11pm. MC/V. ❸

Camping: There are 14 campsites in St-Jean-de-Luz and 13 more nearby. All are slightly separated from the city center, behind the plage D'Erromardie. The tourist office has the addresses and phone numbers of the campgrounds and can make recommendations based on travelers' individual needs. To walk to most of the sites, take bd. Victor Hugo from the center of town, continue along the road as it turns into av. André Ithurralde, then veer left onto chemin d'Erromardie. (20min.) Or take an ATCRB bus headed to Biarritz or Bayonne and ask to get off near the camping. For a quiet and sheltered location, the **Camping Iratzia,** on chemin d'Erromardie (☎05 59 26 14 89; fax 05 59 26 69 69), offers grassy sites 300m away from the beach. Open May-Sept. Reception 9am-12:30pm and 4-7:30pm. Those arriving when the office is closed may set up their tents in an open spot, and return to the reception when it opens. Aug. €5.50 per person, €3.10 per car, €7 per site; July and Sept. €4/€2.50/€5; May-June €3.50/€2/€4. Electricity €3.50. Showers included. Mobile home for 4 people May-June and Sept. €260, July-Aug. €390-550. ❶

🍴 FOOD

St-Jean-de-Luz has the best Basque and Spanish specialties north of the border. The port's famous seafood awaits in every restaurant along the rue de la République and pl. Louis XIV, but expect to pay upwards of €13 per meal. There is a large **market** at pl. des Halles. (Open July to mid-Sept. daily 7am-1pm, mid-Sept. to June closed Su.) For groceries, stop at the **Shopi** supermarket, 87 rue Gambetta (open Sept.-June M-Sa 8:30am-12:30pm and 3-7:30pm; July-Aug. M-Sa 8:30am-8pm, Su 9am-noon; MC/V), or at **8 à Huit,** 46 bd. Victor Hugo (open M-Sa 8:30am-7:30pm, Su 8:30am-12:30pm and 4:30-7:30pm; MC/V).

▨ Buvette de la Halle, bd. Victor Hugo-Marché de St-Jean-de-Luz (☎05 59 26 73 59), has been in the same family for over 70 years and refuses to alter its original menu even the slightest bit to include modern additions such as ketchup. Although this café beside the marketplace appears unimpressive at first glance, it serves the freshest seafood and vegetables in St-Jean, all locally grown based on the season. Grilled sardines €6, *gambas* (large shrimp) €12, *gâteaux Basques* €4, and apéritifs of wild prune Patxaran €3. Open July-Aug. daily noon-3pm and 7-11pm, Sept.-June closed on Su. MC/V. ❷

▨ Pil-Pil Enea, rue Sallagoity (☎05 59 51 20 80) near the post office, is a tiny restaurant serving the finest merlu caught by Europe's only female captain and cooked by her husband. The environmentalist fisherwoman catches all her fish by line, rather than the inhumane net. *Menu* €23, entrées €6-10, fish and meat €10-16. Open M-Sa noon-2pm and 8-10pm, Su noon-2pm. MC/V. ❸

Herria Ostatua, 30 rue Chauvin Dragon (☎05 59 26 29 79), dishes up delicious *menus ouvrier* (worker's menus) from Sept.-June that consist of an appetizer, an all-you-can-eat buffet, and dessert for a flat €10. Catering to local fishermen and burly workers, the restaurant's menu is written only in Basque, but can be translated by the friendly owner. Live music twice a month. Open M-Sa 10am-2am; meals served noon-2:30pm and 7:30-10:30pm. V. ❷

Etchebaster Frères, 42 rue Gambetta (☎05 59 26 00 80), caters to sweet tooths with cherry jam and cream-filled *gâteaux basques* (€6.20-13.50). The traditional pistachio *guernikas* (€1.70) and frosted *gâteaux des rois* (€5.90-11.80) also come especially recommended by the owner. Open Tu-Sa 8:30am-12:30pm and 3:30-7pm, Su 8am-1pm and 4-7pm. V. ❷

⑤ SIGHTS

To see St-Jean-de-Luz at its most striking, follow the walkway on the beachfront away from the river Nivelle to the end of the **Grande Plage.** The path up toward the **Chapelle Van Bree** takes you on a *balade à pied* (footpath) along the edge of St-Jean's cliffsides. From the lookout points, gaze out across the river Nivell over to Hendaye and the Spanish border beyond. In town, the 15th-century **Eglise St-Jean-Baptiste,** rue Gambetta, has a plain exterior but is decorated inside with enormous gold sculptures of saints and apostles. (☎05 59 26 08 81. Open daily 10am-noon and 2-6pm. Mass is held Su 10:30am, Sa 7pm.) It was in this church that Louis XIV married the Spanish princess Maria-Teresa, according to the terms of the 1659 Treaty of the Pyrénées. The treaty was worked out after months of negotiations by Cardinal Mazarin and the Spanish prime minister on the nearby Ile des Faisans or "island of conferences," a "no man's land" jointly owned by France and Spain.

Owned by the same family for over 350 years, the elaborate royal furniture inside the **Maison Louis XIV** has been frozen in time, seemingly awaiting the return of its most famous boarder. It was here that Louis XIV stayed while Mazarin negotiated, and here that he consummated his marriage with Maria-Teresa. Unlike the average royal marriage, this one proved successful; upon the queen's death, the king lamented, *"C'est le premier chagrin qu'elle me cause"* ("This is the first sorrow she has caused me.") (☎/fax 05 59 26 01 56. Open July-Aug. M-Sa 10:30am-12:30pm and 2:30-6:30pm, Su 2:30-6:30pm; Sept. and June M-Sa closes at 5:30pm, Su 10:30am-noon. €4.50, students €3.80. Free 30min. guided tour in French leaves every 30min. July to mid-Sept. Written explanations in English and audio guides in French available upon request.)

◪ SWIMMING WITH THE FISHES

From 1954 to 1956, St-Jean-de-Luz was France's primary supplier of tuna. Fishing boats still leave regularly from quai de l'Infante and quai Maréchal Leclerc, although they are not as fruitful as they once were. To get in on the fun at sea level, stop by the docks near the Maison Louis XIV, where Mairie Rose offers a four-hour **fishing trip** from 8am to noon. (☎05 59 26 39 84 or 06 08 25 49 74; www.bateau-mari-erose.com. Trips leave daily July-Aug. and twice weekly Sept.-June. €25, children €13. Reservations recommended.) If you prefer to leave the fish alive, **Promenade Jacques Thibaud,** sheltered by dikes, provides some of the best **sailing** and **windsurfing** in the Basque region. Farther down the coast, the most popular surfing spot in St-Jean-de-Luz lies beyond the crowded beaches on **plage d'Erromardi.**

◧ FESTIVALS

Summer is packed with concerts, Basque festivals, and the heavily-anticipated championship match of *cesta punta* (www.cestapunta.com. Qualifying series and finals July-Aug. Tu and F at 9pm. Tickets at the tourist office; €8-18.50, students €5-11, under 12 free.) The biggest annual festival is the three-day **Fête de St-Jean,** held on the last weekend in June, when singing and dancing fills the streets. Nearly continuous performances by amateurs and professionals alike liven the *fronton* (arena), while spectators consume fruity sangría and barbecued Basque dishes.

Toro de Fuego heats up summer nights in pl. Louis XIV with pyrotechnics, dancing, and bull costumes. (July-Aug. W 10:30pm, and occasionally Su 11pm.) At the **Fête du Thon** (the first Sa in July beginning at 6pm), the town gathers around the harbor to eat tuna, toss confetti, and pirouette (fish, *gâteau basque*, and wine €10). The madness continues the second Saturday of July with the all-you-can-eat **Nuit de la Sardine** at the Campos-Berri, next to the *cesta punta* stadium (☎05 59 26 02 87 for info). The last festival of the year, the **Fête du Toro,** held on an early Saturday in September, celebrates the region's excellent fish soup.

◪ DAYTRIP FROM ST-JEAN-DE-LUZ: COL DE ST-IGNACE

Basque Bondissant (☎05 59 26 30 74) runs buses to Col de St-Ignace from the green-rimmed bus terminal facing the train station in St-Jean-de-Luz (20min.; July-Aug. M-Sa 3 per day, Sept.-June M-Tu and Th-F 3 per day, W 2 per day; round-trip €4, including train to top €15, children 4-10 €8.50. Office open M, Tu, Th 9am-12:30pm and 1:30-6pm, W and F 9am-noon and 1:30-6pm.)

Ten kilometers southeast of St-Jean-de-Luz, the miniscule village of **Col de St-Ignace** serves as a base for the Basque country's loveliest vantage point. Trains from Col de St-Ignace crawl at a snail's pace along an authentic 1924 *chemin de fer* (railroad) up the mountainside to the 900m summit of **La Rhune.** Each hair-raising turn reveals a postcard-perfect display of forests hovering above sloping farmland, as *pottoks* (wild Basque ponies) return your curious stares and sheep bound down the mountainside. At the peak, chilly air and gusty winds prevail even in summer. (Trains operated by **Le Petit Train de la Rhune.** ☎05 59 54 20 26; www.rhune.com. July-Aug. daily every 30min. 9am-5pm. Mid-Mar. to June and Sept. to mid-Nov. open daily 9:30am until passengers start wearing thin. €11 round-trip. Cash and traveler's checks.) La Rhune *(Larun)* is Spanish soil; shop owners slip easily between French and their native tongue. Those who decide to walk back down from La Rhune should take the longer, roundabout route, as loose rocks on the path make for treacherous footing. Take the well-marked trail to the left of the tracks down to the village of **Ascain** instead of trying to return directly to St-Ignace. Then hike the remaining 3km on D4 back to Col de St-Ignace (1½hr.); or set out directly for St-Jean-de-Luz from Ascain along the busy highway (5km).

ST-JEAN-PIED-DE-PORT

St-Jean-Pied-de-Port is the last stop before the tortuous mountain pass of Roncevaux on the pilgrimage to the tomb of St. James in Santiago de Compostela, Spain. Pilgrims have been making the trek ever since the 10th century, their routes intersecting in this medieval village nestled in the middle of the red Pyrenean hills. First built by Sancho the Strong in the 13th century, the walls of St-Jean-Pied-de-Port have withstood attack from Visigoths, Charlemagne, the Moors, and the Spanish army. Outside the now-crumbling ramparts, visitors can set off on numerous hikes into the gorgeous French and Spanish mountains. The Fôret d'Iraty, a mecca for hikers and cross-country skiers, is only 25km away.

◪ PRACTICAL INFORMATION. Trains leave for **Bayonne** (1hr.; 5 per day, last train July-Aug. 6:50pm, Sept.-June 4:48pm; €7.40) from the station on av. Renaud. (☎05 59 37 02 00. Info office open 6:30am-12:30pm and 1-6:45pm.) **Rent bikes** at Garazi Cycles, 32 bis au Jaï-Alaï. (☎05 59 37 21 79; jean-jacques.etchardy@wanadoo.fr. Bikes €8 per half-day, €13 per day; scooters €17/€29; motorcycles €32/€45. Passport, cash, or credit card deposit. Open M-Sa 8:30am-noon and 3-6pm.) From the station, turn left and then immediately right onto av. Renaud, follow it up the slope, and turn right at its end onto av. de Gaulle. Down the street 40m on the left, the **tourist office**, 14 av. de Gaulle, gives out small maps of the town and sells hiking guides (€6.10) charting the 25 trails in the surrounding region. (☎05 59 37 03 57; saint.jean.pied.de.port@wanadoo.fr. Open July-Aug. M-Sa 9am-12:30pm and 2-7pm, Su 10:30am-12:30pm and 3-6pm; Sept.-June M-Sa 9:30am-noon and 2-6:30pm.) The **police** are on rue d'Ugagne (☎05 59 49 20 10), and the Clinique Luro in Ispoure handles **medical emergencies** (☎05 59 37 00 55). The **post office** (☎05 59 37 90 00), rue de la Poste, has **currency exchange** with no commission. (Open M-F 9am-noon and 2-5pm, Sa 9am-noon.) **Postal code:** 64220.

ⅱ ACCOMMODATIONS. St-Jean offers beautiful rooms at unbecoming prices; you won't find much under €31 per night. The best option is to stay at Mme. Etchegoin's **gîte d'étape ❶**, a popular stopover for pilgrims following the chemin de St-Jacques. The lodging is just outside the city walls, 9 rte. d'Uhart. From the tourist office, walk downhill, cross the bridge, and take the first right on the opposite bank. The street becomes rte. d'Uhart after the city gates. (5min., follow signs to Bayonne.) Twelve spartan bunks await in this 18th-century house, as do six attractive *chambres d'hôte* with handmade quilts, antique furnishings, and hardwood floors. (☎05 59 37 12 08. Open Mar.-Nov. Breakfast €4. Reception 8am-10:30pm. Sheets or sleeping bag €2. Dorms €8; singles €30; doubles €34-39; triples €42-45. All rooms have either personal showers, or access to a communal one. Mme. Etchegoin prefers that you call in advance so that she can be home for your arrival. Cash and check only.) Slightly more elegant than the gîte, the **Hôtel Plaza Berri ❸**, on 3 av. de Fronton, is located in the corner of the old city. Follow the hill down from the tourist office and continue straight through pl. Floquet until it meets the ramparts. Turn left and walk along the walls; the hotel will be on the left. Tastefully decorated rooms are filled with old, wooden furniture and oriental rugs. Directly across from the Fronton Municipal, those on the top floor can sit out on private balconies and watch championship *pelote* games for free. (☎05 59 37 12 79. Breakfast €6. Singles and doubles with shower €35, with shower and toilet €43; triples with toilet and shower €55. Hotel is rarely fully booked. Cash and check only.) **Hôtel des Remparts ❸**, 16 pl. Floquet, is on the same road as Mme. Etchegoin's gîte, but inside the city walls. Large, pastel rooms come equipped with shower, toilet, TV, and telephone. (☎05 59 37 13 79; fax 05 59 37 33 44. Breakfast €5.50. Reception Apr.-Sept. daily 7:30-9pm; Oct.-Mar. M-F only. Singles €38; doubles €41-44. MC/V.)

Quiet **Camping Municipal ❶** rests against a low ivy-covered stone wall by the Nive, 5min. from the center of town, on av. du Fronton. For its price, the campsite has the most central and convenient location of any lodging in St-Jean. From the porte St-Jacques, follow the river upstream 50m to the next bridge. Cross the river; the site is on the left on av. du Fronton. (☎05 59 37 11 19 or 05 59 37 00 92; fax 05 59 37 99 78. Open Apr.-Oct. daily 9am-11pm and 5-7pm. €2 per person, €1.50 per child, €1.50 per tent, €1.50 per car. Electricity €2. Bathrooms and showers are free, although there is no toilet paper.)

◖ FOOD. Farmers bring *ardigazna* (tangy, dry sheep's-milk cheese) to the **market** on pl. de Gaulle. (Open M 9am-6pm.) In July and August, there are also local fairs that bring produce from all the villages nearby; ask for the dates at the tourist office. Bread, cheese and wine are all available at any one of the many small shops that line **rue d'Espagne**. For everyday food, the **Relais de Mousquetaires** supermarket is on the corner of rue d'Espagne and rue d'Uhart. (☎05 59 37 00 47. Open M, W, F-Sa 9:30am-12:30pm and 4-7:30pm, Tu and Th 9:30am-12:30pm. MC/V.) None of the cheap restaurants in St-Jean-Pied-du-Port are spectacular, but there are several cafés and crêperies along the rue de Zuharpeta that offer budget-friendly meals and refreshing sangría. If splurging is an option, the charming little **Restaurant**

Etche Ona ❻, on pl. Floquet (☎05 59 37 01 14; fax 05 59 37 35 69) serves delicious food amid starched white tablecloths and crystal wine glasses. Expertly cooked and garnished with traditional Basque sauces, the duck, lamb, and rabbit (€17-22.50) are truly superb. (3-course *menu* €17, 4-course €25-41. Open July-Sept. daily noon-2pm and 7:30-9pm; Oct.-June closed F. MC/V.)

🔯 **SIGHTS.** Bounded by **Porte d'Espagne** and **Porte St-Jacques,** the ancient *haute ville* of St-Jean consists of one narrow street, **rue de la Citadelle,** which is bordered by houses made from regional crimson stone. The well-preserved remains of the **Citadelle de Vauban** rest at the top of this narrow street, towering over the town and its surrounding farmland. Originally built by the knight Antoine Deville in 1628, the fortress was later reinforced by Vauban during the reign of Louis XIV. In 1750, the citadel housed an impressive 2000 soldiers and actively protected Bayonne and Orthez from the feisty Spaniards lurking across the border. Although the interior of the stronghold has since been converted into an elementary school, visitors can picnic on the grassy ramparts to enjoy a breathtaking view of the town below.

Cowering below the walls of the fortress is the 13th-century **Prison des Evêques,** 41 rue de la Citadelle. Originally built as a municipal prison, the building was used to discipline unruly citadel soldiers during the 19th century and torture French escapees from 1940-1945 during the Nazi occupation. Today, the prison has been converted into a small museum dedicated to the pilgrimage of St-Jacques. (☎05 59 37 00 92. Open July-Aug. daily 10am-7pm; Easter-June and Sept.-Oct. daily 11am-12:30pm and 2:30-6:30pm. €3, children under 10 free.) Rue de la Citadelle returns to the rear of the **Eglise Notre-Dame-du-Bout-du-Pont,** fused with the **Porte St-Jacques** on the banks of the Nive. Once a fortress, the church betrays its past with rocky, low-lit crevices instead of side chapels. Carefully patterned stained glass casts a mist of light over the rest of the simple edifice. (Open daily 7am-9pm.)

🎭🎵 **ENTERTAINMENT & FESTIVALS.** In summer, *bals* (street dances) and concerts offer free entertainment, while Basque choirs and the Basque ball game *pelote* add local color. (*Pelote* June-Sept. M at 5pm at either the Trinquet of the fronton municipal by the campground.) Thursday nights in July and August, traditional Basque folkdances are held in different locations around the town. Once on the eve of Bastille Day and once in mid-August, Basques get buff for the **Force Basque** competition, which includes gritty tug-of-war matches and the hoisting of 150lb. hay bales. Admission around €6.50, but you can peer through vines from the fence for free.

🥾 **HIKE: THE PILGRIM'S ROUTE.** The Spanish border is only a 4- to 5-hour walk from St-Jean-Pied-de-Port along a clearly marked trail. The **GR65** leads you through the Pyrénées toward the Pass of Roncevaux and, a quick 800km later, to Santiago de Compostela and St. James's tomb. To get on the trail from St-Jean, take the rue d'Espagne out from the Porte de l'Eglise. When the road forks, take a slight left onto rte. du St-Michel and continue straight until it becomes rte. Napoleon. You will start to see painted red and white stripes on the telephone poles, the symbol of the GR65. The narrow paved road slopes up the mountainside, past family farms and then into the Pyrénées, where cows, sheep, and wild horses wander. The **Fontaine de Roland** and the **col de Bentarte** signal entry onto Spanish land. The round-trip hike takes about eight hours and scales 1100m up into the Pyrénées; if it becomes too late to turn back, there is lodging near the pass of Roncevaux, about a 2hr. walk past the col de Bentarte. **Amis du Chemin de Saint-Jacques de Pyrénées Atlantiques,** 39 rue de la Citadelle, in St-Jean, offers help, advice, and lodging exclusively for hikers. (☎05 59 37 05 09. Open Mar. to mid-Nov. daily 7:30am-12:30pm and 2:30-8:30pm. Shelter €7 per night.)

PAU

Once the seat of the kings of Navarre, Pau (pop. 78,000) has retained little of its former grandeur. While the château of native son Henri "Edict of Nantes" VI remains in near-perfect condition, the surrounding city has begun to show some signs of wear. Thanks to the nearby Pyrénées, however, Pau benefits from good weather and easy access to several centers of mountain sports. As the capital of the Béarn region, Pau is also the capital of Béarnais cuisine—the city now holds more than 150 restaurants, each serving regional delicacies fit for a king.

■ ♂ **ORIENTATION & PRACTICAL INFORMATION.** The **train station,** on av. Gaston Lacoste, is at the base of the hill by the château. Info office open M-Sa 5:30am-11:30pm, Su 7:15am-midnight. **Trains** go to: Bayonne (2hr., 7 per day, €13.40); Biarritz (2¼hr., 6-7 per day, €14.40); Bordeaux (2½hr.; 9 per day; €24.90, TGV 26.60); Lourdes (30min., 14 per day, €6.10); St-Jean-de-Luz (2½hr., 4 per day, €15.70). CITRAM, 30 rue Gachet (☎ 05 59 27 22 22), runs **buses** to Agen (3hr., 1 per day, €25.60). Office open M-F 8:30am-12:15pm and 2-6:30pm, Sa 8:30am-noon. Société TPR (☎ 05 59 27 45 98), on rue Gachet, goes to Bayonne (2½hr.; M-Sa 2-3 per day, Su 1 per day; €14.10); Biarritz (2¾hr.; M-Sa 2-3 per day, Su 1 per day; €15.20); Lourdes (1¼hr.; M-Sa 5 per day, Su 2 per day; €7.10, under 6 free). Office open M-F 9am-noon and 2-6pm. STAP runs **local buses** (tickets €0.90, day pass €2.50, *carnet* of 8 tickets €5). First bus in any direction M-Sa 6:30am, Su 1:15pm; last bus in any direction M-Sa 8:20pm, Su 7:40pm. The new **Noctambus** is run by the same company but circulates on fewer routes 8pm-midnight. The office is on rue Gachet. (☎ 05 59 27 69 78. Open M-F 8:30am-12:30pm and 1:30-6pm, Sa 9am-noon.) There is also a kiosk on pl. Clemenceau. (☎ 05 59 14 15 16. Open M-F 9am-noon and 2-6pm, Sa 9am-noon.) **Taxis** depart from the train station, pl. Clemenceau, pl. Verdun, the hospital, and the airport. (☎ 05 59 02 22 22. During the day €1.24 per km, at night €1.70, starting rate €2. Approximately €23-25 to go from the train station to the airport. 24hr.) Romano Sport, on the corner of rue Jean-Réveil and rue Castetnau, **rents bikes** (€15 per day), mountain bikes (€22 per day), rollerblades (€8 per day), wetsuits (€10 per day), hiking boots, and mountain equipment. (☎ 05 59 98 48 56. Deposit €100-600 or ID. Open M-Sa 9am-noon and 3-7pm. Cash and traveler's checks only.)

To get to the tourist office and town center from the station, ride the free **Funicular** to bd. des Pyrénées (every 3min.; M-Sa 6:45am-12:10pm, 12:35-7:50pm, and 8:15-9:40pm; Su 1:30-7:50pm and 8:15-9pm), or climb the steep zigzagging path outlined in white fences to the top of the hill. At the top, the **tourist office** is at the far end of pl. Royale, across the tree-lined park from the funicular. They have maps, an **accommodations service,** and copies of *Béarn Pyrénées,* with *gîtes* and camping info, all of which are free. (☎ 05 59 27 27 08; fax 05 59 27 03 21; www.pau.fr. Open July-Aug. daily 9am-6pm; Sept.-June M-Sa 9am-6pm, Su 9:30am-1pm.) **Service des Gîtes Ruraux,** on the corner of rue Maréchal Joffre and rue Gassion in the Cité Administrative, gives advice on mountain lodgings and makes **reservations** for a commission. (☎ 05 59 11 20 64; fax 05 59 11 20 60. *Chambres d'hôte* reservation €3, *gîtes* €15. Open M-F 8:30am-6pm, Sa 8:30am-4:30pm.)

There is a **laundromat** on rue Gambetta (open daily 7am-10pm; wash €3-6.50, dry €0.30 per 4min.) and a dry-cleaning service at **Pressing,** near the marketplace, at 7 pl. du Foirail. (☎ 05 59 30 92 75. €3 per item. Open M-F 9:30am-12:30pm and 3-7pm, Sa 9:30am-12:30pm.) For emergencies, the **police** (☎ 05 59 98 22 22) are on rue O'Quin and the **hospital** is at 4 bd. Hauterive (☎ 05 59 92 48 48). Consult the tourist office or the signs posted on every pharmacy's door for the rotating **pharmacie de garde.** Access the **Internet** at C Cyber, 20 rue Lamothe, past the post office. (☎ 05 59 82 89 40. €0.75 per 10min., €4.50 per hr. Open M-Sa 10am-2am, Su 2pm-midnight.)

The **post office**, on cours Bosquet at rue Gambetta, has **currency exchange** with no commission, and a **Cyberposte**. (☎ 05 59 98 98 98. Photocopies €0.10 per page. Fax services available. Open M-F 8am-6:30pm, Sa 8am-noon.) **Postal code:** 64000.

⊞ ACCOMMODATIONS. Hôtel de la Pomme d'Or ❷, 11 rue Mal. Foch, has bare, spacious rooms, with slanted hallways and old doors that are difficult to lock and unlock. Turn left from the tourist office onto rue Louis Barthou and left again on rue A. de Lassence. Walk through pl. Clemenceau and turn right onto rue Mal. Foch. All rooms but the smallest have TVs. (☎ 05 59 11 23 23; fax 05 59 11 23 24. Breakfast €3.50. Reception 24hr. Singles €18, with shower €23; doubles €21/€23-27; triples with shower €34-36; quads with shower €37-40. Cash and traveler's checks only.) The Pomme d'Or provides the cheapest rooms in town, but couples or larger families may want to try the more upscale two-star **Hôtel Central ❸**, 15 rue Léon Daran. From the tourist office, take a right and walk down rue Louis Barthou until you see rue Léon Daran. The 28 large, spotless rooms are individually decorated and quiet. The renowned author of *Le Petit Prince*, Saint-Exupéry, stayed in room #7 before his rise to fame. All rooms come with shower and TV, and a billiard room and bar with cable TV are available. (☎ 05 59 27 72 75; www.centralhotel-pau.com. Breakfast €6. Reception 24hr. Reservations recommended. Singles €30.40, with toilet €30.40-43.80; doubles €30.40/€30.40-48.40; triples and quads, some with kitchenette and fridge, €55.60. Extra bed €8. AmEx/MC/V.)

⊡ FOOD. Deeper in the heart of the city, is the three-star **Hôtel Montpensier ❹**, 36 rue Montpensier, a large pink stucco building. Follow the directions going to the Hôtel Pomme d'Or, but instead of turning right onto Maréchal Foch, continue straight through pl. Clemenceau to rue Serviez, which becomes rue Léon Daran. Though they lack individualized charm, the rooms all have shower, toilet, TV, telephone and mini-fridge. (☎ 05 59 27 42 72; fax 05 59 27 70 95. Breakfast €6. Reception 6:45am-1am. Reserve well in advance for the cheapest rooms. Singles €35-55; doubles €43-60; triples €62; quads €65. AmEx/MC/V.) About 3km from the train station, the hostel **Logis des Jeunes ❶**, outside Pau, is in Gelos. Shell out €7 to get there by taxi, or take bus #1 (dir: Larrious Mazères-Lezon) to Mairie de Gelos (€0.90). With three bedrooms, this tiny hostel can only support five people at a time. (☎ 05 59 35 09 99. Reception daily 5-9pm. No reservations; call from the train station to see if they have any vacancies. Dorms €8.50, non-HI members €13.60.)

The region that brought you tangy *béarnaise* sauce has no paucity of specialties: salmon, pike, *oie* (goose), *canard* (duck), and *assiette béarnaise*, a succulent platter that can include gizzards, duck hearts, and asparagus. The area around the château, including **rue Sully** and **rue du Château,** has elegant regional restaurants (*plats* €9, *menus* €16). Down the hill, the *quartier du hédas* offers more expensive fare in a fancier setting. Inexpensive pizzerias, kebab joints, and Vietnamese eateries can be found on **rue Léon Daran** and adjoining streets.

Overlooking the pl. de la Liberté and the Eglise Saint-Jacques, the beautiful and modern **Le Saint Vincent ❷**, 4 rue Gassiot, serves €8 *moules frites* and €9 *escargots*. (☎ 05 59 27 75 44. *Menus* €11-22, couscous €10, fish and meat dishes €10-16. Open M-Sa 8am-10pm. AmEx/MC/V.) On a cobblestone street by the château, **Au Fruit Défondu ❸**, 3 rue Sully, serves 10 kinds of fondue—many including typical *béarnaise* fare (€12-15). Don't forget to leave room for the divine chocolate fondue (€12.20), which is meant for two people. (☎ 05 59 27 26 05. Open early July to late Dec. daily 7pm-midnight; late Dec. to early July closed W. MC/V.)

The sprawling, Olympic-sized **Champion** supermarket sits in the new **Centre Bosquet** megaplex on cours Bosquet. (Open M-Sa 9am-7:30pm.) The equally enormous **market** at **Les Halles**, pl. de la République, is a maze of vegetable, meat, and cheese stalls. (Open M-Sa 6am-1pm and 3:30-7:30pm, Sa 5am-2pm and 3:30-7:30pm.

Many vendors choose to shut down during the afternoon slot.) The **Marché Biologique**, pl. du Foirail, offers a variety of organic produce to the health-conscious. (Open W and Sa 8am-noon.)

🅖 **SIGHTS.** Originally built as a fortress in the 12th century, the **Château d'Henri IV** was reshaped and remodeled by a succession of *béarnais* viscounts and famous *navaresse* kings. Henri IV, Napoleon III, and Louis-Philippe all made their mark on the castle, leaving behind a large array of velvet furniture, ornate ceilings, and crystal chandeliers. Now a national museum, the castle displays Henri IV's enormous tortoise-shell crib along with a collection of beautiful Gobelin tapestries. The château is accessible only through 1hr. French guided tours that depart every 15min. (☎05 59 82 38 19. Open daily mid-June to mid-Sept. 9:30am-12:15pm and 1:30-5:45pm; Apr. to mid-June and mid-Sept. to Oct. 9:30-11:45am and 2-5pm; Nov.-Mar. 9:30-11:45am and 2-4:15pm. Last tour 1hr. before closing; English tours by appointment. English brochure available. €4.50, students €3, under 18 free.) The local obsession with Henri IV becomes clear with a visit to the **Musée des Beaux-Arts**, on rue Mathieu Lalanne, where a staircase leads to an enormous tableau of his birth and then to a wall-length depiction of his 1598 coronation. The rest of the museum contains a small collection of modern art and a more impressive collection of 17th- to 19th-century European paintings. (☎05 59 27 33 02. French and English guides available if requested in advance. Open Su-M and W-Sa 10am-noon and 2-6pm. €2, students €1, under 18 free.)

The mild climate makes Pau conducive to botanical flights of fancy, and for a good part of the year the town is covered in flowers and trees of every color and origin, from America to Japan. The best place to sample some of this biodiversity is around the pond in the **parc Beaumont**. Follow the bd. des Pyrénées away from the castle to the Palais Beaumont; the park is just behind the Palais.

🅝 **NIGHTLIFE.** While clubs in the town center cater to an older and more sedate crowd, the foreign bar scene on bd. des Pyrénées are an outlet for the young and lively. The two-story **Galway**, 20 bd. des Pyrénées, provides good old Irish folk music to a mostly anglophone crowd. (☎05 59 82 94 66. Pints of beer from €4. Live music twice a month. Open July-Sept. noon-3am; Oct.-June noon-2am.) Next door an Australian bar, an Irish *brasserie*, and a Russian café serve a stylish mixed crowd of youngsters and 30-somethings. For those looking for more excitement, **Le Contre-temps**, on the corner of rue Lamothe and bd. Barbanègre, has laser lights, a live DJ Th-Sa, and pounding techno music. (Beer €2.20, cocktails from €2.50. Open W-Sa 11am-2am. Closed Aug.)

🅔🅒 **ENTERTAINMENT & FESTIVALS. Cinéma le Méliès**, 6 rue Bargoin, shows artsy films, some in English. (☎05 59 27 60 52; www.cinefil.com. Tickets €5.40, students €4.30, under 12 €3. Closed 4 days in mid-Aug.) Throughout the summer, Pau remains active with numerous festivals and cultural presentations. Starting in mid-June, the **Festival de Pau** brings three weeks of theater, music, ballet, and poetry to the Palais Beaumont and to the Théâtre St-Louis. (Reservations at the tourist office ☎05 59 27 27 08 or from FNAC ☎05 59 98 90 00. €15-40 per concert, €9-15 per child under 12.) The weekend of Pentecost, cars race about the town center during the Formula 3 **Grand Prix de Pau**. Speedy bikes replace cars in mid-July when the **Tour de France** passes through Pau and spectators line the streets to cheer on the competitors. At around the same time, the **Ciné Cité** hosts ten free nights of musical concerts and outdoor films. Country, salsa, blues, and jazz bands perform at around 9pm and are quickly followed by either a recent popular film or an old classic. Contact the tourist office for movie and concert schedules. From mid-July to mid-August, the city hosts a series of strength competitions every Monday and Thursday night during the **Festival de Force Basque**. The **Festival Internacional des Pyrénées** occurs 35km south of Pau in Oloron every other year during the first week of August, when 45 folk ballet troupes from 25 countries storm the city in a celebration of dance and culture. (Info and tickets from the Oloron tourist office ☎ 05 59 39 98 00; www.danseaveclemonde.com. Festival will be held in Oloron in 2004. Tickets around €12.). Trains run to Oloron from Pau's train station (35-45min., 10 per day, €5.70).

PYRÉNÉES

LOURDES

In 1858, 14-year-old Bernadette Soubirous reported seeing the first of what would total 18 visions of the Virgin Mary in the Massabielle grotto in Lourdes (pop. 16,300). Over time, "The Lady" caused a spring to appear beneath Bernadette's fingers, told her to repent, drink, and wash in a nearby stream, and instructed her to "go tell the priests to build a chapel here so that people may come in procession." Today, over five million visitors from 100 countries come annually to this pilgrimage center, toting rosaries and hoping for miracles as they solemnly march, or are wheeled, to the Blessing of the Sick. Lourdes's secular wonders include the medieval fortress that rises from the center of town and the panoramic views from the summit of nearby Pic du Jer rival any neighboring city's attractions. Nestled in the mountain foothills, Lourdes is a gateway to the Pyrénées.

▐ TRANSPORTATION

Trains (☎ 05 62 42 55 53; info office open daily 6am-8:50pm) go from 33 av. de la Gare to Bayonne (2hr., 5 per day, €17.20); Bordeaux (3hr.; 7 per day; €28, TGV €28.50); Paris (7-9hr., 5 per day, TGV €85.80); Pau (30min.; 16 per day; €6.10, TGV €8.50); and Toulouse (2½hr., 8 per day, €20.80). **SNCF buses** run from the station to Cauterets (50min., 3-6 per day, €5.90). **Local buses** (☎ 05 62 94 10 78) run from all points in the city to the Grotto, the Pic du Jer (from which the funicular departs), and the Lac de Lourdes (every 20min. Easter-Oct. daily 7am-6:30pm; €1.50). **Taxis** wait at the train station (☎ 05 62 94 31 30) and the grotto (☎ 05 62 94 31 35) from Easter to October. Rent **bikes** at Cycles Antonio Oliveria, 14 av. Alexandre Marqui, near the train station. (☎ 05 62 42 24 24. Open Tu-Sa 9:30am-7pm. €9.20 per half-day, €18.30 per day, €73 per week. MC/V.)

▐ ▐ ORIENTATION & PRACTICAL INFORMATION

The train station is on the northern edge of town, 10min. from the town center. To get from the station to the **tourist office,** turn right onto av. de la Gare, then bear left onto the busy av. Maransin at the first intersection, cross a bridge above bd. du Lapacca, and proceed uphill. The office is in a modern glass complex on the right. (5min.) The religious heart of Lourdes beats at the **grotto.** Follow av. de la Gare through the intersection, turn left onto bd. de la Grotte, and follow it as it snakes right at pl. Jeanne d'Arc. Cross the river Gave to reach the Esplanade des Processions, the Basilique Pius X, and the grotto. (10min.)

Tourist Office: pl. Peyramale (☎ 05 62 42 77 40; fax 05 62 94 60 95; lourdes@sudfr.com). Friendly polyglot staff distributes maps, info on religious ceremonies, a list of hotels, and brochures about the nearby Pyrénées. Open M-Sa May-Oct. 9am-

7pm; early to mid-Nov. and mid-Mar. to Apr. 9am-noon and 2-7pm; mid-Nov. to mid-Mar. 9am-noon and 2-6pm. Bernadette-related sights are managed by the Church-affiliated **Sanctuaires de Notre-Dame de Lourdes** (☎05 62 42 78 78), which has a **Forum d'Info** to the left, in front of the basilica. Open daily 8:30am-12:30pm and 1:30-7pm.

Youth Center: Forum Lourdes/Bureau Information Jeunesse, pl. de Champ Commun (☎05 62 94 94 00), beyond Les Halles. Helpful info for young travelers, though with a somewhat religious spin. Open M-F 9am-noon and 2-6pm.

Laundromat: Laverie GTI, 10 av. Maransin. Wash €4.50. Open daily 8am-7pm.

Police: 7 rue Baron Duprat (☎05 62 42 72 72). Open daily 9am-noon and 3-8pm.

Hospital: Centre Hospitalier, 3 av. Alexandre Marqui (☎05 62 42 42 42), at the intersection of av. de la Gare, av. Marqui, and av. Maransin. **Medical emergency:** 2 av. Marqui (☎05 62 42 44 36).

Disabled Services: Catholic-inclined guide to facilities *Guide de Lourdes* (€3) is available from the **Association Nationale Pour Integration Handicapés Moteurs** (☎05 62 94 83 88), on bd. du Lapacca. Call first.

Internet: in the social and cultural center in pl. du Champ Commun (☎05 62 94 94 00). €3 per hr. Open daily 9am-noon and 2-6pm.

Post Office: 31 av. Maransin (☎05 62 42 72 00). **Currency exchange** (bills only). **Cyberposte.** Open M-F 8:30am-6:30pm, Sa 8:30am-noon. **Postal code:** 65100.

⚑ ACCOMMODATIONS & CAMPING

Finding a room for €22 in Lourdes is easy. Similar hotels are grouped together—the cheap ones on rue Basse, and the two-stars on av. de la Gare and rue Maransin. Most hotels are clean but drab. The city's massive healing industry has induced many proprietors to improve wheelchair accessibility as well as construct facilities for the visually and hearing impaired.

Hôtel Arbizon, 37 rue des Petits Fossés (☎/fax 05 62 94 29 36). Follow av. Helios away from the station as it curves down the hill. Bear right and under the bridge ahead on bd. du Lapacca. Take the first left uphill after the bridge onto rue Basse; rue des Petits Fossés is the first right. Centrally located, with small but sufficient rooms at low prices. Pleasant owner. No showers available for those in shower-less rooms. Breakfast €4. Reception daily 7am-midnight. Open early Feb. to mid-Nov. *Demi-pension* €20.60-23.70. Singles €13.80; doubles €18.30; triples €22.90; quads €27.50. ●

Hôtel Lutétia, 19 av. de la Gare (☎05 62 94 22 85; fax 05 62 94 11 10; info@lutetia-lourdes.com). A pleasant if somewhat bland mock-château to the right heading away from the train station. 51 clean, comfortable rooms with sink, table, chair, and telephone fill quickly in the summer; call ahead and specify desired type of room. Pricier rooms come with TV. Elegant restaurant on the first floor serves *menus* from €10. Elevator and free parking. Singles €17.30, with toilet €24, with shower €30-36, with bath €37; doubles €21.40/€28/€39/€40. MC/V. ❷

Hôtel du Commerce, 11 rue Basse (☎05 62 94 59 23; fax 05 62 94 89 56; hotel-commerce-et-navarre@wanadoo.fr). Faces the tourist office with a pizzeria on the first floor. Bright, newly renovated rooms all with showers and toilets. Back rooms have view of the château. Breakfast €3.80. July to mid-Oct. singles €31.20; doubles €37.40; triples €44.60. Mid-Oct. to June singles €27.20; doubles €32.40; triples €41.60. MC/V. ❸

Camping and Hôtel de la Poste, 26 rue de Langelle (☎05 62 94 40 35). Small, backyard campground 2min. beyond the post office, has about 12 large spaces with grass and shady trees. The campground also lets 8 pristine rooms in the attached hotel. Breakfast €4.50. Open Easter to mid-Oct. Doubles €22, with shower €25. Camping €2.50 per person; €3.60 per site. Shower €1.30. Electricity €2.50. ●

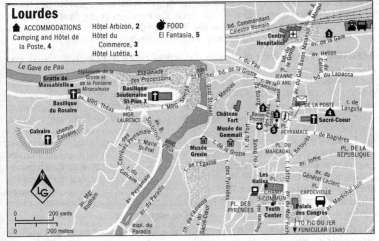

Lourdes

🏠 ACCOMMODATIONS
Camping and Hôtel de
  la Poste, **4**

Hôtel Arbizon, **2**
Hôtel du
  Commerce, **3**
Hôtel Lutétia, **1**

🍴 FOOD
El Fantasia, **5**

FOOD

Find expensive groceries at **Casino** supermarket, 9 pl. Peyramale (☎05 62 94 03 87; open Tu-F 8:30am-1pm and 3:30-8pm, Sa 8:30am-1pm and 3-8pm, Su 8am-1pm), or at the larger **Monoprix** supermarket, 9 pl. du Champ Commun. (☎05 62 94 63 44. Open M-Sa 8:30am-12:30pm and 2-7:30pm, Su 8am-noon.) Produce, flowers, second-hand clothing, books, and cheap pizza are all sold daily at the **market** at **Les Halles,** pl. du Champ Commun. (Open daily 8am-1pm, every other Th until 5pm.) *Boulangeries* line the streets heading past the tourist office and toward pl. du Champ Commun.

Restaurants not affiliated with hotels are few and far between. On the main strip of the **bd. de la Grotte,** many similar restaurants charge similar prices for similar food. Meals, surrounded by religious souvenir shops selling Virgin Mary water bottles, Jesus holograms, and toothbrushes, will cost from €10-15. Slightly cheaper *plats du jour* and *menus* can be found around the tourist office and on **rue de la Fontaine,** just don't expect gourmet fare. Slightly swankier—if still touristy—restaurants are down the steps on both sides of the river Gave, with the nicest views and breeze in town. **El Fantasia ❸,** 5 rue Basse, has a tiny, basic, wholesome Moroccan menu (couscous €10-12, *tagines* €9.50) to relieve *brasserie*-tired palettes. (☎31 40 53 35 45 56. Open daily noon-2pm and 7:30-10pm. MC/V.)

SIGHTS

Most of the religious sights are amazing not in themselves, but for the fervent reactions they incite among pilgrims. **Passeport Visa Lourdes** (€30, children €16) provides access to four Bernadette-related museums, the Fortified Castle and its museum, the funicular to Pic du Jer, and a tourist train ride through town. Ask for details at the tourist office. **Carte Lourdes Pass,** free at the tourist office, gives entrance to two of the previous sights or activities after having visited five others.

GROTTE DE MASSABIELLE. Visitors from around the world shuffle past this small dark crevice in the mountainside at the edge of town, touching its cold rock walls, whispering prayers, and waiting to receive a blessing from the priest on duty. Lines are longest in the late afternoon. Nearby, water from the spring where

Bernadette washed her face is available for drinking, bathing, and bringing home, hence the numerous water bottles sold here. The cave lies by the river on the right side of two superimposed churches, the Basilique du Rosaire and the upper basilica. *(No shorts, tank tops, or food. Fountain and grotto open daily 5am-midnight.)*

BASILICAS. The **Basilique du Rosaire** and **upper basilica** were built double-decker style above Bernadette's grotto. Their pointed steeple, soft grey color, and flags are reminiscent of a fairy tale and look striking against the mountains. The interiors are less elegant. In the **Rosaire,** completed in 1889, an enormous Virgin Mary strikes a maternal pose. The **upper basilica,** consecrated in 1876, has a more traditional interior. The most remarkable space for prayer is the **Basilique St-Pius X,** which is hidden underground, in front of the other two basilicas and to the left of the Esplanade des Processions. Accessible by several wide, unmarked passages, it's a stadium-sized concrete echo chamber designed in the form of an upturned ship. It won an international design prize in 1958. When filled with singing it can be quite gorgeous, though some think it looks more like the parking garage of the Starship Enterprise. Covering 12,000 sq. m, this concrete cavern fits 20,000 souls with room to spare. *(All 3 open daily Easter-Oct. 6am-7pm; Nov.-Easter 8am-6pm, excluding masses at 11am and 5pm, which can be respectfully observed.)*

PROCESSIONS & BLESSINGS. The **Procession of the Blessed Sacrament** and the **Blessing of the Sick** are huge affairs held daily at 5pm, starting in the Basilica St-Pius X. One by one, wheelchair-bound or otherwise infirm pilgrims—often escorted by nuns—receive their blessing. Observers can stand, squeeze onto a bench, or watch from the upper basilica's balcony. "One-day pilgrims" join the procession and march along the esplanade behind rolling ranks of wheelchairs. *(Meet other pilgrims July-Sept. at 8:30am at the "Crowned Virgin" statue in front of the basilica.)* A solemn **torchlit procession** blazes from the grotto to the esplanade nightly at 8:45pm. Pilgrims from all over the world recite "Hail Mary" in six languages and proudly hold banners proclaiming church names and nationalities. Light a candle, available for a few euros in booths by the river Gave. *(Mass in English Apr.-Oct. daily 9am at the Hémicycle, just across the river from the cave in a cavernous concrete building.)*

CHÂTEAU FORT. Practically the only sight in town without a religious connection, the feudal castle overlooks Lourdes from atop a rocky crag. A shuttlecock in territorial disputes between France and England during the Middle Ages, the building dates from the 14th century. The high square tower and well-preserved walls of the château now offer unequaled panoramas of surrounding Lourdes and guard the strange collection of the **Musée Pyrénéen.** The museum displays a series of regional objects including wine barrels, decorated plates, and butter churns. *(☎05 62 42 37 37. Enter by elevator. Open mid-Apr. to mid-Oct. M-Sa 9am-noon and 1:30-6:30pm, Su 11am-6pm; mid-Oct. to mid-Apr. Su-M and W-Sa 9am-noon and 2-6pm. €5.)*

FUNICULAIRE. Just outside of town, a track climbs 1000m up the **Pic du Jer.** Local buses lead to the bottom of the track. Taking this 6min. ride and walking the extra 10min. up to the observatory at the summit gives a stunning 360° view of the surrounding countryside and the town below. Energetic folk can hike up the mountain using the map from the ticket booth. Beware of rapidly descending mountain bikers. *(☎05 62 94 00 41. Buses depart daily every 30min. 10am-6pm. €7.50, children €5.50. Depot on the southern edge of town, at the base of the mountain. Follow the main road, rue St-Pierre, 2km from the center of town by the tourist office. There's also a bus from the ticket booth at the intersection of rue de la Grotte and rue de la Tour de Brie. Round-trip €3.)*

LAC DE LOURDES. Local bus #7 runs to a large, peaceful lake 4km from the center of town, where locals flip off the dock and eat ice cream in the slightly overpriced waterside café. A relief from the hectic town and summer humidity, the lake is a good follow-up to morning tours of the grotto and sanctuaries. *(Buses July-Aug. 4 per day 8:25am-6:30pm; Sept.-June less frequently. By foot, take av. Maransin toward the train station and turn left onto bd. Romain. The street becomes av. Béguere and then rte. de Pontacq. Take a left onto chemin du Lac to reach the water. 30min.)*

MUSEUMS. The **Musée de Gemmail** reproduces famous works of art in the thick, multi-layered stained-glass technique that gives the museum its name. There's an equally large annex near pont St-Michel. *(72 rue de la Grotte. ☎ 05 62 94 13 15. Open Apr.-Oct. daily 9-11:45am and 2-6:45pm. Annex on bd. Père Rémi Sempe. Free.)* Down the street, the **Musée Grevin** is as close as it gets to a Catholic Disneyland. One hundred uncannily lifelike wax figures act out the lives of Bernadette and Jesus. Most impressive is the life-size replica of Leonardo da Vinci's *Last Supper*. *(87 rue de la Grotte. ☎ 05 62 94 33 74. Open daily July-Aug. 9-11:30am, 1:30-6:30pm, and 8:30-10pm; Apr.-June and Sept.-Oct. 9-11:30am and 1:30-6:30pm. €5.50, students €2.70.)*

CAUTERETS

Every morning in Cauterets (pop. 1300), sugared vapors of *berlingots* wafting from the candy stores fill the air while mist rolls slowly off the surrounding mountains. Nestled 930m up in a narrow, breathtaking valley among near-vertical peaks, sleepy Cauterets awakes in May and June to the sounds of a turquoise river rushing beneath its bridges. The melting snows of early summer bring wilderness lovers here to the edge of the Parc National des Pyrénées Occidentales. For serious hikers, the wildly contrasting French and Spanish sides of the Pyrénées are both accessible from Cauterets, and there are dozens of day hikes that range from 1½ to 8 hours. When hiking becomes overly taxing, the *thermes* offer a relaxation program of *remise en forme* to bring hikers back to their former selves.

✴ 🛈 ORIENTATION & PRACTICAL INFORMATION

Cauterets runs lengthwise along the river Gave and is small enough to walk across in 5min. It is accessible only by bus from Lourdes. From the bus station, turn right and follow av. du Général Leclerc up a steep hill to the tourist office at pl. Foch. **SNCF buses** (☎ 05 62 92 53 70) run from pl. de la Gare to Lourdes (1hr.; 6 per day; €5.90, students €4.60. Office open daily 9am-12:30pm and 3-7pm.) **Rent bikes,** as well as in-line skates and ice skates, at Skilys, rte. de Pierrefitte, off pl. de la Gare. (☎ 05 62 92 52 10. Mountain bikes with guide €18-32 per half-day, €40-55 per day, €230-380 deposit; without guide €9.20/€15.30/ID deposit. Open daily 9am-7pm, winter 8am-7:30pm. AmEx/MC/V.) Bernard Sports-tifs, 2 rue Richelieu, next to the tourist office, offers good prices on **alpine ski rentals** and gives discounts to American students. (☎ 05 62 92 06 23; www.bernardsports-tifs.com. €11-16 per day for boots, skis, and poles; €59-83 for six days.)

The **tourist office,** pl. Foch, has a list of hotels, a useful map, and a *Guide Pratique.* (☎ 05 62 92 50 27; fax 05 62 92 59 12; www.cauterets.com. Open daily July-Aug. 9am-12:30pm and 1:30-7pm; Sept.-June 9am-12:30pm and 2-6:30pm.) Their hiking map, *Sentiers Lavanes* (€4), is the best day-hike resource for English speakers, owing to its colorful, comprehensible format. For more hiking info, drop by the **Parc National des Pyrénées** office at pl. de la Gare. The **police** are on av. du Docteur Domer (☎ 05 62 92 51 13). For **medical emergencies,** call ☎ 05 62 92 14 00. Access the **Internet** at **Pizzeria Giovanni,** 5 rue de la Raillère (☎ 05 62 92 57 80; €3 per hr.; open July-Aug. daily noon-3pm and 7-11pm; Sept.-June Th-Su only), or in the basement of the **public library,** 2 esplanade des Oeufs. (☎ 05 62 92 52 45; www.infos@planeticj.com. €5 per hr. Open W-Sa 3-7pm.) The **post office,** at the corner of rue Belfort and rue des Combattants, offers **currency exchange.** (☎ 05 62

THE LOCAL LEGEND

SWEET & SULFUR

Two smells permeate the high Pyrénées from early morning until nightfall. One is the overpowering smell of sulfur rising from natural springs, now home to the famed *thermes* of Cauterets and Luchon. The other is the sweet smell of *Berlingots* candy coming from the *confiseries* that dot the town's main thoroughfares.

These two vastly different smells are historically connected. "Taking the cure" in hot sulfur springs was thought to improve the health of rheumatics, consumptives, and arthritics. The cure included everything from having one's sinuses cleaned with small brushes to taking the water up through the nose and expelling it from the mouth. Around 1840, doctors decided that the healing process would be helped if the patient held a morsel of sugar in the mouth while gargling the hot water. The change held, and France's *thermes* were soon surrounded by *confiseries*.

Today, the *thermes* have gone from pain to pure pleasure. While some of them remain strictly for rheumatics, most offer healing massage therapy, saunas, and relaxing pools for everyone. Others even have small spa and gym areas. Yet the main streets leading toward the sulfurous springs remain sweet with the dozens of shops making and hawking *berlingots*, which are worth a taste either in their hard form, as lollipops, or by the pound.

92 53 93. Open July to mid-Sept. M-F 9am-6pm, Sa 9am-noon; mid-Sept. to June M-F 9am-noon and 2-5pm, Sa 9am-noon.) **Postal code:** 65110.

ACCOMMODATIONS

Gîte d'Etape UCJG ❶, av. du Docteur Domer, 7min. from the town center, is the best accommodation for real mountain travelers in Cauterets. From the Parc National office, cross the parking lot and street and turn left uphill on a footpath underneath the funicular depot. The *gîte* is just beyond the tennis courts. Gloriously located with welcoming hosts, this *gîte* has 60 beds in every possible set-up, from canvas barracks to the eaves of an attic, in addition to leafy campsites. (☎05 62 92 52 95. Kitchen, shower, and sheets included. Reception daily, but hours vary. Open mid-June to mid-Sept. Dorms €8; €3.50 per tent; €6.50 for space in the *gîte*'s tent; bed in bungalow €8.50.) **Hôtel Christian ❸**, 10 rue Richelieu, offers a view of the Pyrénées, darts, and *bocce* for somewhat steep prices, but the buffet breakfast is included. The incredibly gracious owner, whose family has run the hotel for generations, is eager to chat with his guests. Cheaper rooms on the top floor are smaller and darker than the others. (☎05 62 92 50 04; www.hotel-christian.fr. Closed early Oct. to late Dec. Reception daily 7:30am-10pm. Singles and doubles €40-55; triples with shower and TV €67.50; quads with shower and TV €82. MC/V.) Every room at **Hôtel Bigorre ❷**, 15 rue de Belfort, has a balcony with a tremendous view of the surrounding mountains. The rooms are old but spacious, and back-country travelers can leave excess luggage here for a few days. Rue de Belfort runs between pl. de la Gare and pl. Foch, near the tourist office. (☎05 62 92 52 81; www.bigorrehotel.com. Open late May to early Nov. daily; early Nov. to late May on weekends and school holidays only. Reception daily 7:30am-10pm. Singles €15.80, with shower €25.50; doubles €33/€43; triples and quads €48/€65.) **Hôtel de Paris ❸**, 1 pl. Foch, is as close to the action in town as one can get in Cauterets. Decently priced doubles have plush carpets, TVs, and large bathrooms. (☎05 62 92 53 85; fax 05 62 92 02 23. Reception daily 7am-10pm. Doubles €40-43; triples and quads €52-56. MC/V.)

FOOD

The small, beautifully old-fashioned **Halles market**, a few doors down from the tourist office on av. du Général Leclerc, has fresh produce. (Open daily 2-8pm.) An **open-air market** is held in the parking lot next to the Casino. (Open mid-June to mid-Oct. F

8am-5pm.) The local specialty is the *berlingot,* a hard sugar candy originally used by patients visiting the *thermes* to contribute to "the cure." Thirty-five flavors of the candies are prepared by hand and cranked through a magical candy-making machine to the delight of onlooking customers at **A la Reine Margot ❶,** pl. de la Mairie Crown. (€1.40-1.60 per 100g. Delicious swirly lollipops €2-4. Open daily 10am-midnight.) The husband and wife team at **Chez Gillou ❶,** 3 rue de la Raillère, specializes in blueberry and almond cakes known respectively as *tourtes myrtilles* and *pastis des Pyrénées.* (☎05 62 92 56 58. Cakes €5.40. Open July-Aug. and Feb.-Mar. daily 7am-1pm and 3:30-7:30pm; Sept., Dec., and Apr.-June Su-Tu and Th-Sa 7:30am-12:30pm and 3-7pm.) Foie gras and other fancy regional products are sold with a smile at **Chez Gaulhou Dourdois ❷,** 8 rue de Belfort. (☎05 62 82 01 10. Items from €7.70. Open M-Sa 9am-noon and 2-7pm.)

There are few gourmet restaurants in Cauterets, but plenty of hearty food. Several small restaurants with outdoor seating line **rue Verdun.** Paired crêpes and every other kind of snack food imaginable make **Le Ski Bar ❷,** pl. Foch, a popular spot with hikers—or maybe it's the €8 pitchers of sangria. (☎05 62 92 53 83. Main dishes and snacks €3-10. Open M-Sa noon-1am and Su noon-8pm. MC/V.) **La Crêperie Basque ❷,** 8 rue Richelieu, serves simple, delicious *galettes* and crêpes under a pale blue ceiling on a quiet street. (☎05 62 92 51 79. Entrées €6-12, crêpes €3-7. Open M-Sa noon-3pm and 6:30-10pm. MC/V.)

🧭 🔼 SIGHTS & OUTDOOR ACTIVITIES

From av. du Docteur Domer, the **Téléphérique du Lys** cable car (☎05 62 92 03 59) races overhead every 30min. into the nearby mountains. From there, trails lead across the ridge and eventually to the breathtaking Lac d'Ilhéou. (1½hr.) In July and August and during the ski season, the **Télésiège du Grand Barbat** chairlift runs to the **Crête du Lys,** over 1000m above Cauterets. (€9 round-trip, €5 one-way to Crête du Lys, €6 round-trip on the *téléphérique.*) The hike back down from **Crête du Lys** is a medium difficulty trek that passes Lac d'Ilhéou. (1½hr.)

HIKES. Multiple half-day hikes depart directly from Cauterets at a **trailhead** behind the Thermes du César. These include the tough climbs to the **Col du Lisey** and the **Col de Riou,** both of which provide startling views of several valleys (both 3hr. round-trip) and the more relaxing trek to the **Cascade du Lutour** (2hr. round-trip). A **map** (€4) is posted on the main square in pl. Foch and is available at the tourist office. The deservedly popular **Chemin du Cascades** is a steep but waterfall-laden 2½hr. climb from Cauterets. It begins on a staircase on the hill to the right of the Casino (a map is posted here as well), and ends in the national park at the Pont d'Espagne. The €5 **navettes** that depart directly to the Pont d'Espagne make other hikes in the national park easily accessible (see **Parc National,** p. 680).

SULFUR SPRINGS. Cauterets's natural sulfur springs have been credited over the years with curing everything from sterility to consumption. But it's no bubble bath—the doctors here have taken to heart the maxim of "no pain, no gain." Separate sterilized rooms each offer different contraptions for "enjoying" the full effects of the water. The *thermes* also offer a relaxing program of massage for those who don't have what it takes to undergo the full process. For info on the *thermes,* contact **Thermes de Cesar,** av. Docteur Domer. (☎05 62 92 51 60; www.thermescauterets.com. Aerobath-sauna-hydrojet pool €21.50, hydromassage jet showers €29. Open M-F 9am-12:30pm and 2-5pm.) **The Balneo Aladin spa,** 11 av. du Gal. Leclerc, located in a somewhat cheesy pink mall in the town center, has cheaper access to a pool and solarium (€13-17), as well as a jacuzzi, sauna, and hammam. (☎05 62 92 60 00; www.hotel-balneo-aladin.com. Open June-Sept. daily 10am-1pm and 3-8pm.)

🎵 ENTERTAINMENT

Esplanade des Oeufs offers a casual **cinema** (☎05 62 92 52 14) that plays French and foreign films (the latter are mostly popular American imports in their original language) and a **casino.** (☎05 62 92 52 14. Open May-Oct. daily 11am-3am.) The **patinoire** (skating rink) hosts skating nights year-round, mostly near the end of the week, according to a complicated schedule provided by the tourist office. The rink itself can be reached through the parking lot of the train station. (☎05 62 92 58 48. €5.50, children €3; skate rental €2.50.)

PARC NATIONAL DES PYRÉNÉES OCCIDENTALES

One of France's seven national parks, the **Parc National des Pyrénées** shelters endangered brown bears and lynxes, 200 threatened colonies of marmots, 118 lakes, and 160 unique plant species in its snow-capped mountains and lush valleys. Punctuated by sulfurous springs and unattainable peaks, the Pyrénées change dramatically with the seasons, never failing to awe a constant stream of visitors. To get a full sense of the extent and variety of the mountain range, hikers should experience both the lush French and barren Spanish sides of the Pyrénées (a 6- to 7-day round trip hike from Cauterets). But there are plenty of more modest opportunities as well. Jaw-droppingly spectacular views are just hours away from civilization, satisfying those only looking to wet their feet in the wilderness.

AT A GLANCE

AREA: Narrow 100km-long swath along the Franco-Spanish border

CLIMATE: Misty in France, arid in Spain

GATEWAYS: Gavarnie (p. 681); Luz-St-Sauveur (p. 681); Ainsa, Spain (p. 682)

DAY HIKES: Turquoise Lac de Gaube (3½hr. from Cauterets), the Chemin des Cascades (4hr. from Cauterets)

LONG HIKES: Cirque de Gavarnie, passing through waterfalls and lush forests (4-day hike from Cauterets); or continuing into Spain (6-7days from Cauterets)

ACCOMMODATIONS: *Gîtes* (around €11) are available in towns along the GR10; one-night camping permitted in areas at least 1hr. away from major highways

🔧 PRACTICAL INFORMATION

Touch base with the friendly, helpful staff of the **Parc National Office,** Maison du Parc, pl. de la Gare, in Cauterets before braving the wilderness. They provide free info on the park and the 14 different trails beginning and ending in Cauterets. Trails in the park are designed for a range of abilities, from novices to rugged outdoor enthusiasts. The **Haute Randonnée Pyrénées (HRP)** trails offer a more challenging mountain experience. Speak with the folks at the Parc National Office before attempting these treks. Documentary films in French feature aerial views of the local mountains and show 2-3 times per week to advise hikers on the area. (☎05 62 92 52 56; fax 05 62 92 62 23; www.parc-pyrenees.com. €4, children and students €1.50. Open June-Aug. daily 9:30am-noon and 3-7pm; Sept.-May M-Tu and F-Su 9:30am-12:30pm and 3-6pm, Th 3-6pm.)

The **maps** sold at the Parc National office are probably sufficient. (Day-hike maps €6, topographical maps €9-11.) For the Cauterets region, use the #1647 Vignemale map of the Institut de Géographie Nationale. The **Bureau des Guides,** pl. de la Mairie on tiny rue Verdun in Cauterets, runs tours and guides for rock-climbing, canyoning, hiking, and skiing. Medium-difficulty tours are €14-30.50 per person; harder ones €46-140. Tours depart the Cauterets tourist office. (Summer ☎05 62 92 62 02, winter 05 62 92 55 06. Open daily 10am-12:30pm and 3:30-7:30pm.)

Gîtes in the park average €11 per night and are generally located in towns along the GR10. Reserve at least two days ahead, especially in July and August when the mountains teem with hikers. The Parc National office in Cauterets will help plan an itinerary while the **Service des Gîtes Ruraux** (☎05 59 80 19 13) in Pau makes *gîte* reservations. The general rule is that people can camp anywhere in the wilderness for one night, provided they are more than an hour's hike from the nearest highway. Long-term camping in one place is not allowed. Those looking to stay in one place for a couple of days should find a camp zone near a *refuge*. Listen to **Météo-Montagne** for a French weather forecast for nearby mountains (☎08 36 68 02 65; updated twice daily). For **Mountain Rescue**, call ☎05 62 92 41 41.

🎿 SKIING

There is a weekend's worth of skiing available in the Crête du Lys area, accessible by the *téléphérique* in Cauterets (☎05 62 92 03 59). The Cauterets tourist office has free *plans des pistes* (maps of ski paths for all skill levels). Many area resorts are accessible by **SNCF bus** from Cauterets or Lourdes. **Luz-Ardiden** offers downhill and cross-country skiing. (☎05 62 92 30 30; fax 05 62 92 87 19. €20.60, student reductions available.) Farther away, **Barèges** (☎05 62 92 16 01) and **La Mongie** (☎05 62 95 81 81) offer joint tickets for €23.50 per day.

🥾 HIKING

The **GR10** meanders across the Pyrénées, connecting the Atlantic with the Mediterranean and looping through most major towns. Both major and minor hikes intersect with and run along it; for either level of trail, pick up one of the purple maps at the park office (€8.90). The most spectacular local hikes begin at the **Pont d'Espagne** (a 2½hr. walk or 20min. drive from Cauterets). Several **buses** run daily in July and August (every 2hr. 8am-6pm; €3.50, round-trip €5); inquire at **Bordenave Excursions** (☎05 62 92 53 68). The rest of the year, call a **taxi**. (☎06 12 91 83 19. Around €17.) One of the most popular trails follows the GR10 to the turquoise **Lac de Gaube** (1hr.) and then to the end of the stony glacial valley (2hr. past the lake), where hikers can spend the night 2km in the air at **Refuge des Oulettes ①**. (☎05 62 92 62 97. Open June-Sept. Dorms €12.50, *demi-pension* €30.50.) A greener hike lies one valley over along the **Vallée du Marcadau**; the **Refuge Wallon Marcadau ①** provides shelter here. (☎05 62 92 64 28. Open June to late Sept. Breakfast €2.30. Dorms €12.50, *demi-pension* €31.90.) Both hikes are popular as daytrips. The *refuge* is an ideal base for numerous day-hikes to other lakes and *cols* in the area. In May or June, when melting snow swells the streams, the **Chemin des Cascades** (waterfall trail), which leads from the Pont d'Espagne to La Raillère, is sensational. The 4hr. round-trip from Cauterets is a moderate afternoon hike—those who lose the path should keep the river on their left as they ascend the mountain. The **Circuit des Lacs** is a marathon 8hr. hike that includes the Vallée du Marcadau as well as three beautiful mountain lakes.

CIRCUIT DE GAVARNIE

From Cauterets, the GR10 connects to Luz-St-Sauveur over the mountain and then on to Gavarnie, another day's hike up the valley; the round-trip from Cauterets to Gavarnie and back is known as the **circuit de Gavarnie**. These towns are also accessible by **SNCF bus** (1hr. from Cauterets to Luz, 6 per day, €5.90; 2 per day from Luz to Gavernie, €5.30). The Luz tourist office is at pl. du 8 Mai 45 (☎05 62 92 30 30).

Circling counter-clockwise from Cauterets to Luz-St-Sauveur, the **Refuge Des Oulettes ❶** (see **Hiking**) is the first shelter past the Lac de Gaube. Dipping into the Vallée Lutour, the **Refuge Estom ❶** rests peacefully near Lac d'Estom. (Summer ☎05 62 92 72 93; winter 05 62 92 07 18. €8.50 per night, *demi-pension* €26.) The **Refuge Jan Da Lo ❶** is in Gavarnie, near the halfway mark of the loop. (☎05 62 92 40 66. Dorms €8.40, *demi-pension* €22.20.) From Gavarnie, hop on a horse offered by the refuge (€15 round-trip) for a 2hr. trek to the grandiose, snow-covered **Cirque de Gavarnie** and its misty waterfall. During the third week in July, the **Festival des Pyrénées** animates the foot of the Cirque, as nightly performances begin while the sun sets over the mountains. Afterwards, torches are distributed to light the way back to the village. (Tickets available from the tourist office in Gavarnie. €20, students under 25 €17.)

INTO SPAIN & BACK

Both the Spanish and French sides of the range must be experienced in order to get a full sense of the diversity of these mountains. The desiccated red rock of the Spanish side and the misty forests of the French side are accessible on a six- to seven-day hike from Cauterets. Confer with the tourist office in Ainsa, Spain (☎34 974 50 07 07), for reservations at the Spanish *refuges* before attempting this trek. A one- to two-day hike from Pont d'Espagne runs up and over the Spanish border. Descend the far side of the Pyrénées to the village of Torla and hop on one of the buses to the *refuge de Goriz* (☎34 974 34 12 01, call ahead to reserve). A magnificent hike to the snow-capped mountain peaks of **Brèche de Roland,** on the edge of the Cirque de Gavarnie, will start hikers' returns to France the following day. Cut the hike short here at four to five days and take a bus back from Gavarnie to Luz and then to Cauterets; otherwise, it's another rewarding two-day trek back to Cauterets. Climb from the Vallée d'Ossoue to camp among the clouds of the *Refuge de Bayssellance* in view of mount Montferrat before returning to Cauterets along the Vallée de Lutour.

LUCHON

More grandiose and cosmopolitan than other Pyrenean mountain towns, Luchon (pop. 2900) has attracted the rich and famous to its celebrated *thermes* for over two centuries. The baths are the town's main attraction, and the number of senior citizens in the tourist population is correspondingly large. But noisy families, Chanel-swaddled women, and cigarette-toting teenagers all stroll along the boulevards, enjoying the serene atmosphere. Hikers will appreciate that the numerous trails in the surrounding mountains are less crowded than those of the Parc National. A *télécabine* (gondola) ferries skiers and hikers from the town center to the nearby mountain Superbagnères.

■▪ 🔁 ORIENTATION & PRACTICAL INFORMATION. The **train station,** av. de Toulouse, runs. **trains** and **SNCF buses** to Montréjeau (50min., 4-5 per day, €5.80), where connections await to Bayonne, Paris, St-Gaudens, Toulouse, and other cities. Trains also run directly to Toulouse (2hr., 1-2 per day, €16). Info office is open daily M-F 6am-8:15pm and Sa-Su 6am-9pm.

From the station, turn left on av. de Toulouse and bear right at the fork to follow av. Maréchal Foch. At the lions, cross the rotary and bear left, following signs for the *centre ville*. The main **allée d'Etigny** will unfold to the left. A few blocks down on the right is the **tourist office,** 18 allée d'Etigny, which lists nearby hikes and mountain bike trails, as well as a map of the town. (☎05 61 79 21 21; fax 05 61 79 11 23; www.luchon.com. Open M-F 9am-noon and 1:30-7pm, Sa-Su 9am-7pm.) For ambitious outdoor excursions, check in at the **Bureau des Guides,** next to the tourist office, which has info on biking, hiking, rock climbing, and canyon scaling nearby and in Spain. Guided hikes run around €137 per day for a group of 12; canyoning and climbing €228. (☎05 61 79 69 38; bureaudesguides@free.fr. Open July-Sept. daily 10am-noon and 3-7pm; May-June M-Sa 10am-noon and 3-6pm.) **Bike rental** at **Malvina Europe,** 55 av. Foch, is €10 per half-day, €18 per day, with a credit card deposit. They also provide **Internet** for €5 per hr. (☎05 61 74 46 94; malvina@nem.net. Open M-Sa 8:30am-12:15pm and 2-7pm. MC/V.) It's not a bad idea to shop around for **extreme sports;** at least half a dozen outdoor companies base themselves within a half-mile of the tourist office, offering everything from rafting to paragliding. Other town services include a **laundromat,** 66 av. M. Foch (wash and dry €8; open daily 8am-8pm); **police,** at the Hôtel de Ville (☎05 61 94 68 81); a **medical emergency center,** 5 cours de Quinconces (☎05 61 79 93 00); and **Internet** at the **post office,** located on the corner of allée d'Etigny and av. Gallieni. (☎05 61 94 74 50. Open M-F 8:45am-noon and 2-5:45pm, Sa 8:45am-noon.) **Postal code:** 31110.

⌂ ACCOMMODATIONS. Standard budget hotels with rooms under €25 abound in the town center; the tourist office has a list. For nicer rooms, the closest *gîte,* **Gîte Skioura ❶,** is 3km uphill from the tourist office en route to Superbagnères. Call ahead to be picked up. Otherwise, follow cours des Quinconces out of town and up the mountain. During the week, it's more convenient to catch the *car thermal* from the train station allée d'Etigny to the *thermes* and get off at the camping stop (15min., free). Keep walking uphill for 10min. Five large rooms have 40 beds and a fireplace large enough to heat a castle. Some privacy is afforded by cloth partitions between every two beds. During the high season, the *gîte* is dominated by groups. (☎05 61 79 60 59 or 06 81 34 76 10. Breakfast €4. Sheets €2.50. Dorms €12.90.) **La Demeure de Venasque ❶,** located some 2½km up the road from Gîte Skioura, in a large house in the middle of an open field, offers more homey dorm accommodations and every kind of facility imaginable to travelers, including a basketball court, foosball, and a music room. (☎05 61 94 31 96; fax 05 61 94 31 96. Breakfast €4. Dorms €11.)

Across from the train station, the **Hôtel du Baliran ❸,** 1 av. de Toulouse, has first-rate rooms and ornately tiled, modern bathrooms. (☎05 61 79 27 95 or 06 15 41 22 40; fax 05 61 94 31 64. Breakfast €5. Reception 24hr. Singles and doubles with shower €30; triples €36; quads €50. MC/V.) **Hôtel de Sports ❸,** 12 av. Maréchal Foch, just 5min. from the station, has somewhat bland but spotless rooms and caring owners who help guests check email, store luggage, and make reservations for hiking and mountain biking. All rooms have shower and bath. (☎05 61 79 97 80; www.hotel-de-sports.net. Breakfast €5.50. Singles €28-45; doubles €40-50. Prices lower in the low season.)

▷ FOOD. The town **market** is held on Sunday mornings (8am-1pm) in a parking lot to the right of pl. Joffre. The **Casino** supermarket at 45 av. Maréchal Foch is on the way from the train station. (Open M-Sa 8:30am-12:30pm and 3-7:30pm.) The *pâtisserie* **Rino Marseglia ❶,** 9 av. Carnot, has savory quiches and tiny tarts, including the exquisite *tarte aux myrtilles* (blueberry tart). Most of their selections are under €2. (☎05 61 79 18 95. Open M-Sa 7:30am-noon and 2-7pm.) Inexpensive €8-12 *menus* are available at any of the nondescript *brasseries* that line **allée d'Etigny,** many of which become lively bars late at night.

For a slightly more upscale—if not entirely gourmet—experience, try **L'Arbesquines ❹,** 47 allée d'Etigny, which serves fondues from all different regions of France, particularly the Pyrénées, amid dark wooden décor and a multitude of plants. *Menus* €16-30, fondues €12-17. (☎05 61 79 33 69. Open daily noon-2:30pm and 6-11pm. MC/V.)

AQUITAINE

⊡📶 SIGHTS & HIKES. The tourist office has information about hiking paths (1-2½hr.) and mountain bike trails that leave from the **Parc Thermal,** just behind the *thermes* at the end of allées d'Etigny on Superbagnères. An easier option is a 2hr. ramble leading from the Parc to the town market. The truly hardcore can make the 3hr. haul to the top. Alternatively, the **Altiservice** runs a **télécabine** that transports hikers and bikers to the top of Superbagnères. (☎05 61 79 97 00. One-way €4.60, round-trip €7. Open July-Aug. daily 9:45am-12:15pm and 1:30-6pm; Apr.-Sept. Sa-Su 1:30-5pm; ski season daily 8:45am-6pm.) The tourist office has two free hiking and biking maps that indicate the way back down. Also check the Bureau des Guides (see **Practical Information**). Enjoy a soak in the **thermes,** located in the appropriately lavish white marble building at the end of allées d'Etigny. €12 buys access to the 32°C pool and the **Vaporarium,** a natural underground sauna unique to Europe. For this and other programs, inquire at **Vitaline,** found in the Greek temple-like bathhouse of the *thermes.* Tours of the adjacent 18th-century *thermes* depart Tuesdays at 2pm, June through September. (Reservations and info ☎05 61 79 22 97; fax 05 61 79 72 41; www.luchon.com. €3.10, children €1.60. Open mid-Dec. to mid-Oct. daily 4-7pm.)

POITOU-CHARENTES

After adopting Christianity in the 4th century AD, Poitou-Charentes emerged as an influential political and religious center. The 8th century saw Charles "the Hammer" Martel fend off Moorish attempts to conquer the region, but the British ruled it for 300 years starting with Eleanor of Aquitaine's marriage to England's Henry II in the 12th century. In the 17th century, Cardinal Richelieu laid siege to the Protestant stronghold of La Rochelle, relegating it to a century of obscurity until trade with Canada restored it to prosperity. The region now quietly busies itself with fishing, sunbathing, and the drinking of excellent wine.

Poitou-Charentes could be France's best-kept secret. Distinctly influenced by its proximity to the Atlantic Ocean, it is a brilliant collage of coastal towns (**La Rochelle,** p. 705 and **Les Sables d'Olonne,** p. 719), pristine natural sights like the wetlands preserve at ▨**Coulon** (p. 717), the **Marais Poitevin** (p. 717), and the wilds of its countless islands (▨**lle d'Yeu,** p. 721; **lle de Ré,** p. 711; ▨**lle d'Aix,** p. 716). Rich in history, the region encompasses the medieval town of **Saintes** (p. 701), as well as countless châteaux and ancient churches, including those in ▨**Poitiers** (p. 685), **Chauvigny** (p. 692), and **La Rochefoucauld** (p. 698). Those with more youthful sensibilities might enjoy the **Futuroscope** (p. 691) theme park or the mania over comic books at **Angoulême** (p. 692).

Poitou-Charentes is known for its *moules à la mouclade* (mussels in a wine, cream, and egg sauce), and *fricassée d'anguilles* (eels in a red wine sauce). *Escargots* (snails), known locally as *cagouilles* or *lumas,* are prepared with a meat stuffing *(à la saintongeaise)* or with a red wine sauce *(aux lumas).* Finally, no visit to the area is complete without a taste of cognac, provided upon completion of a tour of any of **Cognac's** (p. 698) many cellars and vineyards.

POITIERS

The many renowned churches of Poitiers (pop. 120,000) stand as a testament to the power of the Church here during the early Middle Ages. It was here that Clovis struck a blow for Christianity by defeating the Visigoths in 507 and Charles Martel repulsed the invading Moors in 732. In 1432, when Poitiers was still the capital of France, Charles VII founded the Université de Poitiers. Despite its spiritual origin, this city is now a bustling, businesslike metropolis with plentiful nightlife and cultural events that complement the peace and tranquility that still characterizes the rest of the region.

▣ TRANSPORTATION

Trains: bd. du Grand Cerf. Info office open M-Th and Sa 7am-9:45pm, F 7am-10:45pm, Su 7:20am-10:15pm. To: **Bordeaux** (2hr., 8 per day, €28.50); **La Rochelle** (1¾hr., 8 per day, €18.10); **Paris** (2hr., 6 per day, €53.60); **Tours** (45min., 5 per day, €14.80).

Public Transportation: S.T.P., 6 rue du Chaudron-d'Or (☎05 49 44 77 00). Open mid-July to mid-Aug. M-F 1:30-6:30pm; mid-Aug. to mid-July M-F 9am-noon and 2-7pm. Buses criss-cross the city 7am-8:30pm. One night bus (line #2) runs around the *centre*

Poitou-Charentes

ville and to the University of Poitiers campus (4 per day, 10-11pm). Timetables are at the tourist office and train station. Tickets valid 1hr. €1.20; *carnet* of 5 €4.80.

Car Rental: ADA, 19 bd. du Grand Cerf (☎05 49 50 30 20). From €40 per day. Open M-Sa 8am-6pm. MC/V. **Europcar,** 48 bd. du Grand Cerf (☎05 49 58 25 34). Open M-F 8am-noon and 2-6pm, Sa 8am-noon. AmEx/MC/V. **Avis,** 135 bd. du Grand Cerf (☎05 49 58 13 00). Open M-F 8am-7pm, Sa 8am-noon and 2-5pm. AmEx/DC/MC/V.

Bike Rental: Atelier Cyclaman, 60bis bd. Pont Achard (☎05 49 88 13 25). €9 per half-day, €13 per day. ID deposit. Open Tu-Su 9am-12:30pm and 3-7pm.

Taxis: Radio Taxis, 22 rue Carnot (☎05 49 88 12 34). €11-13 to hostel. 24hr.

■🛈 ORIENTATION & PRACTICAL INFORMATION

Poitiers centers around **place Maréchal Leclerc, place Charles de Gaulle,** and the restaurant- and shop-filled streets between. Buses run from opposite the train station to the **Hôtel de Ville,** pl. Maréchal Leclerc. The *centre ville* is bordered by the Le Clain and La Boivre rivers; parks dot the city's outskirts. *Poitiers et ses environs à pied et à VTT,* available from the tourist office, has hiking and biking trail maps.

Tourist Office: 45 pl. Charles de Gaulle (☎05 49 41 21 24; fax 05 49 88 65 84). Well-labeled maps and lists of hotels and campgrounds. Ask for the brochure "Laissez-vous conter Poitiers." Excellent free walking guide with 3 different circuits around the city available in English. **Hotel reservations** €2.50. **City tours** in French (1½hr.) July-Sept. at 11am and 3pm, each covering different monuments and neighborhoods; English tours Sa afternoons (€5.40, under 25 €3). Open June-Sept. M-Sa 10am-7pm, Su 10am-6pm; Oct.-May M-Sa 10am-6pm.

Money: Caisse d'Epargne, 7 rue Victor Hugo (☎05 49 60 65 56), has **ATMs** and **currency exchange** services. Open Tu-F 9am-12:15pm and 1:30-5:45pm, Sa 9am-12:45pm.

English Books: Librairie de l'Université, 70 rue Gambetta (☎05 49 41 02 05), off pl. M. Leclerc. Wide selection of 20th-century classics, popular fiction, and a bit of Chaucer and Shakespeare. Open M-Sa 9am-7:15pm. AmEx/DC/MC/V.

Youth Information: Centre Regionale Information Jeunesse (CRIJ), 64 rue Gambetta (☎05 49 60 68 81), near pl. Leclerc. Help with jobs, lodging, budget travel, and activity planning. **Internet** for students €0.80 per 15min., €1.50 per hr. Open M-F 10am-1pm and 2-6pm.

Laundromat: 2bis rue de le Tranchée. Open daily 7am-8:30pm. Also at 82 Grande Rue. Open daily 8am-9pm.

Police: 38 rue de la Marne (☎05 49 60 60 00).

Hospital: 350 av. Jacques Caire (☎05 49 44 44 44), on the road to Limoges.

Internet: at the **CRIJ** (see **Youth information**). **Cybercafé LRM,** 71 Grande Rue (☎05 49 39 51 87). €7 per hr., with student ID €4. Open M 10am-8pm, Tu-F 10am-10pm, Sa 11am-10pm, Su 4-7pm. **HTP Games,** 60 rue Carnot (☎05 49 41 49 86). €0.75 per 15min., €3 per hr. Open M 3-8pm, Tu-Th noon-8pm, F noon-1am, Sa 2-10pm, Su 2-6pm.

Post Office: 16 rue A. Ranc (☎05 49 55 50 00). **Currency exchange** with no commission. Open M-F 8:30am-7pm, Sa 8:30am-noon. **Poste Restante:** Poitiers 86000. **Postal code:** 86000.

⚓ ACCOMMODATIONS & CAMPING

The hostel and campgrounds are far from town, but cheap, respectable hotels in the city center and near the train station are reasonable alternatives.

Hôtel de l'Europe, 39 rue Carnot (☎05 49 88 12 00). Sophisticated, spacious rooms with dark wood furnishings face a large, inner courtyard or a garden in the back. Breakfast €6.50. Singles and doubles with toilet and shower in old wing €47-56; singles, doubles, and triples in fancier new wing €72-77. MC/V. ❸

Auberge de Jeunesse (HI), 1 allée Tagault (☎05 49 30 09 70; fax 05 49 30 09 79). Turn right at the train station and follow bd. du Pont Achard to av. de la Libération. At the fork, take a right onto rue B. Pascal, then right onto rue de la Jeunesse and left onto allée Tagault. The hostel will be ahead on the left. (35min.) Or, take bus #7 (dir: Pierre Loti) to Cap Sud (M-Sa every 30min. until 7:50pm, €1.20) from the stop to the right of the train station. Family-oriented, clean hostel with modest communal facilities, a stocked kitchenette, Internet, bike rental, and proximity to local stores and town swimming pool. A large grassy area is generally busy with soccer and volleyball games and afternoon picnickers. 15min. from Futuroscope. Breakfast €2.70, lunch €8, dinner €8. Sheets €2.70. Reception daily 7am-noon and 4-11pm. Bunks in 4-bed rooms €8.50. **Tents** and groundpad available for camping in backyard (€4.80). **Members only.** ❶

Hôtel Jules Ferry, 27 rue Jules Ferry (☎05 49 37 80 14; fax 05 49 53 15 02). To get there from the train station, turn right at the train station onto bd. Pont Achard. Turn left onto rue J. Brunet and left again onto rue Jules Ferry; the hotel will be up on the right. Worn, carpeted rooms with soft mattresses and small but spotless showers. Gracious, friendly hosts make an international crowd feel very welcome. Breakfast €4.50. Reception M-Sa 7am-11pm. Door code for late night entry. For Su reservations, call ahead. Singles and doubles with toilet €22, with shower €28; doubles with bath €33-43; triples €37-46. MC/V. ❷

Camping:

Le Porteau, rue de Porteau (☎05 49 41 44 88), 2km from town. Take bus #7 from near the station (dir: Centre de Gros; 7:15am-7:20pm, €1.20) to Porteau. Tiny, rocky field encircled by roads. Reception daily 7am-10pm. Open mid-June to Oct. 2-person site €7.50; extra adult €2.50, child €1.50; extra car €4.30. Electricity €1.60-2.30. ❶

Camping St-Benoit, rte. de Passelourdin (☎05 49 88 48 55), 5km from Poitiers. Slightly better than Le Porteau (there's grass), but hard to reach by public transportation. From the station, take bus #2, 3, 6, 8, 7, 9, or 11 to Hôtel de Ville. Walk to the bus stop at the corner of rue Carnot and pl. Maréchal Leclerc and take bus #5 (dir: La Varenne; 9:30am-7:20pm) to Rue du Clain. Cross the Rocade Sud-Est and follow rte. de Passelourdin for 1km until reaching the campground. Or take a taxi from the train station (€16-20). Reception daily 8am-noon and 3-8pm. Open July-Aug. 2-person site €8.50; extra person €2.50, child €1.60. Electricity €2.30. ❶

◖ FOOD

In Poitiers, finding chèvre, macaroons, the wines of Haut-Poitou, or lamb from nearby Montmarillon to eat is not difficult to accomplish. The problem is finding a budget-friendly *menu*—most hover around €15-30. Many hotel bars post adequate 3-course *menus* for €10.50-15, and inexpensive pizzerias line the pedestrian streets between pl. Leclerc and Notre-Dame-la-Grande. There is a **market** at **Les Halles,** pl. Charles de Gaulle, which expands to epic proportions on Saturdays (open M-Sa 7am-1pm) and a **Monoprix** supermarket at Ile des Cordeliers on rue des Grandes Ecoles (open M-Sa 9am-7:30pm). **Le Saint Nicolas ❸,** 7 rue Carnot, hidden in a little courtyard with plain walls, prepares delicious French cuisine in the local market. The whole menu looks tempting, but diners can't go wrong with the *plat du jour.* (☎05 49 41 44 48. *Menus* €12, *plats* from €8. Closed W. MC/V.) For a formal meal, the elegant **Le Bistrot de l'Absynthe ❸,** 6 rue Carnot, serves upscale French favorites like *escargot, cuisses de grenouille* (frog legs), and absinthe, straight-up or on an ice cream sundae. The chefs don't shy away from creative combinations, such as an appetizer pairing coffee and almonds. (☎05 46 43 77 52. *Plats* €11.50, lunch *menu* €8.50, 3-course *menu* €20, absinthe €3.80. Open daily 9am-8pm. MC/V.)

◉ SIGHTS

Poitiers's churches, by far the city's most impressive attractions, date from the country's conversion to Catholicism in the 4th century. (All open daily 9am-6pm. Free.) Many hold organ concerts in the summer; check the *Guide des Manifestations* or call *Les Nuits en Musique* (☎05 49 41 21 24) or *Les Concerts du Marché* (☎05 49 41 34 18) for schedules. In addition to the churches, Poitier's Renaissance buildings make it an excellent place to wander.

NOTRE-DAME-LA-GRANDE. Though small, this is one of France's most important Romanesque churches. A scant amount of light filters beautifully through small stained-glass windows, illuminating a vast array of paintings in an otherwise windowless nave. Inside, an original fresco on the choir ceiling depicts Christ in glory, the Virgin and Child, and the Lamb of God in a cruciform. The rest of the interior has been restored in a different style. During the summer, a not-to-be-missed ◼**light show** projects the original polychrome detail onto the façade, reviving the splendor of the original colors and details. *(Pl. de Gaulle, off Grande Rue. Projections daily June-Aug. 10:30pm; early to mid-Sept. 9:30pm.)*

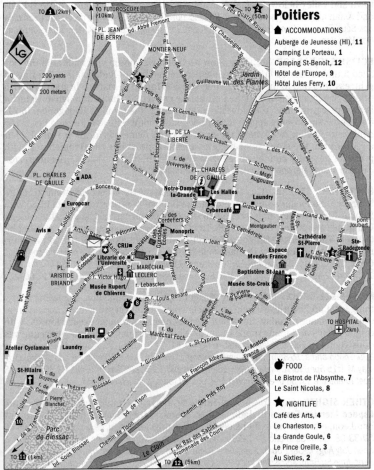

Poitiers

🏠 ACCOMMODATIONS

Auberge de Jeunesse (HI), **11**
Camping Le Porteau, **1**
Camping St-Benoît, **12**
Hôtel de l'Europe, **9**
Hôtel Jules Ferry, **10**

🍴 FOOD

Le Bistrot de l'Absynthe, **7**
Le Saint Nicolas, **8**

⭐ NIGHTLIFE

Café des Arts, **4**
Le Charleston, **5**
La Grande Goule, **6**
Le Pince Oreille, **3**
Au Sixties, **2**

■ CATHÉDRALE ST-PIERRE. In 1162, the construction of the cavernous St-Pierre was funded by Eleanor of Aquitaine and her husband King Henry II Plantagenêt, who lived in the current Palais de Justice. During two hundred years of construction, builders remained faithful to the original plan, constructing a uniformly 12th-century Angevin Gothic cathedral. The church's Cliquot organ (1787-1791) is one of only two extant that predate the Revolution, and its central stained-glass window contains one of France's oldest crucifixion scenes. The interior extends in a seeming eternity of light, space, and clean lines. A careful examination of the columns and the junctions of the wall and the ceiling will reveal 267 of the church's original carvings of people and animals. *(Pl. de la Cathédrale, off rue de la Cathédrale.)*

■ PARC DE BLOSSAC. Paths criss-cross among the Dutch linden trees and secluded areas of this classic 18th-century French- and English-style *jardin*, one of the most beautiful in the region. The park's borders afford beautiful views of the town and valley below. A small but noisy zoological garden houses various birds and Asian mountain goats. *(Rue de Blossac, down rue Carnot, near the river Clain. Open daily Apr.-Sept. 7am-10:30pm; Oct.-Mar. 7am-9:30pm. Jardin Anglais open daily Apr.-Sept. 7am-8pm; Oct.-Mar. 8am-sundown.)*

EGLISE STE-RADEGONDE. The church's bell tower porch was built atop the ravaged foundations of a 6th-century chapel erected by Ste-Radegonde, a Thuringian princess who fled to the church when she was forced to marry a brutish Frankish prince. She later established the first female convent in Gaul. Although its exterior is now nearly in ruins, the church's interior holds the tomb of Radegonde. In AD 587, Christ supposedly appeared to Radegonde on this site and foretold her imminent death, calling her "one of the most precious diamonds in His crown." He left a footprint in the stone floor before vanishing, providing the doomed nun with proof for her story and the abbey with centuries of pilgrims and tourist allure. *(Off rue de la Mauvinière, down the street from the cathedral.)*

BAPTISTÈRE ST-JEAN. This 4th-century baptistry is the oldest Christian structure in France. No longer a sacred building, the Baptistère is now a museum filled with Roman, Merovingian, and Carolingian sarcophagi and capitals, kept by the earliest Christians when they destroyed Poitiers's fine Roman baths, arches, and amphitheater. The interior still contains a 4th-century octagonal baptismal pool surrounded by 12th-century Romanesque frescoes. *(Rue Jean Jaurès, near the cathedral. Open July-Aug. daily 10:30am-12:30pm and 3-6pm; Apr.-June and Sept. Su-M and W-Sa 10:30am-12:30pm and 3-6pm; Oct.-Mar. Su-M and W-Sa 2:30-4:30pm. €0.80, under 12 €0.40.)*

MUSÉE STE-CROIX. This eclectic museum spans four millennia, displaying everything from prehistoric artifacts to Roman coins, medieval sepulchres, and art from the Renaissance to today. Hidden in the basement is a Roman excavation site with original walls and foundations of ancient homes, around which the museum was constructed. *(3bis rue Jean-Jaurès. ☎05 49 41 42 21. Open June-Sept. M 1:15-6pm, Tu 10am-noon and 1:15-8pm, W-F 10am-noon and 1:15-6pm, Sa-Su 10am-noon and 2-6pm; Oct.-May M 1:15-5pm, Tu 10am-5pm, W-F 10am-noon and 1:15-5pm, Sa-Su 2-6pm. €3.50, under 18 free; Tu and the 1st Su of each month free. Guided tours in French on Tu.)*

OTHER SIGHTS. Next to the Cathédrale St-Pierre but a millennium younger, the **Espace Mendès France** is dedicated to science and learning, hosting plenty of hands-on, educational exhibits perfect for youngsters. *(1 pl. de la Cathédrale. ☎05 49 50 33 08. Open Su-M and Sa 2-6:30pm, Tu-F 9:30am-6:30pm. Exhibits in French and English open July-Aug. M-Sa 2-6pm; Sept.-June Tu-Su 2-6pm. Planetarium shows July-Aug. M-F 5pm; Sept.-June Su 5pm. Admission to exhibits €4.50, children €2.50; planetarium shows €6, children €3.)* The **Musée Rupert de Chièvres** displays a collection of Dutch, Flemish, and Italian paintings, many by anonymous artists, and scientific antiquities like the earliest Diderot encyclopedia. *(9 rue Victor Hugo. ☎05 49 41 42 21. Open June-Sept. M 1:15-6pm, Tu-W and F 10am-noon and 1:15-6pm, Th 10am-noon and 1:15-9pm, Sa-Su 10am-noon and 2-6pm; Oct.-May M 1:15-5pm, Tu-F 10am-noon and 1:15-5pm, Sa-Su 2-6pm. €3.50; under 18 free; free Tu, the 1st Su of each month, and June-Sept. Th 6-9pm. Guided tours in French 1 per week, €1.50-3.50. Schedule varies; call for more information.)*

🎵 🎦 ENTERTAINMENT & FESTIVALS

Nightlife in Poitiers is livelier than its size would suggest, particularly during the school year. Locals and students frequent the pubs and restaurants along the side streets of **place Leclerc.** Pick up the booklet *Café-Concerts, Bars avec Animations* at the tourist office for more information.

Le Charleston, 10 rue l'Eperon (☎05 49 41 13 36), is a lively pub with an extensive beer list, pool tables, and karaoke with popular French and American tunes. A steady flow of customers cheers on many a boisterous rendition of "I Will Survive." Beer €4. Open M-F 11am-2am, Sa 2:30pm-2am. MC/V.

Café des Arts, 5 pl. C. de Gaulle (☎05 49 41 14 61), attracts trendy students and couples to its relaxed environment. Patrons people-watch from the bar, with jazz music in the background and a rum punch in hand. Drinks €3-5. Open M-Sa 8:30am-2am.

Le Pince Oreille, 11 rue des Trois Rois (☎05 49 60 25 99), puts its stage to good use, hosting jazz bands, stand-up comedy, and jam-sessions for any musician with the guts to play. Armchairs and painted walls create a welcoming, though dimly lit, atmosphere for a predominantly student crowd. Concerts Th-Sa (€6); free jam-sessions every Tu and W. The bar opens Su Dec.-Feb. at 5:30pm for a "philosophical cabaret" discussion. Drinks from €3. Open Tu-F 5pm-2am, Sa 9pm-3am.

La Grande Goule, 46 rue du Pigeon Blanc (☎05 49 50 41 36). Poitiers's most popular nightclub, pumping house beats beneath the stately Eglise Ste-Radegonde, packs in teens early on and an older crowd later in the evening. Cover €8-10, includes 1 drink; no cover for women before midnight. Drinks €5-8. Open Tu-Sa 11pm-4am.

Au Sixties, 1 rue des Quatres Roues (☎05 49 52 19 44), is a gay-friendly dance club that draws a mix of people, including a large artistic following. It hosts art exhibitions for the up-and-coming several times a year and puts on glitzy cabaret shows the 1st Su of every month. Cover varies. Drinks €5-8. Open Tu-Su 9:30pm-2am.

The **Festival du Cinéma** in March draws film students from international schools for artsy and mainstream showings. Throughout July and August, rock, opera, jazz, and fireworks thunder through town during the **Places à l'Eté** festival. Concerts, mostly free, begin around 9pm three nights per week. A relatively new summer tradition, **La Nuit des Orgues,** organizes a series of mostly free organ performances in local churches from May to October. Contact the tourist office for tickets and details. In late August and early September, a more formal organ festival, **Voix Orgues,** hosts organ players from all over the region. (Call ☎05 49 47 13 61 for more info. Tickets €9-15; book in advance.) "Le guide des manifestations," free at the tourist office, lists all the concerts and shows going in the city.

▶ DAYTRIPS FROM POITIERS

FUTUROSCOPE

Take bus #17 (20min., 18 per day, €1.20) from Poitier's Hôtel de Ville or across the street from the train station, in front of the Printania Bar-Hôtel. Schedules are subject to change. For info, contact STP, 6 rue du Chaudron d'Or (☎05 49 44 66 88) or the tourist office. Buy tickets from the bus driver. Get off at Parc de Loisirs and follow directions to the park entrance. By car, follow A10 (dir: Paris-Châtellerault) to exit 28. The park is also accessible by TGV from Bordeaux (1½hr., 1-2 per day, €35) and Paris (80min., 2-3 per day, €37.50). 10km north of Poitiers, near Chasseneuil. ☎05 49 49 30 80; www.futuroscope.com. Open early Feb. to late Nov.; hours vary, consult the website or the tourist office in Poitiers. €30, children €22; low season €21/€16. All main attractions are included in the price, though the video games on Cyber Avenue require additional tokens.

The Futuroscope amusement park is a slick collection of high-tech film theaters, including spherical and hemispherical screens, virtual reality, high-definition 3-D simulation rides, and the occasional straight-up film experience. A whole building is dedicated to the latest video games. A headset obtained in the Maison de Vienne near the entrance provides the English translation for many films. Those enticed by the late-night laser show will miss the last bus to Poitiers, but hotels and restaurants surround the park.

CHAUVIGNY

*SNCF buses leave Poitiers for Chauvigny from outside the station (dir: Châteauroux; 30min., 5 per day, Su at 4:20 and 8:50pm only; €4.90). Buy tickets in the SNCF train station in Poitiers, on board on return. The bus will stop at pl. de la Poste, in the center of modern-day Chauvigny. The cité médiévale, encompassing all the castle ruins, lies up on the hill. To get there, walk back on rue du Marché in the direction the bus came from. At the end of pl. du Marché, turn right onto rue de Châtellerault. At the end of rue de Châtellerault, turn right onto bd. des Châteaux, which will run to the cité médiévale. The **tourist office** is on rue St-Pierre, a left off of bd. des Châteaux. (☎05 49 46 39 01. Open July-Aug. daily 10am-7pm; Sept.-June M and W-Su 10:30am-12:30pm and 2-6pm. Tours July-Aug. M and W-Su 2:30pm and 4pm; €3.50. Call ☎05 49 46 35 45 in advance for English tours.)*

Chauvigny, 23km from Poitiers, was conquered four times during the Hundred Years' War, razed during the Wars of Religion, and shelled by the retreating Wehrmacht in 1944. Today the beautiful town's tiny medieval citadel and the pretty, restaurant-lined walkways around the tranquil pl. du Donjon make a worthwhile half-day escape from bustling Poitiers.

Five ruined 11th- to 15th-century châteaux create Chauvigny's striking skyline, while farther down, the 12th-century **Eglise St-Pierre** is known for its choir capitals, engraved with dragons, vultures, and images of Satan. The ultra-modern **Espace d'Archéologie Industrielle,** nestled under a glass ceiling in the ruins of the Gouzon keep, showcases regional quarrying, porcelain-firing, milling, and steam-engine activity. There's a great view of the city and countryside below from the museum's glass elevator. (☎05 49 46 35 45. Open Apr. to mid-June and Oct.-Nov. daily 2-6pm; mid-June to Sept. M-F 10am-12:30pm and 2:30-6:30pm, Sa-Su 2-6pm. €4.60, students €3.10, under 14 free. Tours in French July-Aug. Su-M and W-Sa 4:15pm.) The crumbling walls of **Les Géants du Ciel** (☎05 49 46 47 48; fax 05 49 44 10 45), once home to Chauvigny's bishops, now host 60 eagles, falcons, vultures, owls, buzzards, storks, parrots, and countless other winged species. The squeamish should avoid the dark room of *chauves* (bats) that fly unrestrained among visitors. The highlight is a bird show, in which the flock swoops over the city just above the heads of the audience. (Open daily Apr. to early Nov. Shows daily July-Aug. at 11:15am, 2:30, 4, 5:30pm; Apr.-June and Sept.-Nov. at 2:30 and 4pm, with additional shows Sept.-Nov. Sa-Su at 11:15am and 5:30pm. €8, students €5; ruins €3.)

For a truly unique glimpse of the countryside, take a ride on the **Vélo-Rails.** These rail contraptions, powered by pedaling, take passengers along the viaduct that traverses the Vienne River on a 17km loop around the Chauvigny valley. Reservations must be made at least one day in advance. (10 rue de la Folie. ☎05 49 46 39 01. To get there from pl. de la Poste, walk down rue du Marché, cross the Vienne River, and continue straight as the road becomes rue de Poitiers. After reaching rue de la Verrerie, turn right, then left onto rue de la Folie. Open daily July-Aug. 10am-9pm; Sept. and May-June 2-7pm; Oct. and Mar.-Apr. 2-6pm; Nov. 1-5pm; Dec.-Feb. by reservation. 2hr. ride July-Aug. €22; Sept.-June €16.)

From June to August, the **Festival d'Eté** (☎05 49 45 99 10) fills the city with (occasionally free) jazz, dance, and theater performances. Purchase tickets in advance at the tourist office.

ANGOULÊME

A gem unknown to hordes of tourists, Angoulême (pop. 46,000) sits high on a plateau and affords a magnificent view of the Charente river. The cradle of the French paper industry in the 1600s, the town and its ready supply of writing pads brought Jean Calvin here in 1534. Wood pulp is no less an obsession today, for Angoulême reigns supreme as the capital of French comic strip production; countless Lucky Luke and Astérix volumes roll off the town's presses each year and streets are marked with dialogue bubbles and cartoon graffiti. In addition to the town's attractions for the comic-obsessed, the winding hilly streets of the *vieille ville* are filled with modern stores, museums, restaurants, and movie theaters.

⌐ TRANSPORTATION

Trains: pl. de la Gare (☎05 45 69 91 65 or 08 92 35 35 35 for train schedules). Info open Tu-F 9:30am-12:30pm and 1:30-6:30pm, Sa 10am-12:30pm and 1:30-6pm. To: **Bordeaux** (1hr., 10 per day, €18.20); **Paris** (2½hr., 7 per day, €50-60.80); **Poitiers** (45min., 5 per day, €15.80); **Saintes** (1hr., 10 per day, €10.40).

Buses: Autobus Citram goes to: **Cognac** (1hr., 8 per day, €7) and **La Rochelle** (3hr., 2 per day, €16.40). Buses stop at pl. du Champ de Mars. Buy tickets on board. Info at the **Cartrans** office, pl. du Champ de Mars (☎05 45 95 95 99). Open mid-July to mid-Aug. M-Th 2-6:15pm; mid-Aug. to mid-July M-F 9:15am-12:15pm and 2-6:15pm. **CFTA Périgord** (☎05 53 08 43 13), goes from the train station to **Périgueux** (1½hr.; M, F, Su 1 per day; €11.60).

Local Transportation: STGA, in a kiosk on pl. du Champ de Mars. Maps available. Open 7th-27th of each month M-F 1-6pm, Sa 9am-12:30pm; 1st-6th and 28th-end of each month M-Sa 8:30am-6pm. Tickets €1.20, *carnet* of 10 €8.30, one-week pass €10. Buses run M-Sa 6am-8pm and are a good way to get to many of the museums on the edge of town.

Taxis: Radio Taxi (☎05 45 95 55 55), in front of the train station. Meter starts at €2.20, €0.61 per km during the day, €0.90 per km at night. €7 to Auberge de Jeunesse. 24hr.

Car Rental: Ada, 19 pl. de la Gare (☎05 45 92 65 29), right across from the train station, rents cars for €41 per day. Open M-Sa 8am-noon and 2-7pm. **Europcar** (☎05 45 92 02 02), a few doors down at 15 pl. de la Gare, sometimes has special student rates. €45-59. 21+. Can be returned at other locations. Open M-F 8am-noon and 2-7pm, Sa 8am-noon and 2-6pm. AmEx/MC/V.

⊞ 🛈 ORIENTATION & PRACTICAL INFORMATION

The *vieille ville* sits among the ramparts just south of the Charente and southwest of the train station. It is easy to get lost in this maze of streets, so grab a map from the tourist office outside the station.

Tourist Office: 7bis rue du Chat, pl. des Halles (☎05 45 95 16 84; fax 05 45 95 91 76). Provides indispensable city guide with info on restaurants, hotels, museums, and outdoor activities; available only in French, though a few English paragraphs describe the main tourist sites in the *vieille ville*. To get to the main **tourist office** at pl. des Halles, follow av. Gambetta right and uphill to pl. G. Perrot, continue straight up the rampe d'Aguesseau, and turn right onto bd. Pasteur. Keeping close to the rail overlooking the valley, pass the market building on your left, and turn left onto rue du Chat; the office will be on your right. Open July-Aug. M-Sa 9:30am-7pm, Su 10am-noon and 2-5pm; Sept.-June M-F 9:30am-6pm, Sa 10am-noon and 2-5pm, Su 10am-noon. **Kiosk** (☎05 45 92 27 57) by the train station. Open Tu-F 9:30am-12:30pm and 1:30-6:30pm, Sa 9:30am-12:30pm and 1:30-6:30pm.

City Tours: Day and night tours offered through the Hôtel de Ville's **Service Patrimoine** (☎05 45 38 70 79; patrimoine@mairie-angouleme.fr). Enter the main gates of the Hôtel de Ville and cross the courtyard; the office is on the left. 2hr. daytrips leave Mar.-May and Oct.-Nov. Sa and Su at 3pm, June and Sept. daily at 3pm, July-Aug. 3 times per day, Dec.-Feb. at 3pm on select weekends. Tours leave from the Hôtel de Ville. Call the Service Patrimoine or tourist office for more info. €5, children €3.50, family €9. English tours available at slightly higher rates; call in advance.

Budget Travel: Voyages Wasteels, 2 pl. Francis Louvel (☎08 25 88 70 29; fax 05 45 94 01 31). Reductions for students available. Open M-F 9am-noon and 1:30-3:30pm, Sa 10am-12:30pm. **Jet tours,** 5bis rue de Perigeux (☎05 45 92 07 94), also arranges cheap trips with excellent deals on airfare. Open M-F 9:30am-12:30pm and 2-6:30pm, Sa closes at 6pm.

Currency Exchange: The post office (see listing) exchanges money with no commission. For other monetary needs, the **Banque de France** is at 1 rue de Général Leclerc (☎05 45 97 60 00), on pl. de l'Hôtel de Ville. Open M-F 8:40am-noon and 1:30-3:30pm.

Youth Center: Centre Information Jeunesse, inside the Espace Franquin building, 1 bd. Bertholet (☎05 45 37 07 30; www.info-jeunesse16.com), off the rampe d'Aguesseau. Friendly staff provides info on jobs and events, cheap concert tickets, free condoms, and general advice. Open Tu-F 9am-6pm and Sa 2-6pm. **Internet** is €2 for the first hour, but after that requires a €10 1yr. membership.

Laundromat: Lavomatique, 3 rue Ludovic Trarieux, near the Palais de Justice. Wash €3-6.50, dry €0.50 per 5 min. Open daily 7am-9pm. **Washmatic,** 11 rue St-Roch. Wash €3-5.50, dry €1.30-1.60, dry cleaning €1.40-4.60 per item. Open M-Sa 8am-7pm.

Police: pl. du Champs de Mars (☎05 45 39 38 37), next to the post office.

Hospital: Hôpital de Girac, rte. de Bordeaux (☎05 45 24 40 40), not to be confused with rue de Bordeaux. Take the #1 bus (dir: La Couronne Galands) or #8 bus (dir: La Couronne Mairie) from the Hôtel de Ville or pl. du Champ de Mars and get off at the Girac stop. Closer to town is the private **Clinique St-Joseph,** 51 av. Président Wilson (☎05 45 38 67 00).

Internet: The **Musée de la Bande Dessinée** (p. 696) has 10 Internet terminals that can be used free with a museum ticket or for €2 per hour without one. Closer to town, the **Centre Information Jeunesse** provides a great deal for frequent users (see **Youth Center**). Directly below the youth center, in the basement of the Espace Franquin building, the **Espace Culture Multimedia** rents movies and allows tourists 2hr. free Internet, after which they have to buy a €10 1yr. pass to continue their use (☎05 45 37 07 32; open M 1-8pm; Tu-Th, Sa 1-6pm; F 1-8pm).

Post Office: pl. du Champs de Mars (☎05 45 66 66 00; fax 05 45 66 66 17). Open M-F 8am-7pm, Sa 8am-noon. **Branch office,** pl. Francis Louvel, near the Palais de Justice (☎05 45 90 14 30). Open M-F 8am-6:45pm, Sa 8:30am-12:30pm. Both offer **currency exchange** with no commission for US dollars. **Postal code:** 16000.

ACCOMMODATIONS & CAMPING

Cheap hotels are clustered near the intersection of av. Gambetta and the pedestrian district, which slopes downhill from the *vieille ville*.

Hôtel des Pyrénées, 80 rue St-Roch (☎05 45 95 20 45; fax 05 45 92 16 95), off pl. du Champ de Mars. From the train station, follow rue Gambetta until the 2nd large intersection, and take a sharp left. Hotel is at the end of this road on your left. (10min.) Spacious, color-coordinated rooms with spotless bathrooms. Breakfast €5, in room €5.50. Reception 7am-10:30pm. Singles and doubles €23, with shower and TV €30, with shower, TV, and toilet €33-39. Extra bed €7. MC/V. ❷

Hôtel Le Palma, 4 rampe d'Aguesseau (☎05 45 95 22 89; fax 05 45 94 26 66), near the Eglise St-Martial, about 3 blocks up the hill from the train station. Ten rooms decorated with antique furniture lie along a dark, narrow staircase. Quiet atmosphere with friendly owners and an excellent location—5min. from both the train station and the center of town. Breakfast €4.50. Reception M-Sa only; call in advance for Su. Singles €21.50, with shower €28; doubles €26/€33-37. Public toilet and shower available for those in rooms that come equipped with only a sink. AmEx/DC/MC/V. ❷

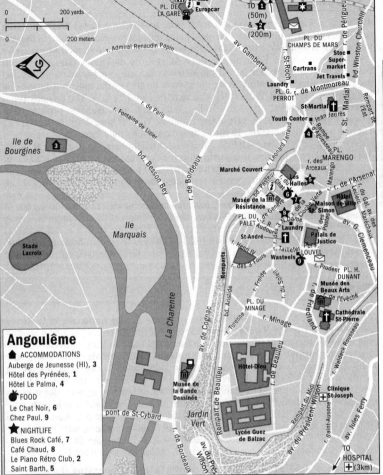

POITOU-CHARENTES

Auberge de Jeunesse (HI), (☎05 45 92 27 50; fax 05 45 95 90 71), on the Ile de Bourgines in the Charente. By foot, turn left out of the train station onto av. de Lattre de Tassigny and take the first left onto bd. du 8 Mai 1945. Just before the big bridge, turn left onto bd. Besson Bey and cross the footbridge. Follow the dirt path beside the river to the left; the hostel is just ahead. (30min.) To get there by bus, leave the station, turn right onto av. Gambetta, and right again onto rue Denis Papin, which crosses over the tracks. Continue straight onto Passage Lamaud, a pedestrian shortcut that leads to rue de Paris. (5-10min.) Turn right onto rue de Paris and take bus #7 (dir: Le Treuil; last bus 8pm; €1.20) to St-Antoine. Bleak modern cement hostel amidst parking lots. Two- to six-bed rooms have maroon metal beds and fiendish press-and-repeat showers with a temperamental hot water supply. Breakfast €3.25. Lockout 10am-5pm. No curfew. Call ahead in summer. Dorms €8.50; doubles €11.85. ❶

POITOU-CHARENTES

🍴 FOOD

The local specialty, *cagouilles à la charentaise* (snails prepared first with garlic and parsley, then with sausage, smoked ham, and spices), can be found in the restaurants of the *vieille ville*. A favorite sweet is the flower-shaped *marguerite* chocolate, named for François I's sister, Marguerite de Valois. Bars, cafés, and bakeries line rue de St-Martial and rue Marengo, but the food becomes funkier and the crowds more interesting along the narrow streets of the quadrant formed by Les Halles, pl. du Palet, Eglise St-André, and the Hôtel de Ville. The recently renovated covered **market** on pl. des Halles sells the town's freshest produce two blocks down rue de Gaulle from the Hôtel de Ville. (Open daily 7:30am-1pm.) There is a **Stoc** supermarket, 19 rue Périgueux, right by the Champ de Mars. (Open M-Sa 8:30am-7:15pm, Su 9-11:45am. MC/V.) For a light meal, **Le Chat Noir ❶** on pl. des Halles serves bruschettas made with the freshest ingredients (€5.25-7), in addition to a variety of sandwiches (€2.40-4.70) and crêpes (€2.40-3.40). The drink menu is also extensive, with a large selection of local cognacs. (☎05 45 75 26 27. Open 11am-midnight. MC/V)

Chez Paul ❸, 8 pl. Francis Louvel, has an unassuming exterior, but opens out to a paradise-themed garden with flowers, candles, sculptures, and a miniature river running through the middle. Excellent regional food served in a summer *menu* (€15.50), or a larger 3-course *menu* (€23). The *brasserie* also hosts non-professional theater every Friday on the stage upstairs. (☎05 45 90 04 61. Open daily 10am-2am. MC/V.)

👁 SIGHTS

MUSÉE DE LA BANDE DESSINÉE. Housed in the **Centre Nationale de la Bande Dessinée et de L'Image (CNBDI)**, this museum is a tribute to Angoulême's leading role in the development of computerized graphics and the *B.D.—la bande dessinée* (comic strips). Presented in colorful rooms that resemble comic books, the exhibits feature French cartoons from the 19th and 20th centuries, including favorites such as *Tintin, Astérix,* and *Popeye.* Entrance to the museum also gives free access to its library and one free hour of Internet access. But it is the extensive book shop filled with comics from all over the world that is by far the best asset of the CNBDI. (*121 rue de Bordeaux. From pl. du Champ de Mars and pl. de l'Hôtel de Ville, take bus #3 or 5 to "Nil-CNBDI" or walk along the ramparts, following the signs. 10min. ☎05 45 38 65 65; cnbdi@cnbdi.fr. Open July-Aug. M-F 10am-7pm, Sa-Su 2-7pm; Sept.-June Tu-F 10am-6pm, Sa-Su 2-6pm. €5, students €3, children €2, under 6 free.*)

MUSÉE DE LA RESISTANCE ET DE LA DEPORTATION. Occupying the one-time home of 16th-century religious reformer Jean Calvin, this museum now chronicles Angoulême's experience under the Nazi occupation, in particular the development and courageous actions of the French resistance fighters, many of whom were captured and tortured to death by Nazis. The horrifying photographs on the second floor display the gruesome experience of the 1180 Jews deported from the Charente region during WWII. The exhibits are all in French, with limited English texts available. (*34 rue de Genève. ☎05 45 38 76 87; fax 05 45 93 12 66; www.museedelarestistance16.fr.fm. Open July-Aug. M-Sa 9am-noon and 2-6pm; Sept.-June M-F 2-6pm. €2.50, students €1.50, children free.*)

MUSÉE DES BEAUX ARTS. Occupying a restored 12th-century bishop's palace, the museum displays a pleasing mélange of media. A labyrinth of 16th- to 19th-century paintings, 19th-century *charentais* archeological digs, North and West African pottery, and locally created sculptures surround one of the museum's prized possessions, Etienne Barthélémy's 1800 *Grief of Priam's Family*. Under renovation at the time of publication, the museum plans to reopen in 2004. *(1 rue Friedland, behind the cathedral. ☎05 45 95 07 69; fax 05 45 95 98 26. Open M-F noon-6pm, Sa-Su 2-6pm. €3, students and children under 18 free, free for all visitors noon-2pm.)*

CATHÉDRALE ST-PIERRE. The elegant 12th-century cathedral of Angoulême is textbook Romanesque but for one main element: the structure was built without internal columns, in order to permit an uninterrupted view of the interior. The original 6th-century structure also lacked windows. Before Byzantine renovations bathed the transept in pale blue light, it was lit only by lanterns. The edifice exerted a considerable architectural influence during the height of religious power, not only on other churches in the diocese, but also on more distant buildings such as Fontevraud in the Loire and Notre-Dame-la-Grande of Poitiers. The intricate façade depicting the Ascension of Christ and scenes from the Last Judgment opens up to a comparatively barren and disappointing interior. *(Pl. St-Pierre. ☎05 45 95 44 83. Open daily 9am-7pm.)*

EGLISE ST-ANDRÉ. The 12th-century church, originally Romanesque, was reworked in a Gothic style. Today it combines paintings from the 16th to the 19th centuries with a massive altarpiece and a superb baroque oak pulpit. The façade was redone in the early 19th century, but the church still retains its original tower and entrance. *(8 rue Taillefer, on the pl. de Palet in the town center. Open daily 9am-7pm.)*

GARDENS AND SPORTS. Angoulême's ramparts and green riverside areas are a refreshing escape from the bustle of the town. At the bottom of av. du Président Wilson, the flowers and waterfalls of the **Jardin Vert** calm visitors. The 4th-century ramparts that surround the town provide a view of the red-roofed houses and green countryside. To kayak (4-14km) on the Charente, call **SCA Angoulême** (☎05 45 94 68 91. €9.10-18.10 per person.) For water skiing, call **CAM's water skiing** (☎05 45 92 76 22. €9 per session. Open June-Oct. daily noon-8pm. Cash or check only.) The tourist office has information on outdoor sports, including water skiing and tennis.

▊ NIGHTLIFE

As the sun sets, folks move toward the cafés on rue Massillon and pl. des Halles, and av. Gambetta comes alive with numerous bars and restaurants. Have a hot coffee or a cold drink at the two-story **Café Chaud**, 1 rue Ludovic Trarieux. Around a wooden spiral staircase, the cushioned orange-striped seats hold mostly locals amid lively music. (☎05 45 38 26 32. Open Su-M and W-Sa noon-2am.) **Blues Rock Café**, 19 rue de Genève on the pl. des Halles, caters to a mature crowd and packs the square outside with drinks, smoke, laughter, and live music every Thursday during the summer months. Extensive salad menu (€5.50-7); beer €2.40. (☎05 45 94 05 98. Open daily 10am-2am.) Further down rue de Genève, the bar at **Saint Barth** has a DJ every night and occasional live music. Crowds rest their drinks on old oak wine barrels in homage to the region's primary industry. (Open daily 11am-2am. Beer €2.50. Happy hour daily 7-8pm. Theme nights on weekends.) A lively crowd and exciting atmosphere justify the hike out to **Le Piano Rétro Club**, near pl. Victor Hugo. (☎05 45 38 16 04. Open W-Sa 11pm-5am. W-Th no cover, F-Sa €10 cover with drink, ladies free before midnight.)

▊ FESTIVALS

Every year, the world-famous **Salon International de la Bande-Dessinée** (☎05 45 97 86 50; www.labd.com) breezes into town the last weekend in January. Over 200,000 visitors spend four days admiring comic strip exhibits throughout town, where

Astérix and Obélix can occasionally be sighted. (For tickets, call ☎08 92 69 00 32 or visit the Hôtel de Ville. €9.20 for one day, €18.30 for all four days, children ages 7-18 €4.60, under 7 free.) The **Festival Musiques Métisses,** 6 rue du point-du-Jour, features live French-African and Caribbean music each year during Pentecost. (☎05 45 95 43 42; www.musiques-metisses.com. Tourist office sells tickets. 4 nights €60, students and ages 16-18 €45, ages 10-15 €35, under 10 free.) The popular **Circuit des Remparts,** 2 rue Fontgrave, revs its engine in mid-September, when antique cars hold free races and exhibitions for three days in the town center (☎05 45 94 95 67), and international pianists of all genres participate in the two-week long installments of the **Festival International de Piano, "Piano en Valois,"** in October and November. (☎05 45 92 11 11. Concerts €12-25, under 26 free.)

In November, **Gastronomades,** a celebration of culinary arts, offers cooking lessons, food displays, and free tastings (☎05 45 67 39 30; www.gastronomades.asso.fr), and **Ludoland** celebrates children's toys and video games. (☎05 45 21 29 02; www.ludo-angouleme.com. Three-day pass €8.) Like many French cities, Angoulême also welcomes all sorts of artistic festivities in the summertime. Call the tourist office after mid-June for info about the **Eté au Ciné,** a series of outdoor films shown during summer evenings, and the **Jeux de Rue,** an open-air theatrical festival with free outdoor performances every Thursday during July and August.

For those who love to wine and dine to the gentle sway of the river, **Les Croisières au pays d'Angoulême** are a series of themed cruises that run July to August. Themes include the paper cruise, which makes a stop at the paper museum, the wine cruise, and the chocoholic cruise. Breakfast, lunch, and dinner cruises are also available. The themes tend to change each summer, but may include fireworks or a Spanish fiesta. Prices range from €15-40, children €5-25. Call the tourist office for info and reservations.

▓ DAYTRIP FROM ANGOULÊME: LA ROCHEFOUCAULD

Get to La Rochefoucauld by train (M-Sa 6 per day, €4.70). From the back of the train station, cross the parking lot to the traffic circle. Go halfway around the traffic circle and keep walking straight for four blocks through the town center. The château is straight ahead. (8min.) The tourist office is at 1 rue des Tanneurs. (☎05 45 63 07 45. Open June-Sept. daily 10am-1pm and 3-7pm; Nov.-May M 2-6pm, Tu-Sa 9:30am-12:30pm and 2-6pm.)

La Rochefoucauld (pop. 3200) has been home to more than 43 generations of the aristocratic Foucauld family. The present **château,** known as the "pearl of Angoumois," was built by Duke Francis II in 1528 on a feudal-era foundation, with twin towers, a medieval fortress, and an elegant chapel on a plateau overlooking the town. The magnificent central spiral staircase, built in 1520 and designed by Leonardo Da Vinci, is a perfect work of Renaissance art. (☎05 45 62 07 42. Open Apr.-Nov. daily 10am-7pm, Dec.-Mar. Su 2-7pm. Open year-round for groups by appointment. €6, ages 4-12 €2.) The surrounding village, which takes its name from the family ("La Roche à Foucauld" or "The Rock of Foucauld"), houses a well-preserved Gothic cloister, **Le Couvent des Carmes** (1329), and a church dating from 1266.

COGNAC

Originally a small medieval town known only as the birthplace of King François 1, Cognac's history was completely transformed in the 17th century with the invention of double distillation. According to French law, crops produced in the Cognac region are the only ones in the world fit to become the liquor that bears the Cognac name. Distilleries today give tours and samples of the sweet liqueur. Anyone except the most passionate liqueur enthusiast will want to daytrip Cognac (pop. 20,000) from Saintes and Angoulême, as there is little else to do in town.

🔁 ☎ ORIENTATION & PRACTICAL INFORMATION. Trains come from Angoulême (40min., 5 per day, €7.30) and Saintes (20min., 6 per day, €4.30). To get to the **tourist office,** 16 rue du 14 Juillet, follow av. du Maréchal Leclerc out of the train station to the first circle and take a right, following signs to the town center. Turn right on rue Bayard and go straight across pl. Bayard onto rue du 14 Juillet. (15min.) The tourist office provides information, maps, and a free accommodations service. It is also the departure point for *Petit Train* tours (May-Sept. every 45min. 11:15am-5:15pm; €5, children ages 5-15 €3), guided visits of the city (July-Aug. Tu and Th 2:30pm; €6.50, under 12 €5), and trips to the local bottle-making and cooperage factories. (☎ 05 45 82 10 71; fax 05 45 82 34 47; office.tourisme.cognac@wanadoo.fr. Office open July-Aug. M-Sa 9am-7pm, Su 10am-4pm; Sept. and May-June M-Sa 9:30am-5:30pm; Oct.-Apr. M-Sa 10am-5pm.) Other services include the **hospital** (☎ 05 45 36 75 75), and **police** (☎ 05 45 82 38 48). The **CIC Banque CIO,** 36 bd. Denfert-Rochereau, exchanges money with a 3% commission and has **ATMs** outside (☎ 05 45 36 84 84; open Tu-F 8:50am-12:15pm and 1:30-6pm, Sa 8:50am-12:30pm). For even better rates, the **post office,** 2 pl. Bayard, exchanges money with a 1.2% commission. (☎ 05 45 36 31 82. Open M-F 8am-5:30pm, Sa 8am-noon.) **Postal code:** 16100.

☎ ACCOMMODATIONS & CAMPING. Staying the night in Cognac, which has no budget accommodations, should be avoided unless necessary. Directly across from the train station, the one-story **Hotel de la Gare ❹** offers clean, modern rooms, all with TV and telephone, for the cheapest prices in the city (☎ 05 45 82 04 15; fax 05 45 82 64 44; hoteldelagare1@tiscali.fr. Breakfast €5. Reservations recommended. Singles with toilet and shower €37; doubles €44; triples €50. Extra bed €7. Handicapped-accessible. MC/V). Three-star **Cognac Camping ❶,** bd. de Châtenay, on rte. de Ste-Sévère, is a 30min. walk from the town. The #1 and 3 buses run from the pl. François I (☎ 05 45 82 01 99; mid-June to Sept., 2 per day; €0.65, under 10 free, 1-month *carnet* €14.80). Get off at Camping. (July-Aug. ☎ 05 45 32 13 32, Sept.-June 05 45 36 55 36. Pool, playground, and fishing. Laundry €4. July-Aug. two people with site, showers, and electricity €13; May-June and Sept.-Oct. €11. Three people with site €13-16. Four- to six-person mobile homes July-Aug. €400 per week; May-June and Sept.-Oct. €100 for three days. MC/V.)

☎ FOOD. Sampling Cognac's famous product doesn't necessarily mean drinking it. Restaurants around **place François I** serve pricey local specialties drenched in the stuff. **La Boune Goule ❷,** 42 allées de la Corderie, is right in the town center at the intersection of rue Aristide Briande. Huge, fresh portions of local cuisine served in an almost American diner setting. (☎ 05 45 82 06 37. Appetizers €4-11, meat and fish €5-13, lunch *menu* €11.50. Open July-Aug. daily 9am-2am, serves food noon-3pm and 7-10pm; Sept.-June open Tu-Sa only. MC/V.) More basic needs can be satisfied at **Supermarket Eco,** on pl. Bayard, right down the street from the tourist office. (Open M-Sa 9am-noon and 3-7:30pm, Su 9-11:45am.) There is an **indoor market** at pl. d'Armes (Tu-Su 8am-1pm), and a lively **outdoor market** brightens pl. du Marché on the second Saturday of each month.

☎ COGNAC DISTILLERIES. The joy of visiting Cognac lies in travelling from one brandy producer to the next, touring warehouses, watching films on the history of each house, and collecting gift-wrapped bottles of liqueur. In the summer, most houses regularly give tours in English; call in advance during the winter.

THE BIG SPLURGE

MIXED DRINKS AREN'T CHEAP

The genius behind each cognac house lies in the finely tuned palate of its "cellar master." Trained for over 20 years, this individual is responsible for tasting and smelling the thousands of *eaux de vies* produced annually by his house. Based on his sampling of the liquid, he must decide the ideal temperature and humidity at which to store the *eaux de vies*, how long each should remain in oak barrels, and at what point they have sufficiently aged and matured. He then mixes hundreds together in order to create a perfect liqueur.

In 2000, Hennessy's (see right) cellar master made the decision to blend together his house's best cognacs, dating back to 1800. The resulting mixture was placed in oval-shaped bottles of solid crystal, designed by perfume manufacturers. Producing a mere 2000 of these millennium concoctions, Hennessy gave it the label "Timeless" and began selling the bottles for a hefty €3200. The cognac became a high-demand item, bought by national governments as diplomatic gifts as well as by wealthy American, Japanese, and Russian collectors and liqueur enthusiasts. Today only 300 of the original bottles remain unclaimed and are being marketed at the discount rate of €2445. Two bottles of the "Timeless" cognac, as well as photographs of the cellar master that created it, are on display in the Hennessy distillery.

Hennessy, quai Richard Hennessy (☎05 45 35 72 68; fax 05 45 35 79 49; quais@hennessy.fr). The industry's biggest player has the longest and most interesting presentation, which includes a trip to "paradise," where the oldest cognacs are kept, a short boat ride along the Charente river, and movies accompanied by dramatic soundtracks. The company has recently launched a popular new vintage called "Pure White," targeted at teenagers, which can be found at every night club. Those with time for only one distillery visit should make this their stop. Tours daily June-Sept. 10am-6pm; Mar.-May and Oct.-Dec. 10am-5pm; Jan.-Feb. call ahead for a reservation. Several excellent English tours per day, call ahead for times. €8 (includes taste of two vintages), €5 (one vintage), students and children under 16 free.

Otard and the Château François I, 127 bd. Denfert-Rochereau (☎05 45 36 88 86), in the Château de Cognac, the 1494 birthplace of François I. The 50min. tour led by guides dressed in medieval costumes begins with the history of the building and ends with a visit to the damp castle cellar where the cognac is produced and stored. The fungus growing on the walls consumes, in vapors, the equivalent of 23,000 bottles each year. Open July-Aug. daily 10am-7pm; Apr.-June and Sept.-Oct. daily 10am-noon and 2-6pm; Nov.-Mar. M-Th 10am-noon and 2-6pm, F closes at 5pm. Last tours leave 1hr. before closing. €4.50, ages 12-18 €2.50, under 12 free, families €9.

Martell, pl. Edouard Martell (☎05 45 36 33 33; www.martell.com), is the oldest of the major cognac houses and ships to cities around the world. The interesting hi-tech tour features a replica of an 18th-century exporting ship and a visit to the founder's elegant and perfectly preserved cottage. Open June-Sept. M-F 9:30am-5pm, Sa-Su 11am-5pm; Oct. and Mar.-May M-Th 9:30-11am and 2:30-5pm, F 9:30-11am; Nov.-Feb. call ahead to reserve. English tours given daily, call for times. €4, students €2.50, under 16 free.

SIGHTS & FESTIVALS. The **Musée Municipal du Cognac,** 48 bd. Denfert-Rochereau, details the history of Cognac and its famous liqueur with regional clothing, ceramics, and viticulture tools. (☎05 45 32 07 25; musee.cognac@alien.fr. Open June-Sept. Su-M and W-Sa 10am-noon and 2-6pm; Oct.-May 2-5:30pm. €3.20, students €1.10, under 18 free.) The Hennessy distillery hosts a **film festival** every April.

OUTDOORS. Cognac's valley provides great **hiking** among vineyards, fields, groves, and forests. The tourist office provides four *Sentiers de Randonnées* maps (€2.30 each, €9.20 for all four) with paths (2-

18km) around Cognac that vary in difficulty; off-trail discoveries include a 13th-century crypt, abbeys, and châteaux. **Canoe Kayak** rents canoes for €6-15 per hr., €13-25 per half-day. (☎06 76 21 06 50; Open mid-June to Sept. daily 9:30am-8pm.) Parks in Cognac include the **Jardin de l'Hôtel de Ville** around the museum, and the large, tree-lined **Parc François I,** northwest of the city center between allée Bassée and allée des Charentes. (Jardin open May-Sept. 7am-10pm; Oct.-Apr. 7am-7pm. Park open 24hr.)

SAINTES

The ancient Roman city of *Mediolanum Santonum*, named for the local Gallic Santon tribe, was founded in the first century AD. Gracefully bisected by the Charente river and connected by a major road to Lyon, this wealthy city served as the capital of Aquitaine for nearly 100 years. It converted to Christianity early and with conviction, and was nearly destroyed in the Wars of Religion. Today Saintes's first-century ruins and impressive cathedrals bear testament to the city's importance during both Roman and medieval times, although they seem out of sync with quiet, modern Saintes (pop. 26,000). With outdoor activities like boating, horseback riding, and fishing, Saintes is a great place to flex one's outdoor muscles and eat good food on the way to larger tourist hubs.

☐ TRANSPORTATION

Trains: pl. Pierre Senard. Info office open M-Sa 9:15am-12:15pm and 2-6:45pm. To: **Bordeaux** (1½hr., 5 per day, €15.20); **Cognac** (20min., 5 per day, €4.30); **La Rochelle** (50min., 5 per day, €10.10); **Niort** (1hr., 5 per day, €10); **Paris** (2¼hr., 6 per day, €52.50); **Poitiers** (1½hr., 6 per day, €22.40); **Royan** (30min., 6-7 per day, €5.70).

Buses: Autobus Aunis et Saintonge, 2 rue des Oeillets (☎05 46 97 52 00). To: **Royan** (1½hr., 8 per day, €7.30). Office open M-F 8:30am-noon and 2-6pm. **Océcars** (☎05 46 00 95 15), in Rochefort, goes to **La Rochelle** (2½hr., 2-3 per day, €9.10). An operator answers calls M-F 8:30am-noon and 2-7pm.

Public Transportation: An €0.85 ticket allows an unlimited number of bus rides up to one hour after its initial purchase. Last train leaves the "Théâtre" stop daily at 7:30pm. Schedules at tourist office or at **Boutique Bus** (☎05 46 93 50 50) in the Galerie du Bois d'Amour, M-Sa 8am-12:30pm and 1:15-7pm.

Car Rental: Budget, 51 av. de la Marne (☎05 46 74 28 11). €171+ per week. 15% discount on weekends. €600 deposit. AmEx/MC/V. 21+. Open M-Sa 8am-noon and 2-6:30pm. **Europcar,** 43 av. de la Marne (☎05 46 92 56 10). €234+ per week. €534 deposit. 21+. Open M-F 8am-6:30pm, Sa 8am-noon and 2-6:30pm. Both allow returns at other locations.

Taxis: at the train station (☎05 46 74 24 24). €0.62 per km plus €2.

Bike Rental: Groleau, 9 cours Reverseaux (☎05 46 74 19 03). €10 per day. No deposit required. Open Tu-Sa 9am-noon and 2-7pm. Cash only.

☒ ☒ ORIENTATION & PRACTICAL INFORMATION

Saintes lies on the Charente River, 25km from Cognac along the La Rochelle-Bordeaux railway line. To get to the **tourist office,** take a sharp left upon leaving the train station and follow av. de la Marne until you hit lively av. Gambetta. Turn right and follow it to the river; the Arc Germanicus will be on your left. Cross the bridge at pont Palissy and continue straight on leafy **cours National.** The tourist office is on your right in a villa set back from the street. (20min.) The hub of the mellow pedestrian district is **rue Victor Hugo,** three blocks to the left after the bridge.

Tourist Office: 62 cours National (☎05 46 74 23 82; fax 05 46 92 17 01; www.ot-saintes.fr), in Villa Musso. Free maps. Organizes walking tours of the city, abbey, and Roman ruins. One **Internet** terminal, €7.40 for 50 minutes, €14.75 for two hours. Open July-Aug. M-Sa 9am-1pm and 2-7pm, Su 10am-1pm and 2-6pm; June to mid-Sept. M-Sa 9am-1pm and 2-6pm, Su 10am-1pm and 2-6pm; mid-Sept.-May M-Sa 9:30am-12:30pm and 2:15-6pm. Tours in French mid-June to mid-Sept. M-Sa. €6 for one tour, €10 for two, €13 for all three; under 16 free.

Money: Banque de France, 1 cours Lemercier (☎05 46 93 40 33). Open M-F 9am-12:15pm and 2-7pm, Su 2-6pm.

Laundromat: L'Arc de Triomphe, rue Arc de Triomphe (☎06 19 17 00 34). Open daily 7am-9pm. Wash €2-5.50, dry €0.30 per 5 min. **Laverie et Cie,** 46 cours Reverseaux (☎05 46 74 34 79). Open daily 7am-9:30pm. Wash €2.70-6.70, dry €0.40 per 5 min. €7-14 washing, drying, and folding service (open Tu-Sa 10am-noon and 3:30-7pm).

Police: pl. du Bastion (☎05 46 90 30 40), or **Gendarmerie,** 17 rue du Chermignac (☎05 46 93 01 19).

Hospital: pl. du 11 Novembre (☎05 46 92 76 76).

Post Office: 6 cours National (☎05 46 93 84 53). **Currency exchange** with no commission. **Internet** €7 per hr. Open M and W-F 8:30am-6pm, Tu 9am-6pm, Sa 8:30am-noon. **Poste Restante:** 6 cours National. **Postal code:** 17100.

▲ ACCOMMODATIONS & CAMPING

Hotels fill for the festivals from early to mid-July; otherwise rooms should be easy to find. Most of the cheap beds cluster on the train station side of the Charente.

■ **Auberge de Jeunesse (HI),** 2 pl. Geoffrey-Martel (☎05 46 92 14 92; fax 05 46 92 97 82; www.saintes.fuaj.org), next to the Abbaye-aux-Dames. From the station, take a sharp left onto av. de la Marne and then turn right onto av. Gambetta, left onto rue du Pérat, and right onto rue St-Pallais. About 25m farther at pl. St-Pallais, turn left through the archway into the courtyard of the abbey. Go straight through the courtyard and out through the arch at the back. The hostel will be on the right. (15min.) A clean, renovated building that feels like part of the abbey itself. Cozy, pine-scented, cabin-like rooms. Breakfast included. Sheets €2.70. Camping €4.20, with breakfast €6. No lock-out or curfew. Reception June-Sept. M-Sa 7:30am-noon and 5-11pm, Su 7:30-10am and 6-10:30pm; Oct.-May until 10:30pm. 2- to 6-bed dorms (single-sex), with showers and toilets, €11.30. MC/V. HI members only. ❶

■ **Au Bleu Nuit,** 1 rue Pasteur (☎05 46 93 01 72; fax 05 46 74 43 80; au-bleu-nuit@t3a.com). Follow directions to the tourist office but continue walking straight on cours National until you arrive at a small rotary. The hotel will be across from you on the corner of rue Pasteur and rue Lemercier. All rooms have long, sheer white curtains, bright bedsheets, and TVs. Rooms vary in size, but some are enormous and come with their own personal terrace. Breakfast €5.50. Reservations recommended in the summer. Singles with toilet €28, with shower €33.50; doubles with shower €37. Extra bed €8. Parking €4.80. AmEx/MC/V. ❸

Le Parisien, 29 rue Frédéric-Mestreau (☎05 46 74 28 92), by the train station. Run by a friendly couple, this hotel has small rooms surrounding a somewhat disheveled garden. Reception 7am-10pm. Breakfast €3-4.50. Call several weeks ahead for July-Aug. Singles €22, with shower €25; doubles with showers €32 (€22 in low season). Extra bed €7. MC/V. ❷

Camping Au Fil de L'Eau, 6 rue de Courbiac (☎05 46 93 08 00; fax 05 46 93 61 88), 1km from the town center. From the train station, follow directions to the hostel until av. Gambetta and turn right onto quai de l'Yser after crossing the bridge. The campsite is

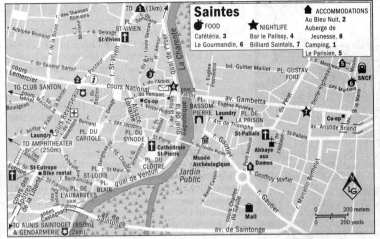

Saintes

🍴 FOOD
Cafétéria, 3
Le Gourmandin, 6

★ NIGHTLIFE
Bar le Palissy, 4
Billiard Saintals, 7

🔺 ACCOMMODATIONS
Au Bleu Nuit, 2
Auberge de
Jeunesse, 8
Camping, 1
Le Parisien, 5

half a mile farther on the right. (25-30min.) By bus, take #2 (dir: Ormeau le Pied) from the train station; get off at Théâtre and catch the #3 (dir: Magezy), to Port Larousselle (Piscine) (25min., €0.85). Three-star site by the Charente, next to pool (free for campers) and mini-golf (€4). Fence makes it feel safe. Individual lots are crowded, but there are an on-site market and *brasserie*. Some buildings wheelchair-accessible. Reception July-Aug. 8am-1pm and 3-9pm; mid-May to June and early to mid-Sept. 9:30am-noon and 4-8pm. €4.10 per person, €2.50 per child, €4.20 per site; car included. Electricity €3.10. Locked parking €3.30. Lockout for cars 10pm-7am. MC/V. ●

🍴 FOOD

Menus in Saintes flaunt the region's seafood, *escargot* dishes, and *mojettes* (white beans cooked in Charenté). Start things off with *pineau*, a sweeter relative of Cognac. Saintes is blessed with plenty of family-run restaurants and bars, especially in the pedestrian district by rue Victor Hugo. The town also holds **markets** on pl. du 11 Novembre, off cours Reverseaux (Tu and F), near Cathédrale St-Pierre (W and Sa), and on av. de la Marne and av. Gambetta (Th and Su), all 7am-1pm. On the first Monday of every month, the cours National and the av. Gambetta host **Le Grand Foire**, an open-air market that sells everything, including clothes, sunglasses, and purses. A huge **Leclerc** supermarket and general store are on cours de Gaulle near the hostel. (Open M-Th and Sa 9:30am-7:15pm, F 9am-8:15pm.) A smaller **Co-op** supermarket can be found on both rue Urbain Loyer, off cours National (open M-Sa 8:30am-12:30pm and 3-7:30pm), and at 162 av. Gambetta, near the train station. (Open M-Sa 8am-1pm and 3:30-8pm, Su 8am-1pm and 5:30-8pm.)

For sit-down fare, try the friendly **Le Gourmandin ❸,** av. de la Marne, near the station. In nice weather, the enclosed outdoor seating provides a respite from the city bustle. Sit under an umbrella in a quiet courtyard next to a small man-made waterfall. (☎ 05 46 93 01 16; fax 05 46 74 37 90. Entrées €7.50-19. Open Tu-F noon-1:30pm and 7-9:30pm, M and Sa 7-9:30pm. MC/V.) A hot, cheap meal is available at **Cafétéria du Bois-d'Amour ❶,** 7 rue du Bois-d'Amour, off cours National in the Galérie Marchandise, a pay-by-the-plate cafeteria, offering €1-4.50 appetizers and €4-7 *plats*. (☎ 05 46 97 26 54. Open daily 11:30am-12:30pm and 6:30-10pm, and 11:30am-10pm for salad. Cash only.)

THE LOCAL LEGEND

HEADY FASHION

Many distinct headdresses have evolved throughout France over the many centuries. Country tailors let their creative inspiration loose on these bonnets, completely unconstrained by city fashions. The remarkable adornments visible in old photographs and on display in museums and festivals throughout the country are the impressive result.

One of the most enduring of these headdresses is the white *quichenotte* worn by French women until well after the second world war. The *quichenotte* has become a trademark of the area along the coast of the Gironde, and can be viewed in any local museum that features old rural clothing. Made of lace or thin cloth, the bonnets served to protect female farmers' delicate skin from the hot coastal sun. Legend has it that the *quichenottes* got their name when invading English soldiers burst into the vineyards surrounding the Angoumois and Saintonge regions and surprised the women working in the fields. In an effort to defend themselves from the advances of the aggressive soldiers, the story goes, the women pulled the large wings of their headdresses over their mouths and screamed "kiss not!" in their best English. In honor of these chaste farmers, the name *quichenotte* was given to the famous white bonnets.

◎ SIGHTS

Built in 18AD as a gateway into the city, the Roman **Arc Germanicus** rises on the right bank of the river in honor of Emperor Tiberius and his nephews Drusus and Germanicus. Although originally located at the entrance to a bridge that crossed the Charente, the arc was moved to the right bank of the river when it began to lose its stability in 1843. The bridge it had been built across was replaced with the sturdier **pont Bernard Palissy.** This bridge, lined with international flags, serves as a modern triumphant entryway into the old Roman town of Saintes.

A little farther down the river is the **Jardin Public,** which offers refuge to travelers in the form of shaded benches next to its colorful flower beds. A peaceful mini-zoo in the center houses a few small goats, deer, rabbits, and birds. Next door, on esplanade André Malraux, the small **Musée Archéologique** displays a collection of Roman funeral monuments and marble statues, as well as the remains of a first-century chariot. (☎05 46 74 20 97. Open June-Sept. daily 10am-7pm; Oct.-May M-Sa 10am-5pm, Su 1:30-5pm. €3.50 ticket includes year-long admission to the **Musée du Présidial,** the **Musée de L'Echevinage,** and the **Musée Dupuy-Mestreau;** under 18 free.)

Rue Arc de Triomphe, which becomes rue St-Pallais, leads to the Romanesque **Abbaye-aux-Dames.** Built in 1047 as a convent for Benedictine nuns, the abbey led a quiet life for a while—some Gothic touch-ups here, another gallery there—until plagues, fires, and wars prompted centuries of constant construction and renovation. During the anti-religious fervor of the Revolution, the abbey was shut down and temporarily used as a prison. Today, it serves as the musical and cultural center of the town of Saintes and displays frequent exhibitions by local artists in its bright **Salle Capitulaire.** The pinecone-shaped belltower of the connected **Eglise Notre-Dame** dates from the 12th century, when Eleanor of Aquitaine aided the nuns during renovations. Climb to the top to scan the stunning horizon or check out contemporary tapestries depicting the six days of the Creation. Unlocked doors, winding stairways, and isolated passageways welcome leisurely wanderers. See the *L'Abbaye aux Dames: Eté* pamphlet at the tourist office for information on the week-long concert held every July. (☎05 46 97 48 48. Exhibition and ramparts open May-Sept. daily 10am-12:30pm and 2-7pm; Oct.-Apr. Su-Tu and Th-F 2-6pm, W and Sa 10am-12:30pm and 2-7pm. Church free. Abbey €3, students and under 16 free. Tours in French June 23 -Sept. 19, €6. Concerts €13-43.)

Across the flower-lined pedestrian bridge on rue St-Pierre the impressive **Cathédrale St-Pierre** towers over the town. Renovations transforming the 12th-century Romanesque church into the Gothic style were halted by the Wars of Religion; the steeple and portal were left unfinished. (☎05 46 93 09 92. Open daily 9am-7pm.) Turn away from the center of town and descend the steps of less traveled rue St-Eutrope, which crawls through tree-lined fields to the **crypt** of the saint who is the road's namesake. Known as the saint of recovery, **St-Eutrope** lies in a crypt treasured by many for its healing powers. Joseph de Compostela paid a visit to the crypt on his way to Santiago. (Open daily 9am-7pm.)

Follow the path from St-Eutrope as it curves to the left and turn right onto rue de La Croix Boisnard. The road leads to the **Arènes Gallo-Romaines,** now a crumbled and peaceful amphitheater in a residential neighborhood. Built in 40AD, the structure seated the 20,000 spectators who flocked to see gladiators fight to the death or slaughter wild animals. Don't bother paying the €1 admission: the view from outside the fence is just as good. (Open June-Sept. 10am-7pm; Oct.-May M-Sa 10am-5pm, Su 1:30-5pm.)

🎵 🎭 ENTERTAINMENT & NIGHTLIFE

Come nightfall, Saintes's cafés and pubs are great places to unwind with an evening of conversation and sunset-watching. Enjoy a game (€1) and a beer (€2) at **Billiard Saintais,** 126 av. Gambetta. (☎06 83 46 02 37. Open Tu-Su 2pm-2am. Cash only.) Where rue Gambetta runs into pont Palissy you'll find **Bar Le Palissy,** a gathering place for students who listen to jazz or rock. The bar also offers karaoke on Thursdays and occasional live music. (☎05 46 74 30 65. Beer €2. Open M-Sa 11am-2pm, Su 3pm-2am. AmEx/MC/V.) Those with cars can dance up a storm with partying students at **Le Santon,** Ste-Vegas, on rte. de Royan. In summer, the adjoining **swimming pool** provides a respite from steamy body heat. (☎05 46 97 00 00. Cover for both club and pool €7 with a soda, €8-9 with alcohol. Open daily 11pm-5am.)

⬛ FESTIVALS

For ten days in mid-July, the **Festival de Folklore en Charente Maritime** celebrates international folk music, food, and dance. The Arènes Gallo-Romaines host the opening and closing events. (☎05 46 97 04 35; www.jeux-santons.net. Some events free, others up to €30.) At the same time, be sure to join the **Académies Musicales** celebration, in which more than 28 classical music concerts are packed into 10 days at the Abbaye aux Dames. (☎05 46 97 48 30; fax 05 46 92 58 56; www.festival-saintes.org. Tickets €13-43, under age 18 free for one concert. Pass for the entire festival €360, students and children under 26 €265.) Childcare is offered at €3.25 per hour. (☎05 46 92 59 96. Reserve 24 hours in advance.)

LA ROCHELLE

Though it cannot boast of beautiful beaches or sandy shores, La Rochelle (pop. 80,000) does have one great claim to fame—fish, and lots of it. The town's reputation as one of France's best-sheltered seaports helped to create its fortune, but it also nearly destroyed it: France and England fought over the town during the Thirty Years' War, and Cardinal Richelieu was so upset with the city's support of England and the Huguenots during the 17th-century invasion of the Ile de Ré that he besieged the town for 15 months, starving three quarters of its citizens to death. Having survived its rocky past, La Rochelle now entices visitors to its shores with medieval architecture, its proximity to some of the most perfect isles off the French coast, quirky museums, and excellent seafood restaurants.

POITOU-CHARENTES

🖪 TRANSPORTATION

Trains: bd. Maréchal Joffre. Info office open M-F 9am-7pm, Sa 9am-6:30pm. To: **Bordeaux** (2½hr., 5 per day, €21.80); **Nantes** (2hr., 5 per day, €20.40); **Paris** (3 hr., 5 per day, €51.70); **Poitiers** (1½hr., 8 per day, €17.50). With a reservation, Eurail passes will reduce all train rides to €1.50-3.

Ferries: Boats run to **Ile d'Aix** (Inter Iles ☎05 46 50 51 88, fax 05 46 41 16 19; **Croisières Océanes,** office on cours des Dames, ☎05 46 50 68 44, fax 05 46 44 52 69; see p. 717 for prices). **Bus de Mer** (☎05 46 34 02 22) shuttles between the old port and les Minimes (July-Aug. every 30min. 9am-11:30pm, Apr.-June and Sept. every hr. 10am-7pm; July-Aug. €1.70, Sept.-June €1.50; children under 5 free). **Le Passeur** (☎05 46 34 02 22) provides transportation between the two Bus de Mer stations (daily every few minutes June-Sept. 7:45am-midnight, Oct.-Mar. 7:45am-8pm, Apr.-May 7:45am-10pm; €0.60).

Buses: Océcars (☎05 46 00 95 15) sends buses from pl. de Verdun to **Royan** (2½hr., 3 per day, €11) and **Saintes** (4 per day, 8:25am-7:15pm, €9.10) via Rochefort. Buy tickets from driver. **Info office** at pl. de Verdun open M-F 8:45am-12:15pm and 2:15-6:15pm. Eurail passes not accepted.

Public Transportation: Autoplus (☎05 46 34 02 22) serves the campgrounds, hostel, and town center (every 20 min., 7am-8pm, €1.20), and nearby towns. Tickets for rides within the city can be bought from the driver, but traveling farther away requires a stop at the pl. de Verdun office. Open M-F 7am-6pm. Provides transit maps and schedules.

Taxis: pl. de Verdun (☎05 46 41 55 55 or 05 46 41 22 22). €7 from train to hostel.

Bike Rental: Vélos Municipaux Autoplus (☎05 46 34 02 22), off quai Valin (open May-Sept. M-Sa 7am-7:30pm, Su 1-7pm) or in pl. de Verdun, near the bus station (open July-Aug. daily 7:30am-7:30pm, Sept.-June M-Sa 7:30am-7pm and Su 1:15-7pm). Free with ID deposit for 2hr., €1 per hr. thereafter.

Car rental: On av. Gal. de Gaulle, under 50 yards from the train station: **Budget** (☎05 46 41 35 53; fax 05 46 41 55 26; open M-F 8am-noon and 2-7pm, Sa closes at 6pm), **Hertz** (☎05 46 41 02 31; open M-F 8am-noon and 2-7pm, Sa closes at 6pm; AmEx/ MC/V), **ADA** (☎05 46 41 02 17; fax 05 46 50 67 75; www.ada.fr; open M-Sa 8am-noon and 2-7pm; MC/V), and **Rent-A-Car** (☎05 46 27 27 27; fax 05 46 28 33 66; open M-F 8am-noon and 2-7pm, Sa 8am-1pm and 2-6pm). Expect to pay €30 per day.

🖪🖪 ORIENTATION & PRACTICAL INFORMATION

La Rochelle spreads from café-lined **quai Duperré** in the **vieux port** to the boutique-filled **vieille ville** inland. Opposite the *vieille ville*, to the south, is the more modern area of **la ville en bois** ("Wooden Village"), which, despite its name, is a complex of industrial buildings, storage houses for boats, and several museums, including the excellent **aquarium** (see **Sights**). Farther to the south is a little strip of beachfront, **Les Minimes.** To get from the train station to the **tourist office,** head up av. du Général de Gaulle to the first square, pl. de la Motte Rouge, and turn left onto quai du Gabut. The tourist office is on the left, in the quartier du Gabut. (5min.)

Tourist Office: pl. de la Petite Sirène, quartier du Gabut (☎05 46 41 14 68; www.larochelle-tourisme.com). Multilingual staff sells a useful French brochure with maps and info (€0.50) and an abbreviated version in English and 8 other languages (€0.20). Sign in window lists festivities. 2hr. **walking tours** of the *vieille ville* depart July-Aug. M-Sa at 10:30am (€6, children €4) and 1hr. horse-and-carriage tours leave daily at 2:30pm (€8, children €6). **Night visits** led by costume-clad locals leave every Th July to mid-Sept. (8:30, 9, and 9:30pm; €8, students and children €6). Reservations are required for the carriage and night tours; call the tourist office. Most tours are in French, but English tours can occasionally be arranged in advance. Also offers hotel **reservation service** for an additional €2. Open July-Aug. M-Sa 9am-8pm, Su 11am-5pm; June and Sept. M-Sa 9am-7pm, Su 11am-5pm; Oct.-May M-Sa 9am-6pm, Su 10am-1pm.

Money: Banque de France, on the corner of rue Réamur and rue Léance Vieljeux (☎05 46 51 48 00), has an ATM. Open M-F 8:30am-noon and 1:30-3:30pm. **Crédit Lyonnais,** 19 rue du Palais, also provides 24hr. **exchange machines.**

Youth Center: Centre Départemental d'Information Jeunesse (CDIJ), 2 rue des Gentilshommes (☎05 46 41 16 36; cdij17@yahoo.fr). Apartment and job listings. Open M 2-6pm, Tu-F 10am-noon and 1:30-6pm. **Internet** €0.80 for ½hr., €1.60 for 1hr., €8 for unlimited use for one year.

Laundromat: Laverie Vague Bleue, 4bis quai Louis Durand, corner of rue St-Nicolas. Open daily 8:30am-8:30pm. Wash €3.80-€7, dry €1, detergent €0.50. W 8:30am-12:30pm: prices reduced by €0.70.

Police: 2 pl. de Verdun (☎05 46 51 36 36).

Hospital: rue du Dr. Schweitzer, 24hr. emergency entrance on bd. Joffre (☎05 46 45 50 50). English-speaking staff.

Internet: Cyber Squat, 63 rue St-Nicolas (☎05 46 34 53 67). €0.80 connection fee, €0.10 per min., €4.60 per hr. Open Tu-F 11am-midnight and Sa noon-midnight. Also has video games and a fax machine (€2 for the first page, €1.80 after that).

Post Office: 6 pl. de l'Hôtel de Ville (☎05 46 30 41 30). **Currency exchange** offered free of charge, outdoor ATM, and **Cyberposte.** For **Poste Restante:** "Hôtel de Ville, 17021 La Rochelle." Open M-F 8:30am-6:30pm, Sa 8am-noon. Main office at 52 av. Mulhouse (☎05 46 51 25 03), 50 yards from the train station. Open M-F 8:30am-7pm, Sa 8:30am-noon. **Postal code:** 17000.

ACCOMMODATIONS & CAMPING

Cheap beds in town are limited, especially during the summer, when rates are higher; make reservations in early June for trips in July and August. The rates listed below are for the high season.

Hôtel Terminus, pl. de la Motte-Rouge (☎05 46 50 69 69; fax 05 46 41 73 12; www.tourisme-francais.com/hotels/terminus). Victorian wallpaper and cascading white curtains create a romantic ambiance in this hotel, complete with a sunny lounge on the first floor and an elegant breakfast room. Breakfast €5.70. Enclosed private parking available. Singles and doubles with toilet €40-49, with shower and satellite TV €49-60; triples and quads €64-70. MC/V. ❹

Hôtel Atlantic, 23 rue Verdière (☎05 46 41 16 68; fax 05 46 41 25 69). With its drippy faucets and cramped rooms, the two-star Atlantic is not as elegant as its more upscale counterparts. However, the hotel's excellent location and unbeatable prices make it one of the best bargains in town. Open mid-Mar. to Nov. Singles €28, with shower €37-44, with shower and toilet €51-53. Breakfast €4.50; parking €5.50; animal €3. Reduced prices in low season. ❷

Hôtel Henri IV, 31 rue des Gentilshommes (☎05 46 41 25 79; fax 05 46 41 78 64; henri-iv@wanadoo.fr), on pl. de la Caille, off rue du Temple, in the heart of the *vieille ville*. Quarters may be tight in these floral bedrooms with brown- and orange-tiled bathrooms, but the location is prime and there's a cheery dining room with a giant photograph of sunflowers. Breakfast €5.50. Singles and doubles with toilet €34-37, with toilet and shower €42-46; triples and quads €54-68. Rates are reduced about €5 in low season. MC/V. ❸

Hôtel de Bordeaux, 43 rue St-Nicolas (☎05 46 41 31 22; www.hotel-bordeaux-fr.com), off quai Valin. Great location with 22 renovated rooms in yellow and blue. Breakfast €6. Reception 8am-9:30pm. May-Sept. singles and doubles with toilet €55, with shower €65, with toilet and shower €74. Nov.-Apr. singles and doubles with toilet €33-36, with shower €38-41, with toilet and shower €43-46. Extra bed €10. AmEx/MC/V. ❸

Centre International de Séjour, Auberge de Jeunesse (HI), av. des Minimes (☎05 46 44 43 11; fax 05 46 45 41 48). A 30min. walk along the water from the SNCF station. Keep to the port edges, navigate through the marina, and look for the white 2-story building on your left. No signs are visible from this angle. Alternatively, take bus #10 (dir: Port des Minimes) from av. de Colmar, 1 block from the station, to "Lycée Hôtelier" (M-Sa every 20min. 7am-7:45pm, €1.20). After disembarking, take a right onto av. des Minimes and look for the *auberge* set back from road on the right. Enormous and impersonal, the hostel offers dimly lit 2- to 6-bunk dorms, with rusty furniture and stained stucco walls. Breakfast included (7-9am). Restaurant overlooking the marina sells meat and salad for cheap (€2.50-€5, 7-8:45pm), but should be a last resort. Laundry room. Internet €0.20 per min. Reception Apr. to mid-Sept. 7am-midnight, mid-Sept. to Mar. 8am-12:30pm and 1:30-7:30pm. Lockout 10am-2pm. Code for entry after 11pm. Reserve ahead. Dorms €12.50; singles €18. €3 more for non-HI members. ❶

Camping Municipal du Soleil, av. Michel Crépeau (☎05 46 44 42 53). A 10min. walk from the city center along the quai, following av. Marillac to the left at its junction with allée des Tamaris. Or catch bus #10 (dir: Port des Minimes). Crowded, friendly and close to the port. Open mid-June to mid-Sept. Reservations suggested. One person and car €7; extra person €3.20; children €2.20; electricity €3.70; 24hr. shower free. The tourist office has information on more beautiful but remote island campsites. ❶

⬛ FOOD

The *fruits de mer* are always ripe in La Rochelle; follow the fishy smell to the **covered market** at pl. du Marché for fresh seafood and produce. (Open daily 7am-1pm.) **Monoprix** is on rue de Palais, near the clock tower. (Open July-Aug. M-Sa 8:30am-9pm and Su 9am-noon, Sept.-June M-Sa 8:30am-8pm.) **Co-ops** operate at 41 rue Sardinerie (open Tu-Sa 8:30am-1pm and 3:30-8pm, Su 9am-1pm and 5-8pm) and at 17 rue Amelot (open M 3:30-7:45pm, Tu-Sa 8:30am-12:45pm and 3:30-7:45pm, Su 9am-12:30pm). Restaurants crowd the *vieille ville* along **rue St-Jean** and the quai.

A Côté de Chez Fred, 30-32 rue St-Nicolas (☎05 46 41 65 76). This little seafood place physically surrounds its supplier, Poissonnerie Fred; you can watch the fish being prepared through an open window. *Plats* €9-22. Don't skip the fish soup (€6.10). Open Tu-Sa 12:15-2:30pm and 7-10pm. MC/V. ❸

Au San Remo Pizzeria, 15 rue St-Jean du Pérot (☎05 46 41 43 68). Along with 24 different pizza options (€6.80-9.60 for large portions), this restaurant serves many local favorites including mussels, duck, and rabbit. 3-course *menu* (€11.60) is a great bargain. Open M-Sa noon-2:30pm and 7pm-midnight. AmEx/MC/V. ❷

Le Cedre, 22 rue des Templiers (☎05 46 41 03 89). Although not the only source of kebabs in the city, this Lebanese restaurant offers fresh vegetables, quality bread, and a shaded outdoor seating area perfect for people-watching. A variety of sandwiches, kebabs, and hamburgers €3-5; fries €2-3. Open daily 9am-3pm and 7-10pm. ❶

👁 SIGHTS

A mere €6.60 buys combined admission to the Musées d'Orbigny-Bernon, du Nouveau Monde, and des Beaux Arts. Joint tickets are available at the tourist office or at any of the three museums, valid for one month.

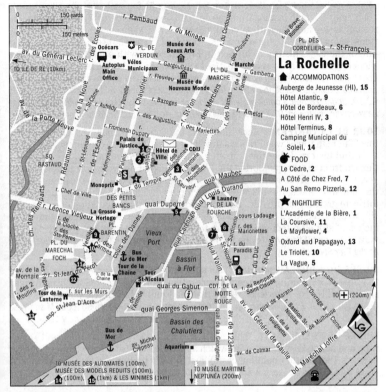

POITOU-CHARENTES

La Rochelle

🏠 ACCOMMODATIONS

Auberge de Jeunesse (HI), 15
Hôtel Atlantic, 9
Hôtel de Bordeaux, 6
Hôtel Henri IV, 3
Hôtel Terminus, 8
Camping Municipal du
  Soleil, 14

🍴 FOOD

Le Cedre, 2
A Côté de Chez Fred, 7
Au San Remo Pizzeria, 12

⭐ NIGHTLIFE

L'Académie de la Bière, 1
La Coursive, 11
Le Mayflower, 4
Oxford and Papagayo, 13
Le Triolet, 10
La Vague, 5

OLD TOWN. The pedestrian *vieille ville*, dating from the 17th and 18th centuries, stretches beyond the whitewashed townhouses of the harbor to a glitzy inland shopping district sprinkled with museums. The 14th-century **grosse horloge** (great clocktower) is worth strolling by, but the archeological exhibit inside has little to offer. Also of note is the intricately decorated white stone façade of the Renaissance **Hôtel de Ville,** with the prominent statue of its builder, Henry IV. *(45min. French tours of the interior July-Aug. daily 3 and 4pm; Sept.-June Sa-Su 3pm. €3.10, students and children €1.60.)*

⬛ AQUARIUM. This not-to-be missed, thematically-decorated aquarium is home to a whopping 10,000 marine animals, kept in habitats that simulate environments from the French Atlantic coast to the tropical rainforest. Audio tours offered in French, Spanish, Italian, and English (€3.50) provide fascinating fish tales to accompany the awe-inspiring visual displays. The aquarium makes a perfect rainy-day activity, but be prepared for crowds of people with the same idea. *(Bassin des Grande Yacht, next to the Musée Maritime. ☎ 05 46 34 00 00. Open daily July-Aug. 9am-11pm; Apr.-June and Sept. 9am-8pm; Oct.-Mar. 10am-8pm. €11, students and children €8. Groups of over 20 people get slightly discounted rates. Free parking. Wheelchair accessible.)*

TOUR ST-NICOLAS & TOUR DE LA CHAÎNE. Now the defining characteristic of La Rochelle's landscape, these 14th-century towers on the port once guarded the town from attack. When hostile ships approached, guards closed the harbor by raising a chain between the two towers. Now unfit for such use, the 800-year-old chain lines the path leading from rue de la Chaîne to the tower. Tour St-Nicolas, on the left as you face the harbor, continues to impress visitors with its thick fortifications and narrow, dizzying staircases. Tour de la Chaîne houses a fascinating timeline of the city's history (with text in French only) with a model of the town in Richelieu's day. *(St-Nicolas ☎ 05 46 41 74 13; Chaîne 05 46 34 11 81; fax 05 46 34 11 83. Both towers open July-Aug. daily 10am-7pm; mid-May to June and early to mid-Sept. daily 10am-1pm and 2-6pm; mid-Sept. to mid-May Tu-Su 10am-12:30pm and 2-5:30pm. €4.60, ages 18-25 €3.10, under 18 free. Combined ticket including Tour de la Lanterne €7, with ferry passage between the two towers €10, ages 18-25 €6.50; Oct-Apr. free first Su of the month.)*

TOUR DE LA LANTERNE. Accessible from the Tour de la Chaîne by a low rampart, this 70m high tower was France's first lighthouse. The 15th-century structure has a morbid history. It became known as the **Tour des Prêtres** after 13 priests were thrown from the steeple during the Wars of Religion. In 1822, four Carbonari sergeants were imprisoned here before being executed in Paris for conspiring against the monarch. Along the 162 steps to the top hold, the stone walls are carved with intricate graffiti that provides remarkable historical documentation of castles and shipwrecks, recorded by the detainees within the tower. At the summit, only three inches of stone protect visitors from their own free-falls, but on a sunny day, the view extends all the way to the Ile d'Oléron. *(☎ 05 46 41 56 04. Same hours and prices as the Tour St-Nicolas.)*

MUSÉE DU NOUVEAU MONDE. This museum explores European perceptions of the New World during the Age of Exploration. Portrayals of colonialists, African slaves, and Native Americans reveal that the French thought New-Worlders were bestial savages. *Plus ça change...* *(10 rue Fleuriau. ☎ 05 46 41 46 50. Open M and W-Sa 10:30am-12:30pm and 1:30-6pm, Su 3-6pm. €3.50, students and children under 18 free.)*

MUSÉE DES BEAUX ARTS. This museum has works by Rembrandt and Delacroix, and a nice Fromentin series which appears on the town's postcards. Look for Signac's 18th-century painting of the bustling city harbor. *(28 rue Gargoulleau. ☎ 05 46 41 64 65. Open Su-M and W-Sa 2-5pm. €3.50, students and children under 18 free.)*

🎵 📷 ENTERTAINMENT & FESTIVALS

La Coursive, 4 rue St-Jean-du-Perot, hosts operas, jazz and classical music concerts, traditional and experimental plays, dance performances, and art films. *(☎ 05 46 51 54 00; fax 05 46 51 54 01. Open M 5-7pm, Tu-Sa 1-8pm.)* During the summer, **quai Duperré** and **cours des Dames** are closed to cars and open to mimes, jugglers, musicians, and an outdoor market. *(May-June Su noon-8pm, July-Sept. daily 10pm-midnight.)* Though its name may raise expectations of port-swilling patrons discussing 17th-century philosophy, **L'Académie de la Bière** on the rue des Templiers is actually a lively cross between an Irish pub and a French outdoor café. *(☎ 05 46 42 43 78. Open daily 10am-2am. Beers €2.40-2.80.)* Next door, relaxed **Le Mayflower** sells a potent €3.80 rum concoction. *(☎ 05 46 50 51 39. Open daily 6pm-2am.)* Along the waters of the old port, the dressed-down folks at **La Vague,** 16 quai Duperré, sip cocktails amidst the surf boards and parasols. *(☎ 05 46 30 53 19. Open daily 10pm-2am.)* For a cool place to hang out on a summer night, head to the **cour du Temple,** a lively square tucked away off rue des Templiers.

The crowd is young at the twin nightclubs **Oxford** and **Papagayo Discothèque,** behind the restaurant Richard Coutanceau on the plage de la Concurrence. Oxford offers a wild night of dancing under a giant disco ball, while Papagayo is a fun-filled party complete with fake palm trees and 80s music. The streets leading to the clubs are dark and isolated at night: they should not be traveled alone. *(☎ 05 46 41

51 81. Su karaoke nights and free admission for women before midnight. Cover €6. Open Su-M and W-Sa 11pm-5am.) Decked with gaudy palm trees and mirrors, **Le Triolet,** 8 rue des Carmes, gets a lot of yuppies very tipsy on 94 different kinds of whiskey. This *discothèque's* eclectic soundtrack doesn't heat up the dance floor until late. (☎05 46 41 03 58. €10 cover includes one alcoholic drink or two virgin ones. Open M-Sa 11pm-5am; July-Aug. also open Su.)

La Rochelle's popular festivals attract art-loving, sun-seeking mobs like nowhere else. During the last week of June and the first week of July, the city becomes the Cannes of the Atlantic with its **Festival International du Film de La Rochelle.** Fans come from Paris to stay up all night watching films. (☎05 46 51 54 00 for information or 01 48 06 16 66 for reservations; fax 05 46 28 28 29. All 100 films €77; 3 films €15; one film €6; under 21, 10 films €29. For tickets, write to 16 rue St-Sabin, 75011 Paris.) Without batting an eyelash, La Rochelle turns around and holds its **FrancoFolies,** a massive six-day music festival in mid-July that draws francophone performers from around the world. (☎05 46 50 55 77; www.francofolies.fr. Event tickets €8-40.) To round out the month, the end of July brings a 10-day **theater festival** on quai Simenon. (☎05 46 34 33 75.) During the 2nd week of September, hundreds of boats in the Port des Minimes open their immaculate interiors to the public for the **Grand Pavois,** a boat competition known as "the foremost floating boat show in Europe." (☎05 46 44 46 39; www.grand-pavois.com.) The **marathon** runs through town at the end of November. (☎05 46 44 42 19. For information, write to Res le Platin, 2 Perspective de l'Océan, BP 97.)

NEAR LA ROCHELLE

ROCHEFORT

The modern town of Rochefort (pop. 27,000) was a sparsely populated marshy area along the **Charente River** until Louis XIV took possession of it in the 17th century and transformed it into the greatest royal dockyard in France. One of Rochefort's biggest draws is its maritime history, although its geographical center has shifted away from the river to the **place Colbert,** a large square surrounded by old white stone buildings, tiny brasseries, and a few small, intimate museums.

⁊ PRACTICAL INFORMATION. Trains connect Rochefort with La Rochelle (20min., 5 per day, €4.70), Saintes (30min., 7 per day, €6.70) and Bordeaux (2hr., 6 per day, €18.70). Rochefort is also easily accessible by taking **Ocecars,** which shuttle between the *gare routière* and La Rochelle (line #51; 1hr.; M-Sa 8 per day, Su 2 per day; €4.80) and Saintes (line #60, 1hr., M-Sa 6 per day). **Citram Littoral buses,** pl. de Verdun, bring travelers to Le Château on l'Ile d'Oléron (☎05 46 82 31 30; line #10; 1½hr.; M-Sa 8 per day, Su 2 per day; €6.50.) For more information, the **tourist office** on av. Sadi Carnot is extremely helpful. (☎05 46 99 08 60. Open July-Aug. 9:30am-7pm; Sept.-June M-Sa 9:30am-12:30pm and 2-6pm.)

⁊⁊ ACCOMMODATIONS & FOOD. In the heart of Rochefort, the two-star hotel **▨Roca-Fortis ❸,** 14 rue de la République, offers quiet, sunny rooms, but beware the mosquitoes from the garden courtyard below. (☎05 46 99 26 32; fax 05 46 99 26 62; www.hotel-rocafortis.com. Breakfast €5, in room €6. Singles and doubles with TV €28, with shower €39, with shower and toilet €49. Rates lower Sept.-June. Extra bed €8. MC/V.) Several houses down, at 20 rue de la République, is the bright, colorful, and extremely clean **Auberge de Jeunesse ❶.** (July-Aug. ☎05 46 99 74 62; Sept.-June 05 46 82 10 40. Breakfast €3.30. Sheets €3. Reception July-Aug. 8-10am and 5:30pm-midnight; Sept.-June 9am-noon and 2-6pm. Dorms (single sex)

POITOU-CHARENTES

€8.60; singles €12.60; tent sites €5.) If the office is closed, go to the **Office Municipal de Jeunesse (OMJ)**, 97 rue de la République. (☎05 46 82 10 40. Open M-F 9am-noon and 2-6pm, Sa 2:30-5:30pm.)

For a tasty meal, Rochefort locals recommend **Le Cap Nell ❸**, 1 quai Bellot, overlooking the small harbor. The combined *bistrot* and grill serves fresh seafood, along with duck and peppered steak. 3-course *menu* €15-21. (☎05 46 87 31 77; www.capnell.com. Open July-Aug. daily noon-2pm and 5-7pm; Sept.-June Su-M and Th-Sa noon-2pm and 5-7pm, Tu-W noon-2pm. MC/V.)

◪ SIGHTS. In homage to their naval past, residents of Rochefort have begun construction of an exact replica of **L'Hermione,** the vessel which transported Marquis de Lafayette to the aid of George Washington and the American colonies in 1780. The reconstruction is expected to be finished in 2007 and will sail to Boston shortly thereafter. Guided tours of the worksite demonstrate the craft of 18th-century blacksmiths and carpenters. (☎05 46 87 01 90. Tours Apr.-Sept. 9am-7pm; Oct.-Mar. 10am-6pm; €6, ages 8-16 €3, under 8 free.)

One of the first buildings constructed to accommodate Louis XIV's new incoming fleet was the 373m long ropery, the **Corderie Royale.** At the time of its opening in 1669, it was Europe's longest factory, allowing workers to twist hundreds of bales of hemp into sturdy naval ropes. Closed in 1926, the ropery was torched in 1944 by departing German troops and remained idle until its reconstruction in 1976. Since then, the old factory has been restored to its original condition and now houses a **library,** the **Chamber of Commerce and Industry,** and the **Musée de la Marine,** an interesting museum dedicated to the maritime history of Rochefort. (☎05 46 87 01 90; www.corderie-royale.com. Open daily Apr.-Sept. 9am-7pm; Oct.-Mar. 10am-6pm. €4.60, children €2.)

Perhaps the most fascinating of Rochefort's smaller museums is the **Maison Pierre Loti,** 141 rue Pierre Loti, which exhibits the exotic collection of curiosities accumulated by the magician and naval officer, Loti. Eccentric to the extreme, this Rochefort resident transformed the rooms of his house into a Turkish lounge, an Islamic mosque, and a Gothic chamber. The museum can only be seen through guided tours. (☎05 46 99 16 88. Tours July to mid-Sept. daily every 30min. 10am-5:30pm; mid-Sept. to June Su-M and W-Sa every hr. 10:30-11:30am and 2-4pm; €7.50, students and children 8-18 €3.90.) Detailed dioramas at the **Musée des Commerces d'Autrefois,** 12 rue Lesson, depict the average day of various French workers between 1890 and 1940. (☎05 46 83 91 50; www.museedescommerces.com. Open daily July-Aug. 10am-8pm; Apr.-June and Sept.-Oct. 10am-noon and 2-7pm; Nov.-Mar. 10am-noon and 2-6pm). The impressive 176m long steel and iron **Pont Transbordeur,** 10 rue du Docteur Pujos, stands farther down the Charentes. Designed by engineering genius Ferdinand Arnodin, the bridge was built in 1900 from the same materials as the Eiffel Tower. (☎05 46 82 18 77; caprtourisme@wanadoo.fr. 1hr. guided tours given at varying times throughout the year; €1.80, children 5-11 €1).

ILE DE RÉ

Ile de Ré, dubbed "Ré La Blanche" for its 70km of fine, white sand beaches, is a sunny paradise just 10km from La Rochelle. Connected by a bridge to the mainland, the 30km long island combines one of Europe's largest nature preserves, with extensive paved bike paths, pine forests, farmland, vineyards, and bustling towns with huge stretches of untouched sand. Though only 15,000 people live on the island year-round, July and August bring crowds to the main town of **St-Martin-de-Ré** and to the beaches on the island's southern coast.

TRANSPORTATION. Just driving across **pont La Pallice** costs a steep €16.50 in round-trip tolls from June to mid-September. (Mid-Sept. to May €9; €2 for motorcycles and scooters year-round.) **Walking** and **biking** are easy alternatives to driving, and cycling from La Rochelle to Sablanceaux takes less than an hour. The ride is a bit tough going up the 4km long bridge, but well worth it, as the trails on the island are marvelous, with great coastal views. From pl. de Verdun in La Rochelle, head west on av. Maréchal Leclerc and follow road signs to Ile de Ré until the bike path appears on the left.

The city **buses** also provide a viable means of transport, as lines #1 and 21 (dir: La Pallice) go as far as Sablanceaux, the first beach on the island after the bridge. Make sure the bus is going to Sablanceaux: some buses on lines 1 and 21 stop before crossing the bridge. (20 min., every 20 min., €1.20.) For ventures beyond Sablanceaux, **Rébus** is a convenient way to travel between pl. de Verdun

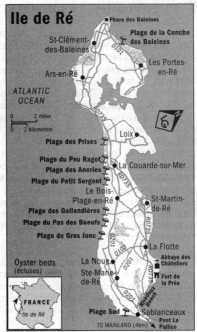

Ile de Ré

and the villages on Ré, including St-Martin (45min., 10 per day, €4.60) and Les Portes (1½hr., 8 per day, €8), at the northern tip of the island. (☎05 46 09 20 15. Info office at 36 av. Charles de Gaulle in St-Martin. Open M-F 8:30am-noon and 2-5:30pm.)

Once on Ile de Ré, there are plenty of places to rent bikes in each village. **Cycland** has branches in Rivedoux, La Flotte, St-Martin, Le Bois-Plage, Ars, Les Portes, St-Clément, and La Couarde. (☎05 46 09 08 66. Bikes €3.50-5 per hr., €7-9 per day. Deposit €100-200, by check or cash. Open daily July-Aug. 9am-7pm; Sept.-June 9:30am-1pm and 2-7pm. Bikes rented at La Flotte, St-Martin, or Le Bois-Plage can be returned at any of those three towns. MC/V.)

PRACTICAL INFORMATION. The largest and most centrally located town on the island, **St-Martin-de-Ré** (pop. 2650) is the best starting place for exploring Ile de Ré. St-Martin's **tourist office,** on quai Nicolas Baudin, has a free map of the island's bike trails. Walking tours (June-Sept. Tu at 10:30am; 2hr; €5.50, children €2) depart from the tourist office. Horse and carriage tours (June-Sept. Th at 10am; 1½hr.; €8, children €4) begin at the **Parking Vauban.** (☎05 46 09 20 06; fax 05 46 09 06 18; ot.st.martin@wanadoo.fr. Open July-Aug. M-Sa 10am-7pm, Su 10am-1pm; Sept.-June M-Sa 10am-noon and 2-6pm, Su 10am-noon.) The best location for **currency exchange,** with a 1% commission, is at **Crédit Agricole,** 4 quai Foran, on the port. (☎05 46 09 20 14. Open Tu-F 9am-12:15pm and 1:30-6pm, Sa 9am-12:45pm.) Other services include: **police** (☎05 46 09 21 17); **Pharmacie Dubreuil,** rue de Sully (☎05 46 09 20 43; open M-Sa 9am-12:30pm and 2:30-7:30pm), and the **post office,** pl. de la République. (☎05 46 09 20 14. Open M-F 9am-noon and 1:30-3:30pm, Sa 9am-noon.) **Postal code:** 17410.

⌂ ACCOMMODATIONS & CAMPING. The attractive winter prices of the hotels in Ré go way up in summer, as hotel owners know there will be a steady stream of tourists ready to pay higher fees. St-Martin's understaffed **Hôtel Le Sully ❸**, 19 rue Jean Jaurès, offers wood-paneled rooms on a busy pedestrian street for the cheapest prices available on the island. (☎05 46 09 26 94; fax 05 46 09 06 85. Breakfast €4.80. Code for entry after 2:30pm. Reservations recommended. Singles or doubles with shower €38, with toilet and shower or bath €45; Oct.-May €30/€37; extra bed €8. MC/V.) The smaller surrounding towns also provide suitable accommodations. **L'Hippocampe ❸**, 16 rue Château des Mauléons, in **La Flotte**, 4km east of St-Martin and 9km north of Sablanceaux, has small, modest rooms. (☎05 46 09 60 68. Breakfast €5. Reserve months ahead. Singles and doubles €35, with shower €40, with shower and toilet €45. MC/V.) Campsites are plentiful on Ile de Ré, but those between the bridge and St-Martin-de-Ré become crowded in July and August. Those seeking solitude should head to beachside **La Plage ❶**, 408 rte. du Chaume, near St-Clément. (☎05 46 29 42 62. Open Apr.-Sept. Reserve months in advance. Two people with tent €15, €5 per extra person; €32.50 per car per week; electricity €31 per week.) Gorgeous, thickly forested **Camping Tamaris ❶**, 4 rue du Comte D'Hastrel, is right near **Rivedoux's** center and one of the island's most popular spots. (☎05 46 09 81 28. Open Easter-Sept. 1-3 people €12, €4 per extra person, children under 7 €2; electricity €3.50.)

☐ FOOD. Most towns have pizzerias and *crêperies* as well as **morning markets**, which are listed in full in Ré's tourist packet. St-Martin's indoor market is off rue Jean Jaurès, by the port. (Open daily 8:30am-1pm.) Two supermarkets sit just east of St-Martin on the road to La Flotte: **Intermarché**, 4 av. des Corsaires (☎05 46 09 42 02. Open M-Th 9am-12:30pm and 3-7:30pm, F-Sa 9am-7:30pm), and **Super U**, 23 rue des Salières. (☎05 46 09 42 80. Open M-Sa 9am-7:30pm.) A cluster of tasty, albeit pricey, restaurants surround the port in St-Martin and overlook the colorful fleet of fishing boats below. The **Marco Polo**, 6 quai de Bernonville, offers a superb penne with black olives (€6.50) in addition to a selection of fresh seafood and an array of traditional desserts (☎05 46 09 15 92. Three-course *menu* €11.50-€22.30. Open daily noon-midnight.)

☒ NIGHTLIFE. St-Martin has a surprisingly outsized nightlife for its diminutive size. Port-side vendors stay open until 11pm or midnight during the summer to accommodate the late-night tourists, while locals shuttle between the bars and discos all night. **Le Cubana,** on Venelle de la Fosse Braye, is a lively bar with rum-infused drinks that accompany thumping Latin rhythms. (☎05 46 09 93 49. Open July-Aug. daily 10pm-2am; Mar.-June and Sept.-Oct. M-Sa 10pm-2am; Nov.-Feb. F-Sa 10pm-2am.) Behind a mysterious locked door next to the Cubana, the **Boucquingham** blasts techno and hip hop into the wee hours of the morning. (☎05 46 09 01 20. Open July-Aug. daily 11pm-5am; Sept.-June F-Sa 11pm-5am.) Across town is **Le Bastion,** cours Pasteur, a wild all-purpose grill, pizzeria, nightclub, and disco. This seaside establishment hosts weekly theme nights during the summer. (☎05 46 09 21 92. €8 cover for men before 12:30am, after 12:30 €10 cover for all. Cover includes one drink. Open July-Aug. daily for food 5-7pm and for dancing 11pm-5am; Sept.-June M-Sa.) Farther down the island, on Rivedoux plage, **L'An Fer,** pl. de la République, cranks out the beats from 11pm to 5am every Friday and Saturday night. (☎05 46 09 30 90. €10 cover.)

☒ TOWNS & SIGHTS. Between Sablanceaux and beachy La Flotte are the ruins of the 13th-century **Abbaye des Châteliers**. First built in 1156, the abbey was destroyed during the Wars of Religion as Ré passed back and forth between Catholic and Protestant hands. The abbey was abandoned in 1574, and many of its stones were taken to build the Fort de la Prée in 1625. The ruins now stand in an isolated field, visible from the bus from Sablanceaux to La Flotte. **La Flotte** (pop. 2700) is the island's most typical fishing town, with a bustling port and pedestrian area. **Maison du Platin,** av. du front de Mer, 4 cours Félix Faure, details the history of the island's fish and salt industries and features photographs of Ré's earliest residents. The museum conducts walking tours in French of the old quarters, port, and nearby oyster farms (€4.50, children €2.50), as well as bike tours of the **Abbey des Chateliers** and the **Fort de la Prée** (90min.; €5.30, children €2.50). Schedules vary; call for information. (☎05 46 09 61 39. Open Apr. to mid-Nov. M-F 10:30am-12:30pm and 2:30-6pm, Su 2:30-5:30pm. €3.50, ages 7-18 €2, under 7 free.) Hour-long tours of the medieval fishing beds, teach visitors about the **écluses à poissons,** teach visitors about the island's fishing traditions. The stone walls of the beds, which lie along the southern coast's beaches off Sablanceaux, were erected to trap fish with the waning tides. Wear boots! (Times vary with tides. Call ☎05 46 37 47 50 for a schedule.)

St-Martin lays claim to a port built by Vauban and a citadel built by Louis XIV in order to protect Ré from the invading English. The citadel now serves as an active prison, with around 500 inmates. The 15th- to 17th-century Renaissance gallery of the **Hôtel Clerjotte,** on av. Victor-Bouthilier, houses the **Musée Ernest Cognacq,** which is devoted to the history of the island and displays such exhibits as model ships, old paintings, and archeological finds including an enormous elephant skull. Visitors to the museum in 2004 may be lucky enough to catch the temporary exhibit documenting St-Martin native Nicolas Baudin's visit to the *indigènes* in Australia c. 1800. (☎05 46 09 21 22. Open July-Aug. daily 10am-7pm, Sept.-June M and W-F 10am-noon and 2-6pm, Sa-Su 2-6pm.) Just up the hill from the quai rests the imposing 15th-century **Eglise St-Martin.** Originally constructed in the Romanesque style, the church has been built and destroyed so many times in religious wars that its outside and interior now have no stylistic relation. At sunset the view of the entire island from the top of the belltower is even more breathtaking than usual. (Open daily July-Aug. 9:30am-midnight, Sept.-June 9:30am-sunset. Admission to church free, belltower €1.50, ages 11-15 €0.75, under 11 free; guided tours €2.30, children 11-15 €1.50. Binoculars are available for €0.75 with an ID deposit.) On the way up the island, stop by **Ars** to admire its 17 windmills, dismantled in the 19th century when a phyloxera plague wiped out the island's chief crop. Nearing **St-Clément-des-Baleines,** watch for the blinking red light of the **Phare des Baleines,** built in 1854. Standing 57m high, the lighthouse is one of the tallest in France and directs boats over 50km away. Climb its 257 stairs for a great view of the ocean. (Open daily Apr.-June 10am-7pm; July-Aug. 9:30am-7:30pm; Sept. noon-6:30pm; Oct.-Mar. 10:30am-5:30pm. €2, ages 7-12 €1.)

🚲 **BIKES & BEACHES.** It's easy to rent a bike in any island town and pedal along the paths, coastal sidewalks, and wooded lanes spread out across the island. Although trails to St-Martin along the southern half of Ile de Ré are often packed, crowds thin out to the north. The *Guide des Itinéraires Cyclables,* available from island tourist offices, describes five 10-22km paths. One of the island's best trails begins in Le Martray, just east of Ars, and runs along the northern coast through the island's trademark salt marsh and bird preserve, a wetlands sanctuary home to herons and rare blue-throated thrushes. The marsh is worth visiting in the summer, but winter's really the time to see it—20,000 birds stop by on their migration from Siberia and Canada to Africa. Other bike paths lead you through forests, beside beaches, and to other island landmarks.

The major attraction of the island is, of course, its splendid beaches. Slather on some sunscreen and shake off all inhibitions at the bathing-suit-optional **plage du Petit Bec** in **Les Portes-en-Ré.** To avoid that full-body glow, head to the pine-fringed dunes of **plage de la Conche des Baleines,** near the lighthouse just off the Gare Bec.

Both beaches, at the northern tip of the island, are huge and free from the crowds that fill beaches on the western coast. The sea off the exposed north coast tends to be dangerous, and the shores rocky; for better swimming, try the long strip of beach along the southern shore, beginning at **La Couarde.**

ILE D'AIX

Smaller and less accessible than Ré, Aix (pop. 200) is almost entirely free of the souvenir shops and fast food stands that cover most towns in this region. Aix sees its fair share of visitors (300,000 per year), but this island maintains the feel of unspoiled wilderness. Just 3km long and barely 600m wide, the island has back-woods trails perfect for quiet hiking and tiny coves set into the rocky, shell-covered coastline. The best beaches are along the southwest coast near the lighthouses. As one of the only coastal islands with no highway to the mainland, Aix rarely sees any cars. To get here, it's ferry or bust.

On the island, stop at the **Point Accueil** (☎06 75 28 38 66), immediately on your right as you leave the port, and pick up a free map and brochure. **Horse carriages** one block farther up conduct historical tours of the island in French. (☎05 46 84 07 18. 50min.; €6, under age 10 €5.) *Crêperies* and snack shops in town rent **bicycles** to tourists who want to explore the island. (Approx. €3.50 per hr., €8.50 per day. ID deposit.) Additionally, pedestrians can walk around the island in a mere two hours, and some of the most beautiful spots are accessible only by foot.

One of the most striking sites dates from the time Aix hosted Napoleon in 1815 three days before he was exiled to the island of Ste-Hélène. The house in which he stayed was transformed into the **Musée Napoléonien** in 1928. Today it contains a small but impressive collection of portraits and Napoleon relics, including a dress worn by his first wife, Josephine, and 40 clocks stopped at 5:49, the time of his death. The **Musée Africain** next door presents an ethnographical and zoological exhibition on Napoleon's Egyptian campaign and contains African war booty such as a stuffed dodo bird. (☎05 46 84 66 40. Both open June-Sept. daily 9:30am-12:30pm and 2-6pm; Apr. and Oct. Su-M and W-Sa 9:30am-12:30pm and 2-6pm; Nov.-Mar. Su-M and W-Sa 9:30am-12:30pm and 2-5pm. Separate admission €3, ages 18-25 €2.30, under 18 free. Combined admission €4, ages 18-25 €3.) The **Fort Liedolt**, built by Napoleon to protect this tiny but strategically located island off the coast of France, housed German prisoners during World Wars I and II and was later used as a summer camp for children, until the government purchased it in 1980 for use as a historical monument. (July and Aug. tours in French available through the tourist office; 6 per day, 11am-6pm; 1hr.; €2.80.)

Ile d'Aix's only hotel, **Hôtel Napoleon ❹,** on the corner of rue Gourgaud and the place Austerlitz, is expensive, but the rooms are spacious and peaceful. (☎05 46 84 66 02; fax 05 46 84 69 70. Breakfast €6.50. Singles and doubles with shower €55, with shower and toilet €60; *demi-pension* for two people €88-96.) Next to the port, quiet **Camping le Fort de la Rade ❶** offers a uniquely picturesque camping experience inside the red-poppy-filled ruins of a fort. (☎05 46 84 28 28; fax 05 46 84 00 44. Open May to mid-Sept. Visitors arriving after the reception is closed are welcome to enter on their own but must be sure to pay in the morning. €5.60-7.70 per tent, €4.10 per person, €2.60 per child aged 2-10. Animals €2.10. Prices slightly lower May-June and Sept.)

The few restaurants on Aix tend to be pricey. The **bakery** on rue Gourgaud sells cheap sandwiches, and a little grocery store just across the street has all the essentials. In the middle of the island, on rue Le Bois Joly, the classy restaurant **Les Paillotes ❹** beckons. Satisfied diners feast upon lamb and fresh seafood in an elegant shaded courtyard. 3-course *menu* €15-25.50. (☎05 46 84 66 24; fax 05 46 84 23 25. Open daily 9am-11pm. AmEx/MC/V.) The cheerful restaurant **Pressoir ❸,** just down rue Le Bois Joly, is run by a bunch of young fishermen with perpetual five-o'clock shadows. Enjoy fresh *moules frites* on the terrace for €9.70. *Menus* €16.50-22. (☎05 46 84 09 37. Open July-Aug. daily noon-2pm and 7-11pm; May-June and Sept. daily noon-2pm and Sa-Su 7-11pm. AmEx/MC/V.)

In the summer, **ferries** link Aix to La Rochelle. **Inter Iles,** on the Espace St-Jean d'Acre, runs boats to the island along routes that circle Fort Boyard, the former prison and stronghold. (☎05 46 50 51 88. 1-1¼hr.; 2 ferries per day. MC/V.) Similar service is provided by **Croisières Océanes,** cours des Dames, in La Rochelle. (☎05 46 50 68 44. 45min.-1hr.; 2-8 per day. Ask about *Journées Promotion,* when prices dip to €12. V.) Both companies charge €21 round-trip, €17 half-day round-trip; ages 4-12 €11/€9.50, under 4 €3.50.

MARAIS POITEVIN

Stretching from Niort to the Atlantic just north of La Rochelle, this natural preserve of marshland has been nicknamed *la Venise Verte* (the Green Venice) for the serene canals that wind through it. Visitors biking along the banks or punting on the canals pass weeping willows, purple irises, herons, herds of cattle, and the occasional rustic home. At its origin by the Sèvre Niortaise river, graceful trees form an overhanging canopy, and duckweed carpets the water's surface, making the canals look like grassy paths. Toward the coast, lush greenery gradually gives way to the dry marsh. The canals control flooding, ensuring that small-scale farming remains the region's primary industry.

Though well worth the trouble, the Marais is not a very convenient daytrip, so consider spending a night here. Most towns are tiny and inaccessible by public transportation. From **Coulon,** travelers can rent bikes or boats to travel along the river, visit other towns, and see the landscape of the wetlands. The tourist office in Coulon provides info and sells a great walking and biking map, the "Pays du Marais Poitevin des Deux-Sèvres Carte Touristique" (€6).

COULON

The winding streets of tiny Coulon (pop. 2200) run alongside the canals of the Marais, making the town an ideal starting spot for a boat into the Marais. **CASA Autocars,** 11-13 chemin du Fief Binard (☎05 49 24 93 47), arrive from Niort's *gare routière* (next to the train station) and its central pl. de la Brèche (30min.; M-Sa 7 per day, no buses Su and holidays; €2.40, students €1.80). Take bus #20 (dir: Coulon/Marais Poitevin).

Once here, the most practical way to penetrate farther into the Marais is by boat or bike. Though many hitch, *Let's Go* does not recommend it. Head to the **tourist office,** 31 rue Gabriel Auchier, for general info about hiking and bicycling tours and for a complete list of the area's *chambre d'hôtes* and campsites. (☎05 49 35 99 29. Tourist office open July-Aug. daily 10am-1pm and 2-6pm; call for low season hours. Hotel and chambres d'hôtes reservation service €2. Hiking tours €4.) Bike, canoe, and punt rental locations pepper the town, especially along the river. An **ATM** is located at **Crédit Agricole,** pl. de l'Eglise. The **post office,** 17 rue Gabriel Auchier, right next to the tourist office, offers currency exchange. (Open M-F 8:30am-noon and 3-5pm, Sa 9-11:30am.)

Though more expensive than bikes, boats are well worth the extra money and are the best way to experience the Marais. Boats are rented in 15 different boat rental locations in the 12 towns along the river. Although most explore the area on their own, a few companies offer guides who instruct travelers in the marsh's history and secrets. Stirring the waters releases methane gas trapped below; theatrical guides will prod the water to light a fire right on the surface. In Coulon, **Le**

Trigale, 6 rue de l'Eglise (☎ 05 49 35 14 14), will supply a private boat and boatsman, though none of the guides speaks English (1-2½hr., 1-7 people €26-64). The nautically inclined can rent a boat and navigate themselves (1-7hr., €13-48, MC/V). Many other vendors offer similar deals, usually €1-2 cheaper down the river.

Hotels are expensive in Coulon, but many *chambres d'hôte* rent rooms from €40 for two people. **Le Central ❹,** 4 rue d'Autre-mont, the least expensive hotel in town, has classic, cottage-style décor and a location close to the city center. (Breakfast €5.40. Make reservations Tu-Sa. Singles and doubles from €40. MC/V.) Three-star **Camping de la Venise Verte ❶,** 2km outside of town, is embedded in lush greenery. Follow the river west from Coulon to reach the campground. Hiking and biking tours are organized through the campground. Canal-side sites, a pool, and canoe and bike rental are available. (☎ 05 49 35 90 36; fax 05 49 35 84 69. Open Apr.-Oct. Reception daily July-Aug. 8:30am-noon and 2-8:30pm.; Sept.-Oct. and Apr.-June 9:30am-12:30pm and 3-9pm. Tours €5. 2 adults, car, tent, and electricity €16.60; low season €14. Children €1.50-4.20. 4- to 5-person bungalows €47 per night. MC/V.) **Camping de La Garette ❶** is another well-equipped campground with showers, a pool, laundromat, and a location right on the water. Located in the little village of **La Garette,** it is 3km south of Coulon. (☎ 05 49 35 00 33. Bike and canoe rental available. Open May to late Sept. €3 per site. €3 per person, €2 per child, €1.50 per car. Electricity €2.50.) Right next to the campsite is the origin of an 8km hike through marshy forests that runs past the two-door houses (one for land, one for water) unique to the area. La Garette is just after Coulon on CASA bus #20. Get off at La Garette—Centre des Loisirs. Continue walking in the direction of the bus, past the horse stables, until reaching the camp.

While in Coulon, take a moment to visit **La Maison des Marais Mouillés,** pl. de la Coutume, for a comprehensive look at the history and development of the Marais wetlands region, presented through artifacts, botanical displays, old photographs, and art exhibits. During July and August, the *maison* also offers a 3hr. guided boat tour of the Marais in French with a 45min. boat segment and a 6.5km walk through the wetlands. (☎ 05 49 35 81 04. Reservations required for tour. Open July-Aug. daily 10am-8pm; May-June and Sept. M-F 10am-noon and 2-7pm, Sa-Su 10am-1pm and 2-7pm; Nov. daily 2-7pm; Dec.-Feb. daily 10am-noon and 2-7pm. €5, students €3.80. Boat tours €13, under 16 €7.80. 1 tour per day.)

Every August, the **Festival du Marais Poitevin** brings music and dancing to a different town in the area each weekend. (☎ 05 49 35 99 29. Ticket prices vary; some events are free. Call for detailed schedule.) The **Fête Maraichine,** in the first week of July, features a parade of traditional boats down the river. The **Rally canoë-kayak** attracts 2000 boats racing down the Marais during one day at the end of June.

OTHER SIGHTS OF THE MARAIS

About 35km from Niort, the ruins of the 12th-century **Abbaye St-Pierre de Maillezais** peep out from among the trees. Within the crumbled walls, on uneven and shifting marshland, are the monks' ruined 13th-century kitchen and living quarters, as well as the tombs of several dukes of Aquitaine. The closest public transportation is the train station in **Fontenay-le-Comte,** which is accessible by **SNCF buses** from the *gare routière* in Niort (45min., M-Sa 10 per day, €5.80). Once in Fontenay-le-Comte, take a taxi the remaining 12km. The only alternative is to rent a car in Niort and follow N148 (dir: Nantes). About 7min. past Oulmes, signs point to the parking lot for the abbey on the left. (☎ 02 51 00 70 11 or 02 51 50 43 00. Open July-Aug. daily 10am-7pm; Sept.-June M-Sa 9:30am-12:30pm and 1:30-6pm, Su 10am-7pm. Free tours in French every hr.) Farther west, just north of La Rochelle, is the little inlet known as the **Baie de l'Aiguillon,** one of the largest shellfish-producing regions of France; oyster- and mussel-collecting still supply its livelihood. Bordered to the east by a nature reserve and by sparkling water to the west, **Aiguillon-sur-mer** is a small vacation resort set amid salt marshes and swamps. Aiguillon is serviced by **Sovetours** (☎02 51 95 18 71) and is accessible by bus from La Rochelle, although the schedule makes it impossible to take a daytrip, so visitors may have to camp out. (Bus 1¾hr.; 6:45pm, return 10:20am; €13.40). Just east of Aiguillon sits a **nature reserve** at St-Denis-du-Payre, with trails to the winter residence of greylag geese and wigeons, and the summer home of storks, redshanks, and the occasional spoonbill. Thousands of birds drop by during migratory periods in spring and autumn. Aiguillon has many campsites which serve as bases for the bay and the nature reserve. The **municipal campgrounds**, rte. de Lyon, are just outside of town on a lake. (☎02 51 56 40 70. Reception daily 8am-1pm and 2-7pm. Open Apr.-Sept. €4.50 per person, €3.20 per child; €4.50 per site. Electricity €3.70.)

LES SABLES D'OLONNE

Les Sables d'Olonne was once a port outlet for Olonne, the region's capital; however, when its harbor silted up, it became useless for shipping, and Olonne abandoned it. Les Sables today is popular with French vacationers for its beautiful beaches, hotels, and restaurants, though it is especially enjoyable as a center for water sports, fishing excursions, and hikes through the marshlands. With ocean to the west, secluded surf to the north and south, and marshlands to the east, this beach town has a landscape for every taste.

■■ **ORIENTATION & PRACTICAL INFORMATION.** The **train station** is on av. de Gaulle. (Open M 5:15am-8pm, Tu-Sa 6:30am-8pm, Su 7am-8:30pm.) To: La Rochelle (2hr., 5 per day, €17.30) via La Roche-sur-Lyon; Nantes (1½hr., 6-7 per day, €16.10); Paris (5hr., 6 per day, €57.80). The bus station is next door. Sovetours (☎02 51 58 28 51) sends **buses** to La Rochelle (3¼hr., 9am, €17) and Fromentine. (2hr., 2 per day, €12.30. Office open M-F 8:30am-12:30pm and 2:30-6:30pm, Sa 9:30am-noon.) La Sabia, 95bis rue de la Croix Blanche (☎02 51 23 54 88), runs **ferries** to l'Île d'Yeu. (Apr.-Sept. 3 departures daily 7:30am-7pm; call for exact times and low season schedule. Round-trip €33, children €22.) **Local TUSCO buses** run to area beaches. (☎02 51 32 95 95. Buses 7:30am-7:30pm. Ask at the tourist office for a map and schedule. €1.10, *carnet* of 10 €7.70.) For **taxis**, call Radiotaxi Sablais (☎02 51 95 40 80). Holiday Bikes, 66 promenade Clemençeau, **rents bikes.** (☎02 51 32 64 15. Bikes €8-9 per day, scooters €38-€55, motorbikes €50-€120; €80 deposit. Open June-Sept. daily 10am-12:30pm and 2-7pm. AmEx/DC/MC/V.)

The **tourist office**, 1 prom. du Maréchal Joffre, a 15min. walk from the train station, has a friendly staff that provides excellent regional and local maps. The "Randonées" brochure is full of info on 16 area hiking and bike excursions. The office also makes **hotel reservations** and books boat tours. (☎02 51 96 85 85; www.ot-less-ablesdolonne.fr. Boat tours July-Aug. daily 3 and 4pm. Open July-Aug. daily 9am-7pm; Sept.-June M-Sa 9am-12:30pm and 1:30-6pm, F opens 10am, Su 10:30am-12:30pm and 3:30-6pm.) The **Centre d'Information Jeunesse**, in the Hôtel de Ville at pl. du Poilu, has services ranging from **Internet** (with *télécarte*) to apartment listings. (☎02 51 23 16 83. Open M-Th 9am-noon and 2-6pm, F 9am-noon and 2-5pm.) **Crédit Industriel de L'Ouest**, 1 av. Carnot, **exchanges** traveler's checks at good rates. (☎02 51 96 82 11. Open Tu-F 8:45am-12:30pm and 1:45-6pm, Sa 8:45am-12:30pm.) Other services include: **laundry** at Lavarie des Salines, 3 rue Nicot (☎06 89 63 45 23; open 7am-9pm), **police** at 1 bd. Blaise Pascal (☎02 51 21 19 91); a **hospital** at 75 av. d'Aquitaine (☎02 51 21 85 85); and **Internet** at Le Quizz Café, 24 promenade Clemenceau (☎02 51 95 91 01; €4 per hr; open daily 10am-midnight). The **post office**, 65 rue Nicot, **exchanges currency.** (☎02 51 21 82 82. Open M-F 8:30am-5:45pm, Sa 8:30am-noon.) **Postal code:** 85100.

ACCOMMODATIONS & FOOD. On the street left of the train station, **Hôtel les Voyageurs ❸**, 16-17 rue de la Bauduère, at pl. de la Gare, has modern rooms with wood floors, bright vinyl furniture, and a tiny, clean bathroom. (☎02 51 95 11 49; fax 02 51 21 50 21. Breakfast €5.40. Singles and doubles with shower and toilet €38.50-44; triples with bath €48. Extra bed €5-10. MC/V.) For an inexpensive hotel along the water, one block from the beach, try the recently opened **Hôtel L'Etoile ❸**, 67 cours Blossac, whose mid-sized, homey rooms have wicker furniture and an organic feel. (☎02 51 32 02 05. Open Easter to Sept. Call ahead for reservations. Singles with sink €26; doubles with shower €30-39. MC/V.) Among the few budget options in the city, **Hôtel de Départ ❸**, 40 av. du Général de Gaulle, near the train station, offers 13 simple, small rooms with well-maintained furnishings above a *brasserie*. (☎02 51 32 03 71; fax 02 51 32 03 71. Breakfast €5. Doubles €26-30; triples €34-39. MC/V.) Les Sables's many **campgrounds** are listed at the tourist office and easily accessible by public transportation.

There's a **covered market** in the 19th-century art nouveau **Les Halles,** between rue des Halles and rue du Palais. (Open late June to mid-Sept. daily 8am-1:30pm; mid-Sept. to late June Tu-Su 8am-1:30pm.) There are also two **Intermarché** supermarkets, a small one on bd. de Castelnau and a larger one on bd. de l'Ile Vertime. (Both open M-Sa 9am-8pm, Su 8:30am-1pm.) The *brasseries* and *crêperies* along the plage du Remblai serve the cheapest food in town, though many of them have fairly low culinary standards. For a more complete meal, try the Porte de Pêche and its nearby *quais*, which overflow with restaurants serving whatever the boats have brought in. **Le Port ❷**, 24 prom. Georges V, specializes in grilled fish (from €13) and has affordable *plats* (€7-15) as well. (☎02 51 32 07 52. Entrées €7-8. Open daily noon-2pm and 7-10pm. MC/V.) For a good plate of traditional French cuisine, **L'Albatros ❸**, pl. de Strasbourg, serves a menu of grilled fish and delightful salads in a more polished environment than that of many of the surrounding options. (☎02 51 32 03 80. *Plats* €9-12, *menus* €14. MC/V.)

SIGHTS. There are a few interesting sights hidden among the postcard racks and plastic sea pails, although they pale before the lure of the beach on a sunny day. The **Musée du Coquillage**, 8 rue du Maréchal Leclerc, near the Porte de Pêche, is one-of-a-kind. The overstuffed shelves display thousands of intricate, beautifully colored shells and corals gathered by a local sea diver for his once private collection. Crowded glass cases hold treasures from deep-sea dives across the world. (☎02 51 23 50 00. Open daily June-Aug. 9am-8pm; Sept.-May 9:30am-12:30pm and 2-7pm; Sept.-June closed Su morning. €6, under 12 €3.50.) The **Musée de l'Abbaye Ste-Croix,** rue de Verdun, occupies a wing of a restored 17th-century Benedictine abbey and presents a hodgepodge of regional artifacts, folk crafts, and modern and contemporary art, most notably the work of Victor Brauner and Gaston Chaissac. Be sure to stroll by their collection of boat portraits for a subtle history of sea commerce in Les Sables. (☎02 51 32 01 16. Open Tu-Su mid-June to Sept. 10am-noon and 2:30-6:30pm; Oct. to mid-June 2:30-5:30pm. €4.60, children €2.30; first Su of every month free.) **La Chaume,** the promontory across the channel from the center of town, has two monuments along its *quais:* the 18th-century **Château St-Clair,** whose cloud-scraping Tour d'Arundel is visible from a distance; and the restored **Prieuré St-Nicolas,** a 17th-century priory, 18th-century fort, and contemporary art gallery. On the mainland, **Notre-Dame-de-Bon-Port,** pl. de l'Eglise, is a rare blend of Gothic and Baroque style.

EXCURSIONS & BEACHES. Sables Tours (☎02 51 96 85 85) books regional excursions, sports, and entertainment. The tourist office distributes a free foldout brochure in French with about 10 hiking and biking trails *(randonnées),* that

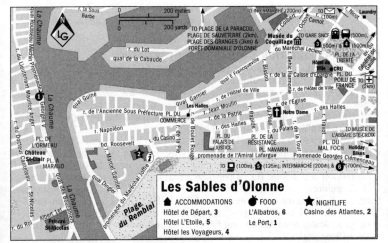

Les Sables d'Olonne

♠ ACCOMMODATIONS	♦ FOOD	★ NIGHTLIFE
Hôtel de Départ, **3**	L'Albatros, **6**	Casino des Atlantes, **2**
Hôtel L'Etoile, **5**	Le Port, **1**	
Hôtel les Voyageurs, **4**		

traverse its dunes, forests, and beaches. In July and August, the office also posts daily listings of local tennis tournaments, concerts, and organized beach volleyball games. Guided boat trips, canoeing, surfing, sailing, diving, and other water sports are also available. The closest **hiking** trail to Les Sables starts about 1km north of the train station. From the station, follow rue Georges Clemenceau until it intersects rue du Doctor Charcot; signs indicate the beginning of an 18km trail that winds through the Vendée countryside and its tiny villages to a beautiful church at Olonne-sur-Mer.

The city's beaches live up to its name (*sables* is French for sand). **La Grande Plage,** a beautiful 3km strip of beach close to the *centre ville*, is the largest and most crowded of Les Sables's offerings. A popular surfing spot, **plage de Tanchet,** is right beyond La Grande Plage, walking along the beach away from the tourist office. Bus #8 also runs to Tanchet. For more solitude, take bus #2 to La Chaume's **plage de la Paracou** (disembark at Le Large), another good beach for surfing, though it is known for its dangerous waters. Following the coast north from Paracou, beachgoers will encounter two uncrowded beaches with great surf. **Plage de Sauveterre** is 1½km north of Paracou, while **plage des Granges** is another kilometer farther on. Nudity lies in between. ▨Lots of nudity. Adventurers may enjoy the **Forêt Domaniale d'Olonne** just east of here, where huge dunes tumble from dry woodlands into the sea.

Nightly during the summer, **Les Remblais,** the widest strip of the boardwalk, becomes a pedestrian walkway with organized concerts, outdoor theater, jugglers, clowns, and marionette shows. The tourist office distributes a complete schedule of events. For the big spender, the nearby **Casino des Atlantes,** 3 bd. Roosevelt, features blackjack tables, slot machines, and a piano bar. During the summer, the casino puts on ritzy shows with dinner on most nights. Call for a schedule. (☎02 51 32 05. Open until 3am.)

ILE D'YEU

Bordered on all sides by clear water, the Ile d'Yeu (pop. 5000) has a vast array of landscapes crammed onto one island—dense mini-forests; wide, flat beaches; stony paths; and sprawling oceanscapes. Despite the rush of tourists who flood the island in July and August, many secluded spots remain, away from the public beaches. Ferries unload passengers from the mainland at Port Joinville, home of marine-wear boutiques, retiree-filled restaurants, and banks: all the prerequisites for a day out on the island.

⌂⚐ TRANSPORTATION & PRACTICAL INFORMATION. The small seaside town of **Fromentine** is the easiest base from which to reach the islands. Sovetours **buses** run between Fromentine and Les Sables. (☎02 51 95 18 71. 2hr., 2 per day 8am-6pm, €12.30.) To get from the *gare routière* to the *gare maritime*, where **ferries** depart, cross pl. de la Gare and turn left onto the av. de l'Estacade. The *gare maritime* is at the end of this road. Two **ferry** companies shuttle visitors from Fromentine to **Ile d'Yeu**: Vedettes Inter-Iles Vendéenes (VIIV), 9 av. de l'Estacade (☎02 51 39 00 00; www.ile-yeu.com; 4 per day; roundtrip €27, students €22.50, children €19; MC/V) and Compagnie Yeu Continent, 3 av. de l'Estacade, near the *gare maritime* (☎02 51 49 59 69; www.compagnie-yeu-continent.fr; office open M-F 9:30am-noon and 2-5pm; 1hr.; 4 per day; round-trip €26.50, students and seniors €21.40, children €19; AmEx/MC/V). Rates change for overnight stays. SABIA **boats** leave Les Sables from quai Rousseau-Méchin in Port Olona for Ile d'Yeu. (☎02 51 23 54 88; fax 02 51 21 33 85. Apr.-Sept. 1hr.; 2 per day 7-10am; round-trip €33, children €22.) Make reservations and ticket sales on the Internet, through company ticket offices or the tourist offices in Fromentine, Nantes, and Les Sables.

Biking is the best means by which to explore; the entire island can be covered in 4-5hr. if the temptation to stop and swim can be resisted. The numerous paths range from sandy to boulder-strewn; fortunately, bikes in Port-Joinville are built for the back roads. Expect to pay €5 per hr. or €12-14 per day. **La Roue Libre,** 4 rue Calypso (☎02 51 59 20 70), offers a range of bikes in many different sizes and rents scooters as well. Another spot, right next to the docks, is **La Trottinette,** rue de la Chaume, which rents everything from bikes to minivans. (☎02 51 58 70 42. Reservations recommended. MC/V.) Most rental places will store bags and provide a map of suggested routes. The **tourist office,** rue du Marché, distributes biking and hiking itineraries of varying lengths, with extensive directions and historical descriptions of sights in English and French. (☎02 51 58 32 58. Open July-Aug. M-Sa 9am-6:30pm, Su 9am-12:30pm; Apr.-June and Sept. M-Sa 9am-noon and 2-6:30pm, Su 9am-noon; Oct.-Mar. M-Sa 9am-noon and 2-5:30pm, Su 9am-noon.)

⌂ ACCOMMODATIONS. Though accommodations on Ile d'Yeu are expensive, some are worth the price. The charming two-star **Hôtel L'Escale ❸,** 14 rue de la Croix du Port, is about a 5min. walk from the quai at Port Joinville, on a quiet street. Sunny, rustic rooms look out on a lovely flower-filled courtyard. Kids will love the family rooms with lofts. (☎02 51 58 50 28; http://site.voila.fr/yeu_escale. Singles and doubles with shower and toilet €35-47; triples and quads €47-50. MC/V.) The island's crowded **campground ❶** is near the beach at Pointe de Gilberge, 1km from the port, enclosed by a calm expanse of beach on one side and tennis courts and horse stables on the other. (☎02 51 58 34 20. 4 people with 2 tents €10; €1.80 per extra person; €2.50 per car.) During the summer, many visitors camp illegally, though *Let's Go* does not recommend it. Fresh, cheap food is available from the **outdoor market** on quai de la Mairie. (Open M-Sa 9am-noon or 1pm.) The **Casino** supermarket, 31 rue Calypso, is 2min. from the port. (Open Tu-Th 9am-1pm and 2:30-7pm, F until 7:30pm, M and Sa 9am-7:45pm, Su 9:30am-12:30pm. MC/V.) There are seven **campsites** in Fromentine; its tourist office (across the street from the bus station) has a list. **Camping la Grande Côte ❷,** on the rte. de la Grande Côte, a few hundred meters from Fromentine and the beach, has a pool, bike rental, laundry, food services, and a full activities calendar. This popular site gets crowded in the summer. (☎02 51 68 51 89. Open May to mid-Sept. Two people and car €9.80-17; additional person €3.40-5. Electricity €3.20.)

■ **EXCURSIONS.** There are three easy **bike circuits** of the island, all originating from Port Joinville. The shortest, a 12km path, runs to the island's southern port and back in 2½hr. Its highlights are **Port Meule,** with its 11th-century chapel and tiny dock, and ■**Pointe du Châtelet,** a beautiful seascape vista overlooking the tall ruins of the 14th-century **Vieux-Château.** The château was used as a fortress in the 16th century, until it was abandoned by Louis XIV. The remarkable remnants stand crumbling on the craggy coast, accessible by bike path alone. (Tours in French July-Aug. daily 9am-7pm; late June and Sept. noon-5:30pm. €2.80, children €1.30.) Both lie just south of Joinville and feature gorgeous sea cliffs; mossy, marshy inlets; and brightly colored local fishing boats. The longest route (5½hr.) circles the island, passing Renaissance churches, picturesque ports, and ■**plage des Conches,** a perfect stretch of shore with soft sand and calm waters that goes on for miles. One of the most popular bike itineraries (4½hr.) travels into the center of the island, stopping 2km southeast of Port Joinville at the 18th-century church in **St-Sauveur,** where bright stained-glass windows illuminate a dark, musty interior. Along this route lies the flat, sparkling **plage des Sapins,** very popular with windsurfers. The route then curves around to the south coast, where cliffs rise in all directions. **Plage Anse des Soux,** enclosed by looming cliffs, is a great place for an early afternoon siesta. The 4½hr. path then leads back to Joinville, but bikers can also continue west to the **Grand Phare,** a 20m tall lighthouse on the island's highest "hill," to get a view of the island from above.

POITOU-CHARENTES

DORDOGNE, PÉRIGORD, & LIMOUSIN

A landlocked position and lack of famous attractions have long left this region out of the limelight. It therefore offers peaceful, unadulterated countryside; tiny villages among valleys and woods of oak; and charming, tranquil cities. While Paris was occupied by the English in the 15th century, ▨Bourges (p. 726), now the area's largest city, served as France's capital and benefited from the lavish attentions of the king's financier, Jacques Cœur, who built a string of châteaux through the heart of Berry. During WWII, resistance movements throughout the region resulted in the destruction of many small villages, such as frozen-in-time ▨Oradour-sur-Glane (p. 737), the site of France's worst massacre. Despite this bleak history, the region has long been an artistic breeding ground, producing painter Auguste Renoir, dramatist Jean Giraudoux, and novelist George Sand. The tradition of porcelain production, centered in medieval **Limoges** (p. 732), completes this varied artistic inheritance. Limousin's idyllic scenery is dotted with occasional remnants from the Middle Ages, such as the 12th-century **Abbaye de Noirlac** (p. 731). Less stressful than the Loire Valley, Berry is perfect for relaxed exploration of the still-inhabited châteaux of the Route Jacques Cœur, including **Château de Meillant** (p. 731), **La Verrerie** (p. 732), and **Maupas and Menetou-Salon** (p. 732), all easily accessible from tiny, medieval **St-Amand-Montrond** (p. 731).

The bucolic scenery of Périgord, whose green countryside is splashed with yellow sunflowers, steep chalk cliffs, and ducks paddling through shady rivers, has an exceptionally rich history. A trove of Neolithic art has been preserved in its numerous prehistoric caves, many of which are easily accessible from **Périgueux** (p. 737). Excavations at **Les Eyzies-de-Tayac** (p. 742) have uncovered more stone-age artifacts than in any other place on earth, and the painted caves of ▨**Lascaux** (p. 746) are the most extensive and best preserved in the world. The **Grotte de Font de Gaume** in Les Eyzies-de-Tayac and the **Grotte du Pech-Merle** (p. 756), 25km from **Cahors** (p. 754), also contain extraordinary original paintings which visitors can explore up close. The caves open into a spectacular rural countryside, with poplar-lined rivers, valleys strewn with sunflowers and carpeted by wheat fields, and feudal châteaux like **Castelnaud-la-Chapelle** (p. 746). The area's mountainous geography has produced such dramatic clifftop and hillside towns as ▨**Domme** (p. 749), **Collonges-la-Rouge** (p. 752), ▨**Rocamadour** (p. 752), and ▨**St-Cirq-Lapopie** (p. 756); **Sarlat** (p. 743) is more noteworthy for its well-preserved medieval architecture. **Brive-la-Gaillarde** (p. 749) serves as an important hub for exploring the Quercy and Dordogne regions. Périgord has recently become one of the most popular destinations for French tourists, who enjoy the close contact with nature, food, and history that the region affords.

The region specializes in *poulet en barbouille*—chicken roasted over a fire, cut in pieces, and then simmered in a creamy sauce made of its own blood, cream, egg yolk, and liver. Limousin is also renowned throughout France for its beef and

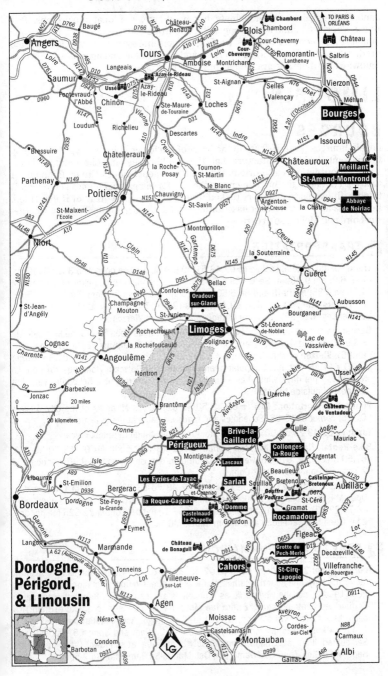

DORDOGNE

lamb, both garnished with walnuts, honey, chèvre, and local mushrooms. *Tripoux*, a regional lamb's tripe specialty, is particularly well known. Périgord is famous for its *cèpe* mushrooms, truffles, walnuts, honey, and chèvre. Its farmland produces most of France's strawberries, and the area's abundant poultry farms are renowned for their foie gras (duck- or goose-liver pâté).

LIMOUSIN

BOURGES

Lovely Bourges (pop. 80,000), in the heart of the lower Loire valley, is marked by flamboyant Gothic architecture, half-timbered houses, and charming medieval streets. Bourges's wealth originated in 1433, when Jacques Cœur, financier of Charles VII, chose the humble city as the site for his palatial home. The region is filled with exquisite châteaux tucked into a thick forest worthy of Robin Hood. Bourges is also a convenient base for daytrips to the beautiful villages of Charité-sur-Loire and Mehun-sur Yèvre.

⎚ TRANSPORTATION

Trains: pl. du Général Leclerc (☎02 48 51 00 00). Info office open M 5:30am-9:30pm, Tu-F 6:05am-9:30pm, Sa 6:05am-6:45pm, Su 7:30am-11pm. Ticket office open M 4:25am-8:35pm, Tu-Th and Sa 5:50am-8:20pm, F 5:35am-9:30pm, Su 7am-9:35pm. To: **Nevers** (1hr., 11 per day, €9.40); **Paris** (2½hr., 5-8 per day, €24); **Tours** (1½hr., 10 per day, €16.80). Many trains require a change at **Vierzon.**

Buses: rue du Champ de Foire (☎02 48 24 36 42). Office open Sept.-June M-Tu and Th-F 8-9:30am and 4-6pm, W and Sa 8am-noon. To: **Châteauroux** (1¾hr., 1-3 per day, €4.90); **Vierzon** (1¼hr., 3 per day, €3.80); and nearby villages. Tickets €1.35, *carnet* of 10 €11.45. The most popular nearby village is **St-Germain** (take bus #4 from La Nation; 2-4 per day), which has a bowling alley and several pubs. Schedules vary, but are posted outside the station.

Public Transportation: CTB (☎02 48 50 82 82) serves all areas of the city. Tickets €1.15, *carnet* of 10 €8. Schedules and maps available at the tourist office.

Taxis: (☎02 48 24 50 00). 24hr. €5 from the train station to tourist office.

Bike Rental: Narcy, 39 av. Marx-Dormoy (☎02 48 70 15 84; fax 02 48 70 02 61). €7.50-8 per day, €16 per weekend. Credit card deposit. Open M-F 9:30am-noon and 2-7pm, Sa 9am-noon and 2-6pm.

Car Rentals: Ucar, 21 av. Jean Jaurès (☎02 48 70 63 63). Cars from €35 per day. Open M-F 8am-noon and 2-6pm, Sa 8am-noon. MC/V. **Hertz,** 4 av. Henri Laudier (☎02 48 70 22 92), near train station. Cars from €57.10 per day. Under 25 €25 fee per day. 21+. Open M-F 8am-noon and 2-6pm. AmEx/MC/V.

⁊ PRACTICAL INFORMATION

Tourist Office: 21 rue Victor Hugo (☎02 48 23 02 60; www.ville-bourges.fr/tourisme), facing rue Moyenne near the cathedral. Cross the street in front of station and follow av. Henri Laudier into the *vieille ville* as it becomes av. Jean Jaurès. Bear left onto rue du Commerce. Continue straight onto rue Moyenne, which leads to office. (18min.) Or catch bus #1 (dir: Val d'Auron, €1.10) to Victor Hugo. **Accommodation booking** €1. 1½hr. **walking tours** in French July-Sept. daily 10:30am and 3pm; €5, students €3. Self-guided illuminated night tours mid-July to mid-Aug. at sundown. Office open Apr.-Sept. M-Sa 9am-7pm, Su 10am-7pm; Oct.-Mar. M-Sa 9am-6pm, Su 2-5pm.

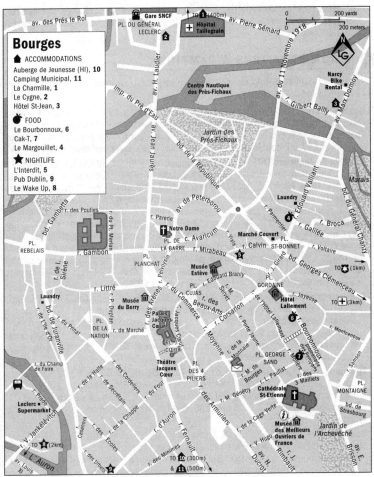

Bourges

🏠 ACCOMMODATIONS
Auberge de Jeunesse (HI), **10**
Camping Municipal, **11**
La Charmille, **1**
Le Cygne, **2**
Hôtel St-Jean, **3**

🍴 FOOD
Le Bourbonnoux, **6**
Cak-T, **7**
Le Margouillet, **4**

⭐ NIGHTLIFE
L'Interdit, **5**
Pub Dublin, **9**
Le Wake Up, **8**

Laundromat: Laveromatique, 117 rue Edouard Valliant (☎06 72 77 32 05), and 15 bd. Juranville (☎02 48 67 41 49). Open daily 8am-8:30pm.

Police: (☎02 48 55 85 00), rue Mayet Genetry.

Hospital: 145 rue François Mitterrand (☎02 48 48 48 48).

Crisis Lines: SOS Médecin, ☎02 48 23 33 33. **SOS Femmes Victimes de Violence,** ☎02 48 21 05 34.

Pharmacy: Pharmacie du Progres, 27 rue Moyenne (☎02 48 24 00 41). Open M 2-7pm, Tu-F 9am-12:30pm and 2-7pm, Sa 9am-noon and 2-6pm. The **pharmacie de garde** is posted in the windows of all pharmacies.

Internet: Médiathèque, bd. Lamarck/Parc St-Paul (☎02 48 23 22 50). Free at the library; 30min. time limit. Open July-Aug. Tu-F 12:30-6:30pm, Sa 9am-noon; Sept.-June M-W 12:30-6:30pm, Th 12:30-8pm, F 12:30-6:30pm, Sa 10am-5pm. **Esprit Club,** 81 rue Gambon (☎02 48 24 71 12). €5 per hr. Open daily 11am-12:30am.

Post Office: 29 rue Moyenne (☎02 48 68 82 82). **Currency exchange. Cyberposte.** Open M-F 8am-7pm, Sa 8am-noon. **Poste Restante:** 18012 Bourges Cédex. **Postal code:** 18000.

ACCOMMODATIONS & CAMPING

Bourges's cheapest hotels are outside the city center. Summer visitors should phone ahead for reservations.

Hôtel St-Jean, 23 av. Marx-Dormoy (☎02 48 24 70 45; fax 02 48 24 79 98), a 10min. walk from both the train station and the center of town. A lovely hostess lets clean, carpeted rooms with excellent showers. Elevator. Breakfast €4. Singles €22, with shower and toilet €27.50; doubles €26/€33.60; triples with shower and toilet €42.70. V. ❷

Auberge de Jeunesse (HI), 22 rue Henri Sellier (☎02 48 24 58 09; fax 02 48 65 51 46), 10min. from town center. From station, take av. Henri Laudier to av. Jean Jaurès, and then to pl. Planchat. Follow rue des Arène as it becomes rue Fernault. At a busy intersection, cross to rue René Ménard. Turn left at rue Henri Sellier, and walk approx. 1 block. Hostel is on the right, set back behind a brown and white building. (25-30min.) Or take bus #1 (dir: Val d'Auron; daily 6am-6pm) to Conde. Cross the parking lot to the right and take the paved footpath to the left that crosses the park patch ahead. Continue straight down rue Vieil Castel. Hostel is across the street, 30m down a driveway slightly to right. Bar, laundry, kitchen, parking, and bare but clean 3- to 8-bunk rooms, some with showers. Grassy yard overlooks a small river. Breakfast €3.30. Sheets €2.80. Reception daily 8-10am and 5-10pm. Beds €8.40. ❶

Centre International de Séjour: La Charmille, 17 rue Félix-Chédin (☎02 48 23 07 40; fax 02 48 69 01 21). From station, cross over the tracks, up rue Félix-Chédin. (5min.) La Charmille—half hostel, half *foyer*—is a skater's heaven, with bowls, ramps, and skating classes in summer. Social atmosphere among predominantly teenage guests. Spotless rooms, all with shower. Breakfast included. Meals €8.60. Laundry. Singles €15; larger rooms €11.70 per person. MC/V. ❶

Le Cygne, 10 pl. du Général Leclerc (☎02 48 70 51 05; fax 02 48 69 09 91). Across from the train station, a 15min. walk from center of town. Rooms are cozy and well kept, with shower and toilet. Elevator and attached restaurant. Breakfast €5.50. Parking €3. Singles and doubles €27-35; triples €40; quads €49; *demi-pension* for 1 person €40, 2 people €52. ❸

Camping Municipal, 26 bd. de l'Industrie (☎02 48 20 16 85; fax 02 48 50 32 39). Follow directions to *auberge* (see listing) continuing on rue Henri Sellier, then turn right on bd. de l'Industrie. Landscaped 3-star campground in a riverside residential neighborhood, a 10min. walk from the city center. Free swimming pool nearby. Reception daily Sept.-June 8am-9pm; June-Aug. 7am-10pm. Open mid-Mar. to mid-Nov. €3.10 per person, €1.70 per child; €3.10 per tent; €4.40 per car. Electricity €2.60-4.10. ❶

FOOD

The outdoor tables on **place Gordaine** and **rue des Beaux-Arts** fill with locals during the spring and summer. For a touch of elegance, try the tasty regional cuisine in the many timber-framed restaurants on **rue Bourbonneux** or **rue Girard.** Look for specialties such as *poulet en barbouille* (chicken roasted in aromatic red wine) and *oeufs en meurette* (eggs in red wine). The largest **market** is held on pl. de la Nation (Sa morning); another livens up pl. des Marronniers (Th until 1pm). There is a smaller **covered market** at pl. St-Bonnet. (Tu-Sa 7:30am-1pm and 3-7:30pm, Su 7:30am-1pm.) The huge **Leclerc** supermarket, rue Prado off bd. Juranville, provides supplies for ambitious chefs. (Open M-F 9:15am-7:20pm, Sa 8:30am-7:20pm.)

▧ **Cak-T,** 74 prom. des Remparts (☎02 48 24 94 60; www.cak-t.com). Beautiful storybook tearoom nestled along a lavender-lined passage between rue Bourbonnoux and rue Molière. Outdoor terrace in summer. A hidden treasure full of gentle music, flowers, lace, and delicious desserts (€3.50-4.60), including a dessert *dégustation* (€4.60). Tea €1.90-3, coffee €3. Open Sept.-July Tu-Sa 3-7pm. ❶

Le Margouillet, 53 rue Edouard Vaillant (☎02 48 24 08 13). Vibrantly colored restaurant serves up Caribbean cuisine in an airy island atmosphere. *Menus* (€13-19) change weekly, but the restaurant's specialty is créole fish (€10-13). Open Tu-F noon-2pm and 7:30-11pm, Sa and M 7:30pm-11pm; closed Su. MC/V. ❸

Le Bourbonnoux, 44 rue Bourbonneux (☎02 48 24 14 76). This stately restaurant serves rotating regional gourmet *menus* (€12-28) on a charming timbered street. Open M-Th noon-2pm and 7:30-9:45pm, Sa 7:30-9:45pm, Su noon-2pm. MC/V. ❹

⌖ SIGHTS

▧ **CATHÉDRALE ST-ETIENNE.** Built in the 13th century, St-Etienne is a magnificent example of the ornate French Gothic style, comparable to Paris's Notre Dame. Stunning stained-glass windows illuminate the marble interior with red and blue tones. The church is free, though tickets are required to visit the simple cathedral crypt and climb St-Etienne's northern tower for its splendid view of the city. *(Cathedral open daily Apr.-Sept. 8:30am-7:15pm; Oct.-Mar. 9am-5:45pm. Closed to tourists Su morning. Crypt and towers open May to mid-June daily 9:30am-12:15pm and 2-6pm; July-Aug. 9:30am-6pm; Sept.-Apr. 9:30am-12:15pm and 2-5:15pm. €5.50, students €3.50. Mass June-Aug. M-F 6:30pm; Sept.-May M 6:30pm and F 9am. Grand Mass Su 11am.)*

PALAIS JACQUES-CŒUR. This mansion was commissioned in 1443 by Jacques Cœur, finance minister to Charles VII. His palace was intended to flaunt his personal fortune to his high society guests, but he was imprisoned for embezzlement in 1451, years before its completion. The palace now lies unfurnished, but exquisite carved mantelpieces, gargoyles, and a heavily decorated chapel remain. *(10bis rue Jacques-Cœur. ☎02 48 24 06 87. Visit by guided French tour only. Open daily July-Aug. 9:30am-5:45pm, tours every 45min.; Sept.-Apr. 9:45am-4:15pm, tours every hr.; May-June 9:45am-5:15pm, tours every hr. English text available. €6.10, ages 18-24 €4.10, under 18 free.)*

MUSEUMS. Bourges has several small, free museums with regionally focused exhibits. The **Musée des Meilleurs Ouvriers de France,** in the Hôtel de Ville, is

ON THE MENU

DUCK, DUCK, GOOSE

Périgord prides itself on its *cuisine du canard* and the excellence of its foie gras, and with good reason: it all tastes delicious. The duck and the goose are spread on every menu from Périgueux to Cahors. What follows is a quick cheat sheet on the many ways you might be served duck or goose.

The bird can be bought whole at *marchés au gras,* but popular cuts are commonly served at restaurants. The most sought-after is the *magret,* duck or goose breast, which can be served grilled, sliced, and covered in a pepper sauce with delicious sautéed potatoes, or *pommes sarladaises. Confit,* cooked thighs and wings preserved in fat, can be bought at any duck gourmet shop in the region, though they are also easy to make and store at home. They are often served sautéed in garlic. *Mique* is a traditional dumpling soup with duck stock.

The delicacy of the region, though, is foie gras, a gourmand's dream come true. As part of an age-old method, foie gras, fattened goose or duck liver, is produced by force-feeding ducks a few weeks before they are sent to the butcher's block. The prized treat is often served in a *terrine de* foie gras, marinated in liqueur and baked slowly, or lightly fried. Poultry lovers rejoice—and give those chicken-weary tastebuds a rest.

perhaps the most unique. Each year the French government bestows a medal of honor, the Meilleur Ouvrier, on a select number of artists and workers who produce exceptional work in fields ranging from hairstyling to cuisine to leatherwork. The museum highlights recent winners within a particular craft. The focus for 2004 is basketry. *(Pl. Etienne Dolet. ☎02 48 57 82 45. Open July-Aug. daily 10am-6pm; Sept.-June Tu-Sa 10am-noon and 2-6pm.)* The **Musée Estève** displays the colorful modern paintings and drawings by the local contemporary artist of the same name. *(13 rue Edouard Branly. ☎02 48 24 75 38. Open M and W-Sa 10am-noon and 2-6pm, Su 2-6pm. English explanations.)* The **Musée du Berry** showcases prehistoric, Gallo-Roman, and medieval artifacts excavated from the region. *(4 rue des Arènes. ☎02 48 57 81 15. Open M and W-Sa 10am-noon and 2-6pm, Su 2-6pm.)*

OUTDOORS. The **Jardin de l'Archevêché,** behind the cathedral, has rows of perfectly manicured flower beds, rose bushes, and cone-shaped trees. *(Open daily June-July 8am-10pm; May and Aug. 8am-9pm; Mar. 8am-7pm; Apr. and Sept. 8am-8pm; Oct.-Feb. 8am-6pm.)* The **Jardin des Près-Fichaux,** off bd. de la République, adds a beautiful river to a similar scene. Stroll past Roman ramparts and back gardens on the **Promenade des Remparts,** between rue Bourbonnoux and rue Molière. The dirt pathway along the Marais is supremely tranquil, passing some of Bourges's rural homes.

🎵 🎭 ENTERTAINMENT & FESTIVALS

Bars and cafés pepper the *vieille ville,* but the nightlife is fairly subdued. Crowds of locals gather nightly at **Pub Dublin,** 108 rue d'Auron (☎02 48 26 38 33), for pool and beer from €3 a bottle. Electronic and 80s music sets the scene at **L'interdit,** 5 rue Calvin, a small, social club frequented mainly, though not exclusively by gay men. Knock or buzz to be let in through the locked door. (☎02 48 65 90 57. Open W-Su 5pm-2am.) At **Le Wake Up,** 147 chemin de Villeneuve, a live DJ spins techno and pop rock for teens and early 20-somethings. Play laser tag in the 500m maze of ramps and walls. (☎02 48 67 90 46; www.wake-up-bar.com. Open daily 4pm-1am.)

End the evening with **Les Nuits Lumière de Bourges,** a lovely self-guided tour of Bourges. This tour begins with music and a slide-show on local history, then follows a predetermined route along streets illuminated by blue lampposts. The major monuments are playfully illuminated in different colors for a fantastic nighttime effect. Tours start at the Jardin de l'Archevêché. (June-Oct. Free.)

Over 200,000 ears perk up in April for the **Festival Printemps de Bourges.** Most tickets cost €7-28, but some informal folk, jazz, classical, and rock concerts are free. (Contact the Association Printemps de Bourges at ☎02 48 70 61 11.) Late June to late September brings **Un Eté à Bourges,** a nightly blend of classical and rock concerts and theater. (Tickets €7.50-14, most events free.)

ROUTE JACQUES CŒUR

Jacques may have left his *cœur* in Bourges, but his ego spilled far into the surrounding countryside. The Route Jacques Cœur is a string of 17 châteaux (with a 12th-century abbey thrown in), from La Buissière in the north to Culan in the south. Less ostentatious than those of the Loire, these castles see much less tourism. Many are still inhabited by the families who made them famous and now often delight in giving personal tours. Most of the châteaux in this section can be seen only by tour; the guide often doubles as ticket seller. Those who arrive while a tour is in progress will have to wait at the ticket booth until the tour guide returns. Written English explanations are usually available, although tours in English are not.

Châteaux are relaxing daytrips, but most can be reached only by car or bike. Fortunately, the routes are usually well marked. Arrange lodging in advance. The tourist offices in Bourges (p. 726) and St-Amand-Montrond (see following) have free English maps of the route and info on excursions. Although *Let's Go* specifically lists several fabulous châteaux here, this area is known for its hidden treasures; this list should be considered simply a starting point for further exploration.

ST-AMAND-MONTROND

Forty-five kilometers south of Bourges, St-Amand-Montrond (pop. 12,000) is a good starting point for an exploration of the southern stretch of the route. Though the surrounding châteaux and hectares of hikeable forest are the real draw, the town too deserves some attention. A walking tour organized by the tourist office takes visitors past the city's two medieval churches, **Paroisse de St-Amand** and **Eglise St-Roche.** The ruins of the ancient **Forteresse de Montrond** can be seen from afar, or up close by reservation. (Call ☎02 48 96 79 64 to schedule a visit.) To get to St-Amand, take the **train** from Bourges (45min.-1¾hr.; M-Sa 6 per day, Su 3 per day; €8.40). From St-Amand, it's a long walk (2hr.) or a short bike ride to each of the nearby châteaux. The municipal campground rents **bikes.** To reach the campground from the train station, turn right off of av. Jean Jaurès onto rue Tissier and follow its continuation, Chemin du Près des Joncs. The campgrounds will be to the left. (☎02 48 96 09 36. Open M-Sa 9am-noon and 2-7pm. Bikes €10 per day.) The **tourist office,** pl. de la République, sells maps indicating sights within the city and environs (€1). From the train station, follow av. de la Gare and its continuation, av. Jean Jaurès, which becomes rue Henri Barbusse, to the town center. After 20min., the road runs into pl. de la République; the tourist office is on the left. (☎02 48 96 16 86; fax 02 48 96 46 64. Open M-Sa 9am-noon and 2-6:45pm.)

CHÂTEAU DE MEILLANT

A beautiful 8km bike ride from St-Amand through the **Fôret de Meillant** leads to the foot of this imposing, heavily-spired Renaissance building. In the 15th century, it was purchased by the Amboise family, who imported Italian architects, sculptors, and decorators. Its ornate stone carvings are especially visible on the **Tour du Lion,** the upper part of which was designed by Leonardo da Vinci. Next to the château, a small building contains surprisingly intricate miniature representations of life from the Middle Ages to the 18th century. To get to Meillant from **St-Amand,** take rue Nationale north to the D10. (☎02 48 63 32 05. Open Apr.-Oct. 9-11:45am and 2-6:45pm; Feb.-Mar. and Nov. 9-11:45am and 2-5:30pm. Visits by French guided tour only; English info available. Château and gardens €7, students €4, ages 5-15 €3.)

ABBAYE DE NOIRLAC

Just 4km west of St-Amand-Montrond, the **Abbaye de Noirlac** sits peacefully next to a field of grazing cows. The typically Cistercian abbey has spacious rooms, undecorated arches, and geometric stained-glass windows. Most of the monks' **chapter house** dates from the original 12th-century construction. The abbey hosts annual exhibits on regional arts and specialties; 2004 brings an exhibit on wine-making.

During the summer, the popular **L'Eté de Noirlac** fills the abbey's space with an excellent selection of live jazz and classical music. (☎08 10 02 01 00; www.festivaldenoirlac.com.) To get there from nearby St-Amand, take rue Henri Barbusse to the rue 14 Juillet. After crossing the river, turn left and follow the signs to N144 direction Bourges. (☎02 48 62 01 01. Open July-Aug. daily 9:45am-6:30pm; Apr.-June and Sept. 9:45am-noon and 1:45-6:30pm; Oct.-Mar. 9:45am-noon and 1:45-5pm; Oct.-Jan. Su-M and W-Sa. Ticket office shuts 1hr. before closing. Self-guided tours optional. French tours every hr. starting 10am; July-Aug. no tours noon-1:45pm. English explanations available; call ahead for a tour in English. €5.50, students €4, under 16 €3.)

LA VERRERIE

The 15th-century La Verrerie, set on a gorgeous lake in the Ivoy forest 45km north of Bourges, is one of the most elegant and popular châteaux on the Route. To get to La Verrerie from Bourges, take N940 (dir: Montargis). At La Chapelle, turn right toward Auxerre on rte. 926. After 10km, signs for La Verrerie will appear. Eighteenth-century Beauvais tapestries and hand-carved 16th- and 17th-century tables create an elegant interior. (☎02 48 81 51 60; www.chateaux-france.com/~verrerie.fr. Open June-Aug. daily 9am-6pm; Apr.-May and Oct to mid-Nov. Su-M and W-Sa 10am-6pm. €7, students €5, under 7 free.) Those willing to shell out the money can spend a night in the château for €150-350. Call ahead for reservations. For significantly less, **La Maison d'Héléne ❺**, a lovely restaurant next to the château, serves regional *menus* (€22-36) and a special *carte blanche* (€40), where the chef creates innovative, one-of-a-kind meals. (☎02 48 81 51 60. Open Th-Tu noon-2pm and 7:30-10pm. MC/V.)

MENETOU-SALON & MAUPAS

A bit closer to Bourges and easy to reach by bike, Maupas and Menetou-Salon combine to make the perfect daytrip. Begin with **Menetou-Salon,** 20km north of Bourges. Jacques bought the estate in 1448, but his subsequent imprisonment and the Revolution left the castle in ruins until the 19th century, when the Prince of Arenburg decided to complete it. Though the current prince lives in New York and only visits his hunting lodge four times a year, his personal touches make Menetou a treat. A guided tour unveils the antique splendor of the home with its 297 windows, 24 chimneys, and multiple secret bathrooms. To get to Menetou-Salon from Bourges, take D940 north to D11 and follow the signs to Menetou-Salon. (Estate ☎02 48 64 08 61. Open June Sa-Su 10am-6pm; July-Sept. daily 10am-6pm. Wine tastings available. €8.50, students €4.)

To continue to **Maupas,** follow the signs to Parassy and Morogues. The château is on the left, about 1km before Morogues. Look for the white iron gates tucked away on the curbside. This 13th-century castle is decorated with antique furniture and *faïences* collected by Antoine Agard, whose family has lived there since 1686. The gardens are kept perfectly manicured in the shape of the fleur-de-lys. A 45min. French tour leads through the rooms of the Comte de Chambord, the last legitimate Bourbon pretender to the French throne. (Estate ☎02 48 64 41 71. English translations available. Open mid-July to mid-Sept. daily 10am-noon and 2-7pm; Easter to mid-July and mid-Sept. to mid-Oct. M-Sa 2-7pm, Su and holidays 10am-noon and 2-7pm. €6.50, students €4.50, ages 7-15 €4.)

LIMOGES

For centuries, Limoges (pop. 240,000) has manufactured porcelain and enamel for the French upper class. The trade and its proceeds have given Limoges a graceful beauty. Traces of the city's craft can be seen on the porcelain mosaic fountains, in the small artisan boutiques, and in the intricate carvings on the Gothic cathedral.

▐ TRANSPORTATION

Trains: Gare des Bénédictins (☎05 55 11 11 88), pl. Maison-Dieu, off av. de Gaulle, has been restored to its 1920s art nouveau splendor. Info office open daily 5:15am-11pm. To: **Bordeaux** (3hr., 7 per day, €25.70); **Brive** (1hr., 15 per day, €13.30); **Lyon** (6hr., 1:13am and 1:13pm, €40); **Paris** (3-4hr., 5 per day, €39); **Poitiers** (2hr., 3 per day, €17.70); **Toulouse** (3½hr., 5 per day, €33.10).

Buses: (☎05 55 04 91 95) in the train station. **Jet Tours,** 3 rue Jean Jaurès (☎05 55 32 47 48), and **Bernis Tourisme,** 24 rue de la République (☎05 55 34 30 50), run buses to locations outside the city.

Local Buses: TCL (☎05 55 32 46 46) runs around the city. Info office at 10 pl. Léon Betoulle, across from town hall. Open M 1:30-6pm, Tu-F 8:30am-12:30pm and 1:30-6pm, Sa 8:30am-12:30pm. Ticket €1, *carnet* of 10 €8.50. Tickets available on board.

Taxis: Taxis Limoges (☎05 55 37 81 81 or 05 55 38 38 38) 24hr.

Car Rental: Europcar (☎05 55 04 13 25), in the train station. Open M-Sa 8am-noon and 2-7pm. **Avis** (☎05 55 79 78 25; www.avis.com) is also in the train station. Open M-F 9:45am-1:30pm and 4-6:30pm, Sa 9:45am-1:30pm and 4-6pm.

ORIENTATION & PRACTICAL INFORMATION

Limoges was originally separated by medieval fortifications into two villages: le Cité and le Château. Today, divided only by one city block, the two villages have become the main commercial and tourist sectors of the city. The Cité, surrounding the Cathédrale St-Etienne along the Vienne river, holds the municipal museum and gardens, while restaurants and small porcelain shops fill le Château.

DORDOGNE

Tourist Office: 12 bd. de Fleurus (☎05 55 34 46 87; www.tourismelimoges.com), near pl. Wilson. From the train station, walk left down av. du Général de Gaulle. Cut across pl. Jourdan onto bd. de Fleurus. English-speaking staff has maps and lists of accommodations. **Currency exchange** €6. Themed **walking tours** July-Aug. Tours in English Tu 3:30pm; 1½hr.; €5, children €2. Office open mid-June to mid-Sept. M-Sa 9am-7pm, Su 10am-6pm; mid-Sept. to mid-June M-Sa 9am-noon and 2-7pm.

Money: Banque de France, 8 bd. Carnot (☎05 55 11 53 00). **Exchange desk** open M-F 8:45am-noon. No commission and good rates.

Laundromat: Le Forum des Lavendières, 14 rue des Charseix. Open daily 8am-9pm. **Laverie,** 31 rue de François Chinieux. Open daily 7am-9pm.

Police: 84 av. Emile Labussière (☎05 55 14 30 00 or 05 55 04 50 50).

Hospital: 2 av. Martin Luther King (☎05 55 05 61 23).

SOS Medecin: (☎08 03 06 70 00).

Poison Control: (☎05 56 96 40 80).

Internet: Free at **Bibliothèque Francophone Multimédia de Limoges,** 2 rue L. Longe-queue (☎05 55 45 96 00), beyond the Hôtel de Ville, but long lines. Open W and Sa 10am-1pm and 2-6pm. **Net Center,** 5 bd. Victor Hugo (☎05 55 10 93 61). €3 per hr. Open July-Aug. M-Sa 9:30am-2am, Su 2pm-2am; Sept.-June M-Sa 7:30am-2am.

Post Office: av. Garibaldi near av. de la Libération. **Currency exchange** with no commission. Open M 2-7pm, Tu-Sa 10am-7pm. **Postal code:** 87000.

ACCOMMODATIONS

Hôtel de Paris, 5 cours Vergnaud (☎05 55 77 56 96). From the train station, walk up av. du Gal. de Gaulle about 200 ft. and veer right onto cours Bugeaud, then right again onto cours Vergnaud. Recently renovated, most of the large rooms have tall windows, clean bathrooms, and a charming Victorian air. Breakfast €3.80. 1 single with no shower €23; singles and doubles with shower and toilet €31-47; triples €56. MC/V. ❷

Foyer des Jeunes Travailleurs, 20 rue Encombe Vineuse (☎05 55 77 63 97; fjt.acceuil-2000@wanadoo.fr). From the train station, descend the stairs to the right, then cut across the grass to the street, curving slightly to the right. Rue Théodore Bac is across the street on the left. Walk to pl. Carnot, turn left onto av. Adrien Tarrade, then left onto rue Encombe Vineuse. (15min.) Simple singles and doubles with sinks. Communal TV room, kitchen, and elevator. Breakfast included. Reception 24hr. Open July-Aug., and the rest of the year if there is room. Singles €14; doubles €20. ❶

Hôtel de la Paix, 25 pl. Jourdan (☎05 55 34 36 00; fax 05 55 32 37 06). Walk left down av. Général de Gaulle away from the train station. The hotel is on the far side of pl. Jourdan. Phonographs create a 1920s feel. Breakfast €5. Single with shower €35; singles and doubles with shower and toilet €45-57. AmEx/MC/V. ❸

Camping Municipal D'Uzurat, 40 av. d'Uzurat (☎05 55 38 49 43; fax 05 55 37 32 78). From the train station, take bus #20 (dir: Beaubreuil; M-Sa 6am-8:30pm) to L. Armand. On Sundays, bus #2 (dir: Beaubreuil) to Uzurat. By foot, take av. Général Leclerc from pl. Carnot and follow signs to Uzurat. (1hr.) Walk down av. d'Uzurat until reaching the campground. 5km north of Limoges, beside Lake Uzurat, this is the closest site. Access to tennis courts, mini-golf, and hiking trails. 2 people and tent €9.90, with caravan €11.90; extra person €2.75, child €1.70. Electricity €3.20. ❶

🍴 FOOD

Perhaps the best option for hungry visitors, the stalls of the central Les Halles **indoor market,** facing pl. de la Motte, overflow with fresh cheeses, produce, meat, fish, and baked goods. (Open daily 8am-noon, fewer stalls open on Su.) A larger market (Sa mornings) brightens pl. Carnot. A **Monoprix** supermarket is at 11 pl. de la République. (Open M-Sa 8:30am-8pm.) A huge **Champion** is on av. Garibaldi in the St-Martial shopping mall on the north side of town. (Open M-F 8am-8pm, Sa 9am-8pm.) The most interesting restaurants are well-hidden. Among them, 🖼**Au Paradis du Jus de Fruit Naturel ❶,** 5 rue Jules Guesde, serves excellent fresh juices (€2.60-5.20) with playful straws. The friendly owner suggests the best fruit combinations. (☎05 55 11 98 46. Open M-Sa 10am-7:30pm.) **Paul ❶,** on the corner of rue St-Martial and rue Jean Jaurès, is an excellent bakery with a range of breads, sandwiches (€3-5), and pastries. (☎05 55 34 60 82. Open M-Sa 7am-8pm.) Restaurant by day and busy bar by night, **La Bibliothèque ❸,** 7 rue Turgot, lives up to its name with chic mahogany stools, candelabra chandeliers, and shelf after shelf of leatherbound books. (☎05 55 11 00 47. Pastas, salads, and entrées €8-17. Open daily 11am-2am. MC/V).

Restaurants around the medieval rue de la Boucherie offer more gourmet dining. **L'Amphytron ❸,** 26 rue de la Boucherie, serves traditional French food in a converted 13th-century home. (☎05 55 32 36 39. *Menus* from €16. Open M and Sa 7-10:30pm, Tu-F noon-2pm and 7-10:30pm.) For a cheaper meal, look to **rue Haute-Cité,** near the cathedral, for *crêperies, brasseries,* and even an Indian restaurant.

👁 SIGHTS

MUSÉE NATIONAL ADRIEN DUBOUCHE. This beautiful national museum houses the largest ceramics collection in Europe, spanning centuries. An excellent video presentation traces modern porcelain production from clay to gilded decoration. The large Chinese plate with a dragon in its center, dating from 1345, is one of the most valuable pieces of china in the world. *(8bis pl. Winston Churchill. ☎05 55 33 08 50; www.musee-adriendubouche.fr. Open Su-M and W-Sa July-Aug. 10am-5:45pm; Sept.-June 10am-12:30pm and 2-5:45pm. €4, ages 18-25 and Su €2.60; 1st Su of the month and under 18 free.)*

MUSÉE MUNICIPAL DE L'EVÊCHÉ. Also known as the Musée de l'Email (enamel), this 18th-century bishop's palace is filled with the city's impressive collections of enameled art dating from the 12th century. The museum also has a small collection of Egyptian art and 19th-century paintings, including five works

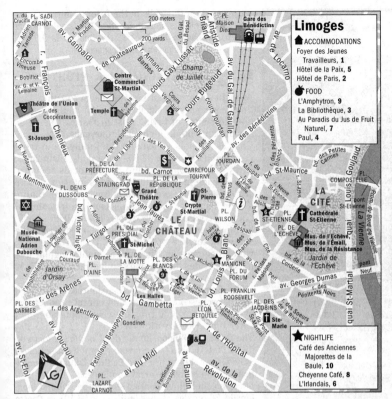

by Auguste Renoir, born in Limoges in 1841. *(Next to the cathedral in la Cité. ☎05 55 34 44 09 or 05 55 45 61 75. Open July to mid-Sept. daily 10-11:45am and 2-6pm; June Su-M and W-Sa 10-11:45am and 2-6pm; Oct.-May Su-M and W-Sa 10-11:45am and 2-5pm. Free.)*

EVÊCHÉ BOTANICAL GARDENS. Surrounding the cathedral, the gardens are a gorgeous oasis on the banks of the Vienne. *(☎05 55 45 62 67. Tours by appointment.)*

OTHER SIGHTS. This beautiful Gothic **Cathédrale St-Etienne,** built on the site of a Roman temple, took over 600 years to complete. *(Pl. St-Etienne. Ask the tourist office for directions. Free French tours M-Sa 11am. Open M-Sa 10am-noon and 2-6pm, Su 2:30-6:30pm.)* For a slice of life as a butcher, visit the **Maison Traditionelle de la Boucherie,** 36 rue de la Boucherie. Guides lead tours through a house in French and broken English. *(☎05 55 34 46 87. Open July-Sept. daily 9:30am-noon and 2:30-7pm. Free.)* Across the street, the 15th-century **Chapel St-Aurelien** still lights candles to honor the patron saint of butchers. Limoges's famous ceramics decorate several remarkable structures, including Les Halles, the nearby Pavilion de Verdurier, and the fountain in front of the *mairie.* To learn more about porcelain production, the **Manufacture Bernardaud** offers tours of the factory. *(27 av. Albert Thomas. ☎05 55 10 55 91. Tours June-Sept. daily 9-11am and 1-4pm; Oct.-May by reservation only. €4.)* Another facet of the ceramics tradition thrives at **Atelier Mosaïque,** 17 rue Montmailler, one of the hidden treasures of Limoges. Here, Mr. Soubeyrand de St-Exupery makes and sells delicate mosaics. Mosaics-in-progress surround his work area and finished

THE LOCAL STORY

MOSAICS

The **Atelier Mosaique**, a tiny workshop with the feel of a retiree's basement, is a world away from the businesslike Bernadaud factory nearby. M. Soubeyrand de Saint-Exupery was putting the final touches on a small mosaic when Let's Go interrupted to ask a few questions.

Q: How do you make a mosaic?
A: Ah, you should enroll in one of my classes [laughs]. We use the same technique of *kaolin* enamel on tiles as they do to make the famous Limoges porcelain. Once I have made several different types of tiles, I cut them into smaller pieces and fit them together on a base with cement, according to a design I've planned in advance.

Q: How are your mosaics different from traditional mosaics?
A: The most well-known mosaics come from ancient Rome, Greece, Pompeii, and North Africa. Many have religious themes with gods and that sort of thing, while others are geometrical, for decorating pools and *hamams*. I learned my art in Italy and the Maghreb, so they've influenced my technique.

Q: Why did you come to Limoges?
A: It was destiny. Well, more specifically, it's famous for being the land of porcelain, for the *arts de feu*. It is, in some ways, the natural extension of my mosaics to incorporate other kinds of influences. Mosaic is an art of assemblage. I combine different methods with different styles.

projects adorn the walls in the form of mirrors, jewelry boxes, clocks, and more. See **The Local Story**, at left, for more. (☎05 55 77 73 05. *Open M-Sa 9:30am-10:30pm. 2-week seminars offered continuously.*)

🎵 🎭 ENTERTAINMENT & NIGHTLIFE

At night the streets of Limoges seem to empty out, though a handful of small but popular bars and clubs dot the center of town. Most *brasseries* serve as social hangouts in night. The **Cheyenne Café**, 4 rue Charles-Michels, is usually the loudest and most crowded. (☎05 55 32 32 62. Open daily 10am-2am.) Artsy older people and hip, young locals socialize over French music in the spacious interior of **Café des Anciennes Majorettes de la Baule**, 27 rue Haute-Vienne. Paintings by local artists and shelves of used books decorate the walls. (Open Tu-Th 10am-1am, F-Sa 10pm-2am.) Communal picnic tables spill onto the sidewalk terrace of **L'Irlandais**, 2 rue Haute-Cité, which becomes an Irish pub at night. Regular live music provides the evening's soundtrack. (☎05 55 32 46 47. Open daily 11am-2am.)

The **Grand Théâtre**, 48 rue Jean Jaurès, presents 60 ballet, orchestral, operatic, and choral productions every season, which runs between September and early June. (Reservations ☎05 55 34 12 12. €5-35.) The **Théâtre de l'Union**, 20 rue des Coopérateurs (☎05 55 79 90 00), also has a season from September to May. On weekdays, the five **Centres Culturels Municipaux** put on a diverse array of concerts, theater productions, and films; contact the **Centre Culturel Jean-Moulin**, 76 rue des Sagnes (☎05 55 35 04 10), or **Centre Culturel Jean Gagnant**, 7 av. Jean Gagnant (☎05 55 34 45 49), for more info.

🎉 FESTIVALS

The **Fête de St-Jean**, also known as the **Fête des Ponts**, held at the end of June every year, brings diving, fireworks, water shows, dancing, and various musical performances. The popular **Festival Urb'Aka** (info ☎05 55 45 63 85) heats up the last three days in June with nightly fireworks and concerts. At the end of September, the **Festival International des Théâtres Francophones** features 15,000 French Canadians, French-speaking Africans, and francophones from all over the world. (☎05 55 10 90 10; www.lesfrancophonies.com.)

During the unique street banquet **La Frairie des Petits Ventres** (Festival of Small Stomachs), on the third Friday of October, residents defy the gala's modest title by consuming meat and regional gourmet cuisine in unheard-of quantities.

NEAR LIMOGES: ORADOUR-SUR-GLANE

On June 10, 1944, in a horrible act of brutality, Nazi SS troops massacred all the inhabitants of the farming village **Oradour-sur-Glane**, without warning or provocation, in their relentless quest to rid the countryside of resistors. The Nazis entered at two in the afternoon and corralled the women and children into the church and the men into six barns. At four, a shot was fired, ordering the troops to begin the massacre. The women and children in the church were burned alive; the men were shot, then burned. By seven o'clock, 642 people, including 205 children, had been slaughtered. Most of the SS troops participating in the attack were tried in 1953, found guilty, and then immediately freed as the result of a general amnesty by the French government. Heinz Barth, commander of the unit, is currently serving a life sentence in a German jail. Plaques with heartbreaking messages and pictures adorn two glass tombs that contain the bones and ashes of the dead. The town remains in disturbingly untouched ruins. Train wires dangle from slanting poles and 50-year-old skeletons of cars rust next to crumbling walls. Visitors can walk freely along the main thoroughfare and peer into remnants of each home. Signs indicate the name and profession of each former resident. A small memorial between the cemetery and town displays bicycles, toys, and watches that were all stopped at the same moment by the heat of the fire. Access to the town is gained through, **Le Centre de la Mémoire,** an incredible museum that places the massacre in the context of the Nazi regime with artifacts, timelines, and an informative film, all with English labels. (☎ 05 55 43 04 30. Museum and town open daily July-Aug. 9am-8pm; Sept.-Oct. and Mar.-Apr. 9am-6pm; Nov. to mid-Dec. and Feb. 9am-5pm; May-June 9am-7pm. Museum €6, students and children €4. Free entry to town.)

Not without hesitation, a new Oradour (pop. 2000) has been built next to its obliterated precursor. **Equival** runs a daily **bus** from Limoges (train station, pl. Carmes, or pl. Winston Churchill) to the Centre de la Mémoire. (30min., 4 per day, €3). Schedules are available at the tourist office and the train station.

PÉRIGORD

PÉRIGUEUX

High above the Isle River, the towering steeple and five massive cupolas of the Cathédrale St-Front dominate the skyline of the city of Périgueux (pop. 65,000). The cobblestone town center is rather quiet during the afternoon, but in the evening Périgueux's youth pack the city's bars and clubs. Rich with tradition and gourmet cuisine, the lovely old quarters of Périgueux have preserved significant architecture from the city's past, which goes back to Gallo-Roman times. Travelers with cars might consider daytripping to the caves of Périgord from here rather than from Les Eyzies.

▣ TRANSPORTATION

Trains: rue Denis Papin. Info office open M 5:15am-8:30pm, Tu-Th 5:30am-8pm, F 5:40am-10:15pm, Sa-Su 6am-10:30pm. To: **Bordeaux** (1½hr., 12 per day, €16.30); **Brive** (1hr., 3 per day, €10.30); **Limoges** (1-1½hr., 8 per day, €13.30); **Lyon** (6-8hr., 2 per day, €46.10); **Paris** (4-6hr., 12 per day, €56.60) via Limoges; **Sarlat** (1½hr., 5 per day, €12); **Toulouse** (4hr., 8 per day, €32.60) via Agen.

Buses: in the midst of reorganization, Périgueux's bus service does not have a central office. Buses depart from various stops around town. To **Angoulême** (1½hr.; M-Sa 3 per day, Su 1 per day; €14.10) and **Sarlat** (1½hr., F-Sa 2 per day, €7.70).

Taxis: Taxi Périgueux, pl. Bugeaud (☎05 53 09 09 09). 24hr.

Car Rental: Avis, 18 rue du Président Wilson (☎05 53 53 39 02). Open M-F 8am-noon and 2-7pm, Sa 8am-noon and 2-6pm. MC/V. **Hertz,** 20 cours Michel Montaigne (☎05 53 53 88), a few blocks from pl. Général de Gaulle. Open M-F 8am-noon and 2-7pm, Sa 8am-noon and 2-6pm. AmEx/DC/MC/V.

■🗗 ORIENTATION & PRACTICAL INFORMATION

To reach the *vieille ville* and tourist office from the train station, turn right onto rue Denis Papin and bear left onto rue des Mobiles-de-Coulmiers, which becomes rue du Président Wilson. Take the right just after the Monoprix and walk one block. The **tourist office** is on the left, beside the stone **Mataguerre Tower.** (15min.)

Tourist Office: 26 pl. Francheville (☎05 53 53 10 63; www.ville-perigueux.fr). Free map; walking, *Petit Train,* and bike tours. Two walking tours in French visit either Gallo-Roman sights or Renaissance monuments. Tours tend to be long, but provide entry to otherwise inaccessible buildings. Tours M-Sa 2:30pm and M 9pm. €4.60, students €3.50. Open M-Sa 9am-1pm and 2-6pm. Alternatively, **Espace Tourisme Périgord,** 25 rue du Président Wilson (☎05 53 35 50 24), has excellent free topographic maps, detailed info on travel in Périgord, and lists of campgrounds, *gîtes,* and *chambres d'hôte.* Open M and F 9am-12:30pm and 1:30-5pm, Tu-Th 9am-12:30pm and 1:30-5:15pm.

Money: Banque Tarneaud, 17 rue du Président Wilson (☎05 53 02 46 02) has **currency exchange.** Open M-F 8:30am-noon and 2-6pm. **Societé Général,** 16 cours Michel Montaigne (☎05 53 02 57 00), offers currency exchange at great rates. Open M-F 8:30am-12:15pm and 1:30-5pm.

English Bookstore: Librairie des Livres et Nous, 34 rue du Président Wilson (☎05 53 53 43 02). Open Tu-Sa 9am-12:30pm and 2-7pm. Small collection of the latest paperbacks. MC/V.

Laundromat: Lav'matic, 20 rue Mobiles de Coulmiers, near rond-point Lanxade on the way into town from the train station. Open daily 8am-9pm.

Police: (☎05 53 06 44 44), rue du 4 Septembre, near the post office.

Hospital: Centre Hospitalier, 80 av. Georges Pompidou (☎05 53 07 70 00).

Internet: surf the net in a medieval mansion at **Arena Games,** 11 rue des Farges (☎05 53 53 75 21). Take a sharp left after the tourist office onto rue de la Bride, which becomes rue des Farges. €1 for 15min., €3 per hr. Open M-Th 2pm-midnight, F-Sa 2pm-1am, Su noon-midnight.

Post Office: 1 rue du 4 Septembre (☎05 53 03 61 12); offers **currency exchange.** Open M-F 8am-7pm, Sa 8am-noon. **Poste Restante:** 24017. **Postal code:** 24070.

▐ ACCOMMODATIONS & CAMPING

Hôtel des Voyageurs, 26 rue Denis Papin (☎/fax 05 53 53 17 44), located directly across from the train station. Voyageurs's friendly owner tends to 15 simple, well-worn rooms at great prices. The rooms can be a bit dusty, but they offer privacy for a good value. Reception M-F 7:30am-10pm. Breakfast €3.50. Singles €13; doubles €15, with shower €18. ❶

Les Charentes, 16 rue Denis Papin (☎05 53 53 37 13), facing the train station. Clean, comfortable rooms have a hodge-podge of brightly colored furniture reminiscent of the 1970s. Reserve 1-2 weeks in advance during summer. Restaurant on ground floor serves an extensive organic and vegetarian menu. Breakfast €5. Reception Su-F 7am-10pm. Closed early Nov. and late Dec. to early Jan. Singles with shower €23, with TV €28, with toilet €33. Extra person €4.60. AmEx/MC/V. ❷

DORDOGNE

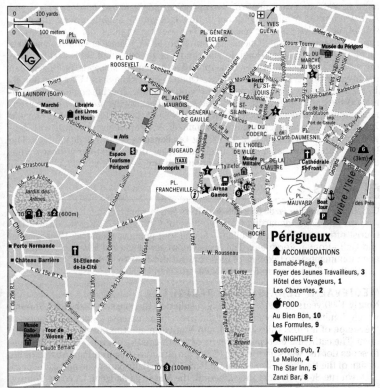

Périgueux

⌂ **ACCOMMODATIONS**

Barnabé-Plage, 6
Foyer des Jeunes Travailleurs, 3
Hôtel des Voyageurs, 1
Les Charentes, 2

🍴 **FOOD**

Au Bien Bon, 10
Les Formules, 9

★ **NIGHTLIFE**

Gordon's Pub, 7
Le Mellon, 4
The Star Inn, 5
Zanzi Bar, 8

DORDOGNE

Foyer des Jeunes Travailleurs Résidence Lakanal, rue des Thermes (☎05 53 06 81 40; fax 05 53 06 81 49). Turn right from the train station onto rue Denis Papin and follow it as it becomes rue Chanzy. Turn left onto av. Cavaignac, then right onto rue Romain. Across the roundabout, take rue Mosaïque until it hits rue de Thermes. Turn right and walk along the train tracks; the hostel is at the end of the street. (25min.) This cramped dormitory in a slightly worn building is conveniently located in the Gallo-Roman section of town. Tiny, clean 2- to 4-bunk dorm rooms with small showers. Reception July-Sept. M-F 9am-6pm, Sa-Su 6:30-11pm; Oct.-June M-F 24hr., Sa-Su 3-5pm. Reserve ahead. Dorms with bedding and breakfast €11.80, with dinner €18.30. ●

Barnabé-Plage, 80 rue des Bains (☎05 53 53 41 45), 1½km away, in Boulazac. From cours Montaigne, take bus #8 (dir: Cité Bel Air, roughly 1 per hr. 7am-7pm, €0.75) to Rue des Bains. It may be faster to walk; from Cathédrale St-Front, head downhill and cross Pont des Barris. Turn left after the bridge onto rue des Prés. The street ends at rue des Bains at the site. (25min.) Riverside site packed in summer. Reception daily 11am-midnight. €2.90 per person, €2.70 per tent, €4.30 per camping car. MC/V. ●

📷 FOOD

The labyrinth of narrow stone streets between cours M. Montaigne and rue Taillefer is lined with regional culinary treasures: foie gras, walnuts, *cèpe* and *girolle* mushrooms, and fruit liqueurs. A stroll down rue Salinière and rue Limogeanne reveals an assortment of *charcuteries, pâtisseries, boulangeries,* and *sandwicheries.* While restaurants in this area can be slightly pricey, the other side of rue Taillefer is more reasonable. For cooking supplies, visit **Marché Plus,** 55 rue du Président Wilson. (Open M-Sa 7am-9pm. MC/V.) There are morning **markets** on pl. du Coderc, pl. de l'Hôtel de Ville, and a larger one on pl. de la Clautre, near the cathedral. (Open W and Sa 8am-1pm.) The behemoth **Monoprix,** pl. Bugeaud in the town center, is impossible to miss. (Open M-Sa 8:30am-8pm.) 🔳**Au Bien Bon ❸,** 15 rue Aubergerie, serves exceptional regional cuisine, specializing in a variety of meat dishes, such as *filet du porc avec sauce bleu.* Try the *menu* with appetizer, main course, and dessert for €14. (☎05 53 09 69 91. Lunch *formule* €10. Open M 7:30-10pm, Tu-Sa noon-2pm and 7:30-10pm. MC/V.) Personalize a *menu* with generous portions for €8.50, €12, or €20 at **Les Formules ❷,** 16 rue des Farges. The herring with potato salad makes a delicious meal, though all their *plats* are wonderful. (☎05 53 03 46 56. Open M-Sa noon-2pm and 7-10:30pm. MC/V.)

🅖 SIGHTS

Gabarre de Périgueux (☎05 53 24 58 80) offers 50min. **boat tours** of the city from mid-June to mid-Sept., departing from the base of Cathédrale St-Front (€6.50). The tourist office provides an excellent walking tour guide to medieval, Renaissance, and Gallo-Roman Périgueux. The only way to get inside the *hôtels particuliers* and monuments is to take one of these tours. (Mid-June to mid-Sept. M-Sa 10:30am and 2:30pm. Tours only in French €4.60, students €3.50.)

MEDIEVAL & RENAISSANCE PÉRIGUEUX

Nearly 1500 years of restoration have resulted in the massive **Cathédrale St-Front,** which dominates the skyline above the river. Five immense Byzantine cupolas in the shape of a cross (like St. Mark's in Venice) make the interior feel light and open. The cathedral incorporates parts of a 10th-century church, and Romanesque frescoes dot the walls. In the late 1800s, the structure inspired Paul Abadie in his design of the Basilique Sacré-Cœur in Paris. (Open daily 8am-noon and 2:30-7pm.)

Down rue St-Front from the cathedral, the **Musée du Périgord,** 22 cours Tourny, is home to one of France's most important collections of prehistoric artifacts, including fossils from Les Eyzies, 2m long mammoth tusks, and an Egyptian mummy whose toes peek out from crusty coverings. There's also a small collection of fine art and regional medieval art. (☎05 53 06 40 70. Open Oct.-Mar. M and W-F 10am-5pm, Sa-Su 1-6pm; Apr.-Sept. M and W-F 10:30am-6:30pm, Sa-Su 1-6pm. €4, students €2, under 18 free.) Walk back to the tourist office to find the crumbling **Tour Mataguerre.** It derives its name from an English captain held in its dungeons for 17 years during the Hundred Years' War.

GALLO-ROMAN PÉRIGUEUX

The few remains of Gallo-Roman Périgueux lie west of the *vieille ville,* down rue de la Cité from pl. Francheville. Particularly impressive is the towering **Tour de Vésone,** built in the first century AD and once part of a huge temple dedicated to *Vésone's* patron god. The tower itself was a *cella,* the center of worship in Roman temples, though now it's little more than a crumbling stone wall. About a quarter of the weighty structure was demolished, supposedly by the last fleeing demons of paganism, although it was more likely dismantled to create the city's defensive wall. (Park grounds open daily Apr.-Sept. 7:30am-9pm; Oct.-Mar. 7:30am-6:30pm.) Next door, the 🔳**Musée Gallo-Romain,** 20 rue du 26*ème* Régiment d'Infanterie, has built an intricate walkway over the excavated ruins of the *Domus de Vésone,* once the lavish home of a wealthy Roman merchant. The museum contains an impressive array of Roman artifacts, murals, and stonework. (☎05 53 53 00 92.

Open July-Aug. daily 10am-7pm; Sept. to mid-Nov., Apr.-June, and Jan. Tu-Su 10am-12:30pm and 2-6pm; mid-Nov. to Dec. and Feb.-Mar. Tu-Su 10am-12:30pm and 2-5:30pm. €5.50, under 12 €3.50. Tours in French July-Aug. daily €2. Audio guide in English €2.) Cross the bridge from the Tour de Vésone and turn left down rue Romaine to reach a cluster of architectural vestiges from the first century through the high Middle Ages. Flowers sprout through the crevices of the **Château Barrière,** a four-story late-Gothic castle. The Romanesque house next door is an example of the use of *spolia*—chunks of ruins incorporated decoratively into new buildings. Both buildings were constructed on the remains of the Roman wall built around the city in AD 275 to defend against the first Norman and barbarian attacks. A fragment of this wall, the **Porte Normande,** is just a few meters away. It is one of the most popular sights in the Roman quarter.

Up rue Romaine, the 11th-century **Eglise St-Etienne-de-la-Cité** was the seat of the bishopric until Calvinist attackers in 1577 destroyed all but the choir and one-third of the nave. Its two impressively wide cupolas are punctuated by small Romanesque windows. (Open M-Sa 8am-7pm.) Barely 40m beyond the church, up rue de l'Ancien Evêché, the crumbling foundations of a **Roman amphitheater** have found new life as a public park, complete with archways and an inviting fountain that becomes a makeshift swimming pool during the summer. (Open daily Apr.-Sept. 7:30am-9pm; Oct.-Mar. 7:30am-6:30pm.)

🎵 🌑 ENTERTAINMENT & FESTIVALS

While the streets may be sleepy, Périgueux's *places* jump with activity. **Place St-Silain** and **place St-Louis** are centers of the city's nightlife with music and outdoor cafés; **place du Marché au Bois** hosts frequent concerts. Bars line the lively cobblestone **rue de la Sagesse.** The sophisticated ◼Le Mellon, 4 rue de la Sagesse, is the coolest place to unwind with a martini. The contemporary lounge also features a cigar bar and upbeat music. (☎05 53 08 53 77. Cocktails €5-6. MC/V.) ◼The Star Inn, 17 rue des Drapeaux, is a classic Irish pub in three large rooms in a restored Renaissance house. (☎05 53 08 56 83. Drinks from €3. Happy hour 8-9pm. Open M-Sa July-Aug. 8pm-2am; Sept-June 8pm-1am.) **Zanzi Bar,** 2 rue Condé, serves jungle-inspired cocktails (from €5) and exotic *tapas* (€6) in an *ambiance tropicale*. Kick things up a notch with their salsa lessons (€5) on Wednesday nights. (☎05 50 50 28 99. Open Tu-Sa June-Aug. 6:30pm-2am; Sept.-May 6:30pm-1am. Salsa class W 8-9:30pm. MC/V.) **Gordon's Pub,** 12 rue Condé, off rue

THE LOCAL STORY

A MIME IS A TERRIBLE THING TO WASTE

Laure Pierre, 26, has been miming ever since she was old enough to walk. Following an unusually lengthy phase of The Terrible Twos, her parents packed her bags and sent her to the prestigious **Ecole Internationale de Mimodrame Marcel Marceau** *in Paris to study the arts of silence, discipline, and finding the way out of an invisible box. Mlle. Pierre currently performs in Périgueux's annual mime festival,* **Mimos.**

Q: How did you become interested in miming?
A: [silence]

Q: What would you say is the relationship between miming and traditional French theater?
A: [silence]

Q: What's the average day like in the life of a mime?
A: [motions incomprehensibly while jumping on one leg]

Q: How has the art of miming evolved since the great age of Marcel Marceau?
A: [scratches toe against ground, clucks, runs in circles with arms flapping]

Q: Who is your greatest influence?
A: [walks into an invisible wall]

Q: Do you get a lot of flack about being a professional mime?
A: [single tear runs down cheek]

Taillefer, is an Irish-style pub with a small terrace and a warm welcome for all. A young, energetic crowd packs the bar late. (☎ 05 53 35 03 74. Beer €2. Open July-Oct. M-F 11am-2am, Sa 2pm-2am; Nov.-June M-F 11am-1am, Sa 2pm-2am. MC/V.)

Macadam Jazz presents free outdoor concerts (July-Aug. Tu). **Son-et-Lumière de Périgueux: La Légende de Saint-Front** illuminates Cathédrale St-Front with an artistic exploration of the area's history. (☎ 05 53 53 18 71. Late July to mid-Aug. W 10:30pm. €13, students €10.) The town quiets down during the first week of August for **Mimos,** the world's leading mime festival. Mime companies from all over the world give phenomenal performances. The big events cost money, but there are free performances and public workshops all over town. (☎ 05 53 53 18 71. Ticketed events €10, students €8.)

LES EYZIES-DE-TAYAC

Les Eyzies-de-Tayac (pop. 900) is the picture-perfect base for travel to the Vézère valley's famous caves (except for Lascaux). A large number of them are less than 20min. from the town center by foot. The beautiful Vézère River next to the town is another way to visit the caves. Reserve a visit weeks in advance, as cave access is limited. With two prestigious museums and the official information center for the region's prehistoric sites, the village is also a good source of information about Neolithic art. The village abounds with prehistoric-themed hotels, duck specialties, and Bergerac wines. The medieval château of the lords of Tayac can be seen from the cliff above the town.

■ ▓ ORIENTATION & PRACTICAL INFORMATION. Trains (☎ 05 53 06 97 22) to: Paris (6-8hr., 3 per day, €46.70); Périgueux (30min., 5 per day, €8.10); Sarlat (1hr.; 3 per day, change at Le Buisson; €9.20). Open M-F 6am-6pm, Sa-Su 10am-6pm. Facing away from the train station, turn right and walk 500m down the village's only street, av. de la Préhistoire, to reach the town center. (5min.) For a **taxi** to the caves, call Taxi Tardieu at ☎ 05 53 06 93 06. The **tourist office,** at pl. de la Mairie, rents **bikes** (€8 per half-day, €14 per day; ID deposit), and offers summer tours to sights within walking distance (€4.50, children €2), lists of caves and *gîtes d'étapes,* **Internet** (€1.60 per 15min.), **accommodations booking** (€1.50) and **currency exchange** at no commission. (☎ 05 53 06 97 05; fax 05 53 06 90 79; www.leseyzies.com. Open July-Aug. M-Sa 9am-7pm, Su 10am-noon and 2-6pm; Apr.-June and Sept. M-Sa 9am-noon and 2-6pm, Su 10am-noon and 2-5pm; Oct.-Mar. M-Sa 9am-noon and 2-6pm.) Other services include: an **ATM** next to the tourist office, **police** in nearby St-Cyprien (☎ 05 53 30 80 00), a **laundromat** at 4 av. de la Préhistoire (open M-Sa 9am-noon and 2-7pm), and a **post office** on av. de la Préhistoire past the tourist office, which provides **currency exchange.** (☎ 05 53 06 94 11. Open M-F 9am-noon and 1:30-4:45pm, Sa 9am-noon.) **Postal code:** 24620.

▐▐ ACCOMMODATIONS & FOOD. Rooms tend to be expensive. The tourist office has a list of private bed and breakfasts in the surrounding area (€25-32 for 1-2 people). Drivers will notice signs along the main roads advertising *fermes* (farms) with camping space (€3-8). Some village homes rent rooms for €23-46 during the summer; look for *chambres* signs, especially on the east end of the town. The Demaison family runs an exceptional ▓**chambre d'hôte ❸,** rte. de Sarlat, 3min. outside town. Six charming rooms are available in their timbered home on the edge of the forest. (☎ 05 53 06 91 43. Breakfast €4.50. Free parking. Reservations required. Singles €25; doubles €35; triples €45-48. Cash only.) In town, try the **Hôtel des Falaises ❸,** av. de la Préhistoire. Spotless rooms have royal blue furnishings and plenty of space. All rooms come with shower, sink, and toilet; larger rooms have a balcony overlooking the garden. The hotel offers more private and homey lodgings in the **annex,** about 100m down the road toward Font-de-Gaume in a large half-timbered building. (☎ 05 53 06 97 35. Breakfast €5. Reception in the bar downstairs 8am-8pm. Doubles €30-35; triples €40. Annex prices same as hotel. MC/V.) For **Camping La Rivière ❶,** rte. de Périgueux, turn left from the tourist office on av. de la Préhistoire. Follow the road for 5min., cross the bridge, and take another left at the gas station. The site offers a snack bar, restaurant, bike rental, laundry, Internet, athletic facilities, kitchen, and a pool. (☎ 05 53 06 97 14; www.campings-dordogne.com/la-riviere. Reception daily 8am-10pm. Open Apr.-Oct. €2.80-4.50 per person; €5-7.20 per site; price varies with season. Electricity €2.80.) Attached to the campsite, a small but luxurious **hotel ❸** inside a 16th-century Périgordian home lets fresh, well-furnished rooms. (Breakfast €4.50. Doubles with shower €30; quads with shower €43. MC/V.)

From April to October, a **market** runs the length of town every Monday 9am-1pm. **Halle des Eyzies,** just past the center of town on rte. de Sarlat, is full of expensive boutiques hawking foie gras, Bergerac wine, and walnut products. Wonderful local art, oils, cookies, and cakes are also for sale here, in addition to every duck, goose, and pork product imaginable. The *gâteau aux noix* and foie gras are not to be missed. (Open mid-June to mid-Sept. daily 9am-noon and 2:30-7:30pm.) A large convenience store, **Relais de Mousquetaires,** by the bridge to Sarlat, sells groceries. (Open M-Tu and Th-F 9am-12:30pm and 3:30-7pm, Su 9am-noon.) Most restaurants in Les Eyzies are expensive, but extremely good. **La Grignotière ❷,** facing the tourist office, serves cheap drinks and sandwiches (€3-4) all day long and a three-course *menu* (€10.80) during mealtimes. The omelettes (€5-8) and salads are particularly delectable. (☎ 05 53 06 91 67. Open daily 7:30am-midnight. MC/V.) **La Milanaise ❸,** av. de la Préhistoire, serves delicious thin-crust pizzas, salads full of *gésiers* and walnuts, and duck plates. Try the inventive Pizza Antilles topped with mango and ham. (☎ 05 53 35 43 97. Salad €3-7, pizza €6-9, *plats* €11, *menus* €10-20. Open for lunch and dinner July-Aug. daily; Mar.-Nov. M and W-Su. MC/V.)

▣ **SIGHTS.** The **Musée L'Abri Pataud** is the site of a prehistoric *abri* (shelter), where reindeer hunters lived over a span of 20,000 years. The museum provides an in-depth explanation of the archeological finds of the region and the types of dwellings built by these early humans. The 18,600-year-old remains of a teenage girl found on the site may represent a transitional link between Neanderthal and Cro-Magnon man. The only way to see the excavation site is through a French tour. (☎ 05 53 06 92 46; pataud@mnhn.fr. Open July-Aug. daily 10am-6pm; Sept.-June Tu-Th and Su 10-11:30am and 2-5pm by reservation. Reserve well in advance. 1hr. visits leave every 30min. English tours for groups of 5 or more by reservation only. €5, ages 6-12 €3.)

The **Musée National de Préhistoire,** in a château overlooking the village, is a generally interesting and periodically dry walk through the prehistoric discoveries in the many caves around Les Eyzies. The remains of a Neanderthal infant lie next to faint stone etchings of bison. Learn how archeologists study these objects and see the actual hearths cavemen used to work with fire. English guide cards are displayed at the entrance of each exhibition room. (☎ 05 53 06 45 45. Open July-Aug. daily 9:30am-6:30pm; Sept.-June M and W-Su 9:30am-12:30pm and 2-5:30pm. Tours 1hr.; 3 per day in French, 1 per day in English at 2pm; €4.50, ages 18-25 €3, under 18 free, 1st Su of the month free.)

SARLAT

Sarlat (pop. 10,500) was a quiet, average hamlet until 1962, when Minister of Culture André Malraux, inspired by the old city's architectural unity and lack of modernization, selected it for a massive restoration project. Three years later, the new

Sarlat emerged—handsomely restored and surprisingly medieval. Since then it has been the setting for films like *Cyrano de Bergerac* and *Manon des Sources*. Flea markets, wall paintings, dancing violinists, and acrobats pack the narrow streets. Sarlat merits a full day's visit, and is the best base from which to explore the Lower Dordogne and Lascaux (p. 746).

▣⊓ TRANSPORTATION & PRACTICAL INFORMATION. Trains (☎ 05 53 59 00 21) rumble from av. de la Gare to Bordeaux (2½hr., 4 per day 6am-7:30pm, €21.40) and Périgueux (3hr., 2 per day M-F 6am and Sa 5:40pm, €13.90) via le Buisson. (Info booths open daily 6am-12:30pm and 1:15-7pm.) CFTA, 15 av. Aristide Briand (☎ 05 53 59 01 48), and Trans-Périgord run **buses** from the train station to Brive (1½hr.; 1 per day July-Aug. Tu, Th, and Sa noon; Sept.-June M-F 6:30am; €6.30) and from pl. Pasteur to Périgueux (1½hr., 2 per day M-F 6am and 12:30pm, €10.20). Sarlat Bus runs **local buses** on two almost identical routes; line A stops at the train station, line B at the roundabout 1 block down rue Dubois. (☎ 05 53 59 01 48. Open M-Sa 8:30am-5pm.) For a **taxi** call ☎ 05 53 59 06 27 or 05 53 59 02 43. (24hr.) **Car rental** is available from Europcar at pl. Tassigny, down the hill from the train station and to the left along av. Thiers walking away from the old city. (☎ 05 53 30 30 40. Open M-F 8am-noon and 2-6:30pm, Sa 8am-noon and 2-6pm. AmEx/MC/V.) To rent **bikes**, try Cum's Bikes, 8 av. de Selves, a block from the youth hostel. (☎ 05 53 53 31 56. Open M-Sa 2-7pm; arrange in advance to return bikes on Su. €8 per half-day, €13 per day.)

For the **tourist office**, off rue Tourny, follow av. de la Gare downhill and turn right onto av. Thiers, which becomes av. Gal. Leclerc, then rue de la République. Bear right on rue Lakanal and left onto rue de la Liberté, which leads to the Cathédrale St-Sacerdos. Next door is the tourist office, in the Ancien Evêché. (15min.) The staff offers **accommodations booking** (€2), **currency exchange** when banks are closed, city **tours**, and an English walking guide. (☎ 05 53 31 45 45; fax 05 53 59 19 44. Open Apr.-Oct. M-Sa 9am-7pm, Su 10am-noon and 2-6pm; Nov.-Mar. M-Sa 9am-noon and 2-7pm. 1-2 **tours** in English weekly Apr.-Sept.; call in advance to arrange. 1-3 tours in French per day. €4, children €2.50.) All banks in Sarlat **exchange currency**, including Crédit Lyonnais, 15 rue de la République. (☎ 05 53 59 20 31. Open Tu-F 8:15am-noon and 1:45-5:15pm, Sa 8:15am-12:15pm.) An **ATM** is opposite the Bishop's Palace on rue Tourny. Other services include: a **laundromat** at 24 av. de Selves (open daily 7am-9pm); **police** at pl. Salvador Allende (☎ 05 53 31 53 17); a **hospital** on rue Jean Leclaire (☎ 05 53 31 75 75); and **Internet** at Le Taverne du Web, 17 rue Gambetta (☎ 05 53 30 80 77; €2.30 for 15min., €5 per hr.). The **post office**, pl. du 14 Juillet, has **currency exchange**. (☎ 05 53 31 73 10. Open M 9am-5:30pm, Tu-F 8:30am-5:30pm, Sa 8:30am-noon.) **Postal code:** 24200.

▮ ACCOMMODATIONS. Sarlat's hotels are expensive, and the hostel is often full in summer. The best option is to book a room at one of the *chambre d'hôtes* (€25-40), close to the city center. The tourist office has a list of *gîtes*, farms, and campgrounds in the surrounding countryside that require a car to get to. The small, laid-back **Auberge de Jeunesse ❶**, 77 av. de Selves, is 40min. from the station, but only 5-10min. from the *vieille ville*. Follow rue de la République until it becomes av. Gambetta; bear left at the fork onto av. de Selves. By bus, walk downhill on rue Dubois and catch line B (dir: Hôpital) to La Pologne. The *auberge* consists of 16 beds in three coed rooms in a large, wooden cabin. There is also a grassy yard for **campers.** Clean bathrooms, a rustic common room, and a stocked kitchen make this a great place to stay. (☎ 05 53 59 47 59 or 05 53 30 21 27. Kitchen access. Reception after 6pm. Reserve ahead. Open mid-Mar. to Nov. Bunks €10 the first night, then €9 per night. Camping €6/€5.) **Hôtel de la Mairie ❹**, 13 pl. de la Liberté, in a lovely, medieval building in the heart of the *centre ville*, offers large, wood-trimmed rooms with clean baths. (☎05 53 59 05 71. Breakfast €5.50. Singles and doubles with shower €35-45; triples €50-65. AmEx/MC/V.) For a quieter night's sleep, the **Hôtel Le Lion D'Or ❹**, 48 av. Gambetta, has refined, spacious rooms, private baths, and high ceilings. (☎05 53 59 00 83. Breakfast €5. Singles €38; doubles and triples €40-46; quad €53. Closed Dec. to mid-Mar. MC/V.) The three-star campground **Le Montant ❶**, 4km from town on D57 toward Bergerac, has hot showers, a bar, laundry, and two pools. (☎05 53 59 18 50 or 05 53 29 45 85; fax 05 53 59 37 73. Open Easter-Sept. Reception daily 9am-8pm. €4.80 per person, €3 per child; €6 per tent, including vehicle. Electricity €2.50.)

🍴 FOOD. Most regional delicacies—foie gras, *confit de canard*, truffles, walnut oil, strawberries, Bergerac wine—can be purchased directly from the farms for lower prices than in town. *Pâtisseries* and *confiseries* sell decorated breads, walnut-and-chocolate tarts, *gâteaux aux noix* (walnut cookies), and chocolate-dipped meringue *boules* the size of grapefruits. A Saturday **market** takes over the city (open 8:30am-6pm); a smaller one fills pl. de la Liberté (W 8:30am-1pm). Follow av. de Selves away from the town center to find the **Champion** supermarket near the hostel on rte. de Montignac (open M-Sa 9am-7:30pm, Su 9am-noon) or stock up at **Petit Casino,** 32 rue de la République (open M-Sa 8am-7:30pm, Su 8am-1pm). The **Auberge des Lys D'Or ❷,** pl. André Malraux, behind the Maison de la Boétie, offers fish or duck specialties in a gourmet atmosphere. Their two-course *formule* (€8), with a *plat* and dessert, is the best deal in town, available until 8pm. Try the *canard aux pêche* for a taste of regional cuisine. (☎05 53 31 24 77. Open daily noon-10:30pm. *Menus* €12 and €17.20. MC/V.) **Le Petit Borie ❸,** 3 rue des Oliviers, hidden in one of the crooked *centre ville* alleyways, crafts delicious, home style favorites like sautéed potatoes and spicy mustard over ham. (☎05 53 31 23 69. Open M-Sa noon-2pm and 7-11pm. *Plats* €7-19, *menus* €11-25. MC/V.)

🎬 SIGHTS. The golden stone buildings of the *vieille ville* are the city's most interesting features, but the landscaped forest and fountains of the **Jardin Public du Plantier,** bd. Henri Arlet, run a close second. Most sights are to the right off rue de la République when entering the town from the station. The 16th-century neo-Gothic **Cathédrale St-Sacerdos,** to the right of the tourist office, was recently renovated. Behind it, the conical **Lanterne des Morts** (Lantern of the Dead) has served as a chapel, charnel-house, election site for city consuls, and gunpowder magazine. Across the street from the bishop's palace, the **Maison de la Boétie,** a tall, gabled house, has carved pilasters and detailed window transoms typical of the Italian Renaissance. The windows are composed of hundreds of tiny glass panels. The building was the birthplace of writer Etienne de la Boétie, a key figure in Renaissance efforts to reconcile Catholics and Protestants.

🎭🎪 ENTERTAINMENT & FESTIVALS. Every weekend, street performers and musicians converge on pl. de la Liberté, crowding cafés with boisterous audiences. Young locals meet in the polished **Le Bataclan,** 31 rue de la République, a glitzy bar and *brasserie* with delicious, inexpensive food. Noisy rock and a carefree crowds spill onto the streets from within. (☎05 53 28 54 34. Drinks €3-5, *plats* €8-9. Open daily 7am-2am. MC/V.) **CinéRex,** av. Thiers, occasionally screens V.O. foreign films. (☎08 92 68 69 24. Foreign films €5.50, French films €7. Cheaper M and W.) During the last two weeks of July and the first week of August, Sarlat hosts the well-attended **Festival des Jeux du Théâtre,** which features open-air performances, comedies, musicals, and panel discussions. (☎05 53 31 10 83; fax 05 53 30 25 31. Tickets €15-21. Students get 20% off with ID.) The second weekend in September brings the flower contests, picnics, and events of the **Fête des Fleurs** to the Jardin Public du Plantier.

DORDOGNE

▶ DAYTRIP FROM SARLAT: CASTELNAUD & LES MILANDES

Castelnaud-la-Chapelle, 10km from Sarlat, snoozes in the shadow of its yellow-stone château, the largest in the region. During the Hundred Years' War, Castelnaud was won and lost seven times. To visit the castle, walk from in the post office parking lot, through the village, following signs for *piétons.* (10min.) The castle houses a 13th- to 17th-century armory and a behemoth catapult. Videos demonstrate the uses of these weapons, while full-scale replicas surround the castle outside. Tour guides share gruesome tales of warfare in the middle ages, and audience members can dress in medieval garb during live demonstrations. (☎ 05 53 31 30 00; www.castelnaud.com. July-Aug. 6 tours in French per day, 2-3 tours in English per day. Call in advance for low season English tours. Demonstrations July-Aug. daily 11:30am-1pm and 2-6pm. Open daily July-Aug. 9am-8pm; Feb.-Apr. and Oct to mid-Nov. 10am-6pm; mid-Nov. to Jan. 2-5pm; Dec. 10am-5pm. Château and museum €6.40, ages 10-17 €3.20, under 10 free; adults €3.20 before 1pm.)

The elegant Renaissance **Château Les Milandes,** 5km from Castelnaud, was built by François de Caumont in 1489 to satisfy his wife, who wanted a more stylish home than the outdated fortress of Castelnaud. Centuries later, cabaret singer Josephine Baker fell in love with the neglected château's pointed roofs and gables, purchased the property, and created a "world village" to house and care for children she had adopted on her international tours. Tours of her homey living space include a museum devoted to her life and times. A falconry show, complete with handlers in medieval garb, takes place 2-4 times per day on the lawns. (☎ 05 53 59 31 21; www.milandes.com. Tours off season only. Falconry show Apr.-Oct.; call for schedule. Open daily July-Aug. 9:30am-7:30pm; June 10am-7pm; Apr.-May and Sept.-Oct. 10am-6pm. €7.50, students €6.50, ages 4-15 €5.50.)

CAVES OF THE VEZERES VALLEY

NEAR SARLAT: LASCAUX

The most famous prehistoric cave paintings line the ceilings of **Lascaux,** "the Sistine Chapel of prehistory." A couple of teenagers stumbled upon them in 1940 while chasing after their runaway dog. Lascaux closed to the public in 1963 because the humidity from millions of visitors bred algae and mini-stalactites that ravaged the paintings that nature had preserved for 17,000 years. Today, visitors line up Disneyland-style to see **Lascaux II,** which duplicates practically every inch of the original. The new paintings of 5m tall bulls, horses, and bison are brighter than their ancient counterparts, but were crafted with identical natural powders, derived from the soil in the original caves. While there is a distinct lack of ancient mystery, Lascaux II compensates with one of the best guided cave tours in the valley. Watch for a deer whose eyes seem to follow the viewer, a horse sprawled on his back on a nearby rock, and a herd of galloping elk.

The Lascaux caves are 2km from **Montignac** (pop. 3000), 25km north of Sarlat along D704 and 23km northeast of Les Eyzies on D706. The Montignac **tourist office** (☎ 05 53 51 95 03), pl. Bertram-de-Born, shares a building with the Lascaux II **ticket office.** (☎ 05 53 05 65 65. Reserve 1-2 weeks ahead. Open from 9am until tickets sell out. French and English cave tours 40min; €8, ages 6-12 €4.50. Advance tickets ☎ 05 53 51 95 03. Open July-Aug. 9am-7pm; Feb.-June and Sept.-Dec. Tu-Su 10am-noon and 2-5:30pm. MC/V.)

In the nearby town of Thonac, **Le Thot, Espace Cro-Magnum,** rte. D706, is a museum that serves as a great introduction to Lascaux and prehistoric discoveries in the area. The center paints a sweeping picture of ancient life, from family groups and hunting scenes to the making of cave art. An informative short film in French with English subtitles explains how Lascaux II was constructed. Engaging displays and an animal park behind the complex are perfect for children. (☎05 53 50 70 44. Open daily July-Aug. 9am-7pm; Feb.-June and Sept.-Dec. 10am-noon and 2-5:30pm. €5, ages 6-12 €3. Combined entrance with Lascaux II €9, ages 6-12 €5.)

The **train station** nearest to Montignac is 10km away at Le Lardin. **Taxis** (☎05 53 50 86 61) wait here, and, during the school year (Sept.-June), CFTA (info ☎05 55 86 07 07) runs **buses** from Brive (1½hr.; 1 per day M-F 6pm, Sa 4:30pm; return M-Sa 6:50pm; €5.50); Périgueux (1½hr.; 1 per day M-Sa 12:10pm; return M-F 6:30pm, Sa 1pm; €6.30); and Sarlat (20min.; 3 per day M-F 6am and 12:30pm, Sa 8am; return M-Sa 1:05pm and M-F 7:15pm; €5.70). July-Aug., most CFTA buses run to Montignac from Sarlat and Périgueux (W 7:30 and 9:15am, return 5 and 7:15pm). Découverte et Loisirs in Sarlat runs a **minibus tour** to Lascaux and the Thot Museum once per week. (☎05 65 37 19 00 for reservations and schedule. May-Sept. 1 per week. €42 includes admission to the cave.) Renting a **car** in Sarlat is the easiest option, though making the trip by **bike** isn't too bad, other than a sharp incline out of Sarlat. **Camping Municipal ❶,** with 91 spots, is just outside town on D65. (☎05 53 52 83 95. Open Apr. to mid-Oct. €3 per person; €2.30 per site; €2 per car.)

NEAR LES EYZIES-DE-TAYAC

CAVES WITHIN WALKING DISTANCE OF LES-EYZIES. The **Grotte de Font-de-Gaume,** on the D47 1km east of Les Eyzies (10min. by foot), has faded but spectacular 15,000-year-old friezes, completed over the course of hundreds of years. They are quite technically advanced, using the natural contours of the cave for relief. This is the last cave in the Aquitaine basin with polychrome (multi-colored) paintings that is still open to the public. Locals discovered the paintings in the 18th century but did not realize their importance until two centuries later, by which time several murals had decayed or had been defaced by graffiti. Consequently, the most brilliant colors are deep into the cavern. The scene of a black reindeer licking the nose of a kneeling red cousin is amazingly expressive, but the *voûte* (vault), where 12 bison stampede across the ceiling, is the undisputed highlight. *(☎05 53 06 86 00; www.leseyzies.com/grottes-ornees. Open mid-Sept. to mid-May Su-F 9:30am-12:30pm and 2-5:30pm; mid-May to mid-Sept. Su-F 9:30am-5:30pm. Reservations required. July-Aug. reserve 15 days in advance; Sept. to early June one week in advance. €6.10, ages 18-25 €4.10, under 18 free. 1hr. tours available in English.)*

The **Grotte des Combarelles,** 2km farther down, has lost its paintings to humidity, but the etchings in the "Lascaux of engravings" are spectacular even without color. Over 600 surprisingly realistic carvings depict a range of species, including donkeys, cave lions, and rhinos. Fifty human figures keep watch from the narrow halls of the cave. Small, six-person tours are more personalized than the larger groups at Font-de-Gaume; the tour guides are wonderfully flexible. Reserve far in advance for the summer. *(☎05 53 06 97 72, tickets and reservations 05 53 06 86 00. Reservations required. Hours, prices, and website same as Font-de-Gaume. 1hr. tours in French only.)*

The **Gorge d'Enfer,** just upstream from Grand Roc and 2km from Les Eyzies, is filled with waterfalls, lagoons, and blooming flora. Inside is the **Abri du Poisson,** a shelter which contains the oldest drawing of a fish in France—a 25,000-year-old, meter-long "beaked" salmon. The rendering is so detailed that the salmon's upturned jaw, a sign of exhaustion after spawning, is distinctly visible. *(☎05 53 06 86 00. Same hours as Font-de-Gaume. Reservations required. €2.50, under 18 free.)*

NEARBY NATURAL CAVES. Many nearby caves have fascinating natural sights, especially the █**Grotte du Grand Roc,** 1½km northwest of town along the road to Périgueux. A footpath by the road makes it easy to walk there. (10min.) Halfway up the chalk cliffs, the cave commands a spectacular view of the valley and Tayac's fortified church. It is filled with millions of stalactites, stalagmites, and *eccentriques*—small calcite accretions that grow neither straight down nor straight up. The most remarkable of these formations are a thin, cross-shaped stalactite and an eroded column that resembles Bigfoot's footprint. The cave is naturally a constant, pleasant 16°C, though its humidity is an unpleasant 95%. (☎05 53 06 92 70. Open daily July-Aug. 9:30am-7pm; Apr.-June and Sept.-Oct. 10am-6pm; Feb.-Mar. 10am-5pm. Closed early Nov. to Jan., except during school vacations. 30min. tour in French only, though there are written guides in English. €6.50, children €3.50.)

The **Musée Spéléologie,** 91 rue de la Grange-Chancel, 1km north of Les Eyzies, in the Fort de Roc, was carved into a cliff above the Vézère Valley by English soldiers during the Hundred Years' War. The museum explains the region's cave history with models, documents, and equipment. (☎05 53 06 97 15. Open mid-June to Sept. M-F 11am-6pm. €3, under 16 €1.50.)

CAVES ACCESSIBLE BY CAR OR BIKE. Fifteen kilometers northwest of Les Eyzies in Rouffignac, on the road to Périgueux, **La Grotte de Rouffignac,** or **La Grotte aux Cent Mammouths,** houses 250 engravings and paintings. Etchings of rhinos and horses are interspersed with striking representations of shaggy mammoths. It is one of the longest caves in the area. The guided tour (via train) lasts an hour. (☎05 53 05 41 71; fax 05 53 35 44 71. Wheelchair-accessible. Open daily July-Aug. 9-11:30am and 2-6pm; late Mar. to June and Sept.-Oct. 10am-11:30am and 2-5pm. €3.40.)

Only 12 indistinct figures, less detailed than those in Font-de-Gaume, are visible on the sculptured frieze **Abri du Cap-Blanc,** 7km northeast of Eyzies on D48, but they are outstandingly well-preserved. Hunters etched horses, bison, and reindeer onto the thick limestone walls 15,000 years ago. The exhibit's centerpiece is a 2m-long herd of shuffling animals. (☎05 53 59 21 74; www.leseyzies.com/cap-blanc. Open daily July-Aug. 10am-7pm; Apr.-June and Sept. to early Nov. 10am-noon and 2-6pm. Reservations necessary July-Aug. 1hr. tours in French. €5.60, children €3.30.)

Northeast of Les Eyzies on route D66, the ▧**Roque St-Christophe** is the most extensive cave dwelling yet discovered. Five floors of limestone terraces with about 100 cave shelters rise 80m and stretch over 400m. From 40,000 BC until the Middle Ages, this fascinating sanctuary served as a defensive fort and housed over 3000 people. A pulley system demonstrates how cave dwellers experimented with civil engineering to move objects into the caves. Visit the 11th-century kitchen and peer over the 60m cliff where Protestants sought shelter from a Catholic army in 1580. A 45min. tour describes the cave's ovens, monastic remains, and military defenses. (☎05 53 50 70 45; www.roque-st-christophe.com. Open daily July-Aug. 10am-7pm; Mar.-Apr. and Oct. 10am-6pm; May-June and Sept. 10am-6:30pm; Nov.-Feb. 11am-5pm. Last entry 45min. before closing. €6, students €5, ages 5-13 €3.)

DORDOGNE VALLEY

Steep cliffs and poplar thickets overlook the lazy waters of the Dordogne, which in the Hundred Years' War was a natural boundary between France and English Aquitaine. Numerous châteaux, not as regal as those of the Loire, were built here to keep an eye on the enemy.

During the summer, the valley brims with tourists in canoes, on bikes, and in cars. The fertile area south of Brive is home to tiny hamlets that have never seen a tour bus. A world away from the area north of Brive, its terrain ranges from deep valleys amid rolling hills to towering cliffs of white rock and fields of tall grass. Though visitors can bike the area, it's probably wiser to rent a car. If you rely on trains, make sure your boots are made for walking.

TRANSPORTATION. The valley stretches west from Bergerac, 15km south of Sarlat. Expect to rent a car or get a good bike workout to explore the area well. **Car** rentals are available in Périgueux, Brive, and Sarlat. For **bikers,** Sarlat is the best starting point. It's about 4-6km between each village, and once out of Sarlat, the bike ride along the Dordogne is fairly level. Most villages are built on hills, with the châteaux at the top; the easiest way to see them is to park bikes at the bottom and walk up. Alternatively, Découverte et Loisirs runs through the valley several times a week from Sarlat. (☎ 05 65 37 19 00. €29-44 per person, call for schedule.) Many places rent **canoes** and **kayaks.** At the Pont de Vitrac, near Domme, try Canoës-Loisirs (☎ 05 53 28 23 43) and Périgord Aventure et Loisirs (☎ 05 53 28 23 82). Canoës-Dordogne (☎ 05 53 29 58 50) and Canoë Vacances (☎ 05 53 28 17 07) are at La Roque Gageac, Le Sioux near Domme and Cénac. (☎ 05 53 28 30 81. Open July to mid-Sept.) Tourist offices have schedules and info; prices average €11 per person per half-day, €16 per day. After a course down the river, many companies will pick customers up and return them to the starting point free of charge.

DOMME & LA ROQUE GAGEAC

Domme (pop. 1000), built by King Philip the Bold in 1280 as a defensive stronghold, is reached by bike on a challenging 4km winding ascent. The **tourist office,** pl. de la Halle, sells tickets for all the attractions in Domme, many of which are accessible only on guided tours. (☎ 05 53 31 71 00; fax 05 53 31 71 09. Open daily July-Aug. 10am-7pm; Sept.-June 10am-noon and 2-6pm; phone ahead for Jan. hours.) Excellent guided tours in French explore the dilapidated **Porte des Tours.** Seventy Templar Knights were imprisoned there in 1307 and tortured for nearly 20 years by King Philip IV, who wanted the secret of their hidden treasure. The artistic graffiti they scratched into the walls with their teeth, hands, and fingernails remain, a combination of idiosyncratic Christian iconography and the Islamic and Jewish motifs encountered by the Templars in the Holy Land. (Tours 1hr.; July-Aug. 2-3 per day, Sept.-June 1 per day. €6, children €3.50.) From pl. de la Halle, a cave tour descends into the **Grottes de la Halle,** some of the largest caves in Europe, brimming with stalactites. (☎ 05 53 31 71 00. Cave tours in French and English July-Aug. every 30min. 10:15am-7pm; Apr.-June and Sept. every 45min. 10:15am-noon and 2-6pm; Feb.-Mar. and Oct. every hr. 2-5pm. €6.10, students €5, children €3.20.)

Downstream, **La Roque Gageac** juts out from the base of a sheer cliff, its steep, twisting streets lined with medieval stone houses and untraditional vegetation, from bamboos to palm trees. A tour on a **gabare** affords a perfect view of the châteaux along the Dordogne. (1hr.; every 15min. 10am-6pm. English-speaking guides available. €7.20, children €4.20.) The 12th-century **Fort Troglodytique Aérien,** high above La Roque, commands a spectacular view of the Dordogne river valley. Its position made it an ideal defensive structure which withstood all British assaults during the Hundred Years' War. (☎ 05 53 31 61 94. Open July-Aug. daily 10am-7pm; Apr.-June and Sept. to mid-Nov. Su-F 10am-6pm. €4, students €3, ages 10-16 €2.)

BRIVE-LA-GAILLARDE

When the courageous citizens of Brive (pop. 50,000) repelled English forces during the Hundred Years' War, they earned their town the nickname, *"la Gaillarde"* (the Bold), an appellation which was reaffirmed when Brive became the first French town to liberate itself from the German occupation in 1944. Unpretentious and untouristed, Brive has interesting museums and a peaceful *centre ville.* Old 12th- to 19th-century houses with 1970s highrises create an unusual cityscape that is an inexpensive base for exploring the ancient villages in the Quercy region.

THE HIDDEN DEAL

LE CORRÈZE

In an area where €11 buys no more than a Coke and a stingy *plat du jour* at most eateries, **Le Corrèze ❷** is an extraordinary find. In the middle of Brive-la-Gaillarde, Le Corrèze stands on the corner of rue de Corrèze and rue Toulzac, providing exceptional service, deliciously fresh food, and generous portions.

As you enter this elegantly decorated, quiet restaurant, the entire staff politely welcomes you. There are a variety of *menus*, but the least expensive (€11) will fill even the hardiest eater. The four-course meal starts with a *soupe du jour* highlighting fresh market picks, which is brought to your table in a terrine so that you can serve yourself to your heart's content. The soup is followed by the *plat du jour*, a tempting and simply prepared meat or fish dish, startling in its quality and home-cooked taste. As you begin to wonder how much you can actually eat in one sitting, a tray of cheeses lands on your table for you to help yourself. Be sure to leave a little room for the dessert course, though, which includes such favorites as *crème caramel* or *pêche melbe*. Combined with impeccable service and a wonderfully tranquil environment, the food will make you a loyal fan.

(3 rue Corrèze. ☎05 55 24 14 07. Open M-Sa noon-2pm and 7-10:15pm. 2-course menus €8.50. 4-course menus €11, €15, and €25. MC/V.)

ℹ PRACTICAL INFORMATION

Trains depart from av. Jean Jaurès to Bordeaux (2hr., M-Sa 4 per day, €23.10); Limoges (1hr., 5 per day, €13.30); Sarlat (1hr. including bus from Souillac to Sarlat, 3 per day, €9.40); and Toulouse (2½hr., 5 per day, €24) via Cahors (1hr., 5 per day, €13.20). The info office is open M-F 9am-6:30pm and Sa 9am-5:30pm. **Buses** stop at the train station and in pl. de Lattre de Tassigny, next to the post office. STUB runs within the city (€1), CFTA to surrounding areas, including Collonges-la-Rouge. Trans-Périgord buses (☎05 53 09 24 08) go to Sarlat via Souillac (1½hr., 1 per day, €9). Buy tickets on board. (Office at pl. du 14 Juillet. ☎05 55 74 20 13. Info desk open M-Sa 8:15am-12:15pm and 2-6:15pm.) **Taxis** wait at 9 av. Jean Jaurès. (☎05 55 24 24 24. 24hr.) At 52-56 av. Jean Jaurès are **car rental** agencies Europcar (☎05 55 74 14 41), Hertz (☎05 55 24 26 75 or 01 39 38 38 38), and Avis (☎05 55 24 51 00). **Bikes** can be rented at Sports Bike, 142 av. Georges Pompidou (☎05 55 17 00 84), or Belot Philippe, 141 av. Ribot (☎05 55 86 14 33).

To get to the **tourist office,** pl. du 14 Juillet (☎05 55 24 08 80; fax 05 55 24 58 24) from the station, head down av. Jean Jaurès to the Collégiale St-Martin and cut diagonally across the courtyard of the Collégiale. Veer left onto rue Toulzac, which becomes av. de Paris, and cross the large parking lot. The staff provides maps, an English audio sights guide, bus schedules, and city **tours.** (Tours Tu and Th 10:30am, W 9pm; €4. Audio guide €6. Open July-Aug. M-Sa 9am-noon and 2-7pm, Su 10am-1pm; Sept.-June M-Sa 9am-noon and 2-6pm.) Other services include: **currency exchange** at Banque de France, bd. Gal. Koenig (☎05 55 92 37 00; open M-F 9:30am-noon); a **laundromat** at Lavarie, 39 rue Dubois (open daily 6:30am-9:30pm); **police** at 4 bd. Anatole France (☎05 55 17 46 00); a **hospital** (☎05 55 92 60 00) at bd. Docteur Verlhac; **Internet** at Media Computer, 46 av. du 11 Novembre (☎05 55 17 58 41; €3 per hr.; open M 2-7pm, Tu-F 10am-noon and 2-7pm, Sa 10am-noon and 2-6:30pm), and Ax'tion, 33 bd. Koenig (☎05 55 17 14 15; €2.30 for 15min., €9 per hr; open M 2-7pm, Tu-Su 9am-7pm). The **post office,** pl. Winston Churchill, **exchanges currency** with no commission. (☎05 55 18 33 10. Open M-F 8am-6:45pm, Sa 8am-noon.) **Poste Restante:** "Brive 19100." **Postal code:** 19100.

🛏 ACCOMMODATIONS

To get to the **Auberge de Jeunesse (HI) ❶,** 56 av. du Maréchal Bugeaud, from the station, walk the length of av. Jean Jaurès, cross the street at the bottom, take rue de l'Hôtel de Ville into the old town, and turn right onto rue du Dr. Massenat. Go left onto bd. du Salan, then right onto av. du Maréchal Bugeaud. The small, well-lit two- to four-bunk rooms with firm mattresses and clean hall bathrooms are in a safe, quiet neighborhood minutes from the *centre ville*. (☎05 55 24 34 00; brive@fuaj.org. Breakfast €3.30. Sheets €3.80. Reception M-F 8am-noon and 2-10pm, Sa-Su 8am-noon and 6-10pm. Bunks €8.90. MC/V. **Members only.**) Next to the station, **Bar Hôtel de la Gare ❷,** 65 av. Jean Jaurès, provides small, quiet rooms with pastel décor and clean hall showers. (☎05 55 74 14 49. Singles and doubles with sink €19-21, with shower €26; triples €38. MC/V.) The amiable proprietor of **Hôtel Le Chêne Vert ❸,** 24 bd. Jules-Ferry, rents spacious, well-furnished rooms with tidy bathrooms, some with balconies. (☎05 55 24 10 07. Singles with sink €26; doubles with shower €35-45. MC/V.) **Camping Municipal des Iles ❶** is beyond the youth hostel on bd. Michelet, 5min. from the center of town. Though crowded, it has shower, tennis, pool, and views of the Corrèze river. (☎/fax 05 55 24 34 74. Reception daily 7am-9pm. €3 per person, €1.50 per child; €2.70 per tent. Electricity €2.60-3.80.)

🍴 FOOD

Regional fare, such as foie gras, duck, walnuts, truffles, apples, and cheese are featured on most menus. The town is peppered with gourmet food shops of all kinds. Brive's **market** is on pl. du 14 Juillet and pl. Thiers, just outside the tourist office. (Open Tu, Th, and Sa 8am-noon.) A **Casino** supermarket is at the intersection of bd. Gal. Koenig and av. de Paris. (Open M-Sa 9am-7:30pm.) Cheap restaurants concentrate around **place Anatole Briand** and the cathedral side of **place Charles de Gaulle.** Elegant, family-run **◧Le Corrèze ❸,** 3 rue de Corrèze, prepares wholesome regional fare at great prices (see **The Hidden Deal**). **La Saladière ❷,** 13 rue de l'Hôtel de Ville, touts such goodies as greens, rice, tomatoes, blue cheese, and hummus. (Salads €6-10, *menus* €13 and €19. Open M-Sa noon-2pm and 7-10pm. MC/V.) Laid-back, Parisian-style bistro **Chez Francis ❹,** 61 av. de Paris, has gourmet attitude and walls signed by satisfied customers. (☎05 55 74 41 72. *Plats* €9, *menus* €14-21. Reservations required. Closed Su. MC/V.)

👁 SIGHTS

The **Musée Labenche,** 26bis bd. Jules Ferry, in the beautiful 16th-century **Hôtel de Labenche,** is a lovely example of southern French Renaissance architecture. The red-stone exterior, secluded courtyard, and wide galleries make it one of Brive's most unique spots. Combining art, natural history, and interior decorating, exhibits include ancient coins, busts, old accordions, 17th-century English tapestries, and contemporary art. All signs are in French. (☎05 55 92 39 39. Open Apr.-Oct. M and W-Su 10am-6:30pm; Nov.-Mar. daily 10am-6pm. €4.50, students €2.50, under 16 and last Su of the month free. Tours in French €2. Temporary exhibits free.)

From pl. de la République, rue Emile Zola leads to the **Centre National de la Résistance et de la Déportation Edmond Michelet,** 4 rue Champanatier. Take bd. Koenig to the pl. de la République, turn right on rue Emile Zola, then left on rue Hue, and right onto rue Champanatier. Michelet, a Brive native and Resistance leader, survived internment at the Dachau concentration camp for over a year, then went on to become a minister under de Gaulle. The museum displays photos of women and children on their way to the gas chambers, heartbreaking last letters to loved ones, and other mementos. (☎05 55 74 06 08; fax 05 55 17 09 44. Free audio guides available in French and English. Open M-Sa 10am-noon and 2-6pm. Free.)

The 12th-century **Eglise Collégiale St-Martin,** pl. Charles de Gaulle, named for the iconoclastic Spaniard who introduced Christianity to Brive in the 4th century, marks the center of town. Martin's sarcophagus rests in the crypt.

DORDOGNE

🎵 🔲 ENTERTAINMENT & FESTIVALS

Pub le Watson livens the otherwise lukewarm rue des Echevins with boisterous beer-drinkers outside and in. (☎ 05 55 17 12 09. Beer €2.50-4. Open Tu-Sa 5pm-2am.) A relaxing bar and a smooth drink await at **Brasserie de l'Europe,** 21 av. de Paris. (☎ 05 55 24 19 55. Drinks €3. Open M-Sa 8am-2am. MC/V.) After midnight, 20-somethings fill **La Charette,** 33 av. Ribot, for tepid techno and disco beats. (☎ 05 55 87 65 73. Cover €9.20, Th-F women free. Open Tu-Sa until 3am.)

In mid-August, **Orchestrades Universelles** attracts orchestras, bands, and choirs from all over the world for a celebration of classical, traditional, and jazz music. All performances are free until 9pm on the last evening, when a spectacular gala fetes 750 young musicians in l'Espace de Trois Provinces. (☎ 05 55 92 39 39. Tickets €3.10-15.30.) During the first weekend in November, pl. du 14 Juillet and Salle Georges Brassens swarm with authors from all over France for the **Foire des Livres** (☎ 05 55 92 39 39). Four times a year, from December to February, the streets of Brive host **La Fois Grasses,** a market with the delicacies that make Brive famous: *champignons* (mushrooms), truffles, chocolate, and foie gras.

🔲 DAYTRIPS FROM BRIVE

COLLONGES-LA-ROUGE

Twenty kilometers southeast of Brive, the exquisite, red-rock Collonges-la-Rouge makes visitors wonder if the village is real. Cylindrical towers dangle grapevines as pastures and orchards bask in sunlight. There's nothing to do here but peek around, though one look is enough to understand why this village has been ranked one of the most beautiful in France. For those dead-set on visiting sights, the **Maison de la Sirène** displays a beautiful 18th-century painting of a blonde siren. The *maison* also houses a museum of local history that doesn't quite live up to the splendor of the town (€2). The 12th-century **church** in the town center got a face-lift during the 16th-century religious wars. CFTA buses depart pl. Thiers in Brive. (M-F 4 per day, Sa 7:40am and 12:20pm; one-way €3.10, students under 26 €1.50.)

ROCAMADOUR

*Trains run from Brive to Rocamadour, stopping at the old train station, 4km from town on route N140 (40min.; M-Sa 3 per day 5:35am-1:35pm, Su 1 per day 1:35pm; return M-Sa 8:50am-8:50pm, Su at 1:40 and 7pm; €11.30). The tourist offices provide schedules and tickets, which can also be purchased on board. From the station, a flat, winding road leads to the top of town. (45min.) For a **taxi,** call ☎ 05 65 33 63 10 or 05 65 33 73 31.*

Tiny Rocamadour (pop. 638) is a "verticity," carved into the large chalk cliffs in three sections, one above the other. In the late 12th century, the perfectly preserved body of St-Amadour was unearthed near the town's chapel. St-Amadour was reputed to have been the biblical Zacchaeus, a tax collector who mended his ways after dining with Jesus. As the story grew, so did the miracles, and the town became an important pilgrimage site. Although the town saw much turmoil during the religious wars, it is now one of the most beautiful villages in France, ruggedly carved out of the large chalk cliffs. The private château at its peak is connected to the village by a winding road that runs through the *Cité Réligieuse.*

Millions of believers have crawled on their knees up the **Grand Escalier.** King Henry II of England visited in 1170, and Blanche de Castille dragged her son St-Louis (Louis IX) along in 1244, just before he led a crusading army into the Holy Land. Some pilgrims still come, but most of the kneeling is done by tourists reloading their cameras. At the top is the 12th-century **Cité Religieuse,** an enclosed courtyard that encompasses seven chapels, two of which can be visited without a guide. Its nucleus is the ■**Chapelle Nôtre-Dame**, a silent place of prayer. It contains a black model ship which honors shipwreck victims under the watchful eye of the rare, 12th-century Black Madonna. (Chapel ☎05 65 33 23 23. *Cité* open daily July-Aug. 9am-6pm and 6:30-10pm; Sept.-June 8am-6pm. Mass daily at 11am.) Under Notre-Dame lies the **Crypte St-Amadour,** where the saint's body rested undisturbed until a Protestant tried to set it ablaze during the Wars of Religion. Though apparently immune to fire, the Saint's body could not withstand the assailant's back-up plan: an axe. The remains are preserved next door in the **Musée d'Art Sacré,** alongside paintings, colorful statues, illuminated manuscripts, and other religious art. (☎05 65 33 23 30. Open daily July-Aug. 9am-7pm; Sept.-June 9:30am-noon and 2-6pm. €4.60, students €2.60.) Adjacent to the chapel, the **Basilique St-Sauveur** attracts visitors to its gilt wooden altar. A French-led **tour** takes visitors to the **Crypte St-Amadour** and the **Chapelle St-Michel.** (☎05 65 33 62 61. Tours 45min.; 3 per day 10:30am-2:30pm; €5.50. Open Apr.-Oct. M-Sa 9am-noon and 2-6pm. Free.)

Next to the *Cité* is the zigzagging **Chemin de Croix,** which depicts the 14 stations of the cross in vivid relief. The weak-kneed will appreciate the elevator. (☎05 65 33 67 79. Open July-Aug. daily 8am-10pm; mid-June and Sept. daily 8am-8pm; mid-June and Oct. daily 9am-12:30pm and 1:30-6pm; Nov.-Feb. M-F 9am-noon and 2-5pm. Round-trip from the lower city to the top of the chemin €4; round-trip from the lower city to the *Cité Réligieuse* €3). At the summit rests the 14th-century **château,** inhabited by the chaplains of Rocamadour and closed to the public. Walk along the **ramparts** for great views. (☎05 65 33 23 23. Open daily 8am-8pm. €2.50.)

The **Grotte des Merveilles,** beside the upper tourist office, is a cave of stalactite formations and remnants of prehistoric paintings. Guided French tours (45min.) point out the paintings. (☎05 65 33 67 92. Open daily July-Aug. 9am-7pm; Apr.-June and Sept.-Nov. 10am-noon and 2-6pm. €6.50, children €3.50.) Signs from the upper tourist office point the way (300m) to **La Féerie du Rail,** a fantastic fairground with all the traditional attractions made miniature for children. Every detail down to the last doorknob was constructed by one man over 45,000 hours. Song and dance shows in French with English subtitles (45min.) sell out quickly, so go early. (☎05 65 33 71 06; fax 05 65 33 71 37. Apr.-Sept. 5-8 shows per day; Oct.-Nov. 2 per day 2:45 and 4:15pm. Tickets sold daily mid-July to late Aug. 9am-noon and 2-7pm; late Aug. to early Nov. and Easter to mid-July 10am-noon and 2-6pm. €6, children €4.) The **Rocher des Aigles** shares the plateau with the castle and hosts a 45min. show featuring trained birds of prey. (☎05 65 33 65 45. Open July-Aug. daily noon-6pm, 5 shows; Apr.-June and Sept. M-Sa 1-5pm and Su 1-6pm, 3 shows; Oct.-Nov. M-Sa 2-4pm and Su 2-5pm, 1 show at 3pm. €6.50, children €4.)

Separate **tourist offices** serve the cliff's top (☎05 65 33 22 00; fax 05 65 33 22 01) and bottom (☎05 65 33 62 59; www.rocamadour.com). Each has town guides, **accommodations booking,** maps (€0.75), and **currency exchange** at nefarious rates. The lower office is in the old Hôtel de Ville, the upper in l'Hospitalet, on rte. de Lacave. (Both open daily Sept.-June 10am-12:30pm and 1:30-6:30pm; mid-July to late Aug. 9:30am-7:30pm.) Other services include: **bike rental** at the upper tourist office (€8 per day); **police** (☎05 65 33 60 17; July-Aug. daily, Sept.-June Sa-Su); and a **post office** near the lower tourist office (☎05 65 33 62 21; open M-F 9:30-11:30am and 2-4pm, Apr.-Oct. also Sa 9am-noon). **Postal code:** 46500.

LOT VALLEY

The emerald-green Lot Valley snakes from Cahors to Cajarc, sheltering sunflowers and vineyards between steep cliffs. Buses pass through irregularly, so exploration inevitably involves some hiking—often upwards of 5km. The easiest way to get around is by car. **Quercyrail,** pl. de la Gare in Cahors, runs trains to certain sights in the valley on day excursions, stopping by St-Cirq-Lapopie, depending on the day. (☎05 65 23 94 72. Office open M and W 8:30am-6:30pm, Tu and Th-Sa 9am-6pm, Su 9-10am. Call office for tour schedule. €18-26, ages 4-11 €8.) The Cahors tourist office sells hiking maps (€4.60) of the entire Lot Valley.

CAHORS

Nestled in the crook of the Lot River, Cahors (pop. 20,000) is a budget-friendly base for daytrips to the beautiful villages, vineyards, cliffs, and caves of the Lot Valley. Those who spend a day exploring the town itself, however, will be entranced by its 14th-century Valentré Bridge and medieval quarter.

🖪🛂 TRANSPORTATION & PRACTICAL INFORMATION. Trains leave from av. Jean Jaurès (info booth open daily 6am-8:30pm) to Brive (1½hr., 10 per day, €13.20); Limoges (2hr., 6 per day, €23.30); Montauban (45min., 10 per day, €9); Toulouse (1½hr., 9 per day, €14.70). Voyages Belmon Buses, 2 bd. Gambetta, runs daily full-day **bus excursions** to nearby sights. (☎05 65 35 59 30; fax 05 65 35 22 55. €15.50-32.50). Call Allo-Taxi, 742 chemin des Junies (☎05 65 22 19 42), for a **taxi.** (24hr.) **Rent cars** at **Avis** in pl. de la Gare. (☎05 65 30 13 10. Open M-F 8am-noon and 2-6pm; Sa 8am-noon. AmEx/MC/V.)

To get to the **tourist office,** pl. Mitterrand, bear right on av. Jean Jaurès from the station, cross the street, and head up rue Anatole France. At the end of the street, turn left onto rue du Président Wilson, then right onto **boulevard Gambetta,** the main thoroughfare separating the *vieille ville* from the rest of Cahors. The office will be around the corner on the right. (15min.) The staff **books rooms** (€0.90) and gives **city tours** in French. (☎05 65 53 20 65; www.mairie-cahors.fr. Tours M, W and F 5pm, €5.50. Call ahead for English tour schedule. Open July-Aug. M-F 9am-6:30pm, Sa 9am-6pm, Su 10am-noon; Sept.-June daily 9am-noon and 2-6pm.) **Bureau Information Jeunesse,** in the **Foyer des Jeunes,** 20 rue Frédéric Suisse, offers **Internet,** European travel planning, and résumé assistance. (☎05 65 23 95 90. Internet €0.70 per 15min., €3 per hr., free on W and Sa. Open M-F 9am-noon and 1-6pm, Sa until 5pm.) Other services include: **currency exchange** and **24hr. ATMs** at Banque Populaire, 26 bd. Gambetta (☎05 65 23 50 50; Tu-F 8:30am-12:10pm and 1:30-5:40pm, Sa 8:30am-12:20pm); **laundromats** at 208 rue Clemenceau (open daily 7am-9pm), 265 rue Nationale (open daily 7:30am-9:30pm), and Lavomatic, in pl. de la Libération, next to Hôtel aux Perdreaux (open daily 7am-9pm); **police** next to the Musée de la Résistance at pl. Bessières (☎05 65 23 17 17); a **hospital** at 449 rue Président Wilson (☎05 65 20 50 50); and **Internet** at the youth center Les Docks, 430 allées des Soupirs (☎05 65 22 36 38; €2 per hr; open July-Aug. M-F 10am-noon; Sept.-May Tu-Sa 2-6pm, Th-F also 8-10pm). The **post office,** 257 rue Wilson, has **currency exchange.** (☎05 65 23 35 00. Open M-F 8:30am-6:30pm, Sa 8:30am-noon.) **Postal code:** 46000.

🛏 ACCOMMODATIONS & CAMPING. To reach the **🖪Foyer des Jeunes Travailleurs Frédéric Suisse (HI) ❶,** 20 rue Frédéric Suisse, from the station, bear right onto rue Anatole France (ignore the Auberge de Jeunesse sign) and turn left onto rue Frédéric Suisse. (10min.) Close to all sights, this 17th-century building has coed dorms and comfortable private rooms. (☎05 65 35 64 71; fax 05 65 35 95 92. Breakfast €3.30, lunch or dinner €7.80. Sheets €3.30. Reception M-F and Su 9am-12:30pm and 2-5:30pm, Sa 9-11:30am and 2-5:30pm. 8- to 12-bunk dorms €9 for members; singles and doubles €9 per person.) To get to **Hôtel aux Perdreaux ❸,** 137 rue de Portail Alban, from the station, follow rue Joachim to bd. Gambetta. Cross the street to rue Portail Alban. (15min.) Large, clean rooms have shower and toilet, and some have balconies. (☎05 65 35 03 50. Breakfast €5. Reception 8am-10pm.

Reserve July-Aug. Singles and doubles €28-33; triples and quads €40-45. MC/V.)
The **Hôtel de la Paix ❸**, 30 pl. St-Maurice, in front of Les Halles, is closer to the
action. Follow the directions to the hostel, but continue on rue Frédéric Suisse
through the arch and turn right down rue Caviole. Turn left on rue du Président
Wilson, cross bd. Gambetta, and go downhill to rue Maréchal Joffre, which leads
to the cathedral. Turn right in front of the cathedral, then right in front of Les
Halles. (15min.) Friendly proprietors rent basic, cozy rooms. (☎05 65 35 03 40; fax
05 65 35 40 88. Breakfast €5.50. Reception M-Sa. Singles with toilet €27-31; doubles with shower €33-36, with bath €37. Hall shower €1.50 or bath €4. MC/V.)

Camping "Rivière de Cabessut" ❶, rue de la Rivière, is a three-star campground
near the town center with bar, laundry, pool, athletic facilities, and mini-golf.
From pl. de la Libération, take the second left to rue Pelegry, and turn right at rue
du Pont Neuf; turn left and continue along the river. (35min.) Or, take city bus #5
(dir: Terre Rouge) from the station to Stade Lucien Desprats (8min., M-Sa, €0.75)
and walk the remaining 10min. along the river. (☎05 65 30 06 30; camping-riviere-
cabessut@wanadoo.fr. Reception daily 8am-10pm. Reserve ahead in summer.
Open Apr.-Sept. €2.50 per person, €1.80 per child; €8-10 per site. Electricity €2.)

📳 **FOOD. Open-air markets** liven up pl. Chapou every Wednesday and Saturday
(8am-noon). The first and third Saturdays of the month are particularly grand. The
smaller **covered market** is just off the square. (Tu-Sa 7:30am-12:30pm and 3-7pm, Su
9am-noon.) **Casino** supermarket is on pl. Gal. de Gaulle (open July-Aug. M-Sa 9am-
12:30pm and 3-7:30pm, Su 9am-12:30pm; Sept.-June closed Su); **Champion** is inside
the shopping center at pl. Emilien-Imbert, just off bd. Gambetta (open M-Th 9am-
12:30pm and 2:30-7pm, F-Sa 9am-7pm).

🍽**Au Coeur du Lot ❷**, 71 rue du Château du Roi, offers delicious *crêpes* and *galettes* in hidden courtyard and *cave* cellar rooms. Ask for any concoction in any
language: they will translate it into wonderful food. (☎05 65 22 30 67. *Galettes* €6-
8, dessert €3-6, salad from €3. Open Tu-Sa 7-10:30pm. MC/V.) Off the beaten path,
Le Mephisto ❸, 448 rue Président Wilson, serves hearty food for measly prices.
Pick from its salads (€6.50-11), omelettes (€6), or four-course *menus* (€9,
€11.50, and €15) that include wine and regional duck specialties. (Open M-Sa
7am-7:30pm, T-F until 10:30pm in summer. MC/V.)

🔯 **SIGHTS.** The monumental 14th-century 🏰**Pont Valentré**, credited with staving
off invaders during the 1580 Siege of Cahors, is the city's most impressive sight.
Legend holds that its architect, dismayed by construction delays, sold his soul to
the devil for building materials. When it came time to give the devil his due, the
architect killed all the town's roosters to stop them from announcing the dawn;
caught unawares, the devil was turned to stone by the sunrise. Look carefully to
see the devil clutching a corner of the central tower. The 12th-century **Cathédrale
St-Etienne**, pl. Chapou, is topped by three Byzantine-like cupolas and peppered
with wide medieval murals, and often hosts classical concerts. (☎05 65 35 27 80.
Open daily Easter-Oct. 8am-7pm; Oct.-Easter 8:30am-6pm.)

The grim but poignant **Musée de la Résistance, de la Déportation, et de la Libération
du Lot,** located in the former Bessières barracks in pl. du Gal. de Gaulle, catalogues
the town of Cahors's role in the fight against the German occupation of France, in
part through a series of quite graphic photos. (☎05 65 22 14 25. Open daily 2-6pm.
Free.) In addition to ultra-modern Cahors-themed photography and video art, the
Musée Henri Martin, 792 rue Emile Zola, displays a small number of modern art
exhibits, including classically Pointillist interpretations of Cahors by the Tou-
louse-born student of Delacroix, Henri Martin. (☎05 65 20 88 66. Open Su-M and
W-Sa 11am-6pm, Su 2-6pm. €3, ages 7-18 and over 60 €1.50, under 6 free, first Su
of the month free.)

■ **FESTIVALS.** During the last week of July, Cahors taps its toes to American blues during the **Festival de Blues.** Afternoon and evening blues "appetizers" in coffee shops and bars throughout town are free, as are many of the more formal concerts. (☎ 05 65 35 99 99; www.cahors.bluesfestival.free.fr. Tickets €15-23, students €10; purchase in advance; available after July 3.) **Festival de Saint-Céré** features classical music during the first two weeks of August. (Call tourist office for info. Tickets €17-50.)

ST-CIRQ-LAPOPIE

One of the most beautiful villages in France, tiny St-Cirq-Lapopie (pop. 200), 36km east of Cahors, is built on a cliff ledge, along streets so steep that the roof of one timbered house begins where its neighbor's garden ends. The incredible view from the town's perch recalls St-Cirq's role as a defensive fortress during the 16th century. The entire village of picturesque stone houses dates from the 17th century and is classified as a historical monument, drawing hordes of tourists. Escape the crowds at **Château Lapople,** the highest point in town, offering an impressive view. The village's cultural center, the ◼**Maison de la Fordonne,** chronicles the St-Cirq's rocky history. (☎/fax 05 65 31 21 51. Open daily June-Sept. 9am-noon and 2-7pm; Oct. to mid-Nov. and mid-Mar. to May 10am-noon and 2-6pm; closed mid-Nov. to mid-Mar. €2, students €1.)

To get to St-Cirq-Lapopie by car, follow D653 out of Cahors; turn right on to D662 when you reach Vers. **SNCF buses** run past St-Cirq-Lapopie from Cahors on the way to Figeac (line #10; 45min.; 5 per day, 3 on Su; €5). Ask to get out at Tour de Faure. Cross the bridge and hike 2km uphill to the village. (30min.) The **tourist office,** pl. de Sombral, in the main square, offers self-guided tours in English, French walking tours, and a complete list of hotel vacancies. (☎ 05 65 31 29 06. Open daily June-Aug. 10am-1pm and 2-7:30pm; Sept.-May 10am-1pm and 2-6pm. Tours July-Aug. 1 per day Th-Tu 4pm. €3.50, under 10 €2.50.)

The best beds in St-Cirq are at the *gîte d'étape* ◼**La Maison de la Fourdonne,** a restored 16th-century home with a stocked kitchenette and timbered common room. Pine-paneled three- to five-bed rooms all have baths; some have balconies. (☎/fax 05 65 31 21 51. Bring sheets. Reception same as museum hours. Closed mid-Nov. to mid-Mar., but takes reservations. Reservations required July-Aug. Dorms €11.) **Auberge du Sombral,** in front of the tourist office, has eight elegant rooms with bed-and-breakfast appeal. (☎ 05 65 31 26 08. Singles with bath €46; doubles €62; quint €70. MC/V.) Between the town and the bus stop, the riverside ◼**Camping de la Plage** is close to hiking, swimming, and kayaking sites. (☎ 05 65 30 29 51; camping.laplage@wanadoo.fr. €5 per person. July-Aug. €5 per site; Sept.-July €4 per site. Electricity €3-4. MC/V.) Kalapca Loisirs offers **kayak rental** and books two-to six-day trips with camping or *gîte d'etape* packages with advanced reservation. (☎ 05 65 30 29 51; www.kalapca.com. Canoe €5 per hr. Kayak €7 per hr. MC/V.)

GROTTE DU PECH-MERLE

A few kilometers past St-Cirq-Lapopie on the road from Cahors is the turn-off for D653 and the **Grotte du Pech-Merle,** one of the best-preserved prehistoric caves open to the public. Unfortunately, the nearest bus stop is 7km away in Caberets. Discovered by local teenagers in 1922, the 4km gallery contains paintings between 18,000 and 30,000 years old. Bring a jacket. Reserve one week ahead June through August. Admission includes the adjoining museum. English pamphlets are available. (Grotte ☎ 05 65 31 27 05; pech@crdi.fr. Museum ☎ 05 65 31 23 33. Both open Apr.-Oct. daily 9:30am-noon and 1:30-5pm. 1hr. limit. Tours in French July-Aug. every 30min. €7, children €5.) *Gîtes d'étape* and campgrounds line the road to Pech-Merle.

CORSICA
(LA CORSE)

Corsica has always resisted foreign control. The Corsican people controlled their island from the 9th century until 1284, when the iron-fisted Genoese overtook the island. The Corsican War of Independence, or the Forty Years' War, began in 1729. By 1767, the revered general Pasquale Paoli had declared the island's independence, created a university, a government, a currency, and an army. With Jean-Jacques Rousseau, he drafted the island's—and the world's—first modern constitution. With the Treaty of Versailles, the Genoese were forced to cede control of Corsica to France's Louis XV. Corsica was quickly divided between the nationalist *Paolistes* and the *Populaires*, who swore allegiance to France and the French Revolution, including a certain Carlo-Maria Buonaparte.

Today the **Front de Libération National de la Corse** (FLNC) continues to try bombing its way to independence, though most Corsicans deplore this sort of extremism and question the wisdom of independence, given that France directly provides 70% of Corsica's GNP. French Interior Minister Nicholas Sarkozy proposed increasing Corsican autonomy, but when put to referendum on the island in July 2003, it was narrowly defeated by a 2% margin: only 49% of Corsicans want increased autonomy from France.

Bathed in the turquoise waters of the Mediterranean, the island paradise of Corsica (pop. under 250,000) was dubbed *Kallysté* (the most beautiful) by the Greeks. In the north, deep-green scrub is fringed with rocky outposts and fishing hamlets such as ▓**Erbalunga** (p. 782); to the south, white cliffs dive into a pristine sea around ▓**Bonifacio** (p. 784), a clifftop city with heavy Italian influence. Pine-shingled red mountains tower to the west, while glacial lakes and gorges await and in Corsica's interior. Hikers flock to the mountainous areas of **Porto** (p. 765), the ▓**Gorges de la Restonica** (p. 776), the **Gorges du Tavignano** (p. 777), the **Forêt de Vizzavona** (p. 777), the seaside areas of ▓**Scandola** (p. 767) and **the Capandula** (p. 783), and the wild geological formations of ▓**Les Calanches** (p. 767).

Corsica's main industry is tourism. In summer, hordes of mainland French retreat to the island's renowned beaches and pricey resorts like **Calvi** (p. 767) and ▓**Ile Rousse** (p. 772). ▓**Ajaccio** (p. 760) is the swankiest town on the island, with a kicked-up nightlife and plentiful Napoleonic artifacts, while **Corte** (p. 773) Corsica's only university town, is a hotspot for intellectuals and Corsican patriots. Visitors can find respite from the crowds at capeside **Bastia** (p. 777) or the Greek and Roman ruins at **Aléria** (p. 780), but to avoid the most heavily touristed areas, hike between the tiny hamlets that cling to the rugged coast of the **Cap Corse** (p. 782). The summer climaxes with a double-barreled blast on August 15, when France celebrates the Fête de l'Assomption and Corsicans observe Napoleon's birthday. Tourists depart by September, when the weather is at its best and the waters their warmest. Winter visitors can visit sleepy coastal towns or head inland to ski.

In Corsica, herbs from the *maquis* (an impenetrable tangle of lavender, laurel, myrtle, rosemary, and thyme that grows on Corsica's hillsides) impart a distinct flavor to local specialties. The island's most famous dishes are *sanglier* (wild boar), *brocciu* (ewe's cheese), *gateau de chataigne* (chestnut cake), and *charcuterie corse* (free-range pork products).

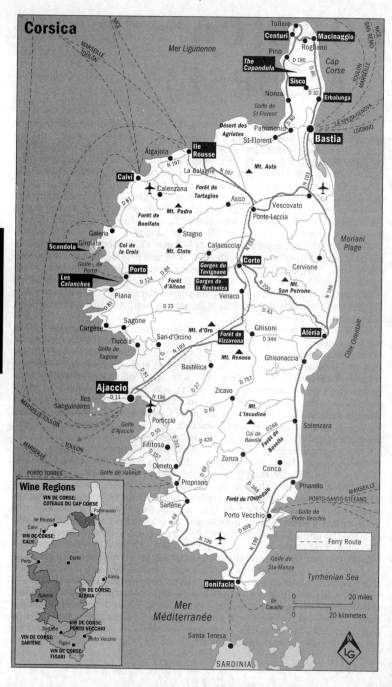

Agence du Tourisme de la Corse, 17 bd. du Roi Jérôme, Ajaccio (☎ 04 95 51 00 00; www.visit-corsica.com), publishes free guides to all of Corsica's accommodations, which are provided free of charge at Corsican tourist offices. Corsica's few budget hotels fill weeks ahead in summer. If it proves impossible to plan far in advance, it's worth calling a day or two ahead in case rooms open up. Campsites lie close to most cities; a ban on unofficial camping is strictly enforced. *Refuges*, or mountain huts, provide little more than a roof over your head; they don't take reservations, but you can usually pitch a tent outside. *Gîtes d'étape* allow advance reservations and offer more comfortable surroundings, including electricity and home-cooking.

✈ INTERCITY TRANSPORTATION

BY PLANE. Air France and its subsidiary **Compagnie Corse Méditerranée (CCM)** fly to Bastia and Ajaccio from Paris (round-trip from €170, students €140); Nice (€120, students €98); and Marseille (€128, students €104). In Ajaccio, the Air France/CCM office is at 3 bd. du Roi Jérôme (☎ 08 20 82 08 20). As with all airfares, hunting around can yield significant savings; inquire at a budget travel agency in France.

BY BOAT. Ferry travel between the mainland and Corsica can be a rough trip, and it's not always much cheaper than a plane. High-speed ferries (3½hr.) run between Nice and Corsica. Overnight ferries from Toulon and Marseille take upwards of 10 hours. The **Société National Maritime Corse Méditerranée** (SNCM ☎ 08 91 70 18 01; fax 04 91 56 35 86; www.sncm.fr) sends ferries from Marseille (€35-53, under 25 €20-40); Nice (€30-41, under 25 €15-26); Toulon (€35-53, under 25 €20-40) to Bastia, Calvi, Ile Rousse, Ajaccio, Porto Vecchio, and Propriano. It costs €40-305 to take a car, depending on the day and the car. During the summer, nine boats cross between Corsica and the mainland, though only three make the trip out of season. SNCM schedules and fees are listed in a booklet available at travel agencies and ports. Corsica Ferries (see below) has similar destinations and prices.

SAREMAR (☎ 04 95 73 00 96; fax 04 95 73 13 37) and **Moby Lines** (☎ 04 95 73 00 29; fax 04 95 73 05 50) run from Santa Teresa, Sardinia to Bonifacio. (3-10 per day depending on the season, €6.80-15 per person one-way; cars €19.70-51.50.) Moby Lines (€15-28) and **Corsica Ferries** (☎ 08 25 09 50 95; fax 04 95 32 14 71; www.corsicaferries.com) cross from Livorno and Savona in Italy to Bastia (€16-33).

⌨ LOCAL TRANSPORTATION

ON WHEELS. Rumor has it that the Marquis de Sade and Machiavelli collaborated on the design of Corsica's transportation system. **Train** service in Corsica is slow, limited to the half of the island north of Ajaccio, and doesn't accept rail passes. Antiquated vehicles travel along winding mountain ridges. **Buses** are more comprehensive and serve the greater part of the island, but be prepared for very twisty roads. If prone to motion sickness, bring medicine. Call Eurocorse Voyages (☎ 04 95 21 06 30) for further info.

Corsica allegedly has the most dangerous roads in France. Those foolhardy enough to rent a **car** should expect to pay at least €44-81 per day or €227-305 per week. The unlimited mileage deals are best. Gas stations are scarce; the police will sometimes help drivers who run out. **Bicycle** rental can be pricey, as can **mopeds** (*mobilettes*) and scooters. Narrow mountain roads and high winds make cycling difficult and risky; drivers should honk before rounding mountain curves.

Hiking may be the best way to explore the island's mountainous interior. The longest marked route, the **GR20**, is an extremely difficult 200km, 14- to 15-day trail that takes hikers across the island from Calenzana (southeast of Calvi) to Conca (northeast of Porto-Vecchio), and requires peak physical fitness and endurance. Do *not* tackle this trail alone, and be prepared for cold, snowy weather, even in early summer. For shorter, less challenging routes, try the popular **Mare e Monti,** a 10-day trail from Calenzana to Cargèse, and the easier **Da Mare a Mare Sud,** which crosses the southern part of the island between Porto-Vecchio and Propriano (4-6 days). All major trails are administered by the Parc Naturel Régional de la Corse, 2 Sargent Casalonga (☎04 95 51 79 00; fax 04 95 21 88 17; www.parc-naturel-corse.com), in Ajaccio, whose jurisdiction encompasses most of the Corsican heartland. For any route, a *topo-guide* is essential. (€14, with shipping €15.30; available for purchase by fax, over the phone, or at a Parc Naturel office.) The guide includes trail maps, *gîtes* and *refuges* listings, and other important practical information. Prospective GR20 trekkers will want to consider buying *Le Grand Chemin* (€15), a more complete guide that includes elevations and sources of potable water. For more info, contact the Parc Naturel.

AJACCIO (AIACCIU)

The largest town in Corsica and the island's departmental headquarters, Ajaccio (pop. 60,000) calls to mind a resort town on the Riviera. With its palm trees and yachts, sunlit buildings, and lively club scene, Ajaccio is a haven for wealthy, well-tanned tourists. Although beaches in Ajaccio itself aren't as breathtaking as those elsewhere on the island, Ajaccio is one of the few Corsican towns with significant museums and considerable urban energy. While Napoleon's birthplace has no shortage of monuments commemorating the little dictator's exploits, Ajaccio's real treasure is the preeminent Italian Renaissance collection of the Musée Fesch.

▐ TRANSPORTATION

Flights: Aéroport Campo dell'Oro (☎04 95 23 56 56), 5km away. Office open M-F 8:30am-12:30pm and 2-6pm, Sa 8:30am-noon. TCA bus #8 shuttles to and from the bus station (€4). Flights to **Nice, Marseille,** and **Paris.** For info call **Air France,** 3 bd. du Roi Jérôme, or **Compagnie Corse Mediterranée** (☎08 20 82 08 20 for both).

Ferries: Depart from *gare maritime* (☎04 95 51 55 45). Open June-Aug. daily 6:30am-8pm; Sept.-June M-Sa 6:30am-8pm and for departures and arrivals. **SNCM,** quai l'Herminier (☎04 95 29 66 99; fax 04 95 29 66 77), across from the bus station, goes to **Marseille** (8½hr., 6 per week); **Nice** (4hr. by day, 10hr. overnight; 1-2 per day). Approximate prices: €30-53, ages 12-25 €15-40. Office open M-F 8am-8pm and Sa 8am-1pm. MC/V. **Corsica Ferries** (☎04 95 50 78 82), in the bus station, runs to **Toulon** (5¾hr.; 1 per day on Tu, W, F, and Su 3pm). €20-33, ages 12-25 €5-18.

Trains: pl. de la Gare (☎04 95 23 11 03), off bd. Sampiero, 400m from the *gare maritime* (toward the airport, away from the city center). Open daily 6:20am-8:20pm. To: **Bastia** (4hr., 4 per day, €23.50); **Calvi** via **Ponte Leccia** (4½hr., 2 per day, €27.30); and **Corte** (2hr., 4 per day, €12.50).

Buses: quai l'Herminier (☎04 95 51 55 45), at the *gare maritime.* Open June-Aug. daily 6:30am-8pm; Sept.-May M-Sa 6:30am-8pm. **Luggage storage** open daily 7am-7pm; €1.50 per bag. **Eurocorse Voyages** (☎04 95 21 06 30) goes to **Bastia** (3hr., M-Sa 2 per day at 7:45am and 3pm, €18) via **Corte** (1¾hr., €11.50); **Calvi** via **Ponte Leccia** (3½hr., July-Aug M-Sa 1 per day at 3pm, €15 to Ponte Leccia; €9 from Ponte Leccia to Calvi on **Les Beaux Voyages;** Sept-June M-F 1 per day); **Bonifacio** (3hr.; M-Sa 2 per day; €20.50); **Porto Vecchio** (3hr., M-Sa 2 per day, €20.50). **Autocars SAIB** (☎04 95 22 41 99) go to **Porto** (2hr.; July to mid-Sept. daily 8:45am and 4pm; May-June and mid- to late Sept. M-Sa 8:45am and 4pm; Oct.-Apr. M-F 7:20am and 4pm, Sa 7:20am and 12:30pm; €11).

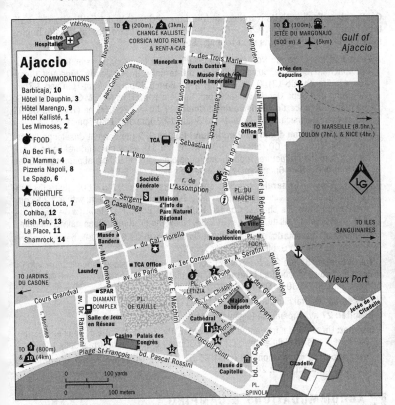

Public Transportation: TCA, 77 cours Napoléon (☎04 95 23 67 70; fax 04 95 50 15 06). Buses run every 30min. Tickets €1.15, *carnet* of 10 €9; available at *tabacs* and on the bus. Buses #1, 2, and 3 go from pl. de Gaulle to the train station or down cours Napoléon. Bus #5 from av. Dr. Ramaroni and bd. Lantivy stops at Marinella and the beaches headed to **Iles Sanguinaires** (7:05am-7:30pm; until 11:55pm July-Aug.).

Taxis: Accord Ajaccio Taxis, pl. de Gaulle (☎04 95 25 06 18) or **Jean-Marc Poli** (☎06 07 25 21 46). About €20 to airport from the city center. 24hr.

Car Rental: Ada (☎04 95 23 56 57), at the airport. Insurance included. 21+. Open daily 8am-11pm. AmEx/MC/V. **Rent-a-Car,** 51 cours Napoléon (☎04 95 51 34 45), in the Hôtel Kallisté, and at the airport (☎04 95 23 56 36). Insurance included. 23+. Open daily 8am-8pm. MC/V.

Scooter Rental: Corsica Moto Rent, 51 cours Napoléon (☎04 95 51 34 45), in the Hôtel Kallisté. Motorbikes from €31 per day, €157 per week. Deposit from €800. 18+. Open daily 8am-8pm. MC/V.

✈ 🛈 ORIENTATION & PRACTICAL INFORMATION

Cours Napoléon, which runs from pl. de Gaulle past the train station, is the city's main thoroughfare. The pedestrian **rue Cardinal Fesch** starts at pl. Maréchal Foch and parallels cours Napoléon. Both are thick with cafés and boutiques. **Place de**

CORSICA

Gaulle, **place Foch** with its Napoleonic fountain, and the **citadel** (still an active military base) enclose the *vieille ville*. The seaside **boulevard Pascal Rossini** begins near pl. de Gaulle and runs next to **plage St-François**.

Tourist Office: 3 bd. du Roi Jérôme (☎04 95 51 53 03; www.tourisme.fr/ajaccio), pl. du Marché. Free maps, bus schedules, and **Internet** with a *télécarte*. June-Aug. theme **tours** in French (€6-12). Open July-Aug. M-Sa 8am-8:30pm, Su 9am-1pm and 4-7pm; Apr.-June and Sept.-Oct. M-Sa 8am-7pm, Su 9am-1pm; Nov.-Mar. M-Sa 8am-6pm, Su 9am-1pm. **Agence du Tourisme de la Corse,** 17 bd. du Roi Jérôme (☎04 95 51 00 00; www.visit-corsica.com). Open M-F 8:30am-12:30pm and 1:30-6pm.

Hiking Info: Maison d'Info du Parc Naturel Régional, 2 rue Sergent Casalonga (morning ☎04 95 51 79 00, afternoon 04 95 51 79 10; www.parc-naturel-corse.com), across from the *préfecture*. Topo-guides for sale and free multilingual pamphlets. Open July-Aug. M-Sa 8am-6pm; Sept.-June M-Sa 8am-noon and 2-6pm.

Money: Société Générale, rue Sgt. Casalonga (☎04 95 51 57 60), just off cours Napoléon, exchanges currency M-F 8:15-11:30am and 1:45-4:30pm, with a 1.2% commission on traveler's checks. **Change Kallisté,** 51 cours Napoléon (☎04 95 51 34 45), in the Hôtel Kallisté, changes at 2-3% below the fixed rate. Open daily 8am-8pm.

Laundromat: Lavomatic, 1 rue Maréchal Ornano (☎06 09 06 49 09), behind the *préfecture*, near pl. de Gaulle. Open daily 7am-9pm.

Youth Center: 52 rue Fesch (☎04 95 50 13 44; josephcorsica@hotmail.com). Info on jobs and housing, and free **Internet** (40min. maximum). Open July-Aug. M-F 8am-6pm; Sept.-June M-F 8:30am-9pm, Sa 1:30-7pm.

Police: rue Général Fiorella (☎04 95 11 17 17), near the *préfecture*.

Hospital: 27 av. Impératrice Eugénie (☎04 95 29 90 90).

Internet: Up to 40min. free at the **Youth Center.** The 2nd-floor **Salle de Jeux en Réseau,** Diamant II, has all-night access. €2.50 for 30min., €4.50 per hr. Open daily 1pm-6am.

Post Office: 13 cours Napoléon (☎04 95 51 84 65). Open M-F 8am-6:45pm and Sa 8am-noon. **Postal code:** 20000.

ACCOMMODATIONS & CAMPING

Ajaccio has many hotels, but prices rival those in Paris. Call far ahead in June-Aug., when rates soar and vacancies plummet. Ask hotels for their absolute cheapest room, then ask if there's anything even cheaper; some hotels keep a couple of older rooms they don't initially list.

Hôtel Kallisté, 51 cours Napoléon (☎04 95 51 34 45; www.cyrnos.com); follow signs from quai l'Herminier. Well-designed rooms with Corsican décor have shower or bath, cable TV, and fan or A/C within walls of exposed stone. Firm beds, elevator, and central location make this the best option. Breakfast €8.50, in room €11. Free luggage storage. Reception daily 8am-8pm. Mar.-July and Sept.-Oct. singles €45; doubles €52; triples €69; Aug. €56/€69/€86; Nov.-Feb. €42/€45/€58. Extra bed €11-20. MC/V. ❹

Hôtel Marengo, 2 rue Marengo (☎04 95 21 43 66; fax 04 95 21 51 26). From city center, walk along the boardwalk with the sea on the left for about 25min.; turn right on bd. Madame Mère, then left onto rue Marengo. Or take bus #1 or 2 to Trottel. Charming rooms by the beach, all with shower, A/C, and firm beds. Breakfast €5.80. Reception daily 9am-10pm. Open Apr.-Oct. July-Sept. singles and doubles €59; triples €69; Apr.-June and Oct. €52/€60. 4 rooms sharing hallway toilet €44-46.50. MC/V. ❺

Hôtel le Dauphin, 11 bd. Sampiero (☎04 95 21 12 94 or 04 95 51 29 96; fax 04 95 21 88 69), between the train station and ferry port, features 39 modern rooms with shower, toilet, and TV, some with sea views. 10 rooms with A/C for an extra €8. Breakfast included. Reception daily 5am-midnight. Check-in 2pm. May-Oct. singles and doubles €54-60; triples €69; Nov.-Apr. €49-54/€66. Extra bed €8. AmEx/MC/V. ❹

Camping:

Les Mimosas, rte. d'Alata (☎04 95 20 99 85; fax 04 95 10 01 77). Follow cours Napoléon away from the city center and turn left on montée St-Jean, which becomes rue Biancamaria and then rte. d'Alata. Continue walking straight on the other side of the roundabout, taking an immediate left onto chemin de la Carrossacia; follow the signs 600m inland to the site. (20min.) Or take bus #4 from cours Napoléon to Brasilia and walk straight to the roundabout, following the above directions. Close to town. Laundry €4. Snack bar. Tennis nearby. July-Aug. €4.80 per person, €2 per tent or car. Electricity €2.80. Prices 10% lower Apr.-June and Sept. to mid-Oct. ❷

Barbicaja (☎04 95 52 01 17; fax 04 95 52 01 17), 4km away. Take bus #5 from av. Dr. Ramaroni, past pl. de Gaulle, to Barbicaja and go straight (last bus 7:30pm). Close to the beach. Laundry €7.60. Bar. Open May-Sept. €5.70 per person, €2.30 per tent or car. Electricity €2.40. ❷

◆ FOOD

The ◼**morning market** on pl. du Marché sells Corsican specialties like chestnut biscuits and sheep cheese. A smaller market opens at pl. Abbatucci, on cours Napoléon. (Both Tu-Su 8am-noon.) A **Monoprix** supermarket is at 31 cours Napoléon. (☎04 95 51 76 50. Open July-Sept. M-Sa 8:30am-7:40pm; Oct.-June M-Sa 8:30am-7:15pm.) A **SPAR** supermarket is at 1 cours Grandval, within the Diamant complex. (☎04 95 21 51 77. Open M-Sa 8:30am-12:30pm and 3:15-7:30pm, Su 8:30am-12:30pm.) Head to the pedestrian streets off **place Foch** towards the citadel for dozens of spots serving local dishes. Pizzerias, bakeries, and panini shops line **rue Cardinal Fesch;** at night, patios on the quai offer affordable seafood and pizza.

◼ **Au Bec Fin,** 3bis. bd. du Roi Jérôme (☎04 95 21 30 52), offers a tasty €13.90 *menu* on its charming terrace. Start with smoked salmon or foie gras, then try the roast veal or *filet de rascasse.* Open M-Sa noon-2pm and 7:30-10pm, F-Sa until 11pm. MC/V. ❸

Da Mamma, passage Guinguetta (☎04 95 21 39 44), off cours Napoléon, is a 41-year-old favorite. Try the *truite aux amandes* (trout with almonds) on the €15 *menu.* A €10.50 *menu* is offered until 9:30pm. Reservations recommended during high season. Open Su-M 7:30-10:30pm, Tu-Sa noon-2pm and 7:30-10:30pm. MC/V. ❸

Pizzeria Napoli, rue Bonaparte (☎04 95 21 32 79), will appease midnight rumblings. *Menus* €11.30-14.50. Pizza €7.30-9.30. Pasta €7-9.80. Open July-Aug. daily 6:45pm-6am; Sept.-June Su-Th 6:45pm-4am, F-Sa 6:45pm-6am. ❷

Le Spago, rue Emmanuel Arène (☎04 95 21 15 71), off av. du 1er Consul. Sleek, modern, and frequented by a smooth young crowd. *Menu* €15. Pasta €12.50-18. Meat dishes €13-16. Open M-F noon-2pm and 7:30-11pm, Sa 7:30-11pm. MC/V. ❸

◆ SIGHTS

Though Ajaccio is perhaps better known for its Napoleon memorabilia, its best museum is the ◼**Musée Fesch,** 50-52 rue Cardinal Fesch, with its stunning collection of 14th- to 19th-century Italian art amassed by Napoleon's uncle Fesch, after he left commerce for the cloth. His treasures include Titian's sensual *Man with a Glove* and Veronese's equally erotic *Leda and the Swan.* Also within the complex is the Renaissance-style **Chapelle Impériale,** the final resting place of most of the Bonapartes—though Napoleon himself is buried at Les Invalides in Paris. The altar displays a crucifix offered by Napoleon to his mother upon his return from Egypt in 1799. (☎04 95 21 48 17. Open July-Aug. M 1:30-6pm, Tu-Th 9am-6:30pm, F 9am-6:30pm and 9pm-midnight, Sa-Su 10:30am-6pm; Apr.-June and Sept. M 1-5:15pm, Tu-Su 9:15am-12:15pm and 2:15-5:15pm; Oct.-Mar. closed Su-M. Museum €5.40, students €3.80; chapel €1.50, students €0.75, under 15 free.)

The **Musée National de la Maison Bonaparte,** rue St-Charles, between rue Bonaparte and rue Roi-de-Rome, the first home of the town's famous megalomaniac now warehouses such memorabilia as the smaller-than-average bed in which the future emperor slept after returning from Egypt. (☎04 95 21 43 89. Open Apr.-Sept. M 2-6pm, Tu-Su 9am-noon and 2-6pm; Oct.-Mar. M 2-4:45pm, Tu-Su 10am-noon and 2-4:45pm. Last tickets sold 15min. before closing. €4, students €2.60, under 18 free.) The glittering **Salon Napoléonien,** pl. Foch, in the Hôtel de Ville, restored in ornate 19th-century style, displays Napoleon's portraits, sculptures, medals, and death mask. (☎04 95 51 52 53. Open mid-June to mid-Sept. M-Sa 9-11:45am and 2-5:45pm; mid-Sept. to mid-June M-F 9-11:45am and 2-4:45pm. €2.30.)

The **Musée à Bandera,** 1 rue Général Levie, provides a comprehensive digest of Corsican history, though the exhibits are incomprehensible without a good understanding of French. (☎04 95 51 07 34. Open July to mid-Sept. M-Sa 9am-7pm, Su 9am-noon; mid-Sept. to June M-Sa 9am-noon and 2-6pm. €4, students €2.50.)

◪ NIGHTLIFE

Unlike most Corsican cities, Ajaccio has its fair share of wild nights. The major clubs are out of town, but can be reached by car or motorbike. **La Cinquième Avenue** is 5km away on rte. des Sanguinaires (☎04 95 52 09 77. Open daily midnight-5am.) **Le Blue Moon** is farther away in Porticcio. (☎04 95 25 07 70. Open July-Aug. daily 11:30pm-5am; Apr.-June and Sept. F-Sa 11:30pm-5am.) **La Place,** Résidence Diamant II, in town on bd. Pascal Rossini, caters to an older crowd in a modern blue-velvet lounge. The DJ mixes American and French hip hop and pop. (☎06 09 07 03 53. No cover. Cocktails €9. Open F-Su 11pm-5am.) Clubs tend to have no cover but a one-drink minimum. Several lively bars crowd **bd. Pascal Rossini,** including **Athena Bar,** where a young crowd grooves to hip hop on the terrace. Beers on tap €2.70, bottled €3.50-6.60, cocktails €8.50. Elaborate ice cream treats €7-8. (☎04 95 21 22 61. Open daily noon-2am.) Those who still have cash to lose can head to the **Casino,** bd. Pascal Rossini. (☎04 95 50 40 60. 18+. Open daily 1pm-4am.) For the latest, check out *Le Rendez-Vous* and *Sortir,* both available at the tourist office.

⬚ **La Bocca Loca,** 4 rue de la Porta (☎06 07 08 68 69). Tasty *tapas* served in a cozy interior with live Gypsy and salsa music. Large terrace has tasteful paintings and palm tree décor. Cocktails €4.50. Sangría €9 per pitcher. *Tapas* €2.50-3. Open Tu-Sa 7pm-2am.

Cohiba, Résidence Diamant II, bd. Lantivy (☎04 95 51 47 05), is a popular *avant boîte* (pre-club scene). A chic crowd fills a sumptuous interior of velvet chairs and dark wood. DJ plays house Oct.-May F and Sa. Open daily 7:30am-2am.

Shamrock, 3 rue Forcioli Conti, off pl. de Gaulle (☎06 09 97 24 82), is a Corsican-Irish pub. Low-key lounging in the green leather interior. Occasional karaoke night W from 9pm. Happy hour daily 5-7pm; 2 draft beers for the price of 1. Open daily 5pm-2am.

Irish Pub, 4 rue Notre Dame (☎04 95 21 63 22), just down the street from Shamrock, provides a livelier pub experience. Loud music plays in a warm setting of green walls and tables designed like beer-bottle caps. Drafts €3-3.50, bottles €4-5. Cocktails €9.50. July-Aug. F-Sa live international music after 11pm. Open daily 6pm-2am.

◙ FESTIVALS

Ajaccio often hosts a summer theater or music festival (call the tourist office for details). August 15 brings the three-day **Fêtes Napoléon,** which commemorates the emperor's birth with plays, a parade, ceremonies, and a huge *pyrosymphonie* (fireworks display) in the bay. But Ajaccio's real mania is revealed during the July and August **Shopping de Nuit,** when stores stay open until midnight on Friday nights as musicians, dance groups, and circus performers ply their trades on the streets.

PORTO

A hiking paradise, the stunning gulf of Porto combines Corsica's most impressive geography: jagged volcanic mountains above a crystalline sea, lush pine groves, and waterfalls pouring into pools. To the north, a marine reserve conceals grottos and rare plants and birds. The heavily touristed town of Porto (pop. 432) is little more than an extended souvenir shop, but lodging is cheap, transportation is convenient by Corsican standards, and the smooth pebble beach is the perfect place to watch the sunset.

ORIENTATION & PRACTICAL INFORMATION

Porto is split into an upper town, **Haut Porto** or **Quartier Vaita,** and a coastal area, **Porto Marina,** where some 15 hotels and restaurants compete for space. D81 connects Haut Porto to Calvi in the north and leads to Ajaccio in the south; the unnamed main road leads from D81 to the port.

Buses: Autocars SAIB (☎04 95 22 41 99). To: **Ajaccio** (2hr.; July to mid-Sept. 2 per day, mid-Sept. to June M-Sa only; €11) and **Calvi** (3hr.; July-Aug. 1 per day, Sept.-June M-Sa only; €16). Purchase tickets on bus. **Autocars Mordiconi** (☎04 95 48 00 04) runs to **Corte** (July to mid-Sept. M-Sa 1 per day, €19). Purchase tickets on board. All buses leave from the top of the main road.

Car, Bike, and Scooter Rental: Porto Locations (☎/fax 04 95 26 10 13), opposite Haut Porto's supermarkets. Cars €60 per day, €305 per week. 18+, with a license for at least 2 years. Scooters €46/€230. License necessary. Bikes €15/€68. Credit card deposit €305 for cars, €610 for scooters. Open Apr.-Oct. daily 8:30am-7:30pm. AmEx/MC/V. **Hertz** (☎06 08 69 75 20), on the left bank. Open daily 8am-8pm. AmEx/MC/V.

Taxis: Taxis Chez Félix (☎04 95 26 12 92).

Tourist Office: (☎04 95 26 10 55; www.porto-tourisme.com), near the marina on the main road. Topo-guide for hikes (€2.30), bus schedules, and info on water sports, boat trips, and lodging. Spotty English spoken. Open June-Sept. daily 9am-7pm; Apr.-May M-F 9am-noon and 2-6pm, Sa 9am-noon; Oct.-Mar. M-F 9am-noon and 2-5pm.

Police: Gendarmerie Maritime (☎04 95 51 75 21), on the port.

Laundromat: Lavo 2000 (☎04 95 26 10 33), on the main road. Wash €7, dry €1 per 5min. Open daily 8am-9pm.

Post Office: (☎04 95 26 10 26), midway between the marina and Haut Porto. Open July-Aug. M-F 9am-12:30pm and 2-5pm, Sa 9-11:30am; Sept.-June M-F 9am-12:15pm and 2-4pm, Sa 9-11am. **Postal code:** 20150.

ACCOMMODATIONS

Porto's abundance of indistinguishable hotels makes the town more affordable than most of the island, although prices rise dramatically in July and August. Make summer reservations well ahead of time. Some of the cheapest accommodations in Corsica are *gîtes* in the pleasant village of Ota, a departure point for many hikes. From Porto, veer right and head uphill at the fork after the supermarkets; follow the signs to D124 and Ota. (1hr.) The bus from Ajaccio to Porto also stops at Ota (15min., 2 per day, €3.10). **Chez Felix ❶** has homey 4- to 8-bed dorms and kitchen access. (☎04 95 26 12 92; fax 18 25. Breakfast €6. Sheets €2. €12 per person, *demi-pension* €29; doubles with bath and *demi-pension* €40. AmEx/MC/V.) **Chez Marie ❶** has modern, spartan dorms with 6-12 beds. (☎/fax 04 95 26 11 37. Kitchen access. Breakfast €5. Beds €12, *demi-pension* €29; doubles with *demi-pension* €29. MC/V.)

Le Panorama (☎04 95 26 10 15), on the main road near the port, is the best value in town. Functional, moderately-sized rooms with huge terraces overlook the marina and beach, all with shower, some with toilet. Reception daily 8am-noon and 3-9pm. July-Aug. singles and doubles €23-25; Apr.-June and Sept.-Oct. €20-23. Extra bed €3. ❸

Bon Accueil (☎/fax 04 95 26 19 50; jesaispas@net-up.com), on the main road a bit farther from the port. Simple rooms, all with shower and toilet, get the job done, even if the mattresses are a little soft. Friendly staff. Breakfast €5.50. Reception daily 7am-midnight. Mid-July to Aug. €43 per person with *demi-pension;* Sept. to mid-July singles and doubles €29-40; triples €35-45. MC/V. ❹

Hôtel Brise de Mer (☎04 95 26 10 28; www.brise-de-mer.com), next to Le Panorama. 20 clean, slightly bland rooms all have shower or bath, toilet, telephone, and balconies. Request a room with a sea view. Bar and TV room. Breakfast €7. Open Apr.-Oct. Singles and doubles €39-49; triples €54; quads €61; *demi-pension* with double €81-84. ❹

Le Lonca (☎04 95 26 16 44; fax 04 95 26 11 83), right next to the post office, lets rooms overlooking the hills. All rooms with shower or bath, toilet, and TV. Reception daily 7am-11pm. Breakfast €6.50. Open Apr.-Oct. July singles and doubles €38-50; triples €60; Aug. €54-69/€79; Apr.-June and Sept. €35-50/€56-60. MC/V. ❹

◤ CAMPING

Le Sole e Vista (☎04 95 26 15 71; fax 04 95 26 10 79), on the right before the supermarkets when entering Porto. 3-star site has shady hillside plots and a rockin' bar. Reception 9am-10pm. Showers included. Laundry €4. 1km from beach. Open Apr. to mid-Nov. €5.30 per person, €2 per tent or car. Electricity €3.20. ❷

Les Oliviers (☎04 95 26 14 49; guy.lannoy@wanadoo.fr), 200m toward Ajaccio on D81. 3-star site. Reception daily 8am-9pm. Showers included. Tennis courts and swimming pool. Scuba diving agency on-site. Open Apr.-Oct. €5.50-6.50 per person, €2.70 per tent, €2.50 per car. Electricity €3. 4- to 8-person fully equipped bungalows €305-793 per week. MC/V. ❷

Camping Municipal (☎04 95 26 17 76) straddles D84 in lower Porto and resembles a poorly planned parking lot, but always has vacancies. Reception daily 8am-9:30pm. Open July-Sept. €5 per person, €2 per tent or car. Electricity €3. MC/V. ❷

◖ FOOD

Two adjacent supermarkets are in Haut Porto on D81: **SPAR** (☎04 95 26 11 25; open July-Aug. M-Sa 8am-8pm, Su 8am-noon and 5-8pm; Sept.-June M-Sa 8:30am-noon and 3-7pm, Su 8:30am-noon) and **Supermarché Banco**. (☎04 95 26 10 92. Open July-Aug. M-Sa 8am-8pm, Su 8am-12:30pm and 4-8pm; Apr.-June and Sept.-Oct. M-Sa 8am-noon and 3-7pm). Prices at hotel restaurants are high and the food mediocre. **La Marine ❶**, on the main road near the marina, is one of the better choices in town, with tasty pizzas from €5.50 and *menus* from €9. (☎04 95 26 10 19. Open Apr.-Oct. daily 11:30am-2:30pm and 6:30-10:30pm.) **La Tour Génoise ❹**, behind the aquarium in the marina, serves more traditional Corsican dishes and fresh fish. There are three *menus* (€15.10-19.70) served until 9pm, with enough options to please any palate. (☎04 95 26 17 11. Open Apr.-Oct. daily noon-2pm and 7-10pm. Wheelchair-accessible. AmEx/MC/V.) Farther up the main road from the port, the restaurant/*discothèque* **Le César ❷** serves appetizing pizza (€6-8), pasta (€6.10-7.30), and salad (€4.60-7.60) that fuels patrons who dance into the wee hours. (☎04 95 26 14 71. Open Apr.-Sept. daily 8:15pm-2am; disco open daily 11pm-5am.) The *gîtes* in Ota (see **Accommodations**) have delicious Corsican specialties (*menus* €17-19), though the 1hr. walk may be too long for some.

HIKES & SIGHTS

GORGES & POOLS & PINES, OH MY. The old mule track from Ota to Evisa is perfect for hikers of all skill levels. This 3hr. trail winds through the deep **Gorges de la Spelunca,** past 15th-century bridges and spots for picnics and swimming. From the stairway to the left of the Mairie (see **Accommodations,** for buses), the trail follows the painted orange rectangles. Spectacular scenery lies near the start of the trail, between the first two Genoese bridges and the **Pont de Zaglia.** (45min.) To walk this shorter section, follow the main road from Ota to the first Genoese bridge and pick up the original orange rectangle trail. (25min.) There are no afternoon return buses from Ota or Evisa; the return hike is about 1hr.

Chestnut trees and 50m pines fill the mountainous **Fôret d'Aitone** between Evisa and Col. de Vergio. This trail, part of the **Tra Mare e Monti,** is famous for its *piscines naturelles,* swimming holes formed by pooling waterfalls. The pools are an hour or so from Evisa; beyond them is a more difficult and secluded trail to Col. de Vergio (6-7hr.), where a *gîte d'etape* marks its intersection with the **GR20.**

LES CALANCHES. The astounding geological rock formations of the Calanches resemble, in the words of Guy de Maupassant, a "menagerie of nightmares petrified by the whim of some extravagant god." Hikes here range from easy-as-pie to do-or-die. The **Château Fort,** in the former category, begins 6km south of Porto on D81; ask the Ajaccio-Ota bus driver to stop at **Tête de Chien.** (30min.) A more masochistic alternative awaits 2km farther south, off D81; the marked trail, which begins near the stadium, climbs 900m to the spectacular 1294m **Capo d'Orto.** (3hr. one way.) From the top of the summit, a trail heads back to Porto.

SCANDOLA. Off-limits to hikers and divers, the caves, grottos, and wild terrain of the **Réserve Naturelle de Scandola** can only be explored by **boat tours** from Porto. **Porto Linea,** next to Hôtel Monte Rosso behind the aquarium, sends a 12-person boat into the reserve. (☎04 95 26 11 50. *Open Apr.-Oct.; reserve ahead in person. 3hr. tour of Scandola €35; 2hr. tour of Les Calanches €20.)* Less intimate but equally spectacular, **Nave Va,** near Hôtel Le Cyrnée, tours Scandola with 50- to 180-person boats. (☎04 95 26 15 16. *Reserve ahead Apr.-Oct. 3hr. €34.)* The reserve's celebrated inhabitants are falcon-like buzzards, whose wailing call is immediately recognizable.

SIGHTS IN PORTO. The *raison d'être* for Porto's hotels and postcard shops is one of Corsica's oldest Genoese towers, the 1549 **Tour Génoise.** A 15min. climb to the top, spectacular views of windswept cliffs drop majestically to the sea. *(Open Apr.-Sept. daily 10am-12:30pm and 3-7pm. €2.50.)* The one-room **Aquarium de la Poudrière,** on the marina, is also worth a brief stop, if only to identify a mysterious dish from last night's dinner. The cave-like space holds a giant stingray and other aquatic creatures from the Gulf of Porto. (☎04 95 26 19 24. *Open daily 10am-7pm. €5.50. Ticket for both the aquarium and Tour Génoise €6.50.)*

CALVI

Sometimes called Corsica's Côte d'Azur, Calvi (pop. 5700) shares some of the best and worst traits of that better-known coastline. Yacht-bound and café-ridden, it is full of souvenir shops and the idle rich, yet it's also stunningly beautiful, with a star-shaped citadel above town and a long, sandy beach below, all against a backdrop of snow-capped mountains. Even if Calvi isn't the most popular Corsican destination, two hostels and an accessible beach make it the most backpacker-friendly town on the island.

CORSICA

▐ TRANSPORTATION

Flights: Aéroport de Calvi Ste-Catherine (☎04 95 65 88 88), 7km southeast of town. Taxi from the town center €20. **Air France** and subsidiary **Air Littoral** (☎08 02 82 08 20) fly to **Lille, Lyon, Marseille, Nice,** and **Paris.**

Trains: pl. de la Gare (☎04 95 65 00 61), on av. de la République near the Port de Plaisance. To: **Bastia** (3hr., 2 per day, €17.80); **Corte** (2½hr., 2 per day, €14.90); **Ile Rousse** (45min., 2 per day, €4.10). **Tramways de la Balagne** also sends trains to **Ile Rousse** (50min.; June-Sept. 10 per day, Apr.-May and Oct. 4 per day; €4.80). Open daily June to mid-Sept. 5:45am-9pm; mid-Sept. to June 5:30am-7:30pm. Purchase tickets at the station or on board.

Buses: Autocar SAIB buses (☎04 95 22 41 99) depart from in front of the Super U and head to **Porto** (2½hr.; July-Aug. 1 per day, May-Oct. M-Sa only; €16). **Les Beaux Voyages,** av. Wilson (☎04 95 65 11 35), leaves from the front of the agency at pl. Porteuse d'Eau. Buy tickets at the office. Open M-Sa 9am-noon and 2-7pm. Buses to: **Calenzana** (July-Aug. M-Sa 2 per day, Sept.-June M-Tu and Th-Sa 1 per day; €5.30), where the famed **GR20** begins; **Bastia** (2¼hr., M-Sa 1 per day, €12.50) via **Ile Rousse** (25min., €3). **Eurocorse Voyages** (☎04 95 21 06 30) runs buses to **Ajaccio** (4hr., M-Sa 1 per day, €15) via **Ponte-Leccia** (€8.50).

Ferries: for info and tickets, call **Agence TRAMAR** (☎04 95 65 01 38), quai Landry, in the Port de Plaisance. Open M-F 8:30am-noon and 2-5:30pm, Sa 8:30am-noon. Both **SNCM** (☎04 95 65 17 77. 3hr.; 7 per week; €30-41, ages 12-25 €15-26) and **Corsica Ferries** (☎04 95 65 43 21. 3½-6hr., 16 per week, €20-33) send high-speed boats to **Nice** and have offices near the Capitainerie du Port de Commerce. Open 2hr. before boat arrivals.

Car Rental: Europcar, av. de la République (☎04 95 65 10 35, airport 04 95 65 10 19). €65 per day, €250 per week. 21+. Open M-Sa 8am-1pm and 2:30-7:30pm, Su until 6:30pm. MC/V. **Hertz,** 2 rue Maréchal Joffre (May-Sept. ☎04 95 65 06 64, airport 04 95 65 02 96). July-Aug from €79 per day, €279 per week; slightly lower May-June and Sept. Under 25 prices slightly higher. 21+. Open M-Sa 8am-8pm. AmEx/MC/V.

Bike Rental: Garage d'Angeli, pl. Christophe Colomb (☎04 95 65 02 13; fax 06 19 09 28 36). €17 per day, €94 per week. €300 or ID deposit. Open Apr.-Oct. daily 9am-noon and 2-7pm; Nov.-Mar. Tu-Sa 9am-noon and 2-6pm.

Taxi: (☎04 95 65 03 10 or 04 95 65 03 10). At the train station. 24hr.

✦ ▐ ORIENTATION & PRACTICAL INFORMATION

The city is manageable in size and easy to walk, connected by one main road that follows the curve of the coast and changes names several times over its course, from **boulevard Wilson** between the citadel and the post office, to **avenue de la République,** to **avenue Christophe Colomb** when leaving the city. The lovely pedestrian **rue Clemenceau** runs below bd. Wilson, parallel to the port.

Tourist Office: Port de Plaisance (☎04 95 65 16 67; www.tourisme.fr/calvi). From the back of train station, turn left; it's on the second floor of the first building on the right. Friendly staff offers a 90min. audio guide of the citadel (€6). 1½hr. guided tours of the citadel in French, English, Italian, or German offered to groups of 6 or more; €7 per person; reserve 2 days in advance. Open June to mid-Sept. daily 9am-1pm and 2:30-7pm; May M-Sa 9am-noon and 2-6pm; mid-Sept. to Apr. M-F 9am-noon and 1:30-5:30pm.

Police: ☎04 95 65 44 77. On Port de Plaisance, to the right of the tourist office.

Laundromat: Laverie, av. Christophe Colomb, in Super U Plaza. Open daily 8am-10pm. **Calvi Clean,** bd. Wilson, has new machines. Wash €6, dry €5. Open daily 7am-10pm.

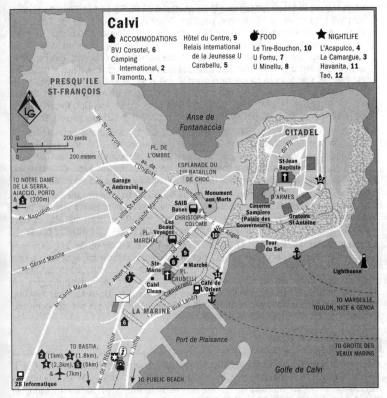

Internet: Calvi 2B Informatique, av. Santa Maria (☎04 95 65 19 25), above the BVJ hostel. €2 for the first 15min, €1 per additional 15min. Open daily 9am-9pm. **Café de L'Orient** (☎04 95 65 00 16), on the port on quai Landry. €1 flat fee, €0.10 per min. Open Apr.-Oct. daily 8am-10pm; café open until 2am for drinks and crêpes.

Post Office: bd. Wilson (☎04 95 65 90 90). Open M-F 8:30am-6pm, Sa 8:30am-noon. **Postal code:** 20260.

▚ ACCOMMODATIONS & CAMPING

Calvi has two of the only hostels in all of Corsica and many hotels, which are cheaper but farther from the center of town. Reserve ahead in summer, especially July. Renting by the week can be cheaper; ask about *tarifs dégressifs* at the tourist office.

BVJ Corsotel "Hôtel de Jeunes," av. de la République (☎04 95 65 14 15; fax 04 95 65 33 72), across from train station parking lot. Friendly staff and ideal location near the center of Calvi make this the best budget option. 2- to 8-bed single-sex dorms with blankets, shower, and sink have high ceilings and plenty of space. Seaside rooms have excellent views. Breakfast included. Reception daily 7:30am-1pm and 5-10pm. No noise after 10pm; curfew and total silence after midnight. Checkout 10am. Reserve in advance, particularly July-Aug. Open Apr.-Oct. Beds €22. ❷

Relais International de la Jeunesse U Carabellu (☎04 95 65 14 16). From the station, turn left onto av. de la République, pass the Super U, turn right at rte. de Pietramaggiore, and follow signs 5km into the hills, until the road forks at a stop sign. Veer left and continue. (45min.) Women may not want to walk the long, deserted route alone. Upon request, owners will pick up guests from the train station or airport. This beautiful, secluded chalet 5km from town has spacious rooms with incredible views of Calvi. The staff allows guests to camp out by request. Families get their own doubles, triples, or quads with private shower; dorms have 10-11 beds each. Breakfast included. Sheets €3.10. Luggage drop-off 24hr. Lockout 10am-5pm. Open Apr.-Oct. Reserve far in advance. Dorms €15.30. Obligatory *demi-pension* July-Aug. €25 per person. ❷

Il Tramonto, rte. de Porto R.N. 199 (☎04 95 65 04 17; www.hotel-iltramonto.com), 800m from town past the citadel. 28 simple, clean rooms have fabulous sea views in addition to shower, toilet, and phone. Breakfast €5. Reception daily 7am-midnight. Open Apr.-Oct. Aug. singles and doubles €49; July €46; June and Sept. €40; May and Oct. €34; Apr. €31. Extra bed €13-16. Excellent balcony rooms €3 extra. MC/V. ❹

Hôtel du Centre, 14 rue Alsace-Lorraine (☎04 95 65 02 01), behind rue Clemenceau, in the heart of Calvi. Friendly manager lets simple, slightly worn rooms with firm beds. Breakfast €4.50. Free luggage storage. Reception 8am-9pm. Open mid-May to early Oct. Singles and doubles €28-37, with shower €31-44; triples €34-46/€37-50. ❸

Camping International, RN 197 (☎04 95 65 01 75; fax 04 95 65 36 11), 1km from town. Walk past Super U and Hôtel L'Onda; immediately past the mini-golf sign, take a right. Relaxed atmosphere and friendly managers. Young people flock here for nearby beach access and on-site bar. July-Aug. bands play all types of music 3-4 nights per week. Showers included. Laundromat across from campsite. Open Apr.-Oct. July-Aug. €5.20 per person, children under 7 €2.60; €3 per tent; €1.50 per car. Apr.-June and Sept.-Oct. €3.70/€1.90/€2.30/€1.30. MC/V. ❶

▣ FOOD

Aside from street-side panini vendors, pickings are slim for cheap food in Calvi. Try the **Super U Supermarché**, av. Christophe Colomb. (☎04 95 65 04 32. Open July-Aug. M-Sa 8am-9pm, Su 8am-1pm; June and early to mid-Sept. M-Sa 8am-8pm, Su 8am-1pm; mid-Sept. to May M-F 8:30am-12:30pm and 3-7:30pm, Sa 8:30am-7:30pm.) Narrow **rue Clemenceau** is filled with specialty food shops and grocers and hosts a **covered market** beside the Eglise Ste-Marie. (Open daily 8am-noon.) Pedestrian alleys have the best food and local ambiance. Cheap pizzerias line rue de la République.

▨ U Minellu, traverse de l'Eglise (☎04 95 65 05 52), prepares an excellent €16 *menu* of Corsican specialties. Start with the *assiette du Minellu*, a medley of fresh Corsican ham and cheese, tomatoes, beets, chick-peas, and hard-boiled eggs. Then sample such local specialties as *sanglier* (wild boar) or *cannelloni au brocciu* (pasta with country cheese). A secluded terrace area offers a satisfying break from the tourist-laden rue Clemenceau. Open July-Aug. daily 7pm-midnight; Apr.-June and Sept. to mid-Oct. M and W-Su noon-2:30pm and 7-11pm. ❹

Le Tire-Bouchon, 15 rue Clemenceau (☎04 95 65 25 41). This rare Corsican wine bar offers 38 regional wines (€1.70-7 per glass), and simple local cuisine, including assortments of cheese and Corsican *charcuterie*. Moderate portions from €5.40. Open Apr.-Nov. M-Sa noon-2:45pm and 7-11pm, Su 7-11pm; Apr. and May closed W. MC/V. ❷

U Fornu, bd. Wilson (☎04 95 65 27 60). Local staple, off the beaten track, has a good €14 *menu*, including *soupe corse* and *raie à la grenobloise* (stingray) and a wide selection of appetizers (€8-13) and main dishes (€11-20). Bread and desserts are homemade. Open daily noon-2pm and 7-11pm, Su closed for lunch. ❷

CORSICA

SIGHTS & BEACHES

The 18th-century inscription, *"civitas Calvi semper fidelis"* (the city of Calvi is always faithful), that crowns the entrance to Calvi's remarkable citadel was bestowed on Calvi by the Genoese in thanks for five centuries of loyalty. Just beyond the entry portal, a welcome center distributes useful free maps and a self-guided audio tour of the citadel, which covers some of the lesser monuments. (☎04 95 65 36 74. Tours in English, French, Italian, and German; 90min.; €6. Open M and W-Su 10am-12:30pm and 4-7:30pm.) Round the first corner and climb the stairs to reach the citadel's center, dominated by the austere **Palais des Gouverneurs.** Once the bastion of Genoese control over the city, today it serves—not without irony—as the mess hall for France's foreign legion. The 16th-century **Cathédrale St-Jean Baptiste** towers nearby, though the church's Baroque domes belie an unusually sparse interior. The 15th-century blue-clad Madonna to the left of the choir, imported from Peru by a wealthy emigré, is the pride and joy of the town's religious sector. (Open daily 9am-7pm.) The **Oratoire St-Antoine,** tucked into the citadel's wall, is largely abandoned, but a decaying 1530 fresco in the upper left corner depicts Christ accompanied by St-Sebastian. (Open daily 10am-6pm.)

Like several other Mediterranean towns, Calvi claims to be the birthplace of **Christopher Columbus.** The local theory is that Calvi expatriate Antonio Calvo returned to his hometown in the 15th century to enlist recruits for the Genoese navy. His nephew Christophe caught his eye, so Calvo brought him with him to Genoa. A **plaque** in the northern end of the citadel marks the ruins of the house where Columbus was supposedly born. The citadel's other famous house sheltered Napoleon and his family in 1793 when they were fleeing political opponents in Ajaccio. At the end of the day, watch the sunset at the far end of the citadel.

Calvi and the surrounding area abound with gorgeous, sandy beaches and a clear turquoise sea. Shallow water allows beach-goers to walk many meters from the coast, and strong winds make for great windsurfing. If the 6km expanse of **public beach** gets too windy, the rocks surrounding the citadel provide secluded and sun-drenched shelter. The **Tramways de la Balagne** (see **Transportation**) run to more remote coves farther out of town.

▉ NIGHTLIFE

The bars on the **Port de Plaisance** are lively on summer nights. Locals come from far and wide to the two open-air nightclubs on the road to Ile Rousse. Signs posted all over town advertise party nights at different spots along the northern coast.

Tao, in the citadel (☎04 95 65 00 73). Piano bar and pricey French/Asian restaurant overlooks the sea. 16th-century architecture, live music, and a romantic garden terrace create an intimate atmosphere. Open June-Sept. daily 7pm-6am.

Havanita, Port de Plaisance (☎04 95 65 00 37). Cuban cocktails served amid Spanish music and palm trees. Tip well; the bartenders need money to buy some actual clothes. Happy hour daily 6-8pm: wine €3, cocktails from €7. Open Apr.-Oct. daily 6pm-2am.

La Camargue (☎04 95 65 08 70), 25min. up N197 by foot. Scantily clad youth bump 'n' grind in one of several discos around outdoor pools, while an over-30 crowd swings in the piano bar. Free shuttles depart for La Camargue from the port parking lot near the tourist office. €10 cover includes one drink. Open July-Aug. daily 11pm-6am; June and Sept. Sa-Su only; piano bar open year-round.

L'Acapulco, on D151, also known as rte. de Calenzana (☎04 95 65 08 03), a right turn 10min. after La Camargue, creates a tropical mood with flaming torches and waterfalls. The club's shuttles leave from the Tour de Sel. €10 cover includes one drink. Open July-Aug. daily 11pm-6am; June and Sept. weekends only; piano bar open year-round.

◘ FESTIVALS

Calvi hosts several festivals, including the **Festival du Jazz** in the last week of June, when over 150 musicians give impromptu performances. (☎04 95 65 00 50. M-F €11, Sa €15.) In mid-September, the **Rencontres Polyphoniques** draw international singers. (☎04 95 65 23 57. Tickets €15-20.) Late October or early November brings week-long **Festival du Vent**, a panoply of artists, scientists, athletes, actors, and human rights activists all converging to celebrate the mystical, omnipresent wind of Calvi and Corsica. For more information, call the tourist office.

ILE ROUSSE

Stretching east from Calvi to the town of Ile Rousse (pop. 3000), Corsica's northern coast is lined with pristine beaches and out-of-the-way coves. The scenery is at its best in Ile Rousse itself; with a powdery beach and clear, opalescent waters, the scenic train ride from Calvi alone justifies the trip. In 1759, Pasquale Paoli, the leader of Corsica before it belonged to France, founded Ile Rousse in an effort to divert trade from Genoese-dominated Calvi. Today, Ile Rousse remains the perfect hub for hikes into the breathtaking countryside of the Balagne.

SNCM sends **ferries** to Nice (3-10hr., depending on the boat; 2-7 per week; €35-40, students €30-35). Call Agence CCR on av. J. Calizi for more info. (☎04 95 60 09 56; fax 04 95 60 02 56. Open M-F 9am-noon and 2-5:30pm, Sa 9am-noon.) The **train station** provides service to Calvi, Bastia, and Ajaccio. (☎04 95 60 00 50. Open daily July-Sept. 6am-8pm, low season 6am-noon and 2-7pm.) Tramways de la Balagne **trains** hug the coast on the way to Calvi. (50min.; June-Sept. 10 per day, Apr.-May and Oct. 4 per day; €4.30. Purchase tickets on train.) Several beaches and campsites lie along the route; the train will stop at any when requested. Few can resist the charm of **Aregno Plage** and its campsite, three stops from Ile Rousse.

No more than 2km across, Ile Rousse is easy to navigate. The town center lies to the right of the train station, while the *gare maritime* and tower-topped peninsula are to the left. To get to the **tourist office** from the train station or ferry depot, walk right for about 5min.; it's in a small office on the opposite side of pl. Paoli. The staff provides a practical guide and information on nearby villages. (☎04 95 60 04 35; www.ot-ile-rousse.fr. Open July-Aug. M-Sa 9am-7pm, Su 10am-6pm; June and Sept. daily 10am-noon and 5-7pm; Oct.-May M-F 9am-noon and 2-6pm.)

Leader's Sport, av. Paul Doumer, rents mountain **bikes**. (☎04 95 60 15 76. Open July-Aug. daily 7am-8:30pm; June M-Sa 8am-7:30pm, Su 8am-12:30pm; Sept.-May M-Sa 9am-noon and 2:30-7pm. €16 per day, €77 per week; €229 deposit. MC/V.) Surf the **Internet** at Cyber One Café, 15bis. av. Paul Doumer. (☎04 95 62 72 91; www.cyberonecafe.com. 16 computers. €1 for 10min., €2.30 for 30min., €4 per hr. Open M-Sa 10am-2am, Su 2pm-midnight.) The **post office** is on rte. de Monticello (☎04 95 63 05 50. Open M-F 8:30am-5pm, Sa 8:30am-noon.) **Postal code:** 20220.

Since Ile Rousse tends to attract moneyed Frenchmen, there's only one budget hotel in town. To find **Hôtel le Grillon ❸**, 10 av. Paul Doumer, go straight on av. Piccioni, beside the tourist office, and take a left. The friendly owners usher guests into light orange hallways and soft pink rooms, all with shower, toilet, TV, and telephone. (☎04 95 60 00 49; fax 04 95 60 43 69. Breakfast €5.20. Dinner *menus* €12.50 and €15.70. Reception daily 6:30am-10pm. Reserve in advance. Open Mar.-Oct. Singles €30.40-46.50; doubles €32-51.80; triples €38.40-57.60. Aug. obligatory *demi-pension* for singles €65.40; doubles €89.80; triples €114.60. MC/V.) Campers generally have more luck. Sites appear fairly regularly all along the Balagne coast, so just hop off the train when you see one that you like. **Les Oliviers ❶** in Ile Rousse is 800m from the town center on av. Paul Doumer, the road to Bastia. The congenial, coastal site offers a snack bar and tiny wooden chalets for two. (☎04 95

60 19 92 or 04 95 60 25 64; fax 04 95 60 30 91; lesolivierskalliste@wanadoo.fr. Laundry €5. Open Apr.-Oct., July-Aug. closed to cars after 11pm. €5.50 per person, €3.50 per tent, €2.50 per car. Electricity €3.50. Laundry €4. Showers free. Chalet doubles July-Aug. €500 per week; Sept.-June €350 per week. MC/V.)

The city's signature covered **market** off pl. Paoli is filled with local fruits, the tentacled and finned catches of the day, and 10 different types of honey. (Open daily 7am-1pm.) On the 1st and 3rd Friday of every month, the market lasts all afternoon. The local **Casino** supermarket on allée Charles de Gaulle takes up where the market leaves off. (☎04 95 60 24 23. Open July-Aug. M-Sa 8:30am-8pm, Su 8:30am-1pm; Sept.-June M-F 8:30am-12:30pm and 3-7:30pm, Sa 8:30am-7:30pm.) The *brasseries* along pl. Paoli specialize in inexpensive pizza and sandwiches. **U Fuccone ❷**, on rue Paoli, offers an excellent three-course, €12 *menu*, which includes such options as warm goat cheese salad, *entrecôte au poivre*, and *tarte au chocolat*. The friendly staff also serves pizzas (€7-8) and pastas (€7.50-11.50) on the well-situated terrace (☎04 95 60 16 67. Open May-Sept. daily 11:30am-3pm and 6:30pm-1am; low season hours vary. AmEx/MC/V.) For a taste of Corsican cuisine, indulge at **U Spuntinu ❹**, on rue Napoléon. The three-course *menu* (€19) includes *cannelloni au broccio* and *veau corse*. This 28-year-old family establishment won't disappoint. (☎04 95 60 00 05. Open mid-Mar. to mid-Nov. daily 7:30-11pm; mid-Nov. to mid-Dec. and early to mid-Mar. M-Sa same hours; closed mid-Dec. to Feb. V.)

CORTE (CORTI)

The most dynamic of Corsica's inland towns, Corte (pop. 6000) blends breathtaking natural scenery with an intellectual flair. Cliffs, gorges, and snow-capped peaks provide a dramatic backdrop for the island's only university, whose 4000 students keep the city's prices low. Known to natives as "the heart of Corsica," the town gave birth to Pasquale Paoli's national constitution. A majority of residents now sympathize with the continent's more moderate politics, but the city is still the center of the Corsican nationalist cause. To show solidarity, most native-born locals speak the island's distinctive dialect, Corse, and sometimes give an icy reception to mainland French. Some visitors, though, will be delighted by Corte's friendly people, authentic cuisine, and singular hikes.

▗ TRANSPORTATION

Trains depart from the rotary at av. Jean Nicoli and N193 to Ajaccio (2hr., 4 per day, €12.50); Bastia (1½hr., 4 per day, €11); and Calvi via Ponte-Leccia (2½hr., 2 per day, €14.90). The station (☎04 95 46 00 97) is open M-Sa 6:30am-8:30pm, Su 7:45am-8:30pm. Eurocorse Voyages **buses** (☎04 95 31 73 76) leave from the *Brasserie Le Majestic* on Cours Paoli for Ajaccio (1¾hr., M-Sa 2 per day, €11.50) and Bastia (1¼hr., M-Sa 2 per day, €10). Autocars Mordiconi (☎04 95 48 00 04), just below pl. Paoli off av. Xavier Luciani, near the Tuffelli parking lot, leave from the train station for Porto (2½hr., July-Sept. M-Sa 1 per day, €19). **Taxis Salviani** can be reached at ☎04 95 46 04 88 or 06 03 49 15 24; **Taxi Feracci** at ☎04 95 61 01 17 or 06 12 10 60 60. **Cars** can be rented at **Europcar**, 2 pl. Paoli (☎04 95 46 06 02. From €81 per day, €282 per week. Credit card deposit. Insurance included. 21+. Open M-Sa 9am-noon and 3-7:30pm. MC/V.)

▗▗ ORIENTATION & PRACTICAL INFORMATION

To reach the town center from the station, turn right on D14 (alias av. Jean Nicoli), cross two bridges, and follow the road until it ends at **cours Paoli**, Corte's main drag. A left turn here leads to **place Paoli,** the town center. At the top right corner,

climb the stairwayed **rue Scolisca** to reach the citadel and the **tourist office,** which provides a useful bus schedule and bilingual brochure that lists popular hikes. **Parc Naturel Régional** expert provides additional info for hikers June-Sept. M-F 9am-noon and 2-6pm. (☎04 95 46 26 70; www.corte-tourisme.com. Open July-Aug. daily 9am-8pm; June and Sept. M-Sa 9am-noon and 2-6pm; Oct.-May M-F 9am-noon and 2-6pm.) Other services include: **Bureau Information Jeunesse de Corte,** rampe Ste-Croix (☎04 95 46 12 48; open M-F 8:30am-noon and 2-5:30pm); a **laundromat** at Speed Laverie (☎06 82 56 08 31), allée du 9 Septembre, next to the Casino supermarket (open daily 8am-9pm); **police** (☎04 95 46 04 81), southeast of town on N200; a **hospital** (☎04 95 45 05 00) at allée du 9 Septembre; **Internet** at Grand Café du Cours, 22 cours Paoli (☎04 95 46 00 33; €1 for 15min., €3 per hr.; open daily 7am-2am) and **Syndrome-Cyber,** 3 av. du Président Pierucci, next to the SPAR supermarket (☎04 95 47 13 32; €1.50 for 15min., €2 for 30min., €3 per hr.; open Sept.-June M-F 7:30am-2am, Sa-Su 10am-2am); a **post office** at av. du Baron Mariani (☎04 95 46 08 20). Open M-F 8am-12:30pm and 1:30-5pm, Sa 8am-noon. **Postal code:** 20250.

⌂ ACCOMMODATIONS & CAMPING

Hôtel-Residence Porette (H-R), 6 allée du 9 Septembre (☎04 95 45 11 11; fax 04 95 61 02 85), near the train station. Head left from the station for 100m. An unattractively converted police station, this budget hotel looks the part, though the pretty back garden is a pleasant surprise. Functional, clean rooms with pastel walls. Sauna (€4), weight room, and restaurant. Breakfast buffet €5. Reception 24hr. Reservations required June and Aug.-Sept. Singles €21, with shower and toilet €29; doubles €29/€39; triples and quads €59. Rooms facing garden €10 extra. AmEx. ❷

Hôtel de la Paix, av. Général de Gaulle (☎04 95 46 06 72; fax 04 95 46 23 84), past Hôtel de la Poste. Recently renovated, this hotel's spacious rooms have pink walls, TV, toilet, and shower or bath. Sleek elevator adds to modern feel. Breakfast €5.50. Restaurant with 3-course *menu* €13. *Demi-pension* available; inquire at time of reservation. May-July singles and doubles €50-57; triples €56-64. Sept.-Apr. singles €39; doubles €43-50; triples €50. Aug. singles and doubles €50-57; triples €62-66. ❹

Hôtel de la Poste, 2 pl. du Duc de Padoue (☎04 95 46 01 37), off cours Paoli. Near the town center. Friendly owner offers 12 rooms with sparkling bathrooms, firm beds, and high ceilings. Breakfast €6. Reception 24hr. Singles and doubles €44; triples €50; quads €57. ❹

Hôtel Sampiero Corso, av. du Président-Pierucci (☎04 95 46 09 76; fax 04 95 46 00 08), in the center of town, 10min. from the train station. 32 spacious rooms with toilet, shower or bath, and telephone, some with small balconies facing the street. Breakfast €6.50. Open Apr.-Oct. Singles and doubles €45-46; triples €64. Extra bed €16. ❹

U Tavignanu, chem. de Balari (☎04 95 46 16 85; fax 04 95 61 14 01). Turn left out of station, right at the fork. Follow allée du 9 Septembre, then the signs at the base of the Citadel, up a steep dirt trail. (20min.) Converted hilltop farmhouse and shaded campsite run by salt-of-the-earth owners. Inaccessible to cars. Breakfast €4, included with *gîte* (4 rooms with 5-6 beds each). Reception daily 7am-10:30pm. Dinner €14. *Gîte* €15, July-Aug. obligatory *demi-pension* €29. Camping €4 per person, €2 per tent. ❶

Camping:

U Sognu, on D623 (☎04 95 46 09 07; fax 04 95 61 00 76). From the top of pl. Paoli, follow rue Prof. Santiaggi around the bend, turn left, and cross the bridge. At the fork, follow the sign and turn right. (10min.) From train station, follow directions to Restonica; after the first bridge, take a left onto D623. Surrounding poplar and olive trees provide little shade, but site has easy access to the nearby stream and scenic views of the *haute ville.* Clean showers and toilets. Breakfast €4.60. Restaurant meals €6.40-10.50. Reception daily 8am-noon and 3-11pm. Closed to cars after 11pm. Open late Mar. to Nov. €5 per person; €2.50 per tent or car. Electricity €3. ❶

Restonica (☎/fax 04 95 46 11 59; vero.camp@worldonline.fr). Follow directions from station to H-R Porette until a sign on the right points downhill to campsite. Crowded site, with showers and a good location. Breakfast €6. Pizza €8. Reception daily 7:30am-10pm. Open mid-Apr. to mid-Oct. €6 per person; €2.50 per tent or car. Electricity €3.50. ❶

FOOD

Place Paoli is the spot for sandwiches and pizza; **rue Scolisca** and the surrounding citadel streets have a good selection of inexpensive local cuisine, with most *menus* around €9-12. **SPAR,** 5 av. Xavier Luciani, is in the town center. (☎04 95 46 08 59. Open July-Aug. M-Sa 7:30am-8pm, Su 9am-noon and 5-7:30pm; Sept.-June M-Sa 8am-12:30pm and 3-8pm, Su 9:30am-noon; Jan.-Feb. closed Su.) The mammoth **Casino** is near the train station on allée du 9 Septembre. (☎04 95 45 22 45. Open mid-June to Aug. daily 8:30am-7:45pm; Sept. to mid-June M-F 8:30am-12:30pm and 3-7:30pm, Sa 8:30am-7:30pm.)

U Museu ❸, ramp Ribanelle, off pl. d'Armes at the foot of the citadel, serves large, tasty portions of regional cuisine on a beautiful, shady terrace. Try the house specialties *civet de sanglier* (wild boar) or *cannelloni au brocciu.* (☎04 95 61 08 36. *Menu* €13.20, salad €6.40-9.20, meat dishes €10.40-14.50, fish dishes €8.40-19.80, pasta €6.90-9.90. Open early Apr. to late Dec. daily 11am-2pm and 7-11pm; Sept.-May closed Su.) **A Scudella ❷,** 2 pl. Paoli, serves delectable regional cuisine. The €9 *menu* includes a double appetizer and dessert, the €11 *menu* a main dish and dessert. (☎04 95 46 25 31. *Plats* €9.20. Open M-Sa noon-2pm and 7-11pm. AmEx/MC/V.) Family-run **A Maniccia ❷,** 7 cours Paoli, is situated in a pleasant *place* beside a fountain. (☎04 95 61 01 69. Local specialties €6.10-9.50, extensive *menu* €13, pasta €6-8, omelettes €4.50-5, crêpes €2.50-6. (Open daily noon-2:30pm and 7:30-10pm.)

SIGHTS

Corte's *vieille ville,* with its steep, barely accessible streets and austere stone **citadel** peering over the Tavignano and Restonica valleys, has always been a bastion of Corsican patriotism. The route up to the old city is dedicated to the town's two heroes: **Pasquale Paoli,** who drafted Corsica's famous constitution and proclaimed Corte the island's capital, and **Jean Pierre Gaffori,** who preceded Paoli as governor until his assassination by Genoese agents in 1753.

In a plain-looking dwelling across from pl. Gaffori, a plaque honors the apartments where Charles Bonaparte, Napoleon's father, lived for two years in the 1760s while serving the Paolian cause.

The **Musée de la Corse,** at the top of rue Scolisca, focuses on Corsica's ethnographic history, moving beyond regional costumes and crafts to deeper issues like the role of tourism on the island. Exhibits are in French and Italian; consider the 90min. English audio guide (€1.50). Admission includes a visit to Corsica's only inland **citadel,** constructed in 1419, with its ancient the dungeon, kitchens, and bathrooms. (☎04 95 45 25 45; fax 04 95 45 25 36. Museum open late June to late Sept. daily 10am-8pm; late Sept. to Oct. and Apr. to late June Tu-Su 10am-6pm; Nov.-Mar. Tu-Sa 10am-6pm. Citadel closes 1hr. earlier than museum. €3-5.30, students €2.30-3.) Uphill from pl. Paoli and left at the Eglise de l'Annonciation is the oldest portion of the 15th-century city walls and a spectacular 360° view from the **Belvedere** that includes the old city, the converging Tavignanu, Restonica, and Orta rivers, and the mountains around Corte.

Corte's surrounding mountains and valleys are striped with countless trails for **hiking** (call the tourist office for maps and trail info, ☎08 92 68 02 20 for weather conditions) or **horseback riding.** Try the **Ferme Equestre Albadu,** 1½km from town on N193 toward Ajaccio. (☎04 95 46 24 55. Reserve at least one day in advance. €13.80 for 1hr., €24.40 for 2hr., €32 for 3hr., €68.60 per day including picnic. 6-night camping trip with guide €533.60; with stay in *gîtes* €701.30.)

▶ DAYTRIPS FROM CORTE

GORGES DE LA RESTONICA

Southwest of Corte, tiny D623 stretches 16km through the Gorges de la Restonica, a high-altitude canyon fed by glacial lakes. The hot-blooded can brave a swim in the gorge's icy water. To get there, descend rue Prof. Santiaggi at the back of pl. Paoli and cross the bridge at the right; head right on D623 at the fork. Follow the signs for Restonica for 2km to the Parc Naturel Régional info office, where a free shuttle *(navette)* whisks hikers 13km up a twisting road to the gorge's summit. The *navette* is only available for groups; individual hikers must access the gorge by car. (Open July-Aug. daily 8am-1pm, return 3-5pm. Call ☎04 95 46 02 12 for detailed schedules.)

Those who only have time for one hike should be sure to tour the **glacial lakes** at the top of the gorge, one of the island's loveliest and least-populated areas, where hikers of all levels can enjoy the magnificent scenery. Take the *navette* to the Grotelle parking lot. To the right, a trail clearly marked in yellow leads to a sheep-pen-turned-snackbar, then crosses the river and steadily ascends to the "most visited lake in Corsica," the circular **Lac de Melo.** (1hr.) This snow-fed beauty lies at 1711m, near the foot of **Mont Rotondo** (2622m), and is surrounded by mountain peaks, including Corsica's highest: **Mont Cinto** (2710m). The trail is designated *facile* (easy), but the climb is steep, rocky, and slippery when wet. Also, temperatures at the top can reach well below zero even when it's 25°C in town. From Melo, the trail continues, marked in yellow, to one of Corsica's largest and deepest lakes, the austere **Lac de Capitellu.** (1930m; 45min.) From here, the trail meets the red-and-white marked **GR20,** Corsica's most famous and most demanding hike.

For a full-day adventure follow the GR20 to the left until it intersects with a trail leading to the **Refuge de Petra Piana,** where hikers can spend the night or continue on to the **Lac de Rotondo.** (4½hr.) Less trodden but equally spectacular is the hike to **Lac de l'Oriente.** Take the free *navette* to **Pont de Tragone** and then follow the marked trail that passes shepherds' houses to the much-photographed lake. (3hr.)

For more info on Restonica's offerings, consult the French-language *Tavignano-Restonica topo-guide* (in bookstores for €11.50) or the tourist office hiking expert. The office also supplies a €5 map with 26 labeled hiking trails.

GORGES DU TAVIGNANO

Less rugged than Restonica, though equally physically demanding and more easily accessible by foot, the Tavignano gorges are filled with waterfalls, natural pools, and picturesque hiking trails. With no road access, it is likely to be less crowded than its better-known counterpart. To get to the trail, head to the back of the citadel and look for signs; the trail is marked in orange. The first 2½hr. of hiking along the Tavignano river leads to the **Passerelle du Russulinu** (902m), a small suspension bridge surrounded by refreshing natural swimming pools and flat, picnic-friendly rocks. Bring sunscreen and wear a hat; there is little shade along the way. Another 3hr. along the same trail leads to the **Refuge de la Sega** (1166m), where hikers can stop to spend the night. The road diverges at this point. To the left, a well-traveled trail passes by ancient *bergeries* (sheep pens) and abandoned shepherd huts, crossing the **Plateau d'Alzo** and ending at the **Pont de la Frasseta**, 8km up on D623 in the heart of the Restonica. (4hr.) To the right, the less traveled trail leads to the heartland village of **Calacuccia,** on D84, 45min. from Corte by car. (4hr.)

FORÊT DE VIZZAVONA

The forests surrounding the town of Vizzavona have some of the most accessible hiking trails on Corsica. Get to Vizzavona via a beautiful train ride. (1hr.; Sept. to mid-July 4 per day, mid-July to late Aug. 5 per day; €5.70). Outside the station, a billboard lists hiking routes. The plunging falls and clear lagoons of the **Cascades des Anglais** provide the best scenery, about 45min. southwest of town along the GR20. The cascade's flat rocks and shaded coves make ideal picnic spots.

BASTIA

Bastia (pop. 40,000), Corsica's second largest city, can often feel impersonal and industrial. The city's huge new port constantly bustles with the arrival and departure of ferries from the mainland and Italy; this and Bastia's proximity to the airport means that many travelers begin their Corsican adventures here. Bastia is more, though, than just a mid-transit stop; it is neither cosmopolitan nor over-touristed, and its crumbling *vieille ville*, lovely citadel, and exquisite Baroque churches give the city a more authentic feel than Ajaccio. In addition, Bastia is the perfect gateway to the must-see Cap Corse.

▉ TRANSPORTATION

Flights: Bastia-Poretta (☎04 95 54 54 54), 23km away. An airport bus (☎04 95 31 06 65), scheduled to coincide with departing flights, leaves from pl. de la Gare, by the *préfecture* (30min., €8). Purchase tickets on bus. Compagnie Corse Méditerranée (☎08 20 82 08 20) flies to **Marseille, Nice,** and **Paris.** 4 flights per day per location.

Trains: pl. de la Gare (☎04 95 32 80 61), to the left of the roundabout at the top of av. Maréchal Sebastiani. Station open M-Sa 6:10am-8:45pm, Su 6:30am-8:45pm. To: **Ajaccio** (4hr., 4 per day, €23.50); **Calvi** (3hr., 2 per day, €17.80); **Corte** (1½hr., 5 per day, €11); **Ile Rousse** (2½hr., 2 per day, €14.70). It is also possible to purchase a 7-day excursion pass for unlimited train travel throughout Corsica (€47).

Buses: Ask the tourist office for a bus schedule. **Eurocorse,** rue du Nouveau Port (☎04 95 21 06 30), runs to **Ajaccio** (3hr., M-Sa 2 per day, €18). **Rapides Bleus,** 1 av. Maréchal

Sebastiani (☎04 95 31 03 79), sends buses to **Porto Vecchio** (3hr.; M-Sa 2 per day, mid-June to mid-Sept. daily; €18.50) via Aléria (1½hr., €11), from across from the post office. Purchase tickets on bus.

Ferries: quai de Fango, next to pl. St-Nicolas; turn left from av. Maréchal Sebastiani just past pl. St-Nicolas. **SNCM** (☎04 95 54 66 90; fax 04 95 54 66 39), by the quai de Fango, sails to **Marseille, Nice,** and **Toulon. Corsica Ferries,** 5bis rue Chanoine Leschi (☎04 95 32 95 95), chug to **Nice** and **Toulon,** and **Livorno** and **Savona** in Italy. **Moby Lines,** 4 rue Commandant Luce de Casablanca (☎04 95 34 84 94; fax 04 95 32 17 94), services **Genoa** and Livorno in Italy. For details on air and ferry connections to mainland France, see **Intercity Transportation,** p. 759.

Car Rental: ADA, 35 rue César Campinchi (☎04 95 31 48 95; fax 04 95 34 96 95), with a 2nd location at the airport (☎04 95 54 55 44). Open M-F 7:30am-noon and 2-7:30pm, Sa 7:30am-noon. It is possible to return cars after-hours. AmEx/MC/V.

Scooter Rental: Toga Location Nautique, port de Plaisance de Toga (☎04 95 34 14 14), near the north quai. Scooters €61 per day, €288 per week; €1220 deposit. Open M-F 9am-noon and 2-7pm, Sa 9am-noon. AmEx/MC/V.

Taxis: (☎04 95 32 24 24, 04 95 36 04 05, or 04 95 32 70 70). €32-33 to airport. 24hr.

■ ☑ ORIENTATION & PRACTICAL INFORMATION

The tourist office is in the center of the action on **place St-Nicolas.** The main thoroughfares are **boulevard du Général de Gaulle,** which runs along the inland length of the *place*, and parallel **boulevard Paoli** and **rue César Campinchi.** Facing the mountains, the old port and citadel are to the left and the ferry docks are to the right.

Tourist Office: pl. St-Nicolas (☎04 95 54 20 40; fax 04 95 31 81 34; ot-bastia@wanadoo.fr), has numerous **maps** of the city and Cap Corse. Ask for a copy of their indispensable bus schedule. Open daily 8:30am-noon and 2-6pm.

Youth Center: Centre Information Jeunesse, 9 rue César Campinchi (☎04 95 32 12 13; fax 04 95 32 50 77; www.crij-corse.com). Friendly staff has info on work, housing, and leisure activities. Free **Internet** for up to 40min. Open M-F 8:30am-noon and 2-6pm, Sa 8am-noon.

Laundromat: Lavoir du Port, 25 rue Luce de Casablanca (☎04 95 32 25 51), just past the Esso gas station. Wash around €6. Open daily 7am-9pm.

Police: rue Commandant Luce de Casablanca (☎04 95 55 22 22).

Hospital: rte. Impériale (☎04 95 59 11 11).

Internet: free for up to 40min. at the **Centre Information Jeunesse** (see **Youth Center**). **Cyber Taz,** 4 cours Pierangeli (☎04 95 31 71 69) offers 14 computers and long hours. €1.50 per 30min. Open daily 10am-2am. **Le Cyber,** 6 rue des Jardins (☎04 95 34 30 34), in the old city. 10 computers. €1.60 for 30min., €3.10 per hr. Open M-Su 9am-11pm.

Post Office: at av. Maréchal Sébastiani and bd. Général Graziani (☎04 95 32 80 70). Open M-F 8am-7pm, Sa noon-7pm; closed W 12:30-1:30pm. **Postal code:** 20200.

⚑ ACCOMMODATIONS & CAMPING

Bastia's hotels are cheaper than those in Corsica's more popular resort towns. Low season discounts and vacancies are common, but from June to September, call ahead. Campsites are far from town but well-serviced by local buses.

Hôtel Central, 3 rue Miot (☎04 95 31 71 12; www.centralhotel.fr). The rooms in this central hotel are large and tastefully decorated. All have toilet and shower or bath. Breakfast €5.50. Reception 7am-11pm. Singles €35-50; doubles €40-80. Extra bed €15. For longer stays, there are fully equipped apartments for €330-610 per week. AmEx/MC/V. ❹

Hôtel Univers, 3 av. Maréchal Sébastiani (☎04 95 31 03 38; fax 04 95 31 19 91). Clean and modern with bright blue and yellow bedspreads. Moderately sized rooms feature large bathrooms, all with shower, toilet. A/C, TV, and phone. Breakfast €6. Reception 24hr. Jan-July singles €55; doubles €65; triples €80; quads €100. Aug-Sept. €65/€85/€95/€130. AmEx/MC/V. ❺

Camping:

San Damiano, Lido de la Marana (☎04 95 33 68 02; fax 04 95 30 84 10; www.campingsandamiano.com), is 5km south of Bastia. Autocars Antoniotti sends buses there from the station near pl. St-Nicolas (☎04 95 36 08 21. June-Aug. daily 8 per day, €2.50). Campsite features tennis courts and a supermarket. Open Apr.-Oct. €5-6 per person, €5.50-6.50 for tent and car. Electricity €3. Avoid the sites close to the road; they tend to be a bit noisy. ❶

Les Orangers, (☎04 95 33 24 09 or 04 95 33 23 65). To get there, take bus #4 from the tourist office to Licciola-Miomo (M-F every 30min., Sa-Su every hr.; €1.15), or follow bd. de Toga parallel to the sea. Small, basic site is 30 seconds from a popular pebble beach. Tennis courts nearby. Open May to mid-Oct. €4.50 per person, €2.50 per tent, €5 per car. Electricity €3.50. Showers free. ❶

🍴 FOOD

Inexpensive cafés crowd **place St-Nicolas.** The best food and most scenic views can be found at the **citadel,** along the **Vieux Port,** and on the broad terraces of the **quai des Martyrs de la Libération** along the boardwalk. Early birds hit the **market** on pl. de l'Hôtel de Ville. (Open Tu-Su 6-11am.) **SPAR** supermarket is at 14 rue César Campinchi. (☎04 95 32 32 40. Open M-Sa 8am-12:30pm and 4-8:30pm, Su 8am-noon.) **U Tianu ❸,** 4 rue Mgr. Rigo, is a hidden bargain (see **Hidden Deal,** at right). Just inside the citadel, **📖Chez Vincent ❸,** 12 rue St-Michel, serves delectable pizzas (€6.90-8.40) on a lovely terrace overlooking the sea. The friendly staff also serves pastas (€7-8), meats (€10-16), and a good selection of local wines. (☎04 95 31 62 50. Open M-Sa 10am-2:30pm and 6:30pm-midnight. AmEx/MC/V.) **Le Pub Assunta ❷,** 4 rue Fontaine-Neuve, in the old town, is a favorite with local youth. Enjoy burgers (€8), salads (€7), and local specialties (€10) on the small terrace, or play pool on the large indoor mezzanine. (☎04 95 34 11 40. Occasional live music in the evenings. Open M-Sa noon-3pm and 6pm-midnight, Su 6pm-midnight). **Chez Mémé ❸,** at the north end of quai des Martyrs de la Libération, specializes in seafood and offers a 3-course Corsican *menu* for €14. The restaurant is simple but pleasant, with a seaside terrace. (☎04 95 31 44 12. Open daily 9am-3:30pm and 6pm-midnight. AmEx/MC/V.) The more formal **La Voute ❸,** 6 rue Luce de Casabianca, near the new port, offers a wide variety of fish (€12-19.50), includ-

THE HIDDEN DEAL

U TIANU

On the second floor of a generic building on a dark, tiny street behind the *vieux port,* U Tianu ❸ is not love at first sight. Ascend the steep red staircase and the first thing you'll notice is the broken-in kitchen that has been serving a loyal local clientele for 21 years. Passing a small, smoky bar area, the friendly owners will usher you into one of two intimate dining rooms. Here, the anonymity of the exterior begins to fade. Old Corsican pictures and posters grace the white stucco walls. Wooden ceiling beams make the rooms feel more like converted barns than old apartments.

With one €19 *menu,* the "deal" of U Tianu may not be as immediately apparent as its seclusion and authentic, unpretentious atmosphere. Your €19, however, will go an incredibly long way: an apéritif of your choice, an entree, main dish, cheese course, dessert, coffee, and digestif, in addition to as much red or rosé wine as you can drink. You will probably be unable to finish it, though not because it lacks in taste. The *menu* is full of down-to-earth but delicious Corsican specialties, including an entree of *charcuterie corse* and main dishes of *veau au corse* (Corsican stewed veal) and *cannelloni au brocciu* (Corsican pasta with local cheese).

(4 rue Mgr. Rigo. ☎04 95 31 36 67. Open M-Sa 7pm-2am. Closed Aug. Cash and traveler's checks only.)

ing grilled *fillet de loup* (€17), and meats (€12.20-19), such as beef, duck, and veal. They also serve pizzas (€6.10-9) and pastas (€8.40-13) in a cave-like interior with yellow walls. (☎04 95 32 47 11, lavoutebastia@aol.com. Open daily noon-2pm and 7-11pm. AmEx/MC/V.) **Le Colomba** ❷ serves 20 varieties of reasonably priced pizzas (€7-9.50), pastas (€5-8), and omelettes (€6.50), and a €13.50 *menu* including salad, pizza, and dessert on a long terrace overlooking the old port. (☎04 95 32 79 14. Open Mar.-Dec. daily noon-3pm and 7pm-midnight.)

👁 👜 SIGHTS & BEACHES

A walk through Bastia's *vieille ville* reveals the town's former glory as the crown jewel of Genoese-ruled Corsica. To the north, the 1380 **citadel**, also called Terra Nova, was the Genoese stronghold on the island. The town's first building, the massive 1530 **Palais des Gouverneurs Génois**, lies just inside the fortified walls of the citadel. Unfortunately, it and the **Musée d'Ethnographie Corse** (an art and natural history museum) inside the Palais, are currently closed for renovations.

Toward the citadel from pl. St-Nicolas on rue Napoléon, sits the **Oratoire de St-Roch**, a small church embellished with crystal chandeliers. A few blocks down is the 18th-century **Oratoire de L'Imaculée Conception**, the entrance of which is paved with stones forming the image of a large sun. During Corsica's brief 1794-1796 stint as an Anglo-Corsican kingdom, the oratory was the home to the British puppet parliament; accordingly it contains a small Italian organ that once played "God Save the Queen" daily. The lavish interior of the church has elaborately painted ceilings, crystal chandeliers, and red-and-gold walls. Open daily 8am-7pm. The 17th-century Neoclassical towers of the **Eglise St-Jean Baptiste**, pl. de l'Hôtel de Ville, dominate the *Vieux Port*. The church's immense, baroque interior, the largest in Corsica, is marked by guilded domes and elaborate *trompe l'œil* ceilings.

Beaches in Bastia are dominated by serious sun-worshipers. To escape the masses, head north to the pebbly turf of **Miomo**, and, farther on, the beautiful sands of the **Cap Corse**. Bus #4 leaves every 30min. from pl. St-Nicolas 6:30am-7pm, traveling as far as Macinaggio three times per day; the closest sandy beach lies between **Erbalunga** (€2) and **Sisco** (€2.30).

🎵 NIGHTLIFE

Bastia is quiet come sunset, with the exception of the nightlife concentrated in the *vieux port*. **Café Wha!**, quai du Premier Bataillon de Choc, stands out with its bright neon sign and cheerful green façade. Always crowded, it caters to a mix of youthful tourists and locals with a wide selection of salads (€7-9) and Tex Mex dishes (€6.60-10) during the day; in the evenings, a hip young crowd drinks margaritas (€5.50) on the outdoor patio. (☎04 95 34 25 79. Live music July-Aug. Th-Sa from 9pm. Open daily 11am-2am.) **La Noche de Cuba**, 5 rue Chanoine Leschi, near the north quai, is a laid-back Latin bar with one of Bastia's few dance floors. On the weekends, it occasionally features live salsa bands. (☎04 95 31 02 83. Cocktails €6.20. Open daily 6am-2am.) Bastia's hottest nightlife option is the faraway **La Marana** area, home to beachside bars and open-air dance clubs like trendy **L'Apocalypse**. (☎04 95 33 36 83. Cover €10, includes one free drink. Open F-Sa 11:30pm-5am; July-Aug. also open M and W.)

🏛 DAYTRIP FROM BASTIA: ALÉRIA

The present-day village of Aléria (pop. 2500), halfway down Corsica's uninspiring eastern coastline, is nothing remarkable, despite its ancient fame. This choice spot—parallel to Carthage and opposite Rome—has seen the rise and fall of five

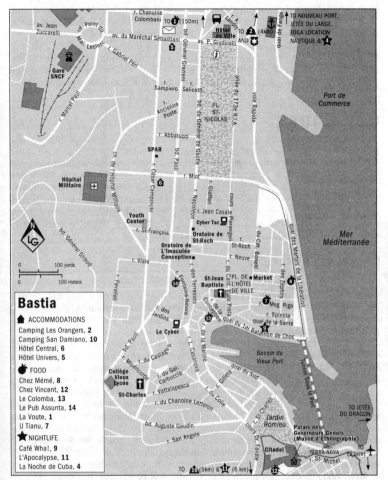

Bastia

🏠 ACCOMMODATIONS
Camping Les Orangers, **2**
Camping San Damiano, **10**
Hôtel Central, **6**
Hôtel Univers, **5**

🍴 FOOD
Chez Mémé, **8**
Chez Vincent, **12**
Le Colomba, **13**
Le Pub Assunta, **14**
La Voute, **1**
U Tianu, **7**

⭐ NIGHTLIFE
Café Wha!, **9**
L'Apocalypse, **11**
La Noche de Cuba, **4**

major civilizations: the Phoenicians, the Etruscans, the Greeks, the Carthaginians, and the Romans. The ancient center of Aléria is set on a hilltop about 1km south of the modern city. The summit has exceptionally long views in both directions, surely one of the reasons the Phoenicians chose to build a settlement there in 565 BC. Today, the fort holds the **Musée Jérôme Carcopino** (☎ 04 95 57 00 92), which houses an impressive collection of Etruscan pottery and Greek and Roman arti-facts—including a cosmetic kit that rivals Marie Antoinette's. The collections are well preserved and nicely presented. Just past the museum is the **Roman city** itself. One shouldn't visit Aléria expecting to find Pompeii—many of the buildings have taken a beating over time, and are little more than the remains of a foundation or the bases of columns, though they are well worth a visit. After passing the ruins of the Greek acropolis, enter the middle of the Roman forum; to the left is a temple to Jupiter, to the right, the extensive baths. Under Augustus, the population of the city swelled to 20,000, almost ten times that of present-day Aléria. Archaeologists have only begun to uncover the city's network of structures. (Museum open mid-May to Sept. daily 8am-noon and 2-7pm; Oct. to mid-May M-F 8am-noon and 2-5pm. Roman city closes 30min. earlier. €2 for both, students €1.)

Autocars Rapides-Bleus (☎ 04 95 31 03 79) run from Bastia (1½hr., M-Sa 2 per day, €11) and Porto Vecchio (1½hr., M-Sa 2 per day, €10) to Aléria's post office. Farther down the road is the **tourist office**. (☎ 04 95 57 01 51; fax 04 95 57 06 26. Open June-Aug. M-Sa 9am-7pm, Su 9am-1pm; Sept.-June M-F 9am-noon and 2-6pm.)

CAP CORSE

Stretching north from Bastia, the Cap Corse peninsula is Corsica's most savage frontier. A narrow road of perilous curves connects the Cap's numerous former fishing villages and marinas and offers breathtaking views of its 80km extent of sharp, jagged coastline. Having largely resisted over-development, Cap Corse is a hiker's dream. In addition to its coastline, its jungle-like forests and *maquis*-covered cliffs are dotted with decaying Genoese towers and hilltop chapels. Nearly every town is an access point for a stunning trail. Unfortunately, there are few budget hotels, and most require guests to pay for dinner with their rooms. Camping is a better option; a handful of sites dot the Cap.

▐ TRANSPORTATION

The best way to visit the Cap is to drive around the entire peninsula, which takes about a day. There are countless places to pull over and explore the coast, including many small, secluded swimming spots. Consider renting a **car** in Bastia (p. 778) or Calvi (p. 768). Be alert and cautious: roads are narrow and winding, and Corsican drivers are fearless. It's best to drive on a weekend, when traffic on D80 thins out; one might also consider starting the trip from the St-Florentine area (the west side of the peninsula), where cliffside roads are less treacherously close to the sea below. To start on the west side from Bastia, take bd. Paoli, then bd. Auguste Gaudin past the citadel onto N199 (dir: St-Florentine). For the east-to-west route, follow the coastal boulevard north from pl. St-Nicolas, following signs for the Cap.

In the high season, it is often possible to see the Cap by **bus tour.** Updated schedules and phone numbers for buses can be found in *Découverte Cap Corse*, an indispensable free guide provided at tourist offices. The cheapest and most convenient way to see the eastern side of Cap Corse is to take public **bus #4** from pl. St-Nicolas in Bastia. The bus leaves for **Erbalunga** (20min.; M-F every 30min., Sa-Su every hr.; €2) and **Marina di Siscu** (30min., every hr., €2.30); it also goes all the way to **Macinaggio** (50min., M-Sa 3 per day, €6.40). Ask nicely and the driver will stop wherever you feel the urge to explore. But keep in mind that most buses serve only the coast; you'll have to hike to the nearest inland village. (☎ 04 95 31 06 65. Service generally daily 6:30am-7:30pm.)

For tourism updates, contact the **Communauté de Communes du Cap Corse**, Maison du Cap Corse, 20200 Ville di Pietra Bugno (☎ 04 95 31 02 32; www.internet-com.fr/capcorse).

ERBALUNGA

The most accessible of Cap Corse's villages, Erbalunga offers a charming afternoon alternative to Bastia's crowded streets. This tiny fishing hamlet, where fishermen drop lines from their coastline houses, shows few signs of the 21st century. Crystal blue waters, white pebble beaches, and flat, secluded rocks make it a sunbather's paradise.

In the hills above, Benedictine monks observe a vow of silence at the **Monastère des Benedictines du St-Sacrement,** passed by a short hike that begins to the right of the restaurant **La Petite Auberge ❸,** where M. and Mme. Morganti serve Corsican specialties, including house seafood (€17), pastas (€8.50-11), and a €16.50 *menu.* The restaurant has also become well known for its delicious couscous, popular among locals. To get there, follow the main road 3min. north of the bus station. (☎04 95 33 20 78. Open daily noon-2:30pm and 6-10:30pm; closing hour varies. Reservations recommended. MC/V.)

Supermarket **SPAR** is across from the bus station. (☎04 95 33 24 24. Open M-Sa 8am-12:30pm and 4-7:30pm, Su 9am-noon.) 2½km south, **Lavasina** holds the famous **Eglise de Notre-Dame des Graces.** Legend has it that a disabled nun from Bonifacio was miraculously granted the use of her legs after praying to an image of the Virgin that hangs in this church. Thousands make an annual candlelit pilgrimage on Sept. 8 to celebrate this miracle.

SISCO

The *Découverte Cap Corse* guide, free at tourist offices, comes with a map listing 21 possible itineraries; hike #9, from **Sisco** (2hr.), is one of the best. Take bus #4 from pl. St-Nicolas to Marina di Sisco (30min., every hr., €2.30) and walk straight on route D32. From Marina di Sisco, follow the painted orange rectangles for a journey that penetrates deep into dense forests and expansive valleys, where a few tiny villages are the only trace of civilization. The path ultimately leads to **Petrapiana,** the intersection of several other routes, but make sure to take a break at **Barriggioni,** just 300m before Petrapiana, and admire the grandiose elegance of the **Eglise St-Martin,** which houses the eerie, bronzed remains of St-John Chrysostomos. From here, it is possible to detour to the 11th-century **Chapelle St-Michel,** perched precariously on a hilltop promontory; just follow the signs from the first church. From here, advance farther to the **Eglise St-Michel;** signs indicating the path are to the left of a grove of ferns near the second church. Though it is impossible to enter the chapel, the striking, panoramic view of the bowl-shaped valley below, sprinkled with Renaissance bell towers, is definitely worth the 1hr. climb. Note that this demanding hike requires a good pair of hiking boots.

Make sure to bring water and food to last the entire route, as the villages on the way do not sell provisions. The tiny village of **Petrapiana** has only three houses. On many routes, several variations of the trail are marked by orange rectangles, though depending upon the season, the vegetation may be too dense to take one or another of them.

MACINAGGIO TO CENTURI: THE CAPANDULA

Crystal-clear waters, white sandy beaches, and deep-green escarpments characterize this "cap of the cap," the arid and windy extreme tip of Cap Corse. Inaccessible to cars, the Capandula is a protected national reserve, the last stop for African migratory birds heading north. Camping is therefore forbidden, but hikers and bikers are blessed by the *sentier de Douaniers,* an extraordinary coastal trail named after the customs officials who first walked it. Beginning in **Macinaggio** or **Centuri,** the 8hr. hike passes by Genoese towers, secluded beaches, dramatic cliffs, and two villages. There are no amenities en route; bring lots of water, durable shoes, and sunscreen.

From the east coast, the trail takes off from **Macinaggio,** the spot to which Corsican leader Paolo Paoli returned in 1790 after 20 years in exile from his beloved island. Forty kilometers from Bastia, this port town is one of the few places that offer supplies and services. The **tourist office,** above the Capitainerie, has small maps of the trail. (☎04 95 35 40 34; sc.macinaggiorogliano@wanadoo.fr. Open July-Aug. daily 9am-noon and 4-8pm; June and early to mid-Sept. M-Sa 9am-noon and 3-7:30pm, Su 9am-noon; mid-Sept. to May M-F 9am-noon and 2-5pm.) The camping is good at **U Stazzu ❶**, just steps from the beach. To get there, follow the signs on the road by the church; the campsite is at the beginning of the *sentier de Douaniers*. (☎04 95 35 43 76. Open Apr.-Sept. €5 per person, €2.50 per tent. Showers free. Fridge/freezer available. No electricity.) Enjoy Cap Corse cuisine at **Ostéria di u Portu ❸**, right on the waterfront. Specialties like *langoustine au muscat du cap*, *haricots à la mode corse*, and the *cap corsini* salad, featuring fresh Corsican cheese and *charcuterie*, are all on the €14 *menu*. The hearty €21 *menu* includes starter, salad, ravioli, veal dish, and dessert. (☎04 95 35 40 49. *Plats* €9-18, fish *menu* €21. Open daily noon-2:30pm and 7-10:30pm.)

The miniature port of **Centuri** at the other end of the trail is one of the Cap's most picturesque spots; sit here at sunset and watch the boats bring in their daily haul of lobsters, mussels, and fish. On calm days, it is possible to swim out from the rocky shores to a small nearby island. **Camping Caravaning L'isulotto ❶**, just south of the town, has lots of amenities, including a bar and restaurant with a €9 *menu*, 200m from the sea. Mini-market and tennis courts also on-site. (☎04 95 35 62 81; fax 04 95 35 63 63. €4.90 per adult, €2.60 per tent, €1.70 per car. Electricity €3.30.)

BONIFACIO (BONIFAZIU)

The fortified city of Bonifacio (pop. 3000) sits high atop steep limestone cliffs, surrounded by strange rock formations that rise from a clear, blue sea. Its stunning landscape, exquisite *haute ville*, and gorgeous crescent-moon beaches make Bonifacio a must-see, despite its astronomical price tags and hordes of tourists.

▐ TRANSPORTATION

Buses: Eurocorse Voyages (Ajaccio ☎04 95 21 06 30, Porto Vecchio ☎04 95 70 13 83) stops by the small ticket and info office in the port parking lot. To: **Porto Vecchio** (30min.; 1 per day, July-Sept. 4 per day; €6.50, €1 for baggage); **Propriano** (1½hr., €11.50); **Ajaccio** (3½hr.; July to mid-Sept. M-Sa 3 per day, Su 2 per day; €20.50) via **Sartène** (1¾hr., €11).

Ferries: *gare maritime* at far end of the port. **SAREMAR** (☎04 95 73 00 96; fax 04 95 73 13 37) runs to **Santa Teresa**, Sardinia (1hr.; Apr. to mid-Oct. 3 per day, mid-Oct. to Mar. 2 per day; €6.70-8.50, cars €19.70-27.90). **Moby** is pricier but has later summer departures. (☎04 95 73 00 29; fax 04 95 73 05 50. July-Aug. 10 per day, Apr.-June and Sept.-Oct. 4 per day. €11-15, cars €22.50-51.50. Office open daily 7am-10pm.)

Taxis: at the port (☎04 95 73 19 08; 06 62 35 79 50; or 06 15 44 31 54).

Bike and Scooter Rental: Corse Moto Services, quai Nord (☎04 95 73 15 16). Scooters €40 per day, €245 per week, €1525 deposit. 18+. Open July-Aug. daily 9am-1pm and 3-7pm. MC/V. **Tam Tam,** rte. de Santa-Manza (☎04 95 73 11 59), 200m from the port on D58, veering away from the citadel. Bikes €12 per day, €75 per week. Open July-Aug. M-Sa 9am-1pm and 3:30-8pm, Su 9am-1pm; Apr.-June and Sept.-Oct. M-Sa 9:30am-12:30pm and 3:30-7:30pm, Su 9:30am-12:30pm. MC/V.

Car Rental: Europcar, av. Sylvère Bohn (☎04 95 73 10 99), at Station Esso just before the port. Cars from €73 per day, €254 per week; credit card deposit. Unlimited mileage and insurance included. 21+. Open Apr.-Oct. daily 8am-7pm, July-Aug. until 8pm. AmEx/MC/V. **Hertz,** on the port (☎04 95 73 06 41), near stairs to the *haute ville*. Cars from €90 per day, €320 per week; deposit from €860. Insurance included. 21+. Open July-Aug. daily 8:30am-1pm and 3:30-6:30pm; Sept.-June closed Su. AmEx/MC/V.

✈ 🛈 ORIENTATION & PRACTICAL INFORMATION

Bonifacio is divided by a steep climb into the **port** and the **haute ville.** The major highway **N198** becomes **avenue Sylvère Bohn** near the entrance to the town. From this direction, the port is visible on the right and the *haute ville* looms above. The main road veers left to become **D58**, leading to nearby beaches. To reach the tourist office, walk along the port and up the stairs before the *gare maritime*.

Tourist Office: corner of av. de Gaulle and rue F. Scamaroni (☎04 95 73 11 88; www.bonifacio.com). Friendly staff offers free maps and guides, and **accommodations booking.** Open May to mid-Oct. daily 9am-8pm; mid-Oct. to Apr. M-F 9am-noon and 2-6pm. **Annex,** on the port. Open July-Aug. daily 8:30am-12:30pm and 4-7pm.

Money: Exchange currency elsewhere. **Societé Générale,** rue St-Erasme, next to the stairs to the *haute ville* (☎04 95 73 02 49), charges €5.30 commission. Open M-F 8:15am-noon and 2-4:50pm.

Laundromat: Le Lavoir de la Marine, 1 quai Comparetti (☎04 95 73 01 03 or 06 85 43 91 29), on the port. Wash €6.10, dry €0.80 per 10min. Open daily 7am-7pm.

Police: at the start of rte. de Santa Manza (D58), just off the port (☎04 95 73 00 17).

Hospital: on D58 toward the beaches (☎04 95 73 95 73).

Internet: Cybercafé, on the port. Exorbitantly expensive, but it's the only option. 3 computers. €0.15 per min., €8 per hr. Open daily 8am-2am.

Post Office: pl. Carrega (☎04 95 73 73 73), uphill from pl. Montepagano in the *haute ville.* Open M-F 8:30am-5:15pm, Sa 8:30am-noon. **Postal code:** 20169.

🏠 ACCOMMODATIONS & CAMPING

Finding a room in the summer is virtually impossible. Camping is by far the cheapest option; many sites also offer affordable lodging in bungalows or chalets. Porto Vecchio has some economy-priced hotels, for those who don't mind daytripping.

Hôtel des Etrangers, av. Sylvère Bohn (☎04 95 73 01 09; fax 04 95 73 16 97), on the road to Bonifacio. Friendly staff lets spare, white rooms with shower and toilet at the cheapest spot in town. Breakfast included. A/C and TV in all but the cheapest rooms. Reception 24hr. Closed late Oct. to late Mar. Mid-July to mid-Sept. singles and doubles €50-72; triples €72; quads €82. Mid-May to mid-July €45-61/€62/€72. Apr. to mid-May and mid-Sept. to Oct. €35-44/€55/€63. Extra bed €10. MC/V. ❹

Hôtel Le Royal, pl. Bonaparte (☎04 95 73 00 51; fax 04 95 73 04 68), in the *haute ville.* 14 modern rooms, with shower, toilet, A/C, telephone and TV, some with sweeping sea views. Breakfast €6.10. Reception 24hr. Reserve at least a month in advance in summer. Early Nov. to late Mar. singles €38.20; doubles €44.30-49. Late Mar. to June and Oct to early Nov. €44-49/€49-59.50. July and Sept. €68.60/€74.70-79. Aug. €91.50/€99-105. Extra bed €15.30. MC/V. ❹

Camping:

L'Araguina, av. Sylvère Bohn (☎04 95 73 02 96; www.corse.sud/camping.araguina), at the entrance to town between Hôtel des Etrangers and the port. Compensates for crowded setup with a proximity to beaches and town. Lively snack bar. Reception daily 8am-9:30pm. Open mid-Mar. to Oct. 4-person bungalows €671 per week, €98 per night. €5.30-5.60 per person, €1.90 per tent or car. Electricity €2.80. Showers free. Laundry €5. ❶

Campo di Liccia (☎04 95 73 03 09; fax 04 95 73 19 94), 4km from the beach and town. The cheapest of a cluster of campsites on the road to Porto Vecchio. Pool, restaurant, ping-pong, volleyball. Open Apr.-Oct. Reception daily 8am-10pm. €4.50-5.80 per person, €1.90-2.50 per tent or car. Electricity €2.50-2.60. Free showers. Laundry available. Cash or traveler's checks. ❶

CORSICA

Camping U Farniente, route de Porto-Veccio (☎04 95 73 05 47; www.camping-pertamina.com), near Campo di Uccia. This 4-star campsite feels like a resort, with 150 *emplacements*, a swimming pool, tennis, ping-pong, volleyball, restaurant, bar, laundry, free hot showers, and free electricity. Open Apr. to mid-Oct. July-Aug. €20.80 for 2 people, tent, and/or car; Apr.-June and Sept. to mid-Oct. €16.80. V. ❷

◖ FOOD

A few supermarkets line the port, including **SPAR** at the start of rte. de Santa Manza. (☎04 95 73 00 26. Open July-Aug. M-Sa 8am-8:30pm, Su 8am-1pm; Sept. and June M-Sa 8am-8pm; Oct.-May M-Sa 8am-12:30pm and 3:30-7:30pm.) The port is filled with mundane restaurants; inexpensive *crêperies* and pizzerias in the *haute ville* serve more authentic Corsican cuisine. **Cantina Doria ❸,** 27 rue Doria, in the *haute ville*, serves hearty regional specialties in a Corsican-themed interior. The €14 *menu* is the best deal. (☎04 95 73 50 49. Open June-Sept. daily noon-2:30pm and 7-11pm; Apr.-May and Oct. Su-W and F-Sa only. MC/V.) Friendly service at **L'Archivolto ❹,** rue de l'Archivolto in the *haute ville*, complements the homey, knickknack-filled interior of this small gem. (☎04 95 73 17 58. *Tapas* for 2 €12.50, *plats du jour* €12.20-14.90. Reservations advised, phone 9-11am or after 5:30pm. Open daily July-Sept. 7:30-11pm; Oct.-June noon-2pm and 7:30-11pm.) **Kissing Pigs ❸,** on the port, specializes in Corsican *charcuterie*, cheese, and wine. (☎04 95 73 56 09. *Menus* €14-20, Corsican club sandwich €6-7, salad €7.50-14. Wine €1.90-5.50 per glass.) **Les Quatre Vents ❹,** on the port past the stairs to the *haute ville*, is a local favorite. Alsacian owners serve fresh seafood in the summer and Alsacian specialties in the winter. (☎04 95 73 07 50. *Menu* €18.50. Meat dishes €12.50-17. Pasta €11-23. Reservations advised. Open July-Aug. daily noon-2pm and 7:30pm-midnight; Sept.-June M noon-2pm, W-Su noon-2pm and 7:30pm-midnight.)

◉ SIGHTS

A marvel of both human and natural architecture, Bonifacio maintains 3km of fortifications above rounded, white cliffs. Make sure to take a **boat tour** of the city. One heads first to Bonifacio's greatest attraction, its multicolored coves, cliffs, and limestone grottos, which are almost as stunning as the clear, turquoise waters. From the water one has a lovely view of Bonifacio's *vieille ville*. Included in the 1hr. tour is a visit to the Dragon grotto *(Sdragonato)*, known for its resemblance to the map of Corsica. The second tour is a shorter version of the *grottes-falaises-calanques* tour, with a detour to the **Iles Lavezzi.** Relax and explore the gorgeous beaches on this nature reserve before catching a return boat. Many companies offer these tours, including **Les Vendettes Thalassa.** (☎04 95 73 01 17 or 04 95 73 05 43. *Grottes-Falaises-Calanques* tour every 30min. 9am-6:30pm, €12. Iles Lavezzi-Cavallo tour 7 departures per day, 3 return boats, last return boat 5:30pm; €25.) **Marina Croisières** offers the same tours for the same prices.

To explore the *haute ville* from within, head up **montée Rastello,** the steep staircase halfway down the port, for excellent views of the cliffs stretching east. Continue up montée St-Roch to the lookout at **Porte de Gênes,** constructed with a drawbridge in 1588 to be the town's sole entrance. Eager to overthrow colonizing Italians, Corsican nationals joined forces with King Henri II to besiege the town, successfully razing the Genoese fortress. The triumphant rebels rebuilt the elaborate **Bastion de L'Entendard** on the ruins of the original. Once a prison, the Bastion now traps tourists; the hokey historical displays are not worth the €2 admission.

After soaking up all this history, head left to pl. du Marché for the best views of Bonifacio's cliffs and limestone formation, **Grain de Sable.** The little mound just out of reach is Sardinia, 12km away. Turn right on rue Cardinal, then left on rue du

Sacrement to reach the **Eglise Ste-Mairie-Majeure,** Bonifacio's oldest building. This 12th-century church guards one of the town's most important objects: a fragment of the **true cross,** stripped from a shipwreck. Continue through the tiny, winding streets to the **cemetery** at the southern tip of the *haute ville.* Like all Corsican burial grounds, it marks the dead with elaborate miniature mausoleums.

🐚 BEACHES

Bonifacio's beaches are hard to reach and harder to leave. The only ones within walking distance of town are intimate but uninspiring; a path leads from Camping l'Araguina to **plage de la Catena** (30min.) and the cleaner and prettier **plage de l'Arinella.** (45min.) The peninsula east of Bonifacio is filled with spectacular beaches, but a car is necessary to reach most of them. From the port, take D58 towards the water; virtually every turn-off leads to a beach. The only beach accessible by bus is the lovely **plage Piantarella. Transports N. Massimi** heads there from the port parking lot. (☎04 95 73 13 16. M-Sa at 9am, 12:30, and 6pm, returns at 9:30am, 1, and 6:30pm. Round-trip €7.) The isolated **Cala Longa,** 8km away from Bonifacio, and **plage Maora,** a large beach in a calm natural harbor, are accessible by car. The turn-off for camping Rondinara, 17km away from town, leads to **plage de Rondinara,** one of Corsica's most famous beaches. Its long, sandy dunes and stunning blue lagoons have been the face of many a postcard.

Even more impressive than the mainland beaches are the pristine sands of the **Iles Lavezzi.** Every company on the port runs frequent ferries (30min.) to this nature reserve, where rock formations and broad fields meet turquoise waters. If spending the day here, be sure to bring water and food; there are no supplies available on the reserve. Just off the island, there is great **scuba diving** along the beautiful reefs. **Atoll,** on the port, past the stairs to the *haute ville,* arranges dives for beginners and experts alike. (☎04 95 73 53 83; www.atoll-diving.com. Open Apr.-Oct. daily 8am-8pm. Dives for beginners €69, for experts €37-59. MC/V.)

CORSICA

APPENDIX

CLIMATE

The chart below gives average temperatures and rainfalls for major French cities. For a rough estimate of Fahrenheit temperatures, double the Celsius and add 32.

Av. Temp. (lo/hi), Precipitation	January			April			July			October		
	°C	°F	mm	°C	°F	mm	°C	°F	mm	°C	°F	mm
Ajaccio	4/13	39/55	7.5	9/19	48/66	5.5	18/29	64/84	7.0	13/22	55/71	9.5
Bordeaux	1.6/9	35/48	6.8	7/17	45/63	6.5	14/27	57/81	5.0	8/19	46/66	9.5
Brest	4/8	39/46	8.8	7/13	45/55	6.3	13/21	55/70	5.0	9/16	48/61	9.0
Cherbourg	4/8	39/46	8.3	6/12	43/54	5.0	14/19	57/66	4.8	10/15	50/59	11.5
Lille	0.5/6	33/43	5.0	4/14	39/57	7.0	13/24	55/75	7.0	7/15	45/59	7.5
Lyon	-1/5	30/41	5.3	6/16	43/61	7.0	14/27	39/81	7.0	7/16	45/61	7.8
Marseille	3/12	37/54	5.0	5/15	41/59	1.5	14/26	57/79	1.5	13/24	55/75	9.3
Paris	0/6	32/43	4.3	5/16	41/61	5.3	13/24	55/75	5.3	6/15	43/59	5.5
Strasbourg	0/4	32/39	6.5	5/15	41/59	8.5	14/26	39/79	8.5	6/14	43/57	6.8
Toulouse	19/26	66/79	6.3	7/17	45/63	3.8	15/28	59/82	3.8	9/19	48/66	5.5

TIME ZONES

France lies in the Central European time zone, which is one hour ahead of GMT. From Easter to autumn, French time moves one hour ahead. Both switches occur about a week before such changes in the US.

MEASUREMENTS

France invented, and still uses, the metric system of measurement. The basic unit of length is the **meter (m),** which is divided into 100 **centimeters (cm),** or 1000 **millimeters (mm).** 1000 meters make up one **kilometer (km).** Fluids are measured in **liters (L),** each divided into 1000 **milliliters (ml).** A liter of pure water weighs one **kilogram (kg),** divided into 1000 **grams (g),** while 1000kg make up one metric **ton.**

1 inch = 25.4mm	1mm = 0.039 in.
1 foot = 0.30m	1m = 3.28 ft.
1 yard = 0.914m	1m = 1.09 yd.
1 mile = 1.61km	1km = 0.62 mi.
1 ounce = 28.35g	1g = 0.035 oz.
1 pound = 0.454kg	1kg = 2.202 lb.
1 fluid ounce = 29.57ml	1ml = 0.034 fl. oz.
1 gallon = 3.785L	1L = 0.264 gal.

APPENDIX

FRENCH PHRASEBOOK & GLOSSARY

FRENCH ESSENTIALS

ENGLISH	FRENCH	PRONOUNCIATION
GENERAL		
Hello./Good day.	Bonjour.	bohn-ZHOOR
Good evening.	Bonsoir.	bohn-SWAH
Hi!	Salut!	sah-LU
Goodbye.	Au revoir.	oh ruh-VWAHR
Good night.	Bonne nuit.	bonn NWEE
yes/no/maybe	oui/non/peut-être	wee/nohn/p'TET-rh
Please.	S'il vous plaît.	see voo PLAY
Thank you.	Merci.	mehr-SEE
You're welcome.	De rien.	duh rhee-AHN
Pardon me!	Excusez-moi!	ex-KU-zay-MWAH
Go away!	Allez-vous en!	ah-lay vooz ON!
Where is...?	Où se trouve...?	oo s'TRHOOV...?
What time do you open/close?	Vous ouvrez/fermez à quelle heure?	vooz ooVRAY/ferhMAY ah kel-UHR?
Help!	Au secours!	oh-skOOR
I'm lost.	Je suis perdu(e).	zh'SWEE pehr-DU
I'm sorry.	Je suis désolé(e).	zh'SWEE day-zoh-LAY
Do you speak English?	Parlez-vous anglais?	PAR-lay-voo ahn-GLAY

OTHER USEFUL PHRASES & WORDS

ENGLISH	FRENCH	ENGLISH	FRENCH
PHRASES			
Who?	Qui?	No, thank you.	Non, merci.
What?	Quoi?	What is it?	Qu'est-ce que c'est?
I don't understand.	Je ne comprends pas.	Why?	Pourquoi?
Leave me alone.	Laissez-moi tranquille.	this one/that one	ceci/cela
How much does this cost?	Ça coûte combien?	Stop/Stop that!	Arrête! (familiar) Arrêtez! (pl.)
Please speak slowly.	S'il vous plaît, parlez moins vite.	Please repeat.	Répétez, s'il vous plaît.
I am ill/I am hurt (m/f).	J'ai mal./Je suis blessé(e).	Please help me.	Aidez-moi, s'il vous plaît.
I am (20) years old.	J'ai (vingt) ans.	Pleased to meet you.	Enchanté(e).
I am a student (m/f)	Je suis étudiant/étudi- ante.	What's this called in French?	Comment-on dit...en français?
What is your name?	Comment vous appelez-vous?	The check, please.	L'addition, s'il vous plaît.
Please, where is/are...?	S'il vous plaît, où se trouve(nt)...?	I would like...	Je voudrais...
a doctor	un médecin	the cash machine	le guichet automatique
the toilet	les toilettes	the restaurant	le restaurant
the hospital	l'hôpital	the police	la police
a bedroom	une chambre	the train station	la gare

with	avec	single room	une chambre simple
a double bed	un grand lit	double room	une chambre pour deux
a shower	une douche	two single beds	deux lits
lunch	le déjeuner	a bath	bain
included	compris	without	sans
hot	chaud	breakfast	le petit déjeuner
cold	froid	dinner	le dîner

DIRECTIONS			
(to the) right	à droite	(to the) left	à gauche
straight	tout droit	near to	près de
follow	suit	far from	loin de
north	nord	east	est
south	sud	west	ouest

NUMBERS			
one	un	ten	dix
two	deux	fifteen	quinze
three	trois	twenty	vingt
four	quatre	twenty-five	vingt-cinq
five	cinq	thirty	trente
six	six	forty	quarante
seven	sept	fifty	cinquante
eight	huit	hundred	cent
nine	neuf	thousand	mille

TIMES AND HOURS			
open	ouvert	closed	fermé
What time is it?	Quelle heure est-il?	It's 11am.	Il est onze heures.
afternoon	l'après-midi	until	jusqu'à
night	la nuit	public holidays	jours fériés (j.f.)
today	aujourd'hui	January	janvier
morning	le matin	February	fevrier
evening	le soir	March	mars
yesterday	hier	April	avril
tomorrow	demain	May	mai
Monday	lundi	June	juin
Tuesday	mardi	July	juillet
Wednesday	mercredi	August	août
Thursday	jeudi	September	septembre
Friday	vendredi	October	octobre
Saturday	samedi	November	novembre
Sunday	dimanche	December	décembre

MENU READER			
agneau (m)	lamb	bière (f)	beer
ail (m)	garlic	bifteck (m)	steak
asperges (f pl)	asparagus	blanc de volaille (m)	chicken breast
assiette (f)	plate	bœuf (m)	beef
aubergine (f)	eggplant	boisson (f)	drink
bavette (f)	flank	brochette (f)	kebab
beurre (m)	butter	canard (m)	duck

bien cuit (adj)	well done	carafe d'eau (f)	pitcher of tap water
cervelle (f)	brain	maison (adj)	homemade
champignon (m)	mushroom	marron (m)	chestnut
chaud	hot	fraise (f)	strawberry
chèvre (m)	goat cheese	miel (m)	honey
choix (m)	choice	moules (f pl)	mussels
choucroute (f)	sauerkraut	moutarde (f)	mustard
chou-fleur (m)	cauliflower	nature (adj)	plain
ciboulette (f)	chive	noix (f pl)	nuts
citron (m)	lemon	œuf (m)	egg
citron vert (m)	lime	oie (f)	goose
civet (m)	stew (of rabbit)	oignon (m)	onion
compote (f)	stewed fruit	pain (m)	bread
confit de canard (m)	duck confit	pâtes (f pl)	pasta
coq au vin (m)	rooster stewed in wine	plat (m)	course (on menu)
côte (f)	rib or chop	poêlé (adj)	pan-fried
courgette f)	zucchini/courgette	poisson (m)	fish
crème Chantilly (f)	whipped cream	poivre (m)	pepper
crème fraiche (f)	thick cream	pomme (f)	apple
crêpe (f)	thin pancake	pomme de terre (f)	potato
eau minérale	mineral water	pommes frites	French (freedom) fries
eau de robinet (f)	tap water	potage (m)	soup
échalot (f)	shallot	poulet (m)	chicken
entrecôte (f)	chop (cut of meat)	pruneau (m)	prune
escalope (f)	thin slice of meat	rillettes (f pl)	pork hash
escargot (m)	snail	riz (m)	rice
farci(e) (adj)	stuffed	salade verte (f)	green salad
faux-filet (m)	sirloin steak	sanglier (m)	wild boar
feuilleté (m)	puff pastry	saucisse (f)	sausage
figue (f)	fig	saucisson (m)	hard salami
foie gras d'oie/de canard	liver of fattened goose/ duck	saumon (m)	salmon
frais (fraiche) (adj)	fresh	sel (m)	salt
haricot vert (m)	green bean	steak tartare (m)	raw steak
huitres (f pl)	oysters	sucre (m)	sugar
jambon (m)	ham	tête (f)	head
lait (m)	milk	thé (m)	tea
lapin (m)	rabbit	tournedos (m)	beef filet
légume (m)	vegetable	truffe (f)	truffle
magret de canard (m)	duck breast	viande (f)	meat

FRENCH-ENGLISH GLOSSARY

Le is the masculine singular definite article (the); *la* the feminine; both are abbreviated to *l'* before a vowel, while *les* is the plural definite article for both genders. *Un* is the masculine singular indefinite article (a or an), *une* the feminine; while *des* is the plural indefinite article for both genders ("some"). Where a noun or adjective can take masculine and feminine forms, the masculine is listed first and the feminine in parentheses; often the feminine form consists of adding an "e" to the end, which is indicated by an "e" in parentheses: étudiant(e).

abbaye (f): abbey
abbatiale (f): abbey church
accueil (m): reception
addition (f): the check
allée (f): lane, avenue
alimentation (f): food
aller-retour (m): round-trip ticket
an (m)/année (f): year
appareil (m): machine; commonly used for telephone
appareil photo (m): camera
arc (m): arch
arènes (f pl.): arena
arrivée (f): arrival
auberge (f): hostel, inn
auberge de jeunesse (f): youth hostel
autobus (m): city bus
autocar (m): long-distance bus
autoroute (f): highway
banlieue (f): suburb
basse ville (f): lower town
bastide (f): fortified town
bibliothèque (f): library
billet (m): ticket
billetterie (f): ticket office
bois (m): forest, wood
boucherie (f): butcher shop
boulangerie (f): bakery
brasserie (f): beer salon and restaurant
bureau (m): office
cap (m): cape
car (m): long-distance bus
carte (f): card; menu; map
cave (f): cellar, normally for wine
centre ville (m): center of town
chambre (f): room
chambre d'hôte (f): bed and breakfast room
chapelle (f): chapel
charcuterie (f): shop selling cooked meats (gen. pork) and prepared food
château (m): castle or mansion; headquarters of a vineyard
cimetière (m): cemetery
cité (f): walled city
cloître (m): cloister
collégiale (f): collegial church
colline (f): hill
comptoir (m): counter (in a bar or café)
côte (f): coast; side (e.g. of hill)
côté (m): side (e.g. of building)
couvent (m): convent
cour (f): courtyard
cours (m): wide street
cru (m): vintage

dégustation (f): tasting
départ (m): departure
donjon (m): keep (of a castle)
douane (f): customs
école (f): school
église (f): church
entrée (f): appetizer; entrance
épicerie (f): grocery store
étudiant (e): student
faubourg (m; abbr. fbg): quarter (of town; archaic)
fête (f): celebration, festival; party
ferme (f): farm
fleuve (m): river
foire (f): fair
fontaine (f): fountain
forêt (f): forest
fronton (m): *jai alai* arena
galerie (f): gallery
gare or gare SNCF (f): train station
gare routière (f): bus station
gîte d'étape (m): rural hostel-like accommodations, aimed at hikers
grève (f): strike, French national pastime
guichet (m): ticket counter, cash register desk
haute ville (f): upper town
horloge (f): clock
hors-saison: off-season
hôpital (m): hospital
hôtel (particulier) (m): town house, mansion
hôtel de ville (m): town hall
hôtel-Dieu (m): hospital (archaic)
île (f): island
jour (m): day
jour férié (m): public holiday
location (f): rental store
lycée (m): high school
madame (f; abbr. Mme): Mrs.
mademoiselle (f; abbr. Mlle): Miss
magasin (m): shop
mairie (f): town hall
maison (f): house
marée (f): tide
marché (m): market
mer (f): sea
mois (m): month
monastère (m): monastery
monsieur (m; abbr. M): Mr.
montagne (f): mountain
mur (m): wall
muraille (f): city wall, rampart
nuit (f): night
palais (m): palace
parc (m): park
pâtisserie (f): pastry shop

place (f): town square
plan (m): plan, map
plat (m): course (on menu)
pont (m): bridge
poste (f; abbr. PTT): post office
pourboire (m): the tip
puy (m): hill, mountain (archaic)
quartier (m): section (of town)
randonnée (f): hike
rempart (m): rampart
rivière (f): river
route (f): road
rue (f): street
salon (m): living room
salle (f): room; in a café it refers to indoor seating as opposed to the bar or patio
semaine (f): week
sentier (m): path, lane
service compris: tip included
soir (m): evening
son-et-lumière (m): sound-and-light show
source (f): spring
supermarché (m): supermarket
syndicat d'initiative (m): tourist office
tabac (m): cigarette shop and newsstand
table (f): table
télépherique (m): cable car
terrasse (f): terrace, patio
TGV (m): high speed train
thermes (m pl): hot springs
tour (f): tower
tour (m): tour
traiteur (m): delicatessen
université (f): university
val (m)/vallée (f): valley
vélo (m): bicycle
vendange (f): grape harvest
vieille ville (f): old town
ville (f): town, city
visite guidée (f): guided tour
vitraux (m pl): stained glass
voie (f): road
voiture (f): car

INDEX

A

Abakanowicz, Magdalena
311
abbeys
  Abbaye-aux-Dames
    (Bayeux) 214
  Abbaye-aux-Hommes 213
  Baume 390
  de Beauport 250
  aux-Dames (Saintes) 704
  de Fontenay 402
  de Fontevraud 306
  d'Hautecombe 468
  de Jumièges 201
  Mont-St-Michel 230
  de Noirlac 731
  St-André 512
  St-Germain 411
  St-Martin de Boscherville
    201
  St-Pierre 718
  St-Vaast 178
  St-Victor 493
  Sénanque 518
abortion 21
Académie Française 85
Académie Royale 83
L'Accueil Familial des
  Jeunes Etrangers 66
Adjani, Isabelle 87
adventure travel 29, 67
aerogrammes 30
Age of Exploration 710
Aguessac 630
Aigues-Mortes 533
airplane travel
  charter flights 40
  commercial airlines 35
  courier 39
  standby 39
airports
  Ajaccio 760
  Bastia 777
  Biarritz 652
  Bordeaux 640
  Calvi 768
  Grenoble 452
  Lille 169
  Lyon 437
  Marseille 485

Nancy 340
Nantes 269
Nice 545
Paris
  Orly 92
  Roissy-Charles de Gaulle 91
Perpignan 620
Toulouse 598
Aix-en-Provence 498
Ajaccio 760
Albert I 564
Albi 605
Albigensian Crusade 597,
  607, 612, 637
alcohol-related holidays 365
Aléria 780
Algeria 73
Alphand, Adolphe 142
The Alpilles 519, 526
The Alps 435–483
**Alsace, Lorraine, and
  Franche-Comté** 338–390
Alternatives to Tourism 56–
  68
altitude, high 20
Les Alyscamps 525
Amboise 290
American Church in Paris 66
American Express 14, 48
  Bordeaux 644
  Cannes 578
  Marseille 487
  Monaco 562
  Nice 546
  Paris 95
  Strasbourg 356
American Institute of Foreign
  Study 61
American Red Cross 19
American University of Paris
  62
Amiens 188
amusement parks
  Antibesland 573
  Disneyland Paris 167
  Futuroscope 691
Anacréon, Richard
  (museum) 225
Angers 307
d'Angers, David 310
Anglo-French wars 276
Angoulême 692

Princess Anne of Austria 645
Annecy 463
Antibes 569
anti-semitism 75
Appellation Contrôlée 67
Appendix 788–792
Aquinas, Thomas 597
  location of ashes 601
**Aquitaine and the Pays
  Basque** 640–684
Arbois 384
d'Arbrissel, Robert 306
Arc Germanicus 704
Arcachon 650
architecture 80–82
Ardier, Paul 290
Argelès 619
Arguin Sandbar 651
Arles 519
Armagnac 79
Armorican Celts 250
Armstrong, Lance 89
Arras 177
Arromanches 220
Ars 715
art nouveau 82, 340, 341,
  343, 344
art schools 63
artificial nature 142, 166
Astérix 692, 696
ATM cards 14
au pair work 65
Augustus 405, 542, 781
authenticity 194
Autun 405
Auxerre 409
Avignon 70, 504
Azay-le-Rideau 301

B

backpacks 29
Baker, Josephine 88
Balabus 94
Ballon d'Alsace 377
Balzac, Honoré de 85, 310
  birthplace 292
de Banville, Théodore 558
Bardot, Brigitte 87
bargaining 16
Baroness de Rothschild 558
Baroque 82

MAP INDEX

MAP LEGEND

✚ Hospital	✈ Airport	🏛 Museum	🏖 Beach
✪ Police	🚌 Bus Station	🏨 Hotel/Hostel	⊓ Gate or Entrance
✉ Post Office	🚆 Train Station	▲ Camping	⋯ Pedestrian Zone
ⓘ Tourist Office	Ⓜ METRO STATION	🍗 Food	▥ Stairs
$ Bank	⚓ Ferry Landing	🛍 Shopping	Subway Line
♠ Winery	✝ Church	★ Nightlife	🚡 Cable Car
▪ Site or Point of Interest	✡ Synagogue	⬛ Internet Café	
🎭 Theater	♜ Bunker/Fort	✝ Monastery/Abbey	
📖 Library	▲ Mountain	⚑ Consulate	LG The Let's Go compass always points NORTH